FOR GOD OR THE DEVIL

A HISTORY OF THE THIRTY YEARS WAR

BY ZACHARY TWAMLEY

WINGED HUSSAR PUBLISHING

For God or the Devil: A History of the Thirty Years' War
by Zachary Twamley
Cover by Jan Kostka
This edition published in 2020

Winged Hussar Publishing, LLC
1525 Hulse Road, Unit 1
Point Pleasant, NJ 08742

Copyright © Zachary Twamley
ISBN 978-1-945430-09-1 Paperback
978-1-950423-41-5 Ebook
LCN 2019954820

Bibliographical References and Index
1. History. 2. Europe. 3. Thirty Year's War

For Anna,

History Friend for Life

CONTENTS

ACKNOWLEDGEMENTS

First and foremost, I have to thank the reader for reading, and for joining me at the triumphant end of this long but immensely enjoyable process. Second, I must thank my publisher Vincent W. Rospond of Winged Hussar Publishing for his patience, dedication and attention to detail when dealing with this work. It is thanks to him that this study is now in your hands, following many years of broken promises, delays and apologetic emails on my part. But that is where the simple task of giving thanks comes to an end. It is impossible for me to recall and pay tribute to every kind word, every piece of advice, every conversation over coffee, which I have been privileged to have with people at all times during the creation of this book, whether they were history academics, podcast listeners, my good friends or my family. Each of these innumerable people made a contribution without which this book would not be the same.

Of course, it is our families who we lean on most during the course of constructing such a book, and ever since my wife Anna learned of my history obsession, she's been unfailingly supportive. I would have been lost without her encouragement and support, but also her genuine interest and advice, over innumerable coffee and pub chats as this work came to life. Her patience, obviously, was regularly tested, especially when it seemed as though this tome would never escape the confines of my brain and land on the pages, never mind the bookshelf! To my family, who have heard of few things other than this book over the last few years, I am as always so humbled and thankful for your help. I must thank my parents John and Angela, whose continued faith in me and enthusiasm for my work never ceased. Special thanks to my Dad, who provided me with a printer where I could pour over the enormous physical manuscript, which he was also brave enough to read and provide invaluable stylistic and editing advice for.

A significant contributing factor to this book has been the morass of podcast listeners and supporters – the so-called 'history friends' – who awaited every bit of news on this book's development with enthusiasm and interest. It would be too simplistic to say that these are mere fans of the podcast – many are valued friends, and many more still have contributed financially to this work. A few months before this book was released, and just as I was beginning my PhD in History at Trinity College Dublin, I announced a campaign on the crowdfunding platform Patreon, where listeners could sign up to support this podcast at a certain level every month, in return for much-deserved acknowledgement for their support. I called this new support tier 'PhD Pal', and invited fans of this show and those that wished to receive a signed copy of the book to sign up. I did not expect much traction, but the response I got was nothing short of astounding, as numerous history friends did sign up, and many others also upgraded their existing level of support to the PhD Pal level.

Per the terms of that PhD Pal tier on Patreon, I committed to noting the names of these supporters in the Acknowledgements section of this book. Yet, I do not wish the reader unfamiliar with these concepts to view this merely as a mechanical process. These people are some of the kindest, most generous and most passionate fans of my work that I have ever known. They will never know how much I value their support and vote of confidence in my projects and career, nor will I be able to fully comprehend my good fortune in finding people like them in the first place. This book is very much a product of their making as a result, because it is made for them, and for those that first requested I examine this fascinating conflict so many years ago. I hope I can do you all justice.

Special thanks to the PhD Pals and supporters who helped to make this book possible

Aaron Barlow, Andreas Haukenes, Andrew Mence, Anthony Klon, Andre F.P. DePlois, Andrew Liffrig, Anto Walsh, Anthony Molloy, Brennan Steele, Bill Carpenter, Brian Frankian, Brian Simmons, Bruce Gudmundsson, Christopher Taylor, Ciaran Murphy, Cody Bronushas , Csaba Suto, Damase Olsson, Darryl Hegel, David Kinsey, David Lund, David Przybyla, Deborah Godspodarek, Deborah Matthews, Derek Upham, Demetrio Munoz, Donna Stevens, Ed Ballinger, Erik Stark, Evan Cannon, Felicity Garde, Francis Luppi-Aquila, Gregory William Troderman, Hamish the Denizen, Ian Perkins, Ira Herniter, James Morphew, Jeff Minor, Jeff Zahnen, Jeremy Curthoys, Jeroen Van Nieuwenhove, Jesper Barnett, Jonas Brandes, John Bauer, John Harding, John Wright, Julie Jones, Kevin Melahn, Khurasan Miniatures, Kim Hamacher, Kyle Walters, Laurence Waring, Laurent Callot, Lee Barkalow, Luke Russell, Madeleine McCrea, Michael Groner, Michael Mulhern, Michael Romahn, Mike Swenson, Paul Doke II, Pawel Lebowa, Philip Idun, Philip Rice, Rebecca Eager, Richard Russell, Rob Caughlan, Rod Sieg, Ronald Henry, Rosa Angelone, Samuel Hettich, Shawn Marincas, Steve DocPinko Cloutier, Sviatoslav Yurash, Tim C, Vidar Stefansson

FOREWORD

I will have been history podcasting for nearly eight years by the time this book is released, to coincide with the 400th anniversary of the eruption of the Thirty Years War. For the uninitiated, you may benefit from a definition of the term "history podcast". In its simplest terms, a history podcast is an audio programme, recorded and edited and uploaded to the internet. The very potential which history podcasting offered appealed to me from an early stage, and the creative and intellectual freedom to research and share was what first moved me to investigate the medium further, and thereafter create my own in May 2012. When Diplomacy Fails, or WDF as it is often referred to in shorthand, was the result of this process. Since 2012, this podcast has given me the opportunity to explore fascinating conflicts and share some truly remarkable stories.[1] It has also provided me with a platform unparalleled in professional and personal terms; in short, without *When Diplomacy Fails Podcast*, it is very unlikely that this book would currently be in front of you.

With the freedom to research what I wanted under the WDF banner, I was quickly drawn to a mysterious conflict set in the first half of the seventeenth century – the Thirty Years War. The Thirty Years War has always enthralled me. As a history podcaster, I have always believed that such a set of wars – that such a *story* as this – would be worthy of my listeners' time and attentions. I was right. The Thirty Years War continues to be one of my most downloaded projects. It was the first major history podcasting project I took on in autumn 2013, and it was thus my greatest challenge to that point. Being not completely familiar with the major themes, the issues at stake or even the general outcome of the war, I covered it in my own time and learned organically as I went on, often at the same pace as the listener who I was attempting to 'teach'. I believed I described the experience to my listeners as 'flying by the seat of my pants'. Nonetheless, it proved an invaluable experience, as eighteen episodes, over twenty hours of finished audio content and countless words later, I had a body of work which I could point to as proof of my curiosity for the relatively unknown, of my taste for the obscure, and of my passion for bringing history out into the open where others could

11

discover it and be enthralled as I was.

Since tackling the Thirty Years War, *When Diplomacy Fails Podcast* went from strength to strength, covering yet more ambitious projects and bringing still more obscure eras of history to the attention of my listeners. Still, I look back on this conflict with a strange kind of nostalgia – just as historians maintain the conflict was a turning point, a watershed moment in the continent's bloody history, so too did my examination of it prove a turning point, and a watershed moment for my passions, my professionalism and of course, my podcast. When the opportunity came to revisit the conflict with fresh eyes many years later, I fell over myself in jumping at the chance. In line with the 400th anniversary of the eruption of the war, I announced that I would completely reimagine my old series from 2013-14, redo them from the ground up, and produce them as a book for everyone to read and enjoy further. I felt I needed no other justification than that to revisit such a fascinating era, but to those who may still be unconvinced, it should go without saying that I have changed a great deal in outlook, maturity and circumstance since I first tackled this era seven years ago. When I first began my investigation of the Thirty Years War, I was a 22-year-old student without a qualification to my name; as of 2020, I am married, with two degrees, a book to my name,[2] and a PhD in History now underway.

After such a long journey back to this era, it is my desire that *all* readers will be able to find something of worth in this book, and that they will come away with a newfound appreciation for the era, just as I did. My aim has been consistent throughout the years – to produce history which enthusiasts of all levels can enjoy. The significant challenge posed by this lofty aim is certainly worth the reward. The range and depth of characters present in the struggle – from the famous, to the infamous, to the relatively unknown – have inspired biographers and world leaders the world over. The interconnected nature of European geopolitics at the time taught historians much about how diplomacy in the seventeenth century worked, just as it provided a crash course to some of those famous contemporaries who learned to swim rather than sink in the fires of war. And then of course, there were the weighted arguments which inspired this armed camp or that, and which produced a dilemma that lent this book its title: would contemporaries choose the side supported by God, or would they veer towards the 'dark side' and fight for the Devil? The Thirty Years War is a conflict which shaped our world, and which left us a legacy that still challenges the historians that attempt to analyse it. More than all of that though, at its heart, the Thirty Years War is a story which has to be read or indeed *listened to* in order to be believed.

Four hundred years on from its original outbreak in May 1618, when those Habsburg officials were first defenestrated, I believe there has never been a better time to add a new study to the already considerable list of tomes which tackle the Thirty Years War.[3] To leave such a legacy for the history enthusiast to enjoy has always been my goal, whether in the realm of the spoken word or of the written. This is history which both *deserves* and *needs* to be known, and it is a narrative which I feel more personally and emotionally invested in than ever before.

Whether it was a European tragedy, a continental crisis or merely a continuous and interconnected series of military contests, understanding the Thirty Years War is essential if we are to appreciate our past. On the surface it may seem disconnected from the modern or better understood conflicts which transformed our world, yet the Thirty Years War is nonetheless filled with real stories of human triumph and adversity, relatable characters, and incredible examples of high drama and endurance. It contains parallels both striking and subtle in their nature to the better remembered or better-known great wars in history. Apocalyptic in its devastation and the terrible impact it wrought upon those it caught in its wide net, it is ours to examine and untangle here in the course of this study; a study which I have wanted to write since I first learned of its remarkable characters, its great battles and its terrible toll.

Zachary Twamley
Wicklow, Ireland
March 2020

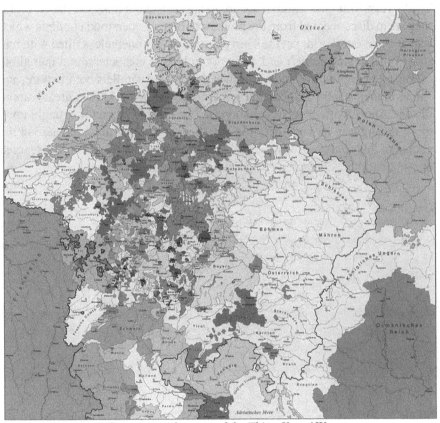

Germany at the start of the Thirty Years' War

INTRODUCTION

When Gustavus Adolphus, the King of Sweden, landed on the Baltic shores of Northern Germany in summer 1630, he was faced with several dilemmas, foremost among them being the need for allies and supplies. Believing that both resources existed in the lands of the Elector of Brandenburg, a ruling prince in the north-east of Germany who happened to be his brother-in-law, Gustavus wrote a strongly worded letter to him, which has been immortalised ever since, with good reason. The Swedish King wrote:

> [The Elector] has to be friend or foe. When I come to his borders, he must declare himself cold or hot. This is a fight between God and the Devil. If my Cousin wants to side with God, then he has to join me; if he prefers to side with the devil, then indeed he must fight me; there is no third way.[4]

If the Elector chose his master the Holy Roman Emperor, then Sweden's King would be his foe, and all of his lands would be ripe for the taking. If he chose to side with his cousin King Gustavus Adolphus, who was stationed with an abundance of soldiers nearby, then Gustavus would still suck his lands dry, but the Elector would at least be permitted to hold onto these lands, if he was lucky. Harrowing indeed was the prospect of turning against his Emperor, the constitutional and traditional figurehead of the Elector's world. Just as there was no 'third way' in Gustavus' mind, so too was there no winning formula for the Elector of Brandenburg. The best he could do would be to choose the lesser of two evils, and at that moment, it was felt wise to accommodate the King that had the power to destroy him and hope for mercy from the Emperor in the future. The Elector of Brandenburg's dilemma was severe, but it was far from the worst position that his German peers faced while the ravages of the Thirty Years War were endured. That unfortunate honour was arguably reserved for the city of Magdeburg.

Magdeburg was proudly Protestant, historically distinctive and culturally important – its rich past also granted it a population of nearly forty thousand, designating it as one of the largest cities of the Holy Roman

Empire.[5] Yet, Magdeburg was also many things to Count Tilly, the Habsburg generalissimo who had surrounded the city in a siege in spring 1631. Above all, Magdeburg was obliged to aid the Emperor, since its people were his subjects, and the Habsburg army which camped outside were the agents of this Emperor. In the months before, Magdeburg had sided with the invading Swedes, and ignored several orders from the Emperor to abandon them at once and provide his soldiers with the aid they needed. Magdeburg was in possession of some badly needed provisions, not to mention coinage, which could keep the soldiery going for a while longer. It was a beacon in a land otherwise stripped bare by years of waste and plunder.

A city like Magdeburg, positioned as it was in such a vital location for the Swedes and the Habsburgs, would never have been able to embrace neutrality, even if its city fathers had wanted to. In this case, Gustavus Adolphus was correct – there was absolutely no 'third way' for Magdeburg. With its allies too far away to help, the Habsburgs stormed the city and wreaked a brutal vengeance upon Magdeburg such as hadn't been seen in European memory. 'The Protestant world wept', wrote one historian, and 'even Catholics were appalled.' A new verb even entered the German vocabulary – *Magdeburgisieren* – to 'make a Magdeburg'.[6]

Daniel Friese was a citizen of Magdeburg, who had moved his family there in 1628 to assume the office of Senior City Clerk. His son Friedrich would later write an account of what happened to them and their world on the night of 20 May 1631. Friedrich recounted the events of that night, when the enemy broke through the defences of the city:

> ...the Imperial soldiers cried in the alleys, 'All is won! All is won!' and hammered on the doors like the devil himself. We poor people were so scared that we nearly died in our houses, prayed and called to God to have mercy. Soon they thumped on our door...the soldiers threatened they would not leave a soul alive unless we opened up. We had to let them in; they soon attacked father and mother and craved money; they were only two musketeers.

Yet, Friedrich's ordeal was not over. As the city began to flood with soldiers, it became harder to keep safe from their desperate quest for booty and plunder, which seemed to run roughshod over all sense of reason and decency. After they were discovered hiding in the family's barn, Friedrich and his younger brothers were brought out by the soldiers as their father came hurriedly to their defence. Friedrich remembered:

> The soldier then came at father with a pickaxe. We children crowded around the soldier, begging and crying that he should please let father live. Christian, my fourth brother, was then a small child who could barely walk and stammer a few words. He spoke in the greatest fear to the soldier: 'Oh please let father live, I'll gladly give you the three pennies I get on Sundays.' Father used to

give each child something each Sunday if he learned a phrase [from the Bible]. This, coming from an unformed and in those days' simple child, touched the soldier's heart, perhaps by God's merciful providence. He immediately changed and then turned to us in a friendly rather than a cruel manner. He looked at us children as we stood about him and said: 'Aye, what fine little lads you are!' because he was a Nuremberger, and then said to our father: 'If you want to get out with your family leave immediately, for the Croats will be here in an hour and you and your children will scarcely survive.'

Friedrich and his family managed to latch onto the soldier here and follow him to the nearest camp just outside the city. The army which had besieged Magdeburg was a multi-ethnic force, and one could expect better treatment from soldiers that hailed from nearby states or cities. Yet Friedrich's journey towards the camp was not free from danger either. He recalled:

On the way a student met mother and ripped the shawl from her body. Another wanted to grab the nanny who was carrying our little sister Anna, but our soldier took her and he let her go again. We saw many dead bodies in the streets, including some women lying quite uncovered...It was a wretched spectacle. We all praised God heartily that he took us from this fire and war.

Eventually, Friedrich and his family made it to the soldier's camp. After the soldier's wife chastised her husband for bringing so many refugees, the soldier quieted her by reasoning that 'he had to rescue the lads, God would grant him booty.' It was at roughly 11PM that night, in their refuge far from the city limits, that the most poignant spectacle of all took place: the infamous torching and sacking of Magdeburg, the city where Friedrich Friese had once called home. Friedrich remembered:

This night at about eleven o'clock, the entire city of Magdeburg was ablaze. Father led us out of the [soldier's] hut so that we could speak of it all our lives. In the camp, which was quite some distance from the city, it was so bright that you could have read a letter by the great glow of the fire.[7]

In a city of tens of thousands, only five thousand would remain in the aftermath. Considering the low survival rate, Friedrich Friese and his family were very lucky indeed to survive the ordeal unharmed, but the city of Magdeburg itself was never the same again. To the inhabitants of Magdeburg, the 20 May 1631 must have seemed like the coming of the apocalypse, yet for the soldiers on the *other* side – those actually partaking in the plundering and looting – they would consider it a great success.

'It is certain that no more terrible work and divine punishment has been seen since the destruction of Jerusalem', claimed one, painting the event simultaneously in both Biblical and inherently just terms. Magdeburg *deserved* what befell it, because the city fathers had for so long flouted the authority of their Habsburg masters. Due to the actions of a select few officials, *all* would suffer. No quarter would be given. 'All our soldiers became rich', the general concluded, 'God with us.'[8] Indeed, Magdeburg epitomised what had already become a common theme of the Thirty Years War; that because of the actions of a select number of citizens, officials or soldiers, everyone in the city, the region or the country would suffer the consequences – regardless of culpability, age, or sex.

How did such a state of affairs become the norm? A generation before, citizens across the Empire would have been horrified at the suggestion that a city such as Magdeburg, where the first truly 'Holy Roman' Emperor Otto I had been buried,[9] should be subjected to such a barbaric, merciless ordeal. The destruction of Magdeburg can partially be explained by the evident brutalisation of the common soldier, who had been desensitised to the horrors of war by that point, after over a decade of conflict. Yet, it can also be understood as an act of punishment, where a besieging army had been refused entry and surrender had been denied, liberating the soldiers from their traditional restraint.[10]

It also deserves mention that the fruits of Magdeburg, a city of plenty, were immensely appealing and desperately required by the Habsburg commander Count Tilly, who had been left essentially to fend for himself when no resources from his master the Holy Roman Emperor seemed forthcoming. At least one historian has remarked that it is highly unlikely – considering his desperate want and need of supplies – that Count Tilly *intended* to destroy the city of Magdeburg,[11] and that the fires which annihilated the city were likely started and spread through accident. Indeed, as Friedrich Friese's account demonstrates, not all enemy soldiers present at Magdeburg were cruel and unfeeling savages, and Friese's 'was not an isolated case amid the horror... other soldiers helped civilians, including clergy, to escape.'[12]

While Count Tilly would not have been thrilled at what had been done to this city, he could not afford to have dwelt upon the horrors for long. He would have reconciled the atrocity in the same manner that Gustavus Adolphus condemned neutrality: that one was either with the Habsburgs and the Emperor, or he was against them. As matters stood in spring 1631, it was not possible to show ample mercy when the needs of his force were so acute, when the enemy was so near and when the pressure was so high. Besides, Tilly could have concluded, Magdeburg had been given several, often generous opportunities, to choose God or the Devil, and because she had chosen the Devil, her people had been faced with scenes taken straight out of hell.

The destruction of Magdeburg is perhaps the most infamous example of the kind of brutality which the Thirty Years War produced. At its core was a theme which would be repeated across the continent many times over; Magdeburg had gambled, she had chosen the wrong side, and she had paid the ultimate price. Whenever a ruler was forced into picking a side, as sometimes metaphorical, sometimes literal, guns were pointed in his direction, damage was always going to be done. Whenever a city tradesman moved from one city to another, and was captured along the way and asked where his loyalties lay, or, even more sensitively, what religious persuasion he subscribed to, that city tradesman was forced to make a choice, and the wrong one could cost him his life. Whenever raiding parties appeared in the distance, did the village's able-bodied men stay and resist, or did they gather all they could and flee, in the process entering the pool of refugees scattered across the countryside?

When Denmark entered the conflict in 1625; when the Swedes entered in 1630; when the French entered it in 1635 – all of these powers made a decision which could well bring the Devil to their lands if they ended on the losing side. In the cases of all these powers, disasters were visited upon them, just as surely as they visited disasters upon the lands and people of Europe. Gustavus Adolphus was right to attest that there was no third way – countless people, villages, towns, families, businesses, farms and, as we saw, entire cities, were torn asunder because they had been pressed against a wall and been forced to make a choice, only to discover in the end that this choice had been the wrong one.

'Whether we win or lose', commented one Lutheran Bohemian nobleman at the time of the Bohemian revolt in 1618, 'our fate will be heavy.'[13] Yet these Bohemians also believed they had little choice but to throw the representatives of their Habsburg masters out of the windows of the Hradschin Castle in Prague, and to engage in open revolt. The alternative was to suffer religious repression and persecution under the intolerant thumb of their new king, soon to be Holy Roman Emperor, Ferdinand II. Certainly, following the three decades of conflict which haunted this act, the Bohemians were easy scapegoats for having started the whole terrible thing. Had they only endured their trials, then Europe would not have had to suffer. Much like the First World War three centuries later though, such ferocious, enraged horrors were not caused and prolonged by a single factor. If the Bohemians had been solely responsible for the Thirty Years War, then this conflict would have ended once their nightmares had been fulfilled, and they were crushed under the Habsburg heel in the early 1620s. Alas, the horrors were not destined to be brief.

Gustavus may have been correct about the absence of a neutral option, but he was wrong to insist that the war was one between God or the Devil; this suggested that there was one side that was inherently more or less evil than the other. Reprisal, atrocity, devastation and horrors followed the armies on all sides, of all nationalities, and at all times. Shortly before the sack of Magdeburg had so horrified his contemporaries, Gustavus Adolphus had overseen a similarly brutal sack of the city of Frankfurt on the Oder –

another city which had chosen the Devil, in Gustavus' mind, and suffered for it. In a conflict where each side believed to be acting with God's blessing, it was hardly surprising that divine rhetoric preceded and followed the divine punishments which were meted out. Win or lose, neither side was willing to permit neutrality: you were either with us, or you were against us; you were either for God or for the Devil. There was no third way, and thus no chance for Europe to pause, until thirty years after the Habsburg officials were first defenestrated, the powers involved staggered, exhausted and dispirited, towards peace.

This is a book about the Thirty Years War. It joins a library of works too innumerable to measure, but positively invaluable for adding to our understanding of such a tangled, fascinating era. Defining this book and what it aims to achieve is a task almost as difficult as writing it in the first place. Much like my idea of the book's length, the vision of 'For God or the Devil' changed over the last several years, but at its heart remains a story which I hope the reader will be able to draw enjoyment and interest from.

This is my telling of the conflict, with a focus on the portions of the struggle which I found particularly captivating. There is less time devoted to specialist studies, such as, for instance, a detailed examination of battles, or the precise minutiae of seventeenth century economics, though exceptions will sometimes be made. Specialist accounts already exist, assessing the contributions of particular leading figures, or the peace congress at Westphalia, or distant but related conflicts outside of the main war in Germany. Those wishing to delve deeper into such topics should consult the bibliography section of this book. In the case of this study, I have no loftier goal than to bring as many of these interconnected threads to the reader as possible. This may be the first introduction one has to the conflict, or it may be one among many other works which have been absorbed and enjoyed. Either way, it is my hope that this narrative will provide something for everyone.

An exhaustive account of the Thirty Years War is impossible, at least not without a team of specialists speaking at least fourteen languages, or in possession of a keen appreciation for the interests of all leaders, all countries, and all people. Scholars have made impressive attempts to create definitive accounts of the Thirty Years War; names like Geoffrey Parker, Peter H. Wilson and C.V. Wedgewood should be suggested to those that want to read more, and to gain from perspectives honed after several decades' worth of experience in study and analysis. I presently lack such experience, nor do I possess any of those fourteen languages required to delve into materials which happen to not be in English. What I do possess is a passion and enthusiasm which I hope is palpable from the following pages. This is a long book, but the aim of all historians that pen such projects is that they do not *feel* long to the reader. At the same time, however, such length is to be anticipated, because the Thirty

Years War, as its moniker suggests, was a very long war indeed. It lasted the lifetime of some individuals; it served as the final exclamation point in the lives of others and served as the baptism by fire for still countless more people.

The Thirty Years War was a conflict which lasted from 1618-1648. Inconsistent in its fury and impact, the conflict was based mostly within the Holy Roman Empire, or for the modern equivalent, across the northern parts of Germany, along the Rhine, in the southeast in the lands of the modern-day Czech Republic, and in portions of the Netherlands, the Baltic, Russia, Poland, Hungary and several other theatres besides. The Thirty Years War itself was a strange beast, because it grew from a Holy Roman constitutional affair into an international and interconnected set of conflicts between the major powers in Europe; principally the Austrian and Spanish branches of the Habsburg dynasty, France, Sweden, Denmark, the Dutch Republic and to a lesser extent, England, Poland and Russia. By its end great swathes of Europe had been utterly devastated, on a scale and with a ferocity never before seen or imagined possible.

Legions of issues were encapsulated within the Thirty Years War. Yet, the conflict was not as continuous or straightforward as its moniker might suggest. Indeed, much like another conflict, the Hundred Years War, the *Thirty Years War* was characterised by the almost cyclical entry and exit of a several powers, the continuation and pausing of several related conflicts, and the dissemination and adoption of several ideals and goals. In the past, its changing nature has led some historians to question the legitimacy of the term Thirty Years War.[14] This was because although the Habsburg family remained a constant fixture, the war plainly spilled into different theatres, and in the case of the Franco-Spanish conflict which emerged from it, the 1648 deadline was totally ignored – a fact which compelled one historian to refer to the Thirty Years War as 'a largely factitious conception which has, nevertheless, become an indestructible myth.'[15]

But the Thirty Years War is *not* a myth – and while we should be wary of tidy titles that make messy conflicts more unnaturally accessible to us, in the case of the Thirty Years War, the title is accurate and fair. The Thirty Years War has its roots in the Habsburg-Bourbon rivalry as much as it has roots in the Reformation, the constitution of the Holy Roman Empire or the Dutch revolt against Spain. Put simply, as an event in history the Thirty Years War defies simple classification. Never before had the intervention of France occurred on such a scale in Germany, or the intervention of the Scandinavian powers been seen in mainland Europe at all. Never before had the Reformation or Counter-Reformation fuelled such a long-lasting conflict. Never before had the constitutionalism of the Holy Roman Empire, or the dynastic ambitions of the House of Habsburg, presented such a compelling list of reasons to continue the war.

Yet, as important as all of these issues undoubtedly were, it would be too simplistic to look to the balance of power, the religious sectarianism of the era, Habsburg greed or the constitution of the Holy Roman Empire as the sole cause for the conflict's intensity and duration. To compensate for the fact that the Thirty Years War encompasses several issues and conflicts at once, it is arguably easier and more appropriate to divide the conflict into four phases, so this is what we have done here. These phases are as follows:

Phase 1: Years of Armed Neutrality and Division; Europe to 1618.[16] *Where issues of religious and constitutional disagreement within the Holy Roman Empire came to the fore.*

Phase 2: Years of Waste and Ruin; 1618-1625. *Where issues relating to the Holy Roman Empire's constitution, and opportunism of the interested powers, provided a major focus.*

Phase 3: Years of Intervention; 1626-1634. *Where states outside of the Holy Roman Empire felt compelled to intervene in the name of their interests and security.*

Phase 4: Years of Coalitions; 1635-1648. *Where the conflict widened as France declared war on both branches of the Habsburgs, which focused the aforementioned issues, exacerbated the intensity of the war across the continent and prolonged its duration.*

These four phases constitute Sections 2-5 of the book, with Section 1 serving as an introduction to the main themes and developments in seventeenth century warfare. This story will be told through references to country-specific case studies, beginning with England, then moving through the French, Dutch and Swedish examples, to see what each power contributed to and learned from military theory and practice. Through this structure, the reader can be familiarised with the more important actors and innovations before beginning the main narrative in Section 2. Alternatively, if warfare is of little interest to the reader, then this section on warfare can be skipped without great consequence to the overall narrative. This story will be chronological, as we follow the course of the conflict while it waxed and waned over the different spheres of Europe for three decades. It is my intention to present the extremities of the conflict as they happened, rather than to cast judgement in every case.

Judging the behaviour of those that acted four centuries ago is a troublesome task, especially considering the stark chasm of difference between the values system of the twenty-first century and that of the seventeenth. Paradoxically though, even while the seventeenth century was very different to our modern world, by putting aside our pre-conceived notions or expectations of human behaviour, we often find that the individuals living through the living nightmare of the Thirty Years War were not so different to us. They feared for the safety of their families, for their personal fortunes and for their lives amidst a constantly worsening crisis which seemed to dominate every aspect of their world.

These fears would prove justified. By the time of the peace treaties at Westphalia in 1648, the population of the Holy Roman Empire would have contracted from roughly twenty million to thirteen and a half million souls. Whole families were destroyed or displaced, villages and towns were annihilated, and the demographic makeup of entire kingdoms was forever altered.[17] At the highest level, such decisions were made by men who had to answer to no one; Princes, Kings and Emperors who wielded the power and influence necessary to command the fates of soldiers, citizens and entire families. Narratives of the Thirty Years War will necessarily examine the aims and actions of such highly positioned individuals, as they controlled the pace and course of the war. At the same time though, we should bear in mind that the consequences of such decisions were borne by the common citizen – the likes of Friedrich Friese, whose family managed, despite the odds, to make it out of Magdeburg alive.

In the case of Magdeburg, a city with a rich history of annoying Emperors with its Protestant sympathies, and in 1631, providing support to the Swedish invader, Ferdinand II's enemies could still argue that notwithstanding Magdeburg's sins, the Holy Roman Emperor was *supposed* to be the protector of such subjects, not the harbinger of apocalyptic punishment against them. Yet, although Magdeburg aroused shock and horror among contemporaries in 1631, it did nothing to lessen the intensity of the war in the years that followed. There was no universal recoiling from the idea of continuing the war, because by 1631, the monster had mutated from its once manageable size to the point that, as the King of Sweden, Gustavus Adolphus then said, 'all the wars that are afoot in Europe have become one war.'[18] Indeed, this interconnectedness of Europe at the time of the Thirty Years War meant that even those powers which did not actively involve themselves – such as Poland, the Ottoman Empire, Russia, Britain, and even Transylvania – still created ripples which were felt in the main conflicts. This fact only increases the challenge to the historian, though it does make the narrative richer and more fascinating as well.

Although the plight of the average citizen will certainly loom into view, my approach will not be concerned with the citizen of the Holy Roman Empire or with Europe per se, but with his ruler. The agreements and negotiations which led certain figures to bring their realm onto one side of the conflict or the other – these will be of great interest to us, and all the while I wish to emphasise, that in Germany's case in particular, it was nigh on impossible to refrain from picking a side, as most of the time, your adversary would pick your side for you by issuing you with a threatening letter, or appearing fully armed outside of your borders. It was, then, a choice of 'God or the Devil', and the consequences for choosing incorrectly were as horrendous as the potential benefits for emerging on the winning side.

The Elector of Brandenburg has already provided us with an example of how hard this choice was to make, having been informed by his brother-in-law Gustavus Adolphus that he must choose between God or the Devil, and that there was no third way, but of course our coverage won't extend just to those beleaguered princes and potentates. We will need to explain how the king of Sweden felt the need to present this impossible choice to the Elector of Brandenburg in the first place, and to do that, we will also have to provide an examination of the aims and motives of the major figures who enthusiastically involved themselves in the war. From the beginning, with Frederick V of the Palatinate and Ferdinand II of Habsburg, two distinct camps were established. Even while the cast of characters changed, the existence of these two stark choices – of opposing the Emperor or fighting for him – would not truly vanish for the next three decades. As powers filtered in and out of these two camps with varying consequences, Europe was brought further and further into an inescapable abyss – the early modern European equivalent of a total war.

And the conflict was *European* by definition, not merely Imperial or German. It was also impacted by circumstances and developments far removed from the continent itself; one needs only to consider, for example, the effect which the Dutch occupation of Brazil had upon Spanish stability in Europe, to see these interconnected theatres manifest themselves. To reflect this reality, the narrative begins in a somewhat unorthodox fashion: not at the moment of the defenestration of Prague, but in the context of the New World, where Cortez faced down the might of the Aztecs. This is to underline the point to the reader that Cortez' masters – the Spanish Empire, led by the Habsburg King of Spain and Holy Roman Emperor Charles V – were a world power of the first rank. Although its power and majesty had degraded by the turn of the seventeenth century, it was still impossible to consider the Habsburg interest without first considering Spain. Spanish money and manpower, indeed, supercharged the conflict as much as the constitutional or religious makeup of the Empire.

Could Spain fight for the Emperor in Germany, while also fighting against its rebels in the Netherlands, and challenging Dutch forces across the world? What would be the impact on the war in Germany if Madrid was to lose to the Dutch in Flanders, or conversely, could a Habsburg victory in Germany render the Dutch position hopeless, and guarantee a Spanish triumph? All this serves only to remind the reader that The Thirty Years War, as we said, defies simple classification – its layers are too numerous and unique to enable the conflict to fit comfortably into a single box. To fully appreciate the significance of the Thirty Years War, indeed, one must work as carefully as possible to unravel these layers and present them to the reader. It is a daunting task, but it is also a task which I have come to relish.

Acknowledgements, Foreword and Introduction Notes

[1] *When Diplomacy Fails* is a history podcast, which means that I produce 'episodes' on certain topics throughout history, which I then release to the listening public free of charge. This hobby of mine has grown substantially over the years, and has played a great role in furthering my passions for history as a discipline. To find out more about this podcast and the work I do for it, make sure to check out the official website at www.wdfpodcast.com

[2] See Zachary Twamley, *A Matter of Honour: Britain and the First World War* (NJ; Winged Hussar Publishing, 2016).

[3] See my bibliography section for notes on further reading and the sources used.

[4] Cited in Christopher Clark, *Iron Kingdom, the Rise and Downfall of Prussia 1600-1947* (London; Penguin, 2007), p. 23.

[5] Geoffrey Parker, *Europe in Crisis 1598-1648* (London; Fontana Paperbacks, 1979), p. 221.

[6] *Ibid*, p. 221.

[7] Account cited in Peter H. Wilson, *The Thirty Years War, A Sourcebook* (New York; Palgrave Macmillan, 2010), pp. 158-163, hereafter *Sourcebook*.

[8] Cited in Peter H. Wilson, *Sourcebook*, p. 146.

[9] Timothy Reuter, *Germany in the Early Middle Ages 800–1056* (MA, Addison Wesley Longman, 1991), p. 148.

[10] Peter H. Wilson, *Sourcebook*, pp. 145-146;

[11] See Peter H. Wilson, *Europe's Tragedy, A New History of the Thirty Years War* (London; Penguin, 2010), p. 469.

[12] Peter H. Wilson, *Europe's Tragedy*, p. 470.

[13] Cited in Wilson, *Sourcebook*, p. 54.

[14] The historian S. H. Steinberg disagrees with the term Thirty Years War, and upholds that the label is a modern one, with no more credence than the War of the Roses moniker. See S. H. Steinberg, *The 'Thirty Years War' and the Conflict for European Hegemony 1600-1660* (London, 1966), pp. 1-2; S. H. Steinberg, 'The Thirty Years War: A New Interpretation', History, xxxii (1947), pp. 89-102. Peter H. Wilson called such a view 'influential but unconvincing', in *Sourcebook*, p. 334. Yet, it is in the 2001 article by Geoff Mortimer that the debate is conclusively decided in favour of the term's validity, so I will apply the term in this work as well. See G. Mortimer, 'Did Contemporaries Recognize a 'Thirty Years War'?', *The English Historical Review*, Vol. 116, No. 465 (Feb., 2001), pp. 124-136. For an additional perspective see Guenther H. S. Mueller, 'The "Thirty Years' War" or Fifty Years of War', *The Journal of Modern History*, Vol. 50, No. 1, On Demand Supplement (Mar.,1978), pp. D1053-D1056.

[15] See N. M. Sutherland, 'The Origins of the Thirty Years War and the Structure of European Politics', *ante*, CVii (1992), pp. 587-625; referenced in this case is p. 587.

[16] This term and timeline is also utilised by Geoffrey Parker in his seminal work on the Thirty Years War. See Chapter IV in the contents page of Geoffrey Parker, *Europe in Crisis*.

[17] C.V. Wedgewood, *The Thirty Years War* (London: Pimlico, 1992), p. 79; Georges Pages, *The Thirty Years War 1618-1648* (London: Adam and Charles Black, 1970), p. 74.

[18] Cited in Parker, *Europe in Crisis 1598-1648*, p. 14.

PART ONE

Seventeenth Century Warfare

Pikemen at the push (1600)

Arquebuser with a rest (1600)

A calvary battle (Anthony Palamedus, 1627)

"I have discovered...a method of getting the musketeers and soldiers armed with harquebuses not only to keep firing very well but to do it effectively in battle order (that is to say, they do not skirmish or use the cover of hedges) in the following manner: as soon as the first rank has fired together, then by the drill [they have learned] they will march to the back. The second rank, either marching forward or standing still, [will next] fire together [and] then march to the back. After that, the third and following ranks will do the same. Thus, before the last ranks have fired, the first will have reloaded, as the following diagram shows: these little dots show the route of the ranks as they leave after firing."[1]

William Lodewijk, contemporary and friend of the Prince of Orange, writing in 1594.

"A young cavalier, desirous of honour and greedy of good instruction, could have learned from this king.... Such a general would I gladly serve, but such a general I shall hardly see, whose custom was to be first and last in danger himself...."[2]

Scottish Colonel Robert Monro observes the behaviour and legend of Gustavus Adolphus, late 1620s.

"Trying to understand seventeenth-century European history without weighing the influence of war and military institutions is like trying to dance without listening to the music."[3]

John A. Lynn, military historian, writing in 1985.

CHAPTER ONE
"Theory in Development"

INTRODUCTION
From Then to Now

Sultan Mustafa II had a plan. The date was 1695, and his Empire of the Ottomans had been at war with Austria, Venice and Poland-Lithuania for over a decade. The state coffers were exhausted, and a stalemate of sorts had ensued, but this did not matter to Sultan Mustafa II. He would adopt the traditions of his predecessors, and lead from the front of the army as all the great conquering Sultans had done before. With his inspirational presence urging the soldiery on, the Ottoman Empire would once more triumph over the heathens that occupied Hungary and portions of the Balkans. Mustafa's plan went against the grain of recent memory – no Sultan had led the Ottoman army from the front since the mid-sixteenth century, and no Sultan had even accompanied the army since the 1660s. The Ottoman palace was full of courtiers and elites that wished to keep it that way, and to monopolise any vestiges of power for themselves. Mustafa had several of them executed, and he turned his full attention to the resurrection of the Ottoman war effort under his name, and he turned his full attention to the resurrection of the Ottoman war effort under his name. It was as he planned on such a grand ambitious scale, that Mustafa was paid a visit by an unusual guest.

The man was a Greek Orthodox Christian, who claimed that he had converted to Islam in secret, and that the Prophet, and Mustafa's father Mehmed IV, had visited him in a dream. They had imparted some words to this Greek man, and he wished to share them with Mustafa at once. Mustafa would never have allowed it, but apparently the Vizier had heard the man's story and believed that what he had to say was worth the Sultan's time. So the Greek convert was brought before Mustafa II, and asked to repeat what he had said. Skipping the less exciting parts, the Greek revealed the part of his dream which would most interest the Sultan. According to his dream, Mustafa's late father had said the following:

Go ye to my son Mustafa...You will be superbly rewarded...Whatever you hear and see here you should convey and tell him...*Inshalla* (god willing), your Sultanate will endure for a very long period. With the aid of the Enduring Truth, during your reign many an enemy domain will be conquered and recovered.[4]

It was just what Mustafa wanted to hear – for the next two years, he met with some moderate successes, until he led over fifty thousand of his men to the worst Ottoman defeat in living memory, at the Battle of Zenta on the Hungary plains. So decisive was the defeat that Prince Eugene of Savoy, the commander of the Habsburg-German-Hungarian allied army that had beaten him, was able to write home to his Emperor and make the following jubilant pronouncement: 'This victorious action drew to a close with the day itself; it was as though the sun decided not to set until it could see and cast its rays on the triumph of Your Majesty's armies.'[5] A triumph indeed, for the Turks were shortly thereafter forced to the peace table, as the allies seized Sarajevo and forced Mustafa's armies out of much of Hungary.

Sultan Mustafa II became utterly despondent after the loss, his initial enthusiasm for command apparently sucked out of him with the totality of his defeat. During the Peace of Karlowitz two years after the battle in 1699, the Ottomans closed out the seventeenth century by reaching a watershed moment of the worst kind. Eugene of Savoy, one of the great tacticians of the age, had so shattered the Ottoman ability to resist, that the Ottoman peacemakers gave formal recognition to the territories they were forced to hand over to the allies, which included portions of the Balkans, of the Ukraine, and some Greek islands. For the first time in Turkish history, the loss of territory was acknowledged, and enshrined in a peace treaty.[6]

With the triumph of Eugene, the military preponderance of the West over the East appeared confirmed. Certainly, there would be cause for celebration, since although the Ottomans were by no means defeated, and actually took back some territories which they had lost in the subsequent decades, the Ottoman Empire would never seriously threaten Western Europe again.[7] Western Europe had arrived, in a process that was neatly marked by the arrival of the eighteenth century the following year. From now on, Europe would become the centre of the world, and enlightenment, overseas expansion, economic boom, cultural refinement, imperialism on a grand scale and incredible technological advancement would follow. Yet, all of these things, and all of the progress and benefit which came from them, were the result of war.

It was this corner of the world map – Western Europe – that would shape the history of mankind as we know it for the next two centuries. In this section of the book, while we will not trace this history up to the Peace of Karlowitz in 1699, we are going to explain how Europe was positioned to supersede the Ottomans at the turn of the eighteenth century. To do this, we must explain how the seventeenth century saw a transformation of Western Europe's military tactics, organisation and technology, all of which greatly improved the capacity for victory. The destruction of the Ottoman army at Zenta and the demoralisation of Sultan Mustafa II may have marked the occasion with an exclamation point, but the Military Revolution had been building for some time.

The scale of warfare, the nature of what it could achieve, the constant onus on the leading figures to improve, the fear of being left behind in the race, the stunning transformations in how war changed, and what this looked like on the battlefield, as much as what it looked like in society – these are all aspects of a thesis developed in the 1950s called the Military Revolution. The Military Revolution provides us with a really useful lens through which we can examine so many previously understudied parts of the puzzle. The military drill; the emergence of mass volley tactics; the development of more advanced fortifications known as the trace italienne; the growth of armies; the development of military bureaucracies to equip and control these armies; the increasing sophistication of Western technology – all of these are issues which the Military Revolution addresses, and in this section of the book, we will investigate them in more detail.[8]

It is often taken for granted that European states went from feudal societies, dependent upon the whims and loyalties of their local lord, to organised, industrialised, militarised societies, capable of fielding and paying for a professional standing army, and kitting it out with the latest in weaponry, supplying it for long periods of time, and educating its leaders with the best in military theory and tactics. Because such developments happened, it is easy to forget that in the space of a few hundred years, everything changed where warfare on the continent was concerned. Not only what weapons Europeans used, but also how their rulers went about summoning the men for battle, and what the reduction in the importance of some units, and the increase in importance of others actually meant for European society – these are facts that are easy to gloss over when we look at the bigger picture.

Yet, even while we examine the bigger picture, we are faced with some unanswerable questions. How did the infantry become so important, at the expense of the knight and the social status he enjoyed? What made certain military leaders so incredibly effective – how do we explain the success of men like Gustavus Adolphus, Ambrogio Spinola, or Count Tilly? How do we explain how a man like Ernst of Mansfield never won a convincing victory, yet was constantly in the employ of Europe's most influential potentates, solely because of his knack for raising an army? We know the names of some important battles in the Thirty Years War – Breitenfeld in 1631, which established Swedish military power; Rocroi in 1643 which did the same for the French, or even before that, the battle of Lutter in 1626, which saw the Catholic-Habsburg forces rout their Danish-German opponents. Yet, unless we can properly get to grips with what these battlefields actually looked like, and what the soldier went through, we will always be disconnected from the events, and the weight of these victories, as much as the weight of other defeats, will be felt far less.

For the sake of clarity, it is worth noting that gunpowder weapons became rapidly more common following the Italian Wars of the 1490s. From that point, the usage of the musket in its primitive form greatly increased, as did the military theory and tactics to go along with its most effective employment on the battlefield.[9] Of course, cannon had already made its presence felt before that time, and Europeans had experimented with cannons of varying size and practicality since the fourteenth century, with the Ottomans famously making use of enormous cannons to break down Constantinople's mighty walls in 1453.[10] Yet it was the usage of the musket in league with the cannon that so transformed European warfare and society as one, and the transformation deserves explanation. To make our point, we will investigate the case study of England in the fourteenth and fifteenth centuries, to demonstrate the feudal system in action, and see how it responded to change and adapted accordingly, so let's begin.

ONE

The Military-Feudal Contract – An English Example

In the middle ages, war was as much a clash between states, as it was a private affair between Kings. Above all though, war was an expensive and immensely complex act, and it should not surprise us to learn that since the sinews of war were money, the pursuit of money by the kings that led their state into war became a full-time occupation as important as organising the troops and stores. Even while wars could be considered a private affair, they had to be paid for and supplied with manpower by the king's public subjects. Considering this, and the fact that, in England for example, the crown's revenues alone were never sufficient to pay for war, the development of the Parliamentary system becomes a great deal easier to understand.

Though he was first among his peers, and selected by God to rule, if a King wished to make war he needed money and manpower contributions from his lords. Since the King alone had less actual power than the sum of his lords and nobles, it was necessary to summon these figures in order to press them for these resources. According to the feudal system, as a knight you owed your King military service, in return for the protection he granted to you and the legitimisation he granted to your position. The nobility were not always knights, because to be a knight meant to distinguish oneself in battle or tournament, and be knighted by the King. Once this immense honour was bestowed upon you, you became a member of a privileged brotherhood with its own rights, reputation, creed and code of chivalry to uphold.[11]

As a knight, you were expected to equip yourself for battle with the finest arms, armour and steed, which was naturally an immensely expensive process. Free knights were logically the richest knights, but knights in service to a lord or noble were also common and could be a great way for the wealthier magnates in the land to demonstrate their prowess and influence. The magnate could travel throughout the land accompanied by his knights and could display his power through demonstrations of pomp and ceremonials.

Some knights bypassed the expense of the creed by pledging their service to one who could afford to equip and house them. They served as tenants when not at war, they could also serve as the household knights of the King, and they were obliged to come running when their master called. In return they received all the honours of a knightly service, without the expense, and they were also a convenient way for the wealthier magnates of the land to raise an army quickly for the king, or even against the King if it came to that.

If said magnate had thirty knights in his service for instance, and rival magnates nearby had similar numbers, then a well-armed, battle-ready force of one hundred or so men on horseback could be mobilised and brought to bear in very quick time. Such results were invaluable, and when multiplied tenfold across the realm, one imagines the sight of the gleaming armour and proud, swaggering elite of the armed forces preparing for campaign. This contract between magnate and the knights in his service was then extended to the King. The King was the head of the feudal system, and the magnate, noble and lord was obliged to provide him with the men at his disposal. In practice things did not always work this way, but feudalism remained a paramount part of English life in the Middle Ages, as the system was perfected and sharpened with the passage of wars and the increasing demands made by kings upon their lords.

With the King's increasing needs came opportunities for the noble class in another sphere, that of education. In thirteenth century England, most knights were illiterate, but this changed ever so gradually as knights became more interested in organisation and administration for their local lord or for their king. To advance in such a society and to further the interests of the knightly brotherhood of which you were a proud member, you had to be able to read and write Latin. The best way to teach knights such valuable lessons was to establish universities and grammar schools across the country. This process was furthered with the additional needs of the government's bureaucracy and the merchant class in mind. How, the King might wonder, do we teach these people how to do their jobs more effectively? The solution appeared obvious, if expensive: We train and educate these individuals, and provide them with an education that will grant them an understanding of the French and English languages, for diplomacy and law-making as much as for later developments in art and theatre.

The improvements and availability of education to those in a position to pay for it granted fresh opportunities to the knightly and noble classes which had not existed before. It spearheaded the transformation of knights from a military caste into one equally concerned with administration, good governance and simple societal advancement. It also made the subsequent developments in musketry technology, and the reduction in the training and military qualifications of the soldier with the adoption of gunpowder weapons far easier to adapt to. If the peasantry were to fill the armies, then that was fine – the knights would organise and mobilise these armies, would arrange for the equipping and direction of these armies, and would foot the bill for their King. As we established, the traditions of feudalism meant that you were obliged to provide these peasants to your King and equip them as you had done for your knights. But since warfare depended on the harvest and the fickle whims of mother nature, it was imperative that these armies were not collected for too long a period at a time, lest the harvest would be uncollected, the productivity of the land would suffer and food shortages would result. Not to mention, as the lord of the land, your incomes would suffer significantly, and plague or banditry could accompany the evils of starvation and want.

The feudal system was eroded not by the chafing of numerous peasants and serfs at the bottom of this pyramid then, but by the advent of developments in education among the privileged classes, which drew them away from war and towards the administrative and bureaucratic positions wherein more power and influence could be amassed without risking one's life. At the same time as this transformation was underway in English society, the development of military technology had also reduced the military potency of the knight, and simultaneously provided new opportunities for the peasant, who could fire a musket with a few weeks' training, and inflict as much damage as a knight after lifetime of service. To make muskets more damaging, you needed more of them, and it just so happened that many peasants would rather serve in your armies then be resigned to the drudgery of agricultural life.

As military technology became more advanced and rendered those heavily armoured knights effectively obsolete, these knights learned that they could further their interests by working within the organs of the state, and by organising these organs in the name of the king, rather than always fighting directly for him. The availability of peasants for the army meant that by and large, the military service of the knight was no longer as important as it had once been. In addition, old feudal traditions meant that you still owed your king allegiance, but since your horse and lance were less effective instruments of war, you transferred this allegiance from the battlefield to the King's administration.[12] Rather than moving those knights in your service from point A to point B, it was now more important that you arranged hundreds, sometimes thousands of men, and that these men were equipped in time. These feats of logistics put the feudal contract under immense strain. The peasants often couldn't afford to equip and feed themselves during battle, which forced the lords to foot the bill. The King had nowhere near enough resources to pay what amounted to a series of private armies popping up across his realm, let alone to pay for and maintain a standing army. This problem became particularly acute because the employment of peasants would detract from the agricultural productivity of the land, so long as the peasant's service was required.

As the complexities of war developed and its demands became more numerous and expensive, the King had greater need of men who understood how warfare worked, and who could arrange the state's resources accordingly. These changes were accelerated by the actual needs of the Plantagenet monarchs, who pursued the Hundred Years War with France – a major departure from the intermittent conflicts waged before the fourteenth century.[13] Yet, this state was still very much bound by the old feudal system, and depended upon the wealthier and more powerful magnates contributing to it. There were many men exactly like these in the kingdom, and when the King wanted something, it was necessary for him to summon these individuals and ask for it, so that all, collectively, knew what was needed and what the King intended to do. Since the King could not organise an entire war by himself, this process provided these figures with an opportunity to bring the King's vision to fruition. The more successful he was in this task, the more royal favours would come his way after the event.

To take us back to England though, it was plain that in the fourteenth and fifteenth century the English lord was now doing more than just footing the bill, he was also taking on an immense risk, and in return, he would surely be entitled to ask for something. Maybe he wanted more influence in his lands; perhaps he desired advancement and influence for his family; it could even happen that in return for raising these forces, the lord would request that he be given command of them as they distinguished themselves in battle – like a kind of legacy of the knightly service once provided by the increasingly pacific warrior caste. Now that the knight and his sons were privileged, educated members of the nobility, it was only natural that families sought influence away from the battlefield and within society itself, leading to intrigues sometimes more deadly than those they had undertaken in war. The historian Peter Reid noted that:

> This development in education amongst the knightly class was one of the factors that gradually changed them from a military elite ready at all times to answer the call of their lord to war, to a group more interested in national and local government as a means to honour and power. For the knight the sword, while still available, was gradually replaced by the pen.[14]

Countless other demands could of course follow, but using the English case as an example, the results bore fruit which would develop in time into the parliamentary democracy and constitutional monarchy of later years. That said, there was no sudden abandonment of the old ways – since nobody was born a knight, to be knighted was, and in some respects remains, a distinction of much honour and was keenly sought after. Then as now though, it became possible to acquire a knighthood not just through battle, but also through distinguished or important service to the King. The King remained critical as a fulcrum of the state's powers, in addition to his position as a fount of patronage and honours. It was up to the King to grant titles, to sell off his land, to award those in his service with honours etc. These rewards were highly sought after, and when combined with tradition it meant that ideas of knightly service, twinned with a romantic nostalgia for the old ways, never truly vanished, even if they became far less practically important in English society and on the battlefield.

Knighthood, much like the organisation and financing of war between the fourteenth and fifteenth centuries, was a constantly changing and evolving system which lacks defining watershed moments or sudden breaks with the past. Because warfare dominated this period in English history, with the Hundred Years' War on one end, and the Wars of the Roses at the other, the English model stands out as a great illustration of how warfare fundamentally altered society, though it is by no means an exceptional case. Warfare instilled a sense of urgency, and a desire for convenience – thus even while Parliament would not be called on every occasion, the King still needed to converse with some of his closest advisors in secret, which led to the creation of privy councils. After close discussion with the Privy Council, it was then that the King's decisions were put to the council of ministers or the Parliament, which were both comprised of the most important lords and nobles of the land.

Warfare changed the contract between King and Parliament during the fourteenth and fifteenth centuries, because it became so all-consuming and eye-wateringly expensive. King Henry V may have been a conquering hero in his time, but he depended upon Parliament for the voting of taxation and men, even with his stunning victory at Agincourt. It was in 1418 that England, with a large portion of Northern France conquered and under its flag, determined that these conquered territories should pay for the occupation and financial burden of the war. However, in spite of these rulings by Parliament, by 1430 Normandy and conquered France were costing more to England than they were bringing in, and Parliament was increasingly asked to foot the bill. The King of England, like the Holy Roman Emperor, did not have enough incomes of his own to support a war in his name without financial help, and this dependence upon his lords, or in the Emperor's case, his princes, provided opportunities in both spheres for concessions, which contributed to the development of the political process.

To make a further comparison, the King was entitled to call out the feudal levy, which would have levied all those who held land direct from the crown into military service. This levy included absolutely everyone – from the knight to the magnate that happened to rent land from the King, and even those spiritual leaders who resided on the royal lands. It was from his lands that the King gained his military power, even if in the English case the King's wealth and military power was often superseded by the combined powers of all of his lords. If we look at the Holy Roman Emperor though, then the situation there was quite similar even while the results were quite different. Since the Emperor was a Habsburg, he drew power and influence from the Habsburg Hereditary Lands, and these provinces and estates formed the bulk of what would become the Austrian Empire.

By the turn of the seventeenth century, the Holy Roman Emperor, prestigious though his title was, depended on his vassals for aid. In the narrow definition of what it means to be an Emperor then, one could argue that this Holy Roman iteration did not quite fit. Ferdinand II, an important figure for our Thirty Years War narrative, could not command the obedience of the princes of the Empire based wholly on his prestigious title or their supposed loyalty, as Charlemagne had done; in addition, Ferdinand II could not rule the Empire as an absolutist monarch, as the enlightened despots of the eighteenth and nineteenth centuries could. Yet, he could rule over his own lands, the hereditary lands, as an absolutist, and demand from them what he liked. This was an important source of power for Ferdinand II as much as his predecessors and successors, but Ferdinand had to be careful not to push these lands too far. The regional assemblies rose up in revolt against him rather than accede to his demanding taxes and repressive religious policies, but so long as he weathered these storms, his lands were his business.

The King of England, on the other hand, owned lands, but could not squeeze them as the Habsburgs could. Strictly speaking, the King could call for the feudal levy and gather those men in his service together; it was more the case that these men that were gathered tended to be insufficient in equipment and training, and put in an uninspiring performance on the battlefield. As a result of these bare facts, the King was led to approve of a system in the late fourteenth century which would incorporate contracts of volunteers for a specified period. This was more reliable than the feudal system, which only summoned men to battle on the basis of their obligation, and in any case could only oblige them to stay in service for forty days at a time. It was therefore essential that volunteers be recruited to serve in the armed forces, but since the King couldn't afford these costs, that was where Parliament came in.

While on the surface this introduction of contracts may appear like the anticipation of a standing army, the reality was less straightforward. Neither the King nor his lords wished to foot the kinds of bills necessary to equip and maintain a well-trained professional force of thousands of men, and while some form of training was instituted, it was nowhere near as organised or efficient as we might expect. There was no clean break with the feudal past simply because an effort had been made to replace the less practical elements of that system. The volunteers were expected to be somewhat proficient with their weapons, but they could also expect to serve alongside what remained of the pool of knights. Serving alongside knights could be beneficial for morale and might help these recruits with the development of their skills. Knights were raised on a diet of jousting, horsemanship and swordsmanship because they had the time and money for such training. This was what had made them such valuable warriors in the first place, and they could pad out the less polished volunteers. Yet, we should note that the basis of their importance rested on their proficiency and skill with weapons – it was no longer enough, in other words, to depend on one's name value alone.

This was because times were changing. New technologies and tactics were emerging which threatened to upend everything which had been learned and valued in the previous centuries. Imagine if a new weapon emerged which enabled even the lowliest volunteer to bypass all the traditional feudal requirements and be as effective a killing machine as those gleaming knights that charged valiantly into battle. With an increasing number of educated knights removing themselves from active military service, in favour of the military bureaucracy or king's administration, and with a precedent set for a volunteer army based on contract and necessitating the approval of Parliament, there was ample room for a significant new development to push the military organisation of the state further into the modern era. When muskets had first appeared on battlefields in the 1410s, there was little indication that this unwieldy, dangerous, noisy and expensive implement would become the most important weapon of war. More than that, muskets and their descendants would engender something more than innovation and discovery – they would help bridge the gap from one era to the other, from the Middle Ages to Early Modern Europe, as the feudal system and its traditions, assumptions and lessons would be upended by the Military Revolution.

TWO

The English World-Beater: From Longbows to Muskets

In 1545, a noted humanist and scholar Roger Ascham wrote *Toxophilus* or 'Lover of the Bow', wherein a proponent of the longbow argued about its benefits to a sceptic.[15] For the sake of English national defence, and for personal development, the longbow was essential, yet Ascham was concerned that, in the mid-sixteenth century, the use and practice of the longbow was in a steep decline. He was far from the only person to think so. Nearly two hundred years before, in 1363, the first of what would prove to be a succession of ordnances were issued, which commanded that on their day of rest or rare holidays, Englishmen should not engage in such wasteful pursuits as football, dice or tennis, but instead they should practice their archery skills. In the mid-fifteenth century, English political writers were writing that 'by law, every man should be compelled' to hone their skills in archery from an early age and should never relinquish these skills for any reason. National defence, it was said, depended upon a pool of men proficient in the longbow. The appropriately named Steven Gunn wrote on the widespread idea of the longbow in English society during the fifteenth and sixteenth centuries, saying:

> Henry VII and Henry VIII defended the longbow with statutes banning the possession of crossbows and handguns by the lower orders; they promoted it with further statutes ordering every householder to keep bows, not only for himself, but for his servants and children, and commanding every adult and adolescent male to use them.[16]

Henry VIII, ruling as he did between 1509-47 when technological innovation was gathering speed, was keenly aware of the threat posed by a reduction in longbow proficiency. It was immensely difficult for Henry, or any one of his peers, to imagine that Englishmen could be equally proficient in any other weapon, or that any other weapon – be it a crossbow or the rudimentary arquebus – would replace the longbow as the symbol of English medieval military superiority. And what a superiority it had been.

From the beginning of the fourteenth to the end of the fifteenth century, English arms were supreme in the British Isles and in France. Conflicts against the Scottish, and in particular against the French during the Hundred Years' War,[17] sharpened the sword of England and enabled her martial Kings such as Edward I but above all Edward III to cement not only the centralised power of the English crown in comparison to its fragmenting French opponent, but also the status of England as a kingdom of tactical genius and innovation.[18] The key to this success did not rest upon the longbow alone, but this formidable weapon certainly rooted itself in the tales of many key victories against the French; especially in the battles of Crecy, Poitiers and Agincourt. Before long, the longbow became something more than a weapon, it became a national symbol.[19]

We are confronted then with two major questions; why did the English decide to swap their longbows for muskets, and why did it take them so long to make this trade off if the new musket was so much more effective? These questions must be answered by looking at the bare facts of the matter – how effective each weapon was at doing damage to an opponent. In his book on the English supremacy at arms in the fourteenth and fifteenth centuries, historian Peter Reid gives us a particularly grim account of a battlefield in the mid-fourteenth century when he writes:

> To be on the winning side certainly led to great profit, but to be the losers generally meant loss of life or horrific wounds: axes, swords, glaives, halberds and pole-axes could all sever limbs, cleave the skull or behead a man. Arrows from the longbow and bolts from the crossbow could penetrate all but the very best plate armour; indeed, arrows were known to penetrate the mail on a knight's thigh, go through the saddle and kill the horse underneath. Primitive handguns, when they appeared, were quite capable of penetrating the best of armours. Many severely wounded men or those who missed their footing would simply fail to get up again because of the press of bodies from others on top of them.

This is certainly a hellish scene, but Reid wasn't quite finished as he noted what the aftermath would have looked like for those involved:

> At the end of a fight a battlefield would be littered with the dead and the dying. The screams and groans of the wounded added to the frenzied shouts of those still fighting, but the cries of the wounded continued long after the battle was done. What happened to them? If discipline in the victorious army was good the first to search the dead and the wounded would be heralds of both sides to identify fallen knights by their surcoats or badges. If the wounded man was a particularly prominent person, he might receive the last sacrament from a priest...Badly wounded men at arms, archers, crossbowmen and billmen were simply despatched with neither ceremony nor mercy. Indeed, as no facilities

existed to cope with them on the scale that might be needed after a pitched battle, and as resuscitation was so primitive and uncertain, probably the most merciful course was to despatch them as swiftly as possible. All of these would be buried in communal burial pits but not before they had been stripped.[20]

Fearsome though this sounds, it would be wrong at the same time to assume that every longbow arrow fared so well against every knight's armour. Chainmail - mail armour which utilised small interlocking rings to block pointed weapons - had repeatedly been proven faulty. Yet, when an arrow fired from an English longbow faced heavier armour, what chance did it have to inflict satisfactory damage, especially when compared to the arquebus or hackbut, as the English called these rudimentary firearms? Thankfully for the sake of scholars and enthusiastic re-enactors everywhere, an accurate study of such a question was made much easier when Henry VIII's vessel *Mary Rose*, which sank off Portsmouth in 1545 and brought down many longbows with it, was discovered and its contents carefully extracted in 1982 by the Mary Rose Trust. Thanks to this extensive work, we have been given an invaluable set of Yew longbows to work with, and many historians since have sought to measure the stopping power of these weapons, with results that may surprise the reader.

By applying a weight of seventy pounds draw on precise replicas made of these bows, we can accurately deduce the average stopping power of an archer in Henry VIII's service in the early to mid-sixteenth century. With this baseline achieved, it was noted that the range of a longbow at this time was between one hundred and fifty and two hundred metres, which was an impressive distance, and roughly akin to the distance which the arquebus and muskets could reach at the same period. When we look closer though, we are greeted with a surprising statistic. The arrows which were fired consistently failed to penetrate three millimetres of plate armour, which was the thickness of a good breast plate or helmet, and which represented the body parts which the longbow man was most likely to target. At ten metres, longbows could not penetrate 3 millimetres of armour, and while they would certainly have winded their target, and could even have knocked him over in some cases with the force of impact, the knight would suffer little more than bruising in almost every case.

If we reduce the armour to two millimetres, then the story changes, but arrows were still only capable of achieving minimal penetration, and not enough even then to inflict a serious wound. At one millimetre in thickness, the damage inflicted increases, as does the effective damage which could be done at a certain range. Overall though, this test demonstrated that longbows were most effective at shorter ranger and against less well armoured targets – obvious facts for sure, but ones which deserve repeating if we are to explain why the longbow was beginning to decline significantly in importance. 'Many disabling wounds and few fatalities' were how the test results were summarised. At the 1513 Battle of Flodden, heavily armoured Scottish pikemen were able to withstand a great deal of the English longbow fire, and even while predictably horrific wounds were inflicted, the kind of destruction inflicted by the weapon one hundred years before at Agincourt was not repeated, nor would it ever be repeated in the same way, so long as the thickness and availability of armour continued to increase in response to the threat which the longbow posed.

In comparison, muskets dating from the 1570s were capable of consistently penetrating armour between two and four millimetres thick at one hundred metres, but it was at fifty metres or less that the damage inflicted by a musket ball became so horrific and significant. Yet, as with the longbow, we would be wise not to generalise too much or present the question as one of straightforward superiority. It depended very much on the musket in question, as well as the skill of the archer, and since neither quality was consistent, we should not take too many great leaps forward in concluding the superiority of one over the other. On a given day, in the first half of the sixteenth century, English longbowmen were more than capable of meeting the challenge posed by muskets. With a minimum fire rate of ten arrows a minute, through the sheer weight of their projectiles, the English archer was greatly feared for the weight of fire he could pour down in comparison to the cumbersome one-shot-per-minute firearm.[21]

Should we be surprised that Henry VIII was very much going against the grain, and apparently the natural progress of technology, by arguing against the obsolescence of the longbow? Sir Charles Oman's vaunted tome, *A History of the Art of War in the Sixteenth Century* was critical of the English for holding onto the 'distinctly obsolescent' longbow throughout the sixteenth century, and much emphasis within Oman's work was placed upon the transformative power of that war-winning weapon, while the English shot themselves in the foot for not adapting firearms earlier.[22] As Dr Gervase Philips noted though, the question of why one state adopts a weapon and another does not is never as simple a case as backwardness or ignorance or a refusal to modernise:

> Military historians have been particularly prone to making such judgements, relying heavily on the concept of "war-winning weapons" as a causal factor in battlefield success. Less attention has been paid to the complex interplay of factors beyond technical performance that have governed the choices surrounding the adoption of particular weapons. A people's chosen tools of war can be a manifestation of economic, political, cultural, and social circumstances, circumstances that defy the simple logic of a new technology displacing an old one. The relationship between the longbow and gunpowder small arms provides an instructive case study in factors relating to technological choice. This is true for military historians in particular, but

the case has implications for all those interested in the remarkable persistence with which past societies have clung to "distinctly obsolescent" tools even after more "sophisticated" technologies had become available. The complexity of the factors relating to the slow replacement of the bow by gunpowder small arms puts at issue any overarching theory of single factor dominance. The transition was chaotic in nature, and incidental changes in surrounding social and political circumstances could have led to a quite different pattern in technology transfer.[23]

The English are an interesting case precisely because of their attachment to the longbow –no other power in Europe was so associated with the use and expertise in the longbow. Furthermore, the practice of fighting and, for that matter, drilling, with the longbow, had been identified by one historian as a major contributing factor towards the development of the musket drills which we will examine later in this section.[24] In comparison to their neighbours, the English were slow to adopt the musket, but their refinement of longbow tactics and the drill to go along with it made a significant contribution to the practice of later gunpowder drills, which borrowed heavily from the earlier English example. To make the best use out of firearms and to emphasise their strengths as projectile weapons, early practitioners of musket volley fire looked to English longbowmen for inspiration.

If it is generally accepted that in the second half of the sixteenth century, the musket began to provide greater advantages in stopping power and range to the longbow, especially as the smaller arquebuses were accompanied by the heavier muskets, then it must also be reiterated that longbows continued to possess one key advantage – their unbeatable rate of fire. Again though, we could ask why it even mattered that more arrows were up in the air, if most of these arrows failed to penetrate the majority of the enemy armour. The answer to this is that not all English longbowmen expected to hit and kill, or even wound, their target. One of their major aims – aside from these obviously sought-after goals – was to disrupt and eventually break the enemy's formation through the sheer volume of dangerous projectiles that were landing around, upon them or within their ranks. The formation of pikes or swordsmen would feel so besieged and beleaguered under this torrent of arrows that they would consistently break ranks in an attempt to better defend their individual persons or attack the source of the arrows, an eventuality for which English arms were always well-prepared. It is not difficult to see the logic of this tactic – it was the equivalent to the later practice of battering the enemy formations with artillery, because even if these shots were far less damaging, the psychological impact was the same.

If one unit in an enemy's army could be consistently targeted and worn down to the point that it charged, then piece by piece, an enemy army could, in such a way, be picked apart. Of course, the enemy was wise to such tactics, and brought up its own archers, crossbowmen or arquebusiers forward to deal with the tactic, not to mention the fact that efforts were made to keep the army out of range of the longbowmen in the first place. Yet, still, from at least the mid-thirteenth century this tactic was an English favourite, and its successful deployment even as late as the 1513 Battle of the Spurs against the French demonstrated not just its staying power, but also the staying power of that tactic's critical component – the longbow.

Such a tactic would have been impossible with muskets, unless of course the firing tactics of muskets were so sufficiently organised that a constant wall of lead would be consistently poured down. Europe would have to wait until the turn of the seventeenth century for such a revolution in firearms tactics to come about, but for now, since a swapping of the bow for the musket meant a removal of this tactic from the English repertoire and a rethinking of their strategy on the battlefield, there was much more at stake than the mere swapping of one weapon for another. In addition, arquebuses could be effectively twinned with the longbow's strengths to graft greater stopping power and range onto English armies, and it wasn't just the English that maintained this tactic. The Venetians, interestingly enough, clung to the use of archers on their Mediterranean warships well into the 1600s, demonstrating that the longbow retained its admirers and its uses.[25]

In the 1590s, a pamphlet war of sorts erupted in Elizabethan England, just as England waged war against the Spanish and Irish in two distinct theatres.[26] Some Englishmen, having served with the Dutch in the Low Countries, maintained that the so-called 'new style' of pike and musket was vastly superior to the old ways of the bow and bill-man, and chalked the incorrect reverence for the longbow at this late stage in the game down to the fact that England had been at peace from the late 1540s to the early 1580s, during which time her military professionalism and theorising had steeply declined. Rather than test out new ideas on the battlefield, old English codgers with their longbows were content to cling to the obsolete ideas of yore, only to receive a short sharp shock when they met the vaunted Spanish infantry in battle during the Dutch War of Independence.

Much like the Thirty Years War would do for European military thought and experimentation, the Eighty Years War provided several opportunities for military theories to be tested and accepted over its long duration. We will see later in this section of the book how Maurice of Nassau, the Dutch leader, revolutionised the use of the musket when, in the 1590s, he and his peers adopted a new means for using the firearm drills in battle. The idea of fire by rank, where one musketeer would fire before engaging in the counter-march to the back of his unit's line, was one pioneered and heavily invested in by the Dutch, to be adopted and perfected by the French, Swedes and English in equal measure.

That the Dutch were arguing about new model musket drills at the same time as the English were arguing about the use of the longbow can seem on paper like a striking gap in military advancement between the two states. However, one theme which will become clear during this miniseries is that idea that the Military Revolution reached every European power at different times and affected its military practices in different ways. Thus, the musket, and its smaller less powerful cousin the arquebus, were hard sells to the English in the first half of the sixteenth century, because they had the rapid fire, cheaper longbow already in circulation, not to mention the tactics to match it.

In addition, it is sometimes said that King Henry VIII feared giving firearms to the disaffected classes, and thus held back with bringing these weapons in on a wide scale. This idea does hold water, but it is also the case that the arrival of a weapon as different as the musket and its spread throughout English society required everyone to overcome old prejudices they may have held about the weapon and its danger to traditional English values. New treatises would have to be issued instructing the English citizen where it was acceptable to brandish and fire such weapons. One such ruling in 1540 limited the use of firearms and chided musketeers for discharging their weapons...

> ...in cities, boroughs and towns, and other unmet places, without having any regard or respect where their pellets do fall... whereby sundry his grace's officers and subjects, being in the high way, in the open street, or in their own houses, chambers or gardens, have been put in great jeopardy of their lives.[27]

In a sense, during the sixteenth century there was a clash between the old values and ideas of Englishness, centred on the longbow, and the increasingly prevalent firearm within English society. Henry VIII's opposition to firearms was based on the idea that criminals would carry them and endanger the unsuspecting populace, while any increase in favour towards firearms would reduce the favour shown towards the longbow. There was no sense in Henry's time that the longbow falling out of favour was somehow part of the natural order of things or of military progress, even while proponents of the new technology, especially later in the sixteenth century, were far from silent.

It would take a long time for the English to essentially forget everything they had learned about love and respect for the longbow. We cannot underestimate either the impact which old legendary tales of victorious English kings, accompanied by longbowmen, had on the English psyche. These were tales which Henry VIII himself was raised on, and the tenacity, skill and bravery of the longbowman formed a great deal of these stories' most appealing parts. How much less heroic or impressive would King Henry V had seemed if he had simply shot his French foe to pieces with superior or equal numbers at Agincourt? It is easy to imagine longbow enthusiasts reminiscing for those better times of the early fifteenth century, back when there was no concept of firearms challenging the longbow, if they appeared on the battlefield at all. Back then, romanticists would muse, Englishmen were real men, they engaged in real wars and they made use of real weapons. By contrast, England's military record was strikingly poor in the seventeenth century, with the exception of Cromwell's triumphs in the 1640s, England's military record was strikingly poor in the seventeenth century.[28]

There is good reason to suspect, in the estimations of the historian Roger B. Manning, that nostalgia for the longbow and suspicion towards the arquebus were both deeply ingrained within English society, and that may have resulted in a delay of the modernisation of an English military bureaucracy such as that seen in France, Spain or the Netherlands during the seventeenth century. As Manning noted, the history and traditions of English feudal and chivalric society did not gel well with the new demands placed upon soldiers in the changing theatres of war:

> The persistence of older values among swordsmen and gallants who disliked missile weapons and clung to the use of edged weapons such as the sword and the pike, and who engaged in individual displays of honour through duelling, challenges to individual combats on the battlefield, and other histrionics, hampered the reception of the technological innovations associated with the Military Revolution and the pursuit of military and political objectives dictated by the needs of state, and often substituted the pursuit of individual honour and glory. This was an assertion that social hierarchies remained more important than military hierarchies in positions of military command and had the effect of delaying the professionalization of the officer classes of the armies of the Three Kingdoms.[29]

That change in society we examined above, where the knights became more concerned with work in the administration rather than in the armies; where firearms replaced the traditional weapons which demanded a lifetime of training and where professional armies replaced the feudal conscript levies, were all very gradual processes in English history, and there was no clear cut moment when the state had an epiphany and did away with the old measures in favour of the new. There seemed a degree of blowback in England against the idea that aristocracy no longer mattered in battle, and that skill mattered more. This can surely be twinned with the overall English tardiness in accepting firearms, since muskets increased equality, whereas knights on horseback, revered longbows and lowly bill-men implied a certain sense of aristocratic, societal hierarchy within even the smallest army that contained these elements.

Indeed, it should be noted that the English clashed badly with their Dutch allies during the early phases of their intervention in the Eighty Years

War. A reason for this came from the English preference for social status over actual merit or skill or even experience, and this caused predictable friction with the Dutch, who were fighting for their lives, not for concepts as vague and ill-defined as chivalry or honour. Even while the Dutch officer corps demonstrated a distinct number of unique skills when dealing with the challenges posed by the new design in fortifications, the trace italienne, for example, the English officers or commanders within their army maintained their distaste for anything other than charging in, lance brandished, while on horseback. That, it was said, was the honourable and determinedly English method, and when accompanied by the longbow there was no better way to make war. Indeed, during Henry VIII's wars such ideas were not as seriously challenged as we might expect, and it becomes easy to understand why English commanders arrived in the Low Countries ready to adopt tactics from 150 years before – many of those that arrived to aid the Dutch had been fed and watered on a diet of books and legends written at that time.[30]

As we alluded to earlier, the pamphlet war between proponents of the musket and the longbow was waged in the 1590s, but the surviving fragments of this struggle provide us with a fascinating window into what Englishmen at this time actually thought of the new and old weaponry. In the mind of John Smythe, whose book *Certain Discourses concerning the Forms and Effects of Diverse Sorts of Weapons* appeared in 1590, it was up to him to argue in favour of the longbow and defend it against the negative press it had recently attracted. Smythe rallied against the praise of the musket and emphasised its dangers and shortcomings – while it was capable of firing up to four hundred yards, this distance rarely brought about any successes. In addition, after a few shots, the weapon was often so hot that the powder could be ignited as soon as it was placed in the musket, causing all sorts of chaos for musketeers as weapons exploded and sometimes shattered into small, lethal pieces apparently at random. Smythe was particularly drawn to the pro-musket side's argument that weather seriously hampered the longbowmen in their craft, whereas it was much easier to keep powder dry. He wrote:

> If in the time of any battle, great encounter, or skirmish, the weather does happen to rain, hail, or snow, the aforementioned weapons of fire can work no effect, because the same does not only wet the powder in their pans and touch holes, but also does wet the match, put out, or at least damp the fire, or does mar the powder in their flasks and touch-boxes…Whereas contrary wise, neither hail, rain, nor snow, can let or hinder the archers from shooting, and working great effects with their arrows.[31]

Yet, while one could find several more sources in support of the longbow, the central points would remain true. Longbows were effective at breaking up formations, they could inflict terrible wounds on an enemy, they could stop a cavalry charge, they were cheaper to maintain and easier to produce, and they were part and parcel of what made England's military prowess so renowned. But even if all these aspects of the longbow are held to be true, then it also follows that a longbow was only as good as the man holding the bow. The arrow would only fly and penetrate as forcefully as the longbow man in question pulled back on his weapon, and he would only be capable of a sufficient draw distance if he was well used to the bow's demanding training regimen.

Thus, we come to an inescapable fact which greets us throughout the sixteenth century. During this period, English proficiency with the longbow declined considerably, because the quality of training declined also, as the historian Thomas Esper recorded in his article examining the replacement of the longbow by firearms in the English army. Esper wrote that: 'Archers as a whole were more poorly trained in the sixteenth century, and especially at the end of it, than they were in preceding centuries; consequently the efficiency of an army of bowmen was reduced.'[32] If a decline in training led to a reduction in the efficiency of the longbow, just at the time that firearms were beginning to become more prevalent and sophisticated, then the question remains – why did training in the longbow decline in the sixteenth century, to the point that longbows were abandoned altogether by the English in 1595? This is what we have now to find out.

The first element of this change in the English way of making war can be explained in the circumstances which greeted those longbowmen when they attempted to take part in England's intervention in the Dutch War of Independence. Since the Eighty Years War consisted mostly of sieges, it followed that weapons suitable for siege warfare would be preferred, and it quickly became apparent that bows were immensely difficult to fire adequately behind the parapet, particularly in comparison to firearms. The English introduction to the revolution in siege engineering, a theme which we will examine later, told them that bows were of little use in these encounters, and that because of the bow's uselessness, Spanish and Dutchman alike had long since adopted the musket for all their encounters.

Yet, it also had to be said that even before the English intervention in the Eighty Years War in 1585, the preceding years had told a story of a gradually declining pool of available archers, from one in three to one in four between 1522-1557. At the same time as this decline was occurring, English armies were making use of muskets within their bands of archers to bring the best of both worlds to bear against their enemies. It was impossible to insulate English armies completely from the creeping pervasiveness of the musket, even while they were slow to adopt it wholeheartedly.[33]

To present the second reason for this decline in the longbow and its replacement by the musket at the end of the sixteenth century, it is worthwhile returning to a point about the available pool of archers being significantly reduced. The reason for this pool reducing was down to a fundamental change in English society. Put simply, the English swapped their favourite sport – archery – for other pastimes and suffered a reduction in longbow proficiency as a result. This was in fact observed by contemporaries at the time of the decline, one of whom opined:

> In my time my poor father was as diligent to teach me to shoot, as to learn me any other thing; and so I think other men did their children: he taught me how to draw, how to lay my body in my bow, and not to draw from strength of the body: I had my bows bought me, according to my age and strength; as I increased in them, so my bows were made bigger and bigger; for men shall never shoot well, except they be brought up in it...But now, we have taken up whoring in towns, instead of shooting in fields.[34]

These were the words of Hugh Latimer, written in 1549, when reminiscing about the decay in English proficiency with the longbow. Latimer may be better known in English history for his martyrdom under 'Bloody' Queen Mary I [r. 1553-1558], but as a renowned man of the Church, his memories of being raised in the longbow are a striking reminder of the prevalence of that weapon not just in the battlefield. It was a way of life, an *English* way of life, but without much great effort being made to deliberately destroy it, this way of life was decaying. Such a decay did not necessarily mean that longbows became less important as a weapon of war – what it did mean was that, as a pastime, practicing the longbow had been usurped by other, arguably more enjoyable and less taxing hobbies like playing dice, or football or other such sports.

If Englishmen had less time to train with the longbow, and if the immediate danger brought on by the sense of constant warfare was subsiding now that the Hundred Years War had long since passed, then it was inevitable that the English should become less proficient overall with the weapon which had once made them famous. When this occurred, it was logical that a replacement should be selected even considering that replacement's clear disadvantages. When we consider that most armies created during the Elizabethan era were formed by conscripting the peasantry into an army and shipping it overseas, it is perhaps not surprising that the old expectations of longbow proficiency were completely lost on this untrained and unenthused peasant stock. These peasants hadn't been raised on a diet of longbow practice, they had been raised on a diet of idle and unlawful games, and thus as longbowmen they were inherently less useful on the battlefield than men from the same class that carried muskets, who could at least be relied upon to fire a consistent weapon a few times. Undertrained peasants suffered from a lack of practice and were mostly unable to pull back the bow in the same way as their ancestors had done one hundred, or even fifty years before by the end of the century.

Thus, the originally impressive stopping power of the longbow was lost, and the weapon itself lost a great deal of its status on the battlefield. If these peasants would not train in their spare time, then it made sense to equip them with a weapon which would bypass these difficulties, and get the job done on the day when it mattered. Of course, this sensible deduction from the problems posed by chronically untrained men were not wholly accepted or acceptable, as we've seen. In the words of one 1591 observation issued by Elizabeth's Privy Council:

> Her Majesty is informed that diverse unlawful games are daily used in most places of this realm and that thereby archery is greatly decayed and in a manner altogether laid aside, being an exercise not only of good recreation but otherwise of good use and defence to the realm, and that in all ages in this land has been specially used, and by laws and statutes necessarily provided for. Wherein though at this time, considering the great charge the subjects do sustain in furnishing themselves with muskets, arquebuses and other weapons both of defence and offense that are now more in use, it should seem a hard course to lay that burden on them which the law in this case does strictly impose, nevertheless her Majesty for very good considerations thinks meet and accordingly has willed us to require you in her name forthwith to take special care that such kinds of exercises, games and pastimes as are prohibited by law, namely bowls, dicing, carding and such like, may be forthwith forbidden... but that instead thereof archery may be revived and practised and that kind of ancient weapon whereby our nation in times past has gotten so great honour may be kept in use, and such poor men whose stay of living with their whole families do chiefly depend thereon, as bowyers, fletchers, stringers, arrowhead makers, being many in number throughout the realm, may be maintained and set on work according to their vocations, and her Majesty's said gracious intent and meaning thereby duly executed.[35]

To summarise then; muskets and other firearms were less than superior to the stopping power, accuracy and rate of fire of a well-trained longbowman, such as had been seen during the glory days of that weapon in the late fourteenth to early fifteenth centuries. Archery was the national sport of England at that time, and this inculcated a degree of respect and reverence for the weapon. If this favourite sport had not been replaced by another, if English society had not become distracted by less martial pastimes, and if England had been involved in more wars in the meantime, which made such consistent practice and proficiency essential, then it is entirely possible that England would not have given up the longbow for the musket, as her European neighbours had done more than a century before.[36] Indeed, for this to have happened, England would have to have continued on as a martial society – like a Spartan centre of longbow training, and it is questionable whether it would have been possible at any stage in English history to police the people to such an extent that the King controlled how the people spent their free time, their Sundays or their holidays.

Still though, the English example of the longbow is deeply fascinating, and the very late adoption, initially unsuccessfully, of the musket and its associated lessons, underlines another key theme in this section of the book. Namely, that in every state where the Military Revolution spread, it landed in each state, influenced its military thinkers, and made its practical influence felt on the battlefield very differently. The story of military technology and its advancement through early modern Europe was thus not one of a straightforward formula involving prowess, expertise and progress, but of idiosyncratic advancement and of the occasionally costly struggle between apparently obvious technological progressions, hampered by equally insurmountable societal traditions and assumptions. England, just like every other state in early modern Europe, brought its own baggage to the table, and had to adapt and evolve according to the laws which this baggage set down. As a window into warfare in the early modern era, the English swapping of the longbow for the musket provides us with an important blueprint for the rest of Europe. It is now time to address the question: what is the Military Revolution?

THREE
The Military Revolution – A Necessary Theory

Michael Roberts was the historian officially responsible for presenting the Military Revolution idea in 1957, and over the following years, another historian of great esteem – Geoffrey Parker – sought to sharpen the theory. In an article assessing whether or not the Military Revolution is a myth, for instance, Parker assesses the accuracy of the theory by listing the major developments on the battlefield which led to so many other progressions. This article, written in 1976, serves as an effective summary of the Military Revolution debate up to that point, and we will draw on this article heavily in this section of the book. Parker writes:

> First and foremost, came a 'revolution in tactics': certain tactical innovations, although apparently minor, were "the efficient cause of changes which were really revolutionary." The principal innovation in the infantry was…the eclipse of the prevailing technique of hurling enormous squares of pikemen at each other in favour of linear formations composed of smaller, uniform units firing salvos at each other; likewise the cavalry, instead of trotting up to the enemy, firing, and trotting back again (the caracole), was required to charge, sabres in hand, ready for the kill.[37]

If men were to be taught to stand and fire into one another without breaking under the terrible strain, and if cavalry were to be instructed on the best ways to charge into their enemy, then they would all have to be trained. Not just training, but the drill in each of these arms of the army would have to be updated and perfected. Similarly, cavalry, while undoubtedly more dashing, operated to a strict code that stated when to charge, who to charge at, what to avoid and when to regroup. On regular occasions, these two arms of the army marched together as one and trained as one unit, so that all men assembled could appreciate the importance of working in tandem, and so that they could see what they could achieve when they were all on the same page, as only the drill enabled them to be. Soldiers were of course trained in the late middle ages, but with the advent of these new drills the bar of professionalism was raised notably higher.

Comparisons between old and new styles of making war deserve mention. To take the familiar English case, armies tended to be comprised of some highly skilled, highly armoured knights, highly trained archers and then the melee infantry – such as bill-men, pike/spearmen or swordsmen. The end result was not a rabble, but it was far from coherent, and could often break down, leaving elements of the system vulnerable. The reason for this degeneration would be the lack of opportunities to train together – these men were not soldiers by trade, they were peasants, or small landowners or noble knights in English society. The importance of their weapons on the battlefield reflected their status in society, and this was largely because soldiers in the late Middle Ages were expected to equip themselves for war, as neither the king nor his nobles individually had the power to pay for a whole army with all of its component parts, not to mention supply the food for the horses, gunpowder for the cannons and rations for the men.

We have seen that knights in England became less important on the battlefield, as they shed their armour for a post in the king's growing administration, or to enrich themselves in burgeoning trades or enterprises. As the knights were extricating themselves from military service, they left behind one of the qualities which made them a warrior caste. They were replaced by men hired on military contracts, on terms quite unlike the feudal contract of obligation which had previously characterised the wars fought by Englishmen. The reason for better contracts was that the feudal system simply did not allow English kings to wrest the necessary commitment from their men that they required. More than that, even while the King was head of the feudal system, he could not compel any of his nobles to commit themselves and their men by a threat of force – he needed something more reliable if wars were to be fought properly.

In the view of Michael Roberts, not only was the Military Revolution thus the ultimate death knell in the coffin of the feudal system, it was also the beginning of something new – those mercenaries and men on military contracts gradually merged into the kinds of armed forces which could commonly be seen by the seventeenth century. According to Roberts' Military Revolution idea indeed, before such innovations took place, (in other words, before 1560) one could find only stagnant, obsolete ideas and ineffectual commanders. We will assess the accuracy of such an assertion later, but for now it suffices to make an important point about how these innovations were even able to take place. Such changes in how battles were arranged and fought can be explained by the weaponization of one substance above all – gunpowder. Without this substance and the weaponization of it, the Military Revolution as Michael Roberts imagined it would not have been possible.

The musket, once an unwieldy weapon, dangerous to its user, became the most important arm of the armed forces, and granted killing power on a new scale to all men in the army – from the average peasant to the richest lord. Since the drill required months upon months of training to inculcate the necessary behaviours and principles into these unthinking unflinching killing machines, it was no longer possible for them to return home, and it was certainly not possible for these men to uproot themselves for war while still providing for their families. Thus, the importance of the drill, adopted thanks to the supremacy of the musket, led to these armies not going home, and becoming instead a paid, permanent force. The standing army was born.

Clearly, this is a summarised version of the change in the military contract; changes which were fundamental to shaping the European relationship with war over 1560-1660. Later in this section, we will be focusing on these changes, how they were felt across Europe, and what implications they had on the ground for that government and its ruler. As we will learn, such changes did not occur all at once, and they were experienced differently and unevenly throughout Europe. For now, though, it is helpful to speak in broader terms to get our points across. Aside from the adoption of the musket drills and the resulting professionalization of armed forces, another aspect, that of improved military strategy, also characterised the Military Revolution. Geoffrey Parker addresses this aspect of theory as he writes:

> With the new soldiers, it proved possible to attempt more ambitious strategies: to campaign with several armies simultaneously and to seek decisive battles without fear that the inexperienced troops would run away in terror. Gustavus Adolphus of Sweden, victor of the Breitenfeld and conqueror of Germany, certainly put these new strategic concepts into effect; according to [Michael] Roberts, he was the first.[38]

As we will discover, it is a bit simplistic and perhaps unfair to credit the likes of Gustavus Adolphus with inventing the search for decisive battles and relying on the experience of his troops as he did so. Yet, it should be said that from at least the late sixteenth century, commanders were more flexible because their soldiery tended to be more reliable. Soldiers would move and act as a battalion or regiment, and they could be expected to depend on one another and, above all, to remember their training. The drill would see many men through the most terrible and trying campaigns, largely by making them focus only on what they had been taught to regurgitate when the times got tough. *Without* this level of training, the kinds of horrific wounds which only mass musket volleys could inflict would never have been survivable.

Forbearance is the technical term for the morale and fortitude of the men, and it could be taught through the drill as much as it could be inspired by a daring, personable commander whom the men would willingly fight for, especially if he had led them to victory before and promised them another chance of enrichment. The expertise of certain commanders like Count Tilly, Gustavus Adolphus and Wallenstein etc. definitely helped to improve the morale of the men, and thus their ability to withstand the horrors of war better than their rivals. And forbearance was an increasingly important element of warfare; to the extent that King Louis XIV of France even weighed in personally on the issue, noting that: 'good order makes us look assured, and it seems enough to look brave, because most often our enemies do not wait for us to approach near enough for us to have to show if we are in fact brave.' This was followed up by Marshal Catinat, one of Louis' most accomplished Marshals, who noted that 'one prepares the soldier to not fire, and to realise that it is necessary to suffer the enemy's fire, expecting that the enemy who fires is assuredly beaten when one receives his entire discharge.' Or, as the historians Williamson Murray and McGregor Knox put it in their book on the *Dynamics of Military Revolution*:

> For seventeenth century generals and military thinkers battle – and infantry combat in particular – had become a test of wills. Victory went to the force that absorbed the worst that the enemy could inflict and still maintained order, rather than the force that inflicted the greatest physical casualties on the other side…The emphasis on taking losses stoically was far from the primitive warrior ethos that commanded headlong attack. The surprising truth is that Seventeenth Century Europe developed a battle culture based less upon fury than upon forbearance.[39]

The increased importance of forbearance was a by-product of the Military Revolution and remained a vital aspect of the drill during the seventeenth century. Although certainly, the central role which bravery or morale played in warfare was by no means a new epiphany, the demands which the new style of warfare placed upon one's psyche were different. With the increased potency of gunpowder arms, standing and enduring the volleys of musket fire replaced the old practice of withstanding the cavalry or pike charge, though these latter tactics did not entirely vanish. The sight of men grinning and bearing the terrible casualties and horrific wounds must have been something to behold, but without constant and consistent training under a reliable commander such qualities of stoicism could never be inculcated in the soldiery. Thus, constant training in the drill was not enough – commanders had to be prepared to innovate and improve upon the accepted drill and tactics, particularly if their counterpart on the battlefield was doing the same. This explains the growth in popularity of war academies, and schools dedicated to understanding and overcoming the perils and challenges of war, to raising responsible and skilled commanders tasked with leading the nation to said war, and by applying a layer of finesse to the whole bloody business. Already in the beginning of the seventeenth century, a familiar practice recognisable in the modern era – that of exchanging military advisors to instruct different states on the latest innovations in tactics and the drill – was becoming more common.[40] From these new ideas came additional theories and schools of thought – what laws of war should be adopted and could a kind of code of laws be implemented during wartime to protect the citizen? This led in turn to new investigations in literature on warfare, new schools of thought and new debates over the following centuries.

If it follows that professional armies required the state to foot the bill for them, or for the state to pay others who would organise these soldiers and foot the bill, then it also follows that military organisation by default would have to improve. The military industrial complex was not quite born, since creating and paying for armies remained immensely expensive, yet the continual, pressing need for armies to fight new wars forced Europeans to challenge themselves and improve how these armies were organised, which led to innovation and a streamlining of the state's bureaucracy to deal with war.

Ministers of war, or defence as they are known today, would be charged with the task of coordinating all the relevant pieces of the puzzle together so that the military machine could work. As a result of this attention, the military machines got a great deal bigger, and an arms race of military machines developed, leading to a dramatic ballooning in the size of armies over the seventeenth century, and all the resulting negative impact this would have on the citizenry, as Parker notes:

> A third component of the Military Revolution theory was a "prodigious increase in the scale of warfare in Europe" between 1560 and 1660. The new strategy, Roberts pointed out, required far more troops for its successful execution: an articulated force of five armies operating simultaneously according to a complex plan would need to be vastly more numerous than a single army under the old order. Fourth and finally, this prodigious numerical increase dramatically accentuated the impact of war on society. The greater destructive- ness, the greater economic costs, and the greater administrative challenge of the augmented armies made war more of a burden and more of a problem for the civilian population and their rulers than ever before.[41]

Countless offshoots of these developments of course followed, but as Parker observed, the original version of the Military Revolution theory put it that 'the four essential ingredients of the theory were tactics, strategy, army size, and overall impact.' It should be reiterated that the Military Revolution theory put forward by Michael Roberts was far from perfect, and while it was a convenient tool for grouping the important developments of European warfare into a one hundred year bundle between 1560-1660, Geoffrey Parker does not take long to find some flaws with this theory, starting with the actual timeline itself.

Parker insists 1560 was not the year that change came suddenly and swiftly to the battlefield and the administration. These changes did of course come, but the theory verges on simplistic through its focus on this wave of change between 1560-1660. In line with this, Parker makes an important point when he takes the starting date of 1560 apart. It was in Renaissance Italy that the kinds of revolutionary change in how armies operated had already taken place, and all this in the thirteenth, fourteenth and fifteenth centuries – not merely in the 1560s. Italian states, confined to such small spaces and competing for such scant resources, engaged on a war on a relatively small scale, but with big, impressive innovations in the gunpowder and military administration spheres. Furthermore, when in the 1490s the French and Habsburgs clashed in North Italy, these European powers were forced to emulate the tactics, strategies and organisational structure of the Italians to get by.

While it may seem strange that this was the case – the Italian city states and micro-republics were hardly great powers, so how did they wield the influence necessary to affect change in their larger neighbours – we need only bear in mind how influential and important the Renaissance was for European thought. The diffusion of Italian ideas around that time was far from unusual. Furthermore, because Italians were able to implement these new ideas on the small and local scale, Europeans outside of Italy were given the chance to experiment and spread these ideas on a far larger scale across their own states. Yet even this does not fully explain the extent or the origins of the Military Revolution.

Considering his expertise as a scholar of Spanish history, it should not surprise us to see Parker highlighting the Spanish example of revolutionary tactics in military organisation and efficiency. Parker makes a strong case for the supremacy of Spanish armies throughout the sixteenth century and considering the prominent position which King Philip II of Spain held throughout his reign in the latter half of the sixteenth century, this claim to supremacy rings true. Spain was nothing without its military machine, which it had developed and matured thanks to its repeated interactions with Italian tactics and technology, and to frequent conflict in the Americas and Europe.

Small groups of men were organised into un*iform regiments or tercios*, to use the famed Spanish terminology, of fifteen hundred to two thousand men, and musketry was a critical part of what made these regiments so effective. The Duke of Alva (1507-1582) was something of a pioneer in this regard. Better known as the Iron Duke in the Netherlands, for his firm hand in putting the Dutch revolt down, the Duke of Alva effectively ensured that musketmen made up a majority of the forces in these regiments, and organised Spanish armies to such an extent that Spanish tercios were ready for any challenge, knew how to react to their enemies, and could meet any threat with similar calmness and tenacity. These innovations made *tercio* a byword for Spanish military supremacy in sixteenth and seventeenth century Europe, and it also enabled the Spanish military machine to remain fearsome and effective long after Spain itself had ceased to properly function. One needs only to observe that in 1634, in the Battle of Nordlingen, a Swedish army drilled in the supposedly more advanced military method perfected during the Military Revolution were in fact defeated by these Spanish *tercios*.

The reason for this was the longevity and innovation of the Spanish Military Revolution in its own right, which had begun and matured several years before anyone else's. Spanish infantry were kept constantly trained by a revolving door of raw recruits into the garrison towns of Naples, Brussels, Milan etc., whereupon they would receive training in the drill by the veterans of the Spanish army already there. These developments all predate Michael Roberts' Military Revolution theory by several years; Spain retained her 'old' tercio tactics in the late sixteenth and early seventeenth centuries because she had already experienced a revolution of her own. Later in this section, we will examine tercio tactics and the development of the pikemen square, in addition to how these measured up when compared to the reforms instituted by Maurice of Nassau. Yet, we should not be content with shining this flattering spotlight on Spain alone. Geoffrey Parker makes the important point that Roberts' Military Revolution overlooks a central fact of European history and warfare, as Parker explains it:

> The simple fact is that, wherever a situation of permanent or semi-permanent war existed, whether in the Hundred Years' War of the later Middle Ages or the Thirty Years' War of the seventeenth century, one finds, not surprisingly, standing armies, greater professionalism among the troops, improvements in military organization and certain tactical innovations.

Seen in this light, it's possible to see Europeans learning not from a Military Revolution necessarily, but from a series of lessons learned after several ruinous wars. Because warfare was such a natural part of the European state system, and because it was so constant, it was only natural that Europeans would search out better ways of conducting themselves. With that in mind, when they encountered people that made war using more effective methods, such as the Italians during the Italian Wars, did it not follow that lessons would be learned here, and applied to their own armies, or that good ideas would be plagiarised, and implemented on a larger scale? All great wartime innovations had not come from sitting around a table and debating the finer points of this weapon or that, but from experimentation on the battlefield and creativity in the attack and defence. Much like every other profession, those that fought and led on the battlefield were standing on the shoulders of giants, or, to be more precise, military leaders learned and gained from the mistakes and successes of their predecessors, and these had only been learned during conflict. Parker underlines this point when he notes that:

> Gustavus Adolphus in the 1620s and Maurice of Nassau in the 1590s were forced to overhaul their armies dramatically because of the disastrous defeats which their predecessors had suffered in the preceding years. For inspiration, it is true, they turned in part to classical writers...but, like other rulers, they also turned to other more successful military practitioners, especially to the generals of Spain. Three of the best English military writers of the reign of Elizabeth...had all served in the Spanish Army of Flanders for several years and held up its practices as examples to others. The war in the Low Countries was a seminary in which many of the great commanders of the German Thirty Years' War and the English Civil War were formed. It is no accident that a large part of the military vocabulary of northern Europe should have come from Spanish.[42]

Warfare, like the progress of history itself, was dynamic and constantly changing, as new strategies, innovations and theories were brought to bear, and commanders were forced to respond to these challenges. Just as the crossbow had enabled the Italian peasant to inflict horrific wounds on enemies of all sizes, so too did the musket now grant any European the chance to do the same. He did not need to undergo a lifetime of training, like the English longbowmen, nor did he need to own land and pay for his equipment, like the knights of the Middle Ages. Instead, all he needed was to present himself to the recruiter where he would be transformed into a killing machine, and whereupon he would handle a weapon which did not distinguish between class, wealth or experience. The strength of this recruit would be found in the damage he could do alongside his peers in the line formation, rather than due to the skills developed after years of training with swordsmanship or horsemanship. This damage could be increased the more that the soldier practiced and drilled with his comrades. The unit rather than the individual became paramount, and the nature of the drill meant that, so long as he was well versed with its tenets, any man could achieve the same exploits as his peer.

Rather than the arrival of a Military Revolution in Europe between 1560-1660, it would be more accurate to note that a revolution in military thinking did take place, but that this began in the 1490s. The onset of the Italian Wars and the European adoption of Italian tactics on a larger scale proved the difference, and these tactics were all made possible by the adoption of the musket and the innovations and creativity which went along with this weaponry. Each such development depended upon the experience and lessons learned during previous years: the innovations did not fall into the laps of the commanders in 1560. In some respects, the most striking innovations in technology and strategy during the period were merely copies or adapted versions of what other peoples, like the Italians and Spanish, had already been doing for several years.

Roberts believed that the arrival of these new tactics made the growth of armies inevitable, thus fostering the development of the more modern professionalised forces in the process. Again though, one should be wary of generalising something as multi-layered and dynamic as military theory. Through his focus on a certain cause and effect formula, however, there were many by-products of the Military Revolution which Michael Roberts' original theory failed to properly emphasise; these included, among others, the importance of forbearance, the diffusion of military literature, the explosion in military education, the building of military hospitals and the resulting schools of expertise which flowed from these developments. In addition, Roberts places little emphasis upon either the development of field and siege artillery, or the most significant result of artillery's dominance – the complete redesign of European fortifications to replace the old castles of the Middle Ages with something more suited to combating cannons of ever-increasing calibre. This development was yet another innovation created by the Italians, and it thus bears the name *trace italienne* – the Italian style of fortifications. It will be our task to examine these innovations in the next chapter.

Chapter 1 Notes

[1] Cited in Geoffrey Parker, 'The Limits to Revolutions in Military Affairs: Maurice of Nassau, the Battle of Nieuwpoort (1600), and the Legacy', The Journal of Military History, Vol. 71, No. 2 (Apr., 2007), p. 339.

[2] Monro, quoted in Roger B. Manning, An Apprenticeship in Arms: The Origins of the British Army 1585-1702 (New York: Oxford University Press, 2006), p. 62.

[3] John A. Lynn, 'Tactical Evolution in the French Army, 1560-1660', French Historical Studies, Vol. 14, No. 2 (Autumn, 1985), pp. 176-191; p. 176.

[4] See R. A. Abou-El-Haj, 'The Narcissism of Mustafa II (1695-1703): A Psycho-historical Study', Studia Islamica, No. 40 (1974), pp. 115-131; pp. 177-118.

[5] Cited in Jeremy Black, Beyond the Military Revolution, Warfare in the Seventeenth Century World (New York; Palgrave Macmillan, 2011), p. ix – preface.

[6] See Rifa'at A. Abou-El-Haj, 'Ottoman Diplomacy at Karlowitz', Journal of the American Oriental Society, Vol. 87, No. 4 (Oct. - Dec., 1967), pp. 498-512; p. 498.

[7] See Michael J. Reimer, 'Ottoman Alexandria: The Paradox of Decline and the Reconfiguration of Power in Eighteenth-Century Arab Provinces', Journal of the Economic and Social History of the Orient, Vol. 37, No. 2 (1994), pp. 107-146.

[8] The Military Revolution was first coined by Michael Roberts in 1955, but was elaborated and developed into its modern form in 1988 by Geoffrey Parker, The Military Revolution: Military Innovation and the Rise of the West, 1500-1800 (Cambridge: Cambridge University Press, 1988); rev. ed., 1999. See also Geoffrey Parker, 'The "Military Revolution," 1560-1660--a Myth?', The Journal of Modern History, Vol. 48, No. 2 (Jun., 1976), pp. 195-214.

[9] This process is examined by Harald Kleinschmidt, 'Using the Gun: Manual Drill and the Proliferation of Portable Firearms', The Journal of Military History, Vol. 63, No. 3 (Jul., 1999), pp. 601-630. We'll return to the question of how firearms became readily available later in this miniseries.

[10] For an account of Ottoman military prowess in brief (we will examine it in more detail later) see Jeremy Black, Beyond the Military Revolution, pp. 13-19.

[11] See Nigel Saul, For Honour and Fame: Chivalry in England 1066-1500 (London; Pimlico, 2012), pp. 1-19.

[12] The development of English military technology is examined in Gervase Philips, 'Longbow and Hackbutt: Weapons Technology and Technology Transfer in Early Modern England', Technology and Culture, Vol. 40, No. 3 (Jul., 1999), pp. 576-593.

[13] See Clifford J. Rogers, 'The Military Revolutions of the Hundred Years' War', The Journal of Military History, Vol. 57, No. 2 (Apr., 1993), pp. 241-278.

[14] Peter Reid, A Brief History of Medieval Warfare: The Rise and Fall of the English Supremacy at Arms 1314-1485 (London; Constable and Robinson, 2007), p. 7. The introduction chapter of Reid's book is an excellent and accessible introduction to these concepts.

[15] A great analysis of this work is provided in Matthew Woodcock, 'Shooting for England: Configuring the Book and the Bow in Roger Ascham's "Toxophilus"', The Sixteenth Century Journal, Vol. 41, No. 4 (Winter 2010), pp. 1017-1038.

[16] Steven Gunn, 'Archery Practice In Early Tudor England', Past & Present, No. 209 (NOVEMBER 2010), pp. 53-81; p. 53.

[17] For further reading on how the Hundred Years War impacted English warfare see: Clifford J Rogers, 'The Military Revolutions of the Hundred Years' War', The Journal of Military History, Vol. 57, No. 2 (Apr., 1993), pp. 241-278.

[18] Clifford J. Rogers, 'Edward III and the Dialectics of Strategy, 1327-1360: The Alexander Prize Essay', Transactions of the Royal Historical Society, Vol. 4 (1994), pp. 83-102.

[19] Peter Reid, The Rise and Fall of the English Supremacy at Arms, bases his book's entire thesis on the idea of English supremacy in comparison to its European rivals.

[20] Both cited in Ibid, pp. 28-29.

[21] Gervase Philips, 'Longbow and Hackbutt: Weapons Technology and Technology Transfer in Early Modern England', Technology and Culture, Vol. 40, No. 3 (Jul., 1999), pp. 576-593; pp. 576-580.

[22] Sir Charles Oman, A History of the Art of War in the Sixteenth Century (London, 1987), p. 381.

[23] Gervase Philips, 'Longbow and Hackbutt', pp. 576-577.

[24] See Harald Kleinschmidt, 'Using the Gun: Manual Drill and the Proliferation of Portable Firearms', The Journal of Military History, Vol. 63, No. 3 (Jul., 1999), pp. 601-630; pp. 606-608.

[25] Gervase Philips, 'Longbow and Hackbutt', pp. 581-582. See also Richard W. Unger, 'Warships and Cargo Ships in Medieval Europe', Technology and Culture, Vol. 22, No. 2 (Apr., 1981), pp. 233-252.

[26] An example of the tactics used against the Irish can be found in G. A. Hayes-McCoy, 'Strategy and Tactics in Irish Warfare, 1593-1601', Irish Historical Studies, Vol. 2, No. 7 (Mar., 1941), pp. 255-279.

[27] Cited in Gervase Philips, 'Longbow and Hackbutt', p. 584.

[28] For one such example of an unsuccessful campaign amidst the Thirty Years War see S. J. Stearns, 'A Problem of Logistics in the Early seventeenth Century: The Siege of Re', Military Affairs, Vol. 42, No. 3 (Oct., 1978), pp. 121-126.

[29] B. Manning, 'Styles of Command in Seventeenth Century English Armies', The Journal of Military History, Vol. 71, No. 3 (Jul., 2007), pp. 671-699; p. 673.

[30] Ibid, p. 674.

[31] Cited in Thomas Esper, 'The Replacement of the Longbow by Firearms in the English Army', Technology and Culture, Vol. 6, No. 3 (Summer, 1965), pp. 382-393; p. 389.

[32] Ibid, p. 390.

[33] Gervase Philips, 'Longbow and Hackbutt', pp. 586-587.

[34] Cited in Thomas Esper, 'The Replacement of the Longbow by Firearms in the English Army', p. 391.

[35] Cited in Ibid, pp. 392-393.

[36] See Ibid, p. 393.

[37] Geoffrey Parker, 'The "Military Revolution," 1560-1660--a Myth?', The Journal of Modern History, Vol. 48, No. 2 (Jun., 1976), pp. 195-214; pp. 195-196.

[38] Ibid, pp. 196-197.

[39] Williamson Murray and McGregor Knox, The Dynamics of Military Revolution, 1300-2050 (New York; Cambridge University Press, 2001), p. 45.

[40] See Parker, Thirty Years War, pp. 184-185.

[41] Geoffrey Parker, 'The "Military Revolution," 1560-1660--a Myth?', p. 197.

[42] Ibid, p. 201.

(Top left) Maurice of Nassau (Michael Jansz v Mierevelt, 1607)
(Top right) William Loderwijk (Michael Jansz v Mierevelt, 1604)

(Top left) Emperor Rudolf II (Hans von Aachen, 1590)
(Top right) Philip II of Spain (Sofonisha Anguissola, 1573)

CHAPTER TWO
"Revolutions in Tactics"

ONE
The Trace Italienne

In the later phase of the sixteenth century, European siege warfare began to move away from its medieval reliance on high, thin stone walls and towards a new approach altogether. Throughout the preceding and indeed the following years, technology had rushed to keep pace with demand; if new cannons were on the scene, capable of knocking down entire structures which had once kept the enemy at bay, then it was necessary for this gap between the offensive and defensive weapon to be bridged. The offensive and defensive weapons did not balance each other out evenly across the continent. However, where historians are agreed is that mid-fifteenth century North Italy was the birthplace of this new approach to defensive warfare.

Michael Roberts' initial explanation of the Military Revolution largely glossed over the idea of fortifications as belonging to the school of significant military developments in the seventeenth century. Roberts focused instead on the armies themselves, and their adoption of new drills and tactics. It took Geoffrey Parker, writing from the 1970s, to make the point that these armies were seriously impacted by the increased toughness of the fortifications which they would have to face. Above all, the appearance of so many sophisticated fortresses necessitated the development of schools of military thought and practice, of engineers capable of besieging them with lines of circumvallation and contravallation, and the transportation of the weaponry necessary for bringing the walls and fortress down. What weaponry would the besieging army bring with them? Generally the list was long and necessarily exhaustive; an abundance of spades to dig trenches and mines, of gunpowder charges used for blowing the mines, small and larger arms for the military contest, and the simple sources of fodder for horses, bread for the soldier, ammunition for the musket.

To meet the challenge of increased organisational efficiency, twinned with the technological sophistication of the cannon, the defender would have to come up with new designs. Some historians, like Geoffrey Parker, emphasise the importance of the trace italienne style, while others, such as John A Lynn, asserted that by the second half of the seventeenth century, if not earlier, the ability of the attacker to succeed had outstripped the ability of the defender to resist. If an army laid siege and was well provisioned, in other words, he would almost always succeed against the defender, no matter how strong his defences. While Parker agreed, he did add that even if this was generally the case, to carry out these successful sieges, a Military Revolution in siegecraft would have to have been engaged with to deal with so many varied sieges.

The Military Revolution was more than merely an adoption of stronger cannons and the defender's response of improving the fortifications, it was also a literal revolution in how states armed themselves, organised themselves and prepared themselves for such sieges. Such preparation was necessary to field the cannons, equip them with gunpowder stores, transport them to the right place, and then to equip the soldiery with the same resources; not to mention the fact that men would have to be trained how to capture these bastions, what the best practices were and what to avoid. As Geoffrey Parker noted:

> The crucial influence on the evolution of strategic thinking in the sixteenth century was the appearance of an entirely new type of defensive fortification: the trace italienne, a circuit of low, thick walls punctuated by quadrilateral bastions. In the course of the fifteenth century it became obvious that the improvements in gun founding and artillery had rendered the high, thin walls of the Middle Ages quite indefensible. A brief cannonade from the "bombards" brought them crashing down.[1]

Parker captured the two most important developments there; the first was the replacement of the high, thin stone walls with lower, thicker earthen walls which could hold their own artillery. The second was to create bastions out from these walls, and to build them in an arrowhead design to eliminate the blind spots which were present in the square or round towers of yore. A major reason why the Reconquista of Spain was so successful against the castles of the Moors, or why the English castles in France fell in quick succession in the latter half of the fifteenth century, was due to the use of cannon trains sometimes containing as much as 180 pieces, being brought to bear against fortifications from a previous era. If Europe was now populated by a system of obsolete castles, then that meant the attackers would have a field day until defensive technology caught up with them, if indeed it caught up at all. The first peoples to realise that a complete revolution in how they defended themselves was necessary were the Italians, whose city state armies had battered each other's forts for hundreds of years, and where the siege was the default method of defeating your enemies. This again is echoed by Parker when he writes:

> Military architects in Italy, where siege warfare was most common, were the first to experiment with new techniques of fortification which might withstand shelling...from about 1450, when it made its first appearance, until the 1520s, when it was fully fledged. It was a development which 'revolutionized the defensive-offensive pattern of warfare', because it soon became clear that a town protected by the trace italienne could not be captured by the traditional methods of battery and assault. It had to be encircled and starved into surrender.[2]

Once it became clear that the new technologies present in the trace italienne were a great leap forward from the old style of defence, Europeans rushed to implement them in their own states and create the kind of fortifications which could actually defend something, rather than merely distract a large army before inevitably falling to his forces. These 'miracle' fortresses were brought to every place where significant conflict would be likely – the Rhine, the Low Countries, the south Coast of England, along the Danube etc. Consequently, it meant that when warfare did come to these regions, such as during the Dutch Revolt or during the wars between the Habsburgs and French along the Rhine valley, sieges became the order of the day. On the other hand, those areas where fortresses were less common, such as the majority of the British Isles, the interior of France or the east of Europe in Poland and into the wilder steppes, pitched battles tended to become *more* important. This did not mean that Britain, France, Poland etc. possessed no fortresses, but warfare was adapted as a result of geography.

When one asks the question of how the Dutch managed to resist the Spanish in the first place, or why the Dutch revolt lasted eighty long years, this question is answered by the plethora of fortresses made in the trace italienne style, and placed in critical points along borders, beside rivers or as anchors of the countryside. The Dutch could not be met and certainly could not be destroyed in a single battle or a seasonal campaign. Instead, an immensely costly and time-consuming process would have to be engaged with every time a fortress in the Dutch or Spanish Netherlands was to be taken, and thus the Spanish military supremacy which was brought to bear on several occasions against the French during the French Wars of Religion was not as immediately obvious or effective.[3] To take this point further, in regions like the wild steppes, where fortresses were uncommon among the tribal or raiding societies that dominated, cavalry became all important instead. Indeed, in portions of Europe where fortresses were less common, and cities dominated – think of the heartland of the Empire for instance – the culture of cavalry taking precedence over all other units on the battlefield took root.

Where fortresses did dominate the landscape though, these were brought up to such a degree of efficiency and sophistication as to defy all but the most equally patient and well-prepared enemy armies sent to seize them. So long as these increasingly important bastions of defence dotted those strategically important portions of the country, it was almost pointless to engage in many pitched battles at all. Most pitched battles took place as an army marched from one fortified place to another, and through the Thirty Years War, the sight of a commander seeking a decisive battle was statistically rare, for the precise reason that such encounters were rarely actually that decisive. Thus, we can consider the regions where fortresses were most important – along the Franco-Flanders border, within the Netherlands and along the Rhine. Later developments in the seventeenth century enabled fortresses to equip more advanced artillery pieces which could strike at a besieging force from long ranges and provided further challenges to the besieger. Developments like these made the work of the French military engineer par excellence Vauban so critical for French security from the 1670s, and his work left a legacy which saved France from total destruction in the twilight campaigns of the War of the Spanish Succession.[4] In addition, the Dutch ability to harness the geography of their flooded lands and hunker down in their fortresses saved their country from becoming an Anglo-French vassal state in the early 1670s.[5]

The prominence of France in these examples provides us with a good opportunity to look at a counterargument levelled against the Military Revolution idea. John A Lynn's expertise in French military history, particularly on Louis XIV's wars in the seventeenth century, distinguishes him as a critical source for measuring the impact of the Military Revolution upon France. Considering this background, we may be surprised to learn that John A Lynn is not wholly convinced of its usefulness. To begin with, Lynn sets forth a list of requirements for a successful fortress in the early modern era of the trace italienne. According to Lynn,

> To be effective in the gunpowder environment of early modern warfare, defensive works had to: (1) protect the fortress from storm by infantry; (2) absorb bombardment without toppling or crumbling; (3) shelter the defenders from attacking fire, and (4) subject the attackers to effective artillery fire.[6]

Bastions played an important role in this procedure, because they provided the defenders with an ideal position that covered all areas the attackers could hide in, and which ensured that lead could be rained down without exception. Bastions, as Lynn points out though, were not as important as the defenders' ability or determination to resist – they were far from magic bullets, and this explains why attackers were able to overwhelm the fortresses if they tried hard enough. Adding ditches, using earthen ramparts, lengthening the depth of the defences and dotting them with artillery all increased the capabilities of the defenders, but if their heart was not in the fight, then surrender was inevitable. A good example of what a determined group of defenders were capable of can be seen in the case of the siege of Vienna in 1683.

It was thanks to the innovations of the trace italienne that Vienna was fortified to such a standard, even while the defences appeared rudimentary on the surface, they were in fact highly effective. Notwithstanding the advantages which they enjoyed though, one observes that the major reason Vienna was saved was not due to the steely determination of the defenders, but due to the famous arrival of a relief army. The Turk, as the attacking force, still managed to beat through each layer of defence, but the point was that this all took time and a great deal of manpower to be expended, long enough for a relief army to save the city and inflict the famous defeat on the Vizier.[7] Only a well-prepared attacking force, with the patience and foresight necessary to account for the challenges of a siege, could hope to be successful.

Yet, it is not so simple that technological innovations led automatically to larger or more professional armies. In Lynn's view, the French case gives one pause for thought. To Lynn, artillery mounted on the walls of the fortress was the most important development, since this had not been possible when castles featuring thin stone walls provided inadequate support for the weight and recoil of the cannon fire. In line with this, Lynn points out that the besieging army established their lines of contravallation – the name given to the trenches dug around the fortress to effectively besiege it – across a wider area not because the fortress was simply big, but because the besieging army was trying to stay out of range of the defender's cannons. To stay out of range, trenches had to be built in a huge circle sometimes a mile or more out from the fortress.

These lines of trenches would keep the defenders locked into their siege, but to be effective, these trenches would have to properly staffed with soldiers, thus driving up demand for more soldiers than normal. Lynn's argument differs from the norm because it challenges the assumption that the scale of the fortress and the challenge it posed required more men, since the trenches had to be built further out from the fortress than they had been before. The point, Lynn says, is to ask *why* these trenches had to be built so far out in the first place. Unless we consider the danger of artillery fire, the resulting revolutions in army size and military organisation do not make sense. According to Lynn then, artillery and the proper use of its power proved the critical ingredient in the resulting Military Revolution.[8]

In the French case, while besieging armies appear large on paper, at an average of 27,500, from the late fifteenth century to the early eighteenth century, this figure did not change all that much. In other words, if the French army was marching to besiege a fortress from 1480-1715, it was generally in the realm of twenty thousand men. One might wonder though, if this number remained relatively stable, then how do we explain the very real explosion in manpower within the French army, from twenty thousand men overall in the late fifteenth century, to nearly four hundred thousand during the War of the Spanish Succession in the first few years of the 1700s? In Lynn's view, the genuine increases in the overall size of the French army are explained less convincingly by the necessity of conducting sieges, since the sizes of the individual besieging force did not greatly increase. Lynn also makes the point that we cannot claim the number of sieges increased the paper size of the French army either, since it was quite unusual for the French to engage with more than one siege per season.[9]

This still leaves the old mystery intact – if the increases in the French army cannot be explained by the increased demands of the siege thanks to the trace italienne, or by the number of sieges, then how else can we explain the significant expansion in Louis XIV's armies later in the seventeenth century? To answer this question, we must adjust our focus from the offensive, and pay more attention to the defensive. In short, Lynn argues that even though the trace italienne did not facilitate an expanded French army, more soldiers were needed *to garrison them*. The trace italienne had resulted in an explosion of not merely army size across France, but also in the building of defensive works in the trace italienne style.

Louis XIV increased his army's size because France had more enemies, and so long as France had more enemies, she needed to defend her lands. At critical choke points, along the Rhine, in the border with Italy, and most importantly of all along the border with the Spanish Netherlands, Vauban's engineering expertise and eye for the perfect defence ensured that France was positively brimming with tough bastions just in time for the War of the Spanish Succession. As Vauban well understood though, it was one thing to pay for all of these fortresses to be built and properly supplied, it was quite another to staff them with enough defenders to make building them worthwhile in the first place.

To prove this point, consider the following figures. In 1666, during the War of Devolution, French army size on paper stood at seventy-two thousand men, of whom twenty-five thousand were said to be involved in garrison duty. By 1678, only a decade later, the size of the French army during the Dutch War had ballooned to 272,000 men, yet of this number, 116,370 of them, as Lynn put it, 'stood behind walls.'[10] This is what we mean when we talk about French army size being 'on paper'; 272,000 was an incredible number of men for France to wield at that time, yet when you consider that over 42% of this army was sitting still, or in other words, engaged in defensive duties, this left the remaining one hundred and fifty thousand or so men in very high demand across the three major theatres.

The historian Jeremy Black has noted that, in his view, the Military

Revolution did not apply to France, and that the massive increases in armies, in addition to the building programme of defensive works and the military bureaucracies which accompanied them can be explained instead by the personality of Louis XIV above all.[11] But more than this, Lynn's facts and figures and his confrontation of the prevailing Military Revolution theory reminds us that across Europe, different circumstances and traditions of geography, politics and a morass of other issues affected how warfare developed and technology progressed. Lynn's emphasis on the French penchant for building trace italienne style fortresses in their problem areas would not have applied to other states that did not have to defend three major border areas, and thus their decision to adopt new military technologies and tactics, not to mention the explanation for the growth of their armies, would have told very different stories.

Lynn's mission to accurately explain not only the reasoning behind the increases in French army size, but also the actual, genuine numbers involved, have made him a scholar of renown in his field. As Lynn has explained, every case was unique, and in the French case, there were far too many variables and inconsistencies over the seventeenth century to definitively prove that the Military Revolution even occurred. The traditional explanation – that Western Europeans, when fighting in North Italy, became impressed with the Italian system, and adopted it for themselves – is less helpful than an analysis of the political and military situation in France at the time.

Nonetheless, this should not lead us to conclude that Geoffrey Parker's interpretation of the Military Revolution held no water when it came to the French – the trace italienne evidently changed everything, even if these changes occurred in France in a unique manner. Even Lynn tacitly acknowledges that the abundance of men for garrison duty still *technically* proves Parker's theory that the trace italienne led to the growth of the French army. Yet, Lynn adds to this concession the point that the process was not as automatic as Parker seems to assume; instead, the French army grew in size because the Bourbons harnessed and improved the fortresses within their realm. In Louis XIV's case in particular, he was bombarded with repeated calls from Vauban himself, the man who stood to gain from a plethora of fortresses existing, that the Sun King should demolish some fortresses to save himself the manpower. As Lynn admitted though:

> Parker has done notable service by drawing our attention to the way in which fortresses influenced the size of standing armies in a given political, strategic, and tactical environment. One of Parker's more provocative assertions, that "the greater part of military expenditure" in early modern Europe was lavished on the defence, does seem to hold, at least in the main.[12]

Further, Lynn provides us with what he believes is the major reason

France expanded its army size. It was not just to garrison the fortresses. Instead, the increases from 1635 under Louis XIII, and which Louis XIV only improved upon, are explained first by the diplomatic isolation of France, and second by the incredibly lofty goals which her administrations under Louis XIII and Louis XIV attempted to achieve. One should consider that in 1635, Cardinal Richelieu's aim was to destroy the Habsburg power base, which he believed was centred upon Spain. Richelieu wanted – and for the sake of French security into the future, believed that he needed – to reduce Spain to a divided, poor and demoralised European backwater. The rise of Spanish power, the result of its military machine, its harnessing of fruits from the New World, the success of the Reconquista and some good fortune thrown in for good measure, was an unprecedented factor in European history, and so long as Spain was in the ascendant, France never could be.

Richelieu and Mazarin, as the guiding lights of French foreign policy between 1635-60, never lost sight of their end goal, but at the same time, one could argue that they engaged in the war with Spain and with their allies during the Thirty Years War with a degree of diplomatic finesse and tact which ensured that French power, even while it increased, did not scare off potential friends or result in the isolation of Louis XIII's realm. In line with this approach to the situation, one can discern that French army size, notwithstanding the uncompromising ambitions of the two Cardinals, remained quite static during their tenure in office. However, it once Louis XIV came to his majority, and sensible Cardinals were no longer around to impart advice, the absolutist Sun King changed everything. As Lynn wrote:

> Military expansion after 1659 was more substantial and more lasting. Louis XIV pursued a foreign policy that marked a very real break with those of the strong first ministers who manipulated the international scene before 1661. Richelieu and Mazarin had succeeded to some degree in isolating their enemies and gaining allies. The strategic lesson that Mazarin imparted to Louis had more to do with diplomatic finesse than naked force. Later, when Louis's brutal methods and obsession with the absolute security of France united the Grand Alliance against him, this seemed a new and catastrophic development. Gone was the standing of France as the guarantor of German liberties, the natural ally of the Dutch, and the occasional friend of England. Louis's foreign policy doomed France to isolation in a hostile Europe.[13]

With several enemies, there emerged fighting on several fronts, and several French armies were urgently required. This naturally resulted in an increase in the total number of men that Louis XIV put in the field. Without these circumstances, Lynn concludes, France would never have had to either engage in such enormous and costly building programmes of so many trace italienne fortresses, nor would France's King have been forced to engender unheard of increases in the size of his army. Lynn's conclusion states that if we are to understand what amounted to the implementation of the Military Revolution in France, we must first understand France's diplomatic position, and how it changed from the Thirty Years War to the War of the Spanish Succession. One of the most important factors in this process was not the arbitrary implementation of a new theory of military development, but the appearance in positions of power of vibrant French personalities, such as Louis XIV and his ministers. Even Louis' own contemporaries recognised this, and how his boorish diplomatic approach made him few friends, but a great target of anti-French propaganda.

> However great the forces of the kingdom, one ought not to imagine that it alone can furnish troops to guard and maintain so many fortresses and at the same time put armies in the field as great as those of Spain, Italy, England, Holland and the Empire joined together.[14]

These were the words of Vauban, the renowned French engineer, who pleaded to the end with Louis to release garrisoned soldiers from the countless fortresses, and even knock some of them down, to be in a position to confront the armies of France's enemies on the field, or at least with more flexibility. As we noted though, Louis ignored him, and not because he was spellbound by the Military Revolution, but because he was a complex character who possessed his own vision for France. 'In a sense', Lynn concludes, 'Louis took heed of Vauban's logic, if not of his conclusions. The Sun King did not sacrifice his fortresses and their garrisons as Vauban proposed, but instead created the four hundred thousand-man army to insure his gloire.'[15] For Louis, the security and glory of France and its King were sufficient to justify the massive size of the army, as much as the number of fortresses. Conversely, the Military Revolution – a device which was coined two hundred fifty years after Louis' death – was not.

TWO
The Growth of Armies – France's School of Hard Knocks

Having examined the impact which the trace italienne had on French defensive strategy, we should look next at what the Military Revolution has to say about the growth and development of the French army. We have touched on some of these ideas before, but it is helpful to examine precisely what Michael Roberts claimed to have occurred. These claims are paraphrased by John A. Lynn, who wrote that Roberts advocated...

> ...a revolution in tactics accomplished by the Dutch stadtholder Prince Maurice of Nassau (1584-1625) and the Swedish king Gustavus Adolphus (1611-32) drove the older Spanish system of massive, unwieldy infantry formations off the battlefields of Europe. New strategy took advantage of well-trained mobile armies to pursue victory, instead of prolonging stalemate. At the same time, standing armies emerged as land forces grew to unprecedented proportions, giving statesmen potent weapons of war for grand schemes. However, the gargantuan armies spawned in the seventeenth century burdened society with crushing taxation, heavy-handed bureaucracies, and all the weighty trappings of absolutism.[16]

This is a familiar argument: the straightforward cause and effect idea, where one set of circumstances leads naturally to another, but the unique conditions on the ground within each state are not considered. In some instances where the Military Revolution can be said to have occurred, there were very different implications for that particular society. Why, for example, did the Dutch refrain from embracing absolutism, but the French did? Both states experienced great changes to their military systems and adopted innovative new methods in warfare with equal relish. In fact, while it is less popularly known, some historians would attest to the fact that absolutist control of the Orange family over Dutch society in the eighteenth century was merely an extension of the kinds of absolutist rule of French kings.[17] Think also of

Cromwell's unflinching absolutist theocracy, or of the enlightened despotism of Frederick the Great, or even the small scale absolutism of the most minor German prince. Michael Roberts claims that the Military Revolution led to absolutism and increased the central control of the state administration, and these claims cannot be simply ignored – notwithstanding the shortcomings of this approach, there are too many convenient coincidences to refrain from assessing Roberts' claims altogether.

If absolutism was the natural outcome of increased army sizes, then one may be justified in ascertaining precisely how great this increase was. Using the 1590s as a starting date, and ending in 1700, the Dutch armed forces grew from twenty thousand to one hundred thousand; the Swedes, from fifteen thousand to one hundred thousand; the English, from thirty thousand to eighty-seven thousand and the French, most impressively of all, from eighty thousand to four hundred thousand.[18] While that French number seems incredible, we have clarified why the French in particular so increased their army size; a combination of a bullish foreign policy which created many enemies, and the need for a well-garrisoned fortress system to defend against these enemies were to blame.[19] Having established these guiding principles, we are drawn to another important set of questions. How, for instance, did the French *actually fight* during the later sixteenth and early seventeenth centuries; did French military innovation and tactics come from within France, or were these ideas imported from the likes of the Dutch Republic or Sweden, and finally, as an aside, we should consider what these points reveal about the Military Revolution. Let's tackle these questions now, with a look first at the kind of cavalry used by France.

'It is better that I should die with arms in my hands, than live to see my kingdom ruined, and myself forced to seek assistance in a foreign country.'[20] These were the words of King Henri IV of France, who assumed the crown of that country following the ruinous wars of religion which ripped France apart. Not only did they rip France apart, they also provided ideal opportunities for the powers of Europe to get involved; the English and Dutch supported Henri, the Protestant candidate from the House of Bourbon, and the Spanish supported the Catholic candidate. This conflict ended in 1598 with the Peace of Vervins between France and Spain, but much would have to be done in time for the next showdown between France and Spain, which King Henri IV of France anticipated in the not too distant future. As it happened, Henri would be assassinated in 1610, and would never get the chance to wage war against the Habsburgs again. Yet, his contribution towards the French army must still be considered if we are to properly grasp how the France's armed forces went from ruined, divided and distraught in the final decades of the sixteenth century, to holding Europe to ransom under Henri's grandson Louis XIV, a century later.

Henri was known as the king who would put himself in danger while on horseback for the sake of inspiring and willing his men onto victory. When the Duke of Parma, Spain's foremost military commander at the time, confronted Henri in a siege outside the town of Aumale in 1592, Parma was heard to remark: 'I expected to see a general; this is only an officer of light cavalry!' The remark implied that the aspiring King of France was something of an amateur, and that he also took great risks while commanding his men. As the historian Ronald S. Love wrote though, Parma was mistaken:

> What Parma failed to grasp…was Henri's appreciation of the pivotal role in warfare of mounted forces, whose battlefield effectiveness he enhanced more than any other commander of his day. He dispensed with obsolete formations for more efficient ones, adapting his weaponry accordingly; he distinguished between types of military horsemen and their specialized functions; and he made original use of the relatively new dragoons. In short, Henri IV was a "cavalry specialist" whose innovations transformed the mounted branch into a far more mobile and deadly force than was available to his Spanish and League enemies, thus making a unique contribution to the late sixteenth-century Military Revolution.[21]

Ronald S. Love was far from the only historian to refer to King Henri IV as a 'cavalry specialist', and the title is important when we consider the trend in Europe at the dawn of the seventeenth century.[22] As we have established, infantry had become the mainstay of the battlefield following the eclipse of knights and their replacement by the cheaper and more numerous pikemen from the early sixteenth century. Henri's decision to transform cavalry into cavalry armed with rudimentary versions of the carbine, and to incorporate them into his army as a separate and distinct unit with its own strengths and weaknesses to play upon, tells a vibrant story.

Henri's example is also fascinating because of how he dealt with the problems of his army, namely, its lack of funds and means to pay for the cavalry he needed. To make up for his lack of coin, Henri encouraged nobles loyal to him to field their own mounts and pay for their own equipment, in return for great gains into the future once victory had been won. This tactic, though it may appear grasping and desperate on the surface, worked well most of the time, but shortages continued to plague Henri, and forced him to make the most of the cavalry that he did have. This determination to squeeze as much efficiency as possible out his rare mounted units led to a dramatic level of innovation among Henri's cavalry. Ronald S. Love notes of these innovations:

> Henri adapted the cavalry tactics and formations of his day to compensate for the problems with his mounted troops and to permit them to fight on a superior footing against their more numerous and better-provided enemies, whatever the circumstances. Specifically, instead of relying upon the essentially medieval

attack...still generally used by other forces (whereby the heavy cavalry would charge with the lance in two thin, extended lines forty feet apart) the Bourbon monarch trained his men to form compact squadrons six or seven ranks deep and to charge with the sword, dispensing with the unwieldy lance and using pistols only in the ensuing melee.[23]

This allusion to the use of the lance by the late sixteenth century highlights the inherent backwardness and archaic nature of cavalry warfare in France at the time; evidently, it was time for a change. The cavalry and its aristocratic roots had been stagnating since the beginning of the sixteenth century, even while the infantry gained an increasing importance on the battlefield and the mass cavalry charges of yore became far easier to parry and block than before. This by no means meant that cavalry charges had become obsolete, nor would they for several hundred years, but it did mean that battles between French cavalry on either side of the Wars of Religion frequently boiled down to clashes with the lance, and unwieldy efforts to close in with the enemy. Unless a breach could be exploited in the infantry, this cavalry was very similar in appearance and tactics to the knights of the middle ages, and they were just as inflexible.

Henri's efforts to change this were not unprecedented, nor was he alone in believing that the old medieval tactic of charging while heavily armoured into other heavily armoured cavalry was in need of change. One of Henri's peers, the Calvinist cavalry commander Francois de la Noue, commented that the emulation of medieval knights and the charge with the lance represented a 'very bad formation'. De la Noue looked upon these lancers as outdated relics of an age before gunpowder, when cavalry was exclusively aristocratic, and noblemen refused from personal honour to ride anywhere but in the front rank. The pride of the nobility, de la Noue believed, meant that the old system was retained at the expense of proficiency, and it was this kind of ideology and traditionalism that King Henri was rallying against.

Thanks to his years of experience commanding cavalry on the battlefield, de la Noue appreciated that the thin extended lines of cavalry were flimsy and difficult to maintain in good order during the charge. Although effective against disorganized feudal levies, they could easily be broken by well-led cavalry or infantry in tighter formations, or simply by rough ground. Moreover, de la Noue argued, the lancer was only capable of striking a single blow in the initial shock, unlike those cavalry armed with pistols that could fire at close quarters six or seven times with greater effect, and in the melee the lance was useless.[24] Indeed, this struggle within French society between the practicalities and demands of warfare, and the desire for status, bravery and reputation, played a surprisingly important role in the development of cavalry tactics. Another historian has noted that:

By the end of the first quarter of the sixteenth century…various factors had combined to challenge the heavy cavalry's primacy. Other types of mounted troops were able to function far more effectively under the evolving conditions of war, but they still were plagued by issues of low status and thus remained an unappealing alternative for most noblemen. Although at least some of the nobles must have recognized that the heavy cavalry was in grave danger of losing its long-standing position as the star of the battlefield, the nobles still were not prepared to adapt by converting to a less prestigious type of mounted service, no matter how effective it might be.[25]

The infantry were equally shaped by the lessons of the Wars of Religion. With less money to go around, the old tactic of the French crown to employ Swiss pike mercenaries was abandoned, and it became necessary for Protestant infantry regiments to find ways to deal with the lack of funds, while still finding the means to defend themselves. This process was actually aided by the prevalence of partisan warfare, since this led to the creation of small units acting independently, who were able to move in flexible formations through the countryside. Partisan warfare was bitter and bloody for sure, but this baptism by fire instilled within French infantry the concept of fighting as companies.

In the Wars of Religion, the tradition was for regiments, the largest formation of companies, to assemble for battle as a single line of squares in which soldiers stood only ten or twelve ranks deep. These company squares were separated by intervals equal to the front of one square. The gaps in the line could be closed in the event of a cavalry charge. Sometimes this arrangement would break down altogether, and large squares might be formed to combat a mass cavalry charge of thousands of horse. As per the rules of warfare at the time, a typical European regiment would field three to five thousand men; however, French infantry usually stood in regimental formations totalling no more than one thousand men, largely because manpower was scarce.

Appreciating this fact, Henri made the *battalion* the official unit of the French army and was forced to compensate for the smaller size of this body of men by removing those gaps between the soldiers, and packing the pike and musketeers closer together. Removing the gaps meant that French infantry could respond better to the orders which were issued, but it also meant that pike and musket could be coordinated better as a fighting force. But how did it look on paper? The pikemen were massed together in the centre of the battalion, flanked on either side by musketeers. On campaign, an average battalion contained about three hundred pikemen and one hundred musketeers. Henri's battalions were also designed to support each other in line or in a checkerboard formation, and to move and operate in tandem rather than what had been the norm with larger regiments.

Henri was wise to appreciate that, while an impressive sight, regiments were not well-suited to the French circumstances. The regiment was full of gaps and contained several independent companies, and the required manpower was rarely on hand to fill the quota and ensure that everyone played their role. Meanwhile, the smaller battalion was of a reasonable size, fielding about half as many men as the regiment, and the men were also packed closer together, increasing each soldier's dependence on his peer.[26] Once Henri began implementing the battalion as the default unit of the French army, its success began to show. Furthermore, the interdependence and cooperation between musket and pike was an innovation which Maurice of Nassau and later Gustavus Adolphus were to perfect.

It is not entirely clear how much influence Maurice of Nassau had on Henri's decision to alter his army's composition to suit its size. It is entirely possible that in France, as in the Netherlands and Sweden, the circumstances on the ground compelled their leaders to make the most out of their position. As John A. Lynn notes though, the fact that these figures were all reforming their infantry tactics, and arriving at similar conclusions, buoyed each decision with a degree of confidence. Lynn wrote: 'In all probability, the work of Maurice was all the more impressive to the French precisely because it reinforced their own tactical development and offered refinements and improvements readily adaptable to French methods.'[27] Frenchmen served in Dutch service to gain a better understanding of these tactics; Marshal Turenne, later a French commander of prime importance for in the later part of the Thirty Years War, and in Louis XIV's wars, was a nephew of Maurice of Nassau, and was raised with the lessons of his uncle close to heart. Even while it cannot be guaranteed that Henri IV copied the Dutch example, it can certainly be said that French military theory was influenced, impressed and encouraged by it. Little wonder that one historian referred to the Netherlands in the seventeenth century as 'the military college of Europe.'[28]

Just as French officers served under Maurice in early in the seventeenth century, so others went to school under Gustavus Adolphus's brief flutter of military brilliance in the 1630s. Claude de Le Touf, baron de Sirot, who later commanded the reserve at the 1643 Battle of Rocroi, gained invaluable experience between 1632 and 1633 with the victorious Scandinavians. Once the French entered the war openly as enemies of the Habsburgs and allies of the Swedes, this contact with Swedish methods brought further adjustments in French tactics. About 1640, Turenne adopted the Swedish practice of marshalling infantry only six ranks deep, which made the line wider and provided greater opportunities for laying down fire. However, just as in the Dutch case, the emulation of some elements of Swedish practices did not mean that the French lazily copied the Swedes. This can be seen in the army composition, for while King Gustavus had increased both the number and offensive importance of his pikemen, Marshal Turenne reduced the number of pikemen to only one third of the entire battalion, adding more musketmen to compensate.[29]

Turenne was in good company with his passion for the musket; no less a man than King Louis XIII (r. 1610-1643) professed to have an intense interest in firearms. As a child of ten, he possessed seven guns, and once he became king, he invested further into this passion, coming into a grand collection of forty individual firearms by the time of his fourteenth birthday.[30] His son and heir, Louis XIV (r. 1643-1715) was equally active in the martial sphere, practicing his command as a young boy by commanding squadrons of soldiers, and emulating his father's example by accompanying the army on several campaigns. 'The King's amusements were all warlike''', wrote one of Louis' contemporaries, who had played as one of the boy soldiers: 'as soon as his little hands could grasp a stick the Queen had a large drum prepared upon which he played continually.'[31] Soon enough, Louis would dispense with practice, in favour of the real thing, with real weapons, real soldiers and real consequences. With this flavour for war, it is to be expected that French kings in the seventeenth century would invest in technological advancement in that sphere. Thanks to the availability of drill manuals published in the 1650s and 70s, we know that by the middle of the seventeenth century, the preferred French method of forming an army was to create two main lines one in front of the other. In the centre of each line would be the infantry, with its battalions standing in checkerboard fashion, and those of the second line standing behind the gaps between battalions in the first. On the flanks stood the cavalry. If the manpower was available, an unofficial third reserve line of the raw recruits or less dependable cavalry and infantry were held, as were the older style of melee cavalry better suited to chasing fleeing infantry down, but vulnerable to musket fire.

Michael Roberts' Military Revolution theory generalises that not until Gustavus Adolphus determined that the cavalry was better suited to the shock tactics of the charge, were the older tactics of the pistol or carbine armed cavalry rendered obsolete. However, even the most brief examinations of literature on seventeenth century cavalry tactics will demonstrate the fact that the consensus about the role of cavalry on the battlefield was frequently subject to change. The utility of cavalry in France had changed, from their appreciated shock value at the head of a heavily armoured charge in the early 1500s, to their adoption of firearms in the mid-sixteenth century, to a return to their roots as shock cavalry by the 1630s.

The changes should not be imagined as abrupt alterations to the way cavalry fought, but as responses to the demands played upon cavalry in a given battlefield. Furthermore, the idea that Gustavus Adolphus pioneered the return to cavalry's more natural roots is somewhat flawed, especially when we consider the consistent debate, even during Henri IV's time, about the best way to make use of cavalry. During the turn of the seventeenth century, cavalry armed with carbines, pistols or other small arms tended to engage in a manoeuvre known as the *caracole*. The caracole turned the cavalry into something little better than faster moving infantry and was immensely wasteful. Lynn describes the manoeuvre and its flaws:

> To perform the caracole, a body of cavalry several ranks deep approached the enemy. The first rank fired its pistols, wheeled about, and rode to the rear of the formation to reload; the succeeding ranks fired and wheeled in turn. By the time the last rank had fired, the first would be ready to discharge its weapons once again. The intention was to blow a hole in the enemy square, but when used against infantry the caracole almost invariably cost the attacking cavalry more than the defending infantry, because infantry muskets outclassed cavalry pistols in range and power.[32]

The solution, it seemed, was to combine the best of both worlds – cavalry would fire as a group from a further distance, and then charge at the enemy to rupture its line. This would demand a level of coordination from the horses for sure, but it would also demand a great deal of the enemy infantry, who would be forced to endure a combination of infantry and cavalry tactics in quick succession. In addition, and a lesson which the French certainly *did not* learn from the Swedes, was that tactic which combined infantry in amongst the cavalry, to provide still more firepower for the initial discharge of the weapons. Then, if the cavalry needed to make a retreat after their initial charge, they could withdraw to a position behind this company of infantry and prepare their charge again. The key was flexibility, and thanks to the ruinous experience of the Wars of Religion, the French army had been through the school of hard knocks and emerged on the other side scarred but well educated and immersed in the arts of war.

Artillery was a similar story. While Gustavus Adolphus' innovations in the realm of artillery are undeniable, the idea that he invented the concept, and that the French copied it, is difficult to support. Indeed, since the early sixteenth century, experimentation with smaller calibres of cannon were the norm, and while the three-pounder artillery most popular among Swedish armies saw extensive French use, most notably during the initial defence of France in 1636 against a determined Spanish invasion, such small pieces became less important. The reason why the smaller but more mobile pieces decreased in importance as the century went on had a lot to do with the trace italienne and popularity of the siege where French soldiers resided. Since the lighter field artillery could not punch through any respectable walls, and since this was what the artillery were needed for, there seemed little reason for the French to lug these small pieces with them.[33] If Henri was something of an innovator when it came to the role of cavalry, and if he did not owe everything to the Swedes in the realm of artillery, then what can one say about his relationship with the infantry drill? To discern the origins of that complex, revolutionary, and modern system, we must engage with its surprisingly ancient source.

THREE
Fire by Rank –
the Surprising Origins Story

1543 was a significant year for Japan. It was in that year that a Portuguese carrack carrying some adventuring vagabonds, armed with arquebusiers in the highly valued Portuguese style, made landfall at Tanegashima, forever changing that island nation's method of making war. While the 1.2 metre smoothbore Portuguese muskets could fire a 20-gram ball to devastating effect, the commissioning of these new weapons alone could not win any warlord the war for Japan. Incredibly enough, while they were only new to the technology, the state of civil war within Japan and the keen desire on the part of each of the competing warlords to best their opponents meant that innovation with these muskets became the order of the day.

This was Sengoku, the warring states period of Japanese history, and it pitted nobles, families and ambitious generals against one another for control of all of Japan. Through these trials, between 1467-1603, Japanese warlords discovered what in Europe was already well known – that muskets had potential, but that they were unwieldy, inaccurate and had an underwhelming rate of fire. When pressed against archers or the samurai, musket-men with their expensive new weapons would be cut to pieces. And yet, the desire for victory and total power moved certain warlords to stick with this European weapon. They would not improve its design; instead, they would improve how it was used.

Oda Nobunaga can be credited with employing one of the most significant innovations in the history of gunpowder warfare, even though he remains virtually unknown. The idea of musket volley fire: where a unit of musketeers several ranks deep would fire by each rank, and where each expended musket would be reloaded in the back of the unit as the next rank fired its weapon, was about as critical an innovation in warfare as was possible for the late sixteenth century. It is thus somewhat incredible that such an innovation first appeared in Japan, the nation most known for its use of the samurai sword. The Japanese employment of volley fire was a reaction to the primacy of the sword and the archer; much like their European counterparts, musketeers were vulnerable to being cut to pieces while they reloaded.

It was Oda Nobunaga's idea to adopt the volley fire tactics of archers, so that a missile of some kind was always in the air. The idea netted him a spectacular victory at the Battle of Nagashino in 1575, where his three thousand musketeers decisively defeated the enemy, armed mostly with disorganised musketeers, heavy cavalry and melee infantry. The message had been sent and received loud and clear – the Portuguese weapons clearly had more potential than even the Portuguese themselves had realised, and now that a better method for emphasising the strengths of the musket had been found, it was only a matter of time before the idea caught on. By 1638, during the final military engagements of Japan's government for two centuries, government forces contained armies which boasted 30% musketeers, all trained in the tactic of firing by rank. Training had been made possible because in the years since the Battle of Nagashino in 1575, Firearm Schools began to pop up across Japan, and incredibly detailed scrolls and manuscripts explaining the best tactics to be employed – the infantry drill – exploded in popularity and number.

Japan is rarely associated with technological innovation. When we think of Japanese history, we are often led to the image of Commodore Perry appearing outside of Japan in 1867 and threatening to blow the paper towns of Japan to smithereens unless the native government opened up for Western trade. Yet, incredible as it sounds, it is entirely possible, given the diffusion of ideas in early modern Europe, that the concept of fire by rank, and of organised volleys in general, was reported by the Portuguese back to their European masters, where it gained a pre-eminence all of its own in the 1590s. So ground-breaking was the Japanese innovation, that Geoffrey Parker has written: 'Volley fire was invented twice in the sixteenth century: in Japan during the 1560s and in the Dutch Republic in the 1590s.'[34]

The development of mass volley fire and its acceptance in Europe, regardless of how important the Japanese example was, or if it was indeed known, is something to behold. Europeans had theorised about changing up the disorganised, inefficient style of musket fire in the second half of the sixteenth century for several years, and thanks to the Dutch revolt against Spain, such ideas were liable to be experimented with. Fighting over fortified towns in a relatively compact region of Europe, the ingredients were present in the Netherlands as they had been present in Japan for some innovative ideas to be birthed and developed on the battlefield. In 1579 Thomas Digges, an Englishman in Dutch military service, wrote his own military treatise and put forward his idea of volley fire in the following way, writing that musketeers should…

...after the old Roman manner make three or four several fronts, with convenient spaces for the first to retire and unite himself with the second, and both these if occasion so require, with third; the shot [musketeers] having their convenient lanes continually during the fight to discharge their pieces.

Digges imagined a group of twenty-five men in each case, in sequence, 'so as the head shall be sure always to have charged [their muskets], before the tail have discharged; and this in a circular march, the skirmish all day continued.'[35] Indeed, the plan which appears so obvious to us now represents the cutting edge of ingenuity and innovation in the final years of the sixteenth century. The idea that men could be properly organised to fire according to a pre-arranged pattern – to a drill – was something close to revolutionary. Two years later, Digges released an updated version of his treatise, this time with the idea that the men at the front would fire, and the ranks behind them would pass forward loaded muskets, and reload them as they were fired, meaning that everyone stood still, and could theoretically be more accurate. As if to answer this challenge, a Spaniard who had spent two decades fighting the Dutch developed similar ideas, and in 1592 put forward the idea that three ranks of five musketeers could fire and alternate the loaded pieces. By reducing the number of men in each unit, it was supposed that they would be more flexible and easier for the melee troops to protect.

Of critical importance was the fact that neither Digges nor his Spanish counterpart could suggest any means by which these men could be trained. There was no concept of a regular training regimen, let alone a military drill to hone the art of firing by rank. In 1594 though, a letter sent by William Lodewick, the governor of the Dutch province of Friesland, to Maurice of Nassau, the famed military commander of the House of Orange, changed everything. After consulting the classics during his evening reading – a tactic not unusual for military leaders of early modern Europe on the hunt for some inspiration,[36] Lodewijk happened upon a tactic discussed by the Roman military theorist Aelian in his great work *Tactica*, from around 100AD, which itself had been preserved by Byzantine scholars from the nineth century. Above all, Lodewijk focused on Aelian's discussion of various types of volley fire, in which ranks of infantry advanced, hurled spears and javelins in sequence, and then retired, a technique known as the 'counter-march'.

The idea of firing – or in Aelian's case throwing the projectile – and then retiring and allowing another rank to do the same while you recovered, had never been properly considered for use with firearms. With a musket, the musketeers would aim and fire their weapons as well as they could, with few goals other than avoiding the cavalry of the enemy and being as accurate as possible. Generally speaking, with some exceptions, little effort had been made to coordinate between the ranks of musketeers, and to fire at the same time as archers would have done, nor was there any effort to arrange any kind of system whereby one group would fire while another waited or reloaded, with the act being swapped around as the battle progressed. The idea was even a bit controversial in Lodewijk's time because of what it would involve – the countermarch, the idea that the infantry that had expended their weapons would march in an orderly queue to the back of their unit, sounded at worst like a recipe for getting your men killed, and at best, it looked like you were retreating and walking away from the enemy. Yet Lodewijk wrote to Maurice in December 1594 nonetheless, saying:

> I have discovered…a method of getting the musketeers and soldiers armed with harquebuses not only to keep firing very well but to do it effectively in battle order (that is to say, they do not skirmish or use the cover of hedges) in the following manner: as soon as the first rank has fired together, then by the drill [they have learned] they will march to the back. The second rank, either marching forward or standing still, [will next] fire together [and] then march to the back. After that, the third and following ranks will do the same. Thus, before the last ranks have fired, the first will have reloaded, as the following diagram shows: these little dots show the route of the ranks as they leave after firing.[37]

Indeed, Governor Lodewijk even went as far as to draw Maurice of Nassau a diagram to demonstrate what was meant. Interestingly, Lodewijk was quite sensitive about the possibility that the idea would make him look bad, and he admitted that it was proving difficult to train the men effectively in this new style. He asked Maurice not to discuss or practice the style in public, 'because it may cause and give occasion for people to laugh, please do it only in private and with friends.' Evidently Lodewijk was a man fearful that his ideas would cost him, yet he remained convinced that they held water.

He had been given great inspiration from the recently translated works of Aelian by Justus Lipsius, who translated several Latin works into Dutch in the 1580s, including these works where the Byzantine Emperor Leo VIII recorded at length his admiration for the tactics used by Aelian in the Golden Age of Rome. Justus Lipsius, the Classical scholar who had translated these works and tied them together in six accessible books by 1590, wrote an entire section on how contemporary European rulers could learn from the wars described by Classical authors. As a scholar obsessed with the Classical method, Justus Lipsius saw sixteenth century infantry in the same light as the infantry of Rome: these infantrymen were the true battle winners, they could do the legwork and they would win the day through their extensive training and expertise.

Lipsius argued that modern infantry must learn to operate in smaller units (like Roman "maniples") as well as to drill with their arms in unison and to march in line with their peers, just as Roman armies had done. 'In all battles,' Lipsius asserted, 'skill and drill, rather than numbers and raw courage, normally bring victory.' William Lodewijk devoured Justus Lipsius' six translated books and dwelt for some time on the section on "Ancient Warfare under Rome", and what modern commanders could learn from it. As a commander with a body of men at his disposal, Lodewijk was in an idea position to test these ideas out, but as we saw, he was wary of what other people would think. He was not so wary that he kept quiet though. Lodewijk wrote to his secretary regularly, who later recalled his master's obsession with the new approach to gunpowder warfare.

> Seeing that the ancient art of war, and the benefits of battle order and speed of wheeling, reversing, turning, closing and extending ranks and files (without breaking), with which the Greeks and Romans had accomplished such splendid deeds, had vanished from the world, and were buried in forgetfulness, and since he could find no veteran colonels and captains from whom he could learn it [Willem Lodewijk] made use of all the leisure allowed by the enemy (who kept him busy) to search out what he could from old books, especially the writings of the Greek Emperor Leo, and therefore constantly drilled his regiment, making long and thin units instead of great squares, and training them to manoeuvre in various ways.[38]

Over the next year, Maurice met with Lodewijk, and the two men discussed and attempted to set out in practice this drill. Of great interest to the two men – perhaps obsession would be the better term – was the behaviour of the Romans. Maurice and Lodewijk continued to experiment, with some amusing results. Lodewijk always thought the end result too messy and uncoordinated in comparison to the legendary organisation and invincibility of the Roman legion. This despite the fact that some Dutch contemporaries believed muskets to be only a passing fascination – incredibly enough, the tactics and weaponry of the Romans were held in such high regard, that some of the advice Maurice and Lodewijk received could be summarised as a return to the roots of warfare, where pikemen, catapults and heavy cavalry dominated. These bizarre pieces of advice thankfully were not fully absorbed by either man, yet they still found it difficult to get the result they wanted out of these new drills.

Again, while consulting the classics, Lodewijk attempted to discern what it was that had made infantry in the Classical Era so formidable, and how their military drill could be emulated for modern times. In further discussions with Maurice, Lodewijk centred upon the example of Cannae, the seismic defeat in Roman history which saw a smaller Carthaginian army massacre its far larger Roman counterpart, in Hannibal's greatest victory. Maurice was interested in this example and what the Dutch infantry could learn from it, so Lodewijk offered to get to work. He first consulted the standard Latin translation of the detailed account of the battle in Polybius's *Roman Histories* but wanted something more detailed. Apparently with little else to occupy him, Lodewijk decided to commission an entirely new translation of the Cannae passage, which shed more light on how Hannibal had fought and won.

This investment seemed to do the trick, because in April 1595 Willem Lodewijk was able to send Maurice a copy of the new translation, with his calculations, and some sketches of the probable battle order in addition to a short treatise on the subject (which naturally cast the Dutch as the victorious Carthaginians and the Spaniards as the annihilated Romans). The following August, with the drills that those classical infantry more clearly spelled out, Maurice and Lodewijk oversaw several weeks' worth of drilling of the Friesland garrison, as the men were put through their paces. The aim was to inculcate in the men the strategy of firing and walking to the back of the line, but also to generally operate together more fluidly, and with greater cohesion and cooperation.

Maurice and Lodewijk wished to accustom the troops both to moving in unison and to seeing musketeers appear to retreat in the face of the enemy, which was no easy feat for men used to associating such tactics with defeat. These lessons were repeated over and over during the autumn months of 1595, until this version of the drill became standard. Four years later, by 1599, this tactic of drilling had spread across the Dutch Republic, and according to an eyewitness in The Hague:

> The new recruits the [Dutch] army assemble two or three times a week to learn keep rank, change step, wheel, and march like soldiers…and if a captain did not give or understand the command, His Excellency told him and sometimes showed him [how do it properly].[39]

Maurice was on his way towards creating something special, and already parallels between his drilling and the Romans were being made. While they drilled with pikes, the Dutch soldiers were referred to as *petites hastati*, in reference to the *hastati* infantry of Republican Roman fame. Those *hastati* were intended to be in Rome's frontlines, and to contain the raw recruits and youngest men, and Maurice seemed content to follow some of these ideas as well. A big test was necessary if the Dutch were to put their drilled forces into action and demonstrate the worth of this new system, not to mention justify the obsession with the counter-march and drill ideas which Lodewijk and Maurice had embraced. Thankfully for Maurice, the war with Spain provided no shortage of opportunities to test his theories out, but he was determined to wait for the perfect moment. In the meantime, refining his already innovative system kept him feverishly busy.

In the course of 1598, Maurice did more than simply revolutionise the way which his soldiers trained, he also altered the composition of his military companies by adding in a great deal more firepower. From this point forward in Dutch military strategy, each company would contain a total of 135 men, this included: thirteen officers and two pages, 45 pikemen, 44 arquebusiers, and 30 musketeers. The inclusion of the two different types of firearm has the potential to cause confusion, so it would be useful to clarify the differences between the two weapons before we proceed. Generally speaking, arquebusiers, sometimes called harquebuses, were smaller handheld firearms, while muskets tended to be larger, and had been devised to puncture armour with their larger calibre. Because of their larger length and weight, muskets tended to come equipped with a fork for balance, which could be stuck into the ground to anchor the musket, but it was also possible for an arquebusier to make use of the fork as well.

To further complicate the picture, the caliver was added into the mix which was intended to be a halfway home between the heavier musket and lighter arquebusiers. The musket even declined in popularity in the mid-sixteenth century due to the decline in armour and the lack of utility for such a heavy, high powered weapon. For whatever reason though, musket began to grow in popularity as a catch all term for firearms. Adding to the confusion, the terms arquebus and musket could be used interchangeably, and the picture was further muddied by the absence of any true regulations during the sixteenth century which would have stipulated the size and weight of the firearm at hand. It wasn't until the later portion of that century that the three broad categories of firearm – arquebus, caliver and musket – began to enter the lexicon of firearms technology, yet even then the terminology varied depending on where one wished to purchase his firearm.

This confusing situation is replicated in the Ottoman Empire, where the *tufek* became the catch-all term for a firearm in the hands of the Sultan's soldiers. This despite the fact that, in the Ottoman Empire as in Europe, the sprawling arms factories throughout the Ottoman Empire meant that manufacturers were bound to make their weapon differently, and depending on the whims of the local commander or the needs of the soldiers and the enemy. Thus, while the *tufek* defied easy classification, Europeans seemed perfectly willing to ignore their own classifications when it suited them to do so.[40] Due to the lack of centralisation in firearms production, it was only to be expected that a lack of consistency would be the result, thus Maurice of Nassau's additional ruling that the weapons of the Dutch army should be standardised proved to be yet another significant stamp which the Prince of Orange made upon the Dutch military.[41] After extensive testing, he determined upon a single "model" for muskets and another for arquebuses, and distributed five examples of each to arms producers. The Dutch producers now knew what to make, while the local commanders, theoretically, knew that they would have to train their men in the use of a much smaller pool of firearms than before, which would lead to a greater mastery and understanding of the weapons they did bring to bear.

With their firearms production somewhat more organised, the Dutch were able to affect a dramatic change in their army's training through an important development – the military drill manual. Maurice of Nassau, together with Count John II of Nassau, were incredibly industrious in their production of the illustrated manual. In 1599 they had secured funds from the States-General to equip the entire field army of the republic with weapons of the same size and calibre, which built upon the progress made in that sphere a few years before. Now the Dutch soldier had only to learn to handle one musket and one arquebus. While this was happening, Count John II of Nassau developed the illustrated manual by painstakingly analysing each movement required to bring the soldier from raising the weapon to making proper use of it.

Each movement was illustrated, so that not just soldiers, but commanders could learn what the different movement patterns were. By absorbing the orders which were barked at them by their captains, Dutch soldiers began to learn from these experiences under the drill, and to hone their skills so that handling a pike or firearm was more a case of hearing an order and then adopting the movement which went along with it. Muscle memory instilled by countless exercises made each one of these admittedly numerous motions easier, so that it became less a question of thinking and one merely of reflex, while *repetition, repetition, repetition* did the rest. There were fifteen drawings for the pike, twenty-five for the arquebus, and thirty-two for the musket, but all of these movements were learned, rehearsed and rehearsed again, so that every man knew where he stood – literally – when it came to a battle.

In 1606-7 these manuals became still more complicated; thirty-two positions for the pike and forty-two for each of the firearms were drawn up, as the step by step guide to bringing your infantry to war was deepened. Rather than have these books remain separate, they were compiled into a book published under Count John's supervision, and it was this book, published in 1607 in Amsterdam and unimaginatively titled *Arms drill with arquebus, musket and pike*, that established the idea of the illustrated drill as a Dutch invention.[42]

So successful was this book that it went through numerous editions in Dutch, French, German, English, even Danish; other states pirated and plagiarized different versions of it, and other efforts still were made to improve upon its instructions, but these were largely unimpressive. Notwithstanding the debate which exists about their practical influence on the Military Revolution, whether the Military Revolution actually existed at all, and what influence the Dutch tactics had on the rest of Europe, it cannot be denied that the Dutch were the first European power to properly put the new ideas of the counter-march into action. Now in Dutch armies, the tactic of the mass volley was perfected and could be readily taught to raw recruits thanks to the availability of these manuals and their clear instruction. Dutch soldiers would fire by rank, then walk to the back of their unit and reload, just as William Lodewijk and Maurice of Nassau's studies had aimed for.

The innovation of the drill was found in the idea that by making a man repeat the same action with his peers time and again, he would become acclimatised to the required movements to the point that he wouldn't have to think, and that he could march into the jaws of death with only the commands of his officer in his ears for comfort. As long as he had his orders, he was safe. It is certainly true that the drill took on a life of its own in the later seventeenth century, with Louis XIV's armies making particular use of the literature. Yet, it is also the case that the Dutch were *not* the first to drill their men; Geoffrey Parker has pointed out that the Spanish tercios of the sixteenth century were professionalised by repeated training regimens which granted them a formidable reputation. John A Lynn has underlined the idea that the French made use of the drill as well, and that they were encouraged by the Dutch example.

Further afield, in Japan for instance, drill manuscripts – rather than the kind of thick manuals as seen in Europe – were published, and the same concepts made their presence felt in these written works as were felt in the Dutch versions. Considering the innovation which the Dutch and Japanese engaged with, almost simultaneously, it would seem, one is left with a curious hole in Japan's development. One cannot help but ask why, if the Japanese were so innovative in developing the mass volley idea, did Japan subsequently fall behind the West in terms of technological sophistication. Why, for instance, did the samurai culture persist in Japan at the expense of the advancement of firearms technology? Or, in other words, what made the Japanese less patient with the weapons than the Europeans?

As it happened, the issue was as much about a lack of patience as it was a lack of expertise. Much of Japan's neighbours lacked native production facilities for these firearms, at least on the scale of Europeans, and thus trade was essential to acquire the necessary materials to continue with production. The Japanese, like the Chinese and Koreans, also had to contend with some fearsome horse-archers in enemy armies, and this led them to expect a great deal from the musket, and that it would be the replacement for the bow that had served them for so long. A great deal of respect for archers existed in Japanese society, as the archers were required to be highly mobile individual fighters, especially if mounted, and they were expected to hit a target at the longest distance with the most accuracy possible. Musketeers were expected to do the same, since they were expected to compete with the archers that had come before.

After some impressive initial showings, most notably at Nagashino in 1575 when three thousand musketeers annihilated a far larger force, expectations were set impossibly high thereafter, and manuscripts drawn up to teach the novice. The problems inherent in the high Japanese expectations of the musket were felt almost immediately. This is noted by the historian Harald Kleinschmidt in his article examining the spread of firearms throughout the world and the increased popularity of the drill to go along with them. Kleinschmidt recorded the high expectations of the Japanese:

> Descriptions showed individual arquebusiers who were expected to shoot with the same degree of precision as archers and who had to be able to fire from a variety of standing, sitting, crouching and lying. These positions were prescribed without concern for technical features, such as the "kick" of the weapon which might have injured the men or at least would have made it difficult for them to shoot accurately. Likewise, men were expected to have ample time for the loading and adjusting the firearms.[43]

Such high expectations were impossible to meet, and the reality, which was far less impressive than had been hoped for, was judged not worth it, as Harald Kleinschmidt continues:

> The social cost of the deployment of portable firearms seems to have been considered too high in Japan, for, after extensive use of portable firearms for about two generations in the sixteenth century, they were banned from the arsenals. Manual drill continued at a few places and firearms were still used as hunting weapons as late as in the eighteenth century. Likewise, cannon and mortars were still being cast in the seventeenth century. But these continuities only confirm that patterns of constrained behaviour did not then emerge as integral parts of Japanese ways of fighting, and thus it made little sense to keep portable firearms in continuing use.[44]

There is a great deal more which can be said about the drill, as well as its social impact on the peoples of Europe. By now we have learned that it is important not to generalise the significance or spread of these reforms in military thinking, especially since they had yet to really make their mark. It was high time they were given the chance to do so. After six years of practice, Maurice of Nassau and William Lodewijk believed they had found the ideal laboratory to test their new innovations. It was time to see if all those years of imagining, reading, studying and practicing had paid off.

FOUR
The Ultimate Test - Nieuwpoort

The army which Maurice of Nassau and others had spent several years reforming and preparing was ready for its first real test. Nieuwpoort and Dunkirk were two Spanish port towns of prime importance to the raiding and piracy industry, which cost Dutch shipping dearly. If these two piracy havens could be removed, then Dutch incomes would increase, but not only that; there was reason to believe that a successful campaign would only deepen the sense of disaffection within the Spanish Netherlands, rousing the people to revolt against Spain and in support of the Dutch Republic. One of the primary motives though, as the subsequent course of events would make clear, was the pursuit of contributions from occupied lands to pay for the on-going war with Spain, and to reduce the tax burden on the Dutch citizenry.[45]

The campaign was significant for other reasons as well. Not only was it Maurice of Nassau's best chance to test his drilled soldiers, since he was in command, but the entire political edifice of the Dutch Republic had been emptied for the sake of the campaign. All thirty of the politicians of the Dutch States-General had come on board the ships for the campaign from 17 June 1600. Had they been captured by the Spanish, then Madrid would have in its hands the commander and head of the Dutch army and navy as well as its government. Why then, were the Dutch taking such immense risks and marching out to meet the enemy, politicians in tow? The answer had much to do with the Dutch confidence not only in their ability, but also in the weakness and instability of the Spanish system.

The Army of Flanders, it was well known, was demoralised, underpaid and isolated. In the 1590s alone, more than twenty mutinies were known to have ripped through the ranks of the Spanish Netherlands army.[46] These soldiers were not merely militia troops, tasked with clinging to the Spanish Netherlands in the name of their King; they were, or at least they tended to be when on their best behaviour, professional soldiers of the highest calibre, renowned and feared throughout Europe for that very reason. The States-

General had banked on the Spanish holding back and not daring to launch any invasion of the Republic, since the revolt among Spanish soldiers that followed would surely lead to the unravelling of the Brussels regime. This was what was believed, and all evidence to the contrary was ignored. These politicians, along with Maurice, ten thousand infantry, 1,200 cavalry and 1,200 ships were supposed to sail around the coast of Flanders and make a direct attack against Dunkirk, but bad weather scuppered these plans. So, forced to improvise, it was decided that the Dutch would march overland to their destination, a distance of roughly eighty miles.

Yet, as it happened, the Spanish were more capable than the Dutch had given them credit for. They launched a counterattack while Maurice was marching south to the first target of Nieuwpoort, and the State General were staying put in Ostend. Both of these towns were along the coast of Flanders, and the primary goal of the States-General at this stage wasn't merely to use this position to block the piracy of the enemy; the ulterior motive, as we learned, was to levy contributions from the enemy lands. This process was accelerated by a series of angry letters which the States-General's members had prepared for the native Flanders towns while at sea. Fire and wrath were promised for these towns loyal to the King of Spain, unless the sword was turned away by the promise of regular gold. Contributions were designed to ease the burden on the home Dutch population, but in addition to this, each of the thirty States-General politicians in attendance at Ostend hoped to get personally rich for their efforts as well. Contrary to the expectations of the politicians in tow, the Spanish did counterattack – perhaps Spain was not as brittle as expected?

By summer 1600, the Spanish Netherlands had indeed been in some trouble. As it happened, the event which saved their regime there *was* the Dutch invasion, since it compelled the government of the Archdukes in Brussels to appeal to the dissenting voices and urge cooperation in the midst of a crisis. This appeal seemed to do the trick – the soldiery would engage with and repel the invading Dutch, and by this action would demonstrate in the plainest terms their worth to the Brussels government, and to the Flemish people. Archduke Albert was on the case, and he had roused nearly eight thousand soldiers to battle – all men of professional stock, and well-versed in the Spanish tercio formation tactic which had won them so much ground in the past.

Albert's stately experience was not inconsiderable, but as usual with Habsburg Archdukes, it was his family pedigree that truly mattered at the time. Albert was the fifth son of a large family, and he counted among his elder brothers the current Holy Roman Emperor Rudolf II (r. 1576-1612), in addition to the future Emperor Matthias (r. 1612-1619), and his father had been Maximillian II, Holy Roman Emperor (r. 1564-1576). After a career, which included being appointed Cardinal at the ripe age of eighteen and viceroy of a newly incorporated Portugal, Albert now faced a serious test of his own, and he was determined not to let the family down by leading through example. Along the way to confront the Dutch, Albert picked up a great deal more men from the loyal garrisons, especially when it was learned that Albert was promising plunder to the men in his employ if they did their duty. By late June, Albert's forces were roughly equal to that of Maurice's, and he was marching northwards to cut between his force and the States-General's officers in Ostend. Incredibly, neither Maurice nor his political masters had predicted such a manoeuvre, as they had bought fully into the idea that the Spanish could not afford to attack, lest Spain would see their unpaid and underappreciated forces melt away before the battle even began.

On 1 July the States-General learned of their predicament – if Albert marched his army to Ostend, he could well put the entire governing apparatus of the Dutch Republic under siege, and perhaps even storm the anaemically defended Ostend before Maurice could arrive. In this crisis the statesmen urgently sent Maurice, according to the official resolution released at the time, 'four or five separate letters' in which, they 'earnestly begged and admonished His Excellency' to put his army in good order and 'not to divide his forces'. This, in short, was a command for Maurice to abandon any previous plans of a siege of Nieuwpoort, one of the first goals of the original campaign, and to fly to the defence of the politicians by meeting the Spanish head on. For his part, Maurice almost certainly resented the fact that 'the States had so explicitly demanded this campaign, as if the Republic could not be preserved in any other way'. Maurice was now forced to respond to the enemy's moves, which was not a good strategic position to be in, and he clearly had no choice but to fight the Spanish, since a withdrawal by sea would have been disastrous.

Various ideas were put forward about the best ways to meet the Spanish in battle, with some urging him to throw up field defences, but Maurice replied that 'he would give battle, that we must strike, that blood must be shed this day, and that he needed no other defence than the pikes and muskets' of his troops. Maurice declared that he 'placed his trust, after God, in the perpetual drilling of his troops' – or, in the words of one of his generals, in 'that skill and dexterity we presumed to excel our enemies in, which was the apt and agile motions of our battalions.' Maurice was keenly aware that all the years of planning and training, all the years of theorising and all the years of investment were about to be put to the test. If he failed, if his men failed to defeat the enemy, then all the naysayers would have been validated, and Maurice's reputation ruined, not to mention the reputations of those men like William Lodewijk who had spent some time studying classical battle methods for the sake of days like these. The circumstances were far from ideal; the ground would be sandy, the numbers of the enemy could not be precisely known, and the pressure from thirty fawning politicians added to the tension, but he had no choice – it was time to place his men at the mercy of the drilling. On 2 July 1600, they lined up to do battle with their Spanish foe.

Before we investigate that battle, it is worth asking an important question – exactly who was this foe that the Dutch under Maurice of Nassau were about to face? We need first to examine what is meant by the tercio, and how it differed from Maurice's forces. The tercios were the first infantry units to make use of pike, musket, sword and arquebus weapons in the same group. Each tercio was composed of a certain number of recruits, interspersed with a core grouping of veterans or old soldiers, designed to keep the whole unit together in times of strain. This method of training the men, by having them learn from the more experienced soldiers within the tercio, was a major feature of the Spanish system, but recruits were also trained in the major troop bastions of Spain's European empire, with Brussels and Milan serving above all as central recruitment and training grounds. The claim normally made is that the Spanish system for training recruits was not as refined or rigid as the drill adopted by Maurice of Nassau, which controlled every aspect of the soldier's movements and which provided step by step instructions for each manoeuvre. Spanish recruits, it was said, learned by osmosis, and by adopting the practices of that aforementioned core of veterans.

Something which gave the tercio its characteristic appearance was the pike. The pike and the men holding them served as the backbone of the tercio, as its main form of melee defence, and theoretically, as a well-oiled machine capable of resisting cavalry charge as much as the charge of soldiery. It was the task of the pikemen to resist, but also to protect, as they shielded the arquebusiers from these same dangers while they reloaded. Such ideas make sense, but it can still seem jarring and somewhat misplaced for pikemen to play such a prominent role in sixteenth and seventeenth century warfare. But the Spanish had not invented the pike or the tight formations of pike squares – that honour belonged to the Swiss. According to Balcus, the Milanese ambassador to the Swiss Confederation from 1500-1504:

> When the Swiss start out to war, they swear a solemn oath that every man who sees one of his comrades desert, or act the coward in battle, will cut him down on the spot, for they believe that the courage and persistency of warriors is greater when they, out of fear of death, do not fear death. They begin a battle after they have formed their phalanx according to the old methods of war, and steadfast and fearless, they are almost indifferent to life and death. They threw away the shield which they had formerly been accustomed to use, like all other nations. They learned through experience that the shield could not in any way withstand the power of the phalanx and the lance.[47]

We have seen the influences of Ancient Rome in the treatises and methods of William Lodewijk and Maurice of Nassau, and here again is evidence that the opponents of the Dutch took their inspiration from warriors who were themselves inspired to 'form the phalanx according to the old methods of war.' A well-disciplined square of pikemen could and did defeat everything in its path – Swiss independence was achieved by the point of the pike when the Dukes of Austria were defeated in successive battles through the fourteenth century. This was the beginning of the Swiss Confederation, powered by ambitious Swiss dukes, and defended by their ingenious use of the eighteen-foot pike. The Swiss legend of efficiency was only matched by their fearsome reputation and bravery – they would challenge a force of any size, would execute any prisoners, any garrisons, which came into their hands. As that above ambassador believed, they were 'almost indifferent to life and death', and Balcus was by no means the only figure to believe so.[48]

Naturally, having learned of the Swiss ability to harness the pike to its full effect, the neighbours of the Swiss began to plagiarise their techniques. But the methods of warfare did not sit still for long. Although Balcus was plainly in awe of the Swiss legend during his service, the opening years of the sixteenth century can in fact be seen as the point when the pike legend began to wear off, thanks in large part to the advent of the firearm. As Frank Tallet recorded:

> At Marignano (1515), La Bicocca (1522) and Pavia (1525) pikemen proved vulnerable to gunfire, and thereafter no army could do without arquebusiers, both to protect its own pikemen and to threaten the enemy's. The proportion of hand-gunners to pikemen rose inexorably, increasing, in the case of the Spanish regular infantry, to one in three by the 1570s and almost parity by 1600, while the Dutch muster lists (unusually accurate records of their type) reveal that by the 1590s an infantry company of 135 men included 74 hand-gunners (44 arquebusiers and 30 musketeers) and only 45 pikemen.[49]

As Tallet notes, the arrival of the more capable firearm did not mean the death of the pike, because arquebusiers and musketeers were still vulnerable to cavalry charge or other infantry as they reloaded. It was therefore evident that a combination of the two arms would produce the best results, and that was what singled out the Spanish for their use of such combined arms. The tercio was the result, but what exactly *was* the tercio? In terms of weaponry, the tercio was designed to emphasise the strengths of the pike and guard the weaknesses of the musket. Leaving men standing in the open while they loaded their weapons was obviously an invitation for a cavalry charge, and thus disaster, so the tercio system enveloped all the defensive postures of a pike with the stopping power and reach of the musket.

In some respects, the idea was not revolutionary – the system was similar to that of medieval armies which had placed the archers behind the frontline of melee soldiers. Archers were vulnerable to other melee soldiers and cavalry, so they effectively followed and stayed behind the cover which the melee soldiers provided. The tercios were a similar formula, except the musket and pike soldiers were tied together and taught to move and fight as one. They fought as squares, but the fact that they moved with their pikes in formation meant that it was sometimes difficult to move at a quick pace, which left them vulnerable in later years to light, mobile artillery that would punch right through their squares.

An average tercio consisted of three thousand men, with musketeers at the front and pikemen holding the hollow centre. The hole in the centre enabled the wounded or reloading men to withdraw into the centre of the square behind the cover of the pikes, and even while the pikemen stood behind the musketeers, and marched with pikes upright, their long weapons would be more than capable of reaching over the shoulders of the musketeers in front of them and stabbing at the enemy. In earlier forms of the tercio, swordsmen armed with javelins would also stand in the centre, and the number of musketeers would be fewer. As the sixteenth century progressed though, the combination of pike and musket was felt to be superior to any other. The tercio squares sometimes drew their musketmen out and lined them up if the opportunity presented itself, but generally formation was kept, and this formation effectively won Spain its European empire. As R. Trevor Davies in his book noted:

> This was the tactical system – simple but frightfully effective – that helped to make Spanish armies invincible, and the models which all Europe sought more or less ineffectively to copy. It is a striking illustration of the rudimentary character of the military mind that it took a century and a half to find an adequate counterblast to this system.[50]

Considered the startling ingenuity of their combat systems, and the staying power of the tercios, it is surprising that Spain was one of the major targets of Michael Roberts' thesis. Evidently, existing as they did on the cutting edge of military innovation, the Spanish had no need of a Military Revolution which replaced their tercios with muskets and focused solely on the volume of fire as the new formations intended to do. As late as the Battle of Nordlingen (1634) the tercio system remained practical and highly effective, in many respects serving as Spain's saving grace. In short, the Military Revolution was far from as simple a case as Roberts claimed in 1957 – while Maurice of Nassau and Gustavus Adolphus brought important new ideas to warfare, in the form of illustrated war manuals and the use of light artillery respectively, it was not axiomatic that these new ideas would supersede the old.

Moving away from the tercio, a reliable method of warfare for over a century, based on principles which could be traced to the high middle ages, could only take place following a period of intensive reflection. Furthermore, it required that the firearm be sophisticated enough to make up for its lack of melee capabilities with the sheer volume of shot it could put down. These latter ingredients – better firearm drills and more technologically advanced muskets – were the *true* factors behind the later Spanish adoption of the fire by rank approach, rather than the ingenuity of Spain's Dutch or Swedish foes.[51]

Yet, it wasn't only Michael Roberts who created the myth of Spanish lethargy and military inefficiency. The historian Fernando Gonzalez de Leon made some important points in his article examining the actual military proficiency of the Spanish Habsburg armies in the sixteenth century, and the role they played in inspiring other military institutions across Europe.[52] Yet, as Fernando Gonzalez de Leon also noted, the actual historical fact of Spanish achievements under the tercio were undermined in some senses by the prevailing generalisation created in some works by Spanish historians themselves. One example, which de Leon gives, is that erroneous picture painted of Spanish infantry in Raffaele Puddu's 1982 study, *Il Soldato Gentiluomo*. De Leon wrote on Puddu's study that:

> His inquiry into the Spanish military ethos of the sixteenth century presents the Spanish officer largely as a crusading cavalier with an abiding love for his sword and a pronounced contempt for modern firearms-in other words, a Don Quixote.[53]

Don Quixote was a character from a novel written in the first few years of the seventeenth century, which told the story of a delusional Spaniard, who goes on a journey to resurrect the ideas of chivalry and knightly customs, and ignores all evidence which paints that nostalgic era of European society as dead and gone. Don Quixote became the perfect archetype of the Spanish soldier, since it was what the rest of Europe knew, even while they also knew that the Spanish had conquered an Empire on which the sun never set, and that Spanish military might had elevated that Kingdom to the first rank of powers by the close of the sixteenth century. The Spaniard was therefore akin to Don Quixote – he was delusional, in denial of the realities of how society had progressed and completely incapable of adapting to the times. His life was a backward one, which longed in vain for the old times, and which did nothing to prepare for the new developments in technology, science or critically, warfare. He struggled hopelessly with the outdated pike, and ignored new developments in the technological sphere, thus making him vulnerable to his innovative neighbours.

To an extent, the myth of Spanish inefficiency laid down in the Military Revolution was the product of the Spanish 'Black Legend'. We need only to look at other impressions of Spain aside from the military generalisations – the Spanish were conservative to a destructive degree, they were champions of the Inquisition, they were ruled by evil and corrupted Kings, they despised personal freedom and loved restrictive absolutism, they loathed hard work and preferred to embrace the siesta while their sprawling empire sank into so many seas. If Spain had been the wasting, lazy and ignorant power that Roberts and others implied, then Spanish might would not have been so feared and loathed during the Thirty Years War, or previously in the sixteenth century. As Geoffrey Parker points out, champions of the Military Revolution often forget that it was the Spanish tercio system which achieved the most shattering victories over its enemies during the conflict; consider the battles of White Mountain in 1620 or Nordlingen in 1634, for instance, and how the primacy of the apparently 'old' Spanish tactics carried the day.[54]

The list of works which examine Spanish tactics and military primacy during early modern Europe are surprisingly few in number, and most tend to be in Spanish, which does nothing to reduce the impressions which English-speaking enthusiasts might have about how Spanish inefficiency was replaced by the Dutch, Swedish and even English examples, the latter example given by Cromwell's new model army.[55] Several treatises written by Spanish officers who fought against the Dutch also testify to what the Spanish valued and looked for in potential recruits, and what made the best officers. As Fernando Gonzalez de Leon noted:

> These treatises...describe the ideal officer, his duties, his behaviour, and his education. The writers constructed a model officer who was certainly an ingenious hidalgo, but very different from the nostalgic and impractical warrior of the Don Quixote tradition. He was instead a soldier who regarded the military as an independent profession in which highly trained technicians earned their commissions through merit, that is, a kind of leader that Maurice of Nassau would have feared.[56]

Indeed, Maurice of Nassau did have a healthy respect for Spanish arms, and he could not have guaranteed that his well-drilled army would be victorious, even while he declared his intentions to rely on their expertise in the weapons and tactics drill. Previous Spanish works and commentaries on the situation emphasised the new for a merit-based officer corps, for constant reform and, interestingly enough, for inspiration to be taken from the examples of 'the ancients', a reference to the classical tactics of antiquity and the staying power of the Roman military example. Just as it had inspired Maurice of Nassau to institute a complex and detailed drilling system, so too had it moved several Spanish military writers to urge aspiring officers to look to past examples for inspiration.

These works appeared over the 1560s and 70s, and in the 1580s, newer, more detailed works on the nature of warfare and what a Spanish tercio commander was expected to do, and the qualities he was expected to possess, were also disseminated. They deserve some mention to demonstrate the parallels between Maurice of Nassau's drilling and the pre-existing Spanish commitment to professionalism and discipline which had carried them so far. One work, published in 1585, the *Mirror of Military Discipline*, was later translated in several languages, and one extract of it reads thus:

> Because the military is such a noble undertaking, it must have its rules and precepts, which are the foundation of the military art. Just as no one can practice medicine, law, or theology who has not studied in those faculties and is [not] learned in those disciplines, so those who are not learned in the military discipline should not be allowed to give orders and lead in war. This discipline serves the officer as a loyal advisor, a light in the darkness and a guide on a difficult and uncertain road.[57]

Other treatises, like 1590's *The Perfect Captain Instructed in the Military Discipline* and the *New Science of Artillery*, or 1592's *Practical Manual of Artillery*, provide highly detailed and technical guides on the best ways of making use of the latest advances in military technology and tactics. These were not, in other words, books produced by a tired and lethargic military system; they were written by professional officers on the cutting edge of military innovation and thinking, and their works were passed about Europe just as the later Dutch illustrated drill manuals would be. The Spanish books emphasised the central importance of artillery, and outlined the essential qualifications of a Spanish officer in military service – notably, aristocratic, noble birth was *not* on the list, and indeed, these works all rallied against the selling of commissions as much as they emphasised the need for a good education in arithmetic, rhetoric and history.

One final example of a published Spanish treatise, released in 1593, further establishes the point. This treatise was entitled *The Science, Discourse, and Rule of the Military* and was written by a twenty-seven-year veteran of the tercios of Flanders who had marched to the Low Countries and fought against the Dutch since the outbreak of the revolt. The veteran's name was Captain Martin de Eguiluz, and while he remains virtually unknown, Eguiluz, according to his books, seems to have invented the entire concept of the military drill which Maurice has been credited for. Considering the fact that Eguiluz' book was released two years before Maurice and his peers began brainstorming about the best way to reform their armies, it is certainly possible that Maurice copied the lessons laid down in this book. Regarding Eguiluz' book, Fernando Gonzalez de Leon commented that:

> Like Maurice…Eguiluz champions constant drill and training for the soldiers, in the style of the ancient Romans, as well as an increase in the number of muskets and musketeers in the tercios. His major claim to fame must rest on his detailed description of the counter-march, considered by many historians

the tactical centrepiece of the early modern Military Revolution. This complex battlefield manoeuvre consisted of aligning long, three-deep rows of soldiers to shoot, yield their place at the front to those behind them, and then to load and come forward to fire again in order to maintain a steady rate of fire. The origin, application, and usefulness of this manoeuvre remain controversial, but most historians, following Roberts, have overlooked Eguiluz and assign the intellectual fatherhood of the counter-march to Maurice of Nassau, even though the publication of Eguiluz' [treatise] antedates Maurice's first letter on the subject by two years.[58]

It is entirely possible that Maurice and his theorising peers were unaware of Eguiluz' work. Considering its striking parallels with the Dutch innovations though, *The Science, Discourse, and Rule of the Military* must be mentioned when talking of military innovation in the era, not least because it has been largely forgotten by so many historians of the period. Indeed, since the era was known for its diffusion of ideas and the enthusiasm for innovation, we cannot ignore the possibility that Maurice or William Lodewijk read Eguiluz' work. What is important to note, however, is that the Spanish government largely ignored these ideas, preferring to stick to what they knew in the tercio rather than reinvent the wheel. Furthermore, the Dutch innovations are no less significant merely because they may have been conceived by someone else first. Where Maurice is wholly deserving of praise is in the realm of publishing, where he commissioned the publication of detailed illustrative manuals that provided detailed instructions and pictures for each stage of every weapon drill. And yet, before commissioning such books or acquiring such a reputation for innovation, Maurice of Nassau would first have to defeat his Spanish nemesis, and it is to that battlefield near the town of Nieuwpoort on 2 July 1600 that we return now.

Sometimes the best perspectives are those given by the enemy, and with this in mind, it is worth hearing the account given after the event by an Italian soldier in Spanish service, who noted that Maurice has assembled and drawn up his troops…

> …very well, placing in front a corps of musketeers and in front of these musketeers some six pieces of artillery. Behind these musketeers stood two more squadrons of over one thousand pikemen, each one with 500 pikes, with the cavalry outside on the wings. All were in very good order. In addition, he placed 70 or 80 musketeers certain sand hills to flank our troops.[59]

On Maurice's side, one of the captain's later gave the following account of the battle:

> Our infantry advanced towards the enemy. The enemy's cavalry, seeing our men advancing in such good order, because they were well supported, wanted to take refuge among their infantry in the dunes; but their own ranks broke and,

seeing themselves still pressed by our cavalry, they decided on headlong flight. The hail of volleys then began to cease.[60]

Fortunately for the Dutch leader, the battle was a victory for Maurice and his well-drilled Dutchmen. Accounts of the battle do not mention the tactic of the counter-march specifically, but they do imply that this tactic was used, and that the Dutch fired their weapons in the front ranks before walking to the back to reload. This is implied in the image painted by the aforementioned Italian, who describes blocks of four thousand musketeers in one unit. Unless these men fired and then went to the back, Maurice would never have allowed them to group together like this, where they would been unable to make the most of their numbers. Firing at what was often point-blank range, the drilled Dutch soldiers held up during even the most horrific stages of the battle, and their use of firepower, with lighter cannon interspersed within the squares of pikemen for instance, as well as the mass volleys of the musketeers, seem to have won the day.

Maurice's packed musketeers fired volley after volley into the Spanish tercios as each man wheeled back into the rear of his formation. The men they fired at were arranged in the traditional Spanish tercio square, with about 1,500 musketeers and 1,500 pikes per square. Clearly from even these numbers, the Dutch would have superiority in fire, but the pikemen which the Dutch did have were left to the side, ready to rush in at a moment's notice, while Maurice's men fired and fired again into the Spanish mass. It was in many respects the clashing of two distinct military styles, and it thus represents a highly significant moment in the history of early modern European battle tactics and military thought.

Whether he invented these tactics or not, what is not up for debate is that Maurice of Nassau managed to leverage them against the Spanish tercios, or, as one Dutch officer put it: 'This victory was wonderful, as much because he [Maurice] won his enemy's territory as because he won it over a victorious enemy, the battle mostly involved Spaniards and Italians, who were esteemed strongest force of the enemy.'[61] The drilling and training of the previous years had massively increased the damage which the musketeers could inflict; Geoffrey Parker records that four thousand Spaniards were killed outright by these tactics – nearly half the force which had come to meet Maurice in battle.

The battle was bloody and immensely loud as well; eyewitnesses were not able to see, thanks to the amount of smoke which rose above the sand dunes around which the battle took place, but they could tell from the noise of the musket and cannons that a serious confrontation was taking place. The experience was an intense two hours in duration, but by its end the Dutch Republic had their champion. Learning from this experience, Maurice became utterly convinced of the primacy of the drill, and went on to find even easier ways to implement it across the Dutch army, eventually settling on the simple illustrated drill manuals, which literally spelled out every movement to raw recruit and instructor alike. Yet, although William Lodewijk had modelled his ideas for the drill on the Carthaginian ability to destroy an army far larger than themselves, Nieuwpoort was not a Cannae.

Maurice had lost one thousand men killed of his own, and many more were wounded. Furthermore, his old problems of supply persisted, so that he was unable to make use of the victory and pursue the defeated Spaniards to Antwerp. In addition, his victory did not create a Spanish rout. A less organised rabble may well have been shattered and disintegrated altogether by this defeat, but the years of discipline and professionalism inculcated in the Spanish soldier, which we must not discount, meant that Maurice's victory was important, but could not force Spain to the peace table. Maurice had simply come to Nieuwpoort with a new way of waging war, but there was no absolute proof that his way was better. In the grand laboratory of military innovation, Nieuwpoort was one test. Thirty-four years later at the Battle of Nordlingen, the Spanish 'old ways' were harnessed to great effect to defeat a Swedish-German army built in the style of Maurice of Nassau. A generation after Maurice of Nassau had changed warfare then, the change was by no means universal, and the Spanish were vindicated for sticking – quite literally – to their guns.

As far as Maurice of Nassau was concerned, he had tried these new tactics and training methods out in the field, and they had paid off, but much still needed to be done if the kind of shattering triumphs achieved by Rome were to be his. We must remember that Maurice was not acting as an instrument of anyone's theory – he was a soldier and an innovator, who simply wanted to defeat the enemy at the lowest possible cost to himself. While he could not have known it yet, the spread of his ideas would produce new innovators and in time, historians and strategists operating with hindsight would reflect that he had been correct. Following the bloody Battle of Nieuwpoort, this was by no means wholly certain, but further opportunities for additional testing abounded, as there were many more bloody battles still to come.

Chapter 2 Notes

[1] Geoffrey Parker, 'The "Military Revolution," 1560-1660--a Myth?', p. 203.

[2] *Ibid*, p. 204.

[3] See Geoffrey Parker, 'Why Did the Dutch Revolt Last Eighty Years?', *Transactions of the Royal Historical Society*, Vol. 26 (1976), pp. 53-72.

[4] On Vauban's improvements to the French defences see: James Faulkner, *Marshal Vauban and the Defence of Louis XIV's France* (South Yorkshire: Pen & Sword Military, 2011).

[5] For more detail on the Franco-Dutch War and the desperate Dutch defensive approach in 1672 see: Carl J. Ekberg, *The Failure of Louis XIV's Dutch War* (Chapel Hill, NC: University of North Carolina Press, 1979), and especially for the Dutch defensive struggle: George Satterfield, *Princes, Posts and Partisans: The Army of Louis XIV and Partisan Warfare in the Netherlands* (1673-1678), History of Warfare (Boston: Brill, 2003).

[6] John A. Lynn, 'The Trace Italienne and the Growth of Armies: The French Case', *The Journal of Military History*, Vol. 55, No. 3 (Jul., 1991), pp. 297-330; p. 302.

[7] John Stoye, *The Siege of Vienna* (Edinburgh: Birlinn, 2000), pp. 187-215.

[8] Lynn, 'The Trace Italienne and the Growth of Armies: The French Case', pp. 304-307.

[9] *Ibid*, p. 311.

[10] *Ibid*, p. 315.

[11] See Jeremy Black, *A Military Revolution? Military Change and European Society, 1550-1800* (Atlantic Highlands, N.J., 1991), p. 98

[12] John A. Lynn, 'The Trace Italienne and the Growth of Armies', p. 318.

[13] *Ibid*, p. 321.

[14] Cited in *Ibid*, p. 322.

[15] *Ibid*, p. 322.

[16] Lynn, 'Tactical Evolution in the French Army, 1560-1660', p. 176.

[17] The end of the Dutch flirtation with absolutism under the House of Orange is examined in H. M. Scott, 'Sir Joseph Yorke, Dutch Politics and the Origins of the Fourth Anglo-Dutch War', The Historical Journal, Vol. 31, No. 3 (Sep., 1988), pp. 571-589. For its beginning see Pieter Geyl, 'William IV of Orange and His English Marriage', *Transactions of the Royal Historical Society*, Vol. 8 (1925), pp. 14-37.

[18] Geoffrey Parker, 'The "Military Revolution," 1560-1660--a Myth?', pp. 206-207.

[19] For both these points see John A. Lynn, 'Recalculating French Army Growth during the Grand Siecle, 1610-1715', *French Historical Studies*, Vol. 18, No. 4 (Autumn, 1994), pp. 881-906; John A. Lynn, 'The Trace Italienne and the Growth of Armies: The French Case', pp. 297-330.

[20] Cited in Ronald S. Love, '"All the King's Horsemen": The Equestrian Army of Henri IV, 1585-1598', *The Sixteenth Century Journal*, Vol. 22, No. 3 (Autumn, 1991), pp. 510-533; p. 512.

[21] *Ibid*, p. 510.

[22] See Sir Charles Oman, *The Art of War in the Sixteenth Century* (London: E.P Dutton and Co., 1937), p. 467.

[23] Ronald S. Love, '"All the King's Horsemen"', p. 514.

[24] See *Ibid*, pp. 515-516.

[25] Treva J. Tucker, 'Eminence over Efficacy: Social Status and Cavalry Service in Sixteenth-Century France', *The Sixteenth Century Journal*, Vol. 32, No. 4 (Winter, 2001), pp. 1057-1095; p. 1057.

[26] See John A. Lynn, 'Tactical Evolution in the French Army, 1560-1660', pp. 177-179.

[27] *Ibid*, p. 180.

[28] J. W. Wijn, 'Military Forces and Warfare, 1610-1648', *The New Cambridge Modern History*, vol. 4 (Cambridge, 1970), p. 203

[29] John A. Lynn, 'Tactical Evolution in the French Army, 1560-1660', p. 181.

[30] See Leonid Tarassuk, 'The Cabinet d'Armes of Louis XIII: Some Firearms and Related Problems', *Metropolitan Museum Journal*, Vol. 21 (1986), pp. 65-122; p. 65.

[31] Quoted in Arthur Hassall, *Louis XIV and the Zenith of the French Monarchy* (New York: G. P. Putnam's Sons, 1895), p. 19.

[32] *Ibid*, p. 182.

[33] *Ibid*, pp. 183-186.

[34] See Geoffrey Parker, 'The Limits to Revolutions in Military Affairs', pp. 331-372; pp. 333-335.

[35] Both cited in *Ibid*, p. 337.

[36] See Donald A. Neill, 'Ancestral Voices: The Influence of the Ancients on the Military Thought of the Seventeenth and Eighteenth Centuries', *The Journal of Military History*, Vol. 62, No. 3 (Jul., 1998), pp. 487-520.

[37] Cited in Geoffrey Parker, 'The Limits to Revolutions in Military Affairs', p. 339.

[38] Cited in *Ibid*, p. 341.

[39] Both cited in *Ibid*, p. 346.

[40] At the risk of complicating the picture further still, Indian sources often recorded crossbows as *tufak* rather than the Turkish for musket *tufek*, which not only suggests a etymological connection but also provides bountiful opportunities to confuse contemporaries in the Ottoman Empire and Mughal Empire alike. See Iqtidar Alam Khan, 'Early Use of Cannon and Musket in India: A.D. 1442-1526', *Journal of the Economic and Social History of the Orient*, Vol. 24, No. 2 (May, 1981), pp. 146-164.

[41] Geoffrey Parker, 'The Limits to Revolutions in Military Affairs', pp. 346-347.

[42] Geoffrey Parker, 'The "Military Revolution," 1560-1660--a Myth?', pp. 201-202.

[43] Harald Kleinschmidt, 'Using the Gun: Manual Drill and the Proliferation of Portable Firearms', *The Journal of Military History*, Vol. 63, No. 3 (Jul., 1999), pp. 601-630; pp. 624-625.

[44] *Ibid*, p. 625-626.

[45] Unless stated otherwise, this account of the Battle of Nieuwpoort is taken from Geoffrey Parker, 'The Limits to Revolutions in Military Affairs: Maurice of Nassau, the Battle of Nieuwpoort (1600), and the Legacy', *The Journal of Military History*, Vol. 71, No. 2 (Apr., 2007), pp. 331-372; pp. 348-370.

[46] Geoffrey Parker, 'Mutiny and Discontent in the Spanish Army of Flanders 1572-1607', *Past & Present*, No. 58 (Feb., 1973), pp. 38-52.

[47] Quoted in John Vincent, *Switzerland at the Beginning of the Sixteenth Century* (Baltimore, 1904; reprint New York, 1974), p. 16-17.

[48] See Frederic J. Baumgartner, *From Spear to Flintlock: A History of War in Europe and the Middle East to the French Revolution* (New York: Praeger Publishers, 1991), pp. 159-161.

[49] Frank Tallett, *War and Society in Early-Modern Europe: 1495-1715* (New York: Routledge, 1997), p. 24.

[50] R. Trevor Davies, *The Golden Century of Spain 1501-1621* (London: Macmillan and Co Ltd, 1967), p. 24.

[51] Tallet, W*ar and Society*, pp. 26-28.

[52] Fernando Gonzalez de Leon, '"Doctors of the Military Discipline": Technical Expertise and the Paradigm of the Spanish Soldier in the Early Modern Period', *The Sixteenth Century Journal*, Vol. 27, No. 1 (Spring, 1996), pp. 61-85.

[53] *Ibid*, p. 62.

[54] Geoffrey Parker, 'The "Military Revolution," 1560-1660--a Myth?', p. 200.

[55] See Roger B. Manning, *An Apprenticeship in Arms: The Origins of the British Army 1585-1702* (New York: Oxford University Press, 2006), pp. 180-261.

[56] Fernando Gonzalez de Leon, '"Doctors of the Military Discipline", p. 62.

[57] Cited in *Ibid*, p. 69.

[58] *Ibid*, p. 73.

[59] Cited in Geoffrey Parker, 'The Limits to Revolutions in Military Affairs', p. 351.

[60] Cited in *Ibid*, p. 353.

[61] Cited in *Ibid*, p. 354.

(Top left) Gustavus Adolphus, King of Sweden 1611 -1632 (Jacob Hoefngel)
(Top right) Albrecht Wallenstein

(Top left) Maximillian I, Elector of Bavaria (Joachim von Sandrat)
(Top right) Johann Tilly (Anthony van Dyck)

(Top left) Frederick V of the Palatinate (Gerard van Honthorst). (Top right) Christian IV of Denmark (Pieter Isacsz, 1612)

(Top left) Johann Georg I of Saxony (Frans Luycx)
(Top right) Gottfried Heinrich von Pappenheim)

CHAPTER THREE
"Perfection and Proliferation"

ONE
Expanding the Dutch Drill

In advancing towards an enemy, musketeers must always give fire by ranks after this manner. Two ranks must always make ready together…and give fire, first the first rank…. As soon as the first [rank] are fallen away, the second [must immediately] present, and give fire, and fall [back] after them. Now as soon as the first two ranks do move from their places in the front, the two ranks next to them must unshoulder their muskets, and make ready…And all the other ranks through the whole division must do the same by twos, one after another.[1]

In such a way did the Dutch States-General describe their newly tried and tested musketry drill. Maurice of Nassau, it seemed, had created something which was well worth talking about. The lessons learned in that campaign of 1600, which ended the following year, were consistently updated over the following years, so that in 1618 the States-General wrote of a reconsidered 'Exercise for musketeers', wherein 'The first two ranks get ready, take aim, and fire (and so on until all the ranks have fired.'[2] Impressive though it certainly was, Maurice's achievements were not felt in the strategic improvement of the Dutch position, but instead in the tactical evolution of the Dutch infantry. The fire by rank, mass volley idea and the restructuring of infantry, in other words, did not lead to an end of the war with Spain. In addition, the horrors experienced by Maurice at Nieuwpoort seemed to have convinced him that discretion was the better part of valour. He would not fight another such pitched battle again for as long as he lived.

One figure who may have influenced Maurice's reluctance was William Lodewijk, the individual who had theorised alongside the Price of Orange to develop the now vaunted infantry drill. Lodewijk was equally, if not more, hesitant, about engaging in another battle like Nieuwpoort, and the following explanation from Lodewijk himself gives a hint as to why. In 1601, Lodewijk had opposed another expedition to Flanders because it involved 'the risk of a battle' and in 1602 he begged Maurice to 'avoid undertaking anything that is not justified on military grounds.' A few weeks later, he sent Maurice the following memorandum:

> We must conduct our affairs so that they are not subject to the risk of a battle, since losing one would immediately bring the prize of the Dutch Republic in its wake...I beg you not to be won over by the false reproaches of those who know nothing about war...Your Excellency should rather remain true to your own judgment, which is not to engage in battle except in extreme necessity... For the zeal I feel towards our country as well as towards Your Excellency, I recommend the last words that Fabius Maximus said on the subject to Aemilius Paulus before the battle of Cannae, [that] if no one shall give [Hannibal] battle this year, the man will remain in Italy only to perish, or will leave it in flight.[3]

This succession of stark warnings held an underlying theme – battles were a risk, and of far less risk were the more common and more decisive sieges which would proceed to characterise warfare in the Low Countries over the coming century. In fact, so absent of pitched battles was Europe, that by 1631 an English observer made the following note about warfare:

> Indeed, our actions in war are nowadays only sieges...of cities. Battles we hear not of, save only a few in France and that of Newport in the Low-Countries. But this manner will not last always, nor is there any conquest to be made without battles.[4]

Such a view would be vindicated later that year, when in September 1631 the Battle of Breitenfeld was fought, and Gustavus Adolphus of Sweden won his greatest triumph, making use of the tactics which Maurice of Nassau had first tested. Yet, while the Englishman quoted above may not have heard of other pitched battles, there were instances before Breitenfeld where the tactics learned from the Dutch were brought to bear. One example is provided by the siege of Esztergom, yet another chapter in the saga of Habsburg-Ottoman wars. It was there in Hungary that Turkish soldiers attacked their Habsburg enemy, making use of volley fire in order to do it. According to the Ottoman secretary of the artillery, who recorded these events in his chronicle, describing perfectly what the musket drill actually looked like:

> In the middle of the field, the Janissary regiments stood in three ranks, each musketeer with matches ready [to fire], and they lined up the big cannons chained in front of the Janissaries. Then, after the first rank of the Janissaries fires their muskets, the second rank fires, too. Afterwards, the rank that fired first bends double and begins to reload their muskets. And as the third rank fires, the second rank in front [of them] bends and prepares their muskets. Then, the first rank stands up and fires their muskets [again].[5]

If the Dutch used these tactics in 1600, and the Turks used them only a few years later, then the question was how such tactics were diffused between different armies in such a short space of time. This indeed is one of the key questions of the entire Military Revolution – how did other powers learn of the trace italienne; how did the transformation of the military contract in early modern Europe spread across different societies; how was the idea of the drill spread, and why did it enjoy more acceptance in some states than others? One historian believed that the desertion of some Habsburg soldiers into Ottoman service explained the diffusion of the musket drill; these soldiers were in fact French mercenaries, who were eager to spread the Dutch ideas around.[6] We know that the Sultan received a letter about the Battle of Nieuwpoort a few months after it had taken place, so he may well have been clued in from that, and adopted the relevant lessons from it. As John A. Lynn wrote:

> Viewed from the French perspective, the Dutch creation of drill in particular rates as an absolutely crucial innovation with profound implications both on the battlefield and beyond it. Drill developed by Maurice and further extended by Gustavus enabled manoeuvre and a rate of fire unknown before. This promise of tactical effectiveness lured French officers to the Netherlands and northern Germany where they might learn the craft of war from the Dutch or the Swedes.[7]

In the vast majority of cases, military training was minimal. Weapon handling and efficiency were taught in the beginning, and once these lessons had been absorbed, soldiers were considered trained. This process could take anything from two weeks to two years, though the average was somewhere in between, and recruits were generally stationed in a place where they would learn from veterans, rather than be inducted into any kind of training camp, per se, though such training camps did exist. There was no sense of a need for constant, regular practice, and surprisingly little was actually done to improve obedience, discipline and good order. These qualities were taken for granted, and little effort was made to inculcate them into the soldier during the limited training. All of this changed with the reforms instituted by Maurice of Nassau, as much because of what this new drill meant for the battlefield as it did for the soldier. In order to complete the detailed movements which would bring the most firepower to bear on the enemy, instruction manuals were developed so that captains could train their men in the drill and ensure their universal proficiency. Yet, to be in a position to hear and obey these orders, not to mention remember them in the heat of battle, were tasks just as difficult and novel to the soldier as the very notion of firing by rank. As John A. Lynn noted, 'It is not stretching a point to say that in the name of tactical necessity, drill ingrained habits of obedience which affected the soldier's conduct and heightened the officers' control on and off the battlefield.'

We have to remember as well as that Maurice's use of the new drill demanded a certain organisation and mental durability from his soldiers. The

Dutch soldiers under his command would have to be capable of marching in step as one. This act of marching together in order was not dissimilar to the tercio tactics of old, however, in Maurice's case, there was more than merely marching that required arranging. Whereas the tercio squares had been defensively sound, they had not been very efficient at bringing firepower to bear, since generally, only the front of the square could fire at the enemy. For the officer commanding the tercio, this meant that he would only have to coordinate a select portion of his men to fire at any one time. In Maurice's new regimen though, *all* Dutch soldiers would be expected to offload their shot in a coordinated, set piece arrangement which ensured that there was always some kind of projectile in the air.

As we have established, the major advantage of the tercio was its defensive soundness, since its square arrangement, with pikes in the centre and muskets at the front, meant that it was ready for anything. Because the Dutch were sacrificing this defensive soundness for greater firepower, it meant they were more vulnerable as a group to the counter-charges of cavalry or even ambitious infantry. Before the bayonet was developed and employed, it was necessary for another unit to take up this role of defence, so this meant that the Dutch soldier would have to be more manoeuvrable, more flexible and simply faster than his opponents. Dutch soldiers would have to be trained to effectively ignore the fire of their opponents, and act according to the instructions laid down in the manuals which were provided. Since no manuals were yet on hand at the Battle of Nieuwpoort for instance, Maurice got to see first-hand the challenges which his new drill faced, as well as the challenges which his soldiers overcame.

The simple act of drilling and training as a unit for several years had instilled a sense of cohesion within the Dutch soldiers on the battlefield which had been absent from their compatriots throughout the preceding years of the revolt. Maurice had transformed the Dutch into professional soldiers, before the Republic could be said to have had an officially institutionalised professional army.[8] This was noticed and acknowledged by the Spanish soldier as much as the Spanish King. The former, a veteran of the army of Flanders, noted in 1616 that:

> It is striking to observe how much better the Dutch soldiers have become than they were in the time of the duke of Alba or the others who have governed these provinces since then: [one of them now] is worth twenty of those back then.

Philip III of Spain was well aware, exclaiming to his viceroy in Goa in 1617 that:

We have tried many times to reorganize our troops in India in the European manner, since experience has shown that without it we have suffered important losses. But now that we are at war with the Dutch, who are disciplined soldiers, it is more important than ever.[9]

By the time of writing this correspondence, King Philip III of Spain would have known that the Dutch revolt had become insurmountable. We will examine the stubborn mindset of the Spanish Habsburgs and their refusal to negotiate with rebels in later sections of this book, but it is worth noting that as the Dutch revolt gathered supporters both at home in the Netherlands and abroad from foreign powers, the Dutch reformed their military capabilities at the same time. At the turn of the century then, just when it seemed as though the allies of the Dutch – the English and French – had made peace with Spain and abandoned them to fight the Spanish alone, the Dutch developed a new method for carrying on this fight which would pay dividends into the future. As Geoffrey Parker noted, when attempting to address the question of why the Eighty Years War lasted Eighty Years, this war had very unimpressive beginnings: 'In 1574 only about twenty towns, with a combined population of seventy-five thousand, remained faithful to William of Orange; Amsterdam, the largest town in Holland, stayed loyal to the king until 1578.'

Even at that comparatively minute size, with all the millions in income and manpower that Philip II of Spain boasted, Madrid could not crush the rebels. If it could not crush them at their weakest state, then how much more incapable of defeating them would Spain be once the Dutch gathered their countrymen together, were led by innovators like Maurice of Nassau, and developed such revolutionary tactics as the drill, before using it against the Spanish for the first time? While the Battle of Nieuwpoort is glossed over today, it was the first, most important test of these new methods and vindicated Maurice's ideas and work in the years before. With the advent of greater firepower being brought to bear on the Spanish, and the increasing demands this placed on the Dutch citizen if he was to carry his instructions out, Maurice authorised several new methods for making the transition from citizen to soldier as seamless a process as possible.

One of these methods was the countermarch, but even after Nieuwpoort, the countermarch continued to pose some problems to the Dutch soldiery. Not only was it the antithesis of the gentlemanly code of honour to be seen to walk away, and to retreat, from the enemy, but it was also an act which required a great deal of bravery. One could very easily be shot in the back as they walked, and we can imagine the Dutch soldier sweating heavily as he counted down the seconds while his back was exposed. Once he reached the rear of his unit to reload, he would be safer, before exposing himself again. The hope, of course, was that by the time it was the turn of the first rank to fire again, the enemy unit would have been so demoralised and ruined by this firing tactic that they wouldn't be able to withstand much more. The spectacle of a constant hail of shot pouring across the field was demoralising and confusing enough, especially in the early days of the tactic when it was not very well known or understood.

To us, it would have been the seventeenth century equivalent of a machine gun, and this high rate of fire guaranteed the reduction in importance of the melee troops as a result. It also made the tactic the talk of Europe, and virtually guaranteed that others would seek to emulate it. Much like the Spanish use of the tercio though, French, Swedish and even English efforts to replicate the drill were admirable, but efforts to duplicate it were not. It would take some time before the culture of drilling instituted by Maurice would spread to other states. However, one aspect which helped this process along was the aforementioned publishing of several illustrated manuals on the drill. The French proved one of the most enthusiastic adopters of the drill, beginning under Louis XIII. By 1629, the French had what was called the *Code Michaud*, which regulated the discipline, administration and regular training of the French soldier, so that he would capable of taking part in the fire by rank drill and countermarching tactics of his Dutch peers.

It was certainly fair to state that the French imitated the Dutch in this regard, but for this they should be admired, since as we have seen in the English case, not every power was so eager to embrace the new reforms. The drill and act of the countermarch brought forth a familiar idea once again – the importance of forbearance. Forbearance was the ability to withstand the fire from the enemy for longer than he could withstand yours. This became critically important with the act of the countermarch, and it required a well-drilled, well-oiled military machine to command the different human pieces on the board and ensure that every piece knew its role. In 1639 Louis XIII established the *Academie royale des exercices de guerre*, a place where captains could send their newly levied men to be drilled and educated in the ways of war. As we know, this process was rapidly accelerated under Louis XIV, who was in many ways Europe's greatest proponent of the drill. Just as he achieved his majority in 1661 Louis XIV issued an ordonnance which required drills take place twice a week, while manoeuvres for entire garrisons were ordered once a month, so as to maintain the training and core lessons. In 1667 the office of Inspector General for Infantry was created and filled by Jean Martinet, whose name has become a byword for rigorous discipline and drill, and who represented yet another bright French light whom Louis was immensely fortunate to have in his employ.[10]

The French adoption of Dutch tactics appeared to suggest that such peoples – followed then by Swedish soldiers under Gustavus – represented something akin to the cutting edge of military thought and practice. On the other hand, the lethargic Spanish, who still bumbled about with their tercio square formations, were easy to malign as backward, and their subsequent decline easy to interpret as part and parcel of their refusal to modernise and reform along with the times. This stark contrast is at the heart of Michael Roberts' thesis in the Military Revolution, yet as Geoffrey Parker and others have noted, Roberts gave too much credit to the Dutch drilling by characterising it as an earth-shattering development. It was not so earth-shattering that the tercios were abandoned, nor was it so earth-shattering that the Dutch won every subsequent battle, and abruptly ejected the Spanish from the Low Countries. Granted, the Spanish famously saw their tercios destroyed by the drilled Swedish and German troops at Breitenfeld, in perhaps the greatest instance where Maurice's ideas were put into practice, but a Spanish-Imperial army more than made up for this defeat at Nordlingen three years later, and by doing so they demonstrated that the tercio was far from obsolete just yet.

Indeed, it was not so black and white a case as the Spanish refusing to modernise – on the contrary, we have seen that several treatises written by experienced Spanish military personnel urged reform and advised on the best new developments in tactics and drill in order to affect such reforms. Of course, the Spanish neglected to implement such reforms, whereas the Dutch under Maurice of Nassau enthusiastically embraced them, but even so, the Spanish did not lag behind. They were enough aware of the importance of the drill books written and illustrated by Dutch authors between 1607-12 to make copies of their own, as did Swedish, Polish, English, French and natives of Flanders.[11]

We might look at these imitations and the resulting imitations of the Dutch drill in action and wonder how and why the Dutch should have let their secret get out – should those illustrated drill manuals not have been state secrets, available only to a select few? Indeed, such a concept as protecting these investments never crossed Maurice's mind, probably because he never believed that keeping such developments secret was going to be possible in the porous courts and armies of the 1600s. All it took, as we saw, was a French mercenary unit transferring itself from Habsburg to Ottoman service for the drill to be known that far east, so one can imagine how easy similar diffusions could take place closer to home. While these organic diffusions may not surprise us, it may actually be surprising to note that the Dutch were quite willing to *sell* their information and expertise in the years that followed their innovations.

The Dutch eagerly sold their knowledge and expertise to any German prince who would buy it, and they made the offer more attractive by including virtually everything in the price, from drill instructors, to the latest manuals. It was the seventeenth century equivalent of a package deal, which any aspiring German rule would have to buy if they did not wish to fall behind, or fall victim to their more advanced neighbours. As Geoffrey Parker wrote:

In 1610 Brandenburg asked for and received 'two Dutch drill masters from the army of Maurice Orange', and Dutch officers soon arrived to drill the militias of Baden, Brunswick, Hessen-Kassel, the Palatinate, Saxony, and Wurttemberg. In 1616, Count Johan of Nassau opened a military academy at his capital, Siegen, to educate young gentlemen in the art of war.[12]

Even to America did the Dutch tactics spread, as Englishmen in Dutch service were chosen to act as governors of the colonies in the New World, and they brought with them Dutch ideas and tactics for training their militias, even while they then served England. This planted the new ideas into the Americas and provided English settlers with invaluable tactics for dealing with troublesome natives as they expanded.

Indeed, it is worth dwelling for a moment on that question of the diffusion of tactics. Geoffrey Parker made the point that the image we have of businesses, for instance, jealously guarding their secrets or formulas or ingredients or blueprints is a relatively new phenomenon. Especially in early modern Europe, the notion that only one state would lead pioneering breakthroughs in technology was never accepted, largely because of the sheer cost involved in spearheading any innovations which were made. The Dutch, for sure, developed and arguably perfected the drill, but by farming this expertise out to their neighbours, they didn't believe that they were strengthening potential enemies, but providing a wide laboratory for experimentation and improvement in these tactics. Not to mention, opening the discourse of these tactics up for greater debate, and hopefully, investment. In addition, we must remember that in the early 1600s, and indeed far before that, it was not abnormal for foreign soldiers to serve in a wide variety of armies, and it could hardly be expected that these soldiers would not talk once they returned home. Even if he had wanted to then, and if he had then he would have represented an anomaly in his era, Maurice of Nassau would never have been able to block the march of military innovation which he had initiated. He would simply have to do his best to keep pace with it, as would everyone else.[13]

Now that we have focused on the developments in terms of military tactics in the seventeenth century, it is largely up to the reader to determine whether or not a revolution took place. One should consider how different a soldier's experience of warfare would have been in each century. A soldier in 1531 would have observed the battlefield of Breitenfeld in 1631 with a sense of wonder, as the stopping power of the firearm was on display for all to see, and the Swedish army appeared to work from a script all their own. On the other hand, Geoffrey Parker would accept that change had taken place, but that such change was far from total. Rather than outmatching the obsolete Spanish tercios, these supposedly revolutionary developments in the drill were soundly defeated by them only a few years after Gustavus' vaunted triumph. The developments were important, but apparently not convincing or effective enough to affect a total transformation in how all armies operated.

The Military Revolution, so it would seem, was shaped by the inclinations of commanders on the ground, yet its lessons were also influenced by the ground itself. In line with this point, John A Lynn also makes the point that the prevalence of revolts in French society necessitated the creation and training of a disciplined French army, which had to be uniquely prepared for revolt at home and conflict with the enemy across his borders. Although it had a shaky start, the French army learned from its experiences during its initial intervention in the Thirty Years War, with the result that France's individual soldiers were that much more disciplined by the 1640s and 50s, than they had been before, thanks to the domination of the military drill. The drill demanded a level of discipline from the Frenchman which would have been unheard of a century before, yet it also made that soldier easier to control, and more likely to follow the orders of his captain, commander or King.

Wars cost a great deal more in 1600 than they had in 1500, and because of this, it was necessary to reform one's financial systems in addition to one's armed forces. This challenge was partially helped by the effective doubling of Europe's population between 1450-1600, and the resulting increases in the tax base, but taxation alone could not pay for the incessant demands of warfare on the state coffers, nor could the pillaging of resources from the New World, as Spain discovered. Mutinies were the outcome of this shortage of funds, and the outgrowth of the military from the economic capacity of European states – we need only to think of Philip II's four bankruptcy declarations in the late sixteenth century, or even the terribly untimely mutiny of the unpaid Swedish army in 1634-35, to see for ourselves the consequences of increased costs in warfare.

If the seventeenth century provides an example of the starkest chasm between income and military commitments, it also contained the point when the trend began to turn in the opposite direction. Much like they initiated the development of the drill, the Dutch innovated their notion of credit, backed up with the overwhelming financial clout of Amsterdam, which became the commercial hub of the world by 1650. The Dutch political system, with its strong financial base, then proved capable of guaranteeing certain loans, and of always paying on time. Acquiring a reputation for solid finance, the Dutch stadtholder William III brought these ideas with him when he became King of England in 1688. Parliament guaranteed the state's debts, the Bank of England was established, and a sophisticated stock exchange was also created. With greater financial organisation, England and the Netherlands proved capable of supporting larger armies on the continent far out of proportion to the population size. If the Thirty Years War had provided the warning against overspending for the sake of short-term gain, then the conflicts which erupted later on in the century, such as the Nine Years War of 1688-97, demonstrated how intertwined state finance and warfare had become.

While these innovations were inherently Dutch, they soon became common practice, and along with the Enlightenment and the opening up of new lands to Europeans, these developments combined to place 'the West' in a position of primacy it had never enjoyed before. Fortunately for them, their soldiers and militias were also armed with the right weapons and trained in the correct style to seize and then defend these precious acquisitions from the natives, not to mention, one another.[14] Considering the revolutions in economics, military drill and military engineering which shadowed the Dutch war with Spain, it may be wondered whether, instead of speaking of a Military Revolution, we should speak of the *Dutch Revolution* which was supercharged by the Eighty Years War.[15] It was from that conflict that so much innovation, experimentation and theorising was sourced, and it was from this platform that Dutch ideas and ingenuity placed their small republic in a position of unrivalled progress, power and wealth.

TWO

The Northern Touch –
Gustavus Adolphus' Innovations

In late May 1630, off the coast of Stockholm and floating on the dark waters of the Baltic, a flotilla was assembling for war. Plainly, an expedition was being prepared. Some fifteen thousand men in all, staffed with officers for the infantry, the cavalry and artillery, and composed of men from the British Isles, from Germany and from Sweden and Finland, the army was a multinational force in many respects, and yet its flags were Swedish, and its commander was arguably the most famous Swede of all time.[16] One Scottish colonel in his service, Robert Monro, would later write:

> A young cavalier, desirous of honour and greedy of good instruction, could have learned from this king.... Such a general would I gladly serve, but such a general I shall hardly see, whose custom was to be first and last in danger himself....[17]

Indeed, any young cavalier could have gained invaluable experience through service with the Swedish King – by 1630, he had certainly taken part in enough campaigns, and during the course of countless battles Gustavus Adolphus had demonstrated his flair for acts of personal bravery, his penchant for innovation and his remarkable skill for command. These qualities, which so distinguished Gustavus as a remarkable man in an era of remarkable men, would also contribute to his death in battle in November 1632 at Lutzen, in Saxony.[18] In short, as his flotilla assembled, Gustavus had fewer than three years left to live, but in the space of that period of time, the King of Sweden would not merely transform the Thirty Years War, he would also propel the Swedish Empire to the pinnacle of its powers. He would defeat the veteran commander of the Habsburgs, twice, and he would ruin the years of supremacy established by the Emperor. By the time of his death, it was evident that the conflict which he had visited for such a short time would never be the same.

Many factors contributed to the legend of Gustavus Adolphus, but the Swedish King would have been nothing without his acumen in the military sphere. Indeed, born into conflict with Sweden's powerful neighbours in the Baltic, a less capable King could have lost his lands and throne, their reign snuffed out never to begin. In 1611 Gustavus' father died; nearly two decades before he had deposed his nephew, the Catholic and Polish Sigismund, and the latter had fled to his homeland vowing revenge. The Polish-Lithuanian Commonwealth, then the most populous state in Europe, was thus positioned as a dynastic enemy of Gustavus from an early stage, and cousin Sigismund was determined to reclaim his birth-right – a struggle he never relinquished his entire life. Coming to the throne as a teenager, the young Gustavus inherited a sparsely populated kingdom of fewer than one and a half million men. During the war with Denmark that Gustavus also inherited, Sweden's manpower shortages were so well known that a rumour had been put about among the Danish soldiery that Swedish women populated the cavalry. Gustavus did not conscript Swedish women – instead he depended upon the vast manpower pool which Germany and the British Isles provided.[19]

That Gustavus inherited a war on several fronts – with the neighbouring powerhouse of the Baltic, in Denmark, with his dynastic nemesis in Poland and with the looming threat of Russia – compelled him to make the best use of the meagre resources he had at hand. Yet, an instant innovator Gustavus was not – like many monarchs of his age, he received minimal military training, and save for a conversation with the cousin of Maurice of Nassau in 1620, there is no direct evidence that he had a true chance to absorb the innovations of the Dutch drill.[20] Certainly, the availability of drill manuals could have made up for such a deficiency, but short of evidence that Gustavus read these manuals, we are reduced to speculation.

If he did read them, he did not heed their ideas, at least not initially. In 1611 Gustavus' conception of the ideal unit of the army was the squadron, conceived to contain a precise number of 408 men, with 216 pikemen forming the central block. On each wing of this block 96 musketeers would stand, with all men standing six rows deep. On occasion, a detachment of 96 more musketeers, used interchangeably for scouting, cavalry support and outpost duty, were also attached to the squadron. We are therefore left with a puzzling, contradictory image, where the supposed master of firepower boasted more pikemen in his squadrons than the Dutch, and used tactics which were closer to the Spanish method than any new innovations. When one considers the circumstances of Gustavus' wars though, the reliance on pike is less surprising than it may first appear.[21] To begin with, conflict with heavy Polish cavalry necessitated the use of pikemen to defend the musketeers, while the weaknesses of the firearm, especially in the harsh climate endured by his men, moved Gustavus to cleave to tried and tested weapons.[22]

It was an accepted part of warfare that the musketeers or arquebusiers needed protection when reloading. A lack of pikemen rendered infantry vulnerable to other pikemen, but above all cavalry charges. 'Pikemen', Colonel Monro insisted

> ...shall ever be my choice when going on execution, as also in retiring honourably with disadvantage from an enemy, especially against horsemen, and we see ofttimes, that when musketeers do disband, of greediness to make booty, the worthy pikemen remain standing firm with their officers guarding them and their colours.[23]

But pikemen were unmistakably in the decline, especially with new technological developments in firearms. Gustavus played no small role in furthering these developments; appreciating the importance of speed and manoeuvrability, the Swedish King endeavoured through the 1620s to reduce the weight of the musket, traditionally much heavier than the arquebus. So heavy was the weapon that it could not be held at an appropriate angle without the use of a fork placed in the ground. Gustavus sought to adjust the length and weight of the musket while retaining its high calibre and stopping power. At the same time, he did away with the fork and replaced it with the so-called 'Swedish feather' – an implement which was really a thin spike that could double as a palisade stake for halting cavalry or, in some cases, as a rudimentary bayonet, thus granting musketeers a more sophisticated form of protection and reducing the need for as many pikemen.[24]

Nor was that all. In the course of watching his men fumble with different quantities of powder used to load their weapons, Gustavus worked to standardise the size of the charge. Some historians report that Gustavus thus invented and sponsored the use of the powder cartridge, with Swedes thereafter adopting bandoliers with these cartridges carried across their shoulders and chest.[25] Other historians are more sceptical, noting the lack of direct evidence for this innovation, and suggesting instead that it was a natural reaction by the soldier to the chaotic circumstances of warfare.[26] Either way, thanks to these innovations, Gustavus' men were equipped with more manageable firearms which could be loaded with greater haste. There remained much to be done before the kind of total standardisation we now take for granted would be possible – Gustavus' men brandished wheellock, matchlock and even some expensive flintlock firearms,[27] and scant regulations on the size of these weapons meant that it was often unclear whether a soldier carried a carbine, a musket or an arquebus.

Occasionally the cavalry made use of innovations to replace their pistoles with the shortened carbines, and wheellock weapons were of great use on horseback, and at night when the element of surprise could be ruined by a bright burning match.[28] While Gustavus' innovations with cavalry and artillery in particular are deservedly renowned (see below) it was equally imperative that the Swedish King honed his infantry, to create the best squadron of foot that could be mustered. As we have stated, Gustavus' army was shaped by the experiences of his wars with his Polish cousin, thus prompting retired American Lieutenant Colonel and historian Theodore Dodge to write that:

> In his wars against the Poles, not above taking a hint from any source, he resorted to the old Roman, or, one might say, the English longbowman's habit of having the men carry sharpened palisades, not for camping, but to erect a defence against the Polish lancers from behind which they could fire upon them. This was a species of survival of the musket-rest; it finally became only an iron-pointed rod; and to it some have ascribed the origin of the bayonet.[29]

Indeed, while he learned from his enemies, he also learned from his mistakes. The squadron which was conceived in 1611 and which contained more pike than musket, was replaced fifteen years later in 1626, with startling results. He changed the composition of his regular squadron, expanding it to four companies of 150 men. Within these four companies, the ratio of pike to musket was adjusted considerably, with 75 musketeers, 55 pikemen and 20 officers. Four companies formed a squadron, and eight companies constituted a regiment, which would be drawn from and paid for by the different provinces of the Swedish Kingdom, at least in theory.[30] Just as startling as the new updates to his army composition was how he planned to make use of the pike and shot. For so long, the pike had been reduced to a mere defensive weapon, lethal for sure, but tasked with serving a specific purpose. Gustavus changed this purpose – he would use the musket to soften the enemy up, and he would then order the pike forward to finish the infantry off. The first part of this process, where the musketeers were intended to prepare the ground for the pike's assault, was made more formidable by another innovation by the Swedish King – fire by rank.[31]

Granted, firing by rank was not a new idea. For the best results from a line of musketeers, it was necessary to coordinate their firepower with the men around them. A properly organised force could send out a wave of shot several times in a minute, but Gustavus Adolphus took this approach to the next level, as the historian Frederic J. Baumgartner noted:

> He recognized that hand-gunners were vulnerable to a hard assault by enemy pike or heavy cavalry, and he realized that the changes he proposed to make in the way hand-gunners fought would increase their vulnerability. Gustavus further appreciated how the pike in the hands of a well-drilled and spirited infantry could be an effective offensive weapon. The opportunity for the pike to reach the enemy's lines and carry home the charge had to be prepared by gunfire. Gunfire would be far more effective if it were a concentrated blast that shattered the enemy's ranks, after which the pike would charge. Gustavus

therefore insisted that his musketeers carry an eleven-pound musket, which was about half as heavy as the standard piece and did not need the fork, and that they learn to fire salvos. His musketeers were formed into six ranks. Once they had loaded and were ready to fire, three ranks combined into one line. The first rank knelt; the second stooped; and the third fired over the top of the other two. At the sergeant's signal they fired simultaneously. The concentrated blast of the three ranks would break up the enemy's lines and give the pikemen openings to exploit in their charge. But if the salvo failed to accomplish the desired result, the pike was needed in strength to defend the musketeers until they had reloaded.[32]

Six lines of between twelve and thirteen men were thus trained and commanded to fire in unison, and to swap places when reloading. Pikemen, furthermore, were on standby to defend a musketeer in the midst of this process, but above all to drive home their weapon into the shattered enemy. The suddenness of this firepower being brought to bear was unlike anything anyone in Germany had seen, and we will note that it was something of a departure from what Maurice of Nassau had conceived as well. What it held in common with the latter's theories was its use of firepower to inflict the most damage – by the time the pikemen moved forward for the attack, the grunt work would already have been done by the murderous projectiles, with the enemy's morale surely in tatters. If the first couple of salvoes did not produce the desired result, the process would simply be repeated. Performing this procedure under enemy fire was very different to proposing it within the safe confines of military doctrine of course, and we imagine that even the most disciplined, organised war machine would have struggled when face to face with other motivated, professionalised armies.

Yet, the Swedish advantage in the sudden volume and density of firepower which they could project gave them the edge over their Polish foes in the remaining year of the war and proved devastatingly effective against the Spanish tercios. The Spanish took some time to adjust the composition of their tercio formations to account for new developments in firearm technology, whereas Gustavus sought to advance the study of said technology to benefit his infantry. Although some tercios did make limited use of the new countermarch technique, such a technique was incredibly difficult to coordinate in units of nine hundred arquebusiers or more, particularly when pikemen got in the way. Michael Roberts even referred to the 'wastage of manpower' in the tercio system, as only the soldiers at the front of the tercio could use their pikes or fire their weapons.

The Swedish model, by contrast, harnessed the full extremity of the musket. On the battlefield, for both systems to clash, we should imagine a tercio of two and a half or three thousand men combatting two Swedish regiments twelve hundred men apiece. With the Swedish technique, as all available firearms were brought forward, the Swedes would possess as many as six hundred muskets, all firing in three coordinated lines, directly into the heart of the Spanish squares. The tercio's limitations would then be on full display, as the weight of fire which could be brought to bear was massively compromised by the restrictive formation. Tens or even hundreds of Spanish infantry could be struck down in a single salvo and multiplied across the line the visual would have been murderous. We should imagine also this fearsome combination in league with the revolutions in musket style, which made the weapon more manageable and versatile, and less unwieldy. Gustavus' eleven-pound muskets packed a serious punch and would have done far more damage to human flesh than the smaller arquebus. It would have appeared and sounded like the seventeenth century equivalent of the rapid-fire machine gun, and before the Battle of Breitenfeld in September 1631, the Spanish had never seen anything like it.[33]

While these changes to the drill and infantry composition were significant, it was when Gustavus combined these innovations with revolutions in the theatre of artillery that the Swedish war machine truly distinguished itself. Notwithstanding the disagreements by historians over the extent of Gustavus' influence on infantry tactics, all are in agreement that the Swedish King transformed not merely how artillery was used, but also how it was viewed and how the artillery gunners thought of themselves. To appreciate the full breadth of this change in the status quo, it helps to briefly examine the position of artillery when Gustavus came to the throne in 1611.

Artillery gunners in the sixteenth and early seventeenth century were the battlefield equivalent of magicians. The secrets of their craft were jealously guarded; tricks of the trade scarcely revealed to those outside the profession, and the profession itself was thankless, immensely taxing and very difficult to access. 'It was still', Michael Roberts noted on artillery, 'in the mediaeval sense of the word at least, very much a "mystery"'.[34] Ballistics being by no means a science in the seventeenth century, range finding was done by mere estimations; adjustments to the range or angle of the gun was made – incredible though it sounds – by bashing in wedges of wood between the gun and its supports to create a rudimentary elevation. Such activity around so many volatile ingredients did not recommend the profession to the faint at heart, and it was horrendously tough on beast as well as man.

This is because before a gun could even be used, it would have to be moved, and this was a process all by itself. To put it in perspective, the heaviest calibre available during the Thirty Years War – the monstrous 48-pounder – required a number of anywhere between thirty-three to thirty-nine horses to pull it. If horses were unavailable in that number, as was often the case, then peasants would be conscripted for this miserable task instead, and the number of men required for the task could run into the hundreds. While dutifully pulling these weapons, horses suffered terribly, with the annual mortality rate of the unfortunate beasts between 20-30% annually. And that was just the weapon itself – the ammunition also required transport or the cannon was useless.

Once again, the unwieldy machinery of the early modern era whirred into action to create ammunition or artillery trains, generally a set of wagons assigned the task of moving the shot from place to place. Again, the task of moving enough ammunition for the varied calibre of guns – sixteen different pieces existed in Sweden when Gustavus ascended to the throne – meant that hundreds of wagons and thousands of horses had to be used. To put it in perspective, when Gustavus arrived to fight the Poles in Livonia in 1625, he brought with him 36 guns, but these weapons required 220 wagons and 1,116 horses to pull the loads. Creating and supplying artillery, in short, was an administrator's nightmare.

The gun manufacturer hardly had a better time of it, since the act of producing large guns remained shrouded in debate, frustrating a common method of production or quality. Technically, gunsmiths were meant to use *gunmetal*, an alloy composed mostly of copper, with some parts tin added. Iron was generally avoided because it was so inconsistent, and could literally explode, creating horrendous scenes where self-inflicted shrapnel wounds tore through the rear of an army. Iron also tended to rust and was often used only on smaller guns as a result. As if this wasn't bad enough, to compensate for its shortcomings and make a reliable iron gun would require a barrel of far larger size than its copper equivalent, which made the 48-pounders impossibly heavy. Broadly, gunsmiths knew of two different classes of gun, the field and the siege guns, but in seventeenth century warfare, that was where classification of any meaningful kind ended. Field artillery in particular was notoriously unwieldy and experimentation with it was minimal, as commanders would rather use the horse or manpower in the front lines. Indeed, the combination of lacklustre accuracy with an underwhelming rate of fire must have made many commanders wonder why they bothered to bring these pieces at all.[35]

That leads us to note that even after such a terribly laborious process, guns remained woefully inaccurate and suffered from a painfully slow rate of fire. The black smoke from the cannon had to be allowed to completely dissipate before firing again, lest they might fire prematurely, and cannons would often be cooled on the battlefield with anything on hand, sometimes water, and occasionally milk or vinegar. The durability of the guns, and their calibre, varied from different manufacturers in different countries, but often, guns would shatter after several shots being fired, or they would fail to ignite. According to some authorities, the average brass gun would last no more than thirty shots before expiring, and on the field if used during a siege or a pitched battle, the rate of fire varied due to countless factors, from the wind to the terrain.

Some have argued that it was possible for a large calibre 24-pound cannon to fire eight rounds an hour – but other estimates claim that a well-trained artillery crew could fire as many as twenty salvos an hour. Others commented that the smaller guns, like Gustavus' three-pounders, could maintain a more regular rate of fire of fifteen consistently, but even this is disputed. Albrecht of Wallenstein, Imperial generalissimo and benefactor of the Emperor, expelled an average of nine shots an hour during the six-hour battle of Lutzen he fought with Gustavus in 1632. Yet Count John of Nassau – the cousin of Maurice – opined that guns would never and should never be called upon to fire more than *five times* in a single battle. Perhaps it was above Count John's imagination to suppose that any commander in his right mind would rely on their heavy cannon to do any more than that.[36]

The Swedish King would dive headfirst into this morass of confusion, mystery and inefficiency. If his aforementioned campaign into Livonia required 220 wagons and 1,116 horses for just 36 guns, then the figures for his 1630 campaign in Germany illustrate the importance of his reforms. Then, when landing in Pomerania, Gustavus brought 72 guns, but he required just one hundred wagons and a thousand horses to move it, a marked improvement on the situation from five years before.[37] The question then is what Gustavus did while he was simultaneously redefining the tactics of infantry and reassessing the behaviour of cavalry, to improve the artillery. One of the earliest acts was to streamline the calibres, which would make everything easier. Rather than sixteen different varieties of shot, by 1630 Gustavus' force fielded just three – the twenty-four, twelve and three pounder varieties. Powder was improved and had to adhere to a national standard, which helped prevent explosions. Iron guns were largely removed or relegated to fortresses, so that only copper guns would be used by the soldiery.

Gustavus also engaged in some covert projects for the sake of increased technological sophistication. In the early 1620s, he commissioned his gunsmiths to operate in secret at Stockholm, and in 1623 a six-pounder gave him hope for future improvements. This secrecy was quite unlike the openness with which Maurice of Nassau had discussed his new drill – evidently, the Swedish King believed he was onto something revolutionary. Shortly thereafter the most famous such gun was born, the three-pounder, or so-called leather gun. While this leather gun is often recorded as a great success, it would be more accurate to note that it was a successful experiment. The weapon was used for barely two years from 1627-1629, before being retired. The main complaint of the Swedish armies, when confronting the Poles on the battlefield, was that the gun was still too heavy to be moved quickly and was too fragile to inflict much damage which made the effort of lugging the pieces along scarcely worth it.

Thus, the gunsmiths returned to the drawing board, and the following year their creation was complete – it was still a three-pounder, but the barrel was now made from the more durable gunmetal, and with a reduced and streamlined carriage, so that the gun remained nearly the same weight as its leather predecessor. The gun could be pulled by a single horse or moved by two or three men at a reasonable pace. At virtually the same time, Gustavus' gunsmiths invented the artillery cartridge, which placed into a single bundle the ingredients necessary for a quick reload; this was a similar idea to the musket cartridge.[38] By reimagining the role and accessibility of artillery, Gustavus changed in a few years what commanders had been struggling with since the advent of gunpowder – how to make effective use of heavy guns. The Swedish King effectively turned the question on its head: commanders would have access to tens of *small* guns, rather than a handful of large pieces. At a range of three hundred metres, the three-pounder was more than equal to the task of ruining the enemy formations, especially when used in vast quantities, as at Breitenfeld in September 1631.[39]

What Gustavus had created, was not merely a more mobile cannon, but the regiment-piece. The Swedish King was not content with bettering the efficiency of the different arms of his forces – he wanted also to integrate them. Artillery would no longer sit, misunderstood and underappreciated, at the rear of the battlefield. Instead, officers would be trained with this regiment-piece, and for the first time, such heavier weapons would be attached to each squadron of six hundred men, with the required experts and engineers present to operate and explain them to the common soldier. This was truly a revolution in combined arms, and Gustavus' adversaries, save arguably for Wallenstein, proved wholly unable to combat the innovation. It was also visibly impressive, as Gustavus arrived not only with an army, but with legions of engineers, gunsmiths, sappers and miners which all had a part to play in the thoroughly integrated army.[40] Gustavus was also fortunate that thanks to an abundance of copper at home, the cost of these improvements to the infantry and artillery did not break the bank.[41]

With its artillery and infantry tactics on par with or surpassing the more elite military forces of Europe, Gustavus turned to the cavalry. Cavalry in Sweden were far from a historical necessity on the battlefield; the rough and hilly nature of the country contributed to the lack of an intensive horsemanship tradition as in France or Britain, and only 3,500 mounted soldiers could be fielded in 1611. Changing the horse breeding culture of Sweden was one mission, but Gustavus also wished to change how cavalry fought, so that they would not engage uselessly in the caracole, exposing themselves to enemy fire as they did so, and nor would they weakly screen and scout for enemy forces. Gustavus wished to replace these tired tactics with those of greater force, a desire reinforced all the more, we imagine, by his sight of the Polish cavalry which cut such an impressive profile. Furthermore, like the other arms he had bettered, Gustavus wanted a greater integration of the cavalry with the infantry and artillery, so that each could support the other.

A powerful charge at the correct moment, Gustavus believed, and his cavalry would more than earn their keep. Some experimentation followed, with dragoons – essentially mounted infantry who could ride to where they were needed on the battlefield before dismounting to fight – imported from Germany. Gustavus believed that by providing the cavalry with two pistoles instead of a carbine or arquebus, they would be able to make greater use of their strengths. They were taught to ride at a gallop, to fire their pistols at speed, and then unsheathe their swords. To be equal to this formidable task, Gustavus employed only cuirassiers, armoured horsemen who would be capable both of disrupting enemy formations with pistole shot, before unbalancing and hopefully routing them in the charge. In comparison to the other arms of his army, Gustavus' innovations in the sphere of cavalry may be the least impressive. Yet, in an era where debate on the best use of cavalry continued to be waged relentlessly, and military theorists seemed to change their mind regularly, the adaption was a useful one, especially in combination with his other improvements.[42]

The Swedish army which landed at Pomerania, in other words, was not merely eagerly anticipated by the Emperor's enemies – it was also composed of state-of-the-art professionals, with integrated military arms, sporting sophisticated technological advancements, and following the latest in infantry tactics. As if that was not enough, to top it all off, it was commanded by one of the most astute, innovative commanders of the early modern era. Much like his predecessors though, he was now compelled to put all of these improvements to the test. All of these improvements would be for naught if Gustavus Adolphus was defeated in his first proper encounter with the enemy, and as he neared the Saxon town of Breitenfeld in early September 1631, it was plain that the world was watching.

THREE

The Murderous Laboratory – Breitenfeld

The armed host which Gustavus confronted on the morning of 17 September 1631 was the proud, powerful and undefeated military arm of a Habsburg supremacy which the Swedish King had had his eye on throughout the 1620s. He had been repeatedly urged during that eventful decade to intervene in Germany, to make some commitment or declaration to the effect that he would support the Protestant powers in their quest against the Emperor. While he was certainly sympathetic to the plight of the rebels, Gustavus' attentions were pulled towards more immediate concerns. His cousin, the King of Poland, continued to claim the Swedish throne after being evicted from it in the final years of the sixteenth century. Since then, Sweden and Poland had waged a Thirty Years War of their own, interspersed with truces and temporary arrangements which would give both sides the opportunity to breathe and recover, before the campaigning season began again.

Just as Gustavus had been urged to save Protestantism, so too had the King of Poland been urged by the Emperor to aid the Habsburg cause; King Sigismund was, after all, a Jesuit-educated Catholic, and what was more, he was the brother-in-law of the Emperor. Thus, while the theatre of Gustavus' Polish Wars had remained distinct through much of the early 1620s, from 1627, as his siege of the critical port city of Danzig (Gdansk) began, the two theatres – the German and the Polish – began to bleed into one another. We might imagine that Gustavus would be happy to see another old enemy, the Danes, suffer catastrophe in their efforts to defeat the Habsburgs, but Gustavus correctly perceived that Habsburg pretentions would not stop at Denmark. Indeed, after Denmark had been effectively overrun by the end of 1626, the Emperor's generalissimo Albrecht of Wallenstein had been granted the grand title 'Admiral of the Baltic and Ocean Seas', and made plans to coordinate with Poles and Spaniards to choke Denmark and inevitably Sweden from its Baltic lifeline.[43]

There was more to this title than mere ceremony – Wallenstein had already sent twelve thousand men to reinforce King Sigismund at Danzig, a force which proved essential as Gustavus was defeated in June 1629, and according to one account, 'was lucky to escape with his life.'[44] Wounded first in the hip and then the shoulder shortly afterwards, Gustavus displayed a disconcerting penchant for placing himself in the firing line, but he would not learn his lesson. Danzig, plainly, was a lost cause, but Gustavus took two things from the whole experience, which dominated the Polish-Swedish War of the late 1620s. First, the Swedish King learned a valuable lesson about the strengths and weaknesses of port cities, lessons which he was shortly to put to great use at Stralsund, one of the last holdouts against Wallenstein's relentless advance through Germany's northern reaches. Second, and in line with this, Gustavus accepted by 1629 that remaining aloof from Germany and ignoring the threat which Wallenstein's swollen army posed to Sweden was impossible.

Within months, he had forced the issue with Poland, defeating Sigismund's forces and noting with satisfaction that his cavalry had distinguished themselves as very near the equal of the Poles. After so many years avoiding a direct cavalry challenge with the superior Poles though, Gustavus had also learned the importance of a well-oiled machine of infantry. His infantry had proved their worth against all manner of enemies, and Gustavus rewarded them by investing heavily in their equipment and reinventing their tactics several times, until he reached the aforementioned conclusions about the best formula for harnessing the power of the foot with the fire-by-rank technique.[45]

Gustavus' new instructions for the infantry were to reduce their depth of rank to three or six men deep, so that his line was longer, but more muskets could be fired in a single salvo. Further, gaps in the ranks were left, so that men had space to reload or retire, and that if they did so they did not disrupt the formation. Shots were fired according to the orders of the officer within the company, and these orders included the now famous arrangement where Gustavus' foot would shoot, in three ranks, standing, stooped and kneeling, with the men also trained to shoot while lying down.[46] The major goal with these innovations was to lay down as much fire as possible upon the enemy. Polish infantry was a lesser concern of Sigismund, whose subjects, especially the nobles, preferred to fight on horseback and break their enemies with a glorious charge. Poland's love of the horse compelled Gustavus to train his men because 'a better-disciplined infantry must be given the means to develop a fire so hot that even if their cavalry were defeated, musketeers and pikemen together would be able to escape annihilation.'

By leading his men through such trying campaigns, and by teaching them to withstand the fiercest mounted enemies, Gustavus ensured his infantry had endured a baptism by fire unequalled in Europe. They were trained, essentially, to cut cavalry to pieces, but since shot did not discriminate, Gustavus rightly believed that such tactics would ruin enemy infantry as well as cavalry. As Michael Roberts appreciated, 'the 'twenties, therefore, saw developments along three lines: the intensification of firepower, the combination of arms and the improvement of cavalry.'[47] When compared to the Imperial-Spanish tactics, the contrast is palpable.

Count Tilly's men were placed up to ten ranks deep, which instantly made it much more difficult for all the firepower of the thousand or so musketeers to match those of Gustavus. From the moment battle was joined, it would seem as though Gustavus had far more musketeers than he in fact did, though it certainly helped that his army of forty-two thousand men outnumbered Tilly's by about seven thousand man, although some sixteen thousands of Gustavus' army was composed of Saxons, reluctant recruits who had only recently joined the fray on Sweden's side, and who could not be wholly depended upon.[48] Certainly, Gustavus was wise not to rely on the Saxons, who fled the field before the battle was done. The illusion Gustavus created, where all men seemed to be firing their weapons at once, was aided by his tactics, rather than by his momentary superiority in numbers. Whereas Tilly's men shot their weapons piecemeal, or according to the traditional tercio drill, Gustavus' fired in devastating, coordinated blocks which shattered the enemy's morale and order. The contrast between the two styles could not have been starker, as Gustavus' infantry operated from a rulebook written in the blood of their Polish campaigns.[49] Years of campaigning had also taught Gustavus the importance of a recognisable, respectable uniform, as he noted:

> Since many will judge contemptuously of the infantry for its clothes' sake, and since thereafter derogatory words may be disseminated in foreign countries concerning the whole army, in the King and country's despite, therefore shall newly conscripted foot soldiers be enjoined to provide themselves with proper clothes instead of their long smocks and peasant attire, wherewith less consideration ought to be had of the material itself, than that the clothes shall be well made.[50]

Alas, while much work was done, the soldiers generally wore uniforms only during parade or inspection, and in any event, by September 1631 the army had been marching around Germany for over a year – though their uniforms had once been crisp, clean and brightly coloured, after such a long period in the field these uniforms would have been virtually unrecognisable. It was hardly surprising that comments were made on the appearance of the Swedish soldiers, who 'having lain overnight on a parcel of ploughed ground, were so dusty, they looked out like kitchen-servants, with their unclean rags', did not present a pretty picture.[51] Their freshly gathered Saxon allies, on the other hand, were 'well clothed, showing robust forms and fresh cheeks, with well-fed horses'.[52] Even Count Tilly's Imperial army showed the Swedes up in this regard, as Dodge recorded:

> In contrast to the rough and rusty Swedes, Tilly commanded a splendid looking set of veterans. His army numbered men who had followed him for years and knew that he had never yet been conquered in a battle. Prominent among these were his Walloons, at the head of whom he took his stand on his white battle-charger, which was known to every man in line. As the rugged old veteran of seventy-two passed along, shouts of "Father Tilly!" rang from battalion to battalion. There was no feeling of uncertainty in the imperial army. That full-throated cheer presaged success.[53]

It would have been an intimidating scene for his men, veterans though they were by this point. But Gustavus knew that even with the unreliable Saxons on his side, the major contrast between his army and Tilly's was not its appearance, but its approach to warfare. The experiences of Poland had not been wholly enjoyable, as Gustavus had been wounded several times, lost many men, and suffered some bitter defeats, but they had taught the Swedish King how to thrive in adversity, and to learn from his mistakes.[54] Tilly, on the other hand, had never lost a battle, and did not expect to start now. Yet if the veteran commander of the Emperor's men had been able to investigate his foe at close range, he would have been able to discern major differences between even the layout of his forces and those of the Swedish King, as Dodge continued:

> Under Gustavus the three arms supported each other much in the modern way. Herein consisted the value of the king's method. His army became a well-designed machine, with all parts operating smoothly, instead of a disjointed mass, whose several parts worked out of time, and failed at the critical moment to sustain one another.[55]

Gustavus had studied the tercio, and determined that the squadron, consisting of four companies of one hundred fifty each, was too small to stand up to it. Thus, three or sometimes four squadrons were combined into a regiment, to create independent blocs of up to two thousand men. These would be a numerical match for Tilly's tercios, but in terms of firepower, Gustavus' foot had no equal. Not only had they been thoroughly versed in the new fire by rank mechanics, but they also had, thanks to recent artillery reforms, as many as twelve regiment-pieces per regiment, all of which were now capable of firing a three-pound ball deep into the mass of the enemy at devastatingly close range. Tilly's artillery, by contrast, were hulking pieces requiring more than 30 horses to shift, and they were positioned to the rear of the line, whereas even in the heat of battle Gustavus' line bore witness to scenes of constantly moving guns, which could be brought to bear so long as three men could be found to drag the 650lb pieces.[56]

We will recall that the goal in bringing this firepower to bear was not merely to decimate the enemy, but in fact to soften his ranks up for the other forgotten innovation of Gustavus' – the offensive charge by the pike. Gustavus' respect for the pike is palpable in the composition of his companies; more than a third of the 150 men brandished pikes, which meant that the unit retained its defensive strength. Unlike Tilly, whose tercios suffered from decreased mobility and reduced fire rates due to their arrangement, Gustavus' companies were prepared for the cavalry charge *and* enemy firepower. Operating in many respects like more flexible version of the tercio with a focus on firepower and offensive tactics, Gustavus' regiment, wrote Michael Roberts, 'represented a combination of some of the advantages of both the Dutch and Spanish schools.'[57]

Thus, even had he been unaware of his rival's reforms, the opening cannonade which announced that the Battle of Breitenfeld had begun would have told Count Tilly that something was very different indeed about the way the Swedish King intended to fight. The sheer volume of firepower which Gustavus' men could bring to bear was nothing short of a revelation, and Tilly's men had no answer for it. The pressure of the initial cannonade actually moved Tilly's left flank to attack at around noon on 17 September, and in such a haphazard manner was the battle opened. By now several hundreds of casualties would have been incurred on Tilly's side, and the noise would have been as unsettling as the smell and sights at hand, nor would this assault on the senses have been enjoyable for the winning side. As Robert Monro, a Scottish officer in Gustavus' service, noted on the battle: 'the smoke being great, the dust being raised, we were as in a dark cloud not seeing the half of our actions, much less discerning, either the way of our enemies, or yet the rest of our brigades.'[58]

We should not imagine a close quarters skirmish, but a wide battlefield stretching across the plain of Breitenfeld, with each army spreading their lines over a mile across. A long winding river flowed along the rear and up towards the right of the Swedish line, while Tilly had Leipzig at his back, and the town of Breitenfeld itself in his sights. Such a large space was only to be expected considering the vast numbers each side had at hand; Gustavus commanded a manpower advantage over Tilly of forty-two thousand men to thirty-six thousand, but the Swedish King was perceptive enough not to rely too heavily on the sixteen thousand Saxons that had recently joined his side under the Saxon Elector. Sure enough, the raw Saxon recruits, having none of the experience of their Swedish allies of the last few years, routed at the height of the battle. In any other battlefield situation, we imagine that the exit of more than a *third* of one's force would have been the beginning of the end, and yet it was not the end; for Gustavus, it represented his chance to demonstrate to his adversary what his soldiery were made of.[59]

Gustavus had ridden across his battle lines earlier in the morning, and we are told that he gave speeches to his men, which are recorded later in this book. Thanks to the wound he had received in his shoulder when warring in Poland, he refrained from wearing armour, preferring instead the more streamlined riding coat, and a hat with a green feather. Demonstrating the fearlessness which had been on full display in Poland, Gustavus by no means planned to sit to the rear of his battle order where he could direct traffic. From the beginning, the King was in the thick of the fighting, directly leading cavalry charges and rallying his troops. There was no need for any kind of single conductor for the Swedish forces, as the men were well-trained and experienced enough to know their roles and follow the instructions of their individuals generals, who were attached to the regiments and squadrons of cavalry, and whose names would, in some cases, become famous later in the war.

In any case, the Swedish King had ensured that his battle line was sound in the planning stages, and he trusted his men to follow the orders of their superiors. In a sense then, it would be incorrect to imagine Gustavus as a commander in the classical sense, directing every movement from a perch far from the dangers of battle. Rather, it would be more accurate to imagine Gustavus as having established the blueprint which his subordinates would follow, while he involved himself where he was needed. To appreciate both the nature of the battle and Gustavus' victory at Breitenfeld, it helps to compare how the two armies were arranged.

The Swedish King's battle line was spread over a mile, and consisted of two lines, with a reserve for each. Gustavus commanded the right and centre, while the Saxons held the left. In preparation for the uncertainties of battle, Gustavus had learned to keep men at hand in the event of a disaster, a decision which would effectively save the battle, as we will see. In the centre of his first line were four regiments at roughly two thousand men apiece, with each regiment boasting its own general for coordination of the men, who stood at six ranks deep, and several regiment-pieces which quickly established a superiority of fire over the enemy. The reserve of the centre in the first line consisted of cavalry, and spaces were provided in between each of the regiments to permit these horses through. 4,100 horse waited for orders on the right flank, and as he had learned to do in previous battles, Gustavus interspersed his cavalry with some 1,200 musketeers. At the front of this impressive line was the main battery, consisting of 12 heavy field guns, likely of the twelve-pounder variety.

Gustavus' second line was a similar story, but with three rather than four regiments. He retained the cavalry interspersed with musketeers, and the smaller but still significant reserve of cavalry and musketeers behind the main line. The second line was thus slightly smaller, and possessed no heavy guns at its centre, but the regiments retained their regiment pieces, moving them forward in the initial cannonade. The Swedish King thus possessed close to thirteen thousand foot arranged into regiments in his centre, and a few thousand other musketeers were dotted along the line, supporting cavalry, defending artillery or preparing to march and plug any gaps. Gustavus had been concerned before the battle about a shortage of pikes, so a few regiments, such as the two thousand Scottish under the command of James Ramsay which stood in reserve of the first line's centre, contained no pikes at all, but were protected by cavalry.[60]

There is some uncertainty over what kind of battle order Gustavus faced, owing to the controversy surrounding the Imperial line. Some maintain that Count Tilly commanded two lines, but greater evidence points to a single line, with a reserve designed to capitalise upon the flanking manoeuvre which he planned to utilise, and which had served him to such devastating effect ten years before at the Battle of White Mountain.[61] And flanking would surely be easy since Tilly possessed an intimidating four groups of three tercios, which contained between fifteen hundred to two thousand men apiece, adding up to a centre of twenty-four thousand men at a maximum, but probably closer to eighteen thousand. Whatever the precise number, Tilly's use of a single line meant that his army could reach further across the horizon than the Swedes, making a flanking manoeuvre seem tantalisingly possible.[62]

Tilly placed his cavalry in similar masses of about one thousand men, ten ranks deep on the flanks. Tilly's guns were all concentrated in the middle of the battle line but would be at a distinct disadvantage once his men needed to move ahead of their cannons. This lack of guns, and a lack of coordination among the tercios, would cost Tilly dearly. As Roberts noted: 'The Swedish battle order, indeed, appeared as something quite different from anything that had been seen on a German battlefield before; and it was no wonder that the Saxon allies viewed it with undisguised astonishment.'[63] The attack was begun by Pappenheim, an impetuous and impatient cavalry commander who took charge of five thousand horse on Tilly's left flank to charge at Gustavus' right, a fatal mistake, as musketeers were in wait, knitted as they were in among the cavalry commanded by Johan Baner, later a distinguished Swedish commander in his own right. Baner demonstrated a resilience and brilliance which boded well for Sweden's future, as he resisted *seven charges* from Pappenheim's men before the latter was forced to withdraw, with Baner in hot pursuit.

The positioning of musketeers within the cavalry had proven the difference, as they cut cavalry to pieces and completely blunted any sense of panic which Pappenheim may have hoped to inflict. It was a reassuring beginning to the battle, but a mile over on the other side of Gustavus' line, the disaster which all had feared came to pass, as Saxony's raw recruits were unnerved and scattered by a similar cavalry attack. Within half an hour, Gustavus' left flank had been completely exposed by the rout and Tilly, who had watched in extreme irritation as his hot-headed cavalry commanders had charged ahead without his blessing, now attempted to reassert his authority by commanding an envelopment of the area, where Imperials outnumbered Gustavus' men more than three to two. Now was the moment of truth for the Swedish King and his soldiers – with this terrible event having come to pass, the question of how they would react next meant everything.[64]

Fortunately for Gustavus, his second battle line was prepared behind the first, and the exit of the Saxons was rectified by pulling forward a distinguished brigade of two thousand Scottish musketeers and an equal number of cavalry, who more than adequately plugged the gap which the hasty Saxon Elector had left.[65] On another critical point in the battle, a detachment of Scottish infantry and cavalry under Colonel Robert Monro captured Count Tilly's artillery, effectively dooming the already beleaguered Imperial force. Monro would later claim that this act won the battle for the Swedish King, and that the latter was not afraid to confess as such. According to Monro:

> ...the victory and the credit of the day, as being last engaged, was ascribed to our Brigade, [who], being the reserve, were thanked by his Majesty for their service, in public audience, and in the view of the whole Army, we were promised to be rewarded.

For these reasons, one historian has noted that 'Although the king showed skill in reacting to the sudden change in battleplan, he was entirely dependent on the Scottish troops for the successful outcome of his orders.'[66] This was of course true, but these same Scottish troops, like their German and Swedish counterparts, had been thoroughly trained and drilled by Gustavus, and proved so devastating because they functioned as part of a well-oiled machine that the Swedish King had created. This is not to claim that the victory was entirely down to Gustavus – he depended upon his subordinates to harness the best of their men and to take advantage of the situation, and the average foot soldier would have faced terrifying scenes of slaughter and carnage regardless of what side he was on. seventeenth century warfare had progressed markedly in technology and innovation, but at the end of the day, warfare still required the soldier to engage in the same haunting and bloody business as their ancestors.

The fast-moving Scottish had been complemented by the actions of one Gustav Horn, another distinguished Swede, who commanded a reserve of horse to block the Imperial approach. Gustavus' commanders were able to predict the attempted flanking manoeuvre not just because they had learned of the Saxon exit, but also because they could see Tilly wheel his tercios in the centre in an attempt to capitalise. Still, in front of the Swedish centre, Lennart Torstenson, the final in a trio of quality Swedish commanders, continued to instruct the heavy batteries to lay down murderous fire on the Imperial army, which only increased the pressure upon Tilly to act. Tilly's flanking act was too predictable, and as Horn's cavalry, supported by musketeers, pushed the attack back, it was the Imperial line that was now exposed. Seeing their heavy investment peter out in the face of a barrage of musket balls, Gustavus arranged his right flank, which had earlier absorbed the charge from Pappenheim, to counter charge.

As they did so, the horse under the command of Johan Baner aimed for the exposed Imperial batteries which were to the rear. They fell upon these with a cold-blooded charge, striking the Imperial gunners down where they stood and, crucially, commandeering the weapons for themselves. Tilly's position was now dire. His men faced into the teeth of Swedish regiments who continued to pour down an unheard-of volume of musket and light gun fire into his ranks; his cavalry wings had either been routed or pulled away, and now on his rear, the artillery had fallen into enemy hands. When the formerly Imperial guns began to ignite, and inflict horrific wounds upon his twelve tercios, Tilly knew the battle was lost.[67] Indeed, it had been lost from the moment he had arrived, thanks to the disparity in firepower alone. As one English observer of the battle described the new Swedish method of fire by rank:

> ...you pour as much lead into your enemy's bosom at one time as you do the other way at two [or six] several times, and thereby you do them more mischief...and astonish them three times more, for one long and [continued] crack of thunder is more terrible and dreadful to mortals than ten interrupted and several ones.[68]

Indeed, the combination of relentless small arms fire with field guns had proved the difference. Bodies of men were left obliterated on the battlefield, and those that survived sported horrific wounds. The casualty figures are as wide-ranging as the figures provided for the size and composition of the two armies, but there is no doubt that the Imperial losses were horrendously grave. Tilly seems to have suffered as many as seven and a half thousand killed or wounded, and six thousand prisoners, whereas Gustavus lost only a little more than two thousand men. The loss was compounded by Gustavus' ability to absorb many of these prisoners into his ranks, swelling his numbers to the further detriment of the aged and now wounded Imperial commander.[69] Yet Breitenfeld was more than just the story of a great victory, and it was more, still, than the triumph of new military tactics against tried and tested methods.

So significant was the victory, in fact, that Gustavus Adolphus can be credited with ending on an afternoon the Habsburg supremacy which had characterised the first half of the Thirty Years War. Never again would the Emperor's position be so unassailable or free from threat as it had been during the glory days of the late 1620s. The Swedish King had fired his first bullet into the heart of the Habsburg colossus, and in the process had laid the foundation stone of the Swedish Empire. This was realised by Johan Salvius, a Swedish chronicler and statesman, who noted in the aftermath of Breitenfeld that:

> Ragged, tattered and dirty were our men besides the glittering, gilded and plume-decked Imperialists. Our Swedish and Finnish nags looked but puny, next their great Germans chargers. Our peasant lads made no brave show upon the field, when set against the hawk-nosed and moustachioed veterans of Tilly. Yet they were mindful how that with victories continual they had made near the whole circuit of the Baltic Sea, driven the Muscovite into the innermost deeps of Sarmatia, and to the Polack prescribed laws. And as for all the same cullions whom they are now to meet in open field, had they not bundled them out already – not from one or two, but from all the strong places that were in Rugen, Pomerania, the most of Mecklenburg, and the whole Mark of Brandenburg? Wherefore they had the less reason to think twice about oppugning them now, when they had no wall to their defence, but were girt only by a little breastplate of iron about their bodies. And thereupon they fell to, and basted the enemy's hide so briskly, that at last he had no choice but to yield.[70]

Indeed, the Emperor's men had no choice but to yield to the Swedish King. Having reached the pinnacle of innovation and harnessed the very best which tactical and technical innovations had to offer him, Gustavus Adolphus had passed his first great test. In this murderous laboratory, at the virtual half-way point of the Thirty Years War, a watershed moment had been passed in seventeenth century warfare.

Chapter 3 Notes

[1] Cited in Geoffrey Parker, 'The Limits to Revolutions in Military Affairs: Maurice of Nassau, the Battle of Nieuwpoort (1600), and the Legacy', pp. 356-357.

[2] Cited in *Ibid*, p. 357.

[3] Cited in *Ibid*, pp. 357-358.

[4] Cited in *Ibid*, p. 358.

[5] Cited in *Ibid*, p. 359.

[6] Caroline Finkel, 'French Mercenaries in the Habsburg-Ottoman War of 1593-1606: The Desertion of the Papa Garrison to the Ottomans in 1600', *Bulletin of the School of Oriental and African Studies* 55 (1992), pp. 451-471.

[7] John A. Lynn, 'Tactical Evolution in the French Army, 1560-1660', p. 187.

[8] Details provided here on Dutch innovation and reform in the drill are examined by John A. Lynn, Tactical Evolution in the French Army, 1560-1660', pp. 187-190.

[9] Both cited in Geoffrey Parker, 'The Limits to Revolutions in Military Affairs', p. 356.

[10] John A Lynn, 'Tactical Evolution in the French Army', p. 190.

[11] Geoffrey Parker, 'The Limits to Revolutions in Military Affairs', pp. 363-364.

[12] *Ibid*, p. 364.

[13] *Ibid*, pp. 365-366.

[14] See Geoffrey Parker, 'The "Military Revolution," 1560-1660--a Myth?', pp. 211-213.

[15] Mahinder S. Kingra, 'The Trace Italienne and the Military Revolution During the Eighty Years' War, 1567-1648', *The Journal of Military History*, Vol. 57, No. 3 (Jul., 1993), pp. 431-446.

[16] John L. Stevens, *History of Gustavus Adolphus* (New York: G. P. Putnam's Sons, 1884), pp. 267-268.

[17] Monro, quoted in Roger B. Manning, *An Apprenticeship in Arms*, p. 62.

[18] See Peter H. Wilson, *Great Battles – Lutzen* (London; Oxford University Press, 2018).

[19] See Nils Ahnlund, *Gustav Adolf, the Great*, trans. Michael Roberts (Princeton: Princeton University Press; American-Scandinavian Foundation, 1940), pp. 36-46.

[20] See Michael Roberts, *Gustavus Adolphus: A History of Sweden 1611-1632*, vol. II (London: Longmans, Green and Co. Ltd, 1958), p. 199.

[21] For more on these wars from 1611-29, see Stewart P. Oakley, *War and Peace in the Baltic, 1560-1790* (New York: Routledge, 1992), pp. 42-79.

[22] See Roberts, *Gustavus Adolphus*, pp. 219-220.

[23] Quoted in C. R. L. Fletcher, *Gustavus Adolphus and the Struggle of Protestantism for Existence* (New York: G. P. Putnam's Sons, 1890), p. 125.

[24] *Ibid*, p. 124.

[25] Baumgartner, *From Spear to Flintlock*, p. 252.

[26] Roberts, *Gustavus Adolphus*, p. 227.

[27] Although more innovative, archaeological evidence points to flintlock weapons being in limited use since at least 1580. See: Barry C. Kent, 'More on Gunflints', *Historical Archaeology*, Vol. 17, No. 2 (1983), pp. 27-40; p. 28.

[28] See Fletcher, *Gustavus Adolphus*, pp. 124-125.

[29] Theodore Ayrault Dodge, *Gustavus Adolphus: A History of the Art of War from Its Revival After the Middle Ages to the End of the Spanish Succession War, With a Detailed Account of the Campaigns of the Great Swede, and of the Most Famous Campaigns of Turenne, Condé, Eugene and Marlborough* (Houghton, Mifflin and Company, 1895), p. 60.

[30] Fletcher, *Gustavus Adolphus*, p. 125.

[31] Baumgartner, *From Spear to Flintlock*, pp. 251-252.

[32] *Ibid*, p. 252.

[33] See Roberts, *Gustavus Adolphus*, pp. 173-178.

[34] *Ibid*, p. 228.

[35] *Ibid*, pp. 229-230.

[36] See *Ibid*, p. 229, especially footnote 2 where Roberts compared the opinions of various experts on rate of fire.

[37] *Ibid*, p. 230.

[38] *Ibid*, pp. 232-233.

[39] See Boyd L. Dastrup, *The Field Artillery: History and Sourcebook* (Westport, CT: Greenwood Press, 1994), p. 181.

[40] Fletcher, *Gustavus Adolphus*, p. 121.

[41] Roberts, *Gustavus Adolphus*, p. 234.

[42] Dodge, *Gustavus Adolphus*, pp. 64-68.

[43] Oakley, *War and Peace in the Baltic*, pp. 59-64.

[44] Parker, *Europe in Crisis*, p. 214. See also chapter 12 of this book.

[45] *Ibid*, pp. 65-66.

[46] See Geoffrey Parker (eds.), *Thirty Years War* (London: Routledge, 1997), pp. 185-186.

[47] Both quoted in Michael Roberts, *Gustavus Adolphus*, p. 247.

[48] Wilson, *Europe's Tragedy*, pp. 475-476 notes that Count Tilly lost control over his force, and this played a pivotal role in his triumph. When accounting for the rout of the Saxons under his nominal command, however, and his ability to seize victory in spite of this setback, it seems reasonable to conclude that tactics, rather than numbers, were what won the day.

[49] Dodge, *Gustavus Adolphus*, p. 75.

[50] Quoted in Roberts, *Gustavus Adolphus*, p. 237.

[51] Quoted in Wilson, *Europe's Tragedy*, p. 472.

[52] Stevens, *History of Gustavus Adolphus*, p. 323.

[53] Dodge, *Gustavus Adolphus*, p. 285.

[54] See Roberts, *Gustavus Adolphus*, pp. 245-246.

[55] Dodge, *Gustavus Adolphus*, p. 81.

[56] Dastrup, *The Field Artillery: History and Sourcebook*, p. 11.

[57] Roberts, *Gustavus Adolphus*, p. 250.

[58] See Frank Tallett, *War and Society in Early-Modern Europe*, p. 45.

[59] Baumgartner, *From Spear to Flintlock*, p. 254.

[60] See Roberts, *Gustavus Adolphus*, pp. 250-251.

[61] See Dodge, *Gustavus Adolphus*, pp. 285-286.

[62] Robert, *Gustavus Adolphus*, p. 253; Dodge, *Gustavus Adolphus*, p. 286.

[63] Roberts, *Ibid*, p. 253.

[64] Dodge, *Gustavus Adolphus*, pp. 289-290.

[65] Alexia Grosjean, "6: Scotland: Sweden's Closest Ally?" in *Scotland and the Thirty Years' War, 1618-1648*, ed. Steve Murdoch (Boston: Brill, 2001), pp. 157-158.

[66] *Ibid*, p. 158.

[67] See Dodge, *Gustavus Adolphus*, pp. 290-292.

[68] Quoted in Roberts, *Gustavus Adolphus*, p. 259.

[69] These figures are used by Matusiak, *Europe in Flames*, p. 313; Dodge, *Gustavus Adolphus*, p. 293; Baumgartner, *From Spear to Flintlock*, p. 255; Parker, *Europe in Crisis*, p. 223; Roberts, *Gustavus Adolphus*, p. 537.

[70] Quoted in Roberts, *Gustavus Adolphus*, p. 537.

(Top left) A Turkish Janissary
(Top right) Bethlen Gabor (Hungarian National Museum)

Soldiers plundering (Sebastian Vranc, 1620)

CHAPTER FOUR
"The Exceptions and the Exceptional"

ONE: Eastern Influences: The Turkish Factor

TWO: Standing Armies – the Habsburg Experience

THREE: Besiegers and Besieged – Mantua and the Isle of Re

FOUR: seventeenth Century Warfare and Society – a Retrospective

ONE

Eastern Influences – the Turkish Factor

The Turk, contrary to what his Christian neighbour would have you believe, was absolutely ahead of his time where military technology was concerned. The Ottomans also dealt with enemies in some very different theatres – Safavid Persia was to the east, the Mamluk Turks were in Egypt, steppe enemies were further afield, border skirmishes could be found in the Caucasus and of course the Christian empires of Europe were encountered with blistering frequency as Turkish power and influence spread forth from the Balkans. As the Turk fought its enemies, it also dealt with warrior cultures that viewed gunpowder weapons very differently.

Safavid Persia thought firearms cowardly, and only reluctantly made use of cannons. Similarly, the Mamluk Turkish Empire in Egypt, Palestine and Syria was rapidly overcome in a succession of stunning triumphs in the second decade of the sixteenth century thanks in large part to the Mamluk aversion to gunpowder weaponry, in a culture which placed more value on prowess on horseback, and less on organised infantry tactics. In a similar vein did the Spanish defeat the Aztecs, as the latter revered a warrior culture which emphasised the bravery and skill of the individual, rather than on the collective tactics of any army, a factor which made the Aztecs and other such warrior cultures, in the words of the historian Jeremy Black, 'vulnerable to forces that placed an emphasis on more concerned manoeuvres and on anonymous combat, particularly those forces employing firepower.'[1]

The Ottomans responded to the varied tactics and fighting styles of their neighbours by combining several different units together into one army. Thus it was possible to see them employ Crimean Tartars against European powers in the Balkans with as much enthusiasm as they emphasised gunpowder infantry volleys against Safavid Persia, and the implementation of different tactics and soldiers necessitated the development of a highly efficient and organised bureaucracy which could properly move the soldiers from one corner of the empire to another, and equip them with the appropriate weapons. It was vital that the logistics were sorted out in this regard, especially in the event of sieges which required consistent pressure and enough resources to keep the besiegers maintained in good health and spirits.

We know that the Ottomans employed cannons against the Byzantines during the successive sieges of Constantinople (between 1394 and 1402, 1422, 1453), at Salónica (1422, 1430), Antalya (1424), Novo Brdo (1427, 1441), Smederevo (1439) and Belgrade (1440).[2] The Ottomans also engaged in several sieges over the sixteenth century, famously in Rhodes, Crete and Malta, and even while not all were successful, it was clear to the West that the Turk possessed an unparalleled talent for bringing the most effective elements of its armed forces to bear.[3] They were forced, as conquerors, to take what was not theirs, so it isn't surprising that the Ottomans developed an intricate system for making the most of the siege. They were also pioneers in the act of actually using cannons during a siege, since it was only from the 1420s that cannons were used with much consistency in siegecraft by Europeans.[4] Similarly, the Turk had been familiarised with gunpowder weaponry since the middle of the fourteenth century, and from the 1380s, made regular use of the most primitive of such weapons while rampaging through the Balkans.[5]

At the same time though, as we alluded to earlier, the Ottomans were highly flexible on the battlefield, and made great use of different fighting styles within the same army. Combining the strengths of the forces at their disposal, and understanding where the weaknesses of their enemy lay, enabled the Ottomans to utterly destroy the cream of Hungary's armed forces at the Battle of Mohacs in 1526. During that battle the Turks made use of horse archers, field artillery, matchlock musketmen, heavy cavalry and a wagon fort tied together by chains to anchor the central Ottoman line. Even during the earlier Ottoman-Hungarian wars of the 1440s though, primitive muskets, what the Ottomans called the *tufek*, were used in battle.

The *tufek* can tend to cause a bit of confusion though, because while they are often referenced in Turkish sources, the term is quite imprecise, in the same way that the word 'gun' or 'musket' can be used to mean legions of different firearms. The end result of this confusion and lack of clarity means that it is often difficult to know what the calibre or statistics of the Ottoman firearms were, but we do know that from the early 1400s, references to the *tufek* in Turkish armies increased dramatically.[6]

It is worth considering the fact that the low fire rate of the musket in comparison with the horse archer – one shot could be fired from a musket in the time it took a horse archer to fire six arrows – greatly influenced the Turks and other empires in the Caucasus, in Mongolia, in India or in South Asia which saw a prevalence of horse archer tactics. The pike and musket combinations which Europeans were perfecting in the first half of the seventeenth century were virtually absent in the East and in the Orient. A culture of making use of the horse archers in the successor states of the Mongols, such as the Crimean Tartars, also played a significant role, along with the traditions of seasonal raiding that made horsemanship essential in the region. It was not practical for the Mughal Empire of India, to take another example, to make use of the slow moving pikemen formations when their enemies would be fielding swarms of horse archers that would simply cut them to pieces. At the same time though, in some areas of India, the climate was not well suited to the breeding of horses, and more of a reliance was placed upon heavy cannons or rudimentary gunners, which their rivals would have to match.[7]

The Ottomans were also eager to learn and were perfectly willing to adopt the tactics of their rivals. During their earlier invasion of Hungary in the 1440s, the Ottomans encountered the wagon fortress for the first time, a tactic which involved chaining several wagons together as an anchor of the defensive line, often positioned atop a hill or some other strategic position, and fortified with crossbowmen or, increasingly, arquebusiers. While the Ottomans' quick adoption of firearms and the wagon tactic is notable, where their example stood out lay in their early integration of specialised gunpowder infantry into their standing forces. From the 1390s on, preceding their rivals by centuries, the Ottomans actually established a specialised corps of permanent salaried troops who were experts in the manufacturing and handling of firearms. In the last decade of the fourteenth century the Ottomans employed artillery gunners paid with military fiefs, and a generation later began to employ salaried cannoneers. This professionalization of their armies clearly predated their European rivals, who had not begun to integrate gunpowder weapons consistently into their armed forces, and who had yet to fully professionalise their armies or establish a standing army on anything more than a strictly seasonal basis.

Ottoman Sultans predictably got in on the act, and from the mid-fifteenth century onward a separate unit of armourers were employed in the Sultan's household troops; they were tasked with looking after and in some cases carrying the weapons of the Janissary infantry. In the second half of the fifteenth century, organisation had reached a point whereby a wagon service within the army had developed, whose job was to manufacture, repair, and operate war wagons in campaigns, as well as to set up the chain linked war wagons which the Turk had copied from the Hungarians. In addition, the Ottomans had a less exciting relationship with their larger guns – whereas Western sources record names and elaborate decorations for the bigger artillery pieces, the Ottoman sources do not. While the craftsmen of firearms were skilled and respected individuals, in the Sultan's realm he was also a soldier and was as likely to fire the weapon as he was to sell it. In these circumstances the aesthetic qualities of an arquebus were not as important as a man's ability to competently use it.

Parallels exist between Ottoman and Western armies thanks to the advent and rise of the Janissaries in Ottoman service. The status and establishment of this military caste is shrouded in myth, and the mere mention of Janissary often conjures up images of young Christian boys being ripped away from their mother's breast and trained for war under a militant version of Islam for the rest of their lives. Regardless of the truth of these ideas, we do know that the Janissaries emerged in the latter fourteenth century, and that they were a product of the child levy system known as the *devshirme*, which Sultan Murad I instituted as a form of blood tax over non-Muslims.[8] The Janissaries were trained in the use of the recurve bow, sword and shield, but were quickly equipped with the *tufek* after the spread of gunpowder weapons into the army.

Unlike Europeans though, the Ottomans only granted the privilege of wielding firearms to the elite in society, which was what the Janissaries gradually became. Unlike the knights of European stock, the Janissaries had the humblest of beginnings, but after establishing a reputation for themselves, they took on the trappings of power in Ottoman society. Like a mixture between a warrior caste of knights, Rome's Praetorian Guard and Jewish pariahs in European society, Janissaries applied their reputations in warfare to create great business opportunities for themselves once they had been released from their service. As the child levy system was relaxed in the seventeenth century, the Janissaries were replaced by regular conscripted soldiers, and the peak of their prowess and reputation seems to have been during the fifteenth and sixteenth centuries, before greed and opportunism overcame the professionalism and Janissaries became just another element of the Ottoman army.

> And in the middle of the field, the Janissaries stood in three ranks, each musketeer with matches ready [to fire] and they lined up the bigger [wagons], chained to one another, in front of the Janissaries. Then, after the first rank of Janissaries fires their muskets, the second rank fires, too. Afterward, the rank that fired first [kneels] and begins to reload their muskets. And as the third rank fires, the second rank in front [of them] bends and prepares their muskets. Then, the first rank again stands up and fires their muskets.[9]

In such a way did a Turkish contemporary record the tactics of the Janissaries' volley fire in 1605 outside the fortress of Esztergom in Hungary. References to such a specific form of volley fire reminds us of the kind of orderly fire by rank tactics of European armies later in the seventeenth century, and it suggests that the Ottomans participated in the Military Revolution which brought these tactics about. However, it is also worth considering the possibility that the Janissaries behaved like their European counterparts and emulated a volley drill because their once legendary status as individually capable warriors had significantly diminished. For the sake of preserving some measure of cohesion among the Janissaries, and to keep their skills with the musket up to date, these Janissaries evolved with the times, rather than abruptly adopt the superior tactics of their European neighbours.

It was also the case that, even while musketry remained important, the Ottoman armed forces boasted significant horse archer and even regular archer units as well, which could often inflict horrific wounds on their enemies far outside the realm of possibility for the one-shot-per-minute musket armed Janissaries. During the so-called Long War between the Habsburgs and Turks, fought between 1594-1607, the Ottomans often brought superior archery skills to bear against the enemy. In one battle in particular, the Battle of Mezőkeresztes in October 1596, archers were of more use to the victorious Turks than muskets. This despite the fact that the use of archers of the battlefield in the late sixteenth century flew in the face of the idea that the Military Revolution had embraced all civilised powers. Conversely, it could also be used to prove that the Ottomans were backward and not with the times, and that this was why they stooped so low as to use a medieval weapon like the bow. Yet, horsemanship and the skills associated with archery remained important facts of life for the steppe peoples upon whom the Ottomans relied for auxiliaries, right up to late eighteenth century. Such facts remind us that the Military Revolution looked very different and developed very differently depending on geography, traditions and culture. The unique status of the Janissaries necessitated military drills to keep that strata of the army in tip top condition, yet this does not at all mean that the Turks abruptly dropped the other auxiliaries which still made use of comparatively primitive weapons on paper, but which granted them such a fearsome reputation in reality.[10]

This fearsome reputation was well-earned and was a product of the lifestyle which these auxiliaries endured while not at war. To address this point, one should consider the practice of raiding. In the West, raiding was less common, except to procure supplies, whereas in the wilder east, raiding was a fact of life, and the Ottomans harnessed these traditions for their military machine. The historian John A Lynn, wrote on this idea that:

> The art of war in seventeenth century Europe passed through a transformation so fundamental that scholars have proclaimed it a Military Revolution. Changes in everything from tactics to institutional hierarchies gave armies many of the characteristics now recognised as modern. After initial advances credited to the Dutch and Swedes, the French led the wave of change during the second half of the century...[11]

But where did this leave the Ottomans? Were they condemned to follow the Europeans like sheep, and even to steal their guns? Not so, according to the historian Gábor Ágoston. Agoston has written extensively on the shape and development of the Ottoman armies, and rallies against the myths often perpetuated about the Ottomans – that their armies required firearms beyond the manufacturing capacity of the state, so many were simply stolen from the Christian West; that the Ottomans couldn't craft the specialised cannons themselves, and remained stuck in the medieval era with their enormous unwieldy cannon instead.

These myths underline a point which we addressed in Chapter 1, where the reality of battle in a given region was that it was not practical to 'modernise' in the Western sense, since this would mean placing underperforming muskets in the hands of men who were more adept with their traditional weapons. The Ottomans understood this point, and their favouring of muskets and their handling by only the most elite demonstrates the respect they held for these weapons.[12] It would not be until the nineteenth century that firearms would have reached a point as to surpass all old weaponry.

At the start of the 1600s, muskets were becoming widely adopted as the basic firearm of the infantry, but they boasted several unfortunate disadvantages for the soldier which would have to be addressed by mixing in a steady supply of shock melee troops. Thus, pikemen were introduced in increasing numbers to provide support against cavalry and to serve as a defence against charging infantry from the opposite side. Pikemen tended to occupy the centre of the battalion and would be flanked by files of musketeers on either side. It is also worth emphasising the unreliability of the matchlock musket which was then commonly available. Vauban, the grandfather of the French network of defences, was able to speak of 'a thousand fire accidents because of the match', and this was hardly surprising considering the complex, careful process which loading, preparing and firing a matchlock musket involved.

A lock would ignite the powder charge with a lighted match, which was normally a cord of flax or hemp. Yet the best most musketmen could manage was one shot per minute, and in the midst of battle, while suffering the horrific wounds of the musket ball projectiles, and trying to maintain morale, the musketeers would be faced with the equally demoralising fact that up to *half* of all shots misfired. In addition, everything acted up when the weather was bad, and sometimes the powder could be of a lower quality, or the match would go out without good reason, forcing the musketeer to light it again with the powder already prepared. Accidents were about as common as successful shots against the enemy, but it was at least easier to train someone with this weapon than with a longbow or recurve bow, and it did require less effort, even if it was less technologically straightforward than the simple bow and arrow mechanism.[13]

Considering these points, it often was not practical to kit out one's auxiliaries with the matchlock weapon, nor was it productive to attempt to train a man on horseback with a matchlock pistol when the bow was far more effective, and formed part of the identity of the raiding Tartars and Caucasus auxiliaries which the Ottomans employed. It was also going to be expensive to provide these auxiliaries with firearms made by the state, and the expense was surely pointless if the horse-archer came equipped with his horse and bow already. On the completely opposite end of the scale though, the Ottomans were among the pioneers of metallurgy, being one of the first empires to establish a state sponsored arsenal in Constantinople the same year the city was conquered by Sultan Mehmed II in 1453. As the historian Gabor Agoston noted, the Constantinople arsenal…

> …was one of the first arsenals in late medieval Europe to be built, operated, and financed by a central government, in a time when European monarchs obtained their cannons from artisanal workshops. The Istanbul foundry cast hundreds of cannons annually and could easily ramp up production during major wars, a sign of adaptability. For instance, whereas in 1676 the foundry manufactured only forty-six pieces, between July 1684 and June 1685, at the beginning of the long war against the Holy League (1684-1699), it cast 785 cannons, mainly small field pieces.[14]

Indeed, the churning out of the small cannons by these production centres makes a lie out of the idea that the Ottomans were hopelessly behind or overburdened by their massive, immovable cannon, and never adapted these hulking pieces for proper warfare. The Ottomans did have artillery for specific purposes, just as they had auxiliaries for specific enemies, and understood that in warfare it was critically important to maintain a degree of flexibility. One of the greatest problems for Ottoman armies wasn't necessarily innovation or ingenuity, rather, it was the challenge in developing a uniform, centrally organised military administration that would provide each soldier with a coordinated training regimen. These problems affected the Ottomans for the same reason that they possessed such varied armies – their neighbours, as well as their vassals and auxiliaries, possessed weapons, military cultures and tribal traditions of their own which often superseded any effort to create a unitary military ordnance. Throw in the contributions made by mercenaries, who came equipped with their own weapons and kept to regiments all of their own within the army, and the situation becomes still more convoluted.

This, as we said, does not at all mean to suggest that the Ottomans lagged behind technologically; on the contrary, the production of a wide variety of field cannon and the use of flexible mass volley and horse archers must single the Turks out as *pioneers* in military technology. Janissaries could also expect to take muskets of varying size with them on campaign depending on the fighting style of the enemy or the forces they would bring to bear, as well as the conditions they would be expected to fight in. Habsburg and Hungarian commanders considered the Ottoman muskets to be of better quality, with greater accuracy, longer range and more stopping power than their European equivalents. As if to qualify this claim, in Ming China during the 1590s a treatise was passed which accepted the superiority of Ottoman muskets over Portuguese muskets and favoured the former musket in the event of trade.

A primitive version of the bayonet even entered Ottoman service in the first two decades of the seventeenth century, and it took the form of a long, straight knife which was stored in the butt of the gun. This could be plugged into the barrel of the gun once it had been fired and would protect the musketeer from cavalry or melee infantry. The varied circumstances of the Ottoman domains meant that a soldier who was equipped for anything was essential, as Gabor Agoston wrote:

> While the Ottomans were late in introducing the bayonet en masse, the above information indicates that the vulnerability of the gunner after he fired his weapon, mainly to swift cavalry charges, was a concern among the Ottomans, and that they experimented with possible countermeasures, including combination weapons similar to the one described in the Chinese treatise.[15]

That the Ottomans were pioneers thus cannot be in doubt. It would not be until the final years of the seventeenth century that a bayonet and the drill to accompany it would spread across European military practice. This process made the infantry more flexible, and effectively doomed pikemen to the dustbin of history, yet whether Europeans accepted the Turkish innovation or not, it is important to recognise the contribution to military technology and innovation which the Ottomans definitely made. This contribution seems to have stalled when it came to fortification techniques though, largely because the Ottomans had no need for the kind of bastions which Western European rulers depended upon. The Long War between the Habsburgs and Turks was waged between the 1590s and 1606, and to defend against their fearsome enemy, along their Hungarian border with the Ottomans, the Austrian Habsburgs had constructed several fortresses in the trace italienne style. Yet, as Jeremy Black appreciated, it was one thing to build, and quite another to adequately defend:

> The Ottomans were able to capture many of the fortresses recently modified by the Austrians using the cutting-edge Italian expertise of the period... Thus, rather than providing a paradigm leap (or revolution) forward in the defensiveness of Christendom, it is necessary to consider the advances in fortification, like other developments, in terms of particular circumstances, and not least to remember that defences were only as good as their defenders and logistical support. Although the Ottomans had no equivalent to the trace italienne, nor to the extensive fortifications built in the Austrian-ruled section of Hungary, as well as along the coasts of Naples and Sicily against Barbary raids, they did not require any such developments as they had not been under equivalent attack.[16]

It would be unrealistic to expect the Ottomans to develop and adapt their military tactics and army composition in the same way as the West, because the Ottomans, while they faced the Habsburgs, also faced very different challenges across the vast spread of their domains. Their Empire developed and contracted according to circumstances which were very different to those faced by empires in the Christian West. As the two theatres entered down different historical paths, and came into new experiences as the century progressed, the gap between Western and Eastern military technologies and tactics became more evident. But then, the Turk could not be counted out; Ottoman armies remained a potent threat, and even after the 1699 Peace of Karlowitz effectively halted the Empire's westward expansion, European contemporaries could hardly be certain that the Sultan's armies would not menace them again.

TWO

Standing Armies –
the Habsburg Experience

The impact of 'revolutions' upon the military was a palpable feature of the seventeenth century, but warfare had an additional impact upon the development and administration of many states caught in the crossfire. One such entity was the hereditary lands of the Habsburg Holy Roman Emperors, which included a considerable swathe of South-Central Europe, based on Austria, and propped up by the Kingdom of Bohemia. Of particular interest to us in this portion of the story is an Emperor who was central to the course of the Thirty Years War, Ferdinand II. The journey which Emperor Ferdinand II (r. 1619-1637) endured was a stark one: in the beginning of his reign he was too weak even to instruct his vassals to act without considerable bribes, yet, by the end of his life, his dynasty's hereditary lands had been reinforced, consolidated and recast. Thanks to the ravages of war, Emperor Ferdinand would effectively bring the Austrian Empire to life, and he would do it thanks largely to the creation of a standing army.

If explaining the origins of the Austrian Empire is an exercise not for the faint of heart, then explaining how that Empire acquired and then developed its army is a still more demanding task. Depending on whom you ask, the Austrian army was a lazy and unprofessional institution, rotten to the core with corruption, outmatched by its rivals and burdened with a myriad of national and cultural problems. Or, perhaps it was a brilliantly trained and led army, which pushed the Turk away from Europe, expanded the Habsburg patrimony into the Balkans, and was characterised by such military geniuses as Eugene of Savoy. In the opening paragraph of his book on the Austrian army from 1619-1918, historian Richard Basset writes:

'Austria', the Austrian writer Hermann Bahr wrote, 'has not been lucky with its biographers.' If this is the case for Imperial Austria as a structure, it is also true for the Imperial and Royal army whose efforts supported the Empire for so many centuries. Perhaps it was Talleyrand who set the tone for later nineteenth and twentieth century disparagement with his famous quip that 'Austria has the tiresome habit of always being beaten.'[17]

156

One doesn't have to look particularly far for a negative opinion on the Habsburg Monarchy, and in some cases, the criticisms are justified. Much like the other multi-national empires of the nineteenth and twentieth centuries, the Habsburgs faced grave challenges which undermined the powers of the centre and eventually caused the whole edifice to splinter into disparate parts. Considering these insurmountable problems, one could be forgiven for asking how the Habsburgs managed to last so long. Emperor Ferdinand II (r. 1619-1637) did much to centralise the Habsburg Hereditary Lands, which was an important step towards creating what would become first the Austrian and then the Austro-Hungarian Empire. Ferdinand II was, as C. V. Wedgewood noted, the 'creator of the Austrian, not the restorer of the Holy Roman Empire.'[18]

However, pivotal though he was, the question of the Habsburg Empire's longevity is answered less by the Emperors that led it, and more by the armies which defended it; thus, we must turn our attention to the creation of the Austrian army. By investigating its origins and tracing its development from such humble beginnings, perhaps the Habsburgs' ability to adapt and improvise will become more apparent. Regardless, as a key player in the conflict, it is important to explain how the Habsburgs made war in the seventeenth century. This investigation will require us to ask what came before this Austrian army was grown, in addition to the challenges it faced, and of course, what the costs of creating this army was to the Habsburg family, both in terms of sheer financial burdens and lost prestige.

Although it wouldn't be until Albrecht of Wallenstein was enlisted in 1625 as Emperor Ferdinand II's personal mercenary that the Austrian Habsburgs would possess an army of their own, the fusion of the military with the dynasty was an event that occurred only a few years before, on a tense and insufferably hot afternoon of 5 June 1619. It was during that afternoon that a few things happened. In a scene which we will return to later in the book, a deputation of Bohemian Protestants barged into Ferdinand's Hofburg palace and demanded concessions from their Emperor. Devoid of allies and lacking any proper army of his own, it seemed entirely likely that the beleaguered Ferdinand would accept the demands. This largely forgotten scene in the context of the eventual crushing of the Bohemian revolt is an immensely important one to bear in mind, because it was here, just in the nick of time, that an armed detachment of cavalry led by Ferdinand's brother arrived to save the day.

On this occasion, and for the remainder of the Habsburg Empire's existence, the dynasty's fortunes would be fused with the fortunes of the army. This dynasty would refrain from risking the whole army in battle and would never allow it to be destroyed. The dynasty would consistently seek to reform it, improve it and expand upon it; efforts would be made to draw better leaders and to learn from its mistakes. This was because subsequent Habsburg

Emperors accepted what Ferdinand came to realise on that hot afternoon of 5 June 1619 – that the Habsburg family's position was not based upon the prestige or value of its Imperial title or its Bohemian kingship, but of the power and strength of its armed forces. Ferdinand II, saved from the shame of making an ignominious and unholy concession to his enemies, never forgot the impression which the timely arrival of his brother's cavalry made that afternoon, and he sought to bring this lesson to its logical conclusion – by crafting an army exclusively for the Habsburg family's usage.

Some perspective is needed, so that the reader will appreciate why Ferdinand's army was created in the first place. Our story begins when Ferdinand arrived in Graz, Styria in 1595 on Easter Sunday after finishing his Jesuit education in Bavaria, and asked his subjects there to join him in a mass, not a single burgher or townsperson appeared – this wasn't because they disliked Ferdinand, but because Styria, the Catholic Ferdinand's home, was overwhelmingly Protestant. This was true not only for Styria, but also for a great number of the Austrian Estates, those regional assemblies who would be called upon to make local decisions and in certain circumstances levy taxes or soldiers on the population. Ferdinand set to work transforming this situation, and turning his Jesuit education to his advantage to reverse the downward trend of Catholicism in the region. Ferdinand's Counter-Reformation zeal and his later intolerance qualified him as one of the most militant Catholics of his age.[19]

While his efforts did result in an upturn of Catholic converts in the years that followed, what they absolutely did not produce was a sense of loyalty in Austria to the future Holy Roman Emperor. If this fact appears surprising, consider that when the Bohemian revolt broke out in summer 1618, among those principalities to mirror the Bohemian behaviour were Ferdinand's Austrian estates. Even while not all such estates across Ferdinand's hereditary possessions rose up in revolt – one historian estimated that just over a third of his Austrian subjects turned against their Emperor – Ferdinand's powers were still significantly eroded.[20] In addition, while the Habsburg hereditary lands extended to Hungary, Royal Hungary was occupied by the Prince of Transylvania, a vassal of the Ottoman Empire, further undermining Habsburg security.

With the Bohemians engaging in a religiously and politically charged revolution against Ferdinand's authority, his own estates in Austria gathering in opposition against him, and the Prince of Transylvania conquering portions of Habsburg Hungary for himself, we should not be surprised to find Ferdinand prostrate before the cross by the following year, in summer 1619, when that aforementioned deputation from Bohemia came to visit. While he would regain the initiative and then some in time, this remarkable reassertion of Habsburg power was not within Ferdinand's imagination in

1619 – he had only survival on his mind, and he was immensely fortunate that the allies which he did have, such as the Bavarians, did not abandon him like the rest. Thanks to his double marriage with Maximillian of Bavaria's family, it appeared that blood was thicker than water – the Duke of Bavaria would save the Holy Roman Emperor and raise an army to fight for the Catholic interest, as much as the Habsburg.

Most of us are familiar with the story that followed. Maximillian of Bavaria's Catholic League army, which the Duke of Bavaria and other Catholic princes paid for, and which the brilliantly talented Count Tilly commanded, obliterated the enemies of the Habsburgs in the first few years of the 1620s, and completely reversed the initially dire situation of Ferdinand and his family until, as we saw, Gustavus Adolphus checked the Emperor's progress at Breitenfeld. Yet, Ferdinand was faced in each of these occasions with a dilemma akin to a crisis. Above all, he was faced with the uncomfortable truth of his own inherent weakness, especially when it came to the unified and religiously homogenous lands of the Duke of Bavaria. Land was power, but the Holy Roman Emperor had alienated or lost much of his own personal lands by the time the actual war came; indeed, it would be accurate to say that Ferdinand's own hereditary lands and miniature kingdoms turned against him. Without these lands, Ferdinand could not draw taxes, and if he could not draw taxes, he could not pay any army of his own.

Those unfamiliar with the course of the Thirty Years War may wonder how, if Ferdinand couldn't pay for his own army, he was able to persuade Maximillian of Bavaria and the Catholic League to finance one. Surely the Duke of Bavaria wouldn't raise an army and pay for it out of the kindness of his heart? Surely, he would expect payment from the Emperor in return. Indeed, he did, but Ferdinand was fortunate at this point that the Duke of Bavaria accepted payment in kind, rather than actual coin that he did not possess. Ferdinand infamously passed the outlawed Elector Palatine's elector title on to the Duke of Bavaria in lieu of pay, a highly unconstitutional and bitterly resented act in the Protestant camp, once it was discovered. Yet, Ferdinand was also forced to pass Upper Austria into Maximillian's hands, which the newly established elector would be allowed to tax as if these lands were his own, so that he could squeeze the lands in a way that the Emperor could not. Indeed, even had he wanted to, Ferdinand did not have the men in place to do so, and he lacked the soldiers to defend against any repercussions.

Ferdinand weakened and diluted the constitution of the Holy Roman Empire, as much as the reach of his own dynasty, in order to empower the army of his allies and defeat his enemies. Initially, with the newly enshrined Elector of Bavaria firmly on his side, Ferdinand's fortunes soared. However, in the long term, Ferdinand would never be able to win the war against foreign powers without an army of his own, especially if these powers threatened Bavaria, and Maximillian was forced to pull this army out of the field and back to Munich for home defence. The inferred message was thus clear – Ferdinand needed an army to defend and fight for the Catholic and Habsburg position simultaneously, but what he needed was an army which he could command, and which answered directly to him. Enter onto the stage, a Catholic Bohemian of minor noble stock, with a penchant for command and grand ambitions: Albrecht von Wallenstein.

At first glance, there seems little difference between Maximillian's fee and Wallenstein's. Both individuals forced Ferdinand to hand over lands and titles instead of money so long as he lacked the latter, but the distinction is important because Wallenstein's force, or at least some iteration of it, was to remain a fixture of Habsburg society for the next three hundred years, whereas Maximillian of Bavaria's would not. The key difference between Wallenstein's force and Maximillian of Bavaria's force was loyalty.[21] Wallenstein answered to the Emperor, and worked in his interests, answered to him before all others, and obeyed his overarching commands. In return, Wallenstein would expect payment not in money, 'for Ferdinand's treasury was empty', but in lands and titles. Where was Ferdinand to get such lands and titles that did not adversely affect his authority or stain his reputation as had the deals with Maximillian of Bavaria? Conveniently for both interested parties, the Bohemian revolt had created a pool of disenfranchised rebels, whose lands and titles were all ripe for the taking.

Ferdinand, having come close to collapse in summer 1619, found himself only a few years later in a position to drastically and dramatically reorganise the lands of Bohemia and of other German princes on a scale never before experienced by any Habsburg potentate. The significance of this fact is often glossed over when it is noted that Wallenstein was paid with half the land of Bohemia, or that Bohemia itself was totally transformed from the religiously plural medieval kingdom it had once been into the Catholicised, centralised appendage of the Habsburg patrimony. This act, in time, did not merely facilitate the creation of a Habsburg army, answerable to the Emperor, it also enabled successive Habsburg Emperors to consolidate their position in their Hereditary Lands, and craft what we would recognise as the Austrian Empire in the process.

These transfers of land, the reversal of hundreds of years of history, and their replacement with a system that thoroughly benefited the Habsburgs – none of these actions would have been possible without first the defeat of the Bohemian revolt, and then the conquering of these lands by Wallenstein. Ferdinand was keen to ensure that his new generalissimo, who gained a great deal from his partnership with the Habsburgs, remained devoted to his cause, especially as Denmark became involved in the war from the mid-1620s. Denmark had undergone her own Military Revolution, and much like her neighbours had experienced a kind of revolution as the old feudal knights were replaced with a professional cavalry service owned and maintained by the state.[22] Denmark was, as we will learn later in this book, one of the most powerful kingdoms in Europe, and certainly the richest in the Baltic. It would seem that Ferdinand had bitten off more than he could chew, as King Christian IV entered the war backed by numerous enemies of the Habsburgs, including the Dutch, English, and Palatine supporters. But here, Ferdinand's preparations paid off; two armies now marched in Christian's direction, where before only one had been in the field. One of these was the familiar force commanded by Count Tilly, and answerable to the Catholic League, but the other, significantly, was the Emperor's personal force commanded by Wallenstein. Christian was overwhelmed, and chased up the Jutland Peninsula, while his allies fell away. All the while, Wallenstein saw his stock rise the more he helped his master. Indeed, as Richard Basset wrote:

> None benefited more from this unique redistribution [of Bohemian land] than Wallenstein himself, who set about erecting at the heart of Europe, along the strategically vital Bohemian and Saxon frontier, a territory which would furnish him not only with prestige but with the wealth in agriculture and minerals needed to sustain such a vast army. No costs were to be incurred by the Imperial house. All Wallenstein sought was the required charter of authority and the freedom to choose his officers and recruitment depots. The charter was quickly granted by Ferdinand, who also gave Wallenstein the impressive designation of 'General-Colonel-Field-Captain of the Imperial Armada.'[23]

By granting him such sweeping powers, and also by showering him with as many titles as he could find, Ferdinand sought to retain Wallenstein and thus retain that man's standing army which had become the key to Ferdinand's overwhelming success. Indeed, this success proved the downfall of both men, for even while Wallenstein was loyal to his master, he did not approve of all of his master's ends, such as the militant counter-reformation policies Ferdinand sought in the 1629 Edict of Restitution. Wallenstein was made a prince, came to possess three duchies and carved out the position of supreme commander by that same year, so that it was rumoured even the Emperor wouldn't dare to cross him. In the end, Wallenstein proved more vulnerable to the machinations and schemes of jealous former friends than those talents of his enemies, and he was assassinated on Ferdinand's orders in 1634 – hardly the best way for an Emperor to show thanks to his subject.[24]

In any case, the fruit of the curious relationship between Wallenstein and his Emperor was that institution we alluded to earlier – a standing army for the Habsburg Monarchy. This fruit was enjoyed during Ferdinand III's reign as well, and it was this Emperor who clarified the Habsburg family's determination to maintain a standing army even with the conclusion of the

Thirty Years War. Ferdinand III issued a decree in 1649 which announced that of the fifty-two regiments raised during the Thirty Years War, a total of nineteen were permanently maintained and not dissolved along with the rest. While this meant the Habsburgs would be cutting their army more than in half, it also meant that, for the first time ever, the Austrian Habsburgs would possess a standing army twenty-one thousand men strong.[25]

It was this standing army that Wallenstein had created, and which had been nurtured after his assassination into a fighting force loyal above all to the Habsburg family. Notwithstanding the immense difficulties which Ferdinand II and Ferdinand III experienced in keeping this army afloat during the subsequent years, it was never once supposed that it would simply cease to exist. Once Ferdinand II had become used to possessing his own force, he felt crippled without it. Indeed, in 1635, he elected to combine the Catholic League army with his own, and a German Imperial army was the result, its central goal being the ejection of the foreign invader from the Empire's lands. This force counted an innumerable cast of Germans among its ranks, but it answered to the Emperor, and its commanders received its orders from him and him alone.

Reforms in discipline and tactics went hand in glove with the pervading ripples of revolutions underway in Europe at the time, and while the Habsburgs did learn much from their adversaries, the stacking up of defeats in the 1640s was a testament to the fact that the Habsburg core was fracturing. Fortunately, by the 1640s peace was on the minds of most other states, so that Wallenstein's legacy army would not be seen to crumble. Its nucleus limped on even if much of its traits and qualities unique to that generalissimo were forgotten; by 1697, Eugene of Savoy was able to marvel at the quality of the Habsburg cavalry, which he brought to great effect against the Turks during the Battle of Zenta, that battle which opened this section of the book.[26]

The eighteenth century were destined to be years of reform and increasing distinction for Austria's army, and it quickly became impossible to imagine Austria existing without a standing army all year round, while the same could be said for her Prussian, French and Spanish neighbours. Europe had come a long way since the high middle ages, where armies were not held together by much more than limited terms of service or rudimentary contractual obligation to your feudal lord.[27]

Standing armies became the norm for the Austrian Habsburgs, and it must be said that this trend was entrenched within Habsburg habits during the Thirty Years War. Without the connection made between Ferdinand II and Wallenstein, and without, arguably, the epiphany reached by Ferdinand to the effect that his power would depend on an army he could rely upon, the development of the Habsburg Monarchy would have been very different indeed. By the end of the Thirty Years War, while the Austrian Habsburgs had exhausted much of their resources, they had established over their Hereditary

Lands and Bohemia in particular an iron grip which they were to retain for the remainder of their dynasty's reign in the heart of Europe.

Indeed, it must be said that a by-product of Ferdinand's crushing of the Bohemian's revolt and his forceful incorporation of this kingdom into the Austrian family was that the Habsburgs had a far wider and more docile tax base than it ever had before once the conflict ended. In addition to this tax windfall, the historian John A. Mears made the point that Ferdinand's quest to empower Wallenstein and protect his investments led the Holy Roman Emperor to bulldoze over the traditional checks and balances on his authority in Bohemia and the Austrian estates. Ferdinand forbade any independent recruiters from operating in Bohemia, Austria, Silesia or further German lands, which preserved Wallenstein's pool of recruits for years to come. This ruling was incredibly significant, even if it has been mostly forgotten by historians. The old system was resplendent in its headache-inducing complexity and restrictiveness. The old system required that representatives of the estates, whose influence over military affairs reached a peak in the first two decades of the seventeenth century, should regulate the enlistment and quartering of troops, and retained extensive police over their respective territories.

Predictably enough, the rights of the estates in this regard undermined the development of a permanent standing army because, short of purchasing a horde of mercenaries, the only means that the emperors had had to replenish their forces was the conscription of native soldiers, which necessitated first acquiring the approval of the local estates. Under the old system, regional assembles had also acquired regiments and commission officers of their own, and to Ferdinand's chagrin, these forces were largely independent of his control. In the Austrian and Bohemian territories, the estates were technically obligated to provide military assistance to their Emperor at their own expense whenever he was attacked by a foreign enemy. Yet this qualification was important, since the technicality over who attacked first could be thrown in Ferdinand's face as an excuse to not get involved. In addition, those levies that did show up were often of limited value because they served for a very limited time, and even then, only to defend the lands from which they had come. They considered it contrary to their privileges to be compelled to undertake military services outside the borders of their own territories and would thus never be suitable to merge into a large, cross-border standing army loyal to Ferdinand. The men assembled were more loyal to their assemblies or local nobles than the distant Ferdinand, and thus could not be relied upon in battle.

If this explains why Ferdinand was so bereft of soldiers once the Bohemian revolt broke out in 1618 and worsened the following year, then what Ferdinand did over the 1620s transformed the issue altogether. In 1627, in a ruling which effected Bohemia most of all, Ferdinand eliminated these independent actions and entitlements in the Habsburg lands. Henceforth, there was only one figure who mattered when it came to raising soldiers – the Holy Roman Emperor. These repressive policies were a flagrant attack upon the privileges of the Estates, many of whom had only recently rebelled, and would surely not take further restrictions lying down. Fortunately for Ferdinand, by the time of this ruling the Emperor had in his employ an enormous army commanded by Wallenstein, which could be expected to swoop into any trouble spots at a moment's notice. Any disgruntled persons, which included those mercenary captains in these regions, who had grown used to taking advantage of the Emperor's disadvantageous position, were shown the sword or were instructed how they might signal their compliance, and many chose the latter option.[28]

Granted, once the Thirty Years War ended, some concessions were made to those estates and lands which had helped see the Habsburgs through to the end, but nothing like the old system of local checks and balances on the Emperor was ever seen again. While it is true to say that the Thirty Years War loosened the grip which the Habsburgs could be said to hold over the Holy Roman Empire, the Peace of Westphalia actually increased the authority which local princes and potentates had over their own subjects – estates were becoming increasingly weakened at a local level, when paradoxically, the Peace of Westphalia provided for more representative institutions at the top levels of the Empire itself. This transformation in the Empire took some time to be fully felt, but neither Ferdinand II nor his son wasted much time. Ferdinand II in particular paved the way not just for the standing armies which would win so much glory and fame for Vienna, but also the fusing of Habsburg lands closer together, so that in time, this once loosely aligned collection of states became an Empire in its own right. None of this would have been possible without Wallenstein, who not only conquered the Habsburg dynasty's enemies, but also conquered the restrictions placed upon Ferdinand's office.

THREE

Besiegers and Besieged – Mantua and the Isle of Re

The Military Revolution, as we have now learned, concerned not just the transformation of tactics used by soldiers, but also affected the state's relationship with the army, and the design of fortresses which could be used to reinforce the government's authority and defend it against attackers. The trace italienne was a revolution in itself, as castles were replaced with the squat fortresses, boasting interlocking bastions, and thick, low walls with emplaced guns which forced the attacker to bring more men to the action. Sieges were a profoundly important feature of the Thirty Years War, and while pitched battles tend to receive more attention, such events were statistically rare, and it was through the capture or the continued defence of these bastions that the national interest was expanded or preserved.

Considering this, it is worthwhile to examine two cases of sieges in the duration of the Thirty Years War, both of which remain generally unknown, being outside the scope of the central narrative, and taking place within a few years of each other. The first is the siege of Saint Martin, on the Isle of Ré, just off the coast of the more famous French fortress of La Rochelle, which was besieged by an English expeditionary force without success in 1627. The second is the siege of Mantua, which was conducted on and off between 1628-30 as part of the war for the Mantuan Succession. In the former case, we will focus our attention upon the lot of the besiegers, while for the latter, we will assess the fate of the besieged. An examination of these two cases, with very different fates, and from different perspectives, will contribute to the general picture of the Thirty Years War by the end of its first decade. It will also serve as a good introduction to the challenges which siegecraft presented to each side. We begin our examination with the virtually unknown English siege of Re.[29]

The siege on the Isle of Re was conducted for three months over the summer of 1627, and was directed by the Duke of Buckingham, Charles

I's favourite. The siege was significant as one of the few occasions where England committed to an independent military action during the Thirty Years War. Unfortunately for those beleaguered Protestants looking on – and indeed for the Danish king whom King Charles had promised to support – the English axe was swung not at the Habsburg enemy, but at France. Even then, the war seemed to be religiously, rather than politically, motived, and was launched in support of French Protestants or Huguenots who were then buckling under pressure from Cardinal Richelieu's regime. It was Sir George Clarke who wrote in 1958 that if the siege of Re had succeeded, we would never have heard of Oliver Cromwell.[30] Clarke's point was that the mostly unknown siege of Re heaped so much shame and scorn upon the Duke of Buckingham following his failure in summer 1627, that once Buckingham was assassinated in 1628, King Charles I's regime began its march towards collapse. We are not here to discuss the accuracy of this statement, but it does remind us that sieges can sometimes have far-reaching consequences, regardless of their location or result.

Re was an island fortress located nearby La Rochelle, the famed Huguenot stronghold, and its importance was therefore clear. If Re could be seized, then subsequent English operations in aid of the French Protestants in La Rochelle would be far easier to successfully undertake. With a base along the coast of Western France, touching into the turbulent Bay of Biscay, English operations would theoretically be easier to supply and reinforce against any French reprisals. In this respect, the plan for seizing Re made sense – the sandy island had only been seized by the French government in 1625, and so it was possible that it wouldn't be overtly taxing to take back in the name of the rebellious French Protestant Huguenots, who had fought a civil war against King Louis XIII's government since 1621.[31]

This civil war ended with the fall of La Rochelle in 1628, and Richelieu worked thereafter to reassert royal authority in Huguenot regions, while he also dealt with the King's mother, and forged a stable foreign policy based less on religious persuasion and more on the political interests of France vis-à-vis its Habsburg rival in Spain and Austria.[32] In 1627 though, the prospects for success for Richelieu remained tantalisingly out of reach. English foreign policy was focused on the maintenance of the Huguenots in France, and the eventual destruction of this Fifth Column was by no means assured. The historian S. J. Stearns provides us with a good sketch of the Isle of Re, where English troops would have to land, as he wrote:

> The small, sandy, irregularly shaped island on the Biscay coast commanded the harbour of Rochelle, which had been for long one of the major protestant strongholds in the intermittent sixty-year religious civil war in France. By seizing the island, recently garrisoned by French royal troops, the British could, without making a major military effort themselves, encourage the

Huguenots to resume their revolt against their Catholic king, while they raided the rich commerce of Bordeaux to the south.[33]

A fleet of 115 ships with six thousand soldiers on board set sail for this sandy island in late June 1627, and upon landing on 12 July, engaged with the French troops on the ground, forcing them to take refuge in St Martins citadel in the island's centre. This fortress enabled French soldiers to retain their hold over the island and keep a watchful eye on the more important fortress of La Rochelle nearby, which was zealously held by the aforementioned Huguenots. English belief had it that if Re was seized, then Huguenots would be encouraged by this setback of the French government to increase their opposition and the civil war would spread further across the country.

Yet, the newly built citadel of St Martins frustrated this high-minded aim. Though it was not completely finished, building having begun only the previous year, St Martins was strategically and tactically well thought out – the fortress had its back to the sea, with a deep moat on the remaining three sides, and it boasted high walls which went against the grain of regular fortress construction at the time. These high walls served their purpose though, as they enabled the defending French garrison to pour down a hail of fire onto the besieging English who were stuck behind the moat, and to maintain an effective panorama of the English siege works, which were quite minimal owing to a lack of preparation and resources. Indeed, the English had never expected to engage in a siege – the campaign had been characterised by Buckingham in the months before as a brilliantly unexpected skirmish, designed to hamper the French encirclement of La Rochelle and encourage the Huguenots.

What the English army and government got instead was a costly, protracted siege, and thanks to the abundance of French royalists on the mainland, and the low yields of Re's surrounding sandy lands, the only way for Buckingham's force to receive supplies and reinforcements was by sea, following a journey of several weeks and through the often hostile Bay of Biscay. As S. J. Stearns continued, the logistical dilemma was as straightforward as it was intractable:

> To assault St. Martin, even after it had been weakened by siege and artillery bombardment, reinforcements would be needed, for the conventional wisdom called for the attackers to have an advantage of at least three (if not four) to one. As the size of the besieging force increased, however, so would the supply problem. How could enough men be put into the field to win the objective without outstripping the capacity to maintain them there during the time required? It was a logistical problem of classical simplicity. The solution was infinitely complex.[34]

The mission appeared an impossible one, and much lament was poured on Buckingham for not planning ahead and foreseeing the French withdrawal into their pre-existing citadel. The channel in between the island of Re and the French mainland was narrow enough at four kilometres that small boats would be able to slip through the English naval blockade of the fortress and resupply the French garrison. Meanwhile in the English camp, reinforcements arrived from Ireland and Scotland, but these men arrived without their rations, and the original fleet which had set sail in late June had done so with only half the rations normally provided, since the expectation was of a short campaign and certainly not of a siege. Having committed to the action though, Buckingham would have to go the whole hog, and pour more and more men into the barren island as they tightened the chokehold on St Martin's citadel.

Before the reinforcements even arrived, between sailors and soldiers, the English had ten thousand men to supply, with the expectation that this number would swell to as much as seventeen thousand by the end of the summer, perhaps even more. Providing for a force this large in such a desolate place would have been a challenge even had the siege taken place on England's doorstep, but because the siege could only be resupplied over hundreds of miles of open water, the challenge was still more severe, and the prospects of success dwindled with each passing day. Not only were the men engaging in a siege, they were also fighting against the garrison, and were incurring casualties at a rate of between 45 to 60 men a day, figures which were exacerbated by disease and starvation as the problem of provisions became increasingly acute.

After a generation of peace, the Stuart monarchy was also ill-prepared psychologically and administratively for any lasting campaign. Shortages in beer and bread, the staple rations of a besieging army, were felt almost immediately, and there remained a lack of practical experience in England when it came to undertake a siege, as the Dutch or Spanish had from their many years of conflict. The requirements were underestimated, and notwithstanding Buckingham's boundless optimism, even he was aware that the siege would be in trouble before long if matters were not resolved. Resolving them was easier said than done though, especially when the needs of the soldiery were repeatedly misunderstood, and the ships inconsistently sent from home. There seemed to have been the expectation within the upper levels of English government that the old rations left over from 1625 would be sufficient to cover at least half of the requirements of 1627, this despite the fact that reports on the ground, which had plainly been ignored, had complained at the time in another campaign in 1625 that the rations were at that stage rotten and insufficient, and stank out the cargo holds in which they had been stored.[35]

A lack of money at home only added to these problems, and even with the reinforcements from Ireland and Scotland, Buckingham was not confident of success if the fortress was to be successfully stormed. The gradually dwindling French defenders were not being reduced quickly enough, and the conditions on the seas were getting increasingly more treacherous as summer progressed, so that it was doubtful the increasing demands of the besiegers could be met in time. Buckingham's letters home became more panicked and downcast as a result, and he urged a more effective channelling of funds and resources to the garrison, but in vain. As the stately system of supply began to fray at the seams with its own inadequacy, Buckingham was forced to rely on less scrupulous suppliers and contractors, who were happy to take the limited funds he did possess, and to promise great things, but proved ineffective at actually delivering the much needed foodstuffs, munitions and beer.

In early October 1627, a contract was concluded with a circle of untrustworthy fellows to supply the necessary rations for twelve thousand men for four weeks. This eased Buckingham's concerns for a time, but when the goods arrived in a state of complete disorder, rot and pollution, Buckingham knew deep down that the siege was doomed. No proper accounts had been taken of what was even being delivered, and since no bills of lading were filled out, it was a mystery what was on each of the ships. Buckingham also found that a great deal of his suppliers didn't even speak English, which only added to the disaster. By mid-October discussions about ending the siege became increasingly bitter, but Buckingham refused to accept this truth, and certainly refused to accept responsibility, arguing that he had been let down by London, which was partially true, but it was also true that the actual machinery was not in place for the siege which Buckingham had not expected, and which was certainly his fault.

In desperation did Buckingham follow through with a recommendation sent via the Huguenots at La Rochelle, a few kilometres away, that St Martins was now vulnerable to assault after the protracted siege. On 14 October, Buckingham gathered the men available to him – which amount to just four thousand effectives after so many months of starvation and inaction – and made a frontal assault on the fortress in miserable conditions, which turned the area around the citadel into a quagmire of mud and sticky death traps where more French firepower could be focused. Hopelessly outclassed and outmatched, Buckingham then agreed to call off the siege, and watched with further dismay as French troops, perhaps sensing the British weakness, were landed on the island. This added to the urgency now to withdraw and completed the picture of an ineffectual English action – Buckingham could neither organise a successful offensive, nor arrange for a safe evacuation when the tide turned.

All in all, the venture cost the crown perhaps as much as £250,000, and it seemed in addition to have cost Buckingham his life. Reports were surprisingly easy to come by on the on-going siege, so that the public was quite well informed of the humiliating disaster unfolding some distance away. This was far from the legendary English military prowess so revered by folk legends and national histories of the time; instead, it was a messy, uninspired and unrewarding campaign characterised by all the mistakes seasoned siege experts avoided. 'In the last analysis', wrote historian S. J. Stearns...

> ...after allowing due weight to domestic political difficulties, with their considerable impact on war finance, and to policy and command errors, diplomatic, strategic and tactical, the defeat at Re was fundamentally the consequence of trying to wage a campaign that was too large, too complex and too costly for the British administration to support logistically.[36]

After having seen the difficulties faced by the besieger, we now turn our attentions to the advantages that the defender possessed, specifically by examining the fortifications of the Duke of Mantua in North Italy.[37] Some context is required on the situation in the Italian patchwork of states and loyalties first. The Gonzaga Dukes of Mantua died out in 1627, initiating the Mantuan War of Succession between France and Spain, which was in actuality a proxy war, and a final step towards the open war between both crowns in 1635. In that conflict, the French candidate to replace the Gonzaga – the Duke of Nevers, was victorious. That is generally where the story is left in the historiography of the Thirty Years War.[38] However, in our case, it is useful to look in more detail at the system of fortifications which these Dukes maintained, to gain a better appreciation for such fortifications, not just for the importance they held in Northern Italian political and strategic considerations, but also for what these fortifications can tell us about the challenges which even the most powerful armies faced when up against zealous, well positioned and experienced defenders.

From 1530, the Gonzaga dukes of Mantua began investing their monies into raising the newly developed angular bastions and thick, low walls which had become the staple features of the trace italienne. Since Mantua was located in virtually the centre of North Italy, it was only natural that the influences and innovations of the trace italienne reach her leaders. Money permitting, these dukes began adding several formidable new layers to the already impressive natural defences of Mantua, which included the existence of natural lakes on three sides of the city, thanks to the fast-flowing River Mincio which passed nearby the city. Beefing up the defences of this Italian city state and its surrounding lands to such a remarkable extent, it is little wonder that one historian believed that Mantua 'became one of the strongest sites in all of Europe.'[39] Thanks in large part to Mantua's integral position along the Spanish Road, and the surviving Gonzaga brothers' lack of heirs by the 1620s, it was clear that these fortifications would soon be put to their ultimate test.

The Duchy of Mantua, which included both Mantua itself and a fortress owned and maintained by its Duke at Casale in the nearby duchy of Montferrat, were believed to be so formidable that Madrid greatly feared the implications of a French garrison arriving in the region to reinforce the interests of the independent Mantuan Dukes against those of the Habsburgs. Mantua and Montferrat, if sufficiently reinforced, could anchor a Bourbon defence in the centre of North Italy's Po Valley, and enable the French to directly threaten Milan, Turin, Genoa, Bologna and even Venice. Yet, it was also possible that French power, if resurgent in the region, would unite these cities and duchies against the Spanish, and block the Spanish Road which ran through the region, above all through the critical Habsburg satellite of Milan. In 1590, as if anticipating the looming challenges which his patrimony presented, the Duke of Mantua transformed Casale into the most impregnable bastion in Europe by constructing a brand new six-sided citadel in the centre of the city. Whatever came his way in the next few decades, he was confident that the twin fortresses of Mantua and Casale would sufficient to withstand it. Nearly forty years later, all involved would deal with the horrendous consequences of these feats of engineering.

Well defended and safe behind walls he may have been, but the Gonzaga Dukes were quickly learning that the succession was much more difficult to protect. Between 1613-20, as the three remaining Gonzaga brothers struggled with the consequences of their lack of heirs and unwise secret marriages, the Duke of Savoy attempted to move forward with his distant claim to the Gonzaga House's Mantuan and Montferrat possessions. The Duke of Savoy possessed grand ambitions by this point, to not merely seize this portion of North Italy for himself, but also to swing south and seize Genoa, thereby crafting in the Po Valley a position of unparalleled dominance over Italian affairs, free from either Spanish or French interference. Savoy appreciated the fortifications of Casale and Mantua were the keys to his security and success, but his tenuous claim on the succession and his reluctance to actually besiege these fortresses came against him when a more viable candidate for the duchies, the Duke of Nevers, emerged. Nevers had a Gonzaga father and a French noblewoman mother, and immediately set about pressing his claim in the mid-1620s, to the chagrin not only of Savoy, but also of Spain, who soon cooperated to forestall this greater threat to their interests.

As a Spanish-Savoyard army moved to invade Montferrat and besiege Casale, a siege which began in mid-May 1628, as the Duke of Nevers made his way to Mantua. A soldier by trade, Nevers refused to accept the demands of either the King of Spain, or the more distracted pleas of the Holy Roman Emperor, who was then preoccupied by another siege, that of Stralsund, to the far north along the shores of the Baltic. An example of the stunningly interconnected nature of Europe was plain to see in 1628. The Emperor's forces were engaged in the siege of Stralsund on the Baltic; the French with the siege of La Rochelle, and the Spanish-Savoyard forces with the siege of Casale. Whichever one of these sieges was successful first; great ripples would be felt elsewhere.

Thus, if Stralsund fell, the Emperor would be able to engage in his Baltic design and put increased pressure upon the Dutch at sea, in league with Spain. If La Rochelle fell, then the French would be able to divert resources and men to Italy, potentially turning the balance in North Italy in France's favour. If Casale fell, then the Duke of Nevers would surely be forced to accept Spanish-Savoyard demands, and bend the knee. This moment provides as clear an indication as any that sieges played a pivotal role in the course of the Thirty Years War. We are also reminded, and will investigate in more detail later, of the fact that the Thirty Years War caused several related and, in many cases, undeclared wars to erupt throughout its duration. One such undeclared war was that which raged between the Spanish and French in North Italy over the Mantuan Succession, and dragged Habsburg resources away from other critical fronts as a result. In the event, as we know, the Habsburg efforts to plug the gaps was in vain. La Rochelle fell to the French Crown in October 1628, and Cardinal Richelieu wasted no time redirecting the required forces to their new destination – Savoy.

French forces smashed those of Savoy in the Battle of the Susa Pass in March, and a peace with the Duke of Savoy was signed in late March 1629. As per the terms of the treaty, Savoy had to recognise the Duke of Nevers as the rightful Duke of Mantua and Montferrat. But this peace did not last. Spain refused to accept it, and drafted veterans from the Netherlands to take the fight to Casale again. Among their number was the veteran Genoese commander and loyal servant of Spain, Ambrogio Spinola, then in the final throes of his service. After its ally displayed such clear determination to continue the war, in 1630 Savoy returned to the fray on Spain's side.

While Casale continued to resist throughout 1630, enduring a siege lasting nearly six months, Mantua did in fact succumb to a siege led by the Emperor's troops in July 1630, but only because the city's population had been decimated by plague. Mantua was finally in Habsburg hands, but the victory was bittersweet. Because Casale held on in 1630, being relieved in October of that year by a French army, Habsburg planners were forced to take stock of the situation in North Italy and confront some uncomfortable truths. The distraction in North Italy had cost Spain dear; the Dutch were only too keen to take advantage of the respite and began to turn the war against Spain from this point on. But there was worse news in the Empire itself. Having failed to heed the warnings of more experienced and qualified men, Emperor Ferdinand II had rushed to support Spain in North Italy, donating soldiers to the campaign for Mantua, and ensuring that the bastion did indeed fall in summer 1630. By the time his soldiers had helped their Spanish and Savoyard allies capture the disease-ridden super fortress, Gustavus Adolphus had landed an army in Pomerania. Thanks to his Mantuan adventure, the nearest defenders of the Emperor's interests could not have been further from the action.

Worse than this for the Habsburgs, even with Mantua's fall, the Duke of Nevers retained the other super fortress which remained resolute even throughout a siege lasting several bitter months. It was largely thanks to Casale's tenacious defence, and the apparently impregnable position which the defenders found themselves in, that the Duke of Nevers managed to win the war even though he lost the battle for his Mantuan capital. The following year in spring 1631, facing a Dutch resurgence and a Swedish storm, both branches of the Habsburg family agreed to recognise the Duke of Nevers as the rightful claimant to the region, and Madrid and Vienna both turned their attentions to more serious matters. As Gustavus Adolphus rampaged through Germany and the Dutch Republic began to undermine the very fabric of Spanish authority in the Low Countries, the Duchy of Mantua and its tenacious new Duke faded into the background, but the damage to the Habsburg position had already been done. In the case of Spain, the historian J. H. Elliot's judgement feels apt. Elliot noted:

> For Spain the results were an unrelieved disaster. Its intervention in Mantua had antagonized European public opinion, driven the papacy into the arms of the French, strained Madrid's relations with Vienna almost to the breaking point, and wrecked Olivares' grand design for securing peace with the Dutch on terms better than those of 1609.[40]

Where this concerns us most of all though is in the demonstrated sophistication of these fortifications, rather than the actual result of this conflict per se. It is possible to argue that the turning point of the Thirty Years War hinged to a considerable extent on the successful defence of Casale, whose defenders were the embodiment of a tenacious resistance against a larger foe done right, by maximising the advantages which a sound defensive system accrued. This demonstrated the potential power which the besieged possessed, so long as he was properly prepared and provisioned, that is. As the historian Thomas F. Arnold concluded:

> Smaller powers, with less money, population, and prestige than France, Spain, and the other acknowledged great powers, could still use fortifications as the foundation of their states' defences. The sixteenth-century fortifications of the Gonzaga in Casale, as sophisticated as any in Europe, proved capable of militarily supporting the independence of a small state, and diplomatically championing the pretensions of one of the most ambitious and active dynasties of the time.[41]

Thus, as surely as the unsuccessful siege of Re by the English had disastrous political consequences for them at home, the Duke of Nevers' successful use of the fortifications of Casale to his advantage preserved his independence, and ensured that the lucrative duchies in the Po Valley did not fall to Spain and the Habsburg interest. We are thus reminded that in the two sides of the siege, the attackers and the defenders faced certain risks, and by no means were guaranteed success. In both of these examples, that of the Isle of Re and Casale, it was the belligerent power, that is, the attacking army laying siege to a defending fortress, that suffered the most from its loss, but this outcome was far from consistent. Perhaps the Duke of Nevers' greatest boon was his possession of not one, but two super fortresses, so that even when the diseased and depleted shell of Mantua fell to the enemy, Casale could still hold on and preserve the allied hopes. Siege warfare increasingly swung to the advantage of the attacker later on in the century, as Louis XIV's vaunted successes in chipping away at the fortifications of the Spanish Netherlands made clear.[42] In the first half of the century though, and particularly, it seems, in the late 1620s, much hinged upon the outcome of a siege, and the defenders proved more than up to the task.

FOUR

Seventeenth Century Warfare – a Retrospective

The Thirty Years War cut a swathe of destruction through the centre of Europe, so it was perhaps inevitable that a significant portion of its population were caught in the middle of this warpath. The majority of the damage done was caused by prolonged, chronic stripping of the lands by rampaging armies, and the destruction of the old infrastructures that had held these lands in working, productive order, since so many able men had gone to war, been killed, or turned to banditry. Yet these results were to be expected considering the three decades of concentrated suffering which the centre of the continent endured. The men who made the critical decisions, be it Frederick V accepting the Bohemian Crown, Ferdinand II seeking to stop him, the Danes, Swedes or French getting directly involved – all of these decisions were of course decisions of policy, made by the upper echelons of that polity's government. At the end of the day though, there was only ever going to be one method to bring this decision to its conclusion, and that was war.

The war which was unleashed and prolonged within Europe between 1618-1648 has been the subject of constant scholarly debate; everything from its significance, to the military lessons which were learned, to the actual duration, to the importance of the Peace of Westphalia, to the very term *Thirty Years War* itself has come under the microscope. The conflict is difficult to classify because it does not fit into any prearranged boxes; it was a conflict launched and then prolonged for reasons of religion, constitutional politics, opportunism, civil liberties, wealth and security according to its varied actors. The conflict saw mercenaries join the war on one side and end up on another; similarly, some powers were to become mercenary in their behaviour, seen in the example given by Saxony. The Saxon Elector changed his stance on the war *four* times; beginning the war on the Emperor's side, then declaring against Ferdinand, then concluding a truce with him and joining his side again, and finally, when all hope seemed lost, exiting the war at peace with all sides. If contemporaries like John George of Saxony could not decide where

175

they fit into this conflict, then what hope do historians have of conclusively deciding what it all meant?

Measuring the impact of the war is similarly difficult, because the furies which the Thirty Years War released were not felt all at once or equally across the continent. Thus, the debate on the war's precise impact, or measuring its destructive force, continues to deny the historian a satisfying answer. The war was, at different times to different individuals, a constant and terrible bedfellow, or little more than a rumour about a distant event. One need look no further than the Habsburg Hereditary Lands; Emperor Ferdinand II homeland of Inner Austria, with Styria and Carinthia, gained 80,000 and 20,000 new citizens respectively during the period 1600-1650. Against all odds, Royal Hungary gained 100,000 new citizens.[43] In that same time period though, Bohemia's population plummeted by nearly half.[44]

Those communities living along important rivers like the Rhine, Main or Elbe were liable to suffer greater hardship as armies moved up and down these transit and trade routes. On the other hand, some regions suffered terribly in the initial years of the war, only to be largely ignored thereafter. For those that were committed to the war until the final phase, such as Brandenburg for instance, the losses were particularly stark. The urban population in Brandenburg fell from 113,500 souls to just 34,000, while those living in the countryside declined from 300,000 to a desolate 75,000, which transformed innumerable villages into ghost towns. The disputed neighbouring Pomeranian region also suffered, its population contracting from 160,000 to 96,000 between 1630-48.[45]

These numbers do not all necessarily mean that death occurred – more often it was the case that the local population fled from an approaching army, but their exit created additional problems, especially when an influx of refugees arrived in an unprepared city. Outbreaks of disease could then ravage the weakened, malnourished travellers, and spread like wildfire within the city. Unaware soldiers travelling across Germany could then carry the disease to the next breeding ground, leading to outbreaks of particularly virulent strains of bubonic plague and typhus in 1622-23, 1625, 1634 and 1646-50. In some places, the crisis never truly vanished, and plague remained a constant fixture of life, compounding the misery which the average citizen faced. Even non-combatant countries were not safe; as was the case with France in the late 1620s. The storm outside her borders contributed to the spread of plague – it arrived from Metz in 1625, and when the harvest failed in 1627, the starving French peasant died in his millions. We must rely on estimates remain in place of solid figures, but Peter H. Wilson concluded that one and a half to two million French citizens died by the end of that outbreak, out of a population which was at most 20 million strong.

When armies were on the march, they only made matters worse. Germany suffered while Wallenstein gathered his enormous force during the winter of 1625-26, but fared a bit better in 1630-31, thanks mostly to a more bountiful harvest, which could bolster the strength of the citizens. In places where the armies remained stationary for months or years, such as in the case of a siege, the results could be catastrophic. It was in Northern Italy during the War of Mantuan Succession (1627-31), where Milan shed a third of its population, and Mantua lost half. When the armies marching around the disease-ridden plains of North Italy crossed back into Germany in 1631, the southern part of the Empire was re-infected, piggybacking on allied armies as they marched into Bavaria, and from there it spread across the Rhine and back into France, always carried by soldiers moving to and from the frontlines. Some regions never recovered, while others experienced a vast decline in the amount of births in relation to deaths – so it was in Stralsund or Nuremburg, which did not restore their pre-war birth rate until the middle of the nineteenth century.[46]

Prolonged occupation of a given region could bring apocalyptic consequences, as the armies stripped the lands bare, and this brought other dangers, such as successive years of famine, followed by starvation and then disease. In fact, it was through disease that most armies experienced their worst casualties. One in ten soldiers were said to be sick at any one time, and armies on the march could spread disease, and in some cases benefit from it – such as in Mantua in 1630, when the population was decimated by a bout of plague. It is estimated that casualties caused directly from military violence amounted to 450,000. This figure was calculated by adding the casualties from each military confrontation in the war, but it remains contentious and open to debate. So too does the total impact which disease had upon casualties – some estimates place the losses to disease in the 1618-48 period at an eye-watering 1.8 million.[47]

It is very easy to become desensitised to the constant battles, as potentates acted to bring their ambitions to life. In each of these battles though, on the ground, behind the cover of glory, of legend, or of the towering advantages which were taken from successful engagements, there was the soldier – suffering in often grim conditions, fighting using often desperate, inglorious methods, and reaching an outcome which was feared and loathed by those on the losing side. What was more, the sheer ferocity and costliness of the Thirty Years War eliminated any sense of finesse, and certainly of chivalry, which may have been carried over from previous traditions. 'Tactics and strategy in the Thirty Years' War', noted the historian David A. Parrott, 'are perhaps best characterised as being undermined by two persistent failures: in the one case, to break the dominance of the defensive; in the other, to cope with logistical inadequacy.'[48] This was doubly true if it was a siege, rather than a pitched battle, that decided the fortunes of men's ambitions.

We dwelt earlier on the innovations that made siege warfare more sophisticated and advanced in comparison to the conditions of, say, the

Middle Ages.[49] Siege warfare had certainly changed since then, even if the fundamental goal of both parties remained the same, and the struggle remained hideously gory. The likelihood of success for the besieger, and the options at the disposal of the besieged, had simultaneously increased with the innovations under the trace italienne. Siege warfare demanded a more delicate, organised approach, with sophisticated techniques that were tried and tested, such as the digging and manning of thorough trenches, or the starving out of a bastion. Knocking down a fortresses' walls, in other words, would no longer suffice, nor were these newly designed walls as easy to level. The besieger had to be wary of a relief force, just as the besieged had to be mindful of his options, such as additional citadels deeper in the fortress, the best means of resupply and the best methods for harnessing interlocking fields of fire from emplaced gun batteries.

These recent innovations represented significant technological steps forward and should not be ignored. Arguably not since the invention of the trebuchet had the nature of siege warfare been so affected. Much like the design of the trebuchet, indeed, the design of the trace italienne soon spread like wildfire across the continent, or at least to where defensive fortifications were traditionally required.[50] Then again, such sophistication would only ever go so far, since a siege would be won or lost with the meeting of the defender and the attacker, and regardless of the ideas of chivalry or the weaponry used, such a fight was always going to be bloody, bitterly contested and costly. The examples of sieges we highlighted; those of St Martins on the Isle of Re by the English, and of Casale by the Spanish-Savoyard forces in the late 1620s, were traumatic affairs made no less horrible by the arrival of the trace italienne or supposedly more sophisticated siege techniques than had been used before. As had been the intention all along, the trace italienne – with its low, thick, reinforced earthen walls, angled bastions and strategically positioned artillery pieces – made the siege a uniquely dangerous and miserable experience for the besieger.

Hours of digging, of manning huge, endless trenches which were intended to cut off and surround fortresses, and of gingerly approaching hazardous gun emplacements and occasionally rushing through the gauntlet were all within the job description of a besieging soldier. While it was rare for a garrison to resist with all its might – ironic considering how much had been spent on the fortifications in the first place – these acts of desperate resistance did happen, but they only ever happened when the garrison's commander believed they had a genuine chance of success, or that relief was on the way.

Yet even military systems which are upheld as the most advanced and superior to its contemporaries ran into problems with sieges, simply because of the sheer weight of demands placed upon the besieger in comparison to sieges in the past. Britain's New Model Army, for instance, faced a morass of problems during sieges of its enemies across the British Isles. Even while some successes were enjoyed, and garrisons suitably punished by the Protector,[51] this did not mean that sieges had become downgraded to a mere nuisance – they remained a serious challenge, requiring all manner of resources and a firm grasp of coordinated logistics to successfully complete. The English had traditionally favoured the pitched battle over the siege, believing them to be more decisive in a country which possessed few fortresses of the calibre of the continent. This meant that siege warfare's lessons were forgotten and would have to be relearned. With all their royalist enemies in Britain and Ireland hunkering down in fortified positions and towns though, from 1645 it became an essential mission to reduce each of these places one by one, and this proved a task only completed after much hard grit, human lives and of course, time had been expended. Not until the fall of Galway on Ireland's west coast in 1652 were the Civil Wars officially considered at an end.[52]

Considering what we learned about England's shortcomings during the siege on the Isle of Re, it shouldn't surprise us too much to note the difficulties of that same state two decades later in engaging in sieges. The army and the navy were two distinctly important pillars of England and then Britain's military establishment, but due to the country's position on the periphery of the continent, and due to the comparative safety that geography provided from continental enemies, English siegecraft theory and practice lagged far behind its French or particularly Dutch and Spanish neighbours. This is understandable, since practice made perfect, and the English engaged in no sieges at all, aside from the brief intervention on the Isle of Re, between 1604-1645. The Anglo-Spanish War begun under Elizabeth was itself a learning process – it was a sudden, abrupt introduction to the requirements of the siege in the last two decades of the sixteenth century which forced the English to abandonsomething which up to that point they had held onto – the longbow.

The case study we have examined of English reluctance to abandon the longbow in favour of the firearm remains an important part of the story, not just for the technical details, but also for what it tells us about how important actual participation in a war was. Compared to her neighbours, England was in the lower tier of experience, military theory and thus, professionalism and skill. The Dutch were positively aghast when English captains and soldiers began arriving ostensibly to help them in their revolt, only to force upon them incompatible ideas like aristocratic hierarchies on the battlefield and outdated, flawed siege tactics. It was a steep learning curve, and even in the war against Spain (1585-1604), while some gains were made, the English were never so foolish as to engage the vaunted *tercio* infantry on the open plains.

One could hardly learn the lessons of war when one was not at war, especially since the kind of military academies and schools had yet to materialise on the level which they later would. As a result, not only did military technology and its revolutions proceed apace in the region where conflict was most consistent and pronounced – Western Europe – but some historians have even supposed that it was because of this repeated exposure to conflict that the West superseded the East in terms of technological prowess, and went on to colonise the world.[53] It is of course a fascinating idea: to measure the extent to which different technologies were interacted with, and how they impacted the societies and military systems that attempted to harness their power.

And these new systems were created not merely in Europe, but also across the wider world; implications for the Military Revolution and these new technologies on the likes of Russia,[54] Japan,[55] Mughal India,[56] and the Chinese[57] are all deserving of comprehensive studies of their own, but the Military Revolution tends to focus on Western Europe, so that is where our focus has largely stayed fixed. Such details are also most relevant to our wider Thirty Years War narrative and adds additional context to the decisions and 'revolutions' which were furthered by the era's innovators. Military Revolution as a term was first coined by Michael Roberts in 1957, the parameters of 1560 and 1660 were added, and in between this block of one hundred years, Roberts focused on the years 1630-32 as the 'focal point' of the revolution, where Gustavus Adolphus had the greatest impact. Following this study, it was Geoffrey Parker who singled out four changes in the European art of war as crucial.[58] The historian Anirudh Deshpande summarises these most effectively:

> First came a revolutionary change in tactics with emergence of massed archers and organised musketry. Secondly the army size in most states grew markedly. Thirdly more complex and ambitious strategies were evolved to bring these armies into action. Finally, these factors in combination had an important impact on society.[59]

Our discussion of the Military Revolution has revealed several inherent flaws within the theory, but we have also learned that the theory itself has remained dynamic and fluid, as new scholars have added their expertise to the debate. Arguably the most significant contribution to the debate was provided by the historian Geoffrey Parker, who identified the development of the trace italienne fortifications system as a further example of the Military Revolution. Parker, in contrast to Roberts, underlined the importance of the trace italienne design in necessitating the growth of armies, which would be required to properly besiege and seize these places. Parker opined that it was in the field of logistics, rather than tactics per se, that Europeans dramatically improved, stating that 'The states of early modern Europe had discovered how to supply large armies but not how to lead them to victory.'[60]

At the heart of Roberts' theory, notwithstanding the challenges which it has been subjected to, lay the observation about the growth of army size, and what this meant for warfare. This provoked additional comments, from the likes of John A. Lynn, who opined that the true reason for the increase in army size, at least in the case of France, was not the sophistication of the fortresses under the trace italienne style necessarily, but the enhanced firepower of the defenders, who could now reach further into the attacker's trenches with their heavy guns. To avoid these guns, the besiegers were forced to dig trenches from up to a mile out from the walls, compounding the sheer size and scope of each siege operation, and forcing concerned governments to employ more soldiers and engineers to staff these trenches and complete the siege satisfactorily.

The debate may appear like little more than splitting hairs, but through their studies, both Parker and Lynn have added to our understanding of how a siege worked in the era, how the process had changed during these innovative years, and what was demanded of those that accepted the challenge. Regardless of who was correct, there can be little doubt that the trace italienne absolutely revolutionised the way Europeans made war, even if the impact on each state was felt differently. Another important consideration is the sheer importance of the siege in comparison to the pitched battle. While it is true that pitched battles often stick out as the more impressive, triumphant or glamorous in comparison to the drudgery of endless protracted sieges, the reality was that pitched battles were not particularly decisive throughout the seventeenth and into the eighteenth century.

When a defeated enemy could simply withdraw into his fortress, it made far more sense to move against this fortress, rather than engage in a two-step process which would cause greater suffering for the soldiers and elicit fewer tangible results. While it is correct in a sense to question the very concept of decisive battles as too simplistic or reductionist a concept,[61] it would be a great leap on the other end of the scale to claim that warfare produced no truly significant results during the seventeenth century, or that the period can be classified as one of 'limited warfare.'[62] One historian has noted that it is possible to count on one hand the amount of pitched battles that took place between 1547 and 1631, a space of time bookended by the 1547 Battle of Muhlberg, and the 1631 Battle of Breitenfeld.[63]

Not until Napoleon Bonaparte engaged in his own Military Revolution, and the army's ability to destroy its opponents became greater than the opponent's ability to resist or flee, would sieges decline in importance. However, as we have also learned, this reliance upon sieges to defend or expand the realm did not mean that different states made no efforts to improve the abilities or tactics of the fighting man. Statistically, the likelihood of success for sieges increased as the years progressed, because technology continued to advance, but also because the soldier became more disciplined and effective as an instrument of war on the battlefield. Why? Because he had been thoroughly trained and drilled in the proper mechanics and lessons of war, and he understood how to apply these lessons to any problems he encountered.

If we can pinpoint the development of the trace italienne as a fundamentally critical step forward, then the other significant development in military affairs must be considered is the prevalence of the infantry drill. Not only did the innovations of Maurice of Nassau have an impact on the formations which would actually take to the battlefield, but by providing these soldiers with drill instruction manuals; by formulating several detailed drill commands; by training regularly and by conceptualising these ideas into schools of military thought which were then taught in the fledgling military academies – warfare was destined never to be the same again. Maurice and his successors managed to transform a Dutch army comprised of militia into a professional, disciplined fighting force up to the challenge of the Spanish enemy. Again, it must be emphasised that it was largely thanks to Maurice of Nassau's quest to find a better, more effective way to defeat his enemy, that the impetus for developing these new ideas in the first place was felt. Constant warfare was an expensive, merciless school, and a costly way for statesmen and commanders to learn new techniques, but it also forced these commanders to improvise in search of ways to reduce such costs, and this mission was felt to be worth it so long as conflicts dragged on for such a long length of time.

By the time Maurice of Nassau brought his new tactics of the fire by rank musket drill to bear against the Spanish tercio formations at the Battle of Nieuwpoort in July 1600, the Dutch still had more than forty years left in their war against Spain. If they were to survive, they could not afford to remain static in their innovations or research – new ideas would have to be imagined, honed and then tested on the battlefield. Since the laboratory of the battlefield was open to the Dutch for a full eighty years, it is hardly surprising that they, coming to the conflict with no original military theories of their own, and facing down the supreme military power of the world in Spain, felt forced to innovate.

The infantry drill was revolutionary because it required the musketeer to stand in a unit several ranks deep, and to fire his weapon according to a specific command, followed by another command which would involve him marching to the back of his unit, with his back to the enemy as he did so. This last point may appear insignificant to us, but the act of presenting your back to the enemy was one of the major reasons Maurice of Nassau's contemporaries found the concept so distasteful. It was, they believed, too close to the image presented by a retreat. Yet, by moving the vulnerable musketeer to the back of the line and presenting the locked and loaded succeeding line to the enemy,

Maurice managed to pour down a nearly endless wall of firepower. By the time six or seven ranks had fired, the first rank would have reloaded, and would be ready to fire again.

Such a tactic required an immense amount of coordination and practice to get right, but the nucleus of this idea would be carried forward right up to the American Civil War of the 1860s. By that time, it was unthinkable that anything other than firepower, and as much firepower as possible, mattered. Indeed, the coordination and skill required to perfect this tactic was honed by the Dutch affinity for producing drill instruction manuals with convenient pictures, detailing exactly what each stage of the fire by rank drill should look like, in excruciating detail. When it was boiled down on the training yard or indeed the battlefield, captains found that the process was a lot less complicated than it looked – the point, of course, was to build the Dutch soldier regardless of his initial level of expertise or professionalism. A peasant from one of the polder farms of Amsterdam would be able to master the drill just as surely as a veteran of the Polish-Swedish wars – all he had to do was listen to the instructions of his commander, and of course, practice, practice, practice.

The fondness for practicing, indeed the urgent need for practicing if the core tenets of the fire by rank drill were to be absorbed, became a feature of virtually all European armies in the latter half of the seventeenth century. Britain's aforementioned New Model Army was a great example of this adherence to the drill, but so were the armies under Louis XIV, the forces of the Swedish Empire and those of Brandenburg-Prussia once that state came of age with the Great Elector's increased intervention in the affairs of others. Frederick William, the Great Elector, increased Brandenburg's profile by crafting one of the most well trained and effective fighting forces on the continent, and even while they were not the largest, working out at about thirty thousand at most, their reputation preceded them, because they were constantly practicing the drill.[64]

There was a good reason as well for all this practice in Maurice of Nassau's army; the Dutch stadtholder knew his men would be up against the cream of the military crop at the time – the Spanish tercio infantry. Tercios were the Roman Legions of the sixteenth century. The formation consisted of a pike square anchoring the group of men, with musketeers, arquebusiers and in earlier designs, archers and javelin men standing on the outside of the square, ready to fire at the enemy. If the enemy remained stationary and endured the barrage of lead and missiles, they would suffer painful losses, but if they moved to engage the formation head on, then the pikemen would angle their spears, and protect the musketeers etc. at the front from any approaching infantry. Before the Spanish recognised the importance of the musket, swordsmen could even be found in the centre behind the pikemen and would be in a position to rush forward and engage with the enemy if necessary. As time progressed though, swordsmen were phased out in favour of more firepower and musketeers.

The advantage of the tercio was its versatility – it could fight infantry and offset the force of a charging line of cavalry. It was vulnerable to cannon fire, but so was every formation during this period. In addition, the act of moving in a defensive posture meant that tercios moved slowly and had to exercise a great deal of coordination to ensure that all parts of the machine operated efficiently. One should remember that it was the Spanish who perfected and continued to refine the tercio as no other power in Europe could. Only Spain contained the bank of experienced veterans necessary to adequately train more soldiers for the tercio, and thus the Spanish were always going to be the best at using it. Accepting this, Maurice of Nassau moved to create a new formation which would beat the Spanish tercio, rather than attempting to beat the Spanish at their own game.

Thus it was a clash of styles that opened the seventeenth century in the July 1600 Battle of Nieuwpoort, and it was especially fitting that the two military styles destined to clash on that battlefield were commanded by the Spanish and Dutch foes, whose war had so shaped and influenced the development of European relations. Now, having had an impact on European diplomacy, Spanish and Dutch tactics were destined to have an impact on European warfare. Much like the Dutch, the rest of Europe had refrained from emulating the Spanish tercios, recognising that the Spanish had them outmatched in that sphere. However, it was far easier for Europeans to emulate the lessons of the Dutch and their fire by rank tactics, especially once the Dutch began releasing a flood of illustrated manuals related to these innovations over the next two decades. The French, German, Italian and even Swedish versions of the fire by rank drill would all come into their own in the next few years, with Gustavus Adolphus the most famed practitioner of what he had learned from Maurice's example.

An important point which was not lost of Geoffrey Parker though, and which we would do well to heed, was the awkward fact that although progress was made in the field of musket drill, this did not render the vaunted Spanish tercio system of old obsolete. In fact, in the 1634 Battle of Nordlingen, Spanish-Imperial forces decisively defeated the Swedish-German army sent against them, while making use of the tercio system. In the case of Nordlingen, the old had beaten the new, and muskets were by no means reliable or efficient enough on their own at this point to carry the day. The pike as much as the cavalry charge still mattered a great deal, and would continue to make its presence felt until the calibre and reliability of firearms increased, and the bayonet replaced the pike on the battlefield; innovations such as these would not occur, at least in France, until the turn of the eighteenth century, when flintlock muskets and socket bayonets became the norm.

Geoffrey Parker was also keen to note that the Spanish propensity for training in the sixteenth century made them the hardened fighting force for which they became famous, but that the Dutch did make it more accessible to their European peers. The accessibility of the new infantry drill buoyed by a ready-made library of materials which could be used to further the training process – first appearing in 1607 under the watchful eye of Maurice of Nassau's cousin – proved to be one of its greatest advantages. We need only recall the proliferation of the drill tactics across Europe to see the boon to innovation which these manuals represented. One is reminded of the French case, where by the end of the century the drill became so refined and so rigid that soldiers would be expected, not just to hold the line and obey commands, but to move and operate as though stoically disconnected from the world in which they lived, as though they did not see the horrors or experience the traumas of their enemies.

When we imagine the robotic Roman legionaries and the mechanical, unfeeling way in which they replaced their own gaps in the line, the comparisons between the legions and the drill become even more acute. As we learned, Maurice of Nassau and William Lodewijk took a great deal of inspiration from the Roman example, and from the superior discipline of the legionary which enabled him to throw his javelin and then turn, unafraid, to the back of his line as his friend did the same. With the legionary in mind, the drill was conceived and inspired by the larger than life Roman example.[65] Maurice attempted to recreate this act with his fire by rank drill, and in many respects he succeeded, but even he may not have been able to imagine that it would develop into the system which enabled men to face one another, apparently without fear, and sustain such horrific losses at such close range for prolonged periods, as smoke covered the battlefield, the stench of death filled the air, and the cries of wounded men haunted any personal space that remained. Like the legionary of Cesar's Gallic Wars, the soldier would stance unfazed, draw upon his training, and destroy the enemy systematically, without fear or remorse.

Muskets, appearing in the 1550s and packing a heavier punch than the arquebus, began to enter more common usage, and was the preferred firearm by the turn of the century. Muskets were a great deal heavier than their predecessors, and required a forked rest to balance upon, but they did possess the critical stopping power which commanders were so keen to harness. At three hundred paces, a musketeer could kill his enemy, a marked improvement upon both the arquebus and the bow and arrow. The rate of fire was still unimpressive, especially when compared to those older weapons, but this gap in fire rate could be offset by the greater range of the musket, and the convenient fact for commanders and recruiters that 'a good archer required a lifetime of training to produce the necessary stamina and accuracy, whereas a musketeer could be trained in a week.'[66] The only restriction on the recruiter was the availability of these firearms, which tended to be expensive the more sophisticated they became.

Yet, it has to be said that equipping an army of several arquebusiers, pikemen and musketeers was much less expensive than the practice of equipping an army of knights, a fact of war which facilitated larger armies made up mostly of infantry, and a decline in the total importance of the horseman, where once he had been the principle arm of the force. Infantry also became more important as the French and Habsburgs fought against one another during the Italian Wars of the sixteenth century and discovered early on that cavalry made little impact in the tightly packed net of fortresses which they competed for. These fortresses – embracing the *trace italienne* style – bring our story full circle in a sense, because the importance of infantry increased as the siege became more prevalent. Both the French and Habsburgs found that they needed more men to take these advanced fortresses from one another, and that they could field the larger forces of infantry suited for this task with a less money spent than before.

A pikeman, for instance, required a pike, sword and helmet, which cost little more than that man's basic wages for a week, and as Geoffrey Parker noted, 'in some cases even this paltry sum could be deducted from the soldier's pay.'[67] It must have been a miserable experience for the common soldier – dragging your worn body from one tiresome siege to the next – but for the commander or King, the savings made and lessons learned proved invaluable. Indeed, there is good reason to suppose that, following these Italian Wars, which ended in 1559, lessons about the importance of infantry in that theatre were exported to the rest of Europe, alongside the new technological innovations inherent in the trace italienne style. Soon enough, Europeans would copy the Italian model and style, and usher in a new era of siegecraft as they did so.

With the decline in the importance of cavalry, the affordability of infantry and the requirement of large infantry armies to surround and starve out the new trace italienne system of fortifications, armies predictably ballooned in size from the middle of the sixteenth century, and would continue to grow for the next few centuries. In addition to the increase in army size came new demands – the French case, for example, demonstrated the chronic need for manpower to actually garrison all of its important fortifications, a task which required at least 40% of the French army's total size at any one time. Along with the rise in army sizes came the pressing question of how to quickly train them in time for war – the Spanish devised a solution, whereby ten thousand men would always be present and well-trained for warfare through constant practice and drilling.

Because Spain maintained this core of professionals, it was able to meet the challenges to its authority in some varied theatres in the sixteenth century – be it in the Mediterranean or in the Dutch revolt in the Netherlands, or even during Spain's intervention in the Bohemian revolt over 1619-20. Spain set this example – a kind of prototype for the standing armies which were to follow. Not until the second half of the seventeenth century would powers as diverse as the English and Austrian Habsburgs field their own standing armies.[68] To maintain these forces though, a bureaucracy of sorts was required, and was created where none had existed. This growth in the King's administration facilitated the emergence of several important governing systems, and even while these were focused above all on making war, the precedent had been established.

Paradoxically, even while it became cheaper as a whole to raise the large infantry armies, war became more expensive as the years progressed. The individual soldier might have become cheaper, but further, greater demands were placed on the overall army, thanks to the increased sophistication of the siege, and the logistical complications involved in supplying so many thousands of men. In addition, these increased costs could be blamed on inflation and the high price of food, as much as it could be blamed on the high frequency of war in the seventeenth century. The Spanish, for instance, did not enjoy a single calendar year of peace across their Empire during the first half of the seventeenth century – there was always a battle to be fought somewhere, be it on the open Atlantic against Dutch pirates, or in the maze of fortresses along the French border with Flanders. Between 1500-1630, food prices rose fivefold and industrial prices threefold, placing an incredible burden upon the state which few could bear for long. The solution, of course, was to make war less, but this did not appeal to the belligerent continent during the period. Alternatively, one could acquire loans on credit, and on the expectation of incomes earned two or three years into the future. This process was akin to gambling in a sense, because 'guaranteed' revenues were not always forthcoming, especially if that state was already at war, a victim of invasion or subject to an untimely revolt. Some states would save up before launching a war, providing them with a kind of bank to draw upon, but the longer the war lasted, the more pressing the need for more money would be.[69]

When the facilities for paying armies broke down, as they would when a state declared bankruptcy – which Spain did three times in the first half of the seventeenth century, and which France did twice – the armies were left to fend for themselves. This, indeed, was the fatal consequence of Europe's financial backwardness. Nobody in Europe, not even Maximillian of Bavaria, possessed by themselves the financial resources required to pay for a Thirty Years War, and thus it is hardly surprising to note the horrors and ravages of the unpaid, underfed armies who were left behind. Rather than mutinying and dispersing into the countryside, armies would keep together in anticipation of the fortunes to come, and in the meantime, they would take what they needed from the people they came in contact with, and strip the land bare to feed themselves. In addition, they would levy contributions upon the different principalities or towns they marched past and use these monies to acquire much needed resources.

This tactic of levying contributions, in return for a promise to leave the people alone, would be repeated during Louis XIV's wars later on in the century, and provided that French King's coffers with a much-needed boost, just as had been the case during the Thirty Years War. Towns and cities were kept informed by the delivery of several newsletters and pamphlets, which detailed where armies intended to go and when, so that monies could be accumulated to pay them the necessary fees. We should not get too ahead of ourselves though – the capabilities of some wealthier towns and cities to pay contributions did not mean all were in a position to do so. In addition, when armies were on the move, and especially in a hurry, they did not wait to negotiate with a given town for a given sum of money – if the town had been loyal to the enemy in the past, they simply took what they needed, and killed or destroyed what was left. This practice was undertaken by Marshall Turenne, Gustavus Adolphus and Albrecht von Wallenstein in equal measure – there were no exceptions, and little mercy could be expected.

Indeed, we need only to recall the example of Magdeburg to be reminded of the barbaric consequences which could await disloyal citizens, who happened to sit on a fruitful town or city when a beleaguered army waited outside. There was little point in trying to control the starved, angry men who made up such forces, and while Count Tilly was no monster, he could not prevent the kind of vengeance which the soldiers in his employ had been taught to expect. That said, the practice of torching a city, as happened to Magdeburg, was unusual, and almost certainly accidental, since this ruined the possibility that a returning Imperial army in a year's time would be able to find succour within the city's walls. If Tilly had deliberately destroyed Magdeburg, then this veteran commander would have known he was also deliberately destroying his security, his future food supply, and a source of contributions.

In this section of the book, we have learned that even while Europe was nowhere near financially sophisticated enough to pay for them, armies were raised on a scale and with a frequency never before seen, which created the terrible conditions that made the Thirty Years War so infamous. In addition, we have learned that the century was one of immense technological change. Firepower had become increasingly important, a fact seen in Maurice of Nassau's fire by rank drill, but such innovations did not supersede the previous century's tactics instantaneously. Gustavus Adolphus' reimagining of the role of artillery, and the reform of each arm of the Swedish army represent changes in the system that can be classified as truly revolutionary.

The case of Military Revolution which Michael Roberts posited, not to mention the significance which he attributed to the couple of years where Gustavus Adolphus intervened in the Thirty Years War, have since been subject to re-examination. This has led not merely to a newfound appreciation for the truly 'revolutionary' changes, above all in army size, but it has also clarified Gustavus' more significant innovations. Rather than inventing a new method for making war against his enemies, and swelling army size in order to do it, the Swedish King approached the battlefield with a desire to improve the potential of his men. Gustavus' two genuinely more important inventions – the powder cartridge and his reimagining of the role of light artillery on the battlefield – were true revolutions in the military sphere, even if the significance of these innovations can occasionally be lost in the alluring image of genius which Gustavus brings to the table.

Gustavus did, it is true, build upon the infantry drill which Maurice of Nassau had supplied; he trained his men rigorously, and increased their flexibility by adding to their repertoire several new drills that facilitated firing while standing, crouching or lying prone. He also made the most of lessons learned in defeat and while on campaign against the Poles. Gustavus was certainly an innovator, and an immensely capable commander; his reputation should not unduly suffer following a re-examination of the Military Revolution thesis. Some of the contributions which the Swedish King made would themselves subsequently be built upon and can be classified as 'revolutionary' in their own right. But then, one should be cautious not to cling too tightly to such buzzwords. A fact which we keep returning to is that not even Gustavus Adolphus' famed reforms were enough to defeat the 'old' Spanish tercio system in the Battle of Nordlingen in 1634. We are denied a simple case of steady, constant progress, as 'Habsburg troops fighting in traditional fashion inflicted a crushing and decisive defeat on the masters of the new military science, forcing Sweden and her allies to abandon all their conquests in south Germany.'[70] Europeans, plainly, still had a great deal left to learn.

Is it accurate to speak of a Military Revolution? Certainly, the new developments in the trace italienne and the increased size of armies, with a reliance on infantry and firepower, distinguish the seventeenth century from what had come before. In league with these changes came new developments – the growth and maturation of a bureaucracy to command and maintain these forces; the gradual appearance of standing armies in several states; a decline in the importance of aristocratic heavy cavalry; the supremacy of the fortress and the siege, and the refinement of siege methods to counterbalance the strong bastion. At the same time though, we would be wise not to generalise. Western Europe may have seen such innovations take root, but in places where fortresses were less common or administration less sophisticated, the old ways remained in favour. It is hardly accurate to speak of a European-wide Military Revolution, when the likes of England, Poland, Spain and Russia experienced these innovations so differently. Is there much utility therefore in conceptualising a theory like the Military Revolution for the French, Dutch, Swedes and Habsburgs alone?

It would be difficult to argue that the changes which were felt in these states over the seventeenth century were not incredibly significant, and, one could argue that they paved the way for the modernisation of European warfare in the centuries that followed, particularly in the honing of the infantry musket drill. However, it is also true that these developments and innovations were adopted or ignored according to the needs and in some case the geography of the states in question. Since it is true that the Military Revolution emerged from technological innovation, it is reasonable to subscribe to the idea that, as one historian wrote, 'the role of military technology in history can only be fruitfully defined in relation to interactive factors like geography and politics conditioning the environment of early modern warfare.'[71] Or, to coin another phrase, the Military Revolution was what each state made it, according to their immediate needs, traditions and location.

We should also take care when considering the term 'revolution'; this suggests that, throughout the seventeenth century, a fundamental change happened, and brought to an end old traditions and processes. On the contrary, it would perhaps be more accurate to speak of the seventeenth century as a period of ongoing Military Revolutions. The changes underway in how states approached war had not *happened*, therefore – they were *happening*, and continued to happen throughout the century, as states became involved in more wars, and confronted new challenges. The historian Clifford Rogers has argued that while the use of the term 'revolution' can be somewhat weighted, it is possible to observe, between the years 1510-1715, several 'punctuations', which provide a framework for dividing this two-hundred-year period into several eras.[72]

Nor does Clifford stop there. 'Over the five centuries between 1300 and 1800', Rogers noted 'Europe experienced not one but several Military Revolutions, even considering land forces alone, each of which dramatically altered the nature of warfare over a short span of time.'[73] Rather than a single revolution which brought European arms from point A to point B, indeed, innovation and technology waxed and waned over that span of five centuries, with remarkable results. It is in these results, however, that some of the problems with the Military Revolution thesis manifest themselves. How can it be accurate to talk of a Military Revolution between 1560-1660, for instance, but ignore a revolution between 1400-1500, when infantry firearms became more prevalent? How, in addition, can be it correct to ignore the earliest appearance of cannon on the battlefield from the early fourteenth century, which changed how armies approached battle for the first time since Ancient Rome revolutionised melee warfare?

If one looks hard enough, surely revolutions will be found in the military sphere from the beginning of the Renaissance, so where is the utility in narrowing one's scope to the era purely from 1560-1660? Perhaps it is of little use to do so, especially when Rogers was able to pinpoint four individual revolutions between 1300-1800; the 'Infantry Revolution' when heavy shock cavalry were superseded by the pike and longbow; the 'Artillery Revolution' which challenged the superiority of the castle; the 'Artillery Fortress Revolution', which restored the superiority of the fortress and enhanced the power of the defender; finally, Rogers noted that here the 'Military Revolution' fit in the debate, as it brought changes in the drill, in army size and military bureaucratisation. 'We are', Rogers concluded, 'dealing not with one revolutionary change, but with a whole series of revolutions which synergistically combined to create the Western military superiority of the eighteenth century.'[74]

Again though, is the question of 'revolution' merely splitting hairs? Does it truly matter that several revolutions in the military sphere occurred before – surely when we talk of the Military Revolution, those that are interested in the debate will appreciate what we refer to. It may appear like a question of semantics, but there is something more to the question than that. Consider the fact that, by looking for a Military Revolution ever since 1957, historians have ascribed intentions and meaning to developments which, at the time, never acquired such significance. Consider also that warfare was a constantly changing beast – this is arguably seen clearest in the development of cavalry tactics, which changed consistently throughout the sixteenth and seventeenth centuries.

Thus, Maurice of Nassau's infantry drill was imagined as a response to Spanish superiority in the tercio system, and the Dutch need to harness as much stopping power as possible from its soldiers. By the end of the century, the use of the drill had changed – this was not the tactic used solely by a desperate, rebellious Republic, but a constantly evolving and debated method of meeting the enemy. As the technology of the firearm became more sophisticated, so too did the drills which involved the weapon, and the potential stopping power of their manoeuvres. Maurice of Nassau, of course, did not develop the drill or publish his illustrated manuals in order to fulfil a certain theory – he acted and reacted according to the demands placed upon him. If we are not careful, we may forget the actual causes of Maurice's reforms, and view them instead in terms of the purpose they serve for satisfying the terms of the Military Revolution. This danger is a real one, as Rogers concluded:

By attempting to subsume the innovations of five centuries into a single

191

phenomenon, we may be imposing an artificial teleological unity onto a series of inherently distinct, separate developments. And, in doing so, we may be clouding our understanding of a critically important area of history, an area which fully deserves to be studied through the clearest possible lens.[75]

Perhaps the reader may perceive the Military Revolution merely as an artificial construct, and of little use either in helping us understand the developments of seventeenth century warfare, or the significance of Thirty Years War. Lest we forget, Roberts was not criticised merely for inventing this misleading picture of straightforward cause and effect development – his conceptual framework has also been criticised as inaccurate. Thus, Geoffrey Parker, by far the most familiar challenger of the Military Revolution thesis, argued convincingly that Roberts 'had overemphasized the importance of Gustavus Adolphus at the expense of French, Dutch, and Hapsburg developments; underemphasized the importance of siege warfare; and put the starting date of the revolution perhaps half a century too far forward.'[76]

As we have also discerned, the actual force of the 'revolution' in the period which Roberts identifies remains subject to debate, since the innovations and advancements which it implied were not felt evenly across the continent. Furthermore, political context must be taken into account when considering the new innovations on offer. If we consider just our limited window of the Thirty Years War, then the actual extent of the 'revolution' appears even less significant. While it is famous for its pitched battles, by the latter phase of the Thirty Years War military encounters took the form either of sieges or of bloody, mobile showdowns with an abundance of cavalry on both sides.[77] As Simon Adams, in his study on the confluence of politics with tactics, noted:

> Any final conclusions about the Military Revolution must therefore take its political context into account. It was the Thirty Years' War that led to the expansion of armies, not the converse. The relatively minor advances in weaponry and tactics between the development of effective small arms fire in the early sixteenth century and the replacement of the pike by the bayonet at the end of the seventeenth meant that on the tactical level changes were largely variations on a theme. Similarly, the relatively limited size of field armies gave to none of the combatants a decisive advantage.[78]

All of these objections, however, should not mean that the Military Revolution theory is useless. It remains impossible to deny that the innovations implemented during the seventeenth century – in the infantry drill and artillery especially – had a profound impact upon the way in which Europeans made war. Rightly or wrongly, war remained central to the development of Western culture, technology and theory, as Geoffrey Parker opined: 'War, which in the seventeenth century was almost as much the normal state as peace, was a major catalyst of European life and one of the hinges on which the history of the continent turned.'[79]

And war had certainly changed since the previous century; the Thirty Years War provided perhaps the most ideal testing ground for the new ideas, while its furies and high costs compelled statesmen and leaders to harness as much as they could from their populations. Considering his successive challenges to Roberts' thesis, we may be surprised to note that Geoffrey Parker claimed that he had 'failed to dent the basic thesis'. This 'basic thesis', in Parker's view, was that 'warfare in early modern Europe was revolutionized, and this had important and wide-ranging consequences.' Notwithstanding the issues one may have with his approach, one struggles to deny that from 1660 – immediately after the period set down by Roberts – Europeans made war in a vastly different manner than they had in the beginning of the proceeding century.[80]

Furthermore, as we have stated before – one of the great benefits of this thesis for scholars and enthusiasts alike is the veritable flood of literature which emerged following its publication. We are left with nothing close to a consensus, but instead with something arguably more valuable – a treasure trove of published works that examine detailed, specific elements of the thesis, and which apply it to European states in the period on a scale never before seen. This, in my mind, is the true utility of the Military Revolution idea. We owe Michael Roberts a debt because his thesis facilitated – or perhaps provoked is a better term – responses from historians which otherwise would never have materialised, and which fleshed out the historiography of the period. As one historian put it:

> It is true that the problematic of 'Military Revolution' opens the possibility of researching further into questions of historical needs of societies and the mentalities of the peoples involved in warfare. At the same time detailed military history and even salted narratives do enrich social history immensely.[81]

While it has divided opinion, there can be little doubt that the Military Revolution thesis has enriched our understanding of social and of military history. Historians were compelled to answer Roberts' challenge, and because of this, the historian who comes to the debate now, over sixty years since it first began, will be armed with a wide variety of studies and findings. Before Roberts presented his inaugural lecture on the subject of the Military Revolution, it was possible for Sir Charles Oman to claim in 1937 that 'The sixteenth century constitutes a most uninteresting period in European military history'. Before 1957, indeed, the general understanding of seventeenth century warfare and its key lessons were largely unknown, but now, historians and enthusiasts have never been so well-informed. Considering this, perhaps it would not be too much of a stretch to speak of another revolution – this one in seventeenth century military history, which emerged from the fount of debate initiated by Michael Roberts six decades ago.[82]

As John A. Lynn assiduously phrased it, 'trying to understand seventeenth-century European history without weighing the influence of war and military institutions is like trying to dance without listening to the music.'[83] Throughout this section of the book, we have assessed several theories and case studies drawn from the different actors of mostly seventeenth century Europe, and with each new anecdote or deep dive, we have vindicated this truth, and with each new example we reached deeper into this truth. In the background to the diplomatic intrigue, fascinating characters and weighted issues were the battles – the warfare, the gunpowder, the victories, the defeats, the honour and the fame which added so much colour and drama to the whole experience, and which placed an exclamation point upon the bloody process of the seventeenth century. At the core of this process were several lessons which had bubbled to the surface, lessons which were supposed to make killing easier and more efficient, and which would only be built upon later in the century. Now that we have been introduced to this wide range of case studies, of key battles and revolutions in tactics and theory, it is time to investigate the proper narrative of the Thirty Years War.

Chapter 4 Notes

[1] Jeremy Black, *Beyond the Military Revolution, War in the Seventeenth Century World* (New York; Palgrave Macmillan, 2011), p. 14.

[2] Gábor Ágoston, 'Firearms and Military Adaptation: The Ottomans and the European Military Revolution,1450-1800', *Journal of World History*, Vol. 25, No. 1 (March 2014), pp. 85-124; p. 88.

[3] See Bernard S. Bachrach, 'Medieval Siege Warfare: A Reconnaissance', *The Journal of Military History*, Vol. 58, No. 1 (Jan., 1994), pp. 119-133.

[4] Gábor Ágoston, 'Firearms and Military Adaptation: The Ottomans and the European Military Revolution', p. 88.

[5] Djurdjica Petrovič, "Firearms in the Balkans on the Eve of and after the Ottoman Conquests of the Fourteenth and Fifteenth Centuries," in Vernon J. Parry and M. E. Yapp, eds., *War, Technology and Society in the Middle East* (London; Oxford University Press, 1975), pp. 169-172, p. 175.

[6] Gábor Agoston, 'Ottoman Artillery and European Military Technology in the Fifteenth to Seventeenth Centuries', *Acta Orientalia Scientiarum Hungaricae* vol. 47 (1994): pp. 15-48.

[7] Jeremy Black, *Beyond the Military Revolution*, pp. 15-18.

[8] Colin Imber, 'The Origin of the Janissaries', in Colin Imber (eds.), *Warfare, Law and Pseudo-History* (Istanbul: Isis, 2011), pp. 165-171.

[9] Cited in Gábor Ágoston, 'Firearms and Military Adaptation: The Ottomans and the European Military Revolution', pp. 97-98.

[10] *Ibid*, p. 98.

[11] John A. Lynn, 'Forging the Western army in seventeenth century France', in MacGregor Knox, Williamson Murray (eds.), *The Dynamics of Military Revolution, 1300-2050* (New York; Cambridge University Press, 2001), p. 35.

[12] Gábor Ágoston, 'Firearms and Military Adaptation: The Ottomans and the European Military Revolution', pp. 99-100.

[13] John A. Lynn, 'Forging the Western army in seventeenth century France', p. 36. See also David Chandler, *The Art of Warfare in the Age of Marlborough* (New York, 1976), p. 77.

[14] Gábor Ágoston, 'Firearms and Military Adaptation', p. 101.

[15] *Ibid*, p. 107.

[16] Jeremy Black, *Beyond the Military Revolution*, pp. 33-34.

[17] Richard Basset, *For God and Kaiser: The Imperial Austrian Army*, 1619-1918 (Yale University Press; London, 2015), p. 1.

[18] See C. V. Wedgewood, *Thirty Years War* (New York: New York Review of Books, 2005), pp. 174-175.

[19] Peter H. Wilson, 'Dynasty, Constitution, and Confession: The Role of Religion in the Thirty Years War', *The International History Review*, Vol. 30, No. 3 (Sep., 2008), pp. 473-514; p. 485.

[20] Karin J. MacHardy, 'The Rise of Absolutism and Noble Rebellion in Early Modern Habsburg Austria, 1570 to 1620', *Comparative Studies in Society and History*, Vol. 34, No. 3 (Jul., 1992), pp. 407-438; p. 408.

[21] Richard Basset, *For God and Kaiser*, p. 12.

[22] Knud J. V. Jespersen, 'Social Change and Military Revolution in Early Modern Europe: Some Danish Evidence', *The Historical Journal*, Vol. 26, No. 1 (Mar., 1983), pp. 1-13.

[23] Richard Basset, *For God and Kaiser*, p. 18.

[24] Geoff Mortimer, *Wallenstein, The Enigma of the Thirty Years War* (Palgrave Macmillan; New York, 2010), pp. 1-3.

[25] John A. Mears, 'The Thirty Years' War, the "General Crisis," and the Origins of a Standing Professional Army in the Habsburg Monarchy', *Central European History*, Vol. 21, No. 2 (Jun., 1988), pp. 122-141; p. 126.

[26] Richard Basset, *For God and Kaiser*, pp. 58-60.

[27] For an excellent summary of this transition see Dennis E. Showalter, 'Caste, Skill, and Training: The Evolution of Cohesion in European Armies from the Middle Ages to the Sixteenth Century', *The Journal of Military History*, Vol. 57, No. 3 (Jul., 1993), pp. 407-430.

[28] John A. Mears, 'The Thirty Years' War', pp. 132-136.

[29] The main source for the siege of Re in this section is S. J. Stearns, 'A Problem of Logistics in the Early seventeenth Century: The Siege of Re', *Military Affairs*, Vol. 42, No. 3 (Oct., 1978), pp. 121-126.

[30] See G. N. Clark, *War and Society in the seventeenth Century* (Cambridge, 1958), p. 20.

[31] A good background to this religious discontent can be found in Mario Turchetti, 'Religious Concord and Political Tolerance in Sixteenth- and Seventeenth- Century France', *The Sixteenth Century Journal*, Vol. 22, No. 1 (Spring, 1991), pp. 15-25.

[32] W. J. Stankiewicz', The Huguenot Downfall: The Influence of Richelieu's Policy and Doctrine', *Proceedings of the American Philosophical Society*, Vol. 99, No. 3 (Jun. 15, 1955), pp. 146-168.

[33] S. J. Stearns, 'A Problem of Logistics in the Early seventeenth Century: The Siege of Re', p. 121.

[34] *Ibid*, p. 121.

[35] *Ibid*, p. 122.

[36] *Ibid*, p. 125.

[37] The main source used for this section of the chapter Thomas F. Arnold, 'Gonzaga Fortifications and the Mantuan Succession Crisis of 1613-1631', *Mediterranean Studies*, Vol. 4 (1994), pp. 113-130.

[38] For two studies on the backgrou nd to this conflict see the following articles David Parrott, 'The Mantuan Succession, 1627-31: A Sovereignty Dispute in Early Modern Europe', *The English Historical Review*, Vol. 112, No. 445 (Feb., 1997), pp. 20-65; R. A. Stradling, 'Prelude to Disaster; the Precipitation of the War of the Mantuan Succession, 1627-29', *The Historical Journal*, Vol. 33, No. 4 (Dec., 1990), pp. 769-785. We will spend more time analysing the political and diplomatic context of this struggle in the proper body of this book.

[39] Thomas F. Arnold, 'Gonzaga Fortifications', p. 120.

[40] J. H. Elliot, *Richelieu and Olivares* (Cambridge, 1984), p. 112.

[41] Thomas F. Arnold, 'Gonzaga Fortifications', p. 130.

[42] See Ekberg, *The Failure of Louis XIV's Dutch War*, pp. 110-115.

[43] Wilson, *Europe's Tragedy*, p. 788.

[44] Parker, *Europe in Crisis*, p. 23.

[45] Wilson, *Europe's Tragedy*, p. 789.

[46] *Ibid*, pp. 792-794.

[47] *Ibid*, pp. 790-791.

[48] David A. Parrott, 'Strategy and Tactics in the Thirty Years' War: The 'Military Revolution', in Clifford J. Rogers, ed., *The Military Revolution Debate: Readings on the Military Transformation of Early Modern Europe* (Boulder, CO: Westview Press, 1995), p. 246.

[49] A good summary of siege warfare in Medieval Europe is Bernard S. Bachrach, 'Medieval Siege Warfare: A Reconnaissance', *The Journal of Military History*, Vol. 58, No. 1 (Jan., 1994), pp. 119-133.

[50] In my view, trebuchets have been understudied, especially in terms of their overall impact upon the siege. See Paul E. Chevedden, 'The Invention of the Counterweight Trebuchet: A Study in Cultural Diffusion', *Dumbarton Oaks Papers*, Vol. 54 (2000), pp. 71-116; more details on the trebuchet can be found at the following study: W. T. S. Tarver, 'The Traction Trebuchet: A Reconstruction of an Early Medieval Siege Engine', *Technology and Culture*, Vol. 36, No. 1 (Jan., 1995), pp. 136-167.

[51] See Eamon P. Duffy, 'The Siege and Surrender of Galway 1651-1652', *Journal of the Galway Archaeological and Historical Society*, Vol. 39 (1983/1984), pp. 115-142.

[52] See James Burke, 'The New Model Army and the Problems of Siege Warfare, 1648-51', *Irish Historical Studies*, Vol. 27, No. 105 (May, 1990), pp. 1-29.

[53] The 'western superiority' thesis is a fascinating one, but one which we don't have time to properly delve into here. For further reading on this idea see William R. Thompson, 'The Military Superiority Thesis and the Ascendancy of Western Eurasia in the World System', *Journal of World History*, Vol. 10, No. 1 (Spring, 1999), pp. 143-178; Philip T. Hoffman, 'Why Was It Europeans Who Conquered the World?', *The Journal of Economic History*, Vol. 72, No. 3 (SEPTEMBER 2012), pp. 601-633; John France, 'Close Order and Close Quarter: The Culture of Combat in the West', *The International History Review*, Vol. 27, No. 3 (Sep., 2005), pp. 498-517.

[54] See Marshall Poe, 'The Consequences of the Military Revolution in Muscovy: A Comparative Perspective', *Comparative Studies in Society and History*, Vol. 38, No. 4 (Oct., 1996), pp. 603-618; Michael C. Paul, 'The Military Revolution in Russia, 1550-1682', *The Journal of Military History*, Vol. 68, No. 1 (Jan., 2004), pp. 9-45.

[55] See Stephen Morillo, 'Guns and Government: A Comparative Study of Europe and Japan', *Journal of World History*, Vol. 6, No. 1 (Spring, 1995), pp. 75-106.

[56] See Anirudh Deshpande, 'Limitations of Military Technology: Naval Warfare on the West Coast, 1650-1800', *Economic and Political Weekly*, Vol. 27, No. 17 (Apr. 25, 1992), pp. 900-904.

[57] Kenneth M. Swope, 'Crouching Tigers, Secret Weapons: Military Technology Employed during the Sino-Japanese-Korean War, 1592-1598', *The Journal of Military History*, Vol. 69, No. 1 (Jan., 2005), pp. 11-41.

[58] Simon Adams, 'Chapter 10 – Tactics or Politics? "The Military Revolution" and the Hapsburg Hegemony, 1525-1648' in Clifford J. Rogers, ed., *The Military Revolution Debate: Readings on the Military Transformation of Early Modern Europe* (Boulder, CO: Westview Press, 1995), p. 253.

[59] Anirudh Deshpande, 'Limitations of Military Technology', p. 900.

[60] Parker, *The Military Revolution: Military Innovation and the Rise of the West*, 1500-1800 (Cambridge, 1988), p. 80.

[61] One historian that does this is Yuval Noah Harari, 'The Concept of "Decisive Battles" in World History', *Journal of World History*, Vol. 18, No. 3 (Sep., 2007), pp. 251-266.

[62] Limited warfare as an idea is full of holes, especially in the timeline selected by the historian in the following article – that of 1640-1740. The idea that battles were somehow less aggressive, or their aims less total, is lost on conflicts like the Franco-Dutch War (1672-78) where the Dutch fought for their very survival, or even in the latter phase of the War of the Spanish Succession (1701-13) where the French did the same. See John U. Nef, 'Limited Warfare and the Progress of European Civilization: 1640-1740', The *Review of Politics*, Vol. 6, No. 3 (July., 1944), pp. 275-314.

[63] Michael Howard, *War in European history* (Oxford, 1976), p. 34.

[64] See Daniel Riches, 'Early Modern Military Reform and the Connection Between Sweden and Brandenburg-Prussia', *Scandinavian Studies*, Vol. 77, No. 3 (Fall 2005), pp. 347-364. The ideological basis for these tactics remained prevalent into the nineteenth and twentieth centuries, see Steven D. Jackman, 'Shoulder to Shoulder: Close Control and "Old Prussian Drill" in German Offensive Infantry Tactics, 1871-1914', *The Journal of Military History*, Vol. 68, No. 1 (Jan., 2004), pp. 73-104.

[65] See John Keegan, *The Face of Battle* (London: Penguin Books, 1988), pp. 60-64.

[66] Geoffrey Parker, *Europe in Crisis*, p. 68.

[67] *Ibid*, p. 69.

[68] See John A. Mears, 'The Emergence of the Standing Professional Army in Seventeenth-Century Europe', *Social Science Quarterly*, Vol. 50, No. 1 (Jun, 1969), pp. 106-115.

[69] See Parker, *Europe in Crisis*, pp. 69-73.

[70] Geoffrey Parker, 'Chapter 13 – In Defence of the Military Revolution', in Rogers ed. *Military Revolution Debate*, p. 337.

[71] Anirudh Deshpande, 'Limitations of Military Technology', p. 900.

[72] Parker, 'Chapter 13 – In Defence of the Military Revolution', in Rogers ed. *Military Revolution Debate*, p. 340.

[73] See Clifford J. Rogers, 'Chapter 3 – The Military Revolutions of the Hundred Years War', in Rogers ed. *Military Revolution Debate*, p. 76.

[74] *Ibid*, pp. 76-77.

[75] *Ibid*, p. 77.

[76] *Ibid*, p. 55.

[77] Wilson, *Europe's Tragedy*, p. 738, noted that by 1648, the 'ratio of horse to foot was now the reverse of that in 1618' and that of the Swedish field army's total of 37,500, 22,000 of these were cavalry.

[78] Simon Adams, 'Tactics or Politics? "The Military Revolution" and the Hapsburg Hegemony, 1525-1648' in Rogers, ed., *The Military Revolution Debate*, pp. 267-268.

[79] Geoffrey Parker, *Europe in Crisis*, p. 66.

[80] See Parker, 'The "Military Revolution," 1560-1660--a Myth?', p. 214.

[81] Anirudh Deshpande, 'Limitations of Military Technology', p. 900.

[82] See Parker, 'The "Military Revolution," 1560-1660--a Myth?', p. 195.

[83] John A. Lynn, 'Tactical Evolution in the French Army, 1560-1660', p. 176.

PART TWO

Years of Armed Neutrality
-Europe up to 1618-

(Top left) Hernando Cortez (eighteenth century portrait)
(Top right) Ambrogio Spinola (Peter Paul Rubens, 1626)

(Embarkation of the Moriscos in Valencia (Pere Oromig, 1616)

"It is known that, for some time, affairs in the Holy Roman Empire of the German Nation have been growing more dangerous and of more concern, and that the beneficial imperial constitution, in particular the religious and profane peace accepted by the Estates to preserve peace, quiet and unity, have not only been the subject of dangerous misunderstanding, but have been violently attacked and often actually breached. It is much to be feared that if this state of affairs continues much longer, the violence will mount progressively in the Empire so that the peace-loving, obedient Catholic Imperial Estates will be overrun and violated by the troublemakers and consequently nothing less can be expected than further oppression of the old true Catholic religion, the unique route to salvation, and its adherents, contrary to justice and imperial law."[1]

The Catholic League justifies its establishment: Munich, July 1609.

I am very much afraid that the states of the Empire, quarrelling fiercely among themselves, may start a fatal conflagration embracing not only themselves...but also all those countries that are in one way or another connected with Germany. All this will undoubtedly produce the most dangerous consequences, bringing about the total collapse and unavoidable alteration in the present state of Germany."[2]

Maurice, Landgrave of Hesse-Kassel, communicates his concerns to the French government regarding the present state of Germany: 1615.

"The dear old Holy Roman Empire; How does it stay together?"[3]

Tavern drinkers in 'Faust' – a play published in 1808 by Johann Wolfgang von Goethe – ask a pertinent question.

CHAPTER FIVE
"Europe and the Empire"

ONE

Prosperity, Profit, Power

Ever since arriving in the lands of the Aztec Empire, Hernando Cortes had been inundated with great packages of gold, silver and other priceless artefacts. The gifts were meant to pay the price of turning away the Spanish swords from the heart of the Aztec homeland. Yet, it had the opposite effect – in Cortes' mind such prizes were the 'mute but eloquent testimony that there must be more.'[4] The further Cortes ventured inland, the more supplicant vassals he found willing to fight the Aztecs for him and his masters back home in Europe. Whether these native vassals understood who these invaders were or why they arrived at all depended on which tribe or village one asked, yet everywhere Cortes went the news seemed to be the same: gifts and riches beyond his wildest dreams.

Not to be outdone, the Aztec Emperor Montezuma aimed at persuading the Spaniards against venturing any further, by presenting the relentless Cortes with 'an offer of a bribe to leave the country fifty loads of gold for Cortes, five loads for each captain and one for each soldier, and a promise to give the king of Spain an annual tribute.' With modern currency exchanges, it is possibly to roughly value this bribe as high as over one billion dollars![5] If Cortes was tempted to leave with this bribe then and there, he did not show it; he likely appreciated that the longer he stayed, the more he could stand to earn.

Eventually reaching Tenochtitlan – Montezuma's capital upon which Mexico City is built – Cortes experienced the Aztec Emperor's hospitality first-hand. Although Montezuma brushed off Cortes' attempts to evangelise, the Spaniard did receive 'many curious pieces of work of gold, silver, feathers, and more than five thousand very fine dresses of cotton', as well as 'certain pieces of gold and ten loads of fine stuffs which [Montezuma] divided between Cortes and his captains; and to every soldier he gave two collars of gold, each worth ten crowns, and two loads of mantles.'[6] Upon sending out envoys to meet further vassals of the Aztecs, these returned to Cortes to inform him of the immense wealth of the surrounding gold mines, which encouraged

Cortes to press Montezuma for further concessions. By the middle of 1520, the Emperor of the fearsome Aztecs had even sold off his father's jewels in a bid to buy the friendship of this mysterious power called Spain.[7]

Not even this massive collective effort in prize grabbing would prove enough to satiate Cortes' desires, but Montezuma had not yet exhausted his reserves. Bernal Diaz del Castillo, one of Cortes' subordinates, noted how the Aztec Emperor made one last incomprehensibly vast gift of hulking gold statues. So large were these gifts that del Castillo and his men 'were for the space of three days constantly employed in taking it to pieces, from the various manners in which it was worked up; in this we were also assisted by the royal goldsmiths from Escapuzalco.' When the pieces of gold had been separated into more manageable cargo, 'the articles of gold were formed in three heaps, weighing upwards of six hundred thousand crowns, exclusive of the various other valuables, the gold in plates and bars, and the metal in its rough state from the mines.' Del Castillo then noted how the local goldsmiths 'melted down the metal which was in the heaps, and ran it into bars the breadth of three fingers.' Now literally weighed down with more gold than they had ever seen in their entire collectives lives, Cortes and his party received yet another present from Montezuma, which was 'so rich that it was worthy of admiration, exclusive of the jewels and pearls, the beautiful embroideries of pearls and feathers, and the panaches, and plumage, a recital whereof would be endless.'[8]

Finally, as a cherry on top of this golden cake, Cortes acquired the additional prize he had been searching for; although it did not shine like a gold bar, it was just as valuable. After exacting a concession of several thousand acres of land for a private estate, Cortes cloaked his sequestrations in a vague legality by having Montezuma and the chief Aztec lords swear an oath of allegiance to his Catholic Majesty, Charles V, the King of Spain, Duke of Burgundy and Holy Roman Emperor.[9] The world's most powerful ruling potentate had, by the actions of Hernando Cortes, just added a new title to his already long list – Charles V of the House of Habsburg was now Master of the Aztecs, and Lord of the New World.

This King, Emperor, Duke, Lord and Master was born in the city of Ghent in 1500, an apparently perfect point from which to mark his incredible rise.[10] Charles was the deliberate product of some very carefully planned marriages. It was to Charles that the inheritances of several dynasties would fall; the sprawling Duchy of Burgundy from the Valois Dukes that had ruled there, King of Spain from its Castilian House and King of the Romans from his native House of Habsburg. Charles was thus the embodiment, or perhaps more accurately the culmination, of several centuries of Habsburg growth and ambition. Never before and never again would a man of that House possess, and claim to rule over, so much. 'By his presence and by the immense prestige that attached both to his imperial title and to the ideology of power which was fashioned around him', Charles could be expected to utilise this great consolidation of power into his hands to further benefit the Habsburg family like never before. If he could succeed in holding his domains together, the sky was the limit, for he was certainly not bound by the seas so long as Hernando Cortes sent such priceless hauls of gold across the Atlantic. Little wonder that Charles was 'likened to Augustus.'[11] Speaking of his rights, titles and responsibilities in 1521, Charles V said:

> Ye know that I am born of the most Christian Emperors of the noble German nation, of the Catholic Kings of Spain, the Archdukes of Austria, the Dukes of Burgundy, who were all to the death true sons of the Roman Church, defenders of the Catholic Faith, of the sacred customs, decrees and usages of its worship, who have bequeathed all this to me as my heritage, and according to whose example I have hitherto lived.[12]

The religious undertones of this address were both intentional and incredibly relevant in 1521, for Charles was not merely addressing his subjects – he was addressing above all the recent rift caused by the incendiary teachings of Martin Luther.[13] That Charles would be confronted by a religious crisis so early in his reign suggested that, far from universally successful and wholly united against the common foe – in this case the Ottoman Empire – Charles' domains would be drawn instead to wage wars against the French, the Turk and the very princes within the Empire over whom he supposedly ruled.

'Look how much depends on your person', wrote one prominent Cardinal in Charles' day, 'and how you would leave your kingdoms if, for our sins, some disaster should befall you.'[14] Yet, Charles was immensely fortunate to reap the fruits of several Habsburg offspring spread out across the continent that could carry out a great number of the tasks of rule in his name, including his own siblings. The plain fact that Charles could not be in several places at once spoke for the need to appoint regents and viceroys in different portions of his sprawling domains, most notably in Burgundy and Austria, while Charles himself spent most of his time in Madrid. In addition, Charles' four sisters, when they did not rule in his name, married and formed separate branches of the Habsburg dynasty in their own right.

Isabella was wedded to the King of Denmark; Mary was betrothed to the heir to the thrones of Hungary and Bohemia, and Catherine married the King of Portugal. In an effort to further parry the French threat, his elder sister Eleanor was wedded to King Francis I of France. In time, Mary would come to rule as regent over the Netherlands, and Charles' brother Ferdinand would rule in his name in Vienna, eventually providing the progeny that would constitute the 'Austrian' branch of the Habsburg line, while Charles' son Philip would constitute the 'Spanish' branch.[15] It was a stunning display of familial ambition, and demonstrated that, far from content to rest on his considerable laurels, Charles aimed at propelling the Habsburg family to greater heights than ever before.

Considering how incredibly influential and extensive the reach of the Habsburg family was by the early sixteenth century, one would be justified in asking how exactly such a family managed to dominate a continent. For the sake of tying all the disparate threads of the Thirty Years War together, we must take some time to examine the history of this family, and how it reached the height of its powers right at the point when Europe was undergoing profound change, and when threats from the east seemed terrifyingly real. It is a story as much about the curious nature of the Holy Roman Empire, as it is about the similarly mysterious family that came to dominate it. It is a story which begins, surprisingly, not in Germany per se, but in the town of Brugg, in Switzerland.

From relatively humble beginnings, as a Swiss noble family hailing from Habsburg Castle, the Habsburg dynasty bided its time, outmanoeuvred its enemies and acquired a rapidly growing portfolio of disparate estates and territories. The true ascension of the Habsburgs to a position of European predominance reads like a succession of well-planned and opportunistically sought marriages with the great houses of Europe. Frederick III arranged a marriage between his son Maximillian and Mary of Burgundy in 1477, tying the massive region of Burgundy,[16] including its successor state in the Netherlands, to the Habsburg family.[17]

The Valois dukes of Burgundy, a branch of the French royal house, had managed to bring together and rule 'this apparently ramshackle polity, with its contrasting economic and social structures, its several different languages and with its local privileges defended by long-established provincial estates and by solemnly sworn princely charters...'[18] A century later, this marriage would greatly shape the development of Europe, as these same Dutch possessions in the Netherlands declared themselves a sovereign state in 1581, in a revolt against the authority of the King of Spain Philip II – the great-grandson of Maximillian.[19] Elsewhere too, the marriages of the Habsburgs had produced fruit.

Maximillian of Habsburg, born in 1459, proved to be arguably the most expansionist and ambitious leader of his house in living memory. He benefited immensely from the aforementioned marriage between himself and Mary of Burgundy, and their son Philip would go on to marry Joanna of Castile, often saddled with the unfortunate epithet Joanna the Mad.[20] Notwithstanding her sanity, Joanna managed to provide Philip with a son, Charles – who would in time be our Charles V, of so many domains. As Philip married Joanna, so too did Juan marry Margaret of Austria, solidifying still further the Habsburg investment in the Spanish possessions. So it was that when the remaining Spanish heirs died in quick succession by 1500, the two half-Habsburg couples Philip and Joanna, Margaret and Juan, seemed well-positioned to place a Habsburg candidate on that prestigious throne. In 1500 and 1503, Charles and Ferdinand respectively were born, signifying Maximillian's initial positivity had been correct – a Habsburg would sit on the Spanish throne.

At the same time as the 'Spanish strategy' was undertaken, the indefatigable Maximillian plotted also to wed his grandson Ferdinand and his granddaughter Mary to the sister of the King of Hungary and the King of Hungary respectively.[21] The kings of Hungary were also kings of Bohemia, and possessed sprawling domains which stretched into the Balkans. In the interests of his house, Maximillian devised an immensely complex set of marital contracts, whereby extended members of the newly created branches of the Habsburg family would, in the time of their maturity, be pledged to wed designated partners. In addition, Maximillian even went so far as to adopt the sole son and heir of the King of Hungary as his own son – what was even more incredible, he then sought to get this adopted son, Louis of Bohemia, accepted as King of the Romans.[22]

Yet even Maximillian could not have imagined what was about to occur – in 1519 upon the death of the old Emperor the titles passed to his grandson Charles, who had also been confirmed as King of Spain and Duke of Burgundy. Thanks to the incredible expansion of the Spanish Crown in the New World, and the successes and prestige which it would soon enjoy in that sphere, the Spanish Crown now meant entitlement to a glittering overseas empire as well.[23] In the space of a few years then, Charles V of the House of Habsburg became the most powerful ruler on the continent – on a scale not seen since the days of the Roman Emperors of yore.

In the years that followed, Maximillian's ghost continued to stalk the proceedings; the adopted Louis drowned in a river while attempting to flee the disastrous battle of the Mohacs in 1526, leaving Hungary and Bohemia without any monarch.[24] Fortunately for the Habsburg family, the sister of the late Hungarian king had married Ferdinand, the brother of Charles V, while Charles' own sister Mary had also married into the Hungarian royal family,[25] thus enabling the Habsburgs to stake their claim on these extensive Hungarian lands while the Ottoman Empire capitalised upon their victory with an occupation of Budapest from the 1540s. Holy Roman Emperor, King of Spain, Duke of Burgundy, and now master of one of the most formidable medieval kingdoms in Europe, Charles V seemed destined to leave a lasting legacy not merely in the pantheon of the Habsburg family, but in the very fabric of the continent.

Ruling during such a transformative period in the history of his dynasty, Charles V presided over an era of great change, as the Reformation redefined the contract between Emperor and subject.[26] The princely electors, once content to be placated with bribes or promises of another beneficial sort, could now stand on a different religious spectrum to their Emperor altogether. The religious and political upheavals which followed were punctuated by the on-going war with the Ottomans, which continued into the 1540s. All the while, the Emperor was forced to maintain his attention on France, which repeatedly sought to undermine the Habsburg position in Italy and along the Rhine. To Charles' great fortune, Imperial-Spanish forces achieved a crushing victory over French forces, which included the capture of the King of France at the battle of Pavia in 1525, but such successes were short-lived, as King Francis resumed the war and would not make peace until both sides had exhausted their resources several years later.[27] At the same time, Charles' victories in North Italy enabled him to expand Habsburg influence there, even while the sack of Rome in 1527 damaged his reputation somewhat, and predictably enough, infuriated the Papacy.[28]

Victories against France were important, but it was while juggling his dynasty's security concerns in the east and constitutional concerns within the Holy Roman Empire that Charles V was ultimately defeated. Forced to sign a series of religious concessions which recognised the existence of another religious creed in the Empire, Charles sacrificed the unity of his domains, and effectively prevented his subjects from uniting against the common enemy of either France or the Turk. The most notable meeting was the Augsburg Diet in 1530, which seemed to provide for a measure of clarity and unity among the Lutheran princes of the Empire.[29] Yet, not even his critics could deny that Charles had any choice. The Holy Roman Empire seemed to be fragmenting before their very eyes, even as religious warfare also began to bubble over in France, with results that would in time effectively paralyse that country for the remainder of the sixteenth century.[30] In the midst of such turmoil did Charles agree to the Peace of Augsburg in 1555,[31] a landmark religious and political settlement which spoke to the permanence of Protestant Lutherans in the Empire, and seemed to provide a calming elixir to the ruinous religious strife which had to that point run rampant.

Before we go any further it is worth asking something of a loaded question: what exactly was the Holy Roman Empire? At its core, the Empire and the Emperor which led it sourced its legitimacy and authority from medieval agreements and traditions, established in the mists of historical account. The first Emperor, Charlemagne, seems to have been as French as he was German, in that he was King of the Franks before redefining his relationship with power and the papacy on Christmas day, 800AD, when he was crowned the Holy Roman Emperor of the German Nation .It is a mark of the curious legacy Charlemagne left Europe and the world, that both France and Germany (as Kaiser Karl) can claim Charlemagne as their own. Certainly it is likely that the Emperor spoke a dialect of Old High German, but his status as King of the Franks, the stately ancestor of France, complicates matters.[32] In a sense, it seems that Charlemagne himself did us a favour with his act of clarification on Christmas Day, 800AD. He was neither a mere King nor a prince, nor an Emperor in a Byzantine sense – he was the Emperor, the successor to Rome, and he had resurrected the Rome of ancient history by fusing it to the Papacy. In the process, Charlemagne also fused together his physical, dynastic authority as King of the most powerful entity in the West, with the spiritual authority that only the descendent of St Peter could endow.

His polity was *Holy*, because of the Papacy's blessing; it was *Roman*, because of his claims to have succeeded that famous Empire; and of course it was an *Empire* in its own right because Charlemagne had cleaved for himself a realm on a scale never before seen or imagined possible by his contemporaries. Symbolism played a key role in the ceremonials which took place in Rome; Pope Leo III crowned Charlemagne *Emperor* while the latter was wrapped in a tunic and cloak in the style of Ancient Rome. Charlemagne's imposing figure rose once crowned, to tower over the altar of St Peter's, just as he would have towered over the rest of the congregation. With this crowning, the King of the Franks became Holy Roman Emperor, but among his contemporaries and among historians since, it was possible to debate what this actually meant.[33]

Did it mean that Charlemagne had reached the peak of his prowess, the height of his powers? For some theologians, it was as simple as seeing Charlemagne as the Christian Emperor ruling a Christian Empire. To others, Charlemagne's power and majesty was such as to harken back to the days of Ancient Rome, and the eternal city's playing host to this event was certainly no accident. Other admirers believed that because of his incredible victories and earthly achievements, Charlemagne had transcended the title of King, and had become something else entirely.[34] Pope Leo III, for his part, hoped that with this crowning, Charlemagne would become not merely Emperor, but also protector – the physical and military force for Christendom and the Papacy, while the Pope himself would be its spiritual leader.[35]

Charlemagne was a figure of profound importance for European history and development, but like all mortals, he had to die eventually. Upon his death in 814, his lands were divided and settled between his sons and the fragmenting of his life's work soon began in earnest.[36] Notwithstanding the fates of his descendants, what is sometimes obscured within the incredible story of Charlemagne is the fact that this King of the Franks and first Emperor of the West since the Romans was also a scion of the Carolingian House. Carolingian would be the name given to the Empire Charlemagne would leave behind, as his successors grappled with the power vacuum left by his absence. The Carolingian dynasty remained, largely because of the person and mythos of Charlemagne, prestigious and majestic, even as it waned.

The monopoly of this family on the title of Holy Roman Emperor was all but broken within a century of Charlemagne's death, but the story then became one not of what the Holy Roman Empire represented, but of who wore the Imperial Crown, and who held those all-important titles which conferred so much power. The medieval Holy Roman Empire was a story of struggles between competing families who vied for influence and legitimacy as all sought that elusive prize. It was a struggle which began with one dynasty – the Carolingian, and ended with another, the Habsburg, and this latter struggle formed but one element of the conflict which developed into the Thirty Years War.[37]

TWO
The Small Print

The 1555 Peace of Augsburg, known to its contemporaries as the Religious and Profane Peace, is known today for its ultimately doomed effort to ease the religious tensions of the Holy Roman Empire. However, a closer examination of the actual text which constituted the agreement demonstrates that 'the section on confessional differences formed only a small part of a wide-ranging reform package agreed by the Reichstag.' Additional issues were also discussed, such as 'adjusting the public peace, revising imperial tax quotas, and providing new regulations on currency.'[38] Augsburg contained no statements on religious doctrine or the actual expression of faith, instead the major drive was aimed at bringing both Catholics and Lutherans within the same legal framework, so that both would be bound by the same laws and rights, and both creeds would be induced to maintain the peace. Those that drafted Augsburg were tasked with piecing together 'the shattered medieval unity of law and faith'; since religion provided the ultimate guide for all human endeavours, the two seemed indivisible – 'since there could only be one truth, there could only be one law.' Yet, Augsburg declared that both confessional camps could be right – a ground-breaking step, which ultimately proved a step too far.[39]

The religious stipulations of the peace deserve mention, considering the profound impact they were to have on the Holy Roman Empire in the years that followed. First, Lutheranism would be undeniably recognised and accepted as a religious creed within the Holy Roman Empire and would be as legal as Catholicism. Second, these two religious persuasions were then applied to the rulers of the disparate states within the Empire; whichever persuasion the ruler in question happened to be, his entire state and possessions would have to follow.

For example, if the Elector of Saxony was to be a Lutheran, then his subjects would have to embrace Lutheranism also. Minorities in either the Catholic or Lutheran case would not be permitted to worship in public and

211

lacked the rights and protections of their peers who followed the faith of the ruler. This latter point – that 'he who rules decides the religion' – would in time be given its Latin designation, *cuius regio, eius religio*, and became a focal point over the years that followed, especially when accompanied by the *reservatum ecclisiasticum*,[40] a ruling which stipulated that if a Catholic archbishop, bishop or prelate converted to Lutheranism, 'his archbishopric, bishopric, prelacy and other benefices together with all their income and revenues which he has so far possessed, shall be abandoned by him without any further objection or delay', and an individual 'espousing the old religion' would be elected to succeed in his place.[41]

It was Archduke Ferdinand, rather than his brother Charles V, Holy Roman Emperor, who managed to, according to historian Peter H. Wilson, 'convert the temporary arrangements evolving since 1521 into a more stable peace, securing broad acceptance of this as necessary to preserve the cherished imperial unity.'[42] The years before this agreement, taking place in the 1555 Imperial Diet which had been moved to Augsburg, were filled with turmoil, constant religious disagreement and regular bouts of conflict. Augsburg seemed to apply a healing salve to such woes and provided a solution which all could adhere to. Yet, primarily because said Peace was designed to appeal to all, and to grant all the opportunity to interpret its sometimes-vague principles as they desired, the entire agreement was, in the words of one historian, 'rife with inherent contradictions and impracticalities.'[43]

Although the position of princes and Electors seemed clear, the Free Imperial Cities, the knights and the counts were all in something of a limbo, since it was unclear how far each enjoyed the same powers as princes to change the faith of their subjects. The decisions of Augsburg seemed to contradict the position of the Holy Roman Emperor as the political leader of European Christendom. In an effort to cope with such a contradiction, the religious elements of Augsburg were deliberately blurred. As Peter H. Wilson wrote:

> Lutherans were referred to as 'adherents of the Confession of Augsburg', without defining what that meant, while use of words like 'peace', 'religious belief' and 'reformation' were a deliberate attempt to incorporate values that all still shared, yet understood differently. For Lutherans, 'reformation' meant the right of legally constituted authorities to change the religious practice in line with their founder's teachings. To Catholics, it confirmed their church's role in spiritual guidance.[44]

What appears the most glaring omission of the Peace was the status of Calvinism, the other major creed in the Empire by 1618. Augsburg recognised only Lutherans and Catholics, Calvinists were technically outlawed, and had been ignored in 1555 because barely any potentates of any significance adhered to that creed, and John Calvin was himself only beginning his journey to France.[45] Since it was from Lutherans that Calvinists tended to receive the most convicts, confessional dislike between the two Protestant creeds grew to incendiary levels by the turn of the century, and helped facilitate the cause of the Counter-Reformation, which was able to provide a united image of Catholicism in contrast to Protestant disunity and chaos.[46]

From 1555 to 1618, the Peace of Augsburg provided a temporary solution to the immediate religious problems of the Holy Roman Empire. These problems, such as they were in 1555, were made still more urgent as the decades progressed, and issues of interpretation with Augsburg continued to emerge. As Brennan Pursell put it:

> These tensions produced no small amount of mutual antagonism, but it did not lead inevitably to the relentless bloodshed from 1618-1648. The Peace of Augsburg had placated warring confessions in 1555, but it had not prearranged the series of crises that incited and escalated the Thirty Years War. Rather than guaranteeing constitutional paralysis and extensive international interference, the Peace of Augsburg had provided grounds for at least fifty years of what has been called 'unusual constitutional liveliness and openness.'[47]

Indeed, Augsburg has often been blamed for crises which could not have been foreseen in 1555. The conversion to Calvinism of several princes, and two actual Electors in the Empire – the Palatine and Brandenburg Electors – threw a confusing spanner in the works, as some of these rulers attempted to apply the *cuius regio, eius religio* principle, even while Calvinism was temporarily excluded from such stipulations.[48] With the exception of the Cologne War in the 1580s though, few direct attempts were made to challenge the principles of Augsburg. It seemed as though many were content to adhere to its stipulations, so long as the traumatic memories of sectarian conflict remained fresh. As the years progressed though, attitudes hardened, and efforts were made after the 1580s to actively apply the principle of *cuius regio, eius religio* in the lands of certain rulers.[49]

As we shall see, tensions arose as Lutherans were caught out by the pace of the Counter-Reformation, as Calvinism spread and as the religious refugees from all sides further complicated matters. The increased influence of the Jesuits and their sway over the hearts and minds of the Habsburg family in particular also helped to push tensions further to the fore. At one point, Augsburg had represented peace, yet, the population growth of the sixteenth century, the varied interpretations of the peace and the disparate nature of inheritance, dynasty extinction and expansion all contributed to the perceived instability of the religious settlement by the second decade of the seventeenth century. Its failure to permanently heal the rift caused by the Reformation has led some historians to criticise it as doomed from the start, yet it should be said that for at least a generation after 1555, the Peace of Augsburg provided a measure of religious calm when states like France were tearing themselves asunder over the religious and political questions that seemed so intertwined.[50]

Having healed – temporarily at least – the religious rift in the Empire, Charles V, master of more lands than the Habsburg family had ever held or would ever hold again, relinquished power to of the Austrian and Spanish branches of the dynasty to his brother and son respectively. The abdication and subsequent retirement to a religious house fascinated those contemporaries that knew of Charles as the protector of Christendom, yet it was for cynical reasons too that Charles chose to divide his domains.[51] The Habsburgs, contrary to what their lofty title may have suggested, could not wield all the power at once. They had proved terminally unable to rule as the Roman Emperors had once ruled; instead of the unending ambition of Trajan, Charles V had preached sense and reform. Such reform was necessary, he reasoned, if the Habsburgs were to survive this new tide of religious division and chaos which threatened to destroy the very constitution of the Holy Roman Empire itself.

The 1555 Peace of Augsburg had placed a temporary bandage over the wounds of the Holy Roman Empire,[52] but the Peace was continually placed in jeopardy thanks to changing circumstances of the Empire and the escalation of princely rivalries within it. The growth of creeds such as Calvinism – which had barely a presence in 1555 – challenged the fundamental tenets of Augsburg which had declared only Lutheranism and Catholicism to be lawful religious persuasions. Similarly, the *reservatum ecclisiasticum* – which stipulated that a Catholic ruler converting to Lutheranism would have to abandon his lands – evoked fierce debate from the Protestant contingents of the Empire, who claimed that they had never agreed to the clause.[53]

Dynastic and political rivalry between the Duke of Bavaria and the Elector of the Palatinate also coloured relations between the two religious camps, a trend which would escalate dangerously in the first decade of the seventeenth century. As Emperor Ferdinand's successors, Maximillian II (1564-1576), Rudolf II (1576-1612) and Matthias (1612-1619) also learned, security in the east against the threat posed by the Ottoman Turk was only guaranteed if concessions were made to the Protestants in the Habsburg Austrian lands. In return for religious concessions, the Protestants would vote taxes in support of the war effort and peacetime reinforcement.

The support of the Protestants was essential for the Austrian Habsburgs, because the Lutheran creed was supreme among the nobility of Upper and Lower Austria, with as many as 90% of those in Lower Austria converting by 1580.[54] Indeed, as Charles of Styria, Emperor Maximillian II's younger brother, had it put to him by his court preacher: 'The Turkish threat is a blessing to the Protestants; if it were not for that, we would be able to deal with them in a very different way.'[55] Indeed, the lax implementation of the Peace of Augsburg in the Habsburgs' own lands underlined the fact that circumstances often got in the way of that settlement's core tenets. Faced with the expansion and empowerment of Protestants in their lands, a determined effort was made by Maximillian's brothers to affect a reduction in their influence and presence through the Counter-Reformation. Through deliberate and sustained policies, the Protestants would be combatted 'not with sound and with fury, but surreptitiously and slowly; not with words, but with deeds.'[56] Charles of Styria and his brothers died before much work could be done to these ends, but Charles' son Ferdinand, returning from a Jesuit education in 1595, proved more than up to the task.

In the event, the 17-year-old Ferdinand of Styria would affect a striking change in his lands. After visiting the Pope in 1598 – when according to one historian 'he no doubt explained his plan of campaign' – Ferdinand set to work. He ordered all Protestant clergy and schoolteachers out of his lands, oversaw the burning of some ten thousand prohibited books, and established a Reformation Commission to conduct his orders more efficiently. With a single-minded determination, Ferdinand forced some two and a half thousand of his most prominent subjects into exile, taking advantage of the fear instilled in his subjects by the Turkish threat, to the point that one historian noted how 'Ferdinand had managed to revive his grandfather's policy of divide and rule with startling success.'[57]

Yet the success was misleading. Shaped by the increased influence of the Jesuit Fathers, who operated four colleges within the Habsburgs' lands, Ferdinand and his contemporaries became more hardline, severe and less willing to compromise. The attempts to purge his lands of Protestants largely complete, Ferdinand of Styria remained deeply influenced by the Jesuits he surrounded himself with. They preached a 'stern, uncompromising and legalistic faith', and upped the tensions of the region and the nature of religious debate, becoming 'steadily more aggressive' as their policies produced results.[58] Yet the Jesuits did manage to greatly increase the progress and scope of the Counter-Reformation, which by 1590 had brought scores of old Bohemian and Austrian noble families back to Catholicism.

How can we explain the success of the Counter-Reformation? A major reason for the apparent resurgence of Catholicism is found in the clear message and united front that Catholicism could present to the wider world. Protestants, by contrast, seemed doomed to split repeatedly over several issues, and the divided nature of Protestantism, combined with a lack of leadership from one single source, as the Papacy represented, provided further incentives. A second point related to this can be added – the repeated splitting and divisions of different Protestant creeds led also to increased bickering *between them.*

As converts from one creed to another would often identify as Protestant, this meant that Lutherans for example lost the bulk of their converts to Calvinism, a fact which led to resentment and eventually hatred towards the Calvinists. The conversion of Protestants back to the Catholicism of their forefathers also saw a reduction in Protestant control over important schools, pamphlets and printing presses which traditionally spread the Protestant message. With these no longer in Protestant hands, the Catholic voices were normally heard above them, which created a greater awareness and eventually more converts.[59]

Added to this was the very opportunistic creation of several Catholic orders which spoke to the nobleman's place in society. The Jesuits, or to give them their full name, the Society of Jesus, were highly active in their spreading of wealth, in appointing impressive representatives across the different capitals of Europe and in their approaches to influential noblemen – all under the watchful eye and sponsorship of the Papacy.[60] Through the nobles as much as the princes could the Reformation be properly countered, as these individuals were the true actors in society and could serve as conduits for their subjects, who would be compelled to follow suit. This combination of papal-sponsored orders, of maintaining a united front and of approaching and proselytising to the most influential in society proved high effective. With their success they could groom and release intensely motivated princes and potentates to continue and further their work – men such as King Sigismund III of Poland, King Philip III of Spain and, as we have seen, Ferdinand of Styria.[61]

Yet, the Counter-Reformation did not ensure a greater adherence to the whims and authority of the Holy Roman Emperor; in fact, with religious tensions growing following the Peace of Augsburg in 1555, a set of crises concerning that religious makeup, as well as the Holy Roman Empire's constitutional structure, further aggravated the tensions. In 1580s Cologne, an archbishopric and an elector in the Imperial College, the stage was set for a five year war which erupted once the individual ruling there converted to Lutheranism, and refused to abandon his lands as per the *reservatum ecclesiasticum*. This ruling had stipulated that any convert would have to abandon his lands to a Catholic peer, and, so the Catholic potentates claimed, had been agreed to by all sides at Augsburg in 1555, but the Protestants claimed they had never recognised the ruling, and they suspected its authenticity. This War of the Cologne Succession (1583-88) pitted the aforementioned Archbishop-Elector, with his Dutch and Palatine supporters, against the Catholic camp of Ernest of Bavaria – his intended replacement – and Philip II of Spain. Duke William of Bavaria, Ernest's brother, ran up debts of over 500,000 thalers in his fight against the Protestant influence, which would have adversely affected the balance of electors within the Electoral College.[62]

Such events now bring us to the point where we must clarify what we mean when we talk of the Holy Roman Empire and its institutions.[63] We have seen where the Holy Roman Empire came from, but we now need to explain how its institutions and structure actually worked. We are greeted with some important questions, not least of which was the pressing dilemma of how a state as large and unwieldy as the Holy Roman Empire was to be administered. It is also worth considering the office of Holy Roman Emperor, and what powers and responsibilities such an office upheld. Before we begin such a daunting task, it is important to note that, in the words of one historian, 'the Imperial constitution is almost impossible to classify';[64] in other words, the Holy Roman Empire was quite unlike any 'state' that came before it or which has come since. The famous phrase from Voltaire; that it was neither holy, nor Roman, nor an Empire, exemplifies the set of contradictions and challenges posed to historians by a polity which was far from Holy, in no sense Roman and not exactly an Empire, certainly not by the seventeenth century.[65]

On the other hand, there is good reason to approach the Holy Roman Empire with a degree of respect, rather than merely dismissing it as an unsustainable, unworkable polity. When writing on Benjamin Franklin's journey to the Holy Roman Empire in 1766, one historian was able to note that the 'German Federation might have influenced his plan of colonial union' within the Thirteen Colonies; an idea which underwrites the great historic and legalistic impression that the Holy Roman Empire left on its contemporaries. In the case of these contemporaries, the Empire was far from a mere source of intimidation or bemusement on account of its complex inner workings; on the contrary, it was often upheld as the purest form of German government, and part of the natural order of European states.[66] Part of this reverence can be explained by the Holy Roman Empire's longevity, and the impossible task of imagining any other power emerging to take its place. Nonetheless, it is necessary to make some attempt to traverse these challenges, otherwise it will be impossible to understand how this complex polity careened into such a ruinous conflict in 1618.

To begin with, the Holy Roman Empire of the German Nation, to give it its full title, was led nominally by the Holy Roman Emperor. The constitutional basis for the Empire was established in the Golden Bull of 1356, which described the procedure for the election of the Emperor and the constitution of the Electoral College. Within this Electoral College existed seven individuals capable of voting, *conveniently* labelled Electors. The Golden Bull named them as the Archbishoprics of Mainz, Cologne and Trier, with the secular rulers of the King of Bohemia, the Margrave of Brandenburg, the Duke of Saxony and the Count Palatine on the Rhine gaining the remaining votes. The Empire thus takes the form of an elective monarchy, with the seven Electors balancing the authority of the Emperor and ensuring his responsibilities towards the Empire would be respected. These responsibilities included powers to bestow princely titles, to grant legal privileges, to name notaries, judges and members of the Imperial Supreme Court.[67] The Emperor was the designated feudal overlord of the Empire, and, in rank at least, was above all other potentates of the Empire.

In a predominantly feudal polity such as the Holy Roman Empire, the different princes, dukes, archbishops, counts, knights and electors etc. were his *subjects*, even while the Emperor himself could never wield anything close to absolute authority over these subjects – certainly not by our time period of the early seventeenth century. Such actors – from the largest of the Imperial Free Cities to the most miniscule principality – all possessed some form of local representation in their regional assemblies, 'confusingly known as Estates', as one historian sympathetically put it.[68] This structure encouraged local independence, even while, as per the traditional feudal contract, the overlord in the person of the Emperor could call upon his vassals to act. Once called upon, the Emperor could expect a positive or negative response depending on his own power, on the power or status of his subject and on the relationship he enjoyed with them. The more powerful the subject, the less likely it was that he would follow the Emperor's requests to the letter – unless of course, the Emperor enjoyed a good relationship with him, and could find a way to motivate him into acting.[69]

The depth and range of the parallel and associated institutions within the Holy Roman Empire and the terminology, rhetoric and history which went along with them are certainly something to behold.[70] Yet, to begin a deep dive into the complex and detailed minutiae of the Empire's inner workings would delay and frustrate one of the primary aims of this book, which is to present as accessible an account of the Thirty Years War as possible. Here our aim is to clarify and classify as best as we can the elements of the Holy Roman Empire which will be relevant to our experience of the Thirty Years War. With that in mind it is necessary to dwell for a moment on the aforementioned Estates of the Empire.

'Two observations concerning the territorial Diets provide a good starting point', wrote the historian Tim Neu in his article examining the extent of representation which the Estates of the Empire were able to grant their subjects. The first, Neu explained, 'is simply that delegates "talked" – they deliberated, voted, and delivered orations – as long as the Diet was in session.' The second was that 'territorial estates claimed to be representatives of the *Land*; the territory and the subjects.' Neu continued that in light of the realities of the Holy Roman Empire, it is possible to conclude that:

...delegates to territorial Diets talked even though there was almost nothing for them to decide, and even though there were no formal means by which to substantiate their claim to represent the Land and the people. Accordingly, all the talking and all the assertions seem irrational and useless.[71]

Although Neu did not believe it was inherently fair to label the Empire's representative processes as such, it is worth considering the role of the estates in the Empire and whether we can define precisely what the Estates did. Clarifying such questions will make imagining the Empire's complex inner workings that much easier to grasp and will help to explain why the Habsburgs and their enemies acted and reacted as they did. It should be noted first that several watershed moments within the Thirty Years War occurred because they were voted or pushed for by specific Estates; this makes understanding and appreciating what these Estates would have looked like all the more important. When we speak of the Estates in a given region behaving this way or that, what we mean is that large assemblies of men gathered to discuss and debate the pertinent issues of the day, and settled on a specific set of objectives or principles, which could then be presented to their lord. In local issues their lord took the form of the local regional ruler – the archbishop, prince, duke or count etc.

The act of discussing and talking over the issues in the Estates did not mean that these individuals were engaging in a genuinely democratic process. Estates are often simply equated with modern democratic Parliaments, which can often give us an inaccurate impression of what these Estates had the power to precisely do. When we imagine Parliaments, we generally think of democratic systems where said Parliament possesses several important prerogatives and holds a worthy place in the functioning of the state. However, in the seventeenth century and before this was not always the case. The confusion over terminology can be explained with a brief lesson in etymology.

The term "parliament" and its counterparts in other languages is sourced from the French verb *parler* – "to talk". Parliaments were and remain places to discuss and debate the pressing issues facing the members of its assembly. Yet, only since the late eighteenth century did Parliaments become associated with direct political representation. This act of talking did not automatically lead to action on the part of the local ruler, although in most cases the Estates were required to approve taxation.[72] Attendance in the Estates, in short, did not equate to representation of that assembly's views, or the ruler's *acceptance* of such views.[73] The act of talking amongst one's peers was nonetheless viewed as a worthwhile endeavour.

Even if a German noble's participation in his local Estates did not represent a necessarily democratic process, it was a tradition of the Holy Roman Empire's constitutional processes and was thus highly respected. It was a strange contradiction – those that attended the Estates or regional Diets were not accountable to the peasantry or their peers; they were not elected to sit at these Estates, and they were not authorised to pass legislation or act in the ruler's name.[74] Yet, at times, the decisions of the Estates could have monumental consequences, as they took their case to the Holy Roman Emperor himself. This, incidentally, was what happened in Bohemia in 1618, when the Bohemian Estates made several urgent deputations to the Emperors Matthias and then Ferdinand II. Bear with me guys; some additional clarification on 'Estates' as a term is necessary.

As with several of the Holy Roman Empire's associated institutions, where confusion often reigns over their structure and the function, Estates can confound the casual history enthusiast thanks to the multi-layered nature of 'Estates' as a term. Used in a form familiar to students of the French Revolution, Estates referred not merely to assemblies, but also to the different classes of the population. The three Estates of the Empire were the commons, the clergy and the princes and as Peter H. Wilson noted, 'the ideal was an interlocking system in which all should accept their allotted place, because all derived benefit from the functions performed by others on their behalf.'[75]

These three social Estates of the Empire included vast chasms of difference within each Estate; for example, the growth of cities led to the emergence of a wealthier merchant class within the commons, and these merchants resented being lumped together with the common peasant. Similarly, the minor prince was well aware that he was outranked by the Electors of the Empire, but he did not like to be reminded of this fact. In the case of the clergy, prince-bishops and archbishops stood far above the common priest in terms of ranks. All of these variations in status were reflected when it came time to sit in the regional assembly; all were represented in the one room, but one sat on a given bench and in a certain place depending on his social status. For example, in 1498 the clearly insecure Duke of Lower Bavaria successfully petitioned the Electors in the Imperial Diet to reduce the height of their platform so that the ordinary princes of the Empire would not be seated so far beneath them.[76]

Given what we know already about the inner workings of the Holy Roman Empire, it should go without saying that 'the social hierarchy was complex and fragmented',[77] and as the economy, population and religious persuasions of the Empire changed and altered with time, the different social strata became still harder to explain and justify. Economic success in business could mean that a wealthy merchant far outstripped the monetary capabilities of his prince, yet it was this prince in his principality where the merchant operated that stood far above him in the pecking order, even if that prince might well be tempted to rely on said merchant for a loan, or even to appoint him to an important political administrative position within his lands. Furthermore, it is inaccurate to think of princes ruling over a unified territory, and more useful to imagine him in control of certain imperial Estates within his collection of lands. As the ambition and resources of the prince grew, he could incorporate additional lands into his property portfolio.

Through marriage, inheritance and sometimes warfare a ruler could expand his domains, sometimes acquiring additional Estates in the new lands. On occasion then, a ruler could possess several Estates, and therefore several votes in the Imperial Diet. Through such a process could the Electors acquire more power for themselves, yet the expanding princely family would never dream of abandoning the formal Imperial distinctions that made his different Estates unique. The Elector of Brandenburg, for example, would never think to remove the old identities or names of any new Estates he came to possess – it was the possession of these Estates across his scattered lands, rather than the often-underdeveloped lands themselves,[78] that granted him his power.[79]

Within all of these Estates the social hierarchy of the Empire was reflected, and the pecking order reinforced. The opinion of a prince for example was rated far higher than a representative of a Free Imperial City, especially as the City's representative tended to be a commoner, was confined to the back of the hall, and was obliged to stand in certain stages of the deliberations, while other attendees could remain seated. This gave a public face to one's rank within society, and ensured that the three tiered social Estates were represented in all walks of Imperial life; from the Imperial Diet to the smallest of regional assemblies.[80] If the bottom of the pecking order in both society and representation were the commoner, then at the top of the princely imperial order, behind only the Holy Roman Emperor, was the Elector.

THREE
Elections and Electors

The Electors were the 'foundations and fixed pillars of the Empire', and they were tasked with protecting the Empire's constitution and ensuring its stability.[81] It was these Electors that enjoyed sovereign rights over their lands, many elements of which were often spread out and bordered by other princes equally eager to maintain some form of legislative independence. Had the Empire been less of a federation and more of a monarchy, the Electors would never enjoyed such freedoms, but the seven individual rulers were permitted to exercise lordship over their own resources, subjects and lands in any way they saw fit – they were effectively miniature kings, who looked up to the Emperor as their overarching sovereign.[82] As per the terms of the Golden Bull, the Electors were supposed to convene periodically to discuss pertinent issues of defence, religious policy or any other business which required their attentions.

Below the Electors could be found virtually every other actor of the Empire; the minor princes, the knights,[83] the bishoprics and the dukes. These individuals were grouped into ten geographical Circles, which were arranged primarily to organise local defences among the smaller princes. The Holy Roman Empire was thus a strange jigsaw puzzle, constituted of several pieces of varying size and importance. Incidentally, the historian Tim Blanning in his stellar biography of Frederick the Great gives one of the most concise and accessible definitions of the Holy Roman Empire's inner workings. Blanning writes that the Holy Roman Empire…

> …is best thought of as a 'composite state'…whose [individual] rulers enjoyed most but not all of the powers usually associated with a sovereign. They were bound together by the allegiance they owed to the Emperor; their subjection to Imperial law administered by the two Imperial courts, and through representation in the *Reichstag* (Imperial Diet) at Regensburg. The Diet was divided into three 'colleges', the first comprising the…Electors…The second and largest was that of the princes, comprising thirty-four ecclesiastical princes, plus two collective votes shared by about forty monasteries and

abbeys, and sixty secular princes, plus four collective votes shared by 100-odd Imperial counts. The third college consisted of fifty-one 'Free Imperial Cities', the self-governing republics subject only to the authority of the Emperor. The institutional structures had been fixed around 1500 but the world had moved on since then, divorcing power from appearance.[84]

The sheer scale of the Imperial Diet's scope and the vast range of potentates and groups that the institution represented seem impossibly complex. One can imagine the Imperial Diet paralysing itself with mundane matters as the important issues are pushed aside in the name of regional or dynastic squabbles. In a body which attempted to give a voice to so many disparate elements of the Empire, one imagines there were surely no opportunities for every voice to be adequately heard. Yet, the apparently doomed Imperial Diet was not always so unwieldy.[85] Statistically, this is because the Imperial Diet in its full and complete form did not meet all that often, and only in times of need or danger would all members of the three sweeping social Estates – the clergy, commons and princes – be called upon to sit for long and regular periods.

Ideally, the institution was meant to meet and deliberate on relevant issues and challenges as they appeared, yet this mission became massively complicated from the early sixteenth century, as the Reformation turned the Electors – not to mention the individual members of the Estates, Circles and Free Cities – into a house divided along deeply sensitive lines.[86] That being said, the Diet was capable of producing important legislation and ratifying critical agreements, such as the aforementioned 1555 Peace of Augsburg.

The net result of this unfortunate trend towards religious division was that the Diet rarely agreed or reached a consensus on its debates.[87] As Lutheranism spread and further split into conflicting creeds, it drew much of the Electors, not to mention the minor princes and dukes below them, into broad confessional camps. The Holy Roman Emperor – a Habsburg institution since that family had monopolised the office in 1438 – now had to contend with Electors of a different religious persuasion to himself.[88] If the Catholic Habsburgs thus wished to hold onto their Imperial position, they would have to mobilise their supporters and resources, co-opt the support of the Spanish branch of the Habsburg family, and do all they could to cajole, scheme and manipulate their religious and dynastic opponents. As the subsequent years would demonstrate, they were also willing to fight for this monopoly if necessary.

After the crisis in Cologne in the 1580s, the different religious camps within the Holy Roman Empire seemed destined to separate further. The uncomfortable divorce of much of the Empire's lands from the old religion, and the rapid pace of the Counter-Reformation within the Habsburg hereditary lands, created a situation which only bred further religious tensions. Thus, once war with the Ottoman Empire broke out in the last decade of the sixteenth century, the Habsburgs were faced with a situation whereby traditionally unreliable elements within their lands would have to be relied upon. If they wanted to fight the Ottomans effectively, in other words, they would have to call upon the Lutheran and growing Calvinist populations within the Empire.

For this to happen, the Habsburg Emperors would have to grant certain concessions to these same subjects as the price of their aid. Such tactics on the part of the Protestants were far from original – they are strikingly similar to those tactics employed by opportunistic individuals in that other important, but difficult to define polity in Europe, the Polish-Lithuanian Commonwealth. In the case of the Holy Roman Emperor though, these concessions were especially necessary in light of the constitutional paralysis of the Empire's traditional institutions, most notably in the case of the Imperial Diet. Between 1555 and 1603, in spite of the tumultuous events taking place within and without of the Empire's borders, the Diet met only *six* times, reflecting perhaps its inherent inability to deal objectively with that Empire's problems, problems which included the voting of taxation for war against the Ottomans.[89]

Rudolf II held the heavy mantle of Holy Roman Emperor from 1576 to 1612, and during this no doubt exhausting span of nearly forty years faced a myriad of problems in his efforts to mobilise the disparate elements of the Empire against external threats. Unless he called a Diet, the Emperor could not secure taxes for his war against the Turks – this dependence echoes the Habsburgs' contemporaries, as the English model in particular comes to mind; that relationship saw the King dependent upon Parliament for the approval and raising of taxation, and the eventual breakdown of that system led to a uniquely British Civil War from the 1640s.[90] Rudolf would not live to see a civil war per se, but he was dependent upon his subjects for financial support, lest the Turks would run roughshod over Habsburg defences and reach the gates of Vienna, as had happened in 1529.[91]

The historian Geoffrey Parker noted that despite Rudolf's reliance on Protestant taxes and support, he determined to turn against these same elements in Hungary at the first opportunity. Parker noted how 'the Balkans might have been liberated had Rudolf not decided to use the opportunity to engineer a revolt in Transylvania, and to exploit the presence of his armies both there and in Hungary to restore the Roman Catholic Church to a position of supremacy.' This behaviour flew in the face of the religious demographic facts in Hungary – where in 1606 'even papal agents could find only three hundred Roman Catholic clergy in Hungary' and that 'there were no Catholic-controlled towns and virtually no Catholic nobles.'[92] How do we explain Rudolf's behaviour in such circumstances, where the Habsburg Emperor seemed more determined to persecute his own subjects rather than prosecute the war with the Ottomans to a successful conclusion?

One explanation put it that Rudolf was, by the turn of the century, bordering on mental instability, and only the election of his brother Matthias could sooth the tensions and strife within Hungary which he had created. But Hungary was far from the only problem Rudolf had helped cultivate. The Imperial City of Donauworth, located in the Swabian circle of the Holy Roman Empire, had enjoyed a status of joint confessional tolerance between both Catholics and Protestants, in spite of the rapidly dwindling Catholic population there.[93] Problems emerged in Donauworth when in March 1607 Rudolf approved of Duke Maximillian of Bavaria's request to journey to the city in defence of the Catholic populace there, who, it was said, suffered much discrimination and even violence from the Protestant majority. This was followed by an Imperial Ban upon the city in August, which effectively granted Maximillian free reign to do what he pleased.[94]

Travelling with much haste, before the issue could be put to the Imperial Diet, Maximillian invaded the Free City in December, and was then permitted by the Emperor to annex the once independent city into his Duchy, as payment for his services. The plainly unconstitutional nature of this incident did not seem to unduly bother Maximillian, who was himself a 'staunch Catholic' and 'a competent, disciplined, rich prince.'[95] Maximillian was also intensely ambitious, and one of the most influential Catholic potentates of the Empire.[96] We will see more of him later.

It was impossible to deny that the incident at Donauworth reflected terribly upon Rudolf, who was meant to uphold the principles of the Empire. Bavarian Dukes had no business either intervening in a Free City outside of their Duchy, let alone annexing it into their lands. Protestants cried foul, insisting that Rudolf had stood idly by and allowed the travesty to occur. Rudolf, for his part, did himself or his family's image no favours when he 'refused to follow Saxon advice and issue a statement denying his judgement was sectarian.' This is because, as Peter H. Wilson noted, Rudolf's 'inflated sense of majesty prevented him from seeing the need to explain his actions', and so it fell to Maximillian of Bavaria to justify his actions and the Emperor's complicity, in the process 'undermining the Emperor's credibility and raising the spectre of arbitrary rule.'[97]

Rudolf's faux pas had been terribly pricey – not only had the Emperor squandered any goodwill he had cultivated over the last few years, he had also allowed a mere Duke to speak for him. Little surprise that the events at Donauworth 'led to a hardening of religious divisions in Europe'.[98] nProtestant princes were no longer willing to place their trust in the traditional legal and constitutional institutions of the Holy Roman Empire so long as a Catholic majority remained within them. Just as intense debate on the interpretations of the 1555 Peace of Augsburg were taking place,[99] Protestants became harder to find in the Empire's institutions.

The major consequence of the Donauworth incident was that it compelled the Emperor – perhaps moving back into the realm of reality – to bring together the princes of the Empire in spring 1608, with an Imperial Diet. The Diet proved to be the perfect forum for the Protestants to air their grievances in public, as one historian noted how 'many of the Protestants walked out of the Regensburg Diet April 1608, leading to its dissolution. In May 1608, several Protestant princes made an agreement called the Protestant Union. They pledged mutual assistance in case of attack.'[100] Indeed, it was within the text of their contract, signed by the potentates of the Protestant or Evangelical Union, that the Donauworth incident was indirectly referenced as justification for the creation of a joint defensive league between several Protestant princes.

Where once the traditional checks and balances on the actors within the Empire protected one's realm from violence, now it was the case that these same institutions 'have become the subject of a damaging misunderstanding, as well as being broken and illegally opposed by many with hostile and violent actions, so that one is no longer sure of certain aid.[101] Incidentally, the creation of this league provoked a similarly incendiary response from the Empire's Catholic potentates, who established their own Catholic league in July 1609.

The contract of the Catholic League *also* claimed that a 'dangerous misunderstanding' had dislocated the traditional institutions tasked with protecting the Empire's actors, and that 'it was much to be feared' that…

> …if this state of affairs continues much longer, the violence will mount progressively in the Empire so that the peace-loving, obedient Catholic imperial Estates will be overrun and violated by the troublemakers and consequently nothing less can be expected than further oppression of the old true Catholic religion, the unique route to salvation, and its adherents, contrary to justice and imperial law.

In light of such bleak predictions, the Catholic League resolved itself to combine 'defensively to implement and further uphold the Holy Imperial laws, and their beneficial and worthy religious and profane peace, and its associated executive ordinance.'[102]

With the Evangelical Union and Catholic League leading opposing groups of princes and potentates within the Holy Roman Empire, the opportunities for the underlying tensions to erupt into open conflict appeared anxiously numerous. All it would take was an excuse; a spark to light the tinder which would engulf the whole Empire in religious and sectarian flames.[103] Indeed historians tend to use the metaphor of a 'pressure cooker' to describe the tensions which appeared destined to boil over by this point.[104] It was at that moment, just as Duke Maximillian of Bavaria was putting the finishing touches on the Catholic League, that news began to emerge of a new succession crisis in the heart of Germany. The newly built confessional alliances were suddenly required to pick a side, as Duke John William of Julich-Cleves and Berg, count of Ravensburg and Mark, died childless and heirless on 25 March 1609.

John William's possessions included wealthy, religiously diverse populations, whose Estates had agitated in the past for support from likeminded religious powers. Spain, the Dutch, the Elector of Brandenburg, the Elector of the Palatinate and several other minor princes all proclaimed their own vested interests in the affair, which represented the first test of the rapidly arming confessional blocs of the Holy Roman Empire.[105] It remained to be seen whether a calm and cooperative diplomatic effort could ease the tensions this crisis had created, or whether it was *this* succession crisis that was to have the distinction of lighting the metaphorical tinder box – which so many years of rising tensions and divisions had cultivated. As a crisis in the heart of the Empire flared, hundreds of miles away, the King of France and that of Spain also lined up to be counted.

In 1609, according to one historian, 'Europe was too exhausted to fight the Thirty Years War.'[106] This exhaustion would soon dissipate, or at least be ignored, in time for that tragic eruption in 1618, but for the moment, peace treaties and agreements, however temporary, were signed, and conflict avoided. Even as the Holy Roman Empire seemed to be splintering into disparate religious camps, the Spanish, English, Dutch and North Italian potentates were more than a little interested in preserving the peace, rather than jeopardising it. Avoiding conflict was at the top of the list of the King of France and Navarre, Henry IV.

Far from an easy journey to the French crown, Henry had in fact only made his peace with Spain in 1598, wherein Madrid committed to interfere no longer in the French succession. The French and Habsburgs had long made a habit of interfering in each other's business and exploiting the other difficulties,[107] so in the sense that this policy of interference was at end, the 1598 Peace of Vervins was highly significant, not least because it enabled Henry to focus on domestic religious matters, with the result that the Edict of Nantes emerged later in the year.[108] Perhaps now, the new French King would have the opportunity to rebuild his shattered, exhausted Kingdom, and to repair the divisions of the French people which had led them to inflict such atrocities upon one another.[109]

'Henry IV is supposed to have said there were three things he did not believe', wrote the historian Charles Howard Carter, 'that Queen Elizabeth was really a virgin, that the Archduke Albert was a good soldier, and that the king of Spain was a good Catholic.'[110] While Henry may not have been well positioned to pass judgement on the first point, he knew a great deal about soldiering and the difficulties of the religious question. Indeed, Henry's military innovations have been studied by several historians, who assessed his contribution to the Military Revolution in European thought and practice.[111]

In religious terms, Henry knew all too well how the potency of one's faith could instigate devastating conflict; the French Wars of Religion, of which he had played a key role, were only completely brought to a conclusion with Henry's conversion to Catholicism, with the King's famed phrase, 'Paris is well worth a mass.'[112]

The French succession had been a terminal question in France for much of the second half of the sixteenth century, thanks to the destabilising impact of the Reformation on that country, and the reduction in the powers of the ruling House of Valois. The net result of French Wars of Religion was that the country slipped into a religiously charged orgy of violence, but a significant watershed moment was also passed.[113] They also saw France swap the medieval House of Valois for that of Bourbon, and in the process, lay the foundations for the French eclipse of Spain in the decades to come.[114] 'Hindsight tells us that France would replace Spain as the dominant power in Europe', wrote the historian Myron Gutmann, adding that...

> ...even had that been visible after 1598, the continuing domestic difficulties faced by Henry IV and the sheer exhaustion of France after decades of civil war, limited his actions. Surely this conflict was the most important in Europe after 1600, and its settlement in 1659 demonstrated the victory of France.[115]

Henry was faced with a dire strategic situation, as the Habsburgs possessed land to his east along the Rhine, to his north in the Spanish Netherlands, and down south, the Pyrenees guarded the border between the French and Spanish realms. To overcome this disadvantageous situation, Henry would have to ally himself with those smaller powers caught up in Spain's orbit. In addition, the French King would have to always keep one eye on the Holy Roman Empire, to ensure that whatever machinations were concocted by the Austrian Habsburgs, these would not adversely affect his passive aggressive struggle with the Spanish Habsburgs. As he was fighting two branches of the same family, with wealth, power and resources that far outstripped his recovering realm, it was hardly surprising that Henry was drawn to events in the Empire which had left the united duchies of Julich-Cleve-Berg without an heir.

The end destination was far from certain, but to those that lived through these fractious years, it appeared as though Holy Roman Empire was determined to position herself consistently on the edge of a precipice. There was no guarantee that – as she tipped this way or that – the longed-for peace which had arrived in 1555 could hold, just as there was no guarantee that the consequences of any conflict could be kept within the limits of the Holy Roman Empire, or that these consequences would not be hijacked by the other powers, and injected into the other *rivalries* which populated the continent at the time.

FOUR
The French Connection

The Julich-Cleve succession crisis created the latest theatre where all of the continent's elements could stand in opposition to their enemies, and in league with their allies. The French, cooperating with the Dutch, and the Habsburgs, with both branches cooperating together, argued for different candidates to succeed the lucrative but disunited duchies, which stretched across the Dutch border. With the Habsburgs selecting a Catholic candidate, the Franco-Dutch camp selecting a Protestant one, the religious and constitutional tensions endured by German princes within the Holy Roman Empire seemed have been brought out onto the stage of European politics. It was all connected – the antagonism felt by the Dutch and French towards Spain had compelled them to choose a candidate which would not benefit Madrid. Henry IV certainly didn't want to see the Spanish expand their influence and land portfolio in such a sensitive region, and although the Dutch had been in the process of negotiating a truce with the Spanish from 1609, Dutch officials were wholly opposed to the Spanish installing themselves along their southern border for very obvious reasons.

The interconnectedness of these rivalries has led one historian to argue that the Thirty Years War could quite reasonably be framed as beginning in 1609, rather than 1618.[116] While this has not been wholly accepted, since the Julich-Cleve succession crisis resulted in a brief conflict which was quickly contained, another idea did gain acceptance, and frames how we view the Thirty Years War to this day.[117] Among English-speaking scholars and accounts of the Thirty Years War, a western perspective of what transpired between 1618-48, and why it transpired at all, is provided. This perspective links the competing powers and leading figures together in a swirling vortex of violence, military strategy and diplomacy. Different schools of thought exist as to exactly how 'international',[118] 'German',[119] or even 'French',[120] the Thirty Years War was, but as usual with these competing schools of thought, the history is never so black and white, and rests somewhere in between the uncompromising debates.

In the event, the Julich-Cleve crisis didn't merely provide an excuse for the Protestant and Catholic factions to test one another, it also provided the perfect opportunity to persuade hesitant or uncommitted German potentates on either side to join, out of fear of being left in the cold if the crisis did escalate. One figure who was very committed indeed was Maximillian, the Duke of Bavaria. Maximillian of Bavaria (1573-1651) was arguably the most important Duke in the Empire, and he was certainly the most important potentate without an electoral title. Succeeding his father William in 1597, Maximillian would rule Bavaria throughout the Thirty Years War, and would elevate his lands from a mere Duchy to that of an Electorate, largely at the expense of the Elector Palatine, to whom he was distantly related through the Wittelsbach family.

Maximillian was staunchly Catholic and a determined ally of the Habsburgs, and in time, he would tie his fortunes to those of the Emperor Ferdinand II, but at the turn of the century Maximillian was focused on cultivating Bavaria's resources as well as its wealth. This was a task he quickly excelled at. Through 'frugality and firmness', Maximillian of Bavaria would accumulate a small fortune of roughly five million florins by the outbreak of the Thirty Years War, a feat which identified him as a 'formidable figure in European politics'. His political and financial acumen enabled him to wrest still more concessions out of potential allies, such as, most notably of all, the Habsburgs, but he was also in a position quite unlike that of most of his peers on the continent – Maximillian of Bavaria, in the words of Geoffrey Parker, 'had money to put where his mouth was.'[121]

Maximillian had been present to lead the charge to the Imperial Free City of Donauworth, and his occupation of that city in December 1607, followed by the highly unconstitutional annexation of it into Bavaria the following year, illustrated the Duke of Bavaria's lack of scruples when it came to enlarging his domains. His staunch Catholicism had compelled him to take a leading role in the formation and guidance of the Catholic League, yet it was also true that Maximillian's resources were necessary to give this League the power to compete with its Protestant rivals on the Imperial stage.

The advantages Maximillian brought to the table were such that he was able to demand a high price from sympathetic Catholic rulers, and once the Julich-Cleve crisis began in early 1609, those powers who had yet to join, such as the three Rhineland Electors of Mainz, Cologne and Trier, all followed suit. In short, by the end of July 1610, Maximillian had forged, through pressure, persuasion and by the passage of tense developments, a genuine threat to the Protestant Union and a strong platform upon which Catholic policy could stand. His efforts were duly noted by the Catholic King of Spain Philip III, who accepted a position as protector of the Catholic League and sent subsidies to support its further empowering.

Yet the Protestant Union, the rival to the Catholic League, had not been idle while Maximillian so expanded its interests and reach. After they had walked out of the Imperial Diet in April 1608, the disgusted Protestant princes gathered themselves into a defensive league the following month, with the Elector of the Palatinate, the Calvinist Frederick IV as their leader. The Union was composed of Calvinist princes as well as Lutheran cities in the South of Germany, and every other interested or concerned Protestant potentate in between. The Union represented a truce of sorts between Lutherans and Calvinists, who had bitterly opposed one another in the years since 1555, but who collectively, with some exceptions of course, began to value cooperation in the face of the increasing militarisation of the Catholic powers. The 'ultra-Catholic' Ferdinand of Styria, soon to be Emperor Ferdinand II, had presided over the Imperial Diet of 1608, and the Protestants gathered there did not like what they saw.

Their Union soon contained nine princes and seventeen imperial cities, and Frederick IV of the Palatinate was its director, with Christian of Anhalt, a native of the Upper Palatinate, serving as his commander, since it would have been impossible for an Elector to risk his serene person in war. In the event, it seems that the formation of the Protestant Union compelled the Catholics to respond and form their own defensive league, which they did, two years later, but the Protestants would argue fiercely that they had responded to the Catholic aggression and unconstitutional behaviour first, after the Donauworth incident, and that this mess was one of the Duke of Bavaria's making.[122]

This brings our narrative back to the point when, on 25 March 1609, the Duke of Cleves, Julich, Mark and Berg died, leaving these scattered territories without a ruler. These duchies had long been recognised for the wealth and importance; the opportunity to marry into Duke of Cleve's family had compelled Thomas Cromwell to arrange a marriage between Anne of Cleve and Henry VIII. The marriage did not last, and the strategic advantages which Cromwell had anticipated did not materialise, but the episode still says much about how high in the estimations of Europe Cleve's power was believed to be.[123]

As one historian has put it, the late Duke's territories, the duchies of Cleves, Julich, Berg and Mark…

> …were not large but they were densely populated, wealthy, and strategically located astride the Meuse and the Rhine At stake were the borders of the Spanish Netherlands and the United Provinces, a significant stretch of the Rhine, the fate of the developing Counter-Reformation in Cologne and Westphalia, and an important link in the Spanish and Austrian supply lines. The question of succession was a lawyer's dream but a politician's nightmare.[124]

Thanks to marriage and inheritance, Cleves was adjoined to other duchies by 1609 and united under one duke, further increasing its appeal. The Emperor Rudolf II summoned the two claimants to the duchies to solve the quarrel before it escalated, but initially, the succession crisis was not religiously charged. The two claimants, descending through the sisters of the late Duke, were both Lutherans, and thus their rivalry alone would not create friction among the two religious camps or their sponsors. Instead, it was the heavy-handedness of the Emperor, who had sent his cousin Leopold with some troops to the duchies, that inflamed tensions. Leopold had been a cousin of the late Duke, and intended to stake his claim, an occasion which had the potential to cause conflict among not merely the other claimants, but also the rivals of the Habsburgs, who would not have appreciated that dynasty once again expanding at their expense.

It did not seem to have occurred to Emperor Rudolf that a belligerent policy was the last thing his family's image could afford. Not only that, before permitting his cousin Leopold to march on Cleves, the Emperor did not pause to think of the contacts of the two Lutheran claimants. Both claimants could draw on support from the Protestant Union, and the forces of that alliance agreed to attack Habsburg garrisons in the duchies in support of the two claimants, who had both been leapfrogged by the Emperor's boorish behaviour. And the Union was not the only power to begin preparing its forces – the King of France, Henry IV, was also gathering his army in the north-east frontier. The great "what-if" question which has endured ever since is that one which asks – what would have happened to the Thirty Years War if Henry IV had *not* been assassinated while travelling to join his troops on 14 May 1610?[125]

Indeed, Henry's departure at a time when the Catholic League in support of the Emperor, and the Protestant Union in support of the Lutheran candidates were both apparently careening towards conflict seemed to silence that crisis in almost an instant. By September 1610, the duchies would be divided between the two claimants and Habsburg troops would be removed, and that large French army, whatever Henry had planned to use it for, was disbanded. Julich-Cleves did not vanish from the European consciousness; it surfaced again in 1614 when one of the Lutheran claimants converted to Calvinism, and this claimant, who was also the Elector of Brandenburg, occupied the duchy of Julich with Dutch assistance in a fait accompli.

Since the Elector claimant was in receipt of Dutch help, the other Lutheran claimant, the Count Palatine of Neuburg, determined to convert to gain some useful allies also, but he would adopt the Catholic creed. Not only that, the Count of Neuburg also married the sister of Maximillian of Bavaria and seemed in the process to invite a war over the duchies once more. In November 1614 the Treaty of Xanten was signed, which granted

Cleves and the Mark to Brandenburg, with Julich and Berg going to the other, newly Catholic duke. In 1616, matters were complicated again when the Dutch purchased the right off of Brandenburg to defend these lands, which essentially meant the right to occupy them. Through this arrangement, the Dutch would increase the depth of their defences against any Spanish attacks from the Rhine, and the Elector of Brandenburg would be set up to receive regular subsidies and be freed from paying for the defence of these sprawling lands. In such a way were the lands of Electors and Dukes increased and were mutually beneficial arrangements made.[126]

When the Julich-Cleves succession crisis first developed in 1609, King Henry IV had been forced to tread carefully. He had only recently brokered a truce between the Spanish and Dutch, a truce which was to last twelve years, and expire just in time to escalate the conflict in the Holy Roman Empire in 1621. Henry's diplomatic strategy up to 1609 had been to bring about peace and settlement in Europe, and to prepare his country at the same time for any resumption in hostilities which may arise in the future. The French strategy was disarmingly simple – cut the Spanish supply route to its sprawling duchies and dependencies in the Netherlands, along the Rhine and in North Italy. The so-called Spanish Road was the land route which tied these disparate entities to the Spanish crown, and ensured that at a galloping pace, Spanish communiques, reinforcements and supplies could be delivered in what was in this era relatively quick time.

It was impossible for Henry to ignore this route if he wished to undermine the Spanish position – he certainly could not afford to ignore the ten thousand Spanish soldiers in Italy or the fifty thousand in the Spanish Netherlands, not to mention the legions of supplicant German vassals that were kept sweet and cooperative precisely because Spain was capable of reaching out to them. From Milan to Brussels, the Spanish Road remained the lifeline for Madrid's interests, and her government was keen to ensure that it was secured from disruption. Spanish control over Lombardy in North Italy and Lorraine along the Rhine aided this quest for security, as did alliances with the Duke of Savoy and the geographic positioning of the Spanish Netherlands.

France was effectively surrounded and choked until this situation was dealt with, and one of Henry's first acts as King had been to orchestrate a lightning war against the Duke of Savoy in 1600, which enabled France to watch over the Spanish Road and police the critically important passes through the Italian valleys in the name of the Duke of Savoy, even if they could not own and directly administer the land. Henry had achieved such an advantageous deal with Savoy because he had been prepared – Henry had mobilised fifty thousand men and moved them against the Duke's critical bastions in Saluzzo and Bresse before the Duke's Spanish allies could muster themselves in response. In 1601, having acquired the advantages he wanted, Henry established French power in Saluzzo, along the border of Savoy, which enabled him to watch over that Spanish ally as well as keep a vigil on the Spanish Road.[127]

That same year, he accepted Papal arbitration and ended this fantastically successful war. With the opportunity to pounce on the Spanish supply line at the first sniff of war, Henry had done French logistics a great service, and placed Madrid in a serious quandary. Since 1601, Philip III's government was forced to grapple with this dilemma and the threat of France suddenly severing the Spanish Road, but this threat was never realised, even as Spain struggled against the tenacious Dutch foe. By early 1609, the French had helped to mediate a truce, and the pressure on the Spanish Road slackened.

What was Henry's aim in the first decade of the seventeenth century? On the one hand, the strategy of lurking near to the Spanish Road meant that Spain was always wary of the French threat, but on the other, Henry never gained any practical advantages from this strategic triumph. Far from preparing for war, indeed, Henry was mobilising all of France's resources for the sake of peace. A succession of spats between different actors were solved by French mediation; King James I of England and the Papacy had their rift healed; Venice and the Papacy were also made to come to terms, and even the bitter war between the Spanish and Dutch, which will be examined later, was brought to a temporary end.

We could be forgiven for thinking that with this policy of forging peace between his neighbours and settling their disputes, the King of France had decided on a more pacific course. It thus appears somewhat contradictory for Henry to decide in late 1609, after the Dutch-Spanish truce had been signed, to support the Protestant claimants in the Julich-Cleve crisis, even at the cost of war. At the same time, Henry made great efforts to persuade the pope that he was working for the peace of Christendom, while the Habsburgs were clearly interested only in their own political gain. This message went to the other courts of Europe as well. Now, it suddenly seemed as though Henry was preparing for war, and that the King could not make up his mind. On the contrary, France did not want war, but Henry was determined to remain firm on the Cleves question and indicated that he would fight if necessary. Henry was moving carefully. He did not want to push Spain too far. But he had proof that the Spanish were up to no good.

Henry's efforts to secure peace from 1601 can be explained by the exhaustion of his Kingdom, but also by the lobbying on the part of the Papacy to secure a marital alliance between the Habsburgs and France. Anne of Austria was born in 1601, and were she united with the young Louis XIII, then surely Vienna and Paris would come to better terms, with the Spanish Habsburgs following. This initiative found success at first – but then the Pope died, and in the interim the Spaniards seem to drop their approval of the idea, even provoking border disputes and engaging in raids from Lorraine and Flanders into French territory. Henry now had a choice – he could accept the Habsburg intransigence, or he could try to confront and intimidate the Habsburgs by acting aggressively, but with a measure of finesse.

Thus, it is possible to see Henry's intervention in the Julich-Cleve crisis as a means for France to prove its seriousness in seeking satisfaction. Henry would paint the impression that he was willing to start a war with Spain, and that Julich-Cleve was only the beginning. Not only did he build an army and send it to the north-east border, he also created allies, and from these allies more allies like England came knocking once it seemed the King of France meant business. King James agreed to send troops to Cleves-Julich. The pope followed suit and began to put pressure on Spain. Yet Henry kept postponing the departure of his troops. He formally requested permission from the Habsburg Archduke in the Spanish Netherlands to let his troops pass through his lands on the way to Cleves. He even went as far as to set up an elaborate series of public functions in Paris.

Throughout the spring of 1610 Henry dallied, but there is good reason to suppose that this dallying was deliberate. As late as May 1610, before his assassination, it could not be said for sure what Henry's true ends were. There is no proof that Henry wanted to do more in 1610 than stop the recent Spanish pressures, keep the Hapsburgs from the Rhine, and build up a system of alliances – as one French minister wrote on 3 June 1610, shortly after their King's death:

> But if our good master was not dead, he would not have had to bother to cross the Seine; the keys of Julich would have been brought to him. All of Italy would have trembled and begun to rise in his favour.[128]

One historian has noted that with the Habsburgs shifting uncomfortably and giving ground under Papal and diplomatic pressure, France could have acquired its ends peacefully without what may well have been a two-front war. What these ends were is debateable, but if the Julich-Cleve crisis was settled peacefully in the Protestants' favour, then, with France having taught the Hapsburgs a lesson on the Rhine, Henry would have been happy to settle for a marriage alliance with Spain as a means of protection and wait for future developments.[129] Another train of thought stipulates that Henry acted with a different goal in mind – to demonstrate to the minor German princes, now linked together in the Protestant Union, that he was ready to act in their interests. Since the Union had been arranged in 1608, French influence among the recalcitrant anti-Habsburg camp had declined, and this act in the name of German Protestantism could well have sent a clear message.

It is worth noting that where the King of Spain had been accepted as the protector of the Catholic League, King Henry had offered and been politely turned down when he had offered the same arrangement for the Protestant Union. A clear demonstration of his respect for Protestant German constitutionalists would surely reverse this decision, and grant France greater powers to involve itself in Habsburg disputes in the future. If this is what Henry wanted, then he did not say, and while it is not certain precisely what his goal was in stirring up trouble during the Julich-Cleve crisis, it did anticipate the eruption of conflict between France and the Habsburgs in 1635. If his aims were uncertain, then the impact his assassination left on France cannot be understated.

King Henry's death had left a gaping hole in the vitality of French foreign policy. While it is not quite correct to say that the French abruptly became pro-Habsburg, it is true that France entered into a regency which lasted until October 1614, and that French foreign policy was not effectively organised and streamlined until the young King Louis XIII ejected his mother and her meddling friends, and attempted to forge ahead with a policy of his own in 1620.[130] French foreign policy thus turned away from the Holy Roman Empire between 1610-20, but as we mentioned, it would be incorrect to claim that this lack of focus on combating the Habsburgs was a break with policy. On the contrary, there is good reason to suspect that King Henry IV had been orchestrating something of a campaign of peace, and that only the situation in Julich-Cleves moved him to raise an army and march suggestively to the border.[131]

It was in April 1611, less than a year after Henry's assassination, that a marriage agreement was negotiated with Spain. Louis XIII would marry a Spanish princess, and the Spanish prince Philip, later King Philip IV, would marry a French princess. These contracts were agreed in spite of the native protests of the Protestant Huguenots in France, and the anger displayed towards Marie de Medici, the Queen regent, and her foreign favourites. Louis XIII would have to grapple with these problems when he came of age, but between 1610-1614, French foreign policy, while it contracted, did not cease to make an impact upon the continent. By tying France and Spain closer together by marriage, the leaders of these two states were repeating a practice which would provide the two countries with splendid marriages, as well as a war of succession a century later.[132] The removal of Henry blunted the French initiatives enough to ensure that no French invasion of the Rhine would be taking place – the great confrontation between the Habsburgs and Bourbons would be delayed. However, the Spanish were more than occupied by a conflict closer to home, which had exploded out of a revolt in the most prosperous portion of their domains: the Burgundian Netherlands.

FIVE

The Triumphs of Peace

Charles V, Holy Roman Emperor, King of Spain and Grand Duke of Burgundy, was not the only individual to abdicate from his numerous titles in 1555. His sister Mary, the widower of the King of Hungary and the regent of the Burgundian Netherlands region since the early 1500s, had also determined, upon her brother's abdication, to resign her position. She gave the following justification for her decision, anticipating the very difficult relationship which Mary's nephew Philip, King of Spain, was soon to endure with the Burgundian Netherlands. She wrote to her brother Charles that:

> All states under the obedience of a prince should desire above all that he should be most wise and virtuous ... Yet I would say that a person who governs under a prince must be wiser than the prince himself who, governing for himself, has to render account only to God ... But he who governs under another must not only render account to God but also to the prince and to his subjects ... Apart from the consultations all governors have to engage in, here in the Netherlands one has to gain everyone's good will, nobles as well as commons; for this country does not render the obedience which is due to a monarchy, nor to an oligarchic regime, nor even to a republic; and a woman, especially a widow, finds this very difficult to cope with ...; for a woman, whatever her status, is never respected and feared like a man. [If things went wrong in war], one is given the fault; for people hate to have to give from their property, as is necessary in such times ... I could write a volume, listing all the difficulties ... I would not desire to go on governing, even if I were a man ... for, as God is my witness, governing is so abhorrent to me that, sooner than continue with it, I would earn my living.[133]

Succeeding Mary of Hungary was her pious and powerful nephew, Philip II, who was simultaneously King of Spain and master of vast swathes of South and Central American territory. As his uncle Ferdinand advanced the cause of the Habsburg branch in Vienna, Philip persevered in Spain, and in time established a formidable legacy in the pantheon of Habsburg Spanish Kings. During his reign massive overseas expansion would further bolster the prestige and coffers of Madrid, as the Philippines became Spanish and the New World became a hive of Spanish owned gold and silver mines. Such increases in Spanish fortunes are also marked by the so-called 'Black Legend',[134] which surrounded this very Catholic King.[135] Excesses of the Inquisition on the continent and the atrocities committed against the natives in the New World formed the bulk of the accusations against Charles' son, who also had the misfortune to launch a failed armada against England's Queen Elizabeth I in 1588, an act which ensured that a costly war against England would continue for the rest of Philip II's reign.[136] At the same time, the Battle of Lepanto in 1571 was viewed as a major naval victory against the otherwise unassailable powers of the Muslim Turk,[137] who had seemed as insatiable in their quest for land as Hernando Cortes had been in his quest for gold.

Dangerous though Philip II's shortcomings may have been, the greatest and most enduring challenge to the might of Spain began in the most prosperous portion of its Empire – lands once tied together by the marital opportunism of the Dukes of Burgundy, but which branded itself first as a Dutch Revolt and, from 1581, a full blown revolution instigated by the sovereign Dutch Republic of Seven United Provinces. From inauspicious beginnings this revolt would grow, and come under the direction of the House of Orange-Nassau, a traditionally German-rooted noble house with long links of friendship to the Habsburgs.[138] Far from a merely provincial affair, the Dutch would prove as industrious and resourceful at waging war against their former master as they once been in merely supplementing his incomes. Operating on a pre-established naval record which grew up out of the superbly positioned trading hubs of the continent, the Dutch were able to utilise and build upon this expertise and experience to repeatedly frustrate and surprise the Spanish efforts to defeat and reassert their authority over their rebellious Dutch provinces.

'It's setting was distinctive', wrote the historian Herbert H. Rowen, 'the delta formed by the confluence of three rivers, the Rhine, Maas or Meuse, and Scheldt. Here trade and shipping, industry and agriculture all developed in mutual encouragement to the highest level in Northern Europe.'[139] Spain would thus not be fighting a backwater with few traditions of its own; instead it would have to pacify perhaps the most developed portion of the continent. When Philip II ordered the prominent William of Nassau's son captured in 1567, he likely believed that he had impressed upon that once loyal family the importance of their continued service and the dangers of rebellion. Yet, such an act merely spurred William of Nassau, later known as William the Silent, into open rebellion the following year. The Eighty Years War between Spain and its unruly Dutch subjects would not be satisfactorily concluded until early 1648, and by that point the revolt had torn the economic and military might, not to mention the reputation of Spain, completely asunder.[140]

It was the costliest conflict that Madrid engaged in during the period and had an additional distinction of being the longest continuously fought war of the era as well. The Dutch in the North and the Flemish in the South Netherlands had endured their share of grievances, but as was usual during this period, religion sharpened all differences, and these differences had been legion to begin with. There was what one historian has called an 'incompatibility of temperament' between Spanish and Dutch peoples. In his account of the golden age of Spain, historian R. Trevor Davies noted that:

> The Netherlander was everything that the Spaniard was not. The Spaniard was not – and despised – everything that the Netherland was: a trader, a drunkard, a glutton, reputedly indifferent to religion, and, worst of all, essentially a civilian.[141]

From April 1572 to April 1607, and then from April 1621 to May 1648, Spain's incurable Dutch disease consumed the resources and attentions of Philip's kingdom and that of his successors, while the conflict also played a pivotal role in external conflicts throughout its eighty year duration, most importantly for us, during the Thirty Years War.[142]

Yet even before the outbreak of the Thirty Years War, the Dutch Revolt consistently served as a way for the rivals of Spain to strike back at her, sometimes covertly, sometimes out in the open. When war broke out between England and Spain, it was through the Dutch Revolt that Queen Elizabeth invested most of her efforts,[143] just as Philip II sought to undermine the security of England by supporting the Irish rebels in revolt against the English Crown.[144] Yet Philip II's continued intervention in the French Wars of Religion also permitted the Huguenot faction in France, led by the future King Henry IV of France, to ally and aid with the Protestant Dutch as a means to further harm Spain.[145] In addition, the overstretched and overbearing nature of Philip II's designs on his European neighbours compelled both France and England to seek common ground, and work diplomatically against him.[146]

Such outcomes would have seemed unimaginable when Philip II sent his most accomplished general the Duke of Alva northwards to deal with the treacherous Dutch in the early 1570s the Duke of Alva northwards to deal with the treacherous Dutch. The invaluable incomes brought by the Dutch trading cities in Amsterdam, Rotterdam, Antwerp and others were certainly worth fighting for, even had the challenge to Philip II's authority not urgently required an answer. Religious as much as political concerns had moved the Dutch to rebel, yet as a people they had 'always been suspicious of central authority'; a suspicion which Charles V had overcome by treating them gently or appointing conscious regents in his place such as his aunt or sister. Philip II, on the other hand, in the words of Andrew Wheatcroft, 'treated them as he would Spaniards. His approach was invariably harsh.'[147]

The Dutch, unaccustomed to the kind of direct rule planned by Philip, and concerned, rightly as it transpired, that Philip planned to expand the reaches of the Inquisition to extirpate Protestantism from the Dutch lands, determined to raise the standard of revolt.[148]

As a conflict of epic proportions, the Eighty Years War remained in the background of much of Spain's dealings until 1648, and formed a staple concern of its monarch's policies throughout the Thirty Years War, to the point that the French would actually join the Dutch in 1635.[149] As this and other conflicts were waged, Philip II's finances became more strained, and he filed for bankruptcy a total of *four* times during his reign, signifying that chronic financial problems lay deep within his administration, which only became worse as the years progressed.[150] As we have seen in Section 1 of this book, the conflict between Spain and the Dutch also contributed to the development of military theory and strategy, as the necessity of the siege in the concentrated network of fortresses in the region was made clear.[151] As the revolt continued, the Dutch proved as diplomatically active as they were militarily defiant. Treaties of friendship were signed with England (1585), France (1589), the Palatinate (1604) and Brandenburg (1605) – these agreements 'all increased the supply of both men and money to the rebels until the Spanish government was forced to accept that victory in the Low Countries was no longer attainable.'[152]

'God who has given me so many kingdoms has not granted me a son fit to govern them'.[153] This, we are told, was how the ailing Philip II reacted to his son's behaviour. Philip III seemed more interested in galivanting off to his latest pleasure party in this or that duke's house, all the while, all the while neglecting the total control over administration which had made Philip II's reign so formidable. Philip II had been a micromanager, spending hours of the day at his desk arranging and signing off on different reports. He had also been instrumental in shuffling resources and manpower to the different trouble spots of the sprawling Spanish Empire. Philip II had, in short, delayed the decline of Spain which historians would later view as inevitable.

Philip had rejoiced when his son had been born in 1578, but refrained from praising the almighty too much, as many of his children had died in their infancy. Philip III survived though, and although he never enjoyed as strong a constitution as his father, he did outlive the expectations of his father by reaching adolescence and giving his Philip II hope that Spain would be in the hands of a King after all. But Philip was quickly disappointed in his son's progress, or lack thereof. The fair haired and short Philip the younger may have resembled his father in a physical sense, and even retained the famed Habsburg jaw which was to so advertise the family's unfortunate penchant for inbreeding. Yet, short of these physical attributes, and the inbuilt religious convictions, the son was very unlike the father.

He lacked, in the words of R. Trevor Davies, his father's 'energy or dogged tenacity of purpose.'[154] Under no circumstances did the twenty-year-old Philip III plan to confine himself to hours upon hours of lonely study in his office – that was surely what the administrators of the Empire were for. Apparently disinterested in direct governance, Philip III's demeanour fit well with the recent rearrangement of government in the Spanish Netherlands. Now that this region was under the rule of his sister and brother in law – a regime known as the Archdukes after the titles both figures held – Philip III had fewer things to worry about, fewer letters to read and fewer people to see. For his freedom to be complete though, it would be necessary to pawn off his responsibilities in Spain itself, and this intention was suggested only hours after his father's death.

The bags of dispatches were brought into the grieving Philip III, and looking upon them, he laid them down on a sideboard and explained that the Marquis of Denia would look through them in his place. This break with his father's policies had two immediate results; first, it detached Philip III from the day-to-day business of his Empire, and second, it made the aforementioned Marquis of Denia the most important man in Spain. Denia was a charming, tactful man in his fifties by the time his chance came to capitalise upon the influence he had built up over the young Philip. His relationship with Philip III would be a demanding one, but it would also enrich Denia, soon recreated as the Duke of Lerma, beyond his wildest expectations. 'To obtain one's suit', recalled the Venetian ambassador to Spain, 'it is more important to be in favour with the Duke of Lerma than with the king himself...for it truly appears that the king has no other will than that of the Duke.'[155]

The judgement of Lerma normally attempts to balance the ambitious nobleman's chronic overspending and enthusiastic frivolity with the genuine success he enjoyed in foreign affairs. Even while he sent Spain further into the red with lavish parties and celebrations to mark marriages, births or the mere arrival of new ambassadors, Lerma significantly lessened the danger posed by Spain's enemies by arriving at peace with them. He had only arrived on the scene when the peace with France was arranged, and while he made great efforts to damage England further in war, particularly in Ireland,[156] in the end he certainly approved of the initiatives undertaken by the Archdukes to arrive at peace with England. The war with the Dutch, on the other hand, was a thankless, apparently endless conflict which would not be so straightforwardly solved.

It is one the curiosities of history that the Eighty Years War should have lasted as long as it did. It is easy to take for granted now the existence of the Dutch Republic, and to view the Spanish hold over what was then cast as the Duchy of Burgundy as somewhat nonsensical. Of course, we imagine, the Dutch were bound to break free, and to successfully remain free from their

Spanish overlords. Yet, to view the Dutch revolt against the Spanish Crown as such an inevitable success undermines the very characteristics which made that conflict so unique in early modern European history. Consider, for example, the fact that the Dutch rebels rose up against the most formidable power in the world in the mid-sixteenth century, and that their people opposed the supremacy of Spain's most formidable King in Philip II. In the years that followed, there was no guarantee that Spanish might and money would not reclaim the lands which had been lost. On the contrary, it was only once the Dutch managed to take the fight to Spain in the 1580s that concerted support from allies in France and England poured into the country, which made the conflict a European war, rather than merely a Spanish civil issue.

And even with the support of foreign powers, Philip II's determination and singleness of purpose to crush the Dutch and bring them to heel never wavered, except perhaps in the final months of his life when he sought to completely recast Spain's relationship with the Netherlands by appointing the Archdukes. It was because Spain was pulled in so many directions that crushing the Dutch never became feasible; wars with the Turk in the Mediterranean, with the French during their Wars of Religion, against the English and in North Italy all strained the resources of the Spanish Crown, and this was before Philip II had died.[157]

In September 1598, Philip III inherited a Dutch war which had long since ceased to bring returns. The people in the Spanish Netherlands were battered, broke and greatly demoralised, even if their loyalty to Madrid did not falter at the turn of the century, when it seemed that Spain had less to give them than before. The South Netherlandish people, writes Pieter Geyl:

> Were no more than the representatives of a defeated people, impoverished and exhausted. Twice had the South risked a revolt, both times it had been struck down. It had lost its economic prosperity, and its bravest and most enterprising men, who were now steeling the strength of the North. It is not to be wondered at that the idea of a new revolt could not inspire the Brussels States. The spring had been broken. Besides, their impotence was not merely moral, it was physical.

Geyl goes on to cite a contemporary Dutch historian, who wrote in 1614 that:

> The States of Brabant, Flanders etc., mastered by castles and garrisons, had no other means for promoting the peace than their humble remonstrances, setting out how needful peace was to them, wretchedly lamenting about the war and the unpaid soldiery.[158]

Philip III was as eager to see the war continue against the Dutch as his father had been, as much for the sake of his Crown's reputation as because it was what Philip II had done.[159] But Spain was simply drowning in problems, even while the Duke of Lerma maintained a façade of splendour and expense. Not even the coinage of Spain made sense anymore,[160] and a declaration of bankruptcy would surely not be far in coming – Philip II had made *four* such declarations during his reign after all, so what chance did his wayward son have?[161]

An effort to bring the fight to the Dutch amidst their isolation following the peace with France in 1598 delivered the fortress town of Ostend to Spain six years later, thanks largely to the herculean efforts of a new soldier of fortune, Ambrogio Spinola. Spinola was a Genoese nobleman of extraordinary talent and perception, and Philip III at least recognised the value of the man in his service in time to completely undercut the authority of the Archdukes, Philip III's sister and brother in law, who were simply told that Spinola was to have full control over the war effort with the Dutch, and would even succeed to the position of Governor of the Spanish Netherlands in the event that Archduke Albert died. As Pieter Geyl remarked, 'the childless Archdukes were overshadowed by the brilliant stranger who enjoyed the confidence of Spain. Hardly the semblance of independence was left.'[162]

Impressive as Spinola's feats were, they could not achieve miracles. The tit for tat exchange of victories and defeats continued before and after Spinola's appointment. On 2 July 1600, the Battle of Nieuwpoort saw the Dutch army led by Maurice of Nassau defeat its Spanish counterparts, who were led by the Archduke Albert, and although the Dutch didn't achieve their major objectives in the course of that campaign, Maurice's military acumen was undeniable.[163] 'My intent', claimed Philip III, 'is to make myself Lord of the Sea', but the Dutch had other ideas, and correctly perceived the damage which would be done to Spanish interests if their naval interests were undermined.[164]

On several occasions Dutch privateers operated at immense cost to Spain, and when some of these operations achieved stunning successes – such as in 1603 when a Portuguese carrack was captured and its contents sold in auction, to the delight and surprise of the Dutch at home,[165] or in 1607 when a Dutch fleet destroyed 20 Spanish galleons off Gibraltar, or even later on in our story in 1629, when the Spanish silver fleet was captured, and the Dutch used the *fifteen million florins* captured in that exchange to fund a massive expansion in their armies – the Spanish were left reeling, and without an answer.[166]

By the turn of the century the war between Spain and the Dutch had been on-going for more than thirty-five years, and contemporaries could be forgiven for thinking that it would not end in their lifetimes. The intractable differences between both sides can be boiled down to the galling fact, to those statesmen in The Hague, that Madrid still refused to countenance Dutch independence, and still refused to recognise Dutch sovereignty over the Northern portion of the Netherlands which they governed. Until this impasse was breached, there was no chance of a peace being arrived at, let alone for normal relations between the two entities to flourish. The military stalemate and exhausting back and forth between the Spanish and Dutch in the first decade of the seventeenth century did give both sides pause for thought though. Spinola wanted peace, interestingly enough, in order to get back the large sums of money he had advanced to Spain during the course of his command. The Dutch wanted peace because over the course of nine summer campaigns, a few towns had been gained and lost, and all that they had to show for it was a depleted treasury.[167]

That the task of reconquest in the Netherlands was impossible for Spain had been realised even as early as the 1570s had been realised even as early as the 1570s, when Philip II's star was on the ascendant and his power seemed omnipresent. Even in this state of supremacy, Spain was not able to reconquer the territory captured by the Dutch rebels. 'There would not be time or money enough in the world to reduce by force the twenty-four towns which have rebelled in Holland, if we are to spend as long in reducing each one of them as we have taken over similar ones so far', wrote the Spanish commander-in-chief, in October 1574. 'No treasury in the world would be equal to the cost of this war.' Geoffrey Parker summarised the problems with the early phases of the Eighty Years War – problems which the problem with the early phases of the Eighty Years War concisely – problems which remained at the forefront of the Spanish dilemma for the duration of the conflict. He noted:

> The total cost of the Spanish army in the Netherlands between 1572 and 1576, a force of over eighty thousand men at times (at least on paper), was estimated at 1.2 million florins every month. Spain simply could not provide such a sum... [and] while the Spanish field army was occupied in the sieges [of Dutch towns], the 'rebels' were free to attack and capture other strongholds in other areas. Moreover, this siege warfare, with the winter months spent in frozen trenches three years running, was unpleasant for the troops; and the unpleasantness was exacerbated by the inability of the government to pay its soldiers for their heroic service. Inevitably it produced discontent in the Spanish army and both desertion and disobedience grew to alarming proportions.[168]

It should not come as too much of a surprise to note that from the 1570s, the costs of maintaining an army only increased, even as the Dutch improved their own defensive measures, grew more industrious with their assaults against Spanish interests, and developed their armed forces to respond to Spanish threats. Even while the Spanish recaptured a great deal of the South Netherland towns, including the predominantly Protestant Antwerp over 1584-85, the campaigns were more like a plodding, debilitating slog than a triumphant, lightning campaign. Even as Philip II engaged in these battles, he also was at war with England and France until 1598, which meant that fighting and beating the Dutch was even harder than it would otherwise have been.

Supplies and resources earmarked for Flanders would often be diverted to Italy, the Pyrenees or the Rhine, and with the defeat of the Armada in 1588, Spanish naval prowess required rebuilding just at the point when Madrid could least afford such a project. With enemies all over the continent, it was hardly surprising that the once steady pace of Netherlands reconquest took a back seat to the more immediate opportunities in the French Wars of Religion, or the more present threats from English piracy. Shorn of funds and attention, the Spanish initiative in the Netherlands receded into a stalemate, bookended by the unhappy and frequent circumstances of underpaid and demoralised Spanish soldiers in Flanders agitating and chafing from lack of pay, which eroded discipline and military initiative still further in the region.[169]

The lack of a definite victory in Flanders continued despite the fact that Spain was expending a small fortune paying the army there. Between 1580-84 over 17 million florins were sent to the Spanish Netherlands; between 1585-89 almost 53 million; between 1590-94 nearly 61 million and between 1595-99 nearly 79 million.[170] Time and again other concerns subordinated the Netherlands theatre, and successive strategies effectively kicked the Dutch can down the road.[171] The legacies of the past and of Spain's costly commitments contributed to the uninspiring condition of the Spanish Netherlands at the turn of the century. Bankruptcy, mutiny, distraction and other wars had pulled Spain in too many directions to count, and the Dutch had tenaciously ensured that this would be the case, maintaining an active diplomatic relationship with the French, English and even the Ottoman Turks in order to depress the Spanish efforts against them, and dilute Spanish solvency in the process.[172]

Even with Ambrogio Spinola's initiative in taking Ostend or with Maurice of Nassau's efforts to resume the Dutch reconquest of Flanders, the writing was on the wall. Neither side could defeat the other, neither side could continue, and neither side remembered the beginning of the conflict – it had always been a staple fact of European relations, so long had the struggle been in play. The Dutch revolt had always been a convenient means through which Spain's rivals could damage its integrity – indeed, even while Henry IV of France had made his peace in 1598, he continued to support and supply the Dutch against the Habsburgs.[173]

If there was to be any respite, it would have to be arrived at through diplomacy, rather than following a shattering victory on land or sea, which could not be achieved. The pertinent questions were as follows; did the Spanish value their stability and prosperity more than they valued their declared right to rule the Dutch? Would they sacrifice their semblance of authority over the Dutch for the sake of a healthy balance sheet, or at least, a *healthier* balance sheet? Would they lose face internationally in order to gain domestically? By 1607, it was apparent that these questions could not be ignored any longer.

While the ground had been laid by officials hailing from Brabant and Flanders, the actual peace negotiations were clearly in the hands of Madrid. While Philip III's government had authorised a measure of independent action, the negotiation of a truce with the Dutch, and all that implied, was too important an activity to be left in the hands of the Spanish Netherlanders, let alone the Archdukes, was too significant an activity to leave in dreary possession of the Spanish Netherlanders, and certainly not the Archdukes. Ambrogio Spinola would be appointed plenipotentiary and was granted the authority to speak for Madrid and the Archdukes – Philip III had undermined his sister once more, but there was nothing she could do about it. The terms of the peace were already known, insofar as it was known what the Dutch wanted, and what the Spanish would reasonably be expected to give.

Dutch sovereignty was recognised here, rather than at the Peace of Westphalia forty years later as is sometimes erroneously claimed.[174] Yet sovereignty was not the only issue at stake. Extensive trading rights in the Indies were up for grabs, and the Dutch refused to countenance any peace arrangement which would neglect their rights in that theatre. Differences within the Dutch provinces shone several unflattering lights upon the disagreements inherent within Dutch society. There was a war party, led by Maurice of Orange, and a peace party, led by Johan van Oldenbarnvelt, a veteran Dutch statesman of the old school, who was in his sixties at this point when his political career was reaching its peak. Yet even through these two camps there were ideological differences. Some wished to proselytise to the south Netherlanders, and to convert them to Protestantism, others saw the conflict with Spain in uncompromising terms. The Union of Utrecht, declared in 1580, had included *all* of the Netherlands north and south, and by extension, a peace with Spain recognised the Spanish hold on half of the territory which the Dutch had once proclaimed to be free – did this represent a defeat of the revolution?

Just as it was not possible for the Spanish to reconquer the North, so too was it impossible, at least at this juncture, for the Dutch to move seamlessly into union with the Spanish Netherlands. While the region had been battered and sucked dry over the years, the core loyalty to the Spanish Crown was immovable unless the Dutch managed to seriously up the ante in military matters. The region was as dense in population and therefore in towns as the north, if not more so, since agriculture flourished in the Dutch Netherlands. Flanders was better equipped for defence, and the largely Catholic population of Brabant and the Walloon regions could not take the religious toleration of the Protestant Dutch for granted, in exchange for freedom from Spain. The Spanish had in fact sought to acquire guarantees from the Dutch that freedom of worship for Catholics would be allowed in their seven provinces, but the Dutch had said that internal matters were none of their business.

Quarrels between the peace and war party, between the religiously motivated and the realistic, dragged on over 1608, and for many, including Maurice of Orange, it became difficult to imagine what a peaceable Dutch Republic would actually look like. Maurice, as stadtholder and thus military leader of five of the seven provinces, was highly sensitive to the idea that once the conflict had ended and the threat from Spain had receded, the Dutch people wouldn't need him to defend their lands any longer, and thus his influence would be lost and gobbled up by the civilian Oldenbarnvelt. The conflict between Maurice and Oldenbarnvelt would reach its culmination just at the wrong time in European developments, but for now, the matter was greatly aided by the pressure of the English and French, who both played roles in inducing both sides back to the negotiating table.

The idea of a rest and an end to fighting had already found firm adherents in the key Dutch towns of Amsterdam, Utrecht and Rotterdam, and with the province of Zealand following that of Holland, the smaller provinces were then led to agree also. By the end of 1608, Maurice of Nassau was no longer asking for a continuation of the war – he had sensed which way the mood of the people was blowing, and rather than sacrifice his own popularity by going against the grain, he determined to risk the uncertain by agreeing to a peace with a power which he had only ever known as a foe. With the country therefore united behind peace, the diplomats under French service sought to further the negotiations, and by April 1609, the war between the Dutch and Spanish was over...for now.

On every level, the unlikely triumph of the Dutch was an astonishing feat. Regardless of the circumstances, of the distractions endured by Spain or her difficulties in meeting so many enemies at once, this small corner of the continent had managed to resist and then beat back and then actively wound Madrid for long enough that the proud Spanish Empire was forced to make peace. It was indeed more pressing for Spain, rather than the Dutch, that peace be signed, and this was tacitly acknowledged by the fact that the Archdukes were permitted to give into every Dutch demand. Protection for Catholic subjects in the Dutch Republic? Ignored. Dutch access to the Indies trade network? Technically permitted. Recognition of Dutch sovereignty? Granted. To the south Netherlanders, in Pieter Geyl's words, 'the treaty gave nothing but twelve years of rest. How much more did it give to the Northern provinces!'[175] Indeed, the decade of peace-making had been surprisingly successful for Spain, but the scourge of war had by no means been exorcised from the continent. Within and without of the Spanish domains, and in the lands of its Austrian Habsburg cousins, grave signals testified to the possibility that war would return, with a vengeance more terrible than anything anyone had ever seen before.

Chapter 5 Notes

[1] Quoted in Wilson, *Sourcebook*, p. 16.

[2] Quoted in Parker eds., *Thirty Years War*, p. 11.

[3] Quoted in *Ibid*, p. 12.

[4] John Tate Lanning, 'Cortes and His First Official Remission of Treasure to Charles V', *Revista de Historia de América*, No. 2 (Jun., 1938), pp. 5-29; p. 6.

[5] John Tate Lanning, 'Cortes and His First Official Remission of Treasure to Charles V', p. 14, valued the haul at over $5 million, but that was in 1938. Modern currency evaluation is not perfect, but the value can be calculated by taking the economic power of $1 in 1938 and acquiring its modern equivalent, which stands at roughly $212 today; see https://www.measuringworth.com/uscompare/relativevalue.php

[6] Cited in John Tate Lanning, 'Cortes', pp. 14-15.

[7] *Ibid*, p. 15.

[8] Cited in *Ibid*, pp. 15-16.

[9] *Ibid*, p. 16.

[10] See Rolf Strøm-Olsen, 'Dynastic Ritual and Politics in Early Modern Burgundy: The Baptism of Charles V', *Past & Present*, No. 175 (May, 2002), pp. 34-64.

[11] Andrew Wheatcroft, *The Habsburgs: Embodying Empire* (London; Penguin Books, 1996), p. 119.

[12] Cited in *Ibid*, pp. 117-118.

[13] *Ibid*, pp. 116-118. This rift was set to continue and to dominate the affairs of the Holy Roman Empire; see Gottfried G. Krodel, 'Law, Order, and the Almighty Taler: The Empire in Action at the 1530 Diet of Augsburg', *The Sixteenth Century Journal*, Vol. 13, No. 2 (Summer, 1982), pp. 75-106.

[14] Cited in Andrew Wheatcroft, *The Habsburgs*, p. 127.

[15] See *Ibid*, pp. 123-125.

[16] For an overview of Charles the Bold's Burgundian domains see Laetitia Boehm, 'Burgundy and the Empire in the Reign of Charles the Bold', *The International History Review*, Vol. 1, No. 2 (Apr., 1979), pp. 153-162.

[17] Andrew Wheatcroft, *The Habsburgs*, pp. 85-87.

[18] H. G. Koenigsberger, 'Prince and States General: Charles V and the Netherlands (1506-1555): The Prothero Lecture', *Transactions of the Royal Historical Society*, Vol. 4 (1994), pp. 127-151; referenced in this case is p. 129.

[19] Pieter Geyl, *A History of the Dutch-Speaking Peoples 1555-1648* (London; Phoenix Press, 2001), pp. 35-99;

[20] A recent study has disputed the nature of Joanna's madness, see Bethany Aram, 'Juana "the Mad's" Signature: The Problem of Invoking Royal Authority, 1505- 1507', *The Sixteenth Century Journal*, Vol. 29, No. 2 (Summer, 1998), pp. 331-358; see also Salvatore Poeta, 'The Hispanic and Luso-Brazilian World: From Mad Queen to Martyred Saint: The Case of Juana La Loca Revisited in History and Art on the Occasion of the 450th Anniversary of Her Death', *Hispania*, Vol. 90, No. 1 (Mar., 2007), pp. 165-172.

[21] See Paula Sutter Fichtner, 'Dynastic Marriage in Sixteenth-Century Habsburg Diplomacy and Statecraft: An Interdisciplinary Approach', *The American Historical Review*, Vol. 81, No. 2 (Apr., 1976), pp. 243-265.

[22] Andrew Wheatcroft, *The Habsburgs*, pp. 88-90.

[23] A great snippet of correspondence from Charles' agents in the New World, more precisely Mexico City, can be found in Arthur P. Stabler and John E. Kicza, 'Ruy González's 1553 Letter to Emperor Charles V: An Annotated Translation', *The Americas*, Vol. 42, No. 4 (Apr., 1986), pp. 473-487.

[24] Andrew Wheatcroft, *The Habsburgs*, p. 91.

[25] See Daniel R. Doyle, 'The Sinews of Habsburg Governance in the Sixteenth Century: Mary of Hungary and Political Patronage', *The Sixteenth Century Journal*, Vol. 31, No. 2 (Summer, 2000), pp. 349-360.

[26] Charles V's religious attentions were also focused on Spain; see Aurelio Espinosa, 'The Spanish Reformation: Institutional Reform, Taxation, and the Secularization of Ecclesiastical Properties under Charles V', *The Sixteenth Century Journal*, Vol. 37, No. 1 (Spring, 2006), pp. 3-24.

[27] Hayward Keniston, 'Peace Negotiations between Charles V and Francis I (1537-1538)', *Proceedings of the American Philosophical Society*, Vol. 102, No. 2 (Apr. 30, 1958), pp. 142-147.

[28] For a great account of Venice, Habsburg progress in Italy and the French opposition see Robert Finlay, 'Fabius Maximus in Venice: Doge Andrea Gritti, the War of Cambrai, and the Rise of Habsburg Hegemony, 1509-1530', *Renaissance Quarterly*, Vol. 53, No. 4 (Winter, 2000), pp. 988-1031.

[29]An analysis of the Augsburg Confession which emerged from these sets of agreements and debates is found in Robert Kolb, 'Augsburg 1530: German Lutheran Interpretations of the Diet of Augsburg to 1577', *The Sixteenth Century Journal*, Vol. 11, No. 3, 450th Anniversary Augsburg Confession (Jun. 25, 1980), pp. 47-61; Robert Kress, 'The Roman Catholic Reception of the Augsburg Confession', *The Sixteenth Century Journal*, Vol. 11, No. 3, 450th Anniversary Augsburg Confession (Jun. 25, 1980), pp. 115-128. Foreign reaction in Scandinavia is also worth noting, see Trygve R. Skarsten, 'The Reception of the Augsburg Confession in Scandinavia', *The Sixteenth Century Journal*, Vol. 11, No. 3, 450th Anniversary Augsburg Confession (Jun. 25, 1980), pp. 86-98. A relatively recent study examines the Augsburg Confession's influence in South-East Europe; see David P. Daniel, 'The Influence of the Augsburg Confession in South-East Central Europe', *The Sixteenth Century Journal*, Vol. 11, No. 3, 450th Anniversary Augsburg Confession (Jun. 25, 1980), pp. 99-114.

[30]Peter H. Wilson, *The Holy Roman Empire: A Thousand Years of Europe's History* (London; Penguin Books, 2017), pp. 110-115.

[31]For the background to such an agreement taking shape see Nathan Baruch Rein, 'Faith and Empire: Conflicting Visions of Religion in a Late Reformation Controversy: The Augsburg "Interim" and Its Opponents, 1548-50', *Journal of the American Academy of Religion*, Vol. 71, No. 1 (Mar., 2003), pp. 45-74.

[32]Hywel Williams, *The Emperor of the West: Charlemagne and the Carolingian Empire* (Quercus, London; 2010), see 'Introduction'.

[33]See Henry Mayr-Harting, 'Charlemagne, the Saxons, and the Imperial Coronation of 800', *The English Historical Review*, Vol. 111, No. 444 (Nov., 1996), pp. 1113-1133.

[34]His achievements were political as well as military, see: François L. Ganshof, 'The Impact of Charlemagne on the Institutions of the Frankish Realm', *Speculum*, Vol. 40, No. 1 (Jan., 1965), pp. 47-62.

[35]Hywel Williams, *Emperor*, pp. 140-141.

[36]See Matthew Innes, 'Charlemagne's Will: Piety, Politics and the Imperial Succession', *The English Historical Review*, Vol. 112, No. 448 (Sep., 1997), pp. 833-855.

[37]See in particular Richard E. Sullivan, 'The Carolingian Age: Reflections on Its Place in the History of the Middle Ages', *Speculum*, Vol. 64, No. 2 (Apr., 1989), pp. 267-306.

[38]Peter H. Wilson, *Europe's Tragedy*, p. 41.

[39]*Ibid*, p. 41.

[40]See Peter H. Wilson, *Holy Roman Empire*, p. 116.

[41]Cited in Peter H. Wilson, *Sourcebook*, p. 8.

[42]Peter H. Wilson, *Holy Roman Empire*, p. 115.

[43]Brennan C. Pursell, *The Winter King: Frederick V of the Palatinate and the Coming of the Thirty Years War* (Burlington VT; Ashgate Publishing Company, 2003), p. 14.

[44]Peter H. Wilson, *Europe's Tragedy*, pp. 41-42.

[45]Pursell, *The Winter King*, pp. 14-15.

[46]Parker, ed., *Thirty Years War*, pp. 18-19.

[47]Pursell, *The Winter King*, p. 15.

[48]Bodo Nischan, 'Calvinism, the Thirty Years' War, and the Beginning of Absolutism in Brandenburg: The Political Thought of John Bergius', *Central European History*, Vol. 15, No. 3 (Sept, 1982), pp. 203-223.

[49]See Peter H. Wilson, *Europe's Tragedy*, pp. 197-199.

[50]An extensive study on the French Wars of Religion is provided by Kathleen A. Parrow, 'From Defense to Resistance: Justification of Violence during the French Wars of Religion', *Transactions of the American Philosophical Society*, Vol. 83, No. 6 (1993), pp. 1-79. See also James B. Wood, 'The Impact of the Wars of Religion: A View of France in 1581', *The Sixteenth Century Journal*, Vol. 15, No. 2 (Summer, 1984), pp. 131-168. A more focused case study on a specific family's experience during this era can be found in Edwin Bezzina, 'Caught between King, Religion, and Social Ambition: Marc-Antoine Marreau De Boisguérin and His Family (ca. 1560-1680)', *The Sixteenth Century Journal*, Vol. 39, No. 2 (Summer, 2008), pp. 331-356.

[51]See Dom Basil Hemphill, 'The Monastic Life of the Emperor Charles V', *Studies: An Irish Quarterly Review*, Vol. 37, No. 146 (Jun., 1948), pp. 140-148.

[52]Lewis W. Spitz, 'Particularism and Peace Augsburg: 1555', *Church History*, Vol. 25, No. 2 (Jun., 1956), pp. 110-126.

[53]Geoffrey Parker, ed., *The Thirty Years War* 2nd Edition (London; Routledge, 1997), p. 17.

[54]Geoffrey Parker, ed., *Thirty Years War*, p. 5.

[55]Cited in *Ibid*, p. 5.

[56]Cited in *Ibid*, p. 5.

[57]*Ibid*, p. 6.

[58]*bid*, p. 7.

[59]Geoffrey Parker, *Europe in Crisis*, pp. 51-52.

[60]An early history of the Society of Jesus can be found in Guenter Lewy, 'The Struggle for Constitutional Government in the Early Years of the Society of Jesus', *Church History*, Vol. 29, No. 2 (Jun., 1960), pp. 141-160. For some context of their Italian history see Christopher Carlsmith, 'Struggling toward Success: Jesuit Education in Italy, 1540-1600', *History of Education Quarterly*, Vol. 42, No. 2 (Summer, 2002), pp. 215-246. The Jesuits were also active in Ireland in the early seventeenth century, see Stephen Hand, 'David Rothe, the Jesuits and the Counter-Reformation in Ireland, 1600–40', *Studies: An Irish Quarterly Review*, Vol. 103, No. 412, THE JESUITS IN IRELAND: Before and After the Suppression (Winter 2014/15), pp. 393-401.

[61]Geoffrey Parker, *Europe in Crisis*, pp. 52-53.

[62]Geoffrey Parker, ed., *Thirty Years War*, p. 17. See also Peter H. Wilson, 'Dynasty, Constitution, and Confession: The Role of Religion in the Thirty Years War', *The International History Review*, Vol. 30, No. 3 (Sept., 2008), pp. 473-514; especially pp. 507-508.

[63]The most exhaustive account of the Holy Roman Empire and its related institutions is the recent work by Peter H. Wilson, *Holy Roman Empire*.

[64]Brennan C. Pursell, *The Winter King*, p. 12.

[65]Peter H. Wilson, *The Holy Roman Empire*, p. 2.

[66]See Jürgen Overhoff, 'Benjamin Franklin, Student of the Holy Roman Empire: His Summer Journey to Germany in 1766 and His Interest in the Empire's Federal Constitution', *German Studies Review*, Vol. 34, No. 2 (May 2011), pp. 277-286; referenced in this case is p. 284.

[67]A good introduction to the Empire's Supreme Court can be found in Ralf-Peter Fuchs, 'The Supreme Court of the Holy Roman Empire: The State of Research and the Outlook', *The Sixteenth Century Journal*, Vol. 34, No. 1 (Spring, 2003), pp. 9-27.

[68]Tim Blanning, *Frederick the Great, King of Prussia* (London; Penguin, 2016), p. 7.

[69]It also helped when the Emperor managed to marry his children off to potential allies, as had happened between the Austrian Habsburgs and the Duke of Bavaria, when Archduke Charles of the Habsburgs married Maria of Bavaria in 1571, thus linking the Duchy of Bavaria with the Habsburg House for better or worse, and underlining the sense of loyalty which Maximillian of Bavaria, Maria's nephew, felt towards the Habsburg dynasty. See Robert Lindell, 'The Wedding of Archduke Charles and Maria of Bavaria in 1571', *Early Music*, Vol. 18, No. 2 (May, 1990), pp. 253-269.

[70]Some historians have taken isolated cases from the historiography of the Holy Roman Empire in an attempt to give them greater attention in their own studies. The sheer scope of literature and information available on the Empire makes such studies possible, while speaking to the extensive depth of that polity, and how much it is possible to learn from it. See Armgard von Reden-Dohna, 'Problems of Small Estates of the Empire: The Example of the Swabian Imperial Prelates', *The Journal of Modern History*, Vol. 58, Supplement: Politics and Society in the Holy Roman Empire, 1500-1806 (Dec., 1986), pp. S76-S87.

[71]Tim Neu, 'Rhetoric and Representation: Reassessing Territorial Diets in Early Modern Germany', *Central European History*, Vol. 43, No. 1 (MARCH 2010), pp. 1-24; referenced in this case is pp. 2-3.

[72]See Parker, ed., *Thirty Years War*, p. 16.

[73]Tim Neu, 'Rhetoric and Representation', pp. 3-4.

[74]*Ibid*, pp. 4-6.

[75]Wilson, *Holy Roman Empire*, p. 240.

[76]*Ibid*, p. 411.

[77]*Ibid*, p. 243.

[78]Brandenburg-Prussia's lands were among the most desolate and underdeveloped, so the value placed on the estates would have been especially high. See Christopher Clark, *Iron Kingdom*, pp. 1-3.

[79]This whole process is clarified in Peter H. Wilson, *Holy Roman Empire*, p. 413.

[80]Wilson, *Holy Roman Empire*, p. 411.

[81]Pursell, *The Winter King*, p. 13.

[82]It is possible to see the Holy Roman Empire as drifting [or progressing] over the centuries from a feudal to a federal entity, with the latter transformation gradually bringing about a weakening in the power and authority of the Emperor. See Heinz H. F. Eulau, 'Theories of Federalism under the Holy Roman Empire', *The American Political Science Review*, Vol. 35, No. 4 (Aug., 1941), pp. 643-664.

[83]A good study on the activities of the knights of the Empire after 1648 is found in Thomas J. Glas-Hochstettler, 'The Imperial Knights in Post-Westphalian Mainz: A Case Study of Corporatism in the Old Reich', *Central European History*, Vol. 11, No. 2 (Jun., 1978), pp. 131-149.

[84]Tim Blanning, *Frederick the Great*, p. 21.

[85]For an account on the durability of the Empire's decision-making processes in times of great conflict and strife see Winfried Schulze, 'Majority Decision in the Imperial Diets of the Sixteenth and Seventeenth Centuries', *The Journal of Modern History*, Vol. 58, Supplement: Politics and Society in the Holy Roman Empire, 1500-1806 (Dec., 1986), pp. S46-S63.

[86]A specialised two-part study of the impact of the Reformation on the Imperial Free Cities of the Empire helps to place these growing divisions into context. See Hans Baron, 'Religion and Politics in the German Imperial Cities during the Reformation', *The English Historical Review*, Vol. 52, No. 207 (Jul., 1937), pp. 405-427; 'Religion and Politics in the German Imperial Cities during the Reformation (Continued)', *The English Historical Review*, Vol. 52, No. 208 (Oct., 1937), pp. 614-633.

[87]Brennan C. Pursell, *The Winter King*, pp. 13-15 gives one of the most concise accounts of the Empire, its processes and the challenges which faced it over the years.

[88]Geoffrey Parker, ed., *Thirty Years War*, p. 14.

[89]*Ibid*, pp. 14-16.

[90]An iconic two-volume account of Britain's descent into civil war is given by C.V. Wedgewood, *The King's Peace* (London; Collins-Fontana, 1966); *The King's War* (London; Collins-Fontana, 1966).

[91]A good account of the siege with a useful perspective of the growing Lutheran population within the Empire is given in Stephen A. Fischer-Galati, 'Ottoman Imperialism and the Lutheran Struggle for Recognition in Germany, 1520-1529', *Church History*, Vol. 23, No. 1 (Mar., 1954), pp. 46-67.

[92]Geoffrey Parker, ed., *Thirty Years War*, pp. 7-8.

[93]Donauworth and the religious-political background to the crisis is examined in C. Scott Dixon, 'Urban Order and Religious Coexistence in the German Imperial City: Augsburg and Donauwörth, 1548-1608', *Central European History*, Vol. 40, No. 1 (Mar., 2007), pp. 1-33.

[94]See Peter H. Wilson, *Sourcebook*, pp. 10-11.

[95]See Brennan C. Pursell, *The Winter King*, p. 25.

[96]Geoffrey Parker, *Europe in Crisis*, pp. 84-85.

[97]Peter H. Wilson, *Europe's Tragedy*, p. 223.

[98]Geoffrey Parker, *Europe in Crisis*, p. 84.

[99]Peter H. Wilson, 'The Causes of the Thirty Years War 1618-48', *The English Historical Review*, Vol. 123, No. 502 (Jun., 2008), pp. 554-586; especially pp. 507-508.

[100]Myron P. Gutmann, 'The Origins of the Thirty Years' War', *The Journal of Interdisciplinary History*, Vol. 18, No. 4, The Origin and Prevention of Major Wars (Spring, 1988), pp. 749-770; referenced in this case is p. 762.

[101]Cited in Peter H. Wilson, *Sourcebook*, p. 13.

[102]Cited in *Ibid*, pp. 16-17.

[103]J.H. Elliott, 'War and Peace in Europe 1618-1648', in Klaus Bussmann and Heinz Schilling, eds., *1648: War and Peace*, vol. 1 (Munich, 1999), pp. 23-39; see especially p. 23.

[104]Peter H. Wilson, 'The Causes of the Thirty Years War', p. 558.

[105]Geoffrey Parker, ed., *Thirty Years War*, pp. 23-24.

[106]J Michael Hayden, 'Continuity in the France of Henry IV and Louis XIII: French Foreign Policy, 1598-1615', *The Journal of Modern History*, Vol. 45, No. 1 (Mar., 1973), pp. 1-23; p. 4.

[107]D. L. Potter, 'Foreign Policy in the Age of the Reformation: French Involvement in the Schmalkaldic War, 1544-1547', *The Historical Journal*, Vol. 20, No. 3 (Sept., 1977), pp. 525-544.

[108]The background to the Edict of Nantes is examined by Gregory Champeaud, 'The Edict of Poitiers and the Treaty of Nerac, or Two Steps towards the Edict of Nantes', *The Sixteenth Century Journal*, Vol. 32, No. 2 (Summer, 2001), pp. 319-334. The aftermath of the Edict is examined in Katharine J. Lualdi, 'Persevering in the Faith: Catholic Worship and Communal Identity in the Wake of the Edict of Nantes', *The Sixteenth Century Journal*, Vol. 35, No. 3 (Fall, 2004), pp. 717-734.

[109]For an example of these divisions see Barbara Diefendorf, 'Prologue to a Massacre: Popular Unrest in Paris, 1557-1572', *The American Historical Review*, Vol. 90, No. 5 (Dec., 1985), pp. 1067-1091.

[110]Charles Howard Carter, *The Secret Diplomacy of the Habsburgs 1598-1625* (Columbia University Press; New York, 1964), p. 25.

[111]The literature on the Military Revolution is too numerous to list here and has already been extensively examined in Chapter 1 of this book. However, for specific French examples see: Ronald S. Love, '"All the King's Horsemen": The Equestrian Army of Henri IV, 1585-1598', *The Sixteenth Century Journal*, Vol. 22, No. 3 (Autumn, 1991), pp. 510-533; John A. Lynn, 'Tactical Evolution in the French Army, 1560-1660', *French Historical Studies*, Vol. 14, No. 2 (Autumn, 1985), pp. 176-191; Treva J. Tucker, 'Eminence over Efficacy: Social Status and Cavalry Service in Sixteenth-Century France', *The Sixteenth Century Journal*,

Vol. 32, No. 4 (Winter, 2001), pp. 1057-1095.

[112]See Edmund H. Dickerman, 'The Conversion of Henry IV: "Paris Is Well Worth a Mass" in Psychological Perspective', *The Catholic Historical Review*, vol. 63, no. 1, 1977, pp. 1–13.

[113]thirteenthe most infamous example of such violence occurred in 1572 with the St Bartholomew's Day Massacre, see James R. Smither, 'The St. Bartholomew's Day Massacre and Images of Kingship in France: 1572-1574', *The Sixteenth Century Journal*, Vol. 22, No. 1 (Spring, 1991), pp. 27-46.

[114]fourteenthe process of repairing the French state and preparing it for later conflict with its nemeses is examined in Jacob Soll, 'Healing the Body Politic: French Royal Doctors, History, and the Birth of a Nation 1560-1634', *Renaissance Quarterly*, Vol. 55, No. 4 (Winter, 2002), pp. 1259-1286.

[115]Myron P. Gutmann, 'The Origins of the Thirty Years' War', *The Journal of Interdisciplinary History*, Vol. 18, No. 4, The Origin and Prevention of Major Wars (Spring, 1988), pp. 749-770; p. 760.

[116]See S.H. Steinberg, "The Thirty Years War: A New Interpretation', *History*, xxxii (1947), 89-102; *The 'Thirty Years War and the Conflict for European Hegemony 1600-1660* (London, 1966).

[117]For an examination of this debate see J. Theibault, 'The Demography of the Thirty Years War Revisited', *German History*, xv (1997), pp. 1-21.

[118]eighteenthe most renowned proponent of the presentation of the Thirty Years War as an international war is Geoffrey Parker, who has written extensively on the conflict, and who sees it as an extension of the Franco-Spanish and Spanish-Dutch Wars that preceded and followed it. See above all Geoffrey Parker (eds), *The Thirty Years War*.

[119]Peter H. Wilson maintains that the Thirty Years War was a conflict which was fought largely within German borders and largely because of German-Holy Roman causes. Wilson has also written extensively on the conflict, but the best article of his explaining the causation of the war is Peter H. Wilson, 'The Causes of the Thirty Years War 1618-48', *The English Historical Review*, Vol. 123, No. 502 (Jun., 2008), pp. 554-586.

[120]Georges Pages is the French historian who maintained that the Thirty Years War began in the manner that it did and was prolonged for thirty years because of the French influence. He sees France as the lynchpin of the conflict, see Georges Pages, *The Thirty Years War, 1618-1648* (New York, 1971; original 1939).

[121]See Geoffrey Parker, *Europe in Crisis 1598-1648* (London, 1979), p. 84.

[122]*Ibid*, p. 85.

[123]The failed marriage is often linked to Cromwell's execution in 1540 see G. R. Elton, 'Thomas Cromwell's Decline and Fall', *The Cambridge Historical Journal*, Vol. 10, No. 2 (1951), pp. 150-185.

[124]J. Michael Hayden, 'Continuity in the France of Henry IV and Louis XIII', pp. 7-8.

[125]Geoffrey Parker, *Europe in Crisis*, p. 126.

[126]*Ibid*, p. 153.

[127]*Ibid*, pp-123-124.

[128]J Michael Hayden, 'Continuity in the France of Henry IV and Louis XIII', pp. 8-11.

[129]*Ibid*, pp. 11-12.

[130]Geoffrey Parker, *Europe in Crisis*, pp. 128-129.

[131]Myron P. Gutmann, 'The Origins of the Thirty Years' War', pp. 760-761.

[132]The product of the Franco-Spanish marriage would be King Louis XIV, who would marry his Spanish cousin, and provide further justification for contesting the Spanish throne once the Spanish Habsburgs died out in 1700. In that conflict, the War of the Spanish Succession, Louis XIV claimed the Spanish throne for his grandson Philip V, and eventually succeeded following over a decade of war. See James Faulkner, *The War of the Spanish Succession 1701-1714* (South Yorkshire; Pen & Sword Books, 2015).

[133]Cited in H. G. Koenigsberger, 'Prince and States General: Charles V and the Netherlands', p. 128.

[134]For literature on the influence of the Black Legend idea see Katheryn Rummell, 'Defoe and the Black Legend: The Spanish Stereotype in "A New Voyage round the World"', *Rocky Mountain Review of Language and Literature*, Vol. 52, No. 2 (1998), pp. 13-28; Benjamin Keen, 'The Black Legend Revisited: Assumptions and Realities', *The Hispanic American Historical Review*, Vol. 49, No. 4 (Nov., 1969), pp. 703-719; A. Gordon Kinder, 'Creation of the Black Legend: Literary Contributions of Spanish Protestant Exiles', *Mediterranean Studies*, Vol. 6 (1996), pp. 67-78.

[135]Tracing the influence and importance of the Catholic Church in the reign of both Philip II and his predecessors is a task undertaken by Antonine Tibesar in his article 'The King and the Pope and the Clergy in the Colonial Spanish-American Empire', *The Catholic Historical Review*, Vol. 75, No. 1 (Jan., 1989), pp. 91-109.

[136]Hiram Morgan, 'Teaching the Armada: An Introduction to the Anglo-Spanish War, 1585-1604', *History Ireland*, Vol. 14, No. 5 (Sep. - Oct., 2006), pp. 37-43; Edward Tenace, 'A Strategy of Reaction: The

Armadas of 1596 and 1597 and the Spanish Struggle for European Hegemony', *The English Historical Review*, Vol. 118, No. 478 (Sep., 2003), pp. 855-882.

[137]See Andrew C. Hess, 'The Battle of Lepanto and Its Place in Mediterranean History', *Past & Present*, No. 57 (Nov., 1972), pp. 53-73; Elizabeth R Wright, 'Narrating the Ineffable Lepanto: The Austrias Carmen of Joannes Latinus (Juan Latino)', *Hispanic Review*, Vol. 77, No. 1, Re-Envisioning Early Modern Iberia: Visuality, Materiality, History (Winter, 2009), pp. 71-91.

[138]Liesbeth Geevers, 'Family Matters: William of Orange and the Habsburgs after the Abdication of Charles V (1555–67)', *Renaissance Quarterly*, Vol. 63, No. 2 (Summer 2010), pp. 459-490.

[139]Herbert H. Rowen, 'The Dutch Revolt: What Kind of Revolution?', *Renaissance Quarterly*, Vol. 43, No. 3 (Autumn, 1990), pp. 570-590; referenced in this case is p. 571.

[140]Geoffrey Parker, 'War and economic change: the economic costs of the Dutch Revolt', in *War and Economic Development*, ed. J. M. Winter (Cambridge; Cambridge University Press, 1975), pp. 49-71.

[141]R. Trevor Davies, *The Golden Century of Spain*, p. 153.

[142]See Geoffrey Parker, 'Why Did the Dutch Revolt Last Eighty Years?', *Transactions of the Royal Historical Society*, Vol. 26 (1976), pp. 53-72.

[143]Simon Adams, 'Elizabeth I and the Sovereignty of the Netherlands 1576-1585', *Transactions of the Royal Historical Society*, Vol. 14 (2004), pp. 309-319.

[144]See Hiram Morgan, 'Hugh O'Neill and the Nine Years War in Tudor Ireland', *The Historical Journal*, Vol. 36, No. 1 (Mar., 1993), pp. 21-37.

[145]Pieter Geyl, *A History of the Dutch-Speaking Peoples*, pp. 218-226.

[146]For an example of Anglo-French cooperation see Gordon K. McBride, 'Elizabethan Foreign Policy in Microcosm: The Portuguese Pretender, 1580-89', *Albion*: A Quarterly Journal Concerned with British Studies, Vol. 5, No. 3(Autumn, 1973), pp. 193-210.

[147]Andrew Wheatcroft, *The Habsburgs*, p. 153.

[148]See Gordon Griffiths, 'The Revolutionary Character of the Revolt of the Netherlands', *Comparative Studies in Society and History*, Vol. 2, No. 4 (July., 1960), pp. 452-472.

[149]We will examine this development later in Section 5 of this book. See Parker, 'Spain, Her Enemies and the Revolt of the Netherlands 1559-1648', pp. 90-95.

[150]A recent study assesses Philip II's debts in light of new evidence, while it does conclude that Spain filed for bankruptcy more than any other country in the era; a total of thirteen times by 1900. See Mauricio Drelichman and Hans-Joachim Voth, 'The Sustainable Debts of Philip II: A Reconstruction of Castile's Fiscal Position, 1566-1596', *The Journal of Economic History*, Vol. 70, No. 4 (DECEMBER 2010), pp. 813-842.

[151]Mahinder S. Kingra, 'The Trace Italienne and the Military Revolution During the Eighty Years' War, 1567-1648', *The Journal of Military History*, Vol. 57, No. 3 (July., 1993), pp. 431-446.

[152]See Geoffrey Parker, ed., *The Thirty Years War* 2nd Edition (London; Routledge, 1997), p. 2.

[153]Cited in R. Trevor Davies, *The Golden Century of Spain*, p. 229.

[154]*Ibid*, p. 229.

[155]*Ibid*, p. 230.

[156]The most significant of Lerma's acts in the closing years of the war with England was his approval and organisation of the Spanish landing in Ireland, in support of the rebellion led by Hugh O'Neill against Queen Elizabeth I's rule over the country. The literature available on the campaign is extensive. For a summary of this campaign see Frederick M. Jones, 'The Spaniards and Kinsale, 1601', *Journal of the Galway Archaeological and Historical Society*, Vol. 21, No. ½ (1944), pp. 1-43. Another visceral account is provided by G. A. Hayes-McCoy, 'The Tide of Victory and Defeat: II. The Battle of Kinsale, 1601', *Studies: An Irish Quarterly Review*, Vol. 38, No. 151 (Sep., 1949), pp. 307-317; and see also John McGurk, 'The Kinsale Campaign Siege, Battle and Rout', *Seanchas Ardmhacha: Journal of the Armagh Diocesan Historical Society*, Vol. 19, No. 1 (2002), pp. 59-69; John McGurk, ' The Battle of Kinsale, 1601', *History Ireland*, Vol. 9, No. 3, Ireland & Spain through the Ages (Autumn, 2001), pp. 16-2. An account of the plan to regroup and land at Galway is examined in Frederick M. Jones, 'James Blake and a Projected Spanish Invasion of Galway in 1602', *Journal of the Galway Archaeological and Historical Society*, Vol. 24, No. ½ (1950), pp. 1-18. For a debate on why the landing was made at Kinsale see John J. Silke, 'Why Aguila Landed at Kinsale', *Irish Historical Studies*, Vol. 13, No. 51 (Mar., 1963), pp. 236-245.

[157]See Geoffrey Parker, 'Spain, Her Enemies and the Revolt of the Netherlands 1559-1648', *Past & Present*, No. 49 (Nov., 1970), pp. 72-95.

[158]See Pieter Geyl, *History of the Dutch-Speaking Peoples*, p. 246.

[159]J. H. Elliot, 'A Question of Reputation? Spanish Foreign Policy in the Seventeenth Century', *The Journal*

of Modern History, Vol. 55, No. 3 (Sept., 1983), pp. 475-483.

[160]Akira Motomura, 'The Best and Worst of Currencies: Seigniorage and Currency Policy in Spain, 1597-1650', *The Journal of Economic History*, Vol. 54, No. 1 (Mar., 1994), pp. 104-127.

[161]See Mauricio Drelichman and Hans-Joachim Voth, 'Lending To The Borrower From Hell: Debt And Default In The Age Of Philip II', *The Economic Journal*, Vol. 121, No. 557 (DECEMBER 2011), pp. 1205-1227.

[162]Pieter Geyl, *History of the Dutch-Speaking Peoples*, p. 249.

[163]A useful examination of the battle in the context of the debate over Military Revolutions is conducted by Geoffrey Parker, 'The Limits to Revolutions in Military Affairs: Maurice of Nassau, the Battle of Nieuwpoort (1600), and the Legacy', *The Journal of Military History*, Vol. 71, No. 2 (Apr., 2007), pp. 331-372

[164]Cited in Roland Dennis Hussey, 'America in European Diplomacy, 1597-1604', p. 8.

[165]See Peter Borschberg, 'The Seizure of the Sta. Catarina Revisited: The Portuguese Empire in Asia, VOC Politics and the Origins of the Dutch-Johor Alliance (1602-c.1616)', *Journal of Southeast Asian Studies*, Vol. 33, No. 1 (Feb., 2002), pp. 31-62.

[166]Engel Sluiter, 'Dutch Maritime Power and the Colonial Status Quo, 1585-1641', *Pacific Historical Review*, Vol. 11, No. 1 (Mar., 1942), pp. 29-41.

[167]Pieter Geyl, *History of the Dutch-Speaking Peoples*, p. 249.

[168]See Geoffrey Parker, 'Why Did the Dutch Revolt Last Eighty Years?', *Transactions of the Royal Historical Society*, Vol. 26 (1976), pp. 53-72.

[169]For more on the mutiny and breakdown of discipline in the Spanish Netherlands army see Geoffrey Parker, 'Mutiny and Discontent in the Spanish Army of Flanders 1572-1607', *Past & Present*, No. 58 (Feb., 1973), pp. 38-52.

[170]For figures see Geoffrey Parker, 'Spain, Her Enemies and the Revolt of the Netherlands', p. 89.

[171]*Ibid*, p. 87.

[172]It should be said that not all historians are of the opinion that Philip II's debts were insurmountable. See Mauricio Drelichman and Hans-Joachim Voth, 'The Sustainable Debts of Philip II: A Reconstruction of Castile's Fiscal Position, 1566-1596', *The Journal of Economic History*, Vol. 70, No. 4 (DECEMBER 2010), pp. 813-84.

[173]Davies, *The Golden Century of Spain*, pp. 236-237.

[174]Pieter Geyl, *History of the Dutch-Speaking Peoples*, p. 250. The Archdukes signed a statement to the effect that they were ready to negotiate with the Dutch 'in the capacity of, and as taking them for, free lands, provinces and towns, against which they claim nothing.'

[175]For the peace negotiations see Pieter Geyl, *History of the Dutch-Speaking Peoples*, pp. 251-255.

(Top left) James IV/I of England, Scotland and Ireland (John de Critz, (1605)
(Top right) Mehmet III, Ottoman Sultan.

The Diet of Augsburg

CHAPTER SIX
"Storm Clouds Near and Far"

ONE
Isles Divided and United

What God hath conjoined then, let no man separate. I am the Husband, and all the whole Isle is my lawful Wife; I am the Head, and it is my Body; I am the Shepherd, and it is my flock. I hope therefore no man will be so unreasonable, as to think that I that am a Christian King under the Gospel, should be a Polygamist and husband to Two wives; that I being the Head, should have a divided and monstrous Body; or that being the Shepherd to so faire a Flock (whose fold hath no wall to hedge it but the four Seas) should have my Flock parted in two.[1]

The King of England and Scotland had spoken. It was a crisp, cool day on 19 March 1604, and King James I and VI had laid down the gauntlet, as well as the justification, for the unlikely union between Scotland and England, two entities which, only a generation before, had been at one another's throats. Unions under a common monarch were not unheard of in early modern Europe. Poland-Lithuania had fused itself together under this arrangement in the fourteenth century and liked the idea so much that they advanced it even further to a real union in 1569. If those two states – one a formerly Pagan duchy, another a Catholic Kingdom, could set aside their differences and combine themselves together, why not those two island kingdoms Scotland and England?

James continued in his efforts to persuade his audience with a note that 'even as little brooks lose their names by their running and fall into great Rivers…so by the conjunction of rivers little Kingdoms in one, are all these private differences and questions swallowed up.'[2] Through such a metaphor, the new King implied that any outstanding issues or grievances between the two old enemies would be subsumed into the healing balm which was this union. The conclusion was reached then that 'only those unable to live in a well governed Commonwealth, and…delighting to fish in troubled waters' would wish to hinder 'this work, which God in my Person hath already established.'[3]

James' declared dedication to peace was not meant merely to refer to the potential conflicts arising between England and Scotland on matters of sovereignty, history or religion though. The new King of 'Great Britain', a term which his courtiers coined, was equally committed to the mission of making peace with Spain. Five months after this speech to Parliament was made, the Treaty of London had brought peace between England and Spain after a nineteen-year war.[4]

Peace with Spain had been a hot topic in the twilight years of Queen Elizabeth I's reign, and especially once the Peace of Vervins was signed between France and Spain in 1598.[5] With France absent from the conflict, and with the rebellion against English authority in Ireland more than occupying English resources and energies, there was a sense that England's position would be greatly improved if she could settle with that old Spanish foe. After the initial flurry of activity, seen in English support of the Dutch rebels, the defeat of Armada in 1588 and the English Armada the following year, Anglo-Spanish conflict had mostly been confined to the New World, and had not produced much fruit for English strategists. In fact, so tumultuous and in a sense, depressing, was the last decade of Elizabeth's rule, that it has been labelled by some as a 'second reign', distinguished from the first by the lack of progress made in foreign policy or the advancement of English interests.[6]

The 1590s were, in the words of one historian, 'a decade of unusual hardship...reflected in the political and literary culture, of weariness with the old queen's rule.'[7] We are not here to assess the success of Elizabeth's reign or the happiness of her courtiers, but the turn in English foreign policy around the time of Elizabeth's death in 1603 does deserve some investigation. As recently as 1597, Spain had been at war with a coalition of England, France and the Dutch. The three powers were far from natural allies, being held together chiefly by the fear of Spanish power, but holding multiple diverging opinions on other matters, such as whether it was acceptable to still trade with Madrid while in a state of war with her. This question remained an important one because of the Spanish predominance in the New World, and trade with Spain was far more lucrative than any fledgling arrangements made in the Indies.[8]

Trade had been in place between England and Spain since before the Norman conquests, and by the sixteenth century business was booming to such an extent that even royal pronouncements on embargoes, or temporary trading spats did not reduce the appetite. English cloth, grain, tin and lead were exchanged for wine, fruit, oil and increasingly, coin, largely minted from new world silver. With the Dutch and Flemish ports coming under increasing strain as the Dutch revolt progressed, it became far more lucrative to trade with the Spanish directly. Royal pronouncements on restrictions in trade were ignored by many coastal officials, who held English goods and contracts, even if they were technically illegal, in high esteem. One example is given of a merchant, named John, who hailed from London and who illegally sold his ship's cargo at Bayona, a port town in north-west Spain, in 1571. While docked in port, the local justice came on board his ship and obligingly assured John 'that if any commandment should come from the king for the arresting of any English ships, he...should have twenty-four hours warning.'[9]

As much as a history of mutually beneficial trade existed, England had been included in some diplomatic schemes of Philip II, most notably when the marriage contract between himself and Queen Mary was developed in 1554.[10] While much had changed since that time, fifty years later King James would have known that Spain had not and could not always be the enemy of England, especially if the commercial and strategic interests of Britain were to be assured. Far better it would be to begin his reign with a new Spanish relationship, based upon mutual agreement and compromise. He met opposition to this approach from some courtiers who found it hard to break with the old polity of hostility towards Spain for economic, cultural and religious reasons,[11] but James won out in the end.

By 1604, the continent was opening up and its rulers were more aware of the opportunities at stake in the New World than they had been in 1585 when the war between England and Spain began. The Indies were enormously valuable to Spain for trade and royal revenues. One historian noted that:

> The clear annual profit from them in the 1590's was around or eight million pesos ("pieces of eight") – an appreciable amount by contemporary standards, perhaps one quarter the total Crown revenues – and was apparently about only part that was not already, or in large part, encumbered before it was received.[12]

France, England and the Dutch had never been able to match the Spanish monopoly on the New World's opportunities, just as they had never recognised Spain's right to an unchallenged presence there.[13] When Spain combined with Portugal in 1580 though, Philip II was able to claim a genuinely unrivalled hold over the fruits of the New World, as well as the merchant marine necessary to police and carry these fruits back home. English, Dutch and French privateers took it upon themselves to seize some of this wealth for themselves, but no piratical activities were as wildly successful as those made famous by Sir Francis Drake. In the background to this activity was a latent competition between all European powers for better markets and opportunities, and this competition would only intensify as the years progressed.

The alliance with its competitors in France and the Dutch had therefore been a means to an end for England, and that end had been the defeat of Spain.[14] With neither group unable to defeat the other though, and with resources intensely strained on both sides, it was hardly surprising that the

French under Henry IV bowed out of the contest in 1598, followed by a degree of soul searching on the English side. 'Even at its peak', wrote one historian, the war with Spain 'did not command the total support of a united bellicose population, and in particular, men who had spent their lives in trade did not see England and Spain as locked in a cosmic struggle of ideologies.'[15] The war had long since ceased to be profitable, and a train of thought put it that with Elizabeth and Philip II dead, and new sovereigns in both Kingdoms eager to make their mark, peace should not be too difficult to come by. James I, as we have seen, was as eager to portray the union of Scotland and England as divinely ordained, as he was to recast the looming peace negotiations with Spain as part of his divinely ordained mission.

For this mission to be successful though, English propagandists would have to get to work, and would have to paint James' reign as one of peace, and James himself as the King of peace. The goal in these efforts to reimagine the Stuart King was not only to urge patriotic citizens to value the king's image as peacemaker, but also to draw attention to the advantages of being citizens of a peaceful nation. As one urging put it:

> ...pray to Almighty God to make his Majesty as careless of war, as he from time to time in his great judgement shall find peace to be necessary; his people and subjects ever obedient to all his designs and appointments either in war or peace, and his Majesty himself blessed with long life, health and ability to undergo either, as it shall seem best to the divine Majesty. Amen.[16]

James may well have had grand ideas for making peace, and Philip III of Spain may have been eager to conclude his father's war also, but the factors which enabled both men to make this peace had not developed by their own making. One of the commonly cited factors compelling England to make peace – the ending of the Franco-Spanish War in May 1598, was not as critically important in a physical sense is often supposed. This was because King Henry IV, as we saw, never ceased to compete with the Habsburgs or make headaches for them, even if he was technically at peace with both branches of the Habsburg family.[17] The psychological impact on the English was far more impressive, since they now felt the sting of being alone against Spain, with only the Dutch left to carry the war on land. In actual fact, arguably the most important factor in favour of peace was one which was created in the twilight months of Philip II's life.

Understanding that the war with the Dutch was not winnable in its current state, the ailing Spanish King aimed to approach the situation differently, and appointed governors of the Spanish Netherlands to rule in the name of Spain. This division of Spanish authority was revolutionary, but it was not total – Madrid would still have the final say in whatever policy was taken, and she maintained her right to govern the region, including the rebellious Dutch portion, whether the rebels in that part recognised that right or not. But this was a kind of concession on Philip's part, because he was imparting his authority to a new regime which would rule in Spain's name, in a region which had always been directly connected to and administered by the Spanish Crown. That this authority was to be held by his daughter Isabella, and her cousin, soon to be her husband, the Cardinal-Archduke Albert of Habsburg, certainly lessened any reluctance the old King would have had for reducing the total powers of his son.

Philip's genuine hope seems to have been that by granting this autonomy to the Spanish Netherlands, and by granting it the public face of his daughter and nephew, Spanish popularity in the Netherlands region as a whole would increase, and the rebellious Northerners would return to the Spanish fold. It was a naïve hope, not least because of the terms which the new regime in the Spanish Netherlands would be forced to work with. Isabella and Albert, as well as their subjects, were forbidden from trading with the West or East Indies and were also forbidden from trading with the Dutch rebels, as the Spanish-Portuguese unit was forbidden from trading with the Dutch.

These restrictions, which harmed the Spanish Netherlands economically and dampened any prospect of a recovery, also forced the Dutch to take piratical measures to secure their own economic interests. 'The States General decided', said a contemporary Dutch historian in 1614, 'to keep... their seamen at work, to fit out a fleet or armada...and therewith to go against Spain and the Spanish islands, and to pounce upon and engage the Indies fleet, going and coming.' The Dutch fleet achieved much less than was hoped, but the trade voyages to America and the East Indies, already begun, multiplied many times over, and the Dutch became even more of a menace than they had been before Philip II's optimistic effort to reverse Dutch hostility. However, now that the regime of Isabella and Albert had been installed in Brussels, this regime, deemed 'the Archdukes' by historians, distinguished themselves far more effectively than Philip had ever expected.[18]

Although the centre of Spain's universe in the early seventeenth century resided in its Iberian Union, and although the most important threads of Spanish diplomacy led to Madrid, many of Spain's diplomatic activities took place in the Spanish Netherlands. In our time period, there could be counted more high-level 'Spanish' negotiations and international conferences involving Spanish interests in Brussels than in Madrid. A good deal of the actual policymaking done in the name of the Spanish Habsburgs took place there as well. How do we account for this fact – was Brussels usurping the authority of Madrid? Not exactly, it would be more accurate to state that Brussels acted in Madrid's name, and faithfully for her interests. One of the most straightforward reasons for this transferral of power, yet the one which mattered most at this stage of history when European travel was far from polished, was the geographical consideration. Spanish Netherland territory was like an anchor in an area where many of the era's most important events involving Spain took place.

The most obvious of these was the conflict with the Dutch, but the Spanish were also on hand with their army of Flanders during the Julich-Cleves crisis (1609-1610) recently examined. Later in this book, we will see how Flanders and the centre of Spanish administration in Brussels aided the Habsburg interest during the war for the Lower Palatinate, but the opportunities provided by this Spanish hub in Europe's centre of activity did not end there in Europe's centre of activity did not end there. The central position of the Spanish Netherlands in Europe also made the region the communications centre of the Habsburg world. Through Brussels, Madrid received not just its correspondence from England, correspondence which was of profound importance so long as both countries were at war. Brussels was also the gate through which the communications of northern Europe in Scandinavia, as well as the Holy Roman Emperor passed. On occasion, when speed was of the necessity, even the dispatches from Rome would be filtered through Brussels, a fact which put the government of the Archdukes in much closer contact with events, both in the Hapsburg world and elsewhere, than Madrid could hope to be, and in a better position to effectively deal with them.[19]

An interesting point which a historian on the Habsburgs, Charles H. Carter, made in the 1960s, was that once the Spanish Netherlands had been placed in the hands of the Archdukes, it was often more convenient for Madrid to follow the lead of Brussels, and to allow the Spanish Netherlandish tail to wag the Iberian Spanish dog. This was because, as Charles H. Carter perceived:

> ...while "Spanish Hapsburg policy" can still be spoken of properly as mainly Spanish policy, a conspicuous amount of that policy was formulated and executed by Brussels, not Madrid. In sum, the government of the Netherlands, being more concerned than Spain in some matters, being more conveniently "on the scene" in others, and having a right to at least a voice in most, could and did take a large hand, often on its own, in the making and conducting of "Spanish policy."[20]

Carter is careful though in not allowing this idea of Spanish Netherlandish autonomy to get out of hand – this was no anticipation of Belgian independence, just as surely as it was not quite accurate to dismiss the Archdukes merely as sheep to Spain's shepherd. The situation of the Spanish Netherlands was unusual, and its status would remain so right up the point of its reimagining in 1830 as the Kingdom of Belgium. At the turn of the century, the status of the Spanish Netherlands had not developed according to a pre-destined plan. The region was the rump of what had once been Spanish

Burgundy, granted to the Habsburgs and then handed to the King of Spain by Philip II's father in the mid-sixteenth century.

The Netherlands had been cleaved in two by the Dutch revolt, with a mostly Catholic south and mostly Protestant north making religious judgements easier, but not universal. If the religious question was far from straightforward in the Netherlands,[21] then the question of loyalty to the Spanish Crown was far simpler. The Dutch rebels had formed themselves into a republic, with the States General as their master, while the remnants of the old Netherlands in the south remained loyal to the Spanish King, and obeyed the orders of his representative, normally a governor. In fact, there had been a governor in place in Brussels when Philip II conceived of his plan to marry his daughter into the Spanish Netherlands position, but when he had died, his brother Albert assumed the duty in his stead, and made haste for Brussels.

Where the affairs of the Spanish Netherlands are relevant to our narrative now is in the surprisingly active role which Brussels played in bringing about the peace between England and Spain that had seemed so long and desired in coming. Albert and Isabella had conducted a healthy diplomatic relationship with King James I and VI and his Queen Anne for many years before James came to England's throne. Since James had never been at war with Spain in his capacity as King of Scotland, there was immediately an opportunity for peace as soon as he assumed the English throne, but the critical ingredient of a suitable channel to negotiate this peace remained. Archduke Albert took the initiative in this respect, 'dragging a reluctant Spain behind him', in the words of one historian, and forcing Spain to adapt when he sent a body of peace commissioners to London. Spain could not be seen to fall behind its satellite's initiatives, and so the actions of the Archduke, as much as the existing relationship between him and England's new King, helped facilitate an end to the Anglo-Spanish War.[22]

As a daughter of the King of Spain, Isabella would thus be a reigning sovereign in Brussels, but her actual ruling powers would necessarily devolve onto her husband, the Cardinal-Archduke Albert. The two cousins were married, and about the time of Vervins, in summer 1598, shortly before Philip's death, a formal cession was made of the Burgundian lands. They were now in the hands of the Archdukes, even though they of course considered Spanish or overarching Habsburg interests before considering the happiness of the stunted Spanish Netherlands population, which had been laid low in the 1590s by the dwindling Spanish answer and the increasing Spanish requests. Madrid always seemed to need more of everything from her beleaguered Flemish subjects – more soldiers, more money, more taxes, more generous trading arrangements, more sequestered resources.[23]

Everything was directed towards fighting the tripod of hostility which was focused from The Hague, London and Paris, but it was fortunate that in summer 1598 and in spring 1604, two of these combatants were eliminated from this race. This would leave the Dutch rebels alone against Spanish might for the first time in over two decades, and it would also provide ample opportunities for the Archdukes to distinguish themselves in war, as they had done with diplomatically orchestrating the peace with England. Yet, during this period, the Habsburgs were also distracted by another war, and this one with an old enemy, more dangerous than any other which they faced in the West.

TWO
The Turkish Problem

The border between East and West in 1590 was not represented by a line on the map delineating two different spheres of influences, but by a fluid, floating series of interconnected rivers, fortresses and wasteland. There never existed a time when the Holy Roman Emperor and Ottoman Sultan met together and mutually agreed on the border between each of their states. Instead, there was a state of almost constant warfare, be it through skirmishes, raiding parties, initiatives undertaken by minor potentates or full-blown invasions led by the Sultan in person which threatened to upset the weak balance which had been established.

The Ottomans were in by far the stronger position. It was they who possessed the most vassals and could therefore call on the most auxiliaries in the region, and it was also the Sultan who tended to initiate the conflict through a fresh invasion. One historian summarised the strategic position of the Turk by examining its borderlands with Christian Europe – a position reinforced by more than a century of constant conquest and military triumph:

> The northern periphery of in eastern Europe – apart from central Hungary which had been annexed outright – consisted of four vassal states: the principality of Transylvania, whose vassalage followed Ottoman victory at Mohacs (1526); the Principalities and Moldavia, both of which had paid tribute Sultan Mehmed II (1451-81), the Conqueror of Constantinople and the Crimean Khanate, over whose khans established the right of appointment and dismissal from 1475. These entities generally served the Ottoman buffer states on the borders between the Habsburg Empire, Poland-Lithuania and Muscovy.[24]

From this, we can observe that the Ottomans had a strong record of wresting submission from the petty princes of the Balkans, a process which added much to their fearsome reputation and prestige. Still, this appetite for conquest and glory had not been satisfied since 1547, when the Ottomans and the Habsburgs signed a peace treaty that committed the Holy Roman Emperor to pay tribute to the Sultan. Paying for peace was a strategy that the Emperor at the time, Charles V, felt forced to accept, hard as that pill was to swallow, thanks to the morass of other problems facing his authority – not least of which were the repercussions of the Reformation, which divided his realm according to religious persuasion.

The Ottomans had proven an ideal candidate to distract the Emperor long enough for the adherents of Luther's new creed to survive. This pattern – of capitalising on the danger posed by the Turk to wrest new concessions out of their Emperor – was a great boon to the growing number of Protestants in the Holy Roman Empire, and helps to explain the compromise between both groups which followed; that compromise being, the aforementioned 1555 Peace of Augsburg which followed: the 1555 Peace of Augsburg. As Geoffrey Parker wrote:

> This was almost standard procedure: since the 1520s, every Ottoman thrust up the Danube allowed the Protestants to sell their military and financial support for a campaign against the Turks in return for guarantees of religious toleration. As Leopold von Ranke pointed out long ago: without the Turkish threat, German Protestantism would scarcely have survived…The converse is also true: without the Protestant-Catholic schism in the sixteenth century… the Turks would probably not have conquered as much of south-east Europe.[25]

In such a manner were the conflicts of the Reformation connected to the expansion of the Ottoman state, but the legacy of the divisions within Christendom meant that in a Europe once united against the Turkish threat, this defence had long since splintered as religious differences and self-interest dominated. Indeed, much to the chagrin of the Holy Roman Emperor, by the late sixteenth century the old taboo of negotiating with the Turk had long been overcome, and it was not uncommon to see Christian powers contact the Ottomans in the name of an anti-Habsburg agreement. As the historian Franklin L. Baumer put it:

> Something like a "diplomatic revolution" did certainly occur in the relations between the Christian powers and the Turk during the sixteenth century. Beyond dispute is the fact that before the century was out practically all the Christian powers had established embassies at Constantinople and on occasion sought Turkish military aid against Christian rivals.[26]

The idea that the Ottomans were just another cog in the machine of European diplomacy, and not a barbaric force to be wholly maligned and feared, had achieved currency with the King of France's shocking creation of an alliance with Suleiman the Magnificent in the 1520s. With that example of *realpolitik*, Queen Elizabeth of England followed suit later in the sixteenth century and established during a seventeen-year span of diplomatic contact what one historian has called 'the first sustained communication between an

English monarch and a non-Christian ruler.' Indeed, while the Holy Roman Emperor Rudolf II fought a war against the Turk from 1593-1606, Queen Elizabeth was in contact not only with Sultan Mehmed III (who ruled from 1595-1603), but also his mother.[27] Yet, this striking case of the enemy of my enemy is my friend did not prevent Elizabeth's Church from reciting the following prayer during her reign:

> Almighty and everliving God...we thy disobedient and rebellious children, now by the just judgement sore afflicted and in great danger to be oppressed, by thine and our sworn and most deadly enemies the Turks, Infidels, and Miscreants, do make humble suit to the throne of thy grace for thy mercy.

Evidently, the relationship only went so far, and was never destined to be truly amicable so long as the English people associated the Turk with images of the barbaric infidel, and a scourge on mankind. During the reign of James I of England (1604-25), this image of the Turk was not challenged by his court, even though in practice, English trade with the Ottoman Empire sharply increased during these years.[28] Habsburg policymakers may have held a measure of nostalgia for the high point of Christian cooperation against the Ottomans – the Battle of Lepanto in 1571, where a coalition of Christian powers defeated the Turks at sea.[29]

That this battle occurred a generation before this latest outbreak of hostilities did not make the appearance of another Holy League to defend the Habsburgs particularly likely. There was to be no Christian cooperation on this occasion, as the Habsburg family had tied up several of Europe's most important powers. The French, English and Dutch were all at war with the Spanish Habsburgs in 1593, leaving the Austrian branch of that dynasty beleaguered and alone, but not completely. Habsburg negotiations with the Pope had led to the creation of a force of eleven thousand men paid for by the Holy See, and the Spanish King Philip II did send what little money he could spare.[30] In addition, Habsburg diplomacy reached out to those aforementioned Balkan vassals who had come under the thumb of the Sultan during the conquests of the previous centuries: Wallachia, Moldavia and Transylvania.

The question of how war between the Habsburgs and Ottoman Turks was resumed, after a half century of peace – and, for that matter, a recent renewal of the 1547 peace treaty in 1590 – cannot be answered without placing Habsburg-Ottoman relations in context. Something which is important to bear in mind is that the vague border between the two entities was always unsettled, and always contained degrees of conflict which varied throughout the seasons. A Habsburg-Ottoman peace, in other words, did not render the borderlands either silent or safe. This state of constant friction and non-cooperation between the two neighbours can be explained at least partially by the demands of Islamic ideology, as one historian wrote:

Islam, by prohibiting Muslims from shedding the blood of another Muslim, turned pre-Islamic concepts of war outward against the enemies of the faith. Only one kind of war was recognized as lawful, the jihad, or holy war, conducted to expand the domain of Islam…The concept of perpetual war to defend the faith and expand boundaries was inherently compatible with the Ottoman view; it was not, however, consonant with the outlook of their Christian enemies.[31]

Further grounds for conflict were maintained in the competing claims of the Habsburg Emperor and Ottoman Sultan; both individuals claimed to be the successors of Rome, the Emperor by right of appointment by the Pope in 800AD, and the Ottomans by right of conquest, following the seizure of Constantinople in 1453 from Byzantium.[32] With the religious as well as the ideological grounds for hostility well-established, the only factor maintaining peace was the lack of interest either party held in a resumption of a total war. Thanks to a variety of factors though, this lack of interest was destined to change. Following an increasing number of raids across the two borders, an initiative launched by the Turkish governor of Bosnia against some Christian outposts upped the ante and was reciprocated by an assault on a Turkish column, who drowned in large numbers while attempting to flee. These actions looked suspiciously like those undertaken during a proper war, and for the Ottomans to prepare a reprisal effort, and the Habsburgs to defend themselves adequately, the peace treaty would have to be torn up.

The initial manoeuvres revolved around the seizure of important fortresses along the Danube, which watched over the Hungarian plains that served as a kind of wasteland between the two empires. Buoyed by the aforementioned Papal contributions, in 1595 the Habsburgs were able to take the fortresses of Esztergom and Visegrad from the Turks, thereby loosening the latter's hold on Hungary. That same year, the Balkan allies which had been encouraged to join the Christian war effort struck fast. In August 1595, Michael the Brave of Wallachia, one of the petty leaders of these states, inflicted a stunning defeat upon the Ottomans in the Battle of Călugăreni, where he had been outnumbered more than two to one. The victory inspired praise from the Papacy and the Spaniards. Michael followed it up by defeating the Turks again with aid from Transylvania and three hundred cavalry from, of all places, Tuscany. This Italian connection was important, for Italian naval raids against the Ottoman's possessions in the Black Sea had been so successful that Sultan Mehmed III supposedly threatened to kill all Christians in Constantinople, before eventually settling on a mere expulsion of all unmarried Greek men from the city.[33]

Impressive as these victories seemed on paper, the Ottomans maintained a massive superiority in numbers at all times, which was beginning to tell. Sultan Mehmed III sought to take advantage of his superiority in numbers by assembling an army of one hundred thousand men in Hungary, filled by men from all manner of vassals and tributary states, and knitted together by the elite Janissary infantry at their core. The Sultan had known to prepare the way beforehand as well – the army would be accompanied by livestock and would stop along the journey at certain regions specifically tasked with growing rice. Thanks to such preparations, the Ottoman army's staple diet of lamb and rice would be maintained, and the Turk would eat far better than his Christian counterpart – at least, until these stocks ran out.

In 1596 this army had travelled the 500-mile journey with the Sultan at its head, and by late October defeated the Christians near Erlau, in the Battle of Mezőkeresztes – a victory which cut communications between the Austrians and their Balkan allies. This was the great and dashing triumph which the Sultan had sought, and with his name made in battle, he returned to his harem and placed the command in less glamourous hands. The 1590s continued without many more battles of consequence, as both sides sought to consolidate their positions and reinforce the fortresses under their control. The Danube continued to be the most important front, and focused attention on the Hungarian frontier. The real story by the late 1590s was not the action in Hungary, but in those Balkan vassals co-opted by the Habsburgs, of which, Michael the Brave of Wallachia was the most important.

Following his famed victory against the Turks at Călugăreni in August 1595, Michael's star continued to rise. He remained a critically important figure for Orthodox Christians, and as he was fluent in Greek, he styled himself as a successor to the Byzantine Emperors of old. Whether his ambitions truly had gotten out of hand is difficult to discern, but his downfall began in 1599, once the Prince of Transylvania Andreas Bathory was succeeded by his cousin, Sigismund Bathory. Sigismund was the nephew of Stephen Bathory, the Prince of Transylvania who had also reigned as King of Poland from 1576-86. Sigismund's plan was to abandon the new course of Transylvanian foreign policy, and to return instead to the old strategy of allying his country with that of Poland.

Rudolf II, Holy Roman Emperor at the time, could not abide by this about face from Transylvania, especially as the Hungarian frontier remained so sensitive. He therefore determined to authorise Michael the Brave to begin a punitive invasion of Transylvania, in an effort to re-orientate the region back towards the allied camp, and away from a Polish alliance and potential neutrality. Michael the Brave was only too happy to invade his neighbour; in fact, the Wallachian ruler was so enthusiastic that he did not stop at Transylvania but invaded and took control of Moldavia for good measure. Michael the Brave, it appeared, had ambitions to unite the region under his rule, as a kind of anticipation of the state of Romania, which would not come into being for more than 250 years. As Demetrius Ion Ghica eloquently put it:

269

Thus at this period of this glorious reign, Wallachia, Moldavia, and Transylvania were in the hands of Michael – the dream of the eastern Latins was realized for one short moment; but this noble edifice was soon destined to crumble, intrigue and jealousy were fast sapping its foundations, both from within and from without.[34]

Indeed, Michael had gone too far, and his efforts to fulfil his ambitions had thoroughly alarmed the Habsburgs, who did not want to lose control of the region to the triumphant, popular, romantic Wallachian prince. The Poles too were angered, since they had welcomed the prospect of a firm Transylvanian alliance to guard their border against the Ottomans. In spring 1600 then, the Poles invaded Transylvania, while the Turks invaded Wallachia, and Michael, caught in the middle of this pincer, appealed to the Habsburgs. This was more like it for Rudolf II, and with Michael's cooperation, the Poles were driven out of Hungary in several running battles.

Yet Michael was not redeemed; his ambitions were plainly too dangerous for Habsburg stability, and in mid-August 1601 the Wallachian prince was assassinated on the Emperor's orders. 'Thus perished treacherously the bravest warrior who ever fought for the independence of Wallachia',[35] an act which Rudolf was soon made to regret. This rash act had created a power vacuum which only the Turk could fill. Subsequently, the Balkan states of Wallachia, Moldavia and Transylvania succumbed to the Ottomans, and for the next two and a half centuries, remained largely quiescent.

By the turn of the century, much of the initial enthusiasm for war had evaporated, and the Balkan losses only added to the impression that the conflict with the Ottomans should be brought to an end. The Ottomans too were becoming eager to end the war; not only were the costs mounting as stores ran dry and salaried troops demanded more pay, but revolts within the Sultan's household also threatened his authority. Sultan Mehmed III would surely have expected his rule to be absolutely secure – after all, he had taken extra precautions at the time of his ascension in 1595, ordering his 19 surviving brothers and countless sisters strangled. Since Ottoman Sultans had free reign of their own exclusive harem, illegitimate children tended to be a problem for their successors, and Mehmed's father Murad had fathered as many as 130 boys through his concubines, along with an unknown number of daughters, since these were not recorded. Child mortality meant that many of these children did not survive to adolescence, but Mehmed was anxious to ensure that nature was encouraged to go further – he could not afford any threats to his regime.[36]

Yet Mehmed faced a revolt against the domination of this culture of the harem from the Ottoman upper classes, who had lost significant influence in the previous decades. In league with other malcontents in Turkish society, these figures seized the opportunity to take over Constantinople itself in

1603, sending the Sultan, then in his harem, a terrible warning. As if these threats to his regime were not bad enough, to the east of the Ottoman Empire lay another formidable Islamic power – Safavid Persia. At regular intervals, Safavid Persia would attack the Ottomans in the east, while the Habsburgs attacked them in the West.[37] In this respect, the negotiation and cooperation with the Habsburgs was similar to the famed Franco-Ottoman alliance against the Habsburgs, and it proved just as devastating in this instance.[38]

Having been dormant for some time, Persia was enjoying a resurgence under its Shah Abbas the Great, and in the war launched against the Turk in 1603, the Persians overcame the beleaguered and distracted opposition sent against them, deceiving several efforts by the Ottomans to overwhelm them with larger numbers, and delivering a crushing blow in the process to the Sultan's prestige. Pressed on two fronts, Mehmed was eager to make peace with the Habsburgs before the situation worsened. Mehmed died in 1603, at just 37 years old, and was succeeded by his son Ahmed, who ruled until 1617. The brief and tumultuous reign of Mehmed may have been over, but the Sultan's court remained a place of intrigue for many years to come, as the authority and powers of the Sultan were gradually eroded.[39]

Chaos in Constantinople did not prevent the new Sultan from taking advantage of a striking consequence of Habsburg financial disorganisation. In 1599, a small French company of infantry sent to aid the Habsburgs in their war effort defected to the Ottoman side due to want of pay. By the time they arrived in front of the Sultan, their pay had increased fourfold as their price for defection rose with the stakes, and one historian wrote that:

> The sultan was intrigued by their magnificent appearance, as well as by their muskets and arquebuses; when they fired a salute in a manner quite unknown to the Turks, he was so impressed that he sent them a present of money and allotted to them lodgings in Galata. They went around at will, carrying their swords and sporting a white plume in their hats.

Unfortunately for this band of two hundred or so men, the future was not to be particularly bright. Once the peace between the Habsburgs and Ottomans had been agreed to in 1606, they were sent to fight against Safavid Persia, but still allowed to retain their French captain. By 1611, scarcely 80 of them remained alive.[40] The ordeal was deeply embarrassing for King Henry IV of France, since not only did the defection of his forces convey dishonour upon the French reputation, but they also brought into the open the fact that the French had come to the aid of the Austrian Habsburgs, however limited their provision of aid had been. This was problematic for Henry, because he had wanted to maintain the immensely beneficial and strategically important alliance with the Turk.

In the event, this experience did not jeopardise Franco-Ottoman relations, though it does provide a fascinating window into the flexible nature of loyalties during the era, as we meet a group of men 'who were prepared to forsake their cultural roots entirely and seek their fortune in a society which was in popular imagination the antithesis of their own.'[41] Emperor Rudolf II could not afford to lose men, and the cities they guarded, to desertion or defection, but even with the conclusion of the war with the Ottomans in spring 1606, it was plain that great and grave challenges lay ahead.

Rudolf's realm was increasingly split along religious lines, and these divisions made themselves felt during the Long Turkish War, as Protestants agitated to wrest concessions from their Emperor in return for their loyalty and aid. Such a strategy, as we have seen, was one steeped in tradition as much as opportunism by the turn of the century. Calvinist efforts to have their creed legalised were met with resistance and failure from the Catholic core of the Habsburg power base in the Holy Roman Empire. More disconcerting still for the Protestants, the Catholic Counter-Reformation appeared to be gathering pace, as the Catholics maintained their iron grip on the Empire's two key institutions – the Imperial Diet and its Supreme Court. Catholic refusal to redress this imbalance and remodel these institutions to better reflect the religious status quo were met with anger on the Protestant side, and a refusal, from 1601, to recognise any rulings on ecclesiastical questions made by the Supreme Court.

In 1603, these frustrations were not helped by a Catholic refusal to permit more Protestant delegates into the Imperial Diet. The years following 1603 were tense, exacerbated by moments of confrontation, such as when the Catholic duke of Bavaria was allowed to seize the Protestant town on Donauworth, and annex it into his duchy, in 1607. In protest at this act, and at the repeated refusal of the Catholic hardliners to accept Protestant arguments, both Lutherans and Calvinists alike walked out of the Imperial Diet in 1608. This done, there was now no facility for the Protestant princes to receive legitimate redress of their grievances. As if to acknowledge this, the Protestants created their own method of redress – the Evangelical or Protestant Union, in summer 1608.

Since 1555 a peace between the two religious groups had, for the most part, been sustained. Following Habsburg financial and political overextension during the war with the Ottomans, and their resilience against Protestant demands during the campaigning months, this peace had never appeared in so much jeopardy. In 1609, in response to the formation of the Union, Maximillian of Bavaria, having already demonstrated his hardline resistance to Protestant concessions, went further by contributing a large portion of the funds necessary to establish the Catholic League. Two organisations, defined by religion, now roamed in the Empire, and both had apparently scorned the traditional constitutional methods of airing or addressing their grievances, in favour of the sword. The prospects for German unity, stability and safety were far from promising.

THREE
The German Problems

> I am very much afraid that the states of the Empire, quarrelling fiercely among themselves, may start a fatal conflagration embracing not only themselves… but also those countries that are in one way or another connected with Germany. All this will undoubtedly produce the most dangerous consequences, bringing about the total collapse and unavoidable alteration in the present state of Germany. And it may also perhaps affect some other states.[42]

This assessment of the state of the Holy Roman Empire in 1615 came from a minor German potentate – the landgrave of Hesse-Kassel and was communicated to the French government. Considering what occurred three years later, it can seem as though such gloomy predictions were almost too perfect too be true. Yet, in fact, the looming threat of conflict in the Empire was clear for anyone to see. Potentates of all sizes were building up their forces in the second decade of the seventeenth century, and where this was impossible due to local opposition or cost, immense sums were spent instead on vast building projects, to ensure that regions of otherwise low population still managed to boast impressive fortifications, complete with sophisticated bastions, earthen works and specially designed walls in the modern trace italienne style. When English traveller John Taylor visited the city of Hamburg in 1617 for instance, he was shocked at what he saw:

> And when I perceived these fortifications I was amazed, for it is almost incredible for the number of men and horses that are daily set to work about it; besides, the work itself is so great that it is past the credit of report.[43]

The erection of vast fortifications, the expenditure on defensive measures on such a large scale, and the recruitment of armies to man and patrol them – these factors all pointed to a sense of doom which was fast approaching. They suggested that the princes and dukes no longer trusted in either their fellow German or in the constitution of the Empire alone to protect them, and they thus felt compelled to take matters into their own hands. Indeed, by 1617, it was apparent that the two most important institutions for resolving disputes in the Empire – the Imperial Diet and the Supreme Court[44]– had deteriorated, as both bodies were shorn of all the trust that had traditionally accompanied them. Religion facilitated this deterioration, as a succession of confrontations in the sixteenth century had reduced the trust individual princes had for what were once viewed as impartial institutions.[45] Now, it could be said that religion covered all Imperial operations, and made itself felt as an agenda to every concerned prince.

It can seem bizarre to modern readers that a collection of states so diverse in geography, history and now religion could ever be able to exist as one unit, such as the Holy Roman Empire apparently professed itself to be. The nation state – so normal in today's world – was a rarity in the seventeenth century. Rather than states or even countries, it is in some ways more helpful to imagine dynasties laying claim to swathes of territory, which were ruled on the micro level by regional assemblies or estates.

Thus, the Austrian Habsburgs ruled over the Habsburg Hereditary Lands, which in early seventeenth century terminology referred to Austria, Bohemia, portions of North Italy and a slice of Hungary. The Spanish Habsburgs ruled over Portugal, Spain, Milan, Naples, the Spanish Netherlands and vast sections of the Americas. The Bourbon family ruled France and Navarre, but the country of France as we imagine it had not been a unitary state for long, and different traditions of loyalty and religion existed north and south of the country. Similarly, the Stuart family ruled England and Scotland, and laid claim to Ireland, but in the latter's case it was impossible, even with the recent expulsion of Ulster's rebellious Irish Earls, to guarantee loyalty across that island; fledgling colonies in the New World and trading posts in Asia were also operated in the name of the House of Stuart.

We could go on, but in the Europe of 1600, the continent was divided into spheres of influence and claims rather than accepted, delineated borders. With the arguable exception of the Dutch Republic which remained largely unchanged in its size, Poland ruled over Belarus, Ukraine and Lithuania; Sweden ruled over Finland; Denmark ruled over Norway. Far to the East, the House of Romanov was only beginning – from 1613 – to stake its claim to the far-flung territories to its distant east and north, where the borders of Russia would eventually extend. This crash course in seventeenth century statehood demonstrates that, while the Holy Roman Empire is perhaps the most well-known multi-ethnic, multi-religious and multi-layered polity, it was far – very far indeed – from the only one.

Perhaps it is the curious stature of the Habsburg family that draws the eye – consider for instance the fact that in the early twentieth century, it was possible to bemoan the multiple ethnicities which the Austro-Hungarian Habsburgs ruled over, and yet few such lamentations were spared for the German Empire, which ruled over Poles, Czechs, Slovaks, Danes and many more identities besides. A case could be made for the idea that strong leadership and a record of success masked all such questions about the suitability or longevity of a state. While the grounds for the absolutist rule of Austro-Hungarian Empire were certainly established in the seventeenth century though, there can be no doubt that the Habsburg Monarchy of the twentieth century was a great deal more powerful than its seventeenth century model, if we take just the restrictions or prerogatives placed upon that dynasty in its sphere of influence.

This was because the Habsburg family did not and could claim to rule over the Holy Roman Empire. Its position as the traditional family of choice (since 1438) for candidates for the office of Holy Roman Emperor had never enabled it to claim any kind of lordship over the totality of the Empire's subjects, let alone its individual rulers. Since the mid-sixteenth century, Habsburg Emperors had been forced to grant numerous concessions to their subjects in return for support against the Turks – a tradition of give and take which passed into the seventeenth century, as we have seen. These concessions were considerable; representative assembles – the estates – were established in Upper and Lower Austria and were staffed by the increasingly Protestant aristocracy that dominated there.

By 1580, some 90% of the nobility in Lower Austria was Protestant, yet despite the Catholic creed of the ruling Habsburgs, the religion of these nobles did not restrict their political rights, for Emperor Maximillian II had been forced in 1571 to concede freedom of religion to all nobles in Lower Austria in return for their support for taxes to pay for defensive measures against the Ottoman threat. In 1578, the estates of Upper Austria cobbled together a small force of 1,500 to drive the point home to the new Emperor Rudolf II that they expected similar religious rights as their neighbours, and these were promised in return for their support. That same year, in Inner Austria, the Protestant estates agitated for religious freedoms in return for a commitment on their part to maintain a permanent force along the border with the portion of Habsburg-owned Hungary.[46]

On the surface, it might seem as though the very foundations of the Habsburg power base was eroding, for how could this dynasty exercise its powers or leverage its lands if it was consistently held hostage by religiously jealous rebels? The question was a valid one and compelled some leading members of the family to meet in secret in 1579 and pledge no more concessions to the grasping Protestants. Solidarity within the Austrian Habsburg family would be the only way forward; three brothers had inherited four sections of Austria upon the death of their father in 1564. Maximillian II gained Upper and Lower Austria; Charles gained Inner Austria and Ferdinand gained Further (Western) Austria.[47] If these brothers wished to ensure that the splendour and power of their family was maintained, then the malignant, troublesome elements of their homelands would have to be kept in check.

Indeed, it should be emphasised that the religious concessions to the Protestants in Austria contradicted one of the tenets of the 1555 Peace of Augsburg, which had then ended the religious wars in the Holy Roman Empire which the Reformation had ignited. This tenet – termed 'his rule, his religion' or in the Latin *cuius regio, eius religio* – was supported by the principles and expectations of the era: of course, the people should follow the lead of their ruler. It made the Habsburgs appear weak to concede equal rights to both religious blocs in their lands, even while it may appear natural and progressive to modern readers. At this stage though, with the Catholic Church mostly 'moribund' with 'parishes…almost permanently vacant, congregations… abandoned, and the surviving establishments…in an unedifying condition', there was evidently a great deal of work to be done if the Austrian Habsburgs were to restore the position of their religion in Austria, and thus reinforce the majesty and security of their rule.[48]

The Counter-Reformation arrived in Austria with breakneck speed and force once the son of Archduke Charles – that son of Emperor Ferdinand who had been granted Inner Austria in 1564 – came to rule over his patrimony in 1595. Ferdinand of Styria was 17 years old by the time he made his return, after a youth spent surrounded in the influences of Jesuits, under whose guidance both his education and religious outlook were formed. Ferdinand engaged with his mission of eradicating heresy from his lands almost immediately upon the assumption of his duties. Paradoxically, Ferdinand was aided by the Turkish War, which was then on-going, largely because his lands were little more than two hundred and fifty kilometres from the nearest Ottoman triumph.

The fear of the Sultan invading their lands compelled the Protestants in Inner Austria to remain loyal to their young Archduke, and in 1599 Ferdinand set up a Reformation Commission to deal with the Protestants and implement the Counter-Reformation. This began with several bold moves in rapid succession – the burning of thousands of books, the forced exile of 2,500 families, and the forced closure of almost seventy Protestant establishments. These efforts were in fact mirrored to some extent by the Holy Roman Emperor Rudolf II, who took advantage of a peasant uprising to impress upon the aristocracy of Lower Austria the necessity of having the Habsburgs on board. The Protestants and their Lutheran preachers had been unable to stop the peasants from revolting, but the Catholic Habsburgs had, and when combined with an influx of preachers and missionaries from Jesuit establishments, it had the effect of reversing, ever so gradually, the spread of the Reformed faith.

Nobles appreciated the monolithic appearance of Catholic doctrine and administration, in comparison to the divided and quarrelling segments of Protestantism, among this group must be considered the man who would later lead Ferdinand's armies – Albrecht of Wallenstein, who had been born a Lutheran.[49] By converting the leading lights of certain noble families, the Habsburgs could initiate a drip-down process through which the most powerful individuals would become Catholic, and the weaker nobles and peasants would be expelled or shown the advantages that awaited if they followed suit. From this story the Jesuits stand out as an organisation that had a profound influence on not only Ferdinand, but also the actual pace and success of the Counter-Reformation itself. The activity of the Jesuits and their investment in young, influential archdukes like Ferdinand would be repaid many hundreds of times over as Ferdinand reciprocated their investment in his own lands. Jesuits spearheaded the Counter-Reformation and were able to do so mostly from the safety of their Universities, which grew from just four to fifty between the years 1561-1650. In that ninety-year span, the number of full members of the Society of Jesus also grew, reaching 870 fully fledged, keenly zealous members by the middle of the seventeenth century. As Geoffrey Parker has noted:

> The face of Catholicism in the Habsburg lands after about 1580 was moulded to an almost unusual degree by the stern, uncompromising, legalistic faith of the Jesuit fathers. As the more tolerant older generation was gradually removed by death, the temper of religious opinion became steadily more aggressive.[50]

Yet there were limits to how far this Counter-Reformation could go. Not even the Jesuits seemed willing to touch Hungary, which had not even sent a prelate to Rome since 1553. Hungary boasted no Catholic nobles, no Catholic-controlled towns, and a miniscule Catholic Church presence. Yet even despite these facts, Emperor Rudolf engaged in a policy of deliberate confrontation and persecution with the Hungarians under his protection in Royal Hungary, that third of the country under his control. The traditional checks on the powers of a Hungarian King – enacted in the thirteenth century – had been respected by the Habsburg family, as they now held the Hungarian Crown.

The expectation that such traditions would protect them proved unfounded as Rudolf set to work though, exploiting the presence of his armies there in 1600-02 to confiscate the lands of Protestant Hungarian nobles and arrest those that resisted, while many Protestant churches were forcibly returned to Catholic use. In 1604, the Hungarian estates were forbidden from discussing religious matters, and Rudolf personally ordered that heresy in Royal Hungary was to be sought out and purged. Rudolf may have been buoyed by the success he had enjoyed in his Austrian patrimony, but this was far too much for the Hungarians to take. Rudolf reaped what his needlessly provocative policies had sown once Imperial armies were forced to march out of Hungary and down south to meet a Turkish attack in 1605. With the military might absent, so too did the fear evaporate, and the Hungarians became emboldened under a new leader, Stephen Bocskay, who was supported by his fellow Calvinist and Ottoman vassal Bethlen Gabor, the Prince of Transylvania.

Just as the messy Hungarian divorce was underway, Rudolf suffered what must be considered akin to a breakdown. He became more reclusive, and his closest family members began to despair that the ruin of the dynasty was at hand. As was usually the case with the Habsburgs though, crisis was averted with some firm action and consolidation. Rudolf's younger brother Matthias was pegged to succeed him at a meeting in Linz in April 1605, and following this, the Habsburgs hastily recruited an army of loyalists to fight the Hungarian rebels. As if connecting these elements still further to the later narrative, this Habsburg army included such figures of later import as Wallenstein, the Habsburg generalissimo, and Count Thurn, leader of the Bohemian rebels in 1618. After some successes, Matthias was able to conclude a peace treaty with the Turks, using the Hungarians as intermediaries, in June 1606.

The peace agreed with the Ottoman Empire here would hold, against the expectations of many, for more than a generation, and provided the Habsburgs with the eastern security they needed to engage in their European pursuits with their full attention and resources. Yet, while the Turks would remain quiescent, the Transylvanians, Hungarians and even Austrian estates would not. If the Austrian Habsburgs had learned anything from this decade of turmoil, persecution and proselytising, it was that they could get away with extirpating heresy closer to home, and would have to tread carefully outside of it. At the same time though, there seemed little consideration of the possibility that one revolt could lead to another, as happened in 1618, and the enthusiasm for spreading Catholicism at the expense of stability or the rights of one's subjects had certainly not been diminished.

Considering the damage done to the trust and sense of goodwill in the Habsburgs' own lands, the similar damage done to the traditional avenues for redress – the Imperial Diet and Supreme Court – it can appear as a march towards the inevitable conflagration of 1618. Other ill-omens were easily found; in 1599, just as Ferdinand was setting up his Reformation Commission, the lands in the principality of Westphalia were ravaged by Spanish troops in search of food and fodder. The spilling over of the Eighty Years War into the Holy Roman Empire was by no means unheard of,[51] but in this case the affected parties acted to expel the invader with significant consequences.

Those princes in a position to do so within Westphalia attempted to recruit soldiers to eject the Spanish, but these soldiers could not dislodge the more experienced Spaniards, and before long it became clear that the same princes who had attempted to recruit these soldiers did not actually have the money to pay for their service. Realising this, it transpired that the Westphalian princes created a monster, as these soldiers mutinied and wandered the countryside in search of payment in kind. The fiasco cost the princes 400,000 thalers, in addition to the damage done by the Spanish in the first place, and the regional institutions in place to encourage cooperation between these potentates were greatly discredited.[52] By the second decade of the seventeenth century, recall, princes recruited soldiers of their own, resulting in the appearance of an Empire that had apparently transformed itself into one large mustering field, with imposing fortifications rising up from the ground where plentiful soldiers could not be found.

Among these supranational institutions were the aforementioned Imperial Diet and Supreme Court, which represented the hundreds of potentates of the Empire on the macro level, but it is also worth investigating the micro level, represented by the ten effective *Reichskreisse* or Imperial circles, which were composed according to geography. These circles enabled the smaller princes to have their concerns heard, and to debate on a forum which entitled them to a single vote regardless of size or power. In the past, they had also been tasked with raising an army for the purpose of defending the Empire from attack. It was unlikely that all within a circle would agree on a given policy, even less likely that all would be united in religious outlook, and impossible to predict what all ten circles would do in the event of a crisis that consumed the Empire.[53]

We are thus confronted with a Holy Roman Empire in 1608 that appeared more divided than ever before, and less capable of properly dealing with its problems as a collective unit. The whole concept of consensus had broken down, and the religious peace made in 1555 had since been outpaced by the unnatural and unpredictable spread of religious creeds, not to mention the acceptance of a new one – Calvinism. In addition to the paralysis of these institutions and the divisions and mistrust which grew from them, the Turkish War sapped the financial reserves of the Austrian Habsburgs, and the tumultuous nature of the Diet meant that one of key functions – the approval of tax for a war – could not be affected.

Thus, the knock-on effect of the religious quarrels meant that Rudolf, Matthias and then Emperor Ferdinand were unable to reduce this war debt, and an unpaid sum of almost 4 million thalers hung over Emperor Ferdinand II in 1619, just as he was about to embark on another impossibly expensive conflict. That he was already so deeply in debt influenced Ferdinand's later behaviour in the war – since he was not in a position to pay the Duke of Bavaria or the Elector of Saxony for their loyalty, he promised them lands and in Maximillian of Bavaria's case, titles instead. In such a way did the disastrous divisions highlighted by the Turkish War make themselves felt during the Thirty Years War. Yet, while it is true to say that Ferdinand II was deeply in debt, he was far from the only one his contemporaries to owe more than he owned.[54]

Indeed, in the context of the early seventeenth century, the fiscal solvency of Maximillian of Bavaria was the exception rather than the rule, and this even considering the fact that, according to Wedgewood, Maximillian was renowned for his 'meanness' when it came to money.[55] Perhaps Maximillian was wise to be so frugal; Germany not only underwent a great deal of religious division from the end of the sixteenth century into the early years of the seventeenth, she also experienced a severe economic recession. One historian noted that the financial crisis continued beyond 1619 and up to 1623, as those states within the Empire produced their own coins at increasing rates to provide pay or contributions amidst the troubling situation.[56] It is also possible to view the seventeenth century simply as a period of general crisis, as some historians have done.[57]

That the Empire was suffering from intractable divisions was a fact loudly underlined when Protestants walked out of the Diet in Augsburg (1608) and then in Regensburg (1613) in protest at the refusal of the Catholics to address their grievances. Yet this apparent paralysis of the Empire's overarching institutions did not automatically ruin the ability of either princes or smaller regional assemblies to cooperate.[58] In a sense, the Empire became less centralised before the Bohemian revolt broke out, but it is important not to overstate the importance of the Imperial Diet or the Supreme Court at the same time; after all, from 1555-1603, even before it became associated with disorder, the Diet met only six times, and three of these occasions was during the Turkish War.[59] So long as each individual ruler remained responsible, and did not seek to antagonise his opponents, there was no reason for a great conflagration.

It is worth making a note on religious divisions as well, in case the impression is given that members of the different confessions were permanently at one another's throats. The reality was, predictably enough, a great deal more complex. Classifications of the Thirty Years War normally attempt to place the conflict in a confessional or political box, yet we would be more correct to remind ourselves of the facts on the ground in the early seventeenth century. As Peter H. Wilson writes:

> Members of the same church disagreed violently over the proper relationship between belief and action. Even if, for some, the [Thirty Years] War was a holy war in which eternal salvation was at stake, most were less willing to believe that God had called them to arms. They remained more pragmatic. The distinction was not one between the religious and the secular outlook: for both, faith, inseparable from daily life, helped to determine attitudes to law and politics.

Religion mattered everywhere one went, yet it meant very different things to different people, and of course to different rulers. To some, religion was an end in itself, and to others it was only worth spreading if it aided the common good – however, it would be reductionist to take religion out of the equation altogether when examining the march towards the Thirty Years War. After all, it was the presence of such distinct religious disagreements in Germany in the first place that led to the reduction in trust and efficiency necessary for the traditional mechanisms of the Empire to function.[60]

In addition, whether we attempt to explain the actions of Ferdinand II or Frederick V in political, religious, constitutional or international terms, there can be no doubt that either man acted without the firm belief that God was on his side. Ferdinand, indeed, lay prostrate and took succour from the Almighty before facing the Bohemian rebels down; Frederick, upon suffering his worst defeat at White Mountain, was compelled to view the experience as a trial from God rather than as a sign that his cause was doomed. At the same time of course, the religious inclinations of both men did not prevent either from relying on allies of a different religious persuasion to their own when it suited them. The political and the religious were thus mutually dependent, rather than mutually exclusive, influences.[61]

The contradiction inherent in the fact that those in opposing religious camps were as capable of confrontation as cooperation reminds us that a great deal of what occurred in the Thirty Years War was charged by the actions of certain individuals. Such a fact may appear obvious, but it is often lost when confronting the sheer morass of details and apparent warning signs that seem to imply that the Empire, and thus Europe, was heading for a catastrophe either way. Disagreements of course exist on this point, as many historians have attempted to provide their own authoritative account on the outbreak of the Thirty Years War.[62] As this incredibly complex era has already shown us though, this origins story cannot be told without examining all of the contingent parts; indeed, the story of the Thirty Years War would be incomplete without examining its two major protagonists, in both the Habsburg and anti-Habsburg camp.

FOUR

First of his Name

Not even his most reasonable biographer could come to a conclusion about the Elector Palatine's life other than that which stated that he had the 'dubious honour' of enduring 'one of the most disastrous political careers in early modern European history.'[63] Frederick V, the Elector Palatine, was as maligned in the historiography of the conflict, as he was physically in its initial stages. He was cast invariably as 'a pleasure-loving nonentity', according to one historian, 'weak and shallow', in the words of another; a 'wavering indecisive character – not an oak, but a reed incessantly trembling in the wind', said another, with many more similarly harsh judgements to be found.[64] Wedgewood's assessment of Frederick V sticks in the mind the most, largely because it is widely available, and is generally the account which most enthusiasts of the Thirty Years War are introduced to first. Because of this, Wedgewood may well have coloured the impressions of generations of these enthusiasts and conditioned them to see Frederick V in a certain negative light. Wedgewood wrote on Frederick's character:

> Gentle, trustful, equally capable of anger, hatred, or resolution, he strove conscientiously to fulfil his responsibilities although the pleasures of hunting, playing tennis, swimming and even lying in bed were very tempting to him. Ironic fate had given him no vices, and all the virtues most useless to a ruling prince. He was strong neither in body nor in spirit, and the gentle education which had been planned to stimulate his timorous nature and to fit him for the arduous championship of a cause had softened out of existence what little character he had.[65]

Damning and conclusive though this may appear, the character that Wedgewood describes seems based less on actual evidence, and more on her own imagination. Brennan Pursell makes the very important point that the old source from 1645 which Wedgewood cited to support these claims actually refer to an author who was 'apologetic, if not laudatory in tone', towards the Winter King. This 1645 source was from Friedrich Spanheim, a contemporary of the Thirty Years War who was based in Leiden. At no point in the reference to which Wedgewood refers does Spanheim criticise Frederick's want of character or willpower, nor does he mention lying in bed or lacking moral fibre.

Instead, Spanheim notes Frederick's lack of military education, but at the same time underlines the fact that even after everything that happened to him, and all the friends that left his side, Frederick never sought vengeance against them, and behaved nobly throughout his many ordeals. This, apparently, was a man who had 'all the virtues most useless to a ruling prince.'[66] It is important to dwell on matters like Frederick V's character, because it was this very character that led the Elector Palatine to make one of the worst decisions in history, and accept the Bohemian Crown. If one accepts such a blackening of Frederick's character, then it becomes too easy to blame the Elector for what followed, and to neglect the additional causal factors, which were themselves critically important

Because he was definitively on the losing side, we are also faced with some enduring myths about Frederick in addition to the inaccuracies spouted by some historians, some of which developed during Frederick's time, and others that became canon for no reason other than the fact that they were repeated time and again. One notable myth was that Frederick's policy was controlled by his wife, Elizabeth Stuart, the sole daughter of James I and VI of England and Scotland. Elizabeth Stuart, many historians claim, pushed her husband to seize the Bohemian Crown, with the quotable phrase that she would 'rather eat sauerkraut with a king than roast meat with an elector', or the other statement that if Frederick had been bold enough to marry a king's daughter, he ought to have the courage to take a crown. Both lines, in the words of Pursell, 'are creations of Palatine enemies, lack primary documentary evidence, have been refuted in secondary historical literature, and should be permanently dismissed.'[67]

That Frederick has been the victim of some character assas*sina*tion makes an accurate assessment of his character more challenging, but no less necessary. First and foremost, Frederick was a member of the Wittelsbach dynasty, a German family name with extensive roots and a proud history of competition and success, which reached its peak when Rupert, one of the Palatine members of the Wittelsbach family became Holy Roman Emperor in the early fifteenth century. Wittelsbach would rule in Bavaria and the Palatine from the thirteenth century until the end of the German Empire, distinguishing the family and its further branches in the electorates of Trier, Mainz and Cologne as one of profound importance for the history of German culture and development. Even by 1610, when Frederick V's father died, his family name held significant weight, despite its eclipse under the Habsburg sun, which stretched all across the world.

Frederick's identity was affected by more than just his family's name – religion played a further critical role in shaping Frederick's sense of self. The branch of the Wittelsbach family that ruled in the Upper and Lower Palatinate had embraced the Reformation, whereas their cousins in Bavaria remained true to the Old Faith, as had the spiritual electorates of Trier, Mainz and Cologne. To It remained to be seen whether blood was thicker than the holy water, but by and large, the relations between the Wittelsbach family members remained good, and throughout his reign as Duke, up until the eruptions later in the decade, Maximillian of Bavaria was 'extremely friendly to the Elector Palatine.'[68] As was typical with reformed princes of the time, Frederick believed passionately and absolutely in the tenets of his faith. 'Rule me, Lord, according to your word' was his motto, but such an expression should not single out Frederick or his Calvinist faith for ridicule. In the words of Peter H. Wilson:

> His firm Calvinism convinced him of the righteousness of his cause and induced an unshakable faith in ultimate victory…In social and political terms, however, his faith was far from the Spartan puritanism that was then taking root among the inhabitants of English and Dutch towns. He had been chosen for a divine purpose because of his dignity as senior secular elector and his family's honourable heritage in imperial politics.[69]

Frederick believed he had been chosen for a purpose – and that purpose was to defend the German nation against the malignant threat from the Catholic conspiracy powered by the Jesuits and facilitated by the Habsburgs. Note Wilson's designation of Frederick as 'senior secular elector' – this status was a result of Frederick's position within the Holy Roman Empire's constitution as Elector Palatine. According to the terms of the 1356 Golden Bull, which established the system of electors and elections on legal ground, the Elector Palatine 'was the only imperial prince who could claim the prerogative to sit in judgement of an emperor.' The Elector Palatine, alongside the Elector of Saxony, were also charged with serving as Imperial vicars, and sharing control of the Emperor's privileges during the interregnum between an Emperor's death and the election of a new one.

In addition, an Emperor accused of any legal violation – that meant the current Habsburg Emperor – would have to answer to the Elector Palatine, who could exercise these rights at the Imperial Diet, as the Emperor sat in nervous silence. It was virtually unfathomable to imagine Rudolf II, Matthias or especially Ferdinand II answering to Frederick V, but according to the legalities of the Empire's constitution, Frederick was well within his rights to expect this.[70] At the same time, it was not within Frederick's character to lord these privileges over his subjects or princely peers. While he was, in the judgements of the Imperial constitutional at least, unequalled in importance save for the Emperor, in practicality Frederick was vigorous, affable and good-natured.

'I do not like to keep anyone from his happiness and well-being', he declared. When he travelled out of his disconnected territories, most notably to wed Elizabeth Stuart in 1613, he made very positive impressions on those that met him. An avid huntsman – Wedgewood did not base all of her character sketch on thin air – Frederick cut a dashing, confident, accomplished figure to those English onlookers that caught a glimpse of him, with his equestrian skills in particular standing out. Little wonder that an Englishman visiting the Palatinate in 1619 judged Frederick to be 'much beyond his years, religious, wise, active and valiant...esteemed and redowted [sic] in all of Germany... loved and honoured by all his own people.'[71]

Indeed, it is sometimes taken for granted that Frederick should have had the opportunity to marry such an English prize, for it suggested in the future that England would support the Palatinate, and thus Frederick himself, in whatever difficulties he came into. The marriage alliance and the diplomatic consequences which went along with the marriage contract, were negotiated in 1611 when Frederick was just 15 years old and had yet to come into his majority in the Palatinate. We will return to King James' angle in these affairs in the future, but the short version of the story holds that the Protestant King of England and Scotland hoped to balance the hostile forces of Europe and maintain his moniker as a peaceable monarch by fostering a marriage agreement between a Protestant (Palatine) and Catholic (Spanish) power. By so doing, James planned to use his familial influence to offset political strife on the continent and avoid war at all costs.

Seen in the context of the early 1610s, it was not a bad plan. Certainly, peace was what the British people wanted, and James correctly discerned that his kingdom could not afford a major continental entanglement at this time.[72] Having contributed to the ending of the Anglo-Spanish War in 1604, James was keen to ensure that his kingdom was not tied up in such a thankless conflict again. While he married his daughter into the Wittelsbach family, James also signed an alliance with the Evangelical Union in April 1612, that defensive alliance bloc of Protestant German princes of which Frederick V was the technical leader, having inherited the position from his father. This agreement was mirrored by the Dutch alliance with the Union the following year.

Before he had even travelled to meet his bride, in other words, Frederick's position seemed secure: defended zealously by the usual suspects in Europe's Protestant camp. Further ties recommended Frederick as well – his mother was a daughter of William the Silent, that Dutch rebel leader who founded the House of Orange as the Dutch Republic's foremost bastion of anti-Spanish rhetoric and action. By marrying Elizabeth, Frederick also gained a mother-in-law in Queen Anne, the sister of King Christian IV of Denmark, another Protestant notch he could add to his belt. In addition, Frederick's aunt had been the first wife of King Charles IX of Sweden, in 1616, Frederick's sister married the Elector of Brandenburg, another Calvinist potentate in the Empire. These familial ties recommended Frederick still further to lead a Union of Protestant princes in Germany and would later recommend him to the Protestant Bohemian rebels when they attempted to search for a new King.

Frederick was eager to play the role of a Protestant champion, and he was also keenly aware of his position in the Empire as an opposing force against the Habsburgs. Upon landing in England in October 1612, Frederick met with Elizabeth several times, forging a bond which was to last twenty years, and making their engagement official in January 1613, marrying in February. In celebration, the future father-in-law King James threw a wedding banquet, which cost him in excess of £53,000 – a startling anticipation of the kind of financial support he would send his son-in-law into the future. In April, the newlyweds departed for the Palatinate, accompanied by 34 luxuriously decorated carriages and an entourage of four thousand individuals. They reached their destination – Heidelberg – on 7 June 1613.

The symbolism was already strong in the Palatine court, which became increasingly regal as the royal couple made it their home. A tournament was announced, and Frederick dressed in the most provocative of clothing. First, he was Jason the Argonaut, the man who stole the Golden Fleece – the Order of the Golden Fleece being the highest chivalric order in the Habsburg realm. Then he was Arminius, defender of the Germans against the Romans – a blatant conflagration of the Germans versus the Habsburgs, who styled themselves as King of the Romans during the process of being crowned Holy Roman Emperor. Driving the point home further, celebrations and performances depicted the Germans reciting in verse the explanation for why the recent Diet in 1613 had failed. The Jesuits, Capuchins and Spanish interference were all freely blamed.[73]

Before the end of the year, Elizabeth was pregnant, and on New Years' Day 1614, she had born her first child – the first of thirteen. A fascinating aspect of this royal couple's offspring was not merely their legacy – as the modern British Hanoverian line is traced to their children –[74] but also these children's names, which serve as a kind of tribute to their illustrious ancestors, as much as to those that later granted the Palatine family asylum and aided their cause. Thus, their son Maurice (b. 1621) was named for Maurice of Nassau the Dutch Stadtholder, while the more blatant Gustavus Adolphus (b. 1632) was named after the triumphant Swedish King of the same name. Both children tell a distinct story of where the Palatine couple was in its struggle against the Habsburgs, and who their leaned on as their allies. It is clear that both individuals leaned on one another; as any married couple would be expected to.

There can also be no doubt that theirs was an immensely fruitful marriage – the ideal of any marriage contract in any century. It was also fortunate that both Elizabeth and Frederick were in love, and from an early stage. This love and affection is sometimes twisted into the aforementioned falsehood that Elizabeth controlled her weak-willed husband, but the evidence attests more to the fact that Elizabeth, in Pursell's words, 'like a good seventeenth century royal spouse...seems to have tried to serve her husband's political objectives without demanding a role in them.' As Frederick wrote himself to Elizabeth on one occasion:

> I would like to be able to write to you as often, but I have so many other letters to write and so little spare time that it impossible for me. Believe that I do not love you the less for that.[75]

Indeed, Frederick V was a very busy man even before accepting the Bohemian crown in autumn 1619. His responsibilities, which he fully assumed in 1614 after his eighteenth birthday, were extensive, and the challenges legion. On his side, Frederick could rely on his numerous Protestant alliances – with the English and Dutch above all – and his position in the Empire as constitutionally supreme, religiously supported and financially secure. However, as the Thirty Years War was soon to demonstrate, such traditional structures counted for nothing when compared to that all-important, primitive failsafe – raw power. While Frederick was militarily buoyed by his allies in the Evangelical Union, the very nature of his lands counted against him, as the historian Robert Zaller appreciated when he wrote:

> Frederick's own dominions...were uniquely exposed to reprisal. Known collectively as the Palatinate, they consisted of two fairly compact areas of roughly equal size, separated by about two hundred miles on an almost exact line of latitude. The Lower (Western) Palatinate was dissected by the Rhine, and lay athwart Spain's route to the Netherlands, while the Upper (Eastern), lying just above the northernmost thrust of the Danube, bordered not only Bohemia but Bavaria, the most powerful Catholic state in the Empire, and Imperial Austria itself. Geography such as this dictated the most extreme caution in foreign relations.[76]

Frederick's capital, Heidelberg, and the place where he and his family made their home and court, was situated in the Lower Palatinate, and was one of three important towns in the region. Straddling the Rhine and its tributaries, such as the Neckar, Heidelberg, Manheim and Frankenthal all played their purpose, as the University City and capital, and the two fortress towns which protected the confluence of the Neckar and the fertile left bank of the Rhine respectively. It is not critically important to appreciate where all of these territories reside, largely because in our narrative, Frederick is unfortunate to not hold onto them for very long. To build a picture of the Elector Palatine's geographical challenges though, we should bear in mind that distance of two hundred miles which separated the two Palatinates; a striking feature of the Holy Roman Empire's apparently nonsensical statecraft, which as usual, had more to do with the traditions of marriage, inheritance and primogeniture than any deliberate Palatine effort to confuse the reader.

If we imagine the Holy Roman Empire as a square, with the square being superimposed on central Europe and modern-day Germany, then it would be correct to place the Lower *Palatinate* in the middle left of that square, especially if we imagine the Rhine as the border of this square. Note that I said Lower Palatinate, because while the Lower section of his lands was his favourite, and unquestionably the most prosperous, Frederick also had responsibility over the Upper Palatinate, and this chunk of territory was positioned in the centre of the square, surrounded by the Habsburgs to the south, Bohemia to the east and Bavaria to the south-west. Both of these halves supported a population of about six hundred thousand – a not inconsiderable number when one considers that the population of Bavaria, Sweden, Scotland, Saxony and Brandenburg was barely a million, and the likes of Wurttemberg, Hesse and Trier had roughly four hundred thousand. Seen in this light, the Palatinate was in the upper tiers of population density in the Holy Roman Empire, but its practical power was less certain.[77]

While his influence within the Holy Roman Empire was considerable, being in possession of two disconnected portions of territory and just over half a million subjects made Frederick V a far less practically powerful figure than the consequences of his actions might suggest. For some time, Palatine diplomacy had held France close, especially once the Protestant Henry IV came to the throne. Christian of Anhalt, later to come under so much scorn from historians for his reckless diplomacy before the Thirty Years War, fought tooth and nail for the Bourbon King's cause, shelling out for the funds out of his own pocket, to the tune of more than one million reichsthalers during one campaign in 1591. The Palatinate sent men as well; ten thousand Palatine soldiers went to fight for the French Protestants in 1568, in 1576, twenty thousand crossed into French territory, and in 1587, twenty-five thousand men made the journey.

These considerable displays of affinity towards the Protestant cause in the French Wars of Religion placed France deeply in debt to the Palatine court, with the latest loan arranged in 1594 amounting to four hundred thousand florins. The turmoil in France and the opportunities this provided the Palatine to back the winning horse were good incentives for the then Elector Palatines to get involved in French business, just as the Habsburgs had made a habit of doing. Once their candidate converted to Catholicism in 1593 though, a sense of coolness entered into Franco-Palatine diplomacy. This did not reduce the francophone nature of Heidelberg though; in fact, this affinity for all things French – in language, art and culture – was enhanced upon the exile of the Huguenot Duke of Bouillon from 1602, who had been implicated in a plot to assassinate Henry IV. Bouillon was Frederick's uncle, and with his father dying at an early age, Frederick spent much of his adolescence at Bouillon's court in Sedan, which had been made into a centre of Calvinist thought and learning. Two things were inculcated in Frederick from this education – a respect for the Holy Roman Empire's constitution, and a love of all things French.[78]

Frederick's fluency in French and fondness for French customs were replicated in Heidelberg when he returned with his bride in 1613. The language was a convenience, as well as necessity, for Frederick's court straddled the Rhine, and was well within reach of the magnetism of the French court. Visitors from the Netherlands, England, the Empire and of course, France itself, provided the Palatine couple with the opportunity to frame their court as one of splendour and influence. If Frederick was concerned at the apparent decay in the Empire's institutions that would normally ensure peace, then he was also sensible enough to rely on the solid foundations of the 1555 Peace of Augsburg, and the fact that this agreement on the religious division of the Empire had preserved peace for over 60 years, a period of time which, as one historian pointed out, was unmatched until the recent stretch of European peace following the Second World War.[79] This despite the fact of course that the Peace of Augsburg did not officially even recognise Frederick's religious creed, but then Frederick's was not the only accepted loophole.

Frederick was only settling into his majority and celebrating the birth of his first son when the Julich-Cleve crisis drew to a close in 1614. The incident had been the latest spat between the Dutch and Spanish, but the French and Austrian Habsburgs also got involved to support their candidates as well. In spite of the close proximity to Spanish satellite states along the Rhine and in the Spanish Netherlands, Heidelberg did not enjoy formal diplomatic relations with Spain. Such non-engagement with Madrid's agents did not mean that either power was ignorant of the other; instead, it indicates Spain's lack of consideration for Palatine power and influence, an attitude which was justified by the rapid pace with which the Spanish and Bavarians conquered the region in the early 1620s.

Palatine diplomacy and Frederick's marital connections to the Dutch, English, Swedes, Danes and Brandenburgers placed him and his party firmly in the Protestant camp, as if his leadership of the Evangelical Union was not enough of a giveaway already. This had the potential to place him in a camp hostile to Spain once the Twelve Years Truce ended in April 1621, and the Spanish-Dutch War was back on. Indeed, historians such as Wedgewood single out the deadline of the Truce's expiration as the moment when Europe's contemporaries anticipated some great conflagration to erupt, but this by no means necessitated the Empire following the Spanish and Dutch into the abyss.[80]

The fact that, in the end, this peace was not held together had as much to do with the inefficiency of the traditional constitutional checks and balances of the Empire as it did with a troubling fact for the Habsburg family – its Austrian branch was shedding its old guard, to make way for a man who was raised in the most thorough iteration of counter-reformation Catholicism yet. It remained to be seen if this figure would be accepted or shunned, and if the latter occurred, how he would react. His name was Ferdinand of Styria, and he was the last, best hope for the Austrian Habsburgs, even while his very candidacy was a subject of intense division and friction both within the Holy Roman Empire and within the Habsburg dynasty itself.

FIVE
Thick as Thieves

In 1613, the same year that one of the final appeals to constitutional calm failed, as the Protestants walked out of the Diet in Regensburg, Ferdinand was putting the finishing touches on a personal rule in Styria which was as disarming as it was impressive. The Archduke of Styria had displayed a single-minded determination to root out heresy in his lands, starting from the moment he had arrived there in 1595 to assume his inheritance. Ferdinand's aforementioned actions in forcibly removing Protestant clergy, in burning ten thousand books, and even in torturing certain Protestant individuals into relinquishing their hold over their schools, do not paint a particularly pleasant picture of the man who would stand as Holy Roman Emperor for nearly twenty years. Indeed, Ferdinand's very behaviour in his own lands can all too easily be seen as the prelude to what followed in the Thirty Years War. He was the 'silly Jesuited soul' who put religion ahead of realism, and enabled his notorious reputation run ahead of itself, to the point that the Habsburgs' traditional bastions of support dramatically revolted just at the wrong time.[81] Yet, there was also more to the person of Ferdinand than a militant Catholic zealot who forced the Thirty Years War into being.[82]

Ferdinand was a man of contradictions. In the first place, despite his reputation for intolerance, Ferdinand's personality was not so easily classified. Far from the austere or dull Catholic zealot, Ferdinand was personable and pleasant to those he met. There was also a different side to his rule over Styria other than the religiously dogmatic treatises which enabled the Counter-Reformation to flourish there. C.V. Wedgewood provided us with a stellar description of his character when she wrote:

> The Archduke Ferdinand was…a cheerful, friendly, red-faced little man with a reassuring smile for everyone. Frank good nature beamed from his freckled countenance and short-sighted, prominent, light blue eyes…Friends and enemies agreed that an easier tempered man was not to be met with. His rule in Styria was conscientious and benevolent; he had started public schemes

for the care of the sock and destitute and the provision of free legal defence for the poor in the law courts. His charity was boundless; he had a memory for the faces of his humblest subjects and a kindly curiosity into their private troubles.[83]

Such a character sketch does not appear to include the ingredients of a religiously motivated absolutist monster. It has to be added to this that Ferdinand was a devoted family man as well as a devout Catholic, and that this latter quality contributed to his infamy more than any other aspect of his character. Indeed, devotion to his family and to God were often intertwined, as the resident Papal Nuncio in his court, Carlo Carafa appreciated when he recalled that Ferdinand...

...goes to bed at around ten in the evening as is the German custom; he is already up around four in the morning or earlier...Once he has got up, His Majesty goes to the chapel to hear two masses, one for the soul of his first wife, who, though of shaky health, was tenderly loved by the Emperor. If it is a feast day, the Emperor then takes holy communion, for which purpose he goes to the church and hears a German sermon. This is usually given by a Jesuit and lasts an hour. After the sermon he remains at the high altar, usually for an hour and a half, accompanied by specially selected music...On those days that are not feast days the emperor, after attending two masses (something from which he never deviates), spends the rest of the morning and often much of the afternoon in council meetings.[84]

What this extract fails to mention was the quality which Ferdinand and many of his peers held in common at this time – a passionate love of the hunt. However, unlike some of his contemporaries – John George of Saxony for instance managed to record over one hundred thousand kills during his tenure as Elector of Saxony – Ferdinand never allowed his pastimes to hamper his responsibilities as a ruler.[85] This, indeed, was more than what could be said for Ferdinand's own relatives. The years before Ferdinand's acceptance first of the Bohemian Crown and then of the title of Holy Roman Emperor over 1617-19, his cousins in Rudolf II (r. 1576-1612) and Matthias (r. 1612-19) had made their contribution not towards the maintenance of the peace per se, but towards the reduction in the dynasty's power base at home and its reputation abroad.

The Defenestration of Prague in May 1618 is widely regarded as the moment when the Thirty Years War began, yet while this event signalled the beginning of a European catastrophe; it also represented the culmination of years of tension and division within Bohemian society.[86] Since 1609, when the ailing Rudolf II was forced to approve of the Letter of Majesty to appease the Bohemians and ease the tensions in the city of Prague where he had made his home, the country presented problems to the dynasty which was supposed to rule over it. According to the Bohemians, the Habsburg rule over their country was a privilege which they bestowed, rather than a hereditary right, since the Bohemian Crown was elective. Due to Bohemia's critical position in the Empire's constitution as one of the Electors though, its crown was far too important to ever let out of the Habsburgs' hands. To Rudolf and Matthias, concessions to the Bohemians, rather than confrontation, appeared the smarter choice, but this did not prevent either figure from engaging in some questionable practices in private, while putting on a public face of toleration and acceptance of Bohemia's traditional liberties.

'The truth was', wrote one historian, 'Bohemia in the later sixteenth century was in the most dismal confusion'.[87] This confusion was caused by the religious, societal and political divisions of the country, which were exacerbated by Habsburg involvement in Bohemian affairs, and the ambitions of Bohemia's Emperor-Kings to recast their rule in a more secure position. The tensions between the Habsburg Kings of Bohemia and the people of Bohemia reached their peak during the tenure of the three Habsburg Kings that ruled before the Thirty Years War broke out – specifically, between the years 1608-1618.

During the war with the Turks, Matthias had pacified the Hungarians by promising them religious toleration, but this had led to increasingly loud calls from other estates in the Habsburg domains, as the people of Bohemia, Austria and Moravia agitated for similar concessions. When the deputations from the estates in these lands failed to wrest the desired concessions from Rudolf, they turned instead to his brother Matthias. In January 1608 Matthias received the Crown of Hungary in return for his pledges to uphold religious toleration for the Protestants there. In April that same year, the largely Protestant Austrian and Moravian estates received similar guarantees in return for their commitment to raise an army for Matthias so that he could march on Prague and depose his brother. Rudolf relinquished his control over these provinces in June, clinging still to his Imperial title, as well as to Bohemia, Silesia and Lusatia – three of the four provinces which together made the kingdom of Bohemia, the other being Moravia.

Matthias ought to have known better than to stall, in the hopes that the Protestants of Austria, Moravia and Hungary would perhaps forget about their jealously defended religious privileges. Over the summer of 1608 though, Matthias did not implement the religious acts which his subjects had expected, so they took matters into their own hands. By October the estates of Upper and Lower Austria had forged an alliance among themselves, cast as a Confederation to preserve their freedoms, and before long foreign actors, such as Christian of Anhalt from the Palatinate, were getting in touch. This spurred Matthias into action; he confirmed the privileges of the Protestants in Austria, Moravia and Hungary in March 1609.

Back in Prague, the ailing Rudolf was facing renewed pressure from the Bohemians to make similar pronouncements on their religious privileges. As with the Austrians, the majority Protestant Bohemians gathered together to mount pressure on their Emperor and King, and once again, Christian of Anhalt approached. Unwilling to watch his rule decay any further, Rudolf bowed to the inevitable, and signed the Letter of Majesty on 9 July 1609. The Bohemians were granted religious toleration in line with their neighbours in the Habsburg lands, while they also acquired the right to maintain a standing committee of Defensors, which would liaise between the estates in the different regions of Bohemia, and ensure that Rudolf remained true to his promises.[88]

The underlying message was sent that if Rudolf did not keep his word, then the Bohemians would move against him in force; indeed this eventuality came to pass in January 1611, when Archduke Leopold, the younger brother of Ferdinand of Styria and the cousin of Rudolf and Matthias, marched on Prague with seven thousand men. Rudolf's reasoning for allowing his cousin to march into his lands may have been due to the Emperor's anger at being forced to make concessions to Protestants, or it may have been as simple as wishing to reassert his authority over the Bohemian people. The year before, during the Julich-Cleves crisis in 1610, the same Leopold, marching with the same army, had invaded Julich and attempted to create a *fait accompli* for the claimants to the duchies, without success. Here again, the Emperor's cousin appeared to be jumping the gun; the trick did not work in Julich, and it was met with a still more startling failure at Prague.

According to the settlement made with Matthias during the Julich-Cleves crisis, Leopold was supposed to reduce his army's size and move to Passau, where his bishopric was located. Making a great deal of noise about the difficulties of moving an army home over the winter of 1610-1611 though, Leopold asked his cousin if he could quarter his forces in southern Bohemia. The Bohemian estates were greatly concerned that Rudolf might use Leopold's army of seven thousand men against them, so to meet this issue they volunteered provisions for Leopold's force, in the hope that the troublesome Archduke would be on his way before long. In public, Rudolf gave assurances to the Bohemians that Leopold's army would not be allowed in Bohemia, but in private, Rudolf welcomed his cousin in, and seemed indeed to intend to fulfil the worst fears of the Bohemians.[89]

The reaction of the Bohemians was predictably apoplectic. At first in disbelief that Rudolf would effectively lie to their faces, the Defensors of the estates soon set to work organising a defence of Prague, where Leopold appeared to be headed by late January 1611. By mid-February, the Bohemian crown jewels had been moved from Prague, and the Defensors had appealed to Matthias to depose Rudolf and come to their rescue. In the meantime,

Leopold had gathered his forces near White Mountain, curiously close to the spot where, nine years' later, the more infamous Bohemian revolt would be crushed.

Indeed, the incident of the Leopold's invasion of Bohemia created further parallels with the later revolt; arguably the most striking was the practice of defenestration among the citizens of Prague, who turned on several Jesuit institutions and Catholic Churches which had been installed during Rudolf's reign. The uncontrolled chaos which afflicted the streets of Prague – as Leopold's invading force clashed with the hastily assembled Bohemian militia – hinted at the scenes which were to follow the ultimate defeat of the Bohemian rebels in late 1620;. Unsurprisingly, considering their King's track record, the Protestants of Prague in 1611 were desperately fearful and paranoid that the invasion by the Leopold was only one part of Rudolf's plan, and that the other was to take over the city from within. One witness recalled that:

> a shot rang from the top of the Jesuit College onto residents of the Old City, and the common man built it up in his head that a murder spree was about to take place whose purpose was to stamp out his religion.[90]

Leopold's troops proved unfit for the task of seizing Prague, and with rumours of reinforcements led by Matthias in route, they fled the city and returned with Leopold to Passau. Arriving in Prague in March 1611, Matthias agreed to depose his dying brother, and to respect the Letter of Majesty which the Bohemians had so desperately guarded. By May of that year, Matthias was crowned King of Bohemia in a ceremony that directly referenced and specifically confirmed the Letter of Majesty in its charter. The Bohemian Protestants, and everyone in between, it appeared, could rest easy and trust in their new King's promises. Discussions about electing the next Holy Roman Emperor were hosted in Regensburg over September to October 1611, whereupon those gathered debated the finer points of the different Habsburg candidates on offer. The 55-year-old Matthias, as childless as his brother, would not be approved until the following June, after Rudolf died in January 1612 and added an element of urgency to the proceedings.

Had Matthias learned much from the Bohemian trials? Considering its location as the flashpoint for the Thirty Years War only seven years after its initial revolt, it can appear incredible that yet another revolt, this one far more damaging, could have erupted in Bohemia yet again. Motivated by fears about their religious guarantees, the Defensors acted in summer 1618 to defend these privileges, but across Prague and Bohemia as a whole the mood was a great deal more rebellious than it had been in 1611. What had changed in the interim to make the Bohemians so rebellious, and how had these feelings been allowed to so develop, when the Habsburg family had

295

seen first-hand what the penalties were for mismanaging their subjects? Such questions appear all the more mysterious given Matthias' reputation for being soft on Protestants, the forceful eviction of his belligerent cousin Leopold from Prague, and his insistence on replacing his intolerant, stubborn older brother with an individual that better understood the nuances of Bohemian society – himself.

Explaining how the Bohemian revolt erupted in 1618, as much as explaining why this revolt transformed into the Thirty Years War, is an impossible task unless we appreciate what came before. The short answer is that between the years 1612-18, Bohemian society became more anxious for its privileges, and Matthias apparently became more interested in finding loopholes to wrest fresh concessions out of the Letter of Majesty to the benefit of Catholics – he alienated 132 parishes to the Archbishop of Prague during his brief reign, demonstrating that his zeal for Catholicism had by no means waned.[91] This was despite the fact that Matthias knew precisely how costly and damaging the period 1608-12 had been not just for the Habsburg reputation, but also for its already dangerously depleted coffers.

It is worth reiterating the fact that the adventures of Archduke Leopold, as he had moved through Upper Austria and into Bohemia in January 1611, had cost the dynasty dearly. Leopold's soldiers, who had been unpaid in their previous campaigns in both the Turkish War and in the more recent Julich-Cleves War, rampaged across the countryside in search of payment in kind. These soldiers caused 2 million florins worth of damage to the Upper Austrian and Bohemian lands and carted around as much as 269 wagons full of booty while they marched. Leopold's army apparently went rogue, to the point that even this unscrupulous Archduke became embarrassed at its behaviour, and he joined this army outside Prague just in time to watch his cavalry abscond with the limited funds he had raised to pay for his ill-behaved soldiers. With Prague's militia guarding the bridges into the main portion of the city, and his infantry having no hope of payment, Leopold fled the scene, as we saw, in mid-March, before his cousin could arrive.

Again, this experience should have taught the Habsburgs a stern lesson. Where soldiers could not find payment from their masters, they would effectively turn rogue in their quest to acquire it. In addition, while their own personal lands were ravaged by this rampaging army, it is worth underlining that neither Matthias nor Rudolf were particularly quick in acting, because they appreciated that any effective response would require money, and money was in the hands of the estates, who would require religious concessions in return for parting with it. In other words, the Habsburgs watched their own lands burn and people be slaughtered, while they hesitated to grant their subjects the religious toleration they desired.[92] All of these experiences; from the religious unrest in Bohemia, to the bloody revolts in Hungary, to even the Turkish War itself – they all revealed much about the dangers of miscalculation, want of funds and the religious sensitivities of their subjects. They also revealed how desperately vulnerable the Habsburg lands were to attack and invasion by either a Turkish force, a rebellious band of Magyars, or a rampaging Habsburg army in search of payment. These experiences should have been properly absorbed, and the warnings fully heeded, but they were not. Instead, with the immediate problems patched up, the root causes were ignored, as Matthias settled into his short reign as Emperor.

The Brothers' Quarrel is the name given to the contest between Rudolf and Matthias, and it is easy in many respects to view it as a wasteful, unnecessary conflict which only weakened the position of the Austrian Habsburg family, and which facilitated religious concessions to their Protestant subjects which no Catholic Austrian Habsburg, operating according to the terms of the 1555 Peace of Augsburg, could possibly countenance in the long term.[93] Yet the Brothers' Quarrel also obliterated what little credit the two brothers still had; Rudolf's untrustworthiness became notorious, as did Leopold's belligerence. Overall, the experience left the dynasty more critically deep in debt, devoid of goodwill, surrounded by subjects that had been kept loyal only through the bribe of unsustainable religious concessions – in the Habsburg mind at least – and promises which they had no genuine desire to keep.

The Habsburgs had squandered much of the goodwill of their subjects, who now anxiously relied upon promises which had been wrested from their masters under duress. This had not been the case under previous Habsburg Emperors, specifically those that ruled before Rudolf II. Indeed, the Habsburgs became increasingly absolutist and dogmatic in their spread of Catholicism,[94] thanks largely to the heightened activity of the Jesuits, who helped improve the Habsburgs' image, and placed additional powers in their hands. In the past, Habsburg authority had been intertwined with the dynasty's ability to intervene in religious disputes and find an acceptable balance. By the end of the Brothers' Quarrel though, the only measure of Habsburg authority that seemed to matter was the dynasty's ability to forcibly assert its claims and powers over its subjects, who felt equally inclined to resist, since these efforts came twinned with a domineering quest to revive Catholicism under the Counter-Reformation.[95]

One individual who must be credited with at least attempting to solve some of the Empire's problems was Melchior Klesl, Matthias' personal advisor and the Bishop of Vienna. Between 1612-1618, Klesl represented one of the leading lights of Austrian Habsburg policymaking, and a strong advocate for cooperation between the two religiously divided camps. The example given by the late Emperor Rudolf and his replacement can hardly have inspired much faith in Klesl's mission, but this was not from lack of trying on his part. Klesl genuinely laboured to disarm the two confessional alliance blocs during the August 1613 Diet at Regensburg, but as we have seen previously, he was unsuccessful. Klesl wrote private letters to each of the attendees, including Christian of Anhalt, but this gesture did not bear fruit.

It was not only an opportunity to foster cooperation among the moderates, it was also a chance to repair the damage wrought during the stormy session of 1608, whereupon disgusted Protestant princes had walked out of the Diet, and shortly thereafter formed the Evangelical Union. Klesl hoped that if he appealed to the moderates and ratified religious toleration in certain cities, that the extremist parties – vindicated to some extent by the revolts in the Habsburgs' own lands, it has to be said – would be disarmed. To Yet, the extremists were not disarmed, and nor were the two alliance blocks, which had both gone on to connect to further foreign capitals since their establishment five years' before. The further goal of isolating the leader of anti-Habsburg cooperation – the Palatinate – also failed, as Klesl could not rally enough Protestants or Catholics to his side. The Diet essentially solved nothing, and though all involved could not know it yet, it was the final time they would meet in this capacity until 1640.

Klesl's efforts after the event to undermine the Catholic League were rewarded by the creation of a 'Christian Defence' in May 1614, in a bid to recast the league as non-sectarian and open to all. Another Habsburg Archduke was brought in to lead it in tandem with Maximillian of Bavaria, but the latter disapproved of this Habsburg interference, and created his own secret alliance of Catholic powers over the next few months. The original Catholic League was soon disbanded, but this whole process had the effect of neutering the Catholic response to the inflammation of the Julich-Cleve crisis later in the year. Klesl's actions did intertwine the Habsburg dynasty with this new organisation, demonstrating that the Austrian Habsburgs could not stand aloof from such a grouping, but this act could not make up for the bare facts about the dynasty's position by 1614.

Besieged at home by Protestants, shamed after several failed military initiatives, and deeply in debt to legions of soldiers, who could still be seen traipsing bitterly around the outskirts of Vienna in search of pay, the years since the eruption of the Turkish War had not been kind to the Austrian Habsburgs, and a further problem loomed. Far from the distinct problems of the Empire, and near the periphery of civilisation itself, lay the Northern powers of Scandinavia and Eastern Europe. While apparently disconnected from the Austrian Habsburgs dilemmas and Ferdinand's ambitions, in time, this portion of Europe was to make the greatest contribution towards the prolonging of the Thirty Years War, as Germany's populace were set alight by the Lion of the North. Before he made his mark though, this lion would have to grow.

Chapter 6 Notes

[1]Cited in James, 'Speech to parliament of 19 March 1604', *King James VI & I: Political Writings*, ed. by Johann P. Sommerville (Cambridge: Cambridge University Press, 1994), p. 136.

[2]James, 'Speech to parliament of 19 March 1604', *Political Writings*, pp. 132,

[3]*Ibid*, pp. 136–37.

[4]Robert Lawson-Peebles, 'A Conjoined Commonwealth: The Implications of the Accession of James VI and I', *The Yearbook of English Studies*, Vol. 46, Writing the Americas, 1480–1826 (2016),pp. 56-74; p. 60.

[5]Alexandra Gajda, 'Debating War And Peace In Late Elizabethan England', *The Historical Journal*, Vol. 52, No. 4 (DECEMBER 2009), pp. 851-878; p. 851.

[6]John Guy, 'The 1590s: the second reign of Elizabeth I?', in John Guy, ed., *The reign of Elizabeth I: court and culture in the last decade* (Cambridge, 1995), pp. 1-19.

[7]Alexandra Gajda, 'Debating War And Peace In Late Elizabethan England', p. 851.

[8]Roland Dennis Hussey, 'America in European Diplomacy, 1597-1604', *Revista de Historia de América*, No. 41 (Jun., 1956), pp. 1-30; p. 1.

[9]Pauline Croft, 'Trading with the Enemy 1585-1604', *The Historical Journal*, Vol. 32, No. 2 (Jun., 1989), pp. 281-302; p. 282.

[10]Alexander Samon, 'Changing Places: The Marriage and Royal Entry of Philip, Prince of Austria, and Mary Tudor, July-August 1554', *The Sixteenth Century Journal*, Vol. 36, No. 3 (Fall, 2005), pp. 761-784.

[11]Albert J. Loomie, 'Toleration and Diplomacy: The Religious Issue in Anglo-Spanish Relations, 1603-1605', *Transactions of the American Philosophical Society*, Vol. 53, No. 6 (1963), pp. 1-60.

[12]Roland Dennis Hussey, 'America in European Diplomacy', p. 3.

[13]Sanjay Subrahmanyam, 'Holding the World in Balance: The Connected Histories of the Iberian Overseas Empires,1500-1640', *The American Historical Review*, Vol. 112, No. 5 (Dec., 2007), pp. 1359-1385.

[14]Alexandra Gajda, 'Debating War And Peace In Late Elizabethan England', pp. 851-852.

[15]Pauline Croft, 'Trading with the Enemy', pp. 301-302.

[16]Gustav Ungerer, 'The Spanish and English Chronicles in King James's and Sir George Buc's Dossiers on the Anglo-Spanish Peace Negotiations', *Huntington Library Quarterly*, Vol. 61, No. 3/4 (1998), pp. 309-324; pp. 312-313.

[17]Roland Dennis Hussey, 'America in European Diplomacy', p. 7.

[18]*Ibid*, pp. 7-10.

[19]Charles H. Carter, 'Belgian "Autonomy" under the Archdukes, 1598-1621', *The Journal of Modern History*, Vol. 36, No. 3 (Sept., 1964), pp. 245-259; p. 245.

[20]*Ibid*, p. 246.

[21]Catholics remained behind in the Dutch Netherlands and maintained a strange relationship with the King they used to obey and their new masters in the Republic who looked unfavourably upon their religion. See Geert H. Janssen, 'Quo Vadis? Catholic Perceptions of Flight and the Revolt of the Low Countries, 1566–1609', *Renaissance Quarterly*, Vol. 64, No. 2 (Summer 2011), pp. 472-499.

[22]See Carter, *Secret Diplomacy of the Habsburgs*, pp. 12-13.

[23]Geyl, *History of the Dutch-Speaking Peoples* pp. 226-227.

[24]C. M. Kortepeter, 'Ġāzī Girāy II, Khan of the Crimea, and Ottoman Policy in Eastern Europe and the Caucasus, 1588-94', *The Slavonic and East European Review*, Vol. 44, No. 102 (Jan., 1966), pp. 139-166; p. 140.

[25]Geoffrey Parker, *Europe in Crisis*, p. 83; p. 341 Chapter III footnote 1.

[26]Franklin L. Baumer, 'England, the Turk, and the Common Corps of Christendom', *The American Historical Review*, Vol. 50, No. 1 (Oct., 1944), pp. 26-48; p. 27.

[27]Rayne Allison, *A Monarchy of Letters: Royal Correspondence and English Diplomacy in the Reign of Elizabeth I* (Springer; London, 2012), p. 132.

[28]See David M. Bergeron, '"Are we turned Turks?": English Pageants and the Stuart Court', *Comparative Drama*, Vol. 44, No. 3 (Fall 2010), pp. 255-275; pp. 255-256.

[29]An excellent summary can be found in Andrew C. Hess, 'The Battle of Lepanto and Its Place in Mediterranean History', *Past & Present*, No. 57 (Nov., 1972), pp. 53-73.

[30]Geoffrey Parker, *Europe in Crisis*, p. 77.

[31]John F. Guilmartin, Jr., 'Ideology and Conflict: The Wars of the Ottoman Empire, 1453-1606', *The Journal of Interdisciplinary History*, Vol. 18, No. 4, The Origin and Prevention of Major Wars (Spring, 1988), pp. 721-747; pp. 726-727.

[32]Andrew Wheatcroft, *Enemy at the Gates*, pp.

[33]William Holden Hutton, *Constantinople: The Story of the Old Capital of the Empire* (J.M. Dent & Co; London, 1900), p. 172.

[34]Demetrius Ion Ghica, 'MICHEL V., SURNAMED "THE BRAVE," PRINCE OF WALLACHIA. 1593—1601', *The Numismatic Chronicle and Journal of the Numismatic Society*, New Series, Vol. 16 (1876), pp. 161-176; pp. 172-173.

[35]*Ibid*, p. 176.

[36]See Geoffrey Parker, *Europe in Crisis*, pp. 79-81.

[37]It is important to stress that while a Habsburg-Persian alliance did not technically exist, several efforts were made to establish one, and these efforts fostered cooperation notwithstanding the official lack of treaty. See David Robert Stokes, *A Failed Alliance And Expanding Horizons: Relations Between The Austrian Habsburgs And The Safavid Persians In The Sixteenth And Seventeenth Centuries* (PhD Thesis, University of St Andrews, 2014).

[38]On the Franco-Ottoman alliance see De Lamar Jensen, 'The Ottoman Turks in Sixteenth Century French Diplomacy', *The Sixteenth Century Journal*, Vol. 16, No. 4 (Winter, 1985), pp. 451-470.

[39]John F. Guilmartin, Jr, 'Ideology and Conflict: The Wars of the Ottoman Empire, 1453-1606', pp. 727-728.

[40]C. F. Finkel, 'French Mercenaries in the Habsburg-Ottoman War of 1593-1606: The Desertion of the Papa Garrison to the Ottomans in 1600', *Bulletin of the School of Oriental and African Studies*, University of London, Vol.55, No. 3 (1992), pp. 451-471; pp. 465-466.

[41]*Ibid*, p. 465.

[42]Cited in Geoffrey Parker, *Thirty Years War*, p. 11.

[43]Cited in *Ibid*, p. 12.

[44]For a concise examination of the activities of the Supreme Court before the seventeenth century lapse, see Ralf-Peter Fuchs, 'The Supreme Court of the Holy Roman Empire: The State of Research and the Outlook', *The Sixteenth Century Journal*, Vol. 34, No. 1 (Spring, 2003), pp. 9-27.

[45]To accessible accounts of this conflict are provided in Jill Raitt, 'The Emperor and the Exiles: The Clash of Religion and Politics in the Late Sixteenth Century', *Church History*, Vol. 52, No. 2 (Jun., 1983), pp. 145-156; Gabriele Haug-Moritz, 'The Holy Roman Empire, the Schmalkald League, and the Idea of Confessional Nation-Building', *Proceedings of the American Philosophical Society*, Vol. 152, No. 4 (Dec., 2008), pp. 427-439.

[46]See Geoffrey Parker, *Thirty Years War*, pp. 4-5.

[47]A concise account of the rise of the Habsburg family, with a particular focus on Austrian acquisitions, can be found in Jean Berenger and C.A. Simpson, *A History of the Habsburg Empire 1273-1700* (Routledge; London, 2014); see especially chapters 4-14. See also Andrew Wheatcroft, *The Habsburgs*, chapters 3-5.

[48]Geoffrey Parker, *Thirty Years War*, p. 5.

[49]Geoff Mortimer, *Wallenstein*, pp. 11-13.

[50]Geoffrey Parker, *Thirty Years War*, p. 7.

[51]Peter Brightwell, 'The Spanish System and the Twelve Years' Truce', *The English Historical Review*, Vol. 89, No. 351 (Apr., 1974), pp. 270-292; pp. 271-273.

[52]Geoffrey Parker, *Thirty Years War*, p. 13.

[53]Peter H. Wilson, *Europe's Tragedy*, pp. 22-23.

[54]Geoffrey Parker, *Thirty Years War*, p. 15.

[55]Wedgewood, *Thirty Years War*, p. 66.

[56]Charles P. Kindleberger, 'The Economic Crisis of 1619 to 1623', *The Journal of Economic History*, Vol. 51, No. 1 (Mar., 1991), pp. 149-175.

[57]Sheilagh C. Ogilvie, 'Germany and the Seventeenth-Century Crisis', *The Historical Journal*, Vol. 35, No. 2 (Jun., 1992), pp. 417-441.

[58]Geoffrey Parker, *The Thirty Years War*, p. 30.

[59]Pursell, *Winter King*, p. 36; footnote 17.

[60]See Peter H. Wilson, Dynasty, 'Constitution, and Confession: The Role of Religion in the Thirty Years War', *The International History Review*, Vol. 30, No. 3 (Sep., 2008), pp. 473-514; pp. 482-484.

[61]Pursell, *Winter King*, p. 19-20.

[62]Three stellar accounts examining the origins of the Thirty Years War can be found in Myron P. Gutmann, 'The Origins of the Thirty Years' War', *The Journal of Interdisciplinary History*, Vol. 18, No. 4, The Origin and Prevention of Major Wars (Spring, 1988), pp. 749-770; Peter H. Wilson, 'The Causes of the Thirty Years War 1618-48', *The English Historical Review*, Vol. 123, No. 502 (Jun., 2008), pp. 554-586; N. M. Sutherland, 'The Origins of the Thirty Years War and the Structure of European Politics', *The English Historical Review*, Vol. 107, No. 424 (Jul., 1992), pp. 587-625.

[63]Brennan C. Pursell, 'Elector Palatine Friedrich V and the Question of Influence Revisited', *The Court Historian* vol. 6, (2001), pp. 123-139; p. 123.

[64]References cited in Pursell, *The Winter King*, p. 17.

[65]Wedgewood, *The Thirty Years War*, pp. 55-56.

[66]On this revisionist note see Pursell, *The Winter King*, p. 37, footnote 36.

[67]*Ibid*, p. 17.

[68]C.V. Wedgewood, *Thirty Years War*, p. 67.

[69]Peter H. Wilson, *Europe's Tragedy*, p. 247.

[70]Brennan C. Pursell, *Winter King*, p. 17.

[71]See *Ibid*, pp. 17-18.

[72]In 1620, to celebrate James' commitment to peace and to emphasise their anxious hope that he would continue to further this policy, the *Tyumphs of Peace* debuted in London – a play dedicated to the English propensity for peace-making, and James' pivotal role in fostering it. See J. Caitlin Finlayson, 'Jacobean Foreign Policy, London's Civic Polity, and John Squire's Lord Mayor's Show, "The Tryumphs of Peace" (1620)', *Studies in Philology*, Vol. 110, No. 3 (Summer, 2013), pp. 584-610.

[73]See Peter H. Wilson, *Europe's Tragedy*, pp. 247-248.

[74]Specifically, it was Sophie, a daughter of Frederick and Elizabeth, who married the Duke of Hanover, and was declared the heir to the British throne in the early eighteenth century. Her son George of Hanover – Frederick V and Elizabeth Stuart's grandson – would rule as George I.

[75]See Pursell, *Winter King*, p. 22.

[76]Robert Zaller, '"Interest of State": James I and the Palatinate', *Albion: A Quarterly Journal Concerned with British Studies*, Vol. 6, No. 2(Summer, 1974), pp. 144-175; p. 145.

[77]Geoffrey Parker, *Europe in Crisis*, p. 81.

[78]Pursell, *Winter King*, p. 18.

[79]Peter H. Wilson, *Europe's Tragedy*, p. 10.

[80]Wedgewood, *Thirty Years War*, p. 53.

[81]Peter H. Wilson, *Europe's Tragedy*, p. 70.

[82]Peter H. Wilson, 'Dynasty, Constitution, and Confession: The Role of Religion in the Thirty Years War', p. 485.

[83]C.V. Wedgewood, *Thirty Years War*, p. 60.

[84]Cited in Peter H. Wilson, *Europe's Tragedy*, pp. 70-71.

[85]*Ibid*, p. 246.

[86]Myron P. Gutmann, 'The Origins of the Thirty Years' War', pp. 763-764.

[87]Wedgewood, *Thirty Years War*, p. 70.

[88]Geoffrey Parker, *Europe in Crisis*, pp. 90-91.

[89]James R. Palmitessa, 'The Prague Uprising of 1611: Property, Politics, and Catholic Renewal in the Early Years of Habsburg Rule', *Central European History*, Vol. 31, No. 4 (1998), pp. 299-328; pp. 303-304.

[90]Cited in *Ibid*, p. 307.

[91]Geoffrey Parker, *Europe in Crisis*, p. 158.

[92]Peter H. Wilson, *Europe's Tragedy*, p. 240.

[93]The 1555 principle of *cuius regio, eius religio* entitled the ruler to impose his religion on his subjects, or at least to make that religion the official creed of his state. The ruler was not obliged to grant toleration to those subjects that did not subscribe to his creed, but in practice this principle was altered according to circumstance in the half century which followed, particularly as the rise of Calvinism complicated its tenants.

[94]Karin J. MacHardy, 'The Rise of Absolutism and Noble Rebellion in Early Modern Habsburg Austria, 1570 to 1620', *Comparative Studies in Society and History*, Vol. 34, No. 3 (Jul., 1992), pp. 407-438.

[95]Peter H. Wilson, *Europe's Tragedy*, p. 114.

(Top left) Zigmunt Waza, King of Poland-Lithuania (Pieter Soutman)
(Top right) Emperor Matthias (1557 – 1619)

(Top left) Defenestration of Prague – 1618
(Top right) Christian I of Anhalt (Benbur)

CHAPTER SEVEN
"Constructing Catastrophe"

ONE
Northern Tremors

The Peace of Vervins may have ushered in a new era of peace between the Spanish and French in 1598, but in that same year, far to the north-west, off the coast of the Swedish capital of Stockholm, a new era of conflict and hostility was being confirmed instead. Sigismund Vasa, King of Poland and officially still the King of Sweden, was forced to sail away from this latter possession, after failing once again to regain it. It was a bitter pill for the proud Sigismund to swallow, yet it guaranteed that conflict was to be rooted in this region for decades to come.

Sigismund Vasa was the Charles V of the North – he had been born to a Polish mother and Swedish father, and had inherited both realms, even though the Polish Crown was technically elective. Ascending to the throne of Poland and Sweden by 1592, Sigismund seemed poised to unite the two realms and to make the House of Vasa into a name greater than any other in the north. Opportunities for glory, expansion and enrichment abounded, but even as the crown of Sweden was placed upon his head, Sigismund encountered problems. His uncle Charles was a Lutheran, as was much of Sweden's population,[1] whereas Sigismund, according to the wishes of his mother, had been brought up a Catholic, and during some trying times earlier in his life, had been taught to rely on the Jesuits, who remained by his side to the end of his days. In terms of the religious differences amongst his scattered people then, Sigismund was every bit like Charles V, but that was where the similarities ended.

His domains were not quite as large as those of Charles V, but they were certainly an acceptable consolation prize. Poland-Lithuania, Sigismund's first crown, was a composite state effectively ruled by the nobility, which nonetheless boasted an elective monarchy. This complex and multi-layered polity is best known as the Commonwealth, but its nobles also saw themselves as pioneers in advancing the rights of their class, and in avoiding that eternal bugbear of all civilised states – absolutism. The Polish-Lithuanian Commonwealth was the largest state in Europe apart from Muscovy to the distant, wild east, and under its writ were lands almost one million square kilometres in size.

This incredible accumulation of land under the Commonwealth was a result of the haphazard expansion of the Grand Duchy of Lithuania, which was fused to Poland in 1569, as much as it was due to the enterprising ambitions of the Poles themselves, who brought 'democracy' and 'civilisation' to modern day Belarus, Ukraine and Livonia. Livonia was the name given to the Duchy which constituted the modern Baltic States of Latvia and Estonia, and its rich ports and geographically important location had rendered it a hot potato between the relevant powers over the previous decades, with Muscovy, Sweden, Denmark and the eventually victorious Poles all vying for the loyalties of its nobility and the rights over its lands. The last century had been something of a golden age for Polish culture and commerce, as wealthy nobles had increased their land holdings to grow fat and happy on the lucrative grain trade and traded this grain in exchange for finished European goods.

Since the late fourteenth century, Poland and Lithuania had shared the same dynasty, the Jagiellonian, which had held the crowns of Poland, Bohemia, Hungary and Croatia at any one time, and expanded its horizons through marriage efforts which only the Habsburgs would supersede. The looming extinction of this dynasty and fear of mutual enemies, as much as historical traditions and the power of the nobility, compelled the two entities of Poland and Lithuania to transform their union from a dynastic into a real union in 1569, when the Union of Lublin was signed. Among other things, the Union of Lublin was the opportunity for the nobility of both states to band together, as a multinational parliament, the Sejm, was incepted at Warsaw, and religious toleration guaranteed for all. Another critically important decision was that made which made an old concession an official policy – all Kings of Poland would henceforth be elected. Blood claims alone would no longer be sufficient to guarantee the successful ascension to the Polish throne.

By the time Sigismund was elected to that throne in 1587, the nobility of the Polish-Lithuanian Commonwealth had already been ruled by a French King and a Hungarian King, and the maternal pedigree of Sigismund – his mother had been the sister of Poland's last Jagiellonian King – recommended him to the nostalgic Election Sejm. Sigismund was crowned as King Sigismund III of Poland, but for the 21-year-old Prince, this was only the first step. The next was to wait until his father, King John III of Sweden had died. Once that happened, Sigismund obtained the Swedish Crown with far less faffing by the nobility, largely thanks to the efforts of his father John and uncle Charles in bringing the nobility over to their side. Sigismund's father, King John, had been somewhat concerned at his younger brother's growing wealth and influence, which had enabled Charles to carve out a duchy for himself in central Sweden, and to wield a considerable amount of power within Swedish society.

Still, Charles remained loyal to his brother's legacy and to his half-Polish nephew, just as long as Sigismund appointed Charles regent, which placed extensive powers in his uncle's hands while he was in Poland. The stubbornness and ambitions of both men meant that the relationship between uncle and nephew seemed destined to worsen once King John died, and when this happened in November 1592 the cracks began to appear and deepen with each passing year. Neither Sigismund nor Charles went about things particularly amicably – the mutual distrust and the religious differences also did not help matters. Co-opting some elements of Sweden's Diet, in 1597 Uncle Charles outlawed the regency government installed by Sigismund to protect his interests while he was away.

Entreaties to reverse this decision were met with silence, as Charles began reinforcing the extensive portfolio of castles which he held, purchasing additional fortresses from the now deeply divided Swedish nobility. Many of Sweden's noble families did not want to choose, but the quarrel between uncle and nephew forced their hands – most, as it happened, flocked to Sigismund's banners, and with most of the Swedish nobility but fewer strategic advantages, Sigismund returned several times to Sweden with expeditionary forces in order to reclaim his Swedish Crown, which Charles had still not officially usurped. As it happened, Charles was biding his time and preparing the ground for this new branch of the Vasa to rule Sweden. Charles could offer Sweden's nobility a truly Protestant and wholly Swedish line which would serve Swedish interests properly, rather than suffer an absentee King. The trauma of the civil war between the Vasa branches was momentarily breached in 1599 by an interesting offer.

If Sigismund would send his son Wladyslaw to Sweden to be raised as a Lutheran King, then the Swedish Riksdag would accept this and would cease their rebellion against him and would alienate Charles. Sigismund was plainly unable to accede to this demand, placing as he did the demands of the Jesuits – who would never allow Sweden to drift out of the Catholic orbit on their approval – above all other counsel. It was of course doubtful how united behind this proposal Sweden would have been, but in any case, Sigismund dismissed it without too much thought. As a result, Sigismund lost his last chance to save the situation in Sweden, and by extension, he lost his Swedish Crown. By this action, in a little-known family feud in the closing years of the sixteenth century, the House of Vasa was to be divided among its Catholic line, with Sigismund at its head, ruling in Poland, and its Lutheran line, with Charles, crowned in 1604 as King Charles IX, ruling in Sweden. The ambitious union which Sigismund had so hoped for had ended with a messy divorce, and Sigismund himself had to share some of the blame for this turn of events.[2] To King Sigismund's contemporaries, it almost seemed as though, as the Holy Roman Emperor Ferdinand II later reflected, that 'In order to make sure of heaven he has renounced Earth.'[3]

Sigismund and Charles, members of the same family, were now dynastic as much as they were religious enemies, and as the years progressed, this feud between the Vasa branches was sharpened by the foreign policy decisions of each. Both Charles and Sigismund focused their attentions on Livonia, that lucrative corner of the Baltic where great opportunities for trade existed for those willing to seize them. Charles believed himself equal to this task and landed with an army of nearly eight thousand men in 1602 with a view towards taking these Baltic jewels for his burgeoning kingdom. By taking Livonia from Poland, Charles would be able to severely hamper his nephew's coffers, but in this act, the up to now successful Charles overstepped.

In the previous quarrels, the nobility or *szlachta* of Poland-Lithuania were willing to allow the conflict between uncle and nephew to simmer, having nothing much to do with it. The one exception to this rule was the notable occasion when a generous grant of seventeen thousand soldiers was made to Sigismund to reclaim Sweden in 1598, in a campaign which was ultimately unsuccessful.[4] That it was unsuccessful intimated to the Polish-Lithuanian nobles that Sweden could not be retaken, and thus should be let slip out of their King's orbit, but Sigismund bitterly contested this, and this bitterness is what we opened the chapter with, as a dejected Polish King sailed away from the land of his birth, never to return.

It made sense that the Polish nobility had little enthusiasm for helping Sigismund fight against his uncle in what was essentially a dynastic war, a family feud, and little business of theirs. Where Charles overstepped though was when he decided to take the fight to Sigismund by invading Livonia. Not only were these lands under the protection of the Commonwealth, they also happened to house some lucrative estates and manor houses, as well as some important agricultural investments, of the Commonwealth's nobility. Suddenly with their own interests directly threatened by the Swedish upstart, the *szlachta* now did have a reason to fight against Sigismund's uncle, and they did so in one of the most incredible, stunning ways possible.

During the Battle of Kircholm in September 1605, the winged hussars, Poland's elite shock cavalry, were sent in, and in the space of less than half an hour, utterly routed the numerically superior Swedish forces. Charles and the remnants of his army were sent packing, and Livonia was never seriously threatened again. With Charles licking his wounds, King Sigismund of Poland now had the perfect opportunity to put his uncle down once and for all, with another invasion of the land of his birth. At this moment though, Sigismund was forced to re-learn that critical lesson which all Polish Kings were forced to absorb – always keep the nobility on side. Contrary to the impression that their stellar performance at the Battle of Kircholm may have given, Poland's nobility was not happy with their King.

Another formidable aspect of the 1569 Union of Lublin was the confirmation of the noble right to form a Confederation. As a concept,

Confederation has no equivalent outside of Poland, and was a symptom of the near total hold that the nobility held on the Commonwealth's inner and outer workings. To form a Confederation meant to instigate a rebellion against the Polish King in the event that he failed deliberately or otherwise to recognise and respect the privileges laid down in the Union of Lublin's list of demands, named the Henrican Articles after the first elected king, the Valois King Henry of 1573.

In his years fighting against his uncle, King Sigismund had manifestly failed to uphold these demands, even going directly against the wishes and grain of the Henrican Articles on several occasions and displaying the uttermost disrespect to the magnates who held so much power. Sigismund was playing with fire, but never seemed quite comfortable with the idea that he would be held accountable for his actions. In spring 1606 though, only a few months after their shattering defeat of Charles' army in Livonia, a Confederation of nobles rose up in revolt against Sigismund's authority and declared him deposed as penalty for failing to uphold his commitments and capitulations to the *szlachta*.

The nobility's list of grievances was long and not unjustified. Sigismund had engaged in an expensive war with Charles for far longer than the Polish nobility deemed acceptable. He had failed to defeat Charles in the late 1590s and had failed to seize the diplomatic initiative as well, due to his uncompromising Catholicism and dynastic ambition. Speaking of Catholicism, Sigismund had shown himself completely contemptuous of the religious toleration acts passed by the Sejm and guaranteed under the Union of Lublin, favouring Catholics over his Protestants and Orthodox subjects, and outlawing Protestant worship in Krakow altogether. Since the early sixteenth century, the Sejm had declared its rights to control Polish foreign policy, yet Sigismund's militant Catholicism and favour for Jesuits had netted him a second marriage with the sister of Ferdinand of Styria, soon to be Holy Roman Emperor, all behind the Sejm's back and without their tacit approval.

Far from a beacon of tolerance, Sigismund had created through his foreign policy a militant Catholic bloc which, the King believed, would help him regain his Swedish Crown. Sigismund never gave up on either the crown or the religious mission, even though upon his ejection from that kingdom it is estimated that less than 250 Catholics remained in all of Sweden. Influenced by the Jesuits and motivated by his dynastic ambitions of revenge against his uncle above all, Sigismund did not heed the repeated warnings from the *szlachta*, brushing aside their concerns and packing his court with Germans, whom he preferred, further alienating the nobles and magnates who had come to talk with him. If Charles had overstepped by invading Livonia, Sigismund had overstepped mightily by assuming that he could rule as he pleased. To Poland's nobility had graced King Sigismund with the limits of their patience, but now they had had enough. To provide a flavour of his regime, one of the leaders of the Confederation which had been set against him in 1606 was a noble who Sigismund had humiliated by publicly evicting him from his house, and by having his belongings tossed into the street. The shamed noble's only crime was that Sigismund had wanted his house for himself.[5]

In the event, Sigismund proved deftly effective at manipulating and dividing the nobility among religious and ethnic lines, and through this policy of divide and conquer, alongside promises to essentially do better next time and forgive all the guilty, Sigismund's loyalists defeated the Confederation by 1609, and the King's power was largely restored. He had lost the respect of the *szlachta*, but he had their begrudging loyalty since, while they had been fighting amongst themselves, events further afield had taken a volatile course, and they now needed what little leadership he could provide. Indeed, by the time the Commonwealth had settled its internal matters long enough to look outside their immediate bubble, it must have seemed as though all of Scandinavia and Northern Europe was up in arms.

Save the ill-fated Livonian expedition in 1604, King Charles IX of Sweden could have taken advantage of the respite provided by the Confederation against his nephew to take stock of his new reign and consolidate his position. Yet, as the Poles fought amongst themselves, Charles was troubled by an old enemy to the west – Denmark. The history of Danish-Swedish relations was long and bloody even before King Christian IV of Denmark authorised a new conflict against his Scandinavian neighbour. It was Christian's ancestor, Queen Margaret of Denmark, who in 1397 had created something unprecedented – the Kalmar Union. The Kalmar Union constituted a personal union of Denmark-Norway and Sweden-Finland, always under a Danish King.

Thanks to Denmark's dominant economic position, and the right of its kings to inherit the German duchies of Schleswig and Holstein, along the Danish-German border, Denmark quickly overawed its less developed Swedish neighbour. Throughout the fifteenth century the relationship between Denmark and Sweden remained unequal, with the Danes effectively ruling over Scandinavia under the aegis of the Kalmar Union. If it was strengthened, this was only due to the challenge posed by the other power in the Baltic of any consequence, the Hanseatic League, which itself was a grouping of German and Baltic trading towns, who pledged mutual assistance and advantageous trade deals between each other, and who jealously guarded these rights from other powers. Sometimes Swedes took advantage of the threat posed by the Hanseatic League, which always maintained a large and formidable naval presence in the Baltic Sea, to demand more powers for themselves, but the Kalmar Union remained in place until 1523, when King Christian II of Denmark effectively dissolved the Union through his own needless brutality.[6]

In an attempt to halt the endless opposition from Sweden's nobility, Christian II, became involved in the infamous 'Stockholm Bloodbath' in 1520, where over one hundred leading Swedish nobles were executed on trumped up charges of heresy, and which led to the Swedish uprising under an ambitious young nobleman, Gustav Vasa. Gustav Vasa's rebellion successfully cleaved the Swedish lands away from Denmark, and with the crowning of the first Vasa King in 1523, the Kalmar Union was no more.[7] Gustav Vasa hadn't merely dissolved the Kalmar Union, he had also established a new royal house – the House of Vasa, which would maintain an active presence in Northern Europe for the next two hundred years. It was quite a feat, but the mission was not accomplished, largely because Denmark still dwarfed Sweden in virtually every respect – her people were more concentrated, in comparison to Sweden's sprawling populace; her industry and culture was more developed, and was connected to the Holy Roman Empire, whereas Sweden was that distant, rocky northern shore of the Baltic, barbarous, mysterious and at the far limits of what was then considered European civilisation.[8]

The most recent conflict between Denmark and Sweden had ended with a truce in 1570, and peace had been maintained for a generation, with the two powers diplomatically manoeuvring against the other all the while, a process which reached new heights with the fusing of the Houses as King John of Vasa and Catherine Jagiellonian were wed. As the historian Robert Frost wrote, and as we have already seen, 'this attempt to seal the Polish-Swedish alliance was to miscarry badly.'[9]

Back in Poland, Sigismund had emerged on the other side of his civil war in 1609 to acquire an appreciation of his nobility's volatility, but little else. He continued on as normal and refrained from fixing or even addressing the issues which had led to the Confederation in the first place; acts of neglect which would have a terminal impact upon Polish stability and central authority later on in the seventeenth century. Once again though, Sigismund's thoughts quickly turned to foreign policy from 1609, after he was made aware of the opportunities present in his disintegrating neighbour, Muscovy.

Muscovy's entry into the seventeenth century was, in the words of one historian, 'far from auspicious.' After Ivan the Terrible's death in 1584, the Tsardom descended into a shaky series of successions, before degenerating altogether into civil war, aggravated by terrible harvests and dark winters over 1601-03.[10] With the Russian nobility separating into competing blocs, the opportunity was ripe for Sigismund to seize the Tsardom for his family – if Sweden's throne was not practical, then a Russian consolation prize would have to do. Sigismund's incredibly high ambitions and haughty diplomacy seemed justified,[11] and his perceptions accurate, when Polish winged hussars and heavy infantry again routed their opposition in the short Battle of Klushino on 4 July 1610. With that shattering victory, the road to Moscow was open, and Polish soldiers occupied the capital for two full years, acquiring the support necessary for Sigismund's son Wladyslaw to be declared Tsar of Russia around that time.

This stunning achievement suggested that Muscovy would be added to the Polish-Lithuanian Commonwealth, and that the years of Russo-Polish conflict would soon be over. Sigismund would surely have imagined that with the pacification of Russia and the support of her nobles, another invasion of Sweden would be successful, and the ailing King Charles of Sweden would be forced to hand his Kingdom over to its rightful Vasa King. If that happened, Sigismund's realms would constitute the largest continuous stretch of land since the Mongol Empire, and by combining Sweden, Russia and Poland-Lithuania together, he would be able to establish an unrivalled platform of power in the east, complete with sons to succeed him and even greater plans for the future.

As was so often the case with Sigismund though, the grand designs inherent in his plans were betrayed by his own narrow-mindedness and dogmatism. Much as he had stood out like a sore thumb to the Lutheran Swedes, so he also inspired precious little confidence in the Orthodox Russians, and once they overcame the shock of their defeats, Muscovy's patriots rallied against him and the rule of his son. Within a few bitter months, Wladyslaw's Russian title of Tsar was rendered as empty as Sigismund's claim on the Swedish throne.[12] Father and son of the Vasa dynasty would maintain the illusion for the remainder of Sigismund's life that Sigismund was the uncrowned king of a kingdom outside of his reach, and father to a son who would never see Russian soil again, but claimed the Russian crown. By 1613, the Russians had selected their new Tsar, Michael Romanov, and while Sigismund never recognised or accepted it, this development signalled the beginning of the end not merely for his dynasty's ambitions, but for Polish independence itself.[13]

By 1613 indeed, much had changed in Northern Europe. The region had been rocked by several years of tension and conflict, and Sigismund had no reason to suspect that the opportunities for regaining the Swedish Crown had been totally lost. This was because his tenacious uncle King Charles IX had died, leaving a 17-year-old on the throne. According to Swedish custom, a king had to be 24-year-old before he could wield fully the prerogatives of a King, and so long as the young Gustav Adolph II could not, Sweden was vulnerable. It was doubly vulnerable on the other hand because in April 1611, the tensions between Sweden and its old Danish foe had erupted into war, and Christian IV of Denmark had trounced the Swedish forces sent against him, providing an unenviable challenge for the new Swedish King.

At home and abroad, Gustav Adolph was beset by problems. His late father had alienated his noble supporters and created a string of opportunistic new men, who were sure to try and manipulate the young king in the sensitive years before he properly came of age. Swedish administration did boast some bright lights though, in spite of its desperate want for an organised education or training system.[14] Foremost among these was Axel Oxenstierna, who would subsequently rise up the ranks of Swedish government and rein as the Kingdom's undisputed Chancellor for several decades during Sweden's brightest and darkest times. With several capitulations made to the nobility and clergy, King Gustav Adolph set to work halting the Danish advance, while Swedish soldiers also fought the Russians in Livonia and remained on guard constantly against another invasion under Sigismund. The invasion from Sigismund never came, because as we saw, the Polish King was too distracted by his efforts to redefine Russia's relationship with the Commonwealth to interfere in much force in Sweden. This was just as well, because Sweden had proved itself unequal to the challenge of King Christian IV of Denmark's invasion. Had Sigismund freed himself from the Russian commitments earlier, then he may well have found an opportunity to invade Sweden in force. As Geoffrey Parker noted:

> If Sigismund had actually invaded again, as he had in 1598, few would have fought to the death for the young Gustav, or for the memory of his choleric, autocratic father. The junior branch of the house of Vasa was saved not by its own efforts but by Poland's involvement in Russia.[15]

Indeed, so interconnected were the different North European theatres, that King Gustav managed to secure a peace with Denmark at terribly high cost in January 1613, just at the point when Sigismund was finishing up his Russian commitments. The playing field was no means even between these two branches of the House of Vasa, and there certainly remained several opportunities for conflict in the future, but from 1613, a certain watershed moment had been passed. This portion of the continent, almost in a world of its own, did not consider too heavily events taking place in the West, or even in the Holy Roman Empire – there was more than enough to occupy the rulers of Poland-Lithuania, Sweden, Denmark and Russia between them. However, a time would come when this section of Europe would be pulled closer into the morass of the Thirty Years War, and when that happened, the rivalries of the House of Vasa, as much as the experience and reputation of King Gustavus Adolphus, would be dragged with them.

TWO

The Roots of Spain

One could argue that without consideration of the religious element, the outbreak of the Thirty Years War itself does not make sense. It would therefore be unwise if we neglected to examine a similar experience of religious division in the lands of the other Habsburg dynasty – Spain. Over the years 1609-1614, Spain evicted some quarter of a million 'Moriscos', the name given to those Muslims who had been forcibly converted since the Reconquest – *Reconquista* – of the peninsula from the Moors in the late fifteenth century.[16] The impact which this had upon the Spanish sense of identity and security are not to be underestimated, and later Spanish behaviour should be examined with these policies and their consequences in mind.

In the first half of the sixteenth century, the Morisco – translated literally as *Moorish* – remained part of a separate cultural and religious group, distinct in society from their Catholic Spanish neighbours in spite of attempts to fully integrate them. Charles V had made efforts to do away with all their old customs in 1525 but was paid eighty thousand ducats to rescind the edict. Christianity was the only legally accepted religion in Spain, but by paying off the authorities, the Moriscos ensured that deviations would remain the law in private. Charles' wife attempted to follow suit in 1530 but was again bought off by Morisco bribes. That same year the *farda*, a new tax worth twenty thousand ducats a year to the Spanish Crown, was brought in and paid for by the Moriscos, in return for Charles' administration agreeing to look the other way and allow Moriscos to dress and speak the language they liked. Morisco money was even used to reduce the jurisdiction of the Inquisition and avoid some of its worst methods. Occupied as he was with the Reformation, and with being Holy Roman Emperor as well as King of Spain and Lord of the New World, Charles V largely left the Moriscos to their own devices, with the result that, by the time his son Philip II succeeded him in 1555, the chasm between Christian and Morisco had never been more apparent.

Moriscos attended mass only to escape punishment, and still worked in secret behind closed doors on Sundays, revering only Fridays. Moriscos fasted

313

and bathed according to their holy calendar; after baptism, their children were cleaned, the males were circumcised, and all were given traditional Moorish names. The women, once they were married in a public Christian ceremony, were believed to return home with their husband, don the traditional Moorish dress, and receive a blessing from the secret Imam of the village. It was even supposed that when the Moriscos went to give confession on Easter Sunday, they recited the same confession they had given the previous year![17]

The modern Spanish autonomous community of Andalusia in the south of Spain takes its name from *Al-Andalus*, the Arabic name for Islamic Spain. Within Andalusia exists eight separate provinces, and it is in Granada in the south-east of the peninsula where these practices and deceptions were arguably the most transparent, and several decades of lax policing had resulted in the practices being more open secrets than actual secrets. As the final Moorish Kingdom conquered by the Christians in 1492, Granada retained more of its original customs than any other segment of the Castilian Kingdom. Moriscos had far more in common with their relatives across the sea in North Africa than they did with their Spanish countrymen, but populations of Moriscos were known to exist everywhere, from the capital of Andalusia in Seville,[18] to La Mancha in the centre of the country,[19] to the Kingdom of Valencia on the east coast of Spain, where in the late fifteenth century Muslims constituted a third of the population.[20] Communities of Moriscos kept to themselves rather than integrate, and lived as Muslims in the same place that their ancestors had centuries before, regardless of what Madrid liked to tell itself or its King. This was soon to change.

The Inquisition focused the issue of religious difference like never before in Spanish society, and while it was 'neither cruel nor unjust in its procedure and its penalties', being 'more just and more humane than almost any other tribunal in Europe', there were still many stark choices ahead for the Moriscos, but also those Jews who had been commanded to convert or exit the country in 1492.[21] Indeed, both Jews and Muslims maintained private traditions to their own degree, while putting on an outward display of conversion.[22] Yet, the Inquisition had been in place as an independent Spanish institution since 1478, requiring only lip service from the Pope in order to bless its largely autonomous activities.[23] It was not the Inquisition itself that focused attention upon the Moriscos then, but the personality and convictions of King Philip II (r.1555-1598).

Ignoring the example set by his father, Philip went ahead with the edict which in previous years Morisco money had kept at bay. From 1 January 1567, all Moriscos would have to cease their distinctive dress, stop speaking Arabic, and throw out their banned books – all those affected would have three years to comply. It should strike us as revealing that while much of Philip's religious and political advisors urged him onwards, a man of the military, the Duke of Alva, urged restraint. This was more out of caution than out of respect for the religious customs of the Moriscos, as Alva recognised that the edict would force the Moriscos into open rebellion against the Spanish Crown, an event for which the Spanish Empire was not well-prepared.

By 1566, Spain was facing into the earliest phases of the revolt in the Netherlands, and though that revolt was then merely a fringe Calvinist movement not yet granted its later tenacious staying power or innovative Dutch resiliency, with the revolt of the Moriscos beginning in December 1568, it was impossible to view these revolts as anything other than religiously motivated insurrections against Catholic Spanish power.[24] 'Accordingly' as one historian noted: 'when the Moriscos rebelled in 1568, their revolt formed part of a widespread, political and religious movement against the Habsburgs and Catholic Christendom.'[25] Spain was, as R. Trevor Davies noted ruefully, 'curiously weak in the centre', and nowhere was this weakness more clearly on display than in the subsequent breakdown in law and order caused by the revolt of the Moriscos.[26]

It lasted only two years before being crushed in late 1570, yet the tit-for-tat atrocities committed on both sides, and the atmosphere of bitter hatred and suspicion which remained in the aftermath, seemed to guarantee that conflict would resume in the future. In policies which were mirrored two generations later, the mass expulsions from once prosperous provinces left arid deserts in their wake, as the Moriscos took their goods, monies and craft with them to their new homes in North Africa, the Ottoman Empire or elsewhere in Europe. The experience had been a shattering one for Madrid, but it had also been a perilous experience for those Spanish policymakers who looked to Spain's main enemy at the time – the Ottoman Empire. The Christian victory at the Battle of Lepanto two years after the revolt had been crushed did not diminish the palpable threat which the Spanish felt from Constantinople.

The early 1560s had not been kind to Spain militarily or financially, as she had lost several naval battles to the Turks, and much prestige as a result.[27] These encounters with the predominant Ottomans, led at that stage by the resplendent Suleiman the Magnificent (r. 1520-66), demonstrated that Islamic power had not ceased threatening Spanish interests. Had affairs been different, and had the Ottomans been in a position over 1568-70 to land an expedition force on the coast of Spain, then the entire edifice of Habsburg Spain could have crumbled. As it happened, only the frequency of raids from the Muslim corsairs in North Africa increased, and the beleaguered Moriscos sought to sell their Christian captives to these opportunists when the pirates made landfall. This upsurge in piratical activity from Africa's Barbary States following this initial expulsion of the Moriscos (1570-71) foreshadowed what was to come during the larger expulsion of 1609-14.[28]

While we might have expected the revolt of 1568-70 to serve as a warning, the Spanish simply lacked the means to properly solve the Morisco problem. Madrid possessed no Arabic-speaking cohort of priests, which would have been truly necessary if the Moriscos, most of whom lacked Spanish, were to be properly reached. The programmes of school and church building in regions where, historically, the Catholic Church had never been strong, were also projects in expenditure 'beyond the financial strength of any in Europe.'[29] The want of funds impacted the Spanish ability to hire and train priests for the Moriscos lands, which left only the 'dregs of the clerical profession' behind to give instruction.

In addition, the taxes which a Morisco would be required to pay were supposed to cease once they became a Catholic and paid tithe's to the Church. Yet, among certain regions where unscrupulous governors ruled, unfortunate individuals were sometimes forced to pay both the Morisco tax, and the tithe to the Catholic Church once they converted. The contradiction mattered less to these individuals than their desire for funds, yet such behaviour, contrary to the Crown's official policy, only served to engender further resentment. It was often within the financial interest of certain lords or governors to ensure that the Moriscos did not properly convert, so that they kept paying the dues and high taxes, while to save face with the Crown, the tithes were also maintained. Further rulings on the eligibility of certain Moriscos for education and employment added to the negative experience; by barring Moriscos to universities, even those descendants of those that had converted felt marginalised and restricted. And, as Davies noted, once 'every pathway of ambition was closed to them, they found vent for their energies in stirring up discontent and planning conspiracies.'[30]

This is not to say, of course, that all Moriscos attempted to agitate against their Spanish overlords – many did, over time, assimilate and become genuinely devout Catholic Spaniards. Many more, however, were not absorbed because Spain was simply unable to carry out such a policy, and the Moriscos were not given enough incentives to abandon the religion and customs of their ancestors. The danger to Spain was not merely the existence of a fifth column, willing to collaborate with Turks and Moroccan Sultans; it was also the case that, in the east of the country, for instance in the Kingdom of Valencia, attacks by Islamic pirates and slavers became increasingly problematic. So acute was the threat from Mediterranean corsairs that in 1584, the viceroy of Valencia declared his region to be on a war footing. As one historian has written, 'neither the Christian victory at Lepanto, the Hispano-Turkish truce, nor the Ottoman withdrawal from the western Mediterranean following the truce resulted in a contraction of North African piracy against Spain.'[31]

Security depended on the existence of a loyal and plentiful population to defend and garrison the region, and these things were lacking in Valencia, as well as in portions of Andalusia where Moriscos made up a sizable minority. Pirates became more numerous in the 1590s and early 1600s, as Algerian revolts against Ottoman rule released them from the terms of the truce with Spain. In addition, the aforementioned recession and reduction in profits owing to the price revolution compelled Turkish sailors to resort to piracy – already the most lucrative form of warfare – once the truce with Spain had been signed. Compounding this influx of new pirates into the region was the simultaneous entry of large numbers of English and Dutch pirates, whose governments were then at war with Spain, and whose citizens yearned for a way to gain glory and wealth on the open seas.

These individuals from Northern Europe did not just augment the ranks of the Muslim corsairs, they also engaged in more advanced piratical practices and harnessed more advanced technology used by Spain's traditional Muslim enemies at sea, and this combination proved too much for the inadequate Spanish naval defences. The pirate raids which had once been confined solely to the coasts of Spain and around North Africa had extended, thanks to these developments and the increased hunger for booty, to the Atlantic, which inevitably drove up the cost of naval insurance and reduced Spain profits still further.[32]

In 1584, a pirate fleet sailed from Algeria for Spain numbering roughly 2,300 ships; the following year a massive raid carted off the entire Morisco population in the Valencian town of Callosa – no small feat of logistics.[33] This brings us to an important point which deserves underlining – pirates did not merely steal goods and Christian slaves, they also brought Moriscos who wished to escape Spain with them to pastures new in North Africa or the Ottoman Empire. Paradoxically, considering the mass expulsion of the Moriscos over 1609-14, in the preceding years the governors and viceroys of Spain's provinces refused to permit the emigration of the Moriscos. This policy of keeping Moriscos in Spain can be explained as much by the repulsion felt against apostates – those Moriscos who declared their conversion to Catholicism only to lapse – as much as it was due to the fear that an exodus of Moriscos would strip the country of profits, skilled tradesmen and farmers which were necessary to maintain the solvency of the realm. This brings us to the important question of what changed within the Spanish government to lead to the policy of expulsion of as many as three hundred thousand Moriscos between 1609-14. It is this question which will occupy us now.

One development which stands out in the first decade of the seventeenth century was the extent to which foreign powers became involved with Spain's Morisco problem. While cooperation with the Ottoman Empire appears the most natural fit for the Moriscos, their agents were equally comfortable making use of Spain's European enemies to gain advantage. Andrew C. Hess wrote that:

> Philip II and his Spanish officials raised a major issue involving international relations when they charged, in effect, that the Moors in Spain made up a fifth column that aided both the Ottoman advance in North Africa and the Protestant cause in Europe.[34]

Some historians have been expressed scepticism on the point of exactly how diplomatically active the Moriscos were in recruiting Protestant European allies, as well as the French.[35] However, these activities were not insignificant; in 1602 the Moriscos entered into negotiations with King Henry IV of France, and specifically his governor of Navarre. The Moriscos promised a force of eighty thousand men to aid the French in the event that they invaded Northern Spain, while a commitment was also made to hand over three cities to the French invaders. As a sign of their good faith, the Moriscos delivered a sum of one hundred and twenty thousand ducats to the governor of Navarre over 1604-5. Davies records that 'Henry decided to follow the Morisco plan but postponed it for a time as the moment did not appear especially favourable.' Davies also noted that the Moriscos were factored into Henry's plan to intervene in the Julich-Cleve succession crisis in 1610. Indeed, Davies went so far as to note that Henry had been discussing plans to collude with the Moriscos with the aforementioned governor of Navarre in his royal carriage, mere minutes before the King stepped out of this carriage on fourteenth May and was assassinated.[36]

The Moriscos of Valencia also negotiated with the King of Morocco in 1608 and promised him one hundred thousand men if he would supply twenty thousand of his own. Opportunistic Dutch sailors offered their logistical services to enterprises like these, in a further bid to weaken Spain wherever possible, and Spain's Royal Council was deeply disturbed when they learned of such offers – so much so that they sought the means to permanently secure Spain's safety by resolving the Morisco issue once and for all.[37] The existence of such 'grand designs' demonstrate the supremacy of Spain and the interconnectedness of her problems, as her three European enemies in the Dutch, English and French consistently aimed at undermining her by inflaming her domestic crises, based on the philosophy not just that the enemy of my enemy is my friend, but also that Spain's difficulty represented a great opportunity.[38]

Even considering the negotiation of peace with France (1598), England (1604) and the Dutch (1609), the fundamental threat posed by the Moriscos remained acute. The arrival of official peace treaties or truces did not mean an end to piracy or conspiracy, and so the threat posed by the Moriscos remained. It would not be quite fair to view this threat as one of Spain's own making; while it is true that Spanish attempts to incentivise the Moriscos to genuinely convert as a whole failed, it is also true that the Moriscos as a whole never truly accepted their new status, or relinquished their attachment to North African, Ottoman and even Christian European benefactors. Since Spain could not afford to neutralise the Morisco threat organically, and since her government could not remain idle and permit the threat to persist, it followed that a more radical solution would be adopted.

As radical solutions go, the expulsion of the Moriscos was the most merciful and least controversial at the time, especially considering the more terrible options technically available to Philip III's government. The process of deliberation was completed on 30 January 1608, when the Council of State arrived at the decision of expelling en masse the Moriscos from Spain. The difficult decision was made easier for Valencia by the stipulation that all expelled Moriscos there would lose their property to the nobles and lords that undertook the operation.[39] This economic motive seems to have placated the earlier concerns of these lords that the exit of the Moriscos living on their land would significantly reduce their incomes, but it would soon transpire that these concerns had been well-founded. The depopulation of Valencia following the expulsion resulted in a dramatic reduction in the productivity of the land and towns there, an outcome which led one historian to actually separate the periods before and after expulsion as one of expansion and recession, respectively.[40] A further motive for expulsion was the belief in some quarters that an absence of Moriscos would reduce the potency and frequency of those pirate raids launched on the Spanish coasts, as the historian Ellen Friedman noted:

> The expulsion of the Moriscos was not an unpopular action in Spain. Indeed, many people expected it to result in greater security along the Mediterranean coasts, where the indigenous Moriscos were believed to be in collusion with the North African corsairs. In Valencia, which had the largest concentration of Moriscos as well as, coincidentally, the greatest vulnerability to attack, there was a clamour for the elimination of this 'fifth column'.[41]

To Ironically, the opposite happened. Instead of a reduction in piracy following the exodus of local Moriscos, the Spanish found that the piratical attacks increased, often led by dispossessed Moriscos who now knew all about the best places to pillage, and the places where Spanish power was at its most tenuous.[42] [In the face of criticism from certain circles at Spanish policy to evict the Moriscos] The explanation was given that the Moriscos had failed to take advantage of 'the opportunity to convert truly', and while Spanish administrators were incredibly diligent in their task, it was inevitable that confusion and injustice reigned on several occasions.[43]

In addition, the actual numbers of Moriscos expelled, versus the number of Moriscos who managed, through a variety of tactics, to remain behind, have confused the precise amount of Moriscos that were removed from Spain during the five-year period. While it is thus possible to estimate that as many as half a million Moriscos lived in Spain by 1609 if we take the narrow Spanish classification of what it meant to be a Morisco, the figure of one hundred and fifty thousand expelled individuals of that group appears the most accurate tally. Davies even noted that the Spanish were so urgent in their mission to expel Moriscos that they managed, in some cases to send third or fourth generation Catholics into exile in North Africa.[44]

In the context of the turbulent political and religious European climate prior to the Thirty Years War, the Spanish examples of the Dutch revolt and the Morisco threat demonstrate what had become a widely accepted truth among statesmen – that loyalty to the regime and religious difference were not compatible. Such a truism was not an exclusively Spanish construct. Indeed to take two examples; it had been enshrined in the 1555 Peace of Augsburg of the Holy Roman Empire, as much as it had been codified in the Recusancy Acts under Elizabeth I, which made it a legal requirement to worship in line with the Anglican creed until 1650.[45] Attempts across Europe to control the religion of the subject and bring it into line with the ruler were based on the belief that without religious affinity, disloyalty and revolt against the regime would follow, alongside potentially fatal efforts to enlist foreign aid. The revolts of their Calvinist Dutch and Islamic Morisco subjects, and the damaging foreign aid they enlisted from Spain's European rivals, validated this belief, and added to the perception that a religiously diverse kingdom was an unstable one.[46]

It is also worth considering the fact that, on 4 April 1609 – two weeks before an exhausting period of Spanish-Dutch peace-making was brought to a successful conclusion with the signing of the Twelve Years' Truce on 21 April 1609 – the expulsion of the Moriscos as official policy was ratified in Madrid. With one conflict resolved, it seems, the Spanish moved with an almost deliberate sense of purpose into another, and this Morisco policy would not be resolved until 1614. Such activity reminds us exactly how busy and distracted by their internal affairs Spanish policymakers were, even before the country's full involvement in the Thirty Years War. By the end of the mass expulsion process, certain individuals had indeed enriched themselves at the Moriscos' expense, yet, while it is important to keep the impact of the expulsion in perspective, considering the pre-existing decline of eastern Spain in particular, by and large the experience had not been a particularly positive one for Spanish finances.[47]

By the second decade of the seventeenth century, Spain was at peace with its enemies, yet it had expended a great deal of resources and confronted several significant challenges to its religious and political regimes. These experiences must be placed in context, and should be considered in light of the subsequent behaviour of Spanish policymakers, who moved diligently in the years after 1614 to secure Spanish security and prosperity through diplomatic and military means on the continent, starting with the question of the succession in the Austrian Habsburg lands.

THREE
Intervention Hispania

Spanish diplomacy and government, on which hinged much of the fate of Europe in this period, dealt with matters of high policy, and the side it presented to the world was peopled with kings and archdukes, ambassadors and commissioners. In practice, however, it also took place in a world of harlots and spies and mud-slinging mobs, and, not least important, of functionaries fighting their own little wars of bureaucratic advancement, overburdened in any case, falling behind in their work, struggling desperately to get these paper finished before the post departed and (above all) before the next one arrived. Sovereigns and envoys, forming Spanish Habsburg policy and in the process shaping the history of the world, played out the drama centre stage, but the backdrop was made of – paper.[48]

In such a way did the historian Charles Howard Carter deliciously describe the course and nature of Spanish diplomacy at the turn of the seventeenth century. From two key pillars, in Madrid and Brussels, documentation, earnest diplomatic representations and no end of espionage was carried out by Spain and by its allies, rivals and enemies. Protocol insisted that the Spanish, positioned as they were at the top of the food chain, should talk with everyone. The impression was still given that the Spanish Habsburg dynasty was the most powerful and influential in the world, whether or not King Philip III, deep down, possessed the genuine resources or strength to maintain this façade into the future.

The first decade of the seventeenth century – to the relief of those that had watched the silver and gold reserves vanish with astonishing speed – was a time of peace-making. England and the Dutch were transformed from costly enemies into coldly receptive neighbours, who still took every opportunity to chip away and attack Spanish might across the rest of the world. As the Spanish had desperately tried and failed to acquire a total peace treaty, it was understood that the Treaty of London (1604) and Twelve Years Truce (1609-21) only extended to Europe.[49] Of course, an overactive piracy under

321

sponsorship from either government could easily inflame relations, and lead to a resumption of open warfare, an outcome which both King James and the Dutch government were careful to avoid. These two enemies mostly placated, for now, King Philip III's administration turned its attention to domestic matters. The first and most pressing of these matters was the resolution of the Moriscos problem which we examined above, but another issue which also drew in the King of Spain was the question of succession; not in his lands, but in those of his cousins, the Austrian Habsburgs.

Considering the common theme of two Habsburg branches, working in tandem during the Thirty Years War, it may surprise the reader to discover that the Spanish government made serious efforts to place the Spanish Habsburg dynasty on the Austrian seat of power – above all the positions of King of Bohemia, King of Hungary and potentially Holy Roman Emperor – between 1612-17.[50] Indeed, if the negotiations between the two branches of the Habsburg family are mentioned at all, they are normally explained by the Spanish desire to secure its Spanish Road supply line from Milan to Brussels. The Onate Treaty which emerged from these negotiations, in the opinion of some historians, represented a Spanish effort to bargain with its Austrian relatives for strategic stepping stones along the Rhine and Italy – above all in Alsace – rather than a genuine desire on the part of Spain to succeed to any of the Austrian thrones, or to undermine that branch's position in the Habsburg Hereditary Lands.[51]

Clarifying what Spain hoped to gain in its negotiations with its Habsburg cousins is an important exercise because of what it tells us about the Spanish foreign policy aims and concerns during the period just before the outbreak of the Thirty Years War. In her article untangling the complex negotiations, which dragged on for five years, Magdalena S. Sanchez examined the opinion of four key individuals, to discern what the Spanish goals actually were. These four individuals were the commander in the Spanish Netherlands Ambrogio Spinola; King Philip III of Spain; Baltasar de Zuniga, the Spanish ambassador to Central Europe from 1608-17, and finally Juan Hurtado de Mendoza de la Vega y Luna, sixth Duke of Infantado and a councillor of state in Madrid. These four figures all possessed different ideas about what the best policy would be for Spain to pursue, and all were affected by the immediate demands of the jurisdiction in which they served. To properly focus our narrative, we will take first the opinions of Baltasar de Zuniga, since his opinions stand out as the most contrary to the general historical record.[52]

It was Zuniga who emphasised the importance of the Bohemian and Hungarian crowns to Philip III, and he presented these Crowns as a critical steppingstone towards greater Spanish control of Imperial processes. Bohemia was believed to be particularly important in Zuniga's mind, as the Crown of Bohemia conferred a vote on its King, which that King could then use during the election of a new Holy Roman Emperor. In short, Zuniga had identified the best means through which Spain could interfere in the constitutional processes of the Holy Roman Empire and bring about the election of a candidate of their choosing. Zuniga wrote to his King in 1611 to the effect that:

> I believe that one of the most important issues facing Your Majesty in your monarchy is to procure the kingdom of Bohemia for one of the Spanish princes...In order to place one of these princes in these parts it would be very convenient to teach them diverse languages...and a knowledge of German or Bohemian could be a most useful thing in acquiring what one wishes to acquire. For this it would be necessary for Your Highnesses [Philip III's sons] to have German, Flemish, or even Bohemian tutors, and cultivate love and knowledge of these nations. To be a good Castilian is a given for a prince of Castile but the ability to deal confidently with other nations is of infinite value for a prince of the royal house of Spain since the [Spanish] kingdoms and dependencies extend to such diverse provinces. Perhaps the failure to do this in other times has been the cause of great damage.[53]

The major obstacle to Zuniga's schemes were the Austrian Habsburgs, specifically the representatives of Ferdinand of Styria, who recommended Ferdinand's succession to Emperor Matthias, a succession which was further brightened by the fact of Ferdinand's two sons – a boon to any ambitious dynast in the seventeenth century. Philip III, it should be said, was more than capable of mounting a legitimate claim of his own to the succession – he was, after all, the sole surviving grandson of Emperor Maximillian II (r. 1564-1576).[54] At the early stage of the negotiations, the Spanish King aimed high, and hoped to gain the Bohemian Crown before it became evident that the Austrians were not willing to relinquish it. Zuniga was initially positive about the outcome, but was forced to settle on the largely meaningless concession from Ferdinand of Styria that his daughters would come after Philip III's sons in the Austrian succession.[55] This was the best Zuniga could do when it came to transferring the Bohemian Crown from Austria to Spain; by December 1616 he had largely given up on the mission and compromised for the transferral of Italian and Rhineland duchies instead.

As Spain's ambassador to the Imperial court, acting in the name of Philip III, Zuniga's efforts shed remarkable light on what the King of Spain actually wanted. It was in Philip's interest to acquire as many concessions as possible for Spain, but Zuniga's insistence that the Crowns of Hungary and Bohemia in particular were 'without doubt more valuable than the Austrian provinces' helped to focus the issue and underlined not only how well Madrid understood the Imperial constitution, but how strongly the King wished to involve Spain in Central Europe. The acquisition of the Bohemian Crown would provide Spain with a chance to stack any Imperial election in favour of Catholics, while it could also lead, in time, to the election of a Spanish candidate – one of Philip III's sons or grandsons, as the orders of Zuniga optimistically imagined.

It is worth considering another factor which compelled Zuniga to ask for such a high price from the Austrians in return for familial friendship and cooperation. As ambassador to previous Emperors Rudolf and Matthias, Zuniga knew all too well the sense of frustration felt when attempting to negotiate Imperial aid for the Spanish war efforts against the Dutch. Zuniga was also keenly aware that while Madrid had filtered monies into the depleted Imperial coffers, both Rudolf and Matthias had reneged on their duties to defend the Catholic position, choosing instead to roll over in the face of demands from Protestants within their own hereditary lands. It is entirely possible that both Zuniga and his master viewed Rudolf and then Matthias with a degree of hostility because of these capitulations, since they undermined the overall position of the dynasty in Europe. Faced with the spectacle of several capitulations in Bohemia in particular, the pressing need to acquire the Bohemian Crown for Spain takes on a more sinister tone – did Zuniga believe that only Philip III could roll back the concessions which had been made to the Bohemians, Austrians and Hungarians, and that only the King of Spain could whip these recalcitrant heretics into line?

With the Brothers' Quarrel only recently being resolved, it is possible that Zuniga did not wish to provide the Austrian branch with any more opportunities to embarrass the reputation of the dynasty. By taking the Bohemian Crown, not only would future elections be secured for a Habsburg candidate, but the Bohemian insistence on religious freedoms and, equally as insulting, the notion that their crown was elective rather than hereditary, would all be trampled under a deliberate Spanish policy. While this may appear more like speculation than anything else, we are drawn to the recent Spanish track record in their own lands with the expulsion of the Moriscos, and the endless efforts to defeat the Dutch - religious differences, in the minds of the Spanish and many others besides, was easily equated with disloyalty. The Bohemians were disloyal and needed to be brought into line for the overall good of the dynasty and its future security. From this, we can conclude that Zuniga was not satisfied with a narrow definition of Spain as existing within the Iberian Peninsula; instead, as Sanchez wrote, Zuniga 'called for a Spanish monarchy with imperial commitments and even imperial designs.'[56]

Baltasar de Zuniga was an important diplomat in Spanish service, but he was one among several important voices shaping Spanish policy relative to its Imperial cousins. Another important voice among these was Ambrogio Spinola, the Genoese commander of Spain's forces in the Spanish Netherlands. Spinola's world was consumed by talk of the Spanish Netherlands – how to defend them, how to supply them, and who endangered them. He was in favour of any policy which would make the defence and supply of Flanders easier, because it would make his job easier. Thus, Spinola's recommendations read like a laundry list of demands which would insulate the Spanish Road and guarantee the delivery of men and materials to Brussels. The best means by which Spain could insulate its key European supply line was by gobbling up key territories in North Italy and along the Rhine. Alsace and the Tyrol were on the top of the list of territories which Spinola wanted, and by relinquishing his claim on the Imperial succession in favour of Ferdinand of Styria, Spinola evidently believed that his King would be well-placed to receive such concessions.

Arguably the most convincing piece of evidence that pointed towards the single-minded Spanish ambition to preserve its Spanish Road can be found in subsequent Spanish policy. Over 1621-23, Spanish and Catholic League forces would overrun the Palatinate and establish a supremacy around the Alsace region. While they never managed to annex the Alsace region outright, they did move swiftly into the region, fortify it and then ignore all requests to leave.[57] By staying in place, the Spanish guaranteed the safe passage of money, men and materials to the Spanish Netherlands, and it is therefore interesting to note the war turning against the Dutch at precisely this time.[58] By moving directly through the Lower Palatinate, the Spanish found an alternative way to fulfil the desires of Spinola, but as we will see, they also convinced the German Protestants and their external allies that Spanish ambitions had gotten out of control.[59]

Juan Hurtado de Mendoza de la Vega y Luna, the sixth Duke of Infantado, was the leading light of the Spanish Council of State in Madrid and was in regular contact with the King. Though he owed his position to the Duke of Lerma, who acquired the position for him in 1599 to serve his interests, Infantado rose through the ranks to become the leading councillor by 1612. His rise complete, Infantado moved to implement the King's ambitions in the sensitive Austrian negotiations, but he also acted with realistic expectations, and in the knowledge that Spain's resources were not infinite, and she could be overstretched if careful hands were not at the helm. Infantado was initially in favour of the transfer of Alsace, but quickly went against the idea when the sheer complexities of that fief were properly learned.

To swap Austrian for Spanish control may have seemed like a minute detail, but such an operation would actually take Alsace out of the Holy Roman Empire and recast it as merely a cog in the machine of the Spanish Empire. This, Infantado anticipated, would lead to local opposition in the region, and could create more problems for Spain if the Alsatians became as implacable an enemy as the Dutch had become. Thus, Infantado moved away from the Alsatian or Central European objectives and focused his full attention instead on North Italy. Through the acquisition of a few interconnected Italian principalities and towns, Spain could reinforce its supply lines, charge tolls for trade between Genoa and Naples, and even be in a position to cut off the water of several further strongholds should they come under the enemy's control. Infantado, like Spinola, was focused on improving the Spanish Road, but unlike Spinola, Infantado cared more for the potential which a focus on Italy could accrue for Spain and counselled a realistic and conscious approach to the Austrians.[60]

That of course left King Philip III of Spain. How would this King view the opportunity to wrest concessions from his Austrian cousins? Ferdinand of Styria was Philip's second cousin, but these familial ties plainly had not precluded the King from finding ways to squeeze out the concessions he desired. At every step of the negotiations with his Austrian relatives, Philip was assured of his firm grounds for contesting the succession by his jurists. So long as this claim could be reasonably contested, Philip was determined not to relinquish these rights without due compensation. In 1617, Baltasar de Zuniga was replaced in his role as Spanish ambassador and thus chief negotiator by Count Onate, who gave his name to the resulting Treaty. Warning his new negotiator as to his duties and the King's expectations, Philip wrote to Onate in early 1617 saying:

> The count of Onate should be instructed to say to the imperial and archducal ministers that, because of the petitions of the emperor and the archdukes... it would be easy for these crowns...to fall to Archduke Ferdinand...It is convenient to give this reply so as to convince Archduke Ferdinand, the emperor and his brothers not to believe...that this renunciation is to be given them freely. It is convenient that the first step in this negotiation be that those princes think to give [me] compensation.[61]

Any delays in the negotiations were countered by threats from Madrid that Philip would back an alternative candidate to the Hungarian and Bohemian Crowns. Due to Vienna's want of funds, and the fact that it was fighting another war against Venice at this time as well, Philip knew he held most of the cards. If Ferdinand wanted his succession to be approved, and if the Austrians wanted the tap of subsidies to be turned back on, then they would have to grant Philip what he requested. Yet, in Madrid, there seemed little consideration of the possibility that by delaying the question of the succession, a Protestant candidate might emerge for the Bohemian Crown, with potentially disastrous consequences.

The best course of action would have been a speedy resolution of the entire issue, and greater cooperation within the wider Habsburg family to ensure that no external enemies were able to capitalise on their disunity. Alas, Philip III believed in his right to compensation, and believed all the more so in the importance of being confirmed as the leading figure of the Habsburg family. For these facts to be affirmed, Philip pressed the Austrians, and more specifically Ferdinand of Styria, until he got what he wanted. The King of Spain may have pushed harder than he otherwise would have done had he and Ferdinand not been, until relatively recently, tied by marriage. Ferdinand's late sister had been married to Philip III until her death in 1611, just at the moment when a pro-Austrian voice in Madrid would have been of great utility to Ferdinand's cause.

The Onate Treaty of 1617 must be considered a victory for King Philip III, since it granted him virtually everything he had desired. Yet, while Philip won this battle against his Austrian relatives, and gained portions of Italy as well as Alsace, it must be said at the same time that the Spanish King squandered a great deal too. By delaying the question of the succession so long, until almost the final moments of Emperor Matthias' life, Philip ensured that Ferdinand would feel more pressure to accede to his demands. However, it is worth considering that this very delay helped to facilitate the revolt which erupted in Bohemia and Hungary over 1618-19, and that it forcibly removed Ferdinand from the Bohemian throne, thereby precipitating the Thirty Years War.[62]

It would be too simplistic to blame the Thirty Years War on Philip III's quest for compensation of course, but the real damage which Philip did to his family's position must not be understated. From 1615-18, the Austrians were fighting a war against the Venetians, after the Croatian irregulars which served under the Habsburgs banner began to engage in piratical activities on an unacceptable scale. These irregulars – *uzkoks* after the Serbian term for refugees – had made problems for Venice since the late sixteenth century, and the inopportune eruption of the issue into full-blown conflict with Austria forced Ferdinand to expend more resources and send more urgent pleas to Spain for aid. While it is true, as Geoffrey Parker wrote, that the *uzkok* war 'was one of the more bizarre episodes of the early seventeenth century', it is also the case that 'it offered an alarming example of how a minor conflict in a remote corner of Europe could threaten to engulf the whole continent with war.'[63]

Originally, the Austrians had appreciated the activities of the *uzkok*, because they preyed upon Turkish shipping, and thus they undermined the trade of the Ottoman enemy. However, it soon became apparent that the *uzkoks* did not distinguish between Turk or Christian, and the most active other power in the Adriatic, Venice, was soon adversely affected by their behaviour. Initially, the Venetians sought to simply increase spending on their defences, leading to gradually climbing expenses on their escorts, until they reached the impossible cost of 360,000 thalers for the year. Venice had had enough and sought to engage the *uzkok* pirates by attacking and besieging their overlord, Ferdinand, at the city of Gradisca in Inner Austria in December 1615.

Technically, the *uzkoks* were subjects of the Hungarian crown rather than the Austrian Archduke, but the Venetians had little time for such technicalities; they needed to force an end to the ruinous piracy and they were willing to take desperate measures in line with this end. By their attack and the inevitable Austrian response, the Austrians would be forced to come to blows with Venice, yet the Venetians had already engaged in an extensive diplomatic campaign designed to curry favour and support against these piratical agents of the Austrian Habsburgs. Predictably, the other maritime powers became involved, as English and Dutch volunteers sailed to the Adriatic to aid the Venetians in their quest to make the region safer for trade.

With the Austrians attacked and isolated, appeals inevitably would be made to Spain. The need to acquire aid and support from Spain, King Philip well understood, would serve as a further source of pressure in Vienna to accede to his demands. Yet, he could not turn his attentions solely to the Austrians, because by 1615 Philip was aware that events in North Italy had become inflamed thanks to a war of succession in the Duchy of Mantua. Mantua was a well-fortified Italian city state, which claimed territory and key fortresses like Montferrat, but it had long been positioned in a contentious region for the French, Spanish and Savoy, who all claimed spheres of influence and rights of inheritance in the region.[64] In time, the war in Mantua would profoundly impact Franco-Spanish relations,[65] but at this moment, the issue provoked fewer belligerences in Madrid and Paris, and a good deal more scheming instead.

The French moved to induce Savoy to attack Mantua's possessions in Montferrat, and they enjoyed the support not just of the Venetians, who were battling the other Habsburg branch in the *uzkok* war, but also of the German Protestants. The Evangelical Union involved itself in the dispute, and Count Ernst of Mansfeld marched with four thousand such Germans to resolve the dispute in the favour of the Savoyard candidate. Since Spanish forces were besieged in Spanish Lombardy, there was nothing they could do to aid Ferdinand of Styria in the *uzkok* war, and thus the interconnectedness, as well as the dangerous tendency of regional conflicts to spread like wildfire, were on full display.[66]

Indeed, the cooperation of the Habsburgs' enemies – including the Dutch, who were meant to be at peace with Spain for several more years – sent a stern message. Yet, it was the prospect of Calvinist Dutch soldiers arriving in Venice that caused the most anxiety in Madrid. 'Religion and reputation are the two great matters which sustain states', so claimed Madrid's Council of State at the time.[67] A full-blown war with the Dutch seemed on the cards if the Republic did indeed decide to land men in Italy to help Savoy and Venice, such was the danger these men were believed to pose to the Spanish reputation and position. Spanish might have proved insufficient to deter to the Dutch in their schemes, but the war between the two powers was not reignited, as mediation found a way.

The *uzkok* war had piled a great deal of pressure on Austrian negotiators to resolve their issues with Spain quickly, lest Matthias died before they were finished, or the Bohemians and Hungarians selected their own, Protestant kings instead. These were pressing dangers, and the fact that the Onate Treaty was signed the year before the Defenestration of Prague and the eruption of the Thirty Years War, followed shortly thereafter by the formal deposing of Ferdinand as King of Bohemia and the offering of the Crown to a foreign Protestant, is very telling. From the terrible results which came after the Onate Treaty, it would appear that King Philip III, in his quest for satisfaction and to demonstrate his supremacy, cost his dynasty dearly.

The Onate Treaty and the events which surrounded it left the Spanish and Austrian Habsburgs with a great deal of answers, but also some new, arguably more troubling questions. It had not gone without notice that the German Protestants had so readily teamed with France and Savoy during the Mantuan affair, nor had Ernst of Mansfeld's command gone under the radar. Faced with another regional crisis, would the German Protestants be expected to interfere once again? For Ferdinand, the negotiations had been painful and illuminating at the same time – King Philip III was plainly unwilling to give away anything for free, even to his relatives, yet his cooperation and the subsequent peace treaty with Venice in 1618 demonstrated that Spain could and would cooperate militarily with its Austrian cousins. Could this cooperation be genuinely relied upon in the future, particularly if a crisis emerged within the Holy Roman Empire?

Indeed, to the German Protestants, the cooperation with the Habsburgs' traditional enemies provided them with much encouragement, yet it was also noted that Spain did rescue Austria from its unprofitable war with Venice. Had the terms of the Onate Treaty been public knowledge, then there would have been further cause for controversy and concern. Vienna may have received the desperately needed Spanish aid, but this was only after Philip III had received some Italian fiefs and Alsace; the latter of which he would never truly be able to properly incorporate, as we'll see. In return, the Spanish gave their blessing for Ferdinand of Styria to surge ahead with his plans to assume the Crowns of Bohemia and Hungary, and to sit as Holy Roman Emperor in the near future.

This was arguably the most important concession given by Philip III during the negotiations. It meant that Spain would not be able to command all of the Habsburg dominions, as Charles V had done several decades before. It also meant that the two branches would have to cooperate and aid the other, if their interests were to be preserved, and if the counter-reformation was to continue. To King Philip III, the outcome of the Onate Treaty meant something else – it meant that Spain suffered from a kind of identity crisis just at the wrong time. What territory was in the Spanish interest to save, what was absolutely critical to hold onto, and what mattered somewhat less if it was lost or ceded? Was it North Italy, Alsace or Bohemia; was it all three? Since he had been unable to determine the answer to the critical question, and since his subjects acting in foreign capitals had been even less consistent, the King of Spain found that Spanish policy was ill-defined as precisely the wrong time. Or, as Magdalena Sanchez concluded:

> Because this issue remained unresolved, the Spanish government was unable to decide where to concentrate its financial and military resources or which areas to disregard. Consequently, the Spanish monarchy continued to spread its resources thin by becoming involved in the Bohemian Revolt. In 1618, when the Bohemians in Prague threw Ferdinand's two councillors out the window, out too fell Spain's grandiose plans for Alsace and Italy. Gone were Philip's plans for an enlarged, stronger monarchy in clear possession of Northern Italy and Flanders. And the Habsburg house found itself engaged in a ruinous war.[68]

King Philip III of Spain had sought to gain great concessions, by leveraging the advantages he held over his familial allies in Austria. Through this process, King Philip had hoped to strengthen Spain either by vesting her with additional lands and titles, or by fully realising his plans to succeed in Austria, whereupon great gains in Bohemia and Hungary would fall to his dynasty. These ambitions were all wrong-headed, as much as they were great leaps in wishful thinking. They were wishful thinking because Ferdinand could never give up his claims on the Crowns of Bohemia and Hungary, nor could he relinquish his plan to sit on Matthias' throne. In addition, they were wrong-headed not only because the Austrian Habsburg dynasty was in desperate need of succour, rather than demands, from its Spanish relatives; there was also an urgent need to resolve the crisis in Bohemia, bubbling over since 1609, with a firmly designated and supported succession decision.

Just in time, in October 1617, Papal mediation brought the succession crisis in Mantua to an end, by postponing it until the Duke of Gonzaga died – which he did in the late 1620s, triggering the next phase of that conflict. In addition, Ferdinand was named king designate of Hungary earlier in the year, and now possessed the necessary power to order the resettling of those *uzkoks* that had posed so many problems to the Venetians. These two Italian conflicts apparently solved, the reality, beneath the calm surface, was deeply unsettling. The resolution of the Habsburg succession had led to a closer alliance between Madrid and Vienna, just as the Protestant Germans, Dutch, French, Savoyards and Venetians closed ranks against them.

It is worth detailing the content of the Onate Treaty, since this will help to demonstrate its net significance. It was Count Onate who renounced Philip

III's rights to the Imperial succession in his King's name, writing that:

> I, the above-mentioned envoy and empowered representative, by the power of my plenipotentiary authority, confirm and certify in the name of the king my master, and his children, the aforementioned renunciation and cession of the rights derived from his mother Queen Anna. In doing so I renounce in the name of my king and his children all rights, whether those of my master the king, or the young Prince Infant, and of his sons, they possess or will have by whatever means to the aforementioned kingdoms and provinces, in favour of Archduke Ferdinand and his legitimate male heirs, without any restriction, limitation or delay, except subject to the following modification and condition, that a compensation and recompense will be provided in the form of an Austrian province, which one could and would desire, and which will be negotiated as soon as possible, thereby bearing in mind the protection that the House of Austria has found until now in Spain, so that appropriate satisfaction follows for all these good deeds.

In response to this declaration from Count Onate, Ferdinand would add a declaration of his own to the effect that:

> I am convinced that my rights to as well as my conduct towards the kingdoms of Hungary and Bohemia is manifest and well grounded. However, the almighty king of Spain is also of the view that his conduct and declarations towards the same kingdoms is well founded. My position derives from this situation: not merely to avoid any cause for strife and disputes – in view of the current political situation which necessitates a swift settlement of the succession to both these kingdoms and the empire – but also to reinforce and consolidate the bonds of mutual love, beneficent goodwill and blood ties between us, I, Archduke Ferdinand of Austria, in view of the imminent renunciation of all rights of the Spanish King to the aforementioned kingdoms, will grant the said king or his successors everything that is asked of me, that I am able to grant, if I, by the grace of God, receive the dignity of the title of Roman Emperor...

Indeed, Ferdinand was aware that the time for inter-dynastic disagreement was hardly ideal, and that over the five long years that the dispute had simmered, the Habsburgs' problems had grown much worse. As we have seen, while Philip was conceding these titles, he did not intend to do so for free. Ferdinand's declaration contains reference to Piombino and Finale, two fiefs located along the upper western coast of Italy, between Tuscany and Genoa. These would have to be handed over to Spain, but as for Alsace, Ferdinand explained that it was proving difficult to hand this territory over as well:

> I ask His Majesty not to hold it against me that I cannot yet make this available, because so many difficulties and problems arise that prevent me from offering it. However, should the time come, for him to demand this of me, but if

appear neither advantageous nor advisable, I promise to provide appropriate compensation.

There was much talk of keeping the treaty's terms secret, and of hiding from the treaty's public text the fact that Ferdinand was ceding lands to King Philip. But how would this treaty explain Philip's renunciation of his rights on Ferdinand's inheritance if there was no acknowledgement of the ceded territories? Ferdinand provided his own explanation, suggesting that the Onate Treaty could allude to 'the correspondence of law with the public good, as well as the king's tender inclination towards me.' Due to the scandal which would inevitably break were it learned that Ferdinand had ceded several territories to Philip, Ferdinand accepted that it was imperative...

> I must not divulge the aforementioned renunciation and on no account remove or diminish the security of the secret agreement, so that no clauses stand in the way and no connection can be made between the general renunciation and the aforementioned future cession.[69]

Ferdinand was attempting to acquire the renunciation from Philip and to cover his bases. So long as the King of Spain was promised this compensation, he proved willing to renounce his claims on the Bohemian and Hungarian thrones, in addition to the Imperial succession. The Onate Treaty had, after some time, finally achieved its purpose. Harmony and cooperation had returned to the wider Habsburg family, and just in time.

A properly supported and funded succession for Bohemia would have meant that Spain had the means and the time to help Ferdinand prepare the ground, and to impress upon its population the unity and sturdiness of the Habsburg family name. Alas, Philip's decision to delay these processes between 1612-1617 meant that Ferdinand had barely a year to ingratiate himself on the Bohemians, and that when he did so, he failed to make the necessary impressions or take the necessary precautions to ease the concerns of the Bohemian peasantry, nobility and clergy, which were legion.

FOUR
Bohemian Rampancy

Explaining the outbreak of the Thirty Years War on 23 May 1618, as the Bohemians threw three Habsburg councillors out the windows of the Hradschin Castle in Prague, is far from a simple task, as we have seen. It would have been far too reductionist to begin our narrative in 1618 and allude to that Bohemian revolt as the cause of all that followed. Thus, we have examined several threads of the story which, when tangled together, created this long and devastating conflict. We have dwelt for some time on actors apparently separate from Bohemia, as we established the background of Europe in the early seventeenth century.

Such threads will become important in time, but in 1618, those states which we have examined in the past, such as the Dutch, Swedish, English and French, and the men that led them, faded into the background. In their place loomed the Kingdom of Bohemia, that singularly puzzling but also fascinating country, which made an indelible mark on world history. We have watched the problems and challenges mount in Bohemia before 1617, as the Habsburgs managed to misjudge the situation on several occasions and provoke costly revolts in these lands against their restrictive policies.

The most significant of these was arguably that revolt which compelled the then Holy Roman Emperor Rudolf II to approve the Letter of Majesty in 1609, and the subsequent efforts by Rudolf to withdraw this concession after the event provoked another revolt in 1611, which came complete with an immensely expensive invasion of Bohemian lands by the Emperor's cousin.[70] These ruinous mistakes – one of many symptoms of the still more ruinous Brothers' Quarrel between Rudolf and Matthias – provided a preview of what was to come in 1618, when the third Bohemian revolt in less than ten years erupted, this time, pulling the rest of Europe in with it.

In addition to Bohemia's troubles, we have also seen the Austrian Habsburgs' inherent weaknesses become exacerbated by the entrenchment of Protestantism in their hereditary lands. With their subjects being of a different religious persuasion to the dynasty, the Austrian Habsburgs faced an intense challenge if they wished to affect any great taxation schemes, implement any reforms or raise any soldiers. The Estates of Austria, Bohemia and Hungary would cooperate, but only in return for concessions which guaranteed their freedom of religion. Since the late 1590s, Archduke Ferdinand had been reversing these concessions through sheer grit and determination, and the counter-reformation was gathering momentum at last in these all-important lands.[71]

Yet, it was one thing to implement such schemes in Austria, lands where the Habsburg dynasty possessed traditional rights to the land, and the physically imposing presence to match. It was quite another to forcibly implement such policies in lands where the Habsburgs had, only in the last century or so, come into a position of predominance, such as in Bohemia and Hungary. In both of these cases, if the counter-reformation was to succeed, the Habsburgs would have to tread very carefully, and to be mindful of the potential for revolt in both regions if they erred. Hungary and Bohemia contained mostly Protestant populations, and each boasted proud histories as independent kingdoms in their own right.

While the Habsburgs claimed the crown of both Kingdoms, the idea that either crown was the hereditary right of the Habsburg family was immensely contentious. Both crowns were elective, and the candidate for either throne would be required to affirm the religious privileges and freedoms which had been gained in the previous years. Knowing what we know about Ferdinand of Styria and his single-minded determination in reversing the Reformation in his Austrian patrimony, it should come as little surprise to note that Ferdinand built up something of a reputation for himself for this very behaviour. Considering this and considering as well the fact that Ferdinand still managed to acquire for himself the crowns of Bohemia and Hungary, we are drawn to the critical question of how. How did Ferdinand, the 'notorious',[72] 'ultra-Catholic',[73] 'militant'[74] manage to persuade the Bohemians of his suitability for their crown? Furthermore, how did he manage to convince them that he would respect their right to religious difference, even while this was wholly out of character for him?

Answering these questions requires us to resume our analysis of the events which immediately followed the signing of the Onate Treaty in March 1617. With the blessing of Spain assured, it remained for Archduke Ferdinand to acquire the blessing of the Bohemians and Hungarians to succeed to those crowns, before the final succession to the office of Holy Roman Emperor was confirmed. While religious compromise may have been the antithesis of his character, it was not outside of Ferdinand's capabilities to lie, and this simple act, more than any other, guaranteed Ferdinand's succession to the Bohemian throne. He swore an oath to uphold and respect the Letter of Majesty, thereby enshrining the promise of religious freedoms in the Bohemian constitution for one more reign. Following this, Ferdinand was crowned King of Bohemia on 29 June 1617.[75]

Ferdinand's almighty fib was possible for two major reasons. First, the Bohemians had debated since 1614 about the possibility of electing a non-Habsburg candidate to their throne, yet dallied and procrastinated for too long, to the point that no acceptable candidate had been found by 1617. It is not certain whether a quicker resolution of the Onate Treaty would have put this idea to bed once and for all, but regardless, the Bohemians approved of Ferdinand's candidacy after buying into his coronation oaths, which it was expected that no self-respecting King of Bohemia could possibly break. Second, in line with this point, Ferdinand's conscience was cleared by this sin by the rationalising of his Jesuit confessor, who reminded Ferdinand that his soul would not be harmed by the act of lying to heretics, and that political necessity in fact recommended such deception.

Some historians suggest that Ferdinand also made use of the threat of force to get his own way, and that with the Spanish and Austrian branches united, the Bohemians felt compelled to elect him as their King.[76] Perhaps there was an undercurrent of intimidation running through the proceedings, but even while historians may differ in their views on *why* the Bohemians named Ferdinand as their king, all are unanimous in the fact that they did. However, while the end result may appear akin to a forgone conclusion for the Habsburg family, the reality was that Ferdinand's coronation represented not just a victory for the dynasty, but also a defeat of the anti-Habsburg plot to unseat the dynasty not only from its Bohemian appendage, but the Habsburg claim on the Imperial throne itself. More will be said of this later.

That Ferdinand's advisors, and evidently, Ferdinand himself, thought so little of his pledges and consequently of the Bohemian people, stand out to this day. C. V. Wedgewood's account of Ferdinand's apprehension makes for especially striking reading, as Wedgewood wrote that:

> Ferdinand himself hesitated; he did not for one moment contemplate standing by the Letter of Majesty, but he was uncertain whether the time was favourable for making his position clear. He was troubled in his conscience at making even a formal concession to heretics...Some consultation with his confessor convinced him that political necessity did in fact justify a deviation from absolute sincerity, and...he formally guaranteed the Letter of Majesty.

Ferdinand's insincerity was marked still further by the expectation that by conceding these empty promises now, the Habsburg dynasty could wait until the more extremist elements of Bohemian society acted out, and gave Ferdinand the excuse he needed to clamp down on their freedoms and rights. With this goal in mind Ferdinand set to work appointing a regency council for

Bohemia composed mostly of Catholics, despite the overwhelming Protestant inclinations of the population. Ferdinand evidently anticipated that frustration at this injustice would compel the Bohemians to resort to violence; after all, resorting to violence had been a common feature of Bohemia's recent history. Just in case they did not get the point though, Ferdinand sought to drive it home by alienating more lands to Catholic Church and bringing the press of the country within the parameters of state censorship. More restrictive policies were soon to follow.[77]

After so many years of conflict, and much of it in the last decade of Habsburg rule alone, a wise advisor would surely counsel caution and toleration, lest another revolt would surely flare up in Bohemia once again. Indeed, Melchior Klesl was just such a figure who preached toleration and care when dealing with the religious differences and anxieties of the Bohemians. Klesl had been Emperor's Matthias' confessor, and though he had enjoyed the patronage of the Jesuits, he had converted from Protestantism at an early age, and was therefore inculcated with a certain degree of understanding largely absent from his peers. Based in Vienna since the turn of the century, Klesl made a name for himself as the cautious, careful but phenomenally successful Cardinal-statesman in charge of the counter-reformation in that city, and quickly rose to prominence in Emperor Rudolf's court.[78]

Having served in the position as Rudolf's principle advisor, and having gathered together the representatives of the dynasty on that critical occasion in Linz in 1605, where it was decided what should be done about Rudolf's deteriorating mind, Klesl was well-positioned to transfer his service to Emperor Matthias from 1612. As shrewd as he was perceptive, Klesl had urged Matthias to tread carefully in Bohemia and throughout the Empire, accepting the concessions made under duress, and swallowing the bitter pills for the Catholic dynasty, such as the Letter of Majesty, but with Ferdinand's accession, Klesl began to decline in influence and power.[79] Klesl had been a figure of great importance for the Austrian Habsburg administration for nearly two decades, and a much-needed voice of reason during such tense times, but his policy of tolerance where necessary did not gel with that of Ferdinand.

In his efforts to strengthen the dynasty, Klesl had striven to reduce the potential for division and discord in the Empire by dismantling the two confessional blocs, and providing a sincere platform where all could air their grievances – the 1613 Reichstag in Regensburg.[80] While such efforts failed, Klesl did not retreat; he remained active in Habsburg politics right up to the point of his removal, and played an active role in the Habsburg negotiations which constituted the Oñate Treaty. However, Klesl was largely powerless to reverse the perception in Europe that Spanish might alone propped the Austrian Habsburgs up, or that the Austrian branch had itself entered into a terminal decline and was thus vulnerable to intrigue from abroad.

Spanish power had grown, while Habsburg power, and therefore the power of the Holy Roman Emperor and his Empire, had contracted – this impression was not helped by the fact that Emperors had consistently remained aloof from European wars since the Peace of Augsburg, and had preferred instead to focus on the threat from the Ottoman Empire. So far had the Habsburg preponderance declined in the West that Austrian Habsburg envoys could no longer be found in most of the major capitals – for news, they relied upon independent resources like the Fugger newsletters, and for diplomatic representation, a special envoy was sent or the Spanish leaned upon. In Klesl's defence, there was little certainty that the 1606 peace with the Turks would last as long as it did – the peace was renewed in 1615, and Ottoman conflict with Safavid Persia proved a godsend to the thoroughly distracted Habsburgs in the years to come. Not until the 1660s would the Ottomans and Habsburgs come to significant blows once more.

This breathing space from the traditional enemy could not have come at a more opportune time for the Austrian Habsburgs, but certain underlying problems remained unsolved. Emperor's Matthias' position was weakened by several years' worth of concessions to his estates, and even with the gradual tide turning thanks to the counter-reformation, the Austrian base was nowhere near as secure as Klesl would have liked. Consequently, he scaled back his ambitions for Europe, and focused on husbanding resources, allies and guarantees from the Austrian and Hungarian estates. Facing this chronic weakness, it is little wonder that Klesl recommended compromise with the Bohemians as well, since yet another expensive revolt in that pivotal kingdom was the last thing the dynasty could afford, especially when so much depended upon the vote which that Kingdom accrued.[81]

Melchior Klesl had done his utmost to disarm the two confessional blocs in the years leading up to 1618, and he had made no shortage of enemies during these efforts, including Maximillian of Bavaria, who suspected that the Cardinal was seeking to undermine his position. This position had been in decline for some time, thanks in large part to the difficulty Maximillian had with organising and co-opting the support of the Catholic League's contingent parts. In his most audacious act since arguably the seizure of Donauworth, Maximillian sent ten thousand men under the Catholic League's banners into Salzburg, to depose and arrest the Archbishop who ruled there, and put an end to his anti-League schemes. The arrest of his fellow Catholic did Maximillian's reputation no favours, and it demonstrated an important fact which is often lost in narratives of the origins of the Thirty Years War.[82]

While we refer to the two confessional blocs as the Evangelical Union and the Catholic League, neither grouping counted in its ranks all or even most members of its religious persuasion. Peter H. Wilson wrote that the princes of the Empire of all religious persuasions mostly wished to remain neutral – a mission which was to become increasingly difficult in the years to come. In peacetime though, the choice between God or the Devil was not so pronounced; of more importance to most princes than the prospect of religious warfare was the sanctity of the imperial constitution. If all concerned princes scrambled to join the awaiting alliance blocs, then this constitution could be placed in jeopardy, since the fear persisted that 'membership would suck them into conflicts not of their concern' – a valid fear when one examines what followed the Defenestration of Prague.[83]

Arguably the most significant neutral party in this confessional equation was the Elector of Saxony, himself the most powerful and important Protestant potentate in the Holy Roman Empire, with a vote in determining the next Emperor along with the six other electors. John George, the Elector of Saxony, has not fared well in historians' estimations of him – invariably cast as 'Beer George',[84] the feckless drunk; or the tragically ineffectual German leader.[85] Notwithstanding his shortcomings, John George was still important enough to receive a visit from Archduke Ferdinand in summer 1617, shortly after the latter's negotiations with the Spanish had borne fruit.

Having acquired the blessing of Madrid to stand for the Bohemian, Hungarian and Holy Roman crowns, it is significant that Ferdinand moved with Emperor Matthias in Vienna before making a beeline for Dresden, where the Habsburgs would meet first with John George. There was much to discuss, as the Saxon Elector had to be enlightened as to the implications of the agreements made with Spain, but only those ones which were considered palatable. In addition, Ferdinand and Matthias were keen 'to discuss something important concerning the welfare of the Empire' – in other words, the question of whether John George would support Ferdinand's claim to succeed Matthias as Emperor. John George, loyal to the Empire's constitution, but by no means devoid of ambition or cynical displays of opportunism, would be called on again when the time was right. After acquiring the tacit approval from John George, Ferdinand and Matthias then continued to travel towards Prague, the Bohemian capital, and then to Pressburg (Bratislava) the Moravian capital, as Ferdinand's rights to the Kingdom of Bohemia were confirmed, and he was accepted in turn as 'king designate' of Bohemia and Royal Hungary.[86]

By the time Ferdinand was confirmed as King of Bohemia on 29 June 1617 then, he had gone to great lengths in league with Emperor Matthias to lay the groundwork for a painless election to the office of Holy Roman Emperor. The public acceptance of the capitulations of his predecessors was the final step towards the realisation of his Imperial coronation, which would only be actually possible once Matthias died. Ferdinand may well have believed that these concessions to 'heretics' were of far less importance than those concessions he had made to King Philip III of Spain.

It is safe to say that no one within the Habsburg dynasty, or within Europe for that matter, desired the ruinous conflagration which followed Ferdinand's terminal underestimation of the Bohemians' anxieties.[87] Notwithstanding his lack of appetite for a third Bohemian revolt though, Ferdinand still managed to provoke it, and he did so by giving his approval for some very blatant and some other covert violations of the Letter of Majesty. The time has come now to examine exactly what Ferdinand did to provoke the Bohemian eruption, and precisely what rights and privileges he undermined along the way, which made the whole process so insulting and distasteful for the Bohemians.

'This king is no good, we need another', shouted the mob, as they crowded into Prague's Hradschin Castle in the height of summer, in 1609.[88] The Bohemians had assembled in number, to demand the concessions from their King and Emperor, Rudolf II, which had been promised to keep them loyal. This was the Brothers' Quarrel in full display, and its dire consequences were plainly felt, as Rudolf, ailing and fragile, was forced to capitulate to the Bohemians demands. The culmination of these capitulations was the infamous Letter of Majesty, officially conceded by Rudolf on 9 July 1609. With his brother Matthias seizing pledges of loyalty from his other subjects, accepting these sweeping concessions were all Rudolf could do to hold onto what little authority he had left. Ever since 1605 Matthias had been aiming for his position, but Rudolf was determined to resist his brothers' ambition, whatever it cost him or his family. The cost was high, and although Rudolf could not have known it, the Habsburgs would continue to repay it for the next generation.

The concession of the Letter of Majesty was the final domino of concessions to fall in the Habsburg Hereditary Lands, but in terms of the long-term impact it had on the continent, it was by far the most significant. The Bohemians acquired toleration of Protestant worship far beyond those concessions granted to their Austrian or Hungarian peers. 'Henceforth', noted Peter H. Wilson, 'the lords, knights and royal towns were free to choose which Christian confession to follow, and each group could elect ten 'Defensors' to safeguard their rights.'[89] This latter point proved the most important, as it effectively created two governments in Bohemia, with the new government controlled by Bohemia's aristocratic Protestants and ruling parallel to the old Habsburg administration. The Protestant Bohemians also named commanders of their own militia and took over important bastions in the country such as Prague University in a bid to institutionalise their church and protect it from interference.

A constitution for the country was prepared by the Bohemians around the same time, but this was a step too far for the Habsburgs, who never ratified it, and neither Rudolf nor Matthias gave it their approval either.[90] It should also be underlined that these religious concessions were not universally popular in

Bohemian society, since the Bohemians wanted more than mere toleration of their religion – they sought equality for their creed with the Catholics, within a country which was already deeply divided along religious lines. Indeed, religious division within Bohemia, and the option for each of the three estates to select only one religion to abide by, made further sectarianism inevitable, and it also ignored the very real corporate interests of Bohemia's businessmen, peasants and burghers, who cared less for religion than for their own material and societal advancement.[91]

Notwithstanding the shortcomings of the Letter of Majesty, it had established a government within Bohemia which the Habsburgs would not be able to ignore if they wished to avoid future conflict. That said, these Bohemians representatives – the thirty Defensors drawn from the three estates of the towns, knights and nobles – may have been elected by the estates, but they were not constitutionally empowered to act in the same way that the Habsburgs' agents were. Thus, a sense of tension inevitably existed between the old Habsburg regency government, and the newer Bohemian government of the Defensors, since only the former possessed the actual authority to govern the country. This authority lay in the hands of ten regents which the Habsburgs appointed, and by 1617 a mismatch of seven Catholics to three Protestants sat in the Habsburgs' name. The Catholic regents were Bohemian nationals, and could not be accused of being mere creatures of the Habsburgs, but still, the disparity between the religious makeup of the country and the picture the Habsburgs were attempting to paint was blatant and unsettling to many Bohemians, especially once Ferdinand was crowned as their King.

In Ferdinand's defence, it can be argued that a major reason why he believed he could push and provoke the Bohemians without risking a full-blown revolt was due to the mute protests of the Bohemians themselves at the time of his coronation. Only two members of the Defensors raised their voices in protest – one of these was Heinrich Matthias, Count of Thurn, a Lutheran Bohemian nobleman of Italian descent, named as commander of the Protestant militia in the previous years. Count Thurn has been identified as one of the most important radical voices, who only exacerbated the tense situation in his country, leading Bohemia's masses to the Defenestration in May 1618, the scene which ignited the Thirty Years War.

Considering Thurn's extremism and favouring of violence, it is perhaps unsurprising that historians have tended to hold negative views of him. Wedgewood wrote that Thurn 'fancied himself both as a diplomat, a political leader and a general', but that he 'possessed few of the qualities on which he prided himself' and that he lacked 'tact, patience, judgement [and] insight; moreover he was covetous, overbearing and boastful, so that although he had many supporters, he had few friends.'[92] Notwithstanding his negative reputation, Count Thurn would retain a pivotal role in the direction of the Bohemian policy during the revolt and during his subsequent exile, and we will certainly see him again in our narrative.

Ferdinand was the King of Bohemia, but he did not remain in Prague for long, since Vienna was where Matthias resided, and Ferdinand wished to be close to him in anticipation of the Imperial succession. This put distance between the King and his subjects at the worst time, since the Bohemians had grown used to having their King near at hand and would now have to petition the ten regents to discuss their concerns. Ferdinand had wasted little time in reinforcing his position in the country. While he was far from being in a position to extirpate Protestantism from Bohemia, as he had done in Styria, subtle and not-so-subtle decisions were made to undermine the Protestants and, as we said, provoke them into some display of limited violence which could be easily supressed and harnessed.

The alienation of land to the Archbishop of Prague effectively took certain towns and villages out of the hands of the Defensors and placed them under the jurisdiction of the Catholic Church. Through this device Matthias and then Ferdinand had managed to undermine the reach of the Bohemians' authority, and the Bohemians had objected loudly to the exploitation of such loopholes. When the Protestant inhabitants of one town were arrested, and the Lutheran Church in another was torn down in late 1617, the Defensors made formal protests to the regents and to Ferdinand, but these were ignored. By this point, the Catholic regents were ignoring their Protestant peers, and hardline Catholics acted virtually in Ferdinand's name.

From late 1617, new rulings were issued which placed the printed media of Bohemia under censorship, and non-Catholics were prevented from holding any position of consequence in the Habsburgs' administration. Such tactics had been used extensively by Melchior Klesl as a 'soft' method for persuading Protestants to convert in the Austrian lands, but when applied by Ferdinand to Bohemia, the reaction was significantly less quiescent.[93] In Prague on 5 March 1618, a meeting of the Bohemian Defensors called for a redress of their grievances, referring to a long list of infringements against the Letter of Majesty perpetrated by Ferdinand's administration. Emperor Matthias was appealed to directly, as were the estates of the other provinces united under the Bohemian crown – Moravia, Silesia and Lusatia. It was not too surprising to receive a reply in the negative, officially from Emperor Matthias, but delivered through the authority of the Regents, on 21 March, but what *was* shocking to the Defensors was the additional demand, inserted by the normally more perceptive Klesl, ordering the Defensors to disband their assembly, and forbidding them to gather together again in such a manner.

According to the Letter of Majesty which Rudolf, Matthias and Ferdinand had all approved, the Defensors were well within their rights to convene an assembly, and Matthias' reply was thus added to their list of grievances not merely on sectarian, but also on constitutional grounds. Matters proceeded quickly from here – the Defensors agreed that they should meet again on 21 May and called their supporters to return to Prague. This meeting inflamed the pre-existing passions, and the Catholic regents, who were believed to have advised Matthias against accepting the Bohemian petition in March, were loudly condemned. The solution appeared to point to a symbolic, violent protest to demonstrate the full extent of the Bohemians' grievances. A storming of the Hradschin Castle, and a forceful wresting of the desired concessions – in a similar vein to what had occurred nearly a decade before when the Letter of Majesty was conceded by Rudolf – seemed on the cards.

It is debateable whether the Bohemians knew all along what they intended to do on the morning of 23 May, or whether, having arrived at that stuffy, tense location, emotions got the better of those assembled. Either way, in a scene immortalised many times since, two of the Catholic regents, and their secretary, were ejected from the windows of the Hradschin Castle, and the Defenestration of Prague was complete. With this great act of rebellion against the representatives of the Habsburg dynasty, the question of what to do next remained a divisive and problematic one for those Bohemians that had acted. Did they intend to expel the entire Habsburg apparatus from their lands, or merely to demonstrate their anger and negotiate from a position of strength? Either way, the first shot had been fired, not in the quest for justice as the Bohemians had hoped, but in the most catastrophic, ruinous conflict in early modern European history – the Thirty Years War.[94]

FIVE
The Right to Conspire

Christian of House Ascania, more commonly known as Christian of Anhalt, arrived in Dresden, Saxony in 1586. As one of five sons, from a German principality which did not yet accept primogeniture, Christian and his four brothers saw their already small lands be split five ways, to the point that precious little remained for Christian by the death of his father. Such a situation had compelled Christian to travel and seek his fortune elsewhere, and Saxony was his most significant stop off to date. While there he converted to Calvinism, and with a single-minded fervour for his new faith, he embraced all manner of schemes which would help him further its teachings. In 1591, he was provided with an ideal opportunity – he was given the chance to lead a Saxon-Palatine army of German soldiers and mercenaries into France to assist the Protestant claimant to the French throne, Henry of Navarre.

While the army did march, the pledges which Christian had accepted turned out to be empty, and Christian, this 24-year-old prince, was left with a staggering debt of 1.3 million thalers, as well as a harsh lesson not to trust wholeheartedly the commitments made by Germans in times of war. This debt proved so formidable that Christian's descendants would still be making efforts to claim back this debt in the early nineteenth century! Once he absorbed this debt though, Christian moved quickly to distance himself from this sticky situation, making sure, before he left the scene, to get in touch with several members of the Calvinist international. These connections served him well, as they eventually landed him a post as governor of the Upper Palatinate in 1595, a province wedged almost in the centre of Europe, between Bavaria, Bohemia and Saxony. Thus, began the relationship between Christian of Anhalt and the Palatinate which was to become so infamous, and play a considerable role in leading the Palatinate into the Thirty Years War.

From 1595, Anhalt displayed a distinct measure of skill and tact in traversing the sensitive religious divisions of this eastern appendage of the Palatine Electors. Since 1329 it had been in the possession of the Palatinate, but it maintained a separate administration, not to mention a very different economy and climate to its wealthier, more glamorous western neighbour, the Lower Palatinate. Since the Elector tended to remain in Heidelberg, the gleaming jewel of the Lower Palatinate, this meant that any governor of the Upper Palatinate, based in the city of Amberg, would have a great deal of independence. To Christian of Anhalt, this position represented nothing less than an opportunity to prove himself, and by the time the Bohemians threw their Catholic regents out the windows of the Hradschin Castle, Christian had engendered a sense of goodwill and loyalty to the Electoral family which was to prove invaluable in the trials to come. Unsurprisingly, Anhalt's impressive body of work stretching back over two decades had recommended him as an experienced, capable and resourceful statesman to the Elector Frederick IV, and then his son, Frederick V.

Anhalt played an important role in Palatine diplomacy from 1608-1618; he helped to arrange the Evangelical Union under the leadership of the Elector Palatine Frederick IV, and he orchestrated arguably his greatest coup – the marital alliance between Elizabeth Stuart and Frederick V. Through these arrangements, Christian of Anhalt was placing his masters in a position of strength which the Palatinate had traditionally never occupied. Of course, by placing the Palatinate in this position, with its Calvinist Electors and its history of anti-Habsburg intrigue, Anhalt greatly increased the tensions within the Holy Roman Empire. Yet, this contribution to the escalation in tensions and anxiety of the Empire's subjects, and his practical contribution towards the actual outbreak of the Thirty Years War which followed, must be juxtaposed with Anhalt's sincere belief that the institutions of the Empire were biased against Protestants, that they were, in the words of one historian, 'captured by the Jesuits as agencies of the Counter-Reformation', and that the Habsburg monopoly on the office of Holy Roman Emperor was an inherently bad thing.[95]

It is sometimes convenient to blame one figure in particular for the perpetuation of a certain crisis. In Wedgewood's account of Christian of Anhalt for example, we are given the impression not only that the man was a complete fool, but that this fool had Frederick V under his spell. 'In arms, in administration and in diplomacy he showed a superficial excellence', Wedgewood wrote, adding:

> How brilliant for instance had been his management of the English marriage! But he had not paused to consider that a day of reckoning would come when the English King realised that he had been inveigled into a German war. Anhalt's diplomacy, with England, with the [Dutch] United Provinces, with the German princes and later with the Duke of Savoy, was based on a simple principle: he always promised everything. He calculated that when the German crisis came his allies would fulfil their side of the bargain before they called on him to fulfil his. He calculated wrong: when the moment came, not one of his far-sought alliances bore the strain.[96]

Wedgewood added that Anhalt was 'not a man who inspired confidence', that he 'deceived himself' and that Frederick V was 'so obviously in the hands of his minister' that he did nothing without his approval, and thus did nothing to improve the worsening situation in the Empire.[97] For all these shortcomings, Wedgewood could not explain how Anhalt's nonetheless forged ahead with a policy which, for an admittedly brief period, did provide the Palatinate with the most impressive security arrangement it had enjoyed since before the Reformation.

Granted, Anhalt took advantage of the fears and anxieties of the neighbouring German Protestants in many respects. One is drawn in particular to the Donauworth incident (1607-08) where Maximillian of Bavaria invaded and then annexed the majority Protestant town of Donauworth into his Duchy in spring 1608, and began persecuting the non-Catholics that lived there, with the backing of the Holy Roman Emperor. This event caused such consternation that it led to the aforementioned walkout of several Protestant princes during the 1608 Reichstag, and the establishment of the Evangelical Union shortly thereafter.

When reading these events, we are provided with a choice. Either we can believe that the actors responsible for furthering the set of crises which erupted in 1618 acted in good faith, and out of genuine fear for their rights and privileges, or we can condemn them for manipulating the situation, and feigning concern in order to gain more powers for themselves. If one was to apply such a deceitful characterisation to Anhalt's behaviour though, then we must ask what his end goal was. Why did Anhalt believe that gathering as many Protestant princes together was necessary, and why did he consistently attempt to solicit foreign support for the union of Protestant potentates which he was trying to create? Did he strive thus to gain leverage over the Habsburgs, and to force them to relinquish their position under threat of war? Perhaps he acted to increase his own power and enrich himself in the process. Yet, in all these hypothetical possibilities, we must ask again, to what end would Anhalt seek such disruptive goals?

What if, contrary to Wedgewood's opinion, Anhalt was not acting with dishonesty, but acted out of a sense of genuine fear, which had been rooted in the Palatinate since the late 1560s, that a Habsburg Catholic conspiracy, powered by the Jesuits, the Pope and the Spanish, was in play? What if we imagine that instead of gathering allies for an uncertain end, Anhalt was gathering pledges and commitments for a religious war which he believed that the Habsburgs were planning? After moving to govern the Upper Palatinate in 1595, and converting to Calvinism before that, is it not at least feasible that Anhalt himself became persuaded of the possibility that the Habsburgs intended to provoke a religious war in order to further the ends of the counter-reformation, which was then gathering apace?[98]

This is not to state that the Habsburgs *did* desire to launch such a confessional war in the name of the counter-reformation, but if we examine the situation from Anhalt's, and indeed from the Palatine perspective, then one could argue that it becomes easier to understand why Anhalt was convinced of the eternal danger which the Habsburgs presented. The danger which the Habsburgs posed was aimed not just against the religious privileges of Protestants throughout the Empire, but also, but also against the constitution of that Empire, which the Habsburgs would sacrifice in the name of their barely veiled quest for absolutist rule over Germany. Indeed, Frederick V was convinced that Ferdinand intended to violate the Empire's constitution, and his beliefs were vindicated when Ferdinand did indeed secretly displace Frederick as Elector of the Palatinate in favour of Maximillian, in lieu of pay for Maximillian's services during the early phase of the war.[99]

To further understand Anhalt's position, we must also recall the Brothers' Quarrel, and the general inefficiency of Emperor Rudolf in the last two decades of his reign. While we have examined the consequences of this crisis in the Habsburg family already, it is worth looking at another hitherto unmentioned side effect. The Supreme Court of the Holy Roman Empire provided great potential for religious divisions to render it paralysed. Yet, in spite of some incidents during the sixteenth century, the Supreme Court functioned remarkably well up until the 1590s, when Emperor Rudolf II ceased to see to his responsibilities relating to that institution. A purpose of the Supreme Court was to implement legislature which the Reichstag had passed, and as part of this process, the Emperor was required to provide his decision on its conclusions. With Emperor Rudolf absent though, the Imperial Supreme Court was forced to go around in circles constitutionally, as matters passed by the Reichstag into the Supreme Court would simply be passed back to the Reichstag again, since no Emperor was in place to sign off on them.[100]

Rudolf's deterioration was having a noted, adverse effect on the operation of the Empire. It was his family's recognition of this fact, not to mention a desire to conclude the war with the Turks, that compelled the Austrian Habsburgs to first meet at Linz in 1605, and then to do everything they could to gradually cut Rudolf out. In the midst of these crises within the Habsburg family, its international standing notable declined. Faced with revolts in Hungary from 1606-08, in Austria and Bohemia from 1609-11, and finally a succession crisis with their Spanish cousins from 1612-17, the once guaranteed Imperial succession seemed at last to be under threat. If the enemies of the Habsburgs could locate another candidate, then the troubled Austrian Habsburg family would be in danger of losing its foothold atop the food chain of the Holy Roman Emperor, as the Emperor of all the Germans.[101]

All of these factors compelled Anhalt to engage in more active diplomatic negotiations than he had in the past, but it also must have seemed as though the actual situation within the Empire was particularly grave. The aforementioned troubles faced by the Austrian Habsburgs had been significant for another reason – in their time of need, the Austrian, Bohemian and Hungarian estates had all made contact with Christian of Anhalt and the Palatine court. This ensured that Anhalt was kept appraised of their fates, so that when the Habsburgs promised concessions to these subjects in order to make them disperse, he recognised that such concessions could not hold for long. With Archduke Ferdinand's notorious reputation preceding him, and with Rudolf and then Matthias providing no children, it seemed certain that Ferdinand would succeed to the Imperial throne, unless some replacement candidate was found.

Ferdinand's success in extirpating heresy from his Styrian lands and his Jesuit upbringing greatly increased the likelihood that he would challenge the concessions which Rudolf and then Matthias had given to their Hungarian, Bohemian and Austrian subjects. Matthias, for his own part, had never been comfortable with the fact that these subjects had wrested such concessions from him under duress, and he viewed them as illegitimate for that very reason, and consistently attempted, through the wiles of Melchior Klesl, to undermine them. It should also be reiterated that Anhalt had seen the Habsburgs violate their commitments to the constitution and to their subjects in the past. Donauworth was the most striking example, but the incredibly unwise adventure of Archduke Leopold, as he attempted to force the Bohemians to stand down over 1611-1612 were as expensive and ruinous as they were illuminating for Anhalt.[102]

Here were the Habsburgs once again undermining the promises they had made to their subjects; here again were the Habsburgs attempting to use force in their own lands to arrive at the religious settlement which they wanted, rather than the one these subjects wanted. With Protestantism overwhelmingly the majority religion in Austria, Bohemia and Hungary – though the counter-reformation was gathering momentum – Anhalt was likely also perturbed by the sight of the religiously besieged Catholic Habsburgs attempting to restrict the rights of the majority. In addition to these developments and to spark of Donauworth which ignited the Evangelical Union, there was also the Julich-Cleve crisis, which remained unsolved over 1609-14, and threatened to pull the Evangelical Union into a war with the Catholic League, with both sides availing of foreign support.

For a variety of reasons as we have seen, the Julich-Cleve crisis did not spark a major confessional or political civil war in the Empire, however, this does not mean that these events, taken together, did not serve to shape or even confirm Anhalt's convictions. In fact, Anhalt appeared secure enough in his convictions to ignore a potential chance for lasting peace in spring 1617. This latest peace initiative had been the product of Melchior Klesl's diplomacy,

diplomacy which had effectively disbanded the Catholic League by April 1617. That Anhalt did not reciprocate, and dismantle the Evangelical Union, can be explained by several factors, including his inability to trust Klesl, but also to the possibility that Anhalt discovered Maximillian of Bavaria's efforts to forge ahead with a secret alliance of German Catholic potentates.[103]

We should also bear in mind the effect upon Anhalt's psyche that the gradual deterioration in the security of the Evangelical Union must have had. Since it had been established in 1608, with the memory of Donauworth fresh in everyone's minds, the Union recruited some new members, and even though Saxony remained out of reach, its prospects appeared good, and it made a much better showing during the Julich-Cleve crisis than its Catholic counterpart, which splintered apart due to Habsburg interference and distrust of the Bavarians. From 1614 though, the Union began to shed members, and Anhalt was forced to watch as much of his hard work was chipped away by the sheer unwillingness of the Union's members to pay their required fees or contribute the required soldiers. In April 1617, just as the Catholic League officially disbanded, Anhalt endured further setbacks when the Union, by now propped up with Palatine monies, lost Brandenburg and Hess-Kassel, two pivotal members, after their rulers became irritated at the concessions Anhalt had been forced to make to keep the whole edifice together. Anhalt had kept the Evangelical Union together, and, he could note with satisfaction, he had done so in spite of direct orders from the Emperor to disband.

Yet, the Union which limped into 1618, and which Frederick V would rely on the following year, was a shadow of its once enthusiastic, confident self. In order to keep the Union in existence, Anhalt had conceded the right of the Union's members for a veto against any military ventures in the future, and the Union was not required to aid non-members of the Union. Both concessions were individually devastating, but to concede both effectively doomed the Union to paralysis. Even in its original form, the Evangelical Union had not contained a majority of Protestant princes, and lacked Saxony, which reduced its credibility abroad, even with the son in law of the King of Britain at its head from 1614. With these concessions granted though, the Union would be able to remain aloof from any conflict that emerged in the future, and there was also now no danger that a conflict between other Protestant princes would draw the Union in.

In the context of his declining Union, we should not be surprised to see Anhalt turn to more desperate schemes to insulate the Palatinate against the Habsburg conspiracy which he believed in. During the *uzkok* war and the Mantuan War of Succession, Anhalt sent representatives to Venice, Savoy, the Bohemian estates, the Austrian estates and France in order to take advantage of the doubly distracted Habsburgs, but all in vain. By 1617, Anhalt's convictions regarding the coming of a religious war and the presence of an overarching Habsburg conspiracy had not abated, if anything they had intensified, buoyed by the presence of several doom-saying prophecies which many in Europe also bought into.

From the Calvinist academy at Herborn, established in 1584, came several Calvinist preachers convinced that the Habsburgs represented the forces of darkness portrayed in the Book of Revelation. Interestingly, this interpretation was the complete opposite of the official Imperial presentation of Revelation, which saw the Empire as the direct continuation of Ancient Rome, as well as its final phase. One preacher, Johann Heinrich Alsted, declared his belief that the Empire was the fourth, unnamed beast of Revelation, and that its end was nigh. More incredible still was the fate which the likes of Alsted prophesied for the Empire; through his interpretation of Revelation and the Book of Daniel, Alsted became convinced that a southern king would overrun the sanctuary of Calvinism, Lutheranism and all non-Catholic creeds, and force them to renounce their faith, until a king of the north intervened to defeat the southern king and deliver his people.

Considering these stark predictions, and the course of the Thirty Years War which was to follow, with Habsburg triumph and repressive religious policies followed by a successful Swedish intervention by Gustavus Adolphus, the 'Lion in the North', it is hardly surprising that preachers like Alsted later felt vindicated, even if their doom-laden prophesies were not in the majority of Protestant believers. Yet, it should be noted that Alsted was not alone, and his intellectual background granted a veneer of respectability to apocalyptic pronouncements like these. Coupled with Alsted's profile was the increasingly harsh weather brought on by the Litter Ice Age. These weather events culminated in the sighting of Haley's Comet in November 1618, and shortly thereafter more than one hundred pamphlets preaching incoming disaster were published to an eager readership. Sightings of comets and apocalyptic predictions were nothing new for the time, but in combination with the additional tensions, the confessional hostility and the belief in a Habsburg conspiracy, we should not understate the impact of these factors, which may well have compelled radical Protestant preachers and leaders to incite the very disaster they had feared.

With the aforementioned challenges facing the Austrian Habsburgs, above all the childless Emperor Matthias providing no direct successor, as early as Matthias' election in 1612, Palatine diplomacy had worked to place an alternative candidate on the Imperial throne. At the same time, Palatine preachers had published tracts and sermons designed to bridge the gaps between Calvinists and Lutherans, with a view towards preparing for the confrontation with Habsburg Catholicism. Various societies and groups were established within the Palatinate for the very purpose of bringing the different sects of Protestantism together. While she led a military alliance of some Protestant powers, leadership within Protestant German society was also a goal, especially once the concessions to the remaining members of the Evangelical Union rendered that organisation much less effective.

Rather than the machinations of the Habsburgs, it was in fact the opposition of Lutheran Saxony that truly blocked this Palatine initiative. With the centenary of the Reformation celebrated in October 1617, the Saxon Elector John George and his court preacher were together determined to reassert Saxon predominance over German Protestants through the traditional method of defying the Papacy. Luther was celebrated as the German Moses, and his likeness and achievements marked with commemorative medals, in school plays and through several fireworks displays. Saxon policy was to distinguish between honest Catholics that respected the 1555 Augsburg settlement, and those that sought to undermine it and the Empire. This enabled John George to support the Habsburgs as the legitimate possessors of the Imperial title, but also to oppose destabilising confessional quarrels, and the vision of the Jesuits.[104]

For these reasons Saxony had remained aloof from Palatine efforts to round up all Protestants under the banner of the Evangelical Union; John George would display a reverence for traditionalism and peace, rather than make any great efforts to oppose the Habsburgs in league with the Palatinate. Because of Saxony's reputation and standing within the Empire and Europe, it proved immensely difficult for Anhalt to unite Protestants without the Saxon presence. Unity among Protestants was far from an easy task; for example, around the same time of the Reformation centenary celebrations, Württemberg, a member of the Evangelical Union, issued a decree 'that lumped Calvinists...along with Jesuits, the pope, tyrants, and Turks as common threats to the faith.'[105] Many Lutherans regarded Calvinists with still more hostility than Catholics, since the former had diluted the gains made by the reformed church under the 1555 Peace of Augsburg, and Calvinists had also gained at Lutheranism's expense. Indeed, as we have seen, it was this very division within Protestantism that recommended the Old Faith to disillusioned nobles, princes and citizens of the Empire.[106]

Throughout 1617, perhaps due to the Reformation's centenary, the confessional differences between Calvinist Palatinate and Lutheran Saxony were exacerbated, and the court preachers in both regions accused the other of dishonesty and sabotage of the Reformation's legacy. It is significant that Melchior Klesl plans for stabilising the Empire were also adversely affected by this inter-Protestant hostility, since the rhetoric employed by both sides convinced many Catholics that any notion of all Christian Germans banding together for the sake of Imperial unity would not be possible.[107] While Anhalt could despair that Saxony ignored the danger which the Habsburgs posed to Protestantism and the Empire, it was once John George displayed a cynical unscrupulousness in his partitioning of Bohemia that Frederick V would bitterly decry the Saxon short-sightedness and betrayal of Protestantism. Evidently, the sanctity of the Empire was only of interest to John George so long as no risks to his person existed, and he could discern some clear opportunity for personal gain.[108] To Frederick as much as to Anhalt, John George's behaviour represented a disaster for the Palatinate and for Protestantism.

It is often said that Anhalt effectively ran the Palatinate's foreign policy during the period, and that it was his views and fears which moved Palatine diplomats into action, rather than his technical master, Frederick V, the Elector. Indeed, Wedgewood interprets the conflict which followed as flowing from Anhalt's pen and ambitions, portraying the senior Christian of Anhalt as more than capable of manipulating his younger master, who bowed without much resistance to his expertise. Wedgewood also seemed to be on a certain mission to paint Anhalt as a corrupting influence in the Palatine court; an influence which corrupted Frederick from a young age. Wedgewood gives little consideration to the fact that, from the 1560s, the Palatinate had been fixed in opposition to the Habsburgs, and there was no reason why Frederick would have grown up to believe in anything other than that policy and mission which he had inherited from his grandfather.[109]

As Brennan Pursell wrote, there is much to be gained from examining the practical situation which the Elector and Anhalt operated within. Since Anhalt spent most of his time in Amberg, as the governor of the Upper Palatinate, and since Frederick rarely viewed that part of his lands, preferring the more sumptuous surroundings of Heidelberg in the Lower Palatinate along the Rhine, this meant that Anhalt and Frederick were not in each other's company very often. Unless he maintained a consistent relationship with Frederick, there was no way for Anhalt to impose his will upon his prince as he supposedly managed to do. Frederick's signature was required on any piece of documentation Anhalt provided him with, and this meant that Anhalt was never in a genuine position to act independently of the Elector. Frederick may well have been influenced by Anhalt's experience, and he was impressed by learned, talented and resourceful men, which Anhalt certainly was. However, to claim that Frederick had no policy of his own is to misconstrue the Elector's position. Frederick did have a policy; it was the one he had been brought up to promote, and the one which he had come to believe was correct and true. For better or worse, his beliefs were his own to hold, and his mistakes were his own to make.[110]

While the Palatine intervention in the Bohemian revolt represented the culmination of Palatine-Habsburg competition, this competition in itself was not at all new. On several occasions between the 1560s and 1618 the Palatinate had featured on the opposite side to the Habsburgs in various Imperial disputes. In 1591, Christian of Anhalt had even helped to lead a

Palatine army into France in a bid to empower French Protestants against the Austro-Spanish Habsburg Catholic cause. The end goal of Palatine diplomacy was the usurpation of the Habsburg family from their position atop the Imperial food chain, and to recommend a new candidate as Holy Roman Emperor. It may appear only reasonable to attack such policies as deliberately destructive and counter to the prosperity and stability of the German Empire. Had the Palatinate merely acceded to the idea of Habsburg predominance, then, perhaps, the Thirty Years War would never have occurred.

However, we must consider at the same time the very real struggle which the Habsburgs engaged with from the late 1500s with their own subjects, who were largely Protestant. This history of confrontation, tension and concession is one we have already examined, yet it should be reiterated that in their quest to establish as firm a base as possible for their Imperial ambitions, the Habsburgs trod on and undermined the Protestant populations within their hereditary lands wherever possible. Why should these actions by the Habsburgs, which went so evidently against the grain of the wishes of their own subjects – whom the Habsburgs were tasked with protecting – be considered any more legitimate or acceptable than those actions undertaken by Palatine diplomacy to remove the Habsburgs from this position, where it seemed clear that they did not fit?

To this we must add that the Palatinate were by no means the only power to try and affect a change in the leadership of the Holy Roman Empire – France, too, had demonstrated its eagerness to destroy the power base of the House of Austria for its own ends, and King Henry II even made an effort to put himself forward as a candidate for the looming Imperial election in the 1550s as Charles V neared his end. This French intervention in the Empire effectively vanished of course, once the French Wars of Religion forced French Kings to focus their attentions inward.[111] Furthermore, it is often remarked that the citizens of Austria, Bohemia and Hungary made use of threats posed by the Ottomans to wring religious concessions from their Habsburg overlords, in return for pledges to support them in the war. Before such behaviour is criticised as disloyal, we must consider how much the sincere beliefs of these subjects were worth, and if they were worth sacrificing in the name of maintaining the Habsburg supremacy.

Finally, this very supremacy and control over the office of Holy Roman Emperor had only been achieved because the Habsburgs had supplanted their rivals, the House of Luxembourg, in 1438, following several years of strategic marriage and intrigue. The Habsburg family was only the latest dynasty to cling to the important positions and titles which granted it invaluable power and influence in Europe – its position was not sacred. Previous Habsburg efforts did not distinguish that dynasty as somehow predestined to retain this office; there was no guarantee, particularly with the recent troubles and divisions afflicting the family, that the Habsburgs would cling to the office of Holy Roman Emperor until its extinction in 1806, nor was there any way for Palatine diplomatists to predict that the Habsburgs would remain a staple feature of European relations until 1918.

With the benefit of hindsight, it is possible to highlight the Palatine actions as contributing to the conflagration which would follow. In everything Anhalt and Frederick did though, they maintained that they acted with the interests of German Protestants and the Empire's constitution in mind. Anhalt and Frederick had not worked with the Habsburgs' enemies in Europe to destroy what the Palatinate would never be able to win; such pettiness was not within Frederick's character, especially when so much was on the line.[112] Lest this be interpreted as an apologia for the Elector Palatine, it must be emphasised before we reach the more tumultuous portions of this narrative that Ferdinand acted with similar sincerity, conviction and tenacity.

Much like Frederick, Ferdinand believed that he was acting in the best interests of his dynasty and of his faith. He may have made mistakes in realising his vision, but he was not a villain, determined to burn and destroy without a true purpose. Granted, one could argue that Ferdinand was needlessly ruthless to his enemies following his triumph, but there is no indication that a total victory achieved by Frederick's anti-Habsburg allies would have been less intolerant or controversial. Propaganda pamphlets on both sides would try to paint the enemy invariably as the enemy of German liberties, of the true religion and even as the anti-Christ.[113] It is important that we do not place too much stock in such propaganda; the Thirty Years War was a conflict rife with difficult choices and terrible consequences, rather than genuinely one of God versus the Devil as the rhetoric implied.

If Anhalt could not rally all Protestants to his side in the name of combating the monolithic Habsburg influence, then he would have to work to delay the Imperial succession until such a goal was possible. Yet, Anhalt, much like Klesl, was running out of time, as Matthias was already in failing health by the time Ferdinand was confirmed as King of Bohemia in June 1617. The election of Ferdinand as King of Bohemia also appeared to thwart Anhalt's plans to orchestrate a plan against a smooth Habsburg succession, and the Onate Treaty ensured that Spain would now fight to ensure that Ferdinand succeeded Matthias in all his titles. Consider Anhalt's genuine belief in a Habsburg Catholic conspiracy against German liberties; more than a decade of confessional tension; the crippling of traditional means of redress; the confirmation of Anhalt's fears; the splintering of Protestantism still further and the shattering defeats inflicted upon Palatine diplomacy.

It is in the context of these developments that the Bohemian revolt, erupting on 23 May 1618, must be examined. While it was a disaster for the

Habsburgs, to Anhalt, it represented a fresh opportunity – a second chance – to refocus the energies of the anti-Habsburg group, by threatening again the succession of Ferdinand to the office of Holy Roman Emperor. It was to prove an opportunity, tragically, that Christian of Anhalt could not resist.

Chapter 7 Notes

[1]Sweden's relationship with the Lutheran creed is examined by Trygve R. Skarsten, 'The Reception of the Augsburg Confession in Scandinavia', *The Sixteenth Century Journal*, Vol. 11, No. 3, 450th Anniversary Augsburg Confession (Jun. 25, 1980), pp. 86-98.

[2]These events are summarised by Geoffrey Parker in *Europe in Crisis*, pp. 94-98.

[3]Cited in Albert Frederick Pollard, *The Jesuits in Poland* (London, 1892), p. 31.

[4]Robert I. Frost, *The Northern Wars: War, State and Society in North-Eastern Europe, 1558 – 1721* (London; Routledge, 2014), pp. 44-45.

[5]Geoffrey Parker, *Europe in Crisis*, pp. 98-99.

[6]Waldemar Westergaard, 'The Hansa Towns and Scandinavia on the Eve of Swedish Independence', *The Journal of Modern History*, Vol. 4, No. 3 (Sep., 1932), pp. 349-360.

[7]Trygve R. Skarsten, 'The Reception of the Augsburg Confession in Scandinavia', p. 87.

[8]David Kirby, *Northern Europe in the Early Modern Period: The Baltic World 1492-1772* (London; Routledge, 2014), see Chapter 4.

[9]Robert I. Frost, *The Northern Wars*, p. 45.

[10]Carol Stevens, *Russia's Wars of Emergence 1460-1730* (London; Routledge, 2013), pp. 111-112.

[11]For a time, Muscovy and the Commonwealth were allied against Sweden, and in the first few years of the seventeenth century, Tsar Dimitri sent a letter to King Charles IX of Sweden in Sigismund's name, demanding that the Vasa usurper hand the Swedish Crown back to his nephew. Charles ignored the letter, but shortly after this diplomatic highpoint, Sigismund managed to alienate his Russian ally, and supported the rivals to Tsar Dimitri as a means of destabilising the Russian state. See Chester Dunning and Dmitrii Caesar, 'Tsar Dmitrii's Bellicose Letter to King Karl IX of Sweden', *The Slavonic and East European Review*, Vol. 87, No. 2 (April 2009), pp. 322-336.

[12]See Peter B. Brown, 'Muscovy, Poland, And The Seventeenth Century Crisis', *The Polish Review*, Vol. 27, No. 3/4 (1982), pp. 55-69; pp. 59-61.

[13]G. Edward Orchard, 'The Election of Michael Romanov', *The Slavonic and East European Review*, Vol. 67, No. 3 (Jul., 1989), pp. 378-402.

[14]David Kirby, *Northern Europe*, chapter 4, second page.

[15]Geoffrey Parker, *Europe in Crisis*, p. 104.

[16]We do not have sufficient space to examine the *Reconquista* here, but a good account which explains the campaign through the premise of an early Military Revolution is available in Weston F. Cook, Jr., 'The Cannon Conquest of Nasrid Spain and the End of the Reconquista', *The Journal of Military History*, Vol. 57, No. 1 (Jan., 1993), pp. 43-70.

[17]R. Trevor Davies, *The Golden Century of Spain*, pp. 164-166.

[18]See Ruth Pike, 'An Urban Minority: The Moriscos of Seville', *International Journal of Middle East Studies*, Vol. 2, No. 4 (Oct., 1971), pp. 368-377.

[19]See Carla Rahn Phillips, 'The Moriscos of La Mancha, 1570-1614', *The Journal of Modern History*, Vol. 50, No. 2, On Demand Supplement (Jun.,1978), pp. D1067-D1095.

[20]Mark D. Meyerson, *The Muslims of Valencia in the Age of Fernando and Isabel: Between Coexistence and Crusade* (Berkeley; University of California Press, 1991), p. 7.

[21]Davies, *Golden Century of Spain*, p. 13.

[22]For a study which measures the zeal of the converted in both cases see Renée Levine Melammed, 'Judeo-conversas and Moriscos in sixteenth-century Spain: a study of parallels', *Jewish History*, Vol. 24, No. 2 (2010), pp. 155-168.

[23]Davies, *Golden Century of Spain*, p. 11.

[24]. H. Elliott, *Imperial Spain 1469-1716* (New York, 1966), pp. 228-237.

[25]Andrew C. Hess, 'The Moriscos: An Ottoman Fifth Column in Sixteenth-Century Spain', *The American Historical Review*, Vol. 74, No. 1 (Oct., 1968), pp. 1-25.

[26]Davies, *Golden Century of Spain*, p. 166.

[27]Geoffrey Parker, 'Spain, Her Enemies and the Revolt of the Netherlands 1559-1648', *Past & Present*, No. 49 (Nov., 1970), pp. 72-95; pp. 76-77.

[28]Ellen G. Friedman, 'North African Piracy on the Coasts of Spain in the Seventeenth Century: A New Perspective on the Expulsion of the Moriscos', *The International History Review*, Vol. 1, No. 1 (Jan., 1979), pp. 1-16.

[29]Davies, *Golden Century of Spain*, p. 243.

[30]*Ibid*, pp. 244-245.

[31]Ellen G. Friedman, 'North African Piracy on the Coasts of Spain in the Seventeenth Century: A New Perspective on the Expulsion of the Moriscos', p. 2.

[32]*Ibid*, pp. 1-2.

[33]Davies, *Golden Century of Spain*, p. 247.

[34]Andrew C. Hess, 'The Moriscos: An Ottoman Fifth Column in Sixteenth-Century Spain', pp. 5-6.

[35]John Lynch, *Spain under the Hapsburgs: Empire and Absolutism 1516-1598* (New York, 1964), vol. 1, pp. 209-210.

[36]Davies, *Golden Century of Spain*, p. 248.

[37]*Ibid*, p. 249.

[38]See Geoffrey Parker, 'Spain, Her Enemies and the Revolt of the Netherlands 1559-1648', pp. 85-86.

[39]See Gerard Wiegers, 'Managing Disaster: Networks Of The Moriscos During The Process Of The Expulsion From The Iberian Peninsula Around 1609', *Journal of Medieval Religious Cultures*, Vol. 36, No. 2 (2010), pp. 141-168; p. 143.

[40]James Casey also wrote that 'After 1609 the Moriscos were replaced, if at all, by draining manpower from the Christian towns, which fell in strength as a result.' See James Casey, 'Moriscos and the Depopulation of Valencia', *Past & Present*, No. 50 (Feb., 1971), pp. 19-40.

[41]Ellen G. Friedman, 'North African Piracy on the Coasts of Spain in the Seventeenth Century: A New Perspective on the Expulsion of the Moriscos', pp. 2-3.

42*Ibid*, pp. 4-5.

[43]Four families in Valladolid and their experience during the expulsion is worth recounting, see James B. Tueller, 'The Assimilating Morisco: Four Families in Valladolid prior to the Expulsion of 1610', *Mediterranean Studies*, Vol. 7 (1998), pp. 167-177.

44Davies, *Golden Century of Spain*, pp. 250-252.

[45]John Spurr, *English Puritanism, 1603–1689* (London; Palgrave Macmillan, 1998), pp. 117-118.

[46]Not even the Dutch Republic could be convinced to grant toleration to its Catholics, out of suspicion that they would represent a fifth column of sorts in Dutch society, and would agitate for a return to Spanish rule. Appreciating the Dutch intractability on this question, Spanish peace-makers determined to abandon it during the negotiation of the Twelve Years Truce. See Peter Brightwell, 'The Spanish System and the Twelve Years' Truce', *The English Historical Review*, Vol. 89, No. 351 (Apr., 1974), pp. 270-292; pp. 278-280.

[47]Davies, *Golden Century of Spain*, pp. 254-256.

[48]Charles Howard Carter, *Secret Diplomacy of the Habsburgs*, p. 91.

[49]See Roland Dennis Hussey, 'America in European Diplomacy, 1597-1604', *Revista de Historia de América*, No. 41 (Jun., 1956), pp. 1-30; pp. 26-30.

[50]The main source for this information is the excellent article by Magdalena S. Sanchez, 'A House Divided: Spain, Austria, and the Bohemian and Hungarian Successions', *The Sixteenth Century Journal*, Vol. 25, No. 4 (Winter, 1994), pp. 887-903.

[51]See C. V. Wedgewood, *Thirty Years War*, pp. 58-59. Wedgewood wrote that Spinola had been in agreement with the terms of the Treaty long before it was signed in March 1617, but in fact, Spinola was only one opinion of consequence during the proceedings, and other actual ambassadors, not to mention the King of Spain himself, held far more weight.

[52]Magdalena S. Sanchez, 'A House Divided', pp. 888-889.

[53]Cited in *Ibid*, p. 890.

[54]Philip III's mother Anna was the sole daughter of Emperor Maximillian, and the Emperors Rudolf and Matthias had been his maternal uncles.

[55]Bohdan Chudoba, *Spain and the Empire* (Chicago; Chicago University Press, 1952), pp. 195-199.

[56]Magdalena S. Sanchez, 'A House Divided', pp. 890-892.

[57]*Ibid*, p. 893.

[58]Pieter Geyl, *History of the Dutch-Speaking Peoples*, pp. 372-375.

[59]On Spanish military manoeuvres in the Palatinate, see Geoffrey Parker, *Thirty Years War*, pp. 58-59.

[60]Magdalena S. Sanchez, 'A House Divided', pp. 894-898.

[61]Cited in *Ibid*, p. 898.

[62]*Ibid*, pp. 899-901.

[63]Geoffrey Parker, *Thirty Years War*, p. 35.

[64]Thomas F. Arnold, 'Gonzaga Fortifications and the Mantuan Succession Crisis of 1613-1631', *Mediterranean Studies*, Vol. 4 (1994), pp. 113-130.

[65]The Mantuan War of Succession would be reignited in the late 1620s, and would effectively pave the way to French entry into the Thirty Years War. See R. A. Stradling, 'Prelude to Disaster; the Precipitation of the

War of the Mantuan Succession, 1627-29', *The Historical Journal*, Vol. 33, No. 4 (Dec., 1990), pp. 769-785; David Parrott, 'The Mantuan Succession, 1627-31: A Sovereignty Dispute in Early Modern Europe', *The English Historical Review*, Vol. 112, No. 445 (Feb., 1997), pp. 20-65. See also Chapter Four (above).

[66] See Geoffrey Parker, *Thirty Years War*, pp. 36-37.

[67] Cited in Geoffrey Parker, *Europe in Crisis*, p. 156. See also J. H. Elliot, 'A Question of Reputation? Spanish Foreign Policy in the Seventeenth Century', *The Journal of Modern History*, Vol. 55, No. 3 (Sep., 1983), pp. 475-483.

[68] Magdalena S. Sanchez, 'A House Divided', p. 903.

[69] All cited from Peter H. Wilson, *Sourcebook*, pp. 30-32.

[70] See James R. Palmitessa, 'The Prague Uprising of 1611: Property, Politics, and Catholic Renewal in the Early Years of Habsburg Rule', *Central European History*, Vol. 31, No. 4 (1998), pp. 299-328.

[71] See Peter H. Wilson, 'Dynasty, Constitution, and Confession: The Role of Religion in the Thirty Years War', pp. 485-486.

[72] Wedgewood, *Thirty Years War*, p. 73.

[73] N. M. Sutherland, 'The Origins of the Thirty Years War and the Structure of European Politics', p. 588.

[74] Wilson, 'Dynasty, Constitution, and Confession' p. 485.

[75] Peter H. Wilson, *Europe's Tragedy*, p. 260.

[76] J. V. Polišenský wrote that 'in 1617 the combined strength of the Spanish and the Austrian branches of the Habsburg family forced the Estates to accept Ferdinand II as their future king.' See J. V. Polišenský, 'The Thirty Years' War', *Past & Present*, No. 6 (Nov., 1954), pp. 31-43; p. 40.

[77] Wedgewood, *Thirty Years War*, pp. 76-77.

[78] Peter H. Wilson, *Europe's Tragedy*, pp. 66-67.

[79] *Ibid*, pp. 109-112.

[80] *Ibid*, pp. 249-250.

[81] *Ibid*, pp. 242-243.

[82] *Ibid*, p. 250.

[83] See Peter H. Wilson, 'Dynasty, Constitution, and Confession', p. 494.

[84] Peter H. Wilson, *Europe's Tragedy*, pp. 245-246.

[85] Wedgewood, *Thirty Years War*, pp. 62-65. Wedgewood summarises her account of John George's character by concluding acidly on p. 65 that 'It is one of the great tragedies of German history that John George was not a great man.'

[86] See Geoffrey Parker, *Thirty Years War*, p. 37.

[87] Peter H. Wilson, *Europe's Tragedy*, p. 269.

[88] *Ibid*, p. 112.

[89] *Ibid*, p. 113.

[90] J. V. Polišenský, 'The Thirty Years' War', p. 40.

[91] See Peter H. Wilson, 'Dynasty, Constitution, and Confession', p. 485.

[92] Wedgewood, *Thirty Years War*, p. 74.

[93] Geoffrey Parker, *Europe in Crisis*, pp. 158-159.

[94] Parker, *Europe in Crisis*, p. 13; Parker, *Thirty Years War*, p. 42-43; Wilson, *Europe's Tragedy*, p. 271-272;

[95] Peter H. Wilson, *Europe's Tragedy*, pp. 215-216.

[96] Wedgewood, *Thirty Years War*, pp. 56-57.

[97] *Ibid*, p. 57.

[98] Parker wrote that 'to the Palatine leaders, a major religious war seemed inevitable...' see *Thirty Years War*, p. 23.

[99] See Wilson, 'Dynasty, Constitution, and Confession: The Role of Religion in the Thirty Years War', p. 487.

[100] Wilson, *Europe's Tragedy*, p. 218 makes this important point. See also: Ralf-Peter Fuchs, 'The Supreme Court of the Holy Roman Empire: The State of Research and the Outlook', *The Sixteenth Century Journal*, Vol. 34, No. 1 (Spring, 2003), pp. 9-27; pp. 17-26.

[101] Peter H. Wilson, *Europe's Tragedy*, pp. 242-243 notes this often-underrated effect of several years of familial infighting between the two branches of the dynasty, as well as the Brothers' Quarrel itself.

[102] *Ibid*, pp. 239-240.

[103] *Ibid*, pp. 251-252.

[104] *Ibid*, pp. 261-264.

[105] Peter H. Wilson, 'Dynasty, Constitution and Confession', p. 499.

[106] Geoffrey Parker, *Europe in Crisis*, pp. 51-53.

[107] Peter H. Wilson, *Europe's Tragedy*, pp. 264-265.

[108]In 1620, John George agreed to help Emperor Ferdinand in return for the Emperor's pledge to give Lusatia, one of the Kingdom of Bohemia's provinces, over to Saxony. See Geoffrey Parker, *Thirty Years War*, p. 54.

[109]See Wedgewood, *Thirty Years War*, pp. 83-86.

[110]See Brennan Pursell, *The Winter King*, pp. 20-22. Pursell concluded that neither his wife, his court preacher nor Anhalt maintained an overbearing, dominant influence on the Elector, and that Frederick was more than capable of thinking for himself. This conclusion makes sense considering Frederick's active role in administering his Electorate from an early age.

[111]N. M. Sutherland, 'The Origins of the Thirty Years War and the Structure of European Politics', pp. 591-592.

[112]Brennan Pursell, *The Winter King*, p. 18.

[113]John Theibault, 'Jeremiah in the Village: Prophecy, Preaching, Pamphlets, and Penance in thThirtyYears' War', *Central European History*, Vol. 27, No. 4 (1994), pp. 441-460; p. 448.

(Top left) Emperor Ferdinand III (Jan van den Hoeche)
(Top right) Philip III of Spain

(Top left) Leopold V, Archduke of Austria (Joseph Heintz)
(Top right) Johan van Oldenbarnevelt (Michiel Jansz von Mierevelt)

PART THREE

Years of Waste and Ruin
-1618-1625-

"Whether we win or lose, our fate will be heavy. Those that have helped Frederick will stand in a long queue hungry for land and money at our expense, if we win. The anger of the much-maligned Emperor will be upon us if we are defeated. What else can we expect! We have taken from the Emperor that which belongs to him, and to God, and offered it to the Turks."[1]

A Lutheran Bohemian nobleman is overheard in Prague, 1619.

"Spain, the Hercules of European states, whose labours had astonished the sixteenth-century world, weakened and collapsed in the seventeenth century with a suddenness that calls for a careful diagnosis of the disease."[2]

Opening sentence of R Trevor Davies' book Spain in Decline.

"So from this we must notice along with you the special providence and predestination of God, who gives and confers down from above the kings, princes and lords, into the hearts of those, who have to elect them."[3]

Frederick V, Elector Palatine, informs the Bohemian Estates that he will accept the Bohemian Crown: September, 1619.

CHAPTER EIGHT
"The Frightful Beginnings"

ONE
Bohemia in Revolt

With the deed done, and their masters defenestrated, it remained to be seen what the Bohemians would do next. For the third time in a decade, Bohemia's populace had risen against the Habsburgs, and it was entirely possible that, just like the previous two occasions, Habsburg platitudes and concessions would be sufficient to bring Bohemia down from the ledge. On the other hand, there was a great deal of fear and anger swirling around in the Kingdom, and a radical portion of the country were already plotting to evict the Habsburgs altogether. Indeed, it must be pointed out that different shades of opinion existed within the country, with varying degrees of radicalisation accompanying this divide.

Depending on whom one asked, the revolt was launched against the pervasive influence of the Jesuits, of the dogmatic interfering of the Catholic regents, of the Habsburg family's worst elements, epitomised by Ferdinand, or all three. Some radicals refused to recognise Ferdinand as king of Bohemia at all and sought to bypass his authority and petition Emperor Matthias directly. If the Bohemians were confused, then it is understandable that foreign opinion was entirely unsure what to think; was this merely another instance of the Habsburgs losing control of their hereditary lands, or was it something more sinister and unsettling? The revolt's energy and fury would have to be harnessed and the cause explained before the enterprise ran out of steam, and with this in mind, the rebels gathered the three estates of the kingdom – the nobility, the knights and the peasantry – and appointed twelve directors from each segment of Bohemian society.

This group of thirty-six men would serve as Bohemia's provisional government, and one of its most significant acts for historians was the decision to write down the reasons for the revolt in a bid to gain foreign support. The resulting document, the *Apologia*, was surely a litmus test of the Empire's susceptibility to the Bohemian message, but it was also aimed at foreign capitals; Paris, London, The Hague and Italian notables like Venice and Savoy, who had supported the Bohemians in the past. The *Apologia* justified Bohemians' grievances, placed them in context, appeased those that feared all sectarian conflicts would be let loose, and urged the recipients of the letter to aid the Bohemian people in the fight against oppression and injustice. What the rebels appeared to want at this early point in the revolt was not necessarily the removal of the Habsburg dynasty from Bohemia, but a proper apology from Emperor Matthias, in addition to several guarantees. As the *Apologia* put it:

> For a number of years all three estates and inhabitants of the kingdom have faced, suffered and endured all kinds of complaints and hardship, both in political as well as in ecclesiastical matters. These were caused and instigated by evil, turbulent clergy and laity, most notably those of the Jesuit sect whose aim, writings and endeavours have always been directed at fraudulently subjugating not only His Majesty, but also all Protestant inhabitants and estates of the entire kingdom to the Roman See, a foreign power.

Note the main focus of the rebels' vitriol here – the Emperor remained blameless and was as vulnerable as the Bohemians had been to the Jesuit schemes. Much like they had blamed the Catholic regents for the repressive religious policies before 1618, here the Bohemians blame the Jesuits for the actions authorised by the Emperor and undertaken with some enthusiasm by the new Bohemian King. Indeed, the *Apologia* continued to note that the 'enemies of the king, land and general peace have not desisted from striving to negate the peace that was so desired and confirmed, and to further their evil, extremely dangerous and pernicious intentions towards this kingdom and our successors.'

The *Apologia* continued, explaining the shocking defenestration that had occurred two days before this document had been written, by recalling how the Defensors had been ordered to disband when they had gathered earlier in the year to discuss the worsening religious climate. It was bad enough that the genuine grievances of the Defensors should have been ignored, but that they should also be ordered to disband, and be forbidden from ever gathering in such an assembly again – these were rulings which were directly contrary to the Letter of Majesty. Again though, it was written that 'instead of granting our humble petition', the Defensors were 'condemned without any hearing by His Imperial Majesty at the instigation of his enemies...'[4]

Yet again, the Defensors were unwilling to point the finger either at Ferdinand, their new king, or at Matthias, the Holy Roman Emperor. They sought to heap blame onto the people who acted in the Habsburgs' name instead, in the forlorn hope that Matthias would step in and order the Bohemians grievances addressed. It had been Matthias after all that had marched to the rescue of the Bohemians in 1612, and he had sworn to uphold the Letter of Majesty before being crowned King. The explanation for why Matthias had been outmanoeuvred by his minions in this regard, and had been recently unable to protect the Bohemian people, was, according to the *Apologia*, that certain 'enemies' of the King's administration had acted as…

> …destroyers of justice and the general peace, and also because they disrespected the offices and positions they held, and instead used them evilly to weaken the authority of His Imperial Majesty, our king and lord, and to abolish the general peace of this kingdom of Bohemia.

These dishonest individuals had reduced the powers of the King, and gone into business for themselves to affect a great and terrible change in Bohemia, and this was what the Defensors had moved to destroy when they threw the regents out of the windows of the Hradschin Castle. Yet these Defensors, and the new provisional government they had established under the 36 Directors, did not wish for Matthias or, it seems, King Ferdinand, to mistake their intentions or actions. The *Apologia* continued:

> …at our assembly at Prague castle we have established a defence system for the entire kingdom for the good of His Imperial Majesty and this kingdom, our beloved fatherland, as well as to protect our women and children from all danger. And through this action we do not intend anything against His Imperial Majesty as our most gracious king and lord, nor desire inconvenience for those Catholics who are our dear friends and peaceful people. For it is commonly recognised and known that no other secular or ecclesiastical person will be harmed by this action, or will any unrest result, but instead a good peace will be maintained in the cities of Prague and throughout the kingdom…Accordingly, we dare hope that His Imperial Majesty, our gracious king and lord, will not otherwise interpret our actions, nor give credence to other contrary reports about us…Instead, we are of firm hope that, considering the reasons explained above and the sufficiently described crimes of the aforementioned persons, all will see that it was not our intention, nor it is in the slightest to act against His most gracious Imperial Majesty, king and lord, those of the Roman religion or the agreements made with them, and will not only excuse this, but will like us also assist in preserving the common freedoms, territorial privileges and all that serves mutual love and unity.

The *Apologia* concluded with a plea for Matthias to 'excuse us to the entire world';[5] in other words to explain to Europeans that the Bohemian people did not want to depose their King, but that they wished instead to receive some guarantees of the rights they had previously enjoyed, and to be entitled to defend themselves until these guarantees were given. Yet the rebels had already made two grave mistakes. First, His Imperial Majesty referred to Matthias, the Holy Roman Emperor, whom the rebels appeared to think had their interests at heart. Whether the rebel leadership sincerely believed that

Matthias had been effectively manipulated by his intolerant advisors or not is not as important as the fact that Matthias would certainly have revoked the Letter of Majesty if he had been able. Since the concessions had been made by his brother under duress in 1609, Matthias had been keen to undo them, but he had never had the opportunity.[6]

Matthias was not the stalwart ally of Bohemian Protestants which the rebels seemed to think he was – he was instead a Catholic Habsburg and wished to see the Old Faith return to Bohemia as much as Ferdinand did. Hence why Matthias worked so closely with Melchior Klesl in the past to undermine Protestant influence in Bohemia and improve the situation for the Catholics. Second, and another thing Matthias was not, was the King of Bohemia. Something which can be observed from the Apologia was the total avoidance of addressing their King – 'His Imperial Majesty' referred to the Holy Roman Emperor. The rebels evidently intended to ignore their new king and bypass his authority in favour of his cousin. The avoidance of Ferdinand could be explained by a distrust of his more zealous character, but also by an expectation that Matthias would be more likely to listen.

From Vienna, the bypassing of Ferdinand could just as easily be construed as an act of defiance – a deliberate snub against the King these same Bohemians had only recently elected. It is significant that their grievances were addressed to the Emperor rather than their King, and it is doubly significant that it was Emperor Matthias rather than Ferdinand who replied to their *Apologia*. The ailing Matthias evidently wished to clear up any potential confusion – he stood by Ferdinand and the government in Bohemia which ruled in Ferdinand's name, and he would not approve of the Bohemians actions, nor would he humour them with further negotiations. In his reply, written on 18 June 1618, Matthias said:

> Dear subjects. You know what happened to our regents, secretary and dear loyal subjects on Wednesday 23 May and subsequently in the Bohemian Chancellery in our palace and residence in Prague which should be a place of the highest respect and security. And all this because it has been alleged that the Letter of Majesty and the free exercise of religion will be abolished. We want to make it clear to you through this open letter that we have no intention of rescinding the Letter of Majesty, or the agreement between the religions, still less want anyone else to do this, despite what others among the Estates of our Bohemian kingdom may have said. Moreover, we have always intended, and still intend, to preserve all the Estates' privileges, liberties, Letters of Majesty, diet recesses and treaties. Anyone who claims otherwise slanders us before God and the world. Rest assured, dear obedient, loyal and true estates of our Bohemian kingdom, and do not given credence to such falsehoods.

On the surface, this extract reads like a Habsburg attempt to talk the Bohemians down from the ledge. It would have been an easy enough narrative to construct – the radical Bohemians, once again in revolt due to their paranoia and anxiety, rose in revolt for the third time in less than ten years, against a benign regime, only to cause the very calamity which they claimed to fear. By rising up, by hiring soldiers, by arming themselves, they forced the Habsburgs to take action, and thereafter to supress their revolt with brute force, lest the region sank into banditry and desolation. Indeed, the example from 1611-1612, when Archduke Leopold had marched with his troops through Bohemia had testified to the damage which a ravenous army could inflict on an unsuspecting populace, as they carted off and seized everything which was not nailed down. Here, it seemed, the troubled Matthias was urging the Bohemians to disperse, and not to fear a non-existent threat, so that the waste and pillage from before could be avoided. Matthias had learned from the past, whereas the Bohemians had not.

However, on the other hand, if one were to weigh the circumstances in this troublesome kingdom with the actual ambitions which the Habsburgs had for Bohemia, it would be possible to note that even while they went about it the wrong way, the Bohemians were onto something. In the first place, the Habsburgs had worked to chip away at the religious freedoms and influence of the majority Protestant population since Matthias took over as King of Bohemia. These processes only accelerated over 1617-18, when censorship, the alienation of land to the clergy, and the actual destruction of Protestant churches took place. Thus angered, the Bohemians had sought redress, did not get it, and flew into revolt. In some respects, the Bohemians were merely following the script which had worked in 1609 and 1612; then, a show of force had preserved the religious and political independence of the Bohemian people; here, in 1618, the Bohemians sought to make lightning strike a third time.

We also know that Matthias and especially Ferdinand *did* wish to revoke the Letter of Majesty, and that Matthias would have done so if he had been able. Ferdinand's conscience was so haunted by granting these concessions to Protestants that he had to be reassured by his confessors, on the understanding that by confirming the Bohemians' religious rights, he was telling them a lie which he would, in good time, expose. Ferdinand was not acting in good faith, and he searched for the right opportunity to transform Bohemia, as he had transformed Styria. Neither Ferdinand nor Matthias were innocent of the charges levelled against them by the more radical Bohemians; the problem was the absence of evidence, at this stage, detailing the extent of the Habsburgs' plans for reimagining Bohemia. Since many could not bring themselves to believe that the Habsburgs would so deliberately infringe upon their rights, the Bohemians remained divided at a critical time, with a significant portion of the country plainly unwilling to go all the way in deposing the Habsburgs.

For the first year of the revolt then, much work would have to be done to liaise between the different segments of Bohemian society, and to co-opt the varied opinions into a workable government. Since the Habsburgs denied the existence of any plot to remove the Letter of Majesty and revoke the Bohemians' religious freedoms, Matthias inserted in his letter several stern warnings for the Bohemians to disperse, lest they invited a Habsburg response. Matthias did note his desire to return to Prague and 'clear up these misunderstandings with God's help', however, due to ill health on his part, the Emperor promised to send 'capable and prominent individuals' in his stead. Matthias elaborated on the Habsburg position with the following extract, which began conciliatory, and ended with a stiff warning of doom to all those that failed to avail of this chance to repent. It read:

> Since no enemy threatens us as Bohemian king, nor the three estates and all inhabitants, there are no constitutional grounds to raise soldiers to defend the country, and thus no grounds for anyone, whoever they might be, to use the territorial privileges, letters of majesty, ordinances, freedoms, or laws to justify arming. Accordingly, we graciously order you to disband the soldiers you have recruited to prevent further damage, expense and ruin of the common man. Furthermore, no more troops are to be recruited and the militia is to stand down. All subjects of either faith are to stop attacking each other by word and deed, and instead to deal with one another peacefully as friends. We do not doubt that the loyal estates will obey these orders. We will stop our recruiting, that was in response to yours, as soon as all the soldiers have been discharged in the kingdom of Bohemia and the militia stood down. We want to spare our loyal subjects the damage and expense that soldiers cause. If our gracious and paternal warnings and our just orders and instructions are ignored and the soldiers and militia are not immediately disbanded in the kingdom of Bohemia, we will be forced to accept that order and justice are being disregarded. We will be left with no choice, but to take the necessary measures to maintain our authority with the help of the Almighty by whose grace we are your rightful king and master. It will be obvious to all that war and unrest bring great inconvenience, hardship and misery to the poor people. We testify before God and the entire world that we have given no grounds for this situation and are entirely innocent. Those who heed our royal order and remain obedient and do not support the unruly (who will not receive another warning) are assured of our royal grace, protection and good will.[7]

By this point in late June, the Bohemians had already recruited four thousand mercenaries, a number which was to triple by the autumn. These mercenaries were an invaluable temporary solution to the intractable problem of a divided populace and unenthused peasantry; problems personified by the uninspiring result of the militia call-up. According to the Letter of Majesty, every tenth peasant and every eighth burghers were eligible for military service, and taxes due for the Habsburgs would be eagerly redirected to pay for just such a force. Disappointingly for the Bohemians' Directory Government, so few men materialised as a result of the call-up that a reliance on mercenaries and, later, foreign armies, was to become accepted policy. The revolt thus could not accused of being one of a nationalistic nature, but during the murky initial summer months of 1618, this did not make it any less threatening to the Habsburgs, nor for that matter, did it make it very different in character to previous Bohemian revolts.[8]

For the Bohemian rebels, their critical problem was the lack of a leader. No unifying voice emerged to lead the Bohemian people, or to overcome the divisions, or to co-opt the different aims of its populace. Peter H. Wilson has remarked that this lack of a leader prevented the Bohemian revolt from transforming into the Central European equivalent of the Dutch revolt, since no William of Orange was at hand in Prague, as there had been at The Hague.[9] Indeed, as we have seen, the rebels could not decide themselves whether the Habsburg dynasty should be removed, or whether the revolt should serve merely as a message to the Emperor to improve their lot and reinforce their guarantees. These divisions among the Bohemian people were extended to those few Bohemian Protestant noblemen, radicals and moderates, who could not decide how best to harness the energy and passions of the Defenestration of Prague.

At the same time though, it should be added that notwithstanding their lack of a leader, the Bohemians did manage to hold their country together with a provisional government that could paper over the cracks, but this effort could not last. Count Thurn was arguably the most popular and visible of all the radicals, but he did not make any concerted effort to seize power. Without a centralised authority issuing commands, neither Bohemia, nor the outlying provinces in Moravia, Silesia and Lusatia could mount an effective defence. Ill-omens were present almost as soon as the provisional government had been established, for centres of Catholic resistance existed in those townships and fortresses where pockets of the Old Faith had remained intact. The most important of these was Pilsen, and so long as it held out, it made a lie of the Bohemians' claims to be engaging in a united cause.

Thus, Pilsen was designated as one of the militia's first targets, and the toleration which had been proclaimed was notably violated by a decree on 9 June, which demanded that all Jesuits leave the country. On 18 June, as we saw, Matthias issued his response to the Bohemians' *Apologia*, and the stand-off was guaranteed. The Habsburgs could not afford to look weak and bow to the demands of the rebels – for a third time, no less – and the Bohemians could not bring themselves to trust this dynasty which they believed worked in secret to undermine their liberties. If the Bohemians were to keep their revolt alive, they would have to impress upon the Habsburgs the seriousness of their intentions and the danger they could pose to their enemies. For this to happen, the Bohemian estates would have to band together, and the 36 Directors would have to put aside their differences. If these two requirements were lacking, then the rebels could also count on a further invaluable resource – the promise of foreign aid, based on the same branching set of international contacts which had been established in the preceding decade.[10]

The first source of support could be found very close to home indeed. While the Crown was Bohemian, this crown and the kingdom which accompanied it actually incorporated the aforementioned provinces of Silesia, Moravia and Lusatia in a form of confederation. All four provinces hosted their own estates and maintained a dogged determination for freedom of action in local affairs. If the rebels were to be successful in whatever aims they agreed upon, then the neighbouring provinces would have to be brought on side. Otherwise, the Kingdom of Bohemia would fragment, and through these fragmented borders Habsburg soldiers would invade. One can imagine the paralysing sense of dismay which accompanied the news in mid-June that the Moravians were recruiting a force of three thousand men to maintain their neutrality, reduce banditry and grant passage to any Habsburgs who approached. Since Moravia resided along the southern border of Bohemia, the permeability of the kingdom was now plain for all to see.

For all its problems, the rebels did not despair in this grave hour. Instead, they moved to strike with the limited forces at their disposal. Count Thurn was tasked with commanding the bulk of the forces, while he sent subordinates to accomplish other limited tasks like reducing the remaining Catholic towns. Despite the reluctance of the entirety of the kingdom to become involved, these provinces also neglected to send forces against the Bohemian rebels, who achieved their first true success in late November, when Pilsen was taken. The siege and storming of that town was accompanied by a sight which was to become all-too familiar in the months to come. Ernst von Mansfeld – a mercenary commander known for his ability to raise an army and make the most effective use of his paymaster's funds – had arrived at Pilsen with a couple of thousand Swiss mercenaries. These men were veterans of the previous Italian campaigns and had travelled with the blessing of the Duke of Savoy, a known rival of the Habsburgs. After fewer than six months then, the Bohemian revolt had been inflamed and exacerbated by foreign intervention, and not for the last time.

After much petitioning, and no small amount of intimidation, the rebels gained Silesian support and three thousand soldiers which were added to the bank of manpower. This influx of new recruits combined with the success at Pilsen and the arrival of Mansfeld moved Thurn to approve of a daring new tactic – divide and conquer. Thurn would march to Moravia, to compel the estates there to join the Bohemian cause, while Heinrich Schlick, a prominent Protestant Bohemian but an ineffective leader of men, was tasked with marching on Vienna.[11] This was demonstrated by the lack of preparations and discipline which hounded Schlick's march to Vienna – he would never make it, instead being so reduced and depleted by the weather that he was forced to retreat before the weather became insufferable. Vienna had been saved from the revolt, at least for the moment, and the approaching winter seemed to promise a respite. If the Habsburgs wished to be taken seriously though, they would have to engineer some kind of response in the new year, lest Europe would watch as their hereditary lands abandoned them one by one.

On 20 March 1619, Emperor Matthias died. This death signalled that a turning point of sorts had been arrived at. For nigh on a year, the Bohemians had insisted that their revolt was not against the Habsburgs per se, but against their malicious agents, and perhaps against their king. Matthias death meant that Ferdinand would succeed him as Emperor, and once that happened, the Bohemians would be unable to hide from the severity of their mission – for the Bohemian rebels, it would be a turning point because there would be no turning back. That is not to say that Ferdinand did not offer terms – indeed, just before Matthias' death, the two camps had been preparing to assemble under Saxon mediation for talks. However, the mood was soured by decision by some in the rebel camp to view Archduke Albert – then in the Spanish Netherlands – as the rightful heir, and not Matthias.

By mid-April 1619, all pretences to the contrary had thus been forcibly abandoned – the rebels were in open revolt, and whether the majority liked it or not, this rebellion was aimed at nothing less than the total destruction of Habsburg rule in Bohemia. Moravia was dealt with by a determined invasion on 18 April, with a great portion of the Moravian army defecting to the rebels, and the leading moderates that counselled peace ejected. Any remaining undecided elements in Bohemia, Thurn hoped, would be persuaded by another invasion launched against Vienna. If the Austrian Habsburg capital fell, then the dynasty's hold on the people's hearts and minds would surely topple with it. It was a daring plan, which came stunningly close to success.

By late May 1619 Thurn's forces had reached the outskirts of the Imperial capital, and it was correctly believed that Ferdinand had no soldiers on hand to relieve whatever siege the rebels engaged in. With success near at hand, some Protestants on the Viennese town council had conspired with the rebels to divide the spoils, a decision made easier by the news a few weeks' beforehand that Upper Austria's estates had elected to join with the Bohemians in revolt. With the Kingdom of Bohemia as united as it ever would be against the Habsburgs, with Ferdinand shut in and alone in his palace, and with confirmed reports of Transylvania, a Hungarian vassal of the Ottoman Empire, also in revolt, the prospects for the Habsburg regime in Bohemia appeared grim indeed.

TWO

On the Brink

I have weighed the dangers that approach from all sides and since I know of
no further human aid, I asked the Lord for his help. But if it should be the will
of God that I go under in this struggle, so be it.[12]

These were reported to be the words which Ferdinand spoke to his
Jesuit confessor, as the net appeared to close around him, and the forces of
rebellion threatened to extinguish the vitality of his dynasty. To a great many
in Europe, it indeed seemed likely that Ferdinand would 'go under', or that,
at the very least, the Habsburgs should consider the fierce opposition which
this man provoked, and look to another candidate to replace him: 'Was there',
as one historian reasoned, 'from the dynastic point of view, any object in re-
establishing a man whose weakness would be a menace to their prestige and
whose chances of the imperial crown were dwindling?'[13]

Ferdinand would surprise them all, for as he lay prostrate in an exercise
of apparent desperation and futility, help was already at hand. The Protestant
Bohemians, led by Thurn, had marched a long way to meet face to face with
their king, and their journey had been aided by the cooperation of friends in
the Protestant Austrian nobility. This fact would have stung Ferdinand, who
had always equated religion with loyalty, but it would also have significantly
clarified the wider picture. Were he able to survive the confrontation with
the rough, burly confederates who had come so far powered on such raw
emotion, then he could sponsor a justified reaction which would rid his lands
of heresy once and for all, and grant those loyal subjects the rewards they
deserved. First, of course, Ferdinand would have to survive the ordeal.

The date was 5 June 1619, the atmosphere was hot and heavy, and the
mood of the city's populace was tense. Bursting through the doors of the
Hofburg Palace, Thurn and his accomplices marched up the stairs to where
Ferdinand was known to reside. There, in an incredible scene, the arch-rebel
came face to face with the Archduke. The windows were open, as it was

the height of a Viennese summer, and Thurn may well have gestured to the possibility that another Defenestration, more terrible and incendiary than the last, would follow if Ferdinand did not comply with the rebels' demands. One of Thurn's associates produced a list of demands and, according to one account, even grabbed Ferdinand by the collar, forced him into his seat, and barked a demand at him to sign it. Had matters progressed in this fashion, it is hard to imagine Ferdinand resisting for long.

His enemies held all the cards, they had battered their way from the walls of Prague's Hradschin castle all the way to his rooms, and now they were here, with him, and all of his privileges, all of his majesty as the heir to the Habsburg dynasty, had been stripped away. It appeared as though the rebels were in search of another capitulation from the dynasty which claimed to rule over them, which would likely contain even more severe concessions than the Letter of Majesty a decade before. If Ferdinand was conscious of the symbolism, it is not known whether Bohemian lightning would have struck twice. For all of the advantages they held, the rebels had not been able to shut off the city completely from reinforcements.

It is said that just as the rebels effectively held their king to ransom, a clattering of hooves was heard, as four hundred cavalry burst into the courtyard of the Hofburg, and sent a clear message to the rebels in the room above – the Habsburgs were not finished yet. Rushing to the window, the most surprised inhabitant of the room may well have been Ferdinand himself – where had this detachment of Imperial cavalry come from? In fact, they had been sent by Ferdinand's brother, the adventurous Leopold of Tyrol. Leopold's adventures in the Julich-Cleve crisis and in the Bohemian revolt of 1611-1612 had cost the dynasty dearly, but here Ferdinand's brother appeared to atone for his mistakes.

The timeliness of the cavalry's arrival cannot be understated – their appearance alone and the trumpets and banners which accompanied them sent a stern reminder to Thurn and his accomplices of what they were in the process of doing. If they proceeded, it was quite unlikely they would emerge from Vienna with their heads. At the appearance of this disciplined cavalry unit, much of the rebels and the rabble around them had melted away to a stronger position, and Thurn elected to follow them. We can imagine that, leaving the room, he uttered some snide remarks or a disrespectful diatribe, but what is certain is that Thurn left Ferdinand's presence never to threaten him so directly ever again. The high point of the rebellion, it seemed, peaked just as the hooves were heard.[14]

Ferdinand's capitulation or even his death or humiliation on 5 June 1619 would have created a very different path for Central Europe and would almost certainly have terminated the Habsburg hold over its Bohemian, Hungarian and Austrian appendages. The counter-reformation could well have stalled, with Catholicism becoming a 'minority cult practised north of the Alps only by a few scattered and demoralised communities.'[15] Ferdinand had been saved, not, arguably, by his own power but by his family – this was to signal a trend which continued uninterrupted for the near entirety of the Thirty Years War. The Austrian Habsburgs inhabited a region and laid claim to titles which were too important to abandon, but which they were not strong enough to maintain themselves. Thus, Ferdinand would be saved, and the Austrian Habsburgs would be saved, by the power most willing to pick up the considerable tab: Spain.

Ferdinand had been in Hungary, more specifically in Pressburg, the capital of Habsburg Hungary. His mission was to secure the Hungarian throne, after being crowned King of Bohemia and designated as the Imperial successor by his Spanish cousins, as per the Onate Treaty.[16] Although his end goal was the Imperial crown, before he had reached his destination Ferdinand had worked to affect a change in how the Habsburg dynasty conducted its affairs, starting with the leading administrator of that family, Melchior Klesl. A falsehood parroted by several of his enemies put it that Klesl was the one standing in the way of defeating the rebels – in reality, of course, the Austrian Habsburgs' own penury was to blame, but Ferdinand did not see matters that way. Klesl would have to go, and in such a way that the wily statesman would not see the end coming.

Melchior Klesl, in spite of the work he had done to improve the tensions between Protestants and Catholics within the Empire, had made few friends. In a sense this is perhaps unsurprising – to Catholics, Klesl appeared weak in the face of religious opposition, while to Protestants, the Lutheran turned Catholic was a turncoat and loyal sycophant of the Habsburgs, who never truly had their interests at heart. On 1 July 1618, as Ferdinand and his circle celebrated his success in being named King of Hungary, Klesl was shot at during the banquet, and the bullet narrowly missed his head. It seemed likely that Klesl, in spite of some significant efforts, would not be mourned by either side. Indeed, the papal nuncio had informed Ferdinand that Klesl had become something of a liability – imagine the scandal if the Cardinal was assassinated in his post! Far better it was to dismiss him quietly, a task which Ferdinand embraced, at least to some extent.

Klesl was invited to the Hofburg to meet with Ferdinand, Count Onate and Archduke Maximillian, Ferdinand's cousin on 20 July. As soon as Klesl arrived he was ushered into an antechamber, arrested, and quickly transported to Innsbruck. Imprisoning Klesl did not merely give Ferdinand greater control over policy, it also provided a badly needed injection into the Imperial coffers – Klesl's cash and jewels came to over three hundred thousand florins, and were immediately invested into the empty war chest. Emperor Matthias, arguably the only living individual who had the power to stop his cousin from following through with this act, was too feeble and in any case bedridden, so Klesl enjoyed no protections for his years of service. It was too much for Matthias' wife, who rounded on Ferdinand with the acidic quip 'I see clearly that my husband is living too long for you: is this the thanks he gets for having given you two crowns?'

Ferdinand was clearly content to ignore Matthias altogether if it meant removing the problem which he perceived as holding the family back. Yet, this pursuit of the greater good, for the money it provided the dynasty and the powers it vested back into the Archduke, also enabled them to save face. In June 1619, shortly after Ferdinand had survived the besieging of his capital, Melchior Klesl was put on trial and charged with responsibility for virtually every shortcoming of the Austrian Habsburg family, from the Letter of Majesty to the *uzkok* war. The College of Cardinals ratified the guilty verdict, and the fix was in. Klesl was shipped to Rome and lived under house arrest, until his return several years later, when his old vitality had long since vanished.[17]

The Klesl episode was not just a significant turning point in the dynasty's leadership, it was also a telling indication of how Ferdinand intended to rule, and what counsel he planned on listening to. Melchior Klesl was a firm advocate of the counter-reformation, and he had done much to further the Catholic faith in Austria, but he was also a moderate voice and an enthusiastic supporter of peaceful co-existence between the Christian creeds. Now he was gone, replaced by Ferdinand, and by Ferdinand's Jesuit confessor William Lamormaini, who took up his post in Ferdinand's ear in 1624, which he held until Ferdinand's death in 1637. Peter H. Wilson wrote that Lamormaini 'possessed none of Ferdinand's agreeable qualities and exceeded him in religious fundamentalism, coming close to the Protestant stereotype of the malevolent Jesuit conspirator.'[18] This was hardly a person who would inspire trust in the nervous Protestants, or peaceful co-existence in the Emperor.

The decline in moderate voices did not, unsurprisingly, provide Ferdinand with an influx of fresh opportunities to crush the revolt, as he seemed to have expected. With Klesl gone by the end of July, Ferdinand still had to endure another year of worsening fortunes, culminating with the vivid scene of early June 1619. During the course of that year, Ferdinand did not learn any universal truths which helped him to neutralise the Bohemians, nor did he seem particularly capable of pacifying Austria itself, as the Lower Austrian estates joined with the Bohemians in revolt against the Habsburgs. Fear and opportunism drove the rebels on, and foreign intervention appeared to offer these rebels a chance to avenge the creeping counter-reformation and Ferdinand's broken promises. With Matthias dead and Klesl in prison, open revolt was the only resource that these desperate individuals had.

Even as allies of the rebels involved themselves in the Habsburg business, Ferdinand was able to take solace from the fact that the Habsburg family had not abandoned him after all. Contrary to the initially terrifying picture, Ferdinand was not thrown under the bus, largely because of a change in statesmen in Spain, which also affected a change in policy at just the right time. The Duke of Lerma, having held the ear of King Philip III of Spain since his accession two decades before, was finally in the decline. This regime change came courtesy of Baltasar de Zuniga, who returned from Vienna, his duties fulfilled with the conclusion of the Onate Treaty, to find a Spanish political atmosphere ripe for exploitation. Lerma was a close friend of King Philip, but not of all the King's men, and his corruption, arrogance, wastefulness and rumoured debauchery had made him many enemies while he clung tenaciously to power.

When one of Lerma's close allies was arrested for murder in October 1618, this appeared to be the signal to move on the old Duke's position and possessions. The Duke's personal fortune of 44 million thalers should have been enough to convict him alone, and the very public secrets of his sins likely convinced Lerma that to contest his downfall would mean death or exile. Thus, Lerma accepted peaceful withdrawal into the life of a cardinal rather than face the wrath of his enemies, and before the end of autumn 1618, Spanish policy had been transformed.[19] The new regime, led by Zuniga, upheld the importance of maintaining Ferdinand's Austrian dynasty no matter the cost – to lose Ferdinand would be to lose too much even to fathom. Unlike Lerma's late regime, which had counselled abandoning Ferdinand to some degree in favour of dealing once and for all with the pirate menace emanating out of Algiers, Zuniga appreciated the importance of coming to Ferdinand's aid.

Over the second half of 1618, Spain sent considerable sums of money to Vienna. With Lerma's influence on the decline, he was effectively powerless to prevent the dispatch of 200,000 thalers in July, or of 500,000 thalers in September. Lerma's opposition was based off the fear that by injecting the Austrian Habsburg family with funds, Ferdinand would be encouraged to fight to the end, and that this would prolong the Bohemian revolt. Philip III stepped in when in January 1619, it was determined that money alone would not be sufficient to save the Austrian branch; in addition, the Algerian expedition would have to be postponed. As Philip put it – 'because it would be impossible to commit ourselves to both enterprises, and because of the risks involved…if the aid to Bohemia is delayed, it seems unavoidable that we must see to the latter.'

But what did 'seeing to Bohemia' actually mean? Within a few months, it became apparent that it meant Spain would contribute more than just money – if the injection of funds was not enough to shore up Ferdinand's regime, then Spanish professionals would also be sent. In May 1619 indeed, seven thousand of these professionals marched from the Spanish Netherlands, down the Spanish Road along the Rhine, through to Northern Italy and then into Austria. The money was also dramatically increased: by July 1619, shortly after Ferdinand had survived the rebels' ploy for Vienna, Madrid had already sent the Austrian Habsburgs 3.4 million thalers, a sum which was to nearly double to six million by 1624. Evidently, the Spanish, just like the rebels, were going for broke, and neither side felt they could afford to lose.[20]

In early September 1619, further bad news was to come for Ferdinand, as the Prince of Transylvania Bethlen Gabor began his invasion of Habsburg Hungary. Bethlen Gabor was technically a vassal of the Ottoman Empire, and as such was meant to conform to his master's policy. With the Ottoman Sultan then in no position to intervene in the Holy Roman Empire, the Habsburgs may have expected his vassals also to remain quiescent, but the opportunities in Hungary proved too tempting for Gabor to resist. Bethlen Gabor remembered the revolt over 1604-06, when the entirety of Hungary seemed to be slipping from Habsburg grasp and into Transylvanian hands. If Gabor could replicate this success, then he would be renowned throughout Hungary as its Calvinist saviour against Catholic Habsburg tyranny.

In addition, in a theme we will explore more in the future: Bethlen Gabor seemed to have hoped that his increased fame and success would recommend him for a more valuable prize – the Bohemian Crown. Gabor was to be disappointed in the latter field, but he achieved stunning successes, nonetheless. The Englishman John Paget, writing in 1839, was able to remark on the significant legacy and legend which Bethlen Gabor left behind, writing thus:

> As a sign of the times, rather than as a characteristic of the man, it may be mentioned that Bethlen composed psalms which are still sung in Reformed churches, and that he read the bible through twenty times. Two of Bethlen's most constant objects were the banishment of the Jesuits from Transylvania, and the securing the rights of the Protestants in Hungary; but to accomplish the first, he did not hesitate to persecute to the death, and the second seems to have been rather a cloak to ambition than the object in which that ambition centred. The part which Bethlen took in the Thirty Years War gave a European importance to Transylvania such as it never before nor since that time has enjoyed...The engagements of Bethlen with the chiefs of the Thirty Years War, the faithlessness of the Jesuit ministers of the Austrian court, and the discontent of the Protestants in Hungary, together with his own ambition, made the life of this prince a constant series of intrigues and wars. That his character should come out quite clear from such a trial is hardly to be expected; indeed, in the intricate mazes of policy, there seems to have been few paths, however tortuous, which he did not tread; yet it is impossible not to admire the greatness of his designs, the fertility of his resources, his diplomatic skill, and the nobles principles of religious liberty for which he professed to struggle.[21]

Bethlen Gabor would need these qualities if he was to successfully remove the Habsburg presence in their Hungarian domains, which they had eagerly rebuilt since the disasters earlier on in the century. For all of his noble intentions and principles though, Gabor was not above pillaging and burning all the way up to Vienna's gates; indeed, upon his defeat of the last Habsburg Hungarian army in October 1619, Bethlen marched on Pressburg, where Ferdinand had been crowned King of Hungary not eighteen months before. With all of the Habsburgs' Hungarian appendages in his hands, Bethlen took the next logical step in his quest for immortality, and marched on Vienna, placing it under siege for the second time in less than half a year. As he had before, Ferdinand awaited the next trial with crucifix in hand – but things were different this time around.

Habsburg military cooperation had worked wonders for the security and reputation of the dynasty, even if rebel armies remained in the field. Thirty thousand men constituted the Habsburg army, with contingents drawn from Germany, Spain, the Spanish Netherlands and North Italy. This force had been critically important the first time Vienna had been placed under siege in early June 1619; once Thurn had been rebuffed by the timely arrival of those cavalry, the rebels' position had further deteriorated on 10 June with the defeat of Ernst von Mansfeld's forces in the battle of Zablati in Southern Bohemia. This was the event which truly forced the rebels from Vienna's walls, but the arrival and maintenance of this large Imperial army signalled that Ferdinand intended to fight, and that he enjoyed the full confidence of his Spanish cousins.

Another consequence of Mansfeld's defeat was not merely the reduction in the Bohemian rebels' steam, but also the loss of his field chancery, which contained his damning correspondence that had been conducted with such powers as Savoy, the Netherlands, the Venetians and the English. Significantly, the defeat of Mansfeld represented the first Catholic victory in a sea of despair and uncertainty, and it moved both confessions to act with some haste. The Catholic forces within the Empire moved to resurrect the defunct Catholic League, which had been retired in spring 1617 after it had outlived its usefulness. Once again, Maximillian of Bavaria was chosen to lead the League, and the organisation was poised to provide essential support to Ferdinand from the Catholic German princes, whereas before he had relied almost solely on Spanish aid.

Considering Ferdinand's very willing acceptance of this support, and the clear indications of the Bohemian revolt spreading its wings to foreign theatres, it should not have come as too much of a surprise to Ferdinand that the old enemies of the Habsburgs – most of whom had made their presence felt during the *uzkok* war only a couple of years before – should again be acting to undermine the dynasty. It was also a sign of things to come; the impressive Habsburg army could not be in several places at once, and while it had invaded Southern Bohemia in the summer the capital city was left exposed. After several weeks of moving along the Danube, Bethlen Gabor sought to complete his legend with a capture of Vienna, and the imprisonment of the arch-Jesuit Ferdinand. Along the way, Bethlen met with Count Thurn, who added his rebels to the mix. For a short time, Vienna seemed doomed once more, and Ferdinand's earlier protestations to the effect that he was willing to die for the cause appeared close to being fulfilled.

Having entered into an alliance with the Bohemian rebels in late August 1619, both parties may have believed that this was their last, or at least their best chance to wrest the capitulations from Ferdinand that they wanted. Yet Ferdinand had one more ace up his sleeve before he resigned himself to such an ignoble fate – his brother in law, the King of Poland, was in a prime position to launch an invasion of Transylvania. Once this occurred, as it did in late November 1619, Bethlen was forced to withdraw to defend his lands, with Count Thurn also forced to retreat. By acting in this manner, the Poles invited the wrath of the Ottoman Sultan, who was the master of Transylvania, and a terrible punitive invasion of Poland would be launched the following year. But none of this mattered to Ferdinand – he had staved off the destruction of his dynasty yet again, and defended the capital against the malevolent forces of the Bohemian revolt.

The siege of Vienna, limited as it was, was significant for another reason. In the second siege, the rebels and Transylvanians were not merely besieging the King of Bohemia and Hungary; they were also endangering the life of the new Holy Roman Emperor. Since 28 August 1619, when the election of Ferdinand of Styria had successfully passed, the Imperial crown rested on the head of Emperor Ferdinand II. It was a momentous occasion, taking place as it did virtually to the day of another election a century before – that of Charles V, the man who had united and ruled over more Habsburg domains than any other figure in history. Other names had been bandied about at the Imperial election in Frankfurt – the Elector of Saxony and the Duke of Bavaria among them – but the safe bet of Ferdinand won the day.

Yet Ferdinand would not be given long to enjoy his triumph. The aforementioned Bohemian defeat at Zablati on 10 June had been a significant Catholic victory, but the defeat had deeply shaken and then forced the hand of the Bohemians. On 31 July 1619, perhaps spurred on following their defeat, the Confederates of the Kingdom of Bohemia signed one hundred articles which declared the intention of the Bohemian, Moravian and Silesian estates to forge a federal union. What was more: these articles linked the Upper and Lower Austrian estates with this union in a defensive alliance, to be directed against Habsburg encroachment. Ferdinand's loss of so much local support evidently did not dampen his prospects for election to the office of Emperor, yet it was what the Bohemian confederates chose to do on 22 August, a week before Ferdinand was crowned Emperor, that truly shook the Habsburg dynasty, and thereafter the entire continent, to its core.

An announcement was sent out to the relevant capitals on 22 August 1619 that Archduke Ferdinand had been deposed; the Austrian Habsburgs, according to the Bohemians, no longer had any hold on the Bohemian Crown. A week later, completely ignorant of these developments, the Empire's potentates determined to elect the deposed Ferdinand as their Emperor. The deposition of Ferdinand would surely have horrified those present at Frankfurt not only because of the message it sent to Europe about Ferdinand's character and candidacy, but also because of what would follow. The Bohemians would not allow their throne to be vacant for long; surely, in good time, they would offer it to someone.[22]

Whoever took the Bohemians up on their offer would acquire a kingdom up in arms against the Habsburgs, in addition to the prestige and vote in the Electoral College which went along with it. Yet, surely, whoever accepted the Bohemian crown would also force the Habsburgs to engage in a fearsome war to regain what they had lost. Too much was at stake for the Habsburgs to allow the Bohemians to slip from their grasp, and too much had been lost already to allow one more nail to be hammered into the dynasty's cracking self-image. War would thus be certain, and once Europe learned of this latest development in the curious Bohemian saga, the question became one of *who*. Who indeed would be brave or perhaps foolish enough to accept this poisoned chalice, thereby opening Pandora's Box and inviting a war to the last extremity? The candidates lined up or recoiled in horror at the suggestion that they should take the crown, but one figure stood out above the rest. He was the most well-connected Protestant ruler in Europe, and he was also the familial, religious and political enemy of the Habsburg family. His name was Frederick V, the Elector Palatine.

THREE
My Kingdom Come

> If it is true that the Bohemians are about to depose Ferdinand and elect another
> king, let everyone prepare at once for a war lasting twenty, thirty, or forty years.
> The Spaniards and the House of Austria will deploy all their worldly goods
> to recover Bohemia; indeed, the Spaniards would rather lose the Netherlands
> than allow their House to lose control of Bohemia so disgracefully and so
> outrageously.[23]

These were the words of Johan Albrecht, Count of Solms, the Palatine's
ambassador to the city of Frankfurt, who, in this case, was merely fulfilling
his task in communicating the latest news from Bohemia to his master. Did
Frederick read these words? Did he absorb their contents and core message,
and did he read between the lines, and grasp that, perhaps, his ambassador
was also warning him against turning some of the rumours doing the rounds
at the time into truth? We cannot know for sure, but we know that Frederick
V was not ignorant either of the risks involved in accepting the crown, of
the constitutional implications, or of the position this would force the
Habsburgs into. We have seen that some accounts of Frederick paint him as
the indecisive, bumbling fool ignorant of what his advisors – above Christian
of Anhalt – were up to, and what it all meant. Wedgewood even provides us
with several ludicrous images of Frederick never realising what Anhalt was
up to and being completely surprised by the pace of events.

In one scene, Frederick meets with the Evangelical Union at Rothenberg
in late November 1618 and is completely surprised by the objections of the
Protestant princes assembled to the idea of intervention in the Bohemian
revolt. By that point, Palatine diplomacy had already distinguished itself as
one of the best hopes of the Bohemian rebels, and in league with the Duke
of Savoy, the Palatinate provided badly needed monies, in addition to the
mercenary captain Ernst von Mansfeld, whom the rebels were soon to heavily
rely upon.[24] So Frederick and Anhalt had arranged all of that by late 1618, yet
Wedgewood maintains that the Elector was most ignorant of all the princes

assembled as to Anhalt's actual policy – this despite the fact that, as we have learned, Anhalt was no king; any document or decision made on Palatine policy would first need to pass across Frederick's desk.[25] Unless the Elector Palatine did not read the volumes of correspondence which the Bohemian revolt was producing – which is unlikely, since he was plainly interested in its events – then there was no possible way he could have been so uninformed.

In this same meeting at Rothenberg, we are told by Wedgewood that Frederick believed wholeheartedly in Anhalt's protestations that he was merely working for peace in the Empire by intervening in the Bohemian crisis, whereas the other assembled Protestants saw right through Anhalt's scheme for what it truly was. Worse than this, Frederick is portrayed as producing a fantastically naïve scheme to ensure peace in the Empire, whereby the Evangelical Union would arm itself, persuade John George of Saxony to join in, and then present a petition to Emperor Matthias – the ailing Emperor would not die for another four months – which would demonstrate that the German Protestants were prepared, if it came down to it, to use force, even though deep down Frederick did not genuinely want war. Wedgewood notes that Frederick's plan was the 'fruit of youth and optimism', and that Anhalt could have pointed out to Frederick that it would have been impossible due to Saxon hostility to Calvinists. Instead of pointing this out though, Wedgewood claimed that Anhalt 'found it simpler to use Frederick's trivial project as a cover for his private intrigues', and that by taking advantage of Frederick's confidence in him, Anhalt 'could give instructions to ambassadors that certainly never reached Frederick's ears and keep the well-intentioned but incurious prince totally ignorant of the things which were being done in his name.'

Conveniently, Wedgewood then noted that shortly after concocting the scheme, Anhalt cracked and felt forced to reveal it to Frederick, whose trust in Anhalt was 'shaken' but 'not destroyed'. This incredible journey into make believe flies in the face of every fact we know about Frederick and the structure of Palatine government, which always ensured, once he had reached his majority in 1614, that the Elector Palatine would have the final say on whatever came across his desk. This fact alone invalidates much of the story Wedgewood presents, but it was the idea that Frederick could be so stupid and blindly ignorant of Saxon hostility towards Calvinism that truly undermines this version of events. The Evangelical Union, it should be pointed out, had been established with the express purpose of overcoming these disagreements and hostilities – Frederick could not have been ignorant to them even if he had wanted to be, since he led the organisation which was charged with tightening the bonds of long-divided German Protestants.

Furthermore, leadership of this organisation would have revealed that Saxon hostility remained intractable and deep, and Protestant division and caution also remained intense within the Empire. Frederick would only have had to look at the recent history of the Evangelical Union to see that whispers of conflict and pre-existing divisions had been more than enough to whittle down the members and forces of the Union considerably over the preceding years. If the process of merely existing in the tense political and religious climate of the Empire had shown him this, then the notion that he would be surprised when objections were raised against Palatine intervention in Bohemia becomes even less possible to believe.[26] Wedgewood even noted that it was suspicious that Frederick should be in the Upper Palatinate, that portion of his lands which were sandwiched between Bavaria and Austria to the south and Bohemia to the east – lands which he rarely visited by the way – just at the time when Ferdinand was deposed as Bohemia's king in late August 1619.[27] Another historian has written that 'As early as January 1619 Frederick was considering the possibility that he might procure the crown of Bohemia for himself';[28] as we'll see later, the Elector Palatine had been considering the Bohemian question many months before that. Frederick was no fool, and he had not been blindly led to accept a scheme of Anhalt's making; he was aware of the potential of the Bohemian revolt and wanted to be near the action in case matters took a certain course.

It should be added that while the act of offering the Bohemian crown to a figure other than a Habsburg may appear revolutionary, it was a tactic which had been rooted as far back as 1612, when Matthias had assumed the crown. The next time their crown became vacant, the Bohemian Protestants fully intended to offer it to a non-Habsburg. The problem was, they had not selected a candidate for this honour by 1617, when the Habsburg family doubled down on the idea of putting Ferdinand forward. If you recall the negotiations of the Onate Treaty, then you will remember the animated concerns of the Austrians regarding Bohemia. The longer Philip III took to declare his satisfaction in letting Bohemia go, the longer the opposition to the Habsburgs would have to develop a platform for such an opposition candidate. Although most of Europe was surprised by the actions of the Bohemians in August 1619 – when the rebels declared their intention to find a new, non-Habsburg King of Bohemia – this would not have been a bolt out of the blue for either Vienna or Heidelberg. The shock came more from the fact that the Bohemians actually followed through with their daring plan, rather than what the details of that daring plan actually were.[29]

It is important for the sake of context that we do not view Frederick's acceptance of the Bohemian crown in late September 1619 as coming out of nowhere, since doing so underrates the impact which a history of competition, suspicion and downright hostility had between the Palatine and Austrian Habsburg families. Since the conversion of the Palatine Elector to Calvinism in the late 1560s, the Palatinate had become a centre of all that Habsburgs loathed, and with the increase in Jesuit activity and the successes of the counter-reformation, it became dynastically as well as spiritually important to contest the Habsburgs at every possible stage. By reducing the Austrian Habsburgs and by challenging their constitutional position, the succeeding Palatine electors aimed at undermining their strength and gaining allies against their predominance within the Empire.

While one may criticise the Palatinate for provoking the Habsburgs further, it should be remembered that the conflict between the two dynasties contained deep roots, which were greatly affected by the troubling signs of Habsburg aggrandisement. With the Spanish and Austrians working in tandem, France had been overrun with religious warfare and the Dutch rebels locked into a desperate struggle for survival. It is worth reiterating the role which Christian of Anhalt played in supporting the Protestant Henry of Navarre in 1591 during the French Wars of Religion, before taking up his place in the Upper Palatinate a few years later. It would be far too reductionist to claim that Frederick V was somehow influenced by the behaviour and stance of Christian of Anhalt; instead it would be more accurate to denote the decades of opposition to the Habsburgs which Frederick's ancestors had maintained, and the arrival of Anhalt confirmed that Palatine diplomacy vis-à-vis the Habsburgs was not about to change.

Such facts are often lost in the story when examining the Thirty Years War's major flashpoints. There was never any doubt as to where the Palatinate stood on the Bohemian revolt; Frederick made sure of this when he became the first European ruler to recognise the Bohemian rebels' provisional government, and to trumpet their cause. By September 1618, Frederick had begun to put his money where his mouth was, arranging with the Duke of Savoy to split the costs of a force of four thousand men, composed of mercenaries, Germans and veterans of the recent Mantuan War.[30] Again, the significance of this action should not be understated – Frederick was at this point the only German potentate to actively intervene in the Bohemian revolt and contribute directly with military force. These actions were undertaken under the policy guise of aiding the Bohemians in their quest to secure their borders and increase their security, since to declare his intentions outright would have drawn much opposition from the Evangelical Union as well as German moderates like the Elector of Saxony. This, again, is further evidence against the idea that Frederick was tone deaf to the Union's objections or Saxon hostility; much like his family's own rivalry with the Habsburgs, such obstacles were facts he had been prepared to deal with, and which he had dealt with, since assuming his majority.

Christoph von Dohna was a Palatine ambassador, who had been in place in Austria and in Bohemia since 1617, and he was well positioned once the revolt broke out to receive the latest news and communicate it back to his master. It was while Bohemian forces triumphed against the Habsburgs, most spectacularly in the storming of Pilsen in late November 1618, that the notion of Frederick's candidature first began to swirl around the discussions between the ambassador and the Bohemians with some seriousness. In the words of Brennan Pursell – 'the question should not have come as a complete surprise to the young prince.' Indeed, paying keen attention to events in Bohemia as he certainly was, Frederick may even have planned for the rebels to offer him the crown in the near future. Pursell, in his book *The Winter King* which provided such an invaluable revisionist account of the Elector Palatine's personality, career and legacy, noted further on the idea of a Palatine candidate for the Bohemian crown, writing:

> There had been a history of rumours and designs whereby an Elector Palatine would relieve the Bohemian throne of its Habsburg occupant. Both John Casimir and Frederick IV had entertained similar aspirations, but not very seriously. The repeated rebellions in the first years of the seventeenth century had raised the level of these aspirations for Frederick V, which, for some, were becoming expectations by the time of his marriage in 1613...sources show that the Spanish monarch, the papacy, the Venetians, the Imperial court, and perhaps the Ottoman Turks as well had heard rumours of an intended usurpation of Bohemia by Frederick V, which would have made the election of a Protestant Holy Roman Emperor a distinct possibility.[31]

Wedgewood presents Frederick's letters which were written around the time of the Bohemian revolt and sent out to the courts of Europe, and to his father in law in particular, in which the Elector Palatine preached of his desire for peace in the Bohemian affair, as evidence of his confusion, his ignorance of the reality, or even his bad faith, considering what followed.[32] Yet, it is important to denote, as Pursell does, that for Frederick, peace and justice for the Bohemians were not mutually exclusive ideas – to attain the Bohemian peace, Frederick was willing 'to use diplomacy, resort to military means, and submit to no small amount of dynastic opportunism.'[33]

On 25 November 1618, Frederick met with his core advisors, including Ludwig Camerarius, his Calvinist confessor, Anhalt, Count Johan Albrecht of Solms, and other members of his court. The question on everyone's minds was the news passed to Heidelberg by Christoph von Dohna, the Palatine ambassador then in Bohemia. Would Frederick accept or even consider the Bohemian crown, or would he not? Frederick proved himself remarkably wise under the circumstances, and he listened to the counsel of his advisors, who upheld that it would be better to wait and see what happened with the Bohemian succession for the moment, rather than rushing in. Matthias could still be leaned on, and a different candidate for the Bohemians within the Habsburg family could be selected if the revolt went to a certain level. Frederick was also aware of a fact which is sometimes held against him – that the Bohemians were eagerly grasping at the possibility of electing other candidates in Europe, who all recommended or failed to be considered depending on their connections and the potential benefits which the Bohemians could gain from them. Frederick was not stupid – he saw the wisdom behind waiting for a few months at least to see what happened next in Bohemia. Since the strategic position of the Habsburgs in Austria, let alone Bohemia, was quite poor by late 1618, Frederick was losing nothing by mulling the issue over further.

Frederick was also cautious about accepting the Bohemian crown because he recognised the danger inherent in his decision. If the Bohemians offered him their throne, then his Palatinate would surely be set upon by the Austrian Habsburgs, their Spanish allies, and others who were in league with them. There was little point in accepting Bohemia only to lose the Palatinate, but Frederick was cautious for another reason, this one constitutional. If the revolt against the Habsburgs descended into a rebellion against the very notion of their authority, Frederick wanted to be certain that the Bohemians had the legislative power to elect their own king on their own power. In his further efforts to acquire a more complete picture, he inquired about the Habsburgs' abuses of the Bohemians constitutional privileges, and whether the Letter of Majesty genuinely was in danger.

Interestingly, Frederick displayed some concern during his correspondence about the likelihood of being able to guarantee his sons' candidature for the crown in the future – did Frederick wish to transform the Bohemian Kingdom into a hereditary extension of his own power, as the Habsburgs hoped to do? We cannot know for certain, but we do know that the Upper Palatinate bordered Bohemia and uniting the governments of the rebels with that governorship of Christian of Anhalt would not have been the most curious fusing of administrations in European history. Frederick's quest for more information did not rest there though; inquiring about the viability of the revolt, and of the likelihood of its success, he picked the brains of his subordinates so that he was informed about Bohemia's army; its rate of pay, the proportion of infantry to cavalry, its list of officers, and the conditions of the strategic land routes which passed between Bohemia, Passau and Austria. In his communications with the Bohemian estates, Frederick compelled those in revolt to maintain a hearty correspondence with the Dutch and English, as well as the Evangelical Union.

From these actions in late 1618, we can say with some certainty that Frederick was more interested in ensuring the survival and success of the Bohemian revolt than he was in guaranteeing his candidacy for the Bohemian throne. Indeed, one of the major reasons for Frederick's apparent reluctance to wholeheartedly accept the Bohemian crown can be explained not merely by the dangers such a plan posed, but also by the fact that a far more determined and self-confident candidate for the Bohemian throne had put himself forward, and Frederick was willing to support him. His name was Charles Emmanuel, the Duke of Savoy, and he had conducted a policy alongside the Elector Palatine for several months, which aimed at undermining the Habsburgs' in Bohemia for their mutual gain. It could not be said that Frederick's ambitions went further than this for the moment, but Charles Emmanuel's certainly did – he desired not only the Bohemian crown, but also to leverage this acquisition to then become Holy Roman Emperor once Matthias died.

Even Pursell described this as a 'fundamentally unrealistic' plan, but this should not detract from the fact that Palatine-Savoyard diplomacy aimed seriously towards this end. Savoy could supply the Italian veterans who had recently fought in the Mantuan War, and for this invaluable resource Frederick was willing to negotiate and promise whatever it took. In January 1619, Charles Emmanuel offered to send an army of seven thousand men to Bohemia, to provide one and a half million ducats in subsidies, and to allocate Hungary, Alsace and portions of Austria to Frederick, if Frederick declared in return his intentions to approve Savoyard candidacy for the Bohemian and Imperial thrones. To demonstrate his own seriousness, Charles Emmanuel then turned off the tap of subsidies in March to prove just how badly Frederick needed him.

The Elector Palatine received the message loud and clear; Christian of Anhalt was sent to sign the proposed treaty in person, which was done in May, just as the rebels were closing in on Vienna. As it happened, Savoy's promised subsidies never arrived, and by the end of the summer the Duke cut off his subsidies entirely once it became clear that the rebels intended to offer the throne to Frederick instead of him. Still, Palatine-Savoyard diplomacy and Frederick's role in it demonstrated in the starkest of terms how determined the Elector Palatine was to undermine the Habsburgs and interfere in the Bohemian revolt. As we have seen though, it had also underlined Frederick's hesitation in accepting the Bohemian crown – he had even been willing to pass the honour onto someone else.[34]

Shrouded as it was under the ominous clouds of anxiety and conflict, the significance of the Bohemian decision to formally depose Ferdinand as their king should not be understated. A century of solid, continuous Habsburg rule of this elective monarchy, which came so close to a hereditary right, was now apparently at an end. Ferdinand was voted as deposed by a majority of the estates' representatives, and the former king was accused of violating his promises regarding the Letter of Majesty, kidnapping Cardinal Klesl, invading Moravia unlawfully, promoting Jesuit designs and, on top of all that, his rumoured vow to extirpate heresy in Bohemia was also levelled against him. On 22 August 1619, Ferdinand was, according to the Bohemians that had placed him on the throne, no longer the king of their lands and subjects. Their task turned from justifying their deposition, to locating a suitable candidate to stand in Ferdinand's place.

As the Bohemians worked to begin a new era of statehood, Frederick worked to ensure that Ferdinand did not become Emperor. Evidently, he failed in this mission, but it was not from a lack of trying. The Elector Palatine sent petitions to all the important electors; discussing extensive judicial matters with the Elector of Saxony in spring 1619, and meeting with the Elector of Mainz in June. While in the company of the Elector of Mainz, Frederick successfully persuaded or coerced him to postpone the Imperial election for another month, beyond the proposed date on 20 July, and into late August instead. Atop Frederick's arguments against the Habsburg candidature was the danger which transforming the office of Holy Roman Emperor into a hereditary right would pose to the Imperial constitution, and Ferdinand, with his aggressive confessionalism, was a big part of this problem. The Archbishop of Mainz gave cold replies, but Frederick persisted with this avenue of electoral diplomacy.

Much was clearly riding upon the Empire's Electoral College to fulfil its function and elect a new emperor, and while it sat in this weighted position in late August, Frederick wanted to ensure that the grievances of the Bohemians and the integrity of the potential candidates were given proper consideration. A month was the most that those already assembled in Frankfurt would wait though; to the Elector of Cologne, who happened to be the brother of Maximillian of Bavaria, he believed that postponing the election any longer would only serve to aggravate the Bohemian revolt. The Elector of Trier echoed this view, which left only the Electors of Saxony and Brandenburg on the fence; Brandenburg tended to follow Palatinate policy since the Elector's conversion to Calvinism some years before, but John George of Saxony was here committed to maintaining the status quo, and had been troubled by the Bohemian revolt. He supported crushing this revolt, and supported the candidate of Ferdinand, who at this point in the discussions was still the King of Bohemia. Ferdinand, as King of Bohemia and in possession of a vote which would facilitate his accession to the Imperial throne, of course compelled those present to move ahead with the Imperial election.

This left Frederick isolated, and his prospects for success in preventing Ferdinand's succession highly doubtful. Still though, in July 1619, as Frederick made his way to the Upper Palatinate to watch over the Evangelical Union's activities there, and perhaps to secure other Bohemian decisions in the near future, he had a list of instructions prepared for his ambassadors to the looming election in Frankfurt. Four candidates, the most important of whom was Maximillian of Bavaria, provided Frederick with what he believed was a hopeful method of outmanoeuvring Ferdinand's candidature. Of course, Maximillian was more than likely to vote for Ferdinand, his ally in religion and his brother-in-law, and this was a well-known fact, but it was not impossible that Frederick could persuade the Elector of Cologne, Maximillian's brother, and two other electors to support him, then with this majority of four votes, the Duke of Bavaria's accession would be secured.

Again, much like Frederick's other initiatives, the idea of placing Maximillian on the Imperial throne was based in history. Since at least 1616, the Duke of Bavaria appeared a straightforward, reasonable candidate to succeed Matthias – that he was a Catholic, raised upon a diet of Jesuit words and lessons, did not dissuade Frederick from this course, and should dissuade us from categorising the Thirty Years War as a religious conflict at its core. If Frederick truly despised Catholics, then his distant Wittelsbach cousin Maximillian would never have been on his radar; since Frederick despised the Habsburgs unconstitutional and inflammatory behaviour, rather than their religious persuasion, the choice of the Catholic Maximillian was not that radical of a concept for the Calvinist Elector Palatine.

It deserves mention that during the sounding out process of Maximillian, Frederick had travelled to meet with Maximillian in spring 1618. Both men pledged to keep the other informed on the likelihood of confessional conflict in the future, and to work together on pacifying it. Throughout these meetings with the Duke of Bavaria, Maximillian refused to accept the Palatine nomination for the Emperor's seat, based on the fact, as he told Frederick, that the scheme was not worth the risks. To Frederick this indicated that if his success could be guaranteed, then Maximillian would contest the election – it was failure that he feared, rather than going against the Habsburg monopoly per se. 'It is clear', Frederick wrote, 'that the Duke may not refuse it at all if he would see some possibility; they are very envious of the House of Austria.' Interestingly, Frederick had met with Maximillian here, in spring 1618, to talk about the anticipated imperial diet which Matthias was expected to host later in the year, where the Emperor would request support for Ferdinand to succeed him. Thanks to the Defenestration of Prague, these plans had been postponed, but Frederick had evidently not forgotten the conversations that preceded them.

To cut a long story short,[35] Frederick lost the battle against the Habsburgs in the halls of Frankfurt, but before this had been officially confirmed, he learned on 24 August 1619 that the Bohemians, having overthrown their king, were leaning strongly towards the Elector Palatine as their next king. The day after Ferdinand's successful election as Emperor, Frederick learned that, in fact, the Bohemians had chosen him as their next king, and that the vote was overwhelmingly in his favour.

FOUR
Desperate Times

It was on the day of his 23 birthday that the rumours were confirmed – Frederick V would be required to make the most momentous decision of his life, upon which so much would hinge. Most of us, on our 23 birthdays, need only choose where the party begins, but Frederick's responsibilities were far grander than that. Failure could very well destroy his Upper Palatinate, sandwiched as it was between the Bavarian and Austrian lands, while the Lower Palatinate along the Rhine would surely succumb to Spanish invasions. To his pregnant wife Elizabeth, he confessed his anxiety – 'believe that I am very troubled about what to decide', he said, a few days after learning of his nomination by the Bohemian estates. In early September, Frederick left Amberg, the capital of the Upper Palatinate where he had been staying for several months and made his way to discuss the situation with the members of the Evangelical Union in Rothenberg.[36]

The last time Frederick had met his colleagues in the Evangelical Union, the previous year, he had been made aware of their hesitation in interfering too extensively in the Bohemian revolt. Much had changed since that time; with Ferdinand now Holy Roman Emperor, and the Bohemians selecting the head of the Union as their new king, a great deal was now at stake. Unsurprisingly, considering their previous behaviour, strong voices were raised against the policy – were Frederick to accept the Crown of Bohemia he could well drag the names of those Union princes through the mud as he did so, opening them and their lands up for punitive measures on the grounds that they were guilty through their association with the Elector Palatine and his rash decision. However, while we may expect that a current of caution and fear at the prospect of accepting the crown would be present, it would be incorrect to claim that 'nearly all voices were loud against the offer', as Wedgewood does.[37]

The Margraves of Baden and Ansbach were in favour of accepting the crown, as of course was Christian of Anhalt and Ludwig Camerarius, Frederick's confessor. The most significant voices against acceptance were the rulers of Wurttemberg, Hesse and Kulmbach, and the Imperial cities of Ulm, Strasburg and Nurnberg refrained from weighing in on the debate at all. Frederick declared himself undecided and for a month, the Bohemians languished in uncertainty. A vocal supporter of the Bohemian project was Camerarius, who cast the venture in divine terms, and reasoned that God's providence was at work in such situations. Whether Frederick was convinced by this argument, or whether he had determined from the get-go to accept the offer and merely delayed acceptance for a month, we do not know for sure.

What we do know is that for a month, Frederick went to great lengths to investigate the feasibility of the project. From Rothenberg he requested that his chancellor in Heidelberg prepare several dossiers and discussions on the critical points, so that when he returned from his meeting with the Union there would be evidence to examine and fully formed opinions to bear in mind. The status of Bohemia's electoral monarchy; the ease in mobilising Bohemia's soldiery; the condition that the Palatinate in the Lower and Upper regions were, and what defences they could provide; how many soldiers he could expect to have in his employ, and how much danger his lands would actually be in – there were all matters on which Frederick requested more information. Testing the waters diplomatically was also critical, so the Emperor's likely position and strategy, in addition to the allies he would lean on were topics for consideration, and the opinions of virtually all powers of importance, from Lorraine to Denmark to Brunswick, were all to be considered. Far from a clueless, ignorant youth, Frederick had realised for some time that there was 'little sense in taking on a kingdom that could not be legitimately defended.'[38]

It was when Frederick reached Heidelberg in mid-September that matters began to take a certain course. Upon arriving, his wife Elizabeth promised him that her father's support would be forthcoming, since King James, regardless of his actual stance, would be unable to stand aside as his son-in-law ventured down this dangerous path. At the very least, Elizabeth insisted, James would never allow the Palatinate to come under threat, or for his family to suffer humiliation and depredation at the hands of their enemies. Pursell noted that 'earnestly wishing that he could rely on England to defend them in the event of attack, Frederick came to believe it.' Frederick had not simply assumed that English support was guaranteed – he had been persuaded that it would be, and while we may lambast the Elector Palatine's naivety, there were sufficient signals emanating out of the England to build a substantial case for support. Dudley Carleton, England's ambassador to The Hague, noted in September 1619 that:

> This business of Bohemia is like to put all Christendom in combustion...since the revolution of the world is like to carry us out of this peaceable time, it is better to begin the change with advantage than with disadvantage...[For if Bohemia were to be] neglected and by consequence supressed, the princes of

the religion adjoining are like to bear the burden of a victorious army…Where will it stay? God knows, being pushed on by the Jesuits and commanded by the new emperor, who flatters himself with prophecies of extirpating the reformed religion and restoring the Roman Church to the ancient greatness.[39]

The idea that once the Bohemian revolt was supressed, the Protestants of Germany would then come under attack, was one which held considerable weight among even the moderate observers of current events at the time.[40] Furthermore, the Twelve Years Truce was due to expire between the Spanish and Dutch in April 1621, and when that occurred, there was absolutely no guarantee that the Spanish war effort against the Dutch might not spill into the Empire, or that Dutch efforts to engage the Spanish would not involve some Protestant German reinforcement. Even since the Bohemian revolt began the Emperor had made use of the Spanish to reinforce Austria, and the Spanish contribution, in conjunction with the Papacy, had moved Maximillian of Bavaria to help in the resurrection of the Catholic League in July 1619. With these steps taken, and Catholic Europe coordinating itself better than before, it certainly seemed plausible that unless some stand was taken, the Bohemians would be trounced, and the Protestants would be immensely vulnerable.

Britain's Archbishop of Canterbury, George Abbott, was emphatic in his insistence that Frederick should accept the Bohemian crown, and that the King should come to his immediate assistance for whatever he needed. Seeing matters in the form of a great Protestant coalition, Abbott said that British intervention…

> …will comfort the Bohemians, will honour Frederick, will strengthen the Evangelical Union, will bring on the states of the Low Countries, will stir up the King of Denmark…and Hungary, I hope being in that same cause will run the same fortune.

A public collection for Bohemia, in addition to a recruitment drive took place, and general enthusiasm within England remained high, especially among the Puritan communities which had continued to grow. It became possible to see Frederick as the leader of the forces of godliness, sent to overthrow the Antichrist – indeed this image was adopted by the pamphleteers of the day in both England and the Netherlands. As was the case with so many of Frederick's friends and the promises they made though, the actual practical contribution that was made to his cause was small – the recruitment drive yielded only two thousand volunteers, and these were not ready until mid-1620, while the collection of monies for Bohemia was partially sabotaged, it was said, by King James himself.[41]

England was clearly struggling to reconcile its King's curious policy of attempting to champion Protestantism while also preserving peace, a contradictory goal. James was not, as Elizabeth had promised, willing to support Frederick's decision to accept the crown. The legend peddled by Friedrich Schiller is worth repeating, even while we have established that it was based more on his enemy's imagination than actual fact. According to Schiller, it was Elizabeth's condescending demeanour and vague threats which had more of an impact that the actual promises she had made about her father's support. 'Had you', demanded the Electress, 'confidence enough in yourself to accept the hand of a king's daughter, and have you misgivings about taking a crown which is voluntarily offered you? I would rather eat bread at thy kingly table, than feast at thy electoral board.'[42]

Notwithstanding the baseless nature of such statements, it is important not to underrate the impression which the promise of English support had on Frederick's decision-making. His father in law had, for the last year, been attempting to mediate the Bohemian revolt, and position England as the peacemaker of Europe while also seeking a Catholic Spanish marriage to balance the Protestant Palatine one. Elizabeth did not seem to realise that her father would never approve of such an adventurous policy at such an inopportune time – a few months later, once Frederick's acceptance of the crown had been made known, she was even assuring the Bohemian rebels that she would represent their case as best as she could to them. English diplomacy was far more complicated than Elizabeth appreciated, and whether she led Frederick astray or not, reliance on English aid to any serious extent turned out to be a major miscalculation which cost the Elector Palatine dearly.[43]

The Dutch contribution, in addition to the English mirage, was also beginning to disappear. Between May and September 1619, the Dutch sent five and a half thousand men and almost £25,000 to aid the Bohemians in their revolt, yet between autumn 1619 and spring 1621, only a slightly larger sum than this was sent. By the time the Twelve Years Truce had expired, the Dutch had mostly ceased to be a practically useful ally, and the only true military ally Frederick would be able to lean on was the Prince of Transylvania Bethlen Gabor, who reached the high point of his own powers in November 1619 as he besieged Vienna.[44]

In mid-September it was time to make a decision, so Frederick gathered his most important advisors – Camerarius, Anhalt and Johan Albrecht, Count Solms, in addition to the chancellors of the Upper and Lower Palatinate, and the grand chancellor of Heidelberg. History has told us that Frederick's most important advisors were at this point in favour of accepting the Bohemian crown, but for the moment, they left the opposition to speak. A strong case was made for the reasons against acceptance; at Rothenberg, where he had met the Evangelical Union a few weeks before, fourteen points were raised to rationalise refusing the crown, and only six reasons could be found in favour. It remained to be seen if those six points in favour were stronger than the more numerous arguments and more numerous advisors that argued against acceptance. To even the most optimistic of princes, the cause appeared grim.

It was nigh on inevitable, Frederick's advisors said, that once he accepted the crown, the Emperor would charge him with an Imperial crime, and the Imperial ban might even be used against him. Faced with the might of the Habsburgs, who could be expected to stand with Frederick against this menace? There was no precedent for what Frederick was about to do – nobody had ever held the Palatine and Bohemian votes before, and while the Golden Bull of 1356 which established the electoral framework of the Holy Roman Empire did not explicitly allow it, it also did not prohibit it.

The fact that Frederick might embark on a scheme too fantastic even for the constitution to imagine was not necessarily a good thing; there were the more practical things to consider, such as how the Catholics of the Empire would respond – likely with anger, or how the Protestants would respond – likely with jealousy. If Protestants remained cautious and aloof, and if the marginalised Evangelical Union reneged in its duties to aid their leader, then Frederick would left abandoned in his time of need, forced to face a coalition of enemies who were individually eager to bring him down, and collectively determined to punish him for his transgressions. This could be balanced with foreign aid, but before Frederick had even gathered his advisors it was learned that Venice was against acceptance. The Duke of Savoy had gradually lapsed in his enthusiasm for the Bohemian revolt since it became clear he would not be Emperor, and the French King had sent words of encouragement to Ferdinand to crush the Bohemian revolt from the beginning.[45]

Another two arguments were raised against acceptance; first, there was no guarantee that the Bohemians would accept Frederick's son as his heir to that throne. To have requested that Frederick Henry, Frederick's firstborn, succeeded him in Bohemia, would have made a mockery out of the non-hereditary characteristics of that crown which the rebels had declared their zeal for. Second was the more apocalyptic outcome of acceptance – that Frederick's move would initiate a religious war in the Empire, 'Europe's most compelling nightmare', a conflict between rival confessions which could not be won, and which would not end.[46]

Outflanked on the front of reason, those advisors in favour of acceptance cautioned Frederick to take the crown based on pure dynastic ambition. Frederick would be availing of a phenomenal opportunity if he acquired the Bohemian crown and managed to hold it. Until it be guaranteed that he did hold it, Frederick should fob off the Bohemians by explaining his delay and hinting that he would accept once gestures of support had been received from the English, Dutch and Brandenburgers. With a combined effort, they reasoned, Frederick would be able to hold the Bohemian crown, and gradually merge his Upper Palatinate into the Bohemian kingdom to forge a powerful Palatine Protestant entity in the centre of Europe, and of the Habsburg interest. Such a move would open Frederick up to ridicule and possibly attack from the Habsburgs, but it would so massively boost his prestige among the Protestant powers that the risk appeared, to some, actually worth it.

Other arguments were used in favour of acceptance. If the Bohemians were not granted the candidate they desired, and soon, in their desperation they could turn to less savoury allies and pledge themselves perhaps to the Turks in return for security. If they were defeated and destroyed, then Protestantism would surely be crushed in Bohemia, so that the Habsburgs could guarantee their position there for decades to come. Once Protestantism was crushed in Bohemia, surely the malignant forces of militant Catholicism would then focus their combined energies on the destruction of other Protestant communities, the Upper Palatinate first, and Frederick's allies afterwards. By the very fact that his name had been suggested, it seemed unlikely that Ferdinand would ever leave the Elector Palatine in peace again. Was it not better to strike the first blow now while the opportunity presented itself, and the Austrian Habsburgs were then beleaguered and retreating from Bethlen Gabor's invasion? To In the end though, those in favour of the daring scheme counselled Frederick that he should wait until encouraging offers were returned from the English and Dutch before accepting the Bohemian crown.

What happened next is mostly shrouded in myth and hearsay, but what we do know is that Frederick drafted a letter to the Bohemians on 21 September, as did his wife Elizabeth. Within it, Frederick rationalised his election in spiritual terms, making use of a Calvinist explanation for the circumstances which now provided him with a great opportunity. God had pre-ordained whatever followed, whether this was his triumph or his ruin. Frederick insisted he had never sought to be elected by the Bohemians, which was technically true, but a bit misleading, since his ambassador had acted in his name but without his knowledge in Prague since the end of July. Frederick urged the Bohemian estates to pray to God for an orderly outcome to these developments, and that his acceptance would bring glory and honour to his name and all Protestants. Finally, Frederick added that he was waiting for advice from London but that as soon as it came, he would send his decision to the Bohemian estates.

If Frederick's answer had been somewhat vague, then shortly after his and his wife's letters were dispatched, matters became a great deal clearer. It seems likely that Frederick genuinely did wish to wait and see what his father in law had to say, but he felt the Bohemian question more urgently over the last week of September, and this seems to have compelled him to give a definite answer. No doubt Anhalt played a role in emphasising the importance of not hesitating, but an underrated factor may well have been the progress which Bethlen Gabor was making at this time. By late September the Prince of Transylvania had overrun all of Habsburg Hungary and was poised to invade Austria – perhaps, Frederick feared that if he did not accept definitively, then the Bohemians would offer their crown to that Prince, since he seemed most capable of defending their interests.

Whatever his primary motivations for rushing to clear the air, the result was that Frederick waited barely four days between sending a request for advice to King James, and then accepting the Bohemian crown. The implications of this act, as the historian Robert Zaller noted, were problematic indeed for Britain's king:

> If Frederick hoped to compromise the King by this, he had struck well. The young Palatine had publicly consulted James; immediately thereafter, he had accepted the crown: what conclusion was the world to draw? James was furious. Not only had his good faith been impugned, but his relations with Spain, the cornerstone of his entire foreign policy, were placed in jeopardy.[47]

And so, the courier sped to Prague with Frederick's answer in his hands, and, perhaps, the fate of Europe as well. Did Frederick know what he was doing? We have looked at explanations for his behaviour, as have other historians. A divine calling; a criminally stupid mistake; an act of defiance against a dynasty he despised; an error made in youth; a pawn manipulated by ambitious advisors – all of these are plausible reasons, on their own, for rationalising what Frederick did. We can also fairly attest that messages of doom and gloom surrounded this decision – Frederick did not know that he was effectively igniting the Thirty Years War, but he would have been made aware that a conflict would be on the horizon so long as he challenged the Habsburg position in the Empire so boldly and directly in Bohemia. What is largely glossed over is the fact that, militarily, matters had not been going well for the Habsburgs, and worse fortune was yet to come. It is certainly worth considering the possibility that, far from ignorant of the Habsburgs' strategic position, Frederick evaluated the strengths and weaknesses of both sides, and concluded that, at this moment, he stood a good chance of winning.

The foundations of Ferdinand's domestic position were far from secure; he had faced revolt in his Bohemian, Austrian and Hungarian lands, on a scale never experienced by Frederick or his allies. Ferdinand's precious few friends consisted mostly of Spanish men and money, and Bavarian promises, but the most valuable thing Ferdinand possessed was the petrified neutrality of most of the Empire. Few princes felt enthused enough in either cause to fight for their Emperor or the Elector Palatine and wished to remain aloof. While this would pose a grave problem for Frederick within a few years, in the early autumn of 1619, it could also be argued that it provided an opportunity. Surely it was better to launch a coup against the Habsburg enemy now, while the Spanish support was minimal and the Catholic princes' contributions not fully fleshed out. Once the Emperor's allies mobilised, Bohemia would surely be crushed, but if Frederick acted quickly and successfully, then forces within and without of the Empire could well be persuaded that a peaceful conclusion was preferable to a terrible war. Under those circumstances, with enough pressure applied on his weak position, Ferdinand could be forced to capitulate in return for having his Imperial crown guaranteed, and his hereditary lands pacified.

Of course, this represents an admittedly optimistic interpretation of affairs in the Empire. As we know, neither branches of the Habsburg family would ever have allowed such a coup to become permanent. Their position in the Empire depended upon the possession of Bohemia, and thus brute force was the only course open to Ferdinand. Such an interpretation also underrates the capabilities of the Catholic League, which was soon to play a pivotal role in returning the status quo and acting as Ferdinand's sword. Frederick may have believed that the hostility and jealousy between the Bavarian Wittelsbachs and the Austrian Habsburgs was greater than it was in fact.

His acceptance of the crown while the Habsburgs were at the height of their peril, and facing into another siege of Vienna, suggests that the Elector Palatine attributed too much credit to Bethlen Gabor, whose offensive was soon to collapse after Ferdinand outflanked him with an appeal to his brother in law, the King of Poland. The best we can do is to interpret Frederick's actions based on what we know about the situation, and what Frederick knew at the time. What may appear as a hopeless, reckless, immensely irresponsible gamble to us, may have seemed to Frederick like a reasonable risk to take, especially considering the strategic position of the Habsburgs, the promises of his allies and the divinely ordained nature of the whole scheme.

Frederick had officially accepted the crown of Bohemia by 28 September 1619. By that point, it was too late to go back, and Frederick would now have to go all for broke if he wanted to secure the Bohemian crown and guarantee the safety of the Palatine cause. For the moment, this appeared like an achievable goal. Ferdinand was facing rebellion in Bohemia, Moravia and Silesia; his Austrian estates were almost all united against him and with the rebels, and the Hungarian threat grew worse with every passing week. The new Emperor's allies were mostly found in Spanish and Papal money, and some Spanish troops, but these had not proved sufficient to land a killer blow against the rebels. In spite of some victories, notably at Zablati in June – a victory which effectively revived the Catholic League – the rebels remained in strength and in good spirits. Faced with the determined opposition of these rebels, Ferdinand was in no realistic position to meet the challenge posed by his dynastic and political enemy, Frederick V.

Indeed, in some respects, Frederick's decision to lunge forward into the abyss appears bold and brilliant; had it succeeded, and had the forces of militant Protestantism in the Empire triumphed over the brittle command Ferdinand wielded over his lands, then the histories would surely remark on Frederick's genius, rather than his rashness. As matters stood in late September 1619 though, the Emperor's back was against the wall, and he had no choice other than to come out fighting. News of Frederick's acceptance of the Bohemian crown necessarily transformed the Bohemian revolt into a dynastic war – Frederick was trying in this act to directly threaten and then replace the Habsburg supremacy, and if Ferdinand did not stop him, then the glories of the Habsburg family would end with his name.

Frederick threw down the gauntlet to his Emperor, but it seems he did not realise exactly how seriously this threat would be taken, or what resources, powers and men the Emperor would move in order to salvage his position. As weak as Ferdinand was in autumn 1619, he would never be this weak again; a storm was brewing, and over autumn 1619 it moved out of the Catholic nucleus of Europe towards Frederick's lands at an alarming rate. As he had grossly overestimated the zeal and ability of his allies, so too had Frederick underestimated the determination of Ferdinand to resist him, and the actual support he would draw on. Even if, contrary to his coronation oath, the act of resisting Frederick brought foreign troops into the Empire, Ferdinand would do it – he had of course done it on a limited scale already.[48]

Nothing would be held back, no expense would be spared, no mission was more sacred; the livelihood of the Habsburg family was at stake, and nothing could be allowed to prevent Ferdinand from crushing the young Palatine upstart, and teaching him a lesson which no power, Protestant or Catholic, would soon forget. The stage was set, and with his conscience at rest, Frederick moved to claim what was his.

FIVE

Desperate Measures

For so long, the revolt had seemed like a localised, regional affair, but as it progressed, and destabilised the Habsburg hereditary lands, new opportunities opened up for the enemies of the dynasty, and rivals moved to take advantage of the new vulnerability in Vienna. Of course, it would not be enough to denote that Frederick intended to move against Ferdinand, and accept that deposed king's crown, simply because the time was right, and that king had had his day. Nor would it be enough for Frederick to explain that he was only fulfilling his end of a relationship which his ancestors had maintained since the late 1560s, when the Habsburgs and Wittelsbach Palatine family first rubbed each other the wrong way.

To Frederick, the acceptance of the Bohemian crown was a culmination of several years' worth of neglect and wrongdoing on the Habsburgs' part, but it would be somewhat naïve of us to conclude that Frederick did it for the welfare of the Bohemians alone. The Habsburgs had not looked so vulnerable in living memory – their lands were in uproar, and their security seemed imperilled even with Spanish interference. With the Prince of Transylvania approaching, and without the benefit of hindsight, Frederick could be forgiven for thinking that this second siege of Vienna spelled doom for Ferdinand, or at least, it spelled opportunity and a chance to negotiate from a far stronger position than his family ever had before.

With the Calvinist doctrine also egging him on, and portraying the events in divinely ordained terms, Frederick was the instrument of destiny who had the chance to reverse years of Habsburg domination, and restore the office of Holy Roman Emperor, in time, to where it belonged by right of the constitution – not perpetually in the lap of the Habsburgs, but in the hands of the Electors who, with enough work, would be compelled to vote for a Protestant Emperor. The risks were legion, but to Frederick, thanks to a variety of factors, these risks seemed worth the immense promise of the reward which urged him ever onwards.

The risks, indeed, began to mature almost as soon as Frederick had determined to accept the Crown in late September 1619. In the past, Frederick had loudly condemned Ferdinand's lack of scruples where violating the constitution was concerned; chief among his condemnations, both to his peers and to any electors that would listen, was the accusation that the Habsburgs clung to the office of Emperor unfairly, and treated it like a hereditary institution. This was unconstitutional, Frederick exclaimed, because the title of Emperor was granted by the Electors, and not guaranteed by Habsburg might and influence.[49] Brennan Pursell remarked that Frederick did not require dynastic ambition to move him into the anti-Habsburg camp; in other words, he did not oppose the Habsburg candidate out of interest for his dynasty's candidature, or of that of the Bavarian Wittelsbach family. Instead, it was the Habsburg domination of the Empire, seen in their unbroken control over the office of Holy Roman Emperor, which Frederick found so 'repugnant and dangerous.'[50]

Frustrated in his inability to prevent Ferdinand's successful election as Emperor, with even his Palatine delegation being forced to elect him, Frederick must have felt vindicated in his claims that the Habsburg monopoly over the Empire was unconstitutional in addition to being unsafe. Here again, the Habsburgs had manipulated their rivals to ensure that no serious alternative candidate would be put forward, while concerns about maintaining the peace, and not wanting to upset the apple cart, compelled the electors to give their acquiescence. In Frederick's mind, it was the threat of what the Habsburgs would do – launch a war in defence of their family's interests – which moved his electoral peers to remain compliant, and to Frederick, this was not right or lawful. Yet in addition to these convictions, we must also note Frederick's unfortunate character flaws. Rather than indecisive, his most glaring faults in autumn 1619 were on full show – a breath-taking, almost incredible naivety. As Pursell wrote:

> At this time Frederick also manifested a character trait that would contribute much to the development of the Thirty Years War: his tendency to believe what he wished and expect what he hoped for, in other words, an inability to distinguish the probable from the possible. This tendency was to lead to tragically frequent political miscalculations.[51]

In the context of our narrative, this cutting analysis meant that Frederick expected some kind of riposte to Ferdinand's contesting of the Imperial election, and when he was elected unanimously, he then expected that his meagre resources would stand against him. Finally, when Ferdinand managed to maintain himself in Vienna even as the enemy approached, Frederick then expected his allies in the Netherlands, the Evangelical Union, Transylvania, Savoy and especially England to act in concert with him to oppose him properly. Yet this assembling of allies did not materialise – the story of Frederick contains a message of caution: the danger of relying on your allies so extensively, when they stood to lose so much and gain so little by supporting you. Frederick never seemed to fully comprehend what he was asking of these allies; he never seemed to read between the lines of King James' correspondence, and see that his father in law, troubled and torn as he was, could not and would not intervene in the Empire by making war on the Emperor, if he wanted his peace policy to succeed.

Similarly, the Dutch could not afford to move determinedly against the Emperor when war with Spain loomed in the near future, even while they decried Spain's increasingly troubling accumulation of strategically important lands. The Evangelical Union too would never countenance entering into open opposition with their Emperor, so long as the threat to their freedoms from the Habsburgs remained minimal, and they had their guarantees. Other allies told similar stories. With the exception of Bethlen Gabor, whose Transylvanian forces were already in the field, no one was willing to lift a finger to aid Frederick, because in this context, lifting a finger did not mean political or ideological defence of their interests – it meant sponsoring a rebellion and waging a war against their Emperor. Try as he might, Frederick would never be able to motivate his peers to go so far.

The roots of Frederick's downfall was found not just in his underestimation of the situation's many dangers, or of his overestimation of his allies' capabilities – it was also in Emperor Ferdinand's demonstrated ability to transform the situation through a reliance on allies who were willing to bear the risks involved in coming to his aid. This willingness to bear risks, it has to be said, can be explained more by Ferdinand's determination to auction off his possessions, in addition to things he did not own, rather than his ability to somehow inspire reluctant friends to action. The irony is that by rushing to meet the threat which Frederick posed to his noble House, Ferdinand violated the constitution, and displayed the very contempt for the Holy Roman Empire's laws which the Elector Palatine had warned was always part of this militant zealot's nature. Perhaps then, it could also be said that the constitution and the Empire itself meant less to Ferdinand than the successful pursuit of the war, and the defeat of challenges to his dynasty which would grant the Habsburgs a new position of power and authority. Just as he overestimated his allies, Frederick may also have underestimated just how low Ferdinand would stoop to stop him, and this miscalculation was to cost him everything.

This trend first presented itself during a meeting between Ferdinand and Maximillian of Bavaria on 8 October 1619. It was here that Ferdinand reinforced a relationship with the Bavarian Duke – 'his university companion at Ingolstadt and his brother-in-law'[52]– which set the tone for the rest of this three-decade conflict. By this point, matters appeared grave indeed for Ferdinand. On his way back from being elected Holy Roman Emperor at Frankfurt, Ferdinand was informed of the dire situation unfolding in Hungary, where Bethlen Gabor had rolled over all remnants of Habsburg resistance, and been hailed as a liberator by virtually all of Habsburg Hungary's settlements. Seventeen thousand men were camped in south-west Bohemia, and another eight thousand six hundred camped along the Moravian frontier, but closer to home, Ferdinand could muster a paltry five thousand to defend Vienna, and more than half of these were Hungarian 'loyalists' of questionable loyalty. Panicked redistributions of soldiers followed, and a Habsburg advance towards Prague abandoned, when it was learned that against these meagre forces, Bethlen Gabor marched with more than thirty-five thousand men.[53]

Mindful of the great test which was to come, Ferdinand nonetheless saved some time for an aforementioned meeting with Maximillian of Bavaria, where the Emperor, perhaps at his most desperate point, sought to restore some balance to the equation by drawing upon the natural allies of the Catholic League. The League had been resurrected since its disbandment a few years before, in recognition of the severity of the Catholic Emperor's position, and in jubilation at the first great Catholic victory at Zablati on 10 June 1619. The progress and danger of the Bohemian revolt also sharpened the nerves of those Catholic princes who were too small by themselves to stand against any potential contamination of the revolt to their lands. Maximillian of Bavaria was the natural choice for these princes to lead their League, since he had been its original leader, and was the wealthiest potentate in the Empire at this stage.

This latter fact was one which Ferdinand was made keenly aware of, for if he wanted Maximillian's help, the price would almost certainly be high – the richer the prince, the higher one could expect his price to be. Yet, the problem for Ferdinand was that the kitty was virtually empty, not to mention dangerously in the red. Indeed, Ferdinand's financial woes make for almost as much depressing reading as his military woes. Debts relating to military expenses alone had ballooned to 4.3 million florins; the Austrian Habsburgs could expect an annual income of 2.4 million, had spent 5 million to date on waging the war against the Bohemians since autumn 1618, and from their Papal and Spanish allies, in addition to forced loans, they received only 3 million florins. As bad as this mess appeared, the reality under the surface was far worse. Ferdinand was personally in debt to the tune of 20 million florins at the time of his Imperial coronation.

These debts would not soon be settled, since the projected incomes from the Austrian Habsburgs' lands were significantly reduced by the revolt, when the lands and estates expected to pay their taxes were seized by rebels, who had no intention of paying. As a result, incomes plummeted, and expenses skyrocketed. Facing chronic financial problems like these, it was inconceivable that Ferdinand could possibly pay off his allies or overcome his enemies. To achieve these ends, he would have to venture outside the realm of acceptable, traditional, constitutional policy. If the solutions Ferdinand procured seemed distasteful, then they also demonstrated how far he was willing to go to preserve what he upheld to be his birth right, and the lands of his ancestors.[54]

This was Maximillian of Bavaria's great opportunity – to profit from the wretchedness and desperation of his Emperor's position like no other Duke in the Empire could. Evidently, Ferdinand had been mulling over the Bavarian option for some time, since he made a stop in Munich on 8 October, even while he had been informed of the crisis in Vienna. Vienna could wait, because Ferdinand had his mind on a deal which would effectively save his dynasty. Maximillian's strength was not only found in his deep reserves of cash which he had been accumulating for several years, it was also in his leadership of the Catholic League, active for all intents and purposes since August 1619 after spending some months rebuilding.

If Maximillian could be persuaded to lead this coalition of Catholic German princes into battle against the Bohemians, in the name of the Emperor, then Ferdinand's situation would dramatically improve. Funded by the League's members, Maximillian could expect to field an army of over twenty thousand, which would solve so many of the Emperor's grave problems. The critical question remained though of how the penniless Ferdinand would pay Maximillian when he was so deeply in debt and personally dependent on foreign subsidies himself. It was in this question that the crux of Frederick's downfall can be found, several months before the Elector Palatine was even declared an outlaw or had the Imperial Ban pronounced on him. To pay off Maximillian and to enlist this auxiliary as a loyal Habsburg servant, Ferdinand effectively bribed him with land, where money was not available. Upper Austria and the Upper Palatinate were promised to Maximillian, and the Duke would be entitled to wrest taxes and leverage contributions from his stranglehold over these lands until Ferdinand's debt to him was paid. This was controversial enough, but at the Munich meeting Ferdinand also promised to transfer Frederick's electoral title to his Wittelsbach cousin, thus demoting Frederick, the Elector Palatine, to a mere prince in his lands, or those lands he was allowed to keep.

The implications for such a treaty were astounding – Ferdinand was essentially reorganising the makeup of the Electoral College behind the back of the majority of its members, without their consent, and definitely without proper process. It is possible to explain Ferdinand's actions by the desperation of his position, not to mention by Maximillian's ambition, as the Duke fully appreciated the extent to which he had his Emperor trapped. The Bohemian revolt would never be defeated if Ferdinand could not harness the power of his allies, and where these allies were not willing to march for free, they had to be compelled. In return for these controversial promises, Maximillian...

> ...has been requested for the common good of all of us to take over full command of the Catholic defences to which the high Catholic estates of the Empire, His Imperial Majesty, his dynasty, and the endangered lands have been constrained for their own preservation to agree.

The terms of the Treaty of Munich detail exactly how extensive Maximillian's control over the Habsburg war effort was to be:

> His Grace, the Duke of Bavaria, is granted free and absolute direction over the Catholic constitutional and defence system, including recruitment and movement of the troops, whom he will lead in the name of the Almighty for the common good. [Maximillian of Bavaria] regardless of the difficulty of this business, danger and problems, is prepared to commit his own person, his worthy house, land and subjects, and is also prepared to give further proof of his affection and support to His Imperial Majesty, His Royal Highness in Spain and the entire praiseworthy House of Austria to defend the Catholic religion and its adherents amongst the Imperial estates, and to accept the associated heavy burdens, dangers and other consequences and to put the common good above all private interest, and to accept the free and absolute directorship of the Catholic defence system that is entrusted to him, along with the recruitment and leadership of the soldiers in the name of the Almighty, but on the following express condition, that this is to begin once His Grace has actually completed the collection of the necessary money, soldiers and other requirements.

For as long as the Duke of Bavaria needed it, it was declared that Maximillian should have 'the full support with money and troops of all the Catholic Estates as well as that of His Imperial Highness, and that this aid in money in troops will be forthcoming as long as His Grace...deems necessary.' Maximillian was to direct these forces against the enemies of the Habsburgs for as long as it took to eradicate them. However, since by acting, the Duke of Bavaria invited reprisals from the enemies of the Habsburgs – who now became his enemies – the Treaty provided for Maximillian's compensation. 'Therefore', the Treaty reads, 'and particularly because His Grace is likely to contribute well in excess of what is needed for the defence system', Ferdinand and his Spanish allies were obliged:

> ...to refund all the expenses incurred through the military constitution and soldiery (excluding the cost of his own territorial defence militia) provided as assistance to His Majesty, or retained in his own lands according to the circumstances to aid His Majesty...To this end, as much of the Austrian lands are to be pawned to His Grace until the debts are settled.

Further startling stipulations followed; if Maximillian lost Bavarian land and was unable to get it back, he would be compensated by Austrian lands which would be ceded to his person. In addition, if Maximillian managed to seize any lands from the enemy party, these lands could be occupied by him and pillaged for contributions and taxes for the sake of his war effort, and he would not have to return them until these expenses had been paid.[55]

Upon making this deal, and establishing this contract with the Duke of Bavaria, Ferdinand proceeded to Vienna, which was under a shadow of gloom and doom as the Transylvanian-Bohemian army approached, while Maximillian moved to meet with the Catholic League and inform them of their newly assigned task. In time, Maximillian would raise an army of twenty-five thousand men under the auspices of the Catholic League, with its sole purpose being the destruction of Ferdinand's enemies, and the aggrandisement of Maximillian's property portfolio. Illegal and cynical though the Treaty of Munich was, it proved a masterstroke for Ferdinand, who at least had an ace up his sleeve which could be used against the rebellious Bohemians. Before he could reap the fruits of these deals though, the Emperor would have to survive yet another siege.

On 21 November, the Bohemian rebels finally crossed the Danube upstream from Vienna and approached it from the east alongside Bethlen Gabor's forces. As the coalition force moved, news was received that three thousand soldiers commanded by the Lower Austrian estates had cut off Ferdinand's line of retreat from Vienna. The Emperor – who had endured a perilous journey to return to his capital from Munich the month before – was now truly trapped, but the situation was not as grave as it appeared on paper. The approaching horde of enemies possessed no artillery and would thus have to starve out the city. However, the inhabitants had stockpiled enough food to last several months, and the surrounding countryside had been ignited to prevent any opportunities for foraging.

These practical difficulties were exacerbated by the heavy rains, which dampened the morale of the forty-two thousand soldiers that engaged in a loose siege of Vienna. Turkish auxiliaries had been promised by the Grand Vizier, but had not arrived, which added to the mutual distrust between the Hungarians and the Bohemians. Then, disease began to rip through the army, reducing effective numbers by a considerable amount. Barely a week after they had crossed the Danube, on 27 November Bethlen Gabor received word that his lands had been invaded by a Polish army, and less than a week later in early December, the Hungarian forces had moved off, followed by the Bohemians. Ferdinand had survived again, and yet again, he had leaned heavily on his allies – in this case the friendly, but officially neutral King of Poland, his brother in law.

Sigismund III of the House of Vasa was more interested in reclaiming his Swedish birth right than in fully committing his Kingdom to the Thirty

Years War. In any event, it is hard to say whether he would have been allowed to intervene by the Commonwealth's nobility even if he had wanted to. Yet, notwithstanding these issues, or Sigismund's potential bitterness at Ferdinand's inaction during his own troubles in 1617-18, as Livonia was invaded, the King of Poland did recognise that aiding the Emperor was an important investment. Rather than invade Bohemia, Sigismund authorised his commanders to harness the Cossacks – the wilder auxiliary cavalry forces within the Polish army – with an invasion of Transylvania.

Four thousand Cossacks would march into Bethlen Gabor's lands, accompanied by three thousand more Cossacks under Gabor's Hungarian rival. Fortunately for the Prince of Transylvania, much had been done in the previous months to consolidate his position in Hungary, and the challenger found few supporters, being forced to retreat by early December, just as Bethlen marched towards him, unaware that the danger had largely passed. Unable to discern for the moment how serious the situation was, Bethlen approved the Hungarian diet's suggestion to search for a truce with Ferdinand. By mid-January 1620, Ferdinand's Hungarian problem would be solved, for the moment.[56]

Ferdinand got his house in order in good time, and by the end of 1619 was in a much better strategic position than he had been at the beginning of the year. Just as other figures were on the move though, so too was the source of the Emperor's angst – the Elector Palatine. Frederick had begun his journey to his new Kingdom in early October, making first for the Upper Palatinate, which bordered the lands of his enemies as well as his friends. It was while he rested in Amberg, the capital of the Upper Palatinate, that Frederick was confronted by Ferdinand's emissary, who urged him to take part in an Imperial Diet and rescind his acceptance of the Bohemian Crown. By this point, Ferdinand had already met with Maximillian of Bavaria and made the necessary deals in the Treaty of Munich. In any case, Frederick rebuffed the plea, but determined to send an open letter to the relevant courts of Europe which would explain his actions, much like the Bohemians themselves had done in their *Apologia*, but this would not be completed until early November.

Frederick was crowned King of Bohemia in a sumptuous ceremony in Prague on 4 November 1619. His reign was destined to last one year and four days, but there was no guarantee that such an ignoble fate awaited him, or that the demeaning moniker 'the Winter King' would soon be his. Wine flowed in the streets, and coins were thrown liberally to the crowds just as the occasion demanded. If the regime was wafer thin, then it projected a strong, durable veneer which had many in Prague fooled. Three days after Frederick's coronation, his wife Elizabeth was then crowned Queen of Bohemia – this time wine and bread, rather than coins, were issued to the excitable public. Within less than two months, Frederick had gone from scheming Elector to the Emperor's worst enemy and most dangerous threat. He had also become a King, and his wife had become a Queen. Had the circumstances not been so weighted, it would have been quite an achievement to stand as Bohemia's King at just 23 years of age. As Frederick well understood though, the coronation was only half the battle – the war for Bohemia and perhaps for his very existence, was just beginning.

Underneath the pomp, the political considerations of Frederick's decision were already making themselves felt. While Ferdinand, by this point, had not yet rid himself of the threat outside Vienna, by the first week of November 1619 Frederick had been given good reason to become somewhat concerned. He may have been the best-connected Protestant prince, but these connections, much to the dismay of Frederick and Christian of Anhalt, had not borne fruit. The Dutch, whom Frederick was connected to via his mother, could not countenance total support and investment in the Elector Palatine's cause, because they not only expected to resume the war with Spain soon, they also had their own domestic problems to deal with. Dutch strategists were also concerned at Frederick's abandoning of the Rhine Palatinate, which left open a critically important flank to the south that Spanish troops, on their way to attack the Netherlands, could certainly pour through.[57]

The Evangelical Union, another potential supporter, had made its divisions clear, if not its position, in the previous months. Opposing the Emperor was a step too far for many, though they did declare themselves ready to defend against the Catholic League if circumstances required.[58] That left the French, who were torn between Catholic and anti-Habsburg commitments, and the English, where King James had done much to both clarify his distaste for his son in law's actions, and to urge caution. As early as January 1619 James had offered to mediate the Bohemian dispute, and he had been enraged when he learned that Frederick had – without waiting for his reply to a request for advice – accepted the Bohemian crown.

With his allies doubtful and his enemies still besieged, Frederick worked to explain his position to those that would listen. An open letter was the solution and had the potential to inspire potential allies to join his cause, if received with an open mind. Frederick knew what he was asking of those that agreed to join his cause, and from his limited experience in the last few months, he had already seen first-hand just how hesitant and fearful others were to enter into direct, open opposition to the Habsburg family. Frederick was asking these apprehensive powers to risk the ruin of their lands for the sake of a cause which must have seemed far removed from their daily lives. It was therefore necessary that Frederick cast the revolt in just terms, and presented his acceptance of the Bohemian Crown as a means of protecting righteous Bohemians against the unjustified and unconstitutional wrath of the Habsburgs.

Frederick explained how the 'hotheads', were to blame, for they 'preferred to push things to extremes and risk all, rather than abandon their deep-rooted intention of returning everything under the spiritual domination of the Pope and the secular domination of a foreign power.' This was a barely veiled reference to the insidious and disruptive power of the Jesuits, a common theme of the open letter. Frederick continued to note that:

> We can easily see the burden, worry, effort, work and danger during the current persistent warfare and ruined lands that must arise for us, alongside many other considerations. We also do not doubt that sensible people will agree that to accept the offer of a kingdom in such a state demands a far stronger resolution than to refuse a peaceable kingdom, and for this reason many have been praised in the history books. We testify again with a clear conscience that if we had seen the means or certainty that, by repudiating the crown, we might have ended this unholy war, obtained the noble peace and thus adequately secured the entire Roman Empire, then all the goods and honour in the world would not have swayed us, but we would have not only immediately refused the offer of the Bohemian crown, but have done our utmost to this end.

Any criticisms levelled at Frederick's decision-making were thus answered – he had had no choice but to accept, since war would have followed even if the Crown had been refused. If an opportunity for peace had arisen, the Elector Palatine would have been the first individual to harness it. Frederick also elaborated on this idea, by reasoning that if the Bohemian crown had been refused, 'then presumably we would have been blamed, especially by the adherents of the Evangelical religion, for all the subsequent bloodshed and destruction of lands.' If Frederick had not answered the Bohemians' call, then regardless of what they said, the Bohemians would be crushed, and Protestants across the Empire would be next. Again, Frederick looked to the Jesuits as the culprits, without explicitly mentioning them:

> For the aforementioned restless people [Jesuits] have constantly admonished and instigated them [Catholics] to act like this, even using published writings, and have also stated that the little innocents should not be spared, no not even their own children, noble families or land and people. These and various similar threats have been heard constantly.

In addition to the militant Catholic Habsburg Jesuit threat, there was another danger which would arise if Bohemia was seized by a foreign power, and became 'detached from the Holy Empire of the German Nation', a reference to the potential of the Turks to become actively involved in the revolt, and seize Bohemia for themselves. Frederick wrapped up his letter with an appeal to the unity and commonality of Christendom against malignant forces, declaring the intention 'to cultivate and maintain the goodwill, friendship, correspondence and trust of all Christian potentates, electors and estates and principalities', followed by a request for 'friendliness, graciousness and good intentions that they would spring to our aid with both word and deed against all those who, with vile intentions, would set upon us or our kingdom and lands with hostile force.'[59]

Frederick neither knew nor imagined what was in store for his Palatinate or Bohemia. At this early stage, with the Bohemian Crown freshly resting on his head, a sense of optimism may well have crowned his actions and correspondence in spite of events taking place in Hungary, outside Vienna, or within the courts of Europe. Although he could not have known it yet, with some exceptions, Frederick was on his own, and soon he would be faced with insurmountable odds, terrible losses and bitter betrayals. Indeed, this Winter King could not have known that his reign was to last barely a year; for Frederick V, the Elector Palatine though, this was to be the longest, coldest and darkest season of winter he had ever experienced in his young life.

Chapter 8 Notes

[1]Quoted in Wilson, *Sourcebook*, p. 54.
[2]Davies, *Spain in Decline*, p. 1.
[3]Quoted in Purcell, *Winter King*, p. 79.
[4]Quoted in Peter H. Wilson, *Sourcebook*, p. 38.
[5]Quoted in *Ibid*, pp. 39-40.
[6]Peter H. Wilson, *Europe's Tragedy*, pp. 270-273.
[7]Quoted in Peter H. Wilson, *Sourcebook*, pp. 40-41.
[8]Peter H. Wilson, *Europe's Tragedy*, p. 274.
[9]*Ibid*, p. 273.
[10]C. V. Wedgewood, *Thirty Years War*, pp. 80-82.
[11]Wedgewood, *Thirty Years War*, p. 73.
[12]Quoted in Andrew Wheatcroft, *The Habsburgs*, p. 178.
[13]C. V. Wedgewood, *Thirty Years War*, pp. 89-90.
[14]urteenthese scenes are recorded in Richard Bassett, *For God and Kaiser*, pp. 54-57.
[15]*Ibid*, p. 57.
[16]Brennan Pursell, *The Winter King*, p. 47.
[17]Peter H. Wilson, *Europe's Tragedy*, pp. 274-275.
[18]*Ibid*, p. 447.
[19]Geoffrey Parker, *Europe in Crisis*, pp. 164-165.
[20]See Geoffrey Parker, *Thirty Years War*, pp. 44-45.
[21]John Paget, *Hungary and Transylvania, with Remarks on their Condition, Social, Political and Economical* Vol. II (John Murray; London, 1839), pp. 264-266. Access provided with thanks to Google Books.
[22]Geoffrey Parker, *Europe in Crisis*, pp. 162-164.
[23]Quoted in Geoffrey Parker, *Europe in Crisis*, p. 163.
[24]Roy E. Schreiber, 'The First Carlisle Sir James Hay, First Earl of Carlisle as Courtier, Diplomat and Entrepreneur, 1580-1636', *Transactions of the American Philosophical Society*, Vol. 74, No. 7 (1984), pp. 1-202; p. 23.
[25]Brennan Pursell, *The Winter King*, p. 21.
[26]See C. V. Wedgewood, *Thirty Years War*, pp. 84-85.
[27]*Ibid*, p. 95.
[28]Roy E. Schreiber, 'The First Carlisle Sir James Hay', p. 23.
[29]Geoffrey Parker, *Europe in Crisis*, p. 163.
[30]Brennan Pursell, *The Winter King*, pp. 48-49.
[31]*Ibid*, pp. 49-50.
[32]Wedgewood, *Thirty Years War*, p. 84.
[33]Pursell, *The Winter King*, p. 50.
[34]See Brennan Pursell, *The Winter King*, pp. 50-53.
[35]Pursell, *The Winter King*, provides the most complete and detailed account of Frederick's failed efforts to secure an imperial candidate other than Ferdinand, see pp. 65-73.
[36]Brennan Pursell, *The Winter King*, p. 76.
[37]Wedgewood, *Thirty Years War*, p. 97.
[38]Pursell, *The Winter King*, p. 77.
[39]Quoted in Geoffrey Parker, *Thirty Years War*, p. 47.
[40]*Ibid*, p. 47.
[41]See Geoffrey Parker, *Europe in Crisis*, pp. 163-164.
[42]Friedrich Schiller, *History of the Thirty Years War* – translated from German by Rev. A. J. W. Morrison, MA (Harper and Brothers Publishers; New York, 1861), p. 72. Digitised by Google Books with thanks.
[43]Pursell, *The Winter King*, p. 79.
[44]Geoffrey Parker, *Europe in Crisis*, p. 164.
[45]Wedgewood, *Thirty Years War*, p. 82.
[46]Pursell, *The Winter King*, p. 78.
[47]Robert Zaller, '"Interest of State": James I and the Palatinate', *Albion: A Quarterly Journal Concerned with British Studies*, Vol. 6, No. 2(Summer, 1974), pp. 144-175; p. 146.
[48]Pursell, *The Winter King*, pp. 80-81.

[49]See Brennan Pursell, *The Winter King*, pp. 66-67.

[50]*Ibid*, p. 69.

[51]*Ibid*, p. 73.

[52]Geoffrey Parker, *Europe in Crisis*, p. 166.

[53]Peter H. Wilson, *Europe's Tragedy*, p. 290.

[54]See *Ibid*, pp. 294-295.

[55]Extracts quoted from Peter H. Wilson, *Sourcebook*, pp. 56-58.

[56]Peter H. Wilson, *Europe's Tragedy*, pp. 291-293.

[57]C. V. Wedgewood, *Thirty Years War*, pp. 99-100.

[58]Geoffrey Parker, *Thirty Years War*, p. 53.

[59]Extracts from Frederick's open letter are quoted from Peter H. Wilson, *Sourcebook*, pp. 47-52.

Cavalry skirmish (Pieter Snayer)

The Battle of Stadtlohn

CHAPTER NINE
"Habsburgs Triumphant"

ONE
Winter is Coming

It is all too easy to view Frederick's tenure as King of Bohemia as one of inevitable and impending doom. This, indeed, is the narrative presented to us by Wedgewood, who wasted no opportunity to comment bitingly on Frederick, a man who was 'no leader; indeed he was of so blank a personality as to defy all attempts to make him one.'[1] Not only was their new king worse than useless, his advisors and accomplices acted with the utmost ignorance and stupidity, apparently unaware of Bohemia's complexities, and cultural taboos. 'Seldom can such innocent and well-intentioned rulers have made themselves more readily disliked', Wedgewood opined, and continued:

> In Bohemia he scandalised his courtiers and advisors by receiving them always bare-headed, but turning to Anhalt for the answer to every question, by allowing his hand to be kissed far too often, by giving precedence to the Queen in public and letting her appear in dresses which no respectable Bohemian husband would have permitted to his wife.

Frederick's ignorance, apparently, knew no limits; he suggested serfdom should be abolished, thus alienating the lords; he made noise about improving Prague's morality, thus alienating the common people, and he tore down several iconographic displays, thus alienating the spiritual folk. Into mistake after mistake the new king appeared to blunder, displaying 'even less of his usual intelligence', with no rhyme or reason as to his policy, before making a tone-deaf request that the Bohemians should approve of his son's succession by hereditary right.[2] Was there any truth to these accusations? Could Frederick do anything right?

In actual fact, Frederick was nowhere near so foolish or pathetic in his governance of this new kingdom. In one of his first acts as king, he paid a visit to a small community of Anabaptists in the Moravian town of Brunn. Anabaptists were an isolated and loathed sect of Christianity in the early seventeenth century,[3] but Frederick's visit to their community, his tolerant observation of their customs and his warm interactions with their leaders spoke volumes about the kind of king he intended to be. In return the Anabaptists presented the new King and Queen with gifts of fur gloves, an iron bedstead and some richly decorated knives. In a letter Frederick wrote to his wife, he commented not at all on their beliefs or religious practices, but instead upon the welcome he had received, and he added that if these Anabaptists ever visited Prague 'he would visit them quite often.' Frederick had no reason to lie in this letter to his wife; he could have ridiculed them or declared his intention to remove their sect from the country, as Ferdinand had long sought to do, but instead he ignored their religious differences, and focused on the matter at hand – crafting his regime.[4]

It would be wrong to assume that Frederick's cause was doomed from the start. At the time of accepting the Bohemian crown, it certainly appeared possible not only that Ferdinand could be forced to compromise, but also that, following this capitulation, other powers would rush to aid Frederick. It was much easier to defend a country like Bohemia than it was to have to seize it, especially when Frederick remained under the impression that Ferdinand had barely enough men to defend Vienna, let alone launch an expeditionary force into Bohemia. The citizens of Prague would certainly be expected to defend heartily against any semblance of a Habsburg takeover – they would have known, of course, that Ferdinand would offer them no mercies if he retook his crown and the capital with it. This was not to say that, in late 1619, Frederick's cause appeared desperate, rather, it would be more accurate to judge the new regime as stable, relatively secure and defensible, but dependent upon a few factors which, in the end, turned out to be far less reliable than Frederick had hoped.

The first of these was the assumption that the Bohemian estates, having elected Frederick as their king, would now help and support him in his quest to defend the crown from its enemies. The second assumption was that his allies meant what they said, and that they would move to aid him once they possessed what he needed. Further assumptions tie in with these – Elizabeth as the daughter of King James of Britain assumed that her father would never allow the Habsburgs to overrun the Palatinate, even if he was not much bothered about the fate of Bohemia. To permit Frederick's ancestral lands to come under attack would have surely brought dishonour upon the King, for failing to defend his family or their interests.

Subsequent pleas, verging on desperate and incredulous, from the court of the Winter King and Queen, testified to the sad fact that King James was wholly committed to his policy of mediation, and more broadly, to positioning England as the moderating force of a continent brimming with dynastic and religious quarrels. One of the primary means by which James believed such ends could be achieved was through a Spanish marriage, where the future King Charles I would marry a daughter of King Philip III of Spain (see Chapter 6). This search for the Spanish match has come under justified criticism, as it hampered King James' ability to look outside the very narrow box which he had placed his foreign policy. Notwithstanding its shortcomings though, the King had bought into it and refused to be moved from it, and so the daughter and son-in-law were sacrificed in favour of the promises granted to the son and heir.

Europe's Protestants were not as animated as Frederick may have hoped, likely because Bohemia was viewed as a somewhat separate entity of the Empire, and because it had revolted several times before against Habsburg authority. To some of his Protestant peers, Frederick may have seemed like an opportunistic, foolishly daring potentate, who sought to take advantage of what was only the latest – though certainly the most severe – Bohemian revolt. By so acting, his recklessness endangered his religious peers and threatened to aggravate what was the tacitly accepted if contradictory peace achieved in 1555. As difficult as Frederick's efforts to mobilise Protestant support had been up to this point, they became progressively more so once Ferdinand capitalised upon the caution and concerns of the majority of the Empire's Protestant princes, and turned them against the Palatine cause. Indeed, in time, Ferdinand so outflanked Frederick's Protestant banner that the Palatine-Bohemian cause was forced to face down a mostly combined Catholic-Protestant confessional alliance, bound together by its determination to remove any dangers to the peace, as well as, it must be said, promises and appeals which Ferdinand had made to its members' self-interest.[5]

Further problems were discovered when Frederick attempted to acquire some kind of Dutch commitment. In the past, the Dutch had provided considerable sums of money and a not insignificant detachment of soldiers. By late 1619 though, the Dutch Republic was working through the inner struggles of its complex societal and religious issues, which resulted within a few years in the triumph of the House of Orange, but which in 1619 remained raw and unresolved. There was also the concern in the Netherlands, that as the deadline for expiration of the Twelve Years Truce approached – April 1621 – that the Spanish were bound to become more belligerent, and could be expected to seize strategically important crossings or towns in anticipation of the resumption of hostilities. To meet these challenges, it was imperative that the Dutch were not distracted, but also that they possessed some measure of military force which could be quickly applied in response.[6]

'Believe me that the Bohemian war will decide the fates of all of us, but especially yours, since you are the neighbours of the Czechs', remarked a Dutch agent in a letter to an envoy of the Evangelical Union in the summer of 1619. 'For the present we shall seek out all ways of bringing you help... though we have many difficulties to face'. Such difficulties had much to do with the religious turmoil underway in the Netherlands, where a Calvinist

Synod had been established to declare on questions of doctrine, and the letter continued:

> The Synod has indeed decreed the aid which reflects the general feelings of our Reformed Church, but…some of our clergy are resisting with great obstinacy and we have been forced to banish them, and to punish their rebellion when they not obey their authorities…All this is harmful to the Bohemian cause, which we would wish to further at all times.[7]

For their part, the Lutheran noblemen even of Bohemia itself were greatly disturbed by the pace of events. One particularly gloomy individual felt that his countrymen had betrayed their best qualities by behaving in such a desperate and provocative manner, and he believed that the display would only hasten the end of the freedoms which they had enjoyed:

> We have broken our oath and thrown respectable men, who came in the name of the king, out of the window; we did not give them time to pray, let alone defend themselves. We did not even want to listen to Emperor Matthias or King Ferdinand who still offered us peace, forgiveness, our rights and privileges as well as judicial resolution. We allied with the neighbouring lands in and outside the Empire; the Hungarians, the English, the Dutch, the Turks, the devil himself. We besieged Vienna and opened the entire German Empire to the Turks and Tartars as far as it was in our power…Whether we win or lose, our fate will be heavy. Those that have helped Frederick will stand in a long queue hungry for land and money at our expense, if we win. The anger of the much-maligned emperor will be upon us if we are defeated. What else can we expect? We have taken from the emperor that which belongs to him, and to God, and offered it to the Turks.[8]

Frederick had no choice, and would have selected no other option, other than tireless resistance. With this end in mind he sought to impress upon the Kingdom of Bohemia precisely how dependent upon his subjects their new king was, and how he relied upon his people in Bohemia, Moravia, Silesia and Lusatia to fulfil the pledges many had made in the past, and give what was needed for his and for their own security. In line with this aim, Frederick tried first to merge the Bohemian cause with that of the Evangelical Union; the previous extract from a Lutheran Bohemian nobleman should give a clue as to how well this appeal went. In late November 1619 at Nuremberg, Frederick sought to commit the Union and as many Protestant potentates as would join him as possible to the Bohemian cause, and in a fit of optimism, had even invited the King of Denmark to join in the discussion. If the attendance disappointed Frederick, then the pessimistic reception from much of the Union's members was a crippling blow.

This meeting marked the end of illusion for Frederick, as his former allies of the Union launched several justified attacks against him. Frederick had neglected to consult them when he had taken Union troops with him from Amberg in the Upper Palatinate, on his way to Bohemia. He had also diverted English subsidies meant for the Union into his new kingdom's treasury in Prague, and by these actions, left the Union terminally unprepared for any war which might occur. The Union now found its very solidarity undermined, as Frederick's actions had caused its members to splinter into more or less radical segments. To take the wind out of Frederick's sails further, the representatives insisted that the Elector Palatine was no longer in a position to defend the Union's interests, and thus, he must give up his position as commander in chief of the Evangelical Union, along with the monthly salary of six thousand florins which went with it. The best the Union's members would do was to issue a guarantee to Frederick that they would defend his Palatinate in the event of an attack from foreign powers.

The cherry on top of this bitter cake for Frederick then arrived – an envoy from the Emperor, who carried a message from Ferdinand which urged those assembled to disperse, and which also promised to respect the religious privileges of the Bohemians, since nothing was more important to Ferdinand than the urgent restoration of peace. Notwithstanding Ferdinand's scheming and dishonest behaviour in the past, or the fact that he had already made a deal with the Duke of Bavaria to partition the Elector Palatine's lands and transfer his Electoral title, Ferdinand's entreaties only served to undermine and divide the Evangelical Union even further. In contrast to the once divided Catholic League, it was now the Union that was beleaguered, under-supported and demoralised, while the resurgent League possessed a unity of purpose, a respected leader in Maximillian of Bavaria who could expect to be obeyed, and most importantly, a personal assurance from the Emperor himself that the League was now the Habsburgs' instrument within the Empire. Just as they did not know exactly what their Emperor had already done to them, the members of the Union also could not have known exactly how outgunned they already were, and the imbalance was only set to increase.[9]

With his Protestant support evaporating, over the period of December 1619 to March 1620 Frederick travelled through Bohemia on his royal progress. If the Evangelical Union was not to be moved, then perhaps Frederick could base his security and his strength upon the loyalty and adoration of the Bohemian people; in any case, such travels were an expected part of the king's duties. The Bohemian kingdom's federal nature meant that Moravia, Silesia and Lusatia all contained independent estates, customs and languages, which Frederick would have to traverse if he wished to win the loyalty of these subjects. In the recent history of the Bohemian revolt, the Bohemian rebels had discovered how difficult rallying the composite parts of the monarchy together under one banner had been – until they applied the necessary pressure, the other provinces had seemed perfectly willing to throw their lot in with the Habsburgs. The Confederation of late July 1619 simplified these matters, but Frederick was still required to venture to each of these provinces in turn, as though each province was its own realm.[10]

It is easy in a sense to view what followed as a kind of sham, as Frederick's attempts to bribe his new subjects into siding with him against Emperor Ferdinand. As Brennan Pursell quite reasonably pointed out though, if Frederick had not travelled in style and with expense, then this would have cast doubt on the regime's longevity, and few would have sided with him. Frederick had to see his subjects, and he had to be seen, so that they could put a face to the name which they had undoubtedly heard so much of. By ingratiating himself towards his subjects, Frederick was not engaging in dishonest behaviour; he genuinely cared for these people and their freedoms, and he genuinely feared for their futures if Ferdinand was victorious and implemented the victor's peace against them.[11]

After some marching, by early February 1620, Frederick was brought to Brunn in Moravia. Frederick confirmed the Moravian freedoms, and asked in return for the traditional gift, which was normally given to the new king, as well as a redoubling of recruitment – to call up every twentieth man. The Moravian Estates did resolve to give Frederick fifteen thousand Moravian Gulden, but would only be persuaded to recruit fifteen hundred militia for their country's defence, and even then only for six months. This was dispiriting for Frederick, but this turned to fear when it was learned that, not too far from the border, eight thousand Cossacks had poured into Upper Silesia, only a few miles from where the Elector Palatine was staying. Moving on the King of Poland's orders, with the express purpose of hampering Frederick's actions and aiding his brother in law, King Sigismund III of Poland showed himself willing to come to Ferdinand's aid, and may have done more had the Sejm not restricted his freedom of action.

Frederick watched the villages burn not far from his residence, as the Cossacks destroyed the areas they moved through with an unflinching sense of mission. By 13 February, Frederick was making his way towards the north of Moravia, and by 23 February, his progress took him into Breslau in Silesia. While in Breslau Frederick met with his new subjects, heard their grievances, confirmed their privileges, refused their request to expel their Jews, received their homage, and left the estates in Breslau to select their own government officials. Frederick also sought to mediate between the disconcerted Catholics who lived in Breslau, and who had been forced to give an oath of allegiance by the majority Protestant population. Frederick assured these Catholics that he had no interest in eradicating their religious creed, and that he wanted merely to ensure that his regime would not be undermined by those few Catholics who engaged in underhanded politics and plotting.

Frederick also made significant efforts to paper over the cracks between Lutherans and Calvinists, a cause dear to him considering his Anglican wife and Calvinist upbringing. True to his character, Frederick proved a tolerant and warm host, and refrained from forcing any Calvinist teachings upon the subjects he came across. It is true that he offered the Calvinists of Breslau space in the great hall of his royal castle for their church services, but this was because these citizens had no such place of their own to worship. Still, Frederick could not heal the divide, and as late as April 1620, these services were being disrupted by angry Lutheran residents of the city. By that time, Frederick had already been forced to cut short his progress, cancelling a trip to Lusatia where a meeting with John George of Saxony, a fellow Protestant Elector, had been hoped for. By 14 March 1620, Frederick was back in Prague, ready and willing to direct the war effort against what turned out to be a swirling morass of enemies. Ferdinand's camp had evidently grown since Frederick had left on his progress, and if he was not yet aware, then it soon became clear that the scales had tipped determinedly against the Elector Palatine.[12]

The progress can seem like the final desperate act of a fleeting regime, but it should be said that most of Frederick's subjects were happy to see their new Protestant King, and they told him so. Frederick received plenty of gifts, had important conversations with eager nobles, spent time in many manor houses, admired the countryside and certainly partook in the bountiful hunting which was on offer. Frederick also learned how difficult it was to be separated from his wife for nearly four months; he even had to urge her not to get too down during his absence. Writing from Brunn in early February, Frederick had said to Elizabeth:

> I beg you not to let go of yourself, because you do yourself harm and offend God to grieve without reason. In the end one must resolve to want what God wants, and each must follow what he is called to do.[13]

Returning to Prague in mid-March, Frederick enjoyed a joyous reunion with his wife, and on the last day of March the couple celebrated the baptism of their fourth child and third son, Ruprecht. It was of no small coincidence that the last Holy Roman Emperor of Palatine Wittelsbach stock had also been called Ruprecht. This did not necessarily mean Frederick intended to place his son on the Imperial throne, but it did indicate that he planned for a changing of the guard at the top, and that the Palatine family had more than enough historical and dynastic clout to make this change happen. As it happened, rather than usurping the Habsburgs' glory in any sense, Prince Ruprecht would become known to posterity as Prince Rupert of the Rhine, a renowned commander and admiral in English royal service during the Civil War and thereafter during the Restoration Era.

To secure the bright future for his family and Bohemia which he so desired, in April 1620 Frederick managed to secure approval from the Bohemian estates to make his son, Frederick Henry his successor to the Bohemian throne. The Bohemian Kingdom had thus definitively moved from the Habsburg to the Wittelsbach dynasty, yet by this point, Frederick had already been bombarded with bad news, in addition to exhortations from the Empire's princes to abdicate the Bohemian throne and beg Ferdinand's mercy and forgiveness. Much like the Bohemians though, by April 1620, Frederick could not go back. He had promised all the Bohemians their privileges and could not abandon them now, nor could he leave this kingdom after securing its crown for his son and heir, potentially for good.

This advantageous position was worth fighting for, Frederick believed, and for the last few months he had not been forced to fight for it all that much. The Habsburgs, indeed, had been building up their strength, just as Frederick's was sapped and reduced by horrified allies and jealous subjects. Contrary to his epithet, Frederick was still the King of Bohemia even though Winter had ended. While the season had come to end though, a different kind of winter – a reckoning – was still forthcoming. In March 1620, a sweeping representation of the Empire's Catholic and Protestant princes had met with Emperor Ferdinand at the city of Muhlhausen. While there, the electors Mainz, Cologne, Trier, Saxony and Ferdinand – who had ignored the rebels' actions was still proclaimed King of Bohemia – were joined by the Duke of Bavaria and other minor princes, and Brandenburg sent a representative. It was at Muhlhausen that one of the most important steps was taken towards an escalation of the conflict.

If Frederick would not relinquish the Bohemian crown by 1 June 1620, the Emperor Ferdinand resolved to issue the Imperial Ban against him, meaning that the Elector Palatine's lands and those of his allies would be forfeit. Of course, Ferdinand did not expect Frederick to comply – if he had, then this would have seriously complicated the pledges he had made in secret to Maximillian of Bavaria, the man charged with engineering the downfall of his Wittelsbach cousin, in the name of the greater good of the Empire and, conveniently, his dynasty's position. The fix was in, and in spite of these public warnings, Ferdinand was inherently incapable of making peace with the Elector Palatine, thanks to agreements and pledges made behind closed doors. Frederick could decry the unconstitutionality of Ferdinand's behaviour, and note that an Electoral College was required to pass the Imperial Ban – Ferdinand was not empowered simply to request support for the venture from his princely pets and creditors. Proper judicial processes and traditional protocols were required, yet as Frederick was beginning to learn, Imperial law mattered less than the powers that interpreted it.

The omens were already grave that Frederick's downfall had been planned for; on top of everything else, the Spanish had raised an army of more than twenty thousand men, and had it poised, it was said, to overrun the Lower Palatinate along the Rhine. While the Spanish moved, Maximillian of Bavaria, the Catholic League and even the Elector of Saxony were rumoured to have settled their accounts with the Emperor.[14] With his allies silent and absent, and his enemies numerous and circling, the summer of 1620 looked to be a long one for the Winter King. Frederick attempted to gather the pieces on the board which were under his control, and to reign as Bohemia's king as best as he could, however long this reign was destined to last.

TWO
Winter is Here

Noble dear cousin and elector! To continue our well-intentioned and highly necessary correspondence about the disorder, unrest and disobedience in Bohemia and subsequently in the Kingdom of Hungary, we do not want to conceal from you that Bethlen Gabor and Count Thurn, together with their infantry and cavalry, advanced again towards the capital city Vienna over the last few weeks and immediately, the day after our return from our duchy of Styria, having robbed, plundered, burned, ransomed the poor subjects without respect to their person on both sides of the Danube, similarly exercised such great mischief and un-Christian tyranny that has scarcely been heard of. A few days ago the enemy began his retreat, but not before the Hungarians had devastated, plundered and burned everything where they had been quartered and (it is said), stripped the people to their last threads, ruined, cut them down and dragged a great number of them away as prisoners, subjected them to unheard of torture to find money and property, dragged away numerous young lads of twelve to sixteen years old, and so ill-treated pregnant women and other women, that many of them were found dead everywhere on the roads. They pulled ropes around the men's necks so tight that their eyes popped out of their heads. Indeed, this enemy has behaved so terribly everywhere, that one can almost not remember whether such tyranny was ever heard of from the Turks. By such means and with such allies Count Thurn thinks he can save Evangelical liberty.[15]

These were the words of Emperor Ferdinand II, written on 5 December 1619 in a letter to the Elector of Saxony John George. As the Holy Roman Empire's foremost Protestant potentate, John George was trapped between a rock and a hard place with Frederick's acceptance of the Bohemian crown. Concerned for the interests and liberties of the Empire's Protestants, John George was also anxious to ensure that a religious war did not erupt, and he seemed to believe that by following the more cautious path, he could save his lands and countrymen from its worst excesses. This caution and deference to Imperial authority were traits ingrained in John George's character, but they were glaringly absent in his ancestors. In the previous century, during the run up to the 1555 Peace of Augsburg and the conflict known as the Schmakaldic War, the Electors of Saxony played a pivotal role in the fight for Protestant Germans, against the Catholic Habsburg opposition.[16]

Since the hammering of Luther's theses to the church door, the Empire had been set alight with religious divisions. In some portions of Germany, the Netherlands and England, the Reformed faith spread and adopted different forms,[17] and Luther's teachings had an important impact on Bohemia's religious development as well.[18] Frederick III of Saxony was one such ancestor of John George's, who sided quickly with Luther, supporting and defending him against Habsburg attacks. Frederick III, known to most as Frederick the Wise, died in 1525, with much of his country still under the influence of Catholicism. The Electoral title passed to his brother John, and for the next few years, John of Saxony was to transform this Electorate by fulfilling Luther's vision for a new church and solidifying the break with Rome.

According to the German historian Leopold von Ranke, John of Saxony was 'full of that moral earnestness which gives weight and dignity to simplicity of character', adding that he was:

> ...by nature, retiring, peaceful, unpretending; but he was raised to such a pitch of resolution and energy by the greatness of his purposes, that he showed himself fully equal to their accomplishment. When justice and religion were on his side, he knew not hesitation...we know of no prince to whom a larger portion of the merit of the establishment of the protestant church can justly be ascribed.[19]

John of Saxony effectively recast Saxony as the Protestant bulwark of the Empire, in the process presenting Saxon resistance and Protestant resistance to the Emperor Charles V as a divinely ordained quest. Saxony's place in this quest for resistance against the Emperor's mission to return all Germans to the Catholic Church changed as Martin Luther's views on violence and opposition changed with them.[20] John of Saxony was highly active during the Diet of Augsburg, which established the primary confession of the Lutheran creed under the Augsburg Confession in June 1530.[21] In 1532, having helped to establish Lutheranism's main principles and clearly distinguishing their faith from the predominant Catholic creed, John of Saxony died, and was succeeded by his son John Frederick.

Several years later in 1546, religious war broke out in the Empire, with the eruption of conflict between Emperor Charles V and the Schmalkaldic League – a union of Protestant German princes bound together in the name of their religious liberties. Arguably the most important leader of this League was the Elector of Saxony, John Frederick. The war itself did not last long, but its impact, and the opportunities it provided for foreign powers to get involved,[22] were both considerable. As Protestant militias poured into Habsburg or majority Catholic lands, calls went out for Protestant preachers to follow the soldiers, and to convert one's fellow German to the reformed faith. Protestants councillors believed that this conversion process complemented the war effort against the Emperor, and it was emphasised that true believers must...

...first and foremost consider God's word and honour...and let God's word be preached...Such a thing should not be delayed until after the war, for if one undertakes the Christian work of improving the corrupted churches of these poor subjects now, God will grant us victory more quickly and allow the newly won Christians to remain with us.[23]

As we said, the war would not last long in spite of these ambitious goals. In April 1547, during arguably the most important pitched battle of the sixteenth century, the Protestant princes of the Schmalkaldic League were effectively destroyed at Muhlberg. Following this triumph, Emperor Charles V issued the Augsburg Interim, as one historian noted:

The Interim, issued at the command of Emperor Charles V, was meant to bring the Protestants one step closer to Catholic orthodoxy: It combines a Lutheran-influenced doctrine of justification with a Catholic order of liturgy and justifies this manoeuvre by appealing to the unity of the Empire.[24]

However, while the Augsburg Interim was important, and is seen by some as a stepping stone towards the more famous Peace of Augsburg in 1555, which granted parity to the two creeds, another aspect of this story deserves emphasis for the sake of our narrative.[25] During the Battle of Muhlberg, John Frederick of Saxony was captured, after his forces were destroyed. Slashed across the face and imprisoned at Charles V's orders, John Frederick, as one of the most renowned leaders of anti-Habsburg, Protestant opposition, was forced to sign the Capitulation of Wittenberg, whereby he abdicated as Elector of Saxony, and, on the Emperor's instruction, his lands were passed to his cousin, Maurice. This transferral of lands and title from one Elector to his cousin, at a Habsburg Emperor's orders, was to receive its eerily similar encore in the early phase of the Thirty Years War.[26]

In spring 1620, Frederick V, the Elector Palatine, could not have known that this fate awaited him, and he would never sign any equivalent of the capitulation which John Frederick signed. Yet, thanks to a secret agreement between the Emperor Ferdinand II and Maximillian, Duke of Bavaria, this transfer would take place. Frederick would have his lands – the Upper Palatinate – pried from his hands and merged into Bavaria's Duchy. In addition, in perhaps the most striking parallel of all, Frederick V would see his Electoral title be transferred to Maximillian of Bavaria, a man who was, like Maurice of Saxony had been to John Frederick, his cousin.

It is interesting to discern the replacement of the Saxon House of Wettin by the Palatine House of Wittelsbach as the most important Protestant opposing force in the late sixteenth century. The behaviour of Charles V when dealing with his Protestant princely subjects was upheld as evidence of his ambition to tear asunder all that Luther had achieved; in the minds of the Palatine court in 1620, the current Emperor Ferdinand II was not much better. Curiously detached from this latest threat to Protestant durability and the continuance of Luther's work was the Saxon Elector, who ancestors had fought tooth and nail against the Emperor. Surely, after all those courageous and noble Electors of Saxony had been through, John George would strive to emulate their example? It was to Frederick's dismay that John George did not take up this mantle, since he commanded great respect within the more moderate Lutheran circles of Germany. In addition, it was to Frederick's utter disgust and bitterness that, far from remaining aloof, John George of Saxony disgraced his ancestors by making a deal with the Emperor and invading the Kingdom of Bohemia out of naked self-interest.

John George was one of the Thirty Years War's most fascinating characters, because he was one of the few individuals to live through its entire duration. From 1611 to 1656, John George ruled over Saxony from its capital in Dresden, and was forced to make some difficult decisions, as the fortunes of war changed, and Saxony's allies changed with them. While his decisions – to seize the province of Lusatia following a deal with Emperor Ferdinand; to join the Swedish invaders when his lands were placed under threat; to re-join the Habsburg camp once the Swedes had been routed – stick out as somewhat ignoble and opportunistic, it was his very detachment that distinguished this Elector.

John George of Saxony was lazy, a passionate hunter, good humoured and, perhaps most infamously of all, a very heavy drinker. His elder brother Christian II had ruled Saxony for years twenty years, but his health had deteriorated as the size of his beer belly increased. Once, when taking part in a tournament and clad in full armour, Christian dismounted from his horse and, since it was the height of summer, took a long drink of cold beer to cool himself down. It was following this act that Christian was struck by a massive heart attack, and he died soon afterwards. He was just 28 years old. With his elder brother dead, the younger Saxon prince would have to replace him, and so John George took up his brother's titles and responsibilities in 1611. When he assumed his inheritance, there was little indication that John George's health or habits would grant him a better fate, yet, he would rule as Elector of Saxony for forty-five years, during the most important period of that Electorate's life cycle since the religious wars of the previous century.[27]

Wedgewood tells us that John George was a 'blond, broad, square faced man with a florid complexion...he wore his beard in the native fashion, clipped off his hair and understood not a word of French.' Wedgewood, too, lampooned John George for his laziness and idleness during these years, not to mention his drunkenness which, although not a chronic problem, was still enough to arouse remarks from foreign dignitaries; 'he began to be somewhat heated with wine', said one, 'he seemed to me to be very drunk' said another.[28] This, of course, made diplomacy difficult, and John George largely deferred to his council, when he was not listening to the advice of his passionately anti-Calvinist confessor, who had been nicknamed the 'Saxon Pope' and 'New Judas' by Calvinists in return.[29]

In a change of pace, the historian Friedrich Schiller attempted to paint John George's action in a more positive light, by blaming the Emperor's false promises and scheming for ruining the Elector's reputation. Schiller wrote:

> His contemporaries accused him of forsaking the Protestant cause in the very midst of the storm; of preferring the aggrandisement of his house to the emancipation of his country; of exposing the whole Evangelical or Lutheran church of Germany to ruin, rather than raise an arm in defence of the Reformed or Calvinists; of injuring the common cause by his suspicious friendship more seriously than the open enmity of its avowed opponents. But it would have been well if his accusers had imitated the wise policy of the elector. If, despite of the prudent policy, the Saxon, like all others, groaned at the cruelties which marked the emperor's progress; if all Germany was a witness how Ferdinand deceived his confederates and trifled with his engagements; if even the elector himself at last perceived this – the more shame to the emperor who could so basely betray such implicit confidence.[30]

Yet, it would be wrong to absolve John George for what followed, since he was very much complicit in what happened next. Much like Maximillian of Bavaria had made his deal with the Emperor, John George sought also to make his – if he would invade from the north and into the Bohemian Kingdom's province of Lusatia, then he would be allowed to keep it once the fighting stopped. Yet again Ferdinand used land as payment in lieu, and yet again he gained a committed, if self-interested, ally because of it. With armies from the Catholic League in the south under Maximillian of Bavaria and from the north under John George of Saxony all en route, Frederick's strategic position in Bohemia appeared fragile indeed, but it was about to get worse. On 9 May 1620, just over a week since Ferdinand had issued an ultimatum to Frederick to vacate the Bohemian lands and surrender the Bohemian crown, the government of Philip III of Spain sanctioned the dispatch of an army to take part in the fighting once the ultimatum expired on 1 June. Its destination was not Bohemia, but Frederick's homeland in the Lower Palatinate along the Rhine.

Spanish intervention in Frederick's rebellion against his Emperor had been escalating since late 1618, when a governmental change of sorts in Madrid took place. Although King Philip III of Spain possessed absolute power, the importance of the favourite in Spanish politics had not diminished, and since Philip could not be in several places at once, it was often necessary to delegate and lean on one's advisors and administrators. One such individual was Baltasar de Zuniga, who effectively controlled Spanish foreign and domestic policy from 1618 until his death in 1622. At the core of Zuniga's policy was the notion that the Spanish Habsburgs must support their Austrian cousins, and this enabled Zuniga to leave his most important imprint upon Spain: involvement within the Holy Roman Empire and the Thirty Years War. In addition, waiting in the wings was Zuniga's nephew, a man who would soon take up the reins of Spanish government as Count Olivares after 1623.

Spanish involvement in Ferdinand's business had been blatant, consistent, and encouraged. When the Emperor had met with the Duke of Bavaria in early October 1619, Count Onate, the Spanish dignitary responsible for the Onate Treaty of two years' before, had accompanied him. While in the presence of the Emperor and his ally, Maximillian of Bavaria, Count Onate was under pressure to deliver – unless Spain intervened with some force in the Empire, it was unlikely that many Catholic German princes would act. To demonstrate his seriousness, Onate acted promptly and without Madrid's permission – he authorised the immediate dispatch of one thousand cavalry from the Spanish Netherlands to join the Catholic League; he moved Spanish soldiers from Italy to Austria for its defence, and most controversially, he promised the timely intervention in the struggle between Emperor and Elector by invading Frederick's Lower Palatinate along the Rhine, thus cutting Frederick off from his home base.

Of no small interest to Onate was the fact that, with the Rhine occupied and secure, pursuing the continuation of the war against the Dutch would be made that much easier once the Truce expired in April 1621. Count Onate did not stop there though; we know that it was at this meeting on 8 October 1619 that the idea for transferring Frederick's lands and Electoral title to his cousin Maximillian of Bavaria was first developed and agreed to, but Geoffrey Parker claimed that it was Count Onate who imagined this scheme. While meeting with the Emperor in private, Onate devised the explosively controversial plan on the basis that it would spur Maximillian on, but that it was still quite unlikely that Frederick's forces would be sufficiently weak to permit the Duke of Bavaria to achieve all that was planned. Based on this absurd gamble, Onate then proceeded to stack the deck against Frederick further by devising the means through which Spanish soldiers could march against the Elector Palatine. Concerns about the other Protestant power were raised, with Saxony and the Evangelical Union proving to be matters for contention. Both of these questions would have to be resolved, all agreed here, before the war against the Elector Palatine could be properly and enthusiastically waged.[31]

Thanks to these deals made by Emperor Ferdinand, substantial forces from the Catholic League, from Spain and from Saxony were all en route to his lands by summer 1620. Indeed, Frederick's position was hopeless by the time the ultimatum had expired on 1 June. Its expiration had plainly been considered a foregone conclusion in Ferdinand's court – had Frederick capitulated as John Frederick of Saxony had done in 1547, it would have placed the Emperor in a terrible bind. Ferdinand had banked on Frederick's refusal to make peace, and predictably, the Elector Palatine did not disappoint. Compounding Frederick's bad fortune, on 3 July 1620 the Treaty of Ulm was signed. This agreement effectively neutered what remained of the Evangelical Union, and its members resolved to provide no aid to the beleaguered Elector Palatine in return for clemency from their Emperor and a vow of neutrality. These pieces they happily took, perhaps unwilling to believe that their Emperor would go any further than the mere defeat of their former Palatine commander. With this loose end tied up – thanks to the diplomatic intervention of Anglo-French mediators no less, more on this later – Frederick's regime was doomed.

The Treaty of Ulm proved to be the final signal; on 24 July the Catholic League army of twenty-five thousand commanded by Count Tilly invaded the lands of the rebellious Austrian estates, which had pledged themselves as allies to the Bohemians the previous summer. A few weeks later, the Spanish made their move, as an army of twenty-two thousand veterans from the Dutch War led by their renowned commander Ambrogio Spinola marched into the Lower Palatinate on the Rhine. Within six months, much of the country was in their hands, and an incredible windfall of more than thirty towns had capitulated rather than face the unexpected onslaught.

Frederick, located far away in his detached Bohemian kingdom, had no remedy for his peoples' bitter plight. While he retained a Bohemian Confederate army of roughly twenty-six thousand men, this force was demoralised, and had no doubt been provided with whispers from the neighbouring lands about how desperate their position had become.[32] The promised aid had not arrived – Frederick, their King, had not provided the aid and support which his connections had promised. The Dutch had determined to protect themselves rather than risk anything for the Bohemians; the Evangelical Union had paralysed itself rather than face the music, and Frederick's own father in law had elected to undermine his son in law and daughter by reducing what little allies he had left, rather than making any effort to help him. The prognosis was certainly not good.

Limited displays of support from other powers had done much to add to the sense of impending doom in Prague. Gustavus Adolphus, the King of Sweden, had recognised Frederick as Bohemia's King, and initially welcomed the prospect of an alliance with both Frederick's properties and the

Evangelical Union. However, after travelling incognito through Germany for a few months, the King returned home to Stockholm once his mission – the wooing of the sister of the Elector of Brandenburg – was completed. Gustavus was far too occupied with his stop-start conflict with his Polish cousin in any case, but he did provide Frederick with a gift of eight artillery pieces and a cache of ammunition – a reflection, perhaps, of the Swedish King's fascination and later innovation with artillery.

The King of Denmark, Christian IV, proved equally non-committal. Since Christian was the uncle of Frederick's wife Elizabeth, it was hoped that this connection would bear fruit. The Danish King had offered to send four thousand soldiers to Frederick's defence in the past, but the opposition from his council consistently hampered these plans. He would loan Frederick 100,000 thalers, money which he would not get back, but Christian provided little else. The Scandinavian cards spent, Frederick had also turned to the Venetians, who also proved themselves full of warm words, but no genuine desire to entangle themselves in the Empire's conflicts – understandably. Anticipating later developments, Venice did commit to preventing any Habsburg soldiers from passing through its lands or the mountain passes it controlled.[33]

These approaches failed; Frederick undaunted turned his attention to that looming beast in the east – the Ottoman Empire. While apparently an ill-fitting choice for an ally, the Turks fulfilled the age-old principle of 'the enemy of my enemy is my friend.' Their representatives informed Frederick that a massive invasion of four hundred thousand men was planned soon enough to teach the King of Poland a lesson for his invasion of Transylvania in November 1619. In April 1620, Frederick's envoy had a personal audience with the Sultan, and in July, the Sultan's envoy arrived in Prague, and asked to be shown where the Defenestration had occurred. Peter H. Wilson presents what happened next with an undercurrent of shame, noting that Frederick agreed to make Bohemia a tributary state of the Ottoman Empire.[34] Yet, the practice of paying tribute to the Ottoman Empire had only been abandoned by the Habsburgs with the conclusion of the Long Turkish War in 1606 – it did not mean that Frederick was the vassal king of the Turks. What it meant was that Frederick paid money to the Sultan, in return for the Sultan's pledges for assistance.

However, of course, the entire agreement was terribly controversial and damaging to Frederick's character, especially with the repeated references to the threat posed by the Turks from both sides. It was not a wise agreement to make, but Frederick was desperate – he had been abandoned by all of his allies by midsummer 1620. The Sultan's terms were also far better than many of Frederick's European peers, and the Ottomans possessed a strategic position along the Habsburgs' border which he would have been foolish not to exploit, as his enemies were soon to exploit his weaknesses. Still, when news did emerge of his deals with the heathen Turk, this was all too easily accepted as evidence of the Winter King's unfitness for rule and rampant dishonesty. His enemies made much out of this controversy, much as Frederick himself would do once the unconstitutional deals between Ferdinand and Maximillian were discovered.[35]

What followed has been well-documented by other historians. On 8 November 1620, after facing invasions from all sides, the remnants of Frederick's Bohemian-Palatine Confederate army, led jointly by Count Thurn and Christian of Anhalt, were routed by the forces under the Catholic League. It was all over in less than two hours – thirty-three thousand men under Frederick's optimistic banners were easily trounced by the confident and well-paid fifty-five thousand men that faced them. While Frederick's forces had dug in, they could not withstand the barrages and professionalism of the League soldiers, let alone the numbers, and morale had been low for months thanks to troubling rumours and a lack of pay. The triumph was decisive not for the numbers killed, but for the great flight which began in the Bohemian army. Since he had not been expecting a battle, Frederick was taken unawares just as his regime in Bohemia had collapsed. Entertaining English ambassadors at one point in the Hradschin Castle which had now become a noted landmark in Prague, Frederick was drawn to the commotion taking place outside the city limits. Riding out to where his army was encamped, the stream of soldiers towards the city, most of them in a blind panic, told him all he needed to know. Frederick moved to secure his family, but so quick had the enemy arrived, defeated his army and taken control of the field that a panic set in during the evacuation. A great amount of useful and incriminating material was left behind, including Queen Elizabeth's jewels and the damning correspondence between Frederick and the Habsburgs' enemies.[36]

After the battle, Christian of Anhalt would write an extensive, detailed account of the defeat at White Mountain, and attempted to explain to his master where it had all gone wrong. He concluded:

> Your Majesty will understand from this account the real reasons for our defeat and will also understand that the defeat wasn't caused by the enemy's valour, but by their good fortune and the divine help they received. Surely, God wanted to punish us for our sins, mostly because of the awful treatment and bad pay bestowed on our soldiers; seeing that the Estates of Bohemia wanted their ruin and disbandment, those soldiers were reduced to extreme despair and bad behaviour, such that no chief or officer could order them to fight anymore. For me to start a proper explanation of those matters, their faults and imperfections, I would need reams of paper to do them justice. Your Majesty knew about this, even if you couldn't remedy the matter in any way possible to you. However, for this generation of people, all was in vain as the unhappy outcome proved.[37]

The Bohemian revolt was over. With Prague captured by the forces of their formerly deposed king, a new process began – that of fleeing the country, seeking Ferdinand's mercy, or taking advantage of the fire sale of land which was to follow, as exiled, murdered or otherwise absent lords had their lands seized and redistributed. Further afield, a new chapter was also beginning for Frederick – this was to be the long, often lonely and dispiriting road of resistance to the Emperor. His was to be the thankless, often unwelcome cause, which most would rather ignore and return to their lives rather than aid and abet. In the years that followed, Frederick's mission would change, as would his allies, but his presence in the anti-Habsburg camp, and his apparently limitless passion for creating coalitions and sending them Ferdinand's way, ensured that the sun did not set on the Winter King yet.

So how does one account for the whirlwind series of events which culminated at the Battle of White Mountain on 8 November 1620? There is, as we have no doubt learned, no easy or straightforward way to analyse and present all that occurred from the moment the Bohemians defenestrated their Habsburg regents, to the moment when their country appeared helped and naked at the feet of so many enemies. A question which frequently arises when examining these events revolves around the issue of responsibility – was Frederick responsible for what happened next? Was he responsible for the ravages and destruction of the Thirty Years War?

We must establish first and foremost the important clarification – Frederick had no intentions of initiating the Thirty Years War. He had acted opportunistically during his rival's time of misfortune, and he had perhaps acted foolishly, since he had underestimated the wrath of the Habsburgs which would follow this decision. He had also naively assumed that the pledges of his allies were all sincere, and that the English, Dutch, French, Danish, Swedish, Venetian, Savoyard and Evangelical Union's promises made in the past or in recent times were enough to base one's hopes upon. Frederick must also have been motivated by the apparently desperate position of the Habsburgs when he accepted the Crown in late September 1619. By that point, the Hungarian rebels were marching in force through the Habsburg possessions, and were poised to threaten Vienna. Ferdinand had no answer for these challenges, or at least, it may have seemed to Frederick that he didn't. Shrewdly gambling that he would never have a better opportunity to capitalise upon the Habsburgs' weaknesses, Frederick took an immense risk which he believed was worth it, but which in the end proved disastrous.

Next, we must accept that Frederick, rightly or wrongly, upheld to the end that the Habsburgs were a malignant and unwelcome force in the Empire, and that they did not belong in the Imperial office. Frederick was persuaded from an early age, as his father had been before him, that the Habsburgs wished to eradicate Calvinism, Lutheranism and all forms of religious difference from the Empire, and to bend the German princes to their will. He also believed – correctly as it turned out – that Ferdinand would act just as Charles V had, and make unconstitutional deals to get what he wanted, re-shaping the Empire's makeup as he saw fit. Frederick had seen the manifestation of these malignant designs in the years before, thanks to the unfortunately crude and provocative Habsburg implementation of religious policy. Ferdinand of Styria, whose notorious transformation of the largely Protestant population of his duchy was common knowledge in Europe, was upheld by Frederick to be the most egregious offender of all.

That Frederick was arguably wrong to accept the Bohemian crown must be tempered with the fact that Frederick proved right where the Habsburg excesses were concerned. Even before his fall, Ferdinand had made use of unconstitutional deals of a dubious legality to secure his position. While these agreements proved effective, and said as much about Ferdinand as they did about the individuals he made the agreements with, they would enable Frederick in time to mobilise anti-Habsburg feeling against Ferdinand and his family, and they would fill Frederick with a burning desire to right the wrong which had been done to him and which would be done to his countrymen. Frederick's rashness, naivety and opportunism may well have provided the spark which caused the Thirty Years War to erupt, but thanks to Ferdinand's equally unfortunate character traits, this war would not end at White Mountain, and would last another 28 years.

THREE

My Poor Palatinate

'I commend all to God. He gave it me, he has taken it away, he can give it me again, blessed be his name.'[38] In such a way did Frederick reconcile his despair with his faith, following the very trying experiences of the second half of 1620. Spanish forces had occupied the Lower Palatinate's major towns, including Heidelberg, by the end of November 1620, which prevented any succour arriving for Frederick from his homeland, if indeed any would have been possible. The sack of Prague for a whole week had followed Frederick's departure, and since there had been barely any time to prepare their exit, much plunder had been available to the hungry soldiers. One English observer had noted that:

> The loss of soldiers was not much unequal, but the loss of cannon, the baggage, reputation, is the Imperialists' victory who, as it seems, hold Bohemia now by conquest, and all immunities and privileges are now void. And if a new establishment by petition shall be obtained, it will be only the law of the conqueror, who doth already finely call those of the Protestant religion to account for what they have, and put it into safe keeping, so that they taste already their condition to come.[39]

Frederick's first port of call had been to escort his wife and children to safety, and this was achieved by marching steadily towards the mountainous Bohemian-Silesian border and taking refuge in the fortress town of Glatz. They would be safe here for a while at least, since Silesia, unlike Bohemia, Lusatia or Moravia, had not been made to suffer invasion or occupation, at least not yet. Resting until the middle of the month in the fortress town, by 17 November 1620, Frederick made his way to Breslau to speak with the Silesians, but they were not happy to see the man they had once chosen to be their king. In fact, it soon became apparent that they wanted as little to do with him as possible. While some nobles felt bound to the oath they had made to Frederick in the past, others wished to avoid the looming threat of ruin which

John George's nearby Saxon troops, the nearby Catholic League troops, or even a Polish invasion could easily bring.

Frederick had been forced to rely on whoever remained friendly, and one such figure was Bethlen Gabor, the Prince of Transylvania whose activities the year before had caused Ferdinand so much difficulty. Hungary was still in pieces, and its loyalties were divided, but by December 1620 a truce had been arranged with the Emperor, and Bethlen withdrew from Pressburg, leaving that important city on the Danube back in Habsburg hands. Frederick was unaware of these developments as they occurred in the background, but to the Silesian diet they likely would have made little difference. The threats from so many directions, and the tempting offer of Saxon mediation, compelled many nobles to try and dissuade Frederick from further resistance.

Under so many pressures, and aware that the costs of maintaining any sufficient forces in the field at all were becoming impossible to bear, Frederick had no choice but to approve of the Silesian requests. He urged them to remain true to their oath and to the Confederation they had declared in July 1619 in any case, and by mid-December he had left the province. The Silesians wasted little time. By February 1621, Silesia had successfully appealed to the Emperor's mercy and clemency and had officially abandoned Frederick's cause in the process. With Bohemia occupied, Lusatia seized by Saxons, Moravia conquered by the Catholic League and now Silesia pledging itself back to the Emperor, Frederick had officially lost the entirety of his kingdom. While he never dropped the title of King of Bohemia, his kingdom had evaporated. Learning of these successive defeats, Frederick wrote sombrely to Count Thurn:

> We entrust it to the Almighty and accept with patience the reprimand that he sent upon us. May he let everything occur for his honour and for the favour of his believers...We did not force ourselves on Bohemia and Moravia. We could have been well contented with our patrimonial lands, but we put that aside upon their request and honestly did everything in our power for their lands. Now we receive the thanks, that they explicitly agree to a treaty – and after put forward ours for their sake – and subordinate themselves to another. Now whether this is laudable or honest we let the whole world judge. Neither greed nor ambition brought us to Bohemia. Neither poverty nor suffering will make us desert our dear God or do something contrary to honour and conscience.[40]

With this statement of intent, it was evident that Frederick had not viewed his loss at White Mountain as anything akin to the end. If anything, the defeat was a punishment, a sign that he had been too disorganised or had not trusted firmly enough in God's providence. Rather than give up, he would work overtime, and petition every Protestant potentate of any import within the Empire. Somebody, somewhere, would surely sympathise with his cause and be willing to bear the challenges implicit in this cause. And Frederick was determined to cast his resistance to the Emperor – some might argue resistance to reality – as a Protestant or even common cause.

Arriving in Brandenburg where his wife had recently given birth to their fifth child, Frederick was made aware once again that his guests were not particularly pleased to host him. George William of Brandenburg, Frederick's brother in law, was no more able to ignore the Emperor's expressions of displeasure than the smaller non-Electors whose lands Frederick passed through on his way to finding a safe haven or drumming up support. Frederick found the time to communicate with Ernst von Mansfeld, the mercenary captain who had been in the field for several years by this point, and Frederick offered him thirty thousand florins to continue his activities and maintain his army in the field. To the Dutch, arguably his best hope, Frederick wrote letters to Maurice of Nassau, the Prince of Orange, and requested financial gifts, military assistance and the resumption of old subsidies. It is possible that Frederick's new-born son was even named Maurice in a bid to sweeten the deal.[41]

On 29 January 1621, Ferdinand issued the Imperial Ban against the Elector Palatine, effectively making him an outlaw within the Holy Roman Empire. This made it an offence to aid and abet Frederick and would compel all princes to hand him over if he resided on their lands. Thus, Frederick determined that the Empire was no longer a safe place for his family and determined to enter into Dutch exile in The Hague. Frederick's familial connections may well have helped his appeal; his mother was the daughter of William of Orange, and this meant that Maurice of Nassau was his uncle. Nonetheless, the Imperial Ban against Frederick severely undermined his cause and his ability to gain allies, since anyone that helped him would now be guilty by association – this, of course, was what made the device of the Imperial Ban so potent and his ability to gain allies, since anyone that helped him would now be guilty by association. Already Frederick's other allies, including Christian of Anhalt, had been issued with a similar ban, which had the additional effect of making their lands and titles forfeit.

Frederick predictably dismissed the ban as yet another example of the Habsburgs' unconstitutional, disreputable behaviour. To an extent, Frederick had a case, since Ferdinand had not pursued the ban through the traditional process and had instead leveraged his influence among the princes over fourteen months to acquire the necessary approval for the ban. Frederick could decry the act all he wanted, but the fact remained that since his lands and person were now opened to attack, the likelihood of reclaiming his Palatinate, let alone the Bohemian crown had become much more remote. Emperor Ferdinand had justified his ban against Frederick on the grounds that his actions in the past had been notorious, and that his crimes of breaking the imperial peace and of acting illegally in the Bohemian revolt necessitated swift, harsh punishment.

These developments in January 1621 shaped Frederick's policy because it limited his freedom of action. He would need allies before any of his losses could be recouped, but since so few Germans would ever agree to help him, he would have to approach the situation somewhat differently. Frederick's opportunity in this regard came in February when King Christian IV of Denmark hosted a conference of several Protestant princes, as well as several Protestant actors including the English, Dutch and Brandenburg. The only problem for Frederick was that he had never been invited to this conference, in the town of Segeberg, and it was not guaranteed that those in attendance would not elect to simply eject him from the town, or hand him over to the Emperor in return for his favour. Frederick was thus taking a risk, but considering the circumstances, he had little choice.

'Who advised you to drive out kings and seize kingdoms? If your councillors did so, they were scoundrels!' This was the frosty reception Frederick received from Christian IV of Denmark; it was clear that the Danish King blamed Frederick for all that had transpired, and he insisted now that his Palatine nephew abdicate the Bohemian crown, make a formal apology to the Emperor, and return to his home on the Rhine. Frederick could not do all this; in his mind, he was upholding not only his honour, but also the Bohemian constitution and the Empire's constitution. He had been elected, Ferdinand had been deposed, and the Bohemians had had the right to take both actions according to the Letter of Majesty which Ferdinand had agreed to. In a theme which was to be repeated and which had already surfaced, Frederick sought to clarify his opposition to Ferdinand – he claimed his actions 'had absolutely nothing to do with the Imperial Majesty as a Roman Emperor, but only as a duke of Austria.' Frederick's problem was with Ferdinand of Styria, the man that had been elected and then deposed as King of Bohemia; his quarrel was certainly not with Ferdinand II, Holy Roman Emperor. Thus, according to Frederick, this among many other reasons meant that the ban against him was invalid.[42]

The Danish episode had been illuminating, as Christian IV had faced great opposition from the princes and estates in the Lower Saxon Circle, whom he was meant to protect. This opposition demonstrated that the Danish King could not expect to act arbitrarily in the Empire; if he wished to act in his capacity as King of Denmark, Duke of Holstein and protector of the Lower Saxon Circle, he would need the approval and cooperation of these three theatres first. Christian was moved by considerations about the Empire's Protestants, and he did display a streak of militarism which was lacking in his Protestant counterparts – such as King James for example – but for the moment, he would not act. After his rebuke at his uncle's hands, Frederick travelled to

The Hague where he intended to establish his court in exile. He would arrive just as the Twelve Years Truce between the Spanish and Dutch had ended, and the war between these two powers had resumed. Understandably, Frederick saw great opportunities in this resumption of hostilities; he likely suspected that the conflict would not stay separate from his own for long.

Frederick may have entertained hopes about the Evangelical Union, which had been effectively pacified in July 1620. Perhaps, its members could foment enough anger and controversy over the Imperial Ban, and through this avenue, more Protestant princes in the Empire would be moved to aid his cause. Any hopes of this kind were dashed in the Union's stern February meeting at Heilbronn. It was here that, after some discussion, the Imperial Ban against Frederick was tacitly accepted, though a protest was sent. A couple of months later, with the Truce between the Spanish and Dutch soon to expire and Spinola present with a large army, some ingenious manoeuvring on that veteran commander's part enabled the Spanish to coerce the Union to disband. The Mainz Accord was signed between the Spanish and the Union on 1 April 1621, barely a fortnight before the war with the Dutch resumed. As Spinola had been instructed, it was imperative that the Evangelical Union not be in any position to strike Spanish positions in the rear, nor to threaten the Spanish position in the Palatinate along the Rhine. Endowed with a large army in anticipation of the resumption of hostilities with the Dutch, Spinola affected a brilliant bluff against the Union, secure in the knowledge that he had not been instructed to fight its princes, but that they did not know this.

The Mainz Accord proved to be the final document signed by the Evangelical Union. As an organisation, it had been spinning its wheels for some time, and with its ex-commander now disgraced and public enemy number one in the Empire, there was perhaps little else to do other than dissolve the order and return to a passive neutrality, in the hope that all would blow over soon enough. The hope was to prove forlorn, but on 14 May 1621, the Evangelical Union officially became no more. As Wedgewood had written:

> The evidence of immediate danger had been stronger than the fear of disaster to come; without a blow the defenders of the constitution had abandoned their leader and made way for foreigners and adventurers to fight the cause of German liberty on German soil.[43]

The judgement was somewhat harsh – the members of the Union could not have known or even imagined what kind of destruction was to come, nor could they have anticipated that Emperor Ferdinand would go as far as he did. In addition, the Union alone should not have had the responsibility of fighting for the constitution, particularly when its members were only slightly less isolated than Frederick. The King of Denmark would not march, and neither would the King of England, and with a large Spanish army on their border and a renowned general at its head, it is hard to imagine the Union following any other course. Hindsight would give them cause to regret this decision, but hindsight was absent in the fast-moving developments and news bulletins of 1621.[44]

Frederick was soon to learn of the folding of the Union, though since it had abandoned him in July the previous year, it is unlikely he had placed much stock in its activities to begin with. Upon arriving in The Hague in April, Frederick penned one of his numerous letters to his father in law in London, claiming that:

> I will live happily, not being able to look to anyone, after God, for the remedy of my evils than Your Majesty, in whose hands I put myself entirely, desiring to submit my will to his, knowing well that he take to heart the conservation of his children.

Frederick's mention of children may have been unintentional, but his appeals and those of his wife continued to draw upon the issue of family, and of the importance of defending one's kin. Frederick's entreaties to James were in vain though, not because of the King's stubbornness, but because he refused to countenance any compromise. Frederick's submission to any form of mediation was only to occur on his terms and, as Brennan Pursell wrote, 'because he would not damage his honour or admit any fault, it was hardly submission at all.' Frederick continued to be optimistic; when James promised £14,000 for the Palatine army's most urgent necessities and an additional £6,000 for treating those suffering the worst excesses of the war, Frederick fired back a request for £50,000. While the Emperor could not be reasoned with, Frederick did request that James send an ambassador to act in his name, and to treat with Maximillian of Bavaria. Frederick hoped that English pressure would move the Duke to negotiate the return of the Upper Palatinate, which he was then occupying, back to him, but to no avail.

On 5 May, Frederick received a letter from James which read that the English embassy to the Emperor would continue, and London would maintain the pressure on Ferdinand to restore his son in law to his lands on the Palatine. James insisted he was obligated to do so 'by the law of honour and of nature', but he added that Frederick must obey his Emperor and render unto Ferdinand what was Ferdinand's. Perhaps James hoped that if he hammered home the point enough times, his son in law would agree to throw in the towel, admit his mistakes and return to the peaceful system of old. But Frederick, just as before, was unwilling to accept that he had erred, and he allowed this letter to go unanswered. Instead, Frederick seems to have believed that he could achieve better results through military means, and he planned to use what meagre resources in manpower and materials he had at his disposal to bring this vision to life.[45]

The pressure was definitely on though. The Spanish assault into the Palatinate had effectively destroyed Frederick's homeland on the Rhine, and those advisors that remained in Heidelberg had sent him letters warning consistently about the dire situation which faced them. Famine was guaranteed because the peasants had fled; several important towns were under Spanish control; the few thousand troops still in the field suffered from chronic payment problems and low morale as a result. The latest news from England spurred Frederick on; this news seemed to indicate that London's House of Commons, and the James' court generally, were far more belligerent and willing to involve the country in Frederick's struggle than the King himself may have been. Many in court and in the Commons believed that upon Frederick's opposition to the Emperor hung the overall fate of Protestantism. In June 1621 the Commons published a declaration which seemed to support whatever use of force would be necessary to defend 'the true professors of the same Christian religion professed by the Church of England in foreign parts...being touched with a true sense and fellow feeling of their distresses as members of the same body.'

Its members searched for ways to support Frederick's cause – a coalition or alliance headed by the English and Dutch would be organised, and soldiers could be landed and move out from their Dutch base. Such involvement would surely involve England in the recently resumed Eighty Years War and considering James' overarching goals of securing peace in Europe alongside a Spanish marriage (see below) there was no way that King James could possibly agree to such terms. This fact did not deter Frederick from hoping that the Commons would influence the King, or that the latent anti-Spanish feeling accompanied by the anti-Catholic feeling would serve in his favour.[46] Frederick was partially correct, since anti-Spanish propaganda levelled against King James would reach a fever pitch in the coming years, but the Elector Palatine was wrong to anticipate that this would move James away from his course.[48]

The simultaneous death first of King Philip III of Spain and then of Archduke Albert of the Spanish Netherlands left something of a power vacuum in Spanish policy, which was filled by Spinola's desire to complete the conquest of the Palatinate, and in this he was supported by the Isabella, the late Albert's widow. Eleven thousand Spanish soldiers remained in the Palatinate under Spinola, but the new king of Spain Philip IV claimed that he would intercede with the Emperor on Frederick's behalf, largely at James' behest. James' efforts to save his son in law's lands continued during the early summer of 1621, and he had even managed to arrange for a ceasefire in the Palatinate while the English embassy travelled to Vienna. The mission of this embassy was in many senses far too optimistic, but its cause was truly doomed by the sudden appearance on the horizon of Bethlen Gabor, a known ally of Frederick, and the news that, further afield, Ernst von Mansfeld's army of twenty thousand men in the Upper Palatinate had crossed the border into Bohemia.

Emperor Ferdinand could see the villages burning in the distance, and it was very hard for the English embassy to reason that Frederick was willing to stand down for the sake of serious negotiations. James had also claimed that he would promise to control Frederick, and this was exposed as an empty promise as well. Frederick could not be controlled, he would only be guided or advised, and he would certainly not be moved to submit to the Emperor or renounce his past decisions. This act of humbling himself was, noted the head of the English embassy to the Emperor, Simon Digby, that the only sure way to guarantee the return of Frederick's lands. But Frederick would not do it; he clearly favoured risking it all on another campaign to throwing in the towel.

By September 1621 in Vienna, Count Onate was telling Digby that it was better 'to lose no more time here, for that the Emperor was no so incensed against the Count Palatine for that his ministers should be the aggressors in all parts.' Another Habsburg figure in Vienna cautioned Digby that Ferdinand was determined to have 'either a general peace or a general war.' In response to this, Digby did as he had been instructed, and warned that King James was prepared to intervene for the sake of his son in law since it was a matter of honour to restore him. This intervention by James – which in itself was highly unlikely given the King's actual policy desires – would mean an escalation of the conflict in the Palatine, and this was 'very like to set a general combustion in Christendom.' Ferdinand responded by promising to send an embassy to London, where James would be granted satisfaction. On his return home, Simon Digby reflected on the conundrum:

> If yet a constant hand may be held, the business will be overcome to the King's satisfaction, but if the King of Bohemia (Frederick) will suffer his name to be used by those that hitherto hath done, and take those middle ways, of neither relying upon a treaty, nor avowedly making a war, he will be ruined irrevocably, and his enemies have the advantage of doing all things against him upon justifiable pretext.[48]

Following this embassy, Frederick's relationship with his father in law soured. In response to the consistent requests for money from the King of England, and to a refusal to abandon the more unsavoury allies such as Bethlen Gabor of Transylvania, who was on the rampage yet again, Frederick was given a dressing down via letter. James insisted that he had never asked Frederick to abandon his allies, and he added that it would not be possible to supply all the monetary assistance which Frederick asked of him, 'nor with all the revenues of our crown' would it be remotely possible for James to fulfil all that Frederick asked of him, because he asked far too much. James criticised Frederick's efforts to enlist Turkish support for his cause, since inviting Islamic powers into Europe to settle his feud with the Christian Emperor 'could only render him a surfeit of dishonour.'[49]

Frederick had become all the more stubborn because on 21 June 1621, he had learned of yet another example of the Emperor's unsuitability for Imperial rule. Twenty-seven participants in the Bohemian revolt were executed in Prague, including the rector of Prague's University. In addition, the coin was debased, religious freedoms were curtailed, the elective monarchy abolished and a great redistribution of Bohemian land among the remaining nobility began in earnest. These actions horrified and incensed Frederick, and convinced him beyond any doubt that Ferdinand would not stop there; how could it not be guaranteed, even if he submitted in good faith, that Frederick's Palatine would not receive the exact same treatment? The Bohemians had believed themselves safe, but now their King and Emperor moved to recreate that country in his own image, and no power would stand in her defence. The only chance Frederick had was to resist; to rely on Ferdinand's mercy was a greater risk than continuing the war.[50]

In August 1621 Frederick had toyed with the idea of leading an army of exiles and Dutch volunteers to the Palatinate where Spinola was located. Since Spinola refused to extend the truce, it seemed inevitable that Frederick's homeland would once again be subject to destruction and devastation. Moving to Arnhem, Frederick planned to move out, and it was there that he met the twenty-two-year-old Christian of Brunswick, a supporter of the Palatine-Bohemian cause since 1619. Christian was determined to fight for Frederick's cause, and he believed in the Elector Palatine's message that Protestantism depended on the defeat of the Emperor. Christian also professed a curious love for his cousin, the Queen of Bohemia and Frederick's wife, Elizabeth, whom he claimed he would fight for and whose fulfilment he guaranteed.[51]

The process of returning the Palatine family to their rightful homes was a messy and bitter one for any side that had to endure the quartering of unwelcome soldiers, or which had to pay contributions to be left alone. 'God help those where Mansfeld comes!' was a common cry, and hardly painted Frederick, the Count's employer, in the most favourable light. Mansfeld and his always underpaid troops had rampaged across the Empire, into the Upper Palatinate, Bohemia and even Alsace by the end of 1620.[52] Alongside Mansfeld's force of varying size – it reached twenty thousand during favourable seasons – Christian of Brunswick added ten thousand somewhat ragtag soldiers, and another new German ally on the scene: George Frederick of Baden-Durlach, added eleven thousand. 'Thus', Wedgewood noted, 'by the spring of 1622 Frederick's cause fluttered three gallant little flags in defiance of the Emperor.' It remained to be seen if these gallant allies would be enough, or if Bethlen Gabor's seasonal campaigns would do the trick.[53]

To Frederick, an outlaw, an exile and almost completely dispossessed, this resistance gave him a better chance to triumph in the end than any peace treaty or submission ever could. Whether he believed he would swing from the gallows as those Bohemian rebels had done, or whether he simply could not accept admitting any wrongdoing, the fact was that Frederick's rebellion would continue for the foreseeable future. Frederick's causes, despite the odds and pressures against it, had survived some grave defeats, and the total victory which Ferdinand had hoped for remained out of his reach, at least for the moment.

FOUR

Woe to the Vanquished

Writing in 1869, English historian Sir Adolphus William Ward wrote on the aftermath of the Bohemian revolt:

> There could be no doubt as to the fate in store for the vanquished kingdom; and to this day she bears the traces of her reconciliation to the dominion and the faith of the House of Austria Yet I cannot agree…that the Bohemians are to be charged with the responsibility of their country's sufferings. It has been sagaciously observed by the present Emperor of the French [Napoleon III], that men are not justified in resorting to unlawful means, when lawful will better suit the purpose. The Bohemians had before them the choice between submitting to Ferdinand, and rescinding his election to their throne. They chose the latter alternative; and herein they seem to have made no fond calculation. True, they played their venturous game badly; but they could hardly have reckoned on so much weakness in Frederick; so much tergiversation in James; so much backwardness in the Dutch; and so much cowardice in the Union. Nor could they have anticipated so unparalleled, I feel almost inclined to say so heroic, a determination in their opponent.[54]

There was little heroism left in Bohemia. After over a decade of resistance to Habsburg inroads, the rebels that had remained in Prague had exhausted their reserves, as well as their deposed king's patience. Ferdinand forbade any residents from leaving the kingdom, which seemed to indicate that he intended to repair the wretched country and restore it to its old position with the help of those recalcitrant citizens. The rebels who had been unable to escape could only hope that Ferdinand would need them for this task, but they were to be wholly disappointed. Ferdinand aimed at nothing less than the complete reshaping of Bohemia in the Habsburg image, and this task began with removing the vestiges of opposition to his regime; pulling out the weeds which had choked proper Bohemian society.

Elective monarchy was abolished in Bohemia; henceforth the country was to be little more than an appendage of the Habsburg Hereditary Lands, and Bohemian Kings were to be Habsburgs and nothing else. That was not all; Ferdinand fulfilled his other mission when he received the original copy of the Letter of Majesty. The Letter of Majesty had been drafted by Bohemian rebels of a different shade in 1609, and this document had since entitled Bohemians to demand so much from their king, and to act against that king if it proved in their interests to do so. It was said that Ferdinand personally took to this document with a knife, carving it up and effectively killing it.

The message was clear. If there had been doubts before about Ferdinand's sincerity when he had sworn to uphold the Letter's tenets, now there was only fear. Bohemia was flooded with Jesuits, Catholics were empowered, and religious difference was squeezed out. On the night of 20 February 1621, all known rebels in Prague were arrested and confined to Prague's dungeons to await sentencing. Among these prisoners were moderates as well as irredeemable rebels, who had urged caution from the very beginning, only be overruled by the likes of Count Thurn, who had long since saved himself and fled Bohemia.

Ferdinand's vengeance was every bit as fearsome as Frederick claimed it would be. Determined once and for all to extirpate heresy and resistance from this important country, the Emperor had the accused put on trial, with the sentences reaching Vienna at the end of May and awaiting Ferdinand's signature. The arrested individuals had been tried by a special commission, and there was no chance to appeal. More than forty individuals were given harsh sentences ranging from life imprisonment to execution, and with Ferdinand's approval coming shortly after, it was now the task of the gallows to carry out the deed. Contrary to the fears of some in Prague, no rescue mission was launched on the day of execution on 21 June. Symbolically, Saxon horsemen patrolled Prague just in case, but the city as much as the country was plainly beaten. This had been the third and most terrible Bohemian revolt by far, but it seemed certain that it would be the last. Among those heads mounted on pikes on the Charles Bridge was a different appendage: the right hand of former Bohemian commander, Count Heinrich Schlick. Schlick's hand served as a grisly reminder of what would happen to those that declared oaths against their Emperor, and who fought to ensure his downfall.[55]

In his mission to destroy opposition and bring Bohemia securely into the Habsburg fold, Ferdinand effectively destroyed its identity and history. Religion and rebels were not the only concerns of the Habsburgs though; one of the reasons why the recreation of Bohemia proved so effective and enduring was due to the Habsburgs' effective mobilisation of arguably the most important commodity then available to them – land. Richard Bassett wrote that:

As the conflict in Bohemia progressed through the 1620s it provided a once in a lifetime opportunity for a radical reorganisation of wealth and a comprehensive redrawing of the aristocracy. The revolt of the Bohemian nobles brought the House of Habsburg the power of redistribution of a vast and hitherto unprecedented scale. It is estimated that some 670 estates changed hands as vast tracts of Bohemian territory were stripped from the rebels and given to two hundred adventurers and officers prepared to embrace the Catholic faith.[56]

The appropriation of so much land enabled the Habsburgs to assume a critically important position in Bohemian society. Just as they were removing the undesirable elements, they were also able to pose as a fount of patronage to those that promised loyalty. Underneath this apparently ideal strategy though, chronic problems were created. When the land confiscations had begun, Ferdinand felt it necessary to raise some money quickly by selling off the land for 30 million florins. To aid the potential buyers to make this purchase, Ferdinand issued a licence to a consortium of buyers to establish a mint, which then issued debased currency, and created something of a money divide in Bohemia, as citizens distinguished between the old heavy silver coins and the new debased coins, even though this was technically illegal.

Since not all citizens did distinguish, and since 42 million florins' worth of coins were minted between 1621-22 (creating twelve times as many coins with the old standards of silver), the aforementioned consortium became very rich indeed. These new men in Bohemia were Catholic loyalists of the Habsburgs and recognised that great profit could be enjoyed by gobbling up as many of the confiscated estates as possible at knock-down prices. With the influx of coins into their pockets, these men were technically rich, and with the purchase of so many estates, they became rich in land as well as in pocket.

Of course, the unnatural suddenness of so many coins entering circulation backfired in the short and long term; once the coin-heavy new men made enough purchases, they found that their coins were accepted less often, and would not be valued as highly. The debasement of Bohemia's currency compounded the misery in society and religion, and by 1623, as many as one hundred and twenty thousand were said to have fled in spite of Ferdinand's efforts. Between 1616-1650 indeed, the population of Bohemia fell by 50%, and in Moravia, 30%. To Ferdinand it was enough that those who remained became loyal, Catholic subjects, but it would not be hyperbole to state that Bohemia was never the same again.[57]

In times of crisis, certain individuals will always find the opportunity to profit, and arguably the most famous individual to profit from these misfortunes was Albrecht Wensel Eusebius von Wallenstein, a Catholic Bohemian who had taken advantage early of the opportunities inherent in the new regime. In quick time, Wallenstein became one of the largest landowners in Bohemia, and consequently, one of the richest individuals in the country. Wallenstein had come into a small fortune after his elderly wife died in 1614, and from there his fortunes only snowballed. Of the 670 estates made available by the Habsburg victory, Wallenstein was able to purchase more than 70 for himself, to co-opt several others, and all with the use of the debased currency that few wished to touch. Indeed, the debased currency problem was actually spreading to other neighbouring states and has been identified by one historian as a contributing factor towards the economic crisis of the time. To Wallenstein, this was just business, and very good business at that.[58]

In time Wallenstein was to become the Emperor's personal generalissimo, while he would also use the immense profits wrested from his new estates to loan Ferdinand considerable sums of money. Between 1622-24, Wallenstein acquired the Duchy of Friedland in Northern Bohemia, a lucrative compact duchy which encompassed one hundred square miles and which yielded Wallenstein £70,000 a year – this sum was four times the amount which King James could expect to receive from Scotland.[59] 'These fortunes', remarked Kindleberger 'enabled Wallenstein to finance his own army in Thirty Years' War battles at a time when other armies had to rely on booty just to feed their troops.'[60] The relationship between needy Emperor and ambitious subject was soon to produce abundant fruit, as Wallenstein commanded, paid for and supplied Ferdinand's personal army, in return for the patronage by his Emperor and the privileges which he could scarcely have imagined – all of these combined to make Wallenstein, at one point, the most powerful potentate in the Holy Roman Empire, second only to the Emperor himself. As matters stood in 1621, there could be no indication that Ferdinand's subject would so distinguish himself. Instead, Ferdinand was tasked with ensuring the loyalty of that other critical ally, Maximillian of Bavaria.

While Ferdinand worked at ensuring his triumph, Frederick worked to undermine it. By the end of 1621 he could still point to some allies in the field, with arguably the most important being Ernst von Mansfeld. In late October 1621, Mansfeld had marched with his army of some twenty-two thousand men out of the Upper Palatinate in Central Europe, and back towards the Lower Palatinate along the Rhine, where the Spanish presence had put down roots. Mansfeld's men were perpetually short of pay and as a result, perpetually on the verge of mutiny, but the grizzled commander kept his men together long enough to menace the Spanish along the Rhine. Count Tilly, the commander of the Catholic League forces, moved to capitalise on Mansfeld's absence in the Upper Palatinate, and the territory was effectively occupied in Maximillian's name.

If Christian of Brunswick and George Friedrich of Baden-Durlach managed to rendezvous with Mansfeld along the Rhine, then Frederick would boast a force of roughly forty thousand men close to his homeland. The difficulty for these three armies was reaching the Rhine before they were intercepted, but an important event outside of the military sphere occurred which had the potential to be a propaganda coup for the Palatine cause. By August 1621, Maximillian of Bavaria was anxious to receive the compensation for his services which his Emperor had promised. The first of these, the transferral of the Upper Palatinate to his domains, was a work in progress, with Count Tilly on the case as we saw. The second of these was the transferral of Frederick's electoral title to the Bavarian Duke.

Ferdinand was still dependent enough on Bavaria at this stage in the conflict that he felt beholden to the promises he had made – to delay too long might cause still more disastrous problems. Bethlen Gabor was at large in the east, in spite of several peace efforts and truces which had been signed in the past, and Mansfeld remained a threat, albeit a brittle one, to the Spanish on the Rhine, not to mention the other minor commanders who had declared for Frederick. As an English observer noted at the time, 'it may well be judged that this is not a fit season for the Emperor to give the Duke of Bavaria a pure negative.' Indeed, the Emperor sent couriers to Brussels, Madrid, Dresden and other locations declaring that the issue would be raised and hopefully solved at the next Imperial Diet, pending Saxon and Spanish approval. While en route to his destination though, one of these couriers, carrying the damning instructions, was captured by Mansfeld.[61]

Ferdinand's intentions had only been the subject of rumour, rather than canon. This discovery had the potential to change all that. Mansfeld had in his hands a letter written by Ferdinand to Baltasar de Zuniga, the Spanish favourite in Madrid, to the effect that he had verbally promised Frederick's electorate to Maximillian, and that very soon it would be time to fulfil this pledge. At one point during the letter Ferdinand had written 'it is not necessary to trust the king of Great Britain, as much as that he is of the religion, and that one can neither remedy nor make secure these affairs, only if the religion called Calvinism be totally exterminated.' When Frederick learned of this find, he saw it for what it was – a great opportunity to harness the reluctance of some Germans and the hostility of others, by exposing Ferdinand's true intentions.

'God', Frederick wrote, 'the Director of all things and the protector of the innocent, has miraculously discovered the source and the most secret counsels', which seemed to confirm all he had loudly proclaimed before: that the Emperor was not to be trusted, that unconstitutional acts did not concern him. Now the Emperor's behaviour made sense: Frederick had been placed under the Imperial Ban not because this was justified, but because it made the intended transfer easier and more palatable. Indeed, the transferral of the electorate had been but one topic for discussion in this damning cache of correspondence. Within it was the Habsburg proposals for recreating their rule in the Empire under Papal decree, to centralise their rule in Germany and to extirpate heresy wherever possible.[62]

Frederick instructed his court preacher to publish the findings, and this was done under the title The Spanish Chancery, a 178 page document which the Habsburgs roundly condemned as a fake, but which has since been validated by historians.[63] The contents of these letters, and the resulting surge in Palatine pamphlet activity which followed, may well have emboldened Frederick to take a personal role in the campaigning season of 1622. On 22 April 1622, Frederick left The Hague to meet with Mansfeld in the Lower Palatinate. Moving along the Rhine with Mansfeld's army, Frederick was able to experience this form of positional warfare first-hand. Mansfeld's aim remained to combine his force with Christian of Brunswick and George Friedrich of Baden Durlach. With the Elector Palatine heading this polyglot army, in wake of the revelations on the Emperor's ignoble intentions, he would cut a dashing, brave and perhaps even appealing figure for other Protestant Germans and foreign potentates alike. Combined with the impact another Transylvanian invasion could have on Viennese security and Ferdinand's position, Frederick certainly had the potential to turn the tables on the Emperor. What he needed most of all was some kind of military victory.

Unfortunately for Frederick, his allies lacked the professionalism and polish of his adversaries. During a skirmish, Mansfield managed to push back the Spanish commander, Cordoba, in late April, but he proved unable to prevent the two Habsburg allies from combining their armies. In the Battle of Wimpfen on 6 May, George Friedrich of Baden-Durlach was cut off and defeated, effectively eliminating him from the race. Mansfeld and Christian of Brunswick remained, but not for long. With their combined army, the Habsburgs managed to intercept Christian of Brunswick as he attempted to cross the Rhine at a bridgehead called Hochst. At this encounter on 20 June 1622, Christian lost two thousand men, his three cannon and a portion of his reputation, but he retained his treasury and the bulk of his army, and he sped to meet with Mansfeld and Frederick by the end of the month.[64]

By this stage, Frederick had travelled for only two months with his commander, but two months was more than enough. He had arrived in his homeland in high spirits; 'I will have nothing to do with the suspension of arms', Frederick had said to Mansfeld, 'for that would be my ruin. I must have either a good peace or a good war.' While he believed that his enemies would never have come to the peace table unless he had this 'good war'; the Emperor simply was not trustworthy, and the exposing of his unconstitutional promises, not to mention his sectarian intentions, left him to feel he had no choice other than to continue the war against him.[65] Unfortunately, while the campaigning season of 1622 had not been full of disappointments, and he had learned much about the reality of battle, it had not provided him with the results he had hoped for. 'There ought to be some difference between friend and enemy', Frederick had lamented in the summer, 'but these people ruin both alike…I think these are men who are possessed of the devil and who take pleasure in setting fire to everything. I should be very glad to leave them.' Indeed, true to his word, on 13 July 1622, Frederick released both Mansfeld and Christian of Brunswick from his service, and he returned to his uncle in Sedan. It appeared that the Palatine cause had been dealt a crippling blow.[66]

In actual fact, Frederick's rationale had been mostly sound. In months' past, successive offers of mediation and of the coordination of a conference in Brussels to discuss the Palatine matter were proposed by James, but Frederick had refused to countenance these suggestions each time. Some proposals were especially ludicrous and impossible for Frederick to accept – such as the proposal, originating in Spain, that Frederick send his first-born son to Vienna to be raised a Catholic and married to a Habsburg. Once he came of age, then this child of the Habsburg court would be permitted to inherit his father's title. There was no question of Frederick sending his son to Vienna as a hostage, nor was it possible for him to renounce his own title until his son came of age. The idea was unlikely to get even to the planning stage once Frederick learnt of it, but it did seem that, by the summer of 1622, James' repeated overtures were wearing Frederick down.

It was from a sincere desire to get away from Mansfeld's unruly soldiery – which he rightly feared would have their worst excesses attributed to him – that Frederick elected to leave Mansfeld and Christian of Brunswick and release them from his service. In addition, the other important motive was the fact that James had asked Frederick several times for a gesture of goodwill; a sign which the King could use to demonstrate his son in law's genuine desire for peace. Frederick had refused in the past because it would have meant trusting the enemy to refrain from attacking while he also stood back, but in midsummer he evidently had decided to trust in James' ability to make them keep their word. 'May God touch the King's heart, certainly I do everything to content him, but I obtain so little with it', Frederick had lamented on his father in law. As per James' instructions, Frederick empowered an ambassador to act in his name in the upcoming conference in Brussels, while he signed his name in the style of a disinherited prince, deprived of his electorate, rather than the proud Elector Palatine which he had always striven to represent. It was at least possible that Frederick was warming to the idea of peace.

Mansfeld and Christian of Brunswick, though freed from Frederick's service, were not about to embrace new career opportunities. Instead, they resolved to stick together and march towards the next available theatre of war where they could better offer their services – in the Netherlands. Before they got there though, the two commanders seemed content to follow their old paymaster to Sedan. Frederick was not especially happy to see them: Mansfeld and Christian of Brunswick did not like each other and disagreed on where their combined forces should be used. Some of Christian's cavalry mutinied, and when it was learned that this had roused some Huguenots nearby to also revolt, Frederick feared that King Louis XIII of France would blame him, and that King James would be unable to intercede on his behalf. 'I am very embarrassed here because no matter what one does, there is no sympathy', he wrote to his wife. Later, when Frederick had to intervene to prevent Mansfeld and Christian engaging in a duel, he would remark to Elizabeth:

> God granted me a great favour in my not being associated with this army anymore...If God does not extend his hand to them, we will see a bad end to this army...I confess that I would have rather preferred that [the army] had taken another resolution to serve the [Huguenot] Churches of France, and I believe that this could have been better for my affairs, but the soldiers did not want to.

Mercifully for Frederick, his most important ally in the Dutch Republic came to his rescue and commissioned the two commanders to serve against the Spanish. In late August they left Sedan, with Frederick's uncle the Duke of Bouillon even providing them with ten cannons to incentivise their prompt exit. Frederick was free from the association with such reckless men, but he was given dire news shortly thereafter. The English ambassador had written home to James about the Habsburgs' refusal to keep the peace in the Palatinate, and instead, Cossack and Croatian auxiliaries had plundered the Palatinate horribly. The devastation had been led by the Emperor's brother, the perennial adventurer Archduke Leopold.

Furious though he certainly was at this violation of the peace idea, Frederick was to learn later in the summer that Bethlen Gabor had also been pacified. After so many failed truces, Ferdinand sought a conclusive deal with the restless Transylvanian prince that would take him permanently out of the Palatine equation. As early as January 1622, Ferdinand signed a treaty with Bethlen Gabor whereby Bethlen renounced his claims on the throne of Hungary and returned the Hungarian Crown Jewels in return for grants of land, money and titles from Ferdinand. Through this treaty, Bethlen Gabor, the Transylvanian prince, became an imperial prince. At this news the final embers of resistance in Silesia were extinguished, which tied up some loose ends and provided the Emperor with a stable Hungarian frontier at long last.

As he waited in Sedan for more news, short of money and friends, Frederick's Palatine capital at Heidelberg surrendered on 19 September 1622, and before long, its distinguished University had shut its doors, while its Calvinist churches were forcibly closed. Count Tilly, commander of the Catholic League forces, permitted the garrison to march out with full honours, but the city was not spared the unfortunately familiar treatment of plunder and destruction. Mannheim, another important Palatine settlement which boasted an English garrison commander, was abandoned by that same commander when he learned of Heidelberg's fall – there seemed no point in sticking around. Of all Frederick's patrimonial lands, all that remained to him by the end of 1622 was the fortress of Frankenthal, which was itself held by two thousand English soldiers – the only notable military contribution which King James made to his son in law's cause.

Frederick was despondent. He withdrew into his rooms in Sedan and thought only of returning to see Elizabeth in The Hague once again. The conquest of the Palatinate proceeded apace as he wrote in mid-September:

> God may well send me afflictions and it is not the least thing to be far for so long a time from my dear heart, whose portrait I carry so very carefully... may it please God to give us a little corner of the world, to live their happily together, it is all the good fortune that I wish.

Unsurprisingly, having made his plans years before, Ferdinand was unable to grant Frederick any restoration of his lands – the very fear that the Emperor might have to do this had compelled Maximillian of Bavaria to send several urgent letters over the preceding years. But Ferdinand did not want a settled peace as badly as he wanted to see his allies triumphant and his ambitions fulfilled. For this to happen, any approaches in diplomacy would have to be met with impossible requests, until the Palatine cause had so withered and withdrawn that no powers would possibly be able to justify supporting it. In a similar vein to Frederick, Ferdinand believed that the Palatine cause could only be defeated, and Frederick only sufficiently marginalised, once his allies were all defeated in detail. After a year of defeats for Frederick, Ferdinand sought to hasten this process by moving ahead with the plan of transferring the Palatine electorate to Maximillian of Bavaria.[67]

In an anti-climactic, somewhat awkward ceremony on 25 February 1623, Maximillian, Duke of Bavaria became, according to the law set down by the Emperor and those present, the Elector of Bavaria. This was an historic moment, as while matters were to be reorganised in 1648, Bavaria was never to lose its electoral title, leaving a balance of eight electors in the Holy Roman Empire; a number which was to increase to nine with the addition of the Hanoverian elector before the end of the seventeenth century. Ferdinand achieved this sleight of hand by alluding to the concessions he had already made - Saxony had received Lusatia, Brandenburg had been granted extensive rights over East Prussia by the King of Poland Sigismund III, Ferdinand's brother in law – a timely settlement indeed. The Catholic scruples were salved by the capable Papal diplomacy, which emphasised the balance in the Electoral College which was now skewed firmly in favour of Catholics. Once again, Ferdinand had violated the Imperial constitution, and once again, he had got away with it.[68]

Ferdinand had taken a firm step not only against Frederick, but also against the position of political Protestantism within Germany. With Saxony and Brandenburg quiescent, and five Catholic votes now present, there was no chance either for a Protestant Holy Roman Emperor to emerge, or for Frederick's situation to be reversed through that body. That said, Ferdinand had refrained from calling such bodies together during the last several years and had relied for the most part of bribes and private agreements. It was a bitter lesson of Frederick's - and arguably one which he never truly learned – that the Imperial constitution and the traditions it implied were only as strong as the leading forces of the Holy Roman Empire. So long as it suited those in power to ignore its regulations, Frederick's appeals to the unconstitutionality of the Emperor's actions fell on uneasy, but still largely deaf, ears.

We should not doubt Ferdinand's intentions. Having effectively won the battle against Frederick, if not the war, he was confident in his position, and with Spanish and Bavarian monies and men, to affect his goal. With the Palatine threat gone, the most potent challenge to the Catholic Habsburg supremacy had vanished with it. Frederick was an outlaw, an illegitimate contender, and any supporters of his had long since been given good reason to reconsider their decisions. The Lower Palatinate along the Rhine was occupied by Spain, and the Upper Palatinate in Central Europe was occupied by Bavaria. His title was taken from him, his armies had been excused and were fighting in the Dutch War, and the few allies he did have – in England for instance – had failed him time and again.

Ferdinand would have cause to remark

> Disobedience, lawlessness, and insurrection…went always hand in hand with Protestantism. Every privilege which had been conceded to the estates by himself [Matthias] and his predecessor, had had no other effect than to raise their demands. All the measures of the heretics were aimed against the imperial authority. Step by step had they advanced from defiance to defiance up to this last aggression; in a short time they would assail all that remained to be assailed, in the person of the emperor. In arms alone was there any safety against such an enemy – peace and subordination could be only established upon the ruins of their dangerous privileges; security for the Catholic belief was to be found only in the total destruction of this sect. Uncertain, it was true, might be the event of the war, but inevitable was the ruin if it were pretermitted. The confiscation of the lands of the rebels would richly indemnify them for its expenses, while the terror of punishment would teach the other states the wisdom of a prompt obedience in future.[69]

From such an uncompromising mind we must ask whether genuine offers of peace were ever going to flow. Once Frederick had taken that inflammatory step of accepting the Bohemian crown in late 1619, the Emperor was apparently absolved from any notions of foul play, and was instead justified in whatever actions he took. Yet this begs the question, arguably inconsequential by this point, of who exactly was responsible for the escalation of the Bohemian revolt into the war between Frederick and Ferdinand, and later the Thirty Years War. Was it the Elector Palatine, who unwisely accepted the Bohemian crown, knowing or at least suspecting what would follow, or was it Emperor Ferdinand, the uncompromising militant Catholic who refused to permit any kind of peace other than one which saw his enemy surrender unconditionally?

In Geoffrey Parker's mind, it was the Emperor who was responsible for the escalation of the conflict, since Emperor Ferdinand quickly became less interested in compromise, and more interested in total triumph. Parker wrote that given the implacable nature of the Habsburgs' demands and the magnitude of Frederick's defeat, the dispossessed Winter King 'had nothing to lose by continued resistance.'[70] The terms for Frederick's peace were simply too harsh for him or for any self-respecting prince of the Empire to accept, and these terms were only to get more severe as the years progressed. On the other hand, Peter H. Wilson judged Frederick harshly when he wrote on the Elector Palatine's character to the effect that: 'peace foundered on Frederick's refusal to compromise. His defiance encouraged others to remain in the field...'[71] But was Frederick truly to blame for the escalation of the war? The historian Sheilagh C. Ogilvie is more objective when she writes:

> This rebellion became a civil war because both Emperor Ferdinand and Frederick V of the Palatinate appealed to institutions and legitimacy outside the territorial state of Bohemia, although within the composite state of the Empire. The Imperial constitution was invoked as a justification by all participants: by Emperor Ferdinand, as territorial lord, claiming the right to impose fiscal and confessional regulation; by the rebellious Bohemian nobility, claiming protection against Ferdinand's expansionist ambitions as territorial lord; and by protestant Electors and German princes, claiming protection against Ferdinand's expansionist aims as Emperor, particularly his claims to interfere within territorial affairs in matters of religion and internal revolt. With the swing vote in the electoral college at stake, no major German state could afford to remain on the sidelines.[72]

It is sometimes convenient or even useful to distinguish between different periods of the Thirty Years War, and to view different actors as responsible for the transitions between these periods. Yet, the conflict in the early 1620s was not so easily classified. It involved German potentates of varying size and importance, and compelled external powers to exert varying degrees of effort in the name of their allies; whether this was James' unsuccessful diplomatic campaign, Bethlen Gabor's repeated invasions from Hungary, or the King of Poland's timely approaches. The Thirty Years War was still in its early phase when Maximillian was recast as the Elector of Bavaria in spring 1623, but it was impossible to mistake the fact that certain steps were thus being taken, steps which could not be retraced, and which had the danger to inflame passions and tensions, rather than solve them. At the centre of these anxieties could be found the cornerstone of the entire conflict – that terrible rivalry between Ferdinand and Frederick. Having mobilised what few friends and resources he could find, Frederick was effectively spent by 1623, and was mostly out of options. Ferdinand, on the other hand, was just getting started.

Having instituted the changes he had desired, it remained to secure these changes for good, and build upon them wherever possible. Frederick's loud and expected protests washed off the Imperial Chancery, as the Emperor's most important ally was tethered to him for better or for worse. This ally, Maximillian of Bavaria, was certainly happy to cooperate with his Emperor's strategy, because he, like Ferdinand, had now gone too far to step back from the precipice. Anything less than total victory would deprive him of his newly gotten gains and scandalise the Emperor in turn. The coalition of the Emperor, the Elector of Bavaria and the King of Spain was so powerful, that it seemed no other state could combat it, and that Frederick could not possibly stand for long. Soon enough, the dispossessed Frederick would not have to stand alone, as the fearsome coalition of Habsburgs and Bavarians pushed too hard, too far, on too many occasions.

Chapter 9 Notes

[1]Wedgewood, *Thirty Years War*, pp. 101-102.

[2]*Ibid*, pp. 118-119.

[3]An examination of the Anabaptists' origins and beliefs can be found in Robert Friedmann, 'Conception of the Anabaptists', *Church History*, Vol. 9, No. 4 (Dec., 1940), pp. 341-365; Walter Klaassen, 'The Anabaptist Understanding of the Separation of the Church', *Church History*, Vol. 46, No. 4 (Dec., 1977), pp. 421-436. For an examination of the development of Anabaptist sects in the Netherlands see Gary K. Waite, 'The Anabaptist Movement in Amsterdam and the Netherlands, 1531-1535: An Initial Investigation into its Genesis and Social Dynamics', *The Sixteenth Century Journal*, Vol. 18, No. 2 (Summer, 1987), pp. 249-265; in the Tyrol region of the Habsburg lands: Werner O. Packull, 'The Beginning of Anabaptism in Southern Tyrol', *The Sixteenth Century Journal*, Vol. 22, No. 4 (Winter, 1991), pp. 717-726; and a German example in Hesse: David Mayes, 'Heretics or Nonconformists? State Policies toward Anabaptists in Sixteenth-Century Hesse', *The Sixteenth Century Journal*, Vol. 32, No. 4 (Winter, 2001), pp. 1003-1026; John C. Stalnaker, 'Anabaptism, Martin Bucer, and the Shaping of the Hessian Protestant Church', *The Journal of Modern History*, Vol. 48, No. 4 (Dec., 1976), pp. 601-643.

[4]See Brennan Pursell, *The Winter King*, p. 93.

[5]*Ibid*, p. 94.

[6]Geoffrey Parker, *Europe in Crisis*, p. 164.

[7]See Peter H. Wilson, *Sourcebook*, p. 52.

[8]Quoted in *Ibid*, pp. 53-54.

[9]See Pursell, *The Winter King*, p. 97.

[10]The text of the Bohemian Confederation of 31 July 1619 can be found in Peter H. Wilson, *Sourcebook*, pp. 41-46.

[11]Pursell, *The Winter King*, p. 98.

[12]*Ibid*, pp. 99-100.

[13]Quoted in *Ibid*, p. 101.

[14]*Ibid*, pp. 102-103.

[15]Quoted in Peter H. Wilson, *Sourcebook*, p. 54.

[16]For more on the Schmalkald League and its war see Gabriele Haug-Moritz, 'The Holy Roman Empire, the Schmalkald League, and the Idea of Confessional Nation-Building', *Proceedings of the American Philosophical Society*, Vol. 152, No. 4 (Dec., 2008), pp. 427-439.

[17]For a concise examination of Protestantism's spread in Germany see Davide Cantoni, 'Adopting a New Religion: The Case of Protestantism in sixteenth Century Germany', *Economic Journal*, Vol. 122, No. 560, CONFERENCE PAPERS (MAY 2012), pp.502-531.

[18]Frederick G. Heymann, 'The Impact of Martin Luther upon Bohemia', *Central European History*, Vol. 1, No. 2 (Jun., 1968), pp. 107-130.

[19]Leopold von Ranke, *History of the Reformation in Germany*, trans. Sarah Austin (Ungar; New York, 1966; reprint of 1905 edition) vol. 2: pp. 611-612.

[20]Cynthia Grant Shoenberger, 'The Development of the Lutheran Theory of Resistance: 1523-1530', *The Sixteenth Century Journal*, Vol. 8, No. 1 (Apr., 1977), pp. 61-76.

[21]Carl C. Christensen, 'John of Saxony's Diplomacy, 1529-1530: Reformation or Realpolitik?', *The Sixteenth Century Journal*, Vol. 15, No. 4 (Winter, 1984), pp. 419-430.

[22]The French intervened in what was called the Schmalkaldic War, see: D. L. Potter, 'Foreign Policy in the Age of the Reformation: French Involvement in the Schmalkaldic War, 1544-1547', *The Historical Journal*, Vol. 20, No. 3 (Sep., 1977), pp. 525-544.

[23]Quoted in Christopher W. Close, 'Augsburg, Zurich, and the Transfer of Preachers during the Schmalkaldic War', *Central European History*, Vol. 42, No. 4 (DECEMBER 2009), pp. 595-619; p. 595.

[24]Nathan Baruch Rein, 'Faith and Empire: Conflicting Visions of Religion in a Late Reformation Controversy: The Augsburg "Interim" and Its Opponents, 1548-50', *Journal of the American Academy of Religion*, Vol. 71, No. 1 (Mar., 2003), pp. 45-74; p. 48.

[25]See Peter H. Wilson, *Holy Roman Empire*, pp. 559-564. Wilson makes the point that the Interim did not merely anticipate the Peace of Augsburg, but the formation of confessional alliances involving princes and electors had also established a precedent which was to be followed in the early seventeenth century.

[26]See Brennan Pursell, *The Winter King*, p. 103.

[27]Peter H. Wilson, *Europe's Tragedy*, p. 246.

[28]Wedgewood, *Thirty Years War*, pp. 62-63.

[29]Wilson, *Europe/s Tragedy*, p. 264.

[30]Schiller, *Thirty Years War*, pp. 81-82.

[31]See Geoffrey Parker, *Thirty Years War*, pp. 50-51.

[32]Geoffrey Parker, *Europe in Crisis*, pp. 167-168.

[33]Pursell, *The Winter King*, pp. 111-112.

[34]Wilson, *Europe's Tragedy*, p. 294.

[35]See Pursell, *Winter King*, pp. 112-113.

[36]*Ibid*, pp. 114-116.

[37]Quoted in Wilson, *Sourcebook*, p. 67. The full letter can be found on pp. 62-70.

[38]Quoted in Wedgewood, *Thirty Years War*, p. 121.

[39]Quoted in Geoffrey Parker, *Thirty Years War*, p. 55.

[40]Quoted in Brennan Pursell, *The Winter King*, pp. 125-126.

[41]*Ibid*, pp. 126-127.

[42]*Ibid*, p. 129.

[43]Wedgewood, *Thirty Years War*, p. 134.

[44]*Ibid*, pp. 134-135; Parker, *Europe in Crisis*, p. 169.

[45]Pursell, *The Winter King*, p. 136.

[46]Geoffrey Parker, *Thirty Years War*, pp. 56-57.

[47]For a study on accusations of James' appeasement of Spain at this time see: Louis B. Wright, 'Propaganda against James I's "Appeasement" of Spain', *Huntington Library Quarterly*, Vol. 6, No. 2 (Feb., 1943), pp. 149-172.

[48]See Pursell, *The Winter King*, pp. 140-144. This piece quoted from the same, p. 144, and edited for clarity's sake.

[49]*Ibid*, p. 145.

[50]Parker, *Europe in Crisis*, p. 176; Wedgewood, *Thirty Years War*, pp. 145-146.

[51]Pursell, *Winter King*, p. 148.

[52]Quoted in Wedgewood, *Thirty Years War*, p. 143.

[53]*Ibid*, p. 146.

[54]Sir Adolphus William Ward, *The House of Austria in the Thirty Years War* (Macmillan and Co; London, 1869), pp. 52-53.

[55]See C. V. Wedgewood, *Thirty Years War*, pp. 138-140.

[56]Richard Bassett, *For God and Kaiser*, p. 60.

[57]Geoffrey Parker, *Europe in Crisis*, pp. 176-177.

[58]Charles P. Kindleberger, 'The Economic Crisis of 1619 to 1623', pp. 159-161.

[59]Geoffrey Parker, *Europe in Crisis*, p. 178.

[60]Charles P. Kindleberger, 'The Economic Crisis of 1619 to 1623', p. 160.

[61]Geoffrey Parker, *Thirty Years War*, pp. 59-60.

[62]Brennan Pursell, *The Winter King*, p. 150.

[63]Parker, *Europe in Crisis*, pp. 183-184.

[64]Wedgewood, *Thirty Years War*, pp. 149-150.

[65]Pursell, *The Winter King*, p. 165.

[66]Wedgewood, *Thirty Years War*, p. 152.

[67]Pursell, *The Winter King*, 165-184.

[68]Parker, *Europe in Crisis*, pp. 181-182.

[69]Quoted in Schiller, *Thirty Years War*, p. 60.

[70]Geoffrey Parker, *Thirty Years War*, p. 55.

[71]Peter H. Wilson, *Europe's Tragedy*, p. 314.

[72]Sheilagh C. Ogilvie, 'Germany and the Seventeenth-Century Crisis', *The Historical Journal*, Vol. 35, No. 2 (Jun., 1992), pp. 417-441; p. 440.

The Siege of Nieuwpoort

Surrender of Breda (Diego Velazquez, 1624)

CHAPTER TEN
"The Spanish-Dutch Interlude"

ONE: From Truce to War
TWO: Trouble in Paradise
THREE: Delaying Decline

ONE

From Truce to War

In his article on the revolt of the Netherlands, the historian Herbert H. Rowen made the following concise assessment:

A special place in historical studies belongs to those great events that everyone knows of, but few know-at least, know deeply and accurately. In such cases, received notions of sequence, character, causes and results continue to be passed on, unchallenged by any requirement that the explanation fit the facts and that the facts receive explanation. One such great event is the Revolt of the Low Countries in the sixteenth century.[1]

Indeed, if the Dutch revolt against the Spanish can be considered an event which is known of, but not truly known, then certain periods within that seismic event must represent great mysteries. It may be common knowledge that in the late sixteenth century, the Dutch revolted against Spain, and by 1648 they had won this battle, but the interim, and the stretch of twelve years where peace was favoured over war, represents a curious, somewhat unexpected interlude in a struggle where national survival was supposed to be at stake. Unpacking the Twelve Years Truce and its expiration, thus requires some work.

Ever since its conclusion in 1609, the Twelve Years Truce had created something of a stopwatch. Twelve years remained on the clock, which counted down to a resumption of hostilities in a sensitive corner of Europe, and when this countdown was finished, there was no guarantee that powers external to the Spanish-Dutch war would not get involved. After all, the years leading up to the Truce in 1609 had seen no shortage of foreign intervention. The French and English had involved themselves heavily in the Dutch war effort, using the conflict as a means to get back at Spain, and both had paid for it in equal measure: the Spanish supporting Catholic rebels in Ireland, and intervening heavily in the French Wars of Religion and Succession Wars which followed. The Spanish-Dutch War – the Eighty Years War of Dutch resistance to Spanish claims on their sovereignty – had thus demonstrated clear potential for fanning the flames of war in Europe. All eyes were on the expiration date of 1621, with the expectation that the resumption of war would tell a similar story.

Of course, in 1609, nobody had factored in the possibility that Frederick V, Elector Palatine would make his own conflict and story disconnected from the Spanish-Dutch conflict. The focal point of warfare in Europe was not to be the Netherlands then, but the Holy Roman Empire, and more specifically, the Palatinate and Bohemia. The House of Orange was not to be the family of resistance against the Habsburgs; this task was taken by the Palatine House of Wittelsbach. Warfare would not begin in the Netherlands, and its conditions would not fulfil expectations – there would be no siege warfare within a closely connected system of fortresses, but revolts and unrest, which destroyed the countryside of Central Europe. Nonetheless, even while warfare had been a staple fact of European relations for three years by the time the Twelve Years Truce expired in April 1621, there remained potential beyond the original scope of expectations to transform the Spanish-Dutch War not into a regional conflict, but into another appendage of the Palatine War against the Holy Roman Emperor.

For one historian the intensification of conflict from 1621 contributed to the feeling of general crisis at the time, because of 'the coincidence of the outbreak of the Bohemian Revolt and the resumption of the Hispano-Dutch war with the peak of the trade, production and currency problems around 1618-21.'[2] Another historian remarked that the very expansion and continuation of war in Europe beyond 1621 'must be linked to the end of the Twelve-Year Truce and the resumption of hostilities between Spain and the Netherlands in 1621', adding that the Spanish-Dutch conflict had a profound impact upon the war underway in Germany...

> ...because the renewal of hostilities in the Low Countries drained Spanish resources from the commitment to Ferdinand. Moreover, although the Dutch were reluctant to intervene actively before 1621, for fear of prematurely reopening their war with Spain, they gave moderate support to Frederick and his allies after the end of the truce, in order to create diversions which would prevent the Habsburgs from uniting against them. The result, of course, was that neither side of the conflict, in Western Europe or in central Europe, was easily resolved.[3]

Just as the resumption of the war forced Spain to divert resources, so had the Truce enabled Madrid to focus on the defence of Ferdinand's interests alone. As the weeks ticked by and April 1621 approached, the Spanish army in the Southern Netherlands, under the command of Ambrogio Spinola had even affected an ingenious coup whereby, through some deft manoeuvring, he compelled the Evangelical Union to disband. Spain had not been above using the war against Frederick to its advantage – the occupation of the Lower Palatinate long the Rhine was obvious hugely advantageous to Spanish strategic interests, and greatly aided Madrid's ability to fight its war against the Dutch. In this sense, it would be safe to say that the Spanish benefited from the Twelve Years Truce at home, since it enabled its important diplomats and statesmen – among them Count Onate, Baltasar de Zuniga and the Archdukes – to campaign for Spanish interests without worrying about the Northern flank. Without Spanish help, indeed, Ferdinand's task would have been much more difficult, and without the peace with the Dutch, Spain would never have been able to spare so many men for the Emperor's war effort.

While advantages had been gleaned from the Truce, two anxieties remained for Madrid. The first was that the Truce had been damaging in other ways to Spanish interests – especially her overseas commercial and colonial interests, and her prestige. 'If the Dutch were made absolute sovereigns of the lands they occupy, it will clearly be seen as damaging to our reputation', went the advice of King Philip III to his negotiators in Brussels in 1607;[4] by 1621 this idea had gained a life of its own. The second concern was that, as the expiration of the Truce loomed, Spanish statesmen grew more and more concerned that the resumption of the conflict would severely hamper Spanish flexibility and security and may even compromise her efforts in support of Ferdinand. Baltasar de Zuniga, the Spanish favourite and chief minister during the years 1618-1622, himself harboured no illusions on the likelihood of success if the war was resumed, as he wrote in April 1619, two years before the Truce was set to expire:

> We cannot, by force of arms, reduce these provinces to their former obedience. Whoever looks at the matter carefully and without passion, must be impressed by the great armed strength of those provinces both by land and by sea, their strong geographical position ringed by the sea and by great rivers, lying close to France, England and Germany. Furthermore, that state is at the very height of its greatness, while ours is in disarray. To promise ourselves that we can conquer the Dutch is to seek the impossible, to delude ourselves. To those who put all blame for our troubles on the Truce and foresee great benefits from breaking it, we can say for certain that whether we end it or not we shall always be at a disadvantage. Affairs can get to a certain stage where every decision taken is for the worse, not through a lack of good advice, but because the situation is so desperate that no remedy can conceivably be found.[5]

Such a cynical, blunt and pessimistic review of Spain's position in 1619 spoke volumes about the Spanish government's mood at the time. Perhaps more problematic was the fact that Zuniga felt, as did his peers in the Spanish Council of State, that even while a resumption of hostilities with the Dutch would not bring positive benefits, there was no option other than to violate the Truce, since its continuation would only have further degraded Spain's strategic position. Furthermore, while Zuniga here exclaimed how unlikely a victory against the Dutch was, the war would be resumed in April 1621 on this understanding, and without a realistic plan regarding how exactly a victory of any recognisable sort would be achieved. Zuniga knew that Philip III's administration was staring defeat in the face, but he could not imagine any possible means to achieve victory. Zuniga's downcast pronouncements on the situation in Germany echoed those of the Netherlands:

> The situation demands that we should make all those supreme efforts that are normally made when one is confronted by total disaster, attempting to raise all possible resources to provide the archduke with what he is asking for, and attending to all the other matters insofar as it is humanly possible.[6]

To Zuniga, the dilemma was plain, and the solution unclear. If Spain did not intervene with force to support Ferdinand, then not only would the Austrian Habsburgs topple, but Protestantism itself would be invigorated throughout Europe, which would certainly invigorate the Dutch. With Frederick triumphant, King of Bohemia, possessing of two votes in the Electoral College and posing as the champion of Protestantism, was it likely that he would refrain from involving himself in the resumption of the Dutch war with the Spanish, especially considering the Dutch efforts to supply the nephew of their Stadtholder with aid? As Zuniga understood – better than Ferdinand, it would seem – a heavy investment in that troubled Emperor's cause would surely ignite Frederick's passions, sharpen all attitudes and prolong the conflict in the Empire well into the future.

To Zuniga, the choice was either to permit the reduction in the dynasty's power and prestige or provoke a series of interconnected wars which would surely produce the same result in the long run. At this crossroads in policy, Zuniga chose the latter option because at least, in the realm of war, opportunities could present themselves which would not be found in the abandonment of Ferdinand's cause. This choice had the effect of fusing the Dutch and Palatine wars together for Spain and made it impossible for Madrid to abandon Germany just as resources were badly needed for the Netherlands. By 1620, the Spanish had already diverted some soldiers from its Italian and Netherlands possessions, but still Ferdinand was beleaguered, and the pressures from Frederick's allies was proving acute. After some deliberation then, in spring of 1620, Zuniga's policy aims were implemented, and a solid army of twenty thousand men was sent from Spain, not to relieve Vienna or reinforce Hungary, but to attack and occupy the Rhine Palatinate directly.

The significance of this act should not be understated, because this represented the point of no return for Spain. Up to this point Spanish aid had been overt but based more around supporting Ferdinand rather than opening a new theatre of the war in his name. As we saw though, once the ultimatum to Frederick expired in June 1620, a Spanish army led by the veteran Spinola was on the move. This expedition cut the Gordian Knot of Frederick's position in the Empire. Combined with the destruction of the Bohemian-Palatine army at the Battle of White Mountain in November 1620, it rendered his position completely untenable. It seems that Frederick did not expect such a brazen violation of his territory, but it also appears that the Dutch had been fooled as well.

When Spinola's force had first appeared in spring 1620, it was assumed that the Genoese generalissimo would march to Prague and put down the Bohemian revolt once and for all. Spinola's decision to remain on the Rhine and eradicate the potential for an attack on the Emperor from the Palatinate was thus a brilliant strategic coup, but a disastrous move in the long run, because it made compromise completely impossible. It raised the stakes as well, because the Dutch had proved the most significant paymaster of the Bohemian rebels up that point but had refrained from supplying troops. From early 1619 to late 1620, the Dutch provided a subsidy of twenty-five thousand thalers a month, in spite of the conflicts on-going within and without of the Republic at that time.

By summer 1620 then, the Palatine conflict had been treated by both sides as merely the latest in a series of proxy wars between the Spanish and Dutch, but the determined Spanish military involvement made Madrid's intentions clear. Spain had not directly invested so much military personnel in a conflict since the Dutch War, and the very arrival of Spinola – a known figure in Dutch circles – demonstrated that, rather than merely a proxy war, Madrid had turned the Palatinate into the latest theatre of its war with the Dutch. The Dutch, much like Frederick, had underestimated the Spanish resolve to support the Emperor. By providing this support, Spain ensured that Ferdinand could pursue the war on a scale far in excess of what he was capable of, or what his German allies were capable of. Baltasar de Zuniga's decision to draw both branches of the Habsburg dynasty together, regardless of the consequences, meant that, in practice, 'a critical step in turning the revolt in Bohemia into the Thirty Years War had been taken.' Spanish fortunes were now bound to Ferdinand, and since retreat meant defeat, total war and the perpetuation of the most ruinous conflict in the history of early modern Europe proved the only available course.[7]

While the scale of Spanish-Dutch hostility increased markedly after the Spanish intervention in the Palatinate, it would be incorrect to view this Spanish escalation as an overtly belligerent act during a time of peace. Dutch opposition to Spanish policy had not ceased simply because open warfare had ceased. Warfare by other means during the tenure of the Truce – including through diplomatic scheming; by strategic preparations; or, most lucratively at all for the Dutch, privateering in Spain's colonies in the New World, where

464

the Truce did not in fact apply – produced impressive results. The Spanish, as we have seen, focused largely on their European position, and improved it alongside Emperor Ferdinand's campaigns.

The Dutch set their sights further afield and proved so successful at privateering that regular fleets were sent with the express purpose of frustrating the Spanish and diverting their resources. Thanks to the Iberian Union of 1580, both Spanish and Portuguese shipping were liable for attack, and this state of what amounted to open season on the high seas cost Madrid dearly.[8] Geoffrey Parker provided the figure of £100,000-£200,000 in annual losses thanks to the professional piracy of the Dutch – an incredible figure, when we consider that the upkeep of Spain's army in Netherlands was costing them £700,000 per year. The Spanish vulnerability to Dutch overseas attacks would contribute significantly to the rot engendered within the Spanish Monarchy, and its effective collapse into revolt and turmoil in the 1640s.

The Dutch chipped away relentlessly at the Spanish position, to the extent that Madrid diverted considerable resources to shore up its defences in the Americas, and the prospect of abandoning the Philippines altogether was even discussed, so prohibitive were the costs of defending it. If the Philippines was abandoned though, the Spanish feared the prospect of the Dutch occupying these islands and using them as a base to finish off Portuguese trade in the West Pacific once and for all. It was thanks to the extensive piracy of the Dutch that its most renowned colonial interests operated at a significant loss – during the years 1618-21, Mexico sent only £400,000 to the Philippines and a slightly lower amount back to Spain. These sums were lost in the bottomless pit of need and waste which the Spanish system had created. Indeed, as one historian has noted:

> In the discussions at the Spanish Court in 1619-20 over the possibility of renewing the Truce…the strongest and perhaps the decisive argument against prolonging the existing arrangement was the damage which the Dutch were doing to the Indies and American trade.[9]

If the Dutch threat was not dealt with, then Spain would be insolvent purely thanks to the Dutch activities overseas. Operating on this kind of a balance sheet simply was not sustainable, and a resumption of the war in Europe, it was said, was the best means through which Spain could hamper Dutch efforts overseas. Initially, at least, this idea proved to be correct.[10]

The expenses incurred from overseas dangers had also to be measured against the similarly high costs of combating the Dutch influence in Europe. During the Julich-Cleves succession crisis for instance, the Dutch and Spanish supported different candidates and drew in different powers to their side, with the result that soldiers were mobilised and the Austrian Habsburgs were scandalised for acting pre-emptively. The conclusion of this crisis in 1614 enabled the Spanish to focus its attentions on the Imperial succession, and Philip III negotiated with his Austrian Habsburg relatives in a process which was not resolved until 1617. The outcome of these negotiations, the Onate Treaty, provided for extensive Spanish support of Ferdinand once he became Emperor, despite the fact that Spanish finances and attentions were already spread thin. Indeed, the conclusion of the Julich-Cleve crisis was followed quickly by another conflict, the *uzkok* war in the Balkans, and a succession war in Mantua. Both of these conflicts drew in Savoy and Venice, and Dutch aid in money, materials and even warships was forthcoming.

Such conflicts and commitments did not guarantee the eruption of the Bohemian revolt in May 1618, or its escalation in September 1619 when Frederick accepted the crown and turned the event into one of Imperial importance for the Habsburgs. While the Spanish had not wanted the revolt, they saw in its outbreak a chance to reinforce Ferdinand and gain some strategic advantages for themselves, particularly once Frederick was placed under the Imperial Ban (January 1621), and his lands were open for the taking. If Spain could not effectively combat the Dutch abroad, then they would do their best to surround them at home, so that Spanish arms would be in the best position possible to attack the rebels once the Truce expired.

Similarly, since the Spanish were so inclined to use Frederick's war to their advantage, the Dutch were determined to support the banished Elector Palatine, and to house him comfortably in The Hague while his court organised anti-Habsburg schemes. Far more than his father-in-law in London, Frederick's Dutch friends were invaluable to his war effort. Little wonder that three of Frederick's children received names inspired by Republic – Frederick Henry, Maurice and Louisa Hollandia. Elizabeth, Frederick's wife, was perceptive enough to request that the entire States General, the governing body of the Dutch Republic, become Louisa's godparents. A cynic might point out that Frederick and Elizabeth used their children to pull at the heartstrings of the Dutch, but it should be underlined that this act of naming their children after their allies was not undertaken to such an extent in honour of any other ally.

The Palatine family's effective use of its offspring tended to be effective because Frederick himself was related to the House of Orange through his mother, who was the daughter of William the Silent. This made Maurice and Frederick Henry, the Dutch Republic's most celebrated military and civic leaders, uncles of Frederick, and great uncles of his children. It was only to be expected that Frederick would seek to exploit these connections, as he attempted to do with his Danish, English and Brandenburg relatives. Thanks to the looming Dutch conflict with the Spanish Habsburgs, and the interconnected nature of this conflict with that of Frederick, it was only natural that the Dutch would prove so obliging, at least in the first few years.

Yet it should be added that at the time of the eruption of the Bohemian revolt in May 1618 the Dutch were slow to comprehend the gravity of the conflict, or to pledge much significant aid to the rebels. This tardiness was not caused only by a misreading of the Bohemian situation, but by the state of Dutch society in 1618, which was then profoundly distracted by domestic issues.

Not until the end of 1618, when these issues had reached their ugly culmination, would the Dutch be ready and able to intervene in the Bohemian revolt in earnest. It is significant that while the Spanish used the Truce as an opportunity to strengthen their position at home in Europe, but received successive blows to their security abroad, the Dutch suffered the opposite problem. Their piratical activities during this period, as we have seen, distinguished the Dutch as the most competent sailors and most potent threat to Spanish commercialism in the New World. However, within the Dutch Republic, conflicts and tensions which had so long lain dormant as the war against Spain had been pursued were aired and aggravated to the extent that Dutch society appeared to be tearing itself apart at the seams.

The Dutch Republic possessed a unique governmental system all their own. The States General was the governing assembly of the country, which contained at most twelve deputies, nominated and sent from the provincial assemblies of the seven provinces which made up the Republic. Due to its population size, income from trade, and history of supplying the bulk of the monies to pay for the war against Spain, the province of Holland was the most powerful presence in the Republic and in the States General, followed by Zeeland.[11] This order of precedence among the seven provinces created tensions, but the most pressing tensions were provided by the conflict within Dutch society between two political ideas – one being the Orangist ideal, espoused by supporters of the House of Orange, the military leaders of the country, and the other being the Republican or Regent ideal, which sought to reduce the power of the House of Orange and place more power in the hands of the Regents. As one historian put it more eloquently in the nineteenth century:

> The history of the United Provinces, and of Holland especially, from the close of the Spanish rule down to the establishment of the modern monarchy of the Netherlands, is distinguished for its manifestation of a permanent struggle between different opposite principles. Liberty and authority, municipal principle and state principle, republic and monarchy, the spirit of federal isolation and that of centralization, appear to give battle to each other upon a territory itself with difficulty defended from the waves of the ocean by the watchful industry of its inhabitants.[12]

Regents were the ruling class of the Republic – they were only about two thousand in number, but they tended to be the wealthiest citizens of the country and were drawn from 57 of the most important towns. Technically aside from the States-General, the Regents and the regional assemblies was the ruling House of Orange. This House, which currently serves as the monarchy of the Kingdom of the Netherlands, has only been installed as a monarchy in the last two centuries. Before this transformation of the House of Orange's contract with the Dutch people – a decision taken during the Congress of Vienna in 1815 – the House of Orange and the princes it produced enjoyed a vibrant but varied relationship with the ruling apparatus of the Republic. The task of the Princes of Orange was to coordinate the military aspects of the defence against Spain, but for this task to be successful, they required the political support of the States-General, being technically subservient to their authority. This made it necessary for the Princes of Orange to cultivate their own political support base in the country, hence the Orangist party.[13]

In addition to their military role, Princes of Orange tended to occupy the position of Stadtholder, an office which each of the seven provinces contained, as well as the aforementioned military position of Captain-General of the Dutch army and navy. The very office of Stadtholder is difficult to define in the more straightforward political systems of today, and contains few equivalents in European politics.[14] The office was actually inherited from the Spanish system, when the Stadtholder would serve as a regent for the Spanish, with a Prince of Orange – hailing from the Principality of Orange in the south-west of France – tending to occupy the office. The Dutch Revolt, erupting in the late 1560s and crystallising in the 1579 Union of Utrecht, transformed the Stadtholder from a regent of the King of Spain to the leader of the opposition against him.[15] This process was only furthered by his son, Maurice, who declared in 1617 before the regional assembly in Holland that:

> This matter is not to be settled by many orations and flowery arguments but with this (slapping his sword hilt on his word), with this will I defend the religion which my father implanted in these lands, and I will see who shall hinder me![16]

So revered was William of Orange (1533-84) in his position of Stadtholder that he effectively established the reputation of that position for his successors to follow. William's two sons Maurice (1567-1625) and Frederick Henry (1584-1647) only built upon the ideals and traditions of this office, making it their own and leading the Dutch to great victories against the Spanish. Inevitably, the triumphs these men achieved evoked pride and intense passion among the Dutch people, which increased the tension between the Orangists, who wanted their Princes to possess greater powers, and the Regents, who wished to temper it. These tensions culminated at several points in Dutch history, when the Orangists accumulated enough power to purge the Regent ruling class and replace them with Regents loyal to their family's interests – this occurred most violently in 1672, when the leader of the ruling

Regent party and his brother were torn to pieces by the mob, their body parts and genitals cut off and burned.[17]

In 1618 the confrontation between these two elements in Dutch society, the Regents and the Orangists, culminated for the first time, and while no body parts were burned in anger, a significant head was lost. Combined with the heady mix of religious diversity and anxiety over the looming expiration of the Truce with Spain, tensions in the Dutch Republic appeared to be exploding just as affairs in Bohemia were taking on a troubling significance all of their own.

TWO

Trouble in Paradise

'I die not as a traitor!' These were the final words of Johan van Oldenbarnevelt, the advocate of the States of Holland and the pensionary of Rotterdam, shortly before he was beheaded. The high positions in Dutch civic government had not helped Oldenbarnevelt, who for the past two decades had stood as one of the Republic's most important politicians. On 3 May 1619, Oldenbarnevelt's execution was carried out. He had been accused of orchestrating a Catholic plot to overthrow the country's Calvinist Church, and to hand the country to the King of Spain. The charges, fantastic though they may seem for a statesman who was among the most loyal and patriotic of his peers, were sincerely accepted and believed in by the masses, which was what counted at that time.

Maurice of Nassau, Stadtholder of five of the seven Dutch provinces, certainly stood to gain from the removal of the Regents' most visible and renowned representatives. The Orangist Party would now be supreme, by virtue of its ability to fill the power vacuum which Oldenbarnevelt's hasty exit left behind. It also meant that the Calvinist Church was empowered, and that anti-Catholic and anti-Spanish feeling soared just as the Twelve Years Truce was coming to an end. That these developments worked in the favour of Maurice, the military leader of the Republic, must be considered either highly fortunate, or somewhat suspicious.[18]

Certainly, Maurice had ridden the wave of religious anger and passion and had not attempted to ease the anger levelled against Catholics, or to ridicule the conspiracies which emerged from such fanaticism. Those Catholics that had remained in the Republic since the beginning of the Dutch Revolt had always found it difficult to reconcile their faith with the exacting demands of the government, which consistently viewed them with suspicion.[19] Catholics were viewed in many places as the last vestiges of Spanish authority, since the neighbouring Spanish Netherlands to the south made compulsory its adherence to Catholicism, and Protestants there could only be considered

470

a 'negligible minority' thanks to the force of the Counter-Reformation.[20] Catholics could very easily be cast as Spanish spies; this was a trend which began as early as the 1570s, when William of Orange had originally promised religious freedom for all in Holland, but had been forced, following militant displays and unfortunate reprisals, to severely limit the freedoms of the Catholics in the Netherlands.

The founding stages of the Dutch Reformed Church only added to these tensions, because even while this Reformed or Calvinist Church came close to being the state church of the Netherlands – akin to the Anglican, Lutheran or Catholic churches of England, Saxony or Austria respectively – the ruling regent class did not force the population to join in any of the towns. Despite the fact that the Reformed doctrine received the most financial support, with the state paying the wages of the Calvinist preachers, there seemed to be a level of reluctance within Dutch society to compel any sense of religious uniformity. Inevitably, as Christine Kooi wrote, the results of this unwillingness to enforce religious commonality as was done elsewhere – in addition to the flirtations with tolerance, created religious pluralism within the Republic:

> Thanks to this vagueness about the public church's political status (which fell just short of the level of state church) and its limited demographic base of committed adherents, the Reformed congregations occupied an anomalous position in the spiritual life of Holland's cities. For the first time ever, the mayors and magistrates who ruled these municipalities were confronted by genuinely multi-confessional societies dwelling within their city gates. This in turn compelled them, also for the first time, to develop and implement ecclesiastical policies that allowed these differing confessional groups – Reformed, Lutheran, Mennonite, and Catholic – to coexist in relative harmony and good order. The Calvinists demanded an exclusive, confessional, independent public church, but the urban authorities, especially those in Haarlem and Leiden, were inclined to treat them as simply one of several denominations under their jurisdiction, albeit a supremely privileged one.[21]

There seems to have been a measure of sensitivity among Calvinist communities regarding the position of the Church in the country. Calvinist preachers of the Reformed Church were eager to reduce the influence of the other churches were possible, and most of their number wished for the regional assemblies in the different provinces to aid in their mission, without interfering too much in Calvinist business as they did so of course. Interestingly, a policy of de facto toleration included tolerance of Catholics within the state, for the sake of ensuring all would live in harmony and contribute to the overall good of the Republic. Catholics were not, as we have seen, universally liked, trusted or tolerated within the Republic, and as Christine Kooi noted:

For Dutch Roman Catholics, the question was a particularly sensitive one, because the Calvinists could never regard them as just another denomination. Reformed preachers and elders could view secret conventicles of Mennonites and Lutherans with relative equanimity, generally perceiving them more as confessional competitors than as doctrinal antagonists. But the Roman Catholic threat was almost an organic one, imperilling the health of the common body of Christians. Catholics were, as [one] Calvinist widow…put it, "members of the devil" who waged perpetual war on every faithful "member of Christ". The Roman Catholic Church had to be combatted because it was the "false" church.'[22]

Considering the open, tolerant and secular reputation of the Dutch today, such revulsion and burning anger over religious difference can appear absurd. Surely, considering modern Dutch society, the Dutch people must have been historically less passionate or exacting regarding religious difference than their neighbours? Indeed, modern readers are not alone in expecting higher standards of toleration from the Dutch: even during the latter half of the seventeenth century, English settlers in New Amsterdam (before it became New York) expressed surprise at the Dutch unwillingness to grant religious toleration to the incoming Quakers. The resident English settlers, it seemed, expected the Dutch to permit religious freedoms in its New World colonies, just as the Dutch had permitted religious toleration at home in Europe.[23]

The Dutch did contribute something tangible to the religious toleration inbuilt in the American state while they held their New Netherland colony, but the legacy is greatly complicated by the different anecdotes of harsh, theocratic Dutch colonial governors and, of more relevance to our narrative, the glaring example of Dutch religious intolerance in their European Republic.[24] Renowned historian Pieter Geyl addresses this strange, somewhat alien state of affairs:

> The religious disputes which dominate the history of the Republic during the Truce are foreign to the present-day reader. His first reaction is one of dismay at this squandering of so much passion on such incomprehensible issues. When he has browsed a little in the musty library of polemics bequeathed by legions of theologians and divines, he is at a loss to choose between astonishment and disgust at the virulence with which these Christian fell upon each other, and at the dry as dust argumentations, cram-full of quibblings and hair-splittings, with which they to approach the eternal verities. This of course, means that we of the present…find its theological terminology hopelessly antiquated.[25]

The religious dispute which had rocked the Dutch Republic began as early as 1610, and was initially unconcerned with Catholicism, and moved more by fierce debate within Calvinist theology. The competing religious camps, their beliefs and the emotions which were evoked need not detain us too much, especially since other historians have spent a great deal of time focusing on these struggles already. One such historian, Jasper van der Steen, summarised the core of the religious disagreement conveniently for us:

> Around 1610, a religious quarrel broke out about the Reformed doctrine of double predestination between two professors of theology in Leiden: Jacobus Arminius and Franciscus Gomarus. The disagreement between the two men was ostensibly a matter for academics only, but in fact it almost dragged the state into civil war.[26]

The question of how this academic debate led to Johan van Oldenbarnevelt's death is answered by the pace with which this issue of doctrine became politicised. The disagreement within the Calvinist Reformed Church and the identification by preachers with one side or the other, led to the creation of two camps named after the figures who led the debate – Arminians and Gomarists. Arminians were in the minority, and so they issued a remonstrance to the States of Holland in January 1610 requesting protection for their sect. Oldenbarnevelt, then at the height of his powers, took their side, for the sake of the greater harmony of the state – let the Arminians say what they wanted, if it made them happy and reduced the likelihood of conflict. Unfortunately for Oldenbarnevelt, Gomarists disagreed with this premise of tolerance, since it divided the Reformed Church and upset their orthodox sensibilities. Maurice of Nassau, Stadtholder of Holland, took the side of the Gomarists, and the stage was effectively set, yet there was as of yet no sign that any kind of terrible consequences would be the result of whatever confrontation might have followed.

In 1613, Oldenbarnevelt attempted to paper over the cracks which were emerging, by co-opting the Pensionary of Rotterdam, Hugo Grotius, to pen the *Resolution for the Peace of the Churches*.[27] This was adopted by the States of Holland the following year, and with this stroke, the leading political figure in the Netherlands seemed to give his stamp of approval to differences of opinion within the Republic. It was imperative, for the civic and political unity of the Republic, that religious questions should not divide the people, particularly since the war against the Spanish enemy had only been put on hold. Yet for Oldenbarnevelt, his role in bringing this peace about had effectively tarnished his reputation. In spite of the monumental success that this Twelve Years Truce had represented for the Dutch, those that were unaware of the realities of the conflict believed that their country had been manipulated into making peace with the enemy at the wrong time.

Maurice of Nassau had initially been vocal in his opposition to the Truce, but he had eventually accepted the will of the majority. As the historian Carl Bangs wrote:

Maurice opposed the truce on personal and military grounds, although he was happy enough to have the support of the Calvinists, even though their theology probably confused him. The truce threatened his military successes, and military success was the path by which he sought to achieve political sovereignty. Opposition to the truce became a passion with him.[28]

His opposition had not been forgotten by those citizens against the Truce, who increasingly identified with the Gomarists, and who whispered that Oldenbarnevelt, far from acting in the country's interests in 1609, had in fact acted in secret consultation with Spain. The ruling Regents were guilty of no such crime, and the Truce had been welcomed eagerly in many sections of the countryside where war had exhausted and impoverished enterprise and trade. It was relatively easy, nearly a decade later, to forget about the war's privations, and to turn against those responsible for the current peace. Oldenbarnevelt, a sympathiser of Arminius, and his Regent peers, were transformed into traitors of the state, and in a short time, the narrative became one far removed from the academic confessional debate – it was now superimposed onto the more important questions of foreign policy, of war with Spain, and of the historical memory of what the Dutch had so far accomplished.

By 1617, attitudes had hardened still further. Arminians were now known as Remonstrants thanks to their presentation of the Remonstrance to the States of Holland in early 1610, while the Gomarists were known as the Counter-Remonstrants. The abundance of titles and names only served to widen the chasm between both sides, and each became identified – rightly or wrongly – with distinct political views in addition to their religious outlook. Through the development of such assumptions, which grew from concerns into fears, Dutch society began to divide against itself. When Oldenbarnevelt called Maurice of Nassau to The Hague in a bid to quell dissent and restore order, Maurice refused, reasoning that the princely guard which Oldenbarnevelt requested he used was meant only for his personal protection.

The Hague was a majority Arminian city, but that had not prevented the Gomarists from demanding extensive rights – the same rights they refused to Arminians in the other towns and cities of the Republic. In mid-July 1617, when Maurice openly attended a Gomarist service, Oldenbarnevelt got the message, and through his political clout he passed the Sharp Resolution which empowered civic leaders to employ mercenaries who would enforce the official policy of toleration, mandated in the ruling passed by the States of Holland in 1614. Oldenbarnevelt had not helped his self-image by supporting the French policies levelled against the Huguenots, an act which – while taken in the interests of Dutch political strategy – did the advocate no favours with the mob. It became relatively easy to cast Oldenbarnevelt as the pro-Spanish, pro-Catholic schemer who plotted with his circle to overthrow the sovereign Republic and install a Spanish regent. Maurice, troublingly for Oldenbarnevelt, did not strive to defend his colleague, in spite of their cooperation in the past. Perhaps the Stadtholder had sensed that there was political capital to be made in the conflict to come.[29]

'The original cause of this disorder is easily discovered to be Arminianism: the effects will be faction in the state, and schism within the church'. These were the words of Sir Dudley Carleton, the English ambassador in The Hague. Carleton was passionately in the Gomarist, Counter-Remonstrants camp, and this was demonstrated in his correspondence home to London. Carleton added: 'The factions begin to divide themselves betwixt His Excellency and monsieur Barnevelt, as heads, who join to this present difference their ancient quarrels'.[30] This observation proved to be astute, for Oldenbarnevelt would live and die not on the decisions made regarding religious policy per se, but because of the inherent conflict and tension within the Dutch Republic, which were founded upon the competition between the Regents and the Stadtholder and, more recently, on the question of the Truce.

Maurice disagreed with Oldenbarnevelt on many aspects of Dutch foreign policy, and this example of disagreement trickled down into the supporters of both camps and fuelled the assumptions which both camps held of the other. The next step in the conflict was to present a certain interpretation of history. To the Counter-Remonstrants, the Remonstrants were corrupting the version of Calvinism which all Dutchmen had fought for during the Revolt against Spain. By corrupting the creed, they were corrupting the memory of the conflict, and manipulating it for their own ends.[31] If the version of Calvinism which had been accepted originally was now lost, then so too would the invaluable lessons and traditions of the Revolt, and to be replaced by what? Gomarists saw in the Arminian creed the intrusion of heretical ideas such as 'salvation by works' and the reduction of God's sovereign will in their lives. Such heresies appeared suspiciously like the doctrines of Catholic teaching, especially to those orthodox Calvinists who looked to extirpate that creed from the entirety of the Republic. Perhaps in Arminianism, Catholicism would creep back into the country through this safe avenue, and from there, Spanish Habsburg influence and control would follow.

By making such views about their doctrinal opponents public, the Counter-Remonstrants may not have expected much of a response, but they got one. Since Oldenbarnevelt was known to empathise with the Arminians, even if he did not profess his whole belief in their tenets, the advocate was able to make use of his influence to instigate a great pamphlet war levelled against the Gomarists. In short, the Arminians attempted to secularise the Dutch Revolt as a way of legitimising their movement, and to undermine what they viewed as the extremism of their Calvinist countrymen, who they still considered their brothers in Christ. William of Orange, the father of the nation, had rallied against such extremism after all, and he had not launched his revolt against Spain for religious reasons alone; instead, the Remonstrants claimed, the first Prince of Orange had fought Spain for political and national reasons. The war had not been launched for Calvinism, but so that the Dutch would be free. These ideas were far too scandalous to go unanswered.

Now that the Arminians had made use of his father's name for their pamphlets, Maurice had no issue with the Counter-Remonstrants using William of Orange for their purposes as well. An anonymous pamphlet disputed the Arminian findings, and noted that the furtherance of Calvinism had been central to the Prince's motives for rebelling against Spain, adding:

> If he [the author of the previous Arminian pamphlet] were to research the many old writings, commissions, and instructions by the Prince of Orange in the years 1567 [to] 1572, and subsequent years, until he was killed so cruelly and murderously…he would find this to have been his chief aim, above all to further the honour and service of God, to protect the oppressed Christians, and maintain the privileges and liberties of these lands.[32]

As if the debates could not contain any more exaggeration or dubious comparisons, the tempo was greatly increased by the publication of a pamphlet which compared Oldenbarnevelt to the Duke of Alva, the infamous figure of Dutch history who had been sent to the Netherlands to crush the revolt in its early phase, and who had executed many thousands of Dutch citizens in his quest. The Iron Duke, as he was known, still evoked passionate reactions from those citizens who heard his name, and while enforcing the comparisons between Alva and Oldenbarnevelt may appear shrill and ridiculous to us, propaganda and rumour greatly abetted the exercise. In one 1618 Counter-Remonstrant print, *Image of the Old and New Time*, Oldenbarnevelt is depicted as seated, while a figure to his left whispers what is assumed to be unsound advice in his ear. The caption depicted two individuals examining the image and read:

> 'Hang on! Who do I see there? Hey mate, look at it, how well it is cut.' 'Hey let us have a look: is it not Barnevelt? The illustrious president, full of power and great force?' 'Tis a president alright', his friend replies, 'but he is named the duke of Alba.'

In this particular print, one could actually swap the head of Oldenbarnevelt for that of the Duke of Alva by flipping over the top of the image. This inventive design proved highly effective at reinforcing the message which the Counter-Remonstrants were creating. The latter part of the aforementioned print traced the dialogue between the two individuals, who debated for a few sentences on the similarities between Oldenbarnevelt and the Duke of Alva, before a third figure entered into the discussion and assured both of his friends that, in fact, there was little difference between the Iron Duke and Oldenbarnevelt after all. The implications of propaganda tracts liked these were as explosive as thcy were deadly for Oldenbarnevelt and his allies.[33]

The outcome of this conflict led to the above opening scene, but the implications of it did not end with Oldenbarnevelt's death in May 1619, as he sought in vain to protest his innocence in the face of so many ludicrous charges. Maurice of Nassau, the individual who had done much to rouse the population against Oldenbarnevelt, must have known that the advocate of Holland was not the second incarnation of the Duke of Alva. Indeed, he must also have known that Oldenbarnevelt had by no means been the sole Regent in favour of the Twelve Years Truce, and that the Republic, while it unravelled at home, had made great progress abroad, largely at Spain's expense. The very vitriolic situation, and the implications of his decision to side determinedly against the civic leader of the Republic placed Maurice in an unprecedented position of power and influence, and added a great deal of credit to his already impressive reputation, for he was the man who rooted out the traitor, and who brought the heresy to an end, and now he would be the figure to lead the Dutch people to victory against Spain once more.

The Reformed Calvinist Church was greatly empowered and vindicated by its pursuit of the struggle against Arminians, who were unilaterally outlawed and expelled from the country in the aftermath. Thereafter, the Reformed Church made great efforts at installing its authority in every facet of Dutch life, this time with only limited success. Pieter Geyl wrote that a spiritual war was declared 'on all ancient folk-customs which seemed to perpetuate a popish love of tradition, or which gave expression to an unchristian enjoyment of life', and in these acts, the public were urged to take part. However, as Geyl noted thankfully, fundamentalism of this kind was not allowed to triumph, because even as the Dutch had largely accepted the incompatibility of the Arminian creed with the Calvinist doctrine, and even while Oldenbarnevelt had been disposed of with suspicious ease, the Church would never be able to usurp those activities or enterprises for which the Dutch were known. Theocracy did not replace commercialism, although a Puritanical strain of Calvinism did put down roots in the countryside and within smaller towns, while the more cosmopolitan cities remained immune to such penetration. In the context of the Eighty Years War with Spain, the narrowing of the religious field of vision, and the encounter with the Arminian heresy made the Dutch people more, rather than less likely, to oppose Catholicism in all of its forms. This meant that any future union with the Southern Spanish Netherlands, if it came, would be fraught with religious dissension and conflict – a fact which Madrid proved all too willing to play up.[34]

The historian Kimberly J. Hackett concluded that: 'The language of Dutch patriotism, invoked to censure Oldenbarnevelt's supposed actions against the state, was the same as that employed to rail against the truce in 1609 and, later, to call for the renewal of war in 1621.' In foreign capitals, the reaction to Oldenbarnevelt's fall varied. King James had instructed his ambassadors to fall in line with the majority view, a line which ambassador Sir Dudley Carlton adhered to willingly, but the French were less confident. Louis XIII's ministers mostly evacuated The Hague during the worst of the violence, and they did so with feelings of profound shock and distaste. Oldenbarnevelt had been a reliable and stable civilian leader, and French relations with the Republic, while uneasy so long as the Huguenots chafed under the Catholic French King, were mostly good.[35]

Any sense of foreboding or the fear that fundamentalism would now be given free rein in the country at the expense of French interests were soon quashed though. One of the guiding features of the demonstrations against Oldenbarnevelt was its anti-Spanish quality, a feature which the French ministers, thinking ahead to the inevitable conflict with Madrid, certainly valued. Indeed, with Maurice of Nassau now greatly empowered, it seemed inevitable that the Dutch and Spanish would not renew the Twelve Years Truce before it expired in April 1621, as some had feared. Instead, the Dutch Regent government, now populated with personnel selected and approved by Maurice, was virtually guaranteed to put an end to the Truce with a resumption of the war.

Perhaps Maurice believed that the end of peace would give him the ultimate opportunity to cement his legacy in the Republic, and further strengthen his House of Orange at the expense of civilians like Oldenbarnevelt who might appear in the future. A successful attack against the major pressure points of the Spanish Netherlands would net Maurice glory and renown, and would enable him to reach new heights of power as the commander of the Netherlands' forces – its Captain-General and Stadtholder. As it transpired, the transition from peace to war was not destined to be smooth.

THREE
Delaying Decline

Pieter Peck was the Chancellor of Brabant, and as such was a high ranking official in the Spanish Netherlands, who could be expected to speak in the name of his masters in Brussels and Madrid, and to act in their interests. It was too significant to ignore his diplomatic mission to The Hague in the spring of 1621, on the very eve of the expiry of the Twelve Years Truce and the resumption of hostilities with Spain which were expected. Some anticipation surrounded Peck's arrival, and when he stood before the States-General in the Dutch capital, there was much interest in what he was about to say. Could this Spanish servant be here to offer genuine terms, or proper concessions, or some form of agreement which would heal the last four decades of bitterness?

Peck's presentation started off well. He spoke with great emotion of the interests of 'the Netherlands, our common fatherland', a reference no doubt to the desire on both sides of the Netherlands divide to reunite their country under one flag. Then, however, things quickly went downhill. He invited the States-General to come to a settlement 'under acknowledgement of the natural sovereigns', which of course, meant the Archdukes, and consequently, the King of Spain. 'No wonder', Pieter Geyl recounts, 'their High Mightinesses [in the States-General] listened to him with head shakes and signs of amazement.' No wonder indeed, for it seemed that Peck, this intelligent and perceptive individual, had been sent to The Hague on a fool's errand, with a mission to simply make the Dutch see sense, in the typically ignorant style of Spanish government.

Peck's mission soon became hotly resented, and he quickly felt his presence unwelcome with this insult. As per diplomatic protocol, he was protected in his exit from the country, and this protection was certainly needed from the enraged populations of Delft and Rotterdam, who had moved to intercept him once they learned of his preposterous demands. It seemed, even after all these years of fighting the Spanish, those same Spanish did not take the Dutch seriously. Or, if they did take the Dutch seriously, they did not appreciate the circumstances, the reality, of the situation in 1621. How could the Dutch possibly have agreed to this request from Peck? How could they simply put themselves in the care of the 'natural sovereigns' as though the bitter history had not occurred? How, indeed, could they trust a word that the Spanish said?

Their enemy's ignorance had left them stunned, but perhaps Peck's snub had been deliberate? Perhaps it had all been a mind-game and a chance for Madrid to demonstrate that they did not take their Dutch enemy seriously? The States-General would not play along, and Peck's embassy was evicted almost immediately. Shortly thereafter, the Truce did expire, the war was resumed and, even more significantly, two figures from an older time died: first Archduke Albert, one half of the Archdukes government in Brussels, upon which the governance of the Spanish Netherlands passed to his widow Isabella. Second, King Philip III of Spain died on the last day of March 1621, whereupon the throne passed to his son Philip IV. 'As though the disasters and disappointments of the previous generation had never been', Geyl wrote, 'this young man preserved inviolate in his mind the pretensions of his father and grandfather.'[36]

Knowing how the second phase of the Spanish-Dutch war panned out, and knowing that this stretch of the conflict cost Spain dearly, ruined her security and effectively guaranteed her inability to comprehensively defeat the French, it can seem like the most irresponsible example of denial that no individual or king or government intervened to stop the madness, and to save the Spanish people any more suffering in this hopeless conflict. Pronouncements about the perceived impossibility of defeating the Dutch were by no means absent from Spanish government circles, and yet the conflict was resumed anyway, with the same vague, impossible goals of subordinating the Dutch to Spanish rule, and of retaking the rebellious provinces in the name of the new King. As the historian Peter Brightwell wrote

> Underlying much of the comment on Spanish behaviour at this time is the feeling that the wise course of action in 1621 would have been for the Spaniards to cut their losses, either by extending the Truce or by winding up the war altogether. In fact, of course, they fought on, to no avail, for another twenty-seven years. The implication is that they never made a rational assessment of their power and capabilities relative to those of the Dutchmen. The business of taking decisions was a matter of espionage, political and court intrigue, ideological claptrap, bureaucratic inflexibility, religious fanaticism - anything, in fact, except rational appraisal.[37]

Indeed, irrational appears in many respects to be the most accurate description of Spanish foreign policy. Either Madrid understood the risks and ploughed onwards anyway, or her government was so completely ignorant of these risks, and so consumed by the idea that nothing had really changed in the Spanish-Dutch relationship, that the war could be won. Either way, the Spanish approach to foreign policy appears ruinous, suicidal even, unless we consider that Spanish policymakers, led by Baltasar de Zuniga, assessed the situation in spring 1621, and concurred that – rather than it being a question of whether or not to renew the war – Spain had no choice but to renew it. To maintain the peace would have spelled doom for the Spanish Empire and for the reputation and prestige of the Spanish Habsburg dynasty. At least in war, the debilitating effects of Dutch piratical enterprise abroad could be combatted by taking the fight to the Dutch in the European homeland. That, at least, was the idea, and initially – at least until a turning point of sorts began to occur from the mid-1620s, this estimation appeared correct.

The Spanish government had not allowed the Truce to expire without offering terms of any kind though. Three points of primary importance were put forward by the new king Philip IV; freedom of worship for Catholics, the opening of the River Scheldt to trade, and the evacuation of Dutch privateers and tradesmen from the Indies. Of these three requests, the final one was the most urgent for Spain, who had paid dearly in the Truce years thanks to the Dutch commitment of resources to piracy. Since they did not have to worry about home defence, more resources in manpower and money could be spent harassing Spanish and Portuguese shipping, which paid dividends for the Dutch, and caused unrelenting havoc for Spain.

Perceptive Spanish statesmen would have noted that the Truce years represented only the culmination of Dutch piracy and intrusion into Hispanic markets overseas – this trend truly began from 1594, when the defensive phase of the Spanish-Dutch War ended, and the Netherlands was made secure against a Spanish reconquest. In that year of 1594 indeed, the Dutch captained half of all ships which passed through the Sound, whereupon the resources and trading cities of the Baltic would be accessed.[38] Evidently, the Dutch were more than accustomed to naval enterprise, and the expertise they exuded in these northern dealings made the Baltic region a theatre of profound importance to their economic interests – a fact which Spain was later to attempt to undermine. Thus, it must be stressed that the Dutch had been giving Spain a run for their money for several decades before the Truce was concluded, and that the Truce, rather than permitting the Dutch to test these new markets, enabled them instead to squeeze more out of them than ever before. The historian Engel Sluiter wrote that:

> Thousands of Netherlanders repeatedly made the American run, and the experience they acquired prepared them to hurl their great challenge against the Iberian powers in America after the renewal of hostilities and the founding of the Dutch West India Company in 1621.

Furthermore, Sluiter concluded that Dutch conflict with Spain and the Spanish response so drained and exhausted the latter's resources, that Madrid proved simply incapable of allocating enough resources to the fringes of its Empire. This reduction in authority on the edges of the realm enabled other powers like England and France to sneak into the Spanish backyard of America, and it helps to explain why the English colony of Virginia was virtually untouched by the Spanish for the entirety of its existence – Spain simply lacked the means to respond to so many threats at once, and her capabilities had been significantly reduced thanks to the war of attrition with the Dutch.[39] The reason why the Truce had provided the Dutch with what in Madrid was considered something of a breather was due to the clause within that Truce, specifically clause four, which read:

> ...the said king understands this to be restrained and limited to the kingdoms, countries, lands and lordships which he has and-possesses in Europe and other places and seas in which the subjects of other princes who are his friends and allies have the said trade by mutual consent; as regards the places, towns, ports and harbours that he holds beyond the said limits, that the lords estates and their subjects may not carry on any trade without the express permission of the said lord king; but they shall be allowed to carry on the said trade, if it seems good to them, in the countries of all other princes, potentates and peoples who may wish to permit them to do so even outside the said limits, without the said lord king, his officers and subjects who depend on him making any impediment in this event to the said princes, potentates and peoples who may have permitted it to them, nor equally to them (i.e. the Dutch) or to the persons with whom they have carried out or will carry out the said trade.

By this clause, the Spanish had acknowledged the Dutch right to trade not only with powers in Europe, but also those European possessions under the Spanish flag, such as the Southern Spanish Netherlands. This was a huge concession, and because of the implications of it, and the weight of advantage it granted to the Dutch during the Truce years, the Spanish government and public proved highly sensitive to its interpretation. Did the clause permit the Dutch to venture into the Indies, and trade with the powers in place there? Did the clause permit the Dutch to encroach on the trade monopoly in these theatres in the modern-day Caribbean and Asian territories which the Spanish and Portuguese had spent more than a century building up? Thanks to the vagueness of the clause, the Dutch were able to interpret it as they desired, and the resulting encroachment and enrichment of these usurpers was bitterly resented in Spain and Portugal.[40]

To these sensitivities we must add a further layer – as per the Papal resolution set forth by Pope Alexander VI in the fifteenth century, all lands and territories outside of Europe were to be divided between the Spanish and Portuguese crowns.[41] Upon this Papal Bull Lisbon and Madrid based their legitimacy and prestige, and they vociferously opposed any challenge or loophole which the other side might exploit to get around it. Any foreign potentates who traded with countries that were not Spanish or Portuguese were chastised as rebels, and so long as they possessed the power to reinforce this position, it remained a formidable means through which the Iberian monopoly over all colonial possessions could be assured.

Of course, since their European peers began establishing colonies of their own, this Papal Bull only remained relevant for a limited time. The loophole chosen by the European powers to make their way into these markets was one which claimed that Spanish-Portuguese exclusivity was only valid in places that these powers were actually the occupying force. A claim and a papal grant were not sufficient to halt the tide of enterprise, adventure and piracy from any European power, least of all their Dutch foe. Within clause four, neither Spain nor the Dutch made any concessions about this technicality – the Spanish continued to claim rights by papal decree, and the Dutch continued to ignore them. As the historian Peter Brightwell noted: 'Both sides probably left the conference table in 1609 believing that they, or their lawyers, had tricked the other with regard to Clause Four.' Of course, when it emerged that both chose to interpret the Truce as they saw fit, accusations of bad faith and manipulation were thrown about. Thanks to the inherent vagueness of the clause which both sides had agreed to though, they only had themselves to blame.[42]

At the same time though, if this examination of the lingo used in treaties has taught us anything, it is that neither the Spanish nor the Dutch expected issues as contentious as trade with the Indies to be resolved with a single agreement. We should remember that this clause was included within the Twelve Years *Truce*, and not the Treaty of Eternal Peace. It was not expected to last longer than twelve years, and if it was to be renewed in 1621, then that was a problem for the negotiators that were present at the bargaining table at that point in time. As a result of this favouring of short-term solutions and deliberate avoidance of any definite resolution, the Dutch established a substantial presence in the Indies, and had wreaked havoc on the Spanish financial markets.

There was absolutely no chance that the Dutch would evacuate these positions, and the Truce years had shown the resolute determination of the Dutch to exploit Spanish overextension and supplant them as the predominant trading power. Spain was therefore determined in its own right to retain their grip on their theoretical right to keep the Dutch out, and to prevent the Dutch presence in the Indies from ever becoming accepted or seen as natural. The more recognition which the Dutch acquired, the harder it would be for Spain to reverse these dangerous new developments. From 1619, when the question of renewing the Truce became a topic for discussion in Spain, the school of thought began to gain currency that the Dutch had been given an easy ride in the previous decade. Had the Truce never been signed, the Dutch would have been far too beleaguered at home to have invested so many resources in the explosion of their commercial interests abroad.

This idea is somewhat flawed as we have seen, since from 1594 the Spanish had proved unable to actually threaten the existence of the Dutch Republic, and it from this point, rather than from 1609, that Dutch intervention in Spanish overseas markets began to increase. On the other hand, while they were mistaken on the origins of the current problem, the Spanish were correct to denote a solidifying Dutch presence in the Indies during the Truce years. It was only to be expected that with the closing of one front in the war against Spain, the Dutch would pursue another with a great deal more energy and enthusiasm than they had before, not least because the option of venturing to the Indies provided a sense of wonder and an opportunity for enrichment which was absent in the European war. The Spanish understood this development and the correlation of peace with their decline and vulnerability overseas, and they were thus presented with two options: either force the Dutch out, or make a demand that they leave the Indies a pre-requisite of a renewal of the Truce.

There was little utility, alternatively, in renewing the Truce and taking the fight to the Dutch in the Indies, as some Spaniards wished to do, simply because the size of the theatres in question were far too large to be given to many long term plans. Communication and access to accurate information was incredibly difficult in such far-flung places, and it was often easier to provide Spanish vessels with vague instructions for them to improvise according the Spanish interests, rather than to issue inflexible demands which could be outdated by the time their destination was reached. A resumption of the European war would focus the issue, and remove what was believed to have been the Dutch advantage from the equation. With the playing field levelled, the Spanish and Portuguese would be better able to defend their overseas interests, and if necessary, portions of the Dutch Republic could be exchanged for these interests in due course.[43]

With the Dutch gone from the Indies, it would not matter that the rebellious provinces remained outside of the King's control, because he could rest assured that the income from his overseas domains would begin to pick up again now that the Dutch pirates and traders were absent. Perhaps unsurprisingly, since the Truce had resulted in something of a free-for-all which the Dutch had greatly benefited from, the concept of abandoning these lucrative tactics was impossible. Not only that, but Pieter Geyl noted that it actually united the Netherlands against the idea of a continued peace altogether, if that was the price Spain requested. Better to resume the war and retain their knife to Spain's colonial interests, even if it meant that Spain would now be working overtime to force the Dutch to spend more on home defence. The greater the threat to the Dutch position in Europe, the more resources and attention they would be forced to allocate to their home defence, and the clock could potentially be turned back, to a period before 1594 when the Dutch Revolt ceased to be a war of national survival for the Dutch, and when their debilitating assaults on Spanish overseas interests had truly begun.[44]

Our analysis must begin with the expiration of the Truce in April 1621. Only a few weeks before, a strategic coup by Spinola had forced the Evangelical Union to dissolve itself, and with this army Spinola refocused his attention on the Dutch once more. By this point the Dutch had learned of the defeat of Frederick V, the Elector Palatine, who had taken up residence in The Hague. If the Dutch wished to remain aloof from Frederick's schemes, and to refrain from provoking the wrath of the Emperor, then they proved incapable of keeping the Winter King on any kind of leash. We will recall that in July 1622, Frederick released Christian of Brunswick and Ernst von Mansfeld, his two most important commanders, from his service. Within a few months, after troubling Frederick to no end in his temporary residence at Sedan, these two commanders and the men who remained at their disposal were hired by the Dutch, who urged them to rush to relieve the siege of Bergen-Op-Zoom, which they did on 4 October 1622.[45]

We will also recall that by autumn 1622, Frederick was relying on King James' policy of mediation to save his Rhineland Palatinate, and he sincerely believed that by refraining from hostilities, the Spanish would also cease from troubling his homeland. But it was not to be. The Spanish had no interest in holding back and sought to make use of their gains along the Rhine to better pursue their war with the Dutch. James, it seems, had not figured this out, and did not realise that the Spanish were playing for keeps when they occupied the Lower Palatinate in its entirety by late 1622.[46] By the end of the year, only the fortress town of Frankenthal remained in Frederick's hands, and this only because the garrison was English. When it was ordered to surrender by James in spring 1623, Frederick officially lost control of his entire Palatinate, with the Rhinish portion occupied by Spain, and the Upper portion further to the east occupied by Bavaria.

The Dutch had been busy in the meantime; with Mansfeld and Christian of Brunswick's combined army proving its usefulness, the decision was made to pay its wages for another few months to keep it in the field. This was great news for Mansfeld and Christian of Brunswick, who had searched for a purpose ever since Frederick had released them from his service. It was also promising news for the Dutch, who could keep Mansfeld in winter quarters over 1622-23 along their border to the south-west, which would keep Spinola off balance. Despite the total loss of his homeland, by the turn of 1623

Frederick had returned to The Hague and was well placed to coordinate a joint offensive against the Habsburgs of both branches, with Dutch support. The Dutch army would hold Spanish attention in the Netherlands, while Mansfeld and Christian would move towards Bohemia, and Bethlen Gabor would strike out from Hungary. He had high hopes, but as usual, such hopes were disappointed.

The Spanish-Dutch border proved relatively quiet in 1623, but this was perhaps the only net positive of Frederick's plan. Once again Mansfeld and Christian of Brunswick worked their way towards Bohemia, and once again Count Tilly strove to meet them in battle. As before, Mansfeld and Christian of Brunswick divided their troops, but this did not necessarily appear to matter, as Christian led twenty-one thousand men. Christian learned that Tilly had aimed at cutting him off by moving through the borders of Lower Saxony, perhaps to send a message to John George of Saxony and the minor princes near his lands. These princes of the Lower Saxon Circle were caught between Tilly's warnings and Christian's urgings, neither of which were particularly friendly. 'Neutral the princes and people were and wished to remain, but they had no choice', Wedgewood lamented, as Christian marched across the countryside. On 13 July 1623, Count Tilly crossed over the border into Lower Saxony, fulfilling his plans to meet Christian before he could reach his destination or link up with Mansfeld.

For his part, Christian sent repeated letters to Mansfeld urging the veteran commander to join him with his smaller army, but Mansfeld refrained from doing so, since he had located secure quarters in the Bishopric of Münster and did not intend to expose himself and place his best resource – his army – at risk. A sense of desperation now entered Christian of Brunswick's actions. He prepared his army not to fight Tilly, but to withdraw to the Netherlands with the plunder that his now reduced army of fifteen thousand had gathered. With insufficient discipline and speed, not to mention being weighed down by their ill-gotten gains, Christian's army was forced to turn around and meet Tilly's in the battle of Stadtlohn on 6 August 1623.[47]

What followed was 'the most decisive of all the Catholic victories', according to Geoffrey Parker, who noted that the carefully coordinated net of agreements and alliances broke apart almost immediately upon the news of Christian of Brunswick's terrible defeat. Christian limped home with only six thousand men remaining, many of whom elected to desert rather than continue serving this luckless man. Tilly would have followed this significant victory with an attack on Mansfeld in Münster, but Mansfeld's defences were too strong for such an act. The ripples of Christian's defeat inflicted another defeat on Mansfeld though, because with that ally of Frederick in retreat, the money for his other allies appeared to dry up. Mansfeld would be forced to disband his army through want of pay in early 1624. Many of these men simply entered Dutch service, but overall, the Dutch effort to coordinate with Frederick had manifestly failed for both parties. Frederick conceded defeat and placed his cause in King James' hands once more.[48]

The Dutch, meanwhile, faced a renewed Spanish onslaught across the frozen rivers in early 1624. Spinola led a large force into the Republic, wasting the countryside and terrifying the populace, and almost reaching Utrecht. By August 1624, the symbolic fortress town of Breda was under siege. One marvels at the rate with which Spain had apparently turned their misfortune around. The key ingredients to Spanish success, it seemed, were those circumstances which had served Madrid so well in the past; both the French and English, for different reasons, were occupied and unable to aid the Dutch war effort as they previously would have. As the Dutch had invested money and effort into Christian of Brunswick, in the hope that he would take the pressure off their frontiers, the Spanish had prepared a multi-layered offensive for the year of 1624. The siege of Breda formed one spoke on this wheel, another was to cut the Dutch off from their lifeline of European trade. The Spanish authorities were convinced that 'Taking away the trade of the Dutch is the most important thing we can do to aid the war in the Netherlands and bring about a favourable settlement.'

To this end, the Spanish had raised a fleet of twenty-four ships to police their ports and prevent any Dutch trade there, while they had also rigorously attacked Dutch shipping in Europe waters, and sunk several fishing vessels. Unable to access their timber, salt or herring, Dutch merchants began to grow uneasy, while shortages prevented the Dutch from making repairs or paying for the resources and manpower that they desperately needed. In May 1624, the Dutch had boldly attacked and seized the capital of Portuguese Brazil, but the Spanish responded quickly, and recaptured this bastion of Iberian colonialism the following year. Emperor Ferdinand had sent soldiers to aid Spinola's siege of Breda, and after beating back several Dutch efforts to relieve the town, Breda surrendered to the Spanish in June 1625.[49]

The notion that Spanish interests at home would be insulated by an all-out assault on Dutch defences was greatly aided by King Philip IV's determination to pursue the war against the Dutch with more vigour than had been done since the days of his grandfather. Unlike Philip III, who had ruled during a period of Truce, and before then, of stalemate, Philip IV sent as much money as he could to the Spanish Netherlands, a tactic which provided Spain with some surprising victories in a region which appeared shorn of all potential triumphs. Perhaps the dark days of self-preservation and desperation had returned after all, and the Spanish plan had paid off?[50]

News of the catastrophic loss of Breda certainly burned the Dutch badly – riots broke out in Amsterdam, Haarlem, The Hague and Delft, as a result of frustration against the lagging war effort as well as the rising tax increases which had been brought in to pay for it. The death of Maurice of Nassau, the fighting father of the Dutch nation, was a further blow. Maurice's successor, his half-brother Frederick Henry, was faced with monumental challenges, yet a perceptive assessment of European diplomacy in this troubled year of 1625 would have revealed that a great deal had changed, with new opportunities opening up in the relevant courts. All was not yet lost. Indeed, even as Frederick's options and allies appeared to dwindle to nothing by late 1623, change was in the air, courtesy of a shift underway in London.

After several years in pursuit of a distinct policy, King James was finally forced to alter his plans after a dramatic series of events convinced him that the end goal – an Anglo-Spanish marriage and alliance treaty – was impossible. Thus enlightened (and certainly spurned), King James endeavoured to work towards a new goal: the creation of the Protestant alliance of European powers which Frederick had for so long urged. The question was, would his father in law create this league in time, before the Habsburg supremacy became too formidable to challenge? One could not say for certain, but with the increase in diplomatic activity it became apparent that, no matter how many times he beat Frederick, Emperor Ferdinand would not be able to end this war. The contest which had begun as a Bohemian revolt had mutated into a constitutional issue, and then a struggle between dynastic rivals. Now, this conflict between Frederick and Ferdinand appeared set to be transformed once again. As new enemies mobilised, Emperor Ferdinand prepared himself by employing a personal army of his own, under a loyal commander. If the stakes were destined to be raised, then he was determined not to shy away from whatever challenges this wretched conflict threw at him next, no matter what it cost him or Germany.

Chapter 10 Notes

[1]Herbert H. Rowen, 'The Dutch Revolt: What Kind of Revolution?', *Renaissance Quarterly*, Vol. 43, No. 3 (Autumn, 1990), pp. 570-590; p. 570.

[2]Peter H. Wilson, 'The Causes of the Thirty Years War 1618-48', pp. 573-574.

[3]Myron P. Gutmann, 'The Origins of the Thirty Years' War', pp. 764-765.

[4]Geoffrey Parker, *Europe in Crisis*, p. 135.

[5]Quoted in Parker, *Europe in Crisis*, p. 171.

[6]Quoted in Geoffrey Parker, *Thirty Years War*, p. 51.

[7]Parker, *Thirty Years War*, pp. 52-53.

[8]A good case study of this commercial rivalry and the damage it inflicted on Portuguese fortunes is examined in Peter Borschberg, 'The Seizure of the Sta. Catarina Revisited: The Portuguese Empire in Asia, VOC Politics and the Origins of the Dutch-Johor Alliance (1602-c.1616)', *Journal of Southeast Asian Studies*, Vol. 33, No. 1 (Feb., 2002), pp. 31-62.

[9]Geoffrey Parker, 'Why Did the Dutch Revolt Last Eighty Years?', p. 64.

[10]Figures provided by Parker, *Europe in Crisis*, pp. 151-152.

[11]A good background to this state of affairs is provided by Erik Swart, '"The field of finance": War and Taxation in Holland, Flanders, and Brabant, 1572—85', *The Sixteenth Century Journal*, Vol. 42, No. 4 (Winter 2011), pp. 1051-1071

[12]M. Esquirou de Parieu and Frederick Hendriks, 'John De Witt; or, Twenty Years' Interregnum in the Stadtholdership of the Seventeenth Century', *The Assurance Magazine, and Journal of the Institute of Actuaries*, Vol. 8, No. 4 (JULY, 1859), pp. 205-231; p. 205.

[13]Parker, *Europe in Crisis*, pp. 141-142.

[14]A notable exception is found in the curious occasion of a Frenchman offering himself as the Stadtholder of the American colonies in the 1770s. See Charles J. Stillé, 'Comte De Broglie, the Proposed Stadtholder of America', *The Pennsylvania Magazine of History and Biography*, Vol. 11, No. 4 (Jan., 1888), pp. 369-405.

[15]fteenthe evolution of the role was quite unique in Dutch society, and the position of Stadtholder was carefully managed, particularly during funerals. See: Geert H. Janssen, 'Political Ambiguity and Confessional Diversity in the Funeral Processions of Stadholders in the Dutch Republic', *The Sixteenth Century Journal*, Vol. 40, No. 2 (Summer, 2009), pp. 283-301.

[16]Quoted in Pieter Geyl, *History of the Dutch Speaking Peoples*, p. 345.

[17]Pieter Geyl, *House of Orange and Stuart 1641-1672*, (London: W&N New Edition, 2001), pp. 386-460.

[18]Kimberly J. Hackett, 'The English Reception of Oldenbarnevelt's Fall', *Huntington Library Quarterly*, Vol. 77, No. 2 (Summer 2014), pp. 157-176; pp. 158-159.

[19]A reminder that one article which examines several Catholic families and their struggles is available: Geert H. Janssen, 'Quo Vadis? Catholic Perceptions of Flight and the Revolt of the Low Countries, 1566–1609', *Renaissance Quarterly*, Vol. 64, No. 2 (Summer 2011), pp. 472-499.

[20]James D. Tracy, 'With and Without the Counter-Reformation: The Catholic Church in the Spanish Netherlands and the Dutch Republic, 1580-1650: A Review of the Literature since 1945', *The Catholic Historical Review*, Vol. 71, No. 4 (Oct., 1985), pp. 547-575; p. 547.

[21]Christine Kooi, 'Popish Impudence: The Perseverance of the Roman Catholic Faithful in Calvinist Holland,1572-1620', *The Sixteenth Century Journal*, Vol. 26, No. 1 (Spring, 1995), pp. 75-85; p. 76.

[22]*Ibid*, pp. 77-78.

[23]Jeremy Dupertuis Bangs, 'Dutch Contributions to Religious Toleration', *Church History*, Vol. 79, No. 3 (SEPTEMBER 2010), pp. 585-613; pp. 586-587.

[24]George L. Smith, 'Guilders and Godliness: The Dutch Colonial Contribution To American Religious Pluralism', *Journal of Presbyterian History (1962-1985)*, Vol. 47, No. 1 (MARCH 1969), pp. 1-30.

[25]Pieter Geyl, *History of the Dutch Speaking Peoples*, p. 326.

[26]Jasper van der Steen, 'Chapter Two: A Contested Past. Memory Wars During The Twelve Years Truce (1609–21)' in *Memory before Modernity: Practices of Memory in Early Modern Europe* by (eds) Erika Kuijpers, Judith Pollmann, Johannes Müller, Jasper van der Steen (Brill, 2013), pp. 45-61; p. 46.

[27]Hamilton Vreeland Jr, 'Hugo Grotius, Diplomatist', *The American Journal of International Law*, Vol. 11, No. 3 (Jul., 1917), pp. 580-606; Jesse S. Reeves, 'THE LIFE AND WORK OF HUGO GROTIUS', *Proceedings of the American Society of International Law at Its Annual Meeting (1921-1969)*, Vol. 19 (APRIL 23-25, 1925), pp. 48-58; Steven Forde, 'Hugo Grotius on Ethics and War', *The American Political Science Review*, Vol. 92, No. 3 (Sep., 1998), pp. 639-648.

[28]Carl Bangs, 'Dutch Theology, Trade, and War: 1590-1610', *Church History*, Vol. 39, No. 4 (Dec., 1970), pp. 470-482; p. 480.

[29]Jasper van der Steen, 'Chapter Two: A Contested Past', pp. 47-50.

[30]Quoted in *Ibid*, p. 50.

[31]This Dutch conflation of national identity with historical memory and religious confession continued well into the seventeenth century. See Charles H. Parker, 'To the Attentive, Nonpartisan Reader: The Appeal to History and National Identity in the Religious Disputes of the Seventeenth-Century Netherlands', *The Sixteenth Century Journal*, Vol. 28, No. 1 (Spring, 1997), pp. 57-78.

[32]Quoted in Jasper van der Steen, 'Chapter Two: A Contested Past', p. 57.

[33]See *Ibid*, pp. 58-60.

[34]Pieter Geyl, *Dutch-Speaking Peoples*, pp. 368-371.

[35]See Kimberly J. Hackett, 'The English Reception of Oldenbarnevelt's Fall', pp. 160-163.

[36]See Pieter Geyl, *History of the Dutch-Speaking Peoples*, pp. 372-373.

[37]Peter Brightwell, 'The Spanish System and the Twelve Years' Truce', p. 276.

[38]Engel Sluiter gives the figure in 1594 of 6,208 ships, of which 3,609 were based in the Netherlands. See: 'Dutch-Spanish Rivalry in the Caribbean Area, 1594-1609', *The Hispanic American Historical Review*, Vol. 28, No. 2 (May, 1948), pp. 165-196; pp. 166-167.

[39]*Ibid*, pp. 195-196.

[40]Peter Brightwell, 'The Spanish System and the Twelve Years' Truce', pp. 278-279.

[41]On this Papal grant see the old but still very accessible H. Vander Linden, 'Alexander VI. and the Demarcation of the Maritime and Colonial Domains of Spain and Portugal, 1493-1494', *The American Historical Review*, Vol. 22, No. 1 (Oct., 1916), pp. 1-20

[42]Peter Brightwell, 'The Spanish System and the Twelve Years' Truce', pp. 279-280.

[43]*Ibid*, pp. 280-281.

[44]Geyl, *Dutch-Speaking Peoples*, p. 272.

[45]Geoffrey Parker, *Europe in Crisis*, p. 175.

[46]Geoffrey Parker, *Thirty Years War*, p. 58.

[47]Wedgewood, *Thirty Years War*, pp. 179-181.

[48]Parker, *Thirty Years War*, p. 61.

[49]Geoffrey Parker, *Europe in Crisis*, pp. 183-185.

[50]See Geoffrey Parker, 'Spain, Her Enemies and the Revolt of the Netherlands 1559-1648', *Past & Present*, No. 49 (Nov., 1970), pp. 72-95; p. 90.

(Top left) George Villiers, 1st Duke of Buckingham (Peter Paul Rubens, 1625)
(Top right) Sir Robert Phelips (Hendrik Gerritsz)

(Top left) Louis XIII, King of France (Philippe de Champaigne)
(Top right) Cardinal Richelieu (Philippe de Champaigne)

CHAPTER ELEVEN
"Imperial Reaches"

ONE: A Perfect Villain

TWO: That's My Prerogative

THREE: The Scales Fall

FOUR: So Many High Hopes

FIVE: A Failure to End

ONE
A Perfect Villain

The background details are now known to us. In 1614, Frederick V of the Palatinate married Elizabeth Stuart, King James' daughter. This marital alliance contains two important caveats which the subsequent storm of conflict has largely obscured. The first point was that James did not marry into the Palatine family to support a war against the Holy Roman Emperor or to upset the Habsburgs. The anti-Habsburg schemes of the Palatine family, if Frederick or his ministers eagerly pressed them upon the Stuart court when the marriage was negotiated, did not factor into James' belief that Frederick was a suitable match.

James did not want a war with the Habsburgs; his marital bond with the Calvinist Palatine Elector was meant to ensure peace within the religious divides of Europe, and above all in the Empire. This is demonstrated by the second caveat; Frederick's match with Elizabeth was only part of what was meant to have been a two-part plan. James had married his daughter to the most well-connected Protestant potentate in Europe; he intended shortly thereafter to marry his son Charles to the proudly Catholic Spanish princess Maria Anna.

In the event, his daughter's marriage to Frederick would entrap English interests in the early phases of the Thirty Years War, causing James no end of problems and headaches, and leading one historian to remark that the marriage into the Palatine family was his 'fatal mistake.' Furthermore, part two of James' plan to balance Christendom upon an English scales was dealt a heavy blow in late 1623, when the negotiations for an Anglo-Spanish marriage fell apart. Shortly after watching his plans for maintaining peace in Europe go up in smoke, James died, to be replaced by his son Charles, a far more active player in Europe. English diplomacy and the king's convictions ensured that London remained a critical actor even if the fully committed English invasion which Frederick so yearned for never came.

The decade between Frederick's marriage to Elizabeth Stuart and the collapse of the Anglo-Spanish marriage negotiations reads very much like a period of increasing English involvement and interest in European affairs, particularly once the Bohemian revolt dragged Frederick into its orbit. That his son in law had entered into open opposition to the Holy Roman Emperor was not a state of affairs which James had foreseen, and he responded to these unsettling developments by urging peace and submission on Frederick's side, while he set to the task of mediating a just peace. Frederick's acceptance of the Bohemian crown had seriously hampered James' plans, because it was impossible to imagine Spain staying out of this conflict between a Habsburg and a Wittelsbach.

For the sake of the Habsburg interest in Europe, Spanish money and materials would surely pour over the Alps and into Central Europe, and if that happened, the marriage partners that James so desired would be facing down his son in law. With his responsibilities and honour so challenged and his attentions so divided, it proved immensely difficult for James to choose one side or the other. He seemed to believe that England would be able to mediate some kind of peace, at least until his plans blew up in his face. Throughout this intensive period, from 1618 to 1623, James faced down rowdy MPs, radical puritans and unfavourable propaganda in his quest to keep England at peace and save some portion of his original plans. As the historian Robert Zaller has noted though: 'It was England's potential weight in the balance of war, and not the sincerity of her desire for peace, which made her a factor – inevitably, a party – in the reckoning on all sides.'[1]

To gain a fuller appreciation of European diplomacy during the period of 1618-25 then, it is important that we dwell for some time on the role of England and of King James in the early phase of the Thirty Years War. The regular correspondence between James and Frederick; the rise of anti-Spanish and anti-Catholic feeling in England; the impact of Anglo-Spanish diplomacy on the initial shape of the conflict, and the role of King James in its development – these are all issues and questions which we must address in the course of this chapter. Moreover, to understand more completely why Frederick's repeated entreaties to his father in law failed, it is necessary to comprehend the lengths to which James had gone to in order to make his dream of the Spanish match a reality. James let go of this dream only very slowly and, predictably enough, only very bitterly, but until he did so, Frederick urged King James incessantly to save his Palatine homeland from destruction, and to save his wife from disgrace.

King James is unsurprisingly a focal point of this chapter, with other important players including the Spanish ambassador to England, Count Gondomar, and other English politicians or courtiers who left us with records or accounts of this fascinating era of British history. We last saw King James solidifying control over the British Isles – the first monarch outside of legend and myth to do so. This significant feat did not grant James a free pass. As the historian Charles Howard Carter noted:

> Almost from birth James lived nearly constantly – and somehow managed to survive – in a vortex of violence, hostility and general mistreatment. More or less continually someone or other was trying, with varying degrees of success and failure, to kidnap him, imprison him, stab him, or blow him up along with all the knights and burgesses of the commons and all the peers of the realm. He was in his own day, and has been since, handled almost as roughly in print.[2]

What has led historians to treat him so roughly? We should consider first the physical characters of the man who would rule as King of England and Scotland. According to the historian Marc L. Schwarz, James was maligned by:

> The strange walk caused by rickets that gave the King a kind of [Charlie] Chaplinesque gait, the tongue that was too big for his mouth which caused him to eat his drinks, the taffeta-like skin which he never washed except for his fingers.[3]

It was enough for the famous satirical tract[4] *1066 and All That* to note that 'James slobbered at the mouth and had favourites: thus he was a bad king.'[5] James was also said to be lacking in moral fibre, and was terrified of plots against his life so that he wore heavy reinforced clothing and had a habit of piling mattresses in front of his door in the event that he believed his life was in danger. On the one hand, such behaviour was understandable considering the trauma which the gunpowder plot must have left upon his mind. To his courtiers though, such behaviour was unacceptable. One noted that:

> King James was the most cowardly man that ever I knew. He could not have endured the life of a soldier or to see men drilled, to hear of war was death to him, and how he tormented himself with fear of some sudden mischief may be proved by his great quilted doublets, pistol-proof, as also his strange eyeing of strangers with a continual fearful observation. His fear of assassination played no small part in his foreign policy.

It may be remembered that James lived and reigned in an era where monarchs could be and were assassinated. One such casualty was James' royal peer, King Henry IV of France, who was assassinated in 1610. On hearing the news of Henry's death, noted a courtier: 'James, refusing at first to believe the news, was profoundly moved, not from love of the French King, for he had none, but from fear and horror of assassination, a horror increased hundredfold because the victim was a king.' This last sentence is important, because in Henry's death James saw a pattern which did not exclude his position or person in the slightest. Henry had been an enemy of the Catholic Habsburg interest, and so he had been removed. If James adopted his policy or behaviour, then hidden Habsburg blades might also find their way to the King's heart across the Channel.

James was so taken by the possibility that he might be next on the hit-list of the Habsburgs that he instructed his travelling ambassadors to remain wary of news regarding any plots against his life. Predictably enough, when news emerged that English ambassadors would pay a high price for such valuable information, dealers in such intel began cropping up at a suspicious rate across the continent. We should bear in mind that knowledge about James' unfortunate relationship with terrible, dramatic plots against him in his realm was widespread, making the exaggeration and subsequent selling of these imagined plots far easier.[6]

To add to the picture of a troubled, paranoid, slobbery domestic reign, James' reputation in the realm of foreign policy is also shrouded in a pall of criticism and controversy. Arguably the root cause of the negative interpretations of James' acumen in this regard come from his relationship with the Spanish ambassador to England, Count Gondomar, who arrived in 1613 and stayed in London – barring a brief absence between 1618-20 – until 1622. Gondomar, it is claimed, wielded an influence over the English King far at odds with his station. Furthermore, the Spanish ambassador manipulated James, and made use of threats from Madrid to force him to do Spain's bidding, at the expense of his struggling son in law, whom Spain wished to destroy. The image of King James meeting Gondomar for the first time with his hat in his hand is thrown back at the King: look here how the craven King of England debases and supplicates himself before the servant of the King of Spain. Yet, as Carter has quite reasonably pointed out, the King "always took off his hat in the presence of an ambassador unless he was mad at him or at his sovereign; James was not being craven, he was only being polite.'[7]

Don Diego Sarmiento De Acura was ennobled as Count of Gondomar in 1617, and he served as Spanish ambassador to England from 1613 to 1622, whereupon he continued to serve in his return home as perhaps the only figure in Madrid who properly understood the English mindset, until his death in 1626. Gondomar served King Philip III at a time when Spain had resolved its issues with the Austrian branch and was determined to come to its aid. This meant involvement in the Empire, and an increase in Spanish influence along the Rhine, as we have seen. To Gondomar, these developments meant that he was tasked with explaining and defending such policies to King James, while James, so long as he desired the marriage alliance which seemed to be on the cards, would have to accept his explanations. As Carter has written:

...what was going to happen in Europe, and to Europe, was very much in the hands of the relatively few men who guided or influenced affairs of state in a few key capitals. None were more important than such men in Spain and England, widely recognized as the heads of 'the two protectorates' over Catholic and Protestant Europe. Gondomar must certainly be counted among these few.[8]

What Gondomar and James accomplished over the years he served as ambassador was nothing short of extraordinary, but then, Gondomar was an extraordinary individual. Carter wrote with his usual prose that in the case of Gondomar: 'There has probably never been a more able diplomat sent to England, nor a more influential one, nor one more passionately hated by so many Englishmen.'[9] This hatred was based largely on the erroneous belief, as we will see, that Gondomar controlled and pulled the strings of James behind the scenes. Gondomar was hated by Englishmen because he manipulated their King, and because, at least until the arrangement collapsed, the Spanish nobleman was very good at his job.

The impression that James was under the Spaniard's evil spell helped to foster the hostile English attitudes towards Gondomar, but as Garret Mattingly had written, and as we will shortly discover, Gondomar's access to the King came less as a result of his schemes, and instead because the Spanish ambassador and King James got along together so well. As Mattingly wrote:

> The real key to Gondomar's success in England lay in his relation to James I. It was not a simple one; certainly, it was not, as has sometimes been represented, just the dominance of a weak character by a strong one; much less, the gulling of a fool by a knave. James was a complex character in whom elements of weakness were surprisingly mixed with traits of real strength; Gondomar, at least, never made the mistake of underrating him. Nor did he achieve his influence at a strike or storm the king's favour with a mixture of bullying and flattery. It was a work of years. In part it was because Gondomar was able to make James like him.[10]

Indeed, there was no sinister secret to Gondomar's success. Both men thoroughly enjoyed the hunt and would spend several hours together during such activities. In addition, the more they grew to enjoy one another's company, the more they eagerly sought each other out. Both men enjoyed discussing history, and Gondomar was understandably alert to any news which James chose to impart. The ambassador and the king thus enjoyed a relationship based on mutual respect, and it certainly helped that James hosted private audiences with resident ambassadors, since Gondomar was able to further his relationship with the King during this process. As James sought more earnestly to secure a Spanish marriage for his son, Gondomar's presence became in turn more sought after, and James relied on him to pass on messages and to remain informed of Madrid's intentions.

While the relationship between Gondomar and James was the most important, we must also consider the often misunderstood or exaggerated base from which Gondomar operated. First, we must provide some context for the records of pensions which the Spanish paid to influential British statesmen. When some historians encountered these lists of Englishmen in Spanish pay, expressions of shock and disgust were issued at the dishonesty and self-interest of those Britons, who shamefully sold state secrets in return for petty Spanish cash.[11] The reality though is far less straightforward, and provides us with an indication of diplomatic protocol at the time. Rather than bribes to favour Spanish interests, these pensions should be viewed instead as a pre-requisite to get anywhere in English court. As one ambassador from the Spanish Netherlands had written, 'in this country, if one wants to negotiate a matter, you have to put up the money.'

The Spanish were competing with Dutch pensions and rightly believed that if they refrained from spending some money or 'tipping' the English, then neither the statesmen nor even the King would be inclined to listen to them. That said, while the list of men (and women) in Spanish pay was long, the payments were often several years in arrears. Most of the money was saved for the heads of James' administration: the treasury lords, chancellors and foreign ministers. This latter point meant that when changes in personnel occurred, the incoming minister would often inherit his predecessor's Spanish pension. Madrid appreciated that a refusal to pay could result in the minister adopting a more hostile than usual outlook towards Spain, but it was also accepted that timely payment was no guarantee that England would be wholly favourable to Spanish designs. Carter compared the system to 'the position of a hapless diner who must "bribe" a surly waiter with tips to avoid getting soup spilled on him.'

An amusing anecdote emerges from this controversy that once James' ambassador to Madrid, John Digby, learned of the existence of this list, he sought to communicate it faithfully to his King. When he presented the list to his King, James expressed surprise that so many Englishmen were in receipt of Spanish pay. As a recipient of a Spanish pension himself, James was more surprised to discover that he was not the only one to avail of such a lucrative scheme. Indeed, Digby only discovered that his King received Spanish money once he deciphered the list, a fact which must have made for a somewhat awkward conversation when Digby set to the task of explaining the document's contents to James.

While it is possible to speak of a 'Spanish party' in James' court – a group which would subsequently become the subject of much ridicule and bad press – the reality was less straightforward. This group contained its measure of Catholics and was moved to argue for friendship with Spain not by a plethora of bribes, but by the fact that their political opponents in Scotland would gain if the alternative, a French alliance, was adopted. Into the latter group we can lump English puritans and opportunistic merchants, who wished to initiate an open, undeclared war against Spain in the Indies. The label 'Spanish party' can tend to obscure the fact that these individuals were by no means unabashedly pro-Spanish, nor were they incapable of changing their minds, as we shall see. Instead, they advocated peace and wished to maintain the status quo, rather than to embark upon a reckless war.[12]

Attitudes were sharpened with the eruption of the Bohemian revolt in May 1618. This direct challenge to Habsburg authority could not go unanswered by Spain, but even while this need for intervention was keenly felt, an anxious eye was kept upon the Dutch. With the Twelve Years Truce due to expire in three years, it was critical that the Bohemian revolt was resolved before that time. This mission was massively complicated by the acceptance by James' son in law of the Bohemian crown in September 1619. At that point, with the Hungarians on the march, Vienna beleaguered and Frederick announcing his intention to march to the Bohemians' defence, the crisis was felt all the more deeply in Spain because Gondomar had left London for a time in 1618, and would not be back in James' presence until March 1620. During that weighted time, the critically important question of what the English would do was difficult to answer.[13]

It was while Gondomar was in Madrid, and while the Bohemian revolt transformed into a conflict which seemed to challenge English religious and moral sensibilities, that the anti-Spanish and anti-Catholic sentiments of James' subjects began to intensify. This process was given a notable boost thanks to the publication of *Vox Populi*, a commentary written by Thomas Scott in 1620. This notorious pamphlet purported to show exactly what went on behind closed doors in Madrid; it claimed to be the actual report that Gondomar had written to his masters in Spain and was tactfully published to coincide with the ambassador's return to London in spring 1620. *Vox Populi* had not been Scott's first foray into the realm of propaganda pamphlets, but it was undoubtedly his most effective and infamous, a fact which is all the more incredible when it is noted that the pamphlet contained not a shred of truth, and yet was wholly accepted as canon by a large number of enraged Englishmen.[14]

The worst confessions and the most insulting assumptions were placed in Gondomar's mouth, and with the immediate success of Scott's pamphlet, Gondomar's comparatively small voice could never have stood a chance. Indeed, Gondomar was justifiably furious at the author, and in the words of the Venetian ambassador, somewhat pleased to see his rival brought so low, *Vox Populi* '...severely castigates the Spanish ambassador here, who therefore foams with wrath in every direction and it is said that he has sent it to the King to make complaint. This has transpired and given rise to much comment.'[15] Average English citizens were not the only ones to come under the spell; country gentlemen and self-styled antiquarian Sir Simonds D'Ewes, a wealthy Puritan MP, was also moved to note in his journal that:

> I perused a notable book styled *Vox Populi*, penned by one Thomas Scott, a minister, marvellously displaying the subtle policies and wicked practices of the Count of Gondomar, the resident ambassador here from the King of Spain, in prevailing with King James for connivance toward the Papists, under the colourable pretence of our Prince's matching with the Infanta Maria of Spain; and that he laboured to accomplish two things, without which the state of England could not be ruined: the first, to breed distaste and jealousies in the King towards his best subjects under the false and adulterate nickname of Puritans, and so to prevent all future parliaments, and secondly, to nourish jars and differences between Great Britain and the United States of the Low Countries, that so being first divided each from the other, they might afterwards be singly and assuredly ruined by Spain and the House of Austria.

Pamphlets such as these were problematic for King James when he was attempting to tread a neutral course. When this neutral course was believed to be the only way to restore Frederick to his Palatinate, Scott's *Vox Populi* jeopardised this plan. Raising the temperature in England to a white-hot intensity, Scott believed his work was done, and individuals like D'Ewes never suspected they had been duped, preferring to believe instead that they had been made privy to the dark secrets which constituted the Spanish way of doing business. As D'Ewes continued:

> But the King himself, hoping to get the Prince Elector, his son-in-law, to be restored to the Palatinate by an amicable treaty, was much in- censed at the sight of it, as being published at an unseasonable time, though otherwise it seemed to proceed from an honest English heart. There was, therefore, so much and so speedy search made for the author of it, as he scarcely escaped the hands of the pursuivants, who had they taken him, he had certainly tasted of a sharp censure: for the Spanish Ambassador himself did at this time suppose and fear the people's eyes to be opened so far with the perusal of this book and their hearts to be so extremely irritated with that discovery of his villainous practices, as he caused his house for a while...by a guard of men.[16]

It is possible to note some overlapping features in this anti-Spanish propaganda penned by Scott, and in the anti-Regent propaganda penned by Dutch Orangists. In both cases, the suspicious fifth column of Catholics – 'papists' – was singled out for ridicule. Gondomar's aim, so Scott claimed, was to serve England up on a Catholic plate to the Pope and thus to the King of Spain, that Universal Monarch of the world. Thereafter, the Reformed in all sections would be supressed, and the meek English King would remain cooperative so long as he got that Spanish marriage which Gondomar had promised. Scott's aims were to fire up Protestants and to enhance the reputation of the Puritans, just as Catholics and Spaniards were dragged down. It is difficult to say for certain exactly where Scott fit on the religious spectrum, but he claimed to speak for mainstream Protestantism even if his views appear to lean outside of the Anglican creed.[17]

In the minds of the average zealous Protestant Englishman, he had certainly been given reason enough to see Catholics as Spaniards in disguise. The gunpowder plot remained a striking example of papist plotting, and it was imagined that such a violent attack was surely only the first step towards a forcible re-introduction of the Catholic faith to the country, whereupon all closet Catholics in England would rise up and aid the invader in the process. This scenario, nightmarish and impossible though it may sound, was just as likely as Johan van Oldenbarnevelt's guilt had been under the charge of attempting to betray the Dutch Republic to the Spanish enemy he had fought for so many years. Oldenbarnevelt, recall, had been beheaded – could Britain's Catholic population be in for such violent repression as well? A recent article has demonstrated that King James proved adept at balancing the threats he perceived in Catholicism as well as Puritanism,[18] but could he withstand the tide of popular fury if it grew too intense?

Those that bought into such negative views of Spanish intentions overrated Spanish zeal and determination. In reality, Madrid's diplomatic efforts were invested in more enthusiastically than any efforts to blow up the Parliament or the King. Queen Anne of England had, after all, been followed with rumours about her Catholic leanings for much of her life, and her personal beliefs remain somewhat challenging to untangle. Whispers of Anne's closet Catholicism made belief in further unsavoury conspiracies easier, especially for those that had so rounded on James in the first place for his pro-Spanish policy. As the historian Albert J. Loomie noted: 'For the alert Puritan there would be the threat of a papal influence secretly on the king's counsels, and there would be the inference that the mother of the royal children might seek to influence them toward her own view.'[19] Indeed, if the Queen was pulling the Catholic strings unbeknownst to her husband, then that would surely explain the King's apparently unshakable convictions regarding the need for a Spanish marriage. Perhaps it was Anne who desired the marriage, and perhaps this was because she intended to restore her adopted country (Anne was a Danish princess) to the Roman Church?

The King's people could imagine these terrible schemes, but James was determined to pursue the foreign policy which promised the greatest rewards. He had, after all, enjoyed some success and popularity for it in the past. He ended the war with Spain in one of his first acts as King of England in 1604; he brokered a peace between Denmark and Sweden in 1613; he mediated a settlement between the conflicting parties during the Julich-Cleve crisis in 1614, and in 1618 he attempted and failed to secure a lasting peace before the Bohemian revolt got out of hand. He was supported in these ventures by another aspect of the realm's propaganda machine – the theatre, and this time, this organ was directed in his favour.

From the time of his ascension as King to his death, James approved several plays which depicted the King of England as a peacemaker, and which were eagerly lapped up by an enthused English audience. *The Peacemaker* released in 1619; *The World Lost at Tennis* in 1620 and *The Triumphs of Integrity* in 1623 were all written and performed in a manner which portrayed James' diplomatic ability and his desire for peace in a positive light. Another play, *The Triumphs of Peace*, in 1620 came at the perfect time for a King angered at the rise in anti-Spanish sentiment and determined to stay the course. These performances emphasised the horrors of war, the value of peace, and the unquestioned talent of the King for balancing the two questions so skilfully.[20] Yet, even with these aides, James began to find it impossible to stem the tide of anti-Spanish and anti-Catholic sentiment. According to the historian J. P. Kenyon this is not surprising. Kenyon noted that:

> [James'] love of compromise was jarring in a world of violent extremes, and his motto, 'Blessed are the peace-makers,' was inappropriate to a nation which had been in a state of emergency for half a century, and to an era in which the potentiality of military command was still one of the most important attributes of a ruler.[21]

It would therefore be easy to criticise James as tone deaf, and ignorant of the prevailing winds within his kingdom. Indeed, it is a difficult question to fairly answer even today. The horrors of war which James rightly detested notwithstanding, if he had intervened in force to save his son in law, then the Palatinate may have preserved, Spain may have been pushed back, and the Thirty Years War may have been arrested at this early stage. Such a scenario was passionately believed in by Frederick, as well as those bitter courtiers of the King who urged their lord to do something, *anything*, which would show his zeal for his family if nothing else.

His daughter wrote to him in late 1620, urging the King, 'to show himself a loving father to us, and not suffer his children's inheritance to be taken away', and adding 'tell the King that the enemy will more regard his blows than his words.'[22] Yet, even in late 1620 when the Palatine cause was defeated at White Mountain, James would offer no such blows. He continued to listen to the returning Gondomar's advice; he continued to angrily supress the slander set against him; he continued to accept a Spanish pension; he continued to pursue that elusive end, of a marriage with a Spanish princess which would surely solve the problems of his family and of the realm.

TWO
That Is My Prerogative

At some point during the early phases of the Thirty Years War – likely during the winter of 1618-19 – the English statesman, MP and aristocrat Sir Robert Phelips sat down to pen a long letter on the question of the Spanish marriage. The manuscript which was left behind has provided historians with a great resource, for here lay the opinions of King James' contemporaries on one of the most contentious questions then facing English foreign policy.[23] Written as it was in the period just before the disaster at White Mountain, and even before Frederick's acceptance of the Bohemian crown, we may be surprised to observe Phelips defend the policy of a Spanish marriage, as only a patriotic, well-travelled Englishman could. Phelips had travelled to Madrid as part of the English embassy in previous years, and while there he had conversed with several exiled English Catholics, who seem to have made an impression upon him.

Yet, what is remarkable about Phelips is that, while in this early phase of his life he rigorously defended and supported the Spanish marriage mission, from 1620 onwards, Phelips would become the most outspoken critic of the idea, and would even spend time in the Tower for his unfavourable views. Phelips' journey in this regard is of great interest to us, even while the full explanation for his change of heart is not easy to discern today. Phelips gave an assessment of Spanish power, of the desirability of the Spanish marriage, and of England's place in the politics of Europe. His views during the winter of 1618-19 provide a refreshingly calm antidote to the exaggerated image sometimes presented by anti-Spanish English courtiers during the same period. In reference to the rampant depopulation of Spain which had become state policy during the preceding years (recall – the expulsion of the Moriscos during 1609-14 and the demographic impact this policy had), Phelips wrote:

> In Spain there is much want of people, many places depopulated, it being not long since that the Moriscos were expelled, and by reason of their sending and passing so many to the Indies, besides the continual employing others in their wars; but the principal want of this Monarchy is their slender force at sea.[24]

Phelips spent little time discussing the Germans, Dutch or Turks, aside from commenting that the latter were the 'enemy of all Christendom.' However, he did underline the intractability of the Franco-Spanish relationship, and the rivalry of both powers which bled into so many sections of diplomacy, trade and strategy between them. Venice and Savoy were noted to be hostile, as was the Pope, and Phelips thus concluded that, considering her lack of European friends, her scattered domains and her want of security, Spain ought to see sense when examining the English marital alliance. "To establish a security upon this so scattered and dispersed a monarchy," Phelips said, Spain must be strengthened at sea, or at least have its position improved through an alliance with a sea power. Where else could such an ideal ally be found, Phelips noted, than England, 'an island the greatest of the world, fertile and abounding with people, ships and mariners and…most strong at sea.'

Sharing a perspective which may appear amusing considering the later scale and power of the British Empire, Phelips claimed that an Anglo-Spanish alliance would be useful to Spain for another reason: England did not harbour aspirations for an empire which spanned across the globe. England was not, Phelips wrote, distracted by 'pretensions' in half a dozen different corners of the world. Instead, the English…

> …having found by experience that the power to have authority among foreigners is more safe and necessary than possessing foreign dominion, they have, like the tortoise, withdrawn themselves into their own shell from whence they do not upon slight motives sally but yet demonstrate to the world their power to do it when necessary occasions shall be presented to them.

Perhaps considering Phelips' status, it is not surprising to see him greatly overrate the power and influence of King James in Europe, yet his expressions are worth sharing, nonetheless. Phelips wrote that King James…

> in being the head of the Protestants, Calvinists and Lutherans, is as it were the arbitrator of the affairs of Germany, Polonia and Suebia and is little less in France and Holland, and can give or cut the wings to any design of Savoy and Venice. He can likewise hinder or facilitate the election of the Emperor…and lastly it is in his power whensoever it seemeth good unto him to rein and cut short the proceedings and insolences of the rebels in Holland.[25]

After weighing up England's strengths and Spain's weaknesses, Phelips attempted next to balance the pros and cons of the looming marriage treaty with Spain, by examining first its potential negative implications for James, should he become beholden to or friendly with a Catholic power in Europe. Phelips noted:

> As the King of Spain is the head and principal among the Catholic princes, so the king of England is the chief amongst those of his religion, and matching his

son with the Catholic king it may pass that he will relinquish the friendship he holdeth with the Protestant princes, and yet cannot assure himself that ever the Catholics will be unto him so fixed friends as undoubtedly were those of his own profession; and this may not only happen in respect of his foreign alliance but with his own subjects and domestic vassals at home, who, it may be by reason of this marriage may put themselves into a civil war, the lamentable and perilous effects whereof have been more than visibly discerned in France and Germany; and so the king of England, resting himself upon new friendships wanting other and greater foundation save the will and liking of him that makes them, and forsaking his ancient allies and leagues who seem to be more firm and obliged unto him in being all of one and the same sort, doth by this way expose himself to the hazard not only of losing his cloak but all his whole garment likewise.[26]

Strikingly for the time, Phelips went on to argue that, contrary to the messages often poured out from the pulpit, James' power did not rest on the idea that he was the leader of Protestantism. The King drew no prestige from this idea either; instead, James was strong and respected abroad because of the strength of his armed forces. Thus, an alliance with Spain would increase these powers, and they would not reduce England's power because true power in Phelips' mind was not based on James' claim to lead Protestant Europe. There was some weight to this idea: after all, King James had not been selected to lead the Evangelical Union – the Elector Palatine had. Soon, Phelips was to be validated; once Frederick V, as the leader of the Union, attempted to draw from his position and call upon their power, he was abandoned, and so his power evaporated with this failure. James would be immune to such faulty allies, because he made his own power and respect by the force and reputation of his own supreme arms.

As if undermining the concept of James' role as the leader of Protestantism was not striking enough, Phelips went even further when he attempted to draw his King's attention towards the dangers which Puritanism – referred to here as the reformed religion – posed to his reign. Phelips concluded:

Calvinism doth give license and occasion for men daily to invent new opinions which for the most part love new changes and beget tumults, whilst that without such occasions the Catholic faith is always one and the same and more compatible to princes and their states...To conclude, the supposed reformed religion is dangerous to the state of kings, unquiet and turbulent for subjects, safe and secure for none, like unto a vessel without a governor subject to the moving of the winds and waves.[27]

Incredibly, Phelips advocated a relaxation of the penal laws, and to grant more concessions to Catholics in England, since this would insure a sense of gratitude and thence loyalty among them. The King should not fear that these Catholics would try to overreach and grasp at more insidious aims, since they would be so thankful to their King for liberating them from the intolerant policies of the past that they would help him build his kingdom alongside Protestants. Phelips wished to challenge the status quo abroad as well as at home though, and he wrote that 'It doth as well concern England to cast an eye toward the increase and power of the Flemings [the Dutch] on the sea and in the matter of contratation [trading and bargaining].' Phelips was even willing to suggest a scheme whereby England evacuated the Indies to the Spanish, in return for several trade guarantees in Europe. In this scenario, the English would be at loggerheads with the Dutch, their traditional ally against the Spanish, but Phelips evidently believed that this trade off would be worth it in the long run. 'All this', Phelips concluded:

> May be effected and brought to pass by the present marriage, the careful observing the conditions determined, and by the well using of the English merchants to the great glory, authority, augmentation, safety and profit of both crowns, and the general quiet and peace of all Christendom.[28]

Phelips' conclusions bear a remarkable similarity and familiarity to those put forward by Count Gondomar, Spain's ambassador to England. In spring 1619, Gondomar was back home in Spain to report on what he had seen and learned – a return trip which granted *Vox Populi* such scandalous material, as we have seen – and the Spaniard gave his own views on the utility of the marital alliance, as well as Spain's general woes. First, much like Phelips, Gondomar gave his sombre views on the state of Spain and its greatly reduced populace, which created some inglorious sights for the traveller:

> The drop in the population, the poverty and wretchedness of Spain today... which foreigners publish, for traveling through it is more painful and uncomfortable than through any other deserted land in all of Europe because there are no beds or inns or meals because of the oppressions and the taxes paid by the subjects.

Gondomar then gave an incredibly insightful, but also rather downcast interpretation of the state of affairs of Spain, especially in comparison to its apparently more vibrant rivals in the wake of the eruption of the Thirty Years War. Gondomar wrote:

> We are allowing them [England and Holland] to take away our wool, which is the best in the world; and only Spain possesses within its borders olive oil and everything else necessary to make good cloth; and despite this we dress largely in the goods of England, Holland, and other foreign countries. Things such as these and many other things that we don't need they send us in abundance every day and take in exchange our gold and silver and make us useless, for it is like selling wheat from the thresher's floor very cheaply and buying all

year round expensive and bad bread from the bakers; and, to sum up, more than five out of six people are unemployed in business and production, while in England and Holland the unemployed don't number more than one out of a hundred; and this is why they grow as much in wealth, power, and population as we decrease.[29]

Gondomar focused in this case on the trade deficit suffered by Spain, and of the negative impact which the Anglo-Dutch entrepreneurship was having on Spanish incomes. Unlike Sir Robert Phelips, who had focused his criticism largely on the Dutch, Gondomar was frank about the dangers posed to Spanish interests by English and Dutch alike. In a turn of phrase which proves somewhat fantastic to modern readers, Gondomar greatly exaggerated the capabilities of King James at sea when he wrote:

Our ports are full of English and Dutch ships while in theirs there is not a single Spanish one, for they do not allow any foreigner to bring in a load of merchandise without being taxed, and obliged to take out as much from the country...England can easily launch a thousand ships upon the sea in several armadas and squadrons, and 100,000 men in them.

After spending more than five years in London and in the King's company, Gondomar evidently had not managed to grasp the true extent of English sea power, and he seemed to believe, much like Phelips, that England's naval capabilities were sufficient to mount all levels of expeditions against all forms of enemies. Despite their common ground and similar claims, it is unknown whether Gondomar and Phelips ever met. In her examination of Phelips' journey from pro-Spanish to virulently anti-Spanish, the historian Katherine Van Eerde suggested that the two men could have shared informants or researchers when they penned their letters.[30]

The stage appeared set for a wonderful friendship between Gondomar and Phelips – two men who held near identical views, and who could be charged with facilitating the successful conclusion of the Anglo-Spanish marriage. Yet, any such opportunities were torpedoed in the summer of 1619, as Sir Robert Phelips embarked upon a tour of Spain. During this trip, it seems likely that Phelips was made aware of just how intractable the differences between Spain and England were, and just how uncompromising and demanding Philip III's government was content to be. Rather than genuinely interested in the hand of Prince Charles, Spain appeared to be stringing England along so as to upset her potential to influence events. It is not known for certain if Phelips' trip to Spain was the catalyst for his abrupt change of heart, but what we do know is that, from 1620 onwards, his views of Spain and his attitude towards the Spanish marriage seem to have been completely reversed.

The pace of events may also have served to transform Phelips into one of the loudest, most ardent agitators against the Spanish marriage. From August 1619, the Bohemian revolt dragged in the Elector Palatine, and once Frederick had been issued with the Imperial Ban the following spring, and Spanish aid was forthcoming to aid the Emperor, it would have been immensely difficult for Phelips to maintain his original position. Indeed, news of Frederick's acceptance of the Bohemian crown seems to have confirmed Phelips' turn, and in early September 1619, from his home in Somerset, he penned the following letter to an unknown individual; unknown, since the letter is simply addressed to 'my lord.' Phelips wrote:

> There is nothing in these later times hath more prejudiced the state of our affairs than that middle and moderate way in which they have been carried and I dare affirm that the mild course in which we have with other states and treaties proceeded hath given more wounds than we could have received from the strongest or most apparent enemy...I shall wish that this presented [sic] business may not be carried upon the same wheel but that (necessity commanding it) a just and noble war may be preferred before a disadvantaging and dishonourable composition, and I do not doubt but God will bless the work and direct the success to his own glory by confirming and extending his truth to his Majesty's honour, by bringing his virtue and his power into a due esteem in foreign policy and lastly to the safety and happiness of this kingdom by preventing and securing it from the subtle and active desires of the Spanish policy.[31]

It was quite the transformation. England should no longer be content to follow its peaceable policy and should instead force itself into the conflict now underway in Europe, for the sake of James' familial honour as much as England's national interest. This, Phelips insisted, was the only way to arrest the interest of the Spanish policy, a policy which, the previous year, Phelips had wholeheartedly defended. As his Spanish connections had declined, so had another important set of contacts – with those of England's parliamentary party.

Since 1614, Phelips had been in touch with some important figures in Westminster, and penned letters to them as he wrote to his friends in Spain. It was in 1614 that James dissolved Parliament and did not permit it to assemble again until 1621. This gap of seven years made many MPs understandably frustrated, and they waited for the opportunity to leverage their greatest advantage – the appearance of the King before them to request money. The task of tracing the development of Parliamentary relations with the monarch is one far outside the scope of this book,[32] but we can nonetheless pinpoint 1621 as a year of particular importance for King James and his MPs. Thanks to Phelips' letters, we are also made aware of the storm which was brewing in the background in 1620. When James appealed to nobles like Phelips for a grant of money to be made to his daughter Elizabeth and her husband's ill-fated Bohemian government, Phelips was quick to note that he held sympathy for the Winter Queen, but that 'the sense and genius of some gentlemen of quality with whom I casually met' was 'that without a parliament they would not give a penny.' In addition, Phelips wrote that he and his peers genuinely wished to aid Frederick and Elizabeth in their plight, but that first time must be spent on...

> ...the rectifying and settling of things here in England, which now all men saw were both as touching God and man in very great disorder and distemper and they had no hope nor imagination to obtain this but by a parliament.[33]

In spring 1620, James permitted Frederick's allies to recruit for him in England. Just as well he should, since he was allowing the Spanish ambassador to do the same thing as late as 1622; anything less than giving equal treatment to the two recruitment drives would have been a phenomenal scandal.[34] Nonetheless, for Phelips and his parliamentary peers, who had been longing for a chance to sit in Parliament and debate the King's policies, such minor acts were not sufficient. News of Spain's invasion of the Palatinate had sharpened all dilemmas, and with even James in shock at the brazenness of this move, he initially seemed to approve its assembly, but had to be coaxed and persuaded for another month before, finally, on 3 November 1620, the King capitulated: 'At noon never a Lord of the Council could say we should have a parliament, but after a long debate with the King, it was concluded on before night, and the writs are now writing.' Almost immediately, when Parliament assembled, the anti-Spanish opinions of the MPs in attendance became abundantly clear; if the Spanish marriage had been a hard sell before, it was next to impossible to sell it with so many suspicious statesmen loudly declaring their views in a public forum.[35]

In the case of Phelips, it was a very busy time. Here he displayed the full extent of his transformation, as he mounted a sustained attack against 'papists' who Phelips lambasted as 'our deadly enemies'. He also ridiculed the idea that Spanish trade negotiations would produce any net positive results for England, and suggested boycotting Spanish tobacco in retaliation against limited Spanish tariffs on English goods. In November 1621, Phelips was assuring his peers that 'our safety and happiness cannot be secured but by a difference with Spain.' On a session of 3 December, Phelips did not mince words either, declaring 'Wherefore I dare be bold to say that in the match with Spain there is neither honour, profit nor safety.' These were bold words indeed, as Phelips may have suspected, he had gone too far for James' sensibilities. Over Christmas 1621 Phelips was taken to the Tower, where he would spend eight months, being released in the autumn of 1622. In the final analysis of Sir Robert Phelips, Katherine Van Eerde wrote that 'ambition had led Sir Robert to support the Spanish Match; ambition combined with patriotism brought him to oppose it. A sense of self-preservation, however, prevented that opposition from carrying him too far.' Phelips would die in 1638, before he was forced to make the ultimate choice between king or country.[36]

Phelips, indeed, was not the only figure to suffer censure at the King's hand. Thanks to Gondomar's relationship with the King, and thanks to the King's vision of what the Spanish marriage would achieve, not only for his realm, but also for Frederick and his daughter Elizabeth too, James proved unwilling to countenance any semblance of opposition to his plans. This was a time in British political history when even the concept of a political opposition per se was not officially permitted to exist; Parliament existed for the purpose of voting the King money, not to usurp his prerogatives, as James continually feared they would do. That said, James' Privy Council continually, but gently, urged the King to treat his Parliament with respect, and not to dissolve it with bad grace. 'I, for my part, think it a thing inestimable to your Majesty's safety and service, that you once part with your Parliament with love and reverence': these had been the words of Sir Francis Bacon, one of England's keenest political minds, and an essential servant of the King.[37]

Unfortunately for Bacon and those that had moved to persuade James that Parliament would be kept under control, it became virtually impossible to police the speeches of all independently thinking MPs. Parliament effectively broke down, and by the first few days of January 1622, James had announced his dissolution of it, which certainly rankled opinion. Into this situation came Thomas Scott, author of the incendiary pamphlet *Vox Populi*, returned to prominence with his *Second Part of Vox Populi* in 1624. This pamphlet ramped up the vitriol levelled against Gondomar, by imagining him as the villain responsible for destroying Parliament in 1621. Since it was easier to blame this breakdown on a scheming Spanish Catholic ambassador than it was to explain the hidden details of personal interest and opinion which actually led to its collapse, Scott's work proved an immense success. Once more, Gondomar was cast as the unscrupulous schemer leading their King astray, and taking advantage of James' sincere love of peace. The Spaniard had bribed his way into the state's most sensitive secrets; he had the nobility and the court in his pocket; he had bought off or pushed out anyone that had learned the truth.[38]

As the date of Scott's *Second Part of Vox Populi* will attest though, by 1624 James was no longer searching for a successful resolution of the Spanish marriage. On the contrary, he had abandoned that policy altogether, and was instead moving towards a more active anti-Spanish policy in league with the Dutch and Denmark. English gentry from Somerset like Sir Robert Phelips were not the only figures, it seemed, that were capable of changing their minds. James had been persuaded by autumn 1623 that Spain was never going to agree to the marriage alliance treaty he desired, and so he abandoned the idea, and England drifted towards war with Spain. From the sidelines, apparently removed from these Anglo-Spanish entreaties, was the individual who had done so much to add urgency and zeal to the English negotiations – Frederick V, the dispossessed Elector Palatine and King James' son in law.

THREE
The Scales Fall

If anyone asked, they were the Smith brothers. Yet these two men, with their fake beards and suspiciously familiar silhouettes, were travellers of a far more exalted status than their humble moniker suggested. One man was the Marquis of Buckingham, George Villiers, a prominent English nobleman and influential friend of the King. The other was, when one removed the fake beard, unmistakably, but incredibly, that King's son – Charles. The story, fantastic as it appears now, inspired wonder and amazement when it was learned of in the seventeenth century. These two figures, two of the most powerful men in the British Isles, travelled from London to Madrid in spring 1623 without an escort or any significant pomp, and arrived in Madrid on 17 March to the immense consternation and utter disbelief of the Spanish government. After pawning off the English for so long, after delaying the establishment of any solid commitment in spite of James' pleas, under no circumstances had King Philip's administration been led to expect the arrival of the British prince, yet here he stood, and until he received an answer either way, he declared that he had no intention of leaving the country for home. The situation was the equivalent of an ultimatum, and was the nightmare of every crafty statesman, if indeed he had ever possessed the imagination to foresee it taking place.[39]

Before they had left, King James had grappled ceaselessly with the problems of the policy he was pursuing. Anti-Spanish feeling and a phobia of Catholics as a fifth column in the country increased steadily in England since the outbreak of the Bohemian revolt in 1618. As the revolt dragged in the Palatine family and thus James' own family, the extent of the King's dilemma became apparent: his original plan of a dual marriage to the leading Protestant and Catholic families of Europe was threatened because one had been attacked and conquered by the other. Still, James continued to hope that just as Spanish actions threatened his family and the marriage treaty with ruin, taking the hand of Spain in marriage would solve so many of his problems. As Brennan Pursell understood:

511

Having a Spanish princess in London would have increased his influence with the most powerful dynasty in Europe, and her dowry would have relieved his government's debilitating lack of money. Above all he wanted the marriage alliance to lead to a resolution of the Palatine crisis, which would have slowed or even stopped the Thirty Years War in its tracks and improved the dismal relations between Christian confessions in Europe. Yet the contradiction remained: how could the English and Spanish monarchies arrange the union of Prince Charles and the Infanta Maria when Spanish and Austrian Habsburg arms had driven the Electress Palatine, Elizabeth Stuart, her husband, and her family into exile?[40]

How indeed. James faced the challenge of tackling head on the perception among many Englishmen that Spain was tantamount to the anti-Christ, and that Count Olivares and Ambassador Gondomar between them continued to scheme for the overthrow of the Stuart monarchy, the removal of Protestantism and the vassalage of England to Madrid. They had been led towards these stunning conclusions thanks to the sheer weight of propaganda levelled against both Spain and the policy pursued by the King. During the last five years of James' reign, Thomas Scott, the author responsible for the infamous *Vox Populi*, penned an additional twenty-four pamphlets attacking the Spanish and their nefarious schemes. Scott was so effective at imagining the public mood and revealing to the people what they wanted to hear, that his works became renowned in the country among those that feared Spain as perhaps the only source of 'truth' they could access.

One such work released in 1621 was *A Relation Of Some special points concerning the State of Holland*, wherein Scott insisted that the King of Spain was conniving, disingenuous and had successfully manipulated James in his quest to destroy England. Scott insisted that it was the duty of all true English patriots to demonstrate…

> that all treaties of peace and truce to be made with the King of Spain are wholly unprofitable for our state, as whereby the said King only seeketh to abuse us, and suddenly to cast a net over our heads.[41]

Throughout his pamphlet series, Scott drew attention to the necessity of the Anglo-Dutch friendship, and reasoned that, with Spain and the Dutch back at war from 1621, it was imperative England support her Protestant ally in their noble fight. Arguably the second most important running theme was the repeated references to Elizabeth and Frederick, the landless, throne-less couple formerly of Bohemia, who wished desperately to return home and secure their family's safety.[42] Considering the very real importance of the print media at this point in English history,[43] it stands to reason that as the situation worsened in Frederick's camp through 1622, as his lands were occupied and conquered piece by piece, English sympathy with him increased. Thanks to

Scott's works, Englishmen were never allowed forget Frederick's suffering, and were reminded of the scandal which continued so long as King James refrained from acting in his daughter's defence.

James had not invaded in any kind of force; two thousand volunteers under the command of Sir Horace Veer were all that was sent to garrison the Palatine town of Frankenthal. What was more, throughout 1621 and 1622, James repeatedly entreated Frederick to submit to the Emperor, to plead forgiveness, to refrain from attacking the Spanish, to maintain a ceasefire, to give his blessing for negotiations and so many other ideas and schemes which rapidly came to nothing. By the end of 1622 Frederick had effectively lost everything, and his only allies were desperate landless exiles themselves. The promise James had made to the Spanish to resolve the Palatine conflict, and the promise he had made to Frederick to ease his burdens, had both been proven false.[44] Yet, still, this was not for lack of trying on James' part.

Almost exactly a year before his son and the Duke of Buckingham set off on their adventure, in February 1622 James authorised the trip of another English figure to Madrid, this one involving Sir John Digby, the former ambassador to Spain. Adhering to the necessary protocols of a travelling ambassador with plenipotentiary powers, Digby did not arrive in Madrid until June, but he quickly made up for lost time. Thanks in large part to the influence of Count Gondomar, the Spanish Council of State proved eager to cooperate with the Englishman, and Gondomar even recommended, now that he had returned home to Spain, that King Philip IV give James 'complete satisfaction' regarding the thorny issue of the Palatinate and Frederick's position. By the early autumn, the combined campaigns of Gondomar and Digby appeared to be doing the trick: the only issue holding up the proceedings was the question of papal dispensation which, it was said, would hopefully arrive by the spring of 1623.

The success of the negotiations appeared to a forgone conclusion: by January 1623 most of Europe was aware that, sometime very soon, England and Spain would be joined together in marriage. Both James and Philip had been persuaded to offer substantial guarantees; that whoever broke the ceasefire underway in the Palatinate would incur the wrath of either side, and that if Emperor Ferdinand refrained from cooperating with the proposed reinstatement of the Elector Palatine, then Spanish forces would be used against him. Neither of these terms, in the end, could withstand the pace of events, but in autumn 1622 this was not at all clear. King Philip IV, initially hesitant and determined to obey the wishes of his late father and his minister Baltasar de Zuniga that the marriage should not be concluded, began to warm to the idea as 1622 progressed.

In December 1622 Philip assured Digby that the Infanta or Princess Maria would travel to England the following spring, and in February 1623, the Council of State met to select her travelling companions for the journey to meet her husband. Strikingly, in March, King Philip IV wrote in his hand to the Pope, to hurry along the dispensation on the grounds that, if Charles died without issue, then the English crowns would logically pass to Elizabeth and her husband, the Winter King Frederick. This, Philip assured the Pope, would guarantee English hostility to Catholicism, and Philip believed that it would also endanger Spanish interests in Europe. With the crown of England, Frederick would be dispossessed no longer, and he could return to the continent with an army of enthusiastic volunteers, as England flung itself into the void in Frederick's name. This nightmarish scenario required but one ingredient – the death of Prince Charles, which was by no means impossible considering the vulnerable constitution of Charles' elder brother Henry, and the suddenness with which such tragedies could occur.

It is easy to become trapped in the exercise of imagining what might have been, but Philip was above all interested to prevent such an eventuality from happening, and so he wrote earnestly to the Pope 'I entreat Your Holiness to please take a short resolution in this business, which is a matter of great importance to the good of Christendom.'[45] A combination of Prince Charles' impatience and the somewhat surprising acquiescence of the King meant that Philip would not have to wait for the Pope's reply in order to proceed – Charles was coming to him. As far as the question of why James permitted his son to travel to Spain is concerned, we can imagine a combination of factors at play. One of these was Charles' pressing concern for his sister Elizabeth's welfare, which was undermined severely in January 1623 with the transferral of Frederick's electoral title to Maximillian of Bavaria. As far as the King understood it, James made his decision 'partly out of an earnest desire to see his mistress and specially to give a final end to that business that has distracted His Majesty's other affairs for so long a time.' Charles and James both believed that by journeying to Spain, Philip would be forced to follow through with the commitments he had made. The sooner this happened, the sooner Frederick could be reconstituted as Elector Palatine, and Elizabeth would be restored to her rightful place in Heidelberg.

Frederick was indeed dependent upon external forces to restore him, though he protested vigorously against the initiatives leading to the Spanish Match, as he saw in them a guarantee against his restoration rather than for it. The Spanish, with England in their pocket, would prevent him from returning home; they would hardly work in his interests and against the Emperor's for nothing. Yet Frederick also understood that his options were severely limited by 1623. As far afield as Constantinople, where he had sent Count Thurn of all people, Frederick's diplomacy remained dedicated to its optimistic ends, but closer to home neither Mansfeld nor Christian of Brunswick had proved capable of achieving any sufficient victories. As we have seen, by August in the battle of Stadtlohn, Christian of Brunswick's forces were destroyed by Count Tilly's.

One consequence of Christian of Brunswick's actions was that, during his travels, he had moved through the Lower Saxon Circle, which had since resolved to raise eighteen thousand men for its own defence in response. In addition, the other Protestant Electors in Saxony and Brandenburg, so long quiet and malleable to the Emperor's will, took the transferral of Frederick's titles badly. In January 1623, Frederick received word from King Christian IV of Denmark that Denmark would cooperate with England and the Protestant electors to find a new peace plan. Yet, despite these flutters of optimism, Christian recommended that Frederick submit to the Emperor's demands, while also taking the time to criticise his brother in law King James' Spanish negotiations as fruitless. And yet they were not fruitless;[46] they certainly produced more fruit than the King of Denmark's schemes.

While the timing and circumstances had taken them by surprise, the Spanish had planned to some degree to receive Prince Charles. The critical point which emerges from the incident, was that even while they hosted Charles and Buckingham with every honour imaginable, this was predicated on the assumption of why Charles had jumped the gun in the first place. Since the negotiations for the papal dispensation were still underway, Madrid assumed that Charles had arrived because he was content to skip these protocols and convert to Catholicism. This assumption, and Charles' disappointment of it, hit both sides like a bomb, and was the true cause of the breakdown in the agreement and the subsequent English bitterness.

The way Charles and Buckingham were treated in Madrid was something to behold and tells us much about the protocols of the era. Before the elephant in the room of Charles, and possibly even Buckingham's conversion was addressed, Charles was greeted with rapturous enthusiasm by Spanish statesmen and crowds alike. 'Whatever the prince may want will be granted him in accordance with the obligation which his coming has placed upon us', Philip IV commented to Olivares. The day after their arrival on 18 March, Count Gondomar, believed to be the most familiar with English customs and behaviour, was appointed to the Spanish Council of State, with the task of working diligently in favour of the match while Charles was the guest of the King of Spain. On 19 March, Charles was even permitted a rare honour – to be allowed to see his Spanish bride before the marriage ceremony took place. The Infanta was paraded in front of a carriage where Charles sat concealed, and after three trips past his carriage, Charles spoke with Philip IV for over an hour, as Digby translated.

The visit continued to go well, as Philip declared all English prisoners destined for the galleys were to be released – a divine piece of mercy for them no doubt – and for the next week, after welcoming the Prince into Madrid in an official ceremony, Charles settled into his own quarters of the palace. Philip hosted Charles as his honoured, esteemed guest, and made him feel well at home. Back at his actual home, Charles' father hoped that the marital arrangements would be speedily concluded, since this would save Charles having to endure any kind of grand ceremony in the blistering heat of the approaching Spanish summer. From Madrid, Olivares wrote to the apparently incommunicado Pope once again to request that the dispensation be hurried along.

As we said, when it transpired that Charles had no intention of converting, a pall of awkwardness must have hung over the proceedings. It was not merely Spanish ignorance that led Olivares, Philip or Charles' intended to make this assumption; Sir John Digby anticipated that Charles would declare his conversion too, as a tool to facilitate a speedy resolution of the marriage contract, and a speedy resolution of his sister's crisis. As Charles' refusal to countenance this idea became apparent, King Philip attempted to appear unfazed even while his disappointment must have been palpable. Philip wished to emphasise to Charles' father how much Spain appreciated England's aloofness from the years of conflict, and he wished to maintain a healthy relationship with England to continue this very advantageous state of affairs. He thus determined to press ahead with the marriage, and as he worked towards this end, James not only sent a ship full of sumptuous robes for the anticipated wedding, he also, in mid-March, handed the fortress town of Frankenthal, hitherto occupied by Sir Horace Vere's Englishmen, into the waiting arms of the Archduchess of the Spanish Netherlands, Isabella, and her nephew, King Philip IV of Spain.[47]

Back in The Hague, Frederick was furious when he learned of his father in law's willingness to bow to the Spanish yet again. His homeland was officially conquered, and only the intervention of the almighty or of foreign powers would now be able to save it. By this point in the conflict, Frederick displayed himself utterly opposed to James' peace plans, including those involving the Spanish, largely because he could not bring himself to trust King Philip IV after all they had taken from him. His hesitation is understandable, considering the very difficult year 1623 had already been, with the loss of his title in January to Maximillian of Bavaria. Interestingly though, it was this hesitation, later turning to resolute stubbornness, that proved the most unfixable crack in the Anglo-Spanish plan.

For the marriage treaty to work, Philip required Frederick to refrain from making any moves which might jeopardise a ceasefire in the Palatinate. Indeed, on 1 May 1623, while Charles remained occupied with his Spanish mission, a treaty purporting to last fifteen months was signed by James, the new Spanish ambassador to England and the Archduchess Isabella. Shortly afterwards, Emperor Ferdinand also ratified it, and communicated its contents to the Empire's princes; peace was to be maintained with a ceasefire, while in the city of Cologne, the relevant potentates would attempt to work out a solution to the conflict. News of this treaty, and of James' signature upon it, once again angered Frederick. A requirement of it was that Frederick committed himself not to attack the Emperor's forces, and James attempted to impress upon him the importance of this feature of the treaty when it was sent to him to sign in The Hague.

In Frederick's mind, absolving the use of force took any potential wild cards out of his hands, and meant that he would be unable to rely on or aid in any way Bethlen Gabor of Transylvania, his most disruptive and useful ally to the east. Frederick declared that he did not at all intend to 'let ourselves be bound through such slippery means', adding that he was not prepared to abandon the chances which military force could bring, being 'rather much more resolved to pay attention to and to use all good occasions that God may lay in our hands for the maintenance of our righteous causes.' Frederick was not alone – his wife Elizabeth had also lost faith in her father's ability to help their cause: 'for my father hitherto hath done us more hurt than good', she said.

Frederick was desperate to sabotage the Anglo-Spanish arrangements, in the hope that this would set England onto a new course where the anti-Habsburg camp would thereafter be invigorated. The dispossessed Elector simply did not trust treaties anymore, having watched his Palatinate fall completely to the Spanish after restraining his allies the previous year, and watching his sacred, impeachable title be clumsily transferred to the Duke of Bavaria by another piece of paper. Considering his negative experiences with negotiations, and the unfavourable terms which he anticipated would emerge from any negotiations involving the uncompromising Emperor, Frederick believed that the only course open to him was to continue his violent, disruptive, immensely unpopular – in Germany that is – quest. On 4 May 1623, only a handful of days after the agreement which caused Frederick so much consternation and heartache had been made, the Winter King was saved not by James, not by the Emperor, nor by the King of Spain, but by the Pope's reply at long last to the previous requests for dispensation. For James, Charles and Philip alike, it was not good news.[48]

The Holy See declared its appreciation for the urgency of the negotiations and the weight of the issues discussed, but it was also added that several new articles should be impressed upon England, which Philip and James would have to personally guarantee in return for the dispensation. One of these was freedom of worship for Catholics, an impossible demand, and one which Philip had deliberately avoided raising in the past because it would only serve to irk the British King. In this instance though, Philip gave his guarantee to secure these ends, in return for the dispensation which the marriage required. It was a gamble, since it was at least possible that James might agree to some limitation of the restrictions on English Catholics, which included economic penalties, but the problem was this development was not communicated to James, it was communicated to his son Prince Charles, who had not expected under any circumstances to encounter additional demands or to have to bargain for the Infanta's hand.

He had expected delays, what he referred to as 'the worst denial', but it did not seem possible that after all these years of negotiating, and with Charles actually in place, the Spanish King would throw such a curveball his way. Charles and Buckingham both were deeply offended, but while Charles managed to absorb the setback remarkably well, Buckingham did not, and blamed Olivares for the demands. This behaviour angered the Spanish favourite, and from this point onwards the two men never lost their hatred of one another. As a result of this Olivares' attitude hardened, and he became more sceptical about the marriage being successfully resolved. Charles did his best to repair the damage, conversing directly with the Spanish King, and impressing the Spanish generally with his good grace. Through June and July 1623, Charles continued to work through the demands, and after weighing up his options, incredible as it sounds, actually agreed to the Spanish terms.

This meant, in effect, that Catholicism was to be tolerated freely in England, just as the Spanish had always wanted. What was more incredible was that by the end of July 1623, King James acquiesced, and shortly thereafter sent a demand for the immediate restoration of the Palatinate. Evidently, the British King was weary of dragging on the negotiations any longer; let there be toleration in Britain, but the Spanish had better uphold their end of the bargain if it was to be so. While negotiating with the Spanish, James had kept the correspondence with his son in law open as well. He reprimanded, coerced, threatened and attempted to appeal to Frederick's interests as an Elector who would be restored one way or another, but Frederick, at every step, refused to accept James' terms. What was more, he sent his father in law a copy of the letter which had been intercepted the year before, where Ferdinand had written to the Pope promising the Palatine Electoral title to Maximillian of Bavaria.

James simply swatted this aside and ignored it and insisted that he was determined to rely upon the Emperor and the King of Spain, but that English arms would prevail if English diplomacy could not. Meanwhile, Frederick contacted his far-flung allies, and planned to apply more pressure on the Habsburgs with another Transylvanian adventure courtesy of Bethlen Gabor. As we have seen though, Frederick's resistance effectively crumbled with news of Christian of Brunswick's defeat at Stadtlohn on 6 August 1623. At the news of this disaster, Frederick agreed to accept the terms of the ceasefire, but only if the treaty would immediately restore him to the Palatinate: Bohemia, significantly, had been dropped from his demands. Broken by the weight of several years of hopeless resistance, Frederick urged James on towards this end, reasoning that through success, the British King would 'acquire the immortal glory to have done a deed worthy of his royal grandeur and promise.' On 26 August 1623, Frederick agreed to cease his opposition against the Holy Roman Emperor. For all intents and purposes, after a supremely rocky road, it appeared that peace had returned to the Empire, and that all of King James' efforts had not been in vain. Such optimism was to be dashed once more.

It quickly became apparent to Charles that the Spanish did not intend to unconditionally restore Frederick and his sister to the Palatinate, as both James and Charles had originally hoped. When asked about the Palatine issue, King Philip continued to dodge, insisting that Frederick would be dealt with once the marriage was agreed to. This vague undertaking was not at all what Charles had been led to expect and matters soon got worse. The Pope died in late summer 1623, and as a successor was being found, no dispensation could come, which added additional delays. Worse still was the stunning defeat to Charles' hopes, when it was learned that the Spanish Council of State had voted in favour not of unconditionally restoring Frederick to the Palatinate, but of making use of the pre-existing Imperial-Palatine marriage idea, which Frederick had already rejected. Through this deal, Frederick's first-born son would be sent to Vienna, would marry a Habsburg, and when he came of age, he would return to rule his Palatinate. The devil was certainly in the details though; Frederick would not be allowed receive his lands in the meantime, and he would have to pay a ludicrously high sum of six million reichsthalers, while his son would also be raised as a Catholic.

Charles was not put off by the fact that the English delegation in Madrid accepted this approach. Instead he pressed Philip for more palatable concessions, which moved Olivares to announce that 'you should not think that His Royal Majesty [the king of Spain] is willing to leave His Imperial Majesty [Emperor Ferdinand] helpless in all incidental occasions, due to his sister's marriage.' This amounted to a declaration that even with the marriage of the Infanta Maria to Prince Charles, the Spanish would remain determinedly pro-Austrian. Such a declaration would not have been a surprise to any student of history, or to any observant contemporary of the time, but it certainly took Charles off guard. 'Buckingham and Digby will negotiate further about this', Charles replied stonily, in one of the few occasions when he publicly showed his displeasure towards the Spanish during his visit.

Shortly after these disappointments, Charles would depart from Spain, but not before tying up some loose ends. On 7 September 1623, Charles swore to uphold the marriage contract as it then existed, and shortly thereafter, Charles met with Philip IV and urged him one last time to restore Frederick unconditionally. The best Philip could do was to suggest that Frederick might be restored as part of Charles' wedding present. Enough was enough for the Prince of Wales, he departed Madrid and while in the course of his journey, he received Elizabeth's personal ambassador who bore the letter from Charles' brother in law which he had likely been expecting; Frederick, under no circumstances, would accept the Palatine-Imperial marriage deal. Elizabeth urged her brother not to agree to marry the Infanta until a solid commitment had been made for their restoration, which Charles knew by now was impossible for King Philip IV to grant. Charles worked at some stalling of his own and ensured that Sir John Digby did not receive new instructions until the papal dispensation arrived from the new Pope. By then, as Charles well understood, he would be back in England.

A change had gone through Charles' demeanour after these events. His initially calm and pleasant disposition had hardened, and according to Sir Francis Nethersole, the personal ambassador of Elizabeth's who had delivered the letter to Charles, the Prince of Wales 'resolved to make war with Spain when he…was in Spain, rather than…not see [the Elector and Electress] honourably repaired.' For her part, Elizabeth and her husband had not yet been made aware of Charles' dark change of attitude towards the Spanish Match and towards Spain in general. 'I hope his Majesty will one day see the falsehood of our enemies, but I pray God send my dear brother safe in England again and then I shall be more quiet in my mind.'

It would not be for a few agonising weeks that the Palatine couple would learn the truth: the journey of their ambassador Nethersole to Charles had done the trick, and the Prince of Wales was less drawn than ever before towards the Spanish marriage. What was more, having been led right around the bends for the last six months, Charles was angry, and when he learned from correspondence from home that his father James was ill, it may have seemed like something of an ideal opportunity for revenge. Frederick learned of these developments by late September and ensured that his representative was in place in early October 1623 to greet Charles when he landed in Portsmouth. As the Prince of Wales entered London on 6 October, Frederick's representative recorded scenes of a city euphoric with joy – it seemed the people were collectively celebrating the failure of the Spanish match. The notably grave Prince Charles received only the Palatine representative with some warmth, and a donation of three thousand pounds was raised for their welfare.

Still though, in spite of the difficulties and insults, King James was under the impression that the marriage was going ahead, and that the Palatine-Imperial marriage was the best means for Frederick to be restored to his lands. On both cases, James was mistaken. In spite of the assurances from James to Frederick that his son would never have to convert to Catholicism, and that this was the perfect time to make a lasting peace, Frederick would not accept the treaty. Perhaps Frederick realised what James apparently did not – that time was not on the British King's side. With Charles out of Spain, the Spanish continued to drag their heels, likely because of the delays which Charles had deliberately left behind him. James became frustrated at these developments but refused to abandon the idea.

Relentlessly he pursued the Match, convinced that it represented the best, perhaps the only hope, to restore his daughter and son in law. He may well have been right, but intractable problems and stumbling blocks remained. After many delays, the last straw seemed to come in early December when yet another delay for the wedding was announced after the invitations for the wedding had been already sent out, and the Spanish were sufficiently embarrassed to cancel the Infanta's English lessons, and Maria no longer accepted any correspondence from Prince Charles, which had greatly decreased in any case. By this point, Emperor Ferdinand had abandoned the idea of any kind of conference in Cologne, and an eleventh-hour proposal for a Palatine-Bavarian marriage could not salvage the situation either.

James was in something of a crisis, because if he announced that he had given up on the whole idea, then the clamour for a war with the Spanish would undoubtedly increase. On the other hand, pursuing pointless negotiations had become a thankless, tiresome process, and Frederick's constant entreaties were draining James' energies. Meanwhile, Charles wanted to break off the negotiations and prepare for a war with Spain; if Philip IV would not accede to what had originally been agreed, if diplomacy would not return his sister Elizabeth and Frederick to the Palatinate, then a resort to arms would surely be the only recourse. Charles had tried diplomacy, James, without a doubt, had tried diplomacy, but diplomacy had failed. Through a combination of factors, the year which began and contained such high hopes on an Anglo-Spanish match was ending with relations between the two states at their lowest ebb in several years. It was time to fulfil the nightmare the Spanish had for so long sought to avoid; to solidify a wide ranging Protestant alliance, to bolster the Dutch, and above all to return the Palatine family at sword point if necessary, regardless of the consequences either from the King of Spain or from the Emperor himself.

It was time, in addition, to ride the wave of anti-Spanish hysteria which had been bubbling over since the whole wretched crisis had begun. By mid-December 1623, Frederick was informed that James was souring on the Spanish match and intended soon enough to announce the break with Spain. After so many years of turmoil, so many frayed nerves and bitter disappointments, perhaps Frederick's greatest victory – this one of the diplomatic battlefield – appeared to be taking shape. It remained to be seen what 1624 would bring, but as many lords in the English court assured the Palatine representative, it could be expected that, soon enough, things would get better for the Winter King and Queen.[49]

FOUR

So Many High Hopes

'They think that they alone are enough to ruin Spain and to put one hundred thousand men into Flanders, that all ought to obey them at once.' This according to Johan von Rusdorf, Frederick's Palatine ambassador to England, who was sufficiently unimpressed with the extreme optimism of English radicals to offer this view in late 1623. Not only were the pro-war Englishmen infected with optimism bordering on naivety when it came to England's military prospects, but the entire country was not yet united behind a common course and, as Rusdorf put it eloquently, 'when the dogs are unwilling, it is difficult to hunt.' The prospect of hunting was not made any easier by the unfavourable military situation by late 1623.

Thanks to the failure of the marriage negotiations, Spain remained entrenched along the Rhine, and the Holy Roman Emperor retained his Catholic League army, led by the undefeated Count Tilly. Bethlen Gabor of Transylvania, Frederick's most unpredictable but also unreliable ally had, true to form, made peace with the Emperor in mid-November, just before the worst winter conditions settled in. Earlier, Christian of Brunswick had suffered a disastrous defeat at Stadtlohn in August near the Dutch border, and Ernst von Mansfeld had stayed put in his quarters near Alsace and could not hold his unpaid troops together for much longer. If England wished to intervene in Frederick's name, a brand-new alliance would have to be crafted, and this mission would sink or swim in 1624.[50]

Once the two marriage schemes had been abandoned, King James did lean strongly towards a plan which would forcibly restore Frederick to his homeland. Ernst von Mansfeld, who dissolved his army in January 1624 for want of pay, arrived in London in the spring to participate in this plan, and was treated like something akin to a national hero. If he would recruit ten thousand foot and three thousand horse, then the King declared his intentions to provide him with £20,000 per month. Such initiatives seem to suggest that James was all in, but in actual fact, several caveats surrounding his interventionist policy were already making themselves felt. The first was that James would not act alone; he had sent feelers to the French and Dutch, but neither of these powers would act without the English acting first, and James would not act until they did.

Second, because James did not actually want war with Spain, and wanted only to restore Frederick to his lands, the King found his actions greatly restricted. This brings us to our third point, because James could not acquire the monies he needed from Parliament, since British statesmen wanted a war in support of Protestantism. This religiously motivated war would demand an attack on Spain in league with the Dutch, but since James did not wish to embroil his kingdom in such a conflict, he soon found that he was at loggerheads with Parliament yet again. 'It seems', commented the Palatine ambassador Rusdorf, 'that the English advance one step and go three backwards, seeing that they are not so inflamed anymore to declare war against the Spaniards.' With the campaigning season fast approaching and no preparations save the hosting of Mansfeld having taken place, it began to seem increasingly unlikely that 1624 would be Frederick's year.[51]

Inactive though it was on the battlefield, England made 1624 its most active diplomatic year yet. Denmark, Sweden, France, the Netherlands, Venice and Savoy all received ambassadors, and a further diplomatic mission was sent to venture through Northern Germany, with Saxony and Brandenburg being the major targets of this offensive. Frederick established and then maintained a relationship with each of these ambassadors, which granted him greater information about the pace of rumour and events in the Empire. To his horror, Frederick learned that the Emperor intended to call a Diet to confirm the transfer of his electoral titles to Maximillian of Bavaria. Such an act would have made it a great deal more difficult to protest this act in the future, and it prompted Frederick to make another appeal to James...

> ...for the sake of his children, his honour, reputation and promise...because we have followed his Majesty's will and strong threats out of dutiful and filial respect only in the point of the said sequestration [of Frankenthal], but also in all other impositions applied to us, which has, as it were, bound our hands and feet and made the business so burdensome.[52]

Frederick was sure that an Anglo-French force led by Mansfeld would secure his restitution, but for the aforementioned reasons, neither King James nor his royal opposite King Louis XIII of France proved willing to move first. With no monarch willing to stick their neck out for Frederick, the dispossessed Elector was provided with many expressions of goodwill, but little else. Considering this flurry of diplomatic activity engaged in by the British King in the months before his death in March 1625, it would perhaps be unfair to write England off as diplomatically bankrupt, as one historian saw fit to do.[53] Although his high-minded diplomacy failed to wrest the naïve results he wanted, one cannot deny that, in his own way, James did try his best. He was faced with the twin problems at home of a recalcitrant Parliament, which wanted its own way in the potential conflict with Spain, and the familiar threat to stability which continued to grow from the soaring anti-Spanish sentiment, sentiments which were fanned, as before, by public literature, this time in the form of theatre.

A Game at Chess was only the latest scandal to rock Anglo-Spanish relations in 1624, which were already on the rocks thanks to the failed Spanish Match idea. Over 6-16 August 1624, a play with unmistakable undertones and subliminal messages was hosted at London's Globe Theatre. The man responsible for the play was Thomas Middleton, who had his first and last hit with the performance, and what a hit it was. The play was performed nine times in front of sell-out audiences, who were treated to depictions of characters they knew of well. The English, depicted as Whites; with their White King (James I and VI), White Duke (Buckingham) and White Knight (Charles) were contrasted with the Spanish Blacks and the Black King (Philip IV) and Black Knight (Count Gondomar, the former ambassador). By tapping into the anti-Spanish feeling, which was rampant at the time, Middleton's play became the talk of the country.

'All the news I have heard since my coming to town is of a new Play. It is called a *Game at Chess*, but it may be a *Vox Populi* for by report it is 6 times worse against the Spaniard.' This was how John Woolly, the secretary of the English ambassador in Brussels recorded his interpretations of the play, which he had returned to London specifically to see for himself.[54] John Woolly's mention of *Vox Populi* recalled the 1620 pamphlet by Thomas Scott of the same name, which vilified the King of Spain and in particular his ambassador Count Gondomar, who was understandably less than pleased at his unflattering depiction. Indeed, Middleton had read his way through the full extent of the anti-Spanish literature available at the time, and was certainly influenced to shape his play based on these works.[55] Thus in Middleton's play, the aim was clearly to capture the essence of that misunderstood ambassador again – the organisers of the performance even procured some of the ambassador's old clothes to add to the authenticity.[56]

In his reports back to Brussels from London, John Woolly was convinced that someone would be hanged for the play's incendiary contents, but this did not happen. Indeed, Woolly's suspicions and concerns shed some light on the political climate in Britain at the time, and of the prevalence of anti-Spanish feeling within King James' court. Upon learning of the performance, the Spanish did angrily protest its contents and its unflattering message, but in Woolly's opinion – erroneous as it happened – the Master of Revels had signed off on it 'it is thought not without leave from the higher powers, I mean the P[rince of Wales] and the D[uke of Buckingham], and if not the K[ing of Britain], for they were all loth to have it forbidden, and by report laugh heartily at it.' [57]

Although he exaggerated the King's enjoyment of the performance, as we will see, John Woolly was not the only person to see *A Game at Chess* as an arm of English foreign policy, and of an indication from a frustrated King James that he was willing to offend Spain and strengthen his position by rallying the anti-Spanish and anti-Catholic elements to his side. As the historian J. Dover Wilson understood: 'the best interpretation…seems to be that Middleton's A Game at Chess was itself a pawn in the game of foreign policy which Charles and Buckingham were in 1624 playing against the Spanish ambassador.' The true message behind and purpose of the play was more complex; it appears unlikely that the play had any political end in mind, and that Middleton's goal went no further than attaining some level of success in London's drama scene by capitalising upon several themes which were rife at the time in English society; hostility towards Spain, suspicion towards Catholics and even a fear of conversions from the Protestant to Catholic side.[59]

The storyline of the play was essentially a commentary on that infamous diplomatic act of the previous year: Prince Charles' voyage to Madrid in his quest to secure the Spanish Match. In *A Game at Chess* though, Charles and Buckingham did not travel with marriage in mind, but for more 'patriotic' reasons. To break the grip of the Spanish over the King and country, Buckingham and Charles travelled to Madrid, where the Prince of Wales disingenuously declared his love for Princess Maria and pretended to place himself at the mercy of the Spanish court, in a bid to draw out a confession from Spain about Philip IV's true intentions. While in the company of the Spanish, both men made their confessions of 'greed, lechery, gluttony, and ambition', which lulled the Spanish into making similar confessions, and professing the 'real reason' for their instigation of the Thirty Years War – a long-suspected mission to acquire Universal Monarchy.[60]

Thus, *A Game at Chess* managed the simultaneous feat of poking some fun at the Duke of Buckingham – who was at his most popular during this period thanks to his zealous hatred for all things Spanish after the Spanish Match debacle – and also exposing the true intentions of Spain and all its rotten statesmen. Unsurprisingly, the play caused a storm in the diplomatic as much as the domestic theatre. Charged with responding to such affronts was the resident Spanish ambassador, Don Carlos Coloma, who had replaced Gondomar from summer 1622. Initially well-respected and well-treated, with the waning of Spanish influence in the country after the Spanish Marriage scheme failed, ambassador Coloma could not hide his sense of horror at what he had experienced when he attended a performance of *A Game at Chess*. In a series of letters sent to James' court and Madrid, Coloma communicated his serene repulsion and indignation in words which are well-worth recounting here. On 10 August 1624, Coloma wrote to King James' court, then in the country and away from London, saying that:

> Yesterday and today the players called Your Majesty's men have acted in London a play that is so scandalous, so impious, barbarous and so offensive to my royal master – if perhaps his known greatness and the inestimable worth of his royal person were capable of receiving offence from any man, least of all from such vile persons as are usually the authors and actors of such follies – that I am compelled to take up my pen and in a few words and with all I owe Your Majesty, to beg Your Majesty one of two things: either that Your Majesty would be pleased to order the authors and actors of the said play to be publicly punished as an example, by which means Your Majesty will satisfy his own honour and the reputation of the English nation which has been so much smirched by actions that are so vile and so unworthy of honourable men; or that Your Majesty would order that a ship be given me in which I may cross to Flanders with the necessary guarantees granted to ambassadors of other sovereigns and leave to depart instantly. I await indifferently either decision.[61]

It was also up to the ambassador to inform King Philip IV in Spain what he had seen and heard, and he thus added a description of the performance, with a palpable sense of disgust pervading the correspondence:

> The actors whom they call here 'the King's men' have recently acted, and are still acting, in London a play that so many people come to see, that there were more than 3,000 persons there on the day that the audience was smallest. There was such merriment, hubbub and applause that even if I had been many leagues away it would not have been possible for me not to have taken notice of it, and notorious baseness, not merely excessive tolerance, if I had paid no attention to it or neglected it. The subject of the play is a game of chess, with white houses and black houses, their kings and other pieces, acted by the players, and the king of the blacks has easily been taken for our lord the King, because of his youth, dress and other details. The first act, or rather game was played by their ministers, impersonated by the white pieces, and the Jesuits, by the black ones...Besides this, those who saw the play relate so many details and such atrocious and filthy words, that I have not thought fit to offend Your Excellency's ears with them. In these two acts and in the third, the matter of which I do not know in detail, they hardly shewed anything but the cruelty of Spain and the treachery of Spaniards, and all this was set forth so personally that they did not even exclude royal persons. The last act ended with a long, obstinate struggle between all the whites and the blacks, and in it he who acted the Prince of Wales heartily beat and kicked the 'Count of Gondomar' into Hell, which consisted of a great hole and hideous figures; and the white king [drove] the black king and even his queen [into Hell] almost as offensively. All this has been so much applauded and enjoyed by the mob that here, where no play has been acted for more than one day [consecutively], this one has already been acted on four, and each day the crowd is greater.[62]

Within that same letter, ambassador Coloma made an interesting observation when he added that:

> It cannot be pleaded that those who repeat and hear these insults are merely four rogues because during these last four days more than 12,000 persons have all heard the play of *A Game at Chess*, for so they call it, including all the nobility still in London. All these people come out of the theatre so inflamed against Spain that, as a few Catholics have told me who went secretly to see the play, my person would not be safe in the streets; others have advised me to keep to my house with a good guard, and this is being done. Let Your Excellency consider whether I could pass over this in silence…Finally, Sir, nothing else but war is to be expected from these people. Let Your Excellency believe me, I beg and pray, even if for certain reasons it suits us to defer it, our best plan is to show bravery and resolution [now], rather than allow them to increase their strength.

Yet, in spite of his certainty that this play signalled war, a reply from King James assured the ambassador of the royal family's profound shock and horror at the performances' 'great insolence and boldness', adding that in the case of the punishment of the actors and playwright concerned, 'complete satisfaction and content will be given in everything'.[63] The British King insisted that he had not known about the performance until Coloma told him about it, a claim which may strike us as bizarre, but the plea does contain elements of truth. It is unlikely that James feigned surprise in his correspondence with the Spanish ambassador, for he was to ask his courtiers at around the same time why 'the first notice thereof should be brought to him, by a foreign Ambassador, while so many Ministers of his own are thereabouts and cannot but have heard of it'. Again, judging from this reaction, it would appear that anti-Spanish statesmen supported and aided the performance of *A Game at Chess*, rather than either James or even Charles. Indeed, if Charles and Buckingham – considered the leaders of the anti-Spanish faction by this point – had been responsible for the performance, then one is struck by the extent to which their plan to use this play for their anti-Spanish schemes 'misfired.'[64]

Notwithstanding its riotous popularity, *A Game at Chess* was too scandalous for the King to countenance, and after nine performances, on 16 August 1624, the performances ceased. The storm caused by the performance of this play reminds us not only of the progressively anti-Spanish feeling of the British people, but also of the intensely cautious behaviour of King James. It is also worth considering the fact that, thanks to the depictions of the country's most important figures within the play, both Prince Charles and the Duke of Buckingham were identified as leaders of the pro-war camp, although neither man possessed the ability to harness the supposedly prevailing mood of the time. Buckingham seethed with anger at his perceived snubbing by

Count Olivares the previous year, and Charles remained bitter about the abandonment of the Palatine issue during the Spanish Marriage negotiations, but the act of leaping into a war with Spain was not as simple as they might have liked. In addition, the tension caused by James' opposition to the war his subjects wanted was a dilemma exacerbated by the King's struggle with that other pillar of his realm – Parliament.

The Parliament of 1621 had not ended well, either for King James or his subjects. Indeed, James reportedly declared his intention during the tail-end of the 1621 session, to never call another Parliament in his lifetime. This bitterness on the King's part and the criminal proceedings against various MPs can all be explained by the anti-Spanish tone of the 1621 session, which seemed to take the King by surprise. Although in 1622 a recall of Parliament was requested by some, James refused to recall Parliament 'until the success or failure of the Spanish negotiations was indubitably demonstrated or until he could be assured that the commons would display a different spirit.'[65] 1623 told a different story, largely because of the breakdown in the Spanish Match plan, and the return of the invigorated Prince of Wales and Buckingham in October of that year.

1623 had been immensely stressful for the King, and although in that year he was only in his late 50's, the strains of recent years had caught up with him. Perhaps the weighted diplomacy of his son in law had worn him out, or perhaps the father's worries about the peril and disgrace of his daughter's position had caused him to age more quickly. Either way, the historian David Harris Willson was able to note that by late 1623:

> His policy of peaceful diplomacy was now thoroughly discredited, and his habit of yielding to his son and his favourite had now become fixed. Their policy filled him with alarm, and he clung instinctively to friendship with Spain, but his only defence was to sink into a state of distracted inaction which could not last.[66]

Indeed, distracted inaction was an apt phrase to describe James' behaviour, but the Venetian ambassador was also well-placed to provide a comment on the King's state of mind, when he wrote:

> [N]o man living knows what is really passing in the King's mind. He is sagacious, deep, and impenetrable. Some think that he is playing his usual game, having secret objects very remote from external appearances. Others believe that he has an understanding with his son and the favourite, and while they seem on the popular side he follows his ordinary and natural inclinations solely. But the most certain thing of all is that the King will do nothing good unless by force or by fraud.[67]

However, this want of a plan does not mean that MPs had the run of the place once Parliament reconvened in February 1624. Interestingly, an overlooked explanation for the lack of gumption on the part of those members of the Commons to debate on a given policy must be their fear of punishment or prosecution. In 1621, several MPs were placed in the Tower for speaking against the Spanish Match policy, and for loudly criticising the then chosen course – one such figure was Sir Robert Phelips, but he was by no means the only one to suffer such a fate.[68] Those MPs who were assembled in Parliament from February 1624 were certainly interested in discussing matters relating to foreign policy, but they were wary of not straying too far outside the boundaries of acceptable discussion, for fear not just of what would happen to them, but of their King's propensity to forcibly dissolve the Parliament. As if adding substance to such fears, James remarked on 24 March 1624, almost as a veiled warning to those assembled, that he had 'broken the necks of three parliaments one after another.'[69]

The spring of 1624 was full of disappointments and contradictions for those assembled. Prince Charles had distinguished himself in the Parliament of 1621, and it was expected that he and Buckingham would do the same in this latest session, especially considering his father's declining health.[70] Yet, when the Prince of Wales had attempted to monopolise the debate and make promises to the Commons and Lords, these promises were immediately violated by his father, who evidently was not willing to relinquish the reins of power just yet. On 11 March, Charles had announced first to the Lords and then the Commons that the king would ask for no money for his own needs, an announcement which was rendered hollow three days' later, when on the 14 March the King demanded greater subsidies and a payment of debts, while remarking that he remained at odds with the opinions of many of his MPs.

Not only did the King need money, he was also unwilling to abandon the Spanish policy which many of his subjects had come to loath. When, during one assembly, the Archbishop of Canterbury opened proceedings by informing the King of the profound joy of his subjects at the news that he was 'sensible of the insincerity of the Spanish in their dealings with him', James replied by denying that he was any way sensible to such a thing. Any assumptions that Charles would take over the business of handling Parliament, or that war with Spain was virtually inevitable, were dashed with these revelations in the middle of March. As the Venetian ambassador put it at the time, there was 'Nothing [more] more certain than the King's disinclination for a rupture [with Spain]. In fine the King is the same as ever, variable, tricky, inscrutable, determined upon peace, dominated by fear only and the forger of every mischief.'

Subsequently, after Buckingham had literally got down on his knees before the King, James agreed in principle to use any subsidies for a war with Spain rather than for the purpose of settling his debts. However, at the same time he altered the wording of his original request, so that instead of war against Spain, the funds were due to be used 'for this great business', an alteration which some found suspicious. It must be added, even with the confusing negotiations between Parliament and King, the Parliament of 1624 was the most productive of the entire Stuart period. Notwithstanding the tricky issue of war, legislation was passed in abundance, with 35 public and 38 private acts passed. The ineffectiveness of the 1621 Parliamentary session seems to have spurred MPs onward, and there had been much business outstanding from that session which was here dealt with. In short, the 1624 Parliament was definitely productive and highly active, just not in the way some of the more belligerent statesmen might have wanted.[71]

James wished to have his cake and eat it; he wanted to make some sort of impression upon the Palatine crisis, and to make some sort of contribution towards restoring his family to their homeland, but he did not wish to be beholden to the Commons. One of James' commissioners had warned him that relying on Parliament for supply during wartime would 'invite the domination' of that body, while other figures wished to prevent the strengthening of the alliance between Buckingham and Charles, and believed that a war with Spain would catapult both men into an unassailable political position.[72] Thus, the King sought to find a loophole, where a limited war could be had in the name of the Palatinate, and he would not have to depend upon Parliament in order to get it. He found this solution in the Four Propositions, a policy which called for the naval rearmament of England, and the subsequent defence of English coasts, Irish coasts and Dutch coasts.

These Four Propositions were agreed to by Parliament, and money was provided for these tasks. James then cynically appropriated these funds for the continental scheme he desired – an ill-fated mission whereby Ernst von Mansfeld would lead a detachment of British soldiers to the Palatinate, and free it from Spanish and foreign dominion. The scheme pleased nobody. Parliament was opposed because it was too limited, did not ensure war with Spain, and took the question of further supply out of their hands, not to mention the fact that their King had misused the funds which they had voted for, which cannot have helped to heal old wounds of mistrust. Prince Charles and Buckingham, the same, wished to have a wider war with greater implications for cooperation with the French and Dutch, and a more involved war with Spain. In addition, both men misunderstood the actual commitment of Parliament in this regard, which was to lead to much bitterness in later years between the new King and his Parliament, as we will see.[73]

Finally, King James himself soured on the idea not too long after sending Mansfeld and his partially recruited army towards the coast. In the weeks before his death, King James would be forced to accept that Mansfeld's army, reduced by desertion and disease, could not make any significant impact upon the conflict in Frederick's name. This was a bitter pill indeed, but even while 1624 had been a year of false promises, dashed assumptions and disappointments – for the English and Palatine parties alike – 1625 brought the potential for new plans and new alliances to take shape. The dispossessed Elector, true to his character, had by no means given up hope yet.

FIVE

A Failure to End

By the summer of 1625, Count Gondomar was an old and frail man. After having served his country for so many years from London, Gondomar's return to Spain in spring 1622 did not mean that his term of service had ended – the old Count was simply too well-travelled, too experienced and too knowledgeable for King Philip IV to allow his talents to go to waste. Gondomar served instead as something of an advisor on Spanish foreign affairs, with a distinct expertise in English matters. In June 1625, Gondomar felt confident enough to write a stunning letter to Olivares, the leading light of Spanish government and the royal favourite. The letter was so stunning because it captured the theme of Spanish history which has since become accepted as automatic and inevitable – the decline, or, as Gondomar himself put it, *se va todo a fondo* – 'the ship is going down'.

Perhaps it was the recent failure of the Anglo-Spanish marriage negotiations; perhaps it was the successful and highly dangerous conclusion of alternative Anglo-French marriage negotiations; perhaps it was the fact that the war against Frederick in Germany never seemed to end; perhaps it was the looming threat of an anti-Habsburg coalition, which gathered steam following the death of King James in March 1625; perhaps it was simply the dismal state of Spanish finances. Whatever the cause for Gondomar's gloomy correspondence, he met with a surprisingly receptive response from Olivares. Olivares accepted the former ambassador's concerns, but he then added some upbeat reminders of his own. How many elder statesmen had pronounced the decline of their homeland since records began, and how many times did that state flourish for many centuries after such a pronouncement? There was no value to be had in lamenting the end of Spain – indeed; surely there were things to take solace from, even on the strategic level.

Interestingly, Olivares then changed his tone somewhat, by adopting a more realistic, some might say downcast, interpretation of Spain's position in the world. 'From this', the Spaniard began, 'I do not mean to say that these are happy times', nor did Olivares attempt to claim that things were better before Philip IV's reign. However, it seems Olivares was attempting to look on the bright side in summer 1625. There had, at least, been no rebellions in Spain, no mutinies in the armies, and some progress had also been made in the war against the Dutch, with the symbolic Dutch fortress town of Breda shortly due to fall. Olivares finished up the letter by saying:

> And I conclude by saying that I do not consider a constant and recitation of the state of affairs to be a useful exercise, because it cannot be concealed from those who know it at first hand. To make them despair of the remedy can only weaken their resolution, while it cannot fail to have adverse effects on everyone else...As far as I am concerned, your words can do no harm. I know the situation, I lament it, and it grieves me, but I will allow no impossibility to weaken my zeal or diminish my concern. For, as the minister with paramount obligations, it is for me to die un-protesting, chained to my oar, until not a single fragment is left in my hands. But when such things are said where many can hear them, wanton damage is caused.[74]

This striking correspondence, and the resignation with which Olivares seemed to greet the situation, provides us with a window into how contemporaries even in the highest positions of power in Spain viewed their Empire's decline. The Spanish were greatly occupied by the task of keeping up appearances, which explains why, even when past its prime, Spanish power was still very highly rated, and as we have seen in the English case, feared and loathed in equal measure.[75] There would come a time when it would no longer prove possible to keep up appearances, but for the time being, Spanish power remained a vital element of the Habsburg war effort. For a German, Protestant or any other power to combat the Habsburg colossus, they would have to contend also with the military, financial or political might of Spain.

The two branches of the Habsburg family were irreversibly tied together, for better or worse, for the duration of the conflict. This, indeed, ensured that many lesser powers had been scared away from the mission of resistance, and that stronger powers refused to take up this mantle alone. Olivares and Gondomar clearly believed that any sense of a Golden Age had passed, but in spite of these observations, Spain's ability to project its power into the Holy Roman Empire guaranteed, for the moment, that the Thirty Years War must continue. It was only once this ability on Spain's part had fractured, and she had been forced to retreat, that the Habsburgs would display that vulnerability which enabled its enemies to take advantage and push the Emperor back in turn. The Thirty Years War is thus impossible to understand unless we view it as something more than a war pursued and maintained by the Holy Roman Emperor. It was instead a war for wide-ranging, interconnected, mutually dependent interests; Spanish fortunes would dip, Austria's would rise, and vice-versa, but until both Austria and Spain were on the ropes, peace could not return to Europe.

When we thus come to the issue of creating an anti-Habsburg coalition of some significance – a mission adopted with real purpose from 1624 – it is possible to see fear and hesitation mix with the ambition and determination of the allies, as they contemplated the totality of the conflict which surely awaited them. War with Emperor Ferdinand and the Austrian Habsburg influence in Germany also meant a war against Spanish resources and influence, if not also her soldiers. Spain maintained a large army in the Spanish Netherlands, which did battle against the Dutch, and her efforts had been greatly aided by the absorption of the Palatinate along the Rhine. The Palatine acquisition surrounded France in a Spanish fence, but it also deepened the Spanish investment in Germany – something which its statesmen believed their country could ill-afford.[76]

The Dutch war, indeed, was more than enough to occupy her attentions. The Palatine occupation had also torpedoed the Anglo-Spanish marital alliance plans, which in turn meant that England was more likely to join itself more tightly to the Dutch and French. Spanish expenditure in the Palatinate, and later in North Italy, dangerously undermined its Dutch war effort. More disastrously, the unexpectedly lengthy nature of the war in Germany, and the dispossessed Elector's tireless efforts to keep his cause alive in the relevant courts of Europe, meant that Spain would not be freed from these extra entanglements any time soon.

When we ask why the Thirty Years War failed to end with the defeat of Frederick's forces at White Mountain, or after any of the other numerous military defeats which followed, or even from some diplomatic negotiation which might settle the matter, the answer is of course more complex than an issue of heavy Spanish involvement in Germany. Instead, Spanish involvement was a symptom of the overall problem. To help their Austrian cousins, and to advance Spain's strategic interests, the Palatinate had been seized, without any due consideration of the consequences which might follow. Madrid apparently had not counted on King James' determination to restore his son in law's lands, nor had Frederick's stubborn obstinacy been factored into the equation. As a result of their Palatine occupation, Spain sacrificed the marital alliance with England – arguably the best way to keep its enemies apart, and to undermine English support for the Dutch. That the consequences were not worse for Spain had less to do with its capacity for meeting formidable coalitions, and more to do with the inability of these coalitions to cooperate and form a united strategy.

In early 1625, despite much optimism for Frederick's cause, cracks were already appearing in the façade which would play no small role in the great triumph of the Holy Roman Emperor by 1629. As much as they feared the combined powers and influence of the Habsburg dynasty; as much as they loathed the injustice of the Emperor's creeping monopoly on the Empire's constitution and powers; as much as Protestants lamented the progress of the Counter-Reformation, the time was not yet right for a proper fusing of allied interests which could be directed against the two Habsburg branches. When this fusing did at last materialise, it spelt doom for Vienna and Madrid, but until it came, neither the Holy Roman Emperor nor the King of Spain could afford to hold back.[77]

As the Habsburgs closed ranks, so too did their rivals. In June 1624, with their defensive measures falling apart, the Dutch renewed their alliance with the French in the Treaty of Compiegne. Through this agreement, the Dutch agreed to remain at war with the Spanish for at least another three years, and King Louis XIII's administration approved an immediate loan of 480,000 thalers for the desperate Dutch needs, with the promise of further instalments in the future. Around the same time, France renewed its alliances with both Venice and Savoy, reinforcing the two northern arms of Italy against Habsburg encroachment, which was correctly anticipated in the near future. Further developments in France boded well for the anti-Habsburg alliance; Cardinal Richelieu was appointed foreign minister in August, a position which he was to retain for the next two decades.

Capturing the conflict inherent in French foreign policy at the time, Richelieu commented that 'We can neither contribute to the restoration of Frederick because of our Catholic faith, nor deny it without being reproached by our allies.' The war in Germany remained a thorny issue, because Maximillian of Bavaria, supported by the Papacy, seemed open to some form of agreement with the French, but to balance their relationship with Frederick and his allies, Maximillian's new electoral titles could not be recognised. Faced with such difficult choices, Richelieu elected to focus on North Italy instead, and attempted to cut off the Habsburg legs by occupying the critical Alpine passes with Swiss assistance. This move, as we will examine later, was part of a wider plan to prepare for war with Spain, but it had an insignificant impact on the Protestant cause.[78]

The French were evidently becoming more diplomatically active, but France was not yet prepared to officially enter the conflict on Frederick's side. As a result, Ernst von Mansfeld's sponsored adventure to the continent floundered, a development which represented King James' last effective effort to restore his son in law, and not a very realistic one at that. 'God give him constancy and resolve', was how Frederick attempted to pray for Mansfeld's success, but the task proved far outside the realm of his capabilities. Upon landing at long last in the Dutch Republic in January 1625, his English soldiers became much reduced by desertion and disease. By the end of March 1625 Christian of Brunswick, who had joined the hopeful army in a bid to salvage some measure of his shattered reputation, was forced to conclude that Mansfeld's force was unfit for entering Germany in any capacity.

It was only shortly after learning of his army's defeat from the twin evils of disease and want of funds, that King James himself succumbed to disease on 27 March 1625. James' death represented not only the end of an era in English foreign policy, but also the removal of the greatest stumbling block to a determined British intervention in Germany. The dispossessed Elector Palatine certainly recognised this, and after expressing his grief added perceptively that 'nothing consoles us more than the new King's good affection towards us and the common cause.' King Charles I was indeed better disposed towards his sister and brother in law's struggle than his late father had been, but the great hopes for an English rescue would not exactly materialise in spite of this.[79]

Shortly after the Franco-Dutch defensive alliance had been formalised under the Treaty of Compiegne in June 1624, King James had followed suit in the middle of that month with a defensive alliance of his own. As we have seen though, the alliance floundered over the tricky question (for James at least) of the Spanish, and since he refused outright to attack them, the Dutch negotiators quickly lost heart in the English mission. Furthermore, by sending Mansfeld's ill-fated expedition to the Republic, the King effectively spent what little resources he had. Not until late in 1625, with a new King and a hopefully invigorated Parliament, could the British contribution be made alongside their Dutch ally. The Dutch, having lost Breda in late summer of 1625, were more than eager to strike back at their Spanish enemy, and the new Stadtholder Frederick Henry was equally determined not to begin his tenure in office with any further disasters.

An Anglo-Spanish War was technically fought from 1625-30, but in reality, the conflict contained small and insignificant ventures which cost more than they granted and served only to foment dissatisfaction at home. One example of such a venture was the Anglo-Dutch naval expedition against Cadiz which was sent in the first week of November 1625. The enterprise began in high spirits, and its planners envisioned an attack on Spain in Europe and then in the Indies. However, owing to shortages in money and poor coordination, the initiative failed to wrest any significant dividends.[80] This was a dark time for the Dutch as well, and perhaps the only silver lining for that beleaguered Republic was found in the fact that, following the capture of Breda, the Spanish were so exhausted by the eleven month siege that they refrained from undertaking any other military action for the remainder of 1625. Frederick Henry similarly entered winter quarters relatively early as a result.[81] As they rested, the Dutch and English, supported monetarily by the French, would have to recoup their losses and plan, in league with Frederick, for a new campaign in 1626. As we will discover later, these plans were aided by the determined diplomatic expansion of the Palatine scope into Scandinavia, where the Kings of Denmark and Sweden awaited.

Before the incorporation of the Danish King into Frederick's war strategy is examined, we must tie up some lose ends of the narrative. From April to December 1625, the goal of Palatine foreign policy was to capitalise upon the hostility felt towards the Habsburgs in various quarters, and to gather as many powers as possible together for the strike against both the Emperor and the King of Spain. 'The principle goal', Frederick claimed, 'is to halt the ambitious designs of Austria and Spain, and to reconcile the affairs of Germany in their entirety, with the restitution of the Palatinate and of that which it depends on.'

Such statements underlined the fact that the Elector Palatine was not fighting a religious war; at its heart, reasons the historian Brennan Pursell, the war was a dynastic one: a fact demonstrated by the incorporation of so many religiously different powers, from the Calvinist Transylvanians, to the Muslim Turks, to Catholic France, to Lutheran Denmark. If any army could be forged from these powers, then Frederick wished to exit his exile in The Hague and join its course 'to serve the fatherland and the common cause'. Yet, Frederick had learned his lesson from before; the disintegration of Mansfeld's army had demonstrated clearly that unless a force was well-supported diplomatically, militarily and financially, its chance for success was hopeless.[82]

Frederick was eager to lean on his brother in law, the new British King, to lead such an army, and he emphasised Mansfeld's failure as a stain on his and on Charles' honour to get his point across. Both England and Frederick needed to be redeemed if anyone could be expected to believe in and follow their cause, and for this to happen, King Charles must commit himself fully to the task of fighting Frederick's enemies. There could be no half measures, as his father had affected – England must be all in and fully prepared for a long war with the Habsburgs. Frederick was of course asking an awful lot through this campaign, but in case Charles did not bite, Palatine diplomatists focused their efforts on the Lower Saxon Circle and the Danish and Swedish Kings.

By summer 1625, Frederick was justifiably nervous; an Imperial Diet which would make official the transferral of his Electoral title to Maximillian of Bavaria had been postponed in 1624, but it was due to reconvene in August 1625. While this Diet had been advertised by Ferdinand as a chance to restore peace to the Empire, Frederick was adamant that the Emperor had no interest in restoring peace. Furthermore, Frederick was certain that Ferdinand would use the occasion of the innocuous looking Diet to complete the ruin of the Palatine cause, and render it impossible to turn back the clock by enshrining the transfer in Imperial constitutional law. No matter what way he attempted to frame the transfer, Frederick insisted that the Golden Bull alone spoke for the true order of the Empire, and this building block of the Empire 'as a fundamental constitution neither should nor can be changed without the participation and approval of all Estates of the Empire.' Frederick believed that Ferdinand's true motive for calling the Diet was 'to strengthen more and more the party of Austria, Spain and the League for the oppression of German liberty'. As the Palatine court's memorandum on the looming Diet noted on 5 June 1625:

> As for the King of Bohemia, as he has always protested, he also still protests sincerely that he thirsts only for peace, on the condition that it is founded not on the ruin and extirpation (such is the design of the opposing party) but on just and honest conditions, assured of his complete restitution, and of a uniform peace throughout all Germany, offering in this case everything that will not be contrary to his conscience, honour, to the fundamental laws and liberty of the Empire.[83]

In the meantime, King Charles was not simply sitting on his hands and waiting for news of Frederick's latest scheme. English diplomats worked hard towards two major ends in 1625; the first, following King James' death, was the restoration of Frederick through a coalition of as many powers as could be recruited. The second was the more impressive: the replacement of the failed Anglo-Spanish marriage plan with an Anglo-French arrangement. Under the latter scheme, King Charles would be wedded to Henrietta Maria, the sister of King Louis XIII of France. France was open to this arrangement, but would not roll over on religious issues, and for the sake of national honour the French negotiators would demand just as good if not better terms than had the Spanish. The difference in this case was that the new King was more inclined to grant these concessions, because it was not the French that occupied the ancestral lands of a member of the royal family. Initially, at least, English public opinion was not overtly hostile either to the Anglo-French cooperation or to the concept of toleration for English Catholics, but this openness would not last.

Tasked with bringing this marriage treaty to life, and attaining a bride for Charles at last, was Sir James Hay, the First Earl of Carlisle, who arrived in France to much fanfare in mid-May 1624. Not for another year would Charles be married by proxy to Henrietta Maria, and while this marital alliance was critically important both for the Stuart dynasty and for British security, it contained its share of problems and controversies over its duration. In addition, the very fact that it took a full year to conclude spoke to the genuine difficulties and disagreements which Carlisle's mission had run into, be it from Cardinal Richelieu's rise, the question of Catholic toleration, the course of the conflict or protests over money. Notwithstanding these setbacks, after an exhausting year of diplomacy, Carlisle managed at last to acquire the hand of the French princess.[84]

The Anglo-French marriage negotiations revealed much about the challenges facing first the tail-end of King James' diplomatic efforts, and then the new beginning promised under Charles. In both cases, the two Stuart monarchs had much to prove; James did not wish for the final memory of his reign to be a failure, and Charles was determined not to begin his reign with one. Yet, neither man proved capable, during the years of 1624-25, of bringing British power and influence to bear in Europe to any significant degree. This was not, as we have seen, from a lack of ambassadors. A veritable flood of empowered men had travelled to the relevant European capitals in the final year of James' reign, with entreaties from Frederick close behind them. From Venice but with more success in Savoy,[85] the veteran English diplomat Sir Isaac Wake sent home regular dispatches on the viability of the hoped for alliance between such 'mid-European states' as Savoy, Venice, Lorraine, the Dutch and the Swiss.[86]

'Ambassadors', opined one contemporary early in King James' reign...

should have knowledge of many things, especially of philosophy, moral and politic, and before all other, Roman Civil Law; and, moreover, a knowledge of histories will greatly help him, which besides the pleasure of it will increase in him wisdom and judgment in the affairs of his charges, and will make him not to be astonished at anything.[87]

The reality for James' diplomats, unfortunately, was that they were chronically underpaid, and suffered much for it on the expectation that they would be richly rewarded with office when they returned home. This underinvestment in the Jacobean diplomatic service was a symptom of the depleted treasury which Queen Elizabeth had left to her successor after so many years of war with the Spanish and Irish. The shortage of funds for English ambassadors verged on worse than embarrassing at times, especially when it was known that their Spanish counterparts – whatever the shortcomings of those administrations – always ensured their representatives were well provided for, prompting one Englishmen to comment 'God send us some good taste of the like'.[88] Amidst the concerns for the security of their correspondence and the often maddening delays in reply were the further vexations that one would not have enough money to put on a suitable display in hosting, networking or, in the more extreme cases, eating.

Englishmen did what they could to survive these conditions; with one receiving a loan from Count Gondomar before he arrived in London, another receiving a gift from the Spanish which cleared his substantial debts, and another selling off his lands to make ends meet while he languished thousands of miles away in a foreign capital. When examining the grand scope of Palatine diplomacy, or the whims of British Kings, it is sometimes easy to forget that real people, facing silent challenges, did battle in these foreign capitals for influence and agreement with fewer resources than we may expect. The life of an English ambassador, indeed, was far from glamorous in the early seventeenth century. As the historian Maurice Lee Jr concluded on the question though, the reasons for such shortcomings was first of all money, and then the King's inability either to secure or apportion it appropriately:

> It was an age of talented diplomatists; if no Englishman displayed the kind of ability that has made the peerless Gondomar the ideal seventeenth-century ambassador in the eyes of posterity, many of them compare favourably enough with most of their continental counterparts. A number of the successes of Jacobean foreign policy were owing to them, and some of the failures. Most historians have weighed that policy in the balance and found it wanting. If this be a just judgment, then the responsibility lies much more with the government in London than with, its professional agents in the field.[89]

British diplomacy nonetheless worked to successfully conclude an alliance which would reduce their overall military and financial commitment, and guarantee Frederick's restoration. In September 1625 the Treaty of Southampton was signed between the English and Dutch, whereby both powers elected to cooperate offensively and defensively, to free the Netherlands from Spain and to restore Frederick by force of arms. Could this latest Anglo-Dutch effort produce fruit? Not quite, for its major export was the aforementioned Cadiz expedition, which failed miserably. By this point, Britain had entered the war against the Spanish, as her vehemently anti-Spanish people had desired, but when push came to shove, these same people were largely unwilling to make the necessary sacrifices. This, coupled with some further unfortunate misunderstandings, would prove fatal in the end for King Charles.

Before autumn 1625, the King of Sweden had also abandoned the idea of war for Frederick – for the moment at least – and opted instead to resume the war against his Polish cousin in Livonia. The Palatine family closed ranks with the Dutch, as Frederick Henry married Amalia von Solms, the daughter of Frederick's late courtier. By blood, Frederick Henry was Frederick's uncle, but the two men of closer age got on much better than had Frederick with the late Maurice. Frederick's family received a new grand house in The Hague for their property portfolio, but independent Dutch initiatives in Frederick's name were, for the moment at least, superseded by the planned cooperation between the English, Dutch and Danish.[90]

During the autumn and winter of 1625, negotiations between these three powers increased. Christian IV of Denmark was himself eager to intervene militarily in Germany, both for the sake of Protestantism and to ensure that the bishoprics for his sons were not seized by the Emperor's agents. Yet, Christian would not move without sufficient monetary and military support.

This was not forthcoming from the French, or either of the Italian powers, but Charles did provide a gift of £46,000 to the Danish King, who happened to be his uncle, along with promises for a monthly subsidy of £30,000. That Charles would later squirm and wriggle his way out of this commitment was not apparent in the optimistic atmosphere of late 1625. In December 1625 indeed, the Hague Alliance which had long been hoped for was finally signed. By its terms, the Dutch, English and Danish agreed to cooperate militarily in the new year, and to restore Frederick to the Palatinate together.

The plan was the strongest commitment from Frederick's allies that he had yet received, but the Elector Palatine knew better than to place all trust in its success. He had been disappointed before, and he had watched as generalissimos with grand ambitions had crumbled before the challenges of isolation, lack of funds and want of forage. Indeed, only recently had he seen the perennial loser Ernst von Mansfeld fail once again thanks to those very shortcomings. Still though, with these agreements concluded, Frederick's cause was provided with a considerable shot in the arm which promised a great deal. He declared himself satisfied, but all three powers had their own reasons for joining together aside from the noble quest to restore justice to the Palatinate.

The volume of spats and the extent to which each power managed to provide their own interpretation of their responsibilities did not bode well, but for the moment at least, a common fear of the Habsburgs, and the common goal of undermining them in several key areas, held their arrangement together. That the Hague Alliance was brittle and not built to last was confirmed with the first serious defeat of the cause the following year, but for the moment at least, the Hague Alliance resembled something of a victory for Frederick, who had refused to capitulate to the Emperor, or to retire into obscurity. His tenacity had kept the Palatine cause alive, and brought it here to new heights, but it had also prolonged the now distant Bohemian revolt, and it threatened worse disasters if the conflict between Emperor and Elector was not soon resolved. If Frederick hoped for such a quick resolution though, he was to be disappointed; over two decades of the most desperate, destructive, weighted conflicts remained to be fought. By the end of this process, neither Frederick nor his Imperial foe would be left standing.[91]

1625 must be viewed to some degree as a turning point in the Thirty Years War. The year did not represent, as the signatories of the Hague Alliance surely hoped, the turning of the Habsburg tide. For the next few years, and until the arrival of the 1630s, the Habsburgs and Emperor Ferdinand especially were to become so powerful as to defy all expectations, but this feat was only accomplished by significantly raising the stakes. It was then that Cardinal Richelieu accepted the necessity in immediately preparing France for wholescale military intervention in the Empire, against both Austria and Spain.

To aid his King in this noble quest, Richelieu would rely upon the military prowess of the King of Sweden, a Protestant Lutheran King, to fight the Emperor, and the Calvinist Dutch Republic to fight the Spanish. Any semblance of a religious war vanished thereafter, as the conflict became a power struggle between the two coalitions, outgrowing in the process the Bohemian or Palatine roots from which it had originally sprung. As we alluded to earlier, this fusing of interests among the anti-Habsburg coalition was only made possible with the ascent of the Holy Roman Emperor to the summit of his powers, to the extent that this Triple Alliance had no choice other than to cooperate to the end in their mission to lay the Habsburgs low. Historians are united in interpreting the latter half of the 1620s as one of supreme Habsburg triumph on the battlefield, within society and in the church.[92] It will be our task for the next several chapters to account for this ascendency, and to paint a picture of Habsburg triumph unequalled in that dynasty's history.

Chapter 11 Notes

[1]See Robert Zaller, '"Interest of State": James I and the Palatinate', *Albion: A Quarterly Journal Concerned with British Studies*, Vol. 6, No. 2 (Summer, 1974), pp. 144-175; pp. 144-147.

[2]Carter, *Secret Diplomacy of the Habsburgs*, pp. 109-110.

[3]Marc L. Schwarz, 'James I and the Historians: Toward a Reconsideration', *Journal of British Studies*, Vol. 13, No. 2 (May, 1974), pp. 114-134; p. 114.

[4]See Robert Lawson-Peebles, 'A Conjoined Commonwealth: The Implications of the Accession of James VI and I', *The Yearbook of English Studies*, Vol. 46, Writing the Americas, 1480–1826 (2016), pp. 56-74; pp. 56-58.

[5]Walter Carruthers Sellar and Robert Julian Yeatman, *1066 and All That* (Penguin; London, 1960), p. 69.

[6]See Carter, *Secret Diplomacy*, pp. 113-114.

[7]*Ibid*, pp. 115-116.

[8]Charles H. Carter, 'Gondomar: Ambassador to James I', *The Historical Journal*, Vol. 7, No. 2 (1964), pp. 189-208; p. 189.

[9]Carter, *Secret Diplomacy*, p. 120.

[10]Garrett Mattingly, *Renaissance Diplomacy* (Boston, 1955), p. 262.

[11]For one example see Samuel Rawson Gardiner, *History of England from the Accession of James I to the Outbreak of the Civil War*, vol. 1, (London, 1884), pp. 214-215.

[12]See Carter, *Secret Diplomacy*, pp. 126-129.

[13]Robert Zaller, '"Interest of State"', p. 147.

[14]Louis B. Wright, 'Propaganda against James I's "Appeasement" of Spain', *Huntington Library Quarterly*, Vol. 6, No. 2 (Feb., 1943), pp. 149-172; pp. 150-153.

[15]Quoted in *Ibid*, p. 152.

[16]Quoted in *Ibid*, pp. 152-153.

[17]See P. G. Lake, 'Constitutional Consensus and Puritan Opposition in the 1620s: Thomas Scott and the Spanish Match', *The Historical Journal*, Vol. 25, No. 4 (Dec., 1982), pp. 805-825; pp. 807-810.

[18]Kenneth Fincham and Peter Lake, 'The Ecclesiastical Policy of King James I', *Journal of British Studies*, Vol. 24, No. 2, Politics and Religion in the Early Seventeenth Century: New Voices (Apr., 1985), pp. 169-207.

[19]Albert J. Loomie, 'King James I's Catholic Consort', *Huntington Library Quarterly*, Vol. 34, No. 4 (Aug., 1971), pp. 303-316; p. 303.

[20]J. Caitlin Finlayson, 'Jacobean Foreign Policy, London's Civic Polity, and John Squire's Lord Mayor's Show, "The Tryumphs of Peace" (1620)', *Studies in Philology*, Vol. 110, No. 3 (Summer, 2013), pp. 584-610; pp. 587-590.

[21]J. P. Kenyon, *Stuart England*, 2nd ed. (Penguin, New York; 1985), pp. 60-61.

[22]Quoted in J. Caitlin Finlayson, 'Jacobean Foreign Policy', p. 591.

[23]Sir Robert Phelips' observations and the study of his life is provided in Katherine S. Van Eerde, 'The Spanish Match through an English Protestant's Eyes', *Huntington Library Quarterly*, Vol. 32, No. 1 (Nov., 1968), pp. 59-75.

[24]Quoted in *Ibid*, p. 64.

[25]All quoted in *Ibid*, p. 65.

[26]Quoted in *Ibid*, p. 66.

[27]Quoted in *Ibid*, pp. 66-67.

[28]*Ibid*, pp. 67-68.

[29]Quoted in *Ibid*, pp. 68-69.

[30]*Ibid*, pp. 69-70.

[31]Quoted in *Ibid*, p. 72.

[32]One historian that does an excellent job in this very task is Carolyn A. Edie, 'Tactics and Strategies: Parliament's Attack upon the Royal Dispensing Power 1597-1689', *The American Journal of Legal History*, Vol. 29, No. 3 (July., 1985), pp. 197-234.

[33]See Katherine S. Van Eerde, 'The Spanish Match through an English Protestant's Eyes', pp. 72-73.

[34]Albert J. Loomie, 'Gondomar's Selection of English Officers in 1622', *The English Historical Review*, Vol. 88, No. 348 (Jul., 1973), pp. 574-581.

[35]David Harris Willson, 'Summoning and Dissolving Parliament, 1603-25', *The American Historical Review*, Vol. 45, No. 2 (Jan., 1940), pp. 279-300; pp. 293-294.

[36]Katherine S. Van Eerde, 'The Spanish Match through an English Protestant's Eyes', pp. 74-75.

[37]See David Harris Willson, 'Summoning and Dissolving Parliament', p. 279.

[38]P. G. Lake, 'Constitutional Consensus and Puritan Opposition in the 1620s', pp. 817-820.

[39]An immensely useful revisionist account of the meeting is provided in Brennan C. Pursell, 'The End of the Spanish Match', *The Historical Journal*, Vol. 45, No. 4 (Dec., 2002), pp. 699-726. The analysis of the negotiations from the perspective of Frederick are provided in Pursell, *The Winter King*, pp. 195-211.

[40]Brennan Pursell, 'The End of the Spanish Match', p. 702.

[41]Quoted in Louis B. Wright, 'Propaganda against James I's "Appeasement" of Spain', p. 161.

[42]*Ibid*, p. 163.

[43]This trend is explored in Richard Cust, 'News and Politics in Early Seventeenth-Century England', *Past & Present*, No. 112 (Aug., 1986), pp. 60-90.

[44]See Robert Zaller, '"Interest of State": James I and the Palatinate', pp. 150-152; Brennan Pursell, *The Winter King*, chapters 5 and 6.

[45]Pursell, 'End of the Spanish Match', pp. 700-703.

[46]Pursell, *The Winter King*, pp. 196-197.

[47]Pursell, 'End of the Spanish Match', pp. 704-708.

[48]*Ibid*, pp. 709-710.

[49]Pursell, *The Winter King*, pp. 202-205.

[50]Brennan Pursell, *The Winter King*, pp. 210-211.

[51]*Ibid*, pp. 221-223.

[52]See *Ibid*, pp. 224-225.

[53]Glyn Redworth, 'Of Pimps and Princes: Three Unpublished Letters from James I and the Prince of Wales Relating to the Spanish Match', *The Historical Journal*, Vol. 37, No. 2 (Jun., 1994), pp. 401-409; p. 407.

[54]Thomas Cogswell, 'Thomas Middleton and the Court, 1624: "A Game at Chess" in Context', *Huntington Library Quarterly*, Vol. 47, No. 4 (Autumn, 1984), pp. 273-288; p. 273.

[55]Christina Marie Carlson, 'The Rhetoric of Providence: Thomas Middleton's A Game at Chess (1624) and Seventeenth-Century Political Engraving', *Renaissance Quarterly*, Vol. 67, No. 4 (Winter 2014), pp. 1224-1264; p. 1225.

[56]Melissa D. Aaron, *Global Economics: A History of the Theatre Business, the Chamberlain's/King's Men, and Their Plays, 1599–1642* (University of Delaware Press; Newark DE, 2003), p. 120.

[57]T. H. Howard-Hill, 'Political Interpretations of Middleton's 'A Game at Chess' (1624)', *The Yearbook of English Studies*, Vol. 21, Politics, Patronage and Literature in England 1558-1658 Special Number (1991), pp. 274-285; p. 275.

[58]J. Dover Wilson, *The Library*, Fourth Series, 11 (1930), pp. 110-112.

[59]See James Doelman, 'Claimed by Two Religions: The Elegy on Thomas Washington, 1623, and Middleton's "A Game at Chesse"', *Studies in Philology*, Vol. 110, No. 2 (Spring, 2013), pp. 318-349; especially from p. 335.

[60]Cogswell, '"A Game at Chess" in Context', pp. 277-278.

[61]Quoted in Edward M. Wilson and Olga Turner, 'The Spanish Protest against "A Game at Chesse"', *The Modern Language Review*, Vol. 44, No. 4 (Oct., 1949), pp. 476-482; p. 481.

[62]Quoted in *Ibid*, pp. 480-481.

[63]Quoted in *Ibid*, p. 482.

[64]T. H. Howard-Hill, 'Political Interpretations of Middleton's 'A Game at Chess'', pp. 278-279.

[65]David Harris Willson, 'Summoning and Dissolving Parliament, 1603-25', p. 297.

[66]*Ibid*, p. 298.

[67]Quoted in Mark E. Kennedy, 'Legislation, Foreign Policy, and the "Proper Business" of the Parliament of 1624', *Albion: A Quarterly Journal Concerned with British Studies*, Vol. 23, No. 1(Spring, 1991), pp. 41-60; p. 46.

[68]Katherine S. Van Eerde, 'The Spanish Match through an English Protestant's Eyes', *Huntington Library Quarterly*, Vol. 32, No. 1 (Nov., 1968), pp. 59-75.

[69]Mark E. Kennedy, 'Legislation, Foreign Policy, and the "Proper Business" of the Parliament of 1624', pp. 46-48.

[70]Charles was especially effective in the first half of the 1621 Parliament, but less so in its second half. See Richard Cust, 'Prince Charles and the Second Session of the 1621 Parliament', *The English Historical Review*, Vol. 122, No. 496 (Apr., 2007), pp. 427-441.

[71]Kennedy, '"Proper Business" of the Parliament of 1624', pp. 53-56.

[72]David Harris Willson, 'Summoning and Dissolving Parliament, 1603-25', pp. 299-300.

[73]Kennedy, '"Proper Business" of the Parliament of 1624', p. 59.

[74]J. H. Elliot, 'Self-Perception and Decline in Early Seventeenth-Century Spain', *Past & Present*, No. 74 (Feb., 1977), pp. 41-61; p. 41.

[75]J. H. Elliott, 'A Question of Reputation? Spanish Foreign Policy in the Seventeenth Century', *The Journal of Modern History*, Vol. 55, No. 3 (Sept., 1983), pp. 475-483.

[76]The observations of Spanish statesmen on their country's ability to project its power into German, North Italy and Bohemia, and the wisdom of such adventures, are revealed in Magdalena S. Sanchez, 'A House Divided: Spain, Austria, and the Bohemian and Hungarian Successions', *The Sixteenth Century Journal*, Vol. 25, No. 4 (Winter, 1994), pp. 887-903. See also the estimations of Spain's financial policies and her liquidity problems: Akira Motomura, 'The Best and Worst of Currencies: Seigniorage and Currency Policy in Spain, 1597-1650', *The Journal of Economic History*, Vol. 54, No. 1 (Mar., 1994), pp. 104-127.

[77]Wedgewood, *Thirty Years War*, pp. 101-137 examines succinctly the mutual dependence of the two Habsburg branches and the implications of this relationship for Europe during the conflict. See also Geoffrey Parker, *Thirty Years War*, pp. 42-64.

[78]Parker, *Thirty Years War*, p. 63.

[79]Pursell, *The Winter King*, pp. 228-229.

[80]Parker, *Europe in Crisis*, p. 187.

[81]George Edmundson, 'Frederick Henry, Prince of Orange', *The English Historical Review*, Vol. 5, No. 17 (Jan., 1890), pp. 41-64; pp. 56-57.

[82]Pursell, *The Winter King*, pp. 232-233.

[83]See *Ibid*, pp. 233-234.

[84]An excellent analysis of these negotiations is provided by Roy E. Schreiber, 'The First Carlisle Sir James Hay, First Earl of Carlisle as Courtier, Diplomat and Entrepreneur, 1580-1636', *Transactions of the American Philosophical Society*, Vol. 74, No. 7 (1984), pp. 1-202; especially pp. 59-88.

[85]An extensive analysis of Wake's career in Savoy is provided by Vivienne Laminie, 'The Jacobean Diplomatic Fraternity and the Protestant Cause: Sir Isaac Wake and the View from Savoy', The English Historical Review, Vol. 121, No. 494 (Dec., 2006), pp. 1300-1326; especially pp. 1324-1326.

[86]Roy E. Schreiber, 'The First Carlisle Sir James Hay', p. 103.

[87]Quoted in G. B. Harrison, *A Jacobean Journal, Being a Record of those Things Most Talked of during the Years 1603-1616* (London, 1941), p. 37.

[88]Quoted in Maurice Lee Jr, 'The Jacobean Diplomatic Service', *The American Historical Review*, Vol. 72, No. 4 (Jul., 1967), pp. 1264-1282; p. 1279.

[89]*Ibid*, p. 1282.

[90]Pursell, *The Winter King*, p. 236.

[91]Pursell, *The Winter King*, pp. 236-238.

[92]Geoffrey Parker, Peter H. Wilson and C.V. Wedgewood all name a chapter after this period of unrivalled Habsburg supremacy.

PART FOUR
Years of Intervention
-1626-1634-

(Top left) George William of Brandenburg
(Top right) Frederick V and Elizabeth Stuart

Christian of Brunswick

"The king of Sweden…is a new sun which has just risen; young, but of vast renown. The ill-treated or banished princes of Germany in their misfortunes have turned their eyes towards him, as the mariner does to the polar star."[1]

Attributed to Cardinal Richelieu, late 1620s.

"All the trouble is caused by this untimely and strict Catholic Reformation and also by the Imperial Edict concerning the restitution of church lands and the expulsion of the Calvinists…The Imperial Edict has turned all the non-Catholics against us…The entire Empire will be against us, aided by the Swedes, the Turks, and Bethlen Gabor."[2]

Albrecht of Wallenstein makes a gloomy pronouncement of the impact of the Edict of Restitution, in two letters sent over 1629-30.

"[The Elector] has to be friend or foe. When I come to his borders, he must declare himself cold or hot. This is a fight between God and the Devil. If my Cousin wants to side with God, then he has to join me; if he prefers to side with the devil, then indeed he must fight me; there is no third way."[3]

Gustavus Adolphus, in a letter to his brother-in-law the Elector of Brandenburg, summer 1630.

CHAPTER TWELVE
"The Previously Unimaginable"

Eastern Baltic

ONE
For Reasons Unsound

The Kingdom of Denmark drew its power from accidents of geography, history and from the prestige of its dynasty. First, in the case of geography, Danish kings held the immensely lucrative Baltic Sea trade captive, because any vessel which wished to trade in the Baltic would have to pass through Danish waters first. The two channels of water which flow between the two Danish islands of Funen and Zealand are known as the Little Belt and Great Belt respectively, and the latter island holds the Danish capital Copenhagen. In modern Europe, a sophisticated network of bridges and underground tunnels connects Copenhagen with the rest of Denmark, and one can even travel from Copenhagen to the Swedish city of Malmo just across the third channel of water, the Oresund. It was through the Oresund or Sound, that the majority of ships passed, and where the majority of tolls were thus levied.

In the early seventeenth century, the Little Belt, Great Belt and Oresund represented not merely a brilliant strategic advantage, but the monetary benefit was by far the more significant benefit for the Danish state. If any ship neglected to pay these tolls, then the Danish navy, repeatedly enlarged since the sixteenth century, would be used to block access. Generally, the ships did pay, and because they paid, the Danish Crown amassed a private fortune of one and a half million thalers by 1625. All tolls went straight to the King's purse, while his self-sufficient nobility drew their incomes from their landholdings. Significantly, the Danish nobility possessed over half of all arable land in the Empire, even while they represented less than a fifth of the population.[4] The King's relationship with his powerful nobility was largely good, but several decades building upon this relationship had taught the king a few things.

First, the Crown was expected to 'live of its own', meaning that, unlike in Britain for example, Christian was not expected to appear in front of these nobles requesting subsidies or grants for a foreign war. Second, the nobility did not wish to upset the good thing they had going, and while they maintained a curiously medieval system of feudal knightly service into the late 1600s,[5]

551

they were pacific in nature, and wholly suspicious of any foreign schemes. A recalcitrant nobility was not necessarily a problem for a King of Denmark though, because while he was a monarch, he was also a Duke of Holstein and thus thoroughly enmeshed within the Holy Roman Empire.

The Oldenburg was a German family in origin, and while it ruled Denmark, it retained its hold on Holstein, one of the largest and wealthiest German duchies in the Lower Saxon Circle. The twin responsibilities of Scandinavian king and German duke are critically important for us to understand if we are to grasp why Christian IV of Denmark intervened in the Thirty Years War. The distinction between his two regimes are immediately apparent; in Denmark, Christian IV was expected, as we said, to live off his own means, and the powerful Danish nobility, rooted in the Council of the Realm, would be slow to approve any of their King's high-minded machinations if they could not discern a benefit for themselves. By contrast, Christian's rule as Duke of Holstein contained no such restrictions; it could be argued that the King was more sovereign as a Duke of Holstein than he was as King of his Danish realm.

Since the late fifteenth century this balancing act had been maintained, with even different governments – the Danish Chancery and the German Chancery – operating in each region. To phrase this situation another way; the Danish Chancery could not tell the Danish King what to do if he operated in his capacity as Duke of Holstein, rather than as their King. Thanks to his accumulated fortune from the Sound tolls, the Danish King would be able to afford this independent policy, at least for a time. Even when the war would come home to Denmark in time, at its declaration King Christian IV was keen to act in his capacity as the Oldenburg Duke of Holstein, thereby taking the opportunity for protest away from his Danish nobles.[6]

Exactly how powerful was King Christian IV of Denmark? Having achieved his majority in 1596, Christian ruled over one of the most powerful Protestant kingdoms in Europe. Once, Denmark had been the nucleus of the Kalmar Union, which was effectively a United Kingdom of Scandinavia under the control of the Danish King. This Union dissolved in a confusing manner during the first half of the sixteenth century, with its most significant consequence being the release of Sweden from the Danish orbit. The Swedish state was small in population and economically poor, but the Danish Empire also contained some weaknesses, which could be exploited by wary neighbours. As Paul Douglas Lockhart wrote, Denmark laid claim to a great deal, but its power was greater on paper than in fact:

> Since 1536, the kings of Denmark claimed sovereignty over a vast array of territories: the kingdom of Denmark itself, the kingdom of Norway and its vassal-state Iceland, three large and wealthy provinces in present-day southern Sweden (Blekinge, Halland, and Skane), the Faroe Island chain, Greenland, the

German duchies of Schleswig and Holstein, and even tenuously the Orkneys. Collectively, it was not a wealthy kingdom – only the Scanian provinces, the Duchies, and parts of Denmark had anything approaching a prosperous rural economy – and it was sparsely populated: of the only 1.5 million inhabitants overall, 600,000 lived in Denmark.[7]

Christian IV sought to build upon his Kingdom's power and prestige by embarking on a massive armament and ship-building programme, while also looking to the latest in military innovations and tactics then under development in the Dutch Republic. Christian had Count John of Nassau's drill book printed in Danish, in a bid to improve the professionalism and quality of his troops. In time, Christian approved the existence of a professional standing army of four thousand men to train conscripts and peasants alike and planned to subsidise this army with mercenaries in times of war. While he possessed an impressive ability to strike first, thanks to his large purse and the availability of German mercenaries nearby, Christian also sought to secure his lands by building several fortresses.

Denmark owned portions of southern Sweden which ensured that control over the Sound tolls would not be undermined, and to protect these investments, a total of eight towering fortresses were built to secure Scania in the south, while work was also undertaken at Christiana (Oslo) in Norway. Two fortresses were built to secure Copenhagen, three to guard access into Western Holstein, and further works blocked access from the east into the duchy. In the case of his ship-building programme, Christian spent six times more money on his fleet than on the construction of fortresses in his lands, with incredible results. Total tonnage was increased from 11,000 to 16,000 between 1600-25, reflecting a trend towards larger, sturdier warships as Christian adopted the latest and most innovative naval designs.[8]

Christian's core dilemma was provided by the unusual contract between the King and his nobles. A long war would require requests of taxation, which would necessitate making concessions to the nobles, potentially reducing his freedom of action. Christian could – and in 1625 he did – make war in his capacity as Duke of Holstein, but if his personal cash reserves dried up, he would be at the mercy of these nobles, who would likely hold his previous actions against him. What Christian needed was a short, sharp war in Germany or, if he could get it, sufficient support from foreign allies which would provide him with economic independence indefinitely. The Hague Alliance filled this requirement and promises of subsidies from the English and Dutch made Christian a great deal more emboldened than he would otherwise have been.

Christian had gained some brilliant advantages during the 1611-13 war with Sweden. The peace treaty from that conflict had been hugely advantageous to Christian's coffers, as its former vassal was committed to pay exorbitant reparations, which greatly boosted Danish prestige and prosperity. This was the so-called Alvsborg Ransom and required Sweden's new King to somehow round up 1 million reichsthalers, a currency not easily come by in Sweden, lest the Danish occupation of Swedish lands would continue. The sum was equal to four years of Swedish harvests,[9] and it necessitated the creation of a new tax on all citizens aged fifteen and above, which even the Swedish royal family would have to pay, and only soldiers 'on campaigns' were exempt from.[10] The balance was made up by selling copper to its neighbours, and a large Dutch loan for the Swedish crown of 250,000 reichsthalers was also arranged, which eventually enabled the beleaguered Swedes to pay what was owed in 1618.[11]

This conflict effectively shattered Sweden for a decade, and secured Denmark's border with her former vassal for the foreseeable future. The point had been made: Sweden was not up to the task of defeating its old overlord on the field, and its new king would have to pay this ransom or be destroyed. Christian was here at the peak of his powers, and a great deal of optimism seemed to set in, aided by an economic boom which lasted for several more years. Even his crown lands were beginning to become more profitable. After 1615, the king received an annual income of 200,000 reichsthalers from his lands, a figure which steadily increased over the following years.

The stability of Christian's position opened him up to the prospect of loaning vast sums to his nobles, who were then tied into contracts that greatly benefited the Danish Crown and made it less likely that the nobility would publicly criticise its policy. In addition, the tolls leveraged on the Sound meant that Christian was created as the wealthiest Protestant monarch in the world, with a personal fortune behind only the Duke of Bavaria. With his money to spare, he established the Danish East India Company, investing over 400,000 reichsthalers in its maiden voyages and colonies. In the meantime, he increased trade with Iceland, undercut the Anglo-Dutch whaling competition, and established a silk factory at Copenhagen. As impressive as these initiatives and the healthy status of the Crown's coffers were by 1625 though, all such gains were beholden to the bottomless pit of military expenditure, which consumed the vast majority of the Crown's wealth.[12]

By 1625, Christian had been watching the events of the Bohemian Revolt and Palatine war unfold with increasing unease. His familial obligations to Frederick meant that he was willing to offer advice to the man that had married Elizabeth, his niece, but he would go no further than urging Frederick to make some kind of compromise peace. It is significant that, in his capacity as Duke of Holstein, Frederick met with Christian IV during a Segeberg meeting in spring 1621. During their face to face encounter, Christian had admonished Frederick 'who advised you to drive out kings and to seize kingdoms? If your councillors did so, they are scoundrels!' While he had been willing to send a letter of protest to the Emperor regarding the Imperial Ban which had been pronounced against Frederick and his allies, and while Christian did declare his willingness to eject the Spanish from the Palatinate, he would not, at this stage, make war against the Emperor in Frederick's name. The mere suggestion of war had apparently panicked the minor German potentates in the Lower Saxon Circle, and Christian did not wish to rely on these fickle princes for his security during the proposed conflict.[13]

Four years later, Christian's concerns had not significantly changed. He was not wholly confident that the Lower Saxon Circle would support him, and he had therefore sought foreign guarantees in their place. Yet, this recap should underline the important key feature of Christian's decision to intervene in the Empire by 1625. He did not take this decision with the expectation that it would empower his realm against Sweden, or that it would increase his prestige in the Baltic. Christian's concerns were not so narrow, nor could they be, since as we have established, Christian was a German Duke. Thus, when the Emperor acted against Protestants and against the German liberties, he acted against Christian's ability to maintain his freedom of action in the Empire.

Christian's concerns in this regard were as genuine and legitimate as any other German potentate; neither Saxony nor Brandenburg had been thrilled to see the increasingly powerful Emperor expand his authority. The difference between those Protestant Electors was that while they were rooted solely in Germany, Christian IV was also a King in his own right, and theoretically, he could make use of the advantages this position accrued to wage a successful war first and foremost in the German interest. Christian was a German Duke, who would harness his personal power as King of Denmark, avoid the jealous nobles, and emerge victorious with this curious arrangement just as he had done in the previous war with Sweden. That, at least, was the plan.[14]

Two great factors aside from Christian's interest in German liberties also spurred him on. The first was the pressing need to provide bishoprics and lands for his two younger sons. According to Peter H. Wilson Christian was driven 'by his strongly Lutheran sense of family responsibility to provide for two princes who could not inherit the kingdom'. Possession of certain key bishoprics, such as Bremen, the most lucrative, could bring with them further territorial advantages, like the control over rivers and their trade. If enough of these north flowing rivers like the Elbe or Weser were monopolised, then Danish tolls could be placed on them, and the Crown would be further enriched. The further into Germany his influence reached, the more Christian could claim was rightfully his. Through pressure campaigns he wrested declarations of loyalty from the cities of Lubeck and Hamburg and controlled their trade by occupying portions of the rivers upstream and levying tolls.[15]

Aside from his needy sons, Christian was perturbed by the advance of the Habsburgs towards the Baltic, and into majority Protestant lands. As a

Lutheran King, the Counter-Reformation was a feared and loathed initiative, and the public progress of the Jesuits – including one famed trip by a Jesuit to Norway in 1604 – moved Christian to issue a ban on Catholic worship in his realm by 1615. During this decade Christian maintained an actively pro-Protestant foreign policy, announcing his support for the Elector of Brandenburg during the Julich-Cleve crisis. Christian's reputation spoke for itself among Protestants, since he was nominated in the 1612 Imperial election and the 1619 Bohemian election; each time, it was hoped that Christian's moderate Lutheran outlook would ease the tension, but Christian never showed much outward interest for independent schemes that might leave him exposed.[16] It would not be fair to judge that religious solidarity had 'little to do' with Christian's decision to intervene.[17] This is because, in Christian's case, it was fear of Catholic encroachment towards the north, rather than necessarily a desire to defend Protestants across the Empire, which moved him to act.

Christian distinguished himself as the paymaster of Protestant designs, whether they be formulated in the Palatine court, in Berlin or in London. Between 1619-20 alone, he lent 779,000 reichsthalers to his brother in law King James in London, to the Elector of Brandenburg in Berlin, and of course, to Frederick, the Elector Palatine. Following Frederick's defeat at White Mountain, and once Ferdinand's harsh terms became known, Denmark was pulled towards the English and Dutch as a 'natural' ally. Christian did all he could to further this process, even providing official Danish recognition of the Dutch Republic's independence at last in 1621 – a ceremonial act for sure, but one which sent a clear message, nonetheless.

It was during the aforementioned gathering of German and foreign Protestant potentates at Segeberg in spring 1621 that Denmark, along with her allies, sent a stern message to the Emperor. The signal threat to raise an army between them of thirty thousand men to restore Frederick and remove the Spanish was a potent one, but due to circumstances we have previously examined, this early manifestation of European cooperation soon fell apart. King James would pursue no policy that jeopardised his Spanish Match; the Dutch were quickly overcome with the renewed commitments necessitated by the resumption of war with Spain from April 1621, and in Christian's case, his Danish Chancery pressured him heavily to dissolve what few troops he had assembled in the Lower Saxon Circle. The experience was a bitter one for the Danish King and led him to back down from his Segeberg commitments altogether by the summer of 1621. Retreating from the conflict in the Empire, Christian turned inwards and consolidated his position instead. It seemed, having misfired once, the Danish King was not particularly keen to reload his weapon and try again.[18]

However, as a Lutheran and a German Duke, Christian would never have been able to remove himself from the dramatic increase in confessional tension which accompanied the outbreak of war in the Habsburg Hereditary Lands.[19] Christian was too distracted crafting schemes against petty German rules and cities in any case, schemes which would ensure that Danish influence expanded and his sons received their substantial inheritances. Having been gradually drawn into the orbit of the anti-Habsburg camp as the conflict spread across Germany, the war was brought very close to home from 1621, when Christian of Brunswick acquired levies from the Lower Saxon Circle, to the chagrin of Emperor Ferdinand, who had instructed them to expel the vagabond Christian of Brunswick wherever he resided.

The defeat of Christian of Brunswick in August 1623 had not removed the sour taste in both parties' mouths; the Lower Saxon Circle remained suspicious of their Emperor's earlier demands, and the Emperor remained bitter and angry that his subjects had not obeyed his instructions.[20] Christian had been immensely offended at the transferral of Frederick's lands and titles to Maximillian in early 1623 as well, largely because he feared that Christian of Brunswick would have his lands confiscated in retaliation for his rebelliousness, particularly after the latter's defeat. Christian of Brunswick owned land in the Lower Saxon Circle, and Count Tilly, the commander of Catholic League forces, had lurked menacingly on the border with the Circle during the preceding years; it was entirely possible that Emperor Ferdinand could seize Christian of Brunswick's lands and hand them to a Catholic loyalist, as he had done with the Duke of Bavaria. There was a further reason for the Danish King's hostility towards any suggestion of dispossessing Christian of Brunswick – this generalissimo and friend of the Winter King happened to be his nephew!

A familiar pattern had emerged once again over 1623, when Christian had tried to mobilise his Danish Council and the princes of the Lower Saxon Circle to act. Short of some sharp threats, Tilly would surely have entered the largely untouched region of Germany to the south of Denmark. Despite his best efforts, Christian IV of Denmark had signally failed to raise or maintain an army of sufficient size for the defence of the region. The princes of the Saxon Circle had provided insignificant contributions for their own defence, and his nobles had undercut his efforts at every turn to raise an army of even four thousand men. This proved fatal for the safety of the Lower Saxon Circle, who were occupied by Tilly's triumphant army from late 1623, as they entered into winter quarters.

By the spring of 1624, requests from the Diet of the Lower Saxon Circle for Tilly to move on were refused, and the Imperials made some demands of their own. The princes of the Lower Saxon Circle would continue to support Tilly's troops and would contribute men of their own to combat the luckless Ernst of Mansfeld, in addition to his Dutch paymasters. The Spanish

Netherlands would be aided, fortifications as far afield as Hungary would be repaired, and the Catholic League would be hosted without protest. This was too far even for the normally timid and divided princes of the Lower Saxon Circle. They rejected these demands out of hand, and thus invited their Emperor to exact his vengeance.

Instead of vengeance, the Emperor sent an emissary to Copenhagen in July 1624, requesting similar terms. In response, the now angry Christian IV sent the diplomat packing with the stark demand that he could not guarantee peace with the Empire unless Frederick was immediately restored to his Palatinate. Just as the diplomat returned empty-handed, an embassy from King James arrived in the Danish capital. Embittered and backed into a corner after several years unsuccessfully arranging a Spanish marriage, James was much more amenable than usual to a concrete Danish alliance, and Christian, spurned and undermined by the Habsburgs, was eager to cooperate. The building blocks of the Hague Alliance thus laid, subsequent negotiations led Christian's emissary to appear in The Hague the following January, to finalise the details and plan for the conflict which would follow.[21]

Such commitments, as we know, were solidified in the Hague Alliance, a process which Christian became involved in from January 1625, when the negotiations for that alliance first began in earnest. It was while the Hague Alliance was taking shape that Christian became persuaded to the wisdom of intervention, and his allies wasted no time egging the Danish King on. The new King Charles even sent a fluent Danish-speaking ambassador to Copenhagen in June 1625, alongside the first large and promising subsidy from England. If there was more where this bounty came from, then Christian would be completely liberated from ever having to defer to his greedy nobility at all, and he would be able, through his own means and those of his allies, to fund what amounted to a private war.

Christian was on the move from May 1625 and made his way towards his Holstein duchy with a significant body of troops. That same month, he was appointed commander of the Lower Saxon Circle in his capacity as Duke of Holstein, and it was in this position that he pursued the war against the Imperials. Flushed with optimism in the first half of 1625, the Danish council even provided Christian with a grant of 200,000 reichsthalers, a rare thing for the Danish nobility to do. In addition to the apparently secure promises from the critical English and Dutch quarters, Christian marched with an army of twenty thousand German mercenaries and peasant conscripts, in the expectation that he would pick up more levies from the Saxon Circle along the way.[22] Since the Hague Alliance was not finalised, the Danish King was not guaranteed the support of his allies, but his decision to march at this stage did send a severe message to the Emperor and the Duke of Bavaria, who both adopted desperate measures in response, as we will see.

Delays followed over the summer of 1625, even though Tilly's army was smaller than Christian's at eighteen thousand men and was plagued by the twin evils of disease and a lack of forage. As the two sides prepared for confrontation, Christian was thrown from his horse into a seven-metre ditch while inspecting fortifications. The fall was nearly fatal, and while he did recover his strengths, he was incapacitated and depressed during August and September apparently because of the incident. During this lull, both sides suffered further, as more of Tilly's men were lost, and several contingents from the Saxon Circle deserted and returned home. During this period Christian ignored several entreaties from the Elector of Saxony and the King of Spain to mediate.

The Hague quickly became a haven for the failed dreamers of the anti-Habsburg cause, as Ernst of Mansfeld and Christian of Brunswick moved what remained of their followers to the Dutch capital and campaigned for a place in the next round of hostilities. Further reinforcements would arrive into 1626, including eight thousand Scots marching for the honour of the late Queen Anne, the sister of the King of Denmark. While gathering in The Hague, it did not take long for disagreements to arise between the three major allies. The Dutch and British fleets were sent on the ill-fated expedition against the Spanish, which proved to be a catastrophic waste of resources, not to mention a strategic failure. Due to this miscalculation, the Anglo-Dutch paymasters for Christian's army went into arrears before the Danish King had even left to seek battle.[23] This certainly boded ill for the Hague Alliance, but it was nonetheless signed by early December 1625. According to the original document of the Treaty,[24] the signatories felt obliged:

> ...to intervene at the right time to prevent the all too violent and unbearable progress of these bad intentions and oppressions, to restore and conserve the aforementioned freedom, the rights and constitution of the Empire against the foreseeable ruin and to oppose all those who currently or in the future cause such trouble.

Of the sixteen articles which the treaty provided for, the second established the military contributions of the Danes, with 'His Highness the King of Denmark' obliged to 'maintain an army of twenty-eight to thirty thousand foot and seven to eight thousand horses in the field, provided his confederates support him in sufficient and appropriate manner.' It was declared in article six that 'none of the confederates shall leave this alliance, until through God's grace, the above-mentioned peace and order is restored in Germany.' In addition, there was scope for widening the Treaty to include France (article ten), Sweden (article eleven) and Venice and Savoy (article twelve), the Electors of the Empire (article thirteen) and Bethlen Gabor of Transylvania (article fourteen). In addition, it was declared that this Hague

Alliance would not 'alter the agreement made between His Majesty of Great Britain and their Lordships of the States-General [the Dutch], which shall remain unchanged in its present form.' This point (article fifteen) illustrated the strong Anglo-Dutch relationship, but it also hinted that, if the Hague Alliance were to fracture, these two powers would have least have each other in their joint struggle against Spain.

Interestingly, Christian IV would not confirm the Hague Alliance until March 1626, apparently wary of the fact that its foundations were not as solid as they once had appeared. By that point, it could be argued that the Protestant European powers external to the Empire had never been more unified and threatening to Emperor Ferdinand's designs. This may well explain why Ferdinand had not simply stood by and hoped for a miracle in the peace negotiations. Instead, he had worked to appoint a generalissimo in his name, someone separate from all other influences than that of the Habsburg family, and keenly motivated by this sense of mission as well as the chance for personal enrichment and glory. His name was Albrecht of Wallenstein, and he was preparing to confront the house which Christian IV of Denmark had spent the last several years building.

TWO

The Emperor's Benefactor

A satire on the ineffectiveness of the Hague Alliance was making the rounds even before that alliance had the chance to prove itself. In a similar theme to the earlier satire on the aid which the Elector Palatine had received during his campaign for support, this latest satire declared that the King of Denmark would receive the following in his fight against the Emperor:

> England sends one thousand tobacco pipes and four pairs of comedians. Savoy sends one hundred hecklers and twenty mousetraps. Norway sends thirty loads of fish. Switzerland sends one thousand nubile milk maids. Holland sends fifty sacks of pepper it captured in the West Indies. Venice sends one hundred loads of soap and four hundred wineglasses. From Lapland are coming fifteen magicians who can make a good wind and fog, to confuse their enemies when they need to escape. Finland sends two hundred reindeer, so they can make a quick getaway. Greenland sends one hundred seals, so they have something to smear on the boots when they have eaten all the bacon. The Muscovites send one thousand white fox pelts. From France ten Huguenots from La Rochelle to teach them how to be disloyal and rebel against the authorities. Bethlen sends two dozen letters he has exchanged with the Turks and the Elector Palatine's former Confederation, about how to betray Germany...

The list continued in this tone, with increasingly useless pieces of aid offered up, as the King of Denmark's limited options and feckless friends are made abundantly clear. Finally, the ultimate condescending offer of help, it was noted that 'the Emperor sends two guides, Prince Wallenstein and Count Tilly, who can show him [Christian IV of Denmark] the way back to Denmark.'[25] The satire was somewhat unfair, for Christian had been led to believe that his allies would help him and had acted accordingly, as any ally could reasonably be expected to do. The satire was also inaccurate, since, far from unthreatening or innocuous, King Christian IV of Denmark represented the most glaring danger which the Emperor had yet faced.

The danger was felt all the more severely because Count Tilly, commander of the Catholic League, did not seem up to the task of meeting and defeating Christian's forces on the field. Thus, the cutting reference to Tilly and Wallenstein as guides to lead Christian back to Denmark belied the fact that Emperor Ferdinand and his allies felt themselves to be vulnerable. Wallenstein was not hired as a mere guide; he was recruited and promised the moon in return for rescuing the Emperor's cause. His appointment was unconventional, probably unconstitutional and in time, highly controversial, but neither the Emperor nor his Bavarian ally felt they had any other choice.

Despite the effective defeat of the Palatine cause at the Battle of Stadtlohn in August 1623, Frederick's allies limped on in spirit, and the dispossessed Elector never consented himself to any peace short of an unconditional restoration. This resistance – frustrating and maddening though it may have been to the likes of Maximillian of Bavaria, who wished to secure his ill-gotten gains and Elector title at Frederick's expense, or King Philip IV of Spain, who wished to unite his dynasty against the Dutch and perhaps the French – proved essential for keeping the root cause of the war alive. Even while his generalissimos fielded no soldiers, his diplomats continued to work for Frederick in London and The Hague, where Dutch and English aid was repeatedly sought.

By 1624, as Frederick's ambassador attempted to wrest some concession from the assembled Parliament in London, the news of the collapsing Anglo-Spanish match complicated matters for the Emperor, because this meant that his Spanish cousins would not be able to restrain Frederick. The Emperor had further cause for concern closer to home, as rumours of a new Bohemian insurrection, while proved false, were nonetheless unsettling, as were the constant reports of Bethlen Gabor's latest campaign into Hungary. Bohemia, while sucked dry, remained quiescent, and the Prince of Transylvania did not march, but Ferdinand remained fearful of a coalition from outside the Empire. If Ferdinand was fearful, Maximillian was nearing a crisis. He tried to seek a rapprochement with the French, and some of his Capuchin advisors advocated a new international Catholic League which would pacify Europe and rally against the Turk.

Yet he found more success in playing to the equally skittish John George, the Elector of Saxony, who had initially greeted Maximillian's approaches with a distinct coolness. Wary of the unconstitutionality of the Duke of Bavaria's actions, John George had clung to the idea of some form of middle ground in the conflict, and while he remained loyal to the Emperor, he would not provide the recognition of Maximillian's new titles just yet. The Elector of Mainz was sent to meet with John George in July 1624, and during the course of the meeting revealed the cache of newly published documents relating to Frederick's brazen activities while acting as King of Bohemia. The full extent of Frederick's treacherous correspondence, including his negotiations with the Turks, was placed before the sensitive Elector of Saxony, who was won over in this way to the Bavarian side.

Going further, the Elector of Mainz insisted that the King of Spain stood behind the Emperor and the new Bavarian Elector, and that the cause was a just one launched to liberate Germany from war and ruin. Finally, it was insisted that only John George had the power to fulfil the dream of a proper lasting peace, since only with an agreement between the Bavarian and Saxon rulers would Germany be truly secure. This certainly appealed to John George's sense of importance, but it also struck a constitutional chord as well, since it hinted that a third party, one aside from either the Habsburg or the French influence would win Germany the settlement it required. For the moment at least, Maximillian's approaches had done the trick, and the Elector of Saxony continued to tether himself to Ferdinand's cause.

His Electoral brother to the north-east, in Brandenburg, had not seen matters the same way though. George William of Brandenburg moved closer to his familial bonds, rather than to his constitutional obligations, and made an alliance with the Dutch on 23 October 1624. This was the final in a series of agreements cobbled together by the French court, and enthusiastically encouraged by both The Hague and Frederick alike. In June, the French and Dutch had solidified their friendship with the Treaty of Compiegne, which England joined shortly after. On 9 July, Sweden and Denmark came to their own terms, which freed both parties up for conflict with the Poles and Emperor respectively. On 11 July, the French secured the alliance of the Venetians and Savoyards for cooperation in the Val Telline, those critical Alpine passes through which so many Spanish goods, money and men passed (see below). To cap the year off, on 10 November 1624, the Prince of Wales and Princess of France were married in person, and Henrietta Maria, the sister of the King of France, became the Queen of Britain. The net appeared, through all of these agreements, to be closing in on Emperor Ferdinand and the allies upon whom he depended. For all the warning signals 1624 sent to Vienna though, 1625 was to set off alarm bells so deafening that all appeared lost.

Albrecht of Wallenstein had spent the winter of 1624-25 in Vienna petitioning for the big break which would eventually make him famous. Initially, he requested that the Spanish ambassador help him to gain approval for a command in North Italy, but when the Val Telline fell to a joint effort of French, Savoyard and Swiss troops he changed his target, but not his ambition. Emperor Ferdinand received Wallenstein's offer – it was an incredible one; one which the Austrian Habsburg dynasty had never heard before, and likely would not hear again. He offered to raise fifty thousand men on his own expense, a deed which the Emperor would repay directly to him, through loans, lands or titles during the course of his command.[26] The offer was not as brazen as it may have appeared: Wallenstein had experience in dealing with Ferdinand, and especially in lending him aid.

Who was the Germanised Czech nobleman? 'Tall of stature, slender, lean and almost perpetually melancholic', Wallenstein was, as Peter H. Wilson perceived, 'a hard man to like.' Even his friends attested to his unsmiling face and cold, staring eyes, while his general politeness and honour when it came to his marital duties could be contrasted with his propensity for violent outbursts which grew more frequent as he aged. He had been born to Protestant Bohemian parents in 1583 and attempted to enter service in the Habsburg army during the Long Turkish War. A bout of malaria endured during his service in 1605 seems to have inflicted lasting wounds on his health and psyche, so that by 1620, then in his late 30's, Wallenstein was suffering from gout despite his meagre drinking habits and healthy eating regimen – it was a condition which the generalissimo suffered from for the rest of his life.[27]

In 1606, with a tour of Italy under his belt, the suitably impressed Wallenstein had determined to convert to the Old Faith, and for the rest of his life he remained a convinced, committed Catholic, but not necessarily intolerant. Shortly afterwards, he married a wealthy, elderly noblewoman from Moravia, and upon her death, inherited her estates.[28] A contemporary French pamphlet would later judge his shifting personality by opining that he was 'very liberal and when he gave presents he very much rejoiced and indeed was a man who gave the most to him who least expected it, but his gifts were golden snares which indissolubly obliged.'[29] By 1618, on the eve of the Bohemian revolt, Wallenstein was a figure of minor importance in Bohemia, but it was this very revolt that utterly transformed his life, starting with his fortune.

The collapse of the Kingdom of Bohemia into revolt, and the subsequent crushing of this revolt by the Habsburgs, provided first a great cause for fear, and then a terrific chance for the opportunistic. Land was cheap and in plentiful supply having been confiscated on a vast scale from rebels, the dead, the exiled or the inconvenient;[30] furthermore, perhaps most importantly for Wallenstein's interests, the Emperor was selling, and he was hard-pressed for cash. During this period, as the historian Geoff Mortimer explained:

> Cash was key. The Emperor urgently needed it, and raising it was the main objective of the confiscations and property sales. For would-be purchasers this was a considerable difficulty, as it was one thing to be wealthy in terms of land but another to have large amounts of ready cash available. Wallenstein was far from alone in facing this problem, but he was uniquely successful in solving it.[31]

How did he solve it? Wallenstein recognised that since the Emperor provided the honours, signed off on the deeds and granted legitimacy to all deals, it was the Emperor that he should pledge his loyalty to. With this accepted, it did not necessarily matter to Wallenstein that Ferdinand was unable at this moment in time to pay him back for whatever money he lent him. Thanks to the security of his estates in Moravia, Wallenstein was able to raise loans from creditors and bankers for millions of gulden – the currency used in the south of Germany – and with this money loaned, the Emperor would then be in his debt. By raising additional loans, Wallenstein was able not just to loan money to the Emperor, he was also able to purchase more land at knockdown prices and use the security of these new lands to raise additional loans. The pattern, while complex, and detailed in the voluminous correspondence between Wallenstein, his creditors, his extended family and the Emperor, boiled down to Wallenstein's ability to raise cash loans based on his extensive landholdings, forward this money to the Emperor, and then pay off his debts with the income from his lands. Between 1619-23 he had loaned the Emperor a whopping 1.6 million florins, and with Wallenstein's money and Maximillian of Bavaria's army, Ferdinand had crushed his enemies, but there always seemed to be more enemies on the horizon, thus the need for more loans, thus more debt for Ferdinand to accumulate.[32]

Wallenstein's wealth was such that he was able to pay off the interest on his loans, and his stellar record in repaying meant that he was able to acquire a line of credit with relative ease. This left Wallenstein occasionally debt free – this process was a constant fixture of Wallenstein's life – but it also left him with additional opportunities to get in the Emperor's good graces. If he could acquire a reputation as a reliable and able lender for Vienna, then the Emperor's debt to him would only increase. In time, the sums would grow to such an extent that Ferdinand was forced to pay them back in the only way he knew how – in a similar pattern to that adopted with Maximillian of Bavaria, Ferdinand paid off his debts by providing land. Through this process the Duke of Bavaria became an Elector, and Albrecht of Wallenstein, the minor Czech nobleman, became the Duke of Friedland and Mecklenburg.

These opportunities were to come in time, but by 1624, Wallenstein already owned lands equal in size to the counties of Kent and Surrey combined, or about half the size of Massachusetts. From just north of Prague to the Bohemian border, two thousand square miles of productive, unified lands were his. He added to the size of this private empire by selling distant lands, buying up neighbouring estates, and making it more formidable by consistently investing in its improvement. This land was the basis of Wallenstein's power, and throughout his life he excelled or declined based on its prosperity. As Mortimer continues:

> Wallenstein must have had not only tremendous personal energy and commitment but also agents upon whom he could rely, particularly as he still has his military duties to attend to. Still more important was the availability of financial backers ready to assist him in putting up the necessary money.[33]

These 'military duties' form the more famous part of Wallenstein's character; he was not only a fabulously wealthy landowner and the Emperor's favourite loan shark, he was also to be become the Habsburgs' generalissimo, thus granting Ferdinand power and supremacy over all the Empire. Much like his earlier dealings with the Emperor, Wallenstein ensured that he took full advantage of whatever arrangements were made with Vienna. Thus, his offer to harness the power of his lands to raise fifty thousand men in the Emperor's name and to fight solely in the Emperor's interest was in reality an offer to lend his military services to Ferdinand, a loan which, much like the others, Ferdinand was expected to pay back. Wallenstein's financial services and loyalty had already been repaid in 1624, as Ferdinand tapped into his fount of honours to name Wallenstein the Duke of Friedland. That united clump of territory, larger than most principalities of the Empire, was designated the Duchy of Friedland as a result. Wallenstein had thus become the most important landowner in Bohemia, with powers equalled only by some Electors.

This was before he had even led men against Ferdinand's enemies. Wallenstein's tactically constructed power base was now blessed by the Emperor, making it still more significant and important. Master of his estates, Wallenstein ruled over them as something akin to judge, jury and executioner. His landholdings and loans to the Emperor had placed Wallenstein in a remarkable position by spring 1625, and it is significant that Wallenstein's wealth meant that he did not need to concern himself with Ferdinand's shaky record of paying back his creditors. The immediate challenge for Wallenstein was not repayment of Ferdinand's debts, but to make himself so indispensable to the Emperor in the military sphere that the Habsburgs could not endure without him, just as he had done with his efforts in the financial sphere. In short, getting the Emperor to accept his offer was only half the battle, above all he would have to prove himself.

Wallenstein would have ample opportunities to do just that, since the closing of the net around the Emperor by early 1625 compelled Ferdinand and Maximillian of Bavaria to recommend drastic action. In April 1625 the wealthy nobleman was recalled to Vienna, and a convincing argument was made that Wallenstein's offer to make himself the generalissimo of the Emperor should be accepted, lest all of Ferdinand's efforts, and all of Maximillian's ill-gotten gains, would be in vain. To preserve what they had acquired so far, it was believed that taking the ambitious Wallenstein on was an acceptable risk. Ferdinand acted with caution in the first place; he continued to regard Maximillian and the Catholic League as the major driving force of the war. In addition, Wallenstein's force was reduced from fifty thousand to twenty thousand men, a far more manageable and realistic number, and the general was ordered to remain solely in the Habsburg hereditary lands. For the moment at least, Wallenstein's potential would be confined.[34]

With some service in the army, Wallenstein's interest in leading Ferdinand's forces had not come from nowhere. Indeed, in June 1623

Wallenstein had been appointed Major-General and instructed to fight against the forces led by Bethlen Gabor. However, this minor rank, and the very inconsistent nature of the Prince of Transylvania's campaigning, was a far cry from full responsibility for the provision and command of his own army. Again, in spring 1625, as had happened before, Wallenstein's great wealth counted in his favour, and he was able to leverage this power to achieve what he desired. The Spanish ambassador in Vienna, the Marquis de Aytona, was a believer in Wallenstein, but what may have swung the balance in his favour was Maximillian of Bavaria's concerted support.

The newly enshrined Elector of Bavaria had good reason to vouch for Wallenstein – Maximillian had heard unsettling rumours of anti-Habsburg mobilisation, and he was always uncomfortable about the fact that his ill-gotten gains might be snatched away should the Emperor's cause be defeated. Wallenstein and his new army, Maximillian believed, presented the ideal solution to these woes. With a second army in the field, the security of what had thus far been gained would be much greater. Maximillian did not think of the costs involved to his Emperor or to Germany, and in this instance only wanted to preserve his interests through further recourse to arms. Intermittent negotiations with the English and French had produced neither peace nor marital alliances, and on the basis of this failed diplomacy, Maximillian recommended to his Emperor that Wallenstein's offer be accepted at once. To Maximillian, and to Ferdinand, the risk was worth taking if it saved their cause from destruction.[35]

Ferdinand was also eager to assume some kind of leading stake in the war, after delegating to and depending upon Maximillian and the Catholic League for so long. Wallenstein gave him this chance, and if 1625 was the year that the origins of the conflict became lost in its escalation and the threat of foreign intervention, it was also the year that the recruited armies ballooned in size. For Ferdinand to assume leadership of the war's direction, Wallenstein would have to be entitled to recruit an army equal in size to Count Tilly's, the Catholic League's generalissimo. This was permitted in the spring and summer of 1625, and Wallenstein set to work, while Ferdinand shifted men around from Hungary to North Italy to fill in the gaps, and the Spanish even stopped by to recruit some ten thousand men for the war against the Dutch. The conflict had evidently widened far beyond its original regional cause, and while Christian IV of Denmark moved towards his German domains, Tilly was appointed to meet him, while Wallenstein was tasked with meeting Ernst of Mansfeld as the luckless captain descended on Moravia. Both Imperial commanders boasted between forty to fifty thousand men combined, and this number was destined to steadily increase.

Plans for Mansfeld to link up with Bethlen Gabor were not based on solid foundations, as the Prince of Transylvania once again let down his allies. Wallenstein had recruited sixteen thousand men to fight with him, and while this force was supplemented by some veterans from Hungary, the overwhelming majority were ill-proven, and were marching to their first battle. If Wallenstein depended on these men, and they failed him in first confrontation with Mansfeld in the near future, then the result could be disastrous for his career and potentially his life. Wallenstein stepped on countless toes on his way to the peak of his wealth and power, and while many of these toes had been attached to exiled rebels or bitter minor nobles, some had the power to strike back at him.

The unconventional rise of Wallenstein provoked those aristocrats whom he had eclipsed and led to the formation of all sorts of scandalous rumours. The true source and nature of his wealth, as well as his unnatural spell over the Emperor made for particular favourites. No thought was given to Wallenstein's actual vulnerability, which was sourced from his near permanent state of indebtedness. This indebtedness did not matter so long as Wallenstein's estates more than paid for themselves, but what would happen if the war reached these estates, and enemy soldiers ravaged his precious Duchy thereby depriving him of his assets? Such a nightmare was one which Wallenstein would endure, but not for some time yet.[36]

From June 1625, Wallenstein began to recruit in earnest, and occupied the town of Halberstadt in November as his forward base. Almost immediately, he organised a system of levying contributions from the nearby towns and cities. Through these payments, the inhabitants and city fathers could expect to be left alone, but while paying was preferable to the occupation and sacking which might follow a refusal to pay up, the costs were still prohibitive. Nuremburg, one city in Wallenstein's path, paid 440,000 florins throughout the period to Wallenstein's soldiery, in return for the promise of being effectively left alone, with minimal quartering and no recruitment of new soldiers on the city's lands. Lengthy quartering could destroy arable land and suck the region dry of resources, while security would also decrease, and if recruitment drives were initiated, some peasants may leave their farms and leave the land denuded of people for the opportunity at a better life.[37]

At the same time as the Hague Alliance was being confirmed in December 1625, Ferdinand leveraged his position to issue the Imperial Ban against Christian IV of Denmark. As the Duke of Holstein, Christian was now persona non grata in Germany, and any German potentates that offered him support would suffer the same fate as had Frederick's allies in the years beforehand. It was beneficial for the Emperor in the short term that several princes did not heed his warning. By acting expressly against their overlord, there were liable for punishment in the aftermath. Considering Ferdinand's indebtedness to Wallenstein, there was no better way for the Emperor to kill two birds with one stone than to strip rebellious princes of their land, and hand these over to Wallenstein as payment.

While this inflated Wallenstein's property portfolio and his power base, it also caused the rumour mill to work overtime against him. So long as Wallenstein could prove his usefulness; so long as he could defeat the Emperor's enemies, the resentment felt by his aristocratic betters and the suspicion he aroused in Vienna would pale in comparison to his personal glory. As 1626 approached, it was apparent that the King of Denmark and the Emperor's new generalissimo were bound to clash soon. For both men, it was do or die.

THREE

To The Rescue

'They will see the beginning of a revolution'. This was how Frederick V, the dispossessed Elector Palatine, had described the gathering forces of the Hague Alliance, as 1625 turned to 1626.[38] The revolution which Frederick had envisioned involved the gradual accumulation of forces hostile to the Habsburgs, as all rivals put their differences aside and combined against the Holy Roman Emperor and King of Spain's dangerous designs. He imagined the Swedish and Danish Kings putting aside their old wars and pooling their resources in the Baltic; he hoped for the King of France to fight against the Spanish and Austrians in the name of Protestant Germans; he believed that these Protestant Germans could do nothing other than join his cause, after having seen the extent of their Emperor's unconstitutional behaviour, and his wanton ambitions. Frederick had hoped for these things to take place ever since he had entered his exile in The Hague, and he had been disappointed as many times as he had hoped.

This time though, the anti-Habsburg camp appeared to possess the advantage in every respect. His years of pressuring the British to fight in Europe paid off, and King Charles declared against Spain and the Emperor in mid-1625. The Dutch, brought low by their defeats to the Spanish, had formalised their agreements with both France and Britain in the preceding years, and seemed poised to fight for as long as was required. Finally, and most significantly, the King of Denmark, having acquired the solid alliance he had for so long sought, was now firmly set against the Emperor, and was loud in his determination to defend the Lower Saxon Circle, that region just below Denmark, against Habsburg aggression. The unification of the anti-Habsburg camp into the Hague Alliance in December 1625 must be seen as the high point of Frederick's fortunes, as well as of his pressure campaign. For so long he had engaged in the apparently futile task to restore justice to the Palatine and peace to Germany on his own terms, and now this task seemed to have borne fruit. Alas, while Frederick's diplomatic triumph was impressive on paper, it was far less solid in reality.

The German princes, save those that inhabited the Lower Saxon Circle, were hesitant to declare against the Emperor. Saxony had not been willing to turn against Ferdinand, even while its Elector John George had regretted the unconstitutional manner with which the Emperor stripped Frederick of his Electorate, and loathed the spectacle of Ferdinand betraying his promises, and expelling the Protestants from Bohemia after all. As reluctant as John George was to take these objections to their logical conclusion, he was constrained nonetheless to remain on the Emperor's side, for one key reason above all others: like the newly established Elector of Bavaria, John George had gained from choosing the Emperor's side. Lusatia, that province of the Kingdom of Bohemia, had been hastily transferred to him as the revolt had been crushed. Any restitution of the status quo would surely strip John George of these gains, and like Maximillian of Bavaria, he was therefore forced to fight not just for the compromised constitution, but also for his lucrative gains which he feared would otherwise be stripped away.

John George might have switched sides had these gains be guaranteed, but his natural caution prevented him from doing so at least until the forces of the Hague Alliance could prove their strength and achieve some lasting victory which would make switching sides a safe prospect. Not until the stunning intervention of the Swedes would this state of affairs present itself. Until then, John George was not willing to take the risk. His protest letters to Vienna fell on deaf ears, because Emperor Ferdinand knew full well that protesting was as far as the Elector of Saxony was willing to go. This behaviour makes John George something of an inconsequential figure in the Thirty Years War, because he cut neither the brave, defiant figure of Frederick, nor the ruthlessly ambitious image of Maximillian. Instead, he was just John George, the Elector of Saxony, the foremost Lutheran prince of the Empire. In later years, his moderation and caution would have the effect of making him something of a weather vane in the Empire, because when he did change sides, the news inferred that a truly revolutionary change was in the air.[39] Then, Frederick's prophecy regarding the 'beginning of a revolution' was actually realised, but in 1626, this revolution could not arrive so long as the majority of Germany refrained from taking his side.

Caught in the crosshairs of the Habsburgs, the Lower Saxon Circle could not help but feel that they had been given the short straw throughout the early 1620s. Christian of Brunswick had rampaged through their lands, and the Emperor had sent them threatening messages inquiring as to why they had not stopped him from recruiting or quartering his troops, as though they were capable of mustering a force which might enable them to have any say in the matter. Naturally timid, and wholly reliant on the policy of the Danish King who held significant influence over them, the Lower Saxon Circle could not move without either his direction or protection. In early March 1626, having learned of King Christian IV's ratification of the Hague Alliance and believing in his convictions, the Lower Saxon Circle officially abandoned this caution which had for so long distinguished them. In acting, they also abandoned something else – their neutrality.

The Lower Saxon Circle was geographically far from the incendiary events of the Bohemian revolt, and they were more concerned with and affected by events in the Baltic than with the constitutional feud between Elector and Emperor. Nonetheless, their efforts to remain aloof from the conflict had been in vain; by 1621, Christian of Brunswick had come to them, and the members of the Circle were then caught between a rock and a hard place, as Ferdinand made clear his displeasure, and quartered Count Tilly on their borders in case they did not get the message. Like John George of Saxony, the Lower Saxon Circle wished above all to be left alone, but unlike John George, these unfortunate princes did not have a choice – the question of whether to side with God or the Devil had been chosen for them.

While the Lower Saxon Circle contained significant cities such as Brunswick, Hamburg, Luneburg, Lubeck and Bremen, some of these cities were themselves trapped between their loyalty to the Emperor as free cities, and the power of the Danish King. Furthermore, there was the greatly declined, but still notable influence of the Hanseatic League – 'one of the most remarkable confederations which the world has ever seen'[40] – a medieval confederation of North German and Baltic trading cities, which had been established at Lubeck.[41] This confederation of cities had competed in the past with Denmark, England and the Dutch, and once held considerable monopolies over Baltic trade.[42] 'It is necessary to carry on navigation, it is not necessary to live' had been but one of many Hanseatic proverbs, which reveal to us precisely how focused upon commercial ventures, even at the cost of personal well-being, the towns of the Hanseatic League had been.[43]

The Reformation had reached the Hanseatic League as well, and added to the sense of identity which the individual cities felt.[44] In spite of their size, they preferred independence to closer union, which made them proud and culturally distinctive, but also vulnerable to a powerful invader. King Christian IV had already forced Hamburg to declare its loyalty to Denmark, or at least to the Duke of Holstein, and the rivers Elbe and Weser upon which the Hanseatic League had so prospered were, by 1625, under the near complete control of the Danish King.[45]

In an effort to take advantage of the decline of the Hanseatic League, some efforts were made by the Imperialists in spring and summer 1625 to bring the League over to its side, as part of a wider scheme to extend Habsburg power to the Baltic. The plot misfired owing to the weakness and jealousy of the late League, which contained only a handful of cities that were capable of taking part in such ambitious scheme. Those powerful cities that remained wished to conserve their independence rather than risk ruin in alliance with the Habsburgs. In spite of this lack of progress here, and the clear message which its failure sent to Vienna and Madrid, this idea would later be resurrected.[46]

The legacies of history aside, neither the shadow of the Hanseatic League nor the Lower Saxon Circle which housed its core German cities would be strong enough to face down the might of the Holy Roman Emperor alone, especially considering the demonstrably harsh penalties which any losers would be forced to endure should their desperate fight fail. For this reason, neutrality was the preferred option, but the Lower Saxon Circle is one of the most glaring – though by no means the first or final example – of a region being forced to choose between God or the Devil. Unfortunately for the Circle's peasants, traders and city fathers, their dilemma was of little concern to either party.

Emperor Ferdinand, for his part, had already mapped out the succession of his sons to its many bishoprics: a crushing victory over the Circle would simply guarantee that he could have whatever bishopric he desired. It was to defend similar appointments which King Christian had already made for his sons that the Danish monarch marched. In a Mandate communicated on 4 March 1626, the Lower Saxon Circle officially announced its decision to prepare for war. For the sake of providing us with a window into the psyche of the Circle, it is worth detailing that Mandate here:

> The worthiest, serenest, worthy, serene and well-born princes and Estates etc. of the worthy Lower Saxon Circle…are in no doubt that it will be well-known both within the Holy Roman Empire and beyond that their highnesses the princes and Estates have been compelled by the most pressing circumstances to establish a defence force in accordance with the authority and guidelines of the Holy Imperial Executive Ordinance and Recesses, and that they have not only agreed this, but have immediately informed His Roman Imperial Majesty, our most gracious lord, as well as others, to avoid all mistrust and suspicious thoughts and hostile impressions, and have done this properly in writing from an upright open German heart to say that such a force is purely defensive and not to harm his Roman Imperial Majesty, the Holy Empire or its electors, princes and Estates, but entirely and singularly for the protection and defence of this worthy Lower Saxon Circle and to be used as a highly necessary assistance for the hard–won liberty in religious and profane matters, together with the traditional exercise of the Augsburg Confession as the highest jewel that princes and Estates in this world could have, as well as to ward off all threatening developments and hostilities.

The Augsburg Confession referred to the definition of the Protestant religion in 1530, and the fear that this creed was in danger permeated this Mandate. We should note the tone of the Mandate as well – there was an almost crippling desire not to offend anyone, least of all the Emperor, since Ferdinand had sent a flurry of stern messages and warnings to the Circle in the past. Next we see the Mandate declaring its legitimacy by reasoning that the decision to arm had been taken by other powers:

> This is also a path that other princes and Estates have followed since the start of the Imperial reign of his Roman Imperial Majesty and those of this Circle do with due devotion, love, loyalty and obedience and will insist to their graves and for all eternity that such an upright German declaration of the Circle will neither harm nor offend anyone in the slightest.

Next, we are provided with a brief history lesson by the Mandate, as the Circle's members attempt to explain their dilemma and thereby justify their decision to arm. The summary provides us with a stark reminder of the devastation caused by the Emperor's armies to his own lands and people, behaviour which was certainly equalled by the Emperor's rivals in the years to come. The sense of despair which was felt by the Circle is palpable in this Mandate, since on the one hand we feel its members desperately wished to remain on the Emperor's good side, but at the same time, on the other hand, they wished to defend themselves against future attacks launched in the Emperor's name. As the Mandate continued:

> In July of last year 1625 the Bavarian and League Lieutenant General…Count von Tilly, followed by…[Albrecht von Wallenstein the Duke of] Friedland, with their large armies, invaded the said Circle, first in the worthy principality of Brunswick, then in the archbishopric of Magdeburg and the bishopric of Halberstadt, and violently attacked fortresses, cities, towns, villages and noble houses, occupied and plundered them, not sparing the churches and houses of God, tyrannically stole not only the property and means of subsistence of many thousands of innocent subjects and their wives and children, but also in many cases their honour, bodies, lives and health, and burnt a great number of beautiful houses, villages, monasteries, farms and mills and other buildings to the ground and in short behaved so gruesomely in the Circle that one would not have expected the same from the hereditary and arch enemy of all Christianity.

After having detailed the devastation inflicted by the Emperor, next it was insisted that all such activities had been undertaken solely to remove the Augsburg Confession from the region, and to restrict or abolish the German liberties which accompanied it:

> And all this occurred with no more reason than blatant pretexts that were used to disguise the long held intention to exterminate from the reformed archbishoprics and bishoprics of this Circle the Augsburg Confession, that is the sole means of salvation, the godly, precious, true religion. Such procedures not only grossly violate the proper and traditional liberty in religious and profane matters, but also completely contravene the Holy Imperial fundamental laws and constitution and stamp on all legal order together with German liberty…

The Mandate ends with an instruction twinned with a warning for all soldiers serving either in Tilly's or Wallenstein's army to leave them immediately, and not to fight against the lawful recruits of the Lower Saxon Circle. Those that disobeyed this Mandate's instruction would be liable, we are told, to the most severe penalties. This reveals much about the regionalist mindset of the Circle's members, as well as the illegitimacy which they attached to the two armies commanded by Tilly and Wallenstein. The Mandate concluded:

> Therefore, the princes and Estates of this worthy Lower Saxon Circle to save their Christian conscience through this public notice and letter hereby remind and warn on their lives, honour and property all officers, horsemen and soldiers who are serving in both opposing armies and who are bound by vassalage of other duties to a prince and Estate of this Circle, to leave both opposing armies as open enemies of the Circle within a month of this present date and go home. If they fail to do so and continue to serve against the worthy Circle they are expressly warned that the natives amongst them will be punished without restraint on their bodies, honour and property with the loss of all rights and jurisdictions, while the foreigners will be treated as unchristian persecutors of their fellow believers and will be granted no quarter.[47]

While providing us with a fascinating and appropriate window into the struggles which Germans everywhere grappled with, the aim of the Mandate was a failure. The Emperor's armies would not turn back, and neither could the King of Denmark. Though they had not wanted the war and loathed the idea of picking a side, the war had spread to within their borders nonetheless, and now this diverse group of German towns, princes, cities and bishoprics would be forced to choose whether they liked it or not. Grave though the choice seemed, the prospects for success were at least not all gloomy by the time this Mandate was sent in early March 1626.

By that time, the Prince of Transylvania marched in cooperation with the Hague Alliance. He had also mobilised his diplomats, and as usual, promised great things to his receptive allies. Were he given 40,000 reichsthalers a month, Bethlen Gabor promised to maintain an army of eight thousand foot and twelve thousand horse, which he would lead to Bohemia and Silesia, and then link up with Ernst of Mansfeld. By combing their forces, Bethlen and Mansfeld would pose a formidable threat to the Habsburg position in Hungary, but the Prince did not stop there. As if anticipating the future diplomatic shenanigans, Bethlen advised that the King of Poland should be distracted by employing Muscovy to strike against her. This initiative could also enlist the aid of the Tartars, who would supply tens of thousands of horsemen for the common cause. All that was required to bring this incredible plan to fruition was money, lots and lots of money, supplied by the members of the Hague Alliance but mostly, it appeared, by King Charles and the Dutch.

Christian of Denmark gave his assent to the scheme, but since he was already in receipt of subsidies himself, he was in no position to play the role of paymaster to the Prince of Transylvania. Furthermore, Christian had been occupied enough by the events of 1625, and his near-death experience, which had slowed his overall progress to evict the forces under Tilly from the Lower Saxon Circle. Both armies had engaged in limited skirmishes against the other, but it seemed clear that 1626 would be the year when the most weighted engagements occurred. Christian was anxious to defend the Lower Saxon Circle against Habsburg encroachment, since his power as Duke of Holstein, the inheritance of his sons, and the maintenance of the Lutheran creed would all be in jeopardy if he could not.

Unfortunately for Christian IV, the Hague Alliance was already in danger, and his allies were already in debt to him. By May 1626, Charles would be in debt to the tune of £240,000, a result of the terminal inability of Charles' kingdom to pay the subsidies which had been promised. According to Frederick's ambassador in London, King Charles simply lacked the money required to pay, and further problems abounded in his kingdom. The Duke of Buckingham was becoming increasingly unpopular, to the point that Parliament stonewalled any talk of raising subsidies for foreign wars so long as he would not be impeached. Frederick regretfully noted that 'the revulsion in the land against the Duke is so great that it hinders much good', and he was correct. Not only would Charles' Parliament refuse to grant him the necessary funds, but public opinion was also splintering over the deepening crisis in France, where the French government attempted to crack down on the rebelling Protestant Huguenots, in a crisis which would drag on for another several years.[48]

France's Foreign Minister Cardinal Richelieu was indeed in something of a bind. A great strategic coup had been achieved in the spring of 1625, when the Duke of Savoy had occupied the Val Telline mountain passes with French assistance. The Val Telline is known today for its great skiing holidays and hot springs, but in the seventeenth century this valley pass in Lombardy, along the border with the Swiss, formed a critical artery along which the Spanish Road's traffic flowed. This initiative had been planned as per the Treaty of Paris from two years before, which had committed Venice, France and Savoy to expel the Spanish from the Val Telline and block the Alpine passes to the Habsburgs. Lombardy, a Spanish possession, was anchored on the Italian powerhouse of Milan, a hub of Habsburg-Italian ambitions,[49] which also included Tuscany in its net.[50]

The Spanish supported the Milanese and the French supported the Duke of Savoy, and both sides quarrelled over the pieces of territory which were held in between. In later years, one such piece, Mantua, would actually cause a proxy war between the French and Spanish, and have profound implications for the Habsburg position in Europe, but in 1625-26, talk of the region focused on the French-sponsored severing of the Val Telline passes. The complex conflicts between the inhabitants of the region and their neighbours need not contain us; it suffices to note instead that with the Val Telline[51] out of Spanish hands, Madrid simply could not move men or money through its Spanish Road up to the Spanish Netherlands, or the Rhine.

Even worse for Spain, with England entering the war against her in mid-1625, the prospects of supplying these same regions by sea became still more remote. With the lifeblood of Spain's European Empire reduced to a trickle, the impact on its soldiers and power projection would begin to tell. Furthermore, so long as Spain could not properly harness its colonies or move its resources, it could not support the Emperor either. This was recognised by Ferdinand, as he chose to lean more heavily on the likes of Wallenstein to compensate. The urgency of the disaster was plain, and not for the last time, Spanish planners worked to liberate the passes from the French, but by the following year, domestic affairs in France worked in their favour.[52]

The prospect of Huguenot rebellion had never seemed distant in France, but its eruption in 1625 and the subsequent worsening of France's domestic situation forced Richelieu to make some tough choices (see below). One of these, as it transpired, was the evacuation of French troops in the Val Telline to defend the Crown. This event took place in the spring and summer of 1626 and demonstrated the interconnected nature of European strategy and politics. With the Spanish Road open once more, Madrid could reconnect itself to its bastions in the Spanish Netherlands and on the Rhine. Not until the Huguenot fortress of La Rochelle was captured in 1628 did Cardinal Richelieu possess anything close to a free hand to intervene in the Empire, and thus, between 1626-28, France effectively withdrew itself from external affairs, a development which seemed to spell disaster for King Christian IV of Denmark, as well as the Dutch.

Despite his original intention to defend the Habsburg Hereditary Lands, and in particular his extensive landholdings in Bohemia, from the wandering excesses of Ernst of Mansfeld, in April 1625 Wallenstein's job description was given a significant upgrade. Wallenstein was to be 'chief over all our troops already serving at this time, whether in the Holy Roman Empire or in the Netherlands', and Ferdinand ordered him to create 'a field army, whether from our existing units or from newly raised regiments, so that there shall be twenty-four thousand men in all.'[53] This hulking force marched towards the Lower Saxon Circle in August of that year, when King Christian was convalescing from his terrible fall. Wallenstein's arrival and quartering of his troops in the fringes of the Circle near Count Tilly's forces promised ruin for the inhabitants, and according to the above Mandate, ruin was the sentence which was duly carried out.

Wallenstein and Tilly spent the winter of 1625-26 in close proximity, before the former moved on to intercept Mansfeld. The pressure was certainly heavy on both sides, but Wallenstein possessed a key advantage of outnumbering his opposite, and Mansfeld, taking for granted the experience of his troops, squandered his final encounter with the enemy as he had all others. Dessau Bridge was the name of Wallenstein's first and arguably most important triumph. The battle took place on 25 April 1626, and resulted in the elimination of Mansfeld's army from the race – another significant blow to the Hague Alliance, and thus the anti-Habsburg cause, had once again been dealt, but it was business as usual for Mansfeld, who responded to the defeat by venturing down south towards the Adriatic.

Apparently imbued with a mission to recruit Venice and the Turks to the cause, Mansfeld caught a bout of the plague and died in November. His death marked the departure of one of the most significant representatives of Frederick's cause, but it was not the final death of such a representative in that eventful year. Christian of Brunswick, as an optimistic third prong of the anti-Habsburg cause, had been caught and defeated in detail over the summer while attempting to outmanoeuvre Tilly along the River Weser. Prematurely aged, the 28-year-old Christian appeared much older than his actual years, and this additional defeat proved to be the final nail in his surely frail constitution. He died in Wolfenbüttel in mid-June 1626, and upon further investigation, according to Catholic sources, it was supposedly discovered that his vitals had been consumed by a gigantic worm.[54]

During the previous month in May 1626, the Habsburgs and their allies sent representatives to a conference in Brussels aimed at accelerating cooperation between the two branches of the dynasty. As had occurred before, disagreement reigned. The Emperor's representative wished for the Spanish to intervene in force against the Danes, the Spanish wanted the Emperor to send forces against the Dutch and to declare against them. Further conflict was engendered between Spain and Bavaria, as the Spanish wished to use the Lower Palatinate as a peace offering to entice England to the negotiating table; for this to occur they required the Bavarians evacuate the territory, which Maximillian refused to do. Any overarching Catholic alliance failed to materialise on the base of these disagreements. Despite the considerable successes Madrid had enjoyed in 1625, there was no desire to enter the war with Denmark, particularly as the conflict with England raged on.

A silver lining had been the ratification of the Treaty of Monzon in March, which made the temporary Franco-Spanish détente and the French evacuation from the Val Telline official. Through this agreement, France confirmed its intention to abandon the Hague Alliance, destroying any possibility that King Christian of Denmark would be propped up by French subsidies in the process. Thus, even while they would not wage war against

Denmark, and even though Spain could not persuade the Emperor to make war on the Dutch, the inter-Habsburg cooperation had again produced critically important fruit. The Danish King, once so threatening, was now more isolated than ever.

The axe fell on King Christian's hopes and dreams at the Battle of Lutter on 26 August 1626. It was there that Count Tilly proved his worth for the Catholic Habsburg cause once more, as his forces shattered the Danish-German army in a single battle, and blunted Christian's offensive capabilities for good. Christian fled back to Denmark, with the Catholic League in hot pursuit. The defeat of Christian's forces granted the Catholic League something akin to free reign in the Lower Saxon Circle, and the unfortunate inhabitants of the region were to suffer much from the demands of the invader over the next few years.[55]

The defeat was as shattering as that of Christian of Brunswick had been at Stadtlohn almost exactly two years before. Much like his Danish namesake, over 1621-23 Christian of Brunswick had endeavoured to rally the Lower Saxon Circle to his side, but his defeat had fostered anxiety and timidity among them in the aftermath. This had momentarily passed with King Christian of Denmark's arrival, but now that he was also defeated, there seemed no great defender of the Protestant cause in place. The only option left was to fall at the mercy of the Emperor and the invader and hope against hope for the best outcome.

By August 1626, with the major armies of the anti-Habsburg cause defeated, and two of the main antagonists of the Habsburgs dead, the Hague Alliance had apparently been smothered in its cradle. Worse for the enemies of the Habsburgs, the English were distracted and penniless, the French succumbing to their Huguenot rebellion and unable to help, and the Val Telline was open to Spanish traffic, it appeared, for good. 1626 was indeed a brilliant year for the Habsburgs, and a rewarding one for Emperor Ferdinand. On the other hand, news of these decisive defeats after hopes had been raised so high cannot have been easy for the exiled Frederick to endure. Somehow, he maintained his composure, and worked against all currents to maintain some semblance of the anti-Habsburg league. These defeats, while unbearably bitter pills, were merely trials in his walk of faith, and he would not abandon this walk now, nor ever. So long as he lived, so did the resistance to the Habsburgs, and so did the righteous cause.

FOUR
Creating Supremacy

The dispossessed Elector Palatine greeted the news of Christian IV's defeat with sombre self-reflection and a declaration of his faith in the eventual triumph of his good cause. Admitting wrongdoing was impossible on Frederick's part, having come so far playing the same song of the Emperor's unconstitutional behaviour and the Habsburg family's pretentions to European domination through the repressive Jesuits. If capitulation was impossible, then it remained for Frederick to hold out, and to justify this resilience in turn. He attempted to bolster the shattered spirits of the King of Denmark, by writing the following to Christian in early September 1626:

> Although God, the Most High Prince of War, often lets dark clouds cover his own, he also still tends to them finally, gladdening them once again with the loving rays of his sun, and release the weather of his wrath over the enemies of his church and the oppressors of common liberty; just as when you suppose you will either be ruined, or at least will not continue, and you must recognise that you can do no more than what is allowed you from on High, as such things already in many places express the good hope that the Almighty will perhaps compensate Your Highness for the loss suffered, to His honour, and for the consolation of so many hard oppressed souls, for thus then we pray to him with all our heart.

Evidently, Frederick maintained a belief in a warrior God, a belief he reinforced in his own personal writings when he sought to reconcile his defeats, saying:

> One must let time run its course, until the Lord God may supply guidance and means for this purpose: for the good hope that He may not allow the common Protestant cause and those liberties, having been obtain at such great costs, to be oppressed.

If Frederick feared the spectacle of oppression in the Empire, then he was right to fear. Emperor Ferdinand did not view the conclusion of the campaigning season as the end of Count Tilly's objectives, nor would Wallenstein be now retired simply because no enemy existed in the field. Ernst of Mansfeld was gone; Christian of Brunswick was gone; Christian IV of Denmark was in headlong retreat up the Jutland peninsula. If he genuinely desired peace, Ferdinand could have acquired it. Like Frederick, the Emperor wanted peace on his own conditions, and he was inflexible on these conditions just as Frederick would not be moved on his. Since compromise was equated with weakness, or worse, an admission of wrongdoing, it was impossible in late 1626 for either side to contemplate a negotiated settlement unless the full extent of their demands was accepted.

Both men were as bad as the other in this regard, the difference was that Ferdinand, on the winning side, quite reasonably expected Frederick to admit defeat and thus be more amenable to giving at the peace table. The Emperor and the Elector did in fact engage in limited peace overtures, and since 1625 the Duke of Lorraine and of Wurttemberg had voiced their opinion to the effect that it was high time Frederick submitted, and save Germany further destruction. Frederick would only submit to his Emperor if Ferdinand fully and unconditionally reinstated him in the Palatinate. This, of course, Ferdinand could not do, because he was actively using Frederick's lands to pay off his debts. Thus, the only way Frederick could rule the Upper Palatinate (occupied by Bavaria) or the Lower Palatinate (occupied by Bavaria and Spain) would be through some kind of cash indemnity which would absolve Ferdinand of his debts to Maximillian of Bavaria, and satisfy at the same time the Spanish.

From Madrid, peace overtures to London had been forwarded, and it seemed at least possible that Spain would be willing to end its war with England and use the Palatinate as the prize to lure King Charles to the peace table. But Charles could not afford to be drawn, so long as the restitution was bound to come with unsavoury terms and conditions which would compromise his bargaining power with his Parliament. So long as Parliament maintained such a vehement dislike of the Duke of Buckingham, and so long as Charles refused to dismiss him, it was unlikely that Parliament would hear their King's proposals in any case. The Spanish would not relinquish the Rhine Palatinate without good reason, since it had proved a boon to their strategic interests in their war with the Dutch. With the war proceeding well in the Netherlands, King Philip IV was willing to use the Palatinate to buy off Britain, and open up trade between the two nations again, but he would not give it away without some incentive. Frederick's ties to Britain, once considered so valuable, had thus complicated matters considerably.

It was rumoured that after Lutter, a truce would be arranged between the parties, but Frederick advised his ambassador in London not to agree to any such proposals for truce based solely on promises from either side. At this point in his life, having received so many successive disappointments,

Frederick needed deeds rather than words. He could not afford to trust the promises of the Spanish or Austrian Habsburgs, especially when they stood to gain from his submission. If Frederick retired at this point, the Habsburgs would have been in a position of unquestioned supremacy in the Empire and in Europe, and with the Spanish Road open, the traditional rivals distracted and the Dutch war going in Spain's favour, there seemed no reason to imagine this power reducing.[56]

Who was there to enforce any terms on the Emperor, or to hold him to account? So long as the two armies of Tilly and Wallenstein were in the field, he would be able to do as he liked. Considering the powers which both of these commanders held, it is somewhat surprising to see Wallenstein writing to the Emperor on the subject of a lasting peace, before the battle of Lutter had even taken place, in June 1626. Interestingly, Wallenstein's motives for doing so were based on the fear that, if Ferdinand did not quit while he was ahead, stopping the war would be impossible in the near future. One could only triumph so many times before he incurred the united wrath of all his wronged opponents. Wallenstein, as a commander but also a landowner of great significance, was concerned to protect his interests. As he wrote:

> I hereby obediently enclose to Your Imperial Majesty what has been communicated with General Count Tilly. You will graciously see from this what position the enemy is in. My humble opinion in this would be that it would currently be best and bring more advantage and higher reputation if Your Imperial Majesty negotiated peace with them, because the enemy will get more help from various quarters and his forces will greatly increase, so that he will perhaps not accept later what he would more easily be persuaded to agree to now, and this evil might not be stopped later.[57]

It was a prophetic warning, and one which the Emperor failed to heed. Certainly, after the victory at Lutter, Wallenstein quieted down about a negotiated settlement, and focused instead on the task of increasing his army's size to truly massive proportions. Over the autumn of 1626, Wallenstein had been vocal about his need for more monetary support from the Emperor – it seemed that not even a private citizen of his immense means could maintain an army indefinitely. Unfortunately for Wallenstein, the Emperor was in no position to provide any money for his soldiers, and requests to levy a new tax in the Hereditary Lands was met with protest in Bohemia and Moravia. Little wonder that Wallenstein exclaimed in frustration in late 1626

> It is sufficient for the Emperor that I have provided him with an army the likes of which no one has had before, and for which he has still not laid out a single farthing…It is not possible to do with an unpaid army what a paid one will do.[58]

Wallenstein was also aggravated by the legion of armchair generals back in Vienna who took every opportunity to criticise him openly and to scrutinise his tactics. With his victory at Dessau Bridge in April 1626 outshone by Tilly's defeat of the Danish King at Lutter a few months later, Wallenstein found that even as he wintered in his Prague palace then under construction his lines of credit were close to exhaustion, his health was beginning to fail and a wave of opinion was forming against him in Vienna. All three of these problems followed Wallenstein for the rest of his life, but regardless of his objections and personal problems, the Duke of Friedland knew he had a job to do, and he travelled to Vienna in spring 1627 to arrange a new campaign. After enduring for many months, the burden of isolated command, Wallenstein fell ill almost as soon as he began his journey and did not meet with the Emperor's people until May.

On 23 May 1627, after a brief audience with the Emperor, Wallenstein left Vienna never to return. The journey had taken a lot out of him, and given him few causes for optimism, but problems further afield demanded his attention. Contrary to expectations, by spring 1627, King Christian IV of Denmark had raised an army of thirty thousand men in Holstein, which was too large for Tilly to reckon with alone. It was time for Wallenstein to confront the Danish threat head on. Perhaps by doing so, total victory, payment of his debts and the silencing of detractors would follow. Geoff Mortimer describes Wallenstein's mindset as well as his plan for the new campaigning season:

> Despite his illnesses and frustrations Wallenstein prepared thoroughly for the campaign of 1627. Central to his planning was to ensure that when he eventually confronted Christian, he would have the superior force at his disposal, while still having enough other troops to deploy against threats elsewhere. Hence, he set out to build his army up into the largest early modern Europe had thus far seen, of the order of one hundred thousand men in total. His growing reputation also enabled him to attract outstanding officers to strengthen his higher levels of command.[59]

The threats elsewhere which Wallenstein feared were found in Transylvania and Silesia. In both cases, the significant leaders of the forces there – Bethlen Gabor and Ernst of Mansfeld respectively – had either retired or died, but Wallenstein could not guarantee that Mansfeld's headless army would not return with plunder on its mind, or that the Prince of Transylvania's military career was in fact over. Exhausted and prematurely aged by years in the saddle, Bethlen Gabor died in November 1629 having just reached his 50th birthday, but the campaign of 1626 was destined to be his last. Wallenstein needed forces for these potential threats, and he also needed soldiers on hand to deal with another, potentially catastrophic intervention – that by the King of Sweden, Gustavus Adolphus. After making some noise about the desire to intervene in 1625, Gustavus had refrained from doing so in the end, and chosen to make war against his Polish cousin instead.

This resumption of that long simmering conflict netted the Swedish King some incredible successes, including much of the Baltic States' lucrative ports. Harnessing the power of these ports and investing the income from their tolls in military upgrades and recruitment, Gustavus seemed to have found the key to success in his war with the Polish King. For Wallenstein, the news of Gustavus' success was grave indeed, since it suggested that an arranged peace would soon be in the offing, and when that occurred, the Swedish King would be free to intervene in the German war.

If Sweden intervened before Denmark could be decisively defeated, then the Habsburgs could face the apocalyptic prospect of war with all of Scandinavia. In Wallenstein's view, war with Sweden was nigh on inevitable, but to delay the entry of her king into the conflict, he was authorised to supplement the Polish army with some units from his hulking force. This move, while strategically clever, would in fact be used by the Swedish King as one of his pretexts for war with the Emperor in 1630, but Wallenstein needed to think in more immediate terms. The immediate danger of a Swedish intervention while the King of Denmark maintained thirty thousand men in the field was obvious, and it made the need to eject King Christian from the war all the more urgent.[60]

Due to Wallenstein's adventure to Vienna and Christian's need to repair and recruit his forces for a new campaign, the campaigning season of 1627 started quite late, in mid-July, in spite of the great issues at stake. Before the campaigning began in earnest though, the dispossessed Elector Palatine made use of another opportunity to achieve peace at the negotiating table. This latest conference took place over July 1627 and was hosted in the town of Colmar in Alsace. It was the fruits of the anxious labours of that same Duke of Alsace and the Duke of Wurttemberg, who had together urged Frederick to the peace table but to no avail. Here at Colmar, they hosted representatives from Frederick and the Emperor in what had been billed as a new initiative for an Empire-wide peace. Shortly after opening though, it became apparent that this conference would fail to achieve peace just like all the others.

Yet, despite its ill-fate, the Colmar Conference was significant because in this instance, Frederick went further than he ever had before. His representatives made it known that he would renounce his claims on Bohemia, would ask for no indemnity from the Emperor in spite of the ruined state of his Palatinate, that he would swear fealty to Ferdinand so long as this did not humiliate his Electoral dignity and that, most interestingly, he was willing to share the Electoral Palatine title with Maximillian of Bavaria, so long as it lasted only until Maximillian's death. On the other hand, Frederick's agents refused to accept the Emperor's demand of religious toleration for Catholics – this would, after all, have violated the terms of the 1555 Peace of Augsburg. As the Emperor had made clear on several occasions previously though, since

Calvinism was not recognised by the Augsburg settlement, its privileges did not apply to the Calvinist Elector.[61]

This narrow-minded view was unfortunate, and also tricky to rationally apply, since Frederick was not the only Calvinist Elector – George William of Brandenburg also subscribed to that creed. In addition, Frederick's refusal to countenance any indemnity for the Emperor came from a mood of necessity as much as of defiance. Frederick's lands had been ravaged and pillaged by the invading Bavarians and Spanish, with the former exacting extensive contributions as recompense for the Emperor's debt to Maximillian. Frederick had given as much ground as he possibly could without compromising his honour, and his representatives were vocal in their insistence that the Palatinate must be restored unconditionally. One called the negotiations 'an inextricable labyrinth' and expressed his fears that unless some common ground was established between the two sides, a proper peace would not be reached at Colmar.

What Colmar required was a mediator more powerful and effective than the Dukes of Alsace and Wurttemberg. Unfortunately for the peace of Europe, the usual suspects in France, Britain and the Netherlands were all occupied, and neither side would have trusted the Papacy to remain impartial in any case. Once it became obvious that no such agreement would be reached, Frederick consoled himself in his anger by pronouncing loudly that he accepted no responsibility for the failure. He had never been as agreeable or flexible as he had been at Colmar, and yet the Emperor had refused to countenance even the smallest of compromises. Like Frederick, the Emperor evidently believed that through war, he could gain better terms. Unlike Frederick though, Ferdinand was not willing to consider anything but the unconditional surrender of his foe, and the complete supplication of the Palatine family to his will. This was not just playing hard to get; it was tantamount to a deliberate torpedoing of the peace negotiations before they had even a chance to make progress.

Ferdinand's intransigence can be explained not only by his faith in the strength of Wallenstein's swollen force (see below), but also in the due processes of the Empire which were sure to work in his favour. An Electoral Diet was due to take place at Muhlhausen in October 1627, whereupon the transferral of Frederick's titles were to be officially confirmed, and the Emperor's uncompromising conditions for Frederick's surrender would be given the blessing by all the Empire's potentates, including, bitterly for Frederick, the Calvinist George William of Brandenburg. Knowledge of this looming Diet had put some urgency into the Palatine negotiators at Colmar, but because the Emperor knew of its likely decisions, he chose to string Frederick along at the July meeting rather than commit to anything.

For Frederick, the tough pill to swallow of the failed Colmar Conference was accompanied in quick succession by the choking unfairness of the

Muhlhausen Diet. At Muhlhausen, Frederick's worst fears were confirmed, as were the Emperor's requests. By this point, in October, Wallenstein's large army had begun to tell on the nerves of those assembled. On the surface, the Emperor made demands which had been tacitly agreed to before by his Electoral subordinates, but in secret, commitments had been made with Maximillian of Bavaria to relinquish the Electoral title of the Palatinate to him and his descendants, permanently excluding Frederick and his family from the Palatine succession. Even Ferdinand knew this was a bridge too far, and he thus kept it secret from the two Protestant Electors. By February 1628, Frederick would learn that the Upper Palatinate had been granted to Maximillian for life, and that it had essentially been stripped away from his Palatine inheritance. These blows in succession were deeply felt, but much worse was to come for the exiled ex-Elector.

The continued campaigns of Christian IV of Denmark are largely forgotten by the histories, and with good reason. Nothing of consequence was achieved after Lutter, and although his impressive army took to the field in summer 1627 with much apparent promise, thanks to the failed promises of Denmark's allies it was unpaid and demoralised, and Christian knew he would not be able to rely long upon it. His decision to return to Holstein and draw what he could from his personal Dukedom was a good idea on paper, especially as the Danish Chancery refused to provide the funds for a new campaign. Their king, having launched his war as the Duke of Holstein and marched as the Lower Saxon Circle's president, would lose his personal war from this position if they had anything to say about it.[62]

Unfortunately for Christian, his allies abroad were not the only ones to fail him. He happened to host several exiles in his army, and one of these was Count Thurn, the figure who had been so instrumental in the Defenestration of Prague almost a decade before. Thurn was a passionate rabble rouser, but he was a useless soldier, and his task of defending the Elbe River was abandoned, as Thurn determined instead to retreat further northwards. With the Elbe crossing abandoned, the mission of defeating the Danish King would be far easier for Tilly and Wallenstein.

By September 1627, the two commanders had arrived in Holstein, and overran Christian's personal holdings within two weeks, exacting lucrative contributions as they did so. Christian's response was to retreat further up the Jutland peninsula, but any hopes that his subjects would repel the Imperialists were in vain, as both Danish and German peasants actually fought *against* the King's men during the retreat, in anger and despair at the terrible chasm into which he had thrown them. As Tilly and Wallenstein encountered successive Danish fortresses throughout Holstein, the garrisons determined to surrender rather than fight. Many had not been paid, and since the bulk of Christian's army was made up of Germans anyway, a great number joined the ranks of the invader in search of better pay and more reliable contracts. Christian's army dissolved as he retreated further northwards. By 28 September, the main Danish camp had been compromised, and on 16 October, the last fortress guarding the entrance to the peninsula surrendered. The road was now open for a massive Imperialist invasion of the Danish heartland. Christian, utterly shattered, retreated to his inaccessible islands through the harnessing of his kingdom's final asset, its navy, and he waited in his capital to weather whatever other storm may come, be it invasion or, he hoped, a favourable peace.[63]

The year 1627 spelled doom for the Danish King's resolve. The task of fielding his armies had been rendered impossible by the silence which greeted Danish requests to its allies in the Hague Alliance to fulfil their end of the bargain and provide the promised subsidies. Without these subsidies, Denmark was alone to face the Habsburg might, which would have been an unwinnable prospect even without Wallenstein's army of one hundred thousand men dominating the field, crowding his fortresses and choking his freedom of manoeuvre. Had King Christian appreciated fully exactly how far Wallenstein had been instructed to go, he might have suffered a breakdown. Wallenstein and Tilly had met with stunning success, and their enormous army dwarfed any that their rivals could match, but their mission did not cease with the defeat and expulsion of the Danish King from Northern Germany.

Instead, Wallenstein was encouraged to pursue a line intimated earlier by the Spanish – the so-called Baltic design, which would provide the Habsburgs would a secure base in the Baltic, from which point all their enemies could be defeated in detail. The scheme excited the Spanish, because in Madrid, Count Olivares envisioned it as the best way to defeat the Dutch and surround them on all fronts. To Wallenstein, the plan had appeal because it would hamper the Swedish King's activities and enable the Emperor to inflict a decisive defeat on King Christian, perhaps through a naval landing near Copenhagen.

Wallenstein aimed to make this Habsburg dream a reality by harnessing the power of the Hanseatic League who, we recall, had been approached by the Habsburgs in 1625 with a similar offer, but had turned it down. Now at the height of their powers, the proposal was offered again, and Wallenstein concocted a series of new campaigns to make further Habsburg aggrandisement possible in 1628 while the Hanseatic League received greater coercion to join. As we will discover shortly, the Baltic design was a bridge too far for the Habsburgs, but for now, it suffices to note the striking correspondence undertaken by Wallenstein in the name of this scheme.[64]

In October 1627, as Holstein was overrun by Imperial troops, Wallenstein penned a letter to King Sigismund of Poland, who as we learned was supplied by some contingents from Wallenstein's army earlier in the year to keep the Polish-Swedish war in motion. Wallenstein attempted to build upon this relationship by approaching the Polish King about the Baltic design. By 1627, although Poland had lost the lucrative Baltic ports to Sweden, she still possessed considerable assets in Pomerania and Prussia, and extensive economic interests in the Baltic, most significantly in the port of Danzig, the Commonwealth's wealthiest and most populous city.[65] Thus, Wallenstein's approaches sought to unify the Holy Roman Emperor with his Polish brother in law in this design; he would appeal to Sigismund's self-interest by detailing the benefits to Poland should the King join in with it. The correspondence is worth recounting not merely for what it says about the interconnected nature of the Thirty Years War, even at this relatively early stage, but also for what it says about the Polish King's insatiable ambitions. Wallenstein began with a letter on 28 October 1627, in which he wrote:

> We report to Your Majesty that we are already busy collecting a large fleet to pursue those who disturb Christianity. We hope that Our Lord will, as till today, support the just cause, now that Your Majesty is willing to join your ships to ours and bring them to a safe port. Therefore, we report that we have captured the town of Wismar, this is the foremost harbour in the Baltic Sea, so that Your Majesty can now send them there in better security.

Had Wallenstein successfully orchestrated a scheme whereby Polish ships would be lent to the Habsburgs for the Baltic design? As it happened, King Sigismund required little convincing – he was already on board, but he had far more in mind than the mere pooling of naval power. What he envisioned was the total destruction of their enemies, and the expansion of the war to all theatres. King Sigismund of Poland responded on 10 November to say that:

> We have received word that Your Grace, thanks to divine grace and support, has achieved a remarkable victory over His Majesty the Emperor's enemy, the King of Denmark, in the principality of Holstein. This is not only pleasant and agreeable to us, but most welcome. We did not want to neglect congratulating Your Grace on such a happy success and to thank the Almighty and to pray that he will graciously permit Your Grace to prosper in such a work that is most necessary to our Catholic religion and to the due extirpation of all the most damaging enemies. We also do not want to omit telling Your Grace that certain reports have arrived that Denmark is currently seeking a peace with His Majesty the Emperor and eagerly wants this. However, this is not pleasant to us, since such peace negotiations will not only do more harm than good to His Majesty the Emperor and the King of Spain, but also to ourselves.

Why, we may ask, would the Emperor's peace with the Danish King disadvantage the King of Poland, who was not even formally involved in the conflict? Sigismund continued to enlighten Wallenstein:

Because, with God's help, victory is in His Majesty and Your Grace's hands and, because the [enemy] population is greatly afraid, by continuing the campaign one can easily obtain the Sound and other places, and so conquer the entire Kingdom of Denmark with such a powerful fleet. Furthermore, this will help the King of Spain be more powerful than his enemies, and so much more easily and quickly provide help and assistance to the King of Spain, from whom we have already had some consolation that we might recover our Kingdom of Sweden. Because matters can be judged by Your Grace's customary discretion, we entrust them to Your Grace with due affected and ask your advice how assistance against Sweden could be sought from His Majesty the Emperor in the manner of the consolation that we have received from the King of Spain, so that once this has been received, Sweden can also be attacked from this side.[66]

The implications for what Sigismund suggested here were nothing short of breath-taking. First, he advised Wallenstein not to make peace, but to use the fleet acquired from this Baltic design to actually conquer Denmark and presumably depose its King. Second, Sigismund inquired about promises made by the King of Spain about Sigismund's recovery of Sweden, and insisted that if the Emperor would also grant such guarantees, and declare against Gustavus Adolphus, then Sweden would be attacked and destroyed from all sides, and Sigismund would be able to take back what was rightfully his – the Swedish crown which his uncle had stolen from him, and which his cousin now kept warm.

Contrary to Sigismund's striking plan, the Emperor was in no position to declare against the Swedes, and Wallenstein likely interpreted these offers as nothing more than an attempt by Sigismund to entangle the Habsburgs in his unsuccessful war against Gustavus Adolphus, without any tangible benefit to their position. Indeed, Sigismund offered no practical guarantees or support of his own through this correspondence – he offered neither to declare war on the Dutch, nor to declare war on the Danes. King Sigismund's activities had not crossed the path of Wallenstein or of the Emperor for the final time though, and in spite of his apparent selfishness, the key role Poland played in occupying Sweden was recognised by Wallenstein as well as the French, with incredible results later in the war. For now, the Swedish-Polish war remained an isolated if distantly related conflict to that waged in the Emperor's name, but Wallenstein was convinced that it could not remain so indefinitely.

FIVE
Troubling Patterns

I can say of this lord that his mind is agile, active and far from tranquil…That he yearns for many things that he does not reveal outwardly. He will certainly be merciless, without brotherly or marital affection, respecting nobody, dedicated completely to himself and his own ambition…He will endeavour to attain many dignities and vast power – and thus he will attract many great and secret enemies, most of whom he will defeat…It appears that he will have a special charm for many people and that he might become the head of a company of conspirators.[67]

This was the horoscope which the famed astronomer Johannes Kepler gave for Albrecht of Wallenstein in 1608. In many respects, it is typical of the vague and reaching predictions of the time, but it is nonetheless a striking indictment of Wallenstein's character, which by 1628 was becoming part of the common conversation of Europe. The Duke of Friedland had been phenomenally successful, and he managed to destroy virtually all vestiges of resistance to the Habsburgs in Northern Germany. Over the winter of 1627-28, his enormous army in excess of one hundred thousand men had been quartered in the mostly unspoiled lands of the Danish King's Jutland peninsula. If 1627 had been a year of mopping up the last gasps of King Christian IV's resistance, then 1628 would have to be the year that this Habsburg victory was convincingly confirmed.

The Emperor's prestige was not the only factor at stake; by 1628 Wallenstein had exhausted nearly all lines of credit, and the exorbitant costs of maintaining such a massive army had the potential to actually bankrupt him. The danger to the Empire and to Wallenstein himself which would follow if these hundred thousand unpaid men went on a rampage was part of the reason why the Emperor continued to ignore all protests about the army's size or the generalissimo's ambitions. One figure who observed these ambitions with great fear was the Marquis of Aytona, the Spanish ambassador to Vienna. On 12 February 1628, Aytona wrote to King Philip IV on Wallenstein's character, fortune and the danger he posed, in a communique which has since become immensely quotable:

> The Emperor has taken Mecklenburg from the last descendants of the old princely house that had joined the King of Denmark and given it to the Duke of Friedland [Wallenstein]. Although [Wallenstein] maintains that peace is within his grasp, I suspect that this gift will push it further away. The Duke is very powerful. One must be thankful that he is satisfied with these possessions, that are admittedly extensive and significant. The Emperor, through his generosity and by ignoring all warnings, has made the Duke so powerful that doubts must arise; he is now the only commander, leaving the Emperor with little more than his title. [Wallenstein] constantly presents himself as the most loyal servant of the imperial family, and indeed is such, but only as long as they do not disturb his current absolute power. At the slightest objection to his plan there will be no safety from him, because his nature is so terrible and moody that he often does not know how to control himself.[68]

We can discern several striking aspects of this communique even before considering the remarks on Wallenstein's character. The first is the confirmation by the Spanish ambassador of what had been long standing rumours up to that point – to pay Wallenstein's debts, the Emperor determined to transfer a new Dukedom to him, this one being Mecklenburg, whose dukes fought on the side of the Danish King. The second is the strange way which Aytona framed this transfer, referring as he does to the generosity of the decision. Mecklenburg, in spite of what Ferdinand would claim, was not his to transfer to anyone he liked in such an arbitrary manner. The act was a significant step up from the Emperor's previous practices of transferring land to pay his debts, and it was far from certain that all would approve of the act.

Finally, Aytona's note that Wallenstein was the sole commander underlined the fact that Wallenstein's rank now outstripped Count Tilly's of the Catholic League. This was a deliberate promotion by the Emperor to reduce his dependence upon either the League of Maximillian of Bavaria. Predictably enough, Maximillian did not appreciate being usurped in the pecking order, and, although once he approved of Wallenstein's appointment, from late 1627 he began to add his voice to the growing number of voices calling for Wallenstein's dismissal. One letter sent by the Emperor to Wallenstein in late February 1628 underlines the immediacy of the confiscations of rebel property across the Empire, and the major motive for doing so: the desperate want of hard currency which Ferdinand needed to pay off his debts:

> We have graciously resolved and decided, that all those confiscations and punishments incurred by the participants of the recent unrest and rebellion in the Holy Roman Empire who have had their fixed and movable property seized by our deputised commissioners, that these are to be used exclusively

to pay the army entrusted to you and not to be used for any other purpose. In order that this can be put into effect, it is our gracious wish that you assist our commissioners with the confiscations so that these can be seized, valued and converted into cash. However, those debts and liabilities of the various properties are to be assessed and those that are found to be justified are to be repaid first, before the rest is used to pay our soldiers in future. Discretion and moderation are to be used to ensure that no one, either from the delinquents or the creditors, feel that they have been dealt with too harshly or have cause for complaint. You know well what to do to secure our grace and we remain yours with imperial and royal grace and also good wishes.[69]

The Emperor was not partaking in a one-off tactic to satisfy immediate needs; he was pursuing a policy which had served him well in the past, and of which he fully recognised the inherent value. As previously discussed, Ferdinand had been transferring the land of 'rebels' and 'delinquents' as soon as it was in his power to do so. Frederick's Upper and Lower Palatinate had been parcelled up between the Spanish and Bavarians, with the latter receiving the Upper Palatinate against the debts of ten million reichsthalers which the Emperor owed to Maximillian. Ferdinand thus paid off his debts by apportioning land which was not his to give; he had a demonstrated history of doing so, and little choice other than doing so, if he wished for his allies to remain loyal. Wallenstein's gift of Mecklenburg was certainly not the first instance of this policy, but for several reasons it was by far the most egregious. As Geoff Mortimer reminds us though, it is important to place such appropriations in context, especially if we are tempted to blame Wallenstein for the transfer:

> Ferdinand never had enough cash to pay for the crippling costs of the war, and so he turned to property, first his own and then that confiscated from others, which he used initially as security and later as outright payment for his debts…The Emperor, not Wallenstein, was the originator of these measures… Ferdinand was prepared from an early stage to manipulate the strict forms of Imperial legality in order to override property rights, and Mecklenburg fits into that pattern.

That it had indeed become a pattern by 1628 was deeply disconcerting not just to perennial neutrals like John George of Saxony, but also to the greatest benefactor of the pattern, Maximillian of Bavaria. It is indeed the case that Wallenstein accepted the transfer, and that he had campaigned for it in the past, but again, it is important to place these actions in context as well. Wallenstein was not eager to acquire another Duchy for the mere sake of it. He had, as we have seen, crippling debts of his own to pay, since he was effectively carrying the financial burden of the war. Even with his noted reputation for paying on time, the lines of credit he possessed on the security of his lands, and the organised system which made him one of the wealthiest men in the Empire, Wallenstein quickly discovered, as King Christian IV of Denmark had, that a private fortune was all too easily exhausted by the privations of war, especially when that war required an army in excess of one hundred thousand men.

Mecklenburg was a strategically important duchy sandwiched between Pomerania in the east and Holstein in the west. It contained several ports which tapped into the Baltic trade, with Wismar being the most significant. It was therefore a lucrative duchy with great potential, especially for a man like Wallenstein who was caught up with the scheme of developing a fleet for the Habsburgs in the Baltic. Wismar provided an ideal opportunity for this, and by deposing the rebellious Dukes of Mecklenburg, Wallenstein would also be given an ideal opportunity to squeeze these new lands in order to pay his considerable debts. Furthermore, his swollen portfolio would serve as collateral for brand new loans on the security of his new landholdings. These practical considerations were of far greater importance to Wallenstein than the personal ambition of acquiring another duchy.[70]

It was just as well that Mecklenburg was available to pay off Wallenstein's creditors and to help him raise new funds, for there much work still to be done. To fulfil his Baltic ambitions which the Spanish and Austrians hankered after, it would be necessary to establish some kind of dominion over the Baltic states which surrounded its seas. Mecklenburg was an important step in this direction, but another was the Duchy of Pomerania which bordered Mecklenburg to the east. If Mecklenburg was an important prize, Pomerania and the loyalty of its Duke Bogislaw XIV were essential. Pomerania straddled the Baltic Sea, and contained several important ports, one of which was Stralsund. In many respects, the status of Stralsund as the supposed turning point in the Thirty Years War is overstated. Militarily, Wallenstein's failure to take this stubborn city had little impact on his position. Politically though, it enabled more enemies to come out of the woodwork in Vienna, and before long, Wallenstein was sacrificed by his Emperor for the sake of political and hereditary interests. Before we address that portion of the famous tale though, we must first examine the campaigning season of 1628, and discern where Stralsund fit into it.

As he had done before, Wallenstein spent the winter in his Prague residence. With Christian IV of Denmark stuck on his islands, there was a great deal less urgency in the campaigning season than there had been before. The bulk of Wallenstein's army occupied the Jutland peninsula, and the next step appeared to be the invasion and siege of Copenhagen, for which he would require a fleet. With this in mind, Mecklenburg became a convenient base for launching such naval operations, and a fleet of twenty-four ships was under construction. By now, virtually all of Northern Germany was open to the quartering of Wallenstein's soldiers – the only way to escape this undesirable situation was to pay off the commanders. In some case, these payments, known as contributions, were preferable to actually billeting soldiers, since hard cash was what was needed. Thus, when approaching the Duke of Pomerania in November 1627, Wallenstein had negotiated to provision a portion of his army quartered there on organised intervals. The alternative, as Duke Bogislaw understood, was that Wallenstein's soldiers would ravage his duchy looking for food if it was not provided to them.

It was therefore preferable to the Duke to arrange for a settlement which would keep everyone happy and protect the integrity of his lands, though of course human nature meant that some privations would occur. Facing no rivals, it was also inevitable that the soldiery would become bored and idle if not given anything to do. When boredom struck, regimented training would only go so far, and if the contributions system broke down for whatever reason, there was little Wallenstein or Tilly could do to prevent their subordinates leading the charge against the untapped wealth of certain regions. These consequences aside, Wallenstein was preparing for a campaign which would finish off the Danish King and also potentially bring the Swedish monarch to the negotiating table. A landing at Copenhagen would send a clear message to Gustavus Adolphus, one which the Swedish King had already learned of thanks to Wallenstein's interference in his Polish War (see above).

The Baltic design would grow and expire based on the whims and ambitions of the two perspectives in Vienna and Madrid. In Spain, Olivares made any Spanish support of a Habsburg Baltic adventure contingent on the Emperor issuing the Imperial ban against the Dutch, which would in time enmesh Ferdinand in that wretched Eighty Years War. Obviously, Ferdinand wished to avoid this conflict at all costs, but he would not refrain from stringing Spain along. First, he reminded Madrid that Spain had ceased its subsidies to Vienna since 1621, a message which was heard loud and clear: by February 1628, two and a half million florins continued to be delivered to the Emperor's court. Second, the Emperor insisted that Mecklenburg and Pomerania provided sufficient bases for the Baltic design, and he named Wallenstein the Captain General of the Oceanic and Baltic seas in spring 1628.[71]

King Philip IV could not force the Emperor to make war on the Dutch, but he could make it known that Ferdinand was expected to join him in the conflict at some point. Certainly, with Wallenstein close to eliminating the Danish King from the race, it is understandable why the Spanish were so anxious to see Wallenstein turn these men against the Dutch Republic – a force of one hundred thousand men could easily cause the collapse of Dutch resistance across the board. If this was coupled with the aforementioned Baltic design and the pooling of ships from Poland, the Hanseatic League and Spain, then the entirety of the enemies of the Habsburg dynasty would be extinguished. The two prongs of this dream would flounder for different reasons; the Emperor would never have been able to wrest approval from the princes of the Empire, and certainly not Wallenstein, to declare war on the Dutch. Furthermore, the defeat of the Danes did not entail the dissolution of Wallenstein's massive army: Ferdinand had another plan for it – to impose upon the people the terms of the religious settlement which he would develop.

At his capital in Stettin, Duke Bogislaw XIV of Pomerania was far from being in a position to offer much resistance himself. He was sandwiched himself between two masters: The King of Poland and, to a lesser extent, the Elector of Brandenburg. With the arrival of Wallenstein's army, Duke Bogislaw endeavoured to keep the generalissimo away from the heartland of his duchy by first promising ready deliveries of supplies for the troops, and then by recommending that he billet his soldiers at Stralsund instead. The suggestion of Stralsund would kill two birds with one stone for the Duke; first, it would mean that Wallenstein would not need his capital for the Baltic design and would hopefully leave Stettin alone. Second, it would put some manners on the recalcitrant residents of Stralsund, who had a history of resisting the demands of their duke.[72]

Wallenstein sent his second in command, the eminently capable Hans-Georg von Arnim, a native of Brandenburg, to acquire the necessary supplies from Stralsund. From January 1628 Imperial interest in the city increased. Initially, the proposed contributions were set at eighty thousand thalers, and Stralsund's city council, constituted mostly of rich merchants fearful of their livelihoods, paid the first instalment of thirty thousand thalers relatively promptly. But that was all that would be paid. An undercurrent of discontent and a spirit of resistance began to enter Stralsund which Wallenstein does not seem to have counted on. Arnim offered to drop the requirement of garrisoning the port city if its council would pay him a one-off sum of one hundred and fifty thousand thalers, and he took a provocative step towards making his seriousness known. One of the city's outlying islands, Danholm, was occupied by Arnim's troops in early February, and their guns were now turned on the city from several angles. In previous instances, cities had surrendered after enduring fewer inconveniences, but Stralsund was not like other cities.

The city was positioned on a triangular island and was separated by several lagoons and marshland. Its inhabitants had long since recognised the city's potential as an impregnable fortress, and the defences, which geography enhanced, made them feel heavily fortified. Significantly for Wallenstein, a great portion of defensive works had been erected in the spring of 1628; a further ill-omen was the author of these fortifications. After the city had determined to resist, Arnim's forces were expelled from Danholm in the mouth of the city's harbour, and Arnim's army of eight thousand faced an unexpected crisis. By the end of April 1628, Stralsund had invited foreign detachments into the city, and Swedish engineers helped to make the aforementioned improvements to the defences.

One thousand mercenaries were added to the two and a half thousand-man militia, and another one thousand Swedish, Danish and Scottish soldiers arrived during May. Arnim was reinforced by six thousand soldiers of his own in mid-May, but Stralsund's greatest advantage was its free access to the sea, which the Habsburgs were unable to impede. In spite of the great plans to establish a fleet in the Emperor's name, Wallenstein had not been able to make one materialise by this point. Thus, reinforcements and fresh provisions arrived throughout these months which kept the city in good spirits. Danish and Swedish ships patrolled the harbour, in line with their agreement to defend the city in unison which had been arranged in April. Meanwhile Arnim's soldiers suffered as the countryside was stripped bare and disease ripped through their ranks. Wallenstein made the decision to intervene in the siege personally, and wrote to the Duke of Pomerania on 17 June to the effect that:

> His Roman Imperial Majesty's Field Marshal Hans George von Arnim has reported to us how the inhabitants of Stralsund persist in their obstinacy. Accordingly, we have no choice but to attack them in order to extinguish the fire before it does great harm to the Holy Roman Empire and Your Grace's land, and since we have arrived [in Frankfurt] already and have rested 2 days, we want to set out for Stralsund at once. We hereby report to Your Grace that the regiments that have marched from the Empire across the Elbe, as we as those that were in Upper and Lower Lusatia, have been ordered to proceed to Stralsund immediately. In order to preserve better discipline and prevent the complete ruin of the country, we amicably request that Your Grace makes arrangements to provide the troops with the necessary sustenance. And since our artillery is currently in Holstein far from Stralsund, and it would take a long time to arrive during which the country would be burdened with the war, we accordingly request equally amicably that Your Grace provide whatever cannon, ammunition and entrenching tools the said Field Marshal Arnim requests. We hope to bring the inhabitants of Stralsund to due obedience in short time and save Your Grace's lands from ruin. You will be doing His Imperial Majesty and the Holy Roman Empire a loyal and affectionate service and we will also be obliged on this occasion.[74]

Whatever results Wallenstein had hoped for, the help was insufficient to make much of a difference. On 20 June 1628, Sweden's most significant contribution to the Thirty Years War yet came in the form of a flotilla of Swedish ships and soldiers. By 7 July, Wallenstein was in place with twenty-five thousand men. This, he hoped, would be enough to starve the city out and force a peace; if not it would have to be stormed. By this point, the city had already pledged itself to its new Swedish overlords. For the next 187 years,

Stralsund would serve as a Swedish base in Pomerania, but the needs of the city were too urgent in 1628 for its city fathers to worry too much about what their long-term future would hold. After associating themselves with the Habsburgs' enemies, they would be liable for harsh treatment unless a suitable deal was made.

Wallenstein would try and seize the city by force first. Over a three-day period, Stralsund came under the full attention and fury of the Duke of Friedland and Mecklenburg, but even with his swollen numbers, he could not force a surrender. The city was simply too well defended, especially so long as it maintained a consistent supply line through the sea and could depend upon consistent reinforcements from its new Baltic allies. Wallenstein entered negotiations, but the Swedish officers in place among Stralsund's garrison whipped the defenders into a frenzy and prevented its inhabitants from accepting any compromise. On 31 July, realising that he was getting nowhere and wasting time and resources, Wallenstein broke off the siege. According to one account, Wallenstein genuinely believed the assurances of the Duke of Pomerania, who had told him that he would bring Stralsund to heel himself, and that Wallenstein need not worry. To avoid the 'inevitable bloodbath' which would follow, he thus broke off the siege.[75] According to another version, this was merely a 'face saving excuse' which Wallenstein later gave for his failure.[76]

Either way, by the first week of August 1628, Stralsund was freed from the noose which had threatened it for so long. It stood as the defiant symbol of resistance against the Habsburg tyranny; the exception to the rule of logical, continuous Habsburg progress; it was reimagined as a crushing defeat of Habsburg pretensions, of which a great deal could be made. 'The check', as Wedgewood wrote, 'was more effective morally than physically.' Yet, this moral victory was tremendously important, because it demonstrated that Wallenstein was not invincible, and that even with his gargantuan army, he was vulnerable in certain situations. 'Eagles', as the anti-Habsburg pamphleteers gleefully noted, 'cannot swim.'[77]

As Wallenstein himself recognised though, the withdrawal was significant not only because it was a setback in the long-term plan for Baltic domination by a Habsburg fleet; it was significant because of the identity of the new overlords of Stralsund. For so long, Wallenstein had worked to keep the King of Sweden occupied. During Stralsund though, Gustavus' soldiers had snuck into the city, and in the process granted their king his first German base. It remained to be seen, as he was knee-deep in a war with Poland, what Gustavus Adolphus would do with this base.

The setback was one which Wallenstein quickly rebounded from. He still held just as much land and had lost very little actual men and none of his artillery at Stralsund. His reputation, granted, had been somewhat tarnished, and the critics in Vienna began to speak openly about his flaws, but while Wallenstein loathed these developments, he was calm enough to recognise that a stiff victory would turn this talk around, as it had done before. He would not have to wait long. In the first week of September, King Christian foolishly landed at Wolgast, along the coast of Wallenstein's new Mecklenburg duchy with a few thousand men hoping, it appears, to turn the land against their new lord. The campaign was short-lived and doomed to failure, since Wallenstein still possessed overwhelming numerical superiority. Christian was lucky to escape the encounter, and he fled back to Copenhagen never to threaten Wallenstein again. Shortly after arriving at his capital, the pressures of fickle allies and a hostile nobility, not to mention an empty treasury, became too much for the King, who acquiesced to peace negotiations in earnest.

Thus, the campaigning season of 1628 ended with about as much success as the previous years. The blight of Stralsund aside, Wallenstein had done everything he had set out to do, and with King Christian now welcoming peace overtures, it was likely that he would be permitted to return to his new duchies and begin the process of ruling them soon enough. Wallenstein was still deeply vexed about Sweden's status, though on the bright side, the Swedes had been repelled in their recent Polish campaign without Wallenstein's direct aid. Gustavus had been forced to retreat from his siege of Danzig – a symptom of the back and forth nature of the Swedish-Polish War which had been ongoing for nearly a decade by this stage – but his army remained intact, and the Polish Commonwealth was unable to press the advantage. The King of Sweden had made great gains in the war with his cousin, but by late 1628 he was over five million reichsthalers in debt. The Polish King too, was looking for an out.

This stalemate in the Northern War was exactly the outcome Wallenstein had feared. All that was required now was the announcement of peace talks, and then a treaty, and he would be forced to fight against another northern power which would surely receive foreign help. The reality was worse than Wallenstein in fact imagined. Gustavus was well aware of the implications of his looming peace treaty. Ever since the Thirty Years War had begun, and Frederick V had become an exile, he had kept his eyes on Germany while he battled his Polish foe. If intervention in Germany appealed to his ambitions and sense of adventure, then within the year, it was also to appeal to his religious duty. Much to Wallenstein's dismay, his master the Emperor was soon to cast a great sectarian shadow over the German conflict. Just as the Danish foe was buckling, Ferdinand took a final step towards the logical conclusion which he had been so long working for: the realisation of the Counter-Reformation, bound up in the Edict of Restitution. For the Habsburg dynasty, the Emperor and his generalissimo, it was to prove a step too far.[78]

Chapter 12 Notes

[1]Quoted in Stevens, *History of Gustavus Adolphus*, p. 152.

[2]Quoted in Parker, *Europe in Crisis*, p. 216.

[3]Cited in Christopher Clark, *Iron Kingdom*, p. 23.

[4]See Paul Douglas Lockhart, 'Denmark and the Empire: A Reassessment of Danish Foreign Policy under King Christian IV', *Scandinavian Studies*, Vol. 64, No. 3 (Summer 1992), pp. 390-416; pp. 390-397.

[5]Danish exceptionalism in this regard is examined in Knud J. V. Jespersen, 'Social Change and Military Revolution in Early Modern Europe: Some Danish Evidence', *The Historical Journal*, Vol. 26, No. 1 (Mar., 1983), pp. 1-13.

[6]Paul Douglas Lockhart, 'Denmark and the Empire', p. 396.

[7]Paul Douglas Lockhart, 'Religion and Princely Liberties: Denmark's Intervention in the Thirty Years War, 1618-1625', *The International History Review*, Vol. 17, No. 1 (Feb., 1995), pp. 1-22; p. 4.

[8]Peter H. Wilson, *Europe's Tragedy*, pp. 173-174.

[9]T. K. Derry, *History of Scandinavia: Norway, Sweden, Denmark, Finland, and Iceland* (University of Minnesota Press, Minneapolis, 1979), p. 104.

[10]See Lennart Andersson Palm, 'Sweden's seventeenth century – a period of expansion or stagnation?' in *Institutionen för historiska studier* (Gothenburg, 2016), pp. 5-6. Available: https://gupea.ub.gu.se/bitstream/2077/50820/4/gupea_2077_50820_4.pdf

[11]Michael Roberts, *Gustavus Adolphus* (Routledge; London, 1998), p. 35.

[12]Wilson, *Europe's Tragedy*, pp. 172-173.

[13]See Brennan Pursell, *The Winter King*, pp. 128-129.

[14]Paul Douglas Lockhart, 'Religion and Princely Liberties', pp. 6-8.

[15]Wilson, *Europe's Tragedy*, pp. 175-177.

[16]Paul Douglas Lockhart, 'Religion and Princely Liberties', p. 8.

[17]Wilson, *Europe's Tragedy*, p. 387.

[18]See Paul Douglas Lockhart, 'Religion and Princely Liberties', pp. 11-13.

[19]*Ibid*, pp. 8-9.

[20]Wilson, *Europe's Tragedy*, pp. 385-386.

[21]Paul Douglas Lockhart, 'Religion and Princely Liberties', pp. 16-19.

[22]*Ibid*, pp. 19-20.

[23]Wilson, *Europe's Tragedy*, pp. 390-391.

[24]These extracts taken from Wilson, *Sourcebook*, pp. 92-93.

[25]Quoted in Peter H. Wilson, *Sourcebook*, pp. 94-95.

[26]C.V. Wedgewood, *Thirty Years War*, pp. 188-193.

[27]Wilson, *Europe's Tragedy*, pp. 391-392.

[28]Veit Valentin, 'Wallenstein, after Three Centuries', *The Slavonic and East European Review*, Vol. 14, No. 40 (Jul., 1935), pp. 154-162; pp. 154-156.

[29]Quoted from A.E.J. Hollaender, 'Some English documents on the end of Wallenstein', *Bulletin of the John Rylands Library Manchester*, 40 (1957-58), pp. 359-90; pp. 388-389.

[30]See Richard Bassett, *For God and Kaiser*, pp. 59-61.

[31]Mortimer, *Wallenstein*, p. 46.

[32]Peter H. Wilson, *Europe's Tragedy*, p. 392.

[33]Geoff Mortimer, *Wallenstein*, pp. 45-46.

[34]Wedgewood, *Thirty Years War*, pp. 192-193.

[35]*Ibid*, p. 192.

[36]Mortimer, *Wallenstein*, pp. 48-50.

[37]Peter H. Wilson, *Europe's Tragedy*, p. 402.

[38]Quoted in Brennan Pursell, *The Winter King*, p. 239.

[39]Wedgewood, *Thirty Years War*, pp. 113-115; pp. 158-159.

[40]Cornelius Walford, 'An Outline History of the Hanseatic League, More Particularly in Its Bearings upon English Commerce', *Transactions of the Royal Historical Society*, Vol. 9 (1881), pp. 82-136; p. 82. A highly readable account of this confederation is still the classic work by Helen Zimmern from 1889, *The Hansa Towns and the Hanseatic League*, which has been republished under Paphos Publishers in 2018. See also David Nicolle, *Forces of the Hanseatic League: thirteenth–fifteenth Centuries* (Osprey Publishing; London, 2014).

[41]Rhiman A. Rotz, 'The Lubeck Uprising of 1408 and the Decline of the Hanseatic League', Proceedings of the American Philosophical Society, Vol. 121, No. 1 (Feb. 15, 1977), pp. 1-45.

[42]See the English case in Hyman Palais, 'England's First Attempt to Break the Commercial Monopoly of the
Hanseatic League, 1377-1380', *The American Historical Review*, Vol. 64, No. 4 (July., 1959), pp. 852-865.

[43]See David K. Bjork, 'Three Hansa Towns and Archives: Bruges, Lübeck, Tallinn', *Pacific Historical Review*, Vol. 9, No. 3 (Sep., 1940), pp. 297-306; p. 297.

[44]Heinz Schilling, 'The Reformation in the Hanseatic Cities', *The Sixteenth Century Journal*, Vol. 14, No. 4 (Winter, 1983), pp. 443-456.

[45]Paul Douglas Lockhart, 'Denmark and the Empire: A Reassessment of Danish Foreign Policy under King Christian IV', pp. 403-404.

[46]See Wedgewood, *Thirty Years War*, pp. 195-196.

[47]These extracts were provided by Peter H. Wilson, *Sourcebook*, pp. 95-97.

[48]See Pursell, *The Winter King*, pp. 239-240.

[49]An interesting examination of Milan during the context of the seventeenth century is found in Stefano D'Amico, 'Rebirth of a City: Immigration and Trade in Milan, 1630-59', *The Sixteenth Century Journal*, Vol. 32, No, 3 (Autumn, 2001), pp. 697-721.

[50]See Niccolò Capponi, 'Le Palle di Marte: Military Strategy and Diplomacy in the Grand Duchy of Tuscany under Ferdinand II de' Medici (1621-1670)', *The Journal of Military History*, Vol. 68, No. 4 (Oct., 2004), pp. 1105-1141.

[51]Geoffrey Parker, *Thirty Years War*, pp. 37-38.

[52]Wedgewood, *Thirty Years War*, pp. 191-192.

[53]Parker, *Thirty Years War*, p. 86.

[54]Wedgewood, *Thirty Years War*, p. 202.

[55]See Pursell, *The Winter King*, pp. 241-243.

[56]See Brennan Pursell, *The Winter King*, pp. 244-246.

[57]Quoted in Wilson, *Sourcebook*, p. 97.

[58]Quoted in Mortimer, *Wallenstein*, p. 92.

[59]*Ibid*, p. 96.

[60]*Ibid*, pp. 96-97.

[61]These developments are covered by Pursell, *The Winter King*, pp. 258-260.

[62]Paul Douglas Lockhart, 'Denmark and the Empire: A Reassessment of Danish Foreign Policy under King Christian IV', pp. 407-408.

[63]See Peter H. Wilson, *Europe's Tragedy*, pp. 419-420.

[64]Mortimer, *Wallenstein*, pp. 99-100.

[65]See Andrzej Wyrobisz, 'Power and Towns in the Polish Gentry Commonwealth: The Polish-Lithuanian State in the Sixteenth and Seventeenth Centuries', *Theory and Society*, Vol. 18, No. 5, Special Issue on Cities and States in Europe,1000-1800 (Sep., 1989), pp. 611-630; pp. 612-613.

[66]Both letters quoted in Wilson, *Sourcebook*, pp. 106-107.

[67]Quoted in Wilson, *Sourcebook*, p. 102.

[68]Quoted in *Ibid*, pp. 103-104.

[69]Quoted in *Ibid*, p. 104.

[70]Mortimer, *Wallenstein*, pp. 107-110.

[71]Wilson, *Europe's Tragedy*, pp. 426-428.

[72]Mortimer, *Wallenstein*, p. 101.

[73]Wilson, *Europe's Tragedy*, p. 429.

[74]Quoted in Wilson, *Sourcebook*, p. 107.

[75]Mortimer, *Wallenstein*, p. 102.

[76]Wilson, *Europe's Tragedy*, p. 431.

[77]Wedgewood, *Thirty Years War*, p. 229.

[78]Wilson, *Europe's Tragedy*, pp. 432-433.

The sack of Magdeburg

The relief of Breisach, 1633 (Jusepe Leonardo)

CHAPTER THIRTEEN
"Hubris and Holiness"

ONE: So Many Foreign Threads
TWO: The Sectarian Shadow
THREE: Doing God's Work

ONE

So Many Foreign Threads

The war had been largely favourable for Wallenstein, but the peace would leave a great deal to be desired. Stralsund, that stubborn city, frustrated the attempts of the Habsburgs to establish a Baltic fleet, and with that dream up in smoke for the moment, there was no way to pressure the Danish King in his home islands. At the same time, while he was militarily secure, Christian IV was domestically besieged. A large proportion of his nobility – who had never wanted the war in the first place – had been dragged into the conflict with the Emperor once Wallenstein had invaded up the Danish Jutland peninsula in 1627. While there, Wallenstein secured invaluable quartering for his soldiers, but he also ravaged the lands of this same nobility, and piled pressure upon the Danish King to save his ruined nobles before it was too late.[1]

This pressure proved significant in the end and acting through the Council the nobility leveraged their position to wrest control over foreign affairs from their King. If they had anything to say about it, there would no more 'royal adventures' in their lifetimes. This development would have several consequences for King Christian in the future, but first he had to end the war. As we have seen, Wallenstein was unable to reach him in Copenhagen, and thus achieve the decisive, crushing victory which the Emperor desired. In addition, Wallenstein's concerns regarding the unification of the Baltic against the Habsburgs grew as the months progressed, and the King of Sweden made more progress in his war with Poland. Once the Swedish-Polish War was concluded, Sweden would be free to join its Baltic neighbour in battling the Habsburgs; Wallenstein wanted Denmark to be out of the war before this could happen. Notwithstanding Christian's failure at Wolgast in September 1628, Wallenstein remained fearful of the combined resources of Denmark and Sweden against the Emperor. He was therefore more amenable to compromise at the peace negotiations.

These negotiations had been underway for some time at Lubeck, but as Geoff Mortimer discerned, these were merely negotiations 'after the fashion of the times', whereby...

...each side made wildly unrealistic demands, responded to proposals only after the maximum possible delay, and preferred to argue over protocol rather than substance, all the while hoping that some success of their commanders in the field might improve their negotiating positions.[2]

This tactic of negotiating while fighting reared its disruptive head again two decades later, when the negotiations for the Peace of Westphalia dragged on incessantly as both sides attempted to improve their diplomatic positions by wresting a new triumph from the battlefield. Since September 1627, both Wallenstein in cooperation with the Emperor, and the Catholic League under Count Tilly, had drafted a peace proposal for the King of Denmark to consider. While 1627 had been a year of defeat for the Danish King, it was also the year before Stralsund demonstrated the futility of the Habsburgs' Baltic design. Christian recognised by the winter of 1628-29 that his best opportunity for achieving a favourable peace depended upon his potential to realise the Habsburgs' fears.

His military forces were spent, and he had only his navy left to patrol the Baltic, but Christian's greatest asset was diplomatic. Rather than buckle under the pressure and cave to the Emperor's stringent peace demands, he would make a very public show of meeting with his old nemesis, Gustavus Adolphus, the King of Sweden. If Wallenstein truly feared the possibility of the Baltic uniting against his Emperor, then Christian was determined to go as far as possible towards making the generalissimo believe that this eventuality was right around the corner, whether he intended to go all the way or not. Bluffing, as the Danish King understood, was his best bet.

Exactly what terms could have compelled Christian to make a show of cooperating with his regional foe? In September 1627, and the terms which were still being peddled by early 1629, the Emperor was demanding the following terms be fulfilled before peace would be considered. First, Christian would have to surrender his Imperial offices, which included those bishoprics which he had acquired for his sons. Second, he would have to cede either Holstein or Gluckstadt, the latter being a city founded by Christian in 1617 to compete with the Imperial Free City of Hamburg. Third, he would have to purchase from the Emperor Holstein, Jutland and Schleswig at two million reichsthalers each; incidentally, this was the same total of six million reichsthalers which Frederick V was charged with paying by Emperor Ferdinand several years' before for breaking the peace.

In the negotiations of January 1629, the Emperor urged further concessions, whereby Christian would commit to not interfere in the Empire ever again, he would financially compensate the Emperor for the war and, most impossible of all, he would cede Jutland indefinitely to the Emperor. These severe additions to the already impossible peace convinced Christian that the Emperor and his chief negotiator at the Lubeck conference, Wallenstein, would not give in unless he held some leverage over them.[4] For his part, Wallenstein was wary of demanding too harsh a peace from the Danish King, for two major reasons. First, he feared pushing Christian into the arms of the Swedish King and creating the aforementioned Baltic union against the Emperor, and second, Wallenstein knew that Denmark's Dutch and English allies could not allow such stringent terms to be accepted.

Rather than allow this peace to be agreed, it was highly likely that London and The Hague would rally around Christian and potentially deepen the conflict. The two concerns were thus connected, since Wallenstein above all wished to end the war in time to deal with whatever the King of Sweden planned, and to enjoy his new estates. Wallenstein by no means intended to liberate the Danish King from his war, but he was willing to reduce the burden of the peace. The more favourable peace was to the Danish King, the more likely he was to accept it. Fortunately for Christian, this left him with some opportunities to exploit Wallenstein's fears as well as his generosity. As the negotiations at Lubeck stalled, Christian moved to meet with the King of Sweden at the town of Ulvsback in February 1629, in a bid to impress upon Wallenstein just how close to establishing the nightmare Baltic arrangement Denmark was. The bluff paid off spectacularly and must be considered one of the great successes of Christian IV's war. Although its results were to ease the harshness of the peace terms, the actual atmosphere of the meeting between the two Northern monarchs was, predictably, less than warm.[5]

The scene of the two Baltic foes meeting together to combine against the greater threat is arguably the most striking image provided by C.V. Wedgewood.[6] The scene is one of a dejected Danish King in receipt of a pep talk from his Swedish counterpart, who plies him with encouragement, and of frightful hypothetical scenarios, where Wallenstein secures a fleet and conquers the Baltic for Vienna, eliminating Protestantism and the freedom of both monarchs in the process. In response to Christian's insistence that his kingdom was devastated and had no fight left in it, Gustavus retorted that Sweden had been fighting continuously for thirty years, even inviting the Danish King to feel the bullet in his shoulder as proof of his zeal for the cause. So long as it was the will of God, Gustavus insisted, he would go on fighting, and he urged Christian to do the same.

Christian gave limp, noncommittal replies, always reverting to the reality of Denmark's domestic and fiscal situation. In frustration did Christian ask the fanatical Gustavus, *What business has Your Majesty in Germany?* This question left the Swedish King momentarily stunned. Recovering, Gustavus let loose a reply which approached hysterical proportions, shouting:

> Is that worth asking? Your Majesty can be sure, that be he who he will that does this to us, Emperor or King, prince or Republic or – nay, or a thousand devils – we will so take each other by the ears that our hair shall fly out in handfuls.

This appeal was lost on Christian though, as it was always bound to be, since the Danish King had not travelled to meet with his Swedish rival for any other purpose other than to frighten Wallenstein. Still, regardless of the accuracy of Wedgewood's account, it is worth retelling for its sheer symbolism and its dramatic qualities. Indeed, Wallenstein was compelled first to send more soldiers to reinforce the flagging Poles, and second to agree to the more moderate peace proposals which would bring the Danish War to an end as soon as possible.[6] The Peace of Lubeck was signed on 22 May 1629, and while its terms were far from a triumph for King Christian IV, they certainly liberated him from the most insufferable articles of previous treaties.[7] One historian has even called the Peace of Lubeck 'in many senses a major diplomatic victory' for the Danish King.[8]

By this treaty, Christian preserved his kingdom intact, but was forced to relinquish suzerainty over the North German bishoprics, leaving his sons out of pocket. Christian would not be forced to pay any reparations to the Emperor, but he would have to refrain from interfering in Germany – not that he was in any position to do so in 1629. The war had been nothing short of a disaster, even if the peace terms did not reflect this. Its consequences were felt most sharply in the aftermath of the conflict, as the King was faced with three interconnected dilemmas. The first was that the war had wiped out his private fortune, which rendered Christian unlikely to engage in any independent pursuits as Duke of Holstein anytime soon. In line with the second point, it also made Christian more dependent on his nobility, who were in no mood to play ball after being dragged into a war they had never wanted. With their lands ravaged and scores to settle, the Danish nobility projected their powers and influence into the State Council for the remainder of Christian's reign, and required additional concessions in return for any further steps Christian wished to take.

Trapped by his nobility, Christian was equally isolated abroad, as the third consequence was to invoke the ire of the English and Dutch. Christian could quite rightly have reasoned that this alienation from The Hague and London was unfair, since his kingdom had been led into a war based on promises as per the Hague Alliance, which his partners had demonstrably failed to fulfil. Christian had essentially been left to the wolves as the English focused on their Spanish and French conflicts, and the Dutch rallied against the Brussels government. Meanwhile, the subsidies dried up, and any pretence of strategic cooperation went out the window until they received whiffs of the uncompromising peace terms from the Emperor, which would have left them considerably out of pocket. Thus, the Peace of Lubeck represented the final nail in the coffin of the Hague Alliance, a league which never succeeded in getting off the ground in the first place. Christian may not have mourned the loss of his unreliable allies, which included his family members, but he would have known that the Peace of Lubeck left him with fewer choices if he wished to recoup his losses in the future, as he intended to do.

A little more than a year after the Peace of Lubeck, Christian was forced to watch as his Swedish rival intervened in Germany. This time, a more important paymaster than either England or the Netherlands stepped forward: France. Thanks to French money and the brilliance of the Swedish King, Christian's unhappy destiny was to be eclipsed by his Baltic rival. The Danish-Swedish hostility in turn was extended from the Baltic into Central Germany and beyond. His junior status to Gustavus Adolphus was something King Christian IV would never accept. He took full advantage of the shifting fortunes of war during the 1630s to regain control over the Lower Saxon Circle, and thereby regain the lucrative bishoprics for his sons. Indeed, he did not relinquish his status as the predominant Baltic power lightly; Christian's role in the Thirty Years War was by no means complete, but in 1629, he was forced to fade momentarily from view.[9]

The end of the Danish War in May 1629 did not mean the end of Frederick V's campaign. Incredibly, his war with the Emperor was nearing its tenth birthday, but the dispossessed Elector Palatine strove to remind his remaining friends that the importance and potency of the cause had not diminished with the passage of time. Indeed, as we will see, this cause acquired further baggage with the passage of the Edict of Restitution in March 1629, a document which aimed to turn back the clock in the Empire, empower the Catholic Church, fulfil the Counter-Reformation and stymy perhaps forever the spread of Protestantism. This Edict and its consequences would prove a step too far for many German and foreign potentates alike, as we shall see later, but for now it remains to analyse the considerable diplomatic activities of the various parties in Europe.

The year 1629 began tragically for Frederick V. Weighed down by the dismal failure of the Danish War and the distracted English war effort, Frederick may have feared that his allies would never fully cooperate to reinstate him or his family in the Palatinate. Turning to the King of Sweden gradually in the 1620s, as his best, perhaps his final, hope, Frederick was crushed by a loss closer to home on 17 January, when his first-born son Frederick Henry drowned. He was just 15. The two had been travelling to Amsterdam – incidentally, to gaze at the tremendous Dutch victory in seizing the Spanish treasure fleet – but a larger boat had collided with their own. Frederick had initially opposed his son joining him for the journey but had reasoned in the end that Frederick Henry could benefit from a change of scene.

This decision surely haunted him for the rest of his life but combined with the recurring bouts of bad news from the Empire, it had the potential to send him grieving to an early grave. 'It having pleased God', Frederick lamented, 'to add to my preceding hardships with a new affliction, the pain of which cannot be expressed with the pen.' By the middle of 1629 Frederick was writing to Count Thurn, the most renowned of Bohemia's exiles, to exclaim that 'God has nearly destroyed me through the loss of my most beloved son, which has surpassed all previous agonies.' At the same time he consoled himself through his faith, accepting that:

> It is reasonable that I submit myself to it as to that which is always just and good, though human sense has difficulty comprehending it…Since the hand of the one who governs all things has ordained it so, it is for me to adore Him and to submit myself, hoping his hand will strengthen me and change everything for the better.

As far as Frederick could see with his own eyes, only the timely intervention of the King of Sweden had the potential to 'change everything for the better.' Yet, Frederick was right to hope, for even while his entreaties to the beleaguered English and Dutch were largely in vain, the war in Germany and between Sweden and Poland had come to the attention of France. Cardinal Richelieu, France's eminent diplomatic and stately genius, was on the case. In a supremely delicate balance, Richelieu was engaging in complex diplomatic negotiations with the Swedish and Polish Kings. In time, these negotiations would produce fruit, because they freed Gustavus Adolphus from his Polish preoccupations, and enabled him to refocus his attentions on Germany as Frederick had for so long hoped he would. It was unfortunate that this shift in Swedish attentions had taken as long as it had, but soon enough, the Swedish King was to restore all faith Frederick had lost. By Gustavus' triumphs and Richelieu's intervention, Frederick could believe that God had not left him.[10]

With the conclusion of the war with Denmark, it might have been reasonable to expect that some form of lasting peace would at last arrive in the Holy Roman Empire. After over a decade of warfare, many fortunes had been wiped out; livelihoods had been destroyed; towns and villages laid to waste; atrocities committed and returned in answer; the countryside plundered; the harvests stolen; the people laid low or forced into exile. The German heartland in particular was affected, but the war had not ceased to reach even the remote corners of the Empire. The Lower Saxon Circle had not been spared just because it had been under the protection of the Danish King. The Duchy of Mecklenburg had not been secure simply because it was ruled by a distinguished house. Electoral titles, religious settlements and constitutional traditions evidently meant little to the Emperor so long as the eventual victory was assured and his debts were paid.

Unfortunately for Ferdinand, during 1628-1630, his debts increased as did his foreign commitments. The passing of the Edict of Restitution necessitated keeping Wallenstein's army in the field to impose it on the unwilling princes of the Empire. Wallenstein was far from pleased with the new mission. He was unenthusiastic about the effect which forcing a religious settlement would have not just on Germans, but also on foreign potentates, above all the Swedish and French. The former would be provided with another plank upon which their intervention in the Empire could legitimised, and the latter could use the opportunity provided by the Edict to pose as the friend to all liberty-loving Germans, thereby creating a third party in Germany, perhaps joined by the disenchanted Saxon and Brandenburg Electors.

These concerns were deeply felt by Wallenstein, who gives the impression of wanting to have his debts paid off, to return to his estates, and to prepare to satisfy Sweden so that any elongation of the conflict in Germany would be avoided, and his gains protected. Instead, what Wallenstein found in his Emperor were further demands predicated on his personal supremacy, and while this Emperor had made Wallenstein a Duke two times over, and granted him more power than he could ever have imagined, the conclusion of the Peace of Lubeck marks the beginning of the end of Wallenstein's positive relationship with the Emperor. The deterioration of this relationship was to prove fatal to both men for different reasons, but in summer 1629, Wallenstein was faced with yet another dilemma: the Emperor's demands to provide troops not only to impose the new Edict, but also to help out his Spanish cousins in North Italy.[11]

The War of the Mantuan Succession was a proxy war of the Franco-Spanish conflict that would eventually explode out into the open in 1635, and the conflict over North Italy was itself an extension of the previous skirmishes for influence over the Val Telline Alpine passes which had punctuated the early and mid-1620s. France, with its Italian allies in Savoy and Venice, faced the Spanish-Habsburg Italian allies of Milan and Tuscany, with devastating consequences not only for that portion of Italy, but also for wider Habsburg strategic interests and, more damningly, the Emperor's relationship with the Pope. The French were by no means free to pursue their interests in Italy with their full attention. It is a striking fact of the Thirty Years War that much hinged on the years 1628-30, and arguably 1628 in particular. In that year alone, four important sieges took place – one at Stralsund, as we have seen, another at Danzig in the Baltic by Swedish troops, and another of Mantua, with the fourth and most threatening one for French internal stability being the siege of La Rochelle, the stronghold of the Protestant French Huguenots.

It was in many respects a race to conclude each of these sieges first, and whoever was successful would acquire a distinct advantage over his rivals. This, at least, was what the strategic situation of 1628 seemed to infer, but the actual outcome was less straightforward.[12] It was good news to Vienna and Madrid that the King of Sweden failed in his efforts to seize Danzig, the greatest prize in the Polish-Lithuanian Commonwealth, but it was unfortunate that the Polish King's resources were too depleted to take advantage of this pyric victory. In addition, the Habsburgs lost the siege of Stralsund, frustrating their efforts to realise the Baltic design.

The immediate significance of the Swedish failure at Danzig and subsequent Polish victories is seen in the new force it imbued in the Swedish King to reach a peace with his Polish cousin. After several years of conflict in Poland, Gustavus Adolphus learned but also lost a great deal. He was by no means an undefeated generalissimo, as Count Tilly was; instead he was a demonstrated innovator, and a skilled leader of men on the battlefield.[13] As comfortable as he was in battle, Gustavus was wise enough to accept French mediation in his war. French action here demonstrates not only the wide strategic vision of the French first minister, but also the increasingly international character of the Thirty Years War. Once consigned to a Bohemian revolt, the conflict in the Empire had evidently mutated far outside the confines of its regional box, to the point that French agents were conspiring to welcome the Scandinavian monarch into Germany. This hugely significant escalation in the stakes and scope of the Thirty Years War should not be understated, but this was far from the final instance where concerted diplomatic efforts widened the reach of the war.

The Truce of Altmark was signed on 16 September 1629, and upon its conclusion Sweden and Poland concluded a truce for six years. This provided the King of Sweden with an unparalleled opportunity to intervene in Germany, but as we will discover, he was not content to rely upon the pretences of a truce alone to secure his Polish flank. By September 1629 Gustavus learned of the Edict of Restitution, which helped couch his later actions in religious terms, but it is worth bearing in mind Gustavus' security concerns for the North German shores as a motive behind his intervention. So long as Mecklenburg and Pomerania's ports faced Habsburg seizure or domination, Sweden could never be safe.

We also cannot discount Gustavus' genuine grievances which he held against the Emperor and Wallenstein, for intervening on the side of the Polish King. These motives may be simplified as religion, strategy and vengeance, and to them we can add the more obvious question of ambition, a trait which the King of Sweden certainly possessed. By pushing back the Habsburgs and occupying the Baltic ports, not only would he secure Swedish security, he would also cement his legend and earn glory for his House.[14] While Gustavus Adolphus' motives for intervention in the Holy Roman Empire are important topics for discussion, it must be underlined that French diplomacy made it possible. Cardinal Richelieu's activity in this regard is undoubtedly significant, but it should be placed in the context of his additional interests in North Italy. It followed that a Habsburg court distracted by a Swedish War would not be able to focus its full attention on the Mantuan conflict, and thus the wide scope of Richelieu's diplomatic activities – not to mention the interconnected nature of the Thirty Years War' related conflicts – looms again into view.[15]

In spite of Richelieu's skill, misfortune also stalked the French, as the stakes of the siege of La Rochelle were greatly increased when an English fleet dramatically sailed to relieve the French Protestants in spring 1628. This unwelcome and untimely Anglo-French War led to a temporary rapprochement of sorts between Paris and Madrid, as both courts attended to their most pressing theatres in the Netherlands and at La Rochelle. This reduction in Franco-Spanish tensions lasted only as long as it suited both sides though, and the war in Mantua effectively killed any hope of Habsburg-Bourbon cooperation in its cradle.[16] At the same time, the ability of both sides to claim some form of victory in the conclusion of the Mantuan War must be balanced against the losing efforts of the Spanish against the Dutch – a state of affairs which greatly benefited France, and weakened the overall Habsburg position in the Empire as well.

These interconnected conflicts produced two major results. The first was that they weakened the Emperor, as Ferdinand felt compelled to send soldiers from Wallenstein's army to support the Spanish, just as Wallenstein watched the movements of the King of Sweden with increasing concern. Second, the dual commitment of the King of Spain to fight for his regime in the Spanish Netherlands and in North Italy at the same time eroded his power and his finances still further. This weakening of the King of Spain meant that he was less than enthusiastic about the Emperor's decision to implement the Edict of Restitution on the Empire. Rather than waste soldiers in that contentious endeavour, King Philip IV of Spain believed that the Emperor should instead support his dynasty in the Netherlands and North Italy, where the true threats resided. These disagreements over policy and the precedence of certain issues might have ruptured the Habsburg branches, but for Vienna and Madrid having no choice other than to work feverishly together.

Dependence on Spain was both necessitated and threatened by the worsening situation in Germany, where resistance to Wallenstein's enormous army and the consumption of resources to feed it had long been a bone of contention. Since the Electoral meeting at Muhlhausen in September 1627, where Frederick V's Electoral titles were confirmed stripped, those present had voiced their disapproval of the Emperor's generalissimo's power and his swollen army, which was then as large as 112,700 men. 'Territorial rulers', the German leaders had lamented, 'are at the mercy of Colonels and Captains, who are uninvited war profiteers and criminals, breaking the laws of the Empire.' The Elector of Mainz would go one further in December 1629, when he addressed the pertinent question: if the King of Denmark, the enemy of the Empire, was defeated, then what was Wallenstein's army needed for? As he wrote in his own words:

> Since the Duke of Friedland [Wallenstein] has up to now disgusted and
> offended to the utmost nearly each and every territorial ruler in the Empire;
> and although the present situation has moved him to be more cautious, he
> has not given up his plans to retain Mecklenburg by virtue of his Imperial
> command.

The argument that Wallenstein required the resources of Mecklenburg
to repay the Emperor's considerable debt to him would have fallen on
unsympathetic ears.[17] So long as Ferdinand wanted his son confirmed as his
successor, he would have to fall in line with their wishes, and in March 1630,
the Imperial Arch-Chancellor announced to the seven Electors of the Empire
that their presence would be required at a meeting in Regensburg on 3 June. In
the meantime, during the months between the signing of peace with Denmark
and the assembly of all electors at Regensburg, the Emperor had been busy.
Ferdinand, while he was eager to acquire the necessary concessions, was
equally determined to shape the Empire in his own image, using Wallenstein
as his sword and the Catholic Church as his shield. Whether they liked it or
not, the Emperor expected his enemies to bow.

TWO
The Sectarian Shadow

It was then, for the first time, that we learned from experience…that neither plague, nor war, nor hostile foreign incursions into our land, neither pillage nor fire, could do so much harm to good people as frequent changes in the value of money.

This was the assessment given by a contemporary of Bohemia in 1633, over a decade after the Bohemian revolt had been crushed by the Habsburgs.[18] The provinces of Silesia, Moravia and Bohemia which constituted that kingdom of Bohemia of a bygone age suffered terribly during the Thirty Years War, an obvious fact considering it nursed that conflict into being, but one which deserves emphasis nonetheless. In 1600, with a population just shy of three million, Bohemia was the most prosperous part of the Habsburgs' domains. Fifty years later, the guts of a million citizens had fled or perished, while the kingdom of Bohemia was itself completely recast in a new role.[19] The Kingdom of Bohemia would no longer boast proudly independent institutions or a sovereign crown. Instead, Bohemia was destined to be merely the appendage of the Austrian Habsburg Empire. This was to be the legacy which Ferdinand II left behind, but it was far from the only contribution he made.

Bohemia was fastened to Vienna, its religious pluralism quashed, and its crown was made a hereditary Habsburg institution. To achieve these ends the native Bohemia nobility had been dispossessed and destroyed, and with them went the old culture of Bohemia as well. The power of land became especially important as the coinage became debased, and citizens turned to barter where they could rather than hold onto the worthless copper coins. A theme of economic crisis ripped through Europe in the early seventeenth century,[20] and while one historian has remarked that Bohemia's economic woes were unconnected with those of the rest of Europe,[21] it is still significant that the war exacerbated liquidity problems and caused disastrous inflation across the continent. An oft used example was the financial woes of the Kings of Spain, who declared bankruptcy several times, and endured periodical bouts of financial crisis, above all in 1607, 1627 and 1647, when the cumulative effect of minting so many debased copper coins ruined bankers and shattered confidence in Madrid.[22]

Ferdinand had played his part in this unfortunate procedure in the interest of quickly selling off Bohemian land. To acquire the sum of thirty million florins, which would be used to pay his debts and demobilise the army, the Emperor authorised a scheme whereby mints were permitted to issue millions of coins at a greatly reduced rate of silver content. The immediate result was that the fifteen members of this scheme – which included Wallenstein – bought off their land, and they became wealthy through their possession of that land. However, the coins which they had created to gain these assets then entered circulation in the country, with disastrous consequences. Initially only those rebels or relatives of rebels fled Bohemia, but the cumulative effects of a ruined nobility and worthless currency compelled tens of thousands to leave, in spite of Vienna's warnings against such a journey. The most fascinating demographic impact of this exodus is seen in neighbouring Saxony, where most Bohemian exiles fled. In 1623, the Czech Church in Dresden boasted only a handful of people, but by 1630, the Bohemian exiles were so great in number that Saxon pamphleteers worked to learn the language of the immigrant, so that he could be converted to the Lutheran creed.[23]

Ferdinand found that once he had destroyed the wealth and power of the old nobility, he was able to succeed where his predecessors had failed in building a loyal Bohemian state. In line with this new regime, Ferdinand introduced special institutions to rule them in his name and based his legitimacy on new constitutions which were crafted in turn for Austria (1625), Bohemia (1627) and Moravia (1628). The estates in both Austria and Bohemia had their influence and power greatly reduced, and Ferdinand filled this power vacuum with his own authority. A notable trend is thus apparent when one considers the course of the Thirty Years War; as the Emperor's forces achieved more triumphs and he gained more power; the Habsburg Hereditary Lands were brought more under his absolutist thumb. Significantly we should recall that when creating the Habsburg army Ferdinand was aided by self-interested servants like Wallenstein, who were more than happy to leverage their personal power in Bohemia to the benefit of their Emperor and themselves.[24]

Ferdinand's inherent weakness at the beginning of the conflict and his relative poverty are explained, as we have learned, by the unruliness of the Hereditary Lands in years past, the lack of stable financial assets to pay any personal army, and the absence of an organised structure with which to organise one. Thus, Ferdinand depended upon personal mercenaries like Albrecht of Wallenstein or Maximillian of Bavaria, and he paid both individuals with confiscated land and titles, rather than money. It is therefore possible to argue that Ferdinand's very weakness pushed him into a corner, since to achieve decisive victory against his enemies he had to violate the Imperial constitution by promising land that was not his, and he overcame any objections by making use of the armies which now answered to him. So long as no concerted efforts were made to destroy this strategy, Ferdinand was able to get away with it, and endure the mute protests of the Elector of Saxony, who had himself been paid off by the lands of Lusatia in 1620.

The key problem with depending upon powerful allies, rather than being in possession of that power yourself, was one of conviction. Ferdinand did not wish to merely defeat his enemies and restore the security and prestige of his dynasty to its Hereditary Lands, he also wished to serve as the conduit of the Counter-Reformation. For a time, this desire was met with equal fervour from Maximillian of Bavaria, who had occupied the Upper Palatinate in 1621, and imposed his own version of re-Catholicisation. Catholicism had not been practiced in the Upper Palatinate since the 1540s, which provided the two Jesuits that attempted to celebrate Mass with something of a conundrum when no chalice could be found across the land. The purge of these lands proceeded slowly and carefully, since much of its administration remained in the hands of largely Calvinist officials, who could not be instantly expelled, or the region would fall into anarchy. By 1625, with more of a handle on the situation, the Upper Palatinate's administration was purged. In 1626 Calvinist ministers were expelled, and in 1628, Lutherans were given six months to either convert or to leave the country. By that point, there was no power that could challenge the Bavarian and Habsburg supremacy in Central Europe, but that did not stop the common people from trying.

In Upper Austria, a portion of the Emperor's lands which had a long history of religious independence and opposition to their overlord, a great and terrible revolt was ignited in 1626 when the people were pushed too far. It was caused technically by Bavarian actions, since Maximillian of Bavaria occupied Upper Austria in pledge for his debts to the Emperor. However, since Upper Austria was a part of the Emperor's domains, it meant that Ferdinand had the final say, and from the beginning he wished to extirpate heresy wherever it was found.[25] Upper Austria had possessed a thriving Protestant community for several decades, and its people had even petitioned the Emperor for their own Letter of Majesty in 1612 in reaction to the similar concession to Bohemia.[26] Furthermore, the Upper Austrian estates had entered into an alliance with the Bohemian rebels, and thus went into open rebellion against Ferdinand. Maximillian had crushed this rebellion, since Ferdinand had not the means to police or pacify his own ancestral lands, and the Duke of Bavaria left behind five thousand men to garrison the region.

Maximillian was wealthy, but his resources were not infinite. Rather than pay these soldiers out of his own pocket, he expected the Upper Austrian garrison to wrest its pay from the contributions provided by the local citizens. On top of these contributions, Maximillian was effectively permitted to feed off the tax base of both Upper Austria and the Upper Palatinate. This, the Emperor hoped, would go some way towards paying off the debts he owed to the Duke of Bavaria, and Maximillian thus levied taxes worth 240,000 thalers annually from each territory. Just as matters appeared to be proceeding smoothly though, the Emperor insisted that in the case of Upper Austria, he was not content with the pace of re-Catholicisation. While the example of the Upper Palatinate demonstrated that a population could be peacefully converted, to the Emperor the pace of this process was much too slow for his liking.

Since Upper Austria was technically still the Emperor's land, Maximillian reluctantly agreed to speed up the conversion process. In October 1624 the expulsion of all Protestant pastors and schoolteachers was announced, and intolerance was furthered by the establishment of the Reformation Commission in October 1625. In this microcosm of the Habsburg Hereditary Lands we can see an indication of what Ferdinand planned for the entire Holy Roman Empire, since one of the missions handed to the Reformation Commission was the recovery of all secularised church lands, effectively turning back the clock in Upper Austria to the period before the 1570s when Protestantism first arrived in the region in force. The different structure of the Lutheran and Calvinist creeds lessened the importance of monasteries, and as the Catholic clergy were gradually edged out, these lands were sold to the highest bidder or were occupied by new tenants. This process had taken root all across the Empire, and in some cases, entire bishoprics like Magdeburg had been secularised in this way. To secularise a bishopric meant to alienate the land from the Catholic Church, and to recast the control over the land in terms of the Empire's secular land rights.

By 1629, first and sometimes second-generation German potentates ruled over land which had once been owned by the Catholic Church. The idea that these figures could be removed, and the lands returned to their 'rightful' Catholic owners, was guaranteed to make the inhabitants unhappy. This aside from the fact that the Habsburgs had endured chronic shortages of priests to stock even their new religious order in Bohemia – did Ferdinand have a plan to fill these new Catholic positions in Upper Austria, let alone the entirety of the Empire?[27] Evidently, he did not learn his lesson from the uproar caused by the restoration of Catholic Church land in Upper Austria. The revolt in that unhappy region boiled over in May 1626, after a ruling insisting that all Protestants had to leave the country, and the arbitrary execution of some seventeen parishioners, who had been chosen by lot, was ordered by the Emperor to set an example.

The message was received loud and clear, and the people rose up in revolt just as Maximillian had feared. The rebels found their leader in Stephen Fadinger, a farmer of modest means, who captured the anger and frustration of the people, Catholics and Protestants alike, who had been aggrieved by a fourteen-fold increase in taxation in the previous years. In addition, the citizens of Upper Austria were weary of the presence of the Bavarian troops, and many had suffered to see their savings wiped out with the currency crisis of 1621-23. Fadinger's forces routed an army of Bavarian soldiers in May, and laid siege to the Upper Austrian capital of Linz shortly thereafter. The organisation and zeal of the rebels may have caught the Habsburgs by surprise, but luck was on the side of the Emperor. In July, Fadinger was killed in the trenches of the siege, and his cause withered without its leader. Taking advantage of the circumstances, the rebels had attempted to make contact with King Christian IV, who was then preparing for his doomed initial offensive against the forces of Count Tilly, but with limited success.

Thereafter, the rebels took to the hills, and Maximillian was forced to request that some twelve thousand soldiers be drafted in to root out the guerrillas and put the rebellion down. It was an immensely costly misstep by a harsh administration, and the rebels were able to claim victory in May 1628, when the Upper Palatinate was sold to Maximillian and the Emperor was absolved of his debts to Bavaria in return. With no debts outstanding, there was no need for Maximillian to occupy Upper Austria in lieu of payment, and the region was returned to Habsburg control. As a reflection on the shortage of fully trained priests, the Papacy granted permission for Ferdinand to stock the Upper Austrian parishes with regular clergy, some of whom were newly converted from the Lutheran faith. The sheer lack of priests gave the Emperor little choice other than to rely on men of dubious piety for now, on the understanding that the situation would be rectified within a generation.[28]

In September 1627, the electors sent representatives to meet at Muhlhausen, as the implications for the anticipated defeat of Denmark were considered. It was at this meeting that Ferdinand's envoy communicated his master's wish – it was time to discuss the religious state of Germany, and to redress the injustice done to Catholics in the past, who had suffered the loss of their lands. This was, Ferdinand claimed, 'the great gain and fruit of the war' which he had been mulling over for some time. Perhaps, having learned that native revolts against religious reorganisation could be defeated by the simple application of force, Ferdinand felt confident to challenge the whole of Germany now that his generalissimo was in the ascendant. In any case, the challenge would be far greater, since it would transpire that the Emperor wished to turn back the clock not to the 1570s, as he had done in Upper Austria, but to a generation earlier, when the 1555 Peace of Augsburg had been signed.[29]

It must be remembered that the Emperor was not acting alone; he was spurred on by the Jesuits, and his confessor William Lamormaini, but also by the Catholic party resident at Muhlhausen, who expected some redress for Catholic grievances to come as part of any peace settlement. Indeed, we should bear in mind the virtually unbroken string of Catholic victories since 1620, which had the effect of confirming the Catholic creed as the only true interpretation, and as all Catholic soldiers as God's anointed. This sharpened the confessional element of the war, as the Catholic Habsburgs continued to ride high, creating an important perception, as Peter H. Wilson noted:

> The battle of Stadtlohn was fought on the feast of Transfiguration in 1623, while a shooting star before the battle of Lutter in 1626 was interpreted as a fiery sword pointing towards the Danish forces who were routed the following day. Such incidents could be fitted into a pattern established by the naval victory over the Ottomans at Lepanto in 1571 and seemed to suggest that God had summoned the faithful to holy war against infidels and heretics.[30]

Seen in this light, the preceding years were not merely a triumph for the Emperor and his allies, but a triumph also for Catholicism. Surprisingly perhaps, Ferdinand hesitated in this mission, and sought to gauge the opinions of the other Catholic electors in July 1627 before the Muhlhausen meeting assembled that September. The central message from that meeting was that the Catholics did not wish to eliminate Protestantism – they wished only to see church property returned to its former owners; a simple request which belied the immensely contentious nature of the task. The Elector of Mainz and the newly minted Elector of Bavaria weighed in on the debate, instructing the Emperor in their turn that monasteries, rather than the more controversial bishoprics, should be targeted, while Maximillian of Bavaria cynically requested that only adherents to the 1530 interpretation of the Augsburg Confession should be allowed to enjoy the privileges of the 1555 Peace of Augsburg.

This piece of legislative acrobatics on Maximillian's part was accomplished for the key purpose of excluding all Calvinists from the end settlement. If all Calvinists were excluded, then that meant the dispossessed Calvinist Elector Palatine Frederick would never be able to recoup his lands and titles from the Bavarian pretender. Yet, even with these instructions, the Catholic Electors did not foresee the full extent of the Emperor's plans. They expected merely new guidelines for the Imperial courts to be issued, or for limited restitution of monasteries to take place in lands within the Habsburg sphere of influence. At the Muhlhausen meeting Ferdinand made his grand intentions plain. He certainly wished to do something special for the Catholic Church, regarding himself as a loyal servant of its interests.[31] His envoy at Muhlhausen assured those present that...

...just as up to now we have never thought to let pass any chance to secure the restitution of church lands, neither do we intend, now or in the future, to have to bear the responsibility before posterity of having neglected or failed to exploit even the least opportunity.

There were many opportunities to exploit, now that the victory over Denmark was effectively guaranteed. Those present at Muhlhausen granted Ferdinand the responsibility for drafting a suitable settlement. Again though, Ferdinand seems to have hesitated. Perhaps he was preoccupied with other business, like the unsavoury task of transferring Mecklenburg to Wallenstein in February 1628. Either way, by September 1628, a full year after he had been given approval, the Emperor received an urgent petition to fulfil his promises to the Catholics of the Empire. This seems to have done the trick, and in October 1628, an initial draft of the Edict of Restitution was sent to the Electors of Bavaria and Mainz for comment. It is interesting to denote the tone Ferdinand maintained throughout the pre-amble. The Emperor regarded the Edict not as an inflammatory move against Protestants, but as a way to settle the uneven pace of the Reformation and Counter-Reformation, by returning lands lost to Catholics, outlawing Calvinism, and rolling back the clock to 1555.[32]

While Ferdinand drafted the Edict in an effort to reach a religious settlement, the conclusion of the Danish War and King Christian IV's known desire for peace appeared to give the Emperor a unique opportunity. He was determined not to avenge himself upon his defeated foes but, in his mind at least, resolve the military as well as the religious problems which had long plagued Germany. The varied Christian creeds had spread their roots unevenly and haphazardly across the German states since 1555, and now that he was in the position to do so, the Emperor wished to fix the problems which several decades of organic growth, Protestant zeal and, it has to be said, Habsburg weakness, had caused.

Ferdinand did not wish to write a new chapter in religious war through the development of the Edict. It is reasonable to deduce from the evidence available that the Emperor believed he was doing the right thing both for God and for Germany. A limited redressing of the religious balance and an investigation into the past legalities of land confiscated from the Catholic Church would not have been a scandalous mission. Some Protestants even expected that religious concerns would be at the forefront of any German settlement, and that within these concerns land would be foremost among them. Yet, while it is important to consider Ferdinand's perspective, it is equally impossible to ignore the fact that he should have known better. Certainly, other figures did, even those that had initially supported their Emperor's limited redrawing of the religious map, only to recoil in horror at the full extent of his plans. Ferdinand had also seen for himself the problems which were caused in

1626 in the Upper Austrian case; if he could not force his own subjects to fall in line without first having to quash a bloody rebellion, how could he expect the entire Holy Roman Empire to obey similar instructions?

Rather than the religious ribbon which would nicely wrap up the military settlement with Denmark, the Edict of Restitution resembled petrol poured on a smouldering fire. Whatever moderate expectations that Protestants may have had about the religious adjustments were destroyed by their readings of the final draft. Ferdinand had made some effort to consult Protestant figures, but the Edict which was produced nonetheless contained a blatantly hard-line Jesuit tone, being in many respects a reiteration of the most uncompromising Catholic interpretations of the 1555 Peace of Augsburg. It seems that, in spite of the noble intentions he may have possessed, Ferdinand had allowed himself to be manipulated by the militant Jesuit party in Vienna, not to mention a belief that, having suffered no defeats since the beginning of the war, he was doing God's work, and was thus bound to receive his blessing and protection.

A sectarian shadow had stalked the outbreak of the war since its beginning, but the Edict threatened to shroud its events in confessional conflict, and to sharpen all dilemmas. If he accepted that the Edict was not what all Germans had been expecting, then Ferdinand did not show it. Instead, his demands were similar to before. Strict obedience and adherence to these new instructions were the only course. The path to the Edict had not been straightforward, but now that it was in his hands, the Emperor refused at all costs to let it go.

THREE
Doing God's Work

In some respects, it was an innocuous enough document. It was not declared from the rooftops or pronounced with trumpets, but simply printed in Vienna and passed across the Empire. It was a single sheet of paper, with four columns of writing and the Emperor's signature at the bottom. Appearances were of course deceptive, and ripples of discontent spread out from the Empire as the contents of the Edict of Restitution were digested. In a version printed in Wurzburg, someone had scrawled on the Edict the phrase *Radix omnium mallorum* – the root of all evils. But the controversy by no means stopped there. Almost at the same time as the Edict was circulated, a Jesuit author Paul Layman released a pamphlet of his own as a form of accompaniment, whereby he argued that 'Whatever is not found to have been explicitly granted, should be considered forbidden'. This was nothing less than a demand for Protestants everywhere to prove the legitimacy of their possessions, or to suffer the consequences. In Brandenburg and Saxony, the Empire's most important Protestant Electors, neither George William nor John George could reconcile themselves with its contents and had grown resentful at the presence of Wallenstein's large army near their borders.[33]

What exactly had the Edict of Restitution said? At its core was the intention to turn back the clock to the 1555 Peace of Augsburg – which itself had applied to the status quo of 1552. To do this, any land which had been secularised or lost by the Catholic Church since that date was to be returned. Much attention was also placed on a particularly tricky article of the 1555 Peace – the *reservatum ecclesiasticum*. This article had stipulated that if a Catholic ruler converted to Protestantism, he would have to abdicate from his offices, and a Catholic would replace him. Understandably, the Protestants of Germany fiercely objected to this, and had not recognised it in the final form of the 1555 arrangement, whereas their Catholic counterparts had. Because they had not recognised or accepted it, Germany was awash with, in the Catholic opinion, 'illegitimate' rulers and dynasties sitting on bishoprics and estates which should not have been theirs in the first place.

Another three points about the Edict are worth examining. The first is that the Edict banned all forms of Christianity save for Lutheranism and Catholicism. This, as we learned, meant that the dispossessed Calvinist Elector Palatine, Frederick V, would not be able to return to his lands, and thus Maximillian of Bavaria would be safe. It also meant, of course, that several Germans were now breaking the law, including the Calvinist Elector of Brandenburg, George William. The Edict seemed not to concern itself with the sheer messiness of its implications – how were Calvinists across the Empire to be treated, and was it even possible to evict them all?

This brings us to our second point, that by providing the ironclad Catholic interpretation of the 1555 Peace of Augsburg, Ferdinand missed the entire point of that peace. In 1555, with so many years of conflict behind them and so many issues still unresolved, what was needed was a peace agreement which all could agree upon. Thus, the end result was that the Peace of Augsburg was deliberately ambiguous, and this was arguably its greatest strength, because every prince could claim some kind of victory within its contents. By steamrolling over the sensibilities of 1629, Ferdinand was also ignoring the valid concerns of those that had agreed to the Peace of Augsburg in 1555. And these concerns were more, not less, pronounced in 1629 than they had been then.

Finally, a striking aspect of the Edict was the question of whether Ferdinand even had the authority to issue it. The sweeping declarations therein gave no hint of the shaky constitutional ground which the Emperor was on, but it is worth noting that no Imperial Diet was ever called to ratify it. Ferdinand acted and legitimised the Edict purely on his own powers. By doing so he gave further demonstration of his willingness to bypass the traditional checks and balances on his office, while also appealing to the constitution whenever it suited him. By virtue of his own authority, Ferdinand laid down the gauntlet to all who would oppose this incontestable Edict. To the end, Ferdinand would maintain that the agreement of the Electors at the Muhlhausen meeting in September 1627 had provided this authority, but we will recall that even the Catholics present at that meeting had expected something far less incendiary than what the Emperor actually produced.[34]

And what Ferdinand produced was incendiary for sure, but it was also 'little less than revolutionary'.[35] The Edict opened with an innocent enough paragraph:

> We, Ferdinand the Second, by the grace of God, elected Holy Roman Emperor, etc., offer our friendship, grace and all goodwill to all and every elector, prince [etc.] and all other of our and the Empire's subjects and faithful followers regardless of dignity, estate or being. It is without question all too well known that our beloved fatherland the German Nation has long suffered from damaging disagreement and destruction.[36]

This extract reminds us of Ferdinand's intention to arrive at a peaceful solution by ending the 'damaging disagreement and destruction' – yet it is fair to say that he signally failed in this quest. After justifying the Catholic position, criticising the Protestants for breaking the 'Religious and Profane Peace', insisting that the 'followers of the Augsburg Confession refuse Catholics the same rights they demand themselves', the Edict presented its most infamous intentions.

> So we are determined for the realisation both of the religious and profane peace to despatch our imperial commissioners into the Empire; to reclaim all the archbishoprics, bishoprics, prelacies, monasteries, ecclesiastical property, hospitals and endowments which the Catholics had possessed at the time of the [1552] Treaty of Passau and of which they have been illegally deprived; and to put into all these Catholic foundations and endowments duly qualified persons so that each may get his proper due without unnecessary delay...We therefore command to all and everybody under punishment from the religious and public peace that they shall at once cease opposing our ordinance and carry it out in their lands and territories and also assist our commissioners. Such as hold the archbishoprics and bishoprics, prelacies, monasteries, hospitals, benefices and other ecclesiastical property, shall forthwith vacate them and return and deliver them to our imperial commissioners with all their appurtenances. Should they not carry out this behest they will not only expose themselves on grounds of notorious disobedience to the Imperial ban under the religious and profane peace and to the immediate loss of all their privileges and rights without further sentence or condemnation, but to the inevitable real execution of that order and be distrained by force...We mean this seriously.[37]

Ferdinand was serious indeed, for on 24 March 1629, a few days before the Edict was made public, he had authorised both Tilly and Wallenstein to use the forces at their disposal to compel the leading figures of the Empire to fall in line. Since both commanders possessed soldiers far in excess of anything which any objectors to the Edict could field, it was only inevitable that the Edict itself felt more like an opportunistic method of conquering Protestant lands, than a legitimate way of arriving at a peace which all could be content with. That said, one figure who declared his satisfaction with the Edict was Pope Urban VIII, a surprising development in some respects, since Urban had long since distanced himself from the Habsburgs, cancelling the Papal subsidy to Vienna in 1623. Nonetheless, Urban declared on 5 May 1629 that:

> Our soul has been filled with a marvellous joy by the recent Edict of Your Majesty which orders the sectaries to return to the priestly estate the ecclesiastical lands they have long held and in which are contained other provisions (which we bless) that remove obstacles that have up to now held back the Catholic restoration. When we reported these developments in secret consistory [i.e. of the cardinals] the apostolic senate rejoiced and praised your

well-deserving piety, desirous that the reward of your noble action will be [more] victorious. Thus heresy will have learned that the gates of hell to not prevail against the church which legions of angels and the arms of powerful Austria so happily defend. How closely you have hereby bound the soul of the pontiff to yourself...our nuncio will declare to Your Majesty in more magnificent fashion.[38]

Appearances were again deceptive though, because even as the Pope seemed to loudly approve of this bold step, we notice that, unlike the language of the Edict, no mention of the 1555 Peace of Augsburg was ever made. This is because, incredible though it may sound, the Papacy did not recognise the Augsburg settlement, because this would have involved officially recognising the schism in Christendom and the Protestant creeds it produced. He would later distance himself from the Edict, and deny that he had ever approved of it to begin with; this despite the fact that William Lamormaini, Ferdinand's confessor, had written to the Pope and exclaimed 'no Roman pontiff has received such a harvest of joys from Germany since the time of Charlemagne.' Urban would have disagreed; an air of resentment clouded the Papal examination of the Edict. While Rome's agents could declare themselves agreeing in principle with the advancement of Catholicism, Ferdinand never sought their advice when creating the Edict. In the Emperor's view, this was because the Edict was a judicial, not a spiritual matter, and Rome had no jurisdiction.[39]

Ferdinand had a point, because even though religion was the measuring stick, the immediate result of the Edict would not be the rescuing of souls, but the reapportioning of land. Predictably, land where Lutheranism was relatively new, and had taken off in popularity after 1555, were bound to be the most affected. Austria and Bohemia, already pacified and forcibly converted, would have put up some form of protest, but as we have learned, Ferdinand had undertaken what should be considered a trial run of the Edict in these lands. Land owned by the Church was returned, Protestants ordered to leave, and Catholics were greatly empowered. On a smaller scale, Ferdinand's Styrian homeland had also suffered the same fate in the late 1590s. Evidently, these three instances were not singular errors in judgement, but a pattern, and one which the Emperor was determined to apply to all of Germany.[40]

Ferdinand could claim that he was not only acting on his lawful authority as Emperor, but also simply enforcing the terms of the Peace of Augsburg, which had incorrectly been allowed to lapse. Again though, this claim was exposed as disingenuous for whoever had actually consulted that same treaty arrangement. Its strength was in its ability to please, not to enforce. Not even Charles V, simultaneously King of Spain and Holy Roman Emperor, felt powerful enough to remove Protestantism by force. After nearly a century of German princes being left to their own devices, the results of Christendom's organic spread and fragmentation posed an even more formidable problem, and yet the single-minded Emperor pressed relentlessly on. While he could not ban Lutheranism outright in Germany, he could push it back to its 1555 status, before Habsburg weakness and the zeal of the Reformation caused the new creed to explode in popularity. Ferdinand himself had seen that all forms of protest could be overcome with the sword, and thanks to Wallenstein he had plenty of swords on standby. The dispossessing or forced conversion of Austrian and Bohemian nobles was an experience which was now extended to the Empire. Unsurprisingly, those that had rebelled against the Emperor were at the top of the list.

The Lower Saxon Circle – that old Danish sphere of influence – and Westphalia came under the Emperor's care, since Lutheranism had spread there only gradually after 1555. However, this was not all, since scattered across the Empire existed hundreds of convents, monasteries, bishoprics, archbishoprics, abbeys and mere churches that had been purchased from their old Catholic owners, and transformed into new secular principalities or been incorporated to enlarge old ones. The bill of the Edict demonstrated just how much Germany had been transformed in seventy-five years, but the pace of change and the sheer organisational challenge before Vienna did not stymy the Emperor's enthusiasm. Some five hundred pieces of Church land were up for grabs, with Wurttemberg provided with the largest bill of all, losing fourteen large monasteries and thirty-six convents. Other German rulers stood to lose up to a third of their immediate wealth, to be returned to a Church organisation which was itself in no position to return these lands to their 1555 state.[41]

In many of the regions where the old Church leaders had been replaced, no adherents to the Catholic faith remained, and Ferdinand had already faced a legion of priest shortages when attempting to fill even the Austrian and Bohemian vacancies – it is not clear how exactly he planned to fill the new raft of openings for church leaders, who simply did not exist. The Emperor's unfailing conviction drove him on, with the result that, notwithstanding the lack of clergy, within eighteen months some six bishoprics had been returned to the Church, in addition to one hundred convents, with 80 more cases under the Edict's review. It should be emphasised that no distinction was made between loyal or rebellious citizens and rulers, which gave the impression that the whole process was terminally unjust. Why should the clock be so severely rolled back, when those that had lived in 1555 were long since dead? What aims could this policy serve, other than offending Protestants, empowering the Catholics and threatening even loyal servants as rebels?[42]

The pace of the Imperial commissioners only aggravated the tensions. The Edict applied to free cities and to independent figures like Imperial Knights, who owned a smattering of villages or towns. Since these figures were the Emperor's servants, their lands belonged to him, and could be returned at any time to Ferdinand, which meant booting out the old occupants, or forcing them to convert to remain in place. The Knights, much like the free cities, were under the protection of the constitution, but Ferdinand had demonstrated that he had no interest in adhering to the rule of law so long as it suited him to circumvent it.

The Imperial commissioners turned their attentions to other weak parties, like the free cities of Augsburg, Heilbronn, Dortmund, Nordlingen, Kempten, Rothenburg and so many others which had been Catholic in 1555 but had since been converted. In some of these cities it was difficult even to find Catholics – were these now to be appropriated and returned so arbitrarily to that key year of 1555 as well? Furthermore, since three generations of nobles had matured in some of these cities, their expulsion would mean the effective destruction of that city's economic and administrative functions. Multiplied over a wide variety of former Catholic cities, this would result in nothing less than the collapse of social order and the undermining of what little native economic activity still flourished.[43]

The Emperor even seemed willing to dispense with old allies. According to the terms of the Edict, the Electors of Saxony and Brandenburg both stood to lose three secularised pieces of church land apiece. This went directly against the agreement which Ferdinand had made with John George of Saxony in 1620, when he had promised the Saxon Elector that his lands would be safe and untouched if he joined his Emperor in putting down Frederick's rebellion. John George had gained Lusatia for his troubles but was now faced with the prospect of existing in isolation in an opposition party too small to achieve anything or accepting the unacceptable. Actions like these proved that Ferdinand cared little for previous arrangements when he considered the 'bigger picture'.

This bigger picture was of little interest even to those in Ferdinand's close circle. Anton Wolfradt, the Bishop of Vienna from 1631, warned at this early stage that such a hostile Edict directed towards Protestants could only serve to alienate them, arouse feelings of bitterness and desperation, and prolong the war which Ferdinand sought to end. Others in Vienna floated between feelings of lukewarm enthusiasm and fear about the implications for foreign potentates, who might use the opportunity which the Edict presented to intervene in Germany and prolong the war by that means. While he may have genuinely believed that he was doing God's work, this very work had the potential to destroy the Empire from the inside out, and at precisely the wrong time. As Peter H. Wilson wrote:

> Issued in 1629, the Edict was a political miscalculation of the first order: it alienated Saxony in the critical months prior to Sweden's intervention. Though Lamormaini influenced the decision to issue the edict, it also reflected Ferdinand's legalist interpretation of the imperial constitution and was intended

to lower, not heighten, the tension.[44]

If Ferdinand's spiritual advisors were largely against the Edict, and if moderate Catholics came to loathe it as well, then it is hardly surprising how dangerous and inappropriate Wallenstein felt the Edict to be. Already torn towards one venture he did not believe in in Italy, the Emperor now demanded Wallenstein use his army – as many as one hundred and fifty thousand men according to some estimates – to aid the Imperial commissioners in enforcing the Edict. But Wallenstein did not want to use his men for this purpose. If the Emperor had no use for him he wished to be dismissed once his debts and the wages of his soldiers were paid. If a campaign was what Ferdinand wanted, then some form of holding action against the King of Sweden, recently liberated from his Polish War, was surely a wise strategic move.

Policing the Empire and supplanting traditions built upon generations of history and belief were not within his job description though, and he refrained, at least for a while, from imposing the Edict on anyone. Fortunately for Wallenstein and the Emperor the mere presence of his soldiers in the Protestant North was coercion enough, but Tilly's Catholic League Army soldiers were employed more often than not, further exacerbating the sectarian tensions already felt.[45]

Wallenstein wrote increasingly anxious letters to the Emperor cautioning him of the dangers of the new policy. Over the winter of 1629-30 he sent two letters to Vienna, the first insisting: 'All the trouble is caused by this untimely and strict Catholic Reformation and also by the Imperial Edict concerning the restitution of church lands and the expulsion of the Calvinists.' In a second letter, Wallenstein would add: 'The Imperial Edict has turned all the non-Catholics against us…the entire Empire will be turned against us, aided by the Swedes, the Turks and Bethlen Gabor.' Bethlen Gabor's death in 1628 did not deter Wallenstein from making this point; so long as the Emperor pushed, there was no guarantee that someone else, perhaps someone powerful, would not push back.[46]

The opposition from the Protestant Germans, Papacy and even moderate Catholics may not have taken Ferdinand by surprise, considering the fact that he had authorised his best generalissimos to use force in anticipation of the disruption and opposition to the Edict. However, opposition from his cousins in Madrid must have come as a shock, especially since the Jesuit influence in Spain was exceedingly strong. Unlike Ferdinand though, King Philip IV of Spain could not afford to ignore political consequences, and he advised the Emperor to 'find a more suitable outlet for his piety and zeal.' Such advice should not lead us to imagine that Spain was a beacon of tolerance; as he had done many times before, Philip merely wished to influence Ferdinand to pacify his German subjects, so that he would be in a better position to help him in the

Netherlands or in Italy. From Italy the commander of Ferdinand's soldiers, Collalto, warned his Emperor and Wallenstein that the Edict undermined the Habsburg effort in the Mantuan War. Convoluted efforts were even set in place in Spain to remove Lamormaini and reduce the confessional venom which that man poured into the Emperor's ear. For the moment at least, these efforts were unsuccessful.[47]

Despite the affront to their sensibilities, and in many instances their rights, Protestant and Catholic alike did not rise up in any organised fashion against their Emperor, as the French Huguenots had recently done. Whether the failure of that venture was fully appreciated or not, the Imperial constitution was sufficiently robust for the Empire's key potentates to rely on it rather than on the application of force. Even those Catholics who stood to gain from the Edict wished to have it weighed against the Emperor's actual legal position and capacity to issue such commands. Furthermore, the majority favoured examining each individual case on its merits, rather than the blanket restitution proclaimed by the Edict – the Elector of Saxony and, in time, Maximillian of Bavaria, were both among this camp.

It is interesting to discern three points from the Empire's reaction. The first is that, even among Protestants, some form of restitution of secularised land was expected. Critically though, it was expected that these lands would be taken from rebellious subjects, such as Halberstadt, where Christian of Brunswick had hailed from, or Magdeburg, whose administrators had declared for the King of Denmark. The concept of restitution was not what they objected to then, but the arbitrary, sweeping nature of the Edict, which failed to discern friend from foe, and failed to consider the results of treating so many innocent Germans like criminals. The second point is that the Peace of Augsburg remained the measuring stick of all that followed and would remain the Empire's guidebook for dealing with religious questions for some time. Requests to examine each case involved weighing the demands of the Edict against the stipulations and directives of the Peace of Augsburg, implying that the latter treaty from 1555 still commanded legitimacy and respect.

The third and final point concerns the belief which began to pervade Germany in the aftermath of the Edict – that Ferdinand's efforts to roll back the clock were just the beginning, and that rather than settle either for the Edict or the 1555 Peace of Augsburg upon which it was based, their Emperor deep down wished for nothing less than the elimination of Protestantism, and the establishment of an absolutist, Habsburg regime in the Empire.[48] Fear of this ambition provoked some passionate displays over the following months, and granted the Protestant pamphleteers an invaluable supply of propaganda to fire across the continent. Ferdinand may have believed that he was acting according to the literal interpretation of that defining peace agreement from 1555, but to his critics, and largely in the opinion of posterity, the Edict of

Restitution was a careless ploy for dominance launched by a man at the apex of his personal powers and influence. These views would mature in time, but the invasion by the King of Sweden would help to sharpen all dilemmas and perceptions of what Ferdinand had done.[49]

It is worth emphasising that no evidence exists of Ferdinand's intentions to extirpate Protestantism or establish a centralised, absolutist monarchy in Vienna in place of the traditional Empire. What Ferdinand did, he did in pursuit of his single-minded quest to achieve justice and righteousness for his family and for Germany. A conservative at heart, it may well have genuinely troubled his conscience that the rulings of the Peace of Augsburg had been allowed to lapsed, had been manipulated or ignored altogether, and perhaps he believed that by reinforcing his strict interpretation of the 1555 Peace, he was making things right, and making the Empire stronger.[50] Regardless of his motives, what mattered in the end was how he was perceived, and while moderates were willing to tolerate some change, the simple, glaring fact is that the Edict went too far too fast. It is also fair to deduce that, as the Emperor, Ferdinand ought to have anticipated the Edict's potential for torpedoing what was perhaps the last chance to make lasting peace in Germany before Gustavus Adolphus invaded.

Once the Empire was in disagreement, and fragmented in its opinions over the Emperor's character and the safety of their rights, 'the door was wide open', as Peter H. Wilson has asserted, for a foreigner to enter the scene and acquire moral support.[51] The first steps towards the shattering of German political unity came from the moderates, and John George of Saxony, whether he realised it or not, effectively led the way. From October 1629, he was in talks with his Brandenburg counterpart to host a meeting, where some united front would be formed to safeguard their rights and ensure fair assessment in any judgements relating to Edict which followed. The message which the Elector of Saxony gave was one of pacific, cautious action, and not one of angry, defiant resistance against his Emperor's poor policy choices.[52] Yet, as John George was soon to learn, by late 1629 it had become increasingly impossible to tread a middle course in the Holy Roman Empire. The Holy Roman Emperor had made sure of that.

Chapter 13 Notes

[1]Paul Douglas Lockhart, 'Denmark and the Empire: A Reassessment of Danish Foreign Policy under King Christian IV', pp. 409-411.
[2]Mortimer, *Wallenstein*, p. 103.
[3]Paul Douglas Lockhart, *Denmark, 1513-1660: The Rise and Decline of a Renaissance Monarchy: The Rise and Decline of a Renaissance Monarchy* (Oxford University Press; Oxford, 2007), p. 170.
[4]Paul Douglas Lockhart, 'Denmark and the Empire', p. 410.
[5]The meeting is also examined in Stewart P. Oakley, *War and Peace in the Baltic, 1560-1790* (Routledge; London, 1992), pp. 63-66.
[6]The scene is recalled in Wedgewood, *Thirty Years War*, pp. 242-243.
[7]The full text of the treaty is available in Wilson, *Sourcebook*, pp. 97-99.
[8]Lockhart, 'Denmark's Intervention in the Thirty Years War, 1618-1625', p. 21.
[9]See Lockhart, 'Denmark and the Empire', pp. 410-412.
[10]Brennan Pursell, *The Winter King*, pp. 261-262.
[11]Mortimer, *Wallenstein*, pp. 111-114.
[12]Wilson, *Europe's Tragedy*, p. 424.
[13]Francis J. Bowman, 'Sweden's Wars, 1611-32', pp. 360-369.
[14]An examination of the Swedish King's motives and ambitions when intervening in Germany is provided in M. Roberts, 'The Political Objectives of Gustavus Adolphus in Germany 1630-1632', *Transactions of the Royal Historical Society*, Vol. 7 (1957), pp. 19-46.
[15]fteenthe fascinating layers of Richelieu's diplomacy with respect to the Baltic and East will be examined later, but those interested should track down the highly illuminating account of the Truce of Altmark in B.F. Porshnev, *Muscovy and Sweden in the Thirty Years War 1630-1635* ed. Paul Dukes, trans. Brian Pearce (Cambridge University Press; Cambridge, 2012), pp. 8-11.
[16]Geoffrey Parker, *Thirty Years War*, pp. 94-95.
[17]*Ibid*, pp. 90-91.
[18]Geoffrey Parker, *Thirty Years War*, p. 81.
[19]Peter H. Wilson, *Europe's Tragedy*, p. 788.
[20]entiethe most extensive examination of this crisis is provided by Charles P. Kindleberger, 'The Economic Crisis of 1619 to 1623', *The Journal of Economic History*, Vol. 51, No. 1 (Mar., 1991), pp. 149-175.
[21]See Arnost Klima, 'Inflation in Bohemia in the Early Stage of the seventeenth Century', in Michael Flinn, ed., *Seventh International Economic History Congress* (Edinburgh, 1978), pp. 375-86.
[22]Charles P. Kindleberger, 'The Economic Crisis of 1619 to 1623', p. 152.
[23]Geoffrey Parker, *Europe in Crisis*, pp. 176-177.
[24]*Ibid*, p. 178.
[25]Geoffrey Parker, *Thirty Years War*, pp. 81-82.
[26]Peter H. Wilson, 'Dynasty, Constitution, and Confession: The Role of Religion in the Thirty Years War', p. 485.
[27]See Wedgewood, *Thirty Years War*, pp. 172-174.
[28]Parker, *Thirty Years War*, pp. 82-84.
[29]*Ibid*, p. 87.
[30]Wilson, Dynasty, 'Constitution, and Confession', p. 496.
[31]Wilson, *Europe's Tragedy*, pp. 446-447.
[32]Parker, *Thirty Years War*, pp. 87-88.
[33]Geoffrey Parker, *Thirty Years War*, pp. 88-89.
[34]Peter H. Wilson, *Europe's Tragedy*, pp. 448-449.
[35]Wedgewood, *Thirty Years War*, p. 233.
[36]Quoted in Wilson, *Sourcebook*, p. 114.
[37]Quoted in *Ibid*, p. 117.
[38]Quoted in *Ibid*, pp. 117-118.
[39]Wilson, *Europe's Tragedy*, p. 449.
[40]Geoff Mortimer, *Wallenstein*, p. 111.
[41]Parker, *Thirty Years War*, p. 88.
[42]Parker, *Europe in Crisis*, p. 216.
[43]Wedgewood, *Thirty Years War*, p. 233.
[44]Wilson, 'Dynasty, Constitution and Confession', p. 496.
[45]Mortimer, *Wallenstein*, pp. 112-113.

[46]Parker, *Europe in Crisis*, p. 216.
[47]Wilson, *Europe's Tragedy*, p. 449.
[48]*Ibid*, pp. 450-453.
[49]Brennan Pursell, *The Winter King*, pp. 266-268.
[50]*Ibid*, pp. 262-263.
[51]Wilson, *Europe's Tragedy*, p. 453.
[52]*Ibid*, p. 452.

(Top left) Frederick Henry of the Netherland
(Michiel Jansz von Mierevelt). (Top right) Philip IV of Spain

(Top left) Admiral Piet Hein (Jan Daemen Cool, 1629)
(Top right) Cardinal Mazarin (Pierre Migna)

CHAPTER FOURTEEN
"War's Unending Hand"

ONE: Dutch Deliverance
TWO: God Has Left Spain
THREE: Lifelines From France
FOUR: Italian Stallions
FIVE: It's All Connected

ONE
Dutch Deliverance

Frederick Henry was to serve as the leader of the Netherlands for twenty-two eventful years, but the bleak early months of his service in 1625 must be considered a baptism by fire of the first order. In April 1625, Frederick Henry had been summoned to the bedside of Maurice, the dying Stadtholder of the Dutch provinces. His half-brother Maurice urged the forty-five-year-old Frederick Henry to take a wife and to secure the future of the House of Orange. Frederick Henry obliged, and married into the court of the dispossessed Elector Palatine. Amalia von Solms was the daughter of one of Frederick V's late officials, and she was to serve the new Stadtholder with love, loyalty, and several children – exactly what a military and naval leader with a vaguely defined job description required.

Only a few days after a quiet wedding service, Maurice of Nassau died. Two months later, Breda, a fortress on the frontier of Brabant, which guarded the roads to Utrecht and Amsterdam, fell to the Spanish. The Dutch people, shorn of their beloved Maurice – a man of Dutch as well as European reputation, having earned plaudits as a skilled tactician and military innovator – were struck low by news of the loss of Breda. Breda had been one of Maurice's most famed successes after all and losing it at the same time as its conqueror cannot have been an easy series of developments to swallow. But the Dutch people had endured far worse. Frederick Henry needed his people to persevere. Further afield, outside of the troubling local bulletins, there was good reason for the new Stadtholder to be anxious. The Dutch War with the Spanish – a conflict rooted several generations before – appeared destined to widen, and to engulf Germany, Scandinavia and Britain with it.[1]

While it was a year of defeat and darkness, in other respects 1625 promised much for the future of the Dutch Republic, as new opportunities presented themselves. The events leading to that year had been troubling indeed. The Austrian Habsburgs, supported by the Spanish and Bavarians, had overrun the Rhine and the Palatinate, had put down the Bohemian revolt and installed a triumphant Catholicising regime in its wake. The Spanish had gained much by their intervention, and now clung to a more secure position on the Rhine than they had ever before held. The German war had spilled over into the Netherlands, most notably in 1623, when forces under the command of Ernst of Mansfeld challenged Ambrogio Spinola's siege of Bergen-op-zoom. There was great potential for further spill-over, thanks to Madrid's incessant demands on Vienna to become properly involved in the war with the Dutch – demands which increased in frequency as the 1620s progressed.

Throughout these years of Habsburg victory, the French, English and Germans had been quiescent. In London, a Spanish marriage was constantly under negotiation, as King James sought desperately to reach an agreement whereby Prince Charles would be wed to a Spanish princess. In France, though a formal defensive alliance had been concluded, it was difficult to believe in any likelihood of French support so long as consistent Huguenot rebellions racked the French administration, then coming under Cardinal Richelieu's control. Elsewhere, there seemed a shortage of promises or commitments which might have persuaded hesitant powers to get involved. The Scandinavian kingdoms had great potential, but neither Denmark nor Sweden was content to enter the war in Germany alone. Thus, to ensure the containment of the war in Germany, to isolate and disadvantage the Spanish, and perhaps to also liberate themselves from the burdens of maintaining the exiled Palatine family, Dutch policy called for the formation of an alliance between parties possessing mutual interests and anxieties. By 1625, despite the grave situation which the Republic faced, circumstances had finally aligned to make this alliance a reality.

The Hague Alliance was the result of these agreements and favourable circumstances, and while this coalition was destined to disintegrate with the defeat of Denmark, it seemed to promise a great deal. During the summer of 1625, as the Dutch grappled with the successive losses of Maurice and of Breda, King Charles formalised the war between England and Spain. By the end of the year, an Anglo-Dutch naval expedition would be launched against Spain, and Denmark would confirm its position in the ambitious new alliance, with additional promises of French financial support forthcoming as well. These developments certainly boded well, but while the Dutch proved adept at weathering the storm, efforts at cooperation left much to be desired. The leading lights of the Hague Alliance – King Christian IV of Denmark, Christian of Brunswick and Ernst of Mansfeld – were defeated in succession over 1626.

More troubling was the English and French retreat from the commitments they had made to the alliance; the French pleading Huguenot revolts at home, King Charles pleading lack of money and an uncooperative Parliament. The Habsburgs appeared immune to such woes, as Ferdinand crushed uprisings in his Hereditary Lands and consolidated his authority there. The Emperor had even managed to pay off his considerable debts to Maximillian of Bavaria, and the policy of confiscating rebel land was expanded as allies were enriched and enemies exiled. By 1628 it was apparent that the Habsburgs would again be victorious in Germany, and the employment of Albrecht of Wallenstein demonstrated the extent of the Holy Roman Emperor's new powers, fragile though they were.[2] Closer to home, the Dutch saw their economic life threatened by an invigorated Spanish naval blockade, as Dutch ships were blocked from entering major ports, and attacks by privateers increased, driving up shipping and insurance costs.

One of the Republic's greatest success stories had been its ability to leverage its geographic position in Europe and become the dominant fulcrum of Atlantic and Baltic trade. North Sea herrings, Baltic grain and local cheeses provided essential dietary needs, complemented by Dutch entrepreneurship in Scandinavian resource exploitation, and advantageous copper and timber monopolies in Sweden. Ruthless determination, adventurism and no short of opportunism had enabled the Dutch to impede the Spanish trade in the Indies to their great benefit. The Dutch had been so successful in replacing the Spanish in the Indies game that the terms of the Twelve Years Truce had urged Dutch evacuation of this theatre as the only acceptable grounds for a peace deal. Spain had been in no position to enforce this stipulation in 1609, and the Dutch had effectively run amuck in the New World, a state of affairs which had cost Madrid millions, and engendered discontent in Portugal.

It was to reverse all of these negative trends that a sweeping new set of Spanish plans were implemented following the expiration of the Truce in 1621. The Rhine and Maas Rivers would be blockaded; extensive forts would be built in the Indies to increase their defensiveness; a trading company would be established at Seville to fight the Dutch monopoly in Baltic trade; a royal Spanish fleet would be docked in Antwerp, where it could target Dutch trade more effectively, and privateers from Dunkirk would be empowered and increased in the havoc they could wreak against Dutch interests in home waters. A focus on cutting the Dutch lifeblood – trade – was believed to be more sensible and less expensive than resuming the land war, as Spinola had requested. For a time then, the years immediately after the expiration of the Truce contained scant events of much consequence. Indeed, with the exception of Breda, the Spanish attempted no vast time-consuming, expensive sieges of the kind which had long been synonymous with the Eighty Years War.

'Profound brains firmly trust that this is the only means to make the water snails of Holland pull their Horns into their Shells, whence they will be pricked with a pin'. This was the judgement of Antwerp's newspaper in spring 1622, echoed by a letter which that newspaper carried, that purported to be from a resident of The Hague, who said 'The Ships of the Flemish Coast harm us in the Apple of our Eye. If this continues our nails will be clipped to the flesh.' Encouraging the residents of the loyal Spanish Netherlands to venture. onto the seas and fight their rebellious neighbours, the Brussels administration appealed to their citizens' thirst for wealth, arguing that 'some Seamen have become so rich with Booty that they can henceforth live as hearty and wealthy as Lords, so that the arrival of stout Fellows daily increases.'

Thus, began arguably the most effective arm of the Spanish war against the Dutch – the employment of privateers from Dunkirk to sever and chip away at the commercial business of the Republic. With expertise in traversing shallower waters that the Dutch had not yet mastered, these Dunkirkers were a significant thorn in the side of the Republic for as long as the Spanish could maintain the pressure on land. The silver lining for the Dutch in the midst of these far sighted Spanish plans for their destruction was the key fact that while Madrid planned for a war to the last extremity, such a commitment was the last thing their strained coffers could afford.[3] His allies had been most disappointing, and the reasons for despair had been legion, but once the storm had passed, Frederick Henry found that his old enemy had lost a great portion of her durability and strength. He assigned himself the task of taking advantage of Spain's weakness, and wresting the initiative from Spinola's tired hands. It was a position he would not relinquish for the remainder of his life. By the late 1620s, the startling fact was that while the Holy Roman Emperor had never been more supreme in his triumph and powers, the King of Spain saw his regime veering towards the abyss.

While it would be upheld in Madrid as a triumph, the capture of Breda in June 1625 following a ten-month siege was in reality, more of a pyric victory. Even as the Habsburg dynasty appeared supreme, by peeling back the surface layers, one could discern that all was not well in the Castilian Monarchy. The core root of the problem was economic; during 1621-27, arguably the most dominant military years for the Spanish in Europe, taxation doubled, and borrowing increased by 500%. The sheer size of the bill due for the Dutch War – a major act of which had been the seizure of Breda – had also gotten drastically out of hand, as Madrid was forced to more than double its expenditure in the Netherlands, from 1.5 to 3.5 million ducats. Even the cost of equipping and defending the critically important Atlantic fleet – which had responsibilities for protecting and chaperoning the treasure fleets from the Americas – had grown to 1 million ducats; a price soon to increase still further with the coming catastrophes and Dutch victories in the region.

The sheer severity of the Spanish woes prevented Madrid from coordinating any advanced strategy with Brussels after the death of Maurice of Nassau and the loss of Breda sapped Dutch morale.[4] Further problems followed; while the English failed to pursue the war with vigour after the failed Cadiz expedition in late 1625, their declaration of war on Spain meant that Spanish vessels could not recuperate in English waters on their way to the

Netherlands. They would have to run the gauntlet, whether they came from the New World or from Spain, which granted the awaiting Dutch a major advantage.[5]

Advantageous though it was, the Spanish managed to make remarkable progress in the local naval war, especially considering the lack of direct investment in the theatre. The key to Spanish success in this regard was the mettle and ingenuity of the privateers from Dunkirk, who we encountered earlier. In autumn 1625, the Dunkirk privateers were granted a wealth of opportunities to strike the Dutch directly thanks to the ill-fated Cadiz expedition. In regular circumstances, the Dutch would have kept Dunkirk under a tight blockade, but with their vessels cooperating beside the English, the net around this bane of the Dutch was momentarily loosened. The effect was immediate; within two weeks in October, the privateers had sent more than 150 fishing vessels and 20 protection boats to the bottom of the sea. They also captured 1,400 sailors, which in turn forced the Dutch to employ costly convoys as the Spanish had done, to protect their investments in the herring fisheries. The total cost for the Dutch during the most intensive portions of this privateer campaign ran into the tens of millions and represents a forgotten success story of the hardy South Netherlands inhabitants. Impressive though the victory was, the tide was plainly moving against Brussels in other theatres.[6]

For the Dutch then, the Hague Alliance was immensely beneficial, and the weight of the challenge soon began to tell in Spain. We must bear in mind that even as Brussels urged Madrid to send more money, men and materials, Spanish soldiers were on hand along the Rhine, had responsibilities to tend to in Italy, and had to police vulnerable possessions in the Americas. It was only inevitable that with so many fronts to guard, Spanish power would be spread too thin. In early February 1627, King Philip IV encapsulated the decline by declaring bankruptcy. This had been the culmination of several years' worth of economic somersaulting, as Madrid took out loans from credit based on the income they expected to make in the near future. The problem for Spain was thus similar to that faced by Wallenstein – a lack of readily available cash. The Spanish went to extreme measures to keep the lights on, but by forcing the balance sheet so deeply into the red, the Genoese bankers upon whom Spain relied grew ever more nervous.

The declaration of bankruptcy did nothing to ease the genuine fears these bankers had about Spain's liquidity problems, and it was apparent that loans would be much harder to come by in the future. Thus, Madrid relied upon new sources of income – the converted Muslims and Jews who had remained in the country after the earlier expulsions as well as an opportunistic Portuguese banking syndicate. These loans were based upon the promise of income from the usual Spanish sources, which meant that severing any of these sources could be tantamount to disaster. Just how vulnerable Spanish finances were to sudden fluctuations became painfully evident within less than two years. By 1627 though, King Philip IV and his favourite, Olivares, believed they had little choice. The war against the Dutch and the campaign in Germany had to be pursued to its logical conclusion. The hope, as we will see, was that the newly triumphant Emperor, having quashed the Danes, would intercede on the behalf of Spain, perhaps paying Madrid back for the recent bailout Ferdinand had received during the heady days of the Bohemian revolt.[7]

In 1625 Olivares had declared with apparently boundless confidence that 'God is Spanish and fights for our nation these days', but less than a year after this statement, it was clear that God had delivered the Dutch rebels, and not their Spanish masters.[8] The causes of the decline were multi-layered, but rather than address them, Madrid sought other explanations for the recent misfortune. The defeats were not signs of Spanish weakness, but that Spain had forsaken God – if it were to repent and remove its many sins, then God would be obliged to smile upon Spain once more. If the explanation was grounded more in superstition than in fact, it should be added that such 'sins' were not hard for any self-aware Spanish official to find. Contemporaries commented with some alarm on the rise in corruption, on the lack of sexual morality even among some clergy, and of the religion hypocrisy within the Church fathers. Scandals regarding embezzlement, waste and idleness focused more on the individual responsible and less on the system which had facilitated it. In addition, it was easy to blame other countries for their corrupting influence. The first singled out the troubling habit of men deciding to wear their hair long – a 'contagion from England' – as a symptom of the Spanish illness. Purge the illness, and the victim would be cured and make a full recovery – but where to start?[9]

Getting to the bottom of the Spanish plight, and employing officials brave enough to initiate genuine reform from the top down was impossible so long as the country remained locked into a succession of conflicts. The most pressing of these conflicts was the Dutch War, although Madrid would involve itself in North Italy from late 1628, an act which stupefied the aged veteran Spinola, who had been drip-fed aid from Spain for several years. Spinola had been a boon for the Spanish, and before the conclusion of the Twelve Years Truce, he had worked hard to seize several key fortress towns. These were all retaken by Frederick Henry between 1626-28, and Spain could offer nothing in response. Had Spinola been empowered to mount sufficient operations against the demoralised Dutch following the fall of Breda, then an impressive triumph or at least a more favourable peace could have been wrested from that wretched corner of Europe at long last. Alas, it was not to be.

The Dutch were hurting, and their people had grown tired of the state of war which drove up taxes, reduced their security and had brought nothing but gloom since the expiration of the Truce in 1621. 'Do me the honour of believing', wrote one Dutch official to Cardinal Richelieu in spring 1626, 'that never were we in a more critical and hazardous condition; it is more than time for you to stretch out your hand.' This request would be heeded by Richelieu, but it would also be complicated by the outbreak of an untimely Anglo-French War. Dutch opinion in 1626 would soon be buoyed by better news – Frederick Henry celebrated the birth of a son in May, and the town of Oldenzaal, a centre of ammunition and stores was captured in August – but evidently, an atmosphere of uneasiness was present in the Republic.[10] This mood, Frederick Henry set himself the task of shaking by the accumulation of triumphs to put steel back into the people; a mission made that much easier by the virtual collapse of Spanish resistance from 1628.

As per the terms of their 1624 alliance, the French had been obliged to provide 1 million florins a year to the Dutch – 7% of the Republic's expenditure. These subsidies were critically important for helping the Dutch get a leg up on their Spanish enemy, and it made good strategic sense for Richelieu to approve such large gifts, since the Dutch had an integral role to play in the great act to come.[11] Unfortunately for the coordination of Franco-Dutch strategy, the plan was complicated by the eruption of a new front, an Anglo-French War, which centred on the French Crown's siege of La Rochelle (see below). With wanton foolishness, the Duke of Buckingham forced the conflict into being, and with wanton weakness, King Charles allowed it to proceed. The conflict was plagued by problems from the start for Buckingham, and it stripped the English of what little military prestige they still had, after so many years of failed peace-making and the lacklustre commitment of soldiers to fight for Frederick V.

On the island of Re, just offshore from La Rochelle, the English learned first-hand how difficult and complex siege operations far from home had become. Utterly failing in his quest to relieve the Huguenots, Buckingham returned home after this dismal venture, only to fall victim to an assassin's bullet.[12] The Anglo-French episode also complicated matters for the Dutch, since the aforementioned letter to Cardinal Richelieu requesting that the wily French minister would 'stretch out his hand' was answered by a request for Dutch aid against the Huguenots. In the initial phase of the siege, before the English had arrived, the ramifications of crushing Protestants in foreign lands was damning enough for the Calvinist Republicans, but once the English involved themselves, it became a question of choosing between the French ally of 1624 or the partner in the Hague Alliance. In the event, the Dutch chose neither; her sailors refused to man the naval expedition to La Rochelle, and at the same time, Anglo-Dutch relations began to sour over competition in new markets overseas, a sign of things to come.[13]

The year of 1627 had not been all about the complexities of Anglo-Dutch and Franco-Dutch diplomacy. Frederick Henry made good progress in his methodical reduction of the outlying fortresses in Spanish hands. Having seized Oldenzaal in August 1626, he turned his attention thence to Grol the following July. Grol (now known as Groenlo) was a vital hub of trade and guarded the marshy plains along the south-eastern Dutch border with the Holy Roman Empire. Although small in size, Grol was a formidable fortress, positioned as though on an island and surrounded by a deep moat which was regularly fed by the water table. Adopting a tactic harnessed by Spinola at Breda, Frederick Henry made extensive use of long, sprawling lines of circumvallation 16 kilometres in length, to prevent any escape for the Spanish garrison within. The strict enforcement of the siege did the trick and Grol surrendered in mid-August, handing Frederick Henry his most impressive victory yet, and the first truly significant Dutch victory since the expiration of the Twelve Years Truce.[14]

By 1629, the Dutch were able to afford an army of seventy thousand professionals, backed by fifty thousand militiamen and a navy manned by eight and a half thousand persons. The rising power of the Dutch navy – inflated by its propensity for hoarding timber stores and adding consistently to its trade fleet since 1621 – was necessary if the Dutch were to retain their hold on the Baltic.[15] We will recall that the Habsburg scheme for severing this Dutch monopoly misfired, but not before the Dutch and all of Scandinavia had been given a significant scare. After Stralsund stubbornly refused to yield, it became apparent to Wallenstein and gradually to Madrid that the Baltic could not at this point be tamed. Thanks to the combined power of Austrian and Spanish Habsburg force, as well as the overwhelming threat to any regional power which Wallenstein's thousands represented, both Olivares in Madrid and Ferdinand in Vienna had been able to dream big, and to imagine a continent overcome by their influence, with a presence in all the vital seas. The Baltic design proved a step too far, but the frustration of that scheme was more than merely a temporary setback. Habsburg pretensions would never rise so high again.

TWO

God Has Left Spain

The Spanish had been spotted. Loaded down with all their treasures, they were at their most vulnerable, so this was where the Dutch admiral decided to strike. They had already encountered the Spanish off of Cuba, but the bulk of the booty had escaped before it could be caught. Now, with the sun setting, here the enemy was again, hunkered down in the protection of Mantazas Bay, some ways east of Havana. The Dutch outnumbered their foe by a large margin, so victory was never in doubt. What mattered more was the speed of their attack; they needed to move against the Spanish before there was a chance to burn the precious cargo or scuttle the ships. The Dutch admiral counted nine Spanish ships in total, and he knew that they contained, potentially, a great haul for his country. On board, if his intelligence was correct, were the fruits of the Spanish silver mines. Capturing this prize could swing the war determinedly against the Spanish, especially considering how intensely Madrid depended upon the regular shots in the arm from the Americas.

If this were a large-scale naval battle, few admirals would have contended these waters with the sun about to set. The Dutch admiral hoped that a proper battle would not commence and anticipated more of a smash and grab than a fearsome naval encounter. The Spanish were outnumbered more than three to one, so it would have been suicide to fight back. The best hope they had was to surrender or to flee, but the true concern was that in the process of undertaking their preferred strategy, the Spanish would destroy their precious cargo, deadening the impact of the triumph. The Dutch admiral decided he could not risk it – he would attack at once. The thirty-one Dutch vessels opened fire and moved to intercept the Spanish ships before they could respond. The Spanish sailors crumbled under the onslaught, with many jumping into the water rather than staying to contest the enemy warships.

When the smoke settled, the Spanish were gone, and their wares... were almost completely intact. The encounter had been well worth it after all, but exactly how valuable was this haul? The counting began, and amidst the shouts and shrieks of the Dutch sailors, the incredible reality began to dawn on the admiral, Piet Hein. The men counted 80,000 kg of silver, thousands of animal hides, dyes and sugar from the surrounding islands. It was no wonder the enemy had attempted to flee – this was not just any valuable convoy, it was *the* convoy, carrying the silver which was meant to return the blood into the veins of Spain in time for the next payment on its debts. The precious silver was essential to keep the creaky payments system propped up, but Admiral Piet Hein had just severed this artery, with potentially catastrophic consequences for Madrid, and the Spanish war effort.

More than the cost to the enemy though, was the momentous boon to the Dutch fortunes. Piet Hein had been sent out in summer 1628 to find the Spanish treasure fleet, like so many of his peers before him who had braved treacherous conditions in the name of plunder and glory. Unlike his predecessors, Piet Hein had succeeded on a scale never before imagined possible. Initial estimates put the total value of the haul at 11 million florins, but it may have been worth much more. Now that he had captured it, Hein would have to guard this floating financial supernova all the way home – this, incredibly, he also managed to do. The Spanish lost their chance to seize back their lost fortunes, and Admiral Hein ignored the English attempts to claim some for themselves. Evidently, word of the haul was spreading, and it spread all the way home. Hein successfully parried the remaining threats and guided the haul in Amsterdam to a rapturous hero's welcome. It was precisely the pick me up which the Dutch Republic needed, and they were determined to make the very most out of it.

The proceeds of the treasure haul were spread surprisingly evenly among the Dutch. First to receive their share were the shareholders of the West India Company, which had made the venture possible in the first place by financing Hein's initial journey. These shareholders certainly made their money back, receiving a 75% dividend for their troubles. Hein was awarded six thousand florins, a small fortune, as well as gold medal commission especially for this daring exploit. The soldiers even gained from the triumph, receiving seventeen months' wages in advance, buoying morale and increasing confidence in their leaders that there was more where that came from.

The impact was felt almost immediately in Spain. With the bankruptcy announced the previous year, Olivares had hoped to effectively wipe the slate clean and restore confidence in Spanish power once more. Piet Hein's triumph destroyed this hope at a stroke, because it demonstrated how precarious Spanish finances remained. Without the promise of the annual injection of silver, concerns among Spain's unfortunate lenders increased, and the sailors responded to the Dutch daring in their own way. Rather than contend the seas with the Dutch in the expected periods, they would seek to avoid the

Dutch and protect their precious cargos by travelling later in the year, during hurricane season. There were good reasons for avoiding the most perilous weather conditions while at sea, but this option was sourced from desperation.

Alas, the abandonment of regular sailing schedules inflicted defeats of its own; the weather battered successive Spanish treasure fleets, as the Crown lost 5 million florins in 1631 and nearly 4 million florins in 1641 during particularly terrible storms. Left with no other choice, the government seized a third of the privately imported silver in 1629, which did them no favours among entrepreneurs and brave sailors, who committed to fudge their numbers in the future to avoid such seizures again. The seizure of private silver was a drastic step, but again, King Philip IV's administration felt it had little choice. As bad as the loss of so much money was at Piet Hein's hands, it was when the Dutch determined to harness this sudden influx of money for a determined campaign in 1629 that matters truly became desperate.[16]

Frederick Henry had his eyes on s'Hertogenbosch, the second largest city in Brabant after Antwerp, and the centre of Catholic propaganda and missionary work in the South Netherlands. It was a dramatic, daring move, and one which the Stadtholder had been planning for some time. Learning the lessons of the siege of Grol from the previous year, trenches were dug around the formidable city in April, and the besiegers settled in for a long siege. Behind the walls and protected by three strong outworks was a garrison of nearly five thousand men, supported by two thousand militia. It was destined to be a hard slog, and like Frederick Henry had done when the Spanish had besieged Breda a few years before, the Spanish were likely now to launch some form of diversionary attack into the Republic to compel him to break off the siege. Frederick Henry knew that whatever the Spanish did, he would have to stand firm.

The seizure of Spanish treasure had enabled the Dutch government or States-General to spend vast sums of money on increasing the size of the army. This resulting superiority in force was one advantage which Frederick Henry knew he had over the Spanish garrisons which the impoverished and beleaguered Brussels government could no longer pay for.[17] Another advantage was the absence of the traditional commander of the South Netherlands forces, the marquis Spinola. Spinola had not been killed in action or carried off by disease; instead, the grizzled veteran chose to bear a far more loathsome cross – he would travel to Madrid and plead for the government of Count Olivares and King Philip IV to forge a peace treaty with the Dutch, before further losses had to be absorbed.

Since 1628, Spinola had been of the opinion that peace with the Dutch was essential if Spain was ever to reap some benefit from its continued occupation of the South Netherlands. A journey to Madrid was hardly a prospect to fill one with excitement, particularly since Spinola expected the

Council of State to blame him for the recent losses of Oldenzaal and Grol. Spinola had further grounds to appeal for peace though; he had learned of the new Spanish commitment to the unfolding war in Mantua, a conflict which Spain could hardly afford. After requesting greater investment in the Dutch War for so long, it must have been phenomenally frustrating for this experienced commander of men to watch more resources be sucked into an Italian vortex.

As unable as Spain was to pursue the Dutch War to any successful conclusion so long as it was so heavily committed along the Rhine, it was impossible to imagine that Spain possessed the resources to open a new front now in Italy. The shortages and weaknesses of the Spanish system had forced Spain to lean heavily on both Wallenstein and Emperor Ferdinand, as we will see, but while the latter was willing, the former was adamant that the Habsburgs could not afford so many theatres of war at one time. As commanders with experience in maintaining a war in the field, both Wallenstein and Spinola understood that the resources which were available were not infinite, and if the Emperor did not exhaust his reserves personally, he would exhaust them out of a sense of obligation to the Spanish, who seemed out of touch with reality.[18]

No less a figure than Pieter Paul Rubens, the famed painter, was on hand to serve Spain as a diplomat during these years. Rubens' career was punctuated by the necessity to make peace with the Dutch before the worst excesses of the war ruined the Netherlands altogether. Furthermore, Rubens like Spinola was adamant that Spain's policy of severing the Dutch trade routes and blocking the key rivers was having an adverse effect on the subjects of Spain as well as the Dutch. The decline and gloom present in the South thanks to these severe restrictions were exacerbated by the constantly hiked taxes, news of Dutch victories and, recently, the aftershocks felt following the capture of the treasure fleet by Piet Hein. Reflecting the gloom of Antwerp, a once great trading city and hub of the Netherlands, Rubens remarked in late 1628: 'This city languishes like a consumptive body which is gradually wasting away. Every day we see the number of inhabitants decreasing, for these wretched people have no means of supporting themselves either by manufacture or by trade.'

Both Rubens and Spinola had valid points, but Madrid did not seem to be listening. Throughout 1628 Spinola had worked to reduce the Spanish demands, so that a lasting truce of some kind might be reached with the Dutch before it was too late. In April 1628 the Spanish were still insisting that the Dutch would have to desist from trading with the Americas – an impossible demand – before peace could be considered. Why, indeed, would the Dutch even consider such terms when the fortunes of the war were finally going their way? Indeed, this was Spinola's point, and by September 1628 it was digested, but only partially. The Spanish would offer terms and clung to a Dutch guarantee of religious toleration for Catholics, another impossible demand, and one which they refused to countenance themselves in their own lands. The talks collapsed before they had begun, and Spinola was close to despairing by the time 1629 dawned.[19]

It was an incredibly busy period of the war. Far to the North, the Swedes and Poles were in the process of concluding their war, which had handed lucrative new ports to the Swedish King but had not been as triumphant as he had hoped. In France, the Huguenot fortress of La Rochelle had been captured at long last, ending the threat posed to Cardinal Richelieu's regime by any fifth column religious dissidents. Just as the siege was concluding outside La Rochelle, Piet Hein was capturing the largest Spanish treasure fleet which had ever fallen into Dutch hands. From Mecklenburg, Albrecht of Wallenstein stepped up efforts to conclude a peace with the King of Denmark and end the war with that Northern potentate before Sweden could intervene in force. He advised moderate terms, and eventually prevailed over the vengeful circle around the Emperor. The Emperor was himself busy putting the finishing touches on the Edict of Restitution (see above), a document which would soon change the landscape of the Holy Roman Empire. In North Italy, the Spanish siege of Casale, a critical fortress of Mantua, stalled amidst a lack of supplies and harsh weather; Spanish power was spread far too thin, just as Spinola had warned, and matters were about to get worse.

The widening of the Thirty Years War meant that Spain was in no condition to contest a determined new campaign in the Netherlands. With morale in the toilet, no money arriving for the army in Flanders between October 1628 and May 1629, and Spinola still in Madrid, it appeared that the Spanish Netherlands might capitulate as a whole to the invader. Although the population had long since outgrown their initial affection for the Spanish governess Isabella, aunt to King Philip IV of Spain, Frederick Henry knew that s'Hertogenbosch could still be expected to put up a robust defence.[20] While his forces would eventually swell to one hundred and twenty thousand men, he had arrived outside the fortress city with only twenty-eight thousand. Interestingly, the Stadtholder's army was composed of several foreign contingents. In his memoirs Frederick Henry wrote that of the eighteen regiments in his army, only three were Dutch, the rest were English, French, German, Scottish and Walloon. These soldiers had been hired, and depended upon the Stadtholder to coordinate regular pay with the Dutch States General, but they tended to be fond of their commander, who was careful to provide them with kind words and to share in their burdens wherever he could.

Arriving outside s'Hertogenbosch on 30 April 1629, the sight must have been seriously impressive. S'Hertogenbosch was a kaleidoscope of interlocking rivers and streams, fortified by thick, heavy walls, impenetrable moats and three tough layers of defences in depth, which guarded the few routes in and out of the city. Marshland surrounded s'Hertogenbosch, so that forage was difficult to come by and conditions had the potential to become quite miserable for the besiegers if Frederick Henry was not careful. What the world was beginning to learn was that Frederick Henry was careful, arguably too careful, in preparing the siege works. Under the sun of late spring the soldiers toiled to craft the necessary trenches which would choke the city into surrender, while the inhabitants within the walls prepared for a showdown which they were confident would transpire favourably for them. s'Hertogenbosch had a vibrant history of repelling the invader, but even if this task was too demanding, it was thought certain that Spain would send reinforcements to save them. Surely, neither Madrid nor Brussels could afford to allow this beacon of Spanish defence in the region to fall.[21]

Shorn of funds and soldiers, the Spanish made use of diplomacy rather than military force in an attempt to save s'Hertogenbosch. With Wallenstein concluding his Danish War, it was thought that the time had come for Ferdinand to denounce the Dutch as breakers of the peace and commit to the destruction of that Republic alongside Spain. This idea, which had done the rounds since 1625, was transformed into a shrill and consistent request by 1628. It initially seemed as though this petitioning had done the trick; Wallenstein was moved to send twenty thousand men for the relief of s'Hertogenbosch in June. Yet, despite this promising start, the Spanish could not make up their minds. After having opened the war in Mantua, Olivares found that his gamble to conclude that conflict before the French had captured La Rochelle had manifestly failed. Now he was forced to make a choice, and in the end, Olivares chose to redirect Wallenstein's contingent away from the Netherlands, and down south to Italy in July,[22] just as Frederick Henry's men had breached the last line of defences, and were within twenty-five metres of the city's walls.[23]

While the cause appeared bleak indeed for Madrid, Brussels had not given up all hope. In anticipation of the arrival of Wallenstein's contingent of twenty thousand men, the Archduchess had ordered that as many as possible be scraped together to join him. Together, these two armies would invade the Dutch Republic, forcing Frederick Henry to make a choice just like Spain had done. This force departed Brussels in mid-June, and while it lost its chance to link up with the redirected Imperials, made towards the relief of s'Hertogenbosch instead. The Spanish scouts arrived near s'Hertogenbosch to discover that Frederick Henry had expected them and had done something incredible to protect his siege. Diverting the rivers nearby, Frederick Henry had guided them around his camp, so as to create, in effect, a set of canals which would defend his men from any relieving force.

This feat of engineering took just under three weeks to complete and characterised the Stadtholder as a man of profound skill and perception.

The Spanish force, frustrated by the great difficulty of their task after a few attempts to storm the Stadtholder's position, turned to the original plan and launched an invasion of the Dutch interior. Having invested so much in the siege, Frederick Henry refused to be moved by troubling reports of Spanish successes, as their soldiers pushed to within forty kilometres of Amsterdam. As he expected, the Dutch eventually rallied, and the Spanish exhausted their supply lines, so that by late August their invasion had been repulsed. By that point, s'Hertogenbosch was virtually in Frederick Henry's hands.

He had achieved another coup even before that bastion of Brabant had fallen to him. Thanks to the scraping together of so many garrisons to constitute the invasion force, Spain had left some of its fortresses dangerously undermanned. One of these fortresses, Wesel, was a town of the utmost importance, because it guarded one of the few Rhine crossings in the region. At 4AM on 18 August, a detachment of Frederick Henry's army arrived undetected outside Wesel and seized it after a brief skirmish. The fall of Wesel threatened Spanish communications and supply lines, particularly for that force which had invaded the Dutch interior. While the capture of Wesel was celebrated with enthusiastic salvos of gunfire in the Dutch camp, the defenders of s'Hertogenbosch recognised that the end was near, while Brussels worked to evacuate as many soldiers as it could before they were cut off.

Through these careful, coordinated attacks, Frederick Henry had delivered successive, decisive blows to the Spanish Netherlands regime, and he had gained a great prize in s'Hertogenbosch as well, a prize which had eluded his half-brother Maurice during the latter's attempt to seize the city in 1601. The triumph of the Stadtholder was complete upon the surrender of the city on 14 September 1629. With great anticipation in some parts, and fear in others, the question was now one of what Frederick Henry would decide to do next. Would he march directly against Brussels, sue for an advantageous peace, or gobble up additional fortresses? News on the mood in the Spanish Netherlands, Frederick Henry would have been told, was that the Prince of Orange would be welcomed in Brussels with open arms, but he could not be so sure.[24]

A notable visitor to s'Hertogenbosch during the ceremonial handover of the city was Frederick V, the dispossessed Elector Palatine. A guest of the Dutch since 1621, Frederick had felt compelled to observe the siege works at s'Hertogenbosch several times during the siege's five-month duration. Frederick visited with ambassadors, princes, generals and more, and took time during the summer to stay with his family in a holiday home provided by further Dutch generosity. It is entirely possible that Frederick's activity was his attempt to keep his mind off the recent accident which had claimed the life of his first-born son, also called Frederick Henry after the Stadtholder of the same name. In addition, Frederick may have believed that he could make himself somewhat useful in the Dutch operations, and that his participation would be more worthwhile than lamenting over the failure of the Hague

Alliance.

True to his character, Frederick did not see the ending of the war between Denmark and the Emperor as the conclusion of the struggle. Instead, he was confident that the King of Sweden had a pivotal role to play in his restoration and the application of justice. If the failures troubled him more than usual, then it did not hamper his activity, but it did make him a touch more cynical. After watching the carefully crafted Hague Alliance splutter and die amidst the needless English declaration of war on France, Frederick resigned himself to having lost the entirety of his influence in King Charles' court. Frederick did not even bother recommending one English officer outside s'Hertogenbosch for promotion, since all of his previous letters to London had been ignored. Even though the Dutch War was not his central preoccupation, and a resumption of hostilities in his name in Germany was preferable, it is still significant that this wandering, dispossessed figure chose to stand side by side Frederick Henry when s'Hertogenbosch was surrendered.

It was a symbolic nod towards the unwritten rule of the conflict in Europe at this point; that even where the connection between the different wars had not been made official, the undeclared war would always be fought so long as mutual interests overlapped. Frederick was interested in seeing Spain brought low, since this would weaken the Emperor, which would in turn brighten his prospects for restitution. With Ferdinand so supreme after the defeat of Denmark, and with the Edict of Restitution transforming the religious dimension of the Empire, it was likely of some solace to Frederick that he was able to take part somewhere, in some act that disadvantaged the Habsburg dynasty. In practical terms, the Dutch victory meant nothing for his dreams of restoration – Frederick would have to wait a bit longer for that dream to resurface again.[25]

Frederick was correct in some sense. The fall of s'Hertogenbosch did inflict a crippling blow against the Brussels administration which had to be immediately contained. The war which Spain had initiated in Mantua could now no longer be reinforced by soldiers from the Netherlands – these had been wasted in the recent campaign. This would place further strain on the Emperor's manpower reserves and left a great burden upon Ferdinand to purse the war in Italy – a war which he did not need to fight – to its successful conclusion, regardless of expense. Fears of a lack of available funds instituted a striking turnaround in Spanish policy over the months following the loss of s'Hertogenbosch. Gradually, Spain abandoned several of its positions along the Rhine and below the Dutch Republic, handing some of these over to the Catholic League. With Spain's Dutch War no longer spilling into Germany, it was easier than before for the Dutch to keep to themselves, and to refrain from provoking the Empire to make war. Consequentially, it was that much harder for the Emperor, under Spanish pressure, to make a case against the Dutch as disturbers of the peace, and to argue for a war against them on that basis. The knock-on effects of s'Hertogenbosch for Habsburg strategy were therefore considerable, but closer to home in the Netherlands, the results were even more profound.[26]

> Never have these provinces been more bitter in their enmity towards Spain. If the Prince of Orange and the rebels were not kept by their fanatical intolerance from granting liberty of worship and from guaranteeing their possession of church property to the clergy, then a union of the loyal provinces with those of the North could not be prevented.

This was the opinion of a Spanish official, describing the dire situation facing Brussels by late 1629. It was accurate for two major reasons. The first was that the Spanish administration had lost considerable public support as the successes against the Dutch in the field dried up, the taxes increased and, now, the Dutch triumphs accumulated. The old government of the Archdukes, under Isabella and Albert, was a distant memory since that administration folded after the latter's death in 1621. Since then, the Spanish Netherlands had been ruled by two juntas, one consisting of empowered Spanish officials, another of hand-picked local elites. This bypassed the Council of State, the traditional council of appeal and administration, and it irritated those who served that institution, because the two juntas frequently went behind their backs, or neglected to consult them at all.

These quarrels about governance were exacerbated by the tarnished record of those that clung to power at the region's expense, as the population was led into successive disasters and defeats. The Archduchess Isabella had once been a loved figure for her demonstrated piety and work to better the country, but patience with her and the regime she represented was quickly exhausted once it was brought home to the people that she could not protect these once loyal provinces from the exactions and demands of Madrid. Yet the above extract revealed that while everything appeared gloomy indeed, the people of the Spanish Netherlands would not throw down their arms and invite the Prince of Orange to Brussels, for one key reason – wherever Frederick Henry's triumphs spread, so too did the efforts to establish Calvinism and displace the Catholicism which resided there.[27]

It is important to pause to consider the nature of the religious divide in the Netherlands. In many respects, the case is similar to that of Germany, with a Protestant north and the Catholic south. This religious divide ensured a degree of separation which continued well up to the point of unification. Similarly, in the Netherlands it was religious questions that compelled Protestant merchants and tradesmen to emigrate in their tens of thousands to the cities of Amsterdam and The Hague, just as the Catholic priests and disgruntled citizens of s'Hertogenbosch and the surrounding region of North Brabant made a choice between staying put or travelling from their homes to where their religion was protected and practiced. In the North and South

Netherlands, tolerance was a hot button issue – we have seen the Spanish insist upon it during any peace talks that had been opened.

When the Kingdom of the Netherlands was established in the aftermath of the Congress of Vienna in 1815, fusing the two blocks of the Netherlands together appeared to make strategic, geographic sense. Yet, the breakdown of this arrangement and the Belgian Revolution that followed clarified the situation: despite living as neighbours for hundreds of years, the inhabitants of the North and South Netherlands were no closer to living in harmony in 1815 than they were in 1629. Frederick Henry could conquer as many formidable fortresses as he liked, and he could, if he was brave enough, make a move on Brussels. Unless he made some supreme effort to win the hearts and minds of the Spanish Netherlands populace though – starting with the confirmation of religious freedoms – there was no way that the Brussels administration could fall. If they would not fight for Spain or its King, the Flemish, Walloons and Brabanters would collectively fight to preserve their right to worship as Catholics.

These Catholics watched in indignation as the Calvinists in The Hague sent their uncompromising demands to the new citizens in their fold. Rather than freedom, these new citizens would have to conform. This inflexibility in religion cost Frederick Henry his best opportunity to unify the two blocks of the Netherlands together under his rule. The Stadtholder realised too late the importance of religion to the new citizens, and even then, with the Calvinists left in control following the disruptions of earlier years he was largely powerless to object.[28] Had he objected with enough vigour, history may have played out very differently. Yet it is a significant fact of the period that while religion did not underline all aspects of the Thirty Years War – nor could the conflict be classified as a holy war with much accuracy[29] – religion played a pivotal role in shaping the fortunes of both sides.

The uncompromising Calvinism of the Dutch government prevented a total victory in the Netherlands and the ejection of the Spanish from the region; conversely, the pronouncement of the Edict of Restitution and the rise of militant Catholicism guaranteed that Protestant Germans across the Empire would fight back, using whatever means necessary to protect their positions and freedoms. Frederick Henry was but an instrument in one theatre of this process, but he was a supremely important one. His triumphs had undermined the Habsburg supremacy in Germany, the Netherlands and in North Italy, right at the time when the King of Sweden and the French loomed on the horizon, and the Emperor's subordinates planned on taking him to task. Before the Emperor's position was challenged in 1630 though, the situation in North Italy had to be dealt with. Having played a not insignificant role in undermining the Habsburgs there, other forces were at work that were determined to make Mantua just the latest in a series of costly miss-steps for the dynasty's plummeting fortunes.

THREE
Lifelines From France

> With some writers he is above humanity, — with at least as many, far beneath it ; and lastly, the man, his policy, his power, together with the personages he was mixed up with, and the times he lived in, have proved so attractive to novelists and play-writers, that Richelieu has taken a place and a colouring in the minds of general readers, which no sober and honest biographer can hope to remove or equal.[30]

This is how William Robson begin his biography of Cardinal Richelieu in 1875. The challenge which faced Robson is no less impressive than that which faces any historian who undertakes a mission to unwrap the nuances and complexities of a character from history.[31] Cardinal Richelieu was indeed a complex person. This 'son of an obscure and poor widow in Poitou' rose to establish a premiership which brought France into its glory years.[32] He was neither too vain nor too naïve to avoid appointing a successor, Cardinal Mazarin, who carried on his work at the King's side.[33] He was a visionary and a playwright.[34] He fought tirelessly against the court practice of duelling, out of a belief that the tradition impugned upon the absolutist traditions of French royal power, rather than due to any moral compunctions.[35]

He was a Cardinal, appointed by Rome, yet he allied France with Protestants in order to bring down the great enemy of Bourbon France, the Habsburgs. While he fought alongside the Lutheran King of Sweden and Calvinist Dutch Republic, he worked to supress the French Protestant Huguenots and reduce their political privileges.[36] He has been called, and is widely considered, a political genius of the first order, responsible for transforming the disadvantageous position which France found herself in the early seventeenth century. As one biographer succinctly phrased it:

> After the premature death of Henry IV it was Cardinal Richelieu who beyond all others succeeded in detecting the frailties of the enemy; more than anyone else this political genius knew how to split the power of his opponent, how

to rally new enemies against it, to stir up all that was most dangerous in it as a force for self-destruction, to encompass its downfall methodically and unremittingly through the encouragement he gave to the canker which long before had begun to invade the huge body of the Spanish Empire.[37]

Richelieu accepted from the beginning that the fulfilment of his ambitions depended upon royal favour, and he would make his name empowering this royal family at the expense of the Spanish Habsburgs. Yet, his domestic battles are as remarkable as his exploits in foreign policy, since before he acquired the reins of the latter, he first needed to establish himself and his regime on secure foundations. Richelieu reinforced the absolutist power of King Louis XIII, defeated rival power blocs such as those led by the King's mother, and most infamously, destroyed the bastion of the Huguenots upon the seizure of La Rochelle. These acts were all a means to an end; that end being, the confrontation of Spain on the European stage, on a scale not seen in history.

Richelieu would guide France into war with both branches of the Habsburgs, but before we reach that point of our narrative, it is important to address how Richelieu established his regime, the challenges he overcame at home, and the proxy wars he fought in the build up to the great showdown with the Habsburgs in 1635. This story will be abbreviated for the sake of necessity, but visiting it should grant us a better understanding of Richelieu's motives, and the context of his policy decisions.[38] As a figure that will be part of our story for some time, it is only fair to provide the reader with a proper introduction to the man who played such a pivotal role in French history, and in the shaping of the Thirty Years War.

The assassination of King Henry IV in 1610 robbed France of its dynamic, guiding force just as Europe was dividing into armed camps.[39] The assassination could have facilitated disaster, or another resumption of the Wars of Religion which had shattered the old position of France. Yet, for a variety of reasons, the removal of Henry did not mean the end of his policies at home or abroad. With Louis XIII only a child, the most important task was the establishment of a regency, a task which was fulfilled by Henry's widow Marie de Medici. Marie allied herself with Henry's old advisors and proved adept at balancing the ambitions and inclinations of these figures for the next seven years, until Louis XIII came of age. By acting with impressive speed, Marie managed to cut off the nobility and princes of the blood, who could have acted as her competition. Marie's grip on power was assured, and she did not relinquish it without a great struggle, one which would cost her the relationship with her son.[40]

In October 1614, the regency government made a statement of its foreign policy goals and concerns before the Estates-General. Within the speech, delivered by the Chancellor, several important points were highlighted.

Speaking for an hour, it was a commitment to peace, rather than to any conflict in the near future, that was communicated as the priority. The speech can be considered a kind of balancing act, where France would consummate alliances and treaties with several states, support the interests of Protestants and Catholics in the Holy Roman Empire, and promote amicable relations among the states of North Italy and within the Swiss Cantons. England, Scotland, Spain, Savoy, Venice – all these powers and more were mentioned. Recent conflicts in the Julich-Cleves crisis, and between the Duke of Savoy and Mantua over the issue of Montferrat, had brought forward the importance of an informed, effective diplomacy. Concluding his speech, the Chancellor insisted that French policy had preserved the dignity of France, and that no deal had been made which would compromise the prestige of the Crown.

Taken alone, the speech before the three estates of France represents an important snapshot of French policy on the eve of the Thirty Years War. Yet, the speech is important for another reason. While several contemporaries noted only the duration of the speech, and did not concern themselves much with its contents, one figure present who did make an actual copy of what the Chancellor had said was a deputy of the First Estate – the clergy – the bishop of Lucon, Richelieu.[41] At this point in his life, Armand Jean du Plessis had yet to take on the red robes of a Cardinal, or even to acquire the reputation which would enable him, within the decade, to assume the premiership of France at his King's discretion. Richelieu was born in Paris on 9 September 1585. Born in the final days of the Valois monarchy, he would set himself the task of making the Bourbon monarchy every bit its superior.[42]

Richelieu did not acquire the Cardinalate until 1622, yet he had been no stranger to the Church before that date. His family had a claim on the bishopric of Lucon, and the young Richelieu abandoned plans for a career in the French army to fulfil the wishes of his late mother and lay claim to its offices. Before long, it was evident that Richelieu was talented, driven and intelligent. He applied himself diligently to the task of learning theology, immersing his mind in the inner workings of clerical administration, and bringing some notoriety and prosperity to the bishopric which he called home. His progress made an impression, and his arrival in the Estates General of France in 1614 brought his talents to the attention of Marie de Medici. This proved only the beginning of a life constantly in tune with the French royal family, and with the Queen mother able to recognise ability when it was present, Richelieu was appointed Secretary of State in 1617. The situation facing Richelieu in the international arena was captured most eloquently by Henri de Rohan, a leading French noble who would later fight against Richelieu as military leader of the Huguenots. Rohan assessed the situation thusly:

There are in Christendom two powers like opposite poles, on whom peace and war between other states depend: the house of France and Spain. Spain, with her sudden vast increase of strength, can conceal from no one that her aim is supreme power in Europe and the erection of a new world monarchy in the Occident. The house of France must provide the equipoise. The others powers ally themselves with one or the other of these two great states, each in accordance with its own interests.[43]

The assessment was concise and greatly simplified, but it was also clear to any student of foreign policy that analysed the situation in 1617. France was still recovering from her earlier trials, and Spanish power was everywhere dedicated to keeping France weak and maintaining the Habsburg dynasty at the summit of its powers. There was nothing for France to do for the moment but to bide its time, repair its defences, and prepare for the showdown which was certain to come in the future. Yet, Richelieu was not yet in a position where he could guide French foreign policy. Amidst the eruption of the Bohemian revolt the following year, France was in turmoil over the machinations of court parties, led by Marie de Medici on the one hand and King Louis XIII, who had recently come of age, on the other.

The tension between mother and son had reached such a point that Richelieu was required to mediate between the two parties. In August 1619, his mediation appeared to have paid off, and the Treaty of Angouleme was signed, bringing to a halt any conflict between either party's supporters. And just in time, since Richelieu was faced with the eruption of the first of many Huguenot revolts in 1620. This revolt ended following the inconclusive siege of Montpellier in 1622, and the Treaty of Montpellier granted the Huguenots their fortresses of Montauban and La Rochelle as well as religious rights. So long as the Huguenots retained these fortresses, they would be in a position to threaten the integrity of the kingdom, yet the Crown did not seem equal to the task of delivering a comprehensive defeat to the Huguenots, at least not yet.[44] It should be pointed out that Richelieu did not wish to destroy the Huguenots out of any sense of religious fervour; instead, he was driven by the need to stabilise the realm and take from the hands of the rebellious that excuse which religion might offer.[45]

An interlude between the first and second Huguenot revolts enabled the French government to focus its attentions on foreign policy, specifically two issues loomed into view. The first was the opportunity provided by the breakdown of Anglo-Spanish negotiations, which fostered discussion and negotiation between London and Paris over the potential union of Henrietta Maria, the sister of King Louis XIII, with Prince Charles.[46] The negotiations proved fruitful in the end, far more so than those arranged between Charles and the Infanta Maria, who was wed instead to the future Ferdinand III, the son of Emperor Ferdinand. The negotiation of the marriage contract reflected the renewed French interest in outmanoeuvring Spain by taking advantage of her failures. Yet, it also reflected Richelieu's views on foreign policy, which he was later to elucidate in his *Political Testament*, saying:

> States receive so much benefit from uninterrupted foreign negotiations, if they conducted with prudence, that it is unbelievable unless it is known from experience. I confess that I realised this truth only five or six years after I had been employed in the direction of your affairs. But I am now so convinced of its validity that I dare say emphatically that it is absolutely necessary to the well-being of the state to negotiate ceaselessly, either openly or secretly, and in all places, even in those from which no present fruits are reaped and still more in those for which no future prospects as yet seem likely. I can truthfully say that I have seen in my time the nature of affairs change completely for both France and the rest of Christendom as a result of my having, under the authority of the King, put this principle into practice – something up to then completely neglected in this realm.[47]

To maintain an open and productive correspondence with as many powers as possible was for Richelieu one of the major lessons he had learned from diplomacy as he then understood it. By maintaining relationships with a host of states and potentates, one possessed more options when it came time to formulate important foreign policy decisions. The universal truth of diplomacy was even applied to Franco-Spanish talks for a brief period over 1626-28, when the foolhardy foreign policy decision of the Duke of Buckingham to intervene in the siege of La Rochelle (see below) led England to declare war on France.

Waging an unsuccessful war against France and Spain simultaneously must be considered a forgotten disaster of King Charles' reign,[48] but it did force Richelieu to improvise and adapt to the circumstances. In the strange circumstances which the English declaration of war had created, France and Spain were technically allies, since they faced the same enemy in England. To overcome the common foe, Richelieu was not above fostering even a temporary détente between Paris and Madrid to facilitate a smoother pursuit of war against England. His pragmatic attitude towards foreign affairs granted him the flexibility to pick his battles and postpone others until the time was right. The negotiation of the marriage treaty with England was the first introduction many foreign officials had to Richelieu's abilities, and until the conclusion of said negotiations, the Cardinal distinguished himself. As the historian Robert E. Shimp explained: 'Combining the qualities of stratagem, finesse, ruthlessness and fixity of purpose, the Cardinal was beginning to turn statecraft into a highly specialized occupation, an occupation in which he had no equal in Europe.'[49]

Speaking of picking his battles, the second initiative which Richelieu pursued was the occupation of the Val Telline, that critically important

Alpine valley which housed the Spanish Road. Occupying the Val Telline and cooperating with the locals in the region granted France an impressive strategic position and suggested that France was preparing to become more active in the developing conflict in Germany as well. The Duke of Savoy had encircled Genoa and the Spanish Road was cut, which greatly hampered Spain's ability to supply its forces in the Spanish Netherlands, who were in the process of besieging Breda. At the same time, it was known that France had promised financial aid to the newly formed Hague Alliance of Denmark, England and the Netherlands – this before, of course, the collapse of English foreign policy led to the alienation of Anglo-French relations.[50] Richelieu had been named Cardinal on 5 September 1622, a prelude to his assumption of another office, the premiership, two years' later, and he had plainly wasted no time making his presence felt in foreign affairs.[51]

Considering these feverish activities and the constant presence of rumours, Madrid, Brussels and Vienna would surely have wondered when the declaration against them would come from France. Yet Richelieu knew that the bare facts of the moment prevented France from making such a herculean commitment to the developing Thirty Years War. He had taken advantage of opportunities to undercut the Habsburgs, and he remained committed to supporting the enemies of Spain, above all in the Netherlands, but the weighty declaration of war against the Habsburg dynasty would be delayed for another decade. So long as the fifth column of the Huguenots remained at large, secure in their fortresses, the integrity and security of France would never be safe. Thus, Richelieu moved to erase the political independence of the Huguenots once and for all; he would reduce the potency of their bite by pulling their most formidable teeth.

At the top of this list was La Rochelle, the bastion of the Huguenots for generations. With this goal in mind, French defensive works surrounding La Rochelle had not been taken down, and had in fact been reinforced, while the French Royal Navy was said to be preparing an attack on the Huguenot bastion to eliminate the threat once and for all. Amidst such rumours and frustrated at the Crown's lax application of the earlier Treaty of Montpellier, the Huguenots launched their second revolt in early 1625. The new revolt was characterised largely by naval actions; the Huguenot fleet sailed to Brittany, smashed the royal fleet at Blavet in January, and seized the island of Re just off the coast of La Rochelle. Louis XIII was forced to respond, and Re was taken from the Huguenots following a campaign in September.[52] By spring 1626, a new treaty, the Treaty of Paris was signed, and peace appeared at last to have arrived in France.

The revolt had given Richelieu a nasty shock. It had erupted with sufficient force to necessitate relinquishing the Val Telline, as these Crown soldiers were badly needed elsewhere. The incident had confirmed his earlier belief that the Huguenots would never give the Crown peace, and that they had to be destroyed. Henri du Rohan and his brother Benjamin, two of the leaders of the second revolt, had ostracised themselves from the French Crown, and the latter figure even went into exile in England. Richelieu's distrust of both men, exacerbated by the rumours that they had opened negotiations with Spain, moved the wily Cardinal to act. With the King's army engaging with the Huguenots throughout 1625, Richelieu initiated a pamphlet campaign to complement the military. Interestingly, throughout the course of this pamphlet campaign Richelieu levelled attacks at militant Protestants fighting for the Huguenot cause, but he also saved some venom for the Jesuits, accusing both of undermining the French realm. In the meantime, Richelieu worked earnestly to bring the second revolt to an end.[53]

The Treaty of Paris was, much like the first peace treaty, only a temporary fix. Richelieu was more than ever convinced that France would be unable to pursue a determined policy so long as the Huguenots could hold the King to ransom. They would have to be dealt with, and the only true means to destroy their power was to attack their main bastion directly at La Rochelle. Even before the arrival of Protestantism to France, La Rochelle had distinguished itself as a city determined to acquire independent rights and to govern free from royal interference. The city was granted political and economic privileges which set it apart from others; it owed fealty to no overlord save the King of France, and its citizens enjoyed extensive tax exemptions, while benefiting from the fruits of a budding trade network. As early as 1207, the citizens were even exempted from having to suffer the quartering of a royal garrison in their midst.

These privileges fluctuated with the centralisation and consolidation of the Valois monarchy in the early sixteenth century, but by and large, the citizens of La Rochelle proved adept at weathering these changes to their contract with the King and reversed many of them through negotiation. For example, when a reorganisation of the King's lands removed the city's exemption from taxation in 1535, the citizens bided their time and simply purchased this privilege back from the Crown twenty years later. With the eruption of the Wars of Religion in 1562, La Rochelle was caught in a difficult position. Should her mostly Protestant citizens support the cause of Condé, the Protestant King of Navarre, or should they remain loyal to the French Crown? In the event, the citizens of La Rochelle felt forced to choose Condé's standard, thanks to the perceived threat which the garrisoning of a royal army nearby posed. Fearing that these soldiers of the Crown intended to force Catholicism upon them, in 1568 the citizens of La Rochelle elected to fly into open rebellion. From this point until the capture of their city sixty years later, La Rochelle was a bastion of French Protestantism with a history of defiance, independence and enterprise to match.[54]

By late 1626, it was apparent that Europe was undergoing a kind of change. In Germany, the forces of Wallenstein and Count Tilly had dealt the first of many decisive blows to King Christian IV of Denmark, and the supremacy of Emperor Ferdinand was slowly being established. In the Netherlands, the Spanish onslaught had stalled due to lack of funds, a situation which was exacerbated by the renewed Spanish interest in the Mantuan succession the following year. Charles Gonzaga, the Duke of Nevers, had a valid claim on the Mantuan inheritance, which the Spanish planned to contest alongside the opportunistic Duke of Savoy, notwithstanding Spain's inability to afford another conflict. Gonzaga had had an interesting career even before he journeyed to North Italy to claim what was his by right of inheritance. He had led the French Royal Navy during its loss to the Huguenots in the Battle of Blavet in January 1625, but this was not destined to be the last time that his fate was tied up with that of the Huguenots.

As Nevers travelled, plots were underway in England to resurrect the Huguenot revolt, and empower the French Protestants against the Crown. Neither King Louis XIII nor his indefatigable minister could allow this to happen, but one thing at a time. If France was to contest the encroachment of Spain into Mantua in league with the Duke of Savoy, she would first have to resolve her domestic woes, which were epitomised in the insufferable defiance of the citizens of La Rochelle. By hook or by crook, Richelieu knew that city would have to be taken for the Crown – then and only then could France focus its energies on Italy. The arrival of an English force in summer 1627 on the island of Re, off the coast of La Rochelle, joined by that Huguenot exile Benjamin de Rohan, simplified matters – before anything else was attempted, this foreign army would have to be ejected from French soil. Richelieu's career, and perhaps his life, depended on his odds of success, while his King depended on him now more than ever before.

FOUR

Italian Stallions

The Treaty of Paris had brought the second Huguenot rebellion to an end in spring 1626, but it had not removed that malignant threat which lurked in the background of the French state. It was impossible to imagine France ever being secure until it solved its Huguenot problem, but the problem was considerable, and what was worse, it was providing opportunities for foreign actors to weigh in on the debate. Spanish diplomacy was intelligent and devious, as Spanish Catholic figures promised help and sustenance to the French King in his quest to remove the heretics once and for all. Behind the scenes, Count Olivares worked to stir up the passions of both sides, in the hope that the old Catholic League of the French Wars of Religion would resurface, granting Spain a pillar to stand on inside France, as it had done in the final decades of the sixteenth century.[55]

On the opposite end of the spectrum, the English and Dutch chafed with their French neighbours as the Protestants were squeezed into a tighter position. Ships meant for La Rochelle had been blocked in Amsterdam, and Dutch sailors refused to take any action against their brethren in that troubled French city. The English were more proactive. Benjamin de Rohan, one half of the de Rohan brothers that had led the Huguenots in the past, had fled to London after the Treaty of Paris was signed. There, among sympathetic Protestants, de Rohan worked on a campaign of a different kind – the hearts and minds of the British people. Thanks in no small part to the rise in anti-Catholic feeling, exacerbated by the recent marriage of King Charles with the Catholic Henrietta Maria,[56] the opportunistic Duke of Buckingham found that this was the ideal time to leverage public opinion, and launch a concentrated strike at the French outside La Rochelle. Religious fervour, rather than common or strategic sense, motivated this latest foreign policy initiative of King Charles; it was to prove every bit as disastrous as the previous efforts.

Richelieu did not wish to break with the English or Dutch in any fashion. The latter, at least, were too preoccupied with their Spanish war in the Netherlands to launch any ill-advised adventures, but Richelieu had heard many rumours about English intentions, none of which he liked. In England, Benjamin de Rohan was cheered in the streets, and public opinion had reached such a fever pitch that King Charles refused to return the French ships captured by de Rohan to his brother in law's government. Rather than go against the grain, Charles seems to have been willing to ride the wave of public sentiment, on the expectation that Parliament would – this time for sure – provide financial support for the war they clamoured for. He did not meet with Rohan, suggesting that he wanted to maintain some handle on his own policy, but he never saw fit to hold Buckingham back from the ludicrously optimistic enterprise he embarked upon in late June 1627, when the Duke set sail for La Rochelle.

Richelieu had expected the English since February 1627, and he had considered the Treaty of Paris of February 1626 as only a temporary measure even then. With the co-leader of the Huguenots plotting and scheming among willing disciples, Richelieu could not imagine any course other than a resumption of hostilities – a third Huguenot rebellion in less than a decade. This time though, the Huguenots would fight for their political privileges, they would not be granted new ones. The Crown would seize La Rochelle and put an end to the machinations of that wretched fifth column once and for all, however long it took. Only with the bastion of the Huguenots in the King's hands could Richelieu feel confident examining any additional policies. The calls for action had been many, from scheming allies as well as well-meaning Papal nuncios and Habsburgs. They had urged Richelieu to destroy La Rochelle, with some believing the act would fail, thereby ruining the Cardinal, or that it would succeed, and empower Catholicism. Richelieu had simply not been strong enough, nor had the King's forces been ready. 'Patience', Richelieu had said to a Papal nuncio in late 1625, following a request to crush the Huguenot centrepiece, 'I must go on disobliging the world for a while yet.' The arrival of Buckingham's fleet off the coast of La Rochelle on 10 July 1627 simplified matters. Richelieu was finished with disobliging the world; he was at last ready for the showdown with the Huguenots.[57]

It was the historian Sir George Clark who said that if the campaign at Re succeeded, the world may never even have heard of Oliver Cromwell. It was thus inferred that the failure of Buckingham's force on this miserable, sandy island during the summer months of 1627 facilitated the weakening and then the collapse of King Charles' regime by the 1640s.[58] Discerning such an automatic course of events in so minor a campaign may be a touch hyperbolic, but there is no denying that the Re campaign was a disaster of the first order for the English military reputation, for King Charles' regime and, fatally, for the Duke of Buckingham, who was assassinated shortly after returning home. It is also difficult to imagine how the venture could have been successful, or what kind of lasting impact an English victory would even have had on the besieged Huguenot city. Surely, if frustrated at La Rochelle in 1627-28, Richelieu would simply order the soldiers back to its walls within a few years? The expectation is well-founded, but it does not take into consideration the potential impact on French public opinion such a failure would have had; would King Louis, angered by his minister's failure, have sacked Richelieu?

We can never know whether France would have reacted as violently to the failure of the Re campaign as the English people did, but what we do know is that the enterprise was doomed from a very early stage.[59] It was also quite unlike previous operations within the Thirty Years War, as England acted virtually alone and without even the promise of aid from other powers. Buckingham had counted on the Dukes of Savoy and of Lorraine, but the former was soon to be very busy, and the latter would never have acted against France without considerable help.[60] To put this English adventure in perspective, King James had failed to act independently for the entirety of the early phase of the war, but his son approved a venture which could only isolate his realm, and upon which all likelihood of success depended.

King Charles was already attempting to pursue a lacklustre war with Spain, which Parliament had voiced approval for, only to refrain from financial support. What made this Stuart monarch believe that a war with France was the solution to his troubles, or that Parliament would behave any different than it had done in the past? Charles seems to have believed he had little choice, but he also placed far too much confidence in Buckingham, a childhood friend, and the same man who had been with him all through the Spanish marriage fiasco. For the moment, Charles bought into the story Buckingham was telling, but not for long.

Richelieu did not seek to understand Charles' motives; it was only important for him to appreciate what this trend in English public opinion meant for France. The marriage between a French princess and British King had been meant to set in motion negotiations for an alliance, but neither side proved willing to compromise in the required areas, and the religious issue remained a thorny one in Britain, especially considering the recent Anglo-Spanish negotiations that had preceded the outbreak of war between both parties. Ironically, Buckingham had been the staunchest supporter of an alliance with France, to be directed against Spain, and one historian noted that Buckingham 'had become convinced of the absolute necessity of French assistance for the imminent war with Spain and the recovery of the Palatinate.'[61]

It is also worth considering Buckingham's person motive for orchestrating the war – revenge. Richelieu had advised his King against even allowing Buckingham back into the country to discuss an alliance, a slight which the vainglorious Buckingham took personally, allegedly declaring in response 'Since I am refused admittance into France, as an ambassador desirous of bringing peace, I will force an entrance, in spite of the French, as the leader of an army bringing war.' Henri de Rohan, a major benefactor of the English involvement, or so it seemed, commented acidly on Buckingham's personal interference in King Charles' foreign policy, saying:

> This is the way that silly court affairs cause the convulsions of kingdoms. The interests of favourites are generally the origin of the evils with which peoples are affected; they not unfrequently make use of their masters to increase their own fortunes, and sometimes even to revenge their private quarrels.[62]

Richelieu had not blocked Buckingham for the sake of watching him sulk, but because English and French interests were misaligned. The declared English mission to restore Frederick V was a compelling reason to search for external aid, but the Cardinal was not ready to make war in Spain in 1624, 25 or 26 – he could only be ready once the Huguenots were dealt with. This hesitation was a major cause of the failure to conclude a French alliance, even while the French and British royal houses did intermarry. Taking irony a step further, when Buckingham found the French unwilling, he then moved to inflame the very elements which had prevented Richelieu's complete acceptance of an English alliance in the first place. The wrong-headedness of this policy was on full display, as England made another enemy it could not afford, and the King felt powerless to work against the tide of public opinion which had reached such a fever pitch of anti-Catholic feeling.

Thus, the appearance of Buckingham and his fleet outside La Rochelle on 10 July 1627 was the result of several factors, but it could mean only one thing for Richelieu. The Huguenot problem having significantly widened, with a new enemy on the scene, it was even more urgent that La Rochelle be seized, and these Huguenots crushed. If this French problem continued to drag on into the future, there was nothing preventing other powers from taking advantage, and from following the English example of using the Huguenots as a springboard into the vulnerable underbelly of the realm. In the past, the Rohan brothers had been promised military aid and money from Spain, and Richelieu justifiably feared that the English action was only the beginning, but he need not have worried. Spain was quickly entrapped within the Mantuan affair, and in spite of Buckingham's grandiose blandishments and promises, the 2,500 French soldiers held out on the island of Re, while Buckingham exhausted his supplies.

By 30 August 1627, Buckingham had sent an optimistic ultimatum to the commander of French forces holed up in the fortress of St Martin on Re, writing: 'As I do not wish to subject you to greater hardships, I offer you and your garrison an honourable withdrawal…I should be sorry to employ the extremer measures which I have at my disposal.' But his French counterpart was defiant, writing in response to the effect that:

> The courtesy of Your Highness is known to the whole world, and as it is guided by clear judgment, those who achieve honourable deeds can above all reckon on your approval; and I know no better deed than to lay down my life in the service of my King.

Buckingham's bluff had failed. The surprisingly stiff French resistance on this island in the mouth of La Rochelle's harbour had thwarted him before he even managed to land in support of the actual fortress city.[63] The Huguenots within, initially amazed that the English had indeed showed up, were aghast when they learned of Buckingham's exit by the end of the year. With the English absent, it was possible for Richelieu to orchestrate a concentrated blockade of La Rochelle, severing its lifeline to the sea, and hastening its surrender. Yet it was an anxious wait for this surrender to come. As the months ticked by in 1628, Richelieu was made painfully aware that the siege of La Rochelle was costing France its freedom of action at precisely the wrong time.

Many miles to the south, the Spanish had taken advantage of the French preoccupation with their Huguenot problem by provocatively declaring against the new Duke of Mantua, Charles Gonzaga, also known as the Duke of Nevers. Nevers was well connected to the French monarchy and was the preferred French candidate to succeed in this North Italian enclave. He was also the lawful choice, but this did not matter to Spain. Seizing an opportunity, Olivares acted to reinforce Habsburg influence in the region, and by so doing accelerated the decline of Spain, dampened the Holy Roman Emperor's triumph against the Danes, and left the door effectively open for the King of Sweden.

> I have just heard with extreme sorrow of the death of His Highness Duke Vincenzo [of Mantua]...Deeply though I have respected all my patrons, I particularly had friendly feelings towards His Highness...because I hoped that by his kindness I might have the capital that provides my pension...but my fate, which has always been fickle rather than happy, has deigned to give me this great mortification.

With such language did the Italian composer Claudio Monteverdi reflect upon the death of the Duke of Mantua and Montferrat in late 1627. While Monteverdi was more concerned for his pension, having played in the court of Mantua until 1613 before moving to Venice, a 'great mortification' was en route which would far outmatch a lost pension. War, famine, plague and the loss of a quarter of North Italy's population was to follow Vincenzo's death, as Spain and France competed for influence and power in the region.[64] Duke Vincenzo had been a compromise candidate, a former clergyman, and a scion of the Gonzaga family which had ruled in the two duchies of Mantua and Montferrat since the mid-sixteenth century. The conflict which erupted in 1627 was in fact a continuation of that which had emerged fifteen years before, and which centred on the Gonzaga family's rights of inheritance.

The nuances of the story require some appreciation if we are to grasp what motivated the sequel. In 1613, Duke Vincenzo's elder brother Ferdinando had withdrawn from the clergy in order to rule the Duchies. This was acceptable to the Spanish and Austrian Habsburgs, as the region would revert to Habsburg control following the extinction of the Gonzaga line, but the Duke of Savoy was not pleased. The Duke of Savoy embarked on a war in the name of Ferdinando's sister, whom the Duke argued had a stronger claim due to Mantua since she had never disavowed her inheritance and entered the Church.[65] The Duke was by no means fussed by the rights of women; he was more interested in the fact that this daughter of the late Duke was his granddaughter, and he thus stood to inherit Mantua and Montferrat once the Gonzaga family expired.

The war which followed lasted for three years, with Spain eventually conceding defeat in the miserable sieges of North Italy.[66] The French mediated a peace in 1616, where the status quo ante bellum was agreed to. For the moment, it seemed, all were content to kick the can down the road and to allow Ferdinando to inherit the duchies. In 1626, when Ferdinando died, it seemed possible that war would flare up in the region again, but this was avoided by simply passing Mantua to his younger brother Vincenzo, who, unfortunately, died a year later on 26 December 1627. With the two Gonzaga brothers dead, the Duke of Savoy believed it was time to cash in on his family ties, and he claimed Montferrat, with its strategically vital fortress of Casale as his inheritance. The Spanish governor of Lombardy had long been watching the Mantuan situation, and reported on the death of Ferdinando to Madrid, urging action. He then contacted the Duke of Savoy, and successfully merged the interests of Savoy and Spain together.

It would be in Spain's interest to occupy Mantua; an eventuality planned for during the first war of 1613-16. Since the Holy Roman Emperor was the Duke of Mantua's overlord, and since the King of Spain acted in tandem with the Emperor, the argument for occupying Mantua until further notice appeared to speak for itself. Yet, there was a problem with this plan, and with the schemes of the Duke of Savoy to cleave away Montferrat for himself. While the direct male descendants of the first Dukes of Mantua and Montferrat had died out, another candidate existed. This was the French-born Charles Gonzaga, the cousin of Duke Vincenzo I, whose death in 1612 had sparked the first Mantuan War. Charles Gonzaga, known under his French title the Duke of Nevers, had distinguished himself in wars against the Huguenots, but he had also tasted misfortune, leading the King's fleet to a defeat in the Battle of Blavet of January 1625.

Nevers possessed a valid claim on Mantua and Montferrat, but his ascension to the duchies would represent a grave setback for Spain, especially if the French were able to pull the strings of Nevers' new regime. Nonetheless, on 11 January 1628, while the French tightened the noose on La Rochelle, the word from Madrid was that both King Philip IV and Count Olivares were willing to bow to Nevers' superior claim. This acceptance of Nevers lasted only a few hours, before some important news woke Spain up from its slumber, and in the process doomed North Italy to become a battlefield. By the afternoon of 11 January, letters from the governor of Spanish Lombardy revealed that Nevers had worked for several years to secure his succession to Mantua and Montferrat, but that in the process he had committed several grave procedural errors.

What happened next set the tone. Rather than communicate these developments and put the issue up to debate, Olivares insisted that Nevers' unscrupulous behaviour rendered his claim, if not void, then certainly dubious. In the meantime, Olivares claimed, Spain would hold onto the duchies, perhaps until the matter was resolved, or perhaps for good if there was no resolution to be found. Montferrat, as per the governor of Spanish Lombardy's insistence, would go to Savoy. Contrary to what some historians have claimed, the Mantuan incident was not merely an example of Spanish opportunism; the crisis contained more layers than that. At its heart was the question of legitimate succession; since Nevers was not of the direct line, it was reasonable to expect Nevers to offer some compensation to any counter claimants, since this was the custom of the day.

Unfortunately, the process of succession was confused by the traditional sovereignty which the Holy Roman Emperor held as the overlord of Mantua. Matters were complicated further by the acquisition of Montferrat, which was only added to the Duke of Mantua's portfolio in 1533. Indeed, the rulers of Mantua had only been recast as Dukes by Emperor Charles V in 1530.[67] With the tradition of rule less than a century old in Mantua, it was reasonable to anticipate that the extinction of the direct Gonzaga line would sew confusion. As the historian David Parrott appreciated, confusion was akin to the middle name of the Gonzaga's regime in North Italy:

> There was no unified Gonzaga 'state' of Mantua, but a patchwork of lands ruled over by different branches of the Gonzaga family, whose competing claims and contentions, traditional rights and overlapping jurisdictions ensured that there could be no clear and unambiguous notion of family sovereignty. There was certainly a main family branch – the dukes of Mantua and Monferrato – but no clear consensus about the hereditary rights and sovereign status of this branch in relation to the other Gonzaga family lines.[68]

Within the Duchy of Mantua existed seven miniature slices of territory all belonging to distant Gonzaga branches, and while the fortress city of Mantua was owned by the senior member of the dynasty, the other lesser relatives did not sit idly by, and actively involved themselves in European politics wherever they could. The presence of so many pieces of inheritance and family claims guaranteed that disputes among the House of Gonzaga over who owned what were inevitable. These had the potential to flare up into war, and thus the overlordship of the Emperor was essential for keeping everyone in line and maintaining peace in the region. A long history of appeals to the Emperor had been established by the Gonzaga family before Count Olivares decided to act in the Emperor's name. Olivares was acting with history on his side, but it was the bluntness of his instruments and the wrong-headedness of his approach that caused problems, rather than its inherent illegality.

This division of the Duke's lands is reflected again in the curious joining of Mantua and Montferrat together. Mantua was sandwiched between several different Italian states within the inner centre of North Italy. Venice was to the east, the duchy of Parma and Modena to the south, and Milan to the west. On the other hand, Montferrat was located on the other side of Milan's borders, itself sandwiched between the Duchy of Milan and Duchy of Savoy, with Genoa to the south. Over the years, moreover, Savoy had repeatedly contested the Duke of Mantua's right to hold Montferrat, and the Savoyard Ducal House had even married into the Gonzaga family in an attempt to solve the dispute, muddying the waters still further. Mantua and Montferrat were thus disconnected and had never been naturally joined together as one political unit, nor could they practically be so long as Milan, the centre of Spanish influence in Italy, existed between them. Mantua and Montferrat, in this sense, were no different to the patchwork of states present in the Holy Roman Empire, and the lineage was no less confusing for those involved.[69]

In any event, the succession disputes over Mantua and Montferrat mattered less in their essence than what this dispute moved either side to do. In Olivares' mind, the dispute was sufficient to send in soldiers and to take Casale, the impregnable capital of Montferrat, until the Emperor's requests were satisfied. Nevers, wishing to retain both duchies in their entirety, resisted Olivares' requests. On 15 January 1628, having consulted the theologians who provided the rubber stamp for Olivares' plan, the King of Spain was set on a collision course with both Nevers and with France.[70] The conflict which followed was not one which either France or Spain could afford, yet in both cases Richelieu and Olivares believed reputation was on the line. Spain was standing up for the Emperor's sovereign rights over the duchies, which had to be respected. France was standing up for the policy which prevented any more Italian territory coming into Spanish hands.

It is also worth considering a key fact which must have factored into Olivares' calculations; in January 1628, with France occupied in its siege of La Rochelle, there seemed no time like the present. An invasion of the two duchies would answer the question of Nevers' inheritance before Richelieu had a chance to formulate a response or spin any webs. The key takeaway from this observation though is that Olivares miscalculated how much longer and how completely France was paralysed with the Huguenots. By October 1628, the Huguenot bastion would have fallen to Louis, and the following year, in June 1629, a conclusive peace treaty which shattered the political pretensions of the Huguenots was signed. Pockets of Huguenot resistance remained, but the great showdown had been survived, in spite of foreign interference and now, external distractions.

It must be underlined how interconnected the two campaigns were. Nevers had arrived in Mantua on 17 January 1628, having received the blessing of his distant relative, the King of France, to succeed to the duchies. Richelieu knew that France could not spare the soldiers for a campaign to protect Nevers, but he also appreciated that support for Nevers could not be withdrawn without a significant loss of face. Shortly after he had arrived in Mantua, Nevers had sent a request for recognition by Emperor Ferdinand, who was at that point busy enough with the creation of a Baltic design and the ultimate crushing of Denmark. Around the same time, as we saw, King Philip's advisors approved Olivares' scheme to contest the succession by force, with the help of Savoy, who had interests in Montferrat.

Indeed, it is relatively easy to make a case for the strategic interests of the King of France, the King of Spain and the Emperor in the region. Olivares had already decided on the course of action when he learned that Nevers had refused the Emperor's request to hand over Casale as compensation.[71] Recall, this request from the Emperor was not abnormal given the indirect line of succession which Nevers' claim was sourced from. Had Nevers agreed to relinquish the Montferrat appendage, it is possible that the Emperor and King Philip would have ironed out the outstanding issues and there would have been no need to resort to war. With the French occupied and the Spanish buckling under the reinvigorated Dutch, it could be argued without much difficulty that neither side was in a position to go to war.

However, just as the confused pattern of inheritance enabled the Emperor to request compensation, it also provided Nevers with the vague justification to resist all claims to partition his territories. The kaleidoscope of sovereignty disputes, stately opportunism and dynastic confusion produced an uncertain platform from which to launch the next phase of the Habsburg-Bourbon rivalry. In spite of the desires of both sides and the restrictions applied by common sense though, standing down from Mantua proved impossible. Unfortunately, resorting to force in Mantua did not produce a satisfactory decision for either side. Instead, it created a vortex, into which all resources and manpower – not to mention any sense of an overall strategic plan – were to be sucked.[72]

FIVE

It's All Connected

We are reminded by the historian Thomas F. Arnold of the strikingly interconnected nature of this phase of the Thirty Years War. Placing the situation in its military context, Arnold wrote:

> The military situation in Europe in the summer of 1628 essentially depended on three sieges: the Spanish siege of Casale in Montferrat, the imperial siege of Stralsund in Pomerania, and the siege of Huguenot La Rochelle by the royal army of Louis XIII. As long as Casale withstood, the independence of the duke of Nevers was assured. If Stralsund fell to the emperor, then the Baltic design of Olivares could be put in motion and a united Habsburg effort mounted against the Dutch. The fall of Stralsund would also expedite the appearance of an imperial army in Italy. If La Rochelle fell to Richelieu, then a French relief army, following the historical French pattern of intervention in Italy, could cross the Alps to raise the siege of Casale. Until La Rochelle fell, the duke of Nevers would be on his own.[73]

Another incident of profound importance for the Spanish war effort was the terrific feat of the Dutch admiral Piet Hein, who captured Spain's treasure fleet on 8 September. As we have seen, the seizure of this shining flotilla was an unmitigated disaster for Spain, and a shot in the arm for the Dutch which would pave the way for the siege of s'Hertogenbosch a few months later. Thus, Spanish intervention in Mantua alongside the Duke of Savoy in March 1628 reads something like the attack on Pearl Harbour launched by the Japanese – Spain essentially had 'six months to run wild', and their inability to conclude the war in Mantua before this fiasco was suffered played havoc with the wider Spanish war plans.[74] In the Spanish case though, Olivares' discovery of this fact came abruptly and at the worst possible time. It guaranteed that Spain would have to depend on the Emperor more than ever, a fact painfully confirmed by the loss of s'Hertogenbosch in August 1629. By that point, indeed, Imperial support for the Spanish in North Italy steadily increased – the war had been significantly widened.

Before the conflict in North Italy had even begun a significant development had taken place. This was the reorientation of Savoy away from France and towards cooperation with Spain. Charles Emmanuel was the Duke of Savoy from 1580 to 1630, a fifty-year period of great change, conflict and contradiction. Switching sides at least three times in an official warlike capacity, Charles Emmanuel had grand ambitions for his strategically placed duchy, and hoped to transform it into a kingdom by playing off the Spanish and French against one another, in a bid to make himself indispensable. His tactic showed flutters of success, but Charles Emmanuel was occasionally overconfident and careless, such as during the siege of Geneva in 1602 which was an embarrassing failure, his stop-start intervention in the early phase of the Bohemian revolt, or the unsuccessful attack on Genoa along the Mediterranean coast in 1625. In this latter conflict, Charles Emmanuel had worked alongside the French, but he was burned by the 1626 Treaty of Monzon which handed the Val Telline back to Spain and established Spanish hegemony over much of North Italy.

Charles Emmanuel blamed Cardinal Richelieu for these setbacks, though the Cardinal himself had been forced to compromise in North Italy so that he could respond to the new Huguenot rebellion – a consistent symptom of French weakness which was still being grappled with in 1628. Yet, while his relationship with France soured, it should also be underlined that the Duke of Savoy was opportunistic and had been watching the succession crisis of the Gonzaga family unfold in Mantua and Montferrat for some time. Savoy had long yearned for Montferrat and had married into a descendent of that Duchy's ruling family several decades before to strengthen this claim.

The Duke of Mantua and Montferrat had granted the Duke of Savoy limited territorial compensation, in the hope of pacifying him, but there remained little to stop Charles Emmanuel from taking advantage of the situation once Duke Vincenzo II died in late 1627. Sandwiched between the borders of Savoy and those of Milan, Montferrat appeared to be ripe for the taking, and impossible for the new Duke of Mantua to defend. Incidentally, Charles Emmanuel's plan to coordinate this campaign of expansion alongside the Spanish campaign to restore its reputation proved to be a miserable failure, and the stronghold of Casale, the capital of Montferrat, turned out to be the most impregnable nut which either Savoy or Spain had yet encountered.[75]

French diplomacy had worked hard to retain its Savoyard friend following the unpopular Treaty of Monzon in 1626, even attempting to partition the two duchies, and give Savoy Montferrat at the accession of the Duke of Nevers, but to no avail. Cardinal Richelieu thus appreciated that the conflict would be pursued against Savoy as well as Spain, but that the former might prove the softer target, and its Duke may prove amenable to switching sides once again, if given sufficient incentives.[76] Another claimant on the

Mantuan territories, the Habsburg-supported Duke of Guastalla, provided the King of Spain and the Emperor with a declared war aim and a potential puppet ruler in the aftermath of a successful war. This contingency plan suggests that the Habsburgs had not intervened for the sake of their reputation and the norms of inheritance alone; they evidently planned to rule over the Duchies in some capacity once the French candidate had been ejected.[77]

An additional pretext for war in the Habsburg camp had been provided by Nevers' hasty confirmation of his position as the Duke of Mantua and Montferrat before acquiring the blessing of the feudal overlord of these duchies, the Holy Roman Emperor. After having married the daughter of the late Duke and proclaimed himself Duke of the two territories, it was only then that Nevers informed Ferdinand what he had done. This was unacceptable not only because Nevers had moved so quickly, but also because he had plainly neglected the terms of the contract which the two duchies had with the Habsburg dynasty. Much like the aforementioned expectation of compensation which Nevers frustrated, he also frustrated the initial offer of compromise, largely because it was such a stiff demand. Nevers could receive his Emperor's recognition of his title as Duke of Mantua, but only if he handed over Casale to Spain. Nevers' refusal to hand over that towering fortress compelled the Spanish to make it the aim of their campaign. By mid-May 1628, Casale was under siege.[78]

While the Spanish and Savoyards moved against Montferrat, during the spring and early summer of 1628, Richelieu was tightening the noose around La Rochelle. So long as this bastion of the Huguenots was intact, Richelieu believed that neither he nor his King would have any peace. The actions of the Spanish in North Italy made it plain to him, as had been made painfully obvious in the past, that Spain was not above taking advantage of French difficulties to make opportunities for itself in sensitive theatres. It was imperative that the Cardinal remained transfixed on the task at hand and ignore the Spanish adventures in North Italy as best as he could.

This was easier said than done, for Richelieu faced grave challenges in addition to that brave and durable garrison within La Rochelle's shrinking confines. The positive mood in December 1627, as the remnants of the English force had withdrawn, had given way to impatience and ill rumours by the following spring. Richelieu had done much to keep the besieging army in good spirits, with a regular wage paid every forty days, and free bread as standard, but morale was slipping, nonetheless. As he grew exhausted with the pace of the siege, difficulties emerged with King Louis XIII, who wanted on the one hand to visit the site of the siege, but who did not wish to undermine his Cardinal by doing so too many times.

Then, there were the intrigues of the Queen Mother to consider, as Marie de Medici seemed to have taken it upon herself to scheme against Richelieu now that he had outgrown her patronage. In January 1628, a significant visitor arrived at the besieger's camp – Ambrogio Spinola, the aged but still formidable Spanish commander, who had achieved much fame for his exploits against the Dutch. Known as an expert on siege warfare – with the capture of Breda in 1625 being his crowning achievement – Richelieu saw fit to pick the brains of this individual over the best means of cutting the coastal city off from the rest of the world. Spinola was also informed that France strongly disproved of Spanish efforts to intervene in Mantua, and Richelieu warned that France would fight for the Duke of Nevers if required. Richelieu was here preaching to the choir; Spinola loathed the overstretched Spanish foreign policy adhered to by Count Olivares back in Madrid. He wished above all for the King of Spain either to make peace with the Dutch and be done with that wretched business, or to refrain from making any additional commitments, and focus entirely on Frederick Henry's resurgent campaigns.

In the event, Spain straddled the dangerous line of doing neither; she did not make peace with the Dutch and made it plain that her interests lay above all in North Italy, a message which was received loud and clear in The Hague, to Spinola's intense dismay. The overlapping interests not merely of different war theatres, but also of the commanders within these theatres, reminds us that by the late 1620s it was no longer possible to point to a single conflict which housed the Thirty Years War, as had been possible from the outset of the Bohemian revolt. Instead, that revolt had transformed into a morass of related conflicts, with all parties rushing to accomplish their mission in one theatre so that they could focus on the next. Spinola understood that once the French were finished at La Rochelle, they would turn to meet the Spanish in Mantua, as Richelieu had just told him. Time was therefore of the essence, but speed did not seem to be in Spain's vocabulary by this point of the war. Madrid ignored the veteran commander's urgent pleas to restrict their military commitments and pursued the war in Mantua.[79]

To triumph over the Huguenots, La Rochelle would have to be seized, yet this task was easier said than done thanks to the historic strength of that city's geographic position. Coastal cities required not only a besieging army on land, but also a navy to cut the city's ties to the sea. It was vital that La Rochelle's access to the sea was severed, so that the city would be forced to rely on its own provisions. These stores had been significantly reduced thanks to the support which the citizens of the city had provided to Buckingham's ill-fated army. In March a scheme to surprise the city by entering through a sewer grate misfired, and in April a delirious English soldier who had gotten lost for nearly three weeks was captured. Sewn into his clothes he had instructions from London which suggested that Buckingham would be back in a few weeks. Before he had left the city, Buckingham had left a few thousand English soldiers behind to aid the garrison, but this force had been much reduced by starvation and disease; demanding higher pay as spring 1628 progressed. Still, the possibility that Buckingham would return with a new fleet and more reinforcements to save his stranded soldiers and rescue the Huguenots evoked new levels of panic and urgency in Richelieu's camp; the Cardinal considered, more than once, abandoning the siege, and blaming the failure on some subordinate.[80]

Amidst fresh rumours of English landings, the King felt compelled to journey from Paris to La Rochelle to put steel into the besiegers, and help Richelieu retain control over the operation. He arrived in reasonable time but was quickly informed of a new development. Against all odds and apparently all sense of reason, on 11 May 1628, a second English expedition had been spotted off the coast of La Rochelle. The urgent prayers of the inhabitants had paid off – here was their English miracle sent by God to deliver them from their plight. The mood of the citizens inside the walls was elevated, and the Calvinist governor rushed from tower to tower to prepare the way for the English fleet, who were expected to crush the blockade and land reinforcements that night. In expectation of this deliverance, some of the city's inhabitants tucked into double rations that evening, their faith in the triumph of the following morning demonstrated for all to see.

A lesser figure could well have lost all hope at the sight of the tenacious, wretched English sticking their nose in the King's business once again. Richelieu was indeed shaken by the incident, but through some organisational acrobatics, he ensured that a steady stream of French reinforcements moved to La Rochelle, giving him a great numbers advantage over anything which the English might attempt. This intensive commitment in manpower, not to mention to requisition of supplies to feed and equip them all, explains why Richelieu believed he could only manage one campaign at a time. The Huguenots had roots established so deep in the history of France, that only a sustained and relentlessly expensive campaign would be sufficient to kill the roots and rid the realm of this menace once and for all. It was a game of endurance, and fortunately for Richelieu, the English fleet was not nearly as formidable as it at first appeared.

Buckingham's rampant unpopularity upon his return home had not prevented King Charles from maintaining his close friendship with him and committing to support the Huguenots whatever the cost. This cause required money, and while the King attempted to paper over the cracks, Buckingham urged him to call Parliament and wrest the money through some form of concession. In the shaky relationship between Parliament and King, this generally meant that Charles would have to hear his MPs' grievances, which he was not fond of doing, but for Buckingham and the cause of La Rochelle he swallowed his objections. He swallowed in vain, for two major issues hampered the new expedition. First, Buckingham would not lead it – this role would be taken by his brother in law. Second, while they appeared impressive offshore, with their gleaming white sails and promisingly plentiful number, the reality was that this new fleet had been hastily gathered, badly organised and even more terribly provisioned.

Buckingham's brother in law was hesitant to the point of paranoid in making any committed attack on La Rochelle; instead he lurked offshore inviting concessions from Richelieu and artificially raising the hopes of the citizens. To further confuse the story, when King Charles discovered that this fleet had achieved next to nothing, he sent orders for Buckingham's brother in law to attack at once. Yet these orders were never received; the second expedition departed from La Rochelle's coast having achieved nothing and arrived back in London in the first week of June depleted, having suffered attacks from pirates and unlawfully seized prizes from England's allies. Buckingham had not thought it possible, but the second attempt had been even more humiliating and disastrous than the first. Charles shut himself away for two days, refusing any food or drink, but he neglected to punish anyone. What was worse, the feckless Buckingham was convinced – despite the evidence of improved fortifications which had been thrown up around La Rochelle to aid the Royal French forces in their siege, and the erection of a dyke which aided their blockade of the city – that he could still achieve victory with a new expedition, the third in less than a year.[81]

Richelieu stayed loyally at his post during these trying days; that famous painting of him at the siege of La Rochelle thus being well-deserved. He did not merely arrive in its closing phase to seek some glory for his name, instead he endured the emotional roller coaster of the experience, even if he was provided with far more luxurious surroundings than the common soldier. Amidst so many rumours of English reinforcements and the apparent refusal of the city to concede defeat, Richelieu's mood invariably endured highs and lows. 'If La Rochelle does not fall now, it will never fall, and the Huguenots will be more unbearable arrogant than ever', Richelieu exclaimed to his King. In late summer he seemed improved, and was plotting for the aftermath, writing again to King Louis:

> If you conquer the city, Sire, Your Majesty will be the mightiest King in Christendom, and its arbiter. After the fall of the city we must raze the fortifications of many other towns as well. But we must keep these plans strictly to ourselves, otherwise we may risk finding ourselves confronted with closed gates.

It was somewhat late in the day to be worrying about how the siege of La Rochelle might influence other Huguenot towns across France. By August, the citizens that remained were surviving by eating the grass which had grown between the unattended cobblestones; the rats had long since been hunted down. Any citizens that begged to be allowed escape the city could be executed by the increasingly desperate city fathers, and were unlikely to receive mercy from the besieging soldiers, who had instructions to drive all refugees back into La Rochelle by sword point, lest they would be broken on the wheel themselves. No quarter could be given; any displays of mercy would only prolong the siege and make the King more vulnerable to external events. Richelieu ensured that the soldiers closest to the city's walls had the most aromatic food, so that the starving defenders of La Rochelle were driven to a state of madness by the hunger pangs.

The city looked increasingly like a ghost town, and it seemed certain that the end was near. The dead could no longer be buried and had to be dragged with ropes over the city walls to prevent the spread of disease, which inevitably ripped through the weakened defenders anyway. Defenders died standing from exposure or sheer weakness, and as autumn approached the death toll climbed even higher. On 18 October, four hundred citizens died from starvation, and thousands died every month. The scene must have been akin to an apocalypse and pursuing the siege to the bitter end can't have been an easy task for the besiegers either, though they at least held the upper hand. Still the city fathers and its Calvinist governor closed ranks and refused to give in. They held out hope for Buckingham's third expedition, a hope which turned out to be not as forlorn as one may have expected.[82]

> By unexampled endurance, La Rochelle has held out now for a year under the tortures of famine, and all this to give Your majesty time to send the promises help...The fact that your fleet appeared at last in spring, and was seen for several days, and sailed away without doing anything or making the slightest attempt to do anything: even this has not shaken the resolution of the citizens... Will future generations read in the history of Your Majesty's reign that the town was destroyed while in your royal hands, and that from the goodwill which Your Majesty assured the citizens he nursed for their cause, the only reward they reaped was the pitiless enmity of their own sovereign, from whom without that goodwill they might have hoped to find mercy.

These were the words of La Rochelle's ambassador to King Charles in late September 1628. By this point, a combination of religious conviction, Buckingham's persuasive arguments and the sheer fact that so much had by now been invested in the operation, Charles was genuinely affected and moved by the plight of the besieged. While his motives for pursuing a war with France while also at war with Spain should be heavily scrutinised, Charles was convinced of the necessity in sending yet another expedition to relieve the enduring Huguenots. Yet the British King was fighting an uphill battle not only against his own courtiers, who were turning against Buckingham, but also against international opinion.

Dutch and Venetian representatives had signalled their approval of the French siege of La Rochelle, and even while Dutch sailors had refused to board ships meant to attack the Huguenot fortress, the official policy of the Dutch government remained one of cauterising the Huguenot wound, so that France could be brought onto a more secure footing, and Spanish power could be combatted more effectively. On 23 August 1628, while talking with friends, Buckingham was fatally stabbed by a disgruntled soldier, who had bought fully into the pamphlet then doing the rounds, which had described the unlucky Duke as the 'viceroy of Satan.' Regardless of his many flaws, Buckingham had been a staple feature of the Stuart court for some time. Charles had grown up with, had travelled with him, had depended upon him, and saw him daily. The news of his murder was whispered to the King as he was in prayer. Absorbing the news, the blood rushed to the King's face, and in a mixture of anger and grief, withdrew to his chambers and flung himself weeping onto his grand bed. His good friend and in many respects his mentor was gone. Richelieu, predictably, lost no sleep over Buckingham's death:

> Buckingham was a man of low birth, of ignoble mind, without honour, without knowledge, ill-born and ill-bred; his father was deranged in mind and his brother so insane that he had to be shut up. He himself stood halfway between madness and sense; he was extravagant, possessed, and without measure in his opinions.

The end of Buckingham meant potentially significant things for the Anglo-French relationship. As Buckingham had been the driving force behind the assaults on La Rochelle, it stood to reason that the enthusiasm for that doomed venture would now fizzle out entirely. Henrietta Maria, the sister of King Louis XIII and the wife of the grieving King Charles, had also loathed Buckingham, and it was her messenger that bore the news of Buckingham's end. Thinking it a trap, Louis initially had the messenger imprisoned, but when the truth was learned, and his origins made clear, the King awarded him with one thousand thalers and sent him on his way. Evidently the French royals hoped that the removal of so vehemently anti-French a figure represented the beginning of a new era in Anglo-French relations. Richelieu simply hoped that it meant an end to English ventures in aid of La Rochelle.[83]

Incredibly enough, Richelieu was to be disappointed. On 3 October 1628 the third and final expedition appeared outside La Rochelle's harbour. This was the most impressive one yet; containing 114 ships, eleven infantry divisions and led by a competent sailor, Lord Lindsey, who had distinguished himself at sea against the Spanish from a young age. This venture appears more like an act of vengeance from a bitterly grief-stricken King than any coordinated campaign, but Richelieu still could not afford to ignore it. During the first week of October Lindsey's fleet attempted to entrap their French counterparts, but the manoeuvres were unsuccessful, and the French coastal defences were too strong. Lindsey faced mutiny from his sailors in spite of the urgency of his mission – that being to bring food to La Rochelle and relieve the suffering of its citizens.

By the first week of October though, it was far too late for a rescue and Lindsey surely knew it. The siege lines which Richelieu had ordered erected in the spring around the city were now impregnable, and the city had lost eight thousand inhabitants through starvation and deprivation since the summer began. La Rochelle was a shell of its former self. Lindsey attempted to offer terms, and to mediate between King Louis and the Huguenots, but neither Richelieu nor Louis were in any mood to permit English interference in this regard. The King demanded capitulation from his subjects and insisted that freedom of worship was only a temporary perk of a timely surrender. By mid-October, Lindsey had to inform La Rochelle's governor that his fleet was not fit for combat owing to mutiny, and by 26 October the remaining inhabitants of the gutted city gathered to bow to the inevitable.

The writing had been on the wall for some time, but with this final English failure, there was no longer anything to hope for, and even less to fight for. A prisoner of the citizens was asked to appeal to the King's mercy, as the city surrendered unconditionally to its predicament at last. Shortly after, Lindsey's fleet sailed away. On 28 October 1628, the surrender of La Rochelle was officially received. The ordeal had taken a year, but it was finally complete. The back of the Huguenots had been broken once and for all. Several approaches for dealing with the city were suggested, revolving around the question of whether mercy should be shown, or whether the city should be made an example of for the remaining Huguenots in the country. Richelieu weighed in on the debate, indicating as he did so where he stood, and what he believed the bigger picture to be:

> Seldom has a prince been given such an opportunity to distinguish himself by his mildness before the world and future ages; mildness and pity are the qualities in which Kings should imitate God, for they can be His true representatives on earth only by good deeds and not by destruction and extermination. Also, the deeper the guilt of La Rochelle, the more glorious must appear the monarch's greatness of heart; he has broken the town's resistance by his invincible arms and forced the rebels to fling themselves on his mercy and that alone; but still greater will seem his victory over himself if he now forgives them. The name of this town will carry his fame over all the world and spread it among future generations.

It was a grand gesture, but the recipients of whatever mercy the King could muster was now greatly reduced. At the beginning of the siege, La Rochelle had stood proud with over twenty-five thousand citizens. By the final days of October, barely five thousand remained.[84]

The capture of La Rochelle did not eradicate French Protestants overnight, nor did it eliminate the possibility of a Huguenot uprising in the future, though it significantly reduced that possibility. In the first place, one of Europe's foremost ports was now under the absolute control of the French crown.[85] In addition, Richelieu now had the leverage necessary to make a lasting peace with the Huguenots, one which would shatter their political autonomy even if their creed remained legal. Making this peace was a balance between dealing a heavy blow to the Huguenots, impressing upon them the errors of their ways, and emphasising the magnanimity of the King's mercy. It was a demanding checklist, but Richelieu achieved it with the Edict of Grace, wherein Protestant worship was permitted, but the Huguenots were prevented from establishing or maintaining any 'state within the state' into the future. This Edict confirmed the Edict of Nantes from a previous generation, and confirmed the central authority of the King of France over all of his subjects. It was signed in late June 1629; a few months after a very different, far less appeasing Edict had been declared law by the Holy Roman Emperor.[86]

The conclusion of the La Rochelle siege in late October meant the effective end of this final Huguenot rebellion, but it also spelled doom for Spanish strategy in Italy. Having banked on Casale submitting quickly to the joint Spanish-Savoyard invasion, the tenacity of Casale's inhabitants, against the expectations of Olivares, meant that Spain was still invested in that siege when La Rochelle collapsed. As early as March 1628, when Richelieu continued to bang his head against La Rochelle's walls, the Cardinal was informed of the Spanish-Savoyard attack on Montferrat. He was kept appraised of events in Montferrat, as that coalition rolled up every outlying town before reaching Casale in mid-May. Richelieu had confidence in the strength of Casale's position, but he did not wish to bet his career upon its relief. He communicated with the Spanish to see if there existed some way to honourably achieve satisfaction for France and Spain. This went against his earlier insistence to Spinola that he would support the Duke of Nevers no matter the consequences, but at the same time they reflect his weakness so long as La Rochelle sucked in so many of the King's men. As negotiations between France and Spain began breaking down, Richelieu informed his King that twenty thousand men would be ready within a couple of weeks to march towards North Italy once La Rochelle fell.

Until La Rochelle ceased to be a problem, Richelieu had more than enough on his plate, and he would have to rely on Casale to hold out against the Spanish onslaught for as long as possible. Disagreements followed in Madrid over these developments, as Philip IV's ministers demonstrated their divided opinions and their agreement with Spinola, while others, like Olivares, insisted that no expense on the reputation of the Spanish realm was too great to spare.[87] It was not until August that the siege of Casale was presented in its full context before the Spanish Council of State, and then the penny dropped for the Spanish King, as he authorised that the fall of that Italian stronghold should be accelerated by any means necessary.

Unfortunately for Philip IV, these urgings were in vain. Autumn brought successive bitter blows to Olivares' administration and to the Spanish psyche, to the extent that it may be considered a turning point of the Thirty Years War.[88] First, the weather around Casale deteriorated, and the roads were transformed into torrents of mud through which only the most tenacious and indefatigable army could march. The Spanish, having sat outside Casale for nearly half a year, had exhausted its reserves, and could not hold on through winter in this state. The decision of the Spanish commander to hold on after all meant that he would be in no state to meet any relief army that materialised in 1629, at least not without some serious backup. This was where the Emperor's forces came in. As the siege of Casale carried on into the winter of 1628, news from thousands of miles away brought intense shame and dismay to Madrid.

The exploits of Piet Hein at the expense of the Spanish treasure fleet was not only a psychological blow, it was a financial disaster because the income from this fleet had already been factored into Spain's debt repayments. With no money coming in, Spain skimped on its wages to the army of the Spanish Netherlands, or what was left of it, during a six-month period from late 1628 to the first half of 1629. During these circumstances, Frederick Henry's meticulous operations outside s'Hertogenbosch excelled, compounding Madrid's failures. Finally, the hammer blow of La Rochelle's capitulation in late October 1628 made it apparent that Spain had lost the race. She would now have to contend with the relief army sent by France, to be expected sometime in spring 1629. Again, considering the grim task of the besiegers to hold on outside Casale during the harsh winter of 1628-29, it was unlikely these soldiers would be equal to the task of meeting any significant French challenge. Thus, the requests of support sent to the Emperor went from a trickle to a flood, as Spanish fortunes during autumn 1628 worsened dramatically. King Philip IV also seems to have decided, in late 1628, to have swallowed his pride with regard to Italy. Together with his ministers, he composed a letter to King Louis XIII which amounted to a surrender, which read:

> In the interests of Christendom and for the peace and tranquillity of Italy, which I have always desired and worked for, I declare that neither now nor in the future will I do anything to impede the duke of Nevers' possession of the dukedoms of Mantua and Montferrat, nor will I threaten in any way the territories of the Christian King or those of his princes and confederates. The said king will [in return] make a similar declaration and will retire his army from Montferrat, Susa, Piedmont and Italy. I promise and swear on my faith and royal word, to observe this and maintain it firmly and truthfully for ever.

It is highly significant that, in the context of a French resurgence following the fall of La Rochelle, the French King refused this overture, thus signalling his willingness to fight it out with Habsburgs forces in this latest Italian war. Having emerged from such a trying period of his reign, Louis seemed content to harness the newfound security which the crushing of La Rochelle granted him. Preparing for a proxy-war with Spain in North Italy was no small commitment, but his minister had evidently informed him that France could manage it. Having spent so many years on the defensive, Richelieu believed that the time was right at last to take the fight to Spain, just when King Philip IV's realm was at its most overstretched, impoverished, and weakened. The interconnectedness of these highly varied war theatres; outside La Rochelle, at the walls of Casale and thousands of miles away at sea under the command of Piet Hein, had never been so strikingly demonstrated.[89]

Chapter 14 Notes

[1]Wedgewood, *Thirty Years War*, pp. 193-195.

[2]Geoffrey Parker, *Europe in Crisis*, pp. 187-190.

[3]See Paul Arblaster, 'Our Valiant Dunkirk Romans': Glorifying the Habsburg War at Sea, 1622–1629', in *News Networks in Early Modern Europe* by Joad Raymond, Noah Moxham eds (Brill, 2016), pp. 586-587.

[4]Peter H. Wilson, *Europe's Tragedy*, p. 434.

[5]Wedgewood, *Thirty Years War*, p. 227.

[6]Wilson, *Europe's Tragedy*, pp. 367-368.

[7]Parker, *Europe in Crisis*, p. 190.

[8]Parker, *Thirty Years War*, p. 92.

[9]See J. H. Elliott, 'Self-Perception and Decline in Early Seventeenth-Century Spain', *Past & Present*, No. 74 (Feb., 1977), pp. 41-61; p. 47.

[10]See George Edmundson, 'Frederick Henry, Prince of Orange', *The English Historical Review*, Vol. 5, No. 17 (Jan., 1890), pp. 41-64; p. 57.

[11]Wilson, *Europe's Tragedy*, p. 434.

[12]See also S. J. Stearns, 'A Problem of Logistics in the Early seventeenth Century: The Siege of Re', *Military Affairs*, Vol. 42, No. 3 (Oct., 1978), pp. 121-126.

[13]Edmundson, 'Frederick Henry, Prince of Orange', p. 57.

[14]*Ibid*, pp. 57-58.

[15]Wilson, *Europe's Tragedy*, pp. 434-435.

[16]See Wilson, *Europe's Tragedy*, pp. 435-436.

[17]George Edmundson, 'Frederick Henry, Prince of Orange', p. 59.

[18]Parker, *Thirty Years War*, p. 96.

[19]Parker, *Europe in Crisis*, pp. 190-191.

[20]Wedgewood, *Thirty Years War*, pp. 240-241.

[21]Edmundson, 'Frederick Henry, Prince of Orange', pp. 59-61.

[22]Parker, *Europe in Crisis*, p. 191.

[23]Wilson, *Europe's Tragedy*, p. 437.

[24]Edmundson, 'Frederick Henry, Prince of Orange', pp. 61-64.

[25]Brennan Pursell, *The Winter King*, p. 262.

[26]Wilson, *Europe's Tragedy*, pp. 437-438.

[27]Pieter Geyl, *History of the Dutch-Speaking Peoples*, pp. 379-381.

[28]*Ibid*, pp. 382-383.

[29]Wilson, 'Dynasty, Constitution and Confession', pp. 512-514.

[30]William Robson, *The Life of Cardinal Richelieu* (Routledge; London, 1875), p. x. With thanks to Google Play E-book Online Store.

[31]A good overview of the bibliography of works on Richelieu is available by William F. Church, 'Publications on Cardinal Richelieu since 1945: A Bibliographical Study', *The Journal of Modern History*, Vol. 37, No. 4 (Dec., 1965), pp. 421-444.

[32]Orest Ranum, 'Richelieu and the Great Nobility: Some Aspects of Early Modern Political Motives', *French Historical Studies*, Vol. 3, No. 2 (Autumn, 1963), pp. 184-204; p. 186.

[33]Mazarin will come under our microscope later on in this book, but a good examination of his character and policies is provided by Geoffrey Treasure, *Richelieu and Mazarin* (London: Routledge, 1998).

[34]Richelieu's vision for maintaining peace in Europe was addressed in the 1642 play of the same name to which he contributed heavily. See Edward W. Najam, '"Europe": Richelieu's Blueprint for Unity and Peace', *Studies in Philology*, Vol. 53, No. 1 (Jan., 1956), pp. 25-34.

[35]Duelling had been outlawed by King Henry IV, but the enforcement of the ban had lapsed after his death. Duelling was such a problem among the French nobility that Richelieu felt compelled to support the ban once he came to power. See Richard Herr, 'Honour versus Absolutism: Richelieu's Fight against Duelling', *The Journal of Modern History*, Vol. 27, No. 3 (Sept., 1955), pp. 281-285.

[36]W. J. Stankiewicz, 'The Huguenot Downfall: The Influence of Richelieu's Policy and Doctrine', *Proceedings of the American Philosophical Society*, Vol. 99, No. 3 (Jun. 15, 1955), pp. 146-168.

[37]Carl J. Burckhardt (trans. and abbr. by Edwin and Willa Muir), *Richelieu: His Rise to Power* (Borodino Books reprint from 1940; Virginia, 2017), p. 4. Google E-book.

[38]Recent biographies of Richelieu do a far better job examining his character and development than I could hope to do in the space I have reserved for him. See Jean-Vincent Blanchard, *Eminence: Cardinal Richelieu and the Rise of France* (Walker Books; New York, 2013); Anthony Levi, *Cardinal Richelieu and*

the *Making of France* (Da Capo Press; Cambridge MA, 2001); Joseph Bergin, *Cardinal Richelieu: Power and the Pursuit of Wealth* (Yale University Press; New Haven CT, 1990).

[39]Burckhardt, *Richelieu*, p. 5.

[40]See J. Michael Hayden, 'Continuity in the France of Henry IV and Louis XIII: French Foreign Policy, 1598-1615', pp. 12-13.

[41]*Ibid*, pp. 14-15.

[42]Burckhardt, *Richelieu*, pp. 4-5.

[43]Quoted in *Ibid*, p. 65.

[44]W. J. Stankiewicz, 'The Huguenot Downfall: The Influence of Richelieu's Policy and Doctrine', pp. 146-147.

[45]Robson, *The Life of Cardinal Richelieu*, p. 63.

[46]For more on this marital arrangement see Robert E. Shimp, 'A Catholic Marriage for an Anglican Prince', *Historical Magazine of the Protestant Episcopal Church*, Vol. 50, No. 1 (March,1981), pp. 3-18.

[47]Henry Bertram Hill (trans.), *The Political Testament of Cardinal Richelieu, The Significant Chapters and Supporting Sections* (University of Wisconsin Press; London, 1961), p. 86.

[48]The disaster exhausted all patience Parliament had both with Buckingham and the King's foreign policy initiatives, and England effectively retreated to her Isles for the remainder of the Thirty Years War. See Carolyn A. Edie, 'Tactics and Strategies: Parliament's Attack upon the Royal Dispensing Power 1597-1689', pp. 215-216.

[49]Robert E. Shimp, 'A Catholic Marriage for an Anglican Prince', p. 7.

[50]See Wedgewood, *Thirty Years War*, pp. 190-191.

[51]Burckhardt, *Richelieu*, pp. 132-133.

[52]Jack Aden Clark, *Huguenot Warrior: The Life and Times of Henri de Rohan 1579-1638* (Springer; The Hague, 1967), p. 120

[53]W. J. Stankiewicz, 'The Huguenot Downfall: The Influence of Richelieu's Policy and Doctrine', pp. 149-151.

54See Judith Pugh Meyer, 'La Rochelle and the Failure of the French Reformation', *The Sixteenth Century Journal*, Vol. 15, No. 2 (Summer, 1984), pp. 169-183; especially pp. 169-177.

[55]Two good sources on this League and the religious conflict which housed it is examined by Elizabeth Tingle, 'Nantes and the Origins of the Catholic League of 1589', *The Sixteenth Century Journal*, Vol. 33, No. 1 (Spring, 2002), pp. 109-128; Mario Turchetti, 'Religious Concord and Political Tolerance in Sixteenth- and Seventeenth- Century France', *The Sixteenth Century Journal*, Vol. 22, No. 1 (Spring, 1991), pp. 15-25.

[56]The negative effect on public opinion which the marriage was beginning to have is examined in Robert E. Shimp, 'A Catholic Marriage for an Anglican Prince', pp. 15-18.

[57]See Carl J. Burckhardt, *Richelieu, His Rise to Power*, pp. 171-177.

[58]See Sir George N. Clark, *War and Society in the seventeenth Century* (Cambridge, 1958), p. 20.

[59]An excellent analysis of the campaign for Re is available in S. J. Stearns, 'A Problem of Logistics in the Early seventeenth Century: The Siege of Re', *Military Affairs*, Vol. 42, No. 3 (Oct., 1978), pp. 121-126.

[60]Burckhardt, *Richelieu, His Rise to Power*, pp. 177-179.

[61]Shimp, 'A Catholic Marriage for an Anglican Prince', p. 11.

[62]See William Robson, *Life of Cardinal Richelieu*, p. 69.

[63]Burckhardt, *Richelieu, His Rise to Power*, pp. 182-183.

[64]See R. A. Stradling, 'Olivares and the Origins of the Franco-Spanish War, 1627-1635', *The English Historical Review*, Vol. 101, No. 398 (Jan., 1986), pp. 68-94; pp. 68-69.

[65]Parker, *Europe in Crisis*, pp. 154-155.

[66]On Gonzaga fortifications see Thomas F. Arnold, 'Gonzaga Fortifications and the Mantuan Succession Crisis of 1613-1631', *Mediterranean Studies*, Vol. 4 (1994), pp. 113-130.

[67]This revisionist perspective is provided in David Parrott, 'The Mantuan Succession, 1627-31: A Sovereignty Dispute in Early Modern Europe', *The English Historical Review*, Vol. 112, No. 445 (Feb., 1997), pp. 20-65.

[68]*Ibid*, p. 26.

[69]*Ibid*, pp. 27-33.

[70]See R. A. Stradling, 'Prelude to Disaster; the Precipitation of the War of the Mantuan Succession, 1627-29', *The Historical Journal*, Vol. 33, No. 4 (Dec., 1990), pp. 769-785; pp. 773-775.

[71]*Ibid*, p. 773.

[72]Peter H. Wilson, *Europe's Tragedy*, pp. 438-439.

[73]Thomas F. Arnold, 'Gonzaga Fortifications and the Mantuan Succession Crisis of 1613-1631', p. 125.

[74]'Six months to run wild' is the short-hand phrase taken from the cautionary advice given by the Japanese Admiral Yamamoto in the prelude to the attack on Pearl Harbour. While completely unrelated to the Thirty Years War, those interested in the quote and its context should read James B. Wood, *Japanese Military Strategy in the Pacific War: Was Defeat Inevitable?* (Rowman and Littlefield; New York, 2007), pp. 22-24.

[75]Peter H. Wilson, *Europe's Tragedy*, pp. 438-440.

[76]David Parrott, 'The Mantuan Succession, 1627-31: A Sovereignty Dispute in Early Modern Europe', pp. 43-47.

[77]*Ibid*, pp. 48-50.

[78]R. A. Stradling, 'Prelude to Disaster; the Precipitation of the War of the Mantuan Succession, 1627-29', pp. 774-775.

[79]*Ibid*, pp. 776-777.

[80]See Carl J. Burckhardt, *Richelieu: His Rise to Power*, pp. 199-214.

[81]*Ibid*, pp. 216-223.

[82]*Ibid*, pp. 224-228.

[83]*Ibid*, pp. 229-235.

[84]*Ibid*, pp. 236-241.

[85]The economic significance of La Rochelle in the context of the Huguenot rebellions, and the extent to which its economic power compelled the French crown to seize it, are issues examined by Franklin Charles Palm, 'The Siege and Capture of La Rochelle in 1628: Its Economic Significance', *Journal of Political Economy*, Vol. 31, No. 1 (Feb., 1923), pp. 114-127.

[86]For more information on the Edict of Grace, also called the Peace of Alais, see W. J. Stankiewicz, 'The Huguenot Downfall: The Influence of Richelieu's Policy and Doctrine', pp. 156-160.

[87]The importance of reputation for Spanish officials and for Spanish foreign policy in general is examined in two articles by J. H. Elliott which we have encountered before. See 'Self-Perception and Decline in Early Seventeenth-Century Spain', *Past & Present*, No. 74 (Feb., 1977), pp. 41-61; 'A Question of Reputation? Spanish Foreign Policy in the Seventeenth Century', *The Journal of Modern History*, Vol. 55, No. 3 (Sept., 1983), pp. 475-483.

[88]R. A. Stradling, 'Olivares and the Origins of the Franco-Spanish War, 1627-1635', pp. 68-70.

[89]R. A. Stradling, 'Prelude to Disaster; the Precipitation of the War of the Mantuan Succession, 1627-29', pp. 778-784.

(Top left) Tsar Michael Romanov
(Top right) Wladyslaw IV of Poland (Peter Paul Rubens, 1620)

A. Sacra Regiæ Maiestas. B. Archiepis: Gnesnen Primas Regni. C.Archiepis: Leopolien D.Episcopi Senatores:
E. Palatini, Castellani, Senatores. F. Magistratus et Officiales Regni et Magni Ducatus Lithuaniae. Senatores.
G. Officiales Curiæ Aulici, et Secretarij RSM. H. Nobil et Regni et Mag.Duc.Lith.

Iacobus Laurus fc 1622. Romæ in Priuilegio SummiPontificis

The Polish Sejm under Sigismund I

CHAPTER FIFTEEN
"Halting the Habsburgs"

_*For God or the Devil*

ONE

Opportunities Lost

It did not take long for the Spanish appeals to the Emperor to bear fruit. In the first week of December 1628, Emperor Ferdinand II wrote to Albrecht von Wallenstein on the question of intervention in the Mantuan War and impressed upon him the importance of the conflict. Note the Emperor's belief that he had been insulted by the Duke of Nevers, a point underlined by Nevers' refusal to consider any compromise or partition of his lands. The letter reads:

> We inform Your Grace of the decision made by the ordinary royal Spanish ambassador at our court...regarding his efforts to remove the French troops from Italy. Although we would not have wanted to use force for this purpose if the Duke of Nevers had not insulted our imperial sovereignty and rejected our recent peace offer, to which both Spain and Savoy had recently agreed, and if he had refrained from invading the Imperial fiefs of Mantua and Montferrat and dismembering the Holy Roman Empire (of which we expect full information within a few days and will report it to Your Grace).

Thus, the Emperor claimed, he had not wanted to act in North Italy, but he had felt compelled to act in the interest of his rights and prerogatives as overlord of the two Italian duchies which Nevers had hastily claimed. Note also Ferdinand's reference to the rejection by Nevers of a peace offer which had been approved by Spain and Savoy; this was the end result of the letter sent by the King of Spain to the King of France (see above) and had been constructed in the first place because both Olivares and King Philip IV of Spain feared the implications of France being able to focus its full attentions on the Mantuan War now that La Rochelle had been dealt with. In short, the peace overtures had been sent during a time of weakness and had been rejected by France and then the French candidate, Nevers, for these reasons.

The toxic blend of offended pride, ignored protocols and opportunism on the part of the Habsburgs motivated the intervention in North Italy, and as a scion of this House, Ferdinand could do nothing but fall in line with the

686

Spanish requests for aid. One should bear in mind that at this point in time, the Emperor had yet to conclude peace with the Danes and had yet to release the terms of the Edict of Restitution. Spanish satisfaction at the conclusion of the former dilemma was mixed with horror at the ripples of controversy created by the latter Edict. Spain's objections to Ferdinand's policies throughout 1629 were not based on moral grounds but were exacerbated by fears that the Emperor would create problems for himself in Germany, and thus be unable to help Spain in North Italy or the Netherlands. The letter continued:

> In these circumstances, we had no choice on account of our imperial office, house and state but to oppose this start and to meet the threatened violence with force and to protect ours and the Empire's rights as best as possible. Therefore, we have warned our dear brother, His Highness the high-born Leopold, Archduke of Austria, to take steps to improve security for this place and to report to us the status of this emergency. Meanwhile, Your Grace will send us your advice as soon as possible, whether it would be appropriate to send the remaining 60 companies of horse and foot that are in the upper Kreise [that is, the Swabian Circle in south Germany], or at least most of them, into Italy as the situation requires, and to replace these with troops from elsewhere, that Your Grace does not need so badly in the lower Kreise. We are in no doubt that you will reflect maturely on the reason for such a necessary move and suggest the best means to us...[1]

This letter captures the essence of what 1628 meant for the Habsburgs. On the one hand, it meant closer cooperation between the Austrian and Spanish branches, symbolised by military and diplomatic assistance as well as the reinforcement of the family ties seen in the marriage of the Infanta Maria with the future Emperor Ferdinand III. On the other hand, by cooperating more closely with Spain, and by committing to defending the dynasty's reputation on several fronts, the Emperor added to the strain placed upon his forces. Worse than that, at a time when he had a real chance to bring about peace in Germany, Ferdinand committed to war in North Italy; a war which would surely be remembered by the French in the future. The King of Spain was pulling the Emperor in too many directions, spreading his forces too thin, right at the moment when a new phase of the war in Germany was about to begin. He was also making new enemies; support for the Spanish war in Mantua angered Pope Urban VIII, who refused to approve of Ferdinand's requests to canonise new saints in Bohemia to replace the old ones. The lack of enthusiastic Papal support right on the eve of the Edict of Restitution was a problem, and as the years progressed, Ferdinand's relationship with Urban VIII only grew worse.[2]

As he indicated in this letter though, Ferdinand believed he had no choice other than to act, since too much was at stake in North Italy to ignore King Philip IV's pleas. A Spanish defeat was as terrible a consequence to contemplate as the reduction in respect for the Emperor's name which might follow if the Duke of Nevers was seen to defy Habsburg authority in its fiefs and get away with it. Such dynastic concerns were needless distractions in Wallenstein's mind though, which was a problem, since the Emperor had requested personally that his generalissimo do as he was told and peel off some soldiers for the Mantuan campaign. Wallenstein had never been quiet about his feelings on the Mantuan affair, and he had weighed in on the conflict early. In March 1628, before the main Spanish-Savoyard army had laid siege to Casale, the Bishop of Mantua had arrived in Vienna on a fact-finding mission, to ascertain whether the Habsburgs would unite against the Duke of Nevers. Reporting back to Nevers, the Bishop recorded some hearsay which, while second hand, at the very least suggests Wallenstein's true feelings on the matter. According to the Bishop of Mantua, he had spoken to Ferdinand's court chancellor, who had been present on the council when Wallenstein had arrived in Vienna during the previous months. While in the presence of the council and the Spanish ambassador, so the chancellor said, Wallenstein had told them that:

> If they wanted to wage a war against Mantua and the Duke of Nevers they should not let the thought enter their heads that they would get a single soldier from him, even if the Emperor himself gave the order. It would be an unjust war, as all the laws of the world supported Nevers.

Wallenstein would have found himself very much in the minority among Habsburg circles if he had vocalised this opinion, but he had never been one to strive for popularity. Instead, he had relied upon his relationship with the Emperor as his personal instrument, and appreciated that so long as there was a war to win, and he was in a position to win it, it did not matter that he did not always agree with the latest policy line. Wallenstein objected on the grounds that Nevers did have the stronger claim in comparison to the Habsburg candidate, the Duke of Guastalla. Putting aside the need to defend the dynasty's prerogatives and Imperial protocol, Wallenstein saw only the naked opportunism of the Emperor and the King of Spain, who wished to score easy points in North Italy at the expense of the German war which he was trying to bring to a conclusion. Objections on grounds of principle were one thing, but we must consider that Wallenstein, the career soldier, was driven most by strategic-military concerns. Wallenstein correctly anticipated that intensive Habsburg intervention in Italy would antagonise the French, and that now they were freed from La Rochelle, France would stop at nothing to avenge itself upon the Habsburgs along the Rhine and in Italy – and all this when Wallenstein expected the arrival of the King of Sweden from the North.[5]

The French commitment to the war in Italy which Wallenstein had feared did not take long to materialise. As if making up for lost time, Cardinal

Richelieu was determined that King Louis XIII himself lead a contingent of men through the winter snows, where the weaker partner of the alliance, Savoy, could be crushed. If this venture was successful, then the Spanish-Savoyard force besieging Casale in Montferrat would be forced to retreat, having exhausted much of its reserves in that year long siege already. Richelieu made his case during a meeting of the Council of State on 26 December 1628. He met with some opposition on what must be considered sensible grounds; by this point, even with La Rochelle's capture, much of the South of France still contained malignant elements, and peace was several months away. Furthermore, the plot to cross over the Alps and fight a campaign in the height of winter without an ally appeared tantamount to suicidal.

Richelieu digested these objections but argued passionately that France could not afford to look weak any longer. Any additional losses would chip further pieces off her once glorious edifice; inaction and caution had been acceptable bedfellows during the worst of the Huguenot troubles, but it was high time now to show the Habsburgs, the Germans and the rest of Europe that French power remained considerable even after all the recent trials. That the campaign was associated with the Val Telline passes also appealed to Richelieu's sense of strategy. Maintaining Mantua and Montferrat as French satellites would work wonders for any future schemes to sever the Spanish Road, and thus undercut Spain during times of war. Italy, Richelieu insisted, was the centre of the world, and must be treated as such. It was a risk, the Cardinal admitted, and the risks were clear to him; 'in this question, only the King himself can decide; the possible dangers are too great.' In response, Louis XIII rose to declare his approval of the Mantuan intervention plan, as well as its importance for the wider strategic aims of his realm. What was more, Louis was adamant that he should lead whatever expedition ventured towards North Italy; the French army and the French King had much to prove, and Louis was as determined as his wily minister to act.[4]

On 15 January 1629, with twenty-two thousand soldiers the French King moved south towards Italy. By 14 February he had reached Grenoble, and by now Richelieu was with him. The heavy snow falls were already restricting French movement even before they had left France behind, but both Richelieu and the King were in one mind about the need to push onwards. By the 1 March, the French were encamped at the entrance to the stunning Susa Valley pass in the Alps – the longest valley in Italy at over fifty kilometres in length – and it was here that some feverish diplomacy with the Duke of Savoy was entered into. Before they crossed through his lands and assaulted his position in the Mantuan war, Louis advised Richelieu to try to reason with the aged Duke. But Charles Emmanuel would not be drawn to compromise; he presented the French representative with a striking set of demands, including that France must openly declare war on Spain and that Charles Emmanuel must be permitted to seize Genoa before Savoy would side with France and freely allow her soldiers safe passage. On the basis of these communications, Richelieu had a declaration of war on Savoy drawn up.

It was said that the Duke acted as though he was at the head of fifty thousand men and Louis only ten thousand. In reality, the French army had been reinforced by the besieging force at La Rochelle and had swollen to thirty-five thousand men. This was more than large enough to meet with the defensive works erected throughout the Susa Valley, which led towards the city of Susa. After several days' march higher and higher into the Alps, the expected resistance from Duke Charles Emmanuel was finally encountered. Francois de Bassompierre, a courtier, military leader and old friend of Henry IV, reported to his King after reconnoitring the land ahead. A defensive line three layers deep was described, and the Duke of Savoy was likely expecting them. Nonetheless, the enthusiastic Bassompierre was eager for battle, and attempted to persuade his King to advance. 'Sire', Bassompierre declared, 'the guests are gathered, the fiddlers are in their places, the maskers are at the door. If Your Majesty pleases, we can begin the dance.' To this Louis replied, 'Are you aware that we have only five pounds of lead in our arsenal?' Bassompierre replied with a laugh, 'This is a fine moment for remembering that. Because the mask is not ready, are we to miss the dance? Let us begin, Your Majesty, everything will go splendidly.' Richelieu added his perspective to the conversation by saying 'Sire, from the expression on the Marshal's face, I think we can count on a fortunate issue.'

Indeed, the battle for the Susa passes had begun, and by its end, the French would be chasing the Savoyard soldiers to the city of Susa, which they would then besiege. On 5 March, the city was taken, and the Duke of Savoy was sent a clear message: the King of France was less than fifty kilometres from his capital at Turin.[5] On 7 March 1629, Savoy made a hasty peace with the French, enshrined in the Treaty of Susa which followed. During this period of French triumph, English diplomatists secured the conclusion of their dismally unsuccessful war as well. By July, the Treaty of Susa had grown to accommodate the conclusion of these two conflicts. Richelieu's first significant foray into peace-making had been met with considerable success. France had achieved its objectives in North Italy, had concluded the dead-end war with England, and now stood to gain from Habsburg overextension.

Meanwhile, their Dutch ally had choked the Habsburgs in the Spanish Netherlands with the siege of s'Hertogenbosch, which was progressing well throughout the summer of 1629. Further afield, the Emperor had made peace with the Danes with the Treaty of Lubeck and apparently brought peace to Germany in the process. Yet the peace was overshadowed by the Edict of Restitution, which outraged moderate Protestants, worried moderate Catholics, and left the militants in Ferdinand's court dissatisfied. Both Wallenstein and his colleague Count Tilly were occupied with the task of implementing the Edict – a task which, we will recall, Wallenstein did without much enthusiasm. However, he did commit to the dispatch of an army towards the Netherlands, with the aim of relieving the siege of s'Hertogenbosch and endangering the Dutch. Within a few weeks though, the Habsburg entanglement in North Italy betrayed this scheme.

The reorientation of Savoyard diplomacy towards the French orbit followed the peace. This disaster was compounded by the failure of the year-long siege of Casale, and the staffing of that fortress with French officers. The Duke of Nevers was not duly pleased about this, but he would have little time to make noise. Following Savoy's ejection from the war, Olivares pressed his King to request that this relief force meant for the Netherlands would be re-routed to North Italy instead. Spain had made its choice, and it had chosen to compete with France in North Italy rather than meet the threat which the resurgent Dutch now posed. Raising the stakes, Olivares felt he had no choice other than to unite the Habsburg war effort against France, in the hope that by achieving victory in Mantua, defeat in the Netherlands and the loss of the Spanish silver fleet the previous year would be forgotten.[6]

In reality, this desperate policy cost far more than it delivered, and brought to an end the pretence of Ferdinand as the arbiter in Italy. With the reorientation of soldiers towards Mantua, and the repeated letters to Wallenstein requesting that he send more, 1629 was turning into a year of heavy commitments for the Habsburgs. While they chopped off the head of one enemy, another two grew up in its place. To Wallenstein, this mutation of the conflict into Germany from a simple beast to a monstrous hydra was not something he could prevent. Having no control over Imperial foreign policy, he could only make his objections known, and resign himself to following the Emperor's requests as far as his capabilities would allow.[7] A letter sent by Wallenstein to the Emperor on 10 October 1629 captures the essence of his dilemma most effectively, and is therefore worth reciting in full here. Wallenstein wrote:

> I now humbly report to Your Imperial Majesty that after all the troops I had to send to the Netherlands and Italy, there are no more than one company of cavalry and three or four foot left in the Empire and among those returning from Denmark, as well as this side of the Elbe. Meanwhile, the few troops that I still have on the other side of the Elbe are in posts where they must remain to keep an eye on things, because Sweden's hostile intentions are becoming clearer by the day. And because these posts are spread across one hundred miles along the coast, not to mention to positions [around Stralsund], as well as posts inland and at points that have to be held, in case the Swede comes, there are no troops I could lead into the field, and I had to borrow eight...companies from Count Tilly in order to strengthen the positions around Stralsund. The men

that Your Imperial Majesty sent to Prussia as aid [for the King of Poland] have been so affected by hunger and grief that there are no more than five thousand left. From this you will see that it is not possible to send the seven thousand or even a company in these circumstances. Since there are everywhere states and others ill-intentioned whose machinations may well cause a general uprising in the Empire and force Your Imperial Majesty to continue the war, no mean can be spared in the coming spring, let along sending reinforcements to the Netherlands, but on the contrary more should be recruited so that yourself, and your kingdoms and lands, as well as the Empire, are not endangered.

Wallenstein's overarching worry of Swedish intervention is palpable in this letter, and his account also brings forward a valid question – where had all the soldiers gone? By October 1629, many had been lodged in garrisons, some had been transferred to the wars in Poland, the Netherlands or North Italy, and a select number had deserted. As the money in Wallenstein's private stores dried up, it became necessary to leverage contributions from larger segments of the population. To do this, he needed to keep increasingly large segments of his army occupied with the tasks of intimidation, collecting contributions and arranging the timely transportation of said contributions to where they were needed most. This was a complex, time-consuming process, and it was far from ideal. Wallenstein would have preferred to have retained his private fortune and pay the debts with his own assets, but such debts had grown so enormously that covering them himself was no longer possible.[8] It was in this trying position that Wallenstein urged the Emperor to speak to the Infanta – the Archduchess of the Spanish Netherlands – and appeal to her on the grounds that she must fight her own battles, because Ferdinand's resources could not afford to fight them for her. Wallenstein continued:

I also hope that the Dutch army will be depleted through the siege of s'Hertogenbosch and, because winter is just before the door, will not be able to do anything more. Therefore, because Your Imperial Majesty cannot spare any men or send them to the Netherlands, Your Majesty should advise the Infanta in good time that she should use the winter to collect sufficient troops in order to resist the enemy better in spring.[9]

Unfortunately, Wallenstein had evidently become the victim of the restricted German postal service, because this request demonstrates that he was uninformed. Unbeknownst apparently to Wallenstein, by 10 October 1629 the Dutch had been in control of s'Hertogenbosch for nearly a month, having captured it after a length siege on 14 September. But while these losses were serious, there was a silver lining which would make itself felt in time. The one major contribution Wallenstein had made to that siege had been redirected, as we have seen, towards the Mantuan War, but this decision did bear fruit. In September these reinforcements arrived to begin a siege of Mantua, the first city of the Duke of Nevers' property portfolio. The task was a formidable one and appeared to be as ill-fated as that siege undertaken against Casale. The Imperial army was forced to abandon the siege altogether during the height of winter in December 1629, thanks to a lack of progress and provisions. For one key reason though, when they returned in May 1630, the siege was a great deal easier. The Imperial army was aided by a new ally – the arrival of plague within the city of Mantua, which effectively gutted the garrison and decimated the ability of the citizens to resist. On 18 July 1630, Mantua surrendered, as did the Duke of Nevers, and the city endured a three-day sack superseded in its horrors only by that of Magdeburg a few months later.[10]

We shall return to the developments of the Mantuan War at a later date, but for now it suffices to note that while the negotiations at Regensburg were underway throughout 1630, this conflict was on the mind of those German princes that attended. The Emperor's willingness to wage war in different theatres, endangering the relationship of these Germans with the French in the process, was difficult to stomach. However, it was the mistaken belief that Wallenstein pulled the strings, and that this generalissimo was the blunt instrument which Ferdinand could never abandon that truly empowered the opposition. The reality was far less straightforward; Wallenstein, as we have seen, was appalled by the increasing range of military commitments which the Emperor pledged his soldiers to. He was also feeling the economic pinch of enduring in a state of war for such long periods, as the incomes from his considerable estates no longer covered the whole cost of maintaining such a vast amount of men in the field.

Above all though, Wallenstein had feared throughout 1629 that the withdrawal of soldiers from Germany towards Italy would leave the door open for the King of Sweden to enter. In addition to all concerns, thanks to the Edict of Restitution, Wallenstein was learning that portions of Germany were going into business for themselves and resisting efforts to implement the Edict wherever this was attempted. Where he had once been an irreplaceable conduit of the Emperor's will, if the rumours were correct, then Wallenstein would soon be little more than a bargaining chip of the Emperor in his looming meeting with his German princes and potentates. Curiously perhaps, Wallenstein was more amenable to the idea of his dismissal than might have been expected, provided he was suitably reimbursed for his service, but at the same time he was perplexed and made ill by the refusal of the court in Vienna to listen to his strategic concerns. In the final analysis, it must be argued that Wallenstein was right to fear the strategic implications of Habsburg overextension just when the King of Sweden was concluding his Polish War. Indeed, Wallenstein was right to fear, and the Emperor was fatally mistaken in his unwillingness to listen.

TWO

Imperial Cracks

From July to September 1630, some of the most important actors in Europe gathered at the town of Regensburg for an Imperial Diet and a congress. Conspicuous in their absence were the two Protestant Electors, Saxony and Brandenburg. Both had already begun to drift away from the Emperor's orbit, thanks in large part to the ill-advised Edict of Restitution which had so alienated them the previous year. The presence of representatives from France and Spain at the congress confirmed its importance though, as did the pace of events outside of its confines. Only a few days after opening, the King of Sweden landed at Pomerania, initiating a journey which would take him to the heights of prestige and fame, as he wrested the peace which Emperor Ferdinand had sought right out of his hands.

Significantly, those assembled at Regensburg were not thinking of Sweden; they were far more preoccupied with the war which remained open, rather than the wars of the future. In April 1630, Ferdinand had outlined his proposals for the upcoming conference. These proposals included a desire to extend the Peace of Lubeck with Denmark throughout Germany, and to bring an end to all forms of conflict within the Empire. Nobody could object in principle to this aim, since all had felt the pinch of this war which had lumbered forward for over a decade. With no enemies in the field, it was hoped that Wallenstein would be dismissed. With the French and Spanish amongst the two thousand individuals in attendance at Regensburg, it was also hoped that the war in Mantua could be concluded, and the Empire could repair its shattered infrastructure in peace.

Having achieved some incredible triumphs, Ferdinand was willing to make a certain amount of peace, but his ulterior motives rubbed the Electors the wrong way, and left him vulnerable to making concessions which he could not afford.[11] In December 1629 Ferdinand had written to his Chancellor in Vienna about organising a compromise peace, urging him to give peace...

...due consideration and reflect reasonably on the current situation in Italy, as well as that in Germany, and how one might deal with the growing power of the States in the Netherlands, and the obstinate intrigues of hostile parties with foreign potentates. I prefer all the more, as I have often indicated, that the Italian differences were settled by amicable compromise, but thereby my imperial authority must on all accounts be preserved and receive due recognition and be assured of its implementation at this time. You will direct all negotiations in accordance with this our intention and direct the council so that the way is open to the amicable compromise I so eagerly await.[12]

As this correspondence indicated though, Ferdinand was only willing to countenance a lasting peace arrangement on his terms. He had authorised the Edict of Restitution in spring 1629, which effectively torpedoed the best opportunity the Habsburgs had to bring all corners of the Empire together, regardless of religious or political outlook. Ferdinand's stance going into Regensburg was that he would give up neither the Edict nor the generalissimo which granted him his power without a struggle. From the beginning it had been made apparent that Protestant opinion was squarely against the Emperor's policies. Taking their time to respond to the Edict and to highlight its disastrous implications for their lands and subjects, the Swabian Circle weighed in on the debate in early 1630. The princes of the Swabian Circle, west of Bavaria, had suffered much from the privations of war and from the stipulations of the Edict of Restitution. The practice of Protestant worship in the Circle, which had grown exponentially since 1555, meant that the land alienated from the Catholic Church was, according to the Edict, ripe for the taking. This was too much for these individuals, who urged the Emperor to reconsider such policies in a letter sent directly to the Imperial Court in January 1630:

We have become anxious that we and other loyal Estates are in dire poverty and are facing immediate ruin, and again voice our concern at the destruction and devastation of the entire Roman Empire to Your Imperial Majesty and humbly beseech your protection, aid and rescue, and meanwhile regard it as advisable to approach you as well, as the foremost loyal council appointed to advise the Empire. It is our diligent view and request, that you will not only take to heart sympathetically the regrettable condition of ourselves and other loyal Estates of the Empire, but also, but from duty to the Empire, as well as for the good of His Imperial Majesty and his dynasty, and for the preservation of the entire Roman Empire, to remind and assist with true advice, without letting up until not only the insatiable burden of war is recognised without, [and that] the loyal Estates together with their subjects are being driven into the ground, despite their patience, through no fault of their own, together with all the misery and evil that entails. Moreover, thanks to the Imperial Edict, we and other Evangelical princes and Estates are threatened with judicial punishments the like of which has neither been heard nor used before in the

Empire, [and] are being de facto deprived of our property that we have held for many years through legal entitlement and inherited from several generations of ancestors. Instead, the directions of the Imperial constitution should be followed to the current situation in the Empire and that such religious and church matters should be dealt with according to the usual custom, as equality and justice should apply to them, as well as the [1552] Treaty of Passau and the (1555) Religious Peace, and everything done differently, and care taken, and matters handled according to the constitutional ways and means so that no one has cause for complaint, but on the contrary the authorised separation and difficulty of the Empire and Estates can thereby be removed.[13]

The Swabian Circle formed merely a snapshot of Protestant opinion within the Empire – it was also to be expected that other Protestants would find their own means of protest in the near future, if they were not listened to here. And yet, Ferdinand was not moved. He would surge forward with the Edict, and he would present steep demands of his own to those assembled at Regensburg before contemplating compromise himself. The Holy Roman Emperor was the master of Germany, thanks to Wallenstein's triumphs and the lack of any formal opposition in the Empire. Aside from the King of Sweden, who in spring 1630 lurked in the background, no potentate possessed the power to contest what Wallenstein had crafted. In spite of this fact though, it must be said that the Emperor's triumphs were not built on particularly durable foundations. The application of force through Wallenstein had been Ferdinand's trump card, but it came with complications. Resentment among the Catholic electors increased so long as Wallenstein's power and importance grew. Despite Maximillian of Bavaria's own responsibility for Wallenstein's position, by 1630 he wished to replace him and his army with that of the Catholic League, and to resume the leverage he had once held over the Emperor.

Maximillian led the opposition to Wallenstein, sponsored the most scandalous rumours about his intentions, and worked as hard as he could to undermine his position. By spring 1630 this was easy enough to do, because now that Wallenstein was forced to rely on contributions taken from the Habsburg Hereditary Lands, he no longer seemed as useful an asset to Vienna. Furthermore, almost because of his triumphs, Wallenstein had elevated Imperial soldiery to such a point that the notion of appointing a successor seemed perfectly possible; it was no longer the case that only Wallenstein could solve the Imperial crisis. Indeed, thanks to Wallenstein's dominance of the military sphere, Ferdinand faced no crises save for those he created himself.[14]

There was one question which Ferdinand felt compelled to answer out of familial duty. Since 1625 Vienna and Madrid had worked closer together, but due to his preoccupation first with Frederick V's machinations, and then the King of Denmark, Ferdinand had been unable to contribute much towards the Spanish war effort in the Netherlands. The princes and electors of the Empire, having no quarrel with the Dutch, would never have countenanced war with such a valued trading partner. It was thus fortunate for the Emperor that Wallenstein was in a position to act as the Emperor's instrument, rather than as a conduit of German policy. Acting independently of the German princes, Wallenstein sent soldiers to intervene in the Polish War, into the Netherlands and finally, towards North Italy during the Mantuan War. He did all this on Ferdinand's instructions, and because his force was independent of the German princes, the Emperor had not needed the permission of these princes to act. This is not to say that Wallenstein had no reservations where any of these conflicts were concerned; he was far more drawn to the prospect of ending the war in Germany and retiring to his considerable duchies in Mecklenburg and Friedland. 'I have received four different and strict orders from the Emperor to lose no time in despatching soldiers to Italy', Wallenstein had noted in August 1629, 'and even though I do not think it advisable I have complied, because His Majesty has commanded it.'[15] By 1630 though, Spain expected more than the commitment of Imperial soldiers to the Mantuan War.

They sought instead the official denunciation of the Dutch by the Empire, and the military intervention of its princes against those rebels, who were charged with breaking the Imperial peace. Certainly, a case could be made that the Dutch had directly or indirectly sponsored most schemes against the Habsburgs – everyone's favourite Winter King continued to use The Hague as his base of operations – but it was equally true that the Spanish had stretched their tentacles into Germany and refused to withdraw. Both the Spanish and the Dutch saw their contribution towards the war in Germany as a way of striking at his foe; neither could afford to completely detach himself from that theatre, especially when there were critical river crossings to guard and quarters to consider. Madrid escalated this policy after the defeats began piling up from late 1628. Unable to strike at the Dutch directly, Olivares wished to lean more heavily on the Emperor for aid, and to push back at the French – the main ally of the Dutch – wherever possible.

For the Emperor to support Spain militarily, he would first need to wrest the declaration of war from the Imperial Diet on the Dutch, and second to send Wallenstein to lead the armies against that stubborn Republic. The problem with this was twofold; the first was that Wallenstein was himself advising against widening the war in Germany by involving the Dutch, and he had intimated in the past to Ferdinand that he did not have the manpower to fight in Germany, the Netherlands and North Italy simultaneously. The second problem was less easy to overcome. Ferdinand needed Wallenstein to command Imperial soldiers, but quickly learned just how unpopular his generalissimo had become. Although he had granted their religion its new position of dominance, trounced all their enemies and turned so many tides, the Catholic Electors did not hesitate to turn against Wallenstein once they felt the generalissimo had served his purpose. It is significant that the Emperor did not put up more of a fight for Wallenstein, just as it is important to explain why Wallenstein did not fight to be retained.

Ferdinand arrived in Regensburg on 19 June accompanied by an imposing retinue intended to demonstrate the power and glory of the Emperor. If the other actors at Regensburg had expected Wallenstein simply to drop everything and accompany his Emperor to Regensburg though, then they were to be disappointed. Although Wallenstein would have been well within his rights to attend – he was Duke of two large and important territories after all – the generalissimo had no interest in exposing himself to the venom which was doing the rounds in the city. 'I have had to make enemies of all the electors and princes, indeed everyone, on the Emperor's account', Wallenstein remarked. 'That I am hated in the Empire has happened simply because I have served the Emperor too well, against the wishes of many.' This estimation of public opinion was accurate, and Wallenstein was certainly careful to keep up to date through an information network which he had established as early as 1623. Wallenstein had more than enough to do without taking time out for a public appearance; he was also in constant pain owing to poor health and frequent attacks of gout which laid him low for several weeks at a time. Wallenstein chose instead to move his headquarters closer to Regensburg rather than to attend in person, and he ensured that his representative was regularly in touch. Still, it is worth considering what might have happened had Wallenstein attended in person, for the simple fact that not a single Elector at Regensburg – not even Maximillian of Bavaria, the proprietor of the rumour mill – had ever met him in person.[16]

Considering the kaleidoscope of interests at Regensburg, it is interesting to discern in the different parties where they stood on the Wallenstein question. In spite of his work in the name of the Edict of Restitution – albeit reluctantly – Wallenstein represented a less straightforwardly militant religious arm of the Emperor than did the forces of the Catholic League under Count Tilly. Since the conflict had begun in the Empire, both forces had remained separate, and Maximillian of Bavaria hoped to be rid of Wallenstein, combine the two forces, and resume his position of influence at Wallenstein's expense. The Protestant Electors – Saxony and Brandenburg – did not approve of the Catholicisation of the Emperor's forces. Wallenstein, whatever the ruin he had brought, was not the Catholic League, and the Elector of Brandenburg issued instructions to his representatives to the effect that they were not to participate in any schemes which might undermine Wallenstein's position. Saxon representatives were issued with similar instructions, with the added caveat that addressing the question of peace would make the maintenance of large armies in Germany irrelevant anyway.

French representatives worked to undermine Wallenstein, because his presence granted the Emperor far more freedom of action and power than Ferdinand would otherwise have had if Maximillian of Bavaria was calling the shots, as he had been up to 1625. Unsurprisingly then, the Spanish backed Wallenstein for this very reason, and both sides were keenly aware that Maximillian of Bavaria was prone to making agreements with France, agreements which could be disastrous if the Catholic League army was somehow subdued through French diplomacy. The French were supported by the Papacy, who wished to weaken Spanish influence in Italy. While those three parties possessed a stake in the negotiations, it was the Catholic Electors led by Maximillian of Bavaria that controlled the proceedings.

On 17 July these Electors intimated to the Emperor that while questions of Universal Peace, a reckoning with Frederick V and the involvement in related conflicts were important, of most importance to them was Wallenstein. It was never more apparent that the Electors blamed the generalissimo for all the evils and ills which the war had caused – the spread of plague, the loss of life, the ruin of harvests, the terror of the soldiery, the destruction of the Empire's infrastructure – these were consequences which Wallenstein had sought to avoid at all costs, since their spread made his job of maintaining so many soldiers a great deal more difficult. Ferdinand tried to appease them with vague promises about improving the organisation of the army, but the Electors returned on 1 August, and delivered their list of complaints about Wallenstein in person, straight into their Emperor's hands. It was a striking gesture of their contempt for the man who had propelled Ferdinand's powers to unimaginable heights.[17]

Ferdinand had long been resilient to the idea of dismissal, for several obvious reasons. Maintaining Wallenstein granted Habsburg power a monopoly in Germany and enabled him to intervene in several theatres at once. It also protected Ferdinand from the schemes of external powers, and thereby protected the Edict of Restitution. By 1630, the Emperor had almost certainly become accustomed to having his own way in the military field, and aside from the shaky early months of the Bohemian revolt, the conflict in Germany had resembled a straight line of Habsburg triumphs all the way to Regensburg. Sacrificing Wallenstein would place this progress in jeopardy, because the army of the Catholic League would not answer directly to him, as Wallenstein had done. Both Maximillian of Bavaria and Count Tilly were perfectly dependable, and had established the first phase of the Habsburg military supremacy by 1625, but Wallenstein was guaranteed to fight for the status quo which he had created, because he had gained so much personally from it, and because of his personal contract of loyalty towards the Emperor and no one else.

Against these advantages though, Ferdinand had to be realistic. He knew from the last few years that Wallenstein had been transformed into a scapegoat. Rightly or wrongly, the Catholic Electors blamed Wallenstein for the widening of the war and its increased costs, even though the generalissimo had acted on the Emperor's orders the majority of the time. Sacrificing Wallenstein might grant the Emperor concessions over the war in North Italy and might wrest a declaration against the Dutch. However, it was clear that Ferdinand would get nowhere in any negotiations until he sacrificed him. It took him less than a fortnight to make the decision. On 13 August 1630, the Emperor released Wallenstein from his service; the subject who had brought his master so many glories and so much power was now a free agent.[18]

With a few exceptions we will investigate below, Ferdinand got very little for his willingness to do away with his most valuable asset. No confirmation of his son as heir to the office of Emperor was made, and no commitment from the Electors regarding a war with the Dutch was provided. The task of leading the new Catholic League-Imperial army was to fall to the dependable Count Tilly, but even this veteran commander would be fighting an uphill battle. The size of the army was reduced significantly to appease the concerns of those in attendance, while the monies put up for the soldiers Tilly did retain was far from sufficient. Faced with shortages in pay, Tilly would be forced to live off the land in Germany, with disastrous consequences for the following year.

'I thank God to be freed from the net. I am glad to my innermost soul about what they have decided in Regensburg, as it means that I can escape from this great labyrinth.' This was how Wallenstein greeted the news of his dismissal on 23 August – it was such a mild reaction that those in attendance at Regensburg were either astonished or convinced that it was disingenuous, and that revenge was in the pipeline. They had long been vexed over the question of what Wallenstein would do once he had been dismissed. Would he lead his soldiers against Vienna? Would he switch sides? Would he join the Swedes? Such Machiavellian schemes were far outside the range of Wallenstein character, not to mention his capabilities. Wallenstein was tired of the campaign and exhausted by the constant political battles. If he was resentful at the way he had been treated, this was more due to the fact that the Emperor had not fought harder for him, and that his exploits had not spoken for themselves, rather than out of any deep seated resentment at having lost the 'power' of the command.

Being the Emperor's instrument had netted him new titles and lands, but they had also cost him great sums of money. Wallenstein's pressing concern by mid-1630 was to somehow make ends meet by arranging for the necessary shipments of cash to reach the right people in time. He and his agents were drowning in debt, and the contributions which the soldiers were meant to levy from the people to make up the difference had dwindled considerably. Dismissal meant that it was incredibly unlikely the Emperor would work in any way to repay his debts – this would be a task which Wallenstein himself would be responsible for. He would have to draw from his lands at Mecklenburg and Friedland and raise lines of credit based on these incomes to settle his debts. Severe though this mission was in late 1630, it was infinitely more impossible once the Swedes began their campaigns the following year; one of Gustavus Adolphus' most symbolic initial acts when sufficiently powerful was to reinstall the old Dukes of Mecklenburg. This added catastrophe on top of catastrophe, and effectively shattered Wallenstein's financial credit, leaving only his reputation behind. His personal banker committed suicide shortly after the Emperor dismissed him.[19]

Wallenstein was not the only figure to be spurned by Regensburg. Frederick V, that dispossessed Elector of the Palatinate, was not allowed representation at the meeting. Ferdinand instead reiterated the demands made at the Muhlhausen meeting of late 1627. For his part, Frederick became still more inflexible, likely due to the anger which had burned resiliently ever since Ferdinand had ignored what Frederick considered his most generous offers. Styling himself as the King of Bohemia once again, and allowing no concessions, it is highly unlikely that Frederick's embassy would have made much of an impression on those assembled had it been granted an audience. Indeed, the Winter King was old news by 1630. As if reflecting the fact that the conflict in Germany had reached a new phase and was teetering on the edge of a new abyss, the Palatine crisis was only of minor concern to the princes at Regensburg. The more pressing issues which that crisis had since spawned were of more interest to them. As Brennan Pursell put it, 'no progress was made toward a resolution of that tired controversy.' Frederick would have to wait for the next phase of the war to begin before he would be in a position to dream of restitution.[20]

Regensburg did not provide Ferdinand with the opportunity to extend the war into the Netherlands, but it did provide him with a platform where the Mantuan War could be settled in the Habsburg favour. The war in North Italy had been a mixed bag for both sides, but both had begun to perceive it as an extension of their rivalry in Europe, rather than an isolated campaign; indeed, the heavy investment from both sides meant that this was no sideshow.[21] In early 1629, a French army had intervened directly, forcing Savoy out of the war and relieving the fortress of Casale in Montferrat. By late 1629 though, Mantua itself was under siege by the large column of Imperial troops which Ferdinand had sent. This army, under the command of Spinola, had to break off their siege of Mantua over the winter of 1629-30, but the spread of plague in the city made the second attempt far easier. By mid-July 1630, Mantua was in the hands of the Emperor's troops.[22]

The loss of Mantua and the decision of the French candidate, the Duke of Nevers, to accept exile in the Papal States, was a crushing blow for French pretensions in North Italy and was a particularly bitter blow considering the previous successes. The Duke of Savoy had also taken the opportunity to re-enter the war, placing Casale once more at risk. That bastion of defence held out resolutely, but back in France Cardinal Richelieu was facing an uphill battle. The situation was exacerbated by the illness of Louis XIII, which effectively paralysed decision making in France, and granted new opportunities for Marie de Medici, the Queen Mother and Richelieu's political adversary, to gain ground at his expense. By the approach of autumn 1630 it was learned that Louis had received the last rites and would be replaced by his brother Gaston as King, an event which would ruin Richelieu's position, and hand the reins of power to the Queen Mother's creatures.

This series of unfortunate events caused Richelieu profound anxiety, but it also meant that those French representatives in Regensburg tasked with arriving at a peace treaty for Mantua received no advice from the King. Ferdinand saw his chance to take advantage of the weak French position and end the war before it could complicate additional Habsburg commitments. The Duke of Nevers would be confirmed as Duke of Mantua and Montferrat, if he would surrender the fortresses of Casale and Pinerolo to Spain – thereby neutering his ability to defend against future incursions – and France would have to renounce its intentions to make alliances with foreign potentates. These terms were encapsulated in the Treaty of Regensburg, and on 13 October 1630, the beleaguered, isolated French officials signed it. All that was required now was for the flailing French administration to ratify this Treaty, and the Emperor would have scored a considerable coup in North Italy, at the expense of France. The vulnerable state of France in October 1630 appeared to render ratification a foregone conclusion, but as all were to discover, Ferdinand's final success was not so easily achieved.[23]

As eventful as Regensburg had been, that meeting did not include the two Protestant Electors to the North. Neither the Saxon nor the Brandenburg Elector had travelled to Regensburg in person as their peers had done (and as tradition required), deciding instead to nominate mere representatives to travel to the gathering, and keep them informed of its deliberations. Instead, in September 1630 they determined to host their own Electoral meeting at the city of Leipzig. With the King of Sweden in Pomerania, hosted at Stettin, the Leipzig convention conjured an impression of division at a time when the Emperor desperately needed unity; it had the effect of casting an ominous shadow over Germany. Leipzig was attended by Protestant potentates of all sizes and creeds – a violation of the Edict of Restitution which left only Lutheranism as a legal faith – but it was not a declaration of war against the Habsburgs. Indeed, it is important for us to appreciate just how desperately those assembled at Leipzig did *not* want to wage war, either in the name of

Sweden or in the name of an alienated Protestant cause. Instead, what most assembled at Leipzig truly wanted was the choice to remain neutral.

Unfortunately for these figures, this choice was taken out of their hands once the King of Sweden landed and the narrative was altered along with him. Gustavus Adolphus' uncompromising stance towards the Edict of Restitution, the Emperor and the restoration of Protestants meant that, in time, all would be forced to choose between 'God or the Devil'. For at least a little while though, Leipzig represented a chance for all frustrated and spurned Protestants in Germany to maintain dialogue with one another and develop some kind of scheme for the protection of their interests, be that military or diplomatic. The Elector of Saxony was in talks with the Elector of Mainz, with the aim of moderating the Emperor's stance vis-à-vis the Edict top of the list.

John George of Saxony had rallied most of the Protestants together into a bloc, so that they could more effectively apply pressure, but his mission was not and had never been to launch a holy war or to justify disobedience of the Emperor. The principle of strength in numbers appealed to John George, and thanks to his activities, Maximillian of Bavaria conceded early in 1631 that the Edict of Restitution could be eased, but much depended on the Emperor before these measures could proceed. Furthermore, John George's moderate policy was undermined by the burden which many of those assembled had already had to bear because of the war. Wallenstein's dismissal in August 1630 had not removed the strain which his army placed on Germany; it had only reduced it. And yet, with the King of Sweden plainly intent on intervention, it was expected that this army under Count Tilly would be increased once again, and the nightmare of previous years would be resurrected. Under these circumstances, those assembled at Leipzig from February 1631 began to vary in opinion. War against the Emperor was unacceptable now, but the recruitment of soldiers to defend their lands from rampaging armies, and to grant them more leverage – these were aims which not even John George could disagree with.

In March 1631, the Leipzig Convention was elucidated by the Protestant Imperial Estates assembled at that city. It was a message to Protestants of the Empire, as well as to the Emperor himself. It resembled a plea for clemency and mercy on the one hand, but a warning against future attacks on the other. It was also a call to action against additional foreign intervention in the Empire – a message directed against none other than Gustavus Adolphus, who wished to style himself as the saviour of Protestant German princes. Gustavus would have to wait for a few months before the Emperor's grave errors granted him the opportunity to take up this standard, but in the first few months of 1631 Gustavus bided his time and waited for the right moment to act.[24] Meanwhile, the Protestants of the Empire, for so long beleaguered and trod on by the Emperor's policies, made their voices heard. They set out a long list of goals, saying:

> We attest before God and the world, that…we seek and wish with peace-loving hearts and souls nothing more than to isolate and resolve all defects thoroughly through amicable compromise, establish true trust as firm peace and mutual concordats, [to] observe that the fundamental [basic laws] and imperial laws do not oppress Germany Freedom, [to] leave the electors and estates with their authority, honours, dignity, privileges, immunities and laws and justice, [and do not] coerce or oppress anyone who lives according to law and justice, [to] end the gruesome disorder, oppression and violence, restore a general, lasting, secure peace, and finally put a stop to the lament, misery, desolation and destruction, and the terrible bloodshed…Their Electoral graces [of Saxony and Brandenburg] have themselves decided from their peaceful hearts that if the amicable compromise is not made the authority and dignity of the Holy Roman Empire will be endangered still further and, God mercifully forbid, will be driven into the ground to the eternal shame and rebuke of the electors and estates. The foreign potentates will also interfere in the affair and bring misery, ruin and destruction to each estate regardless of religion.[25]

While Leipzig was not a declaration against the Emperor, it was a reflection upon his failure to include all actors at Regensburg, and within his vision of a peaceful Empire. At Leipzig, he Protestants declared their intention to step forward in unison in the name of their freedoms and of the constitution, and in doing so displayed both bravery and a unitary purpose which had been sorely lacking since the beginning. Ferdinand had moved individuals like John George of Saxony towards this policy following years of broken promises and harsh missteps, and now he would have to deal with the consequences of a divided Germany just as a foreign potentate lurked and awaited the right opportunity to strike. Ferdinand, it must be said, provided Gustavus Adolphus with this opportunity, for without the Emperor's poor judgement in religious affairs, Germany would never have been so divided against itself, or so vulnerable to exploitation by a foreign conqueror.

Further bad news for the Habsburgs came from another theatre. Notwithstanding the initially impressive settlement over Italy, Ferdinand was soon led to discover that these generous entreaties with France had become irrelevant. In November 1630, it transpired that King Louis XIII of France had exaggerated the severity of his illness, and upon inviting Cardinal Richelieu to his hunting residence for a private audience, the normally unassuming King of France outlined a scheme which he had evidently been developing for some time. It amounted to nothing less than a mortal strike against the Queen Mother and her favourites, and the re-establishment of Richelieu on firmer foundations than ever before. This whirlwind series of events – known as the 'Day of the Dupes' – greatly empowered French foreign policy and put to bed at long last the divisions which had plagued the realm since Henry IV's death. Within the first few months of 1631, Richelieu had repudiated the humiliating Treaty of Regensburg with the Emperor, and the war in North Italy began to swing back in favour of France. The war with the Dutch had drained Spain's ability to project its power in the peninsula, and at the same time, the Austrian Habsburgs were forced to pay attention to the Swedes after having ignored the problem for so long.[26]

The full extent of the Habsburg strategic miscalculation was now apparent. After having sent over fifty thousand Imperial soldiers to North Italy, Habsburg forces in Germany had dwindled to an all-time low.[27] In Leipzig, the Protestants of the Empire, led by the Saxon and Brandenburg example, had created an army of forty thousand, and knit their members together in a defensive alliance by April 1631. In January of that year, Franco-Swedish military cooperation had been formalised with the Treaty of Barwalde, which committed France to sending Sweden's King vast sums of money in exchange for a Swedish commitment to maintain an army of forty thousand in Germany. Even more troubling, in May 1631 the French and Bavarians had signed a secret treaty of their own, the Treaty of Fontainebleau, demonstrating the wily Maximillian's estimation of which way the wind was blowing. Empowered by his King's scheme, Richelieu felt confident to ignore the Treaty of Regensburg, and the Emperor could do nothing in response.[28]

Against these two forces of Swedish and Protestant Germans, and the shaky Bavarians, the Emperor had far fewer options than he had had before the Mantuan War and dismissal of Wallenstein deprived him of his greatest assets. The conference at Regensburg had represented a significant and critical failure for the Emperor and must be considered something of a turning point in the narrative of the Thirty Years War. Maximillian of Bavaria was dominant over Ferdinand's military policy, and Regensburg only served to alienate the Protestants in the North just as a potential saviour was on route.[29] Now, as before, the burden of the war would fall to Count Tilly, whose soldiers were underpaid and demoralised. Backed into a corner, facing new enemies and the threat of reinvigorated Protestants, Ferdinand may have hoped that Tilly would achieve a miracle. Instead, that veteran commander helped facilitate the next phase of the Thirty Years War.

THREE
The Enemy of My Enemy

In 1625, King Gustavus Adolphus of Sweden made a choice. Rather than intervene in Germany as a part of a coalition of powers which included Denmark, England and the Dutch, he would return to the task of fighting his cousin, the King of Poland, in the east. The decision was an understandable one, considering the bitter history between Gustavus and Sigismund III. It was impossible to intervene in Germany so long as the Polish threat loomed; otherwise, the Poles would strike Sweden in the back as it became entangled in the Holy Roman Empire. Gustavus Adolphus had fought a two-front war before; indeed, he had ascended to the throne of Sweden while his country fought Denmark, Poland and Russia simultaneously. He did not want a repeat of that experience again.[30]

For nearly thirty years – since Sigismund Vasa sailed back to Poland in 1598 – Sweden had fought against its neighbours in a string of stop-start conflicts where first its very survival, and then the opportunities for expansion, were at stake. Gustavus' first truly incredible triumph came in 1621, when he landed an army in Lithuania twenty-five thousand men strong – larger than any Sweden had fielded before. The army had to be large, because its target was one of the sparkling jewels of the Polish-Lithuanian Commonwealth – Riga. Boasting over thirty thousand citizens, Riga was three times the size of Stockholm, and contained a sophisticated, prosperous commercial infrastructure which enabled the city to tap into the fruits of the Baltic Sea. The Polish army, thousands of miles away and defending against the full might of the Turks, could provide no answer for this daring Swedish coup. It could not have been known at the time, but the seizure of Riga was only the beginning. From here the King of Sweden began a campaign which netted him several other lucrative Baltic ports, and enabled Sweden, by virtue of its conquests, to take the war more effectively to Poland. The result was even more success.[31]

By 1625, not content with merely renewing the war with Poland, Gustavus wished to foment a coalition against her. Finding much of Europe occupied with the Habsburgs and noting Habsburg support for the Poles at the same time, Gustavus attempted to cast his war with Poland as merely an offshoot of the war against the Habsburg Emperor. He was in regular contact with the Ottomans, traditional enemies of the Poles, and Gustavus recognised the importance of casting his dynastic Vasa conflict with Sigismund III in such a way as to invite foreign aid. The message was simple – by fighting the Poles, Sweden was weakening a critical ally of the Habsburgs, and it thus made sense for the enemies of the Habsburgs to support him in this fight.

Simple though the message was, Gustavus was to express it consistently throughout his reign. In the course of his campaigns against Poland he sought aid from France, England, the Dutch, the Ottomans and even the old enemies in Denmark and Russia. Furthermore, while Gustavus accepted that by weakening Poland one would weaken the Habsburgs, he also believed that the reverse was true, and that by undermining the Holy Roman Emperor, Poland would be disadvantaged. The King of Poland was the brother-in-law of Emperor Ferdinand after all, which only reinforced the dynastic lens through which Gustavus had viewed his Polish War. The Jesuit Catholic background of Ferdinand and Sigismund added further weight to the picture. From an early stage then, Gustavus' perspective on Europe had been shaped by the policies of his relatives, and the friends which his enemies made. In February 1626, he vocalised his perspective on the interconnected state of affairs in Europe, in a letter written to the Russian Tsar. Gustavus said:

> The Roman Kaiser, helped by the Kings of Spain and Poland, has subjected nearly all the apanage princes of Germany, eradicated their evangelical Christian religion and deprived them of lands and people, making himself supreme ruler over all Germany. After this, the Roman Kaiser wants to help the King of Spain to conquer the States of Holland and the Netherlands, and also wants to help the King of Poland to become ruler of the Swedish and Russian states. They have great hopes of accomplishing this aim, and many are already calling Vladislav emperor of all the Northern countries. The Roman Kaiser and the Kings of Spain and Poland think that they have now overcome all the rulers of Christendom. But the King of France, together with the great city of Venice and the Duke of Savoy, have formed a coalition against the above-mentioned powers, and in particular against the King of Spain, and raised up a great force against him in Italy. The King of England, too, along with the rulers of the Netherlandish states, have formed ana alliance against the Kaiser and the King of Spain, and have sent to us, the great King Gustavus Adolphus, and to the King of Denmark, to ask us to join them in opposing the Roman Kaiser and his advisers. To this end the Danish King has gone to war against the Kaiser and now stands with a great army opposing him within Germany, having on his side many of the German apanage princes, who all support him. And in order that the Polish King may not go to the aid of the Kaiser we have now entered the land of Lithuania, so that he cannot help the Roman Kaiser, but the Kaiser

and his advisers will be everywhere ousted and will not be able to realise the wicked design which they have formed against all Christian states.

The letter read like a statement of policy, but it also contained the theme of Russo-Swedish correspondence which was maintained to the end: the war against Poland was not just a war in the name of Swedish interests, it was also a war directed against this 'Roman Kaiser', because by attacking the Polish King, the latter could not provide any aid to the former. The religious undertones of the correspondence are also brought out; the Catholic Emperor and Polish King intend to destroy the Evangelical or Protestant faith, but they also intend 'to crush the Greek faith and persecute all who hold to it.' The Russian Tsar, as the protector of Orthodox Christians, must not allow this to happen. Judging merely from his correspondence in the late 1620s, it was never more apparent that the King of Sweden had chosen his side. His decision to intervene in Germany was not taken off the cuff in summer 1630 but was the result of several years' worth of watching. Behind his dynastic foe the King of Poland stood that terror of Germany, the sectarian Catholic Emperor, and one could not destroy one without defeating the other.[32]

The two themes of religious solidarity and of strategic interest colour Swedish policy and demonstrate the interconnected nature of European affairs at this phase of the Thirty Years War. As the Emperor's victories piled up, the themes became more urgent. Gustavus broached the subject of a coalition of anti-Habsburg forces several times, and urged the Tsar...

...to defend himself as other rulers are defending themselves, to act against the King of Poland and prevent him from helping the Kaiser. Then he [the Emperor] will forget to act against those rulers who stand by their beliefs and will give up his wicked design against our Christian Evangelical and Greek faiths.

The danger which the Emperor posed to all of Christendom was one thing, but the ability of that same Emperor to endanger Sweden in its war with Poland by directly aiding the Polish King was quite another. Emperor Ferdinand, according to Gustavus, was effectively keeping the King of Poland propped up, and the Swedish King even claimed that he 'could have marched unhindered through all Poland with his army', had the Ferdinand not intervened to aid his brother-in-law. Gustavus said in a letter to the Tsar in 1629 that he had not been able to accomplish this comprehensive defeat of his Polish cousin, because of the machinations of the Habsburgs in Poland. Above all, Gustavus emphasised the Emperor's formidable and limitless manpower supply 'which in great strength drew near and laid siege to the town of Stralsund', forcing Sweden to divert its forces from Poland to meet the threat. The Emperor was thus identified as the source of all woes, and as

708

the true enemy of Sweden and of Russia. It was the Habsburg brand of Jesuit Catholic expansion which threatened Swedish and Russian interests far more seriously than Poland possibly could have done alone. As Gustavus wrote:

> The Pope, the Roman Kaiser and the whole House of Austria strive only to become masters of the whole world, and they are very close to succeeding in this…It is certainly known to Your Majesty that the Roman Kaiser and the Papists have brought under their rule most of the Evangelical princes in Germany…[Once the] Kaiser and the Popish conspirators overcome Sweden they will start to try and force the Russian people into submission and extirpate the ancient Greek faith.[33]

The notion that behind King Sigismund III of Poland stood Emperor Ferdinand was one accepted not only by the Swedes and Russians; it was also expanded upon by the French. Cardinal Richelieu viewed Russia as the useful power far in the distance, which would surround the Poles and thereby hamper the strategic unity of the Habsburgs. As a letter from Louis XIII to Tsar Michael put it:

> Although our realms are far apart and divided from each other by many different states with different measures and languages…we wish to maintain our firm, cordial friendship, and love, and true concord and reference [diplomatic relations] with Your Majesty…for the good and advancement of both our crowns and…that a treaty may be made to the benefit of us both.

Interestingly, while the Swedes had worked to find common ground with the Russians in their religious differences which put them at odds with the Catholic Habsburgs and Poles, the Most Christian King of Catholic France would obviously have to find a different approach. With the religious commonality absent, it would be necessary to understate the Catholic aspect of France, and emphasise instead something which Russia and France did have in common – the absolute power of their sovereigns: 'The French obey their King just as the Russians obey and do honour to their Tsar.' It certainly helped that it was in the strategic interests of the Russians to see matters the French way; there was great value to be had in allying with the most anti-Habsburg power of them all. The Tsar's reply to Louis XIII captured this mood in one powerful sentence: 'Our royal persons and powers, when allied, would hold the whole world in awe.'[34]

French and Swedish approaches to Russia were very much in tune with the presentation of Europe as divided into two distinct camps. With the King of Poland, a firm ally of the Emperor, it was impossible to separate either Poland from the Habsburgs, or the war with Poland from the war in Germany. This is an important point to appreciate, since it reminds us how interconnected contemporaries of the Thirty Years War believed their affairs to be. The ambassador which France had sent to Russia, Des Hayes de Courmesnin, furthered these views by underlining the critical points ad nauseum. His correspondence forms a vital, if underrated part of the Thirty Years War narrative, and is worth examining.

> King Louis is at enmity with the Kaiser and with the King of Spain...and he is at enmity with the King of Poland because that monarch is helping the Roman Kaiser, King Louis' foe...and they act in concert with Sigismund, the Polish King, and give him no little aid...And this they [the French] know for certain, that the Roman Kaiser is one with the Polish King, they are friends, the Kaiser's daughter is to marry the heir to the Polish throne, and they help one another. And so let the Tsar's Majesty in friendship and amity with his [the ambassador's] sovereign King Louis stand together with him against their common enemies.

Such appeals were made in the context of the late 1620s, when the war in North Italy had begun and the Habsburgs fought both the Dutch and the Danes. The power of the Habsburgs was spreading, and it was therefore essential that all nations close ranks against them. 'The Poles, who have allied themselves with the House of Austria and have long been hostile to the French King, are in fear lest the Grand Duke [the Tsar] conclude this alliance' [with France]. Just as the Swedish King had done, here the French ambassador makes it plain that his sovereign intends to attack the Emperor in the future. If the Russians were to ally with France and attack the Poles, then they would be in fact attacking the Habsburgs. No means to undermine the Habsburgs could be off limits in this struggle. Thus, we see ambassador Des Hayes pointing to Spanish trade with Persia, referred to as the Orient. These incomes for Spanish coffers went straight into the practice of funding the nefarious wider schemes of the Habsburgs. If one was thus to undercut this trade route, then the Habsburgs and thereby the Poles would also be affected, but how to do it? Des Hayes believed that a land route through Russia towards Persia was the answer:

> It is necessary to check and prevent the Austrian princes from profiting by trade with the Orient, for, as we have pointed out, they used the profits obtained from this source in the past year to hire many soldiers whom they sent to help the Polish King against the King of Sweden, and if the [Russian] sovereign does not stop them from engaging in this trade they will go on helping the Polish King. And it would be better if the [Russian] sovereign were to gain by this trade rather than that his enemies should be enriched by it.[35]

This window into Franco-Russian diplomacy provides as clear an example as is available of that old truism of *realpolitik* – the enemy of my enemy is my friend. Drawn together due to the need for mutual defence against a common enemy, both Sweden and France could gain much from an alliance with the Russian Tsar, just as they had gained much by allying with one another. Indeed, this was also true of the Franco-Dutch relationship, where the French supported the Netherlands in its conflict with Spain, on the understanding that this would weaken the Spanish Habsburgs, which would weaken the Austrian Habsburgs as a result. Not satisfied merely with a Russian alliance, the French envisioned a far-reaching coalition of Eastern states, including the Turks, the Tartars and Transylvania, to be weighed against Poland and the Habsburgs. Furthermore, the French relied upon Transylvanian ambassadors in Moscow and Dutch ambassadors in Constantinople to bring such a coalition about. By 1626 the Poles had intercepted several letters from Sweden which argued for just such a coalition. As Bethlen Gabor, Prince of Transylvania and eternal thorn in the side of the Habsburgs, put it:

> And since these great sovereigns – the Tsar's Majesty, and the Swedish King and their sovereign Bethlen Gabor – are united and mean to act together against their enemies, and the Turkish Sultan Murad intends also, for his part, to oppose those enemies, nobody will be able to withstand these great forces. So as to secure and establish this beforehand, let good alliances be maintained – the enemies of these forces are the King of Spain, the Roman Kaiser and the King of Poland – so as to stand against them and take revenge for their enmity.[36]

These examples demonstrate that the Tsar was not merely a pawn in a Swedish or French game, but that he was an accepted member of an anti-Habsburg coalition, and that, so long as he was hostile towards Poland, he could be no other. The 1618 Truce of Deulino had ended the Russo-Polish War which had been characterised by the effective collapse of the Russian state, the occupation of Moscow by a Polish army and the nomination of King Sigismund's son Wladyslaw as Tsar. The Truce had inflated the size of the Polish-Lithuanian Commonwealth, but it also left a vengeful Tsar to the Commonwealth's east, at a time when the Polish wars with Sweden seemed unending. It was only logical for the dynastic and strategic enemies of Poland to cooperate; indeed, this cooperation was essential if any reduction in Polish power was to be accomplished. That this proved a difficult task was blamed on the succour which Sigismund III received from Emperor Ferdinand, but how important or considerable was this aid?

When presenting his justification for intervention in Germany in summer 1630, Gustavus Adolphus would underline as a *casus belli* the consistent provisions of soldiers, resources and other aid which Wallenstein had granted to Poland.[37] It is worth taking a moment to examine Wallenstein's behaviour in this regard. We have learned that Wallenstein feared the untimely intervention of the Swedish King in Germany, and used the forces at his disposal to bolster the Polish King's resolve, thereby prolonging the war with Sweden and keeping Gustavus distracted in time for a peace with Denmark to be formed.[38] This policy of providing aid to the Poles made good strategic sense, but Wallenstein's foresight was fatally undermined with the outbreak of the Mantuan War, and the Emperor's decision to become entangled in that conflict, stretching Habsburg attentions and capabilities at precisely the wrong time, just as Wallenstein had previously feared.

Yet, Gustavus' ability to profit from the Emperor's misfortune should not detract from the fact that he had been greatly inconvenienced by Wallenstein's previous actions. Indeed, Gustavus' expression of offense at Wallenstein's behaviour was not merely rhetorical hot air. Gustavus had long feared and loathed the spectacle of closer Polish-Habsburg relations, and Wallenstein's timely interventions in the Polish-Swedish War only confirmed these impressions. The practical help which Wallenstein provided was considerable and is most apparent in the generalissimo's decision to lend one of his most skilled subordinates, Hans Georg von Arnim, to the Polish King, along with some eight thousand men under his command. This contingent made its presence felt during the twilight phase of the Polish-Swedish War in May 1629, when Arnim was sent to the Vistula delta.

Arnim's mission was to relieve the pressure on the city of Danzig, the most important city in Poland and one of its few remaining outlets to the Baltic. He was to be joined by Sigismund's thirty-five thousand men, but Arnim soon discovered that his presence was not as welcome in Poland as had been hoped. Sigismund had asked for more men, and Arnim had only travelled to Danzig reluctantly, after Wallenstein had commanded it. The Poles did not provide Arnim with sufficient provisions, and combined with the difficult, marshy conditions, disease and starvation ripped through his ranks. Still though, Arnim played an important role in the battle of Honigfelde in late June. At that battle, Gustavus faced a close call and was nearly captured by the superior Polish cavalry. The Swedish King lost just one thousand men to the Polish-Imperial three hundred, but both sides were by now exhausted. Much of Gustavus' army had been besieging Danzig, but with this loss and the low morale of his troops – not to mention the terminal war fatigue which had set in both sides – the idea of a truce began to seem more appealing.

Even while Gustavus could not take Danzig, he still controlled a great portion of the Vistula plains around the city. Sigismund's nobles were themselves tired of the war, and recriminations between the Poles and Arnim's men were already doing the rounds. Arnim claim that the Poles had fired on his men during the battle and expressed his disgust at the Polish King's failed promises, which had forced his men to eat grass due to their chronic starvation. The campaign represented the most comprehensive attempt at Habsburg-Polish cooperation yet, but it was a diplomatic failure, and left a bad taste in Arnim's mouth, who blamed King Sigismund for the lacklustre results.[39] Still, it is significant that Gustavus Adolphus did not forget the episode; on the contrary it was burned into his consciousness as a prime example of the scheming Habsburgs and their quest to undermine him in his Polish War.

It can therefore be argued that Gustavus did have a legitimate gripe with Wallenstein and his master, since even before the Battle of Honigfelde in June 1629, Wallenstein had sent a trickle of soldiers into Poland to reinforce important towns and bolster depleted Polish divisions. These tactics were all part of Wallenstein's scheme to delay Swedish intervention in Germany by prolonging the Polish-Swedish War, and the strategy evidently found the Emperor's blessing. Gustavus' denial before the walls of Danzig was all the proof he needed. In years past, the Habsburgs had merely been guilty by association. After the final phase of his war with the Poles though, Gustavus saw his fears confirmed. Habsburg support for the Poles did not merely signal the close relationship of those two powers, it also demonstrated that the Habsburgs were inherently hostile to Swedish interests. Arnim's adventure, much like the siege of Stralsund, the Baltic design and the aggrandisement of the Catholic Emperor, were pre-emptive steps taken towards a conflict with Sweden which Gustavus Adolphus would have to be ready for. The only way he could truly prepare for this conflict and meet the Emperor's challenge directly was by ending his struggle with Poland.

After several years emphasising the hostility between Poland and Sweden, as well as the danger which King Sigismund posed to both of their states, one might have expected that the Swedish explanation of their decision to make peace with Poland would be a hard sell in Moscow. As if in anticipation of this difficulty, Sweden sent an envoy to Russia tasked specifically with explaining its position with regard to the Peace of Altmark signed in September 1629. Thanks to the theme of Polish-Habsburg unity though, Gustavus was able to argue that he had already been fighting against their common enemy and that he would continue to do so. The only difference was the face which he confronted on the battlefield; both Poland and the Emperor were the same side of the militant Catholic coin. By fighting the Habsburgs, Gustavus was in fact weakening the Poles. It was to be expected that Poland would send aid to support the Habsburgs, but Gustavus insisted that peace with Poland meant Sweden could invade the Holy Roman Empire and combat the Habsburg problem directly. Thence, the Emperor would be fatally weakened, and the bonds which tied him to the Polish King would be dangerously frayed.[40]

Cardinal Richelieu could not afford to send French soldiers against Poland in support of the Swedish King, but he could provide assistance in the diplomatic sphere instead. A well-timed, skilful mediation mission to the east could capitalise on the war weariness of both Sweden and Poland and guarantee the cessation of hostilities between both parties while granting Sweden the majority of her gains in the Baltic. Thereafter, Sweden would be free to intervene in Germany at last, the Habsburgs would be forced to withdraw from the Mantuan War, and the Franco-Swedish partnership would threaten the Habsburg supremacy at both ends. Yet, what is often forgotten about the French mediation of the Swedish-Polish War is that it was by no means straightforward.

This was demonstrated by Richelieu's decision to send not one diplomat to the east, but two. The first, Hercule Girard, Baron Charnacé, would be sent to meet with the Swedes and the Poles in Pomerania and Warsaw respectively. The second, the aforementioned Des Hayes de Courmensin, was sent to Moscow.[41] The mission of these two French agents would include no shortage of manipulation and misinformation; they were tasked with opening a new front in Germany, and ushering in a new phase of the Thirty Years War. As if reflecting the interconnected nature of the early seventeenth century's related conflicts, it was impossible for the French to proceed without first covering all angles. For the war in the west to begin, the peace in the east would first have to be achieved. This was to prove a task far more complicated and multi-layered than Richelieu could have anticipated.

FOUR

The Peace in the East

The story of Sweden in the 1620s was one of continuous war with Poland; this was a dynastic war, and a war apparently without end. With his cousin sitting on the Polish throne and claiming the Swedish throne with it, it was impossible for Gustavus Adolphus to sit back and do nothing. Poland's power would have to be checked, lest Sweden would never be in peace. A similar peace eluded Richelieu, who believed that unless the power of the Habsburgs was challenged, the Emperor and the King of Spain would run roughshod over all of Europe. In his task to assemble an anti-Habsburg coalition though, Richelieu had been constantly interrupted by troubling events at home, and he had been unable to maintain a sufficient support system. Thus, Denmark was destined to fail, as was the Hague Alliance of 1625 which she had committed herself to. Nothing, indeed, could be done for Denmark, at least not for the moment. With the Peace of Lubeck in spring 1629, the Emperor had effectively removed all opposition to his regime within Germany.

As the events of the previous years had demonstrated, while his power was considerable, and his allies relentless, the façade of Habsburg invincibility was precisely that, a façade. The city of Stralsund had been strong enough to resist the unstoppable Habsburg tide, and if Richelieu took solace from this Habsburg setback, he certainly would not have failed to notice the presence of Swedish reinforcements among the soldiers which had been sent to that city. Gustavus Adolphus, the warrior king of Sweden who ascended the throne during a multi-front war, was a great deal more careful and cautious than we might have expected. He knew better than to throw his kingdom into war with the Empire before the conflict with Poland had been resolved. Thus, Gustavus had sent reinforcements, but the Stralsund incident had not been allowed to serve as the catalyst for open war between the Emperor and the Swedish King.

Sympathising with the plight of the German Protestants – a feeling which only escalated after the Edict of Restitution was unleashed – Gustavus was mindful of the bitter realities of his realm's power. While Swedish gains in the Baltic had been considerable, and her triumphs had wrested several lucrative ports from the Poles, she was nonetheless low on natural resources, lacked the means to exploit what few resources she did have, and was virtually exhausted from nearly three decades of constant war with her larger Polish neighbour. It was an illness which suggested an obvious cure – some foreign potentate would have to intervene and bridge the gap between Sweden and Poland. Foreign interest in the conflict had only increased as the Danish promise had failed, and the Habsburgs surged ahead in the race. In 1627 and 1628, both the Dutch and Brandenburg had worked to broker a peace. It was in the interest of both of these states to do so, but just as he neglected to become involved in the war in Germany in 1625, Gustavus was reluctant to do so at this stage. He believed that more could be gained from continuing the war with his Polish cousin.[42]

And indeed, more was gained. The Polish-Lithuanian Commonwealth was evidently buckling under the strain of the war, and its divided, disconnected magnates had never truly trusted their King in the first place, which made military organisation difficult in the vast country. Furthermore, as the innovative Swedish King marched, the Polish King was beset with urgent requests from his nobles to make peace and institute some military reforms. The once stunning successes of the Polish cavalry were blunted considerably by Gustavus' effective new tactics and use of combined arms.[43] King Sigismund III failed to listen, and his shortcomings compelled Wallenstein to send help from neighbouring Pomerania. It had been in the interest of both men to do so, but the intervention of troops loyal to the Holy Roman Emperor could only bring about the result which Wallenstein feared – by sticking their nose in his business, he now had a legitimate grievance which only war could satisfy.

Military shortcomings notwithstanding, Gustavus engaged in some risky campaigning in 1629 during his efforts to seize Danzig, the premier port of the Baltic. As we saw before, these efforts were repulsed, and with their Imperial reinforcements, the Poles succeeded in driving the King of Sweden back. By now though, the Polish nobility had endured all they could of their King's war. Gustavus too was worn out from the conflict, and his greatest concern was to forge some form of lasting arrangement which would leave him in control of his conquests. The tolls from the Baltic ports of Prussia and Pomerania provided Gustavus with a new source of revenue, but it was still far short of what he would need to make war against the Emperor. Gustavus met with the Danish King in spring 1629 and had seen first-hand what happened to those that were abandoned by their allies. He did not wish to suffer the same fate. It was therefore fortunate for Gustavus that matters in 1629 were a chasm apart from those of 1625, when the Hague Alliance had intervened in Germany with so much misplaced optimism.

Above all was the change in France. Consumed by Huguenot revolts and the intrigues of scheming nobles, foremost among them the King's brother and mother, Cardinal Richelieu was not in a position to wield power in 1625. By 1629 though, not only had his position significantly improved with the defeat of the Huguenots, but French soldiers were actually fighting an undeclared war with the Habsburgs in Italy. Because of this situation, military allies were not merely potential cogs in the anti-Habsburg machine, they were instrumental for taking the burden off of France in Italy and diverting Habsburg attentions elsewhere. With the war in Germany at an end, it was vital for French interests that the Spanish and Austrian Habsburgs be unable to focus the full extent of their powers in the Mantuan War.

The most obvious solution was to simply resurrect the war in Germany, and with Sweden the only power in a position to intervene, it was critical for the sake of French security that the Swedish entry into Germany be facilitated. The war in Italy added a new urgency to French considerations, especially with the arrival of Imperial reinforcements sent by Wallenstein later in the year. As Richelieu recalled in his memoirs, Gustavus Adolphus, 'a new rising sun', had the potential to change everything. According to Richelieu, the King of France…

> …had taken note of this young prince with a view to trying to make use of him in order to divert, in due course of time, the Emperor's main force and to prevent the Emperor from unjustly waging war in Italy and France, and to make him give up, through the terror and damage he would suffer, his design aimed at opposing public freedom…Several princes of the Empire, wrongly despoiled of their states by the Imperial forces…look towards the King of Sweden in their wretchedness, as navigators look towards the North. But he was busy with war against Poland, and, although he lacked neither courage nor ambition, he needed to be freed from that enemy before making for himself another, such as the House of Austria was.[44]

This was the crux of the issue; Richelieu would have to succeed where others had failed and broker a peace between the mortal enemies of the North. Fortunately for Richelieu, he was able to benefit from the exhaustion on both sides which had set in during the year, and it was with the goal of capitalising on this war weariness in mind that Richelieu determined to send an expert on northern affairs, Hercule Girard, the Baron Charnacé, to meet with the relevant monarchs and reach some kind of arrangement. Charnacé was advised, before meeting with the Swedish King, to visit Sigismund III, the King of Poland. By so doing, he could leverage some interesting news which Richelieu had learned against Sigismund – that the Russians were planning to launch a war against the Polish King.

Gustavus Adolphus and his Chancellor Axel Oxenstierna had always believed that King Sigismund of Poland would simply treat any arranged truce as an opportunity to prepare for a new war with Sweden, and once Sweden intervened in Germany Poland would avenge itself upon the distracted Swedes. Charnacé had two cards up his sleeve to combat this justifiable fear. The first was that the French had a resident diplomat in Poland, who had worked with Charnacé to guarantee that the Polish King would keep his word, or, as it was put to Sigismund:

> His Majesty [the King of France] is guided chiefly by the interests of the King of Poland, for if the Swedish King allies with the Muscovite which is his intention, so His Majesty has learnt, such an alliance can bring notable harm to the Polish King.

This expression of concern was in many respects a backhanded warning, that if Poland did break the truce with Poland and make war on Sweden, she would find herself locked in a two-front war. The second tactic which the French could use tied in with the first; in all levels of diplomacy, knowledge was power, and the French had learned that the Russians intended to break the truce which they had signed with Poland a decade before. Thus, through the application of stern warnings and an understanding of the complexities of north-eastern diplomacy, Charnacé believed he would be better equipped to facilitate the truce he desired.[45]

Since 1615, when Muscovy had sent an embassy to Paris, the French had needed to formulate some kind of diplomatic response. While Russia was on the fringes of Europe, it was not so negligible that it could be ignored, especially considering the interdependent nature of Sweden, Poland, Russia and their neighbouring states. Political pressure on Poland could also be increased if France established closer relations with Russia, a point expanded upon by the instructions given to French ambassadors in 1626:

> Besides the advantages that France can draw from these relations with Muscovy through trade, the King will become even more important among the Northern rulers and especially in the eyes of the Polish king who, having no enemy more powerful than Muscovy, will henceforth hold back from promoting the interests of the House of Austria, since His Majesty [the King of France] can also harm him and render services to the Grand Duke of Moscow.

There was, it seemed, no limits to the vision of Richelieu's far-reaching diplomacy, and as we can see, this diplomacy revolved around the Habsburg target. Richelieu had learned of the Russian intention to break their truce with Poland from a convoluted chain of information which originated with the Turkish ambassador in Moscow, who then updated his colleagues in Constantinople. Having made war themselves against the Poles in 1620-21, it was in the Ottomans' interest to leverage the threat which Russia could pose to Poland, and the French ambassador in Constantinople, learning from the excited Turkish chatter in 1628 of Russia's intentions, immediately wrote to Paris informing them of the opportunity. Having been made aware of the use which Russia could now serve for French interests, Richelieu instructed Charnacé to travel to meet with the Polish King and make plain these revelations to him. As Charnacé met with Sigismund in mid-July 1629, he was informed that his colleague, Des Hayes de Courmesnin, had stopped off in Denmark on his way to Russia. Evidently, Richelieu was not content with barely veiled threats or the accumulation of knowledge; he was wanted to facilitate a war between Russia and Poland and believed that sending a diplomatic mission to Moscow was the best way to make this happen.[46]

Interestingly, Sigismund learned of the simultaneous French approach to Poland and Russia and received Charnacé with some hostility because of this. Fortunately, Charnacé had been well prepared by Richelieu in advance should word leak out. Des Hayes' trip to Moscow was presented to Sigismund merely as an economic mission to regulate trade, and indeed Des Hayes was provided with instructions to do just that. Of course, he had also been instructed to compel the Russians to make war on Poland. Sigismund was deeply perturbed by the news which Charnacé had brought about the Russian intentions to make war on Poland soon. Having broken off diplomatic relations since 1622, there was no way for Polish agents to learn of Russian policy; any Polish official that ventured into Muscovy was arrested and treated as an enemy combatant, while Russian officials were treated similarly. It is significant that, upon receiving the troubling French news, Sigismund sought to reverse the downturn in Russo-Polish relations, by sending a great embassy to Moscow. Reaching the disputed border area, this embassy was rudely turned back by Russian soldiers.

This rebuff had an immediate effect on Sigismund. Charnacé had actually left to meet with the Swedish King by the first week of August, having got nowhere with Sigismund in July. He was sent a letter urging him to return to meet with the Polish King, which Charnacé heeded, and he was back in the presence of Sigismund by 6 August. Now, after having used what little bargaining power he possessed, Sigismund was ready to trust the French mediation and make a hasty peace. So long as he remained at war with Sweden, the threat of a two front war would haunt his country's security. Sigismund could not know when the Russian axe would fall, and he showed himself extremely impatient to resolve his differences with Gustavus Adolphus before it did. Thus, Gustavus was permitted to keep all of his Baltic conquests just as he had hoped, and Sigismund put up barely a fight for those lands and cities which he had lost. Little did he know that the Swedish foothold on the Baltic shores was a permanent arrangement.

It was typical of Richelieu's diplomatic approach that while Charnacé was among the Polish King attempting to mediate a peace, Des Hayes was in Moscow attempting to persuade the Tsar that France was doing no such thing.

The French believed that since a Swedish-Polish truce harmed Russia, any news of her role in it should be hidden from view. The end of the Swedish-Polish War could be presented simply as a mutually beneficial arrangement which happened to have come to pass, rather than the fruits of a French diplomatic scheme which it actually was. On the contrary, Des Hayes assured the Tsar, France was aiding Sweden in its Polish War, and her agents were not involved in any mediation. Des Hayes claimed that Charnacé was merely a commercial agent, sent to Poland by France to wrest economic concessions at a time of Polish weakness.[47]

Much like Charnacé's similar claim about Des Hayes to Sigismund, this answer had been prepared in advance by Richelieu, and proved thoroughly effective. The two French agents played both sides, and their exploits also convinced Gustavus Adolphus, who agreed to sign the Truce of Altmark on 16 September 1629. Their work was apparently done. 1629 had been a profoundly busy one for Richelieu, who had made time for these schemes just the moment when the war in Mantua was intensifying. Indeed, Des Hayes' letters and seals were provided by Richelieu in the Savoyard city of Susa before that diplomat set off for his Russian adventure in late April 1629. Only a month later, Richelieu had concluded the war with the Huguenots. The Habsburg peace with Denmark was learned of shortly thereafter, as were the full implications of the Edict of Restitution. Richelieu's failure to block the more unfavourable developments only added to his sense of urgency. He needed to achieve some diplomatic success so that the Habsburg gains would be balanced, and he found this opportunity in the tangled circumstances which the hostile north-eastern powers provided.

Although Richelieu's role in the Truce of Altmark and the Russian preparations for war were considerable, it would be too simplistic to explain these developments by French intervention alone. Indeed, it is worth appreciating the Russian position in these developments, since it was news of the Russian intention to attack Poland before the expiration of their truce which provided Richelieu with so many opportunities to exploit. It would be incorrect to view the Russians as a pawn in the French game, notwithstanding the huge boon to French fortunes which the Russian policy decision provided. Moscow had its own appreciation of European relations, aided by an intelligence and information centre in Novgorod, where press reports from the major capitals were compiled. The Embassies Department within Moscow contained interpreters of the major languages, and these individuals all worked hard and in consultation with each other.

To best combat the machinations of their mortal enemy, Poland, it was vital that Moscow understood who Poland's friends were. Thus, it was well known in Russia that the Habsburgs supported the Poles, and that they supplied them with men and materials – not to mention a marriage – as a sign of their friendship. Foreign ambassadors to Moscow echoed this view of Russia, and it was known that King Sigismund drew much power from Emperor Ferdinand's friendship. If, however, the Emperor could no longer assist the Polish King, then Sigismund would be vulnerable. This logic was expounded by Gustavus Adolphus as we have seen, when he claimed that a war against the Emperor would serve to fatally undermine the position of the King of Poland, but it was also referenced by the Turks. Once Ferdinand became occupied by the war in Germany, foreign observers and particularly Poland's enemies noted the new vulnerability of the Polish King. As the Turkish ambassador in Moscow noted:

> It is known to you, great sovereign, that in Germany there is a great conflict between the Emperor and the Lutherans, so that he is now unable to help the Poles and, on his part, the Sultan has ordered the rulers of Transylvania, Wallachia and Moldavia to attack the Emperor so that he will go on being unable to bring aid to the Polish King.

Any plans for a sweeping anti-Polish or anti-Habsburg coalition did not materialise though, even while the Turks did wage war against Poland, and the Prince of Transylvania, as we have seen, provided no end of headaches for Vienna. It was still within Russia's interests to attack Poland while Sigismund was distracted by his war with his Swedish cousin. Interestingly, while the French had made great use out of the threat of the Russian declaration of war on Poland, it would be up to Sweden to persuade the Russians to make war on Poland by itself. Gustavus would use the argument that Sweden was fighting the same enemy he had been fighting from the beginning – the nefarious Habsburg influence – but he would have to work hard nonetheless to persuade the Tsar to go it alone.[48]

While Richelieu's plan to release Sweden from the Polish War was successful, the second part of his plan met with more resistance. On 21 October 1629 Charnacé arrived in Uppsala for a face-to-face meeting with the King of Sweden. His journey had taken him across the frozen battlefields of North-Eastern Europe and back again, and now he was finally in the presence of the figure whom Richelieu believed was the key to relieving the burden of war on France and turning the war against the Habsburgs. It was pivotal that Gustavus and Charnacé see eye to eye, and that they hammer out some kind of arrangement which would facilitate Swedish intervention in Germany. Charnacé was treated well in the Swedish capital, and his reputation for making a good deal preceded him thanks to his recent work on the Truce of Altmark. After sorting through the anticipated questions of precedence and etiquette, Charnacé attempted to settle down to business, but Gustavus put him off.

It wasn't until November that Charnacé revealed to Gustavus the extent of his powers. King Louis XIII had authorised him to strike a deal with

Sweden's conquering hero, to the tune of 600,000 livres annually, which would certainly solve Gustavus' immediate shortcomings in cash flow. However, the return which Charnacé expected from this subsidy was too high a price for the Swedish King to pay. Charnacé wanted Sweden to expel Spanish troops from the Rhine and to raze their fortresses. He wanted Sweden to combat the Imperial forces under Wallenstein, but to leave the soldiers commanded by Count Tilly of the Catholic League intact, and to refrain from harming Bavaria. Furthermore, under Richelieu's advice, Gustavus was told that the German Protestants would be more amenable to accepting Swedish aid if the Swedish King presented himself as the guarantor of German Protestant freedoms, as well as the independence of the individual princes and cities. Gustavus should therefore pose as the saviour of the Germans, and the answer to the Emperor's absolutist, militant Catholic tendencies which they had feared.

Gustavus was reported to have laughed at these suggestions, before immediately laying into them in turn. He had no intention of playing the role of a French pawn; he would not declare against Spain, when Swedish-Spanish trade was at an all-time high. He would not guarantee Bavaria, when this could damage his relations with the pro-Palatine English. He even questioned the logic in the French attempts to have it both ways; to pose both as the champion of the anti-Habsburg cause, and at the same time to present France as the friend to German Catholics like Bavaria, who would never choose a French King over a German Emperor.

These rebuffs came as something of a surprise to Charnacé. While he would try again, for the moment Charnacé took solace from the fact that, by sheer necessity, Sweden was destined to be a nominal ally of France. 1630 looked set to be the deciding year in Germany as well as North Italy, and Charnacé could not have known that Gustavus would wait until 1631 before formalising his relations with France. In the meantime, having got the peace with Poland that he desired, Gustavus focused on preparing the way for a landing in Germany. Stralsund was reinforced in March 1630, and extensive feelers were sent out to those figures that truly mattered now – the German princes. While he worked to cushion his German landing, he also built upon his Russian insurance policy by closing ranks with Moscow against the Poles. Before he moved with disarming confidence into the next phase of the war, Gustavus wanted to ensure that he had at least either German allies or a Russo-Polish War. In the end, he got both.[49] As the German princes met at Regensburg, the defenders of Mantua prepared for another siege and the Dutch continued their conquest of their Spanish neighbour, the King of Sweden had never been stronger, but he was far from finished yet. It remained to secure the final piece of the puzzle before he could rampage through Germany, and this piece could only be procured from Moscow.

FIVE

The War in the North

Feodor Nikitich Romanov returned to Moscow in 1619, following over eight years in Polish captivity. Feodor had adopted the name Filaret, after he and his wife had been forced to take monastic vows during the Time of Troubles which had plagued Russia in the first decade and a half of the seventeenth century. Henceforth, upon his return to Moscow, Filaret was known as the Patriarch, for not only was Filaret a well-connected and well-travelled Russian nobleman, he was also the father of the new Russian Tsar, Michael Romanov. Returning to his son's side from 1619, this duo worked together to improve Muscovy's position in world affairs, a task which was profoundly shaped by Filaret's experience of Polish hospitality. In 1610, Filaret had travelled to Poland to negotiate with King Sigismund III, but he was imprisoned shortly thereafter once he refused to recognise Sigismund's son as Tsar.

In the war between Poland and Russia which lasted from 1603-18, Filaret had watched his homeland lose everything. Russia's Baltic position went to Sweden, and vast swathes of the Ukraine, West Russian and Belorussian territories which Russia had accumulated over the previous decades went to Poland. The ferocious expanse of Russian power and territory in the sixteenth century over the lands surrounding Muscovy had been the mission of Ivan the Terrible.[50] Filaret now returned to Moscow with a mission of his own – to regain these territories lost to the Poles, so that Muscovy would have her heart restored to her. This mission was to shape how Russia viewed its place in the world, which allies it selected and, incredibly enough, the very course of the Thirty Years War.

In Filaret's mind, Russia had been pushed far back during her misfortune, and she needed to return to her position of predominance over the east one step at a time. While working closely with his son the Tsar, Filaret attempted to engineer a vast coalition of anti-Habsburg states as early as 1620. The logic for this approach was based on the very logic of Polish relations and the perceived foundations of Polish power. The Polish King Sigismund III was closely allied with the Austrian and Spanish Habsburgs; Emperor Ferdinand had married Sigismund' sister, and Poland had intervened against the Habsburg enemy Transylvania in 1619. To regain what had been lost, Russia would have to fight Poland at some point in the future. For this conflict to be a success though, Filaret believed that Russia should not fight it alone. Since behind Poland stood the Habsburgs, Russia should ensure that someone stood behind her as well. This logic was to characterise Russian diplomacy for over a decade, and it made not only the resumption of war between Poland and Russia possible, but also King Gustavus Adolphus' Swedish intervention into Germany in summer 1630.

The Russian ambitions for revenge and resurgence were grand, but in the early 1620s, they were tempered by the realities of the early phase of the Thirty Years War. Filaret and the Tsar found that few powers were willing to listen to Russian entreaties, and that they had more than enough problems of their own. The disappointments and frustrations of the Russians in the early 1620s would certainly have been shared by Frederick V, the dispossessed Elector Palatine, who worked in vain to orchestrate some kind of anti-Habsburg coalition around the same time. The 1618 Truce of Deulino committed both Russia and Poland to a period of peace which could not last, yet there was no sense in breaking this truce without sufficient help. It was well known in Moscow that the Swedes were fighting their own war against the Poles, and that Gustavus' campaigns were frequently undermined by Habsburg intervention and the direct provision of aid to Sigismund.

This pattern of Habsburg aid to Poland during times of Polish difficulty reached its climax over 1627-29, but it posed a formidable threat to Russian security. Frustrated in the early 1620s, Filaret found his influence over his son slipping, and for a time he was replaced by a coalition of Russian nobles or boyars. The tenacious Patriarch was not to be denied though; in the mid-1620s he reasserted his influence and replaced his rivals. Between 1626-1629, Filaret was at the height of his powers, and renewed his mission to upset the Habsburg-Polish apple cart. This mission was made easier by the course of the war in Germany. To the delight of both Frederick V and the Russians, from 1625 the Hague Alliance represented the first concrete anti-Habsburg coalition in Europe. This presented great opportunities for Russia, especially if Sweden were to join in. Alas, Filaret was to be disappointed once more; just as Sweden resumed its Polish War, several diplomats arrived in Moscow seeking Russian support for the Hague Alliance, which at least demonstrated that Russia's anti-Habsburg temperament was known of in the West.

Interestingly, a common theme of this era was that Filaret was not content to allow Russia to be a mere pawn in this game; instead he worked to craft a home for a Russia in the anti-Habsburg camp. Perceiving the division of Europe into the pro and anti-Habsburg camp, Filaret would demonstrate that Russia would make her own way regardless of the diplomatic efforts of other powers. Displaying a keen awareness of European relations from 1626, Filaret inserted Russia into the equation, and believed all issues could be reduced to a single question: are you for the Habsburgs or against them? This approach compelled Russian diplomats to view the Dutch as their allies, even while the Dutch were only at war with the Spanish Habsburgs. It meant that the Ottomans were one of their most important potential allies for the damage the Turk could do to the Austrian Habsburgs' security in Hungary. It also meant that Filaret was more than happy to ally with powers with whom Russia had a score to settle; Sweden had stolen Russia's Baltic possessions from her during the Time of Troubles, but for the moment, she was the lesser evil because she existed within the anti-Polish and therefore the anti-Habsburg camp.[51]

That cliché of 'the enemy of my enemy is my friend' was wholeheartedly accepted by Filaret when it came to relations with Sweden. However, these relations could only go so far. From 1626, when Gustavus Adolphus attempted to appeal to the Russian Tsar for an alliance, and wrote a letter presenting the existence of two camps within Europe, he was, at least to some extent, preaching to the choir. Yet, the history of Russo-Swedish relations contained a great deal of very recent painful antagonism. King Gustavus Adolphus had ascended to the throne while at war with Russia, and his father Charles IX had his own history with the Tsars. At one point, Tsar Dimitri even wrote to King Charles IX urging him to renounce his claims on the throne of Sweden at once, and to return that crown to the rightful King of Sweden, Sigismund III.[52] Incidentally, this correspondence (1605-06) demonstrated the simultaneous hostility and jealously which the Russian Tsar felt for that Polish King, who would not recognise his title of Tsar. Dimitri did not last long as Tsar himself; he was yet another victim of the turmoil which consumed Russia during the Time of Troubles, which only Tsar Michael's ascension in 1613 brought to an end.[53]

The great hostility which Filaret and consequently Tsar Michael felt towards the Polish King was certainly exacerbated not only by the seizure of so much land for the traditionally Muscovite base, but by the disputes over the Russian succession. Until his death in 1634, Sigismund III would maintain his claim on the Swedish and Russian thrones; the former for himself and the latter for his son Wladyslaw. By 1617, Sigismund was one of only a select few of rulers who refused to recognise the Romanovs as anything more than usurpers. Sigismund insisted that the Russian throne belonged to his son, and his refusal to relinquish this claim significantly reduced Poland's diplomatic options, forcing his realm to rely upon the Habsburgs, and forcing the traditional enemies Russia and Sweden to work against him. At the very least, both King Gustavus Adolphus and Tsar Michael Romanov could bond over the fact that the King of Poland refused to recognise their reign as legitimate.[54]

Again though, this bond forged through diplomatic necessity was not sufficient to compel Russian adherence to Swedish schemes. When Sweden did approach the Tsar's agents for an alliance, which included a stipulation that Russia must break the Truce of Deulino, the Russian officials responded vaguely:

> He [the Tsar] will think about how to take vengeance on the Polish King and his country for the wrongs done earlier, but at the present time of truce this cannot be done, because that peace treaty was sealed by great ambassadors with hearts and oaths...but if some wrong, however slight, be committed by the King of Poland or his son, by the Poles or by Lithuanians then, although the period of truce be not expired, our great sovereign, His Majesty the Tsar, will be ready to take action, in advance of its expiry, against Poland and Lithuania, to punish their wrongdoing.

In actual fact, both sides had violated this truce several times since 1619. It was, as the Swedish Chancellor Axel Oxenstierna suspected, merely window dressing to excuse Russian inactivity. Oxenstierna tried again, this time sending a Swedish diplomat in 1627 with powers to persuade Russia to join in a military alliance with Sweden before any Swedish Polish truce was concluded. This initiative also misfired, because Oxenstierna and many historians misunderstood the Russian position. Neither the Tsar nor his father the Patriarch needed to be reminded of the importance of striking at Poland while she was distracted; what they needed instead was a coalition which they could join. This would provide a far more reliable platform from which a war against Poland could be launched. Otherwise, the Tsar quite reasonably feared that Sweden might abandon Russia or even turn against her.

Furthermore, Russia and Sweden were drawn together only by a common enemy; as we have seen, the Tsar had many reasons to resent the power of the Swedish King. Indeed, the only issue separating Sweden from Poland was Gustavus' ready recognition of Michael Romanov as Tsar. Aside from that, Filaret's influence certainly played a role in driving the anti-Polish course in Russian foreign policy, but there was no reason why in the near future this policy might not be reversed or complicated by the growth of the Swedish threat. If Russia was to regain her Baltic territories – which she would surely desire to do once the lands were retaken from the Poles – it was only inevitable that a war with Sweden was to be the result. This war could be postponed for now owing to necessity and the immediate demands of realpolitik, but Russian security demanded greater insurance than such concerns. What she needed above all was another ally, to insulate Russia from the any potential Swedish treachery and to wage a more effective coalition war against the pre-existing coalition of the King of Spain, the King of Poland and the Holy Roman Emperor.[55]

In King Sigismund's court, it was well known that the Russians would not act against Poland without a coalition behind her. Polish diplomacy thus largely ignored any latent Russian threat until spring 1629, when news of the success of the Russians in building this coalition reached Sigismund's ears just as the war with Sweden was reaching a fever pitch. In that period of 1626-29, Russian approaches to France, England, the Dutch and the Danes were stepped up, with the latter believed to be of particular importance in Moscow, since the Danish King was at that point already at war with the Habsburg Emperor. To sweeten the deal and aid its potential allies, the Tsar authorised the provision of subsidies not of roubles or the limited reserves in foreign currency which Russia possessed, but of another commodity altogether – grain. By providing grain to its allies at low prices, this grain could then be sold to the Dutch or invested in the Amsterdam grain exchange in a highly lucrative arrangement.

The Danes were bombarded with such proposals, and for a time the Tsar seemed to perceive King Christian IV of Denmark as the most valuable potential ally, but it was not to be. News of the Treaty of Lubeck which brought peace between the Emperor and the Danish King aroused considerable irritation in Moscow. When Danish diplomats arrived before the Tsar a couple of years later, they were greeted with demands that Russia would only consent to a favourable friendship with the Danish King if Christian first proclaimed his friendship with the King of Sweden. This tactic was designed to repel the Danes rather than accommodate them, and Russo-Danish relations subsequently soured. The Danish card having failed, the Tsar turned to the Dutch, whose far-reaching interest in Baltic trade and control over the grain exchange made them natural economic allies. Politically, the continuous Dutch war with Habsburg Spain, and the knock-on effects this had on the Emperor identified the Dutch Republic as an invaluable member of a potential anti-Habsburg alliance. These Dutch relations were significantly sweetened by the provision of grain and saltpetre at favourable prices, but Dutch unwillingness to make war on the Emperor meant that Russo-Dutch negotiations could only go so far.

Although they made some progress in Western diplomacy, it was in the Ottoman Empire that the Russians truly struck gold. From 1627, the Ottoman Sultan Osman II intimated through his ambassador to Russia that he would be open to an anti-Habsburg alliance. These proposals were received warmly in Moscow, and both Filaret and the Tsar jumped at the chance to incorporate the Emperor's most fearsome foe within their coalition. Russian officials were sent first to Transylvania, with the aim of including the tireless Bethlen Gabor in their schemes. The aim of orchestrating an anti-Habsburg coalition rooted in the east, and consisting of Turkey, Russia, Transylvania and Sweden acquired a new impetus from 1628, when Cardinal Richelieu learned of it through the French ambassador to Constantinople. It was then that the aforementioned embassies to Poland and Russia were launched by Richelieu (see above). Russian diplomatic initiatives had thus aroused French interest, and Richelieu – then occupied with a Huguenot revolt and a looming war with the Habsburgs in Italy – was not ignorant to the damage which Russia could inflict on the Habsburgs' position.[56]

Significantly, news of these diplomatic schemes compelled Gustavus Adolphus to act as well. Where once the Russians had appeared reluctant to break their truce with Poland, her activities since 1626 suggested that a war with Poland was now on the cards. To harness these developments, Swedish diplomats thus followed their French counterparts to Moscow in spring 1629. There they met a Russian court which was far more amenable and friendly to the Swedish requests for alliance. Gustavus asked for fifty thousand quarters of rye to feed his army and asked in addition to be permitted to purchase this at the Tsar's price. To this came the reply from the Tsar's agents: 'Let your King simply write what food supplies he needs, and our great sovereign will let him purchase them, duty free, in the year that the corn comes to ripeness.' The willingness to provide grain at such reduced prices indicated that Russia was serious about forging a closer political union, and indeed the negotiations which followed confirmed this good news.

The records of the Swedish diplomats that had been sent to Moscow shed a great deal of light not only on how the Tsar and Filaret interacted with foreign dignitaries, but also on the extent of Russia's awareness of the European situation by 1629. It must be emphasised that this self-awareness, supplied by an active diplomatic service, made the following agreements possible, because it fortified the Tsar with information and knowledge that he believed he could trust. He no longer felt forced to rely solely on Swedish promises or claims. Indeed, the Tsar was able to inform the Swedish diplomats that a Russo-Turkish agreement had been reached. The record demonstrates clearly the link between the Tsar's decision to break the truce with Poland, and the acquisition of a coalition which Turkey and Sweden would both take an active role in. As Tsar Michael put it in his own words, he had decided:

> ...to help your sovereign and the other Christian sovereigns of the Evangelical faith by all possible means, so that the evil design of the Emperor and the Papists may not succeed...Owing to the wrongs done by the Polish King and his violation of the peace treaty, the great sovereign does not want to wait until the term of the truce expires, but intends to go to war against him and to help your sovereign.

The importance of these developments in spring 1629 must not be understated, nor should the interconnected nature of European relations be ignored. Without the firm agreement with the Ottomans, the Russians would never have felt comfortable to break the truce with Poland and make war in alliance with the Swedes against a common enemy. Without the Russian commitment to make war against the Poles, it is highly unlikely that Gustavus Adolphus would have felt secure enough in his position to make his grand entrance into Germany. Indeed, the conclusion of these negotiations solved several problems for all the powers involved. The Russians were no longer fearful that the Swedes would abandon them now that the Turks were also party to the arrangement, and the Swedes were confident that the Poles would not attack them in the rear when they were engaged in Germany. One could therefore argue without too much exaggeration that an appreciation for the course of the Thirty Years War is impossible without first understanding the complexities of the whole concert of European powers which participated, directly or indirectly, within it.

It must also be underlined that the Russian decision was not motivated either by Gustavus Adolphus' approaches or by Cardinal Richelieu's diplomatic genius. Not only did Russian diplomatic initiatives prove pivotal to the creation of an anti-Habsburg coalition to the east, but subsequent Russian efforts to improve and tighten relations between the Ottoman Empire and Sweden exemplified the far-reaching diplomatic game which the Tsar and the Patriarch were playing. Over 1630-31, Ottoman envoys passed through Russian territory en route to speak with the Swedish King, while Swedish diplomats took the opposite journey, all in the name of a scheme which the underrated diplomatic panache of the Patriarch Filaret and the Tsar had set in motion.[57]

It was hardly surprising that the good news which the Swedish diplomats brought back with them to their King was warmly welcomed. In spite of the Tsar's request that the alliance be kept secret, Gustavus apparently could not contain himself, and for the next several years told anyone who would listen that the Russian Tsar stood alongside him in the anti-Habsburg mission. In his own words, Gustavus said:

> The King is especially glad that the Tsar of Muscovy had promised to help the oppressed Protestants of Germany: many thousands of people have been comforted by this promise, and may Almighty God move the Tsar's heart and mind to carry out the promise he has given.

As the Swedish ambassador in Moscow put it – capturing the essence of Russian propaganda at the time as did so: 'Gustavus Adolphus and his army are the advance wall of Muscovy, its vanguard regiment fighting in Germany for Russia's Tsardom.' By painting the Swedish intervention in such a light, the Tsar brushed off the concerns of the Swedes when they informed him that they had made a truce of their own with Poland in September 1629. Indeed, it seems highly likely that the Tsar knew about the truce even as the French attempted to conceal it from him. Moscow understood and appreciated Sweden's position in the context of its anti-Habsburg struggle far more comprehensively than either the Swedes or French seemed to have given her credit for.

Since she had crafted a coalition against the potent Habsburg threat rather than merely launched a war against the Poles, it did not matter all that much to the Tsar that one element of this coalition determined to wage a war against a single Habsburg actor. After all, this multi-layered anti-Habsburg arrangement had taken shape for some time in Franco-Dutch relations, and in the preceding negotiations of the Hague Alliance. In neither of those arrangements were all members of the coalition at war with all members of the Habsburg camp – i.e. the King of Poland, King of Spain and Holy Roman Emperor – and it is highly likely, considering its participation within and knowledge of European relations, that the Tsar saw his role in the latest anti-Habsburg coalition in the same light. Indeed, as an anti-Habsburg ruler, the Tsar was cognisant of the fact that Sweden would be able to inflict the most damage on the Habsburg centre if she was first freed from her war with Poland. To facilitate this, the Tsar was willing to help the King of Sweden end his Polish War. He did not resent Gustavus' exit from the Polish War because he understood its strategic implications, even while, on the other hand, the Tsar certainly would not have refused Swedish military aid against the Polish King if it had been offered to him.[58]

'And as soon as His Majesty the Tsar begins his war against the Pole, our sovereign will be freer to go to war against the Kaiser', recorded the Swedish ambassador in April 1630. This represented the culmination of the Russo-Swedish negotiations. The arrival of another French delegation in Moscow in May 1630 demonstrated their lack of awareness of the previous Russian activity, by proposing a coalition which was remarkably similar to that which the Tsar had almost concluded. This insult was parried though, amidst further declarations of goodwill from the Turkish Sultan and enthusiastic French offers of support for the scheme. The Russian agent moved to Stockholm and reached the Swedish capital by July 1630. In his hands he held the documentation which confirmed the alliance between Turkey, Transylvania, Russia and Sweden – the Swedish King need only sign it for it to become official.

Yet, the Russian agent was both concerned and comforted to discover that the Swedish King was no longer in Sweden. Concerned because it meant that Gustavus would not yet be able to make the alliance official but comforted at the same time because Gustavus' action demonstrated his faith in the Russian promises without need for the official documentation. Evidently Gustavus had been convinced of the Russian sincerity to fight the common enemy through the dispatches from Moscow of his resident envoy, not to mention the increasingly anti-Habsburg behaviour of Cardinal Richelieu's administration. Seizing the moment, Gustavus Adolphus took it upon himself to act. He was already in Northern Germany by the time the Russian agent arrived in Stockholm to find him absent. In the mind of the Swedish King, more than enough foundations had been established to guarantee a triumph; he must rely now on a successful military campaign, now that the successful diplomatic campaign had been achieved. Gustavus believed that the best way to accelerate the pace of Russian commitment was to demonstrate himself how serious he was about his anti-Habsburg quest. By demonstrating his unshakable faith in the cause, his allies would be compelled to do the same. On 19 May 1630 Gustavus set sail. After so many months of negotiation and preparation, he was more than ready to make his mark.[59]

Russian participation in this act of the Thirty Years War cannot be overlooked if the true range and impact of that conflict is to be appreciated. Without Russian activity, Gustavus' Polish foe would never have been neutralised, and he would never have felt secure enough to intervene in Germany, thereby prolonging the conflict for another eighteen years. On the one hand, Gustavus' caution and willingness to prepare the ground before making war on the Empire demonstrates his patience and foresight. On the other hand, Gustavus was immensely fortunate that the Russian Tsar and the Patriarch Filaret interpreted world affairs in the same black and white terms as he did. Had the Tsar displayed a dual hostility towards Sweden and Poland for their previous attacks on Russia, then one imagines the Thirty Years War proceeding very differently. As it happened though, Gustavus Adolphus was in the right place at the right time to dramatically alter the course of this conflict. His arrival in Germany must be seen as a turning point in that theatre, yet this Rubicon was only crossed with the considerable help of the distant Tsar.

Chapter 15 Notes

[1]Quoted in Peter H. Wilson, *Sourcebook*, p. 108.

[2]See Wedgewood, *Thirty Years War*, pp. 238-240.

[3]See Geoff Mortimer, *Wallenstein*, p. 115.

[4]See Burckhardt, *Richelieu: His Rise to Power*, pp. 286-287.

[5]*Ibid*, pp. 295-299.

[6]See David Parrott, 'The Mantuan Succession, 1627-31: A Sovereignty Dispute in Early Modern Europe', pp. 61-63.

[7]Mortimer, *Wallenstein*, pp. 117-119.

[8]*Ibid*, p. 120.

[9]Both extracts quoted in Wilson, *Sourcebook*, pp. 108-109.

[10]See Thomas F. Arnold, 'Gonzaga Fortifications and the Mantuan Succession Crisis of 1613-1631', pp. 126-129.

[11]Peter H. Wilson, *Europe's Tragedy*, pp. 454-455.

[12]Quoted in Wilson, *Sourcebook*, pp. 109-110.

[13]Quoted in *Ibid*, p. 118.

[14]Mortimer, *Wallenstein*, pp. 125-127.

[15]See *Ibid*, p. 122.

[16]*Ibid*, p. 126.

[17]*Ibid*, p. 127.

[18]*Ibid*, pp. 128-129.

[19]*Ibid*, pp. 129-131.

[20]Pursell, *The Winter King*, p. 266.

[21]David Parrott, 'The Mantuan Succession, 1627-31: A Sovereignty Dispute in Early Modern Europe', pp. 63-64.

[22]Thomas F. Arnold, 'Gonzaga Fortifications and the Mantuan Succession Crisis of 1613-1631', pp. 128-129.

[23]See Wedgewood, *Thirty Years War*, pp. 256-257.

[24]See Wilson, *Europe's Tragedy*, pp. 465-467.

[25]Quoted in Wilson, *Sourcebook* p. 118.

[26]Wilson, *Europe's Tragedy*, pp. 457-458.

[27]Ronald Asch, *The Thirty Years' War*, p. 98.

[28]Pursell, *The Winter King*, pp. 266-267.

[29]Wedgewood, *Thirty Years War*, p. 258.

[30]We have examined the roots of the Swedish-Polish conflict in an earlier chapter, but for two books on the subject readers should track down Paul Douglas Lockhart, *Sweden in the seventeenth Century* and Henrik O. Lunde, *A Warrior Dynasty: The Rise and Decline of Sweden as a Military Superpower*.

[31]Robert I. Frost, *The Northern Wars*, see Chapter 5.

[32]See Porshnev, *Muscovy and Sweden in the Thirty Years War*, pp. 13-14. This underrated book was an invaluable source for this portion of our research.

[33]*Ibid*, pp. 14-15.

[34]*Ibid*, pp. 15-16.

[35]*Ibid*, pp. 16-17.

[36]*Ibid*, pp. 18-20.

[37]We will examine Gustavus' justification for intervention in Germany in a later section, but those interested in reading the Swedish manifesto in its entirety can find it in Wilson, *Sourcebook*, pp. 122-130. See also Pärtel Piirimäe, 'Just War in Theory and Practice: The Legitimation of Swedish Intervention in the Thirty Years War'.

[38]Mortimer, *Wallenstein*, pp. 116-117.

[39]Peter H. Wilson, *Europe's Tragedy*, pp. 432-433.

[40]Porshnev, *Muscovy and Sweden*, p. 15.

[41]*Ibid*, p. 6.

[42]Stevens, *History of Gustavus Adolphus*, pp. 149-151; Stewart P. Oakley, *War and Peace in the Baltic*, pp. 61-67.

[43]This deterioration in the Polish cavalry's effectiveness was an unfortunate trend which continued throughout the seventeenth century. See Alfred P. Brainhard, 'Polish-Lithuanian Cavalry in the Late Seventeenth Century', *The Polish Review*, Vol. 36, No. 1 (1991), pp. 69-82.

[44]See Porshnev, *Muscovy and Sweden in the Thirty Years War*, pp. 2-3.

[45]*Ibid*, pp. 4-5.

[46]*Ibid*, pp. 6-7.

[47]*Ibid*, pp. 8-9.

[48]*Ibid*, pp. 10-12.

[49]See Burckhardt, *Richelieu, His Rise to Power*, pp. 277-281.

[50]A brief but very approachable history of the Romanov dynasty in the context of the early Russian expansions is provided by Simon Sebag Montefiore, *The Romanovs 1613-1918* (Penguin Random House; London, 2016), especially chapter 1.

[51]Porshnev, *Muscovy and Sweden in the Thirty Years War*, pp. 23-25.

[52]See Chester Dunning and Dmitrii Caesar, 'Tsar Dmitrii's Bellicose Letter to King Karl IX of Sweden', *The Slavonic and East European Review*, Vol. 87, No. 2 (April 2009), pp. 322-336.

[53]Geoffrey Parker, *Europe in Crisis*, pp. 111-112.

[54]*Ibid*, p. 113.

[55]Porshnev, *Muscovy and Sweden*, pp. 26-27.

[56]*Ibid*, pp. 28-29.

[57]*Ibid*, pp. 30-31.

[58]*Ibid*, pp. 32-33.

[59]*Ibid*, pp. 34-36.

A contemporary drawing of the battle of Breitenfeld

Axel Oxenstierna

CHAPTER SIXTEEN
"All Changed, Changed Utterly"

ONE
Presenting Salvation

As is bound to occur according to His word, that the jar carries water on the farm until at last it is broken so be it with me ultimately. How often have I been in the midst of blood and danger in the cause of our Swedish Kingdom and yet through God's mercy, even though injured, have been allowed to return? Now I must shed blood one last time. So, before I leave you I commend you, my Swedish subjects, to the protection of Almighty God and desire that we will meet again in His heavenly Kingdom.

This was the King of Sweden's famous address before the three estates of his kingdom on 19 May 1630, a mere month before he left his kingdom, never to return. He addressed the peasants, clergy and burghers in turn, saying first to the burghers that he wished 'that your little cabins may become great houses of stone, your little boats great ships and merchantmen, and that the oil in your cruse fail not.' To the peasants, he declared:

My wish for them is that their meadows be green with grass, their fields bear an hundred fold, so that their barns may be full: and that they may so increase and multiply in all plenteousness that they may gladly and without sighing perform the duties and obligations that lie upon them.

The clergy were roused to remember that they possessed significant power 'to turn and twist the hearts of men', and were encouraged to stick to church doctrine, guarding against the sins of pride as they did so. It was an impressive example which Gustavus Adolphus set for his people – one of courage, tenacity and conviction.[1] Yet, those present at the Swedish *Riksrad* cannot have failed to imagine the fate of another Northern monarch, who had left his kingdom with similar high hopes five years earlier. Gustavus Adolphus was not King Christian IV of Denmark, but there was no guarantee that, when it came down to the brutal finality of battle, his fortunes would not be equally ruined.

Gustavus knew that he was taking a risk. He was taking a risk that he could defeat the experienced and undefeated Count Tilly, the commander of Catholic League forces who had been left to try and gather together the remaining forces in the Empire following Wallenstein's dismissal (which came in August). He was taking a risk that his Kingdom would be able to weather the storm, and that its nobility would not turn on him as Christian IV's had. He was also taking an immense risk when he bargained that the Protestant German princes would support him against their Emperor. Per that latter point, Gustavus knew that he required a manifesto which would help him to explain and legitimise his actions to these same German princes.

It was a long to-do list, but Gustavus had demonstrated that he was not above diplomatic approaches either. Throughout April and May 1630 Imperial envoys had visited Danzig and talked with the Danish King's representatives, who hoped to mediate a settlement. It was there that we glimpse Gustavus' pressing concern – that of security. Axel Oxenstierna captured this in a draft letter to the delegates at Danzig on 12 May 1630, a full week before the King's emotive appeal to the three estates. Oxenstierna wrote:

> The King is well satisfied with the instructions as a whole, but notices that the Chancellor has omitted to bear in mind the most important point of all, namely security [assecuratio]. The Chancellor is accordingly to take care that the King is not engaged to quit Stralsund, or any other place which he may be able to acquire, until all the conditions of peace are carried out by the Imperialists, their armies entirely withdrawn from the Saxon Circles, and everything (especially the coastlands) restored to a secure and peaceable condition.[2]

These conditions for the restoration of the coastlands may appear relatively innocent, but this definition of coastlands included the Duchy of Mecklenburg. Since this was in the possession of Wallenstein this request was unacceptable, as was the notion of Sweden remaining in control of Stralsund, that city which had defied the generalissimo during 1628. Gustavus knew that the Emperor would never accept these demands, but they had not come from nowhere. The minutes of a Swedish Council debate from 4 May 1630 demonstrate that both Gustavus and his subjects weighed up the risks involved in taking the Emperor at his word or retaining their gains at Stralsund as insurance against Ferdinand's bad faith. The minutes read like a kind of watershed moment, where both the King and his councillors accepted that conflict was the only course:

> [One figure] thought that the question was settled by the terms of our treaty with Stralsund, since they laid it down that the King is to withdraw his garrison as soon as the Emperor restores the original state of affairs [in Mecklenburg]... [The King said] our basic war aim is security; and if the Emperor will grant the terms we have proposed, that would be a sufficient guarantee; but if the

King were then to continue his occupation of Stralsund it would look as though he sought to enlarge his dominions. [Others] denied that this would be an adequate guarantee of safety; for if our security is to be assured it must be under our own control, and not in the discretion of the enemy, for…there can be no safety if we hand back any position which we cannot immediately retake…[The King] made the point that it would be iniquitous to deprive the Dukes of Pomerania and Mecklenburg of their hereditary rights for the sake of getting an agreement with the Emperor.[3]

The negotiations went nowhere, and few should have been surprised, since the Swedish King neglected even to send delegates to Danzig to take part. Gustavus had resolved to make war against the Emperor for some time but had delayed the act until it suited him. Now freed from his Polish War and in possession of a landing pad in Stralsund, which Sweden's Council had been persuaded to accept as a Swedish fief for life that same month, Gustavus was tasked with crafting a manifesto which would justify his actions to Europe. The following manifesto was released across the continent in June, but it should not be seen as a necessarily true reflection of the Swedish King's intentions; rather, this was propaganda designed to justify his actions and to shield his policy from criticism.[4] That said, we should not ignore its extensive examination of the perceived wrongs which the King declared he had endured at the Emperor's hands, even if the opening paragraph of the manifesto was not exactly modest:

When we come to the business of war, the first question to be proposed is, whether it be just or not. This is the case at present with respect to that which the King of Sweden has undertaken anew, who may very justly be called great, both for his courage and valour, and for his power, strength and endeavours, and also for all his high and mighty designs, and actions truly worthy of a great King; having for these last years, in order to support and encourage his friends, made war successfully against the Muscovites and Polanders, and then dextrously made peace still for his glory and notable advantage; and some time ago, in a very short time, brought his army into the harbours of the Baltic Sea; having made himself master of all Pomerania, and fortified the places within his conquest, not to extend his limits, and enlarge his bounds, but to deliver his relations and friends from oppression; not by the devastation of countries and cities, but at his own charges and expense, and at the hazard of his own person, as appears by the public accounts, which have spread his fame through the whole universe.

After establishing Gustavus' majesty for all to see, the manifesto proclaimed that 'the Spaniards and the House of Austria have always been intent on a Universal Monarchy', and noted that 'if this brave and generous northern prince had not bestirred himself, and opposed that torrent, she had pushed her ambition and arms to the most distant kingdoms and provinces…'

More specific qualms over Ferdinand's behaviour were also mentioned. Gustavus' letters to Bethlen Gabor, the Prince of Transylvania, were brought up, since Ferdinand's agents had intercepted these in the past 'and after they had been opened, and false glosses put upon them', Gustavus' reputation was 'rendered odious everywhere.' The most justifiable gripe which Gustavus had concerned Wallenstein's consistent and escalating interference in his war with Poland. Stralsund was mentioned as well, a city which Gustavus could not ignore 'without wounding his honour and conscience.'

Gustavus' agents were insulted by their Imperial counterparts when they attempted to participate in the Treaty of Lubeck negotiations, an 'unworthy and dishonourable treatment [which] was held and judged by all nations a sufficient cause of a rupture, and of requiring satisfaction by arms.' The magnanimous King of Sweden resisted this urge though, only to be faced with 'the highest piece of injustice', the invasion of Prussia and the concentrated military intervention into his Polish War by the Imperial commander and subordinate of Wallenstein, Hans Georg von Arnim. Arnim led his contingent against the Swedes, and 'with great diligence' had…

> …harassed that [army] of the King of Sweden in Prussia during the whole summer, whereby he had doubtless suffered the entire ruin of his estates, friends and allies, if God, who is the protector of righteous causes, and the preserver of his innocence, had not taken in his own hand the defence of his cause, having made his enemies justly suffer the evils which they had unjustly prepared and designed against him.

As we know, Gustavus was defeated by the combined Polish-Imperial army, and his forces compelled to retreat from the siege of Danzig. In fact, Wallenstein had provided some twelve thousand men to aid the Polish King, a not insignificant contribution which may well have turned the tide of the entire Danzig campaign.[5] The defeat probably stung all the more, but still it was insisted that the King desired peace, but that 'the enemy had no such intention, considering the frauds and tricks they made use of formerly.' After a long list of the grievances which Gustavus had suffered at the Emperor's hands, the question was put to the reader:

> Seeing all this, is there any person of understanding and sense, not prepossessed with passion and private interest that can deny both by divine and human laws and by the very instinct of nature it is lawful to make use of the means which God puts in our hands to resent and avenge ourselves for so sensible an injury? Especially for Kings and sovereign princes, particularly when their honour and person, the safety of their states, and the good of their subjects are concerned; when all appearance of honour and satisfaction is denied them… Is there anyone, I say, that can blame the most serene King of Sweden for endeavouring by his arms to defend his subjects and friends from such an oppression?[6]

Just in case individuals existed who might object to Gustavus' motives and justifications, the Swedish government ensured that the twenty-three editions and five languages of the manifesto changed with the times and the recipient. It was essential that Gustavus' message be as widely disseminated and as sympathetic as possible to an exhausted Germany and a distracted Europe. Indeed, the wars in the Netherlands and in Italy were more than enough to occupy contemporary attentions, not to mention Habsburg resources. Incredible though it may seem now, by the early summer of 1630 the Holy Roman Emperor Ferdinand II was not watching Gustavus' every move, and neither was he considering the danger the Swedish King posed to Germany – instead, he was focused on the future of his dynasty.

The Imperial Diet at Regensburg was Ferdinand's major concern in 1630, as he sought the confirmation of his son as heir and the declaration of war against the Dutch by the German princes. Ferdinand met resistance and frustration from those assembled at Regensburg; they were frustrated with the behaviour of Wallenstein and some were troubled by the Emperor's actions in North Italy, which seemed to demonstrate that Ferdinand would act independently wherever he liked. Twenty thousand of Wallenstein's men had been sent to prop up the Spanish in Mantua, and the Emperor now demanded more men to aid Madrid in its campaign against the Dutch. The Protestant Electors were conspicuous in their absence, and the shadow left by the Edict of Restitution was impossible to ignore. Convening on 3 July, the Diet at Regensburg was still a vibrant affair, with representatives from all over Europe in attendance. More troubling than what was discussed, of course, was what was not – Gustavus Adolphus landed in Germany on the island of Usedom off of Pomerania just three days later. The Lion in the North had slipped through the back door of the Empire, which Ferdinand's miscalculations had left ajar. As Gustavus knew though, preparing for war with the Emperor and landing in Germany was only half the battle: he would now have to carry the war which he had longed for to a successful conclusion, and for that he urgently needed allies.

One of the gravest initial challenges Gustavus faced in this regard was the counterargument which the Emperor provided to his manifesto. While reduced merely to a war of words at this stage, this confrontation was nonetheless important, because it could blunt the Swedish mission before it had even truly launched. With the exception of the dispossessed Dukes of Mecklenburg and the city of Stralsund, Gustavus had no German allies to call upon. His relationship with the French can be viewed as playing hard to get, as both sides attempted to drive a hard bargain in order to get what they wanted, and only in 1631 would this process reach its conclusion. It was essential for Gustavus that he continued to be seen as the King waging a just war against the Emperor's designs, and yet within that conflict, Gustavus could not declare himself as the saviour of the Protestants, since this might alienate the French and repel those Protestant German leaders who had yet to be tempted away from Ferdinand's orbit.[7]

Gustavus would thus have to tread carefully, and to respond to the Emperors challenges publicly as they appeared. The first challenge did not take long to arrive. On 18 August the Imperial reply to the Swedish King's manifesto was sent, wherein the Emperor said:

> We wish to inform you that we have reliable reports that you have collected a large army of horse and foot throughout this year and have landed on islands belonging to the Holy Empire and are now on its soil and have seized some prominent places, castles and towns in the duchy of Pomerania and levied tolls that lie within our jurisdiction and are resolved on further acts hostile to the Empire.

Ferdinand then understated his past behaviour somewhat when he noted:

> We know that we and the Empire have never harmed you in the slightest throughout our difficult reign, nor caused any misunderstanding that might give grounds for such open hostilities. We are completely baffled why you have effectively begun open war over some difficulties regarding the town of Stralsund that lies on our and the Empire's soil and concern its laws and justice...especially as we feel that such hostilities and unnecessary bloodshed can easily be avoided through the mediation suggested and now obligingly undertaken by the King of Denmark. Unlike you, we have indicated our desire for this and have instructed and dispatched our envoys to the talks.

Ferdinand cannot have been ignorant to the negative impression which policies like the Baltic design, the Edict of Restitution and the intervention in the Polish War must have made on the Swedish King. To say that he was 'baffled' was thus something of a stretch, but Ferdinand did attempt to explain away the past actions in the Baltic:

> We assure you that our military preparations on the Baltic and elsewhere were never, nor are, intended to give you offence. On the contrary, we wish to remain good neighbours with the Kingdom of Sweden and like to continue so provided you do not give further cause otherwise and stop this unnecessary war.

Predictably enough, if Gustavus neglected to evacuate his men from Pomerania, which he had occupied from late July, then Ferdinand declared he would 'be forced to take extreme measures together with the loyal electors and estates of the Empire', before adding 'though we hope it will not come to this.' Ferdinand did make one commendable point though; his claim that he would have 'at least expected according to international law that you would have sent some prior denunciation citing an ostensible pretext or legal cause according to your view prior to this hostile invasion' indicated that, in contravention to the accepted norms of international law, Gustavus Adolphus had not declared war.[8] These principles of international law had only been established relatively recently with the writings of Thomas Aquinas and Hugo Grotius in the preceding years. For the sake of legitimacy however, it was vital that the Swedish King adhere to these accepted norms, and it would have been the antithesis of his character to simply ignore the genuine Habsburg threat which had brought Wallenstein to the edge of the Baltic. Of course, in the Emperor's mind, the Swedish King waged an undeclared war of disputed justice, without having searched for a peaceful way out of his difficulties first.[9]

Gustavus did not desire to wage war merely to seek redress for his grievances, he also aimed to strike at the Habsburgs to prevent them from surging forward to the Baltic again. We have seen before that Gustavus landed in Germany just at the moment when Wallenstein's command was nearing its end, and his army was about to be reduced. The Habsburg scheme for monopolising the Baltic with Polish cooperation had manifestly failed, and the hostility which the Edict of Restitution engendered among the Northern Protestants suggested that Ferdinand would have an uphill battle ahead of him if he wished to constitutionally guarantee his son's succession. Gustavus could not have known in spring 1630, when preparations for his invasion of Germany intensified, that Wallenstein's command was not long for this world, but he certainly benefited from the latter's dismissal. It could be argued therefore that the period of most potent danger for the King of Sweden had passed, especially since he was able to defend himself without fear of a Polish betrayal.

Thus, Gustavus would wage war not due to the immediate danger which the Habsburgs posed, but to prevent them from posing such danger ever again; he would attack the nucleus of Habsburg strength and by doing so, emasculate Ferdinand and force him to roll back the ominous expansion of his authority.[10] Gustavus would have known that his quest for pre-emptive war was supported by the great thinkers of the age. As a reader of Hugo Grotius, the Swedish King was certainly aware of the arguments of Amrecio Gentili, author of *On the Laws of War and Peace* (1589) and Sir Francis Bacon, famed English philosopher and scientist. For his part, Gentili had remarked on the inherent justness of pre-emptive war, saying:

> We ought not to wait for violence to be offered us, if it is safer to meet it halfway...No one ought to expose himself to danger...A defence is just which anticipates dangers that are already meditated and prepared, and also those which are not mediated, but are probable and possible.

Bacon had also weighed in on the debate, stating: 'I shall make it plain; that war preventative upon just fears, are true defensives, as well as upon actual invasions', and while Bacon added that fear is not justified 'out of umbrages, light jealousies, apprehensions', but only 'out of clear foresight of imminent danger', Bacon insisted at the same time that the 'overgrowing greatness' of another state was sufficient ground for offensive war. Hugo Grotius took issue with this presentation of a pre-emptive war as inherently just, but admitted that waiting for one's enemy to strike the first blow was unrealistic and akin to suicide when their intentions had been apparent from the beginning.[11] These elastic conclusions enabled to Gustavus to justify intervention to his court, and even to reason that Sweden had been in a state of public war with the Emperor since 1628, but to justify his actions to Germany with this logic was considered too risky. 'And so, he went forth to carry war into the Empire', wrote the historian A.W. Ward, adding prophetically –

> ...not indeed unaware of the possibility that success might carry him beyond the achievement of his immediate end, or insensible, as his great counsellor Oxenstierna afterwards phrased it, of the fundamental importance of *momenta temporum* [seasons]; but nevertheless intent upon a well-defined purpose from which no obstacle would cause him to swerve.[12]

The decision was not made lightly, and to Gustavus the venture was wholly necessary. Whether it was ambition, revenge, security or religion that drove him forward, the Swedish King was careful to present his intervention in terms that his potential allies would understand. He would proclaim that he had been forced to intervene due to the cruelties inflicted upon the German princes; he was the fearless ruler come to liberate them from the yolk of tyranny and oppression. Gustavus' efforts to legitimise his intervention in Germany were thus multi-layered. It involved first, the publication of a manifesto outlining all the wrongs which the King had suffered at the hands of the Habsburgs. Second, the preparation of the legalistic ground so that both his subjects and potential allies could be assured that his actions conformed with established international law. And third, he had to present a moral narrative within which he was the hero; the salvation of the German people and the defender of the Imperial constitution.[13] Now that we have examined the rhetorical devices which he used, let us now see how these exercises gelled with the political aims of the Swedish King, and what he actually hoped to gain by landing in Germany.

While Gustavus had fought long, challenging wars before, the war against the forces of the Emperor represented a first for him. The enemy he knew was led by Polish hetmans and nobles, awash with cavalry and often punctuated by petty rivalries and jealousies which made the Commonwealth's military efforts less cohesive. By contrast, although Ferdinand's authority took a beating at Regensburg, there was no question of who was in charge. There was also no intention among the Protestant princes of the North to throw off the Emperor's yolk and thereby violate the Imperial constitution, as Gustavus so badly wanted and needed them to do. Without the military and political support of Saxony and Brandenburg, Gustavus' policy could not be vindicated, and he would always be seen as the outsider.

Even with twenty-nine thousand troops by November 1630, a number which included the Swedish garrison of Stralsund, Gustavus faced a considerable military challenge from the Emperor. The spread of Imperial troops in Italy and Germany brought the number to eighty thousand. This was smaller than the numbers under Wallenstein, but it was still nearly three times the size of Gustavus' force. If the Imperials under Count Tilly could combine their forces, and march confidently towards Pomerania without much haste, then a repeat of the Battle of Lutter would surely be on the cards. How did Gustavus plan to rectify this situation? Above all, he desperately required allies from Germany and France. As for the military strategic plan, the Swedish King seemed more than content to hunker down in Northern Germany for the remainder of the year. To march out of his pocket would surely have been suicide, and in fact, it is entirely possible that Gustavus may have become lost – he only possessed detailed maps up to the Saxon borders; Southern Germany was largely a mystery to him.[14]

The Swedish military prowess was considerable, and the King's genius and knack for innovation should not be understated, but this only went so far. Certainly, Gustavus encouraged legends about his men and especially the Finnish cavalry who always rode beside him. That his men did not feel the cold, that they could not break during battle, that the Laplanders rode reindeer into combat – these were all myths which Gustavus was eager to perpetuate, but he invested in some more honest means of improving his army's fortunes as well. While the tactics of mass volley and fire by rank were not his inventions, he was sharp enough to recognise their use. The Swedish army was an example of combined arms, with the infantry, cavalry and artillery working in tandem according to a pre-arranged and consistently practised drill. Gustavus knew that his men had great potential and could net him spectacular victories, but he also knew that this well-oiled machine was not invincible – the most recent encounter of his army had been the defeat at the Battle of Honigfelde against a combined Polish-Imperial force.[15]

It was apparent from the steps which Gustavus had taken that his allies and his objectives would change with the circumstances. 1631 was clearly to be a year of great importance for his campaign. Perhaps, the war would provide him with the opportunities he required to seize victory, or he perhaps he would be forced to withdraw from Germany without having achieved anything,; and then there was the nightmare scenario that he could suffer the same ignominious fate as his Danish peer. With much of Pomerania carved out for his soldiers and the campaigning season effectively at an end by the time the Regensburg meeting wound up, Gustavus' aims for the new year were clear, and are outlined by the historian Michael Roberts:

> The political and religious safety of Sweden required that the Imperialists and Leaguers be pushed as far back into Germany as possible, and somehow or other be prevented from returning; that at least in the two Saxon circles the territorial arrangements revert to those of 1618; that no great power, and especially no great power of a hostile religion, be suffered to control the invasion-ports of Pomerania and Mecklenburg.[16]

To achieve these aims though, Gustavus would have to turn his attentions towards two major aims in 1631. First, he would have to break out of Pomerania and find some way to leverage his position in Germany, so as to recruit Protestants or anti-Habsburg figures to his side. Second, he would have to fight a conclusive battle against the Habsburgs' favourite generalissimo, Count Tilly, if he was ever going to demonstrate his utility to those that were on the fence. These political aims made good strategic sense and were in many respects quite limited. Little could either Gustavus Adolphus or the Holy Roman Emperor have imagined what 1631 would bring.

TWO

Roars of the Lion

From the moment Gustavus Adolphus landed at Usedom in Pomerania, in early July 1630, a clock began ticking which the Swedish King was unable to ignore. This clock whispered ruin and disaster, of shame and humiliation, if he did not manage to wrest alliances and promises of support from the German princes, above all the Protestant actors. It was a clock which threatened to replicate the experience of the Danish King, who had been left high and dry by his supposed allies in 1626, whereupon one by one, promises were broken and contributions unsent. If Gustavus wished to avoid the same fate as his unfortunate Danish neighbour, then he would have to gain a solid support base in Germany and significant foreign aid from an early stage. Without a German base and foreign support, Gustavus would be in no position to launch the invasion of the Empire that he had envisioned, and which he believed was necessary to secure his Kingdom's security.[17]

And yet, while he had landed with sufficient resources to conduct a limited campaign the previous year, Gustavus would be forced to return home if his efforts to canvass for allies proved a failure. As a ruler of a kingdom boasting scarcely more than 1.5 million subjects, scant financial resources and a harsh, underdeveloped landscape, it was to be expected that Gustavus could not go it alone, nor did he expect to. His vision had been one of co-opting both alienated Germans, and external allies, to create a coalition which would deliver the hammer blow to the Emperor that had yet to truly land.

To be fair to Gustavus, since landing in July 1630 he had managed to win some friends – the dispossessed Dukes of Mecklenburg and the Duke of Pomerania, in addition to radical anti-Habsburg crusaders like the Landgrave William of Hesse-Cassel, the latter of whom offered Gustavus three thousand soldiers.[18] These gestures provided reasons to be positive for sure, but the small cast of supporters looked eerily similar to that boasted by King Christian of Denmark, or even Frederick V of the Palatinate before him.[19] Though he had fortified Stettin, wrested an alliance from the aged Duke of Pomerania and cleared a portion of Imperial soldiers from the area, Gustavus was still outnumbered in Germany and accumulating horrendous debts which he could never dream of paying.

Since July 1630, Gustavus had already spent some 2.3 million livres in the few months of campaigning he had managed, yet this only paid for half of the army's expenses. To put this in perspective, the Swedish Crown possessed financial reserves of less than half that amount – not even the recent acquisition of the Prussian ports in the war with Poland, which brought 500,000 livres a year, could put a dent in such a bill. The lesson was thus clear – to break out of his debt, and of his Pomeranian prison, Gustavus earnestly needed to wrest a great victory from the jaws of Habsburg supremacy. The small fry of the Empire simply would not cut it – what the King of Sweden needed was *the* anti-Habsburg power, France, on his side, but this was easier said than done.

It was to Gustavus' great fortune that Cardinal Richelieu finished his quarrel with the Huguenots just in time to turn his attention back towards the Habsburg menace. King Louis XIII of France (r. 1610-1643) had not enjoyed a reign of peace and tranquillity at home – this was surely to be expected given that his father Henry IV had only placed the healing plaster over the religiously divided kingdom by himself converting to Catholicism.[20] With the defeat of the Huguenot stronghold of La Rochelle by 1628 though, and the increased involvement of French forces in a proxy-war with the Habsburgs in North Italy, it was plain that the interests of the anti-Habsburg powers were aligning. For many years, we will recall, France had supported the Dutch in their campaigns against the Spanish. Now, there arrived an opportunity for France to focus its energies against the other significant branch of the Habsburg family, without itself having to directly contend with the forces of the Emperor just yet.

As the Swedish King had lobbied for allies throughout 1630, Richelieu had been at the centre of an upheaval in the French Royal Family's balance of power. In fact, it is worth pausing for a moment to consider the strategic position of France by 1630. On the one hand, France had lost the initiative in North Italy following the capture of Mantua by the pro-Habsburg Duke of Savoy, yet on the other, French diplomacy had scored a succession of triumphs. First, there was the coup of the six-year Swedish-Polish peace, negotiated under the Truce of Altmark in September 1629, which freed up Gustavus to act in the Empire. This freedom was further reinsured by Gustavus' own efforts to secure Muscovy's support against Poland, in addition to an agreement with the Tsar that netted Sweden a lucrative deal worth more than a million livres to sell Russian grain to Amsterdam, but the French role in brokering the peace is still plain to see.[21]

Second, the fortunes of war continued to turn against the Spanish in the Netherlands, following the seizure of the American treasure fleet by Dutch privateers led by Piet Heyn in September 1628. The silver haul from these

For God or the Devil

vessels was worth in excess of £800,000 to the Dutch, but of more importance was the fact that it prevented any money at all from reaching Spain's soldiers in Flanders from late 1628 to mid-1629. The situation was so dire that Ambrogio Spinola, famed Flemish commander and hero of Spanish Habsburg arms, was recalled to Madrid to account for the newly emboldened Dutch rebels, who effectively reconquered Spinola's gains from twenty years before.

Spinola had urged that Spain opt for peace at any price, regardless even of what the Dutch wished to do with Catholics in their midst – previously considered the bare minimum of the demands Spain would make – but peace did not come in 1628, and the following year, their army swollen to more than one hundred and twenty thousand men thanks to Piet Hein's silver, the fortress of s'Hertogenbosch was captured. The seizure of this fortress in September 1629 seriously hampered Spain's ability to project its propaganda into the Dutch Netherlands, as s'Hertogenbosch had been its propaganda headquarters for much of the war up to this point.[22] Spinola, no doubt crushed with disappointment, and dejected following the silence with which his urgings were greeted in Madrid, died before the end of 1630, while besieging the fortress of Casale in North Italy.[23]

A third factor in favour of France's position was the aforementioned submission of La Rochelle, which removed a dangerous fifth column – in Richelieu's mind at least – from attacking the centre of royal power. With the surrender of La Rochelle was followed peace with England shortly thereafter through the Treaty of Susa (24 April 1629), and the conclusion of a war which had been ill-advised and terribly wasteful for King Charles in particular. England also made peace with Spain in November, and with that Treaty, it seemed as though Charles had given up on winning back the Palatinate for his dispossessed brother in law Frederick V, which meant that he had also given up fighting for his sister Elizabeth. Until the Prince of Wales was born in 1630, indeed, Elizabeth of Bohemia was the sole heir to the Stuart dynasty, but this period of English intervention netted no true benefits for a reign which was soon to be infamous for other reasons.

In 1629 though, the failure of Charles' favourite to achieve success outside the ramparts of the Huguenot fortress contributed to the general unpopularity of his whole regime. The Duke of Buckingham, the author of the scheme, was assassinated shortly afterwards, and England retreated across the Channel, effectively absolving itself from any further intervention in the affairs of the Thirty Years War.[24] Richelieu would certainly have preferred to have retained England as an ally, but if given the choice, he was content to watch English prestige sink beneath the waves. The Grace of Alais which solidified the peace with the Huguenots was unmistakably the work of two men, Cardinal Richelieu and his sovereign. Indeed, King Louis even publicly acknowledged as much, noting humbly that 'One must render the Cardinal the honour he deserves; all of the happy successes within and outside the realm have come by his counsels and his courageous judgments.' Not to be outdone, Richelieu then wrote with equal force: 'All [Your Majesty's] subjects vie in their desire to render the obedience that is due him, not only as their king but as the most just, pious, and courageous of all those whom God has given to France up to the present.'[25]

Fourth, the war in North Italy over the Mantuan Succession forced the Habsburgs to prioritise their strained resources, to the benefit of France. Emperor Ferdinand elected to save the Spanish interest in Mantua, rather than in the Spanish Netherlands as had been planned, and twenty thousand of Wallenstein's soldiers were redirected to North Italy, where they would remain until staggering home many months later. While Mantua would be seized, and the war technically a success for the pro-Habsburg Duke of Savoy, even this success brought its own asterisk, as Habsburg forces were far from Gustavus' landing point just at the point when the Imperial commander, Count Tilly, desperately needed them. Furthermore, the disadvantageous treaty which the French negotiators were forced to sign in July 1630 – following the news that the Habsburgs had captured Mantua – was not recognised by King Louis, who took advantage of the distractions within the Empire caused by Gustavus' landing to repudiate it before the end of 1630.[26]

Fifth, and finally, the Diet at Regensburg, which was hosted over the summer and into the autumn of 1630, France had become intertwined with Imperial politics, as Richelieu sent some of his best agents to scope out the situation in Germany, and leverage the French interest. This French interest, sponsored by Richelieu from the beginning, was to present France as the defender of German 'liberties', as the dependable foreign face of a 'third way' in the Empire, between foreign invaders which rankled princely sensibilities, and the Emperor's unbending demands which many resented. As a Catholic power, furthermore, Richelieu felt that France was in a strong position to pose as the champion of German liberties to Catholic German potentates, such as the Duke of Bavaria, as well. During the Regensburg meeting, in fact, one such French agent was reported to have told the Archbishop of Trier – one of the seven electors of the Empire – of King Louis XIII's express wish 'to deliver Italy and Germany from the oppression to which they have been reduced by the manifest violence and ambition of the House of Austria.'[27]

French dignitaries would have been by no means out of place at Regensburg, as representatives from England, Tuscany, Venice and Spain were also in attendance, and even those Protestant Electors in Saxony and Brandenburg who resented the recent passage of the Edict of Restitution sent delegates, who joined the two thousand other dignitaries in attendance. The major outcome of the Regensburg meeting, as we know, was not to confirm Ferdinand III as the Emperor's successor, as Ferdinand II had hoped. Nor could Emperor Ferdinand wrest a commitment from the dignitaries to wage war against the Dutch in support of Spain. All that seemed on their minds was the removal of Wallenstein's hulking host of one hundred and twenty-nine thousand foot and more than twenty thousand horse from Germany.[28] It should go without saying that the dismantling of this force was to the benefit of French security as well as Dutch and Swedish security; with the dismissal of Wallenstein, in fact, command was handed to Count Tilly, and the Empire as a whole was far more vulnerable to invasion than it had been since 1624.[29]

That four great sieges of La Rochelle (September 1627-October 1628), Stralsund (May-August 1628), s'Hertogenbosch (April-September 1629) and Mantua (November 1629-July 1630) should have been tackled in such close proximity and occasionally within the same campaigning season must stand as one of the great accidents of the Thirty Years War. In the same way though, so too can the convergence of French fortunes with those of Sweden be discerned. On 11 November 1630, from his sickbed, King Louis XIII of France made a decision which was to define his reign, his nation and the Thirty Years War. Rather than appease that pro-Habsburg Catholic camp in the country, led by his mother and the so-called *dévots*, Louis determined to ignore that camp, to his mother's utter surprise, and perhaps to the surprise of Richelieu as well.

Encouraging his mother and her favourites to believe their cause was won, this only helped Louis to remove his enemies more easily once they showed themselves. This 'Day of the Dupes', as it has become known, effectively placed the control of French foreign policy within Cardinal Richelieu's hands. King Louis' family had long been a difficulty to King and Cardinal alike; in July 1630, following a succession of bitter betrayals and disappointments, Louis wrote to his brother and heir Gaston to the effect that:

> I object to the little respect you show the queen our mother. I object to the little care you give to keeping the word you have so often and so solemnly given...I object to the disorderliness and debaucheries of your life. [30]

The Bourbon royal family certainly had its troubles then, but after November 1630 these dramas were no longer allowed to disrupt the proper business of running the state. At long last, after having struggled through issues domestic and political since 1624, the Cardinal was in control. By 1630, indeed, Richelieu had secured his position in French politics by creating several 'creatures' of his own – men who owed their position to the Cardinal and who effectively served as his eyes and ears until his death in 1642.[31] The brilliance of Louis' surprise move was matched only by Richelieu's consistent diplomatic finesse, which remained a source of awe for historians and contemporaries alike. 'Richelieu', wrote John L Stevens in 1884...

...knew how to comprehend, and possessed the skill, the persistent and balanced will, to enforce, so much of the plan and policy of Henry as would tend to the unity of France, and render her powerful in the councils of Europe, and an unrelenting enemy of the house of Austria.

Certainly, Richelieu was unrelenting in his opposition towards the Habsburgs – the arrangements with Spain's arch enemy in the Netherlands, and the Emperor's arch enemy in Sweden propelled Richelieu to the forefront of European politics. From the moment he had defeated his enemies and secured his position at home, indeed, Richelieu determined to pursue a course of firm friendship and, soon, military alliance with the Habsburgs' greatest foes, a policy which would extend beyond the Peace of Westphalia. As Stevens continues:

One of the most gifted and capacious minds of the century for statesmanship and diplomacy, time was to show how the cardinal minister and Gustavus Adolphus were to accord in dealing with the issues and deadly struggles on the Rhine, and with the elements of intrigue, ambition, and combat centred around Vienna, with powerful ramifications from one end of Europe to the other.[32]

The first significant step towards the cementing of this policy was the conclusion of the Treaty of Barwalde on 23 January 1631. Per this arrangement, France committed to pay Sweden 300,000 livres right away, and one million livres a year for five years; in return Gustavus swore to leave the Catholic League's forces alone, unless they attacked Gustavus first. This awkward stipulation [Article IX] would not last the year, but it reflected the intention of Richelieu to forge ahead with an agreement with Maximillian of Bavaria, an agreement which would be pursued further with the Treaty of Fontainebleau in May. The professed aim of the Treaty was to finance a war 'for the safeguarding of the Baltic and Oceanic Seas, the liberty of commerce, and the relief of the oppressed states of the Holy Roman Empire.' 'To that end' the Treaty declared, 'the King of Sweden will take up his share of the great burden of the war by bringing an army of thirty thousand infantry and six thousand cavalry at his own expense to Germany and maintaining it there.'[33]

News of the Treaty caused a sensation, but the rationale for it was plain – it was nothing less than the continuation of the cold war with the Habsburgs. Throughout the text, references to a 'common enemy' and the 'great war' were made, indicating that France would one day dispose of the illusion of peace, and make total war on its Habsburg foe. The previous January, after all, when leading another expedition through snowy passes against the rebellious Duke of Savoy, King Louis had proclaimed that 'Since the Spaniards want war, we will ram it down their throats!', but this ramming would have to wait until France was fully prepared. Until Richelieu felt confident to make the cold war with the Habsburgs hot, he was content to strike against her in theatres like Mantua, and through allies like the Dutch and Swedes.[34] This is verified by David Parrott, who wrote:

> Encouraged by these developments, Richelieu's carefully balanced policy was to try to ensure that France's allies could play a major role in the struggle against the Habsburgs, while not being so successful that they might be in a position to break away altogether in order to make a separate peace treaty. To help the allies maintain military pressure on the Habsburgs, France was prepared to pay increasingly heavier subsidies, to lend diplomatic support in disputes with third parties and in the last resort to provide covert military support. Every inducement was provided to keep France's allies in the war, except an open and full-scale military intervention on their behalf.[35]

For the next few years, between 1631-34, Richelieu ensured that France verged very close to outright military confrontation without declaring war on Spain. Richelieu correctly believed that Spain could not afford to open another front, when the war with the Dutch was already ruinous enough. Indeed, within Madrid it was well known and accepted that France was 'the source of all our troubles', yet it was recognised at the same time that, for the moment, the Habsburgs could not afford to usher in a new era of the conflict with what would likely be an all-consuming showdown with France. For the moment at least, it suited all parties involved to keep the conflict covert.[36]

The Treaty of Barwalde therefore represented a determined step towards realising this policy of resistance to the Habsburgs, but its significance should not be underestimated for the Swedish King either – without it, Gustavus' resources, followed by his followers, would have melted away. Another, less obvious intention of the Treaty was to demonstrate a Franco-Swedish desire to restore German 'liberties', and to pose as the joint saviours not merely of the Protestant, but also the Catholic potentates. Gustavus spent some time demonstrating his affinity and respect for the Imperial Free Cities, those city states with long histories of privileges and traditions which the Swedish King proclaimed his determination to uphold. At Stralsund, for instance, Gustavus had relinquished so many rights and privileges to that port city, thereby making it virtually independent, though still clearly within the sphere of Sweden's Empire, and firmly in alliance with the Swedish King.[37]

In February 1631, several Protestant princes in the Empire, including the Electors of Brandenburg and Saxony, met at Leipzig. Throughout the month, the most important of Germany's Protestant potentates discussed the two major issues – the Edict of Restitution and the Swedish landing. Unsurprisingly, they intended to use one against the other. With the pressure caused by the Swedish arrival and the announced support of France, it was possible that with a bit of pressure, the Emperor might be convinced to relax the hated Edict and reverse its tenets. The communique from the meeting, released on 24 March 1631, reads more like a list of requests than a coherent conclusion, but it makes plain the pressure which the Protestant powers felt so suffocated by:

> We attest before God and the world, that we are entirely innocent of all the evil, if this gruesome oppression is not remedied quickly, and we seek and wish with peace-loving hearts and souls nothing more than to isolate and resolve all defects through amicable compromise, establish true trust as [firm peace and mutual concordats], observe that the [basic] and Imperial laws do not oppress German freedom, leave the Electors and Estates with their authority, honours, dignity, privileges, immunities an laws and justice, [and do not] coerce or oppress anyone who lives according to law and justice, end the gruesome disorder, oppression and violence, restore a general, lasting, secure peace and finally put a stop to the lament, misery, desolation and destruction and the terrible bloodshed.

Was it possible to end this 'terrible bloodshed' or 'gruesome disorder'? Indeed, we may interpret the communique as a double-edged sword for Gustavus, since while they protested against the Emperor's policies, the Protestant princes which the Swedish King so badly needed by his side showed no signs of crossing the Rubicon at this stage. Still, the message which they sent to the Emperor deserves to be highlighted, as it represents something of a final warning to Ferdinand II before the Electors of Saxony and Brandenburg did in fact attach their banners to those of Gustavus, however reluctantly they did so. The communique continued:

> Their elector graces [of Saxony and Brandenburg] have themselves decided from their peaceful hearts that if the amicable compromise is not made the authority and dignity of the Holy Roman Empire will be endangered still further and, God, mercifully forbid, will be driven into the ground to the eternal shame and rebuke of the Electors and Estates. The foreign potentates will also interfere in the affair and bring misery, ruin and destruction to each Estate regardless of religion.[38]

Was there any weight to this threat from the Protestant potentates? In all likelihood, not really; the real force of their threat came from the presence of Gustavus rather than from their own resources. Indeed, the Protestants did not even think to mobilise, and nor could they afford to – the Elector of Brandenburg had run up debts nearly £4 million by 1618 alone, while the Elector of Saxony's debts extended to more than 5 million Rhine florins, and foreign debts consisting of over £1 million before the end of the 1620s.[39] Evidently their greatest asset was the Swedish King, and yet they remained neutral in the conflict, unwilling to declare against their Emperor, and unsure of Gustavus' prospects. By early April however, the two Electors did in fact reach agreement on the creation of a defensive alliance, complete with an independent force of forty thousand men, directed at nobody in particular, yet the Saxon and Brandenburg Electors were not to be its financiers – that would be the task of the minor German princes who constituted the Imperial Circles and whose finances were in much better shape. This commitment to protect their territory was known as the Leipzig Manifesto, and added a third party to the morass of German politics which Gustavus would have to navigate. 'So' Geoffrey Parker writes:

> ...supported by none of the major Protestant states, Gustavus marched impatiently up and down the Baltic coast, conquering Mecklenburg and Pomerania so that Swedish control was now complete from Denmark right round to Finland: the Baltic was now a Swedish lake. Gustavus now had achieved the first of the objectives of his invasion. Now he had to secure a settlement that would guarantee Sweden's gains for the future, and for this he required the active support of the two Protestant Electors.[40]

A victory of some kind was needed; a great symbolic triumph would show the two noncommittal Electors that Gustavus was not the Danish King, and if opportunism did not appeal, then the threat of force could always be used. In the spring of 1631 then, furnished with the monies from the recent Treaty with France, Gustavus made for the River Oder where he encountered the large town of Frankfurt. This town was smaller and less symbolically important than its namesake further to the West and straddling the River Main, but it remained an important hub of commerce and a strategic bastion along the River Oder nonetheless. On 13 April, Gustavus engaged in a brief siege and brutal sacking of the town. Alas, Frankfurt on the Main was within the upper tier of German cities, and had never been captured by a foreign invader. A campaign to capture that city was far outside Gustavus' capabilities in early 1631, yet it was nonetheless a glittering prize to aim for, and for several reasons. Since the collapse of the Regensburg Diet, indeed, Frankfurt on the Main had been suggested as a place where Catholics and Protestants might meet and discuss a common policy. This was a further incentive to capture the greater Frankfurt, but not yet.

The garrison at Frankfurt on the Oder was badly paid and demoralised – a reflection, as it transpired, of the wider problem in Germany which Count Tilly's men faced, and which would move Tilly the following month to barge into Magdeburg. Gustavus' forces, buoyed by Scottish mercenaries who would soon become almost as famous as the Swedish King himself, killed 1,700 of 6,400 Imperial garrison in revenge for earlier setbacks in some Pomeranian skirmishes. Such reprisals reiterated Gustavus' message, that he was playing for keeps in Germany, and would allow nothing to stand in his way. Yet, Gustavus' successful quest to capture this still considerable German bastion sent a clear message all by itself, and it demonstrated that Gustavus was capable of breaking out of his Pomeranian base. For the moment though, the River Oder marked the extent of Gustavus' adventures in Germany – after all, he lacked sufficient maps which detailed further reaches of the German country.[41]

The months of campaigning in Pomerania had given the Imperials a bloody nose, but the Swedish King was yet unaware of the importance of Wallenstein's dismissal, and nor did he fully grasp the reason why the once overwhelming Habsburg army did not meet him in a pitched battle. Gustavus was fortunate in his timing, but he was even more fortunate in his allies. Unlike his Danish peer's experience, these allies were to prove dependable and reliable; more than that, they were critical planks of the Swedish King's success.

It took some time before Gustavus learned that Count Tilly had been selected to replace Wallenstein, that the former was gathering up as many of the latter's soldiers as he could afford, and that Tilly had made way towards Saxony, where the undefeated seventy-three year old veteran commander hoped to gain some respite and resources for his depleted soldiery.[42] Rather than inherit the mantle of Wallenstein though, Count Tilly was fated to provide the Swedish King with a far uglier, but also more valuable victory, than that recently won through the Treaty of Barwalde. This victory would be wrested not on the battlefield or in the diplomatic hall, but in the medium of propaganda, from the ashes of Magdeburg.

THREE
Magdeburg

Before I recognise the Papist League
And call it master
I'd rather run into the blaze
Refuse to dance with Charles the Fifth,
I'll stand no more from Tilly too,
And chase the bloodhound through my fire.
Ancient German bravery
Arm yourself for valiant strife,
Earn the crown of constancy.
Innocent chaste maiden I,
Tormented by the bloodhound dire,
Many a mother's child roasted on the fire.
For suffered martyrdom Cologne on the Rhine,
Lauds eleven thousand virgins
I mourn thirty thousand souls!
It must pain any feeling heart,
That babes still suckling at the breast,
By cruel foe into the flames are cast.
[...]
The one dear Swedish hero true
Gave me tons of gold coin too
I praise his name to all the world.
But those who him no passage gave
And severed him from all succour
Must now look to their property.
Bremen, Brunswick through the foe's cunning
Towards Nuremberg too the Bavarian blasts,
Hamburg and Saxony are the last.
The Bavarian speaks pretty words,
But with his troops he strides ahead,
Putting all Lutheran folk to the sword.
Awake, thou German honesty,
And take up arms in my strife,
Thou shalt be praised eternally![43]

This was how a poet, likely a former resident of Magdeburg, described the scene both at Magdeburg, and in the Empire as a whole, by late 1631. Numerous references are peppered throughout the poem; the 'Papist' or Catholic League constituted a major military arm of the Emperor with the dismissal of Wallenstein; 'Tilly' was a clear reference to Count Tilly, the Imperial generalissimo; the 'Swedish hero true' referred to Dietrich von Falkenberg, the Hessian soldier turned Swedish military representative which Gustavus Adolphus had sent to Magdeburg in the spring, once he realised he would not be able to reach the city in time; 'the Bavarian' referred to Maximillian, the former Duke, now Elector, of Bavaria and the Palatinate, who was unquestionably the Emperor's most important German ally.

Few contemporary works capture as eloquently the sheer trauma and pain of the incident, or the rank divisions which pervaded the Empire. This was a call to resist, and for all Protestants to refrain from trusting Bavarians, Tilly, or any other Catholic leader. Those 'eleven thousand virgins' and 'thirty thousand souls' which had been slain underlined the fact that Magdeburg had been a grand and populous city, but there was another side to Magdeburg other than its wealth and importance. It was a centre of Protestant learning and worship, with a rich history of religious independence and opposition to Imperial rule in Germany. In fact, as one author wrote:

> Magdeburg tried to rise in a revolutionary spirit, and so became almost the centre of the entire revolutionary opposition in Germany, and its monstrous destruction proved to be an event of all-German significance, claiming the attention of all the publicists and newspapers, and all contemporaries, near and far. [44]

But what was Magdeburg? It is a city we encountered in the opening section of this book, where the burgher's son Friedrich Friese recalled how hell itself poured into the city, and Magdeburg was sacked and set alight. Friese and his family escaped only thanks to the timely arrival of sympathetic German soldiers, who offered them protection, but others were not so lucky. In many respects, Magdeburg epitomises the central question of this book – would the citizens choose God or the Devil, and what would be the penalty for making the wrong choice? For Magdeburg, the punishment consisted of destruction from which the city never truly recovered. While details of its trade with its neighbours are scarce, we do know that Magdeburg brewed beer and exported it to its neighbours; that it was an important trading centre up the River Elbe; that a substantial portion of East German trade moved through the city's walls. This trade made Magdeburg a wealthy city, but also a divided one.

The war had exacerbated the class tensions within the city, as the wealthy patricians clashed with the merchant burghers, who themselves clashed with the poorer plebeian classes. The latter group, consisting of fishermen, dockers, boatmen and other so-called 'ship folk' who relied on the River Elbe for their livelihood, found that the privations of war had wrecked the river trade. Thus wrecked, 'it's all the same if we die of hunger' became one of many radical rallying cries of this beleaguered lower class, and preachers or unemployed malcontents began to whip them into a frenzy. External events only contributed to the tension; in late 1629, following a failed effort by Wallenstein to besiege Magdeburg, representatives from the Hanseatic League cities of Lubeck, Hamburg, Bremen, Brunswick and Hildesheim supported the burgher classes to overthrow the more moderate patricians, and dominate the city with a new town council.

The inhabitants of Magdeburg were further moved to conflict by the need to remove all Imperialists from the surrounding regions of the city; bands of peasants and unemployed fishermen thus rampaged throughout the countryside, ridding the surrounding small towns, villages or monasteries of the Emperor's men, but the task was mostly incomplete as only a properly supplied army could accomplish the challenging task. Thus, the three classes withdrew behind Magdeburg's walls, and into their own petty squabbles; the patrician nobility escaped if they could, or joined the city's defence, the burghers monopolised their control over the city and the lower classes became more radical. In August 1630, Gustavus sent 'one of his most outstanding military aides', Dietrich von Falkenberg, to advise the city. In Gustavus' mind, Magdeburg was 'the advanced post and base of the whole expedition', and he instructed Falkenberg...

> ...to encourage the administrator of the city...to form some regiments....to secure the city [for Sweden] and in this way prepare a diversion by means of which we can take control of the Elbe...[this diversion] will inspire the disaffected elements and support them in denying the Imperialists all forms of payment...in short it will light a torch from which the flames of universal revolt will spread all across Germany. [45]

By that time, Imperial troops had appeared outside the city limits, and Count Tilly began to make his presence felt, placing the city under a full siege only in March 1631. Thanks to the role Magdeburg played in the religious wars of the 1550s, including its resistance to the entreaties of the Emperor and Maurice of Saxony, the city came to be viewed by its inhabitants as Magdeburg was considered 'our Lord God's chancellery' – a rebellious centre of Lutheran Protestantism in the north of the Holy Roman Empire, which had 'stood up well to the emperor'. While Magdeburg had fallen to the Emperor Charles V in 1551, this had occurred only after a long siege, and only once the rest of Protestant Germany had been moved to resist. Magdeburg, to many, was the spiritual and traditional centre of Protestantism in Germany, and it was therefore essential for Gustavus that he claimed the friendship of this symbolic relic at a time when he was attempted to pose as Protestant Germany's champion.

As early as August 1630, the citizens of Magdeburg were being prepared, if not for martyrdom, then certainly for resistance and great sacrifice. The city's fate – according to some of radical burghers and peasants, led by the Lutheran clergy – was inextricably interwoven with God's plan of salvation and the life to come. It was also predicted that Magdeburg would be a captured and destroyed by a Catholic 'anti-Christ' as divine punishment! Encouraged to see parallels between their experiences and those of Jerusalem by their clergy, the rhetoric and atmosphere in the city became more apocalyptic and intense. 'May God mercifully prevent this from being an evil omen and Magdeburg from going the way of Jerusalem', said Dr Reinhard Bake in his Sunday sermon at Magdeburg Cathedral on 1 August 1630. He preached on the text prescribed for that Sunday, Luke 19: 42-4, in which Christ predicts the downfall of the city of Jerusalem with the following words:

> For the days shall come upon you, when your enemies will cast up a bank about you and surround you, and hem you in on every side, and dash you to the ground, you and your children within you, and they will not leave one stone upon another in you; because you did not know the time of your visitation.[46]

The arrival of Falkenburg in the same month sharpened the rhetoric, but also brought practical benefits. The old Protestant administrator, Christian William, was reinstalled, after being removed from Magdeburg following the passage of the Edict of Restitution. Christian William was determined to work with the Swedes, and was confident that Gustavus would relieve the city before it could be seized. There was a sound strategic reason for installing Christian William in Magdeburg though; access to the city was blocked by the lands of those two stubborn Protestant Electors, John George of Saxony and George William of Brandenburg. Those two Electors had not yet declared themselves for the Swedish invader, though they had committed to raise an army of forty thousand men for their own defence. If Gustavus wanted to reach Magdeburg, he would first need to be granted passage through these determinedly neutral Electors, and it was therefore fortunate that Christian William happened to be the uncle of the Brandenburg Elector.[47]

Surely, for the sake of his kin, George William of Brandenburg would permit Gustavus access through his lands, and the Saxon Elector would follow suit? Alas, Gustavus was to be disappointed, if he had expected any radical alteration in the mood of the two Electors. George William, after all, was his brother-in-law, and if Brandenburg was not to permit him access on that basis, then the Elector's uncle could hardly have been expected to move him. In truth, of course, both the Saxon and Brandenburg Elector quaked at the thought of having to pick a side, and both wished desperately to maintain their neutrality, to avoid the privations of war, and to avoid risking their position. It was dangerous to throw caution to the wind and declare for the foreign invader – the prospects of those that had done so in the past spoke for itself now. No, the only way they would be moved to declare for Gustavus, would be if the Emperor forced their hand through a terrible policy decision, or if Gustavus' position became so insurmountable and immediately threatening to them that they felt they had no choice. As it happened, both such eventualities were to move the two Electors over the following months.

In the meantime, matters did not standstill in Magdeburg while the two Electors stood by, and nor could Gustavus afford to remain idle. To force George William's hand, he captured the Brandenburg fortress of Spandau a few kilometres west of Berlin in early May, and attempted to buy Magdeburg time by intimating to Falkenberg, then entrenched in the city's domestic politics, that the Hessian commander must hold out for another two months.[48] In two months, perhaps, the Swedish King would be able to overcome the opposition of the two Electors, and come to its rescue like a new messiah. Within Magdeburg though, a different kind of prophecy seemed to be playing itself out.

'It would be better not to leave one stone upon another than to submit to the Emperor', went one of the many uncompromising proclamations of the increasingly radicalised leaders of the people, a former brewer who had been ruined by the conditions of the war.[49] And he was not alone. While it would be hyperbole to suggest that a kind of class war had set in within the city, it was certainly the case that the tensions between the major groups had increased. This was only to be expected as the Imperialists closed in, and as news of Gustavus' efforts reached the citizens.[50] Many insisted that Gustavus would relieve Magdeburg, and that to surrender would represent the greatest shame, and a betrayal of the city's history. By mid-May 1631, the city had been under siege for close to two months, and in that space of time opinions had only solidified. Late in the evening of 18 May, recalled by Otto von Guericke, one of the city's councillors, it appeared that the citizens of Magdeburg were on the verge of making some sort of decision:

> ...the council summoned the entire citizenry in their districts and asked whether they should negotiate with General Tilly. The majority in some districts favoured negotiation, some simply left it to the council to decide, while others, especially those who had promoted this business from the outset, refused all talks, expecting help from the King of Sweden at any moment.

On the afternoon of 19 May, Guericke recorded that he climbed a bell tower to gain a better view and noted that the Imperialists were preparing a final assault on the city's battered defences. The immediate threat this posed, the exhausted state of the defenders, and their want of powder, convinced Guericke to appeal to the city council and negotiate thus with Tilly to save Magdeburg from disaster. 'The council', Guericke recorded, 'thought the negotiations with Tilly should begin and a trumpeter was sent [to announce this] to the General.' In the midst of this decision though, who should burst into the room but Gustavus' representative, Dietrich von Falkenburg. Falkenburg, Guericke recalled…

> …interrupted with high-flown assurances of the long-promised relief of the King of Sweden. He urged them again to stick to their promises and to trust him. He declared the danger was not really as acute as they believed. Since relief was only hours away, each hour more they resisted was worth more than a ton of gold. He continued this way for almost an hour…Falkenburg replied that he wanted the Imperialists to attack, since they would be resisted and would suffer badly. Then he continued his speech, until the lookout on the St Johannis [church] spire blew the alarm and unfurled the white war banner.[51]

After debating the issue throughout the night of 19-20 May, it seems that the decision whether to resist or surrender was made for the people of Magdeburg by its besiegers. Unsure of his security, and doubtful, but not willing to rule out the possibility that Gustavus would relieve the city, Tilly was persuaded by one of his subordinates to attack Magdeburg. On the morning of 20 May, as Falkenburg attempted to buoy the morale of the councillors, a ration of wine had been given to the attackers, to boost their morale before the onslaught began. As Guericke's account reveals, the city's defences were extremely worn down following two months of protracted siege, and the mission of the two and a half thousand soldiers and two thousand citizens charged with the defence was virtually hopeless. Yet perhaps the greatest disadvantage of the defenders was that they had been taken by surprise – perhaps the city's councillors had expected a final opportunity for parlay before the attack was launched. This might help to explain Falkenburg's confidence, and declarations that Gustavus was hours away, when in reality, the Swedish King was camped ninety kilometres from the city.

At 8AM, reports that the first soldiers had burst through the city's north gate was learned of, as Croat auxiliaries – the more feared of the Imperialist troops – traversed the shallow Elbe River to break through a poorly defended side gate. Panic spread quickly, almost at the same pace as the fires which started under mysterious circumstances. Much as Napoleon would erroneously be blamed for torching Moscow, so too would Tilly be blamed by Protestant propagandists for mercilessly burning Magdeburg. It was an appealing message for the Protestant diehards, but the reality was more complex, and probably a great deal less exciting. In the chaos of the sacking, which was undeniably terrifying and brutal for the city's inhabitants, fires began in isolated pockets in the city.

By 10AM that morning, after having licked at several burgher houses, a gunpowder store was devoured by the blaze, which soon proved unstoppable. As the fires rampaged across the city, they forced back even the attackers, and Tilly attempted to save the cathedral where some one thousand or so citizens were taking refuge. Another six hundred took refuge in a monastery, and they were all left alone, but they were the lucky ones. An astonishing 1,700 of the city's 1,900 buildings were destroyed, leaving behind a horizon of charred rubble which remained in place well into the eighteenth century. The usual horrors were visited upon Magdeburg's citizens, as children as young as twelve were reported to have been raped; in the mad search for plunder which followed, even a pair of shoes would suffice, but for the soldiers who could find nothing, they often turned to drink or violence. To receive mercy from these soldiers under the circumstances, who had been stationed outside Magdeburg for several months, was a tall order indeed, but a deliberate campaign of rape and violence commanded by Tilly this was not.

We know this, if for no other reason than the destruction of Magdeburg denied Tilly any chance to rest and billet his men, or to wrest contributions from the citizens – the major goal of the campaign to begin with. Indeed, what remained of Magdeburg after the ordeal of 20 May could provide no sustenance for Tilly's men. The burnt husk of a city, which had once housed twenty-five thousand, barely accommodated a fifth of that now. Many would flee in the aftermath, such as Friedrich Friese, who disguised himself as a peasant to avoid being captured for ransom, but as Friese watched his old home crumble into ashes, he would have known that Magdeburg had been effectively killed. A census taken in February 1632 revealed that only four-hundred and forty-nine citizens then lived in Magdeburg, a figure which leaves us to conclude that, whatever the controversy surrounding the event, the sack of Magdeburg must retain the distinction of being the most devastating and total act of the war.[52]

Twelve years into the Thirty Years War, the participants perhaps felt that few acts could shock or move them to action, but Magdeburg was such a shock, and if that city was never the same again, neither was the Empire. Among the slain was Falkenburg, who died early in the battle, and Christian William, the city administrator and uncle of the Elector of Brandenburg. Christian William's body was unceremoniously dumped in the Elbe, alone with several of the more recalcitrant councillors whom the soldiers no doubt blamed for the siege.[53] In the days that followed though, it became difficult to receive accurate reports on what had occurred at Magdeburg, and even when these reports were received, some were reluctant to believe it.

'Prisoners brought here from Magdeburg report that the slaughter continued this morning and the city is completely burnt down, that no building remains but the cathedral', recorded no less a figure than Christian II of Anhalt, the son of that figure who had once stood by the side of Frederick V, the Elector Palatine and 'Winter King'. Christian II had since made his peace with the Emperor, and his palace was situated nearby the slaughter. 'If this mighty and beautiful city has been destroyed in such a short time and reduced to ashes' Christian II continued, 'it is much to be pitied and its downfall to be lamented.' But Christian's pity only went so far – within a few days, he had already begun to capture the difference in view between the two camps of opinion. To Protestants, and to those allies of the Swedish King, Magdeburg was an atrocity without parallel in history, which would have to be avenged, but to the other side, it was a great victory, and the excesses of Tilly's men and the tragic outcome could therefore be excused. After making his peace with the Emperor and regaining his lands, Christian II was eager to make plain, even in his diary, where his loyalties lay. 'I wrote once again in my own hand to Gen. Tilly thanking him warmly for his intercession and congratulating him upon his victory at Magdeburg, desiring a good peace in Germany etc.', Christian wrote, adding:

> It is said that the soldiers of Magdeburg initially fell out with the burghers, but that they were entirely innocent, whereas the citizenry, who were probably twelve times as numerous, made them do too much and would not give them any more bread, even for money. It is quite likely that other injustices, secret sins and [acts of] shame occurred, because the outcome suggests that such a beautiful, powerful city which has flourished since the days of Emperor Otto I could not have met with such an unexpected, rapid [and] terrible end without a particular reason. He sins of the land will mean many changes to the principalities etc...One should not, to be sure, judge [by the outcome] whether a matter be unjust or not, but it is sometimes permitted, especially when one has gained knowledge of something of the [unjust circumstances], which injustice then ravaged the land and people...General Tilly offered them [the people of Magdeburg] mercy on different occasions, but to no avail.[54]

Both sides inevitably worked to blame the other for the event, but at the centre of the disaster were the now homeless citizens of Magdeburg. 'May God have mercy upon us henceforth' recorded one former resident of the city...

> ...for this was a spectacle that has not seen its like in horror and cruelty in many hundred years, for it was beyond all measure. They drove small children into the fire like sheep, sticking them with spears; God knows Turks and barbarians would not have done otherwise.[55]

Just as the Emperor's men worked to portray the event as divine punishment, with weighty comparisons to the destruction of Jerusalem common, so too did the opposite side emphasise that God's judgement had been visited upon the citizens of this 'German Jerusalem'. On the 1 anniversary of the event, a pastor and former resident of Magdeburg delivered a sermon wherein he declared:

> Let us learn: that terrible things tend to happen when a city and fortress is not merely severely besieged by the foe, but also and finally captured by a furious hand; we have seen this in Jerusalem, in Magdeburg and other great cities and fortresses which were taken by force.

Another pastor from Hesse delivered the self-explanatory sermon in August 1631 entitled 'Of the Destruction of Jerusalem...In Pitying Memory of the Destruction of the Ancient, Praise- worthy, Evangelical, Christian City of Magdeburg'. In his sermon the destruction of Magdeburg was regarded as 'more cruel still...than the destruction of Jerusalem' since 'this devastation of a city' was the work not of unbelieving heathens of Babylon but instead those who 'themselves wished to be considered the people of God, as if they were the best friends and protectors of our country'.[56]

The battle lines were evidently being drawn, but there was a surprising lack of movement on the part of the pro-Swedish German broadsheets. 'The reports on these sheets', wrote the historian John Roger Paas, 'are surprisingly straightforward and uncritical of either side, and almost all end with an expressed desire for peace...' One example Paas gives was a mostly neutral broadsheet, which ended with the familiar urging: 'Let Almighty God end all Christian bloodletting, comfort our troubled hearts and give us all sweet peace. Amen.'[57] Scant use was made of the events at Magdeburg by German writers then, though Swedish propagandists did work to emphasise the sins of the Imperialists. The most important such communique which Gustavus released was in fact a new *Apologia* explaining why he had not reached Magdeburg in time. According to one account, the failure was grave indeed, for what it suggested about Gustavus' inability to defend his allies:

> ...it seemed for the moment as if the King of Sweden had come in vain. Loud and high were the accusations against him, raised by those who little understood the difficulties with which he had to contend. He seemed for the moment, to both sides, to be merely a new Christian of Denmark, who would now be only too glad to wriggle out of the war just as that monarch had done. The universal cry of joy raised in Catholic Germany, which, considering the odds against the city, was as ridiculous as it was indecent, and...was echoed back by a wail of terror from the opposite party, and even the imperturbable Wallenstein, on receipt of the news, is said to have hurled a piece of his table furniture at the head of the messenger with the words: "It is a lie!"[58]

Unsurprisingly, the Swedish King heaped blame for the failure upon the shoulders of the two Protestant Electors, who Gustavus could portray as having let their co-religionists down, should he so wish. It was too late for Magdeburg, Gustavus could claim, but there remained time for the two Electors to redeem themselves.[59] If they would not do so, however, the Swedish King was far more emboldened after the sack of Magdeburg to make the decision for them. With greater fury than ever before, he turned his full attention towards the Elector of Brandenburg. Though his uncle lay dead in the River Elbe, the presence of the Swedish army in the outskirts of Berlin proved far more persuasive inducement to attach his banners to those of Gustavus Adolphus, though this process still took some time, and was by no means harmonious, as we will see.

It is often forgotten that among those to be inconvenienced by the destruction of Magdeburg was Count Tilly, who was earnestly relying on the stores of that city to revitalise and resupply his men into the summer, or at the very refresh their coffers with the demanded contributions. When only varying degrees of plunder was the reward, rather than a reliable supply of coin or food, Tilly would have known that the clock was ticking for his men as well. The summer months would be gentle enough, but with the Swedish King waiting in the wings, it was imperative that the veteran generalissimo reinforce his position and secure his supply lines before autumn and winter set in. It was in view of these aims that Tilly made perhaps his greatest, but also understandable, error. Seeing the waste which the war had inflicted on German lands around the Elbe and Oder Rivers, Count Tilly turned his attention to the relatively untouched lands of the neutral, newly armed Protestant Elector, John George of Saxony. Would the Elector of Saxony disarm, and provide Tilly with monies and food according to his Emperor's will? It was time, at long last, for the indecisive John George to make his choice – would it be God, or would it be the Devil?

FOUR
A Season of Choices

Ever since the ticking clock had been set, the Swedish King encountered frustration after frustration in his efforts to move the Germans to support him. He maintained an army of twenty-four thousand men with the support of the French, but actual substantial progress had continued to elude him so long as would be allies remained noncommittal. The war was twelve years old, and the two Protestant Electors in Saxony and Brandenburg whom Gustavus so desperately wished to have on side had seen enough of the conflict to know how quickly affairs could change. Had not Frederick V, the Elector Palatine, seemed so impressive with his cast of allies? Had his friends not besieged Vienna at one point, while the kingdom of Bohemia declared for him? Yet, he had been crushed and was reduced to little more than a burden to the Dutch in his Amsterdam exile. And what of the other significant foreign invader, the King of Denmark? Furnished with a splendid triple alliance in 1625, the future had seemed bright indeed for Christian IV, and yet, the forces of the Emperor had swollen to unimaginable levels, and his kingdom and armies had been systematically destroyed in the late 1620s.

In short, to the two Electors, the record of opposition to the Habsburgs was not encouraging. That they had felt compelled to act and formulate the Leipzig Manifesto in February-March 1631 spoke more to their anger towards the Edict of Restitution than to any deep seated desire on their part to oppose their lawful Emperor, betray the German constitution and side with the invader. This was evident enough by their refusal to side with Gustavus thereafter, but in Emperor Ferdinand II's mind, a position of determined neutrality on their part was not good enough – they would either support him unconditionally, or they would be his enemy. Evidence of the uncompromising position which the Emperor had taken towards these Electors is found in mid-May; before Magdeburg had been sacked, Ferdinand had already issued an imperial decree which declared the Leipzig Manifesto illegal and ordered those partaking in it to disband their troops.

To guarantee their compliance, reinforcements were sent from the recently closed theatre in North Italy, and they enjoyed some success, overrunning Wurttemberg and much of Franconia in the south and south-west of Germany respectively. Perhaps the Emperor anticipated that this new force would dissolve just like the old Protestant Union had in the early stages of the conflict, but if this was his hope then he was to be disappointed. The major goal was to force the reluctant neutrals to resume their contributions to the Emperor's forces, and to renew payment of war taxes which would keep the armies afloat.[60] Unfortunately for the Elector of Brandenburg though, the reach of Imperial forces in the North of Germany was nowhere near as strong as it was in the South. Since late 1630, Imperial garrisons had been withdrawing from Pomerania, leaving several fortresses with anaemic defences. One such fortress, Spandau, had been granted to Gustavus by George William of Brandenburg for the period of a month only, with the purpose, it was understood, of aiding the relief of Magdeburg.

Once Magdeburg fell however, George William displayed little inclination to join the Swedes and avenge his uncle, whose corpse was floating in the River Elbe. Instead, the Elector requested that the Swedish King give Spandau back to him, as the purpose for holding it was no longer applicable. By now surely disenchanted with the Protestant Germans, the Swedish King sent his brother in law something of an ultimatum. 'Unless', Gustavus declared to his George William of Brandenburg on 9 June...

> ...you confirm me in possession of Spandau, I will retire altogether from the war, and, leaving a strong garrison to hold Pomerania for the crown of Sweden, let you and your fellow Protestants defend yourself against Tilly as best you can.

This was nothing less than a threat to leave the recalcitrant Elector to the mercy of the Imperialists, which Gustavus banked would be less than merciful after George William's months of opportunistic neutrality. Incredibly though, the Elector did not cave into the pressure, making a claim instead that he would stand alongside the Elector of Saxony under the Leipzig Manifesto, and essentially take his chances. This seems to have pushed Gustavus into taking serious action. He dutifully evacuated Spandau shortly afterwards, but as he marched his soldiers past Berlin, he finally brought to bear all the military pressure at his disposal.[61] As his cannons were pointed towards the capital, Gustavus sent his brother in law another request for a treaty, this time couched in language, which was far more uncompromising.

'I don't want to hear about neutrality', Gustavus declared. 'His Grace must be my friend or foe...he must declare himself cold or hot', and the Swedish King then added the turn of phrase which was to become famous: 'This is a fight between God and the Devil. If His Grace is with God, he must join me, if he is for the Devil, he must fight me. There is no third way.'[62] Of course, not merely George William, but several other German potentates, had been desperately searching for this 'third way' for some time. And Gustavus' refusal to recognise a neutral party was mirrored in the policy of the Emperor, who had elected to stamp out those signees to the Leipzig Manifesto rather than risk their cooperation with the enemy. After twelve years of war, indeed, too much was at stake for either invader or Emperor to allow a 'third way' to exist in Germany. Neutrality was impossible so long as a foreign king was in Germany, threatening to upend the string of triumphs which the Habsburgs had enjoyed since 1620, or that religious settlement which had been enshrined with the Edict of Restitution. The choice for Germans and their rulers was one of God or the Devil, but it of course depended on one's persuasions and loyalties where one perceived either the Devil or God to reside.

The debate was at least over for George William. Facing such intense pressure, with the 'grinning iron mouths' of Gustavus' cannon pointed at his palace, he could do no other than capitulate. If he did not, proclaimed one of Gustavus' subordinates, 'he would send the Duchess and all the Ladies prisoners to Sweden, and that the Duke should follow.'[63] His decision made for him, George William signed a generous treaty with Gustavus on 20 June 1631. The Elector then worked diligently to draft a letter of explanation to the Emperor, detailing why he had been forced to side with the enemy, and why this state of affairs certainly was not his fault. 'His Majesty of Sweden', George William insisted in his letter to the Emperor, 'already used every opportunity during the Leipzig Convention through letters or envoys to present us with this dilemma: we should either join him or fight him.' Brandenburg was too weak to resist, the Elector insisted: 'Since then imperial troops have abandoned our towns…after feeble defence and evacuated our lands from which they had drawn many millions, claiming they could not trust us.'[64]

At the height of his powers indeed, Emperor Ferdinand had compelled George William to conclude an alliance with him in 1627, whereby ten thousand Imperial troops would be billeted on the lands of Brandenburg, paid for by the Elector. These had been evacuated in recent months though, to join up with Count Tilly, which the Elector not unreasonably claimed now left him utterly defenceless. Recalling Gustavus' arrival outside Berlin, George William noted how he hoped by letting the King into Berlin, 'the business would be easier in those surroundings than when we negotiated through our councillors.' As George William had since discovered though: 'we found that His Majesty of Sweden still insisted on the same points and ignored ours… Instead, he presented harsh counter-demands.'

These demands involved handing any fortresses Gustavus required to his forces; permitting Gustavus to recover war costs from Pomerania; granting Sweden a regular subsidy to pay for its forces and finally, to ratify the alliance with the Duke of Pomerania. Pomerania had long been a sore spot for George William, as he had seemed poised to inherit the childless Duke's lands before Gustavus had arrived and claimed the territory for himself. Faced with Gustavus' military supremacy though, George William had little choice but to accept the unacceptable. However genuine the Elector may have been in this communique to the Emperor, it is evident from it that he was not confidently joining a great crusade against Catholic Vienna. Instead, George William was being forced, against his will, to support his brother in law, and he earnestly hoped that the Emperor would forgive him for it:

> The duty that binds us to His Roman Imperial Majesty [Ferdinand II] and the Empire; the respect we possess amongst our fellow evangelical Estates; even what the imperial and Kreis constitution, the hereditary inheritance pacts and family agreements allow – all this counts for nothing.[65]

Emperor Ferdinand knew only too well that the constitution of the Empire could be brushed aside when one possessed the preponderance of forces – had he not done this exact thing when promising the moon to the Duke of Bavaria, in return for his support against the rebellious Elector Palatine? And speaking of that Duke of Bavaria, Maximillian II had not rested on his laurels while the King of Sweden marched, and Cardinal Richelieu schemed. To ensure his gains in the war against a potential Imperial defeat, Maximillian, not for the last time, sought additional protections from the French. The result was the Treaty of Fontainebleau signed on 30 May 1631, which confirmed previous arrangements and diplomatic manoeuvres in a treaty lasting eight years. Under the terms of the Treaty, Maximillian was compelled

> ...not to provide soldiers or money either directly or indirectly to those who attack His Most Christian Majesty [King Louis XIII of France] and his provinces, nor to allow the recruitment in his [lands] of soldiers against the said King and his provinces, nor to permit friends to provide secretly weapons, cannon and gunpowder to such soldiers.[66]

Such a clause was not merely awkward, in the context of France's alliance with Sweden, and the Duke's record of firm support of the Emperor, it was also virtually obsolete from the moment pen was put to paper. From the moment of Wallenstein's dismissal, the previous autumn, the Catholic League had constituted the main bulk of the forces which the Emperor had sent to meet the Swedish King. The other option for military force resided in the remnants of Wallenstein's army, which had been shipped to North Italy and was only beginning to return to Germany in spring 1631. Thus, Ferdinand would have to rely upon the League, and this League was a Bavarian institution, its soldiers traditionally receiving their pay from the Duke of Bavaria. Catholic League forces had destroyed Frederick V's prospects at the

Battle of White Mountain in 1620; they had marched along the length and breadth of the Danish peninsula, and they continued to be billeted throughout the Empire. The army of the Catholic League under the command of Count Tilly was markedly more acceptable to the Catholic German princes than the independent generalissimo Wallenstein and his ever-increasing force, but its comparatively smaller size brought with it its own problems, even while it made Maximillian more influential than ever before.

It was therefore impossible for Duke Maximillian to abide by the terms of the Treaty of Fontainebleau, lest he wished to take the very confrontational step of withdrawing his Catholic League soldiers from the relevant posts. This would surely have ruined his relationship with the Emperor and could have jeopardised his gains in the Palatinate in the early 1620s, whereupon the transferral of the Electoral title of that territory to Bavaria had been confirmed, and which Maximillian now jealously guarded. Such an overt step was not what Cardinal Richelieu even desired though, since Article VI of the Treaty of Fontainebleau declared:

> Since circumstances require that this alliance and mutual defence pact between His Most Christian Majesty and the Elector of Bavaria must on no account be divulged to others, both sides have agreed that it will not be publicly acknowledged.[67]

If the Treaty was a secret – not for Richelieu to inform Gustavus, nor for Maximillian to inform Ferdinand – and if it was on the whole unenforceable considering the military situation at the time, then one could be forgiven for asking what the purpose in negotiating the Treaty had been in the first place. Peter H. Wilson put it best when he wrote that 'Both parties recognised that the Treaty was unenforceable, but regarded it as a statement of mutual good intentions.'[68] Indeed, the Treaty of Fontainebleau was a step towards a firmer Franco-Bavarian accord which Richelieu believed was essential for undermining the grip of the Habsburg-Bavarian faction on the Empire. As the summer progressed, indeed, it became more and more obvious that the act of preserving peace between the Duke of Bavaria and the King of Sweden would be impossible; soon enough, France would have to make a choice between its two incompatible allies.

The Swedish King faced several unappealing choices himself, none of which seemed destined to deliver to him the loyalty and affection of Protestant Germans that he both desired and needed if a victory against the Habsburgs was to be secured. He had been forced to effectively place a gun at the head of his brother in law, as we have seen, and if not even family could be persuaded to come to his aid, then what likelihood was there that other German strangers would? The deal with Brandenburg had bought him some time, but it was by no means a silver bullet. Until the support of the Elector of Saxony could be confirmed, it was too risky for Gustavus to march into the heart of Germany and challenge Tilly to a conclusive showdown.

Thus, Gustavus set his subordinates into nearby territories to clear out what remained of the Imperial resistance, solidifying his grip over Pomerania and Mecklenburg in the process. He then moved his main army of sixteen thousand men to the River Elbe, where after several days hard work, his army constructed an impressive fortified camp near a small town called Werben. A quick sketch of the position illustrates its suitability for holding out, which was what Gustavus was forced to do throughout July 1631. Situated at a confluence of the Elbe with the River Havel, Werben enjoyed the geographic protection of these waters to the north and east, while a bastion of complex defences had been established to cover the remaining two flanks.[69] The preparations proved essential, for Count Tilly approached with his larger army of twenty-four thousand men on 1 August, but proved unable to break through after two attempts. Gustavus would proclaim that the veteran Imperial commander had lost some seven thousand men in the assaults, but the true number was much smaller.[70]

At long last, the Count and the King had had their first military encounter. It was, for all intents and purposes, something of an anti-climax, as neither actor possessed sufficient means to defeat the other. 'Nothing more ensued but a distant cannonade, and a few skirmishes, in which the Swedes had invariably the advantage', wrote one historian,[71] but the Swedes had at least weathered the storm, and Tilly was forced to move south to a fortified camp of his own, where he sought provisions for his army in desperation. Had Gustavus elected to move out of his camp at Werben and confront Tilly's numerically larger force, then the name of Werben would certainly be more well known today. Yet, as it stood by early August 1631, both men recognised that the time was not yet right for the great showdown.

During August, Gustavus was joined in his camp by William, the Landgrave of Hesse-Cassel, and 'the first sovereign prince in Germany, who voluntarily and openly declared against the Emperor, though not wholly uninfluenced by strong motives.'[72] Finally, here was a German Protestant prince who had come on his own free will, without the threat of Swedish cannons bearing down on his capital. Just as important as this symbolic victory was the practical aid Landgrave William brought in his army of seven thousand men. Gustavus then led a triumphant procession to Mecklenburg, where he oversaw the reinstatement of its old Duke, expelled for supporting the Danish King, and replaced since by Wallenstein. The righting of this wrong in the Empire was an important feather in Gustavus' cap, but it also represented an attack upon the retired Wallenstein.

Even though he no longer served his Emperor in the field, it seemed, the Emperor's enemies were still able to strike back at him. Matters had deteriorated for Wallenstein since his dismissal the previous September; 'I thank God to be free of the net', he had declared when learning of his dismissal following the Diet of Regensburg. Yet his financial resources had dwindled notably since his retirement, and his personal banker had even committed suicide rather than face the pressure any longer. Mecklenburg had been a great boon to Wallenstein's portfolio, but with its recapture by the enemies of the Emperor, Wallenstein was shown just how quickly the fortunes of war could change. Though he remained Duke of Friedland, there was no guarantee that this too would be secure if Gustavus' progress was allowed to continue. For the sake of his own interests, as much as that of Germany then, Wallenstein remained up to date with the situation in the Empire. Though absent from the Emperor's circle, he remained at the other end of the Emperor's letters and cannot have been surprised when the calls for his reappointment began to increase from late 1631.[73]

As August gave way to September, the urgency in Count Tilly's camp had evidently increased. In fact, following the repulse of his force from the camp at Werben, Tilly made for the borders of Saxony where it was hoped the neutral Elector would be persuaded to attach his banners to that of the Emperor. More than merely money or soldiers though, Tilly was desperate to replenish his men after marching through the charred remnants of the Elbe basin for several months. He had received no support from his Emperor, and his orders were often unclear as well. When the rebellious Landgrave of Hesse-Cassel had marched to Gustavus' side, Tilly had refrained from attacking the former to appease the Saxon Elector, a fellow Protestant. Yet, John George of Saxony refused to be drawn, and seemed determined to maintain his army of eighteen thousand recruits. Having watched Brandenburg fall in line with the Swedish invader, John George no doubt intended to be more successful than George William in preserving his position, but his determination only seemed to force Count Tilly's hand. 'In all the days of my life', Tilly complained...

> ...I have never seen an army so suddenly and totally deprived of all that it needs, from the greatest to the small requisite...And I am utterly astonished that the poor soldiers remain so long in such necessity. [74]

After several weeks of balancing precariously on the edge of ruin, Tilly felt he had no other choice than to invade. On 5 September, a great turning point of the Thirty Years War was played out, as Tilly's depleted force followed the lead of all armies before them, and began pillaging, plundering and seizing all they could from the virtually unspoiled Saxon lands. It is easy to imagine that after months of marching over the scorched, empty landscape, Saxony would have seemed like a land of plenty to Tilly's men. Saxony, with its bountiful harvests and gleaming cities, could sustain Tilly well into 1632, but Saxony contained more than just these treasures, it also contained an influential Elector – a leading figure among the German Protestants – and his army of eighteen thousand men which he had raised for just such a purpose as this. As Wedgewood described, the actions of Tilly 'swept the negotiations out of John George's hands' – after attempting to balance between Emperor and Gustavus for so long, John George now had the choice made for him.[75]

He could hardly side with the party which now ravaged his lands; however unpalatable it might be, it was eminently better to side with the invader, which might pile pressure upon the Emperor, than it was to accept his now depressing lot as a besieged Elector. Less than a week after Tilly's men invaded, on 11 September, John George of Saxony concluded an alliance with the King of Sweden. Tilly must have known that this would be the penalty for his invasion; that he invaded and sucked Saxon lands dry despite the inevitable consequences speaks to the veteran commander's desperation. When he had entreated John George to permit his men access to Saxony a few days before, the Elector had replied prophetically 'Now I see that the Saxon sweetmeats, so long spared, are to be eaten; but you may find that they contain hard nuts which will break your teeth.'[76]

Tilly elected to take his chances, and feast on these sweetmeats, but sure enough, the teeth-breaking followed quickly enough, as he added his eighteen thousand raw recruits to Gustavus' twenty-four thousand veterans, thus creating a massive disparity in numbers where once Tilly had the advantage with his army of thirty-five thousand. The terms of the Swedish-Saxon alliance would also have given Tilly reason to pause; it committed Saxony to 'supply the necessary food and forage to His Majesty's army as long as it is in our lands fighting our enemies';[77] to 'not withdraw our troops from his as long as the danger persists, nor make peace without prior consent' and to 'join him with our army and act in concert, standing as one against our common enemies.' The alliance, in short, was everything that Ferdinand had wanted the Elector to give him, but due to a combination of factors, from the infamous Edict to the rapacious nature of the war, John George sided against his Emperor for the first time.

The alliance with the two Electors which Gustavus had sought since his landing in July 1630 was finally his, but it came with several asterisks. Not even Gustavus himself would have admitted that he wholly trusted either Elector. His own brother law had been so fearful of reprimand by the Emperor, and so unsure of Gustavus' position, that he had joined the Swedish King only under the threat of total destruction. John George of Saxony, meanwhile, had attached his forces to Sweden only once he had been forced to by the destruction of his homeland, and the seizure of Leipzig, which fell to Tilly on 15 September.[78] Gustavus was under no illusions, and confessed to a Saxon agent shortly after the Elector's dilemma became so acute:

I am sorry for the Elector...had he heeded my repeated remonstrances, his country would never have seen the face of an enemy, and Magdeburg would not have fallen. Now, when necessity leaves him no alternative, he has recourse to my assistance. But tell him, that I cannot, for the sake of the Elector of Saxony, ruin my own cause, and that of my confederates. What pledge have I for the sincerity of a prince whose minister is in the pay of Austria, and who will abandon me as soon as the Emperor flatters him, and withdraws his troops from his frontiers? Tilly, it is true, has received a strong reinforcement; but this shall not prevent me from meeting him with confidence, as soon as I have covered my rear.[79]

Though he was no confident in John George's reliability, or even in the professionalism of his raw recruits, the numbers which the defection provided Gustavus were still invaluable. The political impact of the two Protestant Electors of the Empire joining sides with Sweden also sent a clear message. It also underlined the religious element of the struggle which remained relevant. Content as many of the smaller princes were to follow Saxony's lead, the possibility that Saxony would do battle alongside the Swedish King, and that they might miss out on the spoils which would follow, served as a powerful motive as well.

Indeed, unwilling to allow the momentum of recent weeks to subside, Gustavus felt confident at long last to abandon his fortified position and wrest from Count Tilly a commitment to meet him in a pitched battle. It had been a season of choices, and now Gustavus made the most important choice of all – where to have this battle upon which the future of Sweden, of Germany, and of the War would depend. He chose the little-known town of Breitenfeld, some eight kilometres north-west of Leipzig. And now the final choice was Count Tilly's – would he confront his nemesis, or would he avoid him now that the Swedish King possessed the numerical advantage? As it happened, for Count Tilly this was not much of a choice at all. He made for Breitenfeld, intending at long last to put to bed the legend of the Swedish King, and to reassert his reputation as the Emperor's foremost generalissimo. The God and the Devil would have their showdown at last.

FIVE
Breitenfeld

If we decide upon battle the stake will be nothing less than a crown and two electorates. Fortune is changeable, and the inscrutable decrees of Heaven may, for our sins, give the victory to our enemies. My kingdom, it is true, even after the loss of my life and my army, would still have a hope left. Far removed from the scene of action, defended by a powerful fleet, a well-guarded frontier, and a warlike population, it would at least be safe from the worst consequences of a defeat. But what chances of escape are there for you, with an enemy so close at hand?[80]

In such a way, we are told, did the Swedish King open the war council summit meeting between himself, the Elector of Brandenburg and the Elector of Saxony in mid-September 1631, as the unlikely allies made their last-minute preparations in the town of Torgau along the Elbe. Torgau is more famous today as the point where American and Soviet forces linked up in the final days of WW2, but in 1631, it was the point of rendezvous for a very different army. Rather than move to prevent the two allied armies from uniting, Count Tilly had elected to seize Leipzig instead, on 15 September. The city had not been well-prepared for a siege, but after a few days of resistance, the gates were thrown open and its residents were treated mostly favourably. Another Magdeburg, Leipzig was not to be, but it was, arguably, a needless distraction which Tilly should have avoided.

He had had to leave one thousand men behind to garrison the city, which further increased the discrepancy in numbers between the two armies. Tilly also possessed fewer guns than the Swedish King; just twenty-six to Gustavus' fifty-six, while Gustavus had been experimenting with artillery relentlessly since his first campaigns against the Poles.[81] Not merely a clash of religious beliefs, this battle was also destined to be a clash of military theory on a scale never before seen. It was a grand showdown between the old tercio system which had won incredible victories for Spain, versus the more flexible manoeuvres pioneered by Maurice of Orange in the opening

775

years of the century. These latter tactics, as we have seen, drew inspiration from Roman tactics of old, and having gone through Dutch and French filters, it was when the Swedish King had applied his own flavour to them that they reached their apex.

Yet there was a notable contrast even within the allied army itself. The Swedes, who 'having lain overnight on a parcel of ploughed ground, were so dusty, they looked out like kitchen-servants, with their uncleanly rags', did not present a pretty picture.[82] The freshly gathered Saxons, on the other hand, were 'well clothed, showing robust forms and fresh cheeks, with well-fed horses'.[83] Skipping breakfast on the morning of 17 September had not helped the Swedish appearance, but beneath the dirt and grit of the Swedish conscript, and his mercenary allies, resided a grim determination and experience which the Saxon recruit sorely lacked, as the coming battle would show.

The army had spent the night of 16-17 September laying on this 'ploughed ground' a few kilometres from the village, and they Gustavus spent much of the morning directing his men to the designated battlefield site. This involved approaching through a marshy area through which a small river, the Lober, flowed. With this marsh at their backs, in front of the Swedish King the plain of Breitenfeld beckoned. Roughly a kilometre away stood Count Tilly's men, and his cannon had already begun firing at the Swedish King's men. As the huge army marched to its destination, Gustavus rode among them, and we are told that he delivered a rousing speech which might lift the spirits of those that were demoralised, hungry, tired or fearful. 'My comrades', Gustavus began:

> If I had to do with men whose sentiments were less known, whose courage was less tried, I might think myself obliged to excite it by words; but I see by your look that it would be at this time superfluous. In reality it is a sword that is necessary to our cause. I ought not and wish not to despise our adversary, nor to represent the struggle with him more easy than it really is. Such a subterfuge would be out of place towards you who have never fled from danger. I avow, then, frankly that we are in front of an enemy very powerful, exercised in deeds of blood, and so accustomed to victory, that, during long wars, he has seldom experienced a reverse. But the more our enemy is covered with glory, so much the more will be the renown to conquer him and gain by a single blow the laurels he has won. All his conquests, all the booty taken by him in so many successful campaigns, will fall at once into our power. You and your soldiers have often said to me in badinage that one can secure his salvation in my service, but not his fortune. It has been thus, because that, passing through devastated countries, and finding ourselves among oppressed allies, it would have been unjust on our part to have thought of amassing riches. Now you have in front of you, for the first time, a camp filled with precious booty, afterwards a road which passes the sumptuous villages and fertile lands of the Catholics. All that is the price of a single victory. That victory can be gained, and will be,

with the aid of God. Our enemy is known to us; and we have tried our swords against a good many of his soldiers…and we know we can conquer them in spite of the arrogance which they affect. I am convinced that you will perform your duty as loyal Swedes. The Saxons, I hope, will defend with courage their country, whose prosperity is principally at stake. But I count on the justice of our cause more even than on our arms and our allies; for we combat, not only for men and human interests, but also for the glory of God, the true evangelical faith, oppressed and almost annihilated by the Papists. The God of all goodness, who has conducted us in so miraculous a manner across seas and rivers, through fortresses and enemies, will give us the necessary force to conquer our powerful adversary. Think…of Magdeburg, whose bloody ruins still smoke, and cry vengeance; think of the thousands of innocent individuals who have been assassinated, and whose blood has gushed out to heaven. The justice of God will chastise these frightful murders, these coarse vices, these hideous crimes. This is why we will attack with courage. God is with us. May these words be our rallying cry; and, with the help of the Almighty, victory will be ours.[84]

It is difficult to assess whether such a speech was even made, or whether it would have been heard above the increasing volume of cannonade, but regardless, the Swedish army was at last prepared. It was now the task of Gustavus Adolphus not to break, but to win the triumph upon which so much depended. Were he to fail, Gustavus would be just another failed interventionist, and potentially, the Counter-Reformation could sweep through Northern Germany like never before. Tilly's legend would reach new heights, and Sweden would surely remove itself from the conflict as quickly as possible. Should he win though, Gustavus kept his goals somewhat modest, intending the victory to induce more Germans to his side, maintain the pressure on the Emperor, and gain *assecuratio* – security – for Sweden into the future. What followed Gustavus' victory at Breitenfeld, of course, was anything but modest, as the Imperial position collapsed, and the Swedish King found that he had Germany in the palm of his hand like no invader before him.[85]

As they had moved into position, Gustavus' men had been subject to several volleys from Tilly's distant cannon, and it was once his line was secure that Gustavus ordered his artillery to answer. 'Our guns answered theirs with three shots for one', was the reported boast of Gustavus after the battle, and the claim was not far off. Immediately, the discrepancy of the two sides' batteries was evident, and it was a discrepancy which would be brought to murderous effect at pivotal stages of the battle. Standing on a slight rise in the Breitenfeld plain, Tilly's men were confident, after having served and won under their veteran commander for more than a decade. Indeed, with the addition of seven thousand tired but experienced soldiers from Mantua in the weeks before, Tilly boasted a force which could justifiably be described as the cream of the Imperial crop. He would certainly not be held back by any deficiencies in training or morale, where, by contrast, Gustavus had been careful to separate his men from the Saxons, and place them on his left flank, while he commanded the cavalry on the right.[86]

It was on this flank that the battle's opening moves were played out. An impetuous cavalry commander by the name of Pappenheim faced Gustavus' horse with more than two thousand of his own, and over the next hour, in seven cavalry charges, Pappenheim learned how Gustavus had earned his reputation. The Swedish horse did not budge, instead absorbing the charges by cycling through their cavalry, who were equipped with pistoles and sabres, and had been bathed in the fire of cavalry combat after years of fighting fearsome Poles – some of the best horsemen in Europe. In spite of the uninspiring results which his charge netted, Pappenheim's action forced Tilly to mobilise his right flank against the Saxons, who were accompanied by their Elector John George. On this flank, the experienced Imperial forces under the command of Furstenberg enjoyed more success, and actually routed the untested Saxons from the field.[87]

This action would have had a far greater impact had both the Saxons and Imperials not abandoned all discipline, and begun pillaging the Swedish baggage train. Yet, it was more unfortunate for Tilly that Furstenberg had marched his cavalry so far ahead of his infantry, which left a few thousand men to march unguarded across the battlefield, only reaching the old Saxon position by 3.30PM, when they were set upon by forces which Gustavus had diverted from his own victorious flank. It was once these tired Imperials were routed that the battle truly turned against Tilly; commanding in the centre, Tilly now found that his men had to turn to face Gustavus' subordinates on their right and left flanks. One of these subordinates, Gustav Horn, charged to where the Imperial artillery battery had been firing for much of the morning, and began to prepare to turn these guns on Tilly's men.

Back in the centre, and the resolve of the Swedes was beginning to tell. As smoke clouded one's vision, cannon shot raked the limbs of men and the choking stench of burning flesh filled the air, it was plain that only the most resolute and well-drilled army could possibly survive. This was certainly the greatest test Tilly's men had ever faced, but it was also the first time they had ever properly encountered Gustavus' infantry tactics. These tactics included doing away with the kind of formations, like the pike and musket tercio squares, that Tilly had perfected. Gustavus' men were more flexible, but also designed specifically to lay down the greatest volume of firepower possible. Swedish soldiers were not compressed into unwieldy squares then, but ranks of men who had been trained to fire their weapons from all manner of positions, using coordinated drills which ensured that there was always a projectile of some kind in the air.

This clash of styles utterly stumped the Imperials, and Tilly was unable to develop an answer for these tactics on the spot. The heavy volume of fire was the perfect answer to the tightly packed pike and musket squares, but the killing blow came once the captured Imperial artillery were moved into position alongside the guns of the Swedes.[88] Thanks to additional revolutions in artillery, Gustavus' lighter guns could be moved by a couple of men, whereas such innovations in the Imperial battery were not fully realised. The result was a slaughter which stole over seven thousand Imperial lives, and six thousand initial prisoners. Tilly was lucky indeed to have escaped, but his reputation for invincibility was among the casualties at Breitenfeld on 17 September. The scale of the victory took some time to sink in, but it was subsequently buoyed by the taking of Leipzig the following day, along with three thousand more prisoners. Having solidified his reputation, many of these prisoners were induced to switch sides and join the Swedish King, in the process turning a great triumph into a turning point of the war.[89]

And this was a turning point, though its potential would be felt in the political and moral spheres, rather than solely in the military. In spite of his considerable losses, Tilly had withdrawn from Saxony through Westphalia and south towards Franconia, where he was joined by forty thousand men and further reinforcements on route from Italy. In Silesia, the Imperials possessed a further twenty thousand men, and this was before the resources of Spain or Bavaria were taken fully into account.[90] In short, Gustavus' victory had not wiped Imperial resistance off the map, nor had he expected one battle, no matter how decisive, to deliver such impossible rewards.

What is truly remarkable about Breitenfeld is that in spite of Tilly's ability to repair his army in the subsequent months, Gustavus found the political situation in Germany utterly transformed. Although Tilly would be back to fight another day, for now, Gustavus had no equal in Germany, and he was effectively free to go where he pleased. 'The thirteen years which had passed since the great conflict began had brought nothing but defeats and humiliation to the Protestants' wrote Andrew Stomberg, adding that now 'in a few hours their status was changed completely: the Swedish king stood in the heart of Germany with a victorious army and there was no army of either the Catholic League or the emperor to oppose him.' According to pious Catholics, it appeared as though 'God had all of a sudden turned Lutheran'. Stomberg continued to note that:

> The prestige of the emperor had received a severe and permanent setback and the Protestants could take heart again. A shout of joy arose from them everywhere...For the Swedish king it meant the rapid accession to his ranks of new allies, both princes and cities, and for the Protestants of Germany it meant the abrogation of the Edict of Restitution.[91]

Gustavus was never so free and victorious as he was for the next few months. Some limitations remained of course; the Swedish King was by no means welcome throughout the Empire, and he still had his shaky Saxon ally to contend with. However, with Tilly licking his wounds to the south, Bohemia and the Rhine were now opened up. In the words of Peter H. Wilson, Gustavus now determined 'to seize as much land as possible before winter closed in.'[92] This race to conquer was supercharged by the news of his victory at Breitenfeld, which spread throughout Germany and soon acquired legendary status.

The production of broadsheets – single sheets of paper containing a single symbolic image, sometimes produced as a short leaflet containing more detail and text – skyrocketed after Gustavus' victory. Protestant pamphleteers increased production by more than 60% after Breitenfeld: of the roughly 250 broadsheets published in 1631, at least 150 appeared following Gustavus' thumping victory.[93] And how was that victory depicted? Generally, they contained stern critiques of Count Tilly, who was depicted as paying for his sins at Magdeburg. Often, it included the image of Gustavus and John George of Saxony side by side – an important picture for building an impression of Protestant unity, particularly after Saxon soldiers had fled the field.

One broadsheet in particular deserves to be underlined. We will recall John George's warning to Tilly of breaking his teeth of the 'Saxon sweetmeats', during the latter's desperate search for provisions in early September. Evidently the reply had entered into common discourse, for a series of broadsheets entitled 'Saxon sweets' appeared several times from late 1631 to early 1632. In this picture, we see John George, Gustavus Adolphus and Count Tilly standing at a table, where several bowls of 'sweets' are depicted. These bowls come with labels such as 'liberty' 'religion' 'dignity' 'territory' and 'Augsburg Confession'. The symbolism continues as John George stands on two pillars labelled 'good cause' and 'infallible hope', while Tilly balances precariously on two stone balls labelled 'deceit' and 'jealousy'.

Further, Tilly is shown reaching out his arms, arms which contain the labels 'avarice' and 'tyranny', to grab the precious bowls of 'religion' and 'territory' which lay on the table. Who comes to the rescue but Gustavus, who is shown thwarting Tilly's outstretched arms with the bowl labelled 'just zeal', while John George also gets in on the action, wielding a staff labelled 'good conscience' to prod at Tilly and force him back away from these precious 'Saxon sweets' which the Protestant leaders evidently hold so dear. At the top of this fascinating show is the phrase 'This confectionary is sacred to us; therefore, we are justly driving you away.' The message which this broadsheet contains is certainly on the nose, but it does a good job recording how Tilly was viewed and how Protestant propagandists wanted their religious brethren to view him. We will note also the importance which the pamphleteers place upon those constitutional aspects of the Empire; on the table, for instance, there are bowls other than those dealing merely with religion, but also the territory, liberty and justice of old German government.[94]

While the depiction of these 'Saxon sweets' is merely a microcosm of the one hundred and fifty or so broadsheets which Gustavus inspired, they tell a distinct story of an Empire which was coming to see the Swedish King in nearly messianic terms. What these broadsheets tell us less about is the opportunity for enrichment and advancement to minor Germans which Gustavus' triumph allowed. Much like his defeated enemies at Breitenfeld petitioned to attach themselves to Gustavus' army, so too did previously neutral German princes begin to solicit, and obtain, appointments in the Swedish army. By doing so, these princes recognised a new status quo whereby the Swedish King, rather than the Emperor, was their ultimate master. Not merely soldiers, but diplomats as well elected to leave their minor German lords behind and work to represent the Swedish King instead. Greater rewards, it was plain, could be found by serving this dynamic new force in Germany rather than one's former employer.[95] The fluidity of German loyalties was an accepted part of this unfolding new phase in the war, as a foreign invader sought to expand his reach and influence as far as it could be projected within the remaining months of 1631, while Tilly was still reeling.

Gustavus' decision to make for the Rhine placed in jeopardy towns and rulers which had previously been insulated by their distance from the front and close proximity to more powerful forces like Bavaria and the Emperor. With both of these entities in retreat though, a power vacuum which Gustavus sought to rapidly exploit brought the Swedish King remarkable gains which he previously would never have imagined possible. Erfurt, one hundred kilometres south-west of Leipzig and home to a University where Martin Luther had once attended, fell to Gustavus on 2 October, followed by Wurzburg on 15 October. This latter town was particularly strong, and boasted Marienberg, a formidable fortress which had been designed to defend the wealthy bishopric from foreign invaders. Evidently, it failed in its task, following a stiff assault on that hilltop fortress. Reportedly, pleas for mercy from the inhabitants were met with shrieks of 'Magdeburg quarter' from the attackers, but just as significant as its capture, was how Gustavus intended to treat Wurzburg in the new vision of Germany which was rapidly taking shape in his mind.[96]

Upon seizing the bishopric and its eponymous capital, Wurzburg lay at Gustavus' feet, but in an open letter to the city fathers, the Swedish king made it known that 'our royal disposition is not at all directed towards such enormities or revenge, but on the contrary…our intention is to re-establish a secure, good and permanent peace in the entire Empire', and therefore, 'we have deemed to make use of the larger part of this diocese…this is our gracious wish.' But the letter continued:

> We also regard it as an unavoidable necessity to take the land and its poor subjects into our royal grace and to put everything into a proper and secure order until all-wise God, according to His good will, directs otherwise to through the desired peace. To this end, we have established a certain territorial government and appointed capable persons to it.

Mild though the tone of the letter seemed in the beginning, this was nothing less than an announcement to the citizens of Wurzburg that their lands would henceforth be annexed into Gustavus' expanding Empire. And what if those residents of Wurzburg refused the King's generous offers of a regime change? Well, Gustavus spoke plainly to them too:

> Now that we have told you your duty, we will take those who are obedient into our royal protection and shelter, and graciously maintain their freedom of conscience and the public exercise of the same, as well as other political rights and jurisdictions, customs and privileges, and to open to them the justice of our already established territorial government. Those that oppose this gracious offer will be dealt with as the situation demands and are warned that such disobedience will be punished severely. [97]

While merely one among likely hundreds of such arrangements which were to be made and rearranged over the remaining years of the war, this open letter serves as a remarkable early indication of how the Swedish King intended to proceed. For how could a foreign invader realistically support himself in the tangle of loyalties and traditions which was the Holy Roman Empire, without rewriting some of the rulebook? At Wurzburg, and many other places thereafter, we see the Swedish King literally remove the bishopric from the Emperor, and therefore the Empire's jurisdiction, placing it instead under a new authority, that of Gustavus Adolphus. Had he stopped there for the year; his record would already have been unparalleled. Yet, after a short rest, Gustavus was on the move again with his irresistible force, following the course of the Main, that major tributary of the Rhine, to arrive in previously unspoiled lands like the Archbishopric of Mainz.[98]

This Archbishopric, which Gustavus captured a few days before Christmas, was immensely important in the constitution of the Empire, because its Archbishop boasted voting privileges in the Electoral college, an honour also bestowed upon the major German potentates like John George of Saxony or George William of Brandenburg. Before he had landed in this electorate and threatened to rework the entire electoral system of the Empire, Gustavus had played the primary role in another triumph. He entered the city of Frankfurt on the Main on 27 November, and was joined there by his Chancellor Axel Oxenstierna, who was charged with honing the administration of the King's sprawling domains and planning for the future. As his Chancellor set to this task, Gustavus made the aforementioned decision to capitalise on the Imperial disorganisation and seize Mainz.

Not merely the Rhine, but also Bohemia lay at Gustavus' feet. Understanding that the opportunity for vengeance a decade in the making was now his, Gustavus instructed his Saxon allies to make for Prague, and after clearing away the anaemic defenders, the city was captured from the Imperialists on 15 November. It did not take long for many of the exiles of the old Bohemian revolt to return – their experiences of the 1618-20 revolt which had ignited the conflict must have seemed like a lifetime ago, utterly detached from the mad disintegration of the old order which the Swedish King's triumph now presented.

Yet beneath the splendour of Gustavus' achievements must have resided several question marks. For one, it had been in the name of the Elector of Saxony, rather than the Swedish king, that Prague had been seized. This was because, following the rupture of the Saxon forces at Breitenfeld, Gustavus had determined to alter his original plans for Germany. Rather than march to Prague and then Vienna personally, as he had planned with John George, he elected to plunder the Rhine basin instead, abandon Vienna, and leave Prague to the Saxons. This change of plan, claims Wedgewood, was because Gustavus had learned he could not trust the Saxons.[99] Yet, it is also possible that another difficult military campaign appealed to Gustavus less than a more comfortable pillaging of Catholic lands, which would certainly have been preferred by his emboldened soldiers.

It is generally known that he lacked maps which detailed the geography of Germany beyond certain points of Pomerania. However, connected to this lack of geographic information was the Swedish King's lack of *demographic* information, seen most notably in Gustavus' failure to comprehend the limits of German wealth. In the course of his spate of conquering down the Rhine and Main, the Swedish King demanded fantastic sums in the hundreds of thousands of thalers, which German cities and rulers could never have paid in full or on time. And whatever was paid, Gustavus always demanded more; 240,000 thalers was demanded from Augsburg in Bavaria in 1632, even though the taxes for the city traditionally raised no more than 50,000 thalers. Wurzburg was ordered to pay 150,000 thalers in October 1631, immediately after it was conquered, a policy which Gustavus applied to other new conquests too, but which completely upset the delicate financial balance in war-torn Germany.

These German towns were rarely capable of producing such enormous sums on such short notice, forcing them to open new lines of credit which they could never repay. Then, after taking on the debt, Gustavus would demand even more; nine months after capturing Wurzburg and taking the bishopric 'into our royal protection and shelter', Gustavus was demanding another 200,000 thalers. When he arrived in Mainz, Gustavus demanded 80,000 thalers from the apoplectic citizens within less than a fortnight – a figure *eighteen times* its usual tax income. By June 1632, after giving 1,500 thalers a week – all the city fathers could afford – Mainz simply ran out of money, and its impoverished neighbours could not afford to loan it more. Gustavus would insist, almost certainly truthfully, that he needed the constant injection of funds to feed the bottomless pit of an army eighty thousand strong by Christmas 1631.

And these costs were only set to increase; by spring 1633 subsidies were only bringing Sweden 2.5 million thalers a year, while the total price tag of its army was nearing ten million thalers annually, a crippling sum which was plainly unsustainable.[100] Thus continued one of the terrible and fundamental problem of the Thirty Years War, where the sheer size of armies more than outmatched the country's capacity to support them. The shortfall would be made up by bleeding the citizens dry.

Yet, it should be said that Gustavus was not unique in his approach to wresting financial sums from his neighbours. The Swedish King was only adhering to a policy of 'contributions' which Wallenstein had first conceived in the late 1620s. Yet, it would seem that while the King's system of contributions suffered from the same problems of wastage and corruption as Wallenstein's had, the latter's had at least been more sustainable.[101] And speaking of Wallenstein, his name was increasingly on the lips of the Emperor and his advisors in 1631, particularly after Breitenfeld had been learned of. Dismissed in autumn 1630 to appease the princes of the Empire, within the year, the Emperor was relying on Wallenstein to reverse the season of disasters which had befallen the Imperial position. Wallenstein, as it happened, was eager to return, for personal as well as political reasons. While Germany had been overtaken by the Swedish advance, Wallenstein's extensive estates in Bohemia and Central Germany lay in the path of the invaders.

If his financial situation had been bad upon his dismissal, a year later it was desperately bleak, to the extent that Wallenstein was 'concerning himself anxiously with sums of money which previously he would scarcely have noticed.'[102] It was plain that the only way to rectify this state of affairs was to bow to the increasingly desperate pleas of his Emperor to return, for it was also clear that he would not be able to rely on the retreating Count Tilly to save his lands and future. Indeed, if Wallenstein wished to avoid becoming a landless refugee, and if he wished to protect the incredible gains in land and titles which his rise in stature had granted, then he could do no other than enter the field again, raise an army on his own reputation, and challenge the might of the Swedish King. Thus, 1632 promised to host a showdown more incredible than 1631; it would be the Lion of the North, versus the Emperor's champion.

Chapter 16 Notes

[1]Gary Dean Peterson, *Warrior Kings of Sweden*, p. 151.
[2]Quoted in Wilson, *Sourcebook*, p. 131.
[3]Minutes from meeting of Swedish Council of State on 4th May 1630, individual quoted first as 'one figure' refers to Gustafsson Oxenstierna, the son of the Swedish Chancellor. All quoted from *Ibid*, pp. 130-131.
[4]Wilson, *Europe's Tragedy*, pp. 461-462.
[5]See John G. Gagliardo, *Germany under the Old Regime, 1600-1790* (London: Longman, 1991), p. 56.
[6]The manifesto is provided by Wilson, *Sourcebook*, pp. 122-130.
[7]Pärtel Piirimäe, 'Just War in Theory and Practice: The Legitimation of Swedish Intervention in the Thirty Years War', *The Historical Journal*, Vol. 45, No. 3 (Sep., 2002), pp. 499-523; pp. 504-506.
[8]This reply is quoted from Wilson, *Sourcebook*, p. 134.
[9]Pärtel Piirimäe, 'Just War in Theory and Practice', pp. 507-508.
[10]Wilson, *Europe's Tragedy*, pp. 462-463.
[11]Pärtel Piirimäe, 'Just War in Theory and Practice', pp. 510-511.
[12]A. W. Ward, G. W. Prothero, and Stanley Leathes, eds., *The Cambridge Modern History*, vol. 4 (Cambridge: University Press, 1902), pp. 190-191.
[13]Pärtel Piirimäe, 'Just War in Theory and Practice', pp. 514-515.
[14]See Wilson, *Europe's Tragedy*, pp. 459-460.
[15]*Ibid*, p. 460.
[16]Michael Roberts, 'The Political Objectives of Gustavus Adolphus in Germany 1630-1632', *Transactions of the Royal Historical Society*, Vol. 7 (1957), pp. 19-46; p. 22.
[17]John G. Gagliardo, *Germany under the Old Regime, 1600-1790*, pp. 55-57.
[18]C. R. L. Fletcher, *Gustavus Adolphus and the Struggle of Protestantism for Existence* (New York: G. P. Putnam's Sons, 1890), p. 138.
[19]Andrew A. Stomberg, *A History of Sweden* (New York: Macmillan, 1931), p. 354.
[20]A good summary of the crisis is provided by Mario Turchetti, 'Religious Concord and Political Tolerance in Sixteenth- and Seventeenth- Century France', *The Sixteenth Century Journal*, Vol. 22, No. 1 (Spring, 1991), pp. 15-25.
[21]See Parker, *Europe in Crisis*, p. 219.
[22]Pieter Geyl, *History of the Dutch-Speaking Peoples*, pp. 375-377.
[23]Parker, *Europe in Crisis*, pp. 190-191.
[24]David Mathew, *The Age of Charles I* (London: Eyre & Spottiswoode, 1951), pp. 54-56.
[25]A. Lloyd Moote, *Louis XIII, the Just* (Berkeley, CA: University of California Press, 1989), p. 204.
[26]David Parrott, *Richelieu's Army: War, Government, and Society in France, 1624-1642* (Cambridge, England: Cambridge University Press, 2001), pp. 100-101.
[27]Quoted in John Matusiak, *Europe in Flames: The Crisis of the Thirty Years War* (The History Press; Gloucestershire, 2018), p. 365.
[28]*Ibid*, loc. 3833.
[29]Gagliardo, *Germany under the Old Regime, 1600-1790*, p. 57.
[30]Quoted in Moote, *Louis XIII*, p. 206.
[31]See Orest A. Ranum, *Richelieu and the Councillors of Louis XIII: A Study of the Secretaries of State and Superintendents of Finance in the Ministry of Richelieu, 1635-1642* (Oxford, England: Clarendon Press, 1963), pp. 38-40.
[32]John L. Stevens, *History of Gustavus Adolphus* (New York: G. P. Putnam's Sons, 1884), p. 159.
[33]Wilson, *Sourcebook*, p. 140.
[34]Moote, *Louis XIII*, p. 208.
[35]Parrott, *Richelieu's Army*, p. 102.
[36]R. Stradling, 'Olivares and the origins of the Franco-Spanish War, 1627–1635', *English Historical Review*, 101 (1986), pp. 68-94; pp. 83-4.
[37]See Porshnev, *Muscovy and Sweden in the Thirty Years War*, pp. 179-181.
[38]Communique from 24 March 1631 quoted in Wilson, *Sourcebook*, p. 119.
[39]See Parker, *Europe in Crisis*, p. 220.
[40]*Ibid*, p. 220.
[41]See Wilson, *Europe's Tragedy*, p. 468.
[42]C. R. L. Fletcher, *Gustavus Adolphus and the Struggle of Protestantism for Existence* (New York: G. P. Putnam's Sons, 1890), pp. 141-143.
[43]Adapted from Wilson, *Sourcebook*, pp. 151-152.

[44]Porshnev, *Muscovy and Sweden*, p. 181.

[45]See *Ibid*, pp. 182-184.

[46]See: Hans Medick and Pamela Selwyn, 'Historical Event and Contemporary Experience: The Capture and Destruction of Magdeburg in 1631', *History Workshop Journal*, No. 52 (Autumn, 2001), pp. 23-48; pp. 23-25.

[47]Wedgewood, *Thirty Years War*, pp. 276-277.

[48]*Ibid*, p. 279.

[49]Porshnev, *Muscovy and Sweden*, p. 185.

[50]The idea that the peasants and lower classes agitated against their betters has been over-emphasised by Porshnev, *Muscovy and Sweden*, pp. 185-190. This focus on Porshnev's part is to be expected, since his work was originally published during the 1960s and 70s Soviet Union. The counterargument to this focus is best provided by Sheilagh C. Ogilvie, 'Germany and the Seventeenth-Century Crisis', *The Historical Journal*, Vol. 35, No. 2 (June 1992), pp. 417-441; especially pp. 424-427.

[51]Quoted in Wilson, *Sourcebook*, pp. 147-148.

[52]See Wilson, *Europe's Tragedy*, pp. 468-470.

[53]Wilson, *Sourcebook*, p. 150.

[54]*Ibid*, pp. 149-150.

[55]Quoted in Hans Medick and Pamela Selwyn, 'Historical Event and Contemporary Experience', p. 30.

[56]See *Ibid*, p. 31.

[57]See John Roger Paas, 'The Changing Image of Gustavus Adolphus on German Broadsheets, 1630-3', *Journal of the Warburg and Courtauld Institutes*, Vol. 59 (1996), pp. 205-244; p. 222.

[58]Fletcher, *Gustavus Adolphus and the Struggle of Protestantism for Existence*, p. 168.

[59]Paas, 'The Changing Image of Gustavus Adolphus on German Broadsheets', pp. 222-223.

[60]Wilson, *Europe's Tragedy*, pp. 470-471.

[61]Fletcher, *Gustavus Adolphus and the Struggle of Protestantism for Existence*, p. 170.

[62]Quoted in Wilson, *Sourcebook*, p. 136.

[63]*Ibid*, pp. 170-171.

[64]Wilson, *Sourcebook*, pp. 136-137.

[65]*Ibid*, p. 137.

[66]*Ibid*, p. 142.

[67]*Ibid*, p. 142.

[68]Wilson, *Europe's Tragedy*, p. 465.

[69]See Fletcher, *Gustavus Adolphus*, pp. 174-175.

[70]Wilson, *Europe's Tragedy*, p. 471.

[71]Friedrich Schiller, *The Works of Frederick Schiller: Historical*, trans. A. J. W. Morrison (London: Bell & Daldy, 1873), p. 150.

[72]*Ibid*, p. 150.

[73]See Mortimer, *Wallenstein*, pp. 127-131.

[74]Quoted in Parker, *Europe in Crisis*, p. 223.

[75]Wedgewood, *Thirty Years War*, p. 285.

[76]Quoted in Parker, *Thirty Years War*, p. 113.

[77]Quoted in Wilson, *Sourcebook*, p. 139.

[78]Wilson, *Europe's Tragedy*, p. 472.

[79]Quoted in Schiller, *The Works*, p. 153.

[80]Quoted in Schiller, *The Works of Frederick Schiller*, p. 154.

[81]Wilson, *Europe's Tragedy*, p. 475.

[82]Quoted in *Ibid*, p. 472.

[83]Stevens, *History of Gustavus Adolphus*, p. 323.

[84]Quoted in *Ibid*, pp. 323-324.

[85]Gustavus' changing objectives before and after Breitenfeld are assessed by M. Roberts, 'The Political Objectives of Gustavus Adolphus in Germany 1630-1632', *Transactions of the Royal Historical Society*, Vol. 7 (1957), pp. 19-46; especially pp. 31-36.

[86]See John Matusiak, *Europe in Flames*, pp. 307-309.

[87]Andrew A. Stomberg, *A History of Sweden*, p. 357.

[88]Fletcher, *Gustavus Adolphus and the Struggle of Protestantism for Existence*, pp. 188-193.

[89]Wilson, *Europe's Tragedy*, p. 475.

[90]*Ibid*, pp. 476-477.

[91]Stomberg, *A History of Sweden*, p. 358.

[92]Wilson, *Europe's Tragedy*, pp. 476-477.

[93]John Roger Paas, 'The Changing Image of Gustavus Adolphus on German Broadsheets, 1630-3', p. 223.

[94]Analysis of this broadsheet is provided by *Ibid*, pp. 223-226.

[95]See M. Roberts, 'The Political Objectives of Gustavus Adolphus in Germany 1630-1632', p. 33.

[96]Wilson, *Europe's Tragedy*, p. 477.

[97]Open letter is quoted in Wilson, *Sourcebook*, pp. 171-172.

[98]Wedgewood, *Thirty Years War*, pp. 295-296.

[99]*Ibid*, p. 295.

[100]Matusiak, *Europe in Flames*, p. 347.

[101]For an analysis of these financial issues see Wilson, *Europe's Tragedy*, pp. 481-483.

[102]Mortimer, *Wallenstein*, p. 134.

(Top left) Johan Baner
(Top right) Gustav Horn

(Top left) Lennart Torstenson (David Beck, 1700)
(Top right) Queen Christina of Sweden (Sebastien Biurdon)

CHAPTER SEVENTEEN
"To Hell and Back Again"

ONE
Cementing the Triumph

In the opening weeks of 1632, a forlorn figure made his way ponderously along terrible roads, following the flow of several major rivers, before arriving in the court of the King of Sweden. As he arrived, this exile, former King and dispossessed Elector must have marvelled at his transformed fortunes. Indeed, it was to be marvelled that after a decade in fierce opposition to the Emperor, Frederick V, the Elector Palatine and former King of Bohemia, was finally in the winner's circle. By late February, Gustavus had reconquered much of the Lower Palatinate, leaving only a couple of fortresses, held by sickly Spanish soldiers, out of reach. Frederick met the Swedish King for the first time at Mainz, shortly after his forces had taken the strategically important Palatine town of Bad Kreuznach.[1]

The town had the distinction of passing into new owners *seven times* during the entirety of the conflict, and its population would dwindle from eight thousand to three and a half thousand souls by the war's end. While Bad Kreuznach's suffering was not unique, German contemporaries evidently empathised with the plight of its inhabitants; the phrase 'He was born at Kreuznach' became a byword for someone who had to struggle with severe hardship.[2] Frederick certainly knew of hardship, but he surely hoped that his plight, like that of Bad Kreuznach, was at an end. Unfortunately, he would be wrong on both counts. Initially, the two men got on well together, with Gustavus even scolding one of his subordinates for failing to address Frederick as the legitimate King of Bohemia. The struggle for the Bohemian crown and the Defenestration of Prague which preceded it must have seemed like a lifetime ago to the Swedish conqueror and his party of exiles, rebels and opportunists, but despite Frederick's total dependence upon him, Gustavus was well aware of Frederick's usefulness to his campaign.

Gustavus' reasoning was simple and captured by a contemporary: 'always it is good, the two Kings should be together, for as Bohemia is protected by Sweden, so Sweden is justified by Bohemia.' In 1629, when he had listed the cast of German princes who would have to be restored to satisfy the *status quo ante bellum*, Gustavus had placed the Winter King at the top of the list. Unless the Palatine problem was solved, Gustavus understood, there could be no opportunity for a lasting peace in Germany. This Palatine problem revolved around several issues; first, the occupation of its major towns and fortresses by Spanish troops, which the strategic situation of 1630-32 was actually helping to solve by itself. Second, there was the problem of Bavaria; with Maximillian being granted the title of Elector, and clearly unwilling to revert to his old position of a mere Duke, it was evident that the two Wittelsbach cousins would have to find some form of compromise. Thus, the presence of Ferdinand II's nemesis in his camp legitimised Gustavus' campaign, but Frederick also boasted important connections with the English and Dutch that the Swedish King was eager to make the most of.[3]

As expected, Gustavus wanted money and a military contribution from Britain, ruled by Frederick's brother in law, the ill-fated King Charles. Gustavus' demands were not politically opportunistic though; in fact, they were motivated by sound military logic. There was little use in clearing the enemy from the Palatinate and placing Frederick back in Heidelberg as though nothing had happened – this would have made Frederick a constant burden on Swedish resources. Frederick lacked any means to defend himself, and his enemies in Bavaria above all were still in the field. It would therefore be necessary to deal with these Bavarian enemies and to defeat Count Tilly once again first. But, as Cardinal Richelieu would have noted, Sweden could not play a role in attacking Bavarian forces, due to the neutrality agreement which Sweden and Bavaria were supposed to enjoy, at least according to the secret Treaty of Fontainebleau. To Gustavus, and evidently also to Maximillian of Bavaria, that Treaty had been little more than a piece of paper. As John Matusiak noted:

> ...the events of the last twelve months had effectively disposed of any such fantasies, after Bavarian money, Bavarian troops and Bavaria's general had helped fight – and lose – the Battle of Breitenfeld. By March 1632 indeed, all thought of Bavarian neutrality was, in Oxenstierna's words, 'sunk' after an incriminating letter from Maximillian to the Emperor was successfully intercepted...[4]

It was with the confrontation of Bavarian forces and Count Tilly in mind that Gustavus led his forces up the Main and towards an encounter with Maximillian. Frederick V accompanied him, eager, no doubt, to watch his Bavarian foe gain some measure of comeuppance. In fact, Gustavus had been moved to act as one of his subordinates, Gustav Horn, had been outmanoeuvred by Tilly's force of twenty-two thousand men at Bamberg on 9 March. After a short encounter, Horn had withdrawn from the town, and while Tilly had not been strong enough to pursue, the defeat had shown Gustavus, and other Germans, that the Bavarians and Tilly were not finished yet. If he wished to maintain his momentum, Gustavus would have to demonstrate that he had not lost a step, and that he could always be depended on to lead his men to victory.[5]

The Bavarians were certainly aware that the Swedish King was on his way. Accompanied by Maximillian, Tilly attempted to anticipate where Gustavus would move next. Since he wished to invade Bavaria, Gustavus would have to contend with the Danube which divided the Electorate, and which would force him to choose between the northern or southern side. Gustavus chose to invade the southern part of Bavaria, because this contained Munich, Maximillian's capital, and the greatest booty could surely be found there. To reach Munich though, Gustavus would have to cross another river, the Lech. On 14 April 1632, Gustavus finally reached the River Lech, and drew his men up opposite Tilly's camp on the far side of the riverbank.

The Lech presented a formidable obstacle, as melted snows and spring rains had caused it to swell to four metres deep in places. Unless he found a place to ford the river, there was no way the Swedish King would be able to get his men across. It was necessary to begin scouting up and down the river for such an opportunity, and Gustavus ensured his cannons kept up a heavy rate of fire just opposite Tilly's camp as he did so. After a while, two potential opportunities were discovered, and Gustavus conceived of an ingenious plan. He made very public use of one crossing further down the river, which compelled Tilly to send men to meet him, but just then, his fast-moving cavalry a kilometre up the river splashed across a hidden ford, and Tilly's detachment was trapped. Tilly wasted little time deciding what to do next – his twenty thousand or so men were outnumbered and outgunned by Gustavus' thirty-seven thousand soldiers, and after a brief encounter, Tilly ordered the retreat.

Or at least, Tilly would have ordered it, had he not been struck with a cannonball in the thigh, and slipped into unconsciousness. Command had then passed to Maximillian, and the Bavarian Elector wasted no time ordering the retreat to Regensburg. Appreciating that he could not possibly defend Munich, and that Regensburg held special significance as the communications hub for Imperial and Bavarian soldiers, Maximillian thus sacrificed his capital to the invaders. Upon crossing at the Lech, with his nemesis in Tilly defeated, one thousand prisoners captured and the Bavarian chancellery on the run, Gustavus took the opportunity to enter Munich in triumph on 17 May.[6]

Among other things, he played tennis with Frederick V in Maximillian's personal tennis court, and he exhumed 119 of the cannons which the Bohemians had lost at the Battle of White Mountain, and which Maximillian had symbolically buried. Maximillian had not left his beloved Bavaria wholly defenceless though, and as he had marched in the retreat from the Lech, he filled the fortresses of Ingolstadt and Regensburg with more men, diluting his own personal defences, but guaranteeing that a Bavarian resistance would be kept alive. In this mission, the Bavarian peasantry did a great deal of heavy lifting themselves, erupting in revolt for the duration of the Swedish occupation, engaging in tit for tat atrocities with the invaders, and sharpening the religious differences of the two sides. A brief appearance by Gustavus in the Munich's cathedral, where he attended a Catholic mass, did nothing to ease these differences.[7]

We imagine that revenge would have tasted very sweet indeed to Frederick, who finally got even with his cousin for deposing him and seizing his lands and titles a decade before. It was a dramatic turnaround, to go from penniless refugee to playing tennis on the personal tennis court of one's greatest foe. However, while the triumphal procession into Munich was hugely symbolic, and spoke of the extent to which the fortunes of war had changed, Frederick's ordeal was far from over. Though he marvelled at Gustavus' energy and successes, noting that he 'would not think of resting, while he was in the field', Frederick was no closer to having a deal for his restoration to the ruined Palatinate hammered out. Indeed, he was beginning to harbour feelings of apprehension towards Gustavus which would only intensify as time went on. 'The King continues to show me plentiful affection; I am negotiating with him. I want to hope that all will go well', he wrote, in a letter to his wife Elizabeth in March.

Shortly after writing this letter, and shortly before he and Gustavus had moved out, Gustavus' first offer was communicated to Frederick. The terms of this offer were, according to Frederick, 'very high', but not impossible to fulfil. Gustavus wanted freedom of worship for Lutherans in Frederick's Calvinist Palatinate; he wanted the right to occupy all Palatine fortresses as long as the war lasted, and he wanted Frederick to acknowledge Gustavus' direction of the war, so that Frederick 'should not depend upon any other king, prince, body or state, but only on His Majesty [of Sweden].'[8] As the historian Michael Roberts has noted in his extensive biographies of Gustavus Adolphus, the Swedish King had no intention of transforming Frederick into a mere vassal of Sweden.[9] What Gustavus wanted was for Frederick to support him, during the war and afterwards, but upon these early impressions of his demands, Frederick did not expect the negotiations with Gustavus to be concluded any time soon, writing to his wife that 'the talks with the King of Sweden will be stretched out endlessly.'

There was also some concern over Gustavus' demands for religious toleration – did these not conflict with the principle of 'whose rule, his religion', as laid down in the 1555 Augsburg settlement? One gets the feeling that Gustavus' demands for toleration, even while they mostly gelled with Frederick's natural inclinations anyway, rubbed the Elector Palatine the wrong way, and this friction continued into the year. At this point, he was hopeful the negotiations would bear fruit, and he was content to travel with Gustavus towards the aforementioned encounter with Tilly at the River Lech, and onto Munich.[10] True to form, Gustavus also wrested more than 160,000 thalers from the residents of Munich during his ten day stay, and by the time he had taken in the sights of that city, his old foe from Breitenfeld, Count Tilly, succumbed to the wounds he suffered at the Lech. In a stroke, after a glittering career and countless triumphs, one of greatest commanders on the Habsburg side was gone. Gustavus could not afford to rest on his laurels, as the removal of one agent of the Emperor merely paved the way forward for another – before the year was out, he would have to confront Wallenstein, who had worked his way through Bohemia, ejected the unreliable Saxons and had rebuilt an army of more than sixty thousand men.[11]

Wallenstein had been busy in early 1632, pushing back John George of Saxony's reeling army – after its poor behaviour and penchant for plunder, the Bohemians were not likely to mourn them.[12] Unwilling to strike the killer blow, as his aim was to detach John George from Gustavus' side rather than destroy him, Wallenstein placed men on the borders with Saxony and Bohemia in early May, while he moved off to confront the Swedish King. While Gustavus' efforts to turn back the clock in Bohemia had failed, his impact upon the Empire, upon the strategic balance in the Rhine, and even upon the war between the Spanish and Dutch was profound. Indeed, his moves along the Rhine in the autumn of 1631 compelled several German potentates there to seek French protection, and one of these, the Archbishop of Trier, successfully did so. As a knock-on effect of Gustavus' Rhineland campaigns and the Dutch successes in the Spanish Netherlands, Madrid had been forced to redirect troops out of Alsace, thus placing that Duchy in danger as well. Rather than allow such a strategically important territory to fall into Swedish hands, Richelieu advocated an invasion of Lorraine in December 1631, which effectively handed the territory to France in the Peace of Vic the following January.[13]

Now that their positions along the Rhine had been seriously compromised, and their supply route to the Spanish Netherlands cut off by the presence of so many Protestant soldiers, Spain's strategic situation had gone from advantageous in early 1630 to ruinous. With the death of their old policy of simultaneously supplying the Spanish Netherlands and surrounding France through the Rhine, the Spanish campaigns against the Dutch died shortly thereafter. The interconnected nature of the Habsburg theatres of war was on full display once more, and after some secret negotiations, some distinguished citizens from Brussels actually made their way to The Hague with a stunning offer. In return for land, money, protection and titles, it was said, many in the Spanish Netherlands would be willing to throw off the

Spanish yolk altogether and unite with the Dutch. Following some talks in this direction, in late May 1632, the Dutch States-General sent a letter to the Spanish Netherlands urging them...

> ...to follow the praiseworthy example of their forefathers in liberating themselves from the heavy and intolerable yolk of the Spaniards and their adherents, and of their own free will to join themselves unto these United Provinces, to which end we offer them our strong and effectual assistance by the army which we have put into the field under the wise and courageous, and withal prudent, leadership of His Excellency, the Lord Frederick Henry, Prince of Orange; and we herewith religiously and irrevocably promise unto the aforesaid provinces that we will conserve and maintain the towns and members of the same, likewise their inhabitants, as well spiritual and secular, of whatever state, quality and condition they may be, in their privileges, rights and liberties, as well as in the public exercise of the Roman Catholic Religion, desiring for ourselves to live, deal and converse with the same as good friends, neighbours and allies.[14]

This was a stunning offer – a guarantee of religious freedom to the citizens of the Spanish Netherlands, in return for their incorporation into the Dutch Republic. What a coup it would be if the Brussels administration could be forced to agree. With Spanish aid far away, and the unpopularity of the war mounting within Brussels and without, there were even rumours that cries of 'Long live the Prince of Orange' had been heard in the streets. To maintain the pressure, Frederick Henry, as the military and political leader of the Republic, determined to lead a large host against Maastricht.

Maastricht, by summer 1632, represented a critical hub whereby the Habsburgs' two wars in the Netherlands and the Empire would be protected. Capture Maastricht, and the Emperor and King of Spain would be cut off from each other like never before. Thus, it is not surprising, though still striking, that in the absence of a Spanish relief force, an Imperial army under the command of Pappenheim made its way to relieve Maastricht once Frederick Henry placed it under siege on 10 June. Considering the Emperor's failure to wrest any declaration of war on the Dutch from the German princes in the 1630 Regensburg meeting, this appeared like a significant step towards a policy which his allies had not countenanced. As it happened though, the movement of armies of different nationalities and the undeclared wars which went with them had become a feature of the interconnected conflicts raging across the continent by this point. It was through such undeclared war, after all, that France and Spain had been able to tear lumps out of each in North Italy, that the Turks had sent their vassals against the Emperor, and Wallenstein had previously sent his men against the King of Sweden during his Polish Wars, and indeed, as Gustavus himself had done when sending soldiers to relieve Stralsund.

Occasionally, they could spark a conflagration, but only when at least one side strongly wished it to, as Gustavus did when he alluded to Wallenstein's intervention in Sweden's wars in the late 1620s as a *casus belli* for him. As the Habsburgs had come to learn by 1632, it all depended on the unfortunate power on the other end of this suspicious military aid, and the Dutch treated the Habsburgs as hostile in both camps, just as the Spanish treated the Swedes as such when their armies appeared outside of their Rhineland garrisons.[15] On this occasion however, Habsburg efforts to swap their armies between unrelated fronts did not work, as the intervention was unsuccessful, and Maastricht did fall on 22 August. 'Following s'Hertogenbosch', noted the historian Pieter Geyl, 'here was another conquest to impress all of Europe; the fame of the cautious but persevering Frederick Henry bade fair to rival that of the dashing Gustavus Adolphus.'

In the event, it was while Frederick Henry besieged Maastricht that the native Spanish government regained control of the situation. Many of the more loyal citizens in the Spanish Netherlands were unwilling to act without the support of France, which failed to materialise, but the series of events which led some to contemplate such extreme action were not easily forgotten. In particular, Dutch offers to tolerate Catholicism made 'a deep impression', and a rebellious enthusiasm for the dynamic Prince of Orange was hard to supress. Considering this, the Governess of the Spanish Netherlands, who happened to be the aunt of King Philip IV of Spain, reacted swiftly. She welcomed back discontented loyalists to Brussels by flattery, reminding them that 'they should disdain a simple States' government, where a loutish and ill-mannered burgomaster can lay down the law.'[17]

When that did not go all the way to appeasing the more recalcitrant nobles, the decision was made to convene the States-General assembly in Brussels on 9 September 1632. This assembly had not met in over thirty years, and its major goal from the beginning was to arrive at suitable peace terms would the Dutch – since they would not join them, and could not beat them, it remained to end the war with them, which had dragged on for nearly seventy years. Madrid, as before, was unwilling to allow the citizens of the Spanish Netherlands to conduct peace negotiations with plenipotentiary powers, and demanded a final say in any probing discussions with the Dutch. The troubles of Spain's European patrimony were not wholly solved though, and there remained a latent school of thought which advocated independence from Spain, rather than union with the Dutch. Still, the differences of opinion between the relevant parties meant that no group was large enough to launch any kind of coup against the lawful Habsburg government, so while the immediate danger had passed, a clear message of the earnest desire which the Spanish Netherlanders had for peace had been sent.[18]

In such a way did the ripples caused by Gustavus' invasion of Germany create great headaches and crises for Spain. By summer 1632 Madrid had lost virtually all of its holdings along the Rhine and was no longer able to threaten France on its eastern border for the first time in several decades. Gustavus' rampage through Germany had been tremendously significant, but had it been wholly successful? On the contrary, according to Peter H. Wilson, Gustavus 'was a victim of his own success during autumn 1631.' The speed and scale of the Imperial collapse in Germany along the Rhine, in Bavaria, and in Bohemia with the initial triumph at Breitenfeld had the effect of opening up a vacuum 'sucking the Swedes and their new allies in all directions, further regionalising the war and hindering coordination.' Just as the Imperials collapsed too fast, so too did Gustavus *expand* too fast, leaving many supposedly conquered areas in fact still populated by formidable fortresses with strong garrisons.[19]

Meanwhile, in places where no Imperial soldiery existed, the Swedes did not ingratiate themselves upon the citizens along the Rhine, in Bavaria or even in Bohemia. By this point in the conflict, it was not difficult to find individuals in Gustavus' army who had been spurned by its initial salvos, or who had lost everything to a Catholic neighbour or rival and now thirsted for revenge. 'The Church lands', Wilson recorded, 'were treated as conquests', adding that:

> Supply arrangements were no more efficient than those of the Imperial and League armies, and Gustavus' famous disciplinary code was ignored by his own officers who took what they wanted. Bad treatment extended to allies. Gustavus made fine speeches on his entry into the important Protestant city of Nuremburg on 31 March 1632, but immediately obliged it to surrender its war material from its arsenal and allow its infantry regiment to be incorporated in his own army.[20]

Gustavus granted titles and land to ambitious subordinates and spurned the idea of restoring or respecting the former inhabitants. He was, according to Geoffrey Parker, 'a force that no one could control', and after Breitenfeld...

> ...a new harshness of speech and rudeness of manner became apparent. The king no longer attempted to disguise his contempt for his German allies, his indifference to the wishes of his foreign supporters, his resentment of any interference with his plans. Having achieved his victories in 1631 almost without help, pride seems to have gotten the better of him in 1632.[21]

Notwithstanding Gustavus' increasing self-confidence, even had the Swedish King boasted the most magnanimous disposition Europe had ever seen, the terrible outcome of the war would have been the same. The invasion of Bavaria blunted some of Gustavus' momentum, especially as his men stayed behind to plunder it as May became June, and the countryside was set alight.

'Your grace would no longer recognise poor Bavaria' exclaimed Maximillian to his brother, 'such cruelty has been unheard of in this war.'[22] Maximillian might well have added that his brother would no longer recognise the war, for it had burst violently out of its initial confines as a Bohemian revolt by the summer of 1632.

By then, both Gustavus and Wallenstein had worked their cruel magic to recruit unsustainable levels of men, with some estimates as high as one hundred thousand on each side. Germany had no way of supplying these two hundred thousand soldiers, let alone the citizens who were trapped in the middle of the divide, and merely wished to survive. The political need had also superseded Gustavus' military strategic requirements; these one hundred thousand men could not be brought to bear at once, but were spread out across Germany, partially as a means of securing the loyalty of other German princes, partially to fulfil the cycle of violence which would maintain pressure upon the Emperor.[23] Alas, after doing his utmost to cement his triumph, it was time Gustavus turned his full attention towards the Emperor's servant. If Wallenstein could be defeated, then nothing would stand in the way of Gustavus and his expanding vision for a Germany under Swedish control.

Swedish triumph had brought Frederick V to Gustavus' side, but these same triumphs forced Wallenstein to get back on his horse, and fight for the Emperor once again. The deal which he made with the Emperor in February 1632 had allowed for a period of service of only three months – an incredibly optimistic clause, because Wallenstein would have known he was the Emperor's last chance. Yet, Wallenstein also knew that he was not in good health, and that campaigning did nothing to improve his painful gout. He also wished to have some sort of option to extricate himself from the command, should he feel the need.[24] By April though, the Emperor's subordinates were making no effort to disguise their belief that Wallenstein would be staying indefinitely.

In the meantime, Wallenstein had conducted an extensive correspondence, supposedly in secret, with John George of Saxony. Moved into opposition due to his Emperor's rash instructions, John George almost certainly never wished to side with the Swedes in the first place, and he had become increasingly concerned at Gustavus' procession throughout Germany. Gustavus could detect this and left the Saxons alone in Bohemia while he moved down the Rhine and into Bavaria. He refused to take John George's men with him for the expected confrontation with Wallenstein, due to their past performance in battle, and the fear that they might defect to Wallenstein at a critical moment. On 16 June, Gustavus erected fortifications outside of Nuremburg, a Protestant city of special strategic importance, as it linked together the Swedish bastion at Pomerania with the Saxon Electorate. Gustavus could not allow it to fall and set six thousand peasants to work emplacing three hundred cannon on the outskirts of the city.

By the time Wallenstein arrived a month later on 17 July, Gustavus' position around Nuremburg was too formidable to challenge. Mindful of his predecessor's failings, Wallenstein determined not to confront Gustavus as Tilly had done at Werben on the Elbe the previous summer, but instead, to prepare an armed camp of his own some ten kilometres away. With a medieval hilltop castle, the Alte Vest, serving as the anchor of his fortified camp, Wallenstein looked to outdo Gustavus in industriousness, constructing a mammoth encampment which put all others to shame. By felling thirteen thousand trees and shifting the equivalent of twenty-one thousand modern truckloads of earth, Wallenstein created what was in effect a fortress sixteen kilometres in circumference.[25]

But that was where the sophisticated tactics ended; for the next few weeks, as the heat of the summer intensified and terrified refugees streamed into Nuremburg in their thousands, a humanitarian disaster threatened. Conditions were nothing short of disgusting, as both camps produced tons of waste, and food shortages combined with the prevalence of rats, flies and disease to produce a situation akin to a nightmare for the average soldier. By mid-August, with neither side budging and reinforcements on route to aid the twenty thousand Swedes, Wallenstein received news that Saxony had invaded Silesia. The move had been conceived by John George to place additional pressure on the Emperor, and wrest from him the peace treaty he desired. To the two encamped adversaries though, the invasion of Silesia had the effect of compelling them to act. Moving out of his base, in the first week of September Gustavus launched several doomed assaults against the Alte Vest which Wallenstein had been expecting once an outlying position had been loudly seized with the aid of the Swedish artillery. The prospects for success were hopeless, and the weather seemed to agree, with a drizzle soaking the wooden pathways and making any act of scrabbling along the slippery wood impossible.

By the time Gustavus pulled away from the Alte Vest, he had suffered some thirty thousand casualties, and possessed only four thousand horses capable of carrying a man, a horrendous, and strangely forgotten blight on the Swedish King's record. The experience must have been utterly debilitating for Gustavus' army; it was demoralising enough to compel eleven thousand men to desert the Lion of the North.[26] Had his roar been expended in that great triumph a year before? Certainly, the anniversary the Breitenfeld triumph on 17 September 1632 would have passed in a sombre mood. The deflating experience of consolidation had proved almost more difficult for the Swedish King than his initial breakthrough – he would need another victory like Breitenfeld if he stood any chance of rectifying the shortcomings of his campaigns in the season. In the meantime, he would winter in the hostile Swabian lands, where Bavarian peasants sharpened their cruel farming implements for a bitter winter of opposition.

The grim picture was interrupted by some troubling, but also exciting news – Wallenstein was marching to Saxony, where he intended to spend the winter. Whatever he had expected Wallenstein to do after the Alte Vest, perhaps he expected him to stay put in his reinforced vantage point, Wallenstein had defied Gustavus' expectations. He had burned his camp on 21 September and made North. After many months of correspondence, the diplomatic line with Saxony had gone dead shortly before the encounter with Gustavus at the Alte Vest. Thereafter, it had become plain that John George of Saxony was determined to make himself a nuisance, and once his forces captured Silesia, even the Emperor was urging Wallenstein to march against Leipzig once again.

Sure enough, the Saxon city was dutifully captured in Wallenstein's name on 1 November, and John George – who had retreated by this point to Torgau – made a point of executing the city's commander in a rage, adding insult to injury by forcing the late commander's widow to pay the cost of the court martial. On 7 November, Wallenstein was joined by his subordinate, Pappenheim on the march to Leipzig, but the two men had no time to catch up. Incredibly, Wallenstein was informed, Gustavus Adolphus had marched a total of six hundred and fifty kilometres at double quick pace in just seventeen days. The advance had cost him four thousand horses, but it re-established the element of surprise which Alte Vest had denied. Now it remained to capture Wallenstein in the net, and Gustavus gained on him over the following days until finally, he could run no longer.

With his eight and a half thousand soldiers, three thousand eight hundred horse and 20 guns, Wallenstein fortified himself twenty kilometres short of Leipzig on the evening of 15 November. The town was called Luzten and contained a smattering of elegant houses in the backdrop of several glittering rivers. It was a beautiful scene, and these two commanders were about to utterly ruin it. Against Wallenstein's wishes, he would now be forced to fight the pitched battle which Gustavus so desperately craved, and the Swedish King was right to be confident, as he outnumbered the enemy with his thirteen thousand foot, six thousand horse and twenty heavy guns. As the sun rose on the morning of 16 November 1632, fog filled the air and obscured the vision of those with even the best eyesight, but regardless, Gustavus insisted on pushing on.[27] Another Breitenfeld surely awaited, and he would smash Wallenstein just as he had smashed Tilly fourteen months before. It had taken far longer than he had wanted, but at long last, the battlefield showdown between the Lion of the North and the servant of the Emperor was about to begin...

TWO
Fatal and Fateful

No engagement of modern times has a greater mass of conflicting records than the battle of Lützen. From the various statements you may sketch out a dozen different theories of the manner in which it was lost and won. It was, however, in the main a simple battle in parallel order, fought out with extraordinary obstinacy, and one whose phases were only those which may always occur in such an action, as the several parts of each line roll forward and back, in response to reinforcements brought up, or to gallant attacks made or repulsed.[28]

This was the introduction retired American General and author Theodore Ayrault Dodge gave to the Battle of Lutzen, in 1890. The controversy surrounding the battle stems mostly from the question of whether it was a Swedish victory or an Imperial victory; more than a century later, Dodge's assertion still rings true. Conflicting reports on what the Battle of Lutzen looked like remain problematic for the historian – even the precise numbers of soldiers on both sides is difficult to pin down. If the historical record is clouded, then so too was the battlefield, as on the morning of 17 November 1632, a heavy fog refused to lift, denying either side a clear line of sight. As battles involving gunpowder tended to do, visibility was further impeded by the abundance of gun smoke hours into the battle. This has created additional conflicting pictures over where each side lined up, what the area of Lutzen looked like, and even what the order of battle looked like for Wallenstein and Gustavus.

Fortunately, we can cut through some of the mythology. Information regarding the number of soldiers, particularly on the Imperial side, have since been filled in thanks largely to the prevalence of Swedish records, which were subsequently accepted as fact by biased accounts, and were then handed down to the reader over the following centuries. These accounts assert the size of Wallenstein's force to be between thirty and forty-eight thousand men, a wildly varied number, and far in excess of what Wallenstein was actually capable of bringing to bear. After having distributed a great number of his soldiers into

Saxony, Wallenstein commanded around 13,900 men, with Pappenheim, his second, on route to reinforce with 5,300 more. These reinforcements were desperately needed, but Gustavus, with his 19,200 men, was also awaiting news of reinforcements from John George of Saxony, before deciding to attack anyway due to his numerical advantage. The exaggeration of the Imperial armies was probably done to add increasing drama to the challenge which Gustavus faced, and to account for the less than stellar outcome of the battle for both sides.[29]

And what was the battle like? At its heart, Lutzen was a bloodbath of the first order. There was nothing pretty, sophisticated or dashing about the way it was fought. Lines of infantry on both sides fired several salvoes, spraying blood and brains on their comrades; sabres and pikes slashed and punctured, disembowelling as they did so; cavalry charged and counter-charged, trampling men underfoot and occasionally subjecting these beats of war to merciless fire, which destroyed horse as much as man; cannon ripped through flesh and bone, sometimes decapitating, sometimes severing a limb in an instant – this was a seventeenth century battlefield, and the chaos and horror which confronted the participant was matched only by the sense of foreboding and terrible responsibility which burdened the commander.[30] It was no wonder pitched battles were rare in the Thirty Years War, especially in comparison to the more decisive sieges. As Gustavus' earlier victory at Breitenfeld had in fact proved, a pitched battle could not win a war, though it could lead to greater opportunities for a successful siege, where more land could be won. Due to the abundance of recruits, indeed, not even the destruction of an army meant the end of the war, particularly when the recruitment pool had enabled both sides to employ as many as one hundred thousand men each. There is something ironic in the fact that after wielding such vast hosts of soldiers for so many months, at the Battle of Lutzen both sides boasted fewer than twenty thousand men each. Twenty thousand, indeed, was the maximum number Gustavus felt comfortable commanding – anymore, said the Swedish King, and it was impossible to coordinate one's men.[31]

And Wallenstein knew well the difficulties of coordination. As he knew just as little of Gustavus' plans as the Swedish King did of his, Wallenstein had attempted to spread his soldiers out, and had seized towns like Halle to the North. Other detachments from Wallenstein's army had moved to occupy several bishoprics, collect contributions, and remove walls to prevent future resistance from the inhabitants. It was by no means clear, in other words, that Wallenstein could have to fight Gustavus at Lutzen, at least not until the morning of 16 November. To compensate for his numerical disadvantage, Wallenstein had taken advantage of several ditches and small anomalies to give his defending musketeers the best strategic position possible. The generalissimo's penchant for establishing a skilful defence had not been greatly tested in the years before, save for the recent experience at the Alte Vest. Here at Lutzen though, in the space of only an evening, Wallenstein had made the most of the terrain at Lutzen to present a formidable challenge to Gustavus.[32] Though he had caught up with him after several days of pursuit, defeating Wallenstein would be another challenge entirely for the Swedish King. Gustavus would not find a trembling foe, mindful of its numerical disadvantage; instead, he found an enemy which greeted his veterans with a grim determination.

What was more, Wallenstein's army was one which had learned the mistakes of Breitenfeld. The aim now was to bring as much firepower to bear on the enemy as possible, so Wallenstein had mostly done away with the larger squares of pike and musket used by Count Tilly to such success before Breitenfeld. He had replaced them with one thousand-man brigades, ten men or sometimes seven men deep, with pikemen standing behind these musketeers and ready to move forward in the ranks in the event of a cavalry charge, or the descent into melee combat. Unwieldy, slow moving squares of pikemen these were not, and we should be cautious when attributing a legendary status to Gustavus' men, while ignoring the equal professionalism of his opponents.[33] Wallenstein's army, after all, would not have been able to withstand the murderous firepower and horrendous conditions of the Battle of Lutzen had it not been a well-oiled machine. As Wallenstein appreciated, well-oiled machines could be clogged up and seize with the advent of battle, so at the end of the day, like so many commanders before him, he relied on the tenacity and forbearance of his men. It came down to a question – how many men could an army lose before it also lost heart? Lutzen would pose this weighted question to both Gustavus and Wallenstein, and the grim conditions of battle would provide the answer one way or another.

True to his previous style at the Battle of Breitenfeld, we are told that Gustavus addressed his Swedish and Finnish soldiers on the morning of the encounter, declaring:

> Beloved compatriots, the day has come for you to show to the world all you have learned in so many campaigns and combats. There is the enemy whom we have so long sought, not intrenched on inaccessible mountains, as at Nuremberg, but standing before you in the plain, not with advantages superior to ours. You know with what care he has hitherto avoided meeting us; and he now accepts battle with reluctance, because he is unable longer to flee. Prepare to show yourselves the brave soldiers you are. Hold firm, stand by each other, and fight valiantly for your religion, your country, and your king; and I will recompense you all, and you shall have reason to thank me. But if you conduct yourselves cowardly, not one of you will repass the Baltic, and again see your native land. May God preserve you all![34]

Then, riding down the battle line, he reached his German captains, and addressed these soldiers:

> My brave brothers and comrades, I urge you, by your Christian belief, your honour, your earthly and eternal welfare, to do your duty as you have always done it since you have been with me; especially since more than a year ago, when, near where we now are, you beat old Tilly. I expect the enemy before you will not escape a like fate. Attack with courage. You go to fight, not only under my eyes, and by my orders, but by my side. I will go at your head and give you the example in exposing my life. Follow me. God, I hope, will give us a victory of which the memory will live with posterity. If not, there is an end of your religion, your liberty, your temporal and eternal welfare.[35]

By contrast, Wallenstein supposedly refrained from addressing his men, not necessarily because he had a 'disagreeable voice' as has been claimed,[36] but because this had never been his style. Instead, the watchword 'Jesus Maria' was established among the troops to distinguish friend from foe in the chaos to come.[37] Indeed, as Richelieu himself had put it, regarding Wallenstein's manner: 'by his sole presence, and the severity of his silence, [he] seemed to make his soldiers understand, that, according to his usual custom, he would recompense them or chastise them.'[38] Words were useful on the morning of a battle, but Wallenstein had accomplished something far more important: he had squeezed as many strategic advantages as possible from the battle site.

Musketeers were placed in ditches which would slow the Swedish cavalry; the main road where the two armies would face each other was dotted with wagons for a better defence; stakes and pointed branches were turned towards the enemy, as had been used at the Alte Vest to murderous effect. Wallenstein was also greatly aided by the stubborn fog which so compromised the view of the Swedish advance guard, though of course, this weather could also hinder his ability to coordinate his soldiers along the mile-long frontline. Possession of skill in coordinating large numbers of men across such a wide front was only possible with experience and by listening to the accumulated wisdom of his subordinates, and Wallenstein was surrounded by such experienced men, such as Piccolomini, who would later distinguish himself against the armies of Louis XIV. For Gustavus too, his list of commanders reads like a veritable who's who of future Swedish military greats, such as Johan Baner, Gustav Horn and Lennart Torstenson, the latter of whom would become most famous for his lightening campaigns against Denmark in the early 1640s, which were so effective that the conflict is often referred to simply as the Torstenson War.[39]

But these considerations were all for the future. As the sun shone weakly through the impenetrable fog at 7.30AM on the morning of 17 November, Gustavus performed his aforementioned speeches, and then marched his army forward. To reach a position where he could properly bring his superiority in numbers to bear against Wallenstein, Gustavus would have to cross the Muhlgraben River. Once he did so, as Wallenstein had predicted, Gustavus' freedom of action would be constrained. If we imagine the battlefield at Lutzen from the Swedish King's perspective, then after lining up in full battle order, the town of Lutzen would be two kilometres forward on the left, having crossed the Muhlgraben River, which flowed northwards under the town and finished in marshland beyond. With these obstacles on his left flank, Gustavus had placed the Flossgraben River behind him. The Flossgraben was a winding river which had been altered to form a canal, so that the inhabitants of Lutzen could easily transport firewood. The Flossgraben flowed at the back of Gustavus' army, before it curved up to his right, so that his army was virtually surrounded by the waters of the Muhlgraben and Flossgraben.

Roughly a kilometre in front of Gustavus was the main road into Lutzen town, and a further kilometre behind that Wallenstein's army was sprawled across a two-kilometre line. What Gustavus could not see from his position was Wallenstein's use of ditches and the environment, such as nearby marshes, to force the Swedes to face him head on. Proper surveying of the battlefield assured Wallenstein that Gustavus' left flank, where the Muhlgraben flowed, had produced a great deal of marshes, and as the river flowed north under the bridge constructed by the citizens of Lutzen, this guaranteed that any effort to outflank the Imperial army by riding around the town would not be possible. Gustavus, indeed, had little intention of attempting such flanking manoeuvres; he was confident that his numerical superiority would carry the day, and Wallenstein's hasty preparations demonstrated that the Imperial generalissimo was anxious about such advantages as well.[40]

The battle was effectively joined at 10AM, after several salvoes from the artillery of both sides, which enabled Gustavus' men to properly form up. Both armies were deployed in two lines, with the best infantry in the first line – Gustavus commanded the Swedish and Finnish horse on the right flank. After a few hours of murderous fire, the Croats on Wallenstein's left fled the field, and it became apparent that the best chance for enveloping Wallenstein would be here. The other side of the battlefield – on Gustavus' left flank – had been rendered impassable thanks to Wallenstein's decision to set Lutzen on fire. A second issue for Gustavus to grapple with was the resulting smoke that the wind blew into the Swedes' eyes, and a third issue was Wallenstein's order of battle, and the fact that the Habsburg commander had concentrated his men most heavily to face Gustavus' left. These factors meant that for the commander of Gustavus' left, Bernhard of Saxe-Weimar, the task of dislodging the Imperials with his three thousand horse was made incredibly difficult. A considerable part of the battle was spent contesting the set of hills next to Lutzen, which Bernhard's men repeatedly tried and failed to seize.

In the Imperial centre line, a fierce bloody battle was fought with the Swedes. The latter were the victors of Breitenfeld, utterly confident in their eventual success, and while they withstood heavy fire from Wallenstein's artillery, answering with their own, routing Wallenstein's centre was proving impossible. The time he had been given the previous night to prepare for Gustavus had paid dividends. Then, in the early afternoon, potential disaster was on the horizon, as the cavalry led by Pappenheim which had moved ahead to capture Halle the previous day had returned, exhausted, on Wallenstein's vulnerable left flank. Pappenheim's return was made possible only by marching thirty-five kilometres through the night, and while his 2,300 horse did not seem like much, they had the potential to turn the tide. They managed to rally the dispersed Croats, and together, this force pushed back the advancing Swedes where Gustavus had once commanded. As the Swedish left flank buckled under the force of Pappenheim's charge, it appears that during this progress Pappenheim himself was hit and mortally wounded.

That the loss of Pappenheim – a dynamic, ambitious and skilled subordinate of Wallenstein's for several years – is not the subject of greater discussion can be explained by the loss of an even greater figure on the same field. Seeing his infantry be repulsed and pushed back across the road, which ran like a red line through both armies, Gustavus returned with all haste to revive the spirits of his men, and it is then that catastrophe seems to have struck. His small party of defenders was set upon, as it became plain that the King was trapped. His retinue worked in vain to save their King, with few left standing by the end. A short time after the exchange, Gustavus was shot, whereupon he finally broke out before being shot again, this time fatally.[41] Much like the smoke and fog hampered the vision of the soldiers, so too has the passage of time, and the presence of so many historical accounts clouded the events at Lutzen. According to the historian John L. Stevens, Gustavus' death was known from an early stage and rather than ruin the morale of the Swedes, it drove them on to victory:

> The death of the king was already generally known, or at least suspected, in the Swedish army. His horse, with its empty saddle, covered with blood, running among the troops, had made known to the Swedish cavalry what had happened to their king. They knew he must have been slain, or was a wounded prisoner in the hands of his enemies. The soldiers of the fallen hero were filled with mingled sentiments of bitter grief, despair, and vengeance. Duke Bernhard made use of this strong feeling of the army, riding through its ranks exclaiming, "Swedes, Finnlanders [sic], and Germans! your defender, the defender of our liberty, is dead. Life is nothing to me if I do not draw bloody vengeance from this misfortune. Whoever wishes to prove he loved the king has only to

follow me to avenge his death." The whole Swedish army, fired by a common enthusiasm, nerved by desperation, advanced to the attack. The death of their king, instead of destroying the courage of these brave troops, excited it into a wild and consuming flame.[42]

Yet, according to other accounts, Bernard was not even aware that the King's death had occurred, nor could Wallenstein have been certain. Meanwhile, many other uncertainties regarding the battlefield still reign – it is not certain if Pappenheim died before or after Gustavus; it is still hotly debated whether Wallenstein made use of one battle line or two; for many years, it was claimed that Wallenstein was carried on a litter, suffering from syphilis, when in fact, it seems more likely that he rode a horse, but suffered terribly from gout.[43] Notwithstanding all these uncertainties, what was not in doubt was that Lutzen had degenerated from a set piece battle with controlled flanks, battle lines and tactics into muddled scenes of unprecedented carnage and slaughter. From the early afternoon, the battle had disintegrated, commanders losing control amidst the poor visibility and confusion which pervaded the field. Upon learning of Gustavus' death, recorded Fletcher, his army plunged headlong into the apocalypse:

> Manoeuvring there was none any longer, it was simply a death-grapple all along the lines. In the first charge the Swedes, maddened by their loss, carried everything before them; the body of their beloved leader was rescued, the hostile guns retaken, and Wallenstein's powder waggons blown into the air... The Swedish footmen died where they stood. The flower of Gustavus's army was cut to pieces. The veterans from the Polish and Livonian wars were not used to running away. Nothing could induce Duke Bernard to retreat, and Torstenson's artillery could still be plied with deadly effect. The Imperialists could get no further than the high road.[44]

Indeed, the battle lines on both sides, spread out over a mile, would have been difficult to coordinate under the best conditions, but as the casualties mounted and desperate news began to filter among the troops, the day was seized by those commanders brave enough either to charge the enemy or resist his attacks. Certain figures like Bernhard of Saxe-Weimar, who reportedly spurred on the Swedish-German left flank to victory before the battle's end, deserve plaudits, but the sheer chaos of the encounter made the gathering of information scarce. Neither side knew how badly the other was affected, until Wallenstein, horrified by the carnage, elected to withdraw before 5PM.

By that point, Bernhard had captured some strategically important hills, and had begun to shell the Imperial centre, but that central line of resistance which Wallenstein had so skilfully created the night before remained resolute. It was an impressive feat, to resist the victors of Breitenfeld for so long, especially when outnumbered, but it was in vain, as Wallenstein's withdrawal, the loss of his cannon and the decimation of more than half of his army meant that Lutzen would by no means be considered a triumph for the Emperor.[45] Nor, of course, could it be considered a triumph for the Swedes. Even had Gustavus survived, Lutzen would have been at best a pyric victory, but his death changed everything about the battle, though it would be another week before Wallenstein was actually able to confirm his death.

Wallenstein could justifiably claim the medal of superior generalship, defending stoutly against great odds, while by contrast, Gustavus attempted to bring his numerical superiority to bear, technically with success, though in the process, the Swedish King seems to have advocated an unimaginative and terribly costly frontal assault of entrenched defensive positions. In response, one could reasonably assert that poor visibility and a lack of good information reduced Gustavus' ability to make good tactical decisions, but this was far from Gustavus' finest hour, and further still from resembling a second Breitenfeld.[46] Wallenstein's army, it was true, was forced out of Saxony in the months that followed, but the celebration of the battle in Vienna made it plain that the deaths of those nameless soldiers and the outcome of that foggy battle mattered less to the war than its greatest casualty. For more than eighteenth months, Gustavus Adolphus had held friends in rapture and appeared to his foes like an invincible punishment from God. But now, he was dead, and with him died the overall control he had wielded over Protestants, Germans, mercenaries, and everyone else in between.

In subsequent years, Gustavus' comrades would remember him. One such comrade in arms was a Scottish officer by the name of Robert Monro, who recalled many years later on the Swedish King:

> Such a General would I gladly serve; but such a General I shall hardly see; whose custom was: to be the first and last in danger himself, gaining his officers' love, in being the companion both of their labours and dangers.[47]

Indeed, Gustavus had shared perhaps too much in the dangers of his men. Had he exposed himself less, had he led from the back rather than from the front of the army, then history would certainly have been different. Unfortunately for the Swedish cause though, Gustavus Adolphus was not the kind of general or King to lead from behind. He would fight in Germany, as he had fought his Polish wars and his wars against Russians and Danes – fully involved, fully determined and often, fully exposed. It was this tradition – of great Swedish warrior kings – which was to be carried forward faithfully, by Gustavus' nephew (Charles X) and great grand-nephew (Charles XII). The tradition was to prove deadly, but also impossible for those warrior kings of Sweden to resist.[48]

Reportedly, none other than Gustavus himself saw his future end in such a manner. In a conversation with his chaplain, as the army converged on Erfurt and rested for a while on 7-10 November, a week before the Battle of Lutzen, Gustavus supposedly confessed: 'Everyone venerates me so, and treats me as some sort of God...the Lord will soon punish me for this.'[49] It is tempting to read too much into such a quote, and to imagine Gustavus predicted he would soon be punished for his hubris, but it is more likely that such a confession, if indeed it was ever made to his chaplain, referred to some misfortune other than his untimely death and the collapse of the Protestant group in Germany. It would have been above Gustavus' imagination to suppose that God would smite him down at the summit of his powers, thereby leaving his people leaderless. Indeed, the leader of God's people was precisely how the German broadsheets had come to depict the Swedish King. As one poet recorded in March 1632:

> Whoever is not stubborn like the Pharaoh,
> Consider how God enticed a cherished hero
> To come here from midnight [i.e. the north].
> He is the consuming fire of our enemy
> Gustavus Adolphus, the king of Sweden,
> Who once received only modest respect.
> Now everyone must admit
> That God can protect us through him.[50]

Nor was this all – other polemics had attempted to use a revisionist approach to all of Gustavus' previous campaigns, be they against Poles, Danes or Russians far removed from the current conflict. This was the purpose of one tract entitled 'The Swedish calling, that is: The dispelling of several incorrect opinions about the current changes in the Holy Roman Empire, and the just reason for it', but that mouthful was only the tip of the iceberg.[51] Another attempted to justify Gustavus' God-like status by presenting him as the literal sword of God, as the fulfiller of several prophecies, and even as a descendant of Noah. Thus one broadsheet was entitled: 'Genealogy, The Royal Swedish Succession from the Flood to present times, compiled by most highly reputed authorities'.[52] By mid-1632 indeed, Gustavus had become so intertwined with this message of Protestant deliverance, that his co-religionists would have found it impossible to imagine the religious struggle without him. Broadsheet after broadsheet depicting Gustavus and his promise of salvation for all Protestants was published during this time, even while Gustavus' military campaigns against the Alte Vest had been frustratingly disappointing. Protestants were encouraged to pray not only for his safety, but also for his help against the Catholic Habsburg tyranny, which only Gustavus was capable of protecting them against. One broadsheet entitled 'A daily greeting in contemplation of the royal portrait' contained the Swedish King's image, and a prayer which was intended to guide the reader. Its first strophe read:

> (O, noble hero, may God protect you,
> And grant you good fortune, blessings and victory
> Against the enemies of Christianity,
> Who for so long have oppressed us.[53]

And we should not assume that Gustavus' death put an end to such proclamations. Instead his death at Lutzen was recast as the sacrifice of the lamb; as the willing martyrdom of a King who faced overwhelming, impossible odds, yet still pushed Protestantism forward onto victory, eagerly paying the ultimate price in order to do so. On broadsheet published in early 1633 for instance, Gustavus is portrayed in an open coffin, with the backdrop of his military victories playing out, as an angel reaches down from heaven, laurel wreath in hand. The laurel wreath, a symbol of triumphing over death, was a powerful message; just as Jesus had conquered the grave, so too would Gustavus, who would rise up as the champion of Protestantism and live forever in the hearts of all faithful men. The lament which accompanied the scene is also worth detailing:

> Behold, the Lord acts in unexpected ways.
> At the height of victory He gives us a sorrowful, odious joy:
> He tears from us through death the one man
> Who with the courage of a mighty lion and by many heroic deeds
> Gloriously saved us from the enemy, when we were nearly lost.
> [...]
> Here a mighty king, the Lord's anointed hero,
> Risked his life without argument or hesitation,
> Just so that we could be free from oppression and fear,
> And was not afraid to shed his own blood.[54]

Because of the divine nature of his victories, the polemicists could do no other than portray his death as an ordained part of God's plan. Religious rhetoric was furiously intertwined with his death, just as it had been with the last few years of his life. It should go without saying that Gustavus' death had caused profound shock among the camp of his followers, and tracts like these could help some mourners find solace in the apparently senseless catastrophe. Thus, one broadsheet promised safety and security well into the future:

> God sends whom he wishes; He also sent him [i.e. Gustavus Adolphus]
> And will continue to act this way. Thus, dear Germany,
> Hold fast to God and act yourself.
> Be thankful to Him at all times and place your deep trust in him.[55]

And another urged Protestants to believe that the King's death was merely a technicality, and that immortality was already his:

Our Swede lives on;
[He, who was] our hope, light and life,
Will bring us peace and freedom.[56]

So dominant were the pro-Swedish propagandists during the period of Gustavus' life, that Catholic counterarguments rarely made an appearance. In fact, the very use of broadsheets to spread one's message and communicate the sins of the other side had scarcely been necessary or possible before Gustavus' triumphs. The intervention of the Swedish King changed all that, and the persistent presence of the Swedish army in Germany for the remainder of the war encouraged the propaganda press to continue in their work. So dominant were the pro-Swedish writers, that it was only after Gustavus' death that Catholic polemists felt confident to answer back and deliver some striking propaganda messages of their own. These broadsheets from the Catholic side, for the most part, depicted the weakness of the Swedish King, and urged Protestants, now that their paper champion was dead, to repent and return to the Emperor's good graces.

Interestingly though, Gustavus Adolphus slips out of the pro-Swedish/ Protestant broadsheets after 1634. The Thirty Years War, it seemed, had moved on without him. Yet, while the broadsheets moved on, the conflict which the late Swedish King left behind retained his unmistakable stamp. Without Gustavus, the conflict may well have ended in 1630; his victories did not merely challenge the Habsburg supremacy, they also created a firm divide in the Thirty Years War which would only become more acute as the conflict progressed. Henceforth, it would be possible to mark Gustavus' intervention as a watershed moment, and to view the years 1618-29 as the period before Gustavus, whereas the period from 1630-48 was after Gustavus, when the Swedish King had acted, and changed everything. And indeed, it was *without Gustavus* that Sweden's German allies, Sweden's Chancellor and Sweden itself would now have to proceed.[57] As Stevens concluded: 'By the enduring force which his genius and character imparted to the Swedish nation, it maintained an influence for nearly a century among the leading powers of Europe much beyond what her natural strength and geographical position gave it.'[58] Indeed, it is possible to mark Gustavus Adolphus' reign as the beginning of the Swedish Empire, and Gustavus' intervention in Germany as the moment of her arrival on the world stage. If the Swedish Empire was just being born, then the Thirty Years War was about to move into its fifteenth year, and into its more destructive, decisive half.

THREE

Out with the Old

On 29 November 1632 at 7AM, Frederick V, the Winter King, the dispossessed Elector Palatine, and engineer of the Bohemian portion of the Thirty Years War, died of a fever. It was an incredibly anticlimactic end for an individual who had served as the face of the German opposition for much of his life. He had hung on every engagement, pinned his hopes and prayers on every campaign, declared his loyalty to each new intervening power, and now he was dead. Had Frederick died sooner, or had Gustavus Adolphus not died two weeks before, then the death of such a pivotal figure in the early phase of the conflict would likely have received greater attention. As it stood by that point in Europe though, any sympathies which were swirling around the ruined countryside were spared for the late Swedish King, and not for the Winter King, whose career was, after all, a great deal less impressive.

Someone who did care a great deal about Frederick's death was his newly widowed wife, Elizabeth Stuart, the sister of King Charles of Britain. 'I am the most wretched creature that ever lived in this world', she cried, 'and this shall I ever be, having lost the best friend that I ever had, in whom was all my delight.' In desperation did she write to her brother, declaring that 'After God', King Charles was her 'sole resource.'[59] Now that Europe's persona non grata was dead, Charles was willing to offer her asylum, yet Elizabeth refused, insisting on maintaining the German tradition of remaining in one's home for a given period of time after the death of a spouse. Yet, Elizabeth would return to Britain in time; she would live to see the Civil Wars consume Britain and execute her brother, and she would live just long enough to see her nephew Charles II embark on his restoration in 1660.[60]

Elizabeth lived a remarkable life, and while she could not have known it, the immensely fruitful marriage she had enjoyed with her late husband would prove vital to the future of Britain's monarchy. Of her brood of thirteen children, several lived to adulthood, among them Prince Rupert of the Rhine, a famed commander in the Civil Wars and Anglo-Dutch Wars; Charles Louis, Frederick's successor as Elector Palatine, and most importantly perhaps,

Princess Sophie. Sophie would marry into the Hanoverian family, and after the Stuart line had virtually died out, Sophie would be heir designate to the British throne, though her death in 1713 ensured that her son George succeeded in her stead. In such an indirect way was the Hanoverian line of monarchs established, and it was made possible by the marriage of the Winter King and Queen. While they would never see Bohemia, their descendants would manage a significant consolation prize.

But while his large family would later secure the future of the British crown, in 1632 it only served to make Frederick homesick. During the summer, it had become apparent that Gustavus would not make a lasting deal with Frederick regarding his restoration to the Palatinate until John George of Saxony was consulted. This was a difficult pill for Frederick to swallow, as John George had never been sympathetic to his cause, opportunistically invading and seizing portions of the Kingdom of Bohemia in the name of the Emperor rather than support his fellow Protestant Elector in 1620. By September, the honeymoon was over, and Frederick left Gustavus' camp for Frankfurt on the Main, where he was told negotiations would continue with the Swedes over his Palatinate's future. Frederick had been greatly depressed by what he discovered – Gustavus wished to cling to the most valuable portions of the Palatinate, and to relinquish the rest only after Frederick himself paid for it.

This was impossible, as the only assets Frederick possessed were those which had been given to him. 'It will be a true penitence that I do here', Frederick said. In early October he wrote to the Swedish King requesting that he be returned to the Palatine on the terms which they had previously agreed, i.e. Palatine support for Sweden, Swedish occupation of Palatine fortresses, and Frederick's commitment to tolerate Lutheranism. 'If [the Swedish King] wants neither the one nor the other, I do not know what I ought to do', Frederick exclaimed. He was totally dependent upon his allies, so after despairing for long enough, he penned yet another letter to his brother in law. Therein he complained about his treatment under the Swedes, the miserable state of his Palatinate and his want of aid. Throughout, Frederick was kept going by the promise that he would be reunited with his family in The Hague in spring 1633. He travelled from Frankfurt to Mainz, and there began corresponding with Elizabeth twice a week, the highlight of his week it seems.

And then, his fortunes seemed to improve; Charles was willing to sponsor an English expedition of eight thousand foot and two thousand horse, to serve under Frederick's personal command. What was more, the Palatine fortress of Oppenheim was willing to swear fealty to him. The Swedish forces were by now far away chasing after Wallenstein in Saxony, so Frederick dared to dream a restoration was possible, and that he could return to heal his scarred homeland. 'I would not stay eight days in Mainz', he wrote to his wife in early November, 'being so extremely tired of it all.' And it was there that his correspondence ended, for just as his fortunes seemed to be improving, Frederick caught the fever which was to kill him. Almost certainly, his genuine exhaustion played a role in weakening his health, which had been stellar for much of his life. By the time Elizabeth read those final words, her husband had passed away. Strangely, Frederick's remains vanished shortly after his death. It is rumoured that his coffin was even desecrated by bandits on route to Sedan, but this is possibly a rumour put about by Vienna.[61] Regardless of the circumstances, the news of Frederick's death just following that of Gustavus would have been sweet indeed for Emperor Ferdinand. Before 1632 was over, his two greatest nemeses had died, and he was the last one standing.

As 1633 dawned, the strategic situation in the Thirty Years War looked very different to the story which had been told in 1632. Lutzen had plainly been a disaster, and not merely for Sweden's strategic position in Germany. Gustavus' premature death at thirty-eight years old had left only a six-year-old daughter, Christina, in Stockholm. Furthermore, the Swedish constitution, such as it was, made no provisions for a regency. As no provision would be made for Gustavus' despondent widow – the sister of George William of Brandenburg – to rule either, it was evident that the mission would be taken by Sweden's aristocracy. From the beginning, Axel Oxenstierna, chancellor during Gustavus' reign, worked to cement his influence on the country. He was largely successful in this task, since even while the nobles might have disliked him, they could not deny the necessity of cleaving to his expertise in such a time of crisis. But Oxenstierna did not gamble on his influence remaining in the ascendant in Stockholm while he was in Germany; he installed his brother as Lord High Steward, with responsibility for Sweden's High Court, while his cousin was named Treasurer. 'This supremacy on the part of one family', wrote Ingvar Anderson, was 'unparalleled since the Middle Ages', and it proved essential for the Swedish war effort, for it 'enabled the Chancellor to carry out his own policy, in which he revealed a combination, characteristic of him, of obstinacy and flexibility.'[62]

As his position at home was secured, Oxenstierna recognised that the most important and pressing task would be to secure the loyalty and continued cohesion of the army which Sweden had maintained, and which Gustavus had formerly led. The grisly aftermath of the battlefield at Lutzen had brought home to soldiery and statesman alike the increasing cost of war on both sides. The Swedish army held the stinking battlefield the next day, where some six thousand of their men had been lost, but what remained of the soldiery returned to Saxony shortly thereafter. Wallenstein had escaped to Bohemia, but four thousand men had been lost, among them distinguished and dependable lieutenants like Pappenheim, whose body was taken to Prague and afforded a Catholic burial complete with all the ceremonials one could expect. Other commanders, like Piccolomini, had been wounded, and Piccoloimin's detachment of arquebusiers suffered casualties as high as 40%. Wallenstein paid for the funeral of his second, but also presided over another funeral, that of his cousin, who had also been struck down at Lutzen. The long hand of death which Lutzen had unleashed seemed to leave no one safe.[63]

The impact of the battle was also felt into the new year of 1633. It was necessary to plan for a new campaign, and on the Imperial side, the understandable impulse was to take advantage of Gustavus' untimely death and the discord this caused in the Protestant camp. Wallenstein, for his part, intended to detach Brandenburg and Saxony from Sweden's side, and resumed the correspondence with John George of Saxony, in addition to a correspondence which was initiated with Axel Oxenstierna. Indeed, in the spring of 1633, it seemed that all sides had found a reason to pause and consider their next move. Diplomatic channels among the Protestant German princes were opened, and the Danish King Christian IV took advantage of the death of his rival to pose as mediator. Initially buoyed by the death of his foes, it took some time for Ferdinand to be worn down and persuaded to compromise, but by July, he had been convinced to offer a suspension of the unpopular Edict of Restitution if the Protestant Electors would return to the Imperial camp. The offer was certainly tempting, and John George would have switched sides in a heartbeat had Swedish soldiers not been so nearby. Efforts to persuade Brandenburg to abandon the Swedes also failed, likely for the same reason, and Axel Oxenstierna knew he would have to move quickly in the diplomatic as well as in the military sphere to prevent any shedding of allies or discussion of peace.[64]

Oxenstierna turned to the political situation first and worked to realise the ambitions of the late Swedish King with the creation of the Heilbronn League in January 1633. The aim of such a League was to provide an alternative to the Catholic League, that body dominated by Maximillian of Bavaria, and serving since 1620 as a significant military arm of the Emperor, alongside Wallenstein's 'imperial' force. But this was not all. Oxenstierna was not thinking merely of his enemies, he was also thinking of his friends. The loyalties of many German princes, especially those Protestant Electors in Brandenburg and Saxony, had been won largely due to the Emperor's intransigence and Sweden's military supremacy. A great deal of Sweden's political security then, rested on its military power, but with the death of Gustavus, Oxenstierna also had to demonstrate to the Germans that an era had not passed, and that Sweden was still a dependable power.

A further concern may have been the creeping involvement of Cardinal Richelieu in German affairs. Richelieu was mindful of the need to maintain a party of opposition to the Emperor in Germany, but there were rumours that Richelieu had viewed the death of Gustavus as a chance to jump ship, and to offer the helm of this opposition party to a more malleable partner, such as Saxony. Heilbronn would nip these rumours in the bud, before a disastrous political decision could be made and Sweden be left without its French paymaster. Subsidies had slowed throughout 1632, as Gustavus had continued to unnerve Richelieu with his expansive ambitions.[65] The historian David Parrott even went as far as describing Gustavus' death as a 'piece of unexpected good fortune', because it granted Richelieu more opportunities. As we have seen though, it also compelled Oxenstierna to act.[66]

After assembling in March, key German figures on the Rhine, in Swabia and Franconia agreed to the sign the treaty formulating the Heilbronn League on 13 April 1633. Notable in his absence was John George of Saxony, who remained aloof from the arrangement, but still officially in alliance with Sweden according to the treaty made in September 1631. Officially, he may have been a friend, but John George had in fact hosted a rival meeting of Protestant German potentates in Dresden at the same time. Aside from George William of Brandenburg, who refused to go against the Swedes, attendance was poor. Evidently, even with the vanishing of their champion, Germans were unwilling to bet against Sweden – its military reputation spoke for itself, and until Swedish forces did suffer a great defeat, there was no reason for these Germans to jump ship. Thus, the terms of Heilbronn obliged the German signatories...

> ...freely and collectively confederate closer with the royal dignity and majesty of the most praiseworthy crown of Sweden under the guidance of its plenipotentiary legate and his excellency the royal chancellor [Oxenstierna]. They agree that all confederates shall be faithful, and give mutual assistance, and protect each other from harm. They will also venture their persons, their lives and their fortunes in the cause, until such time as German liberty, and a respect for the principles and constitution of the Holy Roman Empire, ate once again firmly established, the restoration of the Evangelical Estates is secured, and a just and certain religious and profane peace (which all confederates can enjoy) is obtained and concluded, and also *until the royal dignity and majesty and crown of Sweden has been assured of an appropriate satisfaction.*[67]

This final sentence was probably the most significant stipulation, because it committed the German potentates to make war alongside Sweden until a peace treaty which Oxenstierna deemed satisfactory was made. And if there was any doubt that the Chancellor of Sweden was in charge, the second article of the League declared the desire 'to give a testimony of their high esteem of the Chancellor's excellent qualities, by asking and entreating him to take upon himself the office of Director, for the good of the common cause in its hour of need, and for German liberty.' To further solidify the alliance, it was agreed that 'no confederate shall seek peace separately with the enemy'. We are also drawn to the lack of options granted to these Germans – neutrality was not merely impossible; it was also expressly forbidden per the terms of the League treaty:

> If any confederate, against expectation, does not assist their fellow members or tries to pursue such dangerous policies as becoming neutral (which is henceforth forbidden among the evangelicals) then he will not receive aid from the confederation when he is threatened or attacked by the enemy.[68]

Evidently, it was no longer possible to choose between God or the Devil as Gustavus had once urged – this choice was made for these princes, and they could choose to accept the gracious protection of Sweden or be cast adrift in a hostile country. Other proclamations were of note, such as the claim that the Heilbronn League had 'been forced upon them by the great insolence of the enemy, and is designed as a legitimate means of self-defence', and that:

> The confederates cherish the confident hope that other Evangelical Electors and Estates of the Empire, and also foreign potentates and republics, will not be displeased at this work of salvation that promotes God's honour, conserves the Holy Roman Empire and the Estates and their eternal welfare, but on the contrary that they will take occasion to adhere to and enter so Christian and so just a league and assist it…[69]

It was a forlorn hope that all Protestant potentates would declare their adherence to the League, but Oxenstierna could rest assured that he had gone a long way towards consolidating and legitimising Sweden's position in the Empire among the minor German potentates. Now joined by the forces of the Heilbronn League, who together would be compelled to raise a force of nearly eighty thousand men on their own expense, Sweden could assert its right to lead the war in Germany based on something more than Gustavus' force of personality. Armed with the Heilbronn League, the real goal was to bring the likes of Brandenburg and Saxony into its orbit, but George William refused to be drawn owing to the thorny issue of Pomerania, which Brandenburg had once been promised by the Emperor and which Sweden refused to relinquish.[70] The best George William could do was to attach Brandenburg to an alliance between Sweden and France in October. In the meantime, a general congress was hosted over the summer of 1633 to persuade more Germans to join. Such a congress could only be hosted in the first place because while Oxenstierna had managed to bring these minor German figures under Sweden's thumb, he had also saved Sweden's army.[71]

The Swedish army had spread itself out after Lutzen, as part of the still-enormous force, with the Saxon and Brandenburg contingents, was to operate in Bohemia and Silesia, meeting the army led by Wallenstein. Another part, with the troops of the Hessian and lower Saxon Circle, was to hold Westphalia and protect North Germany from any threats to Sweden's

Pomeranian bridgehead. Finally, Bernhard of Saxe-Weimar, that daring commander who had captured the hills beside Lutzen, was ordered forward into southern Germany with the bulk of the Swedish army. While marching through Thuringia in April though, it was when he combined his forces with those of Gustav Horn outside Augsburg that problems began to emerge. Thanks to the unification of the remnants of Gustavus' old army with the new German recruits, Bernhard boasted a formidable force of more than forty-two thousand men.[72]

And yet, these men had not been paid in full since 1631. Worse, the promised bonuses which were meant to follow battles like Breitenfeld and Lutzen had not arrived either. Bernhard was a capable commander of men, but he was no Gustavus, and his personality could not keep their dissatisfaction at bay for long. Dissatisfied with their lot, the soldiers began acting out, demonstrating a brutality which Bernhard did little to restrain. The unfortunate town of Landsberg on the River Lech – where Gustavus had confronted and fatally wounded Tilly the previous year – was subject to a four-day sacking, and children were recorded to have been among those massacred. However, Oxenstierna appreciated that it was more the officers, rather than the humble grunts, who would have to be appeased. When Bernhard arrived suddenly in Heilbronn in late May, Oxenstierna capitulated, granted a whole range of lands and titles to the army's officers in exchange for loyalty and pledges of continued service.

Yet it was Bernhard himself who received the greatest treasure of all. Apparently, content to copy the policy of the Emperor towards Wallenstein, Oxenstierna signed away vast lands and duchies to Bernhard, and made him Duke of Franconia. Per an arrangement reached in June, Bernhard became one of the most powerful men in the Empire, at least on paper, for it was suspected that Oxenstierna was writing cheques the Swedish army could not cash. A resistance to the Swedish occupation in Franconia had not ceased throughout 1632, and the mostly Catholic citizens of the region were unlikely to be pacified by the arrival of their braggadocios new overlord. Rather than be bogged down by the reward, Bernhard passed governorship of his new Dukedom to his brother, and he continued to serve as Sweden's useful, if somewhat wild pair of hands along the Rhine for several more years.[73]

The Rhine remained a volatile theatre of the war, thanks largely to the sheer number of significant actors swirling around. Of these actors, there was little doubt that France was becoming the most important. Having united behind a common policy, King Louis XIII and Cardinal Richelieu set their sights on the Duchy of Lorraine, a task made increasingly easy thanks to the Duke of Lorraine's refusal to accept a lasting peace.[74] Originally forced to the peace table in summer 1632, Duke Charles of Lorraine had recreated a new army of nine thousand men by August 1633. His newly created powers led him to grow more defiant and influential among German Rhinish princes, but there was a further compelling reason for Richelieu and Louis XIII to authorise another hammer blow on the recalcitrant Duke: he had recently welcomed the disgraced younger brother of King Louis, Gaston d'Orléans, into his court. By 20 September, Nancy, the Lorraine capital, was in French hands, and Duke Charles signed the Treaty of Charmes shortly thereafter. Per the terms of the treaty, Lorraine was subject to French occupation for thirty years, and Duke Charles was pulled once more from the Habsburgs' orbit. It was to prove a strategically vital move to insulate France's eastern frontier along the Rhine, but several additional dangers remained, and would only be aggressively dealt with once the war between Spain and France was allowed to erupt into the open.[75]

'I believe that Sweden wants peace, that she wants to bring her forces home, and to leave the two Electors [of Brandenburg and Saxony] to find their own way out of the labyrinth.' This had been the astute judgement of Wallenstein in the months before Gustavus' death, and he believed it still applied to Oxenstierna's regime. The best way to bring about peace, therefore, was to exploit the rift between Saxony on the one hand and Sweden on the other. On paper, it seemed an easy task. Wallenstein was based in Bohemia, tasked essentially with combating that third of the Swedish army which had been sent to defend the Saxon border with Bohemia, while waiting for an opportune moment to seize land in Silesia. Because of John George of Saxony's proximity to the Bohemian front, his soldiers made up the bulk of the army. Theoretically then, with a reduced Swedish influence, there was never a better time to get at John George and convince him to switch sides. If Saxony could be brought back into Emperor Ferdinand's orbit, then Sweden would have lost a major ally, and the Protestant weathervane would swing back in favour of the Habsburgs.

In this way, Wallenstein attempted to divide and conquer; in June 1633 he arranged a ceasefire with the Swedish-Saxon army that was then invading Silesia. Then, Wallenstein brought some suspicion upon himself by engaging in discussions with the Saxon commander, Hans Georg von Arnim, who had fought for Wallenstein only a few years before. Understandably, the Emperor and Oxenstierna were suspicious in equal measure about these contacts, with the Emperor warned that Wallenstein was searching for a means of switching sides, and Oxenstierna warned that John George, through Arnim, intended to do the same. Throughout the summer the ceasefire endured, but when it ended Wallenstein managed to trap the Swedish contingent of the army, which had been led by a blast from the past – Count Thurn, the former commander of the doomed Bohemian confederate army in 1620. He was to prove just as unsuccessful here, as his army of eight thousand men was cut off and surrendered at the fortified town of Steinau, and Thurn promptly made a deal. This development was devastating, clearing the enemy out of Silesia and providing a monetary boost to Wallenstein's reputation. It also left Wallenstein with a real advantage over Arnim in the field, since Arnim's Saxon army was now the only thing standing in the way of the destruction of Saxony itself. Understandably, following this triumph, Wallenstein reopened negotiations with Arnim, hoping once more to detach Saxony and Brandenburg from the Swedish camp, reducing as a result the activity on the Bohemian front.[76]

Meanwhile, at the town of Oldendorf, west of Hanover, on 8 July, a Swedish force of thirteen thousand attacked and routed an Imperial force of fifteen thousand. This effectively cleared the Imperial army out of Westphalia and Lower Saxony and served as the Saxon-Swedish answer to Wallenstein's success at Steinau. Oldendorf was atypical in the context of the Thirty Years War, as both sides attacked in the beginning of the battle rather than the traditional style where one side attacked and the other defended. After routing the Imperial cavalry, George of Brunswick-Luneburg demonstrated an adept appreciation for flexibility in the attack and overcame the numerically superior Imperial opposition.[77] Though largely glossed over in the war's narrative, this battle was the largest seen in Westphalia during its duration, and Peter H. Wilson called it 'one of the most complete victories of the war', after the Imperial side endured as many as six thousand casualties, to George of Brunswick-Luneburg's three hundred.[78]

But that was not the end of Wallenstein's story in 1633. By the end of the year, indeed, he had become persona non grata in Vienna once again, as a result of developments further afield. While he had been successful in his own theatre, Bernhard of Saxe-Weimar had rampaged through Bavaria in the autumn, capturing Regensburg in mid-November. This was a symbolic and a significant triumph for Bernhard, and for the anti-Imperialist cause.[79] It piled additional pressure onto Maximillian, who petitioned the Emperor to make his generalissimo do something to save his beleaguered Electorate. Little effort was made to congratulate the hard working and unwell Wallenstein, who had routed Sweden's threat to Bohemia, and increased the pressure upon Saxony. The problem with Wallenstein by this point was not necessarily that his record had become lacklustre, instead it seems to have been a simple case of the Emperor's distrust of him, and imagining that he harboured grand, treasonous ambitions, perhaps even for the Bohemian Crown. These suspicions, which we will address later in the book, remain as elusive and mysterious as the campaigning year of 1633. 'In military terms', wrote the historian Geoff Mortimer:

> 1633 was a year in which neither side achieved much of consequence, as although the war did not by any means come to a standstill it was effectively relegated into second place by a convoluted series of attempts to find some basis for peace.[80]

It is not surprising that this lack of consequential battles was the story of 1633, when we consider the Thirty Years War as a whole. Although Ferdinand in Vienna and Oxenstierna at Frankfurt had become frustrated with the lack of progress, it seems to have slipped their minds that the last two years had been an anomaly in the grand scheme of things. That the decisive battles of Breitenfeld, the Lech and Lutzen had all followed one another within fourteen months was not in keeping with the previous pace of the war. In a sense, 1633 was a return to form. And yet, it would prove perhaps the final full year of breathing space which either side would enjoy for the remainder of the war.

The total collapse of Swedish power which Oxenstierna had so feared, Ferdinand had welcomed, and Richelieu had predicted did not take place, at least not yet. Sweden and its German allies were spread out on three major fronts, and they continued to hold too many important bastions of Germany to be discounted. Oxenstierna had solidified and formalised the pact which Sweden enjoyed with the Germans, and this Heilbronn League would have to be confronted if the Swedish grip on the Empire was to be substantially loosened. Swedish commanders were entrenched in Pomerania, in Bavaria and along the Rhine, though they had been mostly ejected from Bohemia. It would take another thumping victory either to resurrect Swedish fortunes, or to crush them once and for all. Through 1633 they had held on, but Ferdinand was mobilising the resources of his family, in Austria and in Spain, and he planned to make 1634 count. An army, courtesy of Madrid, was on its way to Austria, picking up men from Italy as it did so. Its aim was nothing less than the reversal of the Habsburgs' poor fortunes, and with twenty-four thousand under the command of the brother of the King of Spain, the mission was as bold as it was significant.[81] Lutzen had removed Sweden's head, now it remained to extract her heart.

FOUR
Reversals Great and Terrible

The duke of Friedland asserted that all troops of foreign potentates, whether Spanish, French, Swedish or from Lorraine, and all foreigners who did not belong in the Empire, must be expelled in order to restore it to its state during the time of the Emperors Rudolph and Matthias…When I asked to know and write down the specific terms of the peace he would not agree, instead insisting that both armies should march immediately into the Empire, directly against the Swedes, who at that time were the nearest, to remove them.[82]

In such a manner did Duke Franz-Albrecht of Saxe-Luneburg describe Wallenstein's offer to him, made during a meeting in September 1633. Franz-Albrecht, as the second in command of the Saxon commander George von Arnim, was in a unique position throughout the summer and early autumn of 1633 to hear Wallenstein's offers. Yet, the plan mentioned above was outlined by Franz-Albrecht only after news of Wallenstein's death was made known. Franz-Albrecht, in other words, may have been stretching the truth in an effort to change the narrative surrounding Wallenstein's negotiations. Unfortunately for historians, it seems that Franz-Albrecht was far indeed from the only contemporary of Wallenstein's to muddy the truth about what the Imperial generalissimo actually said or offered. The result is that historians have been left with a morass of conflicting opinions and reports on Wallenstein's intentions and character.

Some claim that Wallenstein still burned with revenge at being dismissed in 1630, and that he harboured ambitions for the Bohemian Crown.[83] Others assert the general difficulty in getting to the bottom of the riddles so long as so many conflicting reports were present.[84] Others, like Geoff Mortimer in his work *Wallenstein: the Enigma of the Thirty Years War*, presented Wallenstein's negotiations and his subsequent behaviour as rational, but occasionally weak, motivated less by sinister intentions to defect or betray his Emperor, than by a genuine desire to bring about peace and eject the foreigner from the Empire.[85] Wallenstein had little to gain and everything to lose by abandoning his

Emperor and placing his trust wholly in the dubious Saxons. In October 1633, in the final period of negotiations he had with Franz-Albrecht, Wallenstein signed a declaration made with that Saxon commander for the first and only time since negotiations with him had begun. The agreement was between the two Protestant Electors, Saxony and Brandenburg, and Wallenstein only – the Swedes were excluded, in fact they seemed to be the target of the arrangement signed by the parties, who…

> …seeing the present comprehensive devastation and decline of the Empire have considered ways and means by which this may be remedied, and the Empire and its constituent parts rescued from despoliation by foreign troops and restored to their former prime and well-being.

Thus, both electoral armies were instructed to join with the Imperialist forces and be placed under Wallenstein's overall command:

> In order to achieve the above objectives and through their combined might to restore the stability of the religious and secular peace as it was during the Imperial reigns of Rudolph and Matthias, and under his present Imperial Majesty before these troubles which have arisen, and to maintain the same against anyone who persists in further disturbing it.[86]

But this arrangement with Franz-Albrecht was precisely that – it was not canon until the two Electors agreed to sign it. As Wallenstein surely suspected would be the case, in the replies to these offers received in mid-November 1633, neither John George of Saxony nor George William of Brandenburg would declare their willingness to do so. The reason, they claimed, was due to Wallenstein's poor health – common knowledge in Vienna as much as Dresden. The two Electors did not want to place their eggs in Wallenstein's basket, only for him to die or retire, leaving them vulnerable. Wallenstein's health was deteriorating by late 1633, and his doctors had reportedly given him only two years left to live. However, it is far more likely that neither Elector wished to abandon the Swedes, as the latter remained the more powerful faction, and Wallenstein's position far from certain considering the mostly uneventful campaigning season of 1633.

For both Electors as well, the unpalatable implications of the Edict of Restitution meant that siding with Emperor Ferdinand was impossible until its worst clauses were rescinded, a request blocked repeatedly by the ultra-Catholic counter-reformation faction which had long surrounded Ferdinand at Vienna. Wallenstein had also been vague in his communications with Arnim, while Ferdinand's thirty-four page memorandum detailing the Habsburg position had been explicit. In addition, Wallenstein assumed that by abandoning the Swedes, the two Electors would automatically make war on them in league with the Emperor, whereas Arnim, if he contemplated abandoning his Swedish ally, did so as a means to a different end, that of creating a neutral 'third party' in the Empire, which would stand aloof from the Emperor and his foes.

Notwithstanding the feasibility of remaining aloof by this stage in the conflict, we are led to conclude that the fundamental reason for the failure of these negotiations between Wallenstein and Arnim was a failure to understand what the other side wanted.[87] By November, in any case, the negotiating period was at an end, as was the period of ceasefire. Wallenstein had little to show for it, in fact it seemed to have done his reputation a great deal of damage, as the details of the negotiations were subsequently warped to suit the propaganda of each side. Wallenstein's reputation took a further hit when he failed to save Regensburg from Bernhard of Saxe-Weimar that same month and incurred additional damage when he made the decision to quarter his soldiers in the Habsburg lands for the winter. Ferdinand, outraged at this decision, ordered Wallenstein out to attack, writing to his generalissimo in early December 1633:

> It is my express wish and demand that Your Excellency should immediately turn the army round and proceed towards Passau and the duke of Weimar, march against him, follow him and drive him out, and this is my final decision, upon which I am completely firm and immovable.[88]

Yet, such strong words were not accompanied by a coherent plan. Ferdinand had made no provision for Wallenstein's army if it was to march away from its headquarters at Pilsen and towards Bernhard's army, a distance of several hundred miles. Nor had Ferdinand managed to pay Wallenstein or his men what had been promised in spring 1632. Indeed, Wallenstein was in an even worse financial situation now than he ever had been, and all because of the Emperor's failed promises. His subordinates, who had invested their own funds into the campaign and their soldiers, with the expectation that the forthcoming loot would return such investments, began to become anxious that Wallenstein would not secure their money, and that they would be bankrupted. The machinery of Wallenstein's war machine threatened to grind to a halt altogether if his men were not properly paid – at the beginning of the year, the Swedes had revolted for similar reasons, but the campaigning year of 1633 had not been conducive to large profits. There was great strategic, but very little monetary value, in engaging in negotiations with the enemy, as Wallenstein had done in the summer.

Wallenstein had also not refrained from making plain his objections to the Emperor's policies in a wider sense. Informed of the looming arrival of a Spanish army some twenty-four thousand strong, which would be tasked with marching towards the Rhine and dealing a killer blow to the Swedes, Wallenstein objected, on the grounds that heavy Spanish intervention in the German War would provoke the French to enter the conflict openly in response. In early January 1634, Wallenstein was informed by an Imperial agent that the younger brother of the King of Spain – also called Ferdinand, and entitled the Cardinal-Infante – should be given an escort of six-thousand of Wallenstein's cavalry in order to make it to the Spanish Netherlands where he would serve as governor. Wallenstein was sympathetic, but also realistic – five hundred miles lay between his position at Pilsen and Brussels, and the Swedes or their allies were in the ascendant virtually everywhere. For the younger brother of the King of Spain to suffer capture or worse at the hands of such enemies would have been tantamount to disaster, as Wallenstein explained. When news of his refusal to cooperate with this hare-brained scheme reached the Emperor though, it seemed like just another strike against his record and character.[89]

It was under these circumstances that Wallenstein partook in what later became an infamous scene, that of the Pilsen Oath. Over 11 to 13 January 1634, as the anxieties of the Imperial army under his command mounted, Wallenstein searched both for way out of the command himself, and for a way to achieve satisfaction for his men. As he floated between the two decisions, one of his subordinates orchestrated a unique event, where a document was drawn up pledging the officers under Wallenstein's command to remain loyal to him until he received what was owed to them. In return, Wallenstein committed not to resign the command. Much was said about honour and faithfulness, and much alcohol was also drunk, but as Mortimer explained:

> Stripped of the grand phrases, however, this oath was essentially a symbolic gesture, a warning shot to Vienna rather than an actual threat, and it was neither kept secret nor formally transmitted to the court. As such it had little practical significance, but it did allow Wallenstein's enemies to resurrect and exploit the old fear, dating back to 1630, that he would not go quietly if dismissed, but would turn the army against the emperor and the court. Hence more drastic measures would have to be considered in order to get rid of him.[90]

In context of his previous failings and disobedience, not to mention his more suspicious acts like negotiations with the Saxons and perceived gentleness of former Bohemian exiles like Count Thurn, the Pilsen Oath acquired a notoriousness far in excess of reason, for the Emperor and historians alike.[91] What Wallenstein viewed as a necessary act to keep his men loyal and the army together in the context of scant resources and empty promises from Ferdinand, the latter was told to see as a smoking gun. By 22 January, contact had been made by Ferdinand's subordinates with a coterie of Irish and Scots officers under Wallenstein's command who would be willing to assassinate him. On 24 January, the Emperor signed a patent which released Wallenstein's men from their oaths. On 18 February, the final patent was signed, this one accusing Wallenstein of conspiracy and essentially serving as the official death warrant, though it was not made public for the moment.

Still, those closest to Wallenstein were detached through secret communications, until the scales finally fell from the generalissimo's eyes and he fled to Eger on 22 February. Assuming he would be safe from intrigues there, Ferdinand's agents proved relentless, and in the evening of 24 February, Wallenstein's closest allies were butchered as they sat down to eat dinner. Noting that Wallenstein was not among the dead, the hired blades searched the castle for him, until one of their number, an Irishman by the name of Walter Deveraux, burst through his bedroom door. Wallenstein, having removed his boots, sword and coat, was utterly defenceless, and reports vary on precisely what happened next, but either way, we know Deveraux ran Wallenstein through with a broken pike, after having broken his sword in earlier exchanges.[92] Wallenstein's body was dragged down the stairs into the courtyard, after Deveraux had had the decency to prevent it being thrown out the window. In a flash of conspiratorial violence then, Wallenstein and his inner circle were dead, and his army had lost its leader.[93]

The story of Wallenstein's fate appears on the surface as a strange distraction from the business of 1634, yet it was the culmination of a story which began in 1625, when an ambitious, wealthy Bohemian nobleman rose to prominence following a series of invaluable promises to his Emperor. It must be said that Ferdinand benefited immensely from the service of his generalissimo; with the numerical superiority and loyalty Wallenstein provided, the Habsburgs were able to overwhelm the Danes and inflict the Edict of Restitution upon the Empire. Then, when crisis loomed for the dynasty, Wallenstein's reputation and tactical ability enabled him to frustrate the tide of the Swedish King at Lutzen. It was a remarkable record, buttressed by the apparent moderation with which Wallenstein greeted his mission – refusing, for example, to impose the Edict at sword point, and insisting on offering his criticisms when Ferdinand decided to widen the war into Mantua in 1629 or to welcome in the Spanish in 1633.

While Wallenstein's failing health and naivety in the final days of his life certainly counted against him, it must be said a greater failing was that of Ferdinand. Had the Emperor provisioned him and supported him as promised, Wallenstein's men would have been paid, contented and happy to spend their winters somewhere else other than the stripped Habsburg lands. Ferdinand's willingness to believe the rumours and lies peddled by ambitious and influential men at court; his decision to dismiss him in autumn 1630 just as the Swedes were preparing to launch their campaign; his willingness to believe in those rumours once again when the situation became more difficult in 1633 – all of these shortcomings on the Emperor's part contributed to Wallenstein's fall. Alongside Gustavus Adolphus and Frederick V of the Palatinate, Wallenstein was an experienced figure from an old period of the war. With his removal, the opportunity now presented itself to replace him with someone new. Ferdinand did not mourn his generalissimo long. After acquiring the necessary pledges of loyalty from Wallenstein's men, Ferdinand appointed his son as the commander of the army in late April 1634.[94] A new phase of the conflict had apparently been ushered in.

The arrival of a Spanish army in Germany in the summer of 1634 was the brainchild of one man above all – Gaspar de Guzman, better known as the Count of Olivares to posterity, or simply the Count-Duke to his contemporaries. Olivares' career followed a very similar trajectory in Madrid to that of Richelieu in Paris; both men had had to challenge royals for influence, both men relished and valued their intimate relationship with their respective monarch, and both men were, in their own right, highly accomplished statesmen of the first rank. From 1622-42, Olivares was at the helm of Spanish government and policy, serving as the closest thing to its Prime Minister. Geoffrey Parker, an expert in Spanish history, describes the dizzying lengths Olivares went to in order to remain on top of all that Spain's churning bureaucracy had to offer, writing:

> Olivares rose at five, confessed, roused the king from his slumbers and discussed the day's programme with him. Then he would spend the rest of the day (until eleven at night or later) giving audiences, reading papers, dictating orders. Although he often accompanied the king while hunting, or in his carriage, he worked on the way, giving audiences from the saddle or dictating letters to the coachful of secretaries who followed him. With state papers stuffed in his pockets and even in his hat, "from his bedchamber to his study, from his study to his coach, out strolling, in the corner, on the stairs, he would hear and deal with an infinite number of people."[95]

Busy though he was with the King, Olivares, like Richelieu, also took charge of Spanish foreign policy. And what a foreign policy it was. A lot had changed in the world since Balthasar de Zuniga, his uncle and predecessor in Spanish government, had died in 1622. Then, the Habsburg family was unquestionably triumphant, with only the pithy remnants of Frederick V's allies standing in his way. More importantly to Spain, the Dutch were cowed, and under immense pressure following the expiration of the Twelve Years Truce the year before. Certainly, Zuniga may have gone to his grave confident that he had played no small role in forestalling the decline in Spanish powers which had been so greatly feared in Madrid and Vienna alike. Spain's Golden Age, Zuniga had proclaimed, was not going to go quietly, and it would be up to his energetic nephew Olivares to further the legend. But in spite of his 'ox-like constitution' and evident ability, there was still only so much Olivares could do. 'It is true that the ship is going down' a colleague wrote to Olivares in 1629, 'but under other captains we should have perished much sooner.'[96]

The solution to these problems of the Spanish monarchy was to cleave closer together with the Austrian branch of the Habsburg Empire. What this effectively meant was the Emperor making war upon the Dutch, a task, we will recall, Ferdinand attempted to take up during the Regensburg meeting in the summer and autumn of 1630. Yet, the requests for the German princes to join the Spanish in an attack on the Dutch fell on deaf ears; German Protestants were angered by the recently passed Edict of Restitution, and his allies were angling to get rid of Wallenstein. In such circumstances, there was no room for a joint Habsburg venture to destroy the Dutch Republic. This was an unfortunate development for Olivares, who had long advised the Emperor to make peace with his German vassals for the very reason that it would free them up for a campaign against the Dutch.

The pressure was on for Olivares, who was aware of Frederick Henry's stunning successes from 1629, as a massive haul of Spanish silver was seized, and the Dutch bought an army of more than a hundred thousand men. As the fortresses guarding the Spanish Netherlands toppled, and the very population of that Spanish patrimony threatened revolt, Olivares' requests in the years that followed became still more urgent.[97] Finally, with the transformation of the Empire's strategic situation by 1633 under the guise of the Swedes, the Emperor's weakness provided Olivares with a new opportunity. Not only had these losses made the Emperor more desperate, and thus more willing to accede to Spanish requests in return for aid for his position, but both Emperor Ferdinand and Philip IV, the King of Spain, appreciated that France's increasing activity and involvement in Germany could mean only one thing – soon, surely, her intervention would be made official. When that happened, it was imperative that both branches of the Habsburg dynasty were on the same page.

To put some steel into the Austrian branch, Olivares authorised for the Duke of Feria, a former governor of Catalonia, to lead a small professional force over the Alps and into Germany in early 1634, to be followed by the larger army led by the Cardinal-Infante in the summer. However, the primary aim of this army under the Cardinal-Infante was not to deliver a decisive blow to the Swedes – instead the mission was one to reinforce the Spanish Netherlands, where the late Governess had died. This was part of a two-pronged approach by Olivares, who advocated sending Charles and Ferdinand, King Philip IV's two younger brothers, to Spain's European trouble spots. Charles would go to Lisbon to shore up the Portuguese regime, and Ferdinand would go to Brussels. 'If the news that two members of the royal family are being sent out does not inspire the nation to do its duty', proclaimed Olivares at the time, 'we may despair of ever being able to stiffen our sinews as we ought if we are to beat the enemy and to restore Spain's reputation.'[98] Still, though Brussels had been the Cardinal-Infante's original mission, he took heart from the experiences of the Duke of Feria, who had engaged in 'one of the most brilliant campaigns of the Thirty Years' War. Spanish land communications with Flanders were restored, and a Swedish attack upon Austria frustrated.' With Feria's example already set, the act of delaying his final mission in order to aid the Emperor directly was not too great an ask for the Cardinal-Infante.[99]

With Archduke Ferdinand commanding a force in Silesia, and the Cardinal-Infante Ferdinand moving up from Italy, the Emperor's son was forced to choose, in the midsummer of 1634, where he would go next. Would he rendezvous with his Spanish cousin, or would he stay in Silesia to protect it and Bohemia from the Saxons? In the event, Archduke Ferdinand decided to surprise the Saxons, and abandon the Habsburg Hereditary Lands in favour of combining his army with that the Cardinal-Infante, to create an Austro-Spanish army at a town called Nordlingen. On his way to the fortuitous rendezvous, the Archduke outmanoeuvred the Saxons altogether, capturing Donauworth and Regensburg, thereby restoring contact between Bavaria and the Emperor. These successes placed a great deal of pressure on Bernhard of Saxe-Weimar to act, so once it was made known that Nordlingen was the latest fortified town with a Swedish garrison to come under siege, he made for it followed by Gustav Horn, the Swedish commander.

By 2 September, the Archduke's force of eighteen thousand men had begun their siege of the walled town – a wall which remains fully intact to this day – and they were joined by the Cardinal-Infante's force of fifteen thousand. These thirty-three thousand men dwarfed Bernhard and Horn's approaching army of twenty-five thousand men, but Bernhard's information about this disparity was patchy, and in any event, he felt compelled to attack and dislodge the army of the two Ferdinands, as a victory was desperately needed. While they had busied themselves with a siege of Nordlingen, the two Ferdinands had also found the time to establish a fortified camp nearby. From this fortified camp, they would defend against the tired and demoralised combined force of Protestant Germans and Swedes. The scales were determinedly tipping in favour of the Habsburgs, but this did not deter Bernhard, who banked on the inexperience of the two Ferdinands counting in his favour. On the morning of 6 September 1634, Bernhard and Horn attacked, initiating one of the very few pitched battles in this phase of the war. Even with their advantages, the victory was not easily or cheaply bought by the Habsburgs – for seven hours, reportedly after withstanding fifteen charges, the Habsburg army held out against the kind of murderous firepower and tactics which had by now become a staple of the war.

Disciplined, hardy and tenacious though they were, the enemy's advantages were simply too great, and the defeat turned quickly into a rout when Swedish cavalry became entangled in Bernhard's baggage train. Imperial cavalry did not have to be told to capitalise twice – here at last was the opportunity to break Sweden's strategic position as much as its reputation, and they did not flinch. By the end of the battle, the cream of Sweden's pool of troops had been liquidated, along with thousands of her German allies. The tally is reported to stand at twelve thousand killed or wounded, and four thousand prisoners, but what is not disputed is that Gustav Horn was taken prisoner, adding to the disaster. By the end of the day, the stunned Swedish garrison at Nordlingen had handed over the town. It was a shattering defeat, one more crushing than any since the war had begun. Only the loss at White Mountain in November 1620 had the same immediate impact for the anti-Imperial cause.

Even better for Habsburg propagandists, the triumph had been won not by generalissimos or a second-rate League, but by two leading figures of their respective dynasties. The triumph of the two Ferdinands certainly had a nice ring to it, but the battle continued to ring in the ears of Bernhard all the way to Alsace, where he reached by retreating over the Rhine, leaving Sweden's allies south of the Main utterly exposed and alone. Pitched battles of the kind of Nordlingen were statistically rare in the Thirty Years War, but what a transformative result it had had on the situation in Germany. In the space of a day, all the efforts of Gustavus Adolphus, from the military triumphs to the political penetration of his politics, had been undone. Sweden, save for its remnants in Alsace under Bernhard, and a force in headlong retreat to Pomerania under Johan Baner, now faced a strategic situation very similar to that faced by Gustavus in summer 1630, when he had first made landfall in Germany.[100]

We are told that Nordlingen caused only the second sleepless night of Oxenstierna's life – the first had followed the death of Gustavus two years' before.[101] With the disintegration of her army in South Germany, it could be expected that any allies in that region would be lost to Sweden, and furthermore, that any individuals on the fence would follow. Oxenstierna now rightly began to fear that the previously reluctant Electors in Saxony and Brandenburg would be among those to jump ship. 'I will struggle no longer, but drift where the tide will take me', wrote the Chancellor to Baner in Pomerania, adding 'we are hated, envied, harassed.' Indeed, by the time these words had been put to paper in November 1634, John George of Saxony was already engaging in preliminary negotiations with the Emperor. Nordlingen, it seemed, had given him the push he needed to abandon the Swedes, but more importantly, it affected a change in the policy of the Emperor towards his rebellious vassals and the final religious settlement (see below).[102]

The Habsburg reaction to Nordlingen was equally momentous. News of the victory was greeted with jubilation, and while revelling in their triumph, each Ferdinand proclaimed his fondness for the other. A new era of Habsburg cooperation seemed at hand, and who better to make such cooperation official than Count Onate, the same figure who had negotiated a partition of the

Habsburg lands in 1619? Onate arrived in Vienna shortly after Nordlingen, and negotiated what historians believe to have been an offensive alliance directed against all enemies of the dynasty, including France. By the following spring Olivares would write to Vienna as if confirming this arrangement:

> ...we are still ignorant of the finer points of the German situation, whilst your majesty finds himself preparing at great expense to comply with the requirements of the alliance, in which it is expressly laid down, if not in so many words, that war will be declared against France.[103]

But this war would not be waged by the two Ferdinands – in fact they would never stand side by side in battle again. The Cardinal-Infante resumed his old mission of travelling to Brussels, leaving Germany in the rear-view mirror, though not without some reservations. He would continue to fight the Dutch in the region until his death in 1641, and represented in many respects the last gasp of effective Spanish administration in the theatre.[104] The consequences of Nordlingen were felt not only in Sweden and Vienna, but also in France. Richelieu, essentially, was moved to accelerate his plans for the open break with the Habsburgs, and to preserve in the meantime whatever could be salvaged from the wrecked remains of Bernhard's force. These developments are examined by Martin Hume, who wrote:

> The Cardinal Infante passed on his way triumphant to his new governorship, crowned by the laurels of victory and the plaudits of his countrymen. But his active intervention in the war with Spanish Government troops changed the aspect of the war. The Swedes were no longer the leaders of a federation of Protestants against a federation of Catholics. It was clear to Richelieu that unless with the whole force of France he threw himself into the fray against the house of Austria, not only Protantism in Germany would suffer – for that indeed he cared nothing – but the vital interests of France. And so it happened that when the Cardinal Infante was entering Brussels in pompous triumph, Richelieu had already heavily subsidised the Dutch for an active renewal of their war against him; and within a few months, early in 1635, Spain herself was in the grip of a great national struggle with France, a struggle which extended as time went on from her Flanders dominions to her Italian possession, and from the Franche-Comté to the sacred soil of Spain itself.[105]

Thus, Nordlingen was far more than the Imperial answer to Breitenfeld, it was also a loud, dramatic declaration to the effect that the Swedish part of the war had come to an end. Moved to offset the threat to the Dutch by the invigorated Cardinal-Infante, and to defend its interests in Germany which the reeling Swedes could no longer protect, Cardinal Richelieu and his king embarked solemnly upon a course which was to transform the conflict, and effectively create the Thirty Years War.[106]

For God or the Devil

832

FIVE
From Victors to Vanquished

Axel Oxenstierna had experienced the greatest highs of the Thirty Years War, and he had watched awestruck as his king had transformed not merely the nature of the conflict, but the fortunes of Sweden. Gustavus Adolphus would be immortalised as the man who made the Swedish Empire, and if Oxenstierna failed now, then he would be the Chancellor that lost it. The schizophrenic nature of the war had delivered such momentous highs and lows for the Imperial and the Swedish cause, and the fortunes of war now flowed firmly in favour of the Emperor. The truly important question, in the aftermath of such a devastating defeat, was how Oxenstierna would react. How would he respond to this latest turning point of the war, and could his actions prevent the worst consequences from being realised? Oxenstierna had seen how a single battle could change the narrative of the war – now that he was on the other end of this changing narrative, Sweden would be preserved or torn asunder based on how the Chancellor decided to react. It was a formidable challenge, but that Oxenstierna proved equal to the task of what essentially amounted to damage control explains why Sweden remained an active participant in the conflict until 1648, and how the Swedish Empire was maintained for much longer. None of this was certain in the autumn of 1634 though; the old problems of unpaid soldiery, unreliable allies and strategic disadvantages remained acute, and had only been exacerbated by the shattering loss.

Bernhard of Weimar made his way to Heilbronn with the remnants of his army, some fourteen thousand men in all – 'the great misfortune is so bad it could not be any worse' was the gloomy note he forwarded to Oxenstierna. This gloom was contagious, as news of the loss spread to Frankfurt on Main, where many of the delegates for the Heilbronn League had made their base. Utterly despondent at the loss, several packed up and fled. Oxenstierna urged them to stay, and to help arrange a defence along the Main River, which could serve as an effective barrier between the Imperial and Swedish spheres of Germany. Yet his requests fell on deaf ears, and before long the Imperials had arrived, targeting several of the more important bastions along the winding Main River, such as Wurzburg and Schweinfurt. The Imperial army felt content to divide and conquer; Stuttgart fell on 19 September, Wurttemberg was totally overwhelmed, and the Hessian duke who had conquered it for Sweden beat a hasty retreat.

Even a long-time ally of the Swedes, William of Hesse-Cassel, was close to apoplectic, and noted in November 'the House of Austria wishes to subjugate all Germany, extirpating liberty and the Reformed religion. So in this extremity we must look to France.'[107] Before France could be looked at though, the focus turned to Bavaria and the Palatinate; one by one in autumn 1634, the breath-taking pace of Sweden's conquests in the region were undone by the Imperials, with Regensburg and Donauworth falling in October, and Heidelberg, the late Winter King's capital, captured on 19 November, leaving only its citadel to hold out. That same month, a secret mission by representatives of the Heilbronn League had been sent to Paris, where they made extensive concessions to France in return for French control of their body, to the detriment of the reeling Swedes, who would be effectively pushed out. When Oxenstierna learned of these approaches by his erstwhile allies in December, he determined to absolve himself of the fiction of leadership of the Heilbronn League 'never to return'.[108]

There seemed to be next to nothing that Oxenstierna could do to stem the tidal wave of military losses; it was akin to the collapse of Central Germany after Breitenfeld, or the surrender of Bavaria after the River Lech. And more uncomfortable parallels were to be found in the men Oxenstierna was forced to rely upon. While he had been defeated, Bernhard of Weimar seemed like the only military leader with some grasp of the situation. Gustav Horn, Bernhard's peer during Nordlingen, had been captured by the Imperials, while Johan Baner was cementing his position in a defendable enclave in Pomerania. Bernhard of Weimar withdrew his army from Heilbronn to make a base in Alsace on the left bank of the Rhine, where the friendly neutrality of France could be depended upon. Yet even there he was not safe; while moving to Worms, where the remaining Heilbronn delegates had convened on 2 December, Bernhard was made aware of the mobilisation of the Habsburg resources along the Rhine.[109] Leading the charge was the dispossessed Duke Charles of Lorraine, whose appearance in the Imperial camp suggested that an open breach between the Emperor and the King of France loomed. This merely meant greater opportunities of employment for Bernhard – after all, if Sweden collapsed, he would have no qualms about switching his loyalties to that of France, as later events proved.[110]

Just as devastating for Oxenstierna as the military setbacks were the political gunshots which were fired across Sweden's bow. One significant outcome of Nordlingen was the new opportunity granted to Cardinal Richelieu to fill the power vacuum left by Sweden with that of France. As William of Hesse-Cassel, quoted above, had recognised in November 1634, German Protestants had little choice other than to rely on the promises of the King of France, and yet France had not yet officially involved itself in the German War. As the historian A. Lloyd Moote recognised:

Unless France intervened, Nordlingen spelled the end of the German war – to the advantage of the emperor. Hence Richelieu, with great reluctance but keen understanding, worked toward two new alliances that would prevent Habsburg hegemony at the price of bringing on the war that had been avoided in 1631.[111]

It was necessary to prepare the political ground in Europe before France committed itself wholly to intervention in Germany; it was also to be expected that in the showdown between the Bourbon and Habsburg dynasties, peace would not come to Germany for some time. And yet, the considerations of France had not been foremost in the mind of the Elector of Saxony, when he signed the Preliminaries of Pirna ten weeks after Nordlingen. These agreements between John George of Saxony and Emperor Ferdinand brought to life the possibility which Oxenstierna had for so long feared – that Saxony would abandon Sweden in its hour of need, and that Brandenburg, Hesse-Darmstadt and other renowned German Protestant powers would follow suit.

Indeed, the Preliminaries at Pirna were merely the first step towards what was perceived as the final German peace. The terms were established from early stage; John George would receive Lusatia, that province of the Kingdom of Bohemia which he had been handed in 1620 to buy his loyalty to the Emperor. In return, John George would recognise Maximillian of Bavaria's receipt of the Palatinate, along with the title it accrued. But that was not all; John George would also have to recognise a religious state of affairs in the Empire which was dated at November 1627. This 'normative date' amounted to a turning back of the clock for Protestants and Catholics alike; the Habsburgs' thumping gains in Germany up to that point would be preserved, but the Edict of Restitution which had followed in 1629 would be suspended for forty years. In practice, the Edict would be effectively abandoned, removing in the process a major gripe in the Saxon camp.

In February 1635, Emperor Ferdinand was busy meeting with his theologians and advisors regarding these peace terms. Of the twenty-four men assembled, only six voted against the limited concessions made to the Saxons. Nordlingen was seen as a blessing from God, as vindication for the Emperor's faith in the Catholic cause, and as proof of the wisdom of removing Wallenstein. However, it had also been a desperately urgent victory, amidst a sea of uninspired defeat and retreats. Just as easily as the supremacy now returned to the Habsburgs, it could be taken away with another Breitenfeld. Ferdinand, and the majority of his counsellors, were therefore moved to be cautious and conciliatory – they had apparently learned their lessons of the last few years.[112] If lessons had been learned in Ferdinand's court, then it also seemed like a corner had been turned – no longer were radical Catholics in control of Imperial policy, and no longer would Germans be pitted against one another with religion as the major source of the division. The suspension of the Edict certainly aided this development, but it was also true that Vienna had come to appreciate the importance of making peace with Saxony before the expected intervention from France.[113]

The road to the Peace of Prague, signed on 30 May 1635, was paved with the diplomatic contacts first established between the Emperor and Saxon Elector in spring 1632. Throughout 1633, with Wallenstein's numerous ceasefires making further dialogue possible, the position of Saxony was teased out, but John George could not contemplate abandoning Sweden so long as they seemed the stronger power. Nordlingen changed all that, and enabled John George to depart from the Swedish alliance first formulated in September 1631. John George had empowered Hans Georg von Arnim to negotiate in his stead, and the removal of Wallenstein in February 1634, to be replaced by Ferdinand III in late spring, granted the Saxon a unique opportunity to negotiate directly with the Imperial court. The more moderate, pragmatic tone of the Imperial negotiators, headed by the Emperor's son and heir, indicated that greater progress could be made, but Nordlingen made it all possible. At Pirna in November the bare bones were laid down, and on 28 February 1635 a truce was signed at Laun which formally brought Saxony out of the war. George William of Brandenburg was not slow in following; his resentment over the seizure of Pomerania by Sweden and his fear at being left to face the wrath of the Emperor alone proved compelling indeed.[114]

When news of these truces reached Oxenstierna, he could have no illusions over what it meant – the two Protestant Electors could not be expected to rely on a mere truce for long, and a formal arrangement would surely follow. Sweden's position as leader of Germany's Protestants had already been usurped by France in November 1634; all Oxenstierna possessed was the unreliable Bernhard of Saxe-Weimar on the Rhine, and Johan Baner in Pomerania. Clearly, French acceptance of leadership of the Heilbronn League would pull France further into Germany, and potentially into conflict with the Emperor himself. There were already abundant signals sent out by Paris that she did not intend to remain aloof from the conflict for long. In March 1635, a French army overran the Val Telline, thereby severing the route connecting Spain's Italian possessions with those of Austria. To further compromise the Habsburg ability to reinforce its possessions, control over Alsace was increased, thus removing a vital land route between Lombardy and Flanders.

The Spanish Road was all but cut, but Richelieu was eager to do more than exacerbate Spain's supply problems; on 8 February an alliance with the Dutch was formalised. Greater subsidies were provided, and a provision for the partition of the Spanish Netherlands was even made. With her ally in the war against Spain secured, Richelieu then turned to securing Sweden for the conflict with the Emperor. It was not believed possible to refrain from attacking one branch of the Habsburg family – France would be going all in.[115] As Richelieu later noted:

If it is a sign of singular prudence to have held down the forces opposed to your state for a period of ten years with the forces of your allies, by putting your hand in your pocket and not on your sword, then, when your allies can no longer exist without you, to engage in open warfare is a sign of courage and great wisdom.[116]

Plainly, France's allies could no longer exist without them by spring 1635, and in recognition of this on 28 April, France formalised its alliance with the Heilbronn League and Sweden in the Treaty of Compiegne. A provision of this alliance moved France to make a public declaration of war on Spain and Austria as soon as was possible. Already, twelve thousand French soldiers had been promised to the Germans for the 1635 campaign, and Heidelberg's citadel had been relieved by a force of French soldiers, who effectively saved this final bastion of the Palatinate from falling into Habsburg hands. As had happened in previous Franco-Swedish negotiations though, much was left undefined until a later date – Oxenstierna was left to sweat, almost certainly in a literal sense, as the Swedish Chancellor met with his French counterpart in person to hammer this treaty out. We are told that Richelieu found Oxenstierna 'a bit gothic, and very wily', and we imagine there was some semblance of genuine respect, as these two leaders of the anti-Habsburg cause knew they would have to cooperate.[117] Perhaps it is worth remembering the Cardinal's warnings regarding the pitfalls of diplomacy when it was in less capable hands. As Richelieu has written:

> Just as ignoramuses are not good negotiators, so there are certain minds so finely drawn and delicately organised as to be even less well suited, since they become overly subtle about everything. They are, so to speak, like those who break the points of needles by trying to make them too fine. For the best results, it is necessary that men hold themselves to a middle course. The most successful ones use their keenness of mind to prevent themselves from being deceived, having a care not to use the same means for deceiving those with whom they are negotiating.[118]

But Oxenstierna was himself no 'ignoramus', and his delicate diplomatic style and penchant for thoroughness had singled him out long ago as Sweden's premier statesman, more than equal to the task of meeting with France's foremost Cardinal.[119] The problem was not Oxenstierna's shortcomings, but the weaknesses of his realm, which were becoming more pronounced by the month. It was no secret by April 1635 that Sweden had lost its military supremacy in Germany, and that its very presence south of the River Main was no more. Elsewhere in Germany, hostility towards the Swede was increasing due to the changing tide of opinion and desire for peace. To German figures like John George of Saxony, Maximillian of Bavaria, George William of Brandenburg and many others, the sole power standing in the way of a final peace after more than fifteen years of war was Sweden. Surely, the combined might of all Germany, save for some recalcitrant traitors, would be enough to rid the Empire of the foreign invader.

Indeed, this may have been so, but it was a state of affairs which France absolutely could not allow. For in its looming showdown with the Habsburgs, in Austria and Spain, it was imperative that another power was made to carry the burden of war in the Empire. Powerful though she was, France could not carry this burden alone. Evidently, Nordlingen had moved Richelieu to step up his interventionist plans and become bolder. 'In the space of six months, therefore', Geoffrey Parker writes, 'France had skilfully isolated her enemies before launching an attack on several fronts.'[120] Conveniently for Richelieu, there was even a handy excuse for involving France in the war, provided by the aggressive policy of the Spanish.

Following his triumphant campaign at Nordlingen, the Cardinal-Infante Ferdinand was urged by the Emperor to remain in Germany and aid Austria with its war effort. Unfortunately for Emperor Ferdinand though, the Cardinal-Infante had been given a job to do by Madrid. Since the death of Isabella, the Archduchess of the Spanish Netherlands and aunt of the King of Spain in December 1633, that beleaguered portion of Spain's European Empire had been rudderless, and subject to intrigue from the Dutch. Frederick Henry, the military and political leader of the Dutch Republic, engaged in few new initiatives throughout 1634, but the triumph at Nordlingen would certainly have stung, as would the news that the star of that battlefield, the Cardinal-Infante, was on his way to Brussels, to serve as the new Governor of the province. The arrival of such a dynamic figure could only re-energise the war party in The Hague and make them more agreeable to a treaty with France, which was formally signed in February 1635.[121]

Perhaps it was because of this re-energised Spanish command that Spanish forces increased their activity along the Rhine. On 26 March the Electorate of Trier was invaded by the Spanish, and its archbishop taken prisoner. We may recall that during that early successes of Gustavus Adolphus, several Electoral German leaders had welcomed French protection rather than take their chances with the Swedes. Among those who had sought French protection was this Elector of Trier. As David Parrott explained:

> Despite the ambiguous attitudes of his subjects, the Elector himself had been one of the earliest and most consistent adherents of French protection. His abduction was an outright challenge to the credibility of French military and political guarantees and demanded a French response.[122]

After several months of manoeuvring, of formulating alliances with the Netherlands and Sweden, and securing their frontier along the Rhine through the subjugation of Alsace and Lorraine, it was abundantly clear to Cardinal Richelieu and his King that this deliberate act of provocation could only be answered one way – through war. As Richelieu stated:

> Kings should be very careful with regard to the treaties they conclude but having concluded them they should observe them religiously. I well know that many statesmen advise to the contrary, but without considering here what the Christian religion offers in answer to such advice, I maintain that the loss of honour is worse than the loss of life itself. A great prince should sooner put in jeopardy both his own interests and even those of the state than break his word, which he can never violate without losing his reputation, and by consequence the greatest instrument of sovereigns.[123]

The Treaty with the Elector of Trier was being called into question by the Spanish, and thus the honour of King Louis XIII was on the line. According to his own principles, let alone the traditions of the era, Richelieu could do no other than advise his King to act. The time had come to transform the cold, covert war between the Houses of Bourbon and Habsburg dynasties into an open struggle. On 19 May 1635, a royal herald was sent to Brussels, thus making the Franco-Spanish War official. It would not end in Richelieu's lifetime, or even within the boundaries of the Thirty Years War. That said, it represented a critical step towards the widening of the war, which had for so long been threatened, and was now made fact. The open intervention of France in the war against Spain meant that the conflict ceased to be one defined merely by the latest intervening power; instead, there was now a veritable coalition of states pitted against the Habsburg influence, in Germany and in Flanders, and all across the world. The age of interventions was over, and the age of coalitions had thus begun.

It is unclear whether news of the erupting war between Spain and France reached those assembled at Prague in the month of May 1635. The news was certainly ominous, but it did not mean that war between France and the Emperor was at hand. There was time first to bring to an end the war between the Emperor and his vassals first. The Peace of Prague was published on 30 May 1635, and represents in the first place a watershed moment, in a year of watershed moments. It severed the partnership between many of the most important German princes with the invading foreign powers, and it also compelled them to defend this German fatherland against the invader through war. It was, therefore, not merely a declaration of their intentions to make peace, but also a statement of intent by all concerned, to do all in their power to rid the Holy Roman Empire of the cruel invader through war.[124]

At its core, the Peace of Prague aimed at bringing peace between the Protestant North of Germany, led by Saxony, and the Catholic South, led by the Emperor and Maximillian of Bavaria. It intended to heal the rifts of recent years by making official the transfer of lands and titles and freezing the delicate state of church lands at November 1627, which struck an acceptable balance. Of most concern to us was article 35, which proclaimed:

> Concerning the foreign potentates and nations, in particular the crowns of
> France, Sweden and others, who are neither Imperial Estates, nor members
> of the Empire, nor are currently recognised as such, nor were once formerly,
> and who do not accept this peace, nor will abide by it, His Electoral Highness
> of Saxony, together with other adherents of the Augsburg Confession, electors
> and Estates, if they wish to enjoy this peace, must assist his Roman Majesty
> and the Catholics with their entire strength without any delay to restore and
> recover peace by the power of this treaty, as well as the general Public Peace
> and Imperial ordinances and discuss the ways and means to implement the
> peace agreement.[125]

It was not just a peace treaty then; it was also a contract which bound all
'loyal' Germans to make war on the invader under the Emperor's command
for as long as it took. For this to work, the Emperor recognised that it was
necessary to forgive what had been done in the past, as article 54 declared:

> There is a complete amnesty between, on the one side, His Roman Imperial
> Majesty and allied Catholic Electors and Estates, and on the other His Electoral
> Highness and all other adherents of the Augsburg Confession who were
> previously at war, provided they fully accept this Peace and its implementation
> with ten days of notification of its publication without delay.

It was therefore ruled:

> This covers all that has passed between them during the war since the arrival
> of the King of Sweden on Imperial soil in 1630 and annuls all disagreement,
> displeasure and opposition, regardless of how it occurred, so that neither side
> shall think further ill of the other, nor threat or use action or the law against
> the other. In particular [the Emperor and his allies] will not claim war costs
> or damages from the adherents of the Augsburg Confession, who do likewise
> with His Imperial Majesty.[126]

There would be exemptions from this amnesty though; for one, the
Palatine family, 'Because their suppression caused His Imperial Majesty and
His House such heavy burdens and forced them to leave behind and abandon
several hereditary lands', the Emperor was therefore entitled to wrest
compensation from them, though the Winter Queen's offspring could claim
a pension from the Emperor so long as they submitted.[127] Article 64 stressed:

> ...the high necessity, as well as duty, love and loyalty to the Fatherland, as well
> as the solemn duty and oath binding them to His Roman Imperial Majesty and
> the Holy Empire, to exhort them to publish the current peace treaty in their
> territory and to accept and observe all its points, and then to actually withdraw
> his soldiers from his neighbours' lands, without thereby doing anyone any
> harm, and to combine these troops with His Imperial Majesty's army, and to

maintain no more soldiers than are necessary to garrison their fortified places. In addition, upon acceptance of this Peace Treaty, they are to report how many troops can join the imperial army, and what condition they are currently in.[128]

It was thus a multi-layered peace; not merely a call to all loyal Germans, but also something of an ultimatum, and a census. If Germans adhered to its terms, then Vienna would be furnished with up to date details on how many soldiers they could call upon and their location, so that the defence of Germany would be made much easier. While the document represented a challenge to all Germans to once more choose between God or the Devil, with terrible consequences, the choice was made much easier and more palatable by the notable relaxation of religious rhetoric which had characterised earlier attempts at peace-making. The historian Robert Bireley effectively summarised the Peace of Prague when he wrote:

> Despite its failure to provide a permanent settlement for the problems of the Empire, the Peace of Prague was of major significance for German history. It was a milestone on the way toward religious toleration in Germany. Inasmuch as it ended the most aggressive phase of the Counterreformation in the Empire, it was both a return to the moderate Catholic policy set by Ferdinand I at the time of the [1555] Peace of Augsburg and an anticipation of the [1648] Peace of Westphalia. The Peace of Prague was the grave of the militant ideology that arose in the wake of the White Mountain and played a decisive role in the middle period of the Thirty Years War. The crusading spirit that had departed from Spain and Rome to move north, was now put to rest in Germany as well. The belief that Ferdinand had been specially selected by God and promised assistance to lead the Church to complete triumph in the Empire was no longer to be an effective factor in the formulation of policy. This does not mean that in the future the Emperor would overlook the welfare of the Church. Both Ferdinand II and his son, Ferdinand III, would endeavour to secure all possible benefits for her. But the principle had been established, or perhaps better, re-established, that concessions could be of greater advantage to both Church and Empire. When rational analysis showed this to be the case, they could be made without fear of betraying a divine mission or failing to trust in the Lord. The moderates had gained the upper hand, and they were not to relinquish it.[129]

One of the most notable omissions from the Peace was any reference to giving foreign powers satisfaction – on the contrary, as article 35 had established, these powers would be forcibly ejected if they would not make a peace, and satisfaction was never to be on the table. Thus, the historian Richard Bonney called it a 'Habsburg-dominated treaty, which refused any concessions to Sweden or its dwindling band of exiled Calvinist princes' and added 'The settlement excluded Calvinists from legal rights under the Imperial constitution.'[130] The political implications of the Peace of Prague had not escaped Richelieu's notice: 'The Elector of Saxony has made his peace' the Cardinal wrote, 'but that will have no effect on us save to make us renew our efforts to keep all in train.'[131]

Rather than facilitate peace, indeed, the Peace of Prague guaranteed the continuation of the war, and on a scale probably not fully appreciated at the time by the German signees. Their intention had been to end the war in Germany by banding together and accepting the Emperor's concessions, but instead, they were now compelled to rid Germany of all enemies, which included Sweden, but soon also, France. 'And', wrote Wedgewood, 'if they closed in conflict with France, they must make common cause with the King of Spain.' In other words, Wedgewood concluded, 'the Peace of Prague was metamorphosed into an alliance for war, and those who signed it bound themselves to fight the battle of the House of Austria.'[132]

And just in time too, for with the direct intervention of France against Spain, the aged Emperor needed his German vassals by his side now more than ever – it was only a matter of time before the French declared against the Emperor too. After so many years of uncertain, but certainly hostile, neutrality, a sense of clarity had finally been applied to the situation. As the summer of 1635 beckoned, the new battle-lines were drawn. All the resources of the Habsburg dynasty, in Austria and in Spain, would be pitted against those of France, Sweden and the Dutch. The wars of the last few decades had finally congealed and coalesced, as though according to some well-orchestrated plan, when in fact they had been forged and borne out by the unpredictable highs and lows of this Thirty Years War.

Chapter 17 Notes

[1]Brennan Pursell, *The Winter King*, pp. 270-271.

[2]See Karl Friedrich Wilhelm Wander, *German Proverb Lexicon* Bd. II (F. A. Brockhaus, Leipzig 1870), p. 1615

[3]Pursell, *Winter King*, p. 271.

[4]Matusiak, *Europe in Flames*, p. 320.

[5]Wilson, *Europe's Tragedy*, p. 499.

[6]*Ibid*, p. 500.

[7]Matusiak, *Europe in Flames*, p. 325.

[8]Pursell, *Winter King*, p. 272.

[9]See Michael Roberts, *Gustavus Adolphus: A History of Sweden*, pp. 613-614.

[10]Pursell, *Winter King*, pp. 272.273.

[11]Parker, *Europe in Crisis*, p. 229.

[12]Wilson, *Great Battles – Lutzen*, p. 37.

[13]See Wedgewood, *Thirty Years War*, pp. 298-299

[14]See Pieter Geyl, *History of the Dutch-Speaking Peoples*, pp. 384-385.

[15]For more on this argument see Pärtel Piirimäe, 'Just War in Theory and Practice: The Legitimation of Swedish Intervention in the Thirty Years War', pp. 516-521.

[16]Geyl, *Dutch-Speaking Peoples*, p. 385.

[17]*Ibid*, pp. 386-387.

[18]*Ibid*, pp. 387-388.

[19]Wilson, *Great Battles – Lutzen*, pp. 36-37.

[20]*Ibid*, p. 36.

[21]Parker, *Europe in Crisis*, p. 228.

[22]Matusiak, *Europe in Flames*, p. 326.

[23]Wilson, *Lutzen*, pp. 33-34.

[24]Geoff Mortimer, *Wallenstein*, p. 142.

[25]Wilson, *Europe's Tragedy*, p. 501.

[26]*Ibid*, pp. 504-506.

[27]*Ibid*, pp. 506-508.

[28]Theodore Ayrault Dodge, *Gustavus Adolphus*, p. 393.

[29]See Peter H. Wilson, *Lutzen*, pp. 52-53.

[30]See Robert L. O'Connell, *Of Arms and Men: A History of War, Weapons, and Aggression* (New York: Oxford University Press, 1989), pp. 145-147.

[31]Matusiak, *Europe in Flames*, p. 328.

[32]Mortimer, *Wallenstein*, pp. 169-172

[33]See Wilson, *Lutzen*, pp. 53-54. Wilson claims that tercio squares had 'never used during the Thirty Years War, even by Tilly' (53), yet this conflicts with accounts of the battles of White Mountain (1620), Lutter (1626), Breitenfeld (1631) and Nördlingen (1634). While Wallenstein seems to have adapted his tactics to suit Gustavus' at Lutzen, the tercio was not discredited. It remained a respected method of war for the Habsburgs, and they would use it to great effect at Nördlingen, where their tercios defeated the Swedish army. See Fernando Gonzalez de Leon, '"Doctors of the Military Discipline": Technical Expertise and the Paradigm of the Spanish Soldier in the Early Modern Period', *The Sixteenth Century Journal*, Vol. 27, No. 1 (Spring, 1996), pp. 61-85; Wedgewood, *Thirty Years War*, pp. 371-377.

[34]Quoted in Stevens, *History of Gustavus Adolphus*, p. 412.

[35]Quoted in *Ibid*, p. 413.

[36]*Ibid*, p. 413.

[37]Wilson, *Lutzen*, pp. 59-60.

[38]Quoted in Stevens, *History of Gustavus Adolphus*, p. 413.

[39]*Ibid*, pp. 423-426.

[40]The best map of the battle is provided by Wilson, *Europe's Tragedy*, p. 509, from which all this detail can be deduced. See also Dodge, *Gustavus Adolphus*, p. 392.

[41]Wilson, *Lutzen*, pp. 68-79 provides the fullest account of the battle.

[42]Stevens, *History of Gustavus Adolphus*, p. 417.

[43]See Wilson, *Europe's Tragedy*, pp. 508-510.

[44]Fletcher, *Gustavus Adolphus and the Struggle of Protestantism for Existence*, p. 285.

[45]Ward, G. W. Prothero, and Stanley Leathes, eds., *The Cambridge Modern History*, pp. 219-223.

[46]Wilson, *Europe's Tragedy*, p. 511.

[47]Adapted from quote in Ingvar Andersson, *A History of Sweden*, p. 178.

[48]See Stewart P. Oakley, *War and Peace in the Baltic,* pp. 55-111.

[49]Quoted in Matusiak, *Europe in Flames*, p. 330.

[50]Quoted in John Roger Paas, 'The Changing Image of Gustavus Adolphus on German Broadsheets', p. 230.

[51]*Ibid*, p. 228.

[52]*Ibid*, p. 230.

[53]*Ibid*, p. 237.

[54]*Ibid*, p. 238.

[55]*Ibid*, p. 239.

[56]*Ibid*, p. 243.

[57]*Ibid*, pp. 243-244.

[58]Stevens, *History of Gustavus Adolphus*, p. 426.

[59]See Brennan Pursell, *Winter King*, p. 277.

[60]Antonia Fraser, *King Charles II* (London: Phoenix, 2011), especially chapter 11.

[61]See Pursell, *Winter King*, pp. 275-278.

[62]Ingvar Andersson, *A History of Sweden*, pp. 179-180.

[63]See Wilson, *Lutzen*, pp. 87-89.

[64]See Wilson, *Europe's Tragedy*, pp. 514-515.

[65]*Ibid*, pp. 516-517.

[66]David Parrott, *Richelieu's Army: War, Government, and Society in France, 1624-1642* (Cambridge, England: Cambridge University Press, 2001), p. 105

[67]Quoted in Wilson, *Sourcebook*, pp. 179-180, emphasis my own.

[68]All quoted in *Ibid*, p. 180.

[69]Quoted in *Ibid*, p. 181.

[70]Stomberg, *A History of Sweden*, pp. 370-373.

[71]Wilson, *Europe's Tragedy*, p. 517.

[72]Dodge, *Gustavus Adolphus*, pp. 416-417.

[73]Wilson, *Europe's Tragedy*, pp. 518-519.

[74]Parrott, *Richelieu's Army*, pp. 105-106.

[75]A. Lloyd Moote, *Louis XIII, the Just*, pp. 234-235.

[76]See Parker, *Thirty Years War*, p. 123.

[77]William P Guthrie, *Battles of the Thirty Years War: from White Mountain to Nordlingen, 1618-1635* (CT: Greenwood Publishing Group. 2002), pp. 249-255.

[78]Wilson, *Europe's Tragedy*, p. 523.

[79]Wedgewood, *Thirty Years War*, p. 342.

[80]Mortimer, *Wallenstein*, p. 181.

[81]*Ibid*, p. 188.

[82]Quoted in Mortimer, *Wallenstein*, p. 192.

[83]See Wedgewood, *Thirty Years War*, pp. 343-344.

[84]See Wilson, *Europe's Tragedy*, pp. 535-537.

[85]Mortimer, *Wallenstein*, pp. 194-196.

[86]Both quoted in *Ibid*, pp. 193-194.

[87]*Ibid*, pp. 195-196.

[88]Quoted in *Ibid*, p. 202.

[89]*Ibid*, pp. 206-207.

[90]*Ibid*, p. 209.
[91]See Wedgewood, *Thirty Years War*, p. 345.
[92]See Wilson, *Europe's Tragedy*, pp. 538-540.
[93]Mortimer, *Wallenstein*, p. 232.
[94]Wilson, *Europe's Tragedy*, p. 541.
[95]Parker, *Europe in Crisis*, pp. 232-233.
[96]*Ibid*, p. 233.
[97]George Edmundson, 'Frederick Henry, Prince of Orange (Continued)', *The English Historical Review*,

(Top left) Jan II Kazimierz of Poland (Peter Paul Rubens)
(Top right) Matthias Gallas

Top left) Bernhard Saxe-Weimar (Michiel van Mierevelt, 1630)
(Top right) Gaspar de Guzman, Count-Duke of Oliveres (Diego Velazquez, 1643)

PART FIVE
Years of Coalitions
-1635-1648-

"By now I am nearly at my wits end, but I say, and I shall still be saying on my deathbed, that if the constitutions do not allow this, then the devil take the constitutions, and whoever observes them, myself included. For no man can observe them who has not been abandoned by God, and who is not an enemy of His Divine Majesty, of his king, and of his fatherland."[1]

Count Duke Olivares proclaims his wrath for Catalonia, 1639.

"Well over a year has passed during which I, a pastor, have not been able – in a whole year – to have a dish on my table…Those who were once the most distinguished and richest…are now the poorest. They have carried loads of wood or some corn across the fields for payment or for themselves, barefoot or just in stockings, and without shoes, for they had none, just to earn their bread. I don't want to name them; it is not their disgrace."[2]

Pastor Ludolph laments on his plight: Hesse, 1642.

Can he make peace without even asking me? Does he not owe all his victories to me? Have I not shot down the Swedish king? Have I not conquered Saxony? Have I not earned my reputation in Denmark? How would the battle on White Mountain have ended without me? What glory have I not earned in the battle with Grand Turk? Fie upon you…[3]

An extract from "Horribilicribfrix", a comedy drama by Silesian poet Andreas Gryphius, published in 1664.

CHAPTER EIGHTEEN
"Death and Disaster"

ONE: Ripples to the East
TWO: The Great Showdown
THREE: The Road to Wittstock
FOUR: Death of an Emperor

ONE

Ripples to the East

Are the Polish Crown Prince Wladyslaw and his brothers talking with the
Emperor at the present time, and if so, what about? And will the Emperor help
Crown Prince Wladyslaw and his brothers against Muscovy in some way, and
if so, how? With men or with money? ... And the ambassadors are to discover
whether other states are having fresh discussions with the Polish Crown Prince
and his brothers, and if so, what about? And do any of these states want to help
the Poles against Muscovy, and if so, how do they mean to help? With men or
with money?[4]

While this anxious set of questions was formulated as a kind of
guidebook for the group of Russian agents sent on a 'Great Embassy' to
Sweden in spring 1633, it could just as easily be posed by contemporaries to
any one of the belligerents within the Thirty Years War. It was often difficult to
gain a full picture of the inclinations of particular actors, or to gauge the true
intentions of one's allies. Axel Oxenstierna knew all about unreliable allies:
the Protestant Electors switched sides three times between 1630-35, from the
Emperor to Sweden and back again. But Oxenstierna was equally aware that
Sweden had been profoundly affected by the death of Gustavus Adolphus,
not just in terms of its military position, but also in the diplomatic sphere –
would agreements made by and with Gustavus Adolphus still be honoured
now? The context of the Russian 'Great Embassy' to Sweden is tremendously
important, as it contributes to our understanding of the wider European
situation. As we have seen, the role of Russia in the early 1630s was critical
to Gustavus Adolphus – a Russian war against Poland would guarantee that
King Sigismund would not endanger Sweden while she invaded Germany.[5]

Yet, the second phase of this narrative is less well known, and it began in
January 1633, soon after the death of Gustavus Adolphus had been learned of.
The death of the main Swedish sponsor of the Russian alliance meant that it
would have to be renegotiated or at least reinforced by the Russians again. As
was customary though, the Russian agents were still required to be respectful

towards Gustavus' widow and daughter, who might well be the new agents of Swedish foreign policy. They were required to express their condolences in unambiguous terms, emphasising that 'King Gustavus Adolphus was killed in battle by the soldiers of the enemy, the Emperor', and:

> ...that against the common foes of our great sovereign Majesty the Tsar and His Royal Majesty, against the heretics of the Roman faith, the Papists and the Jesuits, their wrong-doings and persecutions, and for your faith, His Royal Majesty stood forth in his valour, firmly and courageously, and won many a victory over them, and in that war, for his sovereign nature and his faith and for all the people in the German states to have justice, he yielded and laid down his royal life.[6]

Noble though he had been, the authors of these instructions would certainly have preferred if Gustavus had not 'laid down his royal life', for the death of the Swedish King changed everything for Russia. In previous months, an understanding had been established that Sweden would make war on Poland in league with Russia, or that at the very least an alliance with Russia against Poland would be formalised. It was on this understanding that war had been declared by Moscow against the Poles in autumn 1632, with Russia's major aim being the recapture of Smolensk, a town lost to Poland earlier in the century.[7] For that reason, this short war between Poland and Russia is often deemed the Smolensk War, and it lasted only until summer 1634, with Russia ultimately failing to achieve its ends. None of this could be known in spring 1633 though; upon learning of Gustavus' death, the Russian agents were instructed to return to Moscow at once, only for these instructions to be modified, to the effect that the 'Great Embassy' became something of a fact-finding mission for Moscow instead.

What plans had Gustavus made for the rule of Sweden, for the relationship with Russia, or for the direction of the war in Germany, in the event of his death? Furthermore, several worst-case scenarios were conceived of in Moscow, whereby the ultimate fear of a coalition war against Russia, joined by the Emperor, Sweden and Poland, was imagined. What if the weakened Vasa regime in Stockholm was overthrown by one of the Polish King's Vasa sons? What if Wladyslaw or John Casimir managed to seize the Swedish Crown in the name of the Catholic Vasa dynasty, and thereafter turn Sweden against Russia? What if Wladyslaw, the Polish Crown Prince, managed to then claim the three crowns of Sweden, Poland and Russia all at once? Such nightmarish scenarios could not be ignored by the distant and often uninformed Kremlin. The only way to be sure of their security and to avoid another national catastrophe like the Time of Troubles (1603-1618) was for Russians to find out for themselves what the future held.[7]

The Russian embassy arrived in Stockholm on 4 June 1633, bringing the more frantic portion of their journey to an end for the moment. In their letters home to Moscow, read by Tsar Michael and his father, the so-called Patriarch, the Russian ambassadors recorded how they were honourably received by their Swedish hosts, they confirmed that Christina, Gustavus' daughter, was the heir to the Crown, and that the Polish King Sigismund III had in fact died. With Sigismund's death, his sons Wladyslaw and John Casimir would be more concerned with solidifying their position in Poland rather than seizing the Swedish Crown, and sure enough, confirmation of Wladyslaw's election as King of Poland is also provided in the correspondence.

The year 1633 was a mostly uneventful one in the military sphere, thanks largely to the hole which Gustavus' death had left. But, as the Russian agents were learning, Gustavus' death had seemed to move the Poles to act as well; alarming reports had trickled down to the Russians regarding a Polish envoy in Sweden, who had been in Stockholm not too long before to urge the Swedes not to break the truce which had been signed in 1629. Furthermore, the Russians heard that a new ambassador was on the way to Stockholm from Danzig to make this case once again. It was imperative then that the Russians acted first. They tried to find out whether the Polish delegate had made any agreements with the Swedes before, but the Swedish council were cagey, and refused to grant an official audience to the Russians just yet. This was a bad sign, but as the Russians were forced to languish in Stockholm, another envoy, a Swede by the name of Hans Berenson, languished in a lonely room in Moscow.

Berenson was supposed to be Sweden's answer to the Russian embassy; he was meant to confirm the news of Gustavus' death, of Christina's ascension and of hopes for the continuation of the Russo-Swedish alliance. Unfortunately for Berenson though, he had travelled slowly, slower in fact than his courier, who had come bearing the same information, and arrived a month earlier. This courier brought with him news of the Polish approaches which the Russian ambassadors in Stockholm had found so alarming; unlike those ambassadors though, the nobility and the Tsar in the Russian capital were empowered to do something about it. When Berenson arrived at Moscow in the first week of June 1633 then, he found the Kremlin closed to him, and his quarters were bare and bleak. Was he being punished? In fact, he was only being sweated, so that the Russian escort he had been given could find out what he knew.

Further complicating the picture in Moscow was the fact that other figures in Sweden had taken it upon themselves to open a correspondence with the Russians outside of the official governmental channels. One of these figures was the Livonian governor for Sweden's expanding Empire, a man by the name of Johan Skytte. Skytte seems to have ambitions beyond his station, and negotiated privately with the Tsar's uncle, from late 1632 and throughout 1633. He even sent his nephew to Moscow to reinforce this correspondence in July 1633, and before that, Skytte sent several letters which provided additional bits and pieces of information on the situation in Europe to the Tsar's regime. Thanks to Skytte's letters and the early arrival of the Swedish courier of letters, the unfortunate Berenson discovered that the Tsar was far better informed than he had expected, and the Russians generally were wholly suspicious of Swedish intentions.[9]

Above all, the Russians were angry about the reported visits by the Polish agents to Stockholm and wanted clarity on the future of the Swedish-Polish relationship. Now that they had in their hands a man who might be able to shed some light on the overall situation in Germany, the Baltic and the East, it was to be expected that they would hold onto him. Eventually, Berenson was granted an audience by a small circle of Russian nobles. It was true, Berenson said, that Polish agents had been in Stockholm, that Wladyslaw had offered marriage to Queen Christina, and that a truce lasting ten years had been floated as well. However, Sweden had refused these offers – the Swedish Council was adamant that not one of the late Sigismund's sons should get anywhere near the Swedish throne, and Polish access to Russia through Swedish-occupied Livonia had been refused as well.

Berenson's assurances made some impression upon the Russian nobles, but the Tsar still refused to see him until July, when his letters were taken in a brief audience. The letters Berenson bore with him apologised on behalf of all the magnates in Stockholm for the late official notice of Gustavus' death. The excuse given was that the magnates had been so grief-stricken they had been unable to pen such a letter any earlier – a lame excuse in any event – but the truth was that Swedish policy had been shaken in spring 1633 before righting itself, whereupon Swedish officials determined that the old policy with Russia would be pursued. Within Berenson's letters indeed were all the high-minded platitudes one would expect – according to the Swedish authors, Gustavus had died in the fight 'for the Evangelical and the Ancient Greek faiths', while the Catholics, led by the Emperor and the Polish King:

> ...wanted first to conquer the great Kingdom of Sweden and then the great possessions and state of Your Majesty the Tsar, and to crush the Evangelical and the Ancient Greek faiths, and to install instead their accursed Popish darkness.

Yet, the Tsar was not entirely convinced that the 'accursed Popish darkness' was a fate which Gustavus' martyrdom had saved him from. For one, the tenuous confessional aspects of Gustavus' fight were rejected, as it was stated frankly that the Swedish King 'fought for your faith' and died 'for his faith and truth and for all the people of the German states.' If they would not countenance the religious undertones of the message though, then on 5 July 1633 the Tsar and Patriarch did approve of a letter from their side which underlined the political importance of Gustavus' career and of the Russo-Swedish alliance. It was recognised that Gustavus 'fought against the common foes of His Majesty the Tsar and of His Royal Majesty', and it was hoped that the regency of Christina would not break with Gustavus' policy, instead enjoying the same 'firm friendship and love and kindness, with exchange of counsel' as before.[10]

Although the Russo-Swedish relationship was by no means hostile, it was never to realise the high-minded aims which had once been ascribed to it by its advocates, and the reason for this centred upon the Swedish strategic position in 1633, which made any fulfilment of the Russian demands impossible. It was made plain to the ambassadors of the Great Embassy over July and August 1633 that Sweden simply could not afford to make war upon the Poles. The Russians, who were already at war with Poland since the previous August, made use of the threat that if Sweden did not join Russia in its war, then the Tsar would be compelled to make a separate peace with Poland, thus freeing the Poles to make war on Sweden.

But this threat was not believed in Stockholm, for the understandable reason that since the new King Wladyslaw of Poland still claimed the title of Tsar, it would have been immensely impolitic for the actual Russian Tsar to make peace with such an enemy. Wait two more years when the truce with Poland expired naturally, the Swedish negotiators urged, and Sweden would be willing to join Russia's side in a war against Poland. In the summer of 1633, indeed, it may have appeared to these officials in Stockholm as though the war in Germany was by no means lost – only Nordlingen the following September would threaten that prospect – but the offer was still unsatisfactory to the Russian ambassadors, whose Great Embassy came to an anticlimactic end in late August 1633. As a result of these failed negotiations though, the Swedish position was left dangerously imperilled, for just at the moment when Nordlingen shattered the Swedish reputation and position, the Russians did the unthinkable (in Stockholm at least) and made peace with Poland.

The perceptive Polish King Wladyslaw reckoned that the cost of abandoning his claim to the Russian throne was worth it, for the sake of piling additional pressure upon the Swedes. By May 1635, with the Peace of Prague signed, and the grand plans for distracting the Poles up in smoke, there could be no guarantee that a vengeful Poland would not make war following the expiration of the six-year Truce of Altmark, signed in 1629, which had enabled Gustavus to rampage through the Empire. And in Stockholm, this was indeed the fear – Oxenstierna was becoming encumbered with requests from anxious Swedish nobles to abandon the German war and focus on the real threat, the Poles, instead.[11] It seems very likely that Oxenstierna was considering this: 'the Polish War', he wrote later:

> ...is *our* war, win or lose, it is our gain or loss. This German War, I do not know what it is, only that we pour out blood here for the sake of reputation, and have naught but ingratitude to expect...we must let this German business be left to the Germans, who will be the only people to get any good of it (if there is any), and therefore not spend any more men or money here, but rather try by all means to wriggle out of it.[12]

Indeed, this sounds a like a Chancellor exhausted with the very idea of continuing on in Germany, and more interested in tackling a conflict which was rooted in Sweden's dynastic interests. Unfortunately for Oxenstierna, events in the midsummer of 1635 made this option impossible for the moment and made the Swedish position far more critical than ever before.[13]

With the failure of Russo-Swedish negotiations and the end of the Smolensk War, Sweden's Polish flank was exposed, and Oxenstierna could expect a resumption of the war with that power once the truce expired in September 1635. But Oxenstierna had more immediate problems than this – the soldiery, whose pay had been so long in coming, effectively held the Swedish Chancellor prisoner at their camp near Magdeburg in late July 1635. Their grievances revolved around a want of pay, and their anxiety over the ability of Sweden to recompense them for it. Such grievances were made all the more pressing because, according to the terms of the Peace of Prague, all Germans were obliged to join the Emperor's side in ridding Germany of the foreign powers. Barely a tenth of the 'Swedish' army was actually Swedish, and most were Germans, rendered anxious about backpay and conflicted over their duties now that all Germany seemed to have turned against the Swede.[14]

Oxenstierna would have to do something radical and likely against his better judgement in order to mollify the only weapon Sweden still had, her army. The result was the Powder Barrel Convention, signed in early August 1635, and its effects were considerable. Whereas before, Sweden's war aims consisted of territorial gains or some concept of satisfaction, now the payment of the soldiery would be included within these aims. Should Oxenstierna renege on this agreement, and should the army not receive its pay, then these soldiers could be expected to rampage across Sweden until the pay was extracted by force. It was, as Geoffrey Parker noted, 'an appalling prospect', but Oxenstierna had had no choice but to agree.[15] He had explained, according to the document of the Powder Barrel Convention, 'the generally dire situation following the Peace of Prague, that has divided the evangelical Estates and caused such widespread collapse that there is now no human help left than our honourable army.' And yet, continued the Convention:

> If our army was also to go, the entire cause would be lost. The soldiery would not only not be content, but each and every cavalier serving in this army could expect all kinds of unpleasantness, even threat to body, life, hour and property,

not to mention that only insults and ridicule would reward the right-honourable Swedish Crown, His Excellency's beloved fatherland and above all the blood of its most glorious late King.[16]

It was the following paragraph which established the significance of this arrangement – for the first time in the war, the needs and dues of the soldiery were to be included within any consideration of a final peace:

> The only way, other than God, to prevent this and to try and obtain a good, reputable peace, and to provide some satisfaction to the soldiery as well as the right honourable Swedish Crown, was for His Excellency to be empowered by his beloved fatherland and for the soldiery to unite and to stand firmly and resolutely together until we die or God Almighty grants a desirable and honourable peace, either through negotiation or force of arms…Those officers and soldiers who will see this through to the end, should it lead to fighting with the Elector of Saxony and should this cause them suffering or (Almighty God forbid) should they be driven in force from Germany, wish to be assured that their loyal service thus far will be rewarded and their pay settled, or [advised as] to whom they should turn to for this.[17]

It was a polite, almost gentlemanly way of phrasing the situation, but Oxenstierna was under no illusions as to what he had just agreed to. The jeopardy for Sweden was now immense – the Chancellor was effectively banking on one of the Swedish generals pulling another Gustavus and turning the military-political situation around once again. This, at least, was how it seemed, but in reality, Oxenstierna's plans went deeper than that. Throughout 1635, and especially after the conclusion of the Peace of Prague, the Swedish Chancellor had come to accept that Sweden's succour lay not in the hope of another military victory or in a new league of German potentates, but with France.

And Sweden was not the only power to cleave closer to its French ally in light of recent events. The conflict in the Netherlands appeared to be reaching a fever pitch with the arrival of the triumphant Cardinal-Infante in Brussels early in 1635. Basking in the glow of the recent Habsburg triumph at Nordlingen, this new governor of the Spanish Netherlands arrived with great expectations and ambitions, but was soon to discover what his aunt, and so many other governors had learned before him – that the task of maintaining this underfunded and hard-pressed appendage of Spain's European Empire was a thankless task indeed.[18] Although the citizens of Flanders greeted the arrival of an energetic new governor from the royal family with enthusiasm, it soon became hard to mask the gloom which the vibrancy and ambition of the independent Dutch leadership exuded. Attitudes towards any kind of Netherlandish unity, across north and south, were also sharpened thanks to the new campaigning season and the failure of previous negotiations, which prompted one Dutch author to compare the situations of the two Netherlands with some venom:

> If one would speak frankly, one must say: ... States of full age and free of wardship with states still underage, and held in tutelage, in short, freemen with slaves. For who lords it over the others? The King of Spain. Who holds them in tutelage? The King of Spain. Whose slaves are they? *Ad idem*, the King of Spain's. And do you still think it possible to negotiate with these people without first throwing the King of Spain and his Spaniards out of the country? I do not believe it.[19]

Nor was he the only sceptical observer. Frederick Henry, the Dutch leader, had been emboldened by the French alliance signed in spring 1635, which provided for subsidies in return for a commitment from both sides to maintain an army of at least thirty thousand men each. Furthermore, with France's declaration of war on Spain in mid-May, there arrived the potential for true military coordination between the French and Dutch armies.[20] Yet, on the other hand, this ability to coordinate went both ways; it meant that the Spanish could openly collaborate with their Imperial allies, and draw on a much larger manpower pool in Germany now that the Peace of Prague brought most Germans over to the Emperor's side. Indeed, the Count-Duke Olivares was able to announce to the Spanish Council of State with some satisfaction in April 1635, that: 'despite fears that the Imperialists view with disquiet the prospect of a joint war against France, our latest despatches from Germany take the fact of such a war as already accomplished.' During the summer of 1635 this process was underway; while the Emperor had yet to make war officially on France, according to Olivares, this open conflict between France and the two Habsburg branches was only a matter of time. Certainly, by the autumn of 1635 an army of forty thousand men, comprised of Imperial and Spanish veterans from previous campaigns, was under construction – this would certainly give the French a run for their money along the Rhine, and this was only one of many planned strategies for hurting the French along their porous borders.[21]

The conclusion of the Peace of Stuhmsdorf in mid-September 1635 confirmed that war with Poland would be kept on hold for twenty years, but Oxenstierna had been forced to pay a high price for that assurance.[22] Oxenstierna bemoaned that Sweden had been forced to relinquish its control over the Prussian port tolls, tolls which had brought Sweden incomes that were vital to the continuation of the German War. Through this peace, Oxenstierna had ensured that the Emperor would not be able to induce his kin, the new Polish King Wladyslaw IV, to attack Sweden from the east, but the aged Ferdinand II still retained a great preponderance of power over his foes.

The army of eighty thousand Imperial-Saxons which the Peace of Prague had created was merged with the Catholic League, providing new strategic opportunities for the Habsburgs, and John George of Saxony made his defection official when he authorised war to be declared on Sweden in October. The Habsburg army was growing, as the combination of the late Wallenstein's reforms in tactics, the victory at Nordlingen and the terms of the Peace of Prague all had invigorated the Imperial army which Breitenfeld had shattered.[23] The Swedish military grip on the situation, on the other hand, was notably withering. Sweden had lost at least half of the fifty-five thousand men she had conscripted directly from its homeland by 1632, and the ratio of German to Swedish soldiers had only increased since. What had once been a largely Swedish army was now almost entirely a German army, and this German army could only be kept under Swedish control with promises which were difficult to swallow, such as the Powder Barrel Convention of early August, but a firm political-military alliance with France, along with subsidies to match, still eluded Oxenstierna by autumn 1635.[24]

It was plain that the rescue of the Swedish military position would come from its allies, the French and Dutch. However, by autumn 1635 it was less clear what the future actually held for France. They possessed a great pool of taxation, and French financial capacity had increased dramatically from 57 million livres to 207 livres between 1632-35. Yet, impressive though this was, Richelieu was troubled by a pressing lack of professional soldiers, or even experienced commanders to lead them.[25] The Spanish were at least in no doubt as to who was to blame for the decline of their position, as King Philip IV himself declared that:

> The greater number of misfortunes which have occurred and continue to occur in my kingdoms and provinces can justly be attributed to the French... Their aim is well known; to procure the diminution of my greatness, discrediting my forces and objectives as they have always done.

Nor were the French ambitions the solely unpalatable export from Paris; one of Olivares' subordinates was under no illusions over who was to blame:

> Richelieu has offered nothing in satisfaction of our complaints, since his method of negotiation is constantly to lie and deceive. To my mind, whatever kind of agreement we may make with the French, whilst the Cardinal remains in their government it will never be observed.[26]

The formidable military resources which the Austrian and Spanish Habsburgs could bring to bear against France marked a new phase in the Thirty Years War, but they are significant for another reason. 'The failures and near-disaster of the first years of France's open involvement in the Thirty Years War', wrote the historian David Parrott, 'have always presented an historiographical problem for studies of Richelieu's ministry.' While they may present a historiographical problem, or something of a puzzle for us to solve now, in 1635, these circumstances combined to produce the greatest crisis in the reign of King Louis XIII, in the career of Cardinal Richelieu, and in the national memory of the French people. For while Richelieu had approached the preceding years with a unique blend of diplomatic finesse, financial investment and direct military intervention, the years of war were to prove another challenge altogether.

TWO

The Great Showdown

The Netherlands cannot be held if the Imperialists are defeated in Germany...
If the Netherlands are lost, neither the Indies, nor Spain, nor Italy can be
defended...The first and greatest dangers are those that threaten Lombardy,
the Netherlands and Germany. A defeat in any of these three is fatal for this
Monarchy, so much so that if the defeat in those parts is a great one, the rest
of the Monarchy will collapse, for Germany will be followed by Italy and the
Netherlands, and the Netherlands will be followed by America, and Lombardy
will be followed by Naples and Sicily, without the possibility of being able to
defend either.[27]

This gloomy, panicked conception of Spain's interconnected interests,
and the anticipated domino effect which would follow the loss or one or the
other of them, makes for revealing reading. It also sheds some light of the
question of why Madrid felt compelled to fight tooth and nail for a region
like the Spanish Netherlands, which continued to cost Spain as much as £1
million annually to maintain in the current war with the Dutch. The Spanish
understanding of the situation, as King Philip IV explained to his aunt Isabella,
then the Spanish governor of the region, was thus defined as follows:

Although the war which we have fought in the Netherlands has exhausted our
treasury and forced us into the debts that we have incurred, it has also diverted
our enemies in those parts so that, had we not done so, it is certain that we
would have had war in Spain or somewhere nearer.[28]

It was not merely for the sake of propping up these interconnected
theatres of her Empire then, but because of the expectation that the enemies
of Spain were bound to confront her somewhere, and would need to be
confronted themselves, so why not in the Netherlands? Spain would cling to
everything, no matter the cost, because letting go of one front would mean the
eruption of a new war somewhere else, which might well be more expensive
and dangerous than the current state of affairs. Interestingly, the plea was to

the effect that nothing should be lost, but we find few, if any, explanations for how anything should be gained. Nor was there much in the way of optimism from Spain's chief minister, the Count-Duke Olivares. 'Spain's sickness is serious and has become chronic', Olivares wrote as early as 1626, when one could argue that things were proceeding well for the Habsburgs, adding 'We have lost our prestige; the treasury (which is the basis for authority) is totally exhausted; and our ministers are lax, accustomed either not to act or to act slowly and ineffectively.'[29]

It is to Olivares' credit that despite Spain's circling of the metaphorical plughole, the Count-Duke managed to delay what he perceived as the inevitable for several years. There is something to be said for the idea that it was high time Spain cut its losses in any one of the active theatres, and we suspect that in addition to the strategic considerations, questions of honour also compelled King Philip IV to maintain the war in the Netherlands which his grandfather had begun. As the historian Martin Hume wrote:

> ...it never entered the head, apparently, either of Olivares or his master, that these terrible sacrifices were useless to Spain, except that it was a point of honour to hold the Catholic States of Flanders that had been the ancient inheritance of its royal house. Holland was really lost beyond all recovery, though the stiff-necked pride of Castile would not acknowledge it; the religious question in Germany had already practically settled itself, and had left Spain hardly an excuse for fighting for orthodoxy there. All that was needed, even now, for Spain was to eat her unavoidable leek, to recognise facts patent to all the world, and to abandon her impossible pretensions; and peace with France and Holland might have been attained with ease. But through all the suffering and stress, that if continued meant national exhaustion, there was no indication anywhere of the conviction that Spain must voluntarily humble herself or bleed to death.[30]

But it was inconceivable to Olivares that this 'unavoidable leek' should be swallowed or digested at all. Fighting on, as Spain had always done, seemed the only reasonable course. This grim determination had, after all, netted some notable successes; Nordlingen had been possible because Olivares had conceived of a plan to use King Philip's brothers against their enemies. That had been a tremendous Habsburg victory, and the symbolism of the two branches of the Habsburg dynasty coming together on the battlefield to rout the enemy must have put new steel and vigour into Olivares, for upon the French declarations of war, he conceived of yet another bold plan. It was nothing less than Richelieu's nightmare, for it would force France to defend herself on three fronts all at once, and it threatened the utter ruin of the Bourbons if it were to succeed. From three routes – from Catalonia across the Pyrenees, from Alsace over the Rhine, and from Flanders into the north-east of France – would King Louis XIII's domains be invaded.

This was what the historian J. H. Elliot referred to as Olivares' 'master-plan of campaign', and Olivares himself recognised that it would either 'win and finish the war with supreme brevity, or else utterly finish with the Monarchy.'[31] Notwithstanding his realm's decline, Olivares' plan for the campaigning year of 1636 promised to be a grave challenge which Cardinal Richelieu could not possibly ignore. Not merely a challenge to France, Olivares conceived of the three-pronged invasion plan as the best way to ruin the *Dutch*, as he explained to King Philip in November 1635:

> Neither your father nor your grandfather had the opportunity which your majesty is now vouchsafed to settle the affair of Holland with all advantage and prestige. For God has been pleased to place in your majesty's hands the master-key to everything.[32]

Initially though, the French seemed to possess this 'master-key to everything', and Richelieu seemed equally determined to use it. Having declared the war, Richelieu had sponsored its first offensive, and it was an ambitious one. On 22 May 1635, barely a few days after declaring war on Spain, a French army slipped into the Spanish Netherlands and linked up with its Dutch counterpart. The two allied armies, now working in tandem and overtly for the first time since the previous Franco-Spanish War of the 1590s, had as their end goal the seizure of all of Flanders from Madrid. The French and Dutch governments had even conceived of a partition of the Spanish Netherlands between its French and Dutch speaking populations, but in the development of these plans, both allies had acted prematurely. The results of this Franco-Dutch cooperation were not inspiring, though the appearance of the French so quickly after declaring war must have sent a message.[33] Tirlemont in Brabant was seized, but this small town served no strategic purpose, and its sacking by the French and Dutch effectively ruined any pro-French or pro-Dutch sentiments which the beleaguered Spanish Netherlands populace had previously harboured. Henceforth, they would resist the invader with the same grim determination that had driven Olivares forward. A siege of Louvain was thwarted by the loyal defenders, and in late July, Frederick Henry was forced to abandon the ambitious plans of his French ally by rushing to the defence of Schenkenschans. The latter was a critical bastion which defended the borders of Cleves and Gelderland, and also protected a rare crossing of the River Waal, the main tributary branch of the Rhine which flowed through the Netherlands.[34]

The campaign in the Netherlands had been a learning curve for the French army; their first foray into the morass of the Netherlands war had not netted France any genuine benefits, despite the large commitment of twenty-five thousand men which had been sent there. Furthermore, the relationship with the Dutch had been soured somewhat, thanks to perceptions on both sides that their ally had not pulled their weight. The planned campaigns along the Rhine for 1635 produced equally uninspired results, as Charles of Lorraine's small force was not defeated, and nor were the remnants of Wallenstein's army led by Matthias Gallas. Despite grand plans to place an army at the personal command of King Louis XIII, embarrassing shortcomings in the regions of supply and organisation forced Richelieu to abandon much of these plans, and nearly moved him to abandon Alsace and Lorraine. A confession from the French governor of Nancy that anyone who ventured outside the city's walls might be captured by the enemy told its own story – the region was overrun with enemy soldiers.

Evidently, the teething problems which Richelieu had failed to foresee plagued the French army, as did the actual plague itself, which forced the French back from Mainz, and prevented Bernhard of Saxe-Weimar's army of Heilbronn League desperados, German Protestants and mercenaries from making any meaningful attack.[35] Perhaps the only true triumph could be found in the Val Telline, those critical Alpine passes which connected the Spanish with their Italian appendages. Making use of meagre resources and the friendship with the Grisons who controlled the passes, a French army under the Duc de Rohan made remarkable progress, but at the expense of security closer to home. A daring Spanish attack on some of the islands just off the coast of Marseilles provided the enemy with a convenient base to threaten and raid French shipping interests in the Mediterranean. As David Parrott concluded:

> The lessons of the 1635 campaign were clear. In numerous areas, administrative, supply and command failure had undermined whatever initial advantages had been enjoyed by the French forces. However, it was one thing to recognize that these initial setbacks owed so much to organizational weakness, quite another to provide practical responses.[36]

What responses Richelieu did develop for the new campaigning season of spring 1636 amounted to a resumption of the old efforts which had brought failure in 1635. Little did Richelieu seem to realise that Madrid had absorbed the initial salvoes, and that under Olivares' aforementioned 'master-plan of campaign', France would be forced onto the defensive. The three-pronged invasion struck first at Picardy in the north-east of France, where an army under the Cardinal-Infante, that co-victor of Nordlingen, moved across the border from Flanders on 4 July. From there, La Capelle was seized, the River Somme was crossed in early August, and the Cardinal-Infante's force of twenty thousand or so men continued to press onwards, with Paris apparently in their sights.[37]

As his scouts were reported being just twenty-five kilometres away from the capital, the French defence finally stabilised, and the sense of panic which had animated the Parisians mercifully passed. During the crisis of August, Richelieu and Louis XIII had elected to stay put in Paris, and Richelieu had put on a brave face, walking through the streets and greeting with cold indifference any who might plead with him to help them flee.[38] Disaster was averted, and the Cardinal-Infante pulled his men back by the end of August, having come close to seizing another prize, Amiens. Like the Miracle on the Marne of 1914, this blistering invasion of France had seemed unstoppable, but one cannot avoid the conclusion that Richelieu was at least partially to blame for France's unpreparedness. Richelieu had prioritised an invasion of Franche-Comte, a region which straddled France's eastern border, and which had historically been a centre of Spanish defence.

Richelieu imagined that seizing it would sever Spanish strategic plans for the Netherlands and the Rhine, but he had not planned on the Spanish pre-empting this attack with one of their own; instead, Richelieu seems to have expected the Spanish to sit still for another year while French armies were sent against them. The image we have of an overextended Habsburg defence gradually being chipped away by Richelieu's brilliance is certainly tarnished by the events of 1636. Richelieu's lack of preparations was totally exposed, and for a frightful moment, he appeared fatally out of his depth.[39] Fortunately for Richelieu though, the Habsburg high tide had expended itself on the invasion of Picardy, and the grand coordinated plan which Olivares had imagined was never borne out, for a number of reasons.

The first reason was that the Cardinal-Infante's forces gradually retreated from Picardy and Champagne over late summer. The second was that Matthias Gallas, the Imperial commander and key ingredient in the three-pronged plan, took too long to invade Burgundy and threaten Dijon. Due to Gallas' tardiness, he arrived only in mid-September, by which point the panic caused by the Cardinal-Infante had evaporated. Third, and finally, Spain's opening move in the grand plan had been thwarted before it had even begun – there was to be no invasion over the Pyrenees, because the intended base of this operation, Catalonia, proved a most unwilling host. Olivares had wanted the three invasions coordinated so that they complemented each other, and had this happened, the results may well have been a succession of triumphs. Yet, the potency of the plan lay in the multitude of simultaneous threats it would present to Louis XIII's realm; by presenting these threats unevenly, the urgency and force of the Spanish plan was quickly lost, and impressive advances like those undertaken by the Cardinal-Infante were possible less due to the brilliance of the offensive, and more because of the unpreparedness of the opponent.

But there were worse consequences for Olivares than simply the failure of this campaign; as the Count-Duke had claimed when presenting the plan to his King, the choice was either great success or terrible failure, and the heavy investment necessary for making the scheme possible would bring one or the other to Madrid's door. As the course of the conflict was to show, the words of the Count-Duke rang true: 'Sir, this is my opinion', Olivares had declared when presenting the plan,

> ...it would be idle to deceive myself, because I have the feeling that I am going to lose my life - not in the war itself (which would be a happy fate) but merely in the task of making all ready for the struggle. I am so unwell that my head cannot bear the flame of the candle or the light of a window, which seems as strong as the glare of the streets in the August sun. But God may not want my health to improve, nor anything of mine to flourish, except insofar as it represents the smallest hair in the balance of service to your majesty...To my present judgement it seems that this is either to lose everything irretrievably or enable us to save the ship. I would be a traitor not to put things as I find them ... here go religion, king, queen, nation, and all besides with them. And if there is not enough strength, let us die in summoning it, for it is better to die than to fall under the sway of heretics, as I hold the French to be. Thus, everything will come to an end, or Castile will be the leader of the world.[40]

There were to be no half-measures in Olivares' mind; either Spain would be rejuvenated by a successful campaign in 1636, or her decline would be accelerated. Indeed, as Olivares would have known by late 1636, France had not been knocked out by the succession of blows – she was still standing, bruised and stunned, but by no means down and out. Spain had manifestly failed to capitalise upon Richelieu's failures from 1635, and now Madrid was herself open to a counterattack which struck at the heart at Habsburg Spain. Catalonia was the fiercely independent kingdom which itself had been ruled by Aragon, the partner of Castile which together constituted Spain. With its cultural and financial base of Barcelona, Catalonia represented a critical part of the Spanish Kingdom, and its proximity to France, being on the border with the Pyrenees, singled the region out as vital to Spanish security. It was therefore a serious problem that Olivares always seemed to rub the Catalans the wrong way.

The citizens insisted that the demands placed upon Catalonia were unfair, and that Madrid could not possibly expect Catalans to foot such an enormous bill. Unbeknownst to Olivares, the Catalan protests were rooted in fact, as the demands placed upon them were based upon a flawed system of censuses which had massively exaggerated the Catalonian population. Rather than 1 million people, as Madrid believed, Catalonia contained less than half that, roughly 400,000 citizens. The bill presented to Catalonia was therefore far larger than her neighbours, and far more difficult for her to pay. On Christmas Day 1624, the so-called Union of Arms had been presented, with the goal of spreading the burden of the military expenses foremost in Olivares' mind. Each of the provinces would be required to pay a share, and the Count-Duke used the aforementioned system to deduce what was owed.

The numbers discussed were considerable; Catalonia's supposed 1 million citizens were requested to pay an eye-watering 3.7 million ducats, compared to Aragon's 2 million ducats spread over 300,000 citizens, or Valencia's 1 million ducats for its 350,000 citizens. These figures were almost all inaccurate and caused disquiet, but the Catalans were by far the greatest objectors to the plan. Olivares insisted that the sums were used for home defence, and the payments would be spread over 15 years, but even so, Barcelona remained resolute in its refusal to grant King Philip IV a penny.[41] Each time Olivares and his King ventured to Barcelona, they were forced to return empty-handed, and this was the case once more in spring 1636, where Spanish troops were meant to use Catalonia as a staging post for a French invasion from the south. Catalonian citizens, bitter over the demands repeatedly placed upon them, refused to provide the quarters for the mostly Castilian recruits, which were themselves beginning to look increasingly drawn and wasted, as the English ambassador to Madrid recorded:

> I have observed these levies and I find the horses so weak as the most of them will never be able to go to the rendezvous, and those very hardly gotten. The infantry so unwilling to serve as they are carried like galley-slaves, which serves not the turn, and so far short in number of what is purposed as they come not to one of three.[42]

The loss of prestige, money and power represented devastating wounds upon the Spanish psyche, but the weakening of its armed forces could be fatal to the very existence of Spain. Having built its reputation as the premier fighting force of Europe, the withering of Spanish manpower suggested the end was nigh for Madrid. Catalonia could be greatly imperilled if Olivares did not find some way to bind the Catalans closer to Madrid, but the Count-Duke was not in the business of granting concessions. As far as he was concerned, Catalans were betraying their sovereign by refusing to pay him what he was owed – it does not seem to have crossed his mind that Catalans genuinely could not afford the high price tag which he waved in front of them.[43] Nor, it must be said, did Olivares stop to consider the cumulative impact which this wrong-headed approach to troubles subjects might produce, especially since another contingent part of the Spanish Crown, Portugal, was also beginning to splinter and crack under the pressure.

In February 1630, a Dutch fleet appeared off the coast of Pernambuco, the most populous province of the Portuguese colony of Brazil, which also produced 60% of Brazil's sugar.[44] Sugar was the equivalent of a gold mine, despite the labour-intensive process required to bring it from plantation to table, and slaves were therefore required in abundance to make it viable. This was a period of history characterised by the explosion of the slave-trade and the simultaneous enrichment of the slavers and plantation owners. It was especially lucrative for the Spanish and Portuguese, who managed to control the supply of slaves and the markets which required them. From Seville and Lisbon, to the East coast of Africa in Angola, and back to the Americas, money and sugar flowed back to Europe, powered by the appetite for sugar and the ambition of the slavers.

The Dutch interrupted this ideal Iberian arrangement, which had been fused even more closely together once the Spanish and Portuguese crowns merged under Philip II in 1580. From that point, the Dutch faced the formidable combination of the two fleets, but they were also granted irresistible opportunities to take by force what the Portuguese and Spanish had spent decades building. Portuguese national pride and finance was invested heavily in Brazil, and in the sugar -slave trade which had enriched Lisbon in the preceding centuries.[45] As a result, when the Dutch arrived in February 1630 to sever this link once and for all, and when subsequent efforts by the Spanish to eject the Dutch from the Brazil colony failed, it called into question the symbiotic Iberian arrangement. For the next twenty-five years, the Dutch would cling to this Brazilian appendage, shoring up their regime in Pernambuco by appealing to religious minorities like the *moriscos* and resident Jews, the latter of whom were even allowed to establish their own printing press, publishing in the Americas for the first time and urging more Jews to join them in Brazil to escape the persecutions of Madrid and Lisbon.[46] Dutch tolerance, which was certainly politically motivated, nonetheless left a great impression upon the residents of the colony.[47]

The Dutch occupation of northern Brazil was a doubled-edged sword, because not only did it transfer the colony's revenues from the Spanish to the Dutch side of the ledger, it also called into question Spain's ability to defend its Portuguese partner, and increased tensions regarding the idea of a Portuguese divorce from Spain, which would erupt into the open within a few years. Understanding the impact of the occupation, Frederick Henry approved the dispatch of his cousin, Count John Maurice of Nassau, to Pernambuco in October 1636. Three hundred miles of Brazilian coastline came under Dutch hands, and by 1641, Count John had even ruptured the Portuguese hold over the slave trade, by breaking into the slaver port of Luanda in Angola. By that point, Portuguese skirmishes with their Spanish overlords had resulted in a full-blown war of Portuguese restoration, and Olivares had utterly lost control of the situation.[48]

Such a grim outcome could not have been known in autumn 1636 though and following a campaigning season which had sent some firm messages, but drawn no concrete results, Olivares began to contemplate entering negotiations with the French following not even 18 months of open war. Olivares had been moved to adopt this course due to the fear – correctly placed as it turned out – that the inability to focus on regaining Brazil would cost Spain dearly. But there was more to Olivares' sudden turn than this. It is worth considering the possibility that, having fired what was expected to be Spain's best shot, and having missed, Olivares had come to terms with the facts, and these facts were that Spain simply could not afford a full-scale war with France. Further, these facts remind us that the main goal for Olivares had always been the subjugation of the Dutch, or at least the creation of some kind of beneficial arrangement.

We are drawn to the fact that even while his multi-layered campaign against the French appears formidable on paper, it was often referred to in those same papers merely as a diversion. But a diversion against what? So long as France remained to support the Dutch with strength – the Franco-Dutch alliance had been confirmed in February 1635 – it was impossible to imagine Madrid ever forcing the Dutch to the peace table. And, as we know, Richelieu's regime was by no means wholly popular across the country. A string of debilitating defeats might force Richelieu from power, and reinstate the pro-Spanish regime led by Louis XIII's mother, thereby removing the threat France posed to Spain's Dutch War. Eliminate France, Olivares imagined, and the Dutch would be brought earlier to the peace table.

If this was Olivares' plan, then – to strike quickly and sharply at France in order to force her out of the recently made war – then it can be stated the Count-Duke miscalculated disastrously. The campaign against France failed, and only awakened in Richelieu the sense that the defeat of Spain in detail was essential for the sake of French security and expansion.[49] Even worse for Olivares, 1636 can be viewed as the year when the war widened considerably; in March of that year, Sweden and France concluded the Treaty of Wismar, which compelled Richelieu to maintain a proper system of subsidies with the Swedes in Germany and dangled a military alliance in front of Sweden's nose. The treaty was subject to ratification, but it pointed to the enemies of the Habsburgs – the French, Swedes and Dutch – moving closer together, as did the confirmation of the open breach between France and the Emperor.[50]

With France now at war with the Spanish and Imperials, joining with the Dutch in the former and Swedes in the latter theatre, all sides waited patiently for news of a victory which might justify the vast resources which were now invested in this great showdown between the Habsburgs and their enemies. In the first few days of October 1636, Richelieu was informed that the beleaguered Swedes had pulled just such a victory from the jaws of desperation, the Swedish commander Johan Baner defeating a larger Saxon-Imperial army at the battle of Wittstock. It was exactly what the demoralised Swedes needed, and Chancellor Oxenstierna was determined to wrest every bit of political capital out of the victory that he could.

THREE
The Road to Wittstock

Few would have envied the position or the responsibilities of the Swedish Chancellor. Axel Oxenstierna had been in power nearly thirty years by the time news of Nordlingen was received, yet that news had been powerful enough to give the Chancellor only the second sleepless night of his life. From there, it was a matter of picking himself and his country up from its succession of disasters, which only seemed to grow in size as the months progressed. By the autumn of 1635, indeed, Germany was up in arms against Sweden, the Emperor was even more formidable than before, and her one-time allies in Saxony and Brandenburg were now set firmly against her. Further afield, the Polish foe threatened Sweden with an unaffordable second front upon the expiration of the six-year truce which had freed Gustavus Adolphus in 1629 to enter Germany. That must have seemed like a lifetime ago to Oxenstierna; since the fall of the Swedish King at Lutzen the legacy of Gustavus had been his burden to carry, yet he was fortunate in perhaps one major area – the Swedish Council did not question his right to lead, and the Regency which governed the young Queen Christina effectively handed the reins of government to him. The question was, what would Oxenstierna do with these reins?

Where the Count-Duke Olivares had insisted on the need for Spain to maintain its Dutch War, so as to pile pressure on its enemies, Oxenstierna and his colleagues seemed less certain of the utility in continuing the now thankless war in Germany. As a result of this uncertainty, 1635-36 contained many grim predictions for what the future of the war held for Sweden, but it also contained several phases of negotiation not just between Sweden and its French ally, but between Sweden and its German foes. By summer 1636, Oxenstierna felt moved to return to Stockholm to put some steel in the Swedish Council, and news of the victory at the Battle of Wittstock in early October certainly contributed towards this. Before then though, Oxenstierna was forced to maintain Sweden in the war largely by the force of his own personality and his uncompromising vision for what Sweden required before she could extricate herself from the war.

'The fundamental problem', Derek Croxton wrote, 'was that Sweden was in over its head.' Certainly, this seemed to have been borne out by recent events. Swedish influence and reputation had peaked at Breitenfeld, five years before, and yet the high hopes and grand plans which Gustavus had built and Oxenstierna inherited had moved Sweden to commit far more than she was naturally able, and to spend more than she had. Sweden was, in short, puffing out its chest, and had been for several years, but Oxenstierna was fortunate that this chest was strong, since although it had been built on the talent of its King, Sweden's position in the Empire was not so easily removed.[51] For one thing, Sweden still had armies, and though they were short of pay, the soldiers in Swedish service recognised and accepted that, for the moment, Swedish service was better than the alternatives, not least because of the opportunities which it offered to some foreign soldiers. Indeed, one English captain by the name of George Fleetwood entered Swedish service in 1629, and Oxenstierna had been so impressed with the Englishman's service that by 1636, the Chancellor was sending him on a diplomatic mission to King Charles, where it was hoped Fleetwood would be able to obtain some measure of military assistance. At this stage, Oxenstierna had refrained from ratifying the agreement with France, and was keeping his options open. This presented Fleetwood with an incredible opportunity to distinguish himself, as Fleetwood recognised when he wrote to his father:

> I met...the Chancellor [Axel Oxenstierna] on...the 26 October...but the Chancellor being the next day to return back for the ordering of affairs towards Bavaria and the Palatinate, took me with him the night's journey to [Germany], where he presently gave me my dispatch, with letters to the King in all points that I desired, with so great manifestation of his affection that I could not have expected the like, and gave me assurance that whilst he lived he wold be my patron, being very joyful at the good report which he hath heard of my regiment from everyone.[52]

Fleetwood had built such a great reputation for himself through his military service, that the most powerful man in Sweden had taken it upon himself to sponsor his career. Fleetwood was certainly lucky; many of his compatriots would not rise so high in their station, and British soldiers or officers who could not hide behind their high rank suffered a horrendously high casualty rate – this was indeed the story throughout the Swedish army as a whole.[53] Sweden had benefited from its sterling reputation as a foremost military power which Gustavus had built, but even before that King's career captured the imagination of budding adventurers; the likes of King James had shunted off many unwanted Irish levies into Swedish service with the unsentimental note 'there will be a good riddance of them all when they are gone.'[54]

These records all serve to remind the reader that Sweden was fundamentally incapable of raising an army and maintaining it solely of its own power. It had neither the manpower nor the financial resources necessary to fight in the Thirty Years War, and this has been the challenge which moved Gustavus Adolphus essentially to stall for time until he wrested an agreement from the French for subsidies in early 1631.[55] This agreement, however, was only due to last for five years, which meant that it would be due for renewal in early 1636. In practical terms, this meant that the Franco-Swedish deal would be renegotiated, and in negotiations, the stronger power with greater leverage always receives the best deal. Leverage, for Oxenstierna in early 1636, was in desperately short supply. All he possessed was an army of dubious loyalty under Bernhard of Saxe-Weimar along the Rhine, and a smaller force commanded by Johan Baner in Pomerania. Little wonder then that the advice given by the Swedish Council in mid-September 1635 had been particularly gloomy:

> Discussion as to what is to be written to the Chancellor, and whether it would not be advisable for him frankly to pull out of Germany by degrees, and devote his efforts to doing it without loss of security and reputation, and without forfeiting German goodwill: if he can secure something over and above, so much the better.

Interestingly, while the desire to exit the war in Germany was palpable, the Swedish statesmen here evidently wished for some kind of military victory to be seized, which would greatly relax the burden that was felt, as the minutes continued:

> The view was that if the Chancellor should win a victory, we may no doubt hope for reasonable peace terms; if he loses a battle, he will be forced to retire northwards to a place of safety. In the meantime, that he keep in close touch with the French, so that he may shape his conduct according to how things develop. He should make every effort to hang on to the most important places, as far as he can…If he can obtain any territory [at a possible peace], that would be best, if not, to take satisfaction in money, and if he cannot get that, to try every means consistent with reputation and safety to extricate himself from the German business.[56]

As it happened, Oxenstierna was moved to engage in peace talks with his former allies in September 1635, at the town of Schonebeck. Here at least, Oxenstierna was told that neither Saxony nor Brandenburg would make war against Sweden, at least not yet, for although they had signed the Peace of Prague and made their peace with the Emperor, John George of Saxony was willing to engage in peace talks to see if Sweden could be removed peacefully from the war first; this, as we have seen, was what the Swedish Counsellors seemed to want as well. It can be said that in these limited negotiations, Oxenstierna did his best. He requested a cash indemnity, with the city of Stralsund, and John George seemed inclined to agree. Even at this anxious moment, when a lasting peace with Poland had not be attained, Oxenstierna kept his cool when with the Saxon Elector.[57]

But the demands were still believed to be too high; John George refused to let the talks progress any further until Oxenstierna promised to accept the Peace of Prague, but to do so would have hung Sweden's German remaining allies out to dry. This was not how honourable negotiators did business, and so Oxenstierna elected to break negotiations off. There could be no confusion over what this breakdown in diplomacy would mean – John George would feel within his rights to make war on his former ally, thus compounding the sense of isolation which Sweden faced. Sure enough, this was what happened, as on 16 October, Saxony delivered its declaration of war – 'in a document full of involutions worthy of the Saxon Chancery' – as one historian put it. Unwilling to be isolated from his main Protestant ally, George William of Brandenburg followed suit with his own declaration of war in late January 1636.[58]

Peace was made with Poland, and Oxenstierna managed to avoid a two-front war, but the price King Wladyslaw's negotiators were able to demand was predictably exorbitant. After facing down a Russian invasion orchestrated by the Swedes, the Polish King was understandably in no mood to operate with mercy, but he was a touch more pragmatic than his father. He offered to renounce his claims on the Swedish throne in return for compensation, but this was refused, so in 1633 he had renewed an alliance with Emperor Ferdinand and allowed for limited recruiting in the lands of the Commonwealth. By now, knowledge of Gustavus' failed diplomatic initiatives had spread among the Polish nobility, and they were eager to avenge themselves upon the Swedes in their recently acquired Baltic conquests. When the truce expired in September 1635, in other words, Oxenstierna would not be able to rely on a recalcitrant Polish nobility holding its King back.

He had to take the Polish threat seriously, and he sent twenty thousand men under the command of Lennart Torstenson to reinforce the holdings in Prussia as a show of force. Yet Oxenstierna knew Sweden could not afford a German and a Polish War, and Cardinal Richelieu was also mindful of this fact. French diplomatic aid, so useful for brokering the original truce in 1629, came through again here, as Richelieu sent his trusted envoy Claude d'Avaux to Stuhmsdorf in West Prussia for talks. On 12 September, the Polish sword hanging over Sweden was permanently lifted, and a truce lasting twenty years concluded. Sweden relinquished much of the trump cards it had seized in the recent Polish War, and it cannot have inspired Swedish statesmen back in Stockholm that they traded these sure gains in the Baltic, for an uncertain war in Germany.[59]

Indeed, this apprehension is reflected in the minutes of the Swedish Council, as a meeting on 9 October 1635 contained a debate over how to proceed next. In light of the news that peace negotiations with John George of Saxony had broken down, and the expectation that the Elector's determination to make war on Sweden would shortly be confirmed, it was decided that 'a gloss should be put upon it, and the information conveyed in softened terms', when communicating the news to the Swedish people. In addition, it was added that:

> Since the Elector of Saxony wants to drive us out of Germany by force, it is plain that we must prepare to defend ourselves, in particular by providing garrisons and ample supplies for the coastlands, since our main armies are steadily falling back nearer and nearer to the coast.

The minutes record that Per Baner, the brother of Swedish commander Johan Baner then in Pomerania, was of the view that 'we could not simply get out of Germany, as once the King of Denmark did' and therefore 'he could see nothing for it but that we must fight.' This view was supported by Count Brahe, who had been the main Swedish negotiator at Stuhmsdorf. Count Brahe took an incredibly pragmatic, one may even say cold, approach to the current military situation in the Empire, stating:

> ...we could not accept compensation in money and preserve our honour...If the crown of Sweden could obtain satisfaction in land, that would be the best solution...In any case our armies could hardly be paid off for less than 4 or 5 million. It would seem best, therefore, if we cannot reach any respectable agreement with the Emperor, that we go on fighting. If we win a victory, we must exploit it; if we are beaten, then that disposes of the soldiers' arrears, and we can defend the strong places on the coast with the survivors.[60]

Indeed, it would 'dispose of the soldiers' arrears', because the soldiers themselves would be disposed of! These final days before John George made official his war with Sweden on 16 October produced more anxious rhetoric in the Council; on 10 October, one particularly vocal Swede, the Court-Chancellor Johan Adler Salvius, expressed the view that:

> If it does come to a breach with Saxony, our own German troops will desert us. If our army consisted of French, Scots and Swedes, we could no doubt put up a fight, but as it is, our army is entirely composed of Germans. Conscription at home at the moment is out of the question. The Chancellor [Oxenstierna], in his anxiety to escape humiliation, is firmly determined to die over there in Germany, but this will hardly do the country much good: we shall be forced to make peace just the same. The burden of defence will be intolerable in the long run; and in any case peace will have to be made sooner or later.[61]

This was a gloomy picture, tinted with a sense of resentment towards Chancellor Oxenstierna, who was apparently suspected by his peers of seeking martyrdom to avoid facing the music. Oxenstierna was likely aware of this sense of alienation which the Swedish Council felt; as the main director of Swedish policy, it was inevitable that jealousies and suspicion would follow him. Rather than avoid the issue though, Oxenstierna would return to Stockholm, for good as it happened, in summer 1636. First though, the Swedish Council had to digest the news that, indeed, Saxony had declared war upon Sweden, and that the war in Germany was destined to be a far more difficult affair than they had once hoped. Almost immediately, the thoughts of the Swedish Council turned to resignation and a swift exit from the conflict, as they expressed when they gathered on 23 October, a week after John George's shattering declaration:

> It was considered wisest and best to start a negotiation with the Emperor, and extricate ourselves from the German war: if it cannot be done on honourable terms, then let us content ourselves with whatever terms we can get; for the resources of the country are not adequate to the maintenance of great armies…[the Court-Chancellor Salvius added] that we wage war in Germany as auxiliaries, and not as principles. If the principles have now done a deal with the enemy, who can say that we are behaving dishonourably, if we cut ourselves off from the whole business?[62]

This was the ultimate low point of the Swedish position, when it seemed as though everything which could go wrong did. And not just their enemies, but even Sweden's friends, seemed to have it out for them. In November 1635 Bernhard of Saxe-Weimar effectively confirmed his decision to switch sides, and fight for the French rather than the Swedes. Bernhard's loyalties had always been somewhat in doubt, as the man's inherent opportunism and ambition rendered him unreliable, but still, here was a lieutenant of Gustavus leaving Swedish service for the promise of greater rewards elsewhere. Who could guarantee that others would not follow suit? Certainly, the deal Bernhard had been offered was generous: four million livres annually, and a personal stipend of 200,000 livres, so long as Bernhard maintained an army of twelve thousand foot and six thousand horse. Bernhard, like many generalissimos who came before him, was also to be made a landlord at his paymaster's expense: Richelieu promised him the title 'Landgrave of Alsace', and both parties were allowed to remain vague over what that precisely meant.[63]

The more important point for Richelieu was that France now possessed a proxy on the Rhine, and France had demonstrated her predominance in the German question. For Oxenstierna, the pill must have been bitter to swallow, all the more so since it advertised Swedish weakness in the face of French strength. Yet, part of Oxenstierna's skill was knowing when to let such slights go. While a lesser statesman might have let it cloud his judgement and impressions of France, Oxenstierna recognised that France needed Sweden to distract the Emperor's intentions, but he also accepted that Sweden desperately needed France's help. It was important that he not appear too needy or grasping, but Oxenstierna travelled to Wismar in February 1636 nonetheless, with the main goal of wresting some form of agreement from the French which would succeed the old 1631 agreement made at Barwalde.

1636 had opened optimistically for Richelieu; he had yet to face the grand campaign orchestrated by Olivares, and in spring he was planning new offensive campaigns into Alsace, unaware that much of the year's activity would be spent on the defensive.[64] But Richelieu had by no means succumbed to hubris; he was keenly aware that France needed Sweden in the fight against the Emperor, which was soon to be made official. Thus, on 30 March, French negotiators concluded the Treaty of Wismar, and by 11 May, even King Louis had ratified it. The Treaty effectively continued the Franco-Swedish alliance and granted Oxenstierna an instant injection of cash, with subsidies to follow. Interestingly though, perhaps with the concerns of his peers back in Stockholm ringing in his ears, the Chancellor refused to ratify the Treaty due to the clause which would have prevented Sweden exiting the war without French consent. Sweden's position, Oxenstierna believed, required that she had the freedom to manoeuvre, and he could hardly resume negotiations with the Protestant Electors, or the Emperor, if those parties knew that Sweden could only extricate itself from the war with its ally's approval.[65]

By this stage, Oxenstierna had announced the confirmation of the Franco-Swedish alliance, signed for the previous year. This sent a clear message to the Emperor that his allies were closing ranks against him, and it even reached the Danes, who were applying pressure upon the Swedes from summer 1635 to enter into peace negotiations with King Christian IV as mediator.[66] This would have been a gross humiliation for Sweden, and Oxenstierna never intended to accept the offer, but if he refrained from ratifying the Treaty of Wismar as King Louis XIII had done, did that not render the agreement worthless? Not so; the Emperor could not ignore French interference any longer – the French diplomatic corps were expelled from Vienna shortly after Wismar was learned of.[67]

Tensions between the Emperor and the King of France seemed to be escalating, with war the likely outcome, but Ferdinand II actually wished to avoid pulling the French into Germany, correctly interpreting the Franco-Spanish war as the major theatre of interest for Richelieu and for France.[68] This was the case, but since the Emperor aided the Spanish as much as France aided the Swedes, an undeclared war had existed since May 1635 anyway. Historians tend to agree that France was at war with the Emperor while also at war with Spain, though some make the point that a formal declaration was never made. Perhaps it was never made because it was not believed to be necessary. French soldiers made no effort to avoid conflict with Germans loyal to the Emperor, and an active Rhine campaign meant that confrontation between the forces of the French King and Emperor was inevitable. Indeed, part of Olivares' grand strategy for 1636 was to send an army towards Alsace commanded by an Imperial general, Matthias Gallas, and populated by Imperial soldiers. It was therefore impossible, as Richelieu well knew, to separate the Emperor from the King of Spain, or vice-versa, when the two parties had been actively cooperating since the beginning of the war.[69]

One side-effect of the peace with Poland was the influx back to the front of nearly ten thousand soldiers under the command of Torstenson, where they could reinforce Johan Baner then attempting to hold Magdeburg and Pomerania. Baner had engaged in a gradual retreat from the area from May to August, and although his forces had an easier time of it than the French, who were at that point rushing to plug the many holes exposed by the Spanish-Imperial invasions, Baner evidently did not feel comfortable entrusting his men to stand their ground. Instead, the army marched over scorched earth, barren fields and empty villages, passing by the remains of Magdeburg, which was populated by barely 2,500 citizens and had never recovered from its traumatic destruction of five years before. Magdeburg was actually taken by the Imperials in mid-July, to the delight of John George, who had been promised the city and its bishopric under the terms of the Peace of Prague.

With twelve thousand men in early July, Baner had retreated to Werben, that town where Gustavus had once made his fortified camp, but a lack of resources forced him to retreat further west, rendezvousing with Alexander Leslie, a Scottish commander with six thousand men of his own. Collecting and distributing some more forces into Pomeranian garrisons, Baner elected to stake his position on a battle rather than continue the wild goose chase away from the enemy.[70] If his army would not stand, then they did not serve Sweden any purpose anyway, and as that Swedish counsellor had coldly observed the previous year, Sweden would at least have 'disposed of the soldiers' arrears.'

But before Baner could provoke such a showdown, Oxenstierna returned to Stockholm in July, with the goal of reinvigorating the Swedish Council foremost in his mind. On 1 August, the Regency Council released a memo commenting on the developments which Oxenstierna had kept them informed of, proclaiming: 'We have given all these things our careful attention, and having entreated God, have now by His aid reached the following conclusions.' The memo began with the justifications for restoring their German allies as part of any peace settlement – the so-called amnesty dilemma which the Swedes felt compelled to agree to, and the Emperor felt unable to accept. This was, among other things, justified by honour, by the desire to maintain the Lutheran faith, to continue the legacy of Gustavus, to preserve the German liberties, and to keep the Habsburgs from becoming too empowered or returning to threaten the Baltic.

This was the first option; however, considering several factors, like the high costs of the war and her unreliable allies, it was also declared that: '...the Regency and Council do not consider it either reasonable or advisable that we should in the last resort persist with the war for the sake of others', but that as soon as Sweden was compensated and the soldiery contented, she would exit from the war. Many words were then spent on the amount of money Sweden should be entitled to in the event of exiting the war, and it was optimistically believed that the Emperor would grant Sweden some additional harbours as added security. 'Some concessions, as has been said, may well be made on this point of indemnity', the memo resolved, adding that 'it is reasonable rather to give way then at this critical time to deprive the country of its gain, and commit it to a perpetual war, to the advantage of others and the hurt of ourselves.' Evidently, Oxenstierna had not instilled within his peers a desire to continue the war indefinitely, but the next demand rendered any resolution of the war virtually impossible:

> But above all things we must try to obtain the contentment of the soldiery, and relive Her Majesty and the crown of that burden, which should not and must not be placed upon her, since she receives no benefit from them, but rather hurt and extortion. Nevertheless, since it would not be advisable nor honourable to the country to leave the soldiery entirely unsatisfied, the burden must be taken from our shoulders and transferred by agreement to those of the German Estates, and on this we must strictly insist.[71]

This demand for the contentment of the soldiery, however moderate and reasonable it might have seemed to the Swedish Counsellors, amounted to nothing less than a demand for the Emperor to pay off Sweden's army to disband. According to the promises made by Oxenstierna during the Powder Barrel Convention of July 1635, it had been made plain to the Chancellor that the army's officers would take it upon themselves to invade Sweden and make good their pay through other sinister means if money was not forthcoming. Yet, it was impossible for the Emperor to have committed to this idea, and the Swedish Counsellors cannot have been so naïve as to have believed otherwise. As they had stated the previous year, the greatest hope for Sweden lay not in alliances, or in the hope that the Emperor would pay their soldiers to go home, but in achieving a military victory which would send a similar message to that of Breitenfeld. The pressure, in other words, would be piled upon Johan Baner, then moving towards the lakes of Pomerania. If Baner was unable to grasp this triumph, his army succumbing to defeat, then Sweden would be faced with an impossible choice of the wrath of the Emperor, or the wrath of their bitter and unpaid soldiery. Mercifully for Oxenstierna, this was a choice which he was to be saved from having to make.

The road to the Battle of Wittstock on 4 October 1636 had thus been paved with anxious predictions for Sweden's future, great fears of how to deal with their underpaid soldiery, and lamentations about how impossible the dilemma appeared to be. Sweden would either be ruined or saved by the sword, and in a bloody confrontation where Alexander Leslie and his Scots distinguished themselves, the day ended with a victory for Baner. The Saxon contingent had been accompanied by the person of John George, but as at Breitenfeld, the Elector fled the field from an early stage. The Saxon-Imperial force, which varies in size according to the record used, lost an estimated five thousand casualties from its force of nearly twenty thousand, to Baner's three-and-a-half thousand casualties from a force of roughly seventeen thousand. The Saxon baggage and artillery were abandoned to the victors, but the real story, as before, was the effect the confrontation had. It was not necessarily the most shattering of defeats, but its effects were immediate because the Saxon and Imperials split up afterwards, returning home and plundering their way down the Rhine respectively, and panic began to spread in Northern Germany, where George William of Brandenburg determined to evacuate Berlin.[72]

Wittstock was the answer to Oxenstierna's prayers, and it was the foil to the Emperor's string of diplomatic, military and political successes. The tide had apparently been turned, but just as important as what the battle was, was what it was not. Had it been a triumph for the Saxon-Imperial army, then we can deduce having examined the deliberations of the Swedish Council that Oxenstierna would have felt forced to extricate Sweden from the war, taking his chances with the soldiery. The Emperor would have been in a position to exact revenge on those few German potentates that had resisted him, and only France would have stood shakily against a Germany freed from foreign invaders. However grim one imagines this alternative scenario to have been, it must be said that what followed instead was certainly as awful. Although neither Oxenstierna, nor the Emperor, nor Johan Baner could have known it, Wittstock did not only mean a Swedish triumph, it also meant the continuation of the war for another twelve years.

FOUR

Death of an Emperor

A 59-year-old man, prematurely aged beyond his years, lay dying at Vienna on 14 February 1637. This was Ferdinand II, Holy Roman Emperor since 1619, leader of the Austrian Habsburg dynasty, hard-line Catholic, pride of the Jesuits and, some would argue, instigator of a war which had raged across the Germanies for the last two decades. Of course, the war was not so simple that it could all be blamed on Ferdinand II, and there was nothing simple about this man either. To his friends, and even to strangers, he remained cheerful and pleasant, yet to those that defied him he treated with merciless contempt. He removed rebellious families from their historical bases and trampled upon centuries of religious tradition in the likes of Bohemia. He hired and bribed with land fabulously successful generalissimos like Albrecht of Wallenstein, calling on him regularly, only in the end to betray him and order his assassination.

There is no question that Ferdinand was a formidable character; his refusal to compromise netted his dynasty previously unimagined successes, and the Emperor's hold over Germany was raised up to such heights as to make Charles V marvel. The Peace of Prague was perhaps his greatest achievement, for it brought the Germanies together and directed their energies against the invader, rather than against each other. This document had only been made possible following compromise on Ferdinand's part, and the suspension of the Edict of Restitution which had been so inflammatory and caused him so many problems with the Protestant rulers. Once these necessary compromises were made, Ferdinand learned what he should have known all along: that only through the accommodation of the other religious bloc in the Empire could a lasting peace be made. And it was only in death that Ferdinand had achieved, according to one anonymous manuscript, 'that universal peace which he always desired but was never able to secure.'[73]

It cannot be denied that a less dogmatic, fundamentalist, uncompromising Emperor would have brought Germany together earlier and with less bloodshed and suffering. At the same time, we cannot know what the Empire's fate would have been, had Ferdinand not been at the helm. Unsurprisingly, historians have weighed in on the character of the man who personified the greater part of the conflict. Schiller wrote on Ferdinand II that:

> During a reign of eighteen years he had never once laid aside the sword, nor tasted the blessings of peace as long as his hand swayed the imperial sceptre. Endowed with the qualities of a good sovereign, adorned with many of those virtues which ensure the happiness of a people, and by nature gentle and humane, we see him, from erroneous ideas of the monarch's duty, become at once the instrument and the victim of the evil passions of others; his benevolent intentions frustrated, and the friend of justice converted into the oppressor of mankind, the enemy of peace, and the scourge of is people. Amiable in domestic life, and respectable as a sovereign, but in his policy ill-advised, while he gained the love of his Roman Catholic subjects, he incurred the execration of the Protestants. History exhibits many and greater despots than Ferdinand II, yet he alone has had the unfortunate celebrity of kindling a Thirty Years' War; but to produce its lamentable consequences, his ambition must have been seconded by a kindred spirit of the age, a congenial state of previous circumstances, and existing seeds of discord. At a less turbulent period, the spark would have found no fuel; and the peacefulness of the age would have choked the voice of individual ambition; but now the flash fell upon a pile of accumulated combustibles, and Europe was in flames.[74]

Such an account seems rather even handed, even biased, towards the late Emperor; he did not act maliciously, he was not a cruel person, instead he was led astray by fundamentalists in his ear, who fanned the lesser aspects of his character and moved him constantly away from moderate action. Richard Bassett credits him with empowering the Jesuits, but also setting the base for a Habsburg army which later Emperors would copy.[75] It is also worth noting that through the Peace of Prague, the creation of this army was made possible because the Catholic League and Evangelical Union were both folded into it. While he had played no small role in fanning the flames of religious discord, Ferdinand died having rid the Empire of two armed confessional blocs, uniting them under the authority of the Emperor. Henceforth, nationality as Germans, rather than religious identity as Catholics or Protestants, would move his vassals and their subjects. Or this was at least the idea; the war by 1637 had long abandoned its solely religious flavour, if indeed such a flavour had ever moved Ferdinand by itself.[76] Now it was a war motivated by political, strategic considerations, where multi-ethnic and multi-faith states like France, Sweden and the Dutch Republic were armed and set against the Habsburg dynasty – the Peace of Prague had changed the nature of the war, and Ferdinand II had made this change possible.[77]

One could argue that under such trying circumstances, the Habsburg dynasty was actually fortunate to have him, since these were times of immense difficulty, where so much could be transformed in the course of a single day – as Breitenfeld showed. Following shattering defeats such as these, Ferdinand II picked himself up, gave himself to God, and prepared to undo his enemies once again. This tenacity of purpose and faith in his cause meant that a dynasty which seemed doomed in 1619, 1625, 1631 and afterwards did not die, but lasted sustained until 1918. Yet, fortunate though the Habsburg dynasty was to have Ferdinand II, it was to Germany's greater fortune that Ferdinand II's son was not like his father. 'The Roman Empire needs me no more', Emperor Ferdinand is reported to have said on his deathbed, 'for it is already provided with a successor and indeed an excellent one.' This was perhaps Ferdinand's greatest legacy, for he had provided the Empire with a successor that was not burdened by his connections to the Jesuits, nor affected by strong inclinations to usurp Protestant worship; Ferdinand III was moved instead by a singular aim which moved him from the beginning to the end of his equally long reign as Emperor – the quest for peace.[78]

The Emperor's aim to guarantee the succession of his son to the Imperial throne had been a long-running campaign of pressure and favour, but only through an election could such a decision be finalised. For this election to take place, the Electors which we have frequently encountered would have to be present to cast their vote. By 1637, this system of Electors had changed somewhat, thanks largely to the removal of the Palatine Elector, the increased Habsburg control over Bohemia, and the elevation of Bavaria's Duke Maximillian to the status of Elector. These developments had effectively increased the Catholic, pro-Habsburg vote count, yet Ferdinand had still struggled to get what he wanted the last time all the relevant Electors had been present. In the Regensburg Diet, held in the summer and autumn of 1630, for example, the concerned parties spent more time focused on the problematic status of Wallenstein, while the Protestant Electors personally boycotted the gathering, in protest of the Edict of Restitution which had recently been passed.

Here was a new opportunity for the ailing Ferdinand to appeal to his subjects and leave as his final legacy a smooth succession. It opened on 15 September 1636 and remained in session until late January 1637. Through its duration, petitions and envoys from the influential and the weak were sent. It was impossible for external parties to ignore this seminal moment in the Empire's history, or for an opportunity to curry favour with the new Emperor. It was hardly a surprise that the Spanish were heavily involved. Count Onate, the same Spanish official who had negotiated the division of the Habsburg territories in 1617, and remained in Vienna since, paid hundreds of thousands of florins to the Electors of Bavaria, Mainz, Cologne and Trier. These expenses were scarcely necessary, since although neither of the Protestant Electors attended, citing the excesses of the war as an excuse, they still committed their vote to the Emperor's son – it wasn't as though there were any other candidates with similar pedigree or prestige.

Yet the meeting represented more than merely a formality; Ferdinand III was elected as King of the Romans and Emperor on 22 December, but in the background, other less predictable initiatives were sponsored. The money which Count Onate had provided came in handy once the Dutch envoys urged the Empire to declare its official neutrality; that such a request had been necessary at all demonstrates how the lines had been blurred between the issue of war and peace. While in 1630 a declaration of war against the Dutch had not been forthcoming from the Empire, Imperial soldiers had served with distinction alongside their Spanish allies since at least 1621; there was no sense of hesitation, among either the soldiers or their commanders that an official declaration was necessary first. The soldiers simply followed the employment opportunities, and these opportunities followed the beginning of new campaigns. German figures were also heard to demand the return of the bishoprics of Metz, Toul and Verdun, all of which had been occupied by the French – this despite the fact that France and the Empire remained locked into an unofficial war.

When it came to questions of war and peace, clarity was in short supply at Regensburg, yet it was still an important forum and an opportunity to take stock of the situation following a significant recent peace treaty and nearly two decades of war. It is also interesting to see how the prospects for both Protestant Electors changed with the shifting circumstances of autumn 1636. Initially, John George of Saxony sent agents to Regensburg arguing that the best way to rid the Empire of the Swedes was for Protestant Germans to pay them off; this confirmed the Habsburg view that such Protestants had invited the Swedes in in the first place. Yet, as the weeks progressed, this approach became more difficult to pursue. George William of Brandenburg, who was in a weaker position and possessed a smaller army – only eleven thousand strong – than either Bavaria or Saxony, sent agents to insist on an open discussion of the negotiations then underway between the Saxon Elector and Chancellor Oxenstierna.

Paradoxically though, the Swedish victory at Wittstock, one month into the Regensburg Diet, compelled George William to move closer to the Emperor, as one of the first acts of the victorious Swedish army was to occupy Brandenburg and send its Elector into headlong retreat towards his East Prussian appendage. George William remained deeply concerned that the Emperor would hand Pomerania to Sweden in return for a swift peace, an outcome which was both feared and resented, as the childless Duke Bogislaw had promised to bequeath the lucrative Pomeranian Duchy to Brandenburg after his death, until the arrival of the Swedes there in 1630 complicated matters. Resentment over this situation had moved George William to act against the Swedes, and he correctly feared that Oxenstierna would never relinquish Pomerania willingly.

So, in June 1637, George William formalised an alliance with the new Emperor, which compelled both parties to defend the other, and granted financial assistance to Brandenburg's heavily indebted court. Pomerania, unfortunately for George William, remained a hot topic well into the 1640s, and was foremost in the mind of George William's son, Frederick William when the latter sent envoys to negotiate at Westphalia. At the same time, John George abandoned his brief efforts as mediator between the Emperor and the Swedes, once it became plain that the latter were too powerful following the conclusion of a peace with Poland that freed up several thousand soldiers, and the Battle of Wittstock where these men were put to great use. The opportunity for the Germans to avenge themselves on the Swedes had been lost by January 1637, just as surely as the Germans themselves squandered their opportunities here to make a lasting peace for the Empire.[79]

Curiously though, Regensburg had not been the sole moment where a gathering of German officials and foreign dignitaries had taken place. No less a figure than Pope Urban VIII had urged for a peace conference to be held where the interests and resentments of the three major Catholic powers – the Emperor, the French and the Spanish – could be hashed out. Pope Urban had played at mediation before, with some inspiring results; he had sponsored the 1626 Treaty of Monzon which ended the war of the Val Teline passes in North Italy, and followed that with the 1631 Treaty of Cherasco which brought the war of the Mantuan succession to an end. In 1634 then, he tried again, calling all three aforementioned parties to come to Cologne. In the Pope's mind, peace was a noble endeavour, but this was not peace for peace's sake – true enemies of the true Church lurked, so that while believing Catholics had fought one another and died, the infidel Turks and heretical Protestants had gained.

Richelieu might have balked at these requests in private, but as a Cardinal, and as a servant of Catholic France, he could not ignore them. Stalling for time, Richelieu had accepted the invitation in theory, only to expose France's true intentions when the war Pope Urban feared did erupt for real in May 1635. This added a greater sense of urgency to the peace mission, but Richelieu continued to stall out of fear of alienating his Protestant allies, who were not to be given representation at the Cologne Congress. Richelieu did select his main representative for the Congress – Claude d'Avaux, whom we last met facilitating the peace between Poland and Sweden at Stuhmsdorf – yet he sent him to Hamburg in the meantime, where it was hoped d'Avaux could persuade the Swedes to agree to a more permanent, concrete version of the Treaty which they had signed but failed to ratify at Wismar in March 1636.

Nor was this all; King Christian IV of Denmark, still smarting from his loss to the Emperor in 1629, and greatly fearing the rapid rise of his Swedish neighbour, proposed a congress at Lubeck, where all powers would be represented. Landgrave George II of Hess-Darmstadt, the son in law of the Elector of Saxony, had proposed a congress to take place at Breslau in Silesia as early as 1633. With varying degrees of success, these congresses played host to fascinating scenes of scheme and intrigue, where Protestants and Catholics alike sought to peel potential allies away from their respective camps, and plentiful money purses were flashed to make dangerous points. It was all an important prelude to the eventual Westphalia Congress, and the misfired conferences of the mid-1630s taught the participants a series of important lessons, the most important among them being, that one needed to possess some kind of supremacy in military or political power before sitting down to treat. As the late 1630s and early 1640s were to demonstrate, furthermore, potentates were often reluctant to forge concrete plans on the expectation that the status quo – so changeable and unreliable – could change again with the advent of a new military triumph for either side.[80]

These approaches potentially presented some problems for Richelieu, as offers for a separate peace for Sweden remained potent so long as Oxenstierna did not wish to formally tie himself to his ally. Until their alliance was confirmed – and it was not so until 1638 – Richelieu was anxious that Sweden might exit the war prematurely and leave France alone to face the combined might of the Germanies and Spain. It was with some gloom that Richelieu noted in September 1637: 'Everyone is making peace with the Emperor, who is deliberating how to carry the war into France.' He certainly had reason enough to lament French fortunes since the declaration of war against Spain; the war had plainly not gone France's way, with an uninspiring campaign in partnership with the Dutch in 1635, desperate scenes of invasion and panic in 1636, and political disasters further afield as pro-French regimes in Savoy, Mantua and Hesse-Kassel were all toppled. This complicated matters for France in North Italy and Germany, since the Landgrave of Hess-Kassel had been one of Gustavus' earliest and most enthusiastic supporters. Not until 1639 would Hesse-Kassel be confirmed as an ally of France, but Savoy slipped into a four-year civil war from 1637, and Mantua was inherited by a pro-Spanish daughter in law of the late Duke whom France had fought so hard to install in the region in the Mantuan War of Succession.[82]

It may appear somewhat strange that after preparing for the war for several years, Richelieu would be so quick to revert to negotiations with the Spanish in order to bring it to an end. After years of preparing for the final confrontation, should the Cardinal not have been prepared to fight to the bitter end with his Spanish foe? However, we should not be surprised to see Richelieu engage in negotiations so soon after taking the plunge and declaring war. Maintaining continuous negotiations with even his foes was a principle of diplomacy that Richelieu believed so sincerely in, he devoted a whole chapter to it in his *Political Testament*, and it was likely in the year of 1635 that this part biography, part guidebook, was composed. On the subject of continuous negotiation, Richelieu put the matter most succinctly when he wrote that:

> ...it is absolutely necessary to the well-being of the state to negotiate ceaselessly, either openly or secretly, and in all places, even in those from which no present fruits are reaped and still more in those for which no future prospects as yet seem likely. I can truthfully say that I have seen in my time the nature of affairs change completely for both France and the rest of Christendom as a result of my having, under the authority of the King, put this principle into practice – something up to then completely neglected in this realm...He who negotiates continuously will finally find the right instant to attain his ends, and even if this does not come about, at least it can be said he has lost nothing while keeping abreast of events in the world, which is not of little consequence in the lives of states. Negotiations are innocuous remedies which never do harm.[82]

This philosophy was certainly true for the other potentates as well – negotiations could never do harm so long as one protected his party throughout their duration. There was nothing to be lost from investigating the price for peace, and it serves to bear this in mind as the war progressed. There was no uniform plan to drag out the suffering for a tidy thirty years; from the moment it became viable to do so, as we saw, conferences and talk of conferences exploded in frequency. The reason why these congresses failed was not because those present were inherently opposed to peace, but because they believed they could achieve what they wanted more completely through a continuation of the war.

While the diplomats talked and the statesmen schemed, the soldiers did not sit still. France, after absorbing the best of what the Habsburg could throw, was unable to capitalise on the general retreat from Picardy or Alsace. In the summer of 1636, the Spanish had captured, among other towns, Corbie in Picardy, and from September-November of that year, Richelieu and his King mobilised the French army to take it back. The ripples of Wittstock were felt in their camp, as Imperial reinforcements under Matthias Gallas were sent to shore up the Emperor's position in Southern Germany, rather than confront the French in Alsace. This, in turn, freed Richelieu to call on Bernhard of Saxe-Weimar, now a French subject, to donate some troops of his own. The effort to retake Corbie, and thus undo the worst of Spain's triumphs during the troubling initial months of the Spanish invasion, was a success, but it was also a distraction. 1636 thus ended with the French reacting to Spanish initiatives, as Richelieu could not afford to launch any campaigns of his own.[83]

But these setbacks had not marred the confidence of the Dutch stadtholder Frederick Henry. He had cooperated with the French, who promised five thousand handpicked men, to attack Dunkirk in the spring of 1637, and the fleet left The Hague on 7 May to accomplish that daunting task. Dunkirk was a prized port of the Spanish Netherlands, and for the Dutch, it was also the source of legions of headaches, as this was where the Flemish sent out the majority of their privateers to attack their shipping. The ingenious design of their privateer frigates, and the earnest greed of the sailors, singled Dunkirk out as a problem spot for the Dutch as early as 1622, when one political pamphlet observed: 'Here some seamen have already waxed so rich that they may henceforth live like lords in lust and luxury. Wherefore the numbers of brave fellows doth greatly increase day by day.'[84]

Dunkirk had become a place where pirates and even Dutch deserters could make a grand living, and by 1637 it had become too great a thorn in the Republic's side to ignore. His fleet had set out with high hopes, yet almost immediately, Frederick Henry's voyage was met with misfortune, as a terrible storm smashed several of his ships, and left the fourteen thousand soldiers on board badly shaken. As his men became wrecked further by disease, the stadtholder remained true to his reputation, and worked to salvage a ruined plan by improvising. In early July, his forces were landed, and shortly thereafter, they made their way to besiege Breda.[85]

Breda had been the culmination of the Spanish campaign of reconquest in 1625, when the brilliant commander Ambrogio Spinola surged across the outskirts of the Republic, seizing what were previously believed to be safe fortress towns. Among these towns was Breda, the official seat of the House of Orange, and a settlement which was fundamental to the identity of the Dutch Republic. News of its endangerment could not have come at a worse time, for it was in 1625 that the Republic's favourite family was facing something of a succession crisis, and thus a pause in the personal military leadership of the House of Orange. As Frederick Henry's brother Maurice of Orange lay dying, he had rushed to relieve Breda, but the tragic loss of his brother was compounded by the loss of Breda, and morale in the Dutch Republic reached an all-time low level. Some in the Dutch government wished to offer the Spanish a new truce. The situation soon picked up for the Dutch into the late 1620s, but the loss of Breda, being Frederick Henry's first loss, must still have stung. Certainly, it was the last piece of territory which the Spanish still held within the Republic. If the Dutch could expel the Spanish here, with a sharp surprise attack, then surely the Spanish would be face plummeting morale of their own, to the equal of that which so reduced the Dutch twelve years before.[86]

Within days, the siege process of Breda had begun, and Frederick Henry was evidently determined to exorcise his demons. The place was surrounded by ditches, the river was dammed and flooded the countryside, Breda itself was cut off, and the relief army led personally by the Cardinal Infante could not make any headway against the defences which Frederick Henry had erected. Believing the situation to be futile, the Cardinal Infante rode off elsewhere, effectively leaving Breda to its fate. By mid-October this city was firmly in Frederick Henry's hands, but the siege had not been without its casualties. Perhaps surprisingly, the five thousand French soldiers originally earmarked for a siege of Dunkirk had not abandoned the stadtholder when he decided to march on Breda instead, and this is underlined by the loss of a distinguished Frenchman among the allied army. Hercule Girard Charnacé was shot through the head as he led a charge on the Spanish-held walls – an explosive end for a figure better known for his diplomatic exploits as Baron Charnacé, the man who had played a key role in brokering the Truce of Altmark which pulled Sweden out of its Polish War in 1629. Still, it could not be denied that a great triumph for Frederick Henry was at hand, and the historian George Edmundson wrote:

> The fall of Breda caused the greatest joy throughout the united provinces, for it was the last place of importance within their boundaries which was in the hands of the Spaniards. The Netherlanders now felt themselves really masters of their own domain.[87]

Perhaps, the man the Habsburgs needed was their new Emperor, who had led Imperial forces to victory alongside the Cardinal Infante at Nordlingen, after all. Although this triumph had brought him much admiration, Ferdinand III could not debase his authority by serving as a mere commander; this, at least, would surely have been his response for any such request to command. In reality, the danger that the Emperor's office and authority would be irreparably tarnished by a loss he might suffer to a common Swedish commander was the true incentive for Ferdinand III to stay in Vienna – his commanding days were over.

Surveying the position of his dynasty in spring 1637, Ferdinand III could be confident of one fact above all: that the war would not and could not end without at least one other significant Habsburg triumph. In the North in Pomerania, where the Swedes dominated Mecklenburg, Brandenburg and Saxony, even threatening Leipzig, there was much to be done. Yet, Ferdinand would also have been informed of the variety of new theatres in the war; supporting Spain with thirty thousand Imperials on the River Meuse; recruiting sixteen thousand more Germans along the Rhine; twelve thousand men under Duke Charles of Lorraine who might recapture the Spanish Road.[88] These were figures notably reduced from the unsustainable highs of Wallenstein, who had on hand one hundred thousand men or more at a time. It seemed that Ferdinand III had learned several lessons from the war's early years; perhaps his father had taught him a thing or two about leading the Empire. And yet, no education in the world could have prepared the new Emperor for what was to follow – a full decade of warfare, as the schemers talked, the soldiers marched, and his Empire was ripped apart.

Chapter 18 Notes

[1]Quoted in J. H. Elliott, *The Revolt of the Catalans: A Study in the Decline of Spain* (1598-1640) (Cambridge: University Press, 1963), p. 374.

[2]Wilson, *Sourcebook*, pp. 270-271.

[3]Quoted in *Ibid*, p. 263.

[4]Quoted in Porshnev, *Muscovy and Sweden in the Thirty Years War*, p. 216.

[5]Paul Dukes, "7: New Perspectives: Alexander Leslie and the Smolensk War, 1632–4," in *Scotland and the Thirty Years' War, 1618-1648*, pp. 176-179.

[6]Quoted in Porshnev, *Muscovy and Sweden*, p. 214.

[7]See *Ibid*, pp. 71-73.

[8]See Oakley, *War and Peace in the Baltic*, pp. 72-73.

[9]Porshnev, *Muscovy and Sweden*, pp. 219-224.

[10]See *Ibid*, p. 225.

[11]See Andersson, *A History of Sweden*, pp. 181-182.

[12]Quoted in Parker, *Thirty Years War*, p. 140.

[13]irteenthese issues have been summarised for the sake of brevity, but Porshnev, *Muscovy and Sweden*, pp. 226-241 provides the best analysis available.

[14]See Wedgewood, *Thirty Years War*, pp. 385-384.

[15]Parker, *Thirty Years War*, p. 142.

[16]Quoted in Wilson, *Sourcebook*, p. 206.

[17]*Ibid*, pp. 206-207.

[18]Wedgewood, *Thirty Years War*, p. 385.

[19]See Pieter Geyl, *History of the Dutch-Speaking Peoples*, pp. 405-406.

[20]George Edmundson, 'Frederick Henry, Prince of Orange (Continued)', pp. 271-273.

[21]See R. A. Stradling, 'Olivares and the Origins of the Franco-Spanish War, 1627-1635', pp. 82-83.

[22]Jarmo Kotilaine and Marshall Poe, eds., *Modernizing Muscovy: Reform and Social Change in Seventeenth-Century Russia* (New York: Routledge Curzon, 2004), pp. 207-210.

[23]Richard Bassett, *For God and Kaiser, The Imperial Austrian Army, 1619-1918*, pp. 32-35.

[24]See Parker, *Europe in Crisis*, pp. 241-242.

[25]See Moote, *Louis XIII, the Just*, p. 239.

[26]Both quoted in Stradling, 'Olivares and the Origins of the Franco-Spanish War, 1627-1635', p. 84.

[27]Quoted in Parker, *Europe in Crisis*, p. 239.

[28]Quoted in *Ibid*, p. 238.

[29]Quoted in *Ibid*, p. 246.

[30]Hume, *The Court of Phillip IV: Spain in Decadence*, p. 300.

[31]See Elliot, *The Revolt of the Catalans*, p. 309.

[32]Quoted in Stradling, 'Olivares and the Origins of the Franco-Spanish War, 1627-1635', p. 94.

[33]Edmundson, 'Frederick Henry, Prince of Orange (continued)', pp. 271-272.

[34]Geyl, *History of the Dutch-Speaking Peoples*, p. 406.

[35]See Parrott, *Richelieu's Army*, pp. 113-117.

[36]*Ibid*, p. 117.

[37]*Ibid*, pp. 119-120.

[38]Parker, *Europe in Crisis*, p. 252.

[39]Moote, *Louis XIII, the Just*, p. 241.

[40]Quoted in Stradling, 'Olivares and the Origins of the Franco-Spanish War, 1627-1635', p. 92.

[41]See Parker, *Europe in Crisis*, pp. 233-235.

[42]Quoted in Elliot, *The Revolt of the Catalans*, p. 306.

[43]Parker, *Europe in Crisis*, p. 250.

[44]See Geoffrey Parker, 'Why Did the Dutch Revolt Last Eighty Years?', *Transactions of the Royal Historical Society*, Vol. 26 (1976), pp. 53-72; p. 65.

[45]See Filipa Ribeiro da Silva, 'Crossing Empires: Portuguese, Sephardic, and Dutch Business Networks in the Atlantic Slave Trade, 1580-1674', *The Americas*, Vol. 68, No. 1 (July 2011), pp. 7-32; pp. 16-19.

[46]Parker, *Europe in Crisis*, p. 236.

[47]See Stuart B. Schwartz, "Chapter 2: Portuguese Attitudes of Religious Tolerance in Dutch Brazil" in *The Expansion of Tolerance: Religion in Dutch Brazil (1624-1654)*, by Jonathan Israel and Stuart B. Schwartz (eds), (Amsterdam: Amsterdam University Press, 2007), pp. 35-56.

[48]Parker, *Europe in Crisis*, p. 353.

[49]For more on the debate surrounding Olivares' conception of the war with France, see R. A. Stradling, 'Olivares and the Origins of the Franco-Spanish War, 1627-1635', pp. 90-92.

[50]Parker, *Thirty Years War*, p. 142.

[51]See Derek Croxton, *Westphalia: the Last Christian Peace* (New York: Palgrave Macmillan, 2013), p. 48

[52]Quoted in Mary Elizabeth Ailes, 'Power, Status, and Wealth: British Officers in Seventeenth-Century Sweden', *Scandinavian Studies*, Vol. 71, No. 2 (Summer 1999), pp. 221-240; p. 235. Extract is edited for easier comprehension.

[53]See *Ibid*, pp. 236-237.

[54]See E. Bourke, 'Irish Levies for the Army of Sweden (1609-1610)', *The Irish Monthly*, Vol. 46, No. 541 (Jul., 1918), pp. 396-404; p. 399.

[55]Alexia Grosjean, "6: Scotland: Sweden's Closest Ally?" in *Scotland and the Thirty Years' War, 1618-1648*, ed. Steve Murdoch (Boston: Brill, 2001), p. 143.

[56]Both extracts quoted in Wilson, *Sourcebook*, pp. 209-210.

[57]See Croxton, *Westphalia*, p. 49.

[58]See Ward et all, *The Cambridge Modern History* vol. 4, pp. 366-367.

[59]See Wilson, *Europe's Tragedy*, pp. 577-578.

[60]Extracts taken from Wilson, *Sourcebook*, p. 210.

[61]Quoted in *Ibid*, pp. 210-211.

[62]Quoted in *Ibid*, p. 211.

[63]See Wedgewood, *Thirty Years War*, pp. 390-392; Ward, *Cambridge Modern History*, pp. 369-370.

[64]Parrott, *Richelieu's Army*, pp. 118-119.

[65]See Wilson, *Europe's Tragedy*, pp. 579-580.

[66]See Stomberg, *A History of Sweden*, pp. 373-374; Andersson, *A History of Sweden*, pp. 182-184; Wilson, *Europe's Tragedy*, p. 580.

[67]Wilson, *Europe's Tragedy*, p. 559.

[68] *Ibid*, p. 559.

[69]See Jan Glete, *War and the State in Early Modern Europe: Spain, the Dutch Republic, and Sweden as Fiscal-Military States, 1500-1660* (London: Routledge, 2002), p. 187. Glete is one among many historians that claims France declared war on the Emperor, whereas Wilson, *Europe's Tragedy*, p. 559 notes that a declaration was avoided. A more nuanced approach to the question is taken by K. Malettke, 'France's imperial policy during the Thirty Years War', in K. Bussmann and H. Schilling (eds.), *1648: War and Peace in Europe* (3 vols, Münster, 1998), vol. 1, pp. 177-185; especially pp. 182-183. Henceforth, we will work from the assumption that a state of war existed between France and the Emperor, with the expulsion of French diplomats from Vienna in March 1636 marking its undeclared beginning.

[70]See Wilson, *Europe's Tragedy*, p. 581.

[71]All extracts from Wilson, *Sourcebook*, pp. 211-213.

[72]Wilson, *Europe's Tragedy*, p. 583.

[73]See John Matusiak, *Europe in Flames*, pp. 373-374.

[74]Schiller, *The Works of Frederick Schiller*, p. 317.

[75]Basset, *For God and Kaiser*, pp. 66-68.

[76]Wilson, 'The Causes of the Thirty Years War 1618-48', pp. 577-580; Wilson, 'The Role of Religion in the Thirty Years War'.

[77]See Robert Bireley, 'The Peace of Prague (1635) and the Counterreformation in Germany', *The Journal of Modern History*, Vol. 48, No. 1, On Demand Supplement (Mar.,1976), pp. 31-70; pp. 64-67.

[78]Wedgewood, *Thirty Years War*, pp. 396-398.

[79]For all of these developments, see Wilson, *Europe's Tragedy*, pp. 585-587.

[80]For all these peace initiatives, see Croxton, *Westphalia*, pp. 52-61.

[81]*Ibid*, pp. 62-63.

[82]Richelieu, Benny Hill trans., *Political Testament of Cardinal Richelieu*, p. 86

[83]See Parrott, *Richelieu's Army*, pp. 120-121.

[84]Pieter Geyl, *History of the Dutch-Speaking Peoples*, pp. 408-409.

[85]Edmundson, 'Frederick Henry: Prince of Orange (continued)', pp. 272-273.

[86]See Geoffrey Parker, 'Spain, Her Enemies and the Revolt of the Netherlands 1559-1648', *Past & Present*, No. 49 (Nov., 1970), pp. 72-95; pp. 89-91.

[87]Edmundson, 'Frederick Henry', p. 274.

[88]See Wilson, *Europe's Tragedy*, pp. 588-589.

(Top left) Octavio Piccolomni (Justus Sustermans)
(Top Right) Elector Karl Ludwig (Christoph Le Blon, 1651)

(Top left) Charles V of Lorraine
(Top right) Admiral Maarten Tromp (Jan Lierens)

CHAPTER NINETEEN
"The Weight of the War"

ONE: Cruel Tides of War

TWO: Spain is Sinking

THREE: Germany is Aching

ONE

Cruel Tides of War

Emperor Ferdinand III was just 29 years old when he ascended to the Imperial throne, and the mission which lay in front of him was as formidable as it was complicated. After twenty years of war, few in Europe genuinely wished to see it continue, yet fewer still were willing to give way so long as they held a position of some significance. Ferdinand knew that the balance of power was beginning to count against Vienna, or at least balance itself out, now that France had placed itself firmly in the enemy camp. However, with the arrival of France, potentially, came the opportunity to mobilise all of Germany against the traditional foe. What was needed was a coordinated campaign of attack for the late 1630s, which would compromise French security, remove Sweden from Pomerania, weaken the Dutch for Spain, and confirm German solidarity. As Ferdinand was to learn, these tasks were not merely difficult, they were also interdependent and connected.

There now existed several fronts in the war, which Vienna and Madrid would have to devote the necessary attention to. In the north-east of Germany, Johan Baner's Swedish army was quartered, having bought itself sometime after the victory at Wittstock the previous October. Opposing Baner were mostly Saxon and Brandenburg troops, though these were increasingly desperate for Imperial reinforcement since Wittstock. To the north-west, based in Westphalia, the rebellious German figure William of Hesse-Kassel led opposition to the Emperor, and was in touch with France. He faced the forces of Germans loyal to the Emperor, led interchangeably by the Saxons and by Octavio Piccolomini. Above them in the Netherlands, the Dutch continued to batter away at the Spanish, which hampered the latter's ability to contribute much in the northern theatres, but further to the south, and along the Rhine, the Spanish were more active.

First, there was an army under the Imperial Piccolomini, who commanded near Picardy following the invasion of France the previous year. Second, further to the south, the status of Alsace and Lorraine plagued the

French court and provided great opportunities for the Spanish and Imperial forces. Bernhard of Saxe-Weimar, the former Swedish turned French subject, led a motley crew in that region, and was opposed by the Imperial general and former subordinate of Wallenstein, Matthias Gallas. Gallas was supported by Duke Charles of Lorraine, but above all by the nearby Bavarians, and a nervous Maximillian of Bavaria looked on out of fear that the French might spill across the Rhine and into his lands.[1]

Olivares may have intended to retry the ambitious campaigns of 1636, but 1637 was to deny him the chance. The fall of Breda in October 1637 moved Imperial and Spanish forces away from French territory; the Swedish resurgence forced Matthias Gallas to send troops away from the Rhine and into Saxony; Piccolomini, following Spanish pleas, quartered in nearby Luxembourg and watched the Spanish defences, effectively occupying his army of twelve thousand men until late 1639. The need to plug leaks in struggling theatres represented a constant drain on the resources of Vienna and Madrid, and Ferdinand was growing restless for another reason: Spain had failed to provide the subsidy it had promised, and as a result the Emperor did not feel compelled to make any supreme effort in 1637, even if he had been in a position to, which he was not.

It was immensely difficult to take stock of the situation at the different theatres, and more difficult still to coordinate between them. The ravaging of German lands seriously hampered the delivery of post, and it also seems to have reduced the number of men which recruiters could traditionally support. The days of Wallenstein commandeering more than one hundred thousand were long gone; barely five years on from those record highs of recruitment, the Emperor could scarcely boast half that number of effectives.[2] This reduction in soldiers did not result in a reduction in stakes – in fact it made the Habsburg and allied positions more anxious. In spring 1637, Matthias Gallas arrived in Saxony with twenty thousand men. As the commander of the main Imperial army, Gallas had been watching the Rhine throughout 1636, and awaiting the French attack. With the position in Northern Germany acute after Wittstock though, and John George of Saxony seeking to remain calm as the apoplectic George William of Brandenburg scurried off to East Prussia, Ferdinand recognised that something would have to be done if North Germany was not to be lost to Sweden altogether.

In fact, Johan Baner's hold over the north was not as powerful as might have been imagined. He had only fourteen thousand men under his command, and with the approach of a combined Imperial-Saxon army twice that size, it was clear that he would have to avoid its advance. For the next few months, Baner engaged in an ingenious campaign of cat and mouse, as he ditched his baggage train and commandeered its horses to get the edge on the foe. Yet, impressive though his escape over the River Oder to the north-east was, the retreat had cost Baner four thousand men, and it frustrated the potential which Wittstock had suggested for a Swedish resurgence – this would not come until later. Oxenstierna received the news of Baner's struggles loud and clear, initially making an effort to negotiate with the Imperials directly in January 1638, yet these negotiations came to nothing, and the Imperial agent at Hamburg noted that Oxenstierna continued to stall. The reason for this stalling was that the Swedish Chancellor had come closer to a more concrete arrangement with France.[3]

The Treaty of Hamburg was confirmed on 15 March 1638 and established a full alliance between Sweden and France which was to last three years. As per the terms of the alliance, France would supply 400,000 thalers annually, Sweden was confirmed as excluded from the Franco-Spanish War, and Oxenstierna pledged to coordinate diplomacy with France. Oxenstierna still did not trust Richelieu, but he did trust in the value of the sudden cash injection, using it to expand Baner's army based in Stettin to more than twenty thousand men. The impact of the cash was such that by the midsummer of 1638, Matthias Gallas was now the outnumbered party. All Gallas could call upon were a few thousand poorly trained Brandenburg troops, and the ailing Elector George William was more interested in seeing Gallas secure Pomerania for his family than in helping him expel the nearby Swedes. Baner took the initiative, and as Gallas retreated beyond the Elbe, he could not have known that he was retreating from the Swedish base for the final time. The Imperials would not get another chance to endanger Sweden's position again for, just as Gallas was repulsed from the north, further to the west along the Rhine, Bernhard of Saxe-Weimar finally came through for France.[4]

The years 1637-38 had contained a great deal of inconsistent campaigning for Bernhard. As he would not or could not raise more than nine thousand men, the French both reduced their subsidy to him and determined to reinforce his army with their own. Closer to home, in Picardy to the north-east, and in Languedoc in the south of France, a Spanish invasion had been beaten back, but Richelieu continued to delegate control of these matters to their provincial governors, which meant that the expense of these operations would have to be borne by the governors as well, rather than by the royal treasury. Any efforts to do more than expel the Spanish from the extreme south of the country floundered on the usual problems of supply, apathy and bad generalship. The historian David Parrott, analysing the campaigning year of 1637, provided the following astute observations:

> The year marked a low point in French military activity. It presented the cardinal with the possibility of a war that would not necessarily lead to outright defeat, but would lose all momentum under the impact of supply and financial failures, the reluctance of the generals to risk their reputations and their fortunes and the practical difficulties involved in any attempt to exploit

success in one campaign theatre without excessively weakening all of the others. It was this threat of military stagnation, with its consequences both for strategy and for the loss of royal reputation, that drove the ministers to place greater pressure on the individual commanders to undertake more ambitious strategies in subsequent campaigns. Unfortunately, this increased pressure was not matched by any significant improvement in the administrative structure or the resources available for the war-effort.[5]

With 1637 producing little of note, Richelieu had focused on the diplomatic sphere, and continued to sponsor encouraging congresses in Lubeck and Hamburg, which might grant breakthroughs at the peace table where the battlefield was less generous. Yet all these efforts at creating some preliminary peace congress proved to be in vain; the Emperor still hoped to make a separate peace with Sweden; King Philip still hoped for the Emperor to join him against the Dutch; Oxenstierna did not wish to show his hand or commit himself. All the while, undersupplied and underfunded armies marched and pillaged their way along the Rhine, one of which was led by Bernhard of Saxe-Weimar.[6]

Bernhard had made little use out of 1637 but did intend to make greater effort in spring 1638. He found poised against him a seriously understrength Imperial force, which had seen its regiments peeled away to aid the Saxons in the middle Rhine, while further up the Rhine near the border with the Spanish Netherlands, a new invasion by Frederick Henry aimed at seizing Antwerp pulled many Spanish support units away from the Imperial side. These interconnected threats had a serious impact upon the Imperial capacity to defend its position along the Rhine; Bernhard was thus confronted by garrisons defending several fortresses of strategic importance along the daunting river and its plain. One such fortress was Breisach, and during 1638, Bernhard manoeuvred into a position along the Rhine to besiege it. The mission was far from simple, but if he was successful, then France would have established a bridgehead on the other side of the Rhine, and they could use this as a base for further incursions into the Empire, threatening Bavaria above all.

In early March, Bernhard defeated the Imperial army at Rheinfelden, increasing the isolation of Breisach in the process, and paving the way for sieges of Breisach's supporting fortresses up and down the Rhine. In mid-June, Bernhard finally felt confident to draw his cannon before Breisach. Inside this tough nut was Colonel Reinach, a veteran of the Battle of Lutzen, and an experienced commander of men. He had three thousand well-prepared soldiers at his command, complemented by 152 cannons. If Bernhard wanted Breisach, he would have to be prepared not only for a lengthy siege, but also to foil the efforts at relief launched by the Imperials over the rest of the year. An interesting point about these operations is the juxtaposition between the importance of what was at stake, and the small numbers of men used by either side. At Rheinfelden, Bernhard had only six thousand men, as did his foe, while even following French reinforcement in late spring of 1638, his army still numbered no more than twelve thousand men.

Perhaps both sides had come to accept that difficulties in provision and command recommended the use of smaller forces, yet it is more likely that neither side possessed the resources to act in any greater numbers. In the Imperial case in particular, Matthias Gallas was attempting to capture Johan Baner's Swedes in Pomerania while Bernhard laid siege to Breisach. At the diplomatic table, meanwhile, the Treaty of Hamburg was formalised between Sweden and France. Important as Breisach and its command over Alsace was, it seemed as though the rest of the war was passing Bernhard by. If he wanted to confirm the investment France had placed in him, then it was vital he succeed and seize this bastion for his French masters. Fortunately for Richelieu's nerves, this was done by mid-December, as the shattered Imperial garrison was allowed to march out with full honours. Colonel Reinach's men had been through hell, their initially healthy three thousand reduced to just four hundred effectives, and the starved garrison were reduced to chewing the hides of horses and cows to survive.[7]

Emperor Ferdinand would certainly have lamented the loss; Breisach represented the first true loss of Imperial territory to a French regime which had spent previous year's invariably buckling under the military pressure and, so far as Ferdinand was concerned, feigning an urge for peace.[8] Breisach presented a great opportunity for Richelieu to plan for a more impactful Rhine campaign into the new campaigning year of 1639, but it was also a desperately needed piece of good news for a people crushed by taxation and driven anxious by the initial setbacks in the war. By late 1638, after not even a full year of rule, the Emperor was beginning to realise precisely how urgently the Empire needed peace. Following the spat with Spain over unpaid subsidies, and withdrawal of Spanish auxiliaries from the Lower Rhine to fight the Dutch, it surely appeared to the Emperor as though the other branch of the dynasty was not pulling its weight, or abiding by the terms of previous alliances which had been made.

But the Spanish had severe problems of their own, above all in their major war theatre with the Dutch, but also closer to home in Catalonia. This northernmost principality of Spain, with its capital of Barcelona, had been a client of the Kingdom of Aragon, and was difficult even for the medieval Aragonese to bring to heel. Catalonia, uniquely among the Spanish Monarchy which was centred on Castile, had managed to retain its independent culture, and even its language, with some Catalans not even being fluent in Spanish, or able to understand those Castilian officials who came to rule over their region. The intransigence of the Catalans was especially problematic into the late 1630s, as manpower shortages elsewhere in the Iberian Peninsula moved Olivares to request more and more men from Castile's neighbours. However, a further dimension to the problem was one of national security – as the border province with France, a Catalan revolt could throw Spain into crisis, and open a backdoor into the peninsula which France could invade from.

For so long it had been assumed that the Catalans would never go that far, but the resilience of the locals to all Castilian demands, be they taxes or the provision of recruits, certainly put Olivares' back against the wall, and compelled him to imagine worst case scenarios. According to the judgements and figures of the Union of Arms which had been drawn up in the early 1620s, Catalonia was meant to provide a healthy regular income to Madrid, yet as we learned, this income had been calculated in error, and was based on an inaccurate picture of Catalonia's population. The Catalans thus rarely if ever paid what Madrid insisted, they owed, and the recruits they did levy were often disbanded followed rumours that they would be expected to serve in Germany or elsewhere. Reportedly, some Catalans even compelled recruits from neighbouring regions to disband as they marched through their territory. Predictably, Olivares was less than impressed, and he wrote to King Philip IV repeatedly on the matter, saying on one occasion in early 1636 that:

> If Barcelona were to behave as it should [burst out Olivares on hearing of the rejection] the whole province would follow suit...but it attempts to bargain over questions not only of grace but even of justice, to the detriment of the public welfare and of royal authority. And it is impossible not to add that, unless these vassals recover from their present blindness, it will be necessary to take some terrible steps which Your Majesty, in his mercy, has always been anxious to avoid.[10]

But the problem with Catalonia only grew worse, and as Olivares' impatience grew, so did the Catalans become more concerned with their alienation from Madrid. In a secret Junta meeting held in August 1636, Olivares confirmed their fears when he expressed the view that:

> If there were anyone who would dare reduce that province without the presence of Your Majesty (a task which, with Your Majesty's presence, one hopes to God will be easy), he would deserve the greatest imaginable honours and rewards from Your Majesty. And really, it raises serious questions of principle to allow this business to drag on.[11]

Was Catalonia merely a troublesome spot, a blemish on the King's Majesty, or was it something far more sinister? Time would in fact reveal that Catalonia was a far greater threat to Madrid than Olivares could have imagined, but throughout the late 1630s, precious little was done to fix the core problems which underpinned the Castilian-Catalan relationship. The

Duke of Cordoba, the Spanish viceroy for Catalonia, communicated the problem to Olivares in a meeting held in May 1637, saying:

> As regards using the Catalans for their own defence, we shall try to do so by the most subtle methods. But I beg Your Excellency to permit me to tell you that these people are temperamentally so lacking in docility, even when their own welfare is at stake, that even when aware of this they remain suspicious, and will take no action until necessity compels.[12]

By now Olivares had had enough; it was time for Catalans to do their duty, and by hook or by crook, he intended to force them to do so. Since they would only act 'when necessity compels' according to the viceroy, Olivares determined, in the words of the historian J. H. Elliot, 'to give necessity a helping hand.' He would raise an army fifteen thousand strong, composed of six thousand Catalans, and this would be sent against the French in Languedoc, the southern region of the French country, which was traditionally rebellious, and contrarian to the North of France in religion, culture, history and language. Languedoc, in short, was the Catalonia of France, but in seeking to batter his enemy's troublesome vassal with a troublesome vassal of his own, Olivares made a severe miscalculation.

Those six thousand Catalans would be raised, insisted the Count-Duke, on the basis of the proclamation of *Princeps Namque*, which stated that Catalans must rush to the defence of their King. Interestingly though, Catalans had read the fine print of this 11th century proclamation, which had as a pre-requisite that the King should be in Catalonia if it was to be valid. Since King Philip was certainly not present in Catalonia in summer 1637, Catalans used this loophole to absolve themselves of their supposed duty to defend him. This defeat could not be kept a secret; one Spanish official noted how the demand for six thousand recruits had been transformed into six thousand lawsuits, 'which will last for years, while the province looks on and laughs.' Olivares seethed in Madrid, aghast at the opportunism and lack of patriotism of the Catalan people and determined to have his way.[13]

What followed was further disaster for Spain, as its anaemically provisioned army still moved over the Pyrenees and in August 1637 besieged Leucate, a picturesque seaside town on the Mediterranean. There was not a Catalan to be found in the army, yet when Barcelona's council did move to make some show of obedience, the five hundred men they raised marched too late, and the French relieved the town. And even while they had marched, the Catalans had not distinguished themselves, as one Barcelona commander recorded: 'they are dissolute men, quite shameless about stealing hens and sheep...It is all wrong that these soldiers, who are natives of the province, should conduct themselves so badly.' News of the Spanish defeat in late September was received with consternation in Madrid, and even some Catalans began to feel anxious about letting the side down.

Interestingly though, while many citizens proclaimed their intentions to serve the required three months service in the new campaigning season of 1638, the senior officials objected, consulted the constitutional lawyers who informed them of their rights, and continued to try to dodge service. Without the senior nobility on side, Madrid could not expect much in the way of help, and any campaigns launched for 1638 seemed to be doomed to failure once again. Disgusted with receiving the bulk of the blame for the recent disappointments, the Spanish viceroy, the Duke of Cordoba, resigned in late 1637. The question thus remained – who could whip these Catalans into shape in time for a new campaigning season? Or, as some in Madrid feared, was the situation in Catalonia simply irretrievably lost? As Spanish troops wintered in the truculent principality, it was clear that greater tests were still to come.[14]

The war with the Dutch did not sit still over 1637-38 while the Spanish grappled with Catalonia and while Olivares planned his strikes against the French. Indeed, as Richelieu understood it, the Dutch-Spanish War served as the ideal foil to Spanish strategic plans, because just as a small victory or military initiative was seized in one theatre, resources would have to be diverted to account for a setback in another. This was the case, as it happened, with the Habsburg position generally, as we saw many Imperialist soldiers diverted from the Rhine in spring 1637 to protect Saxony once the Battle of Wittstock in October 1636 destroyed the Saxon-Imperial position. Perhaps only in North Italy, where French alliances with Savoy and Mantua collapsed, could the Habsburgs have any claim to genuine success in the period, yet even with the reconquest of the Val Teline, the Spanish Road remained cut, and Spain was denied a direct land route between either Madrid and Vienna, or Madrid and Brussels. It was to be expected then that in both of these theatres, the ability of the Habsburg dynasty to coordinate its campaigns began to decline.

So did the integrity of the Spanish Monarchy itself; the Portuguese remained bitter and its nobility resentful at the failure of the Spanish to return Pernambuco to Portuguese control. Pernambuco was a valuable prize which the Dutch had seized in 1630 and only expanded since. By 1638, Olivares was willing to make serious offers of peace to the Dutch if they would relinquish the region, and promised 5 million ducats if the Dutch committed to hand back Maastricht, Breda and this South American colony.[15] Yet, the Dutch were unmoved; they knew they possessed the advantage, and that the resumption of war with France had severely hampered Madrid's ability to project its power. Not just its power, but also its finances; Spanish monetary aid to Brussels rapidly decreased in the late 1630s as the burdens of war with France increased, and the compact within Iberia fractured. Spain sent nearly 13.5 million florins to Brussels in 1637; 11 million in 1638, and just short of 9 million in 1639. During the particularly grim year of 1643, Spain could spare only 4.5 million florins for Brussels, while the Dutch continued to run rampant.[16]

Such facts and figures suggest that, far from holding out on Vienna, Madrid was struggling even to defend and support its own direct interests in Europe and the New World. The late 1630s must be seen as the culmination of many years of chronic decline in Spanish finance and strength, aggravated by the Dutch ingenuity in the New World and by Frederick Henry's successful campaigns, which had effectively liberated the Republic from any latent Spanish threat by October 1637, with the fall of Breda. Henceforth, Spain was unable to genuinely threaten Dutch independence, and it became a matter of when, rather than if, she would concede defeat. Olivares' multi-pronged campaign against France in 1636 had been bold and creative in theory, but in practice, that grand strategic plan for pushing France out of the war and focusing attention on the Dutch proved to be the final truly promising Spanish initiative of the Thirty Years War.

Indeed, it seemed that the Dutch were as innovative and daring abroad as Frederick Henry was in his siege-craft in the Netherlands; so long as the Dutch usurped Spanish power in Asia, the Caribbean and South America, Madrid was unable to absorb the knock-on effects of such losses. Portugal's nobility had always been an important lobby group, and they were joined by the merchant classes of Lisbon who had a direct financial interest in the Brazilian sugar industry. With Dutch possession of that industry, much of the sheen of Spanish rule wore off, and from the mid-1630s regular petitions from Lisbon to Madrid spoke of the urgent need to take back Pernambuco.[17] It was not from lack of trying that Spain failed in these efforts, but even greater disaster followed in autumn 1639. Olivares, after seeing his efforts melt into pools of disaster, resolved to replicate the grand-campaign strategy of 1636, but this time at sea, and directed solely against the Dutch. On paper, the plan was fearsome – an armada of 80 ships would be sent to destroy the Dutch fleet, thereby endangering the economic lifeblood of the Republic, and freeing the supply routes to Brussels. But the promise of success was illusory; the 80 ships varied greatly in size and quality, and in late October 1639, the superior Dutch Admiral Martin Tromp outmanoeuvred his foe off Dover, in the Battle of the Downs.[18]

The defeat was a bitter one for Olivares. He had spent the majority of 1639 building up the fleet for an attack which he hoped would be the answer to Spain's woes. 1638 had seen Frederick Henry repulsed from Antwerp, but there had been no major initiatives launched by either side in the meantime.[19] Similar to the French case, the Dutch-Spanish experience of 1637-38 was a somewhat quiet period, following the fall of Breda in autumn 1637. Yet, as Frederick Henry appreciated, continuous triumphs were less important than the retention of the major weapons in his arsenal.[20] All he had to do was hold onto Pernambuco and maintain a large army in the Netherlands, and the sapping effect this would have on Madrid would eventually tell. The Battle of the Downs vindicated this idea, and represented arguably the greatest naval victory of the Dutch Republic.[21] Far more important than this triumph at sea though was the succession of disasters which convulsed Spain in the following year. For, if 1639 was the year when Olivares' great plan was destroyed, then 1640 was destined to be the year when the very idea of Spain appeared to be in jeopardy.

TWO
Spain is Sinking

Sir John Pennington had received his orders, but he did not have to like them. As the Admiral of King Charles's hulking fleet, featuring the latest in naval technology, and paid for by the King's infamous ship-money schemes, Pennington led a powerful arm of British authority.[22] Powerful though it was, Pennington's orders were somewhat unorthodox. Unusually for an Admiral in command of such a hefty fleet, Pennington had orders, not to engage in battle, but to prevent two other navies from engaging one another. The task, as it happened, was utterly impossible – Pennington would later thank God that fog and uncooperative winds granted him the excuse to take no action. This English Admiral had no interest in butting between the two navies, one Spanish and one Dutch, just off the coast of Dover. On the one hand was that enormous fleet of 80 ships, sent out by Olivares in mid-September 1639 for the express purpose of defeating the Dutch at sea. On the other hand, here was a powerful and well-led fleet under Admiral Martin Tromp. One power was an ally, the other a nominal ally, and while Pennington was unlikely to have been informed of the diplomatic and strategic circumstances, he was aware that it was difficult to play peacemaker when two armed, floating behemoths wished to fight.

Not even the departure of the son of the late Winter King, Karl Ludwig, could reduce the tension. Karl Ludwig ventured to Alsace, intending to request Bernhard of Saxe-Weimar's personal loyalty – this was a difficult task, and a dangerous one, but we imagine Pennington might have envied the Palatine Elector for the simplicity of his mission. Pennington knew that to order his men to protect Spaniards could invoke mutiny among them, but a forlorn hope was that neither would engage the other – after all, they were in English waters. A week after Karl Ludwig had departed for France, the battle began. This was the Battle of the Downs, but it was less a battle than a massacre. After more than a week blockading the Spanish fleet, Tromp attacked on 21 October, and in the course of the battle, using fireships and superior tactics, more than half of the fleet was destroyed. Those surviving Spanish sailors who desperately sought safety when struggling to shore were met with cold indifference, and sometimes hostility, by the Kentish natives. Returning Spaniards would later complain that Kentish fishermen had plundered and stolen their possessions.[23]

Victory at the Battle of the Downs was a terrific result for Tromp and the Dutch, but it was also a seriously problematic outcome for King Charles. Rumours circulating before and following the Battle demonstrate the kind of regime Charles had come to lead. Suspicions of Catholic sympathies moved some to fear that their King wished to use the Spanish to impose his will on his rebellious subjects, but Charles wanted this less than he wanted to somehow balance the two powers which he had attempted to ally England with.[24] Thanks to Charles' policies though, several issues had come home to roost. The first and most glaring was the King's inability to eject these two foreign navies from English waters. The ship-money levies had been brought about to make Charles 'master' of the seas around Britain since 'it would be very irksome unto us if that princely honour in our times should be lost or in any thing diminished.' Yet no effort was made to defend this honour, as Charles would not allow Admiral Pennington to risk his hulking fleet that had cost him so much. The result was nothing less than embarrassment, as the King was forced to watch while two foreign powers duked it out in his backyard, without having any say in the matter, his weak protests being of no avail.[25]

As Pennington remained apprehensive, Admiral Tromp had been given 'carte blanche' to act as he deemed it necessary by the Dutch government; in fact, he was encouraged to destroy the Spanish as soon as was possible, without paying heed to 'locality or impediments of any kind.'[26] As Tromp wrecked Olivares' brainchild, and the final naval threat to the Dutch Republic, the people of Britain, for the most part, rejoiced, proclaiming that yet another Spanish Armada had been destroyed. Further humiliation for Charles followed, when it was learned that his nephew, the Elector Palatine Karl Ludwig, had been captured and imprisoned on Richelieu's orders. After waiting for so long for Bernhard of Saxe-Weimar to be of use to France, Richelieu was not about to permit the Elector Palatine to steal him out from under his nose. At this time, Prince Rupert of the Palatinate, Karl Ludwig's brother, was also in Habsburg captivity.

Indeed, the Palatine cause had seemed luckless in recent years, and it had faltered apparently for the final time at the Battle of Vlotho in October 1638, where Imperial forces intercepted and destroyed an army meant for the Palatinate.[27] It was there that Prince Rupert was captured, and the imprisonment of Elector Karl Ludwig the following year was a disaster for that cause, but it also represented a black mark of King Charles' reputation.

The interminable story of the Palatinate, which never ceased to bother the Stuart family since 1618, continued to haunt King Charles more than twenty years later. With the death of Frederick V, the Winter King, in 1632, the large family which had grown up around Frederick and Elizabeth, Charles' sister, promised that the Palatine cause would not stay quiet for long.

Sure enough, Elizabeth called regularly upon her brother to act in Palatine interests, and yet in the developing morass of the Thirty Years War, it was difficult for Charles to determine the best course of action. Vlotho seemed to put the Palatine mission to bed, hence Karl Ludwig's desperate mission to co-opt the help of Bernhard of Saxe-Weimar as a proxy of the Palatine cause, but now that mission had gone up in smoke as well, Charles faced a situation where two of his kin were in foreign prisons. His subjects urged him to act, but thanks to two major factors – Charles' diplomatic approach to the Thirty Years War, and the difficult opposition he faced within his Kingdoms – Charles was essentially powerless. [28]

When Charles had come to the throne in 1625, he had seemed a more energetic and bolder monarch than his cautious father. Charles involved England in the Hague Alliance of 1625, which also counted the Dutch and Danes as partners. Notwithstanding the catastrophic failure of that arrangement, which effectively doomed the Danish war effort, Charles did not remain aloof from foreign politics, and he stayed interested in and informed of the latest developments in the Thirty Years War. Thanks largely to the regular petitions of Frederick, his brother in law, Charles was kept updated regarding the growing Habsburg supremacy, and of the thumping triumphs of Gustavus Adolphus. The years since Gustavus' death saw Charles attempt a policy which his father would certainly have recognised – marital alliances with a Protestant and a Catholic power.

With the sea lanes closed thanks to Dutch hostility, the Spanish came to rely more on neutral powers for the security of their shipping, and the English suited this role perfectly. Initially at least, King Philip was willing to pay handsomely for the privilege of using British waters to transport his goods, and this closeness moved Charles to imagine succeeding where he and his father had failed – a Spanish Match. The early 1620s, indeed, had been dominated by the notion that an English prince and a Spanish princess would unite in a marital alliance; a decade later this was flipped around, and Charles' daughter Mary was put forward to marry the Spanish prince. As we have learned though, Spain did not possess much of a surplus for long and, shorn of her other securities, Madrid was forced to cut back on foreign expenditure. The Spanish incomes thus dried up, along with Charles' interest in a Spanish marriage. These developments all took place from the mid-1630s to roughly 1641, when Princess Mary was pledged to Frederick Henry's son William.[29]

In 1639, Charles was at the height of his balancing act. Before the scales fell and he realised that no more money would be had from Spain, the

King enthusiastically pushed for a marital alliance. Charles had a motive for granting the Spanish safe harbour as they sought to shelter from harsh storms which rocked the Channel during the autumn, and he also had a motive for wishing to keep the Spanish and Dutch apart. This was because he planned to marry his younger daughter Elizabeth to the House of Orange, thereby reinforcing England with a two-pronged marital arrangement, and potentially serving as mediator to their ongoing war. Charles was also obsessed with his personal honour, to the extent that he resurrected the concept of 'sovereignty of the seas' in 1634 and used the aforementioned ship-money levy to create a navy to defend this supposed right of British Kings.

A monarch that publicised their intention to rule the seas around their realm, that devises a levy so that a navy can be created to defend them, and who even names one such vessel *Sovereign of the Seas*, would surely be expected to act when two foreign navies engage in battle in these very seas, in full view of spectators on the English coast. Yet Charles refrained from acting because he did not want to risk this fleet in battle, and because his diplomatic negotiations, far from an effective balancing act, had represented the worst of both worlds which only tied him up in knots. The arrival of the two fleets off of Dover was the perfect manifestation of the King's diplomatic and strategic dilemma – he was forced to choose to save one fleet or the other, to choose one ally or the other – but in the end, he did nothing.[30]

We should not imagine that the solution was necessarily straightforward though. Some officials like the Earl of Dorset, the Lord Chamberlain of Charles' wife Henrietta Maria, attempted to dress up the fiasco, arguing throughout that it was only sensible for the King to remain aloof from the convergence of the Dutch and Spanish fleets, regardless of the optics of the incident. The best way for Charles to defend his claim on sovereignty of the seas was to shrink from all challengers who might defeat it. Dorset openly admitted that England was not in the same league as France, Spain or the Netherlands, and when he was informed that the Dutch, Spanish and English fleets had converged off of Dover, he wrote that "if either of the first two have a mind to disprove the King's dominance over these seas, they might as easily overthrow it as dispute it.' Driving home the point further, Dorset wrote:

> I hope the King will at most be but a spectator and stickler between, for I hope God hath not so deprived those that are entrusted as to advise that the King should either confound the Spaniards or assist the Hollander to be greater at sea or the King of France at land. I pray God I may never live to see either of the two last the one to have more potency at sea or the other at land especially in the Low Countries. They want not minds to possess this fayre island. God keep them from means proportionable.[31]

Dorset was realistic about Charles' prospects, and believed England would be best served by allying herself with none of the continent's major powers, including France, whom Charles had actually concluded an alliance with in February 1637.[32] In September 1639, just as the Spanish were arriving, Dorset recorded his perceptive thoughts on the power of France, writing that:

> ...they are grown to that conscience and religion as they believe all to be lawful that by power they can do. They are butt our over-thwart neighbours and can bid us in some parts...God deliver kingdom from ever being under their worse than Turkish tyranny.[33]

Of course, it was one thing to admit these things in private, and quite another for the King to base his foreign policy upon what amounted to an admittance of his own weakness. More infamous than King Charles' diplomatic failings were his failings in domestic politics. The 1639 Battle of the Downs in the context of the Civil Wars, which were to erupt across the British Isles in autumn 1642, may seem irrelevant. Yet, the King's inaction in that incident was another clear manifestation of his powerlessness. He could not risk his navy since he did not wish to seek the funds to pay for another; he could not risk war with either power since he did not wish to ask Parliament for funds to pay for an army.[34] These considerations seriously hampered the King's freedom of manoeuvre, and meant that he could do little more than issue weak protests against the conduct of his neighbours. Being on the losing side, the Spanish were particularly unimpressed with Charles' timidity, as Madrid's ambassador in London noted that the Downs affair had occurred 'in his own port, underneath his own artillery, before the eyes of his own fleet and in spite of his announced intentions...' [35]

By autumn 1639 though, Charles was facing a more immediate problem than the disgruntled opinions of foreign dignitaries. Scotland was close to erupting into full-scale war, a situation aggravated by the King's determination to achieve some form of religious uniformity with the issuing of the Book of Common Prayer in summer 1637.[36] In the preface of the book, the King himself wrote that:

> It were to be wished that the whole church of Christ were one, as well in form of public service as in doctrine...This would prevent many schisms and divisions, and serve much to the preserving of unity. But since that cannot be hoped for in the whole Catholic Christian church, yet at least in the churches that are under the protection of one sovereign prince the same ought to be endeavoured.[37]

This wish would not be borne out though, as the Scots reacted quickly and violently, rioting in Edinburgh throughout the July 1637, creating the National Covenant shortly thereafter, and inviting all Scots to pledge themselves to the document as 'Covenanters'. A Scottish army was created, but it never came to blows with Charles, as a peace was arranged in June

1639. The King may have imagined that the affair would soon resolve itself, but in the meantime, Scotland pulled further away from his authority. Less than a year after the Downs affair, in August 1640, a Scottish army would invade England and in a brief campaign, seize Newcastle. Charles was left utterly humiliated by the shattering loss, and worse for his regime, he was forced to summon the Long Parliament to pay for the financial concessions the Covenanters demanded as the price for peace.[38] The religious concessions were implemented after, and it seemed as though Scotland had gotten away with defying their King.[39]

What followed this disaster is now well known. In the following autumn in 1641, the Irish broke away to form their Confederation of Kilkenny;[40] the autumn after that in 1642, England itself fractured and descended into civil war.[41] Far from being in a position to aid the Palatine cause or choose an ideal candidate for marriage, Charles was in danger of losing his very throne to a revolution of unprecedented scale for the British Isles.[42] While the religious elements underpinning the Thirty Years War appear to have been mostly replaced by the mid-1630s with political and strategic considerations, religious fanaticism was to remain an integral part of the struggle: from the eruption of Scotland's Bishops' Wars in the late 1630s, to the creation of a Commonwealth under Oliver Cromwell's theocratic puritanical dictatorship well into the 1650s.[43]

Charles thus continued his father's regrettable tradition of an ineffectual foreign policy, at a time when the very continent was changing. He had been unable to help his nephew, the Elector Palatine, and following the catastrophe at the Battle of Vlotho it seemed possible that the Palatinate might never be independent again. Yet, Charles' relative lack of a coherent policy towards the Thirty Years War should not lead the reader to imagine that none of his subjects attempted to make their own mark on the conflict. No less a man than Alexander Leslie, a Scot famous for distinguishing himself in Swedish service, wrote to Charles' counsellor in 1636 on the subject of the Palatine cause, exclaiming:

> My lord, if it be that the restitution of the [Elector] Palatine can come no other way but by way of arms, the nearest and most convenient way for His Majesty's project towards the advancement of that interest is be Westphalia, where I should think myself happy to attend His Majesty's commandments, and to do His Majesty service with these people committed to my charge.

Driving the point home further, Leslie added in a personal note addressed to the King himself, and describing his wish to undertake 'the performing of some acceptable service to your Majesty', and that if Charles would only ask, then 'I should accompt my chiefest earthly happiness.'[44] But Leslie would not be given the chance to serve Charles in restoring the Palatine family; instead,

Leslie was to play an altogether different role in the events that followed. After having trained under some of the most innovative commanders and tacticians of the Thirty Years War, including Gustavus Adolphus, Leslie and many of his compatriots returned to Scotland in the late 1630s to put what they had learned into practice, and play a leading role in the creation of a Scottish army which would defend itself against the King.[45]

Initially though, it was by no means certain that Scotland's continental veterans would align themselves against the King. After Charles made his temporary peace with the Scots in late 1640, discussion over how to solve the Palatine problem remained prevalent in the Scottish discourse, and Leslie was among those Scottish nobles chosen to direct Covenanter policy in this direction. Grand plans were envisioned over 1641-42, including the dispatch of an army ten thousand strong from Scotland to cooperate with Sweden in freeing the Palatinate from the Emperor's grasp. Unfortunately for the dispossessed Elector Palatine though, it was noted that Karl Ludwig 'lacks money, not to speak of strength, good counsel and ability', and enthusiasm for a Palatine expedition began to wane. At the same time, the attention of the Scots turned towards the eruption of civil war in England itself, and by late 1643, the Scottish Parliament pledged itself in alliance to its English counterpart. Leslie and his compatriots had chosen to go against the King; the once loyal subject who once viewed service to Charles as his 'chiefest earthly happiness' was now the King's enemy.[46]

At the very least, King Charles still had his fleet, which was more than Count Olivares could lay claim to by late 1639. The year had been a shattering experience, which the Battle of the Downs had only capped off in defeat. Closer to home, King Philip – like his British counterpart – continued to face disobedience in his subjects, which led quickly to disaster in summer 1639, as a French invasion over the Pyrenees took place. The invasion was a success, and Salces, a fortified castle in northern Catalonia, was seized by the French advance in July 1639. 'This is a bad time for those of us who serve the king, and will always be so as long as the ruling ministers are so unfavourable to our nation', proclaimed one Catalan regent in Barcelona, two months before.[47] Olivares would have disputed this claim furiously, using the loss of Salces as irrefutable evidence of the Catalan treachery; the French invasion had not been a surprise, after all, and Madrid had prepared an army to defend Catalonia from the enemy in the spring of 1639.

'Better that the Catalans should complain, than that we should all weep', Olivares had said ominously in June, after sending the recruits from Castile to defend the troublesome province. This new army was tasked with frustrating any French incursions, and the soldiers would be wholly reliant upon Catalan provisions and money as they prepared themselves. However, as it was quartered in the region, the Castilians found Catalans so unwilling to part with those provisions or money to help the troops, that desertion and disease began to plague the entire force. At the right moment, the French arrived, and seized Salces on the frontier of Catalonia, thereby securing an outpost where further attacks could be launched. Olivares was apoplectic when he learned of the disaster:

> By now I am at my wits' end, but I say, and I shall still be saying on my death bed, that if the Constitutions do not allow this, then the Devil take the Constitutions…[we must] settle matters in Catalonia in such a manner that no obstructions are placed in the way of Your Majesty's service…we always have to discover what the customary usage is, even when it is a question of the supreme law [of necessity], of the actual preservation and defence of the province.[48]

Yet the problems only grew worse. Olivares may have viewed the assembly of a powerful armada as the silver bullet to Spain's multi-faceted problems but kitting out such a large fleet was supremely expensive, and not even guaranteed to solve them all. Nonetheless, the fleet set out on 15 September 1639, to be met with utter disaster a month later. Olivares could and did cry foul, blaming King Charles, even though the King had been painfully strict in his observation of neutrality. Admiral Pennington was temporarily imprisoned to satisfy Olivares' demands, but this weak fop to Spain did little to solve the Count-Duke's problems or endear Charles to his subjects.[49]

With this disaster weighing down on his mind, Olivares approached the Catalonian question with even less patience than before in early 1640, ordering the new viceroy to dispense with the Catalonian privileges, ignore the constitutions, and imprison anyone who got in his way. Two counsellors from Barcelona were dutifully locked up, and when Catalonia did not erupt into revolt, Olivares felt confident to poke the bear once more. In March 1640, Olivares ordered that an army of six thousand be levied at the expense of the Catalans, and that Castile would henceforth be unwilling to even share the burden of this army's maintenance. With such a stiff, unbending policy, Olivares believed he was demonstrating the unbending will of Madrid, but in effect, the provocation sent the province over the edge. After a poor harvest and painful drought, Catalans had even less to spare than before, but Olivares refused either to investigate or to listen, even when one Castilian observer reported back the following:

> This province is very different from the others. It contains a villainous populace, which can easily be excited to violence, and the more it is pressed, the harder it resists. For this reason, actions which would be sufficient to make the inhabitants of any other province submit to orders of any kind from above, only succeed in exasperating the inhabitants of this province, and in making them insist more stubbornly on the proper observance of their laws.[50]

The following month, reports were received in Madrid that Catalans had attacked royal regiments, and when these soldiers reciprocated by razing a recalcitrant farmer's village, the situation exploded. By late May 1640, most of Catalonia was in revolt against Madrid, and in June, the rebels stormed Barcelona, killing the viceroy and announcing plans to 'liberate' the rest of the province from Spanish rule. It was "make or break" time for Olivares – it was not too late to save the situation, if he decided now to respectfully deal with the Catalans as loyal subjects. Instead, Olivares ramped up the tensions, announcing his intentions to send in an army to supress the revolt; when this was done, Olivares declared, then the constitutions of the province would be abolished for good measure. This was as disastrous a policy decision as could possibly have been made, and it forced moderates into the camp of the rebels. Even more catastrophically for Olivares, it forced the rebels into the willing, gleeful arms of the French.[51] The Spanish position had plainly collapsed. October 1639 began with Spanish ships sinking beneath the waves; by the following year it seemed likely that Spain itself would sink beneath the tides of history.

THREE

Germany is Aching

It was something of a tradition for the Thirty Years War, that victorious generalissimos should possess great ambition and equally great demands. Wallenstein had absorbed the duchies of Friedland and Mecklenburg; Ernst of Mansfeld had demanded Hagenau in Alsace; several Swedish generals continued to demand German estates, and now Bernhard of Saxe-Weimar seemed eager to add his name to this ledger. The curious fate of Alsace-Lorraine, and its centrality to the Franco-German rivalry in the nineteenth and twentieth centuries, sharpen the debate on Bernhard and his intentions. He was a German soldier in French service, and in early 1639 he wished to keep Alsace for himself; if he died, then the region would first go to his brothers, in the second place to France, and only if a general peace was arranged would it return to the Empire.[52]

While he lived, Bernhard intended to keep Alsace as a fief of his family, and to establish this family on a par with the other allies in the Franco-Swedish camp. It was no small ask – Bernhard demanded control over Breisach, and several other fortified forest towns along the Rhine. This would establish him as a formidable prince, worthy of such a title, but Richelieu was understandably apprehensive about creating a Wallenstein on his doorstep, especially in Alsace, where French pretensions to rule had been harboured for many years.[53] And Breisach itself was an invaluable place, crucial to the furtherance of the French war effort, as A. Lloyd Moote appreciated when he noted:

> The Breisach bridgehead was a splendid acquisition: it covered recent French conquests in Alsace, cut the Spanish supply lines between Italy and the north, and acted as a gate for future French troop deployment with the Swedes against the emperor.[54]

Richelieu did not wish to lose control over the area, so in June 1639 he sent a French general to reinforce Bernhard with several thousand men, and orders to reach an agreement with the generalissimo. Such an agreement would never be made though, as Richelieu's luck turned. The troublesome Bernhard of Saxe-Weimar died of the plague in mid-July. The timing was so perfect for Richelieu that several rumours were put about that he had poisoned Bernhard; these rumours were never validated with proof, but Richelieu certainly did not waste time.

He immediately worked to harness the full control of France over Bernhard's army. Bernhard's lieutenants were told in no uncertain terms that they would never be granted the opportunities to lay claim to lordship, nor did they wish to tempt fate in such a way. Bernhard's relatives also recognised the folly in accepting the inheritance which their brother had left them, and thus, through such a miraculous development, France came into Alsace and the ideal strategic position which Bernhard had made. A Latin pamphlet at the time proclaimed that: 'Untimely and premature death, for such was the decision of God, commanded the hastening foot to stay in the midst of its victorious race, and marked out the limit to his further ambition.'[55]

That a figure as dramatic and controversial as Bernhard of Saxe-Weimar could be felled by something as apparently mundane as a bout of plague underlines an important fact about the state of Germany by the late 1630s. The countryside was devastated after two decades of war, and with the destruction the harvest failed, starvation followed, and disease became empowered like never before. The passage of armies and marauding bands into the same towns or patches of land over and over again had bled the countryside dry in many regions. Law and order broke down, and the word of the soldier became law. What harvests there was to collect was stolen by bands of men, the crops eaten in its rawest form or trampled underfoot in the fields. It was impossible for good forage to be found for the horses, as people in the most deprived areas dug up grass seeds and ate them. Fugitives who had been left on the gallows were said to have been cut down and their bodies eaten by desperate citizens.

In one town a pastor recorded seeing a crazed woman gnawing on the raw flesh of a horse, joined by an equally crazed dog and several birds. Cats, dogs and rats were supposedly sold at the market in Worms, so desperate had the food shortages become. People ate whatever they could find, including acorns, saddles and even one another. Stories of abject terror concerning roaming bands of cannibals did the rounds in several refugee camps along the River Main, where it was said that criminals had developed a method for exhuming the newly buried dead and selling their corpses as food. Some of the more depraved tales were likely fabricated, but there can be no denying that desperation and despair drove many to horrendous extremes.[56]

Compounding the misery was the reaction of the peasantry, who engaged in desperate revolts against their authorities. Along the Rhine, where the situation was most desperate, peasants armed themselves and withdrew into the hills. The rotting corpses and filthy conditions combined with the march of so many soldiers back and forth across the land provided ideal conditions for the germination and spread of disease. According to one account, sickly Spanish soldiers brought a plague to Munich which carried off ten thousand of its citizens. Plague was the nightmarish bedfellow to starvation, which was itself in plentiful supply. With as much as 95% of the population dependent upon the seasonal arrival of new agricultural produce each year, a collapse in this system could be catastrophic. Shortages in food would follow, and price increases in staples like bread would follow that.[57]

In addition to these woes brought about by war, Geoffrey Parker had indicated that Europe was itself suffering from a sudden cooling of its climate in the early seventeenth century, which only served to underline the sense of general crisis that the people suffered through.[58] A bout of plague ravaged Western Europe on average every fifteen years between 1536 and 1670, but one particularly bad dose arrived between 1628-32,[59] and wreaked havoc on the sieges then underway, most notably at Mantua, where the disease proliferated among besiegers and besieged alike, until the latter became so weak that the settlement virtually collapsed at the feet of the former.[60] There was little that even the physicians of the time could do to contain such epidemics; doctors were notoriously ineffective, and a remarkably small proportion of them existed, with services accessible mostly to the wealthiest citizens only.

At the heart of these humanitarian disasters was the scourge of war. War spread plague like no other agent, it destroyed years of prosperity and jeopardised the fragile economies, disrupting trade and ruining the less essential professions like artisans or luxury craftsmen. When soldiers passed through an area, they ate all the food, burned the rest, and demanded monies as contributions. These sums were supposed to serve as a guarantee against excesses by the soldiery, but it frequently was not enough to stop all atrocities. People were haunted by the arrival of these armies on the horizon, and any citizens who did their best to hide or mask their true wealth were liable to severe penalties.[61] The horrors of war were not distributed evenly across Europe during the Thirty Years War, but generally the regions along the Rhine into Bavaria, in Saxony, across Northern Germany and Central Europe in the modern-day Czech Republic, suffered the most.

When Johan Baner's Swedes broke into Bohemia in 1638, it was considered a boon to their fortunes that the surrounding lands had not been spoiled by war for four years.[62] In August 1639, Swedish troops under a new commander, the Brandenburger Konigsmarck, marched into Franconia and raided the suburbs of the towns of Bamberg and Wurzburg; such towns had not seen the enemy on the horizon since 1634, and to see the enemy again would surely have been the equivalent of a gut-punch to the psyche of Germans in the area, who had perhaps dared to hope that the worst of the war's furies had passed them by. These disasters would have compelled Ferdinand to become more active in his peace-making initiatives, but there was still only so much he could do in this regard.[63]

The Emperor's allies were not blind to the crisis which was unfolding before them; after the Peace of Prague Maximillian of Bavaria, arguably the man who had profited most from the war, was urging for the war to be brought to a negotiated end. He did not wish to tempt fate any longer and risk his gains. In 1637 Maximillian engaged in a comprehensive reflection on the situation in Germany, and wrote that:

> ...the costly maintenance of such a strong army running into the twelfth consecutive year had so stressed and exhausted His Imperial Majesty and the electors, princes and estates of the Catholic League that many true-hearted people now felt it better and safer to consider more appropriate means for peace, respite, recovery, stabilisation of conquests...rather than continue the war, for which the means were already noticeably lacking and which would expose what had been recovered, as well as existing Catholic possessions, to the uncertainties of military events...Matters have reached a crisis. The Catholic electors, princes and estates, together with their lands and peoples, have been largely exhausted and have lost the means to continue the war. The Imperialists and Austrians have shoved the burden from their lands onto others. Even the Pope has excused himself from helping the Catholics in the Empire who are fiercely attacked and oppressed by foreign Catholic and non-Catholic potentates and have been reduced to such a condition that they and the Catholic faith are threatened with complete destruction. It is thus appropriate and timely to consider who is to blame for this, so as to promote a peace as good as the current situation permits, and whether it is better and appropriate before God and posterity to take this last means to preserve what remains...or to continue the war that...threatens the total ruin of the aforementioned archbishoprics, bishoprics and Catholic lands, along with the Catholic religion and so many millions of souls.[64]

'Men hunt men as beasts of prey, in the woods and on the way', wrote Sir Thomas Roe, an English ambassador at the time. In Hesse-Darmstadt, nominally an ally of the Emperor, the region was subject to the full force of billeting after the triumph of Nordlingen. So great was the want of resources that ministers in Hesse-Darmstadt recorded losses of thirty thousand horses, one hundred thousand cows and six hundred thousand sheep, while ten million thalers in hard currency was also extracted. And the Swedes were no better, as Mainz had 60% of its wealth and 40% of its population sucked dry, while a quarter of the buildings in the city were levelled for good measure. In Württemberg, occupied by Imperial and Bavarian forces after 1634, 75% of the population was lost.[65] 'The Westphalian estates and poor subjects have unfortunately been almost entirely exhausted and ruined by the heavy billeting and damaging passage of troops for some time', noted one Imperial observer in March 1636.[66] One of these Westphalian estates, in a region called Balve, felt compelled to write to its overlord, the Elector of Cologne, urging their master to protect them, or else the population in the region would be forced to emigrate '...because we have been completely exhausted and ruined by paying the contributions (not to mention the devastating passage of friends and foes and the heavy burden of war).'

The petition continued with the note that 'more than half the farms in this district of Balve are now wasteland and so it has become impossible to continue paying obediently without us all soon being forced to emigrate as beggars.'[67] A major cause of the devastation was not just the presence of armies, but the size of these armies, and their existence all year round, which went against both tradition and, according to the opinions of one pamphlet produced in 1631, common sense. 'So let's just compare the present war with those of the past that were conducted during the reigns of Emperors Maximillian II and Rudolf II', the pamphlet began, 'and you can easily see the considerable difference between the warriors of the past and the soldiers of today.' The pamphlet continued:

> To be brief, you must accept that current military ways are but a shadow of those of the past...Wasn't there a fine universal order in the [Holy] Roman Empire? If there had to be a war between it and its hereditary and open enemies, it had to be done with the advice and agreement of the Electors and Estates. Then each Kreis was assigned and paid its share of the burden, like a general tax, to support the war effort. No one knew anything about extraordinary contributions, extractions and similar extortions. Honourable, brave colonels were appointed, who enjoyed a good name and high standing amongst the cavalry and foot soldiers, and these quickly collected brave men together at the must sites and led them against the enemy. It was rare that a regiment was kept together for more than a year, unless it guarded the frontier; we were discharged before the winter, so that the poor country folk weren't burdened with winter quarters. Today, you hear nothing but billeting, mustering, contributions and other exorbitant matters. The colonels are either foreigners or skivers, swindlers, stone masons, smiths and the like, who, once they have collected enough money and property, pack their bags and leave the others to look out for themselves, especially when the campaign starts.[68]

Some regions suffered far worse than others from this cycle of 'billeting, mustering, contributions and other exorbitant matters.' Brandenburg was one such case; by 1638 the population in Berlin, the capital, had contracted from 12,500 to just 7,500. In the Saxon capital of Dresden meanwhile, the ratio of burials to baptisms changed from 100:121 before 1630 to 100:39 thereafter, with immigration being the only way Dresden could maintain its population.

Thanks to Johan Andrea, a supervisor of Lutheran churches in Swabia, we are provided with a particularly gloomy and human account of the effects of the war; the war, Andrea reminds us, did not produce merely death and destruction, but also terrible loneliness. Andrea noted that of his 1,046 communicants alive in 1630, only 338 remained by 1639: 'Just in the last five years, 518 of them have been killed by various misfortunes', Andrea wrote, detailing the loss of, among others, five intimate friends, twenty relatives and forty-one clerical colleagues. 'I have to weep for them', Andrea wrote, 'because I remain here so impotent and alone. Out of my whole life I am left with scarcely fifteen persons alive with whom I can claim some trace of friendship.'[69]

If the conflict was a horrendous experience for those that lived in Germany, it appeared like the vision of an apocalypse to those foreign observers who had decided – for a variety of reasons – to visit Germany in such desperate times. One such foreign visitor, the Earl of Arundel, determined to engage in a voyage down the Main River in spring 1636. The Main flowed east from the Rhine, in the process bisecting the Holy Roman Empire, and providing the unofficial boundary between north and south Germany; it was across this line that Swedish troops retreated following the disaster at Nordlingen in 1634. Due to the prevalence of conflict in the region, the lands surrounding the Main River were subject to particularly grim trials, and Arundel took it upon himself to record these for his audience back home in England.

> From Cologne to Frankfurt all the towns, villages and castles are battered, pillaged and burnt and every one of our halts we remained on board, every man taking his turn on guard duty. Here we stayed for four days until our carriages were prepared for us to continue our journey...Then, after passing through a wood, we came to a wretched little village called Neukirchen, which we found quite uninhabited yet with one house on fire. Here, since it was now late, we were obliged to stay all night, for the nearest town was four miles away; but we spent that night walking up and down with carbines in our hands, and listening fearfully to the sound of shots in the woods around us...Early next morning, His Excellency went to inspect the church and found it had been plundered and that the pictures and the altar had been desecrated. In the churchyard we saw a dead body, scraped out of the grave, while outside the churchyard we found another dead body. Moreover, we entered many houses but found that all were empty. We hurried from this unhappy place and learnt later that the villagers had fled on account of the plague and had set that particular house on fire in order to prevent travellers from catching the infection.[70]

Arundel's account of this unknown village of Neukirchen was by no means unusual, and Arundel was not above taking advantage of the situation, buying the famous Pirckheimer library for a paltry 350 thalers from its desperate owner 'in consideration of the hard times and the difficulty in obtaining food.' The Pirckheimer library was one of Nuremburg's more fabulous stores, containing the collection of the humanistic renaissance thinker Willibald Pirckheimer (1470-1530), and its contents must have appeared to the stricken Germans as relics from a bygone age.[71] It must have been difficult for many to remember a time when the war was not consuming their daily lives. 'Well over a year has passed during which I, a pastor, have not been able – in a whole year – to have a dish on my table', wrote Pastor Ludolph from Hesse, adding:

> Anyone who has not themselves seen and endured such a state of affairs will not believe what I set down here for remembrance. There continues to be a shortage of cattle, no pigs, not a goose to be found in the village, and even the road is overgrown with grass, corn, oats and barely...Those who were once the most distinguished and richest...are now the poorest. They have carried loads of wood or some corn across the fields for payment or for themselves, barefoot or just in stockings, and without shoes, for they had none, just to earn their bread. I don't want to name them; it is not their disgrace.

By 1652, the demoralised pastor confessed that he 'had to give up maintaining the death registers altogether in such miserable times.'[72] And it is little wonder that pastor Ludolph gave up this mission; population declined at a remarkable rate in the first half of the seventeenth century, aggravated undoubtedly by the privations and extreme nature of a war spanning three decades and crossing into multiple states. Between 1600-1650, the demographic change is startling: Bohemia's population declined from 4 million to 2.5 million; Spain from 7.6 million to 5.2 million; Russia from 11 million to 9.5 million; Italy lost a million citizens in the same period, and Germany's population contracted from 15 million to 11 million.[73] We are led to the narrative provided by Friedrich Schiller in his classic accounts of the Thirty Years War, written in the 1790s. One extract reads:

> ...the misery of Germany had risen to such a height, that all clamorously vociferated for peace; and even the most disadvantageous pacification would have been hailed as a blessing from heaven. The plains, which formerly had been thronged with a happy and industrious population, where nature had lavished her choicest gifts, and plenty and prosperity had reigned, were now a wild and desolate wilderness. The fields, abandoned by the industrious husbandman, lay waste and uncultivated; and no sooner had the young crops given the promise of a smiling harvest, than a single march destroyed the labours of a year, and blasted the last hope of an afflicted peasantry. Burnt castles, wasted fields, villages in ashes, were to be seen extending far and wide on all sides, while the ruined peasantry had no resource left but to swell the horde of incendiaries, and fearfully to retaliate upon their fellows, who had hitherto been spared the miseries which they themselves had suffered. The only safeguard against oppression was to become an oppressor. The towns

groaned under the licentiousness of undisciplined and plundering garrisons, who seized and wasted the property of the citizens, and, under the license of their position, committed the most remorseless devastation and cruelty. If the march of an army converted whole provinces into deserts, if others were impoverished by winter quarters, or exhausted by contributions, these still were but passing evils, and the industry of a year might efface the miseries of a few months. But there was no relief for those who had a garrison within their walls, or in the neighbourhood; ever, the change of fortune could not improve their unfortunate fate, since the victor trod in the steps of the vanquished, and friends were not more merciful than enemies.[74]

Certainly, revisionist accounts of the Thirty Years War, written in the twentieth century, have attempted to challenge the notion that the conflict was wholly ruinous, and Robert Ergang's 1954 work *The Myth of the All-Destructive Fury of the Thirty Years' War* deserves mention among such works.[75] Ergang claimed that much of the information which we have drawn from the destructive history of the conflict comes from imperfect sources prone to exaggeration, with Schiller's works among these, in addition to novels written after the event.[76] One such novel was *Adventures of Simplicissimus*, published in the late 1660s, and focusing on the fate of a citizen of Germany as he endured the horrors of the war. The book was written by the Catholic convert Hans Jacob Christoffel von Grimmelshausen, and its account of the worst excesses of the soldiery were later reproduced word for word, even though the work was not intended to be read as an historical account. One historian has called Grimmelshausen's work 'a simpleton's best-seller', implying that only such a simpleton could be capable of accepting the novel as fact.[77] And, it should be said, some scenes which Grimmelshausen has depicted are particularly incredible, as the protagonist describes a scene where his father was tortured for information:

> …they put him close to a fire and bound him so fast that he could stir neither hand nor foot, and smeared the soles of his feet with wet salt, and made our old goat lick it off, and tickle him that he nearly burst his sides laughing. And this seemed to me such a merry thing, for I had never seen him laugh so much, that I had to laugh too to keep him company, or perhaps to hide my ignorance. In the midst of such glee he had to tell them everything they demanded, and indeed revealed the whereabouts of hidden treasure much richer in gold, pearls and jewellery than might have been expected on a farm.[78]

While a certain amount of scepticism is therefore important when assessing the damage that the war inflicted, historians and enthusiasts alike will be confronted with the dilemma that a complete record or perfectly accurate measurement remains impossible. Certainly, earlier estimates that the war destroyed half or even two thirds of Germany's population has since

917

been replaced with more conservative estimates that place the tally closer to losses of 15-20% in the Holy Roman Empire alone. Yet, this was still the equivalent of a drop from 20 million to 16-17 million by the war's end, a significant demographic change whatever way the figure is presented.[79] Efforts to balance the research of sceptics with the narratives of destruction and despair which accompanied the war has led another historian to conclude that:

> A collective memory of the tragic consequences of the war was created, which validated the experiences of the common people in a way that rarely been done before...The rhetoric of death and destruction was not, therefore, simply a symptom of the war, it became part of the impact the war.[80]

Indeed, a great impact of the Thirty Years War was the scars it left behind on the people of Germany, not just because of the demographic, political and economic transformations which the war brought about, but also because of the narrative these experiences created. The trauma was ingrained in German memory like no other event and would only be surpassed by the modern wars of the twentieth century.[81]

To Emperor Ferdinand III, the full consequences of the war could not be known, but they were certainly felt. By spring 1639, Ferdinand had been informed that the Electors wished to call an Imperial Diet. The Imperial Diet was different from the Regensburg Diets of previous years, in that this gathering would not be tasked with electing an Emperor's successor, but solely with discussing the means by which the war could be brought to an end. Ferdinand was unable to resist these demands, which his father might have rallied against. The aching continent which had hosted so many battles and too many armies was crying out for peace, and the Emperor was no longer strong enough to combat his vassals. The constant draining years of war and ruin had taken their toll, it became increasingly doubtful that a favourable outcome to the war could be had by force of arms alone. Then, once 1640 dawned, this suspicion was confirmed, with the collapse of the Spanish position. The cracks in the Habsburg dynasty were beginning to spread and threatened to fracture everything that had been gained. At the heart of the conflict in the Empire, the German countryside creaked, groaned and prepared itself for yet more disaster.

Chapter 19 Notes

[1]Wilson, *Europe's Tragedy*, p. 589.
[2]*Ibid*, pp. 599-600.
[3]*Ibid*, pp. 596-597.
[4]*Ibid*, pp. 597-598.
[5]Parrott, *Richelieu's Army*, p. 127.
[6]See Croxton, *Westphalia*, pp. 60-65.
[7]The campaign for Breisach is examined best by Wilson, *Europe's Tragedy*, pp. 602-610.
[8]Croxton, *Wallenstein*, p. 66.
[9]See Elliot, *The Revolt of the Catalans*, pp. 311-318.
[10]Quoted in *Ibid*, p. 318.
[11]Quoted in *Ibid*, p. 319.
[12]Quoted in *Ibid*, p. 324.
[13]See *Ibid*, pp. 324-325.
[14]*Ibid*, pp. 325-327.
[15]Parker, *Europe in Crisis*, p. 254.
[16]See Parker, 'Spain, Her Enemies and the Revolt of the Netherlands 1559-1648', p. 92.
[17]Geoffrey Parker, 'Why Did the Dutch Revolt Last Eighty Years?', *Transactions of the Royal Historical Society*, Vol. 26 (1976), pp. 53-72; pp. 64-66.
[18]Geyl, *History of the Dutch-Speaking Peoples*, pp. 413-414.
[19]Edmundson, 'Frederick Henry: Prince of Orange (continued)', pp. 276-277.
[20]Frederick Henry also focused his attention on domestic matters, as the tensions between the Orangist Party and the opposition intensified into the 1640s, see: Jonathan I. Israel, 'Frederick Henry and the Dutch Political Factions, 1625-1642', *The English Historical Review*, Vol. 98, No. 386 (Jan., 1983), pp. 1-27.
[21]Wedgewood, *Thirty Years War*, pp. 414-415.
[22]Pieter Geyl, 'Frederick Henry of Orange and King Charles I', *The English Historical Review*, Vol. 38, No. 151 (July., 1923), pp. 355-383; p. 358.
[23]See C. V. Wedgewood, *The King's Peace: 1637-1641* (London: Fontana, 1970), pp. 273-274.
[24]*Ibid*, p. 272.
[25]See Richard Cust, *Charles I: A Political Life* (New York: Routledge, 2014), p. 191.
[26]George Edmundson, 'Frederick Henry: Prince of Orange (continued)', p. 278.
[27]Wilson, *Europe's Tragedy*, p. 594.
[28]Wedgewood, *The King's Peace*, p. 274.
[29]Simon Groenveld, 'The English Civil Wars As a Cause of the First Anglo-Dutch War, 1640-1652', *The Historical Journal*, Vol. 30, No. 3 (Sep., 1987), pp. 541-566; pp. 542-544.
[30]Cust, *Charles I*, pp. 189-190.
[31]Adapted from David L. Smith, 'The Fourth Earl of Dorset and the Personal Rule of Charles I', *Journal of British Studies*, Vol. 30, No. 3 (July., 1991), pp. 257-287; pp. 274-275.
[32]Parker, *Thirty Years War*, p. 149.
[33]Quoted in Smith, 'Fourth Earl of Dorset', p. 275.
[34]*Ibid*, pp. 276-277.
[35]Quoted in Albert J. Loomie, 'Alonso de Cárdenas and the Long Parliament, 1640-1648', *The English Historical Review*, Vol. 97, No. 383 (Apr., 1982), pp. 289-307; p. 291.
[36]See Charles L. Hamilton, 'The Basis for Scottish Efforts to Create a Reformed Church in England, 1640-41', *Church History*, Vol. 30, No. 2 (Jun., 1961), pp. 171-178.
[37]Quoted in Cust, *Charles I*, p. 242.
[38]See Sarah Waureghen, 'Covenanter Propaganda and Conceptualizations of the Public during the Bishops Wars,1638-1640', *The Historical Journal*, Vol. 52, No. 1 (Mar., 2009), pp. 63-86; pp. 65-66.
[39]Peter King, 'The Episcopate during the Civil Wars, 1642-1649', *The English Historical Review*, Vol. 83, No. 328 (Jul., 1968), pp. 523-537.
[40]See Ethan Howard Shagan, 'Constructing Discord: Ideology, Propaganda, and English Responses to the Irish Rebellion of 1641', *Journal of British Studies*, Vol. 36, No. 1 (Jan., 1997), pp. 4-34.
[41]A good account of the gradual collapse of England is provided by David Cressy, 'Conflict, Consensus, and the Willingness to Wink: The Erosion of Community in Charles I's England', *Huntington Library Quarterly*, Vol. 61, No. 2 (1998), pp. 131-149.
[42]David Cressy, 'Revolutionary England 1640-1642', *Past & Present*, No. 181 (Nov., 2003), pp. 35-71.

[43]Debate continues over the extent to which the Civil Wars were a religious conflict. On the religious debate, see Edward Vallance, 'Preaching to the Converted: Religious Justifications for the English Civil War', *Huntington Library Quarterly*, Vol. 65, No. 3/4 (2002), pp. 395-419; Tim Harris, 'Revisiting the Causes of the English Civil War', *Huntington Library Quarterly*, Vol. 78, No. 4 (Winter 2015), pp. 615-635.

[44]Adapted from Elizabeth and C. Sanford Terry, 'Charles I and Alexander Leslie', *The English Historical Review*, Vol. 16, No. 61 (Jan., 1901), pp. 115-120; p. 119.

[45]Matthew Glozier, "5: Scots in the French and Dutch Armies During the Thirty Years' War," in *Scotland and the Thirty Years' War, 1618-1648*, ed. Steve Murdoch (Boston: Brill, 2001), p. 117

[46]See John R. Young, "3: The Scottish Parliament and European Diplomacy 1641–1647: The Palatine, the Dutch Republic and Sweden," in *Scotland and the Thirty Years' War, 1618-1648*, ed. Steve Murdoch (Boston: Brill, 2001), pp. 81-86.

[47]Quoted in Elliot, *Revolt of the Catalans*, p. 357.

[48]Quoted in Parker, *Europe in Crisis*, p. 258.

[49]Hume, *The Court of Phillip IV*, pp. 324-325.

[50]Parker, *Europe in Crisis*, pp. 258-259.

[51]*Ibid*, pp. 259-260.

[52]James Heywood, 'Narrative of the Transference of the German Weimarian Army to the Crown of France in the Seventeenth Century', pp. 219-220.

[53]David Parrott, *Richelieu's Army*, p. 138.

[54]Moote, *Louis XIII*, p. 242.

[55]Wedgewood, *Thirty Years War*, pp. 409-410.

[56]These scenes are recorded by *Ibid*, pp. 400-401.

[57]Parker, *Europe in Crisis*, p. 22.

[58]See Parker, 'Crisis and Catastrophe: The Global Crisis of the Seventeenth Century Reconsidered', *The American Historical Review*, Vol. 113, No. 4 (Oct., 2008), pp. 1053-1079.

[59]Parker, *Europe in Crisis*, p. 25.

[60]See Thomas F. Arnold, 'Gonzaga Fortifications and the Mantuan Succession Crisis of 1613-1631', *Mediterranean Studies*, Vol. 4 (1994), pp. 113-130; pp. 128-129.

[61]Parker, *Europe in Crisis*, pp. 26-28.

[62]Wilson, *Europe's Tragedy*, p. 614.

[63]*Ibid*, pp. 616-617.

[64]Wilson, *Sourcebook*, pp. 220-222.

[65]Matusiak, *Europe in Flames*, pp. 374-375.

[66]Wilson, *Sourcebook*, p. 240.

[67]*Ibid*, p. 242.

[68]*Ibid*, p. 263.

[69]See Parker, *Thirty Years War*, p. 148.

[70]See Wilson, *Sourcebook*, pp. 268-269.

[71]Matusiak, *Europe in Flames*, p. 374.

[72]Wilson, *Sourcebook*, pp. 270-271.

[73]Parker, *Europe in Crisis*, p. 23.

[74]Schiller, *Works*, p. 399.

[75]Robert Ergang, *The Myth of the All-Destructive Fury of the Thirty Years' War* (Pocono Pines: PA, 1956).

[76]See Kevin Cramer, *The Thirty Years' War and German Memory in the Nineteenth Century* (Lincoln, NE: University of Nebraska Press, 2010), pp. 178-179.

[77]See Gerhard Benecke, *Society and Politics in Germany 1500-1700* (London, 1974), p. 233.

[78]Quoted in Wilson, *Sourcebook*, pp. 274-275.

[79]Parker, *Thirty Years War*, p. 188.

[80]John Theibault, 'The Rhetoric of Death and Destruction in the Thirty Years War', *Journal of Social History*, Vol. 27, No. 2 (Winter, 1993), pp. 271-290; p. 286.

[81]Cramer, *The Thirty Years' War and German Memory in the Nineteenth Century*, pp. 180-181.

(Top left) George of Brunswick-Luneberg
(Top right) Urban VIII (Pietro de Cortona, 1627)

Wallenstein – A scene from the Thirty Year's War (Ernst Croft, 1884)

CHAPTER TWENTY
"The Tide Has Surely Turned"

ONE: Unfriendly Allies

TWO: Year of Disaster

THREE: Against the Habsburgs

ONE
Unfriendly Allies

I say, as I have always said, that there are many arguments to dissuade me from the French alliance. I have had experience of their tricks in former years. They commit hostile acts against us, under a mask of friendship. When we remonstrate with them about taking Breisach, and how they debauched the Army of Bernhard of Weimar, they make long speeches, and trot out excuses, and shrug their shoulders. Our late King often tore his hair at the impertinences he had to put up with from them. But what could he do? Necessity is a great argument, and for a handful of gold one must often sacrifice reputation.[1]

This was how Swedish Chancellor Axel Oxenstierna described the strategic alliance with France in 1640. The very topic of that alliance was a strange, often controversial one, in Oxenstierna's Sweden. Above all, the Chancellor did not want to see Sweden's freedom of action reduced. If an opportunity arose for Sweden to get what it wanted from the Emperor, Oxenstierna did not want France to be in a position to block that opportunity. In short, the Chancellor valued the French alliance, but not so much that he was willing to put Swedish interests on the line to defend it. At least, not yet. In 1638 the Treaty of Hamburg had been signed, but contrary to what is often said about that agreement, it did not commit both sides to make peace as one; instead, it compelled Swedish and French agents to negotiate and *cooperate* together. It was a step up from mere subsidies and military arrangements, but it was not a diplomatic union or a pledge to make peace as one party.

This latter characteristic of the alliance would come once this three-year agreement was up for renewal in 1641. Only then, with peace negotiations already underway in their preliminary stage, would Oxenstierna concede that unifying the French and Swedish war effort in that way was desirable. The situation would likely have been different in 1640 if the French intervention had dramatically changed the strategic situation of the war. But in many respects, with some exceptions such as the capture of Breisach in late 1638, the situation for Sweden had not fundamentally changed. Their main army under Johan Baner remained boxed into Northern Germany, and France was still too pre-occupied with the Spanish commitments to dedicate its powers solely to defeating the Emperor.

Was Oxenstierna looking for the kind of transformative invasions of Germany which the late Gustavus had directed? Such scenes were only eight years old by 1640, yet they seemed a world removed from Sweden's current strategic position, which had forced Baner to manoeuvre around a shrinking theatre as a growing number of Imperial soldiers engaged in the pursuit. Swedish military performance in the late 1630s was hardly glamorous; much like the French, there had been some bright spots, such as Wittstock in 1636 or Chemnitz in 1638, but these victories could not turn the tide. Instead, Baner had served as both a thorn and a distraction; he drew soldiers away from other fronts, such as the Rhine, and enabled the French to take advantage, seen in the capture of Breisach.

With France now established in Alsace, did this mean that, at last, Richelieu would ensure the favour was returned? A significant French distraction, surely, might force the Emperor to divert forces away from Northern Germany and against the French position. Then, perhaps, Baner would be in a position to direct his small army, roughly ten thousand strong, against a vital pressure point. That Baner had been able to spend the winter of 1639-40 in Bohemia suggested that this turn in fortunes was at hand, and yet, by the spring of 1640, the Emperor retained the preponderance of power in the region, and a great French invasion across the Rhine, at least to Oxenstierna's knowledge, had yet to reach the planning stage. Oxenstierna was not the only figure to present a running commentary on the situation by 1640; Richelieu, too, took the time to describe the situation to King Louis XIII in his *Political Testament*, and it is from this great resource which we can take the following interesting titbits regarding French strategy:

> It is an action of singular wisdom to have kept all the forces of the enemies of your State occupied for ten years by the armies of your allies, using your treasury and not your weapons. Then, when your allies could no longer survive on their own, it was an act of both courage and wisdom to enter into open war. This shows that, in managing the security of the kingdom, you have acted like those stewards who, having been careful to save money, know when to spend it to prevent a greater loss.

Richelieu then provided his view on each of the conflicts which France was involved in or had been involved in; the war in Germany was 'virtually unavoidable' since 'this part of Europe had been the theatre where it had opened long before.' Turning his attention to the Spanish Netherlands, Richelieu remarked that although the war there 'did not achieve the success one might have expected', nonetheless, it was still 'impossible not to regard

924

it as advantageous in its aims.' This was certainly a generous interpretation of French progress in that theatre; one might have reasonably expected a Franco-Dutch alliance directed against Brussels to have borne much more fruit after five years of cooperation, but Richelieu was at least correct that the central aims of this theatre were sound – Spain was weakening in its Netherland position, and by applying pressure here, Madrid could not divert resources elsewhere. Richelieu then addressed the war in the Val Teline, where the struggle for those Alpine passes that formed part of the Spanish Road were found. The war there was necessary 'so as to encourage the Italian princes to take up arms by removing their fear of the Germans'.

The war in Italy was also of great importance, as the campaign for getting the Duke of Savoy on side was vital 'because the Milanese, the heart of the States possessed by Spain, was the territory he had to attack.' 'During the course of the war', Richelieu added with some optimism, addressing his King directly, 'nothing went wrong for you without seeming to have happened only for your glory.' Contrary to Oxenstierna's interpretation of events, Richelieu then took the time to explain to his King why France had negotiated and warred in the manner that it did. As far as Richelieu was concerned, the French record in both these respects was flawless, and the reputation of France was spotless because she had honoured her obligations to her allies. Oxenstierna might have disagreed with this interpretation, but it is worth examining what the wily Cardinal said:

> Your Majesty did not enter the war until it was unavoidable and did not leave it until he had to. This observation sheds great glory on Your Majesty, because when at peace France was often urged by its allies to take up arms, though reluctant to do so. And during the war his enemies often proposed a separate peace, but he would never consider it because France could not be separated from the interests of its allies. Those who know that Your Majesty was abandoned by several princes allied to France, and that nonetheless he did not wish to abandon anyone; that moreover some of those who remained loyal let him down in several important matters, yet still received from Your Majesty the treatment they were promised; those people, I say, understand that if the good fortune of Your Majesty is apparent in the success of his endeavours, his virtue is no less great than his good fortune. I know well that if France had broken its word, its reputation would have suffered badly, and the least loss of this kind means that a great prince has nothing further to lose.

Oxenstierna might have taken issue with this interpretation of French policy as inherently honourable, when, as the Chancellor noted, France had 'debauched' the army of Bernhard of Saxe-Weimar, and effectively bribed him into the French camp. That act – of making a French subject out of an army led by the veterans of Gustavus Adolphus – still stung Oxenstierna, but he would certainly have agreed with portions of this final extract, where

Richelieu delicately presented the French military disappointments to date, writing:

> If they consider further the natural frivolity of this nation, the impatience of its soldiers who are little accustomed to hard work, and finally the weakness of the instruments which by necessity you had to use on these occasions – among which I hold the first place – they will have to admit that nothing made up for the failings of your implements except the excellence of Your Majesty, who is the artisan.[2]

From where Oxenstierna was standing, the notion that King Louis XIII's majesty somehow made up for the French military blunders, the underhanded diplomatic tactics or the disappointing returns from having France as an ally, must have rung somewhat hollow. But what Oxenstierna would not deny was that Sweden needed France, and the reverse was also certainly true. The best way to make the most of Swedish military prowess and French finance was to double down in their respective theatres and engage with the enemy; to seize crushing military victories, to flip the Emperor's allies back to their side, and use the strength of French finance to support proxy wars in the various theatres, which would chip away at the Habsburg position.

But neither the Emperor nor the King of Spain were willing to make this mission easy for them. As 1640 dawned, Spain was facing into a domestic crisis in Catalonia which would only get worse, a disenchanted Portuguese populace which were soon to erupt, and an unrewarding Dutch war which was beginning to deteriorate beyond her control. Not even the Cardinal Infante, that hero of Nordlingen now based in Brussels, seemed capable of rescuing the situation. The war with France had been impossible to quickly resolve, as Olivares' best shot misfired in 1636, and Spain was now prevented from directly aiding the Emperor thanks to the severing of those land routes. Not that, as Olivares appreciated, Spain would have had much to spare for Vienna even if the road to the Emperor had been cleared. Perhaps, then, it was time to place Spanish interests ahead of the wider Habsburg dynasty's? Interestingly, this was exactly what the Emperor was mulling over in early 1640.

To begin with, Emperor Ferdinand III had been effectively forced to summon the Imperial Diet, a gathering which had not assembled in twenty-seven years. The last time it had been called, in 1613, confessional hostility had made it grind to a halt. The Evangelical Union and Catholic League had been at loggerheads, and the ailing Emperor Matthias was unable to stem the tide. Ferdinand III had only been a toddler when that scene had taken place, yet he was joined by stalwart allies – Maximillian of Bavaria and John George of Saxony – who had been deeply concerned by those ill-omens, and had lived through the troubling early years of the war.

By January 1640, Ferdinand was able to bring forty-four thousand men to Bohemia, where their main task was to defend against the threatening moves of Johan Baner's smaller force. Due to the necessity of reinforcing garrisons and other measures though, the commander in the region was only able to gather twelve and a half thousand men into a mobile army. In addition to this force, Piccolomini possessed an army of thirteen thousand in Westphalia, near the border of the Dutch Republic, while John George of Saxony maintained an army just over 6,500 strong. Along the Rhine, it was known that Maximillian of Bavaria possessed seventeen thousand men, with an army consisting of ten thousand active effectives defending the Lower part of that river against French incursions. Elsewhere in Northern Germany, Brandenburg's army was effectively wiped out. Not only were the massive hosts of men numbering one hundred thousand strong now a thing of the past, but it was also increasingly difficult for the country to support more than one major operation at a single time. While one theatre became active then, the other was drained of troops, and defence became the order of the day; the dynamism of the war's earlier phases had passed, along with the initial prosperity of the countryside which had been necessary to sustain such campaigns.[3]

The French and Swedes had also been joined by two new German players, who made up for the exit of Brandenburg and Saxony in 1635. George of Brunswick-Luneburg was of the House of Welf (or Guelph), and ruled over lands south of the Danish border. With his capital in Hanover, Duke George's lands were situated in an important strategic position, in the Empire's north-west, and the importance was reflected in the marital contracts of his ancestors, linking the House of Welf with Brandenburg, Denmark and Saxony at various points in its history. Duke George's mother had been a daughter of King Christian III of Denmark (1503-1559), which made him cousin to the current Danish King, Christian IV. By the end of the seventeenth century, Duke George's family would be indelibly associated with the city that he had made his capital, Hanover, and the House of Hanover would provide Britain which its Hanoverian line, thanks to intermarriage with the Palatine offspring of Frederick V and Elizabeth Stuart. In short, Duke George's descendants were destined to play a significant role in history, but in 1640, the aged Duke George was merely one of the upper-mid tier of German rulers who had determined to throw his lot in with the Franco-Swedes, thus frustrating his Emperor's quest for a German peace.

Further to the south of Duke George's domains was the complicated morass of Hesse. Hesse had been divided among four sons in the mid-sixteenth century, but by 1640 half of these lines had died out and been combined with the two main Houses of Hesse. These were Hesse-Darmstadt, which sided with the Emperor, and Hesse-Kassel, which maintained its support first of Sweden and then of France. The lands of Hesse were sprawled across the Main River, and like Brunswick-Luneburg to the north, they occupied a strategically important part of Germany. Unlike Duke George's lands, those of Hesse-Kassel were ruled by the regency of Amalie Elizabeth, who controlled the principality's affairs while her son, Duke William VI, was merely a child. Hesse-Kassel was able to field an army of a few thousand, and Amalie Elizabeth followed Duke George's lead in attaching her soldiers to Johan Baner's army in the spring of 1640.

Eventful though the year was for other theatres, the campaigning season of 1640 in Northern Germany mostly consisted of manoeuvring with little in the way of practical results. The summer was unseasonably cold and wet, and bouts of plague continued to spread, even killing Baner's second wife. Baner was obliged to withdraw from Bohemia and engage in several standoffs with the enemy, but no truly significant engagements took place, and certainly, the balance of power was not fundamentally affected. Emperor Ferdinand had mostly monopolised his influence over south and central Germany, but in the north, as 1640 became 1641, a decisive encounter proved frustratingly elusive. Something which the French and Swedes would have to bear in mind was that even with the lacklustre military returns from 1640, the fusing of Hanover and Hesse-Kassel to the allied cause meant that both would have to be included in a final peace settlement.[4]

While the military situation in Germany did not change in 1640, there was great activity on the diplomatic front. The Emperor would personally participate in one such activity, the Imperial Diet, which was hosted from September 1640 to October 1641. The reasons for hosting such an assembly at Regensburg were legion. Most urgently perhaps, Ferdinand needed money from his vassals to maintain the Imperial armies. Yet, to receive these monies, the Emperor was first required to summon all estates of the Empire, and second, to hear the grievances of these estates. Interestingly, a theme which emerged from the Diet was one of amnesty. For some time, as established in the Peace of Prague five years before, the question of amnesty had animated those Germans who had fought against the Emperor in the war's early phases. Some of those that had made peace with the Emperor in 1635 had been 'reconciled with grievances', insofar as they were now on good terms with Ferdinand, but they had been forced to agree to difficult terms in order to reach that stage.

Yet, other German states, like Brunswick-Luneburg and Hesse-Kassel, had refused to make peace with the Emperor, and actually possessed small but still noteworthy armies of their own. It was these that Maximillian of Bavaria wished to court, by extending the amnesty of the Peace of Prague to them. But other issues abounded; some Catholics did not want to return lands they had been given from rebels, some Protestants believed the earlier concessions did not go far enough, and the issue of the Palatinate remained a sore subject. The Emperor would only turn the clock back as far as 1628, or 1627 at a push, but some demanded that 1618 be the benchmark. Maximillian knew that he would either keep the lands which had been confiscated from other Germans, or he would be compensated for them by the Emperor, thus the burden would fall on Ferdinand whatever the outcome. But like his father, Ferdinand had no way of reimbursing his dissatisfied allies, nor did he know how to make everyone happy with whatever settlement the Diet could produce.

What the Emperor did know, however, was that his coffers needed to be increased if the war was to be pursued. Furthermore, to properly bring the full weight of Germany to bear against the French and Swedes, it was essential that no Germans were left out. But bringing the likes of Hesse-Kassel and Brunswick-Luneburg back into the Imperial fold would mean making promises that seemed quite impossible to fulfil in 1640. Thus, Ferdinand made use of a vague mechanism where the concessions to repenting rebels would be placed under effective suspension until such a date as suited him. Understandably, this rankled Ferdinand's allies, who argued that this defeated the entire purpose of amnesty in the first place – what German rebel would return to the Emperor for the sake of a promise that, at some undefined date in the future, their losses would be made good?

Ferdinand could plead that he had no other choice but to delay restitution – it was difficult enough even to hold an Imperial Diet while a war was underway, and he lacked the resources to make everyone happy – but the criticism proved accurate, as no new converts to the Imperial cause materialised. This fact, combined with the religious grievances and the numerical superiority of Catholic potentates, further hampered the Diet, which dispersed in October 1641 having made no transformative decisions. The Regensburg amnesty, contrary to the Prague amnesty of 1635, would be applicable to all Germans, they needed only to accept it. Yet, the suspension of its terms until all estates had joined the Emperor, and Ferdinand's inability to compromise in the meantime, meant that the war would go on. Indeed, the war had reached the Diet itself in January 1641, when Johan Baner sent several detachments of cavalry to Regensburg where the Emperor was actually present. With the Danube frozen, Baner's forces crossed over and threatened the Emperor's authority more directly than ever before. The emergency passed with the melting of the Danube's ice, but still, it had been a close-run thing.[5]

If Ferdinand could not rely on his German vassals to arrive at a united peace, and if he could not rely on Spain for further financial or military support as Madrid buckled under two sinister revolts, then perhaps the best approach would be to negotiate with the French or Swedes directly, and to work at separating one from the other. The observations of Chancellor Oxenstierna and Cardinal Richelieu certainly did not suggest an unbreakable allied bond. Richelieu and Oxenstierna remained suspicious of one another. The French, as Oxenstierna had opined (see above), seemed willing to let Sweden down and cover their tracks with feeble excuses after the event. The three-year

Treaty of Hamburg would expire in mid-March 1641, and if the Emperor managed to insert his negotiators in between the two allies in the meantime, then he might achieve a diplomatic coup of the first order.

The problem was that Sweden's price for peace was far higher than Ferdinand was willing to pay; it included all of Pomerania, and the Elector of Brandenburg's public acknowledgement of Sweden's right to overlordship of that region. Since Ferdinand was required to defend the interests of Brandenburg according to the terms of the Peace of Prague, the Emperor could not concede Pomerania to Sweden even if he had wanted to. However, as Regensburg was in session, a great wrinkle presented itself. On 1 December 1640, George William of Brandenburg died, to be succeeded by his son Frederick William. The exit of one stalwart participant of the war was a significant event, but more significant still was the man who was now leading Brandenburg in his late father's stead. Frederick William would receive the epithet of 'the Great' in his own lifetime, largely for the exploits he sponsored which propelled Brandenburg to new heights of power.

Power, in early 1641, was perhaps the last thing in Frederick William's grasp, and so he worked towards a simple enough goal on paper – that of removing the most immediate threat to Brandenburg, by making peace with Sweden. This quest, while simple, was in fact brimming with consequences. If Brandenburg exited the war with Sweden, then the Emperor would not feel obliged to fight for her rights in Pomerania. Thus, perhaps, if Ferdinand would consent to handing Pomerania over, Sweden might exit the war, and France would be left alone to face the combined might of the Habsburg dynasty. Unfortunately for Ferdinand, a potential coup was not around the corner; he delayed and procrastinated rather than sacrifice Pomerania, likely because he hoped that Johan Baner, last seen retreating from Regensburg in January, might be defeated and destroyed by Imperial forces.

If Baner could be removed from the equation, then Sweden's position would be greatly undermined, and then the Emperor would only have to part with a small portion of the Pomeranian inheritance. But by waiting, Ferdinand had allowed that precious window of opportunity to close. By April 1641, when the Emperor had decided it was worth ridding himself of Pomerania to also be rid of the Swedes, Oxenstierna's hands were tied. A few weeks before, indeed, the Chancellor had agreed to renew the Treaty of Hamburg, which was done in June.[6] The Emperor had missed his chance to divide his foes; from this point on in the war, neither France nor Sweden could make a separate peace. There would have to be a conference involving both powers, or the war would go on.

TWO
Year of Disaster

In Madrid, in early December 1640, King Philip IV was presiding over a bullfight, which had been hosted to honour the Danish ambassador who was then present. The atmosphere was akin to that of a party, and the war with France, not to mention the troubles with Catalonia, seemed far away. On the outskirts of the palace grounds, a troubled rider arrived, it was said, from Portugal, and made way immediately for the Count-Duke. Why should this courier be in such a hurry to see Olivares? The palace became full of whispers, and witnesses would later claim that the Count-Duke's face became rigid and pale when he was told the news. Few had wanted to believe these rumours as they were put about – Portugal, so it was said, had erupted in revolt, led by John, a privileged Portuguese nobleman from the House of Braganza. Surely it was grave news indeed, if Portugal was in revolt at such a fractious time for the Monarchy, when her resources were already spread so thin? Olivares, of course, could not burden his King with this disaster, and so, visiting him while at play with some of his close friends, the Count-Duke sought to keep up the appearances he had been maintaining for the last few years, and put a positive spin on what had happened.

"I bring great news for your Majesty," he said. "What is it?" asked the King, with little concern. "In one moment, Sire, you have won a great dukedom and vast wealth," replied the minister. "How so, Conde?" inquired Philip. "Sire, the Duke of Braganza has gone mad, and has proclaimed himself King of Portugal; it will be necessary for you to confiscate all his possessions." But this did not please Philip at all, nor had Olivares likely expected it to. 'The King's long face', according to the historian Martin Hume, 'fell longer still, and his brow clouded, for all his minister's jauntiness. He was no fool, and he knew this was tidings of evil moment.' "Let a remedy be found for it", was all King Philip said, returning to his game; and the Count-Duke, as he left the room, must have wondered how he would fix yet another broken spoke on the Spanish wheel.[7]

Contrary to what Olivares claimed, the Duke of Braganza had not gone mad, instead he had risen to the occasion, after years of remaining in the background. John was the eighth Duke of Braganza, and his grandmother had been one of several claimants during Portugal's succession crisis in 1580, which had been settled to the favour of King Philip II of Spain. For the last sixty years then, Madrid had ruled over its smaller Iberian neighbour, sharing in its fortunes and failures at home and abroad. Spanish rule was not necessarily unpopular, but there remained a significant portion of the Portuguese nobility who were opposed to being squeezed to help Spain. One of ways Madrid tended to squeeze Portugal was to order its nobility to lead in the army, and in the summer of 1640 few conflicts were as pressing for Madrid than that in Catalonia.

Ordered to help put the Catalonian revolt down, Portuguese nobles assessed the situation instead, and noted that there had never been a more opportune time to take advantage of Spanish weakness. In seizing the opportunity to revolt, all they needed was a true leader and figurehead who would represent their struggle. In fact, they would need more than this if Portuguese independence was to be guaranteed – they would need a new King who could justifiably establish a new royal dynasty in Lisbon. In their search for candidates, John, duke of Braganza was nominated. At one time a loyal subject of the King of Spain, Duke John was apprehensive, and we are told he was buoyed by his Spanish wife, who encouraged him to seize the throne because she wished to be Queen.

Whatever the true reason for Duke John's seizing of the moment, once he signalled his willingness to be King, the nobles acted quickly, arriving in Lisbon on 1 December 1640, when all of Iberia was ablaze with news of what the Catalans had done. The nobles gathered in Lisbon before travelling by individual carriages to the royal palace, where the Spanish governor resided. These nobles and their retainers overcame the paltry Spanish guards and began proclaiming their revolution. Apparently unable to contain himself, one noble flung open the windows of the palace, and shouted 'Liberty! Liberty! Long live King João IV! The Duke of Braganza is our rightful king! Heaven awards him the crown to revive the realm!' The Spanish representative was taken completely by surprise. She was Margaret of Mantua, the widow of the late Duke of Mantua, but she also boasted other impressive familial ties, with her maternal grandfather being Philip II and her father the Duke of Savoy.

These connections did nothing for Margaret though; she was told by the rebellious nobles that she could either leave through the door or the window. Perhaps envisioning a repeat of a previous defenestration, Margaret did as she was told, leaving the keys to Lisbon behind her. The Portuguese capital was in rebel hands, and within a fortnight, Duke John would be crowned King John IV of Portugal. History knows him as John the Restorer, for his role in reasserting Portuguese independence, and bringing the Portuguese Empire to new heights of power and global reach. Before Portugal could be resurrected though, King John would have to fight against his former master. Indeed, with news of the coup launched by Portuguese patriots having certainly reached Olivares, the Spanish reaction was surely inevitable.[8]

But the Portuguese nobles had chosen their moment well; throughout 1640 the situation in Catalonia had grown graver with every passing day. A successful campaign in January 1640 to roll back the French from the fortress of Salces along the border of Catalonia provided no respite either from the demanding Olivares or for the beleaguered Catalans. In fact, once Salces had been relieved, Olivares wasted no time writing to the Count of Santa Coloma, Spain's viceroy in Barcelona, saying:

> It is undeniable that the Catalans in their present condition are not useful to the Monarchy and are not serving in person or with their possessions. Moreover, there is no province subject to the king, and not even a province outside the Spanish Monarchy, which conducts its affairs in this way, in a manner offensive to everybody and one that sets a very bad example to other vassals... Now, Sir, I want you to tell me the best and cheapest method of getting a good body of Catalan troops – some two or three tercios of two thousand men each. This is a measure that has been adopted in Castile, Italy and Flanders, and is to be introduced into Portugal this year, where we are asking for eight thousand men.[9]

By this early stage, of course, the Portuguese had yet to revolt, and Olivares here was plainly still convinced that the contract which the Monarchy's contingent parts had with Madrid would be maintained. It was above his imagination to suppose that by the end of this year, two significant parties to the Iberian Union would have been peeled off. What Olivares seems to have imagined instead was that Catalonia would fall into line, and that it would do its duty to the Crown by raising a contingent of eight thousand troops. Furthermore, Olivares was equally adamant that soldiers would be quartered in the northern province, not just to quell potential dissent, but also for the sake of security – if the French had invaded once, they would surely do so again. He wrote as much to Count Santa Coloma on 7 February 1640:

> As regards billeting, I must repeat how vital it is to arrange it properly, because it is against all reason that a province or a kingdom should be defended by an army and not be prepared to quarter it. Similarly, it is unreasonable that a king who has no fixed income from a province, should be expected to meet this expense, while the province itself supports neither the king nor the army. And, by your leave, I cannot easily allow myself to be persuaded that a province which has contributed and is contributing nothing, should have less substance than those that are heavily taxed.[10]

Due to the scarcity of veteran soldiers, Olivares wished to take the utmost care of the army which had recently relieved Salces, and he believed it was the duty of the Catalans to aid in this quest. One of Olivares' letters to Count Santa Coloma would even contain the line 'I beg you on my knees, and from the bottom of my heart, to billet that army well', and despite Santa Coloma's misgivings about Catalonian reliability, he professed his willingness to obey with his command. Before long Santa Coloma was receiving urgent letters from governors across Catalonia regarding the bad behaviour of the cavalry and the dangerous stubbornness of the Catalans: 'The entire province has arms in its hands, and many of the soldiers are taking the opportunity to desert because they are in such danger', wrote one such governor, adding that . 'The cavalry is utterly disintegrating.'

This was far indeed from what Olivares had wanted, needed, or expected from the Catalans.[11] Considering the circumstances though, it appears predictable enough; the refusal by the Catalans to give food to the billeted soldiers moved those soldiers to commit great excesses in the name of filling their empty stomachs. This provoked reprisals from the Catalonians, and the relationship only deteriorated further. As one academic sent from Madrid observed at the time: 'As long as food is not assured to the soldiers, it is impossible to keep them under control, because a hungry man must eat off the land if His Majesty does not come to his help.'[12] Santa Coloma did his best to reconcile his conflicting orders; on the one hand he was to pacify the Catalans, on the other, the billeting was to continue. Reprisals escalated, with the Italian contingents proving especially impatient with the Catalans. Priests were murdered, goods stolen, and women defiled. By the end of spring it was clear that the issue had become personal for the Catalan people, but Santa Colona remained determined to follow his orders to the letter, and having no experience of commanding soldiers, he proved utterly out of his depth. He wrote several concerned letters to Olivares warning of the issues, but the Count-Duke remained as resolute as ever, writing in late February 1640 that:

> ...no king in the world has a province like Catalonia...It has a king and lord, but it renders him no services, even when its own safety is at stake. This king and lord can do nothing that he wants in it, nor even things that need to be done. If the enemy invades it, the king has to defend it without any help from the inhabitants, who refuse to expose themselves to danger. He has to bring in an army from outside; he has to maintain it; he has to recover the fortresses that have been lost. And then, when the enemy has not yet been driven out... the province refuses to billet it...Sir, we all admire your wisdom, but we all without exception consider that a viceroy of that province, and especially a native of it, like yourself, should have made an example of these people...Sir, the king our lord is king of Castile, which has billeted troops; he is king of Navarre, which has billeted and is today billeting them. He is king of Aragon, which is doing the same, and Valencia, too. He is king of Portugal, which...

has never objected to billeting. And [among] Milan, Naples, Flanders, the Indies, the Franche-Comté...there is probably no state or province with more liberties and immunities. Not one of these objects to billeting, not only when it is helping in its own defence but even when His Majesty chooses to station troops in it. Should all these kingdoms and provinces follow the example of Catalonia? Really, Sir, the Catalans ought to see more of the world than Catalonia...[13]

This was nothing less than a rant from Olivares, but it proved to be futile. The Catalans wanted neither to compare their privileges to those of their peers in the Spanish Monarchy, nor to 'see more of the world'; what they wanted, in effect was to be left alone. But Olivares could not allow this; in the context of Spain's wars with the French and Dutch, every province had to pull its weight, lest other regions of Spain begin to demand similar concessions. It wasn't as though Olivares desired the war to continue, far from it: 'God wants us to make peace', he wrote in a memorandum for the king in March 1640, 'for He is depriving us visibly and absolutely of all the means of war.'[14]

Indeed, with the exception of some successes in North Italy, the weight of the interconnected conflicts was beginning to tell; grave defeats such as those suffered in the Battle of the Downs the previous October demonstrated that Spain could no longer rely on the professionalism of her military machine to make up for her shortfalls in resources. But the Catalans were by no means determined to revoke their allegiance to King Philip; the officials charged with upholding the Catalan constitutions were caught between a rock and a hard place which was equally as painful. The problem was that as neither side compromised, the options for redress became more radical, Olivares' responses more draconian, Santa Coloma more desperate, and the Catalan officials more extreme.

An unwillingness or inability to negotiate properly meant that communications were delivered and received under the cloud of aggression or atrocity, and when a leading Catalan official was arrested in late March, the situation deteriorated still further. This was followed by a new order to levy Catalan soldiers, and to use the veteran army which had been billeted to coerce the Catalans into the army where necessary. So long as Catalonia remained quiescent, Olivares did not really care about its frustrated privileges – there was far too much at stake to worry about that. Yet, in the first week of May 1640, the atmosphere changed, as a tercio denied billeting clashed with local peasants, and in response, both Olivares and Santa Coloma conceived of an incredibly provocative policy. Some twenty houses owned by the worst rebels in the nearby town, coincidentally called Santa Coloma de Farners, were to be torched, but when the soldiers arrived to find the town deserted, and wine left in some of the houses, there was no way to restrain their wrath. The town was effectively burned to the ground, and news quickly spread to neighbouring regions, whose towns barred their gates to all but Catalonian citizens.

By the middle of May the situation had become so grave that the commander requested permission to withdraw his tercios from Catalonia altogether. His troops burned and looted as they moved, and the misery was exacerbated for the Catalan people thanks to the poor harvest and drought which had plagued the country for many months. In south Catalonia one Spanish official recorded how extensively the situation had now changed, writing to the viceroy on the 20 May that 'We had got these places all settled and content with the billeting, and now they are so transformed that I am in despair, with most of them pretty well determined not to feed the troops, and threatening to kill them.'[15] Indeed, the protests were over, and the revolution for Catalonian independence had begun.

It was around this time, in the midsummer of 1640, that Olivares began pulling in recruits and commanders from across the Iberian Peninsula, and among those to receive the call was John, Duke of Braganza, before his bid for the Portuguese throne later in the year could have been known. As a potential rival to the Portuguese throne, Olivares had been wary of pushing Duke John too far, but in general, this maternal grandson of King Philip II did his duty. For the moment at least, he fell in line with the other Portuguese nobles who had been called to serve. This was part of Olivares' two-pronged strategy of neutralising the Portuguese threat before it erupted; throughout the late 1630s, when French intrigue was thrown into the mix, Olivares needed to be wary of that former rival to Spanish fortunes – a Portuguese war of independence, sponsored by Richelieu's seemingly bottomless pockets, could spell disaster for Madrid.

So, Olivares approached the Portuguese tactfully; among other policies, he replaced Portuguese captains with Spanish ones, he drained the peninsula of Portuguese levies, sending them to Italy or Germany and getting them away from their homeland, and most importantly for the likes of Duke John, Olivares issued a recall of all prominent Portuguese nobles in 1638, and while he stayed in Madrid, Duke John was promoted to Governor of the Arms of Portugal the following year. Olivares hoped that by tying Duke John closer to his overlord, his potential as a revolutionary leader would be tainted, and any aspiring Portuguese nationalists would search elsewhere. Indeed, these tactics certainly imbued a sense of hesitation within Duke John, but at the point when it mattered, he did determine to throw his lot in with the rebels.

Upon learning of the full extent of the crisis in Catalonia, Olivares communicated his intention to make the Portuguese fight the Catalans. This way, the Count-Duke imagined, Spain could kill two ungrateful birds with one stone, and Castile would be spared any further burdens. But the transferral of these very burdens onto the Portuguese populace was what pushed the plotters over the edge, and by late November they had committed themselves to the cause. By this point, Barcelona had been captured by the Catalonian rebels, and the Spanish viceroy, the Count Santa Coloma, had been executed on 7 June as the city fell. With the Catalonian province in revolt, the border with France was now dangerously porous, and the Portuguese swords which were meant for those rebels had been suddenly, shockingly, turned against Madrid. It was the ultimate nightmare, and there was nothing for it but to raise additional levies in the aching Castilian heartland. As 1640 turned to 1641 though, to Olivares' apoplectic dismay, matters only got worse.[16]

Much of this was Olivares' own fault. After so many years following a given policy line – that of confrontation, aggression and intolerance in the face of challenges to Spanish authority – Olivares found that this approach only inflamed the passions of Spain's new enemies, it did not smother the revolts in their cradles as he had hoped. Worse still, those rebels in Lisbon and Barcelona were actively engaging with one another. They concluded an alliance early in 1641, and both Catalonia and Portugal sent out feelers throughout Europe in their search for allies. These efforts bore a great deal of fruit, but it was poison apples for the Count-Duke, whose efforts at intimidating the Catalans by threatening to utterly revoke all their privileges in September 1640 had forced the Barcelona council to use its contacts with the French.[17]

Initially, friendship or alliance with France was not necessarily a forgone conclusion, largely because both Paris and Barcelona laid claim to Roussillon, a province which stretches across the Pyrenees, and boasted historic links with Catalans and Frenchmen alike. In late 1640, French military planners were also busy with a siege of Turin and were using the manpower pool around Languedoc in Southern France to raise an army for that campaign. Whatever soldiers they did send reported to Richelieu that the Catalan rebels were disorganised, more interested in plundering their own lands than combatting the enemy, and too ill-disciplined to constitute a proper professional army.

As the historian David Parrott wrote 'The obvious question in the French Court in the last months of 1640 was whether further military resources devoted to the Catalan rebels would be support for a lost cause.'[18] There were, in other words, several ways for Olivares to weasel his way out of having to face down a French-Catalan alliance in such a sensitive region. The Portuguese revolt erupted at just the right time then, because it helped to reaffirm French commitments in the region. Furthermore, it hinted that Catalonia and Portugal would not merely distract the Spanish and reduce the manpower commitment for France, but that it would also provide new avenues to undermine Spain. These avenues would be heartily pursued in spring 1641.[19]

The first such avenue was military and resulted in the destruction of Olivares' bitter hopes in January 1641. Early in that month, Catalonia was officially placed under the protection of the King of France, and this political coup was twinned with military success, as the army of raw recruits which Olivares had sent to deal with the Catalan rebels was routed in the Battle of Monjuich on 27 January. The Count-Duke's most desperate, urgent bullet had been fired, and it had missed. Now it was only a matter of time before Spain's Dutch and French enemies flooded into these new theatres to capitalise. Olivares was right to fear. The French had shown their hand in Catalonia, and within a few months, Richelieu was confident enough in the fortunes of King John to send a force of ships. These thirty-two vessels joined with the Portuguese, and in August 1641 mounted an attack on Cadiz. Fortunately for Olivares, disaster did not follow, and the defenders repelled the four thousand soldiers that the French attempted to land. That Spain's enemies could strike so close to home was an ill-omen, and a reflection of the dearth of Spanish power; that the allied attack failed suggested that, for the moment at least, the military fortitude of Castile had not been broken, but how much longer could it last?[20]

The story of the Dutch involvement was less straightforward, but equally ominous for Olivares. Here were more enemies pooling their resources to attack the King's domains, and successful or not, these thousands of cuts would eventually result in death. On 10 September 1641, a Dutch fleet of nearly thirty vessels also docked at Lisbon, apparently having missed the Cadiz campaign. While they were waiting for new orders, it was learned that in the new world, Dutch privateers had seized more parts of Brazil and had captured Angola, the latter being Portugal's slave-trading base. These slights served as uncomfortable reminders of the clashes between Portuguese and Dutch interests; King John offered the Dutch an alliance against Spain, but the Dutch decided that they liked their new Brazilian conquests more than they liked the idea of making common cause against their old enemy. At the same time, it was well known that Portuguese nobles had revolted against Madrid partly because it was perceived that Spain had let Portugal's new world possessions go. King John could not be permitted to do the same.

In September 1641 though, these conflicts of interest placed the Dutch admiral in an awkward position, since he was now docked in something very close to enemy territory. Fortunately for him, King John ignored his nobles' pleas and refused to seize the Dutch vessels here, and his admirals were sweet-talked into mounting a new expedition against the Azores instead. Incredibly, once they were in the open sea, the Dutch admiral turned for home, leaving his embarrassed former allies to curse the Dutch yet again. Evidently, the Dutch and Portuguese were destined to endure a relationship closer to enemies than allies, but they at least held the war with Spain in common.[21]

It was surely evident to the Dutch by now that that old enemy did not seem so formidable any longer. With the eruptions so close to home, it was impossible to imagine that Madrid would have men or moneys to spare for any new campaigns in the Netherlands. As a result, Frederick Henry engaged in negotiations designed to increase the prominence and power of the House of Orange, by marrying into the House of Stuart. His son William was wed to Mary in May 1641, and from that moment onwards, Anglo-Dutch history was destined never to be the same again. William had been quite taken with his English bride, confessing in early May that:

> I will tell you how everything is. At first, we were both of us a little serious, but now we are quite at our ease together; I find her much prettier than her portrait: I love her very much and I believe she loves me too.[22]

But love was less important to Frederick Henry than the security of the Republic, security which he believed Britain would help guarantee. Through 1640 to 1641, the stadtholder had been repulsed from Bruges and Hulst, but he had seized the consolation prize of Gennep on the eastern frontier of the Republic. It was while assaulting Hulst though that the interests of Frederick Henry's branch of the House of Orange spotted an opportunity, thanks to the untimely death of another stadtholder, who left vacancies in the other Dutch provinces which Frederick Henry sought immediately to fill with his own branch. That this backfired spoke volumes about the way these provinces jealously guarded their privileges, but it also hinted towards a creeping suspicion of Frederick Henry generally.[23] With his military victories, and the royal marriage of his son, was the House of Orange growing too popular? These questions would be answered, in fact, by the end of the decade, when a new generation was at the helm.[24]

The dissatisfying Dutch returns notwithstanding, Olivares' position in 1641 was still grave. Following the loss in late January at Monjuich, Spanish security was greatly reduced, and the Count-Duke's freedom of action compromised. How was Spain now to combat the two revolts in two corners of its realm? Inevitably, her attentions would have to be focused somewhere, and during the next few years the change would become apparent. Spain was to concentrate on Catalonia and dig in for defence in the Spanish Netherlands and against Portugal. This meant that Spanish power would be directed primarily not against the Dutch, but against the newly proclaimed 'Count of Barcelona' Louis XIII of France. Spain's bitterness, as Derek Croxton observed, was transferred from the Dutch to the French, and just in time for the war to enter its final phase.[25]

THREE
Against the Habsburgs

The first half of 1641 was a year of departures. Three major figures died within weeks of one another, leaving new opportunities for both Habsburgs and allies alike. George William of Brandenburg, a staple of the Thirty Years War since its beginning, had died in December 1640, but his son Frederick William was only in a position to take control of the Electorate's foreign policy once's the late Elector's Catholic advisor Count Schwarzenberg died in March 1641. One month later, Duke George of Brunswick-Luneburg, that ally of Sweden from the House of Welf, who was based at Hanover, also died. One month after that, on 10 May 1641, the worn commander of the Swedish army Johan Baner followed him to the grave. These three deaths in three months had a profound impact upon Swedish and Imperial policy, so it benefits us to examine each case in brief now.

Frederick William would one day be known as the Great Elector, for taking Brandenburg out of the miserable conditions his father had lumbered into by late 1640. The winter of 1640-41 was especially dire, as the region was partially occupied, stripped of all valuable resources, and its people were aching from so many years of incessant warfare. Frederick William succeeded to an inheritance worth an eighth of that which his father had succeeded to in 1619. In the space of twenty years, Brandenburg had been sucked dry, its lands wasted, its ducal buildings collapsing, its people divided, its armies supported by banditry and plunder. First and foremost, Brandenburg needed a figure who would seize the reins of government and work diligently to save the situation. Saving this situation, as Frederick William well understood, involved making a hasty peace with the Swedes, even if this conflicted with previous alliance which his father had made with the Emperor.

Count Adam von Schwarzenberg had been chief advisor to George William, which was in itself a strange arrangement; a Catholic advisor of a Calvinist Elector in a Lutheran Electorate. But George William's experience of the war had been anything but normal; he had been pulled repeatedly between his family ties, his religion, his loyalty to the Emperor and the immediate security of his lands. Gustavus Adolphus' widow was his sister, and thus the new Queen of Sweden his niece – it was suggested on his ascension that Frederick William should thus marry his cousin, trying Brandenburg and Sweden together in an irresistible combination of German and Scandinavian might. This never came to fruition, but Frederick William did dispense almost immediately with any policies save those that directly benefited Brandenburg. He had no love for the Emperor's alliance, nor did he let drop the old feud with Sweden over Pomerania. Instead, Frederick William recognised his position for what it was – trapped between Polish lords, Swedish armies and Imperial constitutions. He could not intervene against one without offending the other, and after pushing out Count Schwarzenberg, who is believed to have died of shock shortly thereafter, the new Elector sought to bring this policy of self-interest to life.[26]

Frederick William had known only war, being born in 1620 when it was already two years old. By the time he died in 1688, Europe was a very different canvas, and Brandenburg was a very different duchy. Few knew of the character or intentions of the 21-year-old Elector in 1641 though; fewer still could have imagined the impact his regime would have on Northern Germany, Scandinavia and Vienna during his 48-year reign. But Frederick William did not keep them in suspense for long; by September 1641, it was learned in Regensburg that Brandenburg had made peace with Sweden. This was a problematic development for Ferdinand, because he had presented the 1635 Peace of Prague and these new negotiations as the opportunity for all patriotic Germans to arrive at peace and eject the foreign invader. With one of the Electors now making a separate peace, Ferdinand's claims to have had the interests of the Germans at heart were undermined. If peace with Sweden was so difficult to reach, then why had the new Elector of Brandenburg been so capable of reaching it? Pamphlets were published, likely on the Elector's instruction, blaming the Habsburgs for their efforts at inflaming the war's worst effects and going into business for themselves. These tracts found an eager audience in Northern Germany, and by autumn 1641 the Emperor was faced with rumours that he was continuing the war for his own personal gain.[27]

Thanks to the death of another German figure though, the Emperor was at least comforted by the defection of Hanover into the Imperial camp. Duke George of Brunswick-Luneburg died in April, to be replaced by his inexperienced nephew, who immediately was cowed by the prevailing Imperial influences of the court to make peace with Vienna and leave Sweden's side. This arrangement did not merely remove a strategically important region from Sweden's orbit – the late Duke's lands straddled along the southern Danish border – it also left Oxenstierna with even fewer allies. Now only the Palatine exiles – who were spread across Europe, fighting for the Dutch, soon to fight for King Charles in England, and fighting for the French – and Amalie

Elizabeth of Hesse-Kassel remained in the Swedish camp. In other words, all of Germany save these two pariahs were on the Emperor's side, which greatly reduced Sweden's political and military options, and Sweden's situation was about to get even worse.

On 10 May, at the town of Halberstadt, in Saxony, Johan Baner died. He had been unwell for some time, and he had been grief-stricken since losing his wife the previous June to one of the numerous recurring bouts of plague. Baner had been ruthless, difficult to like and a heavy drinker. He had not always been successful in battle, and he had plainly failed to wrest Northern Germany from the Emperor's influence by force alone. However, this former subordinate of Gustavus Adolphus had managed to stop the bleeding after 1635, and to maintain Sweden's sole force in the Empire even while the Emperor appeared to gather in strength. Even with virtually all of Germany turned against him, Baner had maintained his small army, which rarely exceeded twenty thousand men. His victories at Wittstock and Chemnitz had intimidated the late Elector of Brandenburg into fleeing to the wilds of East Prussia, while his efforts to reinforce Hesse-Kassel, Hanover and even the French at times demonstrated the commitment of Sweden to the war. If the Emperor needed any reminding, then Baner's appearance outside Regensburg in late 1640 proved his industriousness, even while he was forced to retreat shortly thereafter. Baner was what remained of Gustavus' legacy, and he was a difficult man for a difficult job at a supremely difficult time in Sweden's war effort.

With his death though, there was little time for mourning. The most pressing question was who would succeed him, followed by those familiar questions from the colonels, to the effect of who would pay them. Unlike Oxenstierna's experience from the Powder Barrel Convention, resolution with the Swedish colonels was arrived at quickly, although the notion of a 'Swedish' army was virtually irrelevant now, as barely five hundred of the sixteen thousand soldiers formerly under Baner's command were actually Swedish. This was instead a mercenary German army with a Swedish flavour, seen in the choice of commanders. Oxenstierna did not select any of the Germans who were nominated to succeed Baner, but a sickly Swede by the name of Lennart Torstenson, who was at that moment not even in Germany. The choice might have seemed wrong-headed, but the Chancellor's decision bore fruit later in the year, as Torstenson proved himself the superior even of Baner in terms of his tactical approaches.

It was now that many of the disparate threads of early 1641 were blended together. Oxenstierna was able to take advantage of the truce with Brandenburg to recall the leading colonels and pause campaigning for the moment. Thanks to the renewed treaty with France, which granted increased subsidies, Sweden was able to take out a line of credit, which was extended to the underpaid colonels that were wined and dined in Stockholm. In fact, it was because of rumours of a looming truce between the Emperor and Sweden that Claude d'Avaux, the French agent, agreed to grant an additional 80,000 thalers to the French subsidy. A peace between the Emperor and Sweden had only seemed possible, because Ferdinand had agreed to give all of Pomerania to the Swedes, and he had only done this, because Brandenburg had made peace. Thus, the interconnected nature of these developments created ripples within the war, to the effect that by the second half of 1641, France and Sweden had secured their alliance, Brandenburg was out of the war, and a new Swedish commander was ready to lead his paid army against the Imperials. All the while, the negotiations continued at Hamburg and Regensburg.[28]

1641 saw French attentions pulled in several different directions. The year began with a triumph at Montjuic, on the outskirts of Barcelona, where a French-Catalan force routed the Spaniards. The rest of the year saw Richelieu concentrate his attentions on the Spanish Netherlands, where Arras, the capital of Artois, was seized in July, only to be lost to the Spanish in November,[29] and the Duke of Lorraine made peace in spring only to resume the war in summer.[30] It was a bewildering series of events, and in addition to the Italy front, demonstrated precisely how overextended French commitments had become. In Italy Piedmont and Montferrat had been secured, but Milan remained a powerful hub of Spanish influence, and the French commander simply lacked the resources or vision to make any headway.[31]

In the spring of 1641, in the midst of these interconnected campaigns, the very regime of Louis XIII suffered an incredibly close call, when his army was routed by the Comte de Soissons, a second cousin of the French King and an ally of Spain. Only for Soissons' death during the battle, where he was said to have died from an accidental wound, Louis XIII could have been in danger of being usurped by a Spanish candidate. But the battle of La Marfee itself had been a close call, as it had taken place in Sedan in the north-east of France.[32] The event had shown, first, that several armies campaigning in the region was necessary, as the siege of Arras had continued even as this disaster was sustained. Second, the loss and miracle of Soissons' death thereafter underlined the point that Richelieu had made many enemies in his rise to the top, and that his regime was far from popular among the French people, who were heavily taxed to pay for his policies.[33]

More obvious opportunities for success against Spain seemed to present themselves, but these opportunities netted few genuine gains. The whole point of the Catalan front was to suck in Spanish soldiers, but to save France from additional commitments. Instead, France wasted nearly 30 ships in an abortive attack on Cadiz in league with the Portuguese, and experienced failure once again when they were beaten back from the siege of Tarragona on the Mediterranean coast in August. The Dutch made a similarly unimpressive impact on the Portuguese war, though they would return with a nominal peace treaty to Lisbon in 1642. The Dutch, unlike the French, remained impressive abroad, seizing portions of Brazil and establishing a sphere of influence ranging well into the murky Amazon.[34] Short of propping up these revolts and taking a few reinforced positions along the borders, Richelieu would have had to admit that 1641 had returned very little in the way of triumphs,[35] which likely helps to explain why he was willing to accept the Treaty of Hamburg in late December, which prepared the ground for the peace negotiations in Westphalia.[36]

1641 had been equally uninspiring for Frederick Henry, the Prince of Orange, who had led Dutch armies since 1625. His last great triumph had been at Breda in 1637, and his campaigns since had brought only failure. Notwithstanding Frederick Henry's disappointing returns, his career prospects were at least more positive than those of Philip IV's brother, the Cardinal Infante, most famous for the 1634 victory at Nordlingen. But Nordlingen was a distant memory for the melancholy, prematurely aged Cardinal Infante by 1641. He noted

> ...if the war with France is to continue, we have not the means to take the offensive. The Spanish and Imperial armies are reduced to such a state that they can undertake nothing. The only solution is to establish supporters in France and use them to make the Paris government more amenable.[37]

But this chance had surely passed with the death of Soissons in July 1641, and as the enthusiasm for a revolt against Richelieu fizzled out, so too did the life force of this Habsburg prince fizzle out with it. He had been heavily burdened by the pressures and demands of the war against the Dutch, and the eruption of revolts in Iberia convinced him that he could expect even fewer nuggets of help from Madrid from now on. The Cardinal Infante Ferdinand died a broken, wasted man in Brussels in early November 1641. He was just 31.[38]

Back in Madrid, the Cardinal Infante's brother was having an equally difficult time. The increasingly isolated Olivares, in his late 60s, was learning that it was impossible to pay for a single one of these military theatres, let alone all of them at once. Stopgap measures were again implemented, as the copper currency was reduced to one-sixth of its previous value, and those in possession of silver had even greater demands placed upon them. So desperate was the situation that in spring 1641, as these measures were implemented, 150 people were sent to the Madrid dungeons for their inability to pay all that was asked of them. The situation was indeed grave, as one merchant recorded:

> Trade and commerce were confused, and the prices rose enormously, so that people could not find money for boots and clothes; and even provisions could

not be had, as no one would sell. The copper money was valueless, and people threw it about or forced it upon those to whom they owed money, as the law gave it currency. The agony and desperation of the people were intense, and utter despair consumed the hearts and lives of the people.[39]

Olivares had not merely alienated the suffering working class; he had also pushed several of his aristocratic peers over the edge. On one especially scandalous occasion, the Duke of Medina Sidonia, a brother in law of the new King of Portugal, had attempted to make himself the overlord of Andalusia.[40] The effort misfired, but the writing was on the wall – Olivares was losing the battles abroad in the military sphere, just as he was losing the battle for the hearts and minds of his compatriots. Criticism of his regime became increasingly acidic, as one contemporary recorded his opinions:

> Our Ruler, hesitant, and nearly swamped by the weight of affairs…went around asking how he could pacify Catalonia. If he were to ask me, I should answer that it could be done by leaving it alone; by not always harrying its inhabitants; by not inflicting on them every hour for a full nineteen years, Juntas and decrees and councils, and investigations into their estates and persons; by using temperate words and temperate actions, and treating them in a way that befits the vassals of so illustrious a prince.[41]

The Spanish paralysis complemented the Dutch inaction and the French failures, but in northern Germany, with the arrival of Torstenson as the new commander in November 1641, matters soon began to tilt in favour of the Swedes. Torstenson succeeded to an army which had already proved itself earlier in the year; despite the confusion at its head, an Imperial-Bavarian army commanded by the Emperor's brother and Piccolomini had been defeated in the Battle of Wolfenbüttel in June. The victory was a pyric one, but it demonstrated the potency of the Sweden's military power. After several years of consolidation, defence and manoeuvre, Torstenson was eager to take this power to the next level, combating the Emperor's allies directly, and aiming at the heart of the more prosperous centre of the Empire. First though, on Christmas Day 1641, the interested parties paused to agree on 'the form but not the content' of the peace negotiations, in a process which would only end with the Peace of Westphalia some seven years later.[42]

The Treaty of Hamburg had itself been agreed to only after many years of negotiation and manoeuvre, where affairs on the battlefield and the changing proclivities of German princes moved concessions and opportunities across the board. At different occasions, Richelieu had worked to move a conference involving all of France's allies and enemies into being, while the Emperor had attempted to separate Sweden from France. With the events of 1641 in context, a halfway home between these goals was established. Osnabruck would host the Swedish delegation with Protestant allies, and at Münster the French dignitaries with the Catholic powers gathered, with intermediaries from the Emperor moving between each. The cities were to be neutral, which would certainly help to reduce the military burden on Westphalia, but conspicuous in their absence were the Spanish and Dutch, who had yet to commit to send representatives to Westphalia, their war being separate from that between the Franco-Swedish and Emperor's forces.[43] Notwithstanding these technicalities and setbacks, the announcement was officially made on Christmas Day 1641 to the effect that the Emperor...

> ...wishes to announce to all whom it may concern that after many years of negotiations over the basis to start general peace talks, and after the most diverse difficulties arose from the preliminaries, finally, thanks to divine assistance and the intervention of the authority of the serene King of Denmark as mediator, the following preliminaries have been agreed...[44]

The reader may be puzzled by the appearance of the Danish King in such a prominent position. How had Sweden been persuaded to agree to King Christian IV, a historical rival of the late Gustavus Adolphus, to play a significant role in determining the spoils it would receive in any peace arrangement? Surely the jealous Danes would prevent Sweden getting what it deserved, and would drive a hard bargain just to spite Oxenstierna, for succeeding where they had not in the 1620s? In fact, though these concerns remained in the background for Oxenstierna, he was content, at least outwardly, at Sweden's rival taking charge of the duties of mediation. When Christian had approached the idea of mediation in the late 1630s, these had been rejected on the basis that the jealous Danish King would do all in his power to undermine Sweden and force her to compromise on her war aims.[45]

What had changed since then? Certainly, there had been few friendly gestures sent from either side in the years since Gustavus' death. Denmark and Sweden nearly came to blows in 1638, and the following year an Imperial councillor was spotted in Copenhagen, apparently convinced of his ability to persuade Christian to form an offensive alliance with the Emperor against Sweden. The plan did not get off the ground though, thanks to the restraint upon King Christian's regime which had tightened following the disastrous intervention in 1625. Since then, the Danish Royal Council wielded far more power, and effectively reduced Christian's freedom of action.[46] Christian attempted to rebrand his position thereafter, as a concerned party interested in mediation.

This led to a curious result, where a Danish agent attempted to increase his reputation by claiming that Spain would agree to any treaty made in Hamburg, and that none other than King Christian himself would personally guarantee Spain's position. Never was it explained how Christian might precisely do this, and Christian initially refused, only to agree by the end of

November 1641. It was this personal guarantee, a meaningless and vague device for sure, that persuaded Claude d'Avaux, the French negotiator at Hamburg, to proceed. Spain, d'Avaux believed, would abide by the terms of the Treaty of Hamburg, and if she did not, then at the very least it would cause some headaches for the Danes.[47] Richelieu was certainly concerned that his goal of a universal peace conference hosting all parties would be jeopardised if the Spanish neglected to attend, and it was an odd choice to place the responsibility at Denmark's door.

Nor was the Danish element the sole issue with the Treaty; almost as soon as it had been signed arguments broke out over the language used and the order of precedence, to the extent that Sweden and France had to be issued with separate copies of the document. The French caused further headaches, as Imperial negotiators noticed how they were still referring to Ferdinand III as a mere King of Hungary, rather than as the Emperor. This slight had to be addressed, but it was sign of the pettiness which was to come on both sides. The exhausting, mind-numbing procedures which were necessary to indulge with before coming face to face with one's equal – even down to where one sat at the table – could drag on for hours.[48] The ratification process dragged on well into spring of the new year, in spite of the high-minded declaration that this preliminary peace conference would begin on 25 March 1642.

And of course, there was the confusing layout of the conference itself; why, one may ask, did the conference have to be spread over two cities at all? Certainly, the French would have preferred the one city rather than the complexities of stretching their diplomats into two. The key reason for the separation was that Swedish dignitaries resented the presence of the Pope. The Papacy declared its intention to tolerate Protestantism in the final treaty, but to the Swedes, this smacked of disrespect; that Pope Urban VIII was laying claim to rights which were not his own. The French at least managed to convince the Swedes to reside at Osnabruck, rather than the distant Cologne or Lubeck. Henceforth, the conference would be split between the two cities, but this division came with two important caveats. First, the division was to be political, rather than religious. In other words, those at war with Sweden or interested in the Swedish peace would attend in Osnabruck, and the same was true for Münster with France. Second, per Richelieu's insistence, the two cities would remain part of the one conference notwithstanding the distance between them. This fiction could only be maintained by constant travel between the two places, and so the road linking Münster to Osnabruck was neutralised.[49]

It seems that the parties had thought about this process a great deal, but they were to be utterly unprepared for how long the process took. The date was set for 25 March 1642, but this optimistic goal failed to take into consideration a legion of issues, including matters as simple as the process for

947

issuing passports, which was the responsibility both sides found frustrating and surprisingly complex to attend to. Much is revealed by the fact that the provisional date was missed by more than three years; not until spring 1645 would concrete negotiations at the two cities be hosted with any modicum of intention or sincerity, and even then, the pace of the war still got in the way. Contemporaries recognised that their hand could be massively empowered by a military victory or through the capture of a fortified region or landmark. While in possession of a metaphorical, and sometimes literal gun to the head of one's counterpart, compliance with demands was much more likely. But this said nothing about the general complexity of the whole process, especially when, as we will see, the French and Swedes upped their demands, insisting not just on the presence of the major powers and their allies, but also of every estate – that is, every territorial unit of consequence – in the Empire.[50]

And other events were developing even as the passports went into production. With the conference date set and commitments made, there was more of an impetus than ever before on the commanders to apply new pressures with the goal of wresting fresh concessions. Lennart Torstenson, having taken up the baton of the Swedish army in November 1641, was the perfect man for such a job. He arrived with seven thousand conscripts, and a keen energy to fix the problems the late Baner had left him. For the next four months he repaired the Swedish army, restoring its discipline and endearing himself to the fifteen thousand men under his command. He was joined by another five thousand by the new year, and he reinforced his base at Werben, where Gustavus Adolphus had fortified his army a decade before.

This was not the only echo of the Swedish King; Torstenson learned from his predecessor's mistakes and noted that Baner's invasion of Silesia in 1639 had failed because Baner neglected to seize the fortified places which held the region in rapture. In April 1642 he began this process, launching a new invasion of Silesia, and sending his subordinate Konigsmarck to raid Saxony and keep John George distracted. Strategically, Torstenson could benefit from Saxon exhaustion and the absence of Brandenburg from the equation, but he still had to reckon with the Imperial army. Fortunately for Torstenson, he found that his revitalised army was more than a match for them. The small detachment of cavalry under Konigsmarck which he had sent to raid Saxony reappeared just at the right time to trap and destroy an Imperial relief force of seven thousand men near the town of Schweidnitz on 31 May. Konigsmarck's army of six thousand horse performed valiantly, and the Imperial commander, a Duke of Lauenburg and veteran of Gustavus' campaigns, was run through and killed. The Imperial army virtually disintegrated, with nearly four thousand of its seven thousand men written off as casualties. When Torstenson learned of this triumph by Konigsmarck, he knew he was free during the spring and summer to have his way with Silesia.

But Torstenson was not merely content with Silesia. Sensing an inherent weakness in the Imperial defence, Torstenson left half his army in Upper Silesia while he marched south into Moravia. It had been some time before armies had pillaged the region, and Torstenson found it ripe with new uniforms, food, wine and all manner of other spoils. No Swedish army under Baner had ever moved so far so fast. Olmutz, the Moravian capital, was seized, and a mass exodus of its population south caused panic in Vienna – Torstenson was only two hundred kilometres from the Imperial capital, and he had to be stopped before he spilled into any more of the Habsburg hereditary lands. None other than the Emperor's brother, Leopold William, was on the case. He assembled an army of twenty thousand men, and prepared to confront Torstenson at a familiar place, Breitenfeld, where Torstenson had commanded the artillery of the Swedish King eleven years before.

Torstenson was outnumbered by seven thousand Imperial and Bohemian militiamen, but he knew that this was the Emperor's only army in Germany. If his brother was unsuccessful, then Emperor Ferdinand would be forced either to make great concessions at the peace table or find some other way to placate Sweden's wrath. Either way, Torstenson was determined to stand and fight, and to make this a repeat of Breitenfeld, rather than something closer to Nordlingen. Fortunately for Torstenson, the day was his. Battle was met on 2 November 1642, and the two armies fought at right angles to their positions of a decade before. The ghosts of that battle may well have been palpable, as the Imperial left flank, along with the Saxons, routed in the face of a sudden onslaught from the cavalry at dawn. From that point, Leopold William was on the defensive, and never managed to rally his inexperienced troops to where they were needed.

It was the quality of Torstenson's men, in the end, that proved the difference, but the cost was still high. Torstenson lost four thousand to the Archduke's three thousand, though an additional five thousand of the latter's army were also taken as prisoners, making up the numbers.[51] It was not as spectacular a triumph as the First Breitenfeld, and it was not exactly the thumping, crushing victory which some accounts have suggested, but it was nonetheless a vital turning point in Swedish and Imperial fortunes. In similar scenes to those following Breitenfeld in 1631, Sweden's enemies battened down the hatches, preparing for the worst. Leipzig surrendered to Torstenson's forces, and Maximillian raised the Bavarian militia. Ferdinand urged John George of Saxony to fight on, and he did for the moment, but after that fiasco it was plain that the Habsburgs had no army in Central Germany to combat Torstenson's warpath.

The unglamorous old efforts of Baner were forgotten, as the Swedes seemed to be back on top form once again. News of the triumph resounded across the Empire and Europe, being exaggerated in its scale and impact as it spread. The association of the battlefield with the late Swedish King, and the coincidence that his lieutenant had now achieved a signal victory in that same place certainly helped fan the story, and it certainly gave pause to those dignitaries who might have been on their way to Westphalia. It was an additional disaster for the Spanish, who appreciated that their bond with the Emperor was further loosened, and a separate peace could follow with France if the Swedes marched on Vienna. For Richelieu, the news was vindication that the Swedes were a worthwhile ally to have invested in, and that the tide could in fact be turning for good. Not for the first time or the final time, military victory had changed the narrative of the Thirty Years War.

Chapter 20 Notes

[1]Quoted in Wilson, *Sourcebook*, p. 213.
[2]Richelieu's survey of the situation is provided in *Ibid*, pp. 214-216.
[3]See Wilson, *Europe's Tragedy*, pp. 618-619.
[4]See *Ibid*, pp. 619-622.
[5]See Croxton, *Westphalia*, pp. 71-74.
[6]*Ibid*, pp. 74-76.
[7]The scene is recorded in Hume, *The Court of Philip IV*, pp. 343-344.
[8]See Charles E. Nowell, *A History of Portugal* (New York: D. Van Nostrand, 1952), pp. 148-150.
[9]Quoted in Elliot, *Revolt of the Catalans*, p. 388.
[10]Quoted in *Ibid*, pp. 390-391.
[11]*Ibid*, pp. 393-394.
[12]Quoted in *Ibid*, p. 395.
[13]Quoted in *Ibid*, pp. 400-401.
[14]Quoted in *Ibid*, p. 402.
[15]See *Ibid*, p. 426.
[16]H. V. Livermore, *A History of Portugal* (Cambridge, England: Cambridge University Press, 1947), pp. 278-280.
[17]Parker, *Europe in Crisis*, p. 260.
[18]Parrott, *Richelieu's Army*, p. 146.
[19]*Ibid*, pp. 146-147.
[20]James M. Anderson, *The History of Portugal* (Westport, CT: Greenwood Press, 2000), p. 112.
[21]*Ibid*, pp. 112-114.
[22]Quoted in Edmundson, 'Frederick Henry: Prince of Orange (continued)', pp. 281-282.
[23]*Ibid*, pp. 282-285.
[24]For more on this relationship see Pieter Geyl, 'Frederick Henry of Orange and King Charles I', *The English Historical Review*, Vol. 38, No. 151 (Jul., 1923), pp. 355-383.
[25]See Croxton, *Westphalia*, p. 94.
[26]See Wedgewood, *Thirty Years War*, pp. 271-272; pp. 423-425.
[27]See *Ibid*, pp. 425-426.
[28]See Wilson, *Europe's Tragedy*, pp. 627-629.
[29]Parrott, *Richelieu's Army*, pp. 149-150.
[30]*Ibid*, p. 147-148.
[31]*Ibid*, pp. 150-152.
[32]J. H. Elliot, *The Count-Duke of Olivares: The Statesman in an Age of Decline* (Yale: Yale University Press, 1989), p. 613-614.
[33]Parrott, *Richelieu's Army*, p. 149.
[34]See Engel Sluiter, 'Dutch Maritime Power and the Colonial Status Quo, 1585-1641', *Pacific Historical Review*, Vol. 11, No. 1 (Mar., 1942), pp. 29-41, especially pp. 39-41.
[35]Parrott, *Richelieu's Army*, pp. 154-155.
[36]Croxton, *Westphalia*, pp. 80-81.
[37]Quoted in Matusiak, *Europe in Flames*, p. 380.
[38]Edmundson, 'Frederick Henry: Prince of Orange (continued)', p. 284.
[39]See Hume, *The Court of Phillip IV*, pp. 351-352.
[40]*Ibid*, p. 357.
[41]Quoted in Elliot, *Revolt of the Catalans*, p. 490.
[42]See Wilson, *Europe's Tragedy*, pp. 629-632.
[43]See Croxton, *Westphalia*, pp. 75-80.
[44]Quoted in Wilson, *Sourcebook*, p. 280.
[45]Croxton, *Westphalia*, pp. 53-55.
[46]*Ibid*, pp. 60-62.
[47]*Ibid*, pp. 79-80.
[48]We will return to the question of Westphalian procedure in later chapter, but a good explanation of the situation is provided by Kenneth Colegrove, 'Diplomatic Procedure Preliminary to the Congress of Westphalia', *The American Journal of International Law*, Vol. 13, No. 3 (Jul., 1919), pp. 450-482.
[49]See Croxton, *Westphalia*, pp. 78-81.
[50]See Wilson, *Europe's Tragedy*, p. 55. The general definition provided by historians is that of a territorial

assembly ruling over a portion of land, but for the sake of brevity and ease of access, we will henceforth use 'estate' when referring to those states and microstates who were invited to Westphalia.

[51]See Wilson, *Europe's Tragedy*, pp. 636-638.

[52]Stomberg, *A History of Sweden*, p. 383; Andersson, *A History of Sweden*, p. 183.

(Top left) Georgy Racoczi, Prince of Transylvania
(Top right) Maria Elenore of Brandenburg (Michiel van Mierevelt)

Armand de Bourbon, Prince of Conde

CHAPTER TWENTY-ONE
"A Fractured Dynasty"

ONE: Rocroi

TWO: Torstenson's War

THREE: Maintaining Pressure

ONE

Rocroi

The Prince of Condé was within his rights to have hard feelings. He had been given command of the north-western theatre of France, near the border with the Spanish Netherlands, but the front was expected to be secondary in importance and intensity. The real military theatre of importance in 1643, it was expected, was that of Catalonia, so Condé's instructions amounted to a directive to block whatever expeditions the Portuguese commander, Francisco de Melo, might launch. It was a dull enough appointment for a Prince of the Blood; Condé was, after all, fourth in line to the throne, behind King Louis XIII's infant son. Condé's father had been viewed with suspicion in years' precisely for that reason, especially before a son was born to King Louis in 1638. Now, placed in this secondary front, with few opportunities to make his name, it was not hard to imagine that the inexperienced 22-year-old felt like he was being punished for his father's crimes. Suddenly, and unexpectantly, however, this theatre was to become the centre of a new Spanish initiative to resurrect the old fears of 1636, by launching an invasion of France from Flanders once again. The target of Francisco de Melo's assault was the town of Rocroi.

On 19 May 1643, Condé marched with his twenty-one thousand men to confront de Melo's twenty-three thousand in a risky pitched battle. His advisors had cautioned against such a strategy; pitched battles were unpredictable, messy and often inconclusive, but Condé persisted. Prickly and self-important though he was, Condé was consumed by a self-confidence which was to prove the difference. Beginning at 3AM, Condé assaulted the veteran Portuguese commander with the full force of his army, and the men under his command suffered numerous close calls, but by the end of the battle it was plain that reforms in organisation and tactics had proved the difference. Opposing Condé was the cream of the Spanish crop, with their reserves of heavy infantry laid out in the traditional tercios and daring Condé's men to challenge them. Over a front more than two and a half kilometres wide, the challenge was taken up, and in scenes not dissimilar to those of Breitenfeld, the Spanish infantry were broken. De Melo's spring campaign spluttered to a halt, amidst the loss of more than seven thousand casualties, to the French four and a half thousand.[1]

The victory moved the French to delay their arrival at Westphalia, which opened days later on 23 May 1643, but the battle was significant for additional reasons. The first was that it represented a signal triumph for Condé, who made hearty use of propaganda to emphasise and exaggerate the scale of the victory. Condé returned to Paris soon afterwards to be wined and dined and adored by the Parisians, who were taught to believe in the military prowess of this Prince. Conde attached his army to that of Marshall Jean-Baptiste Guébriant along the Upper Rhine in midsummer, but following this move, the campaign actually turned against the French. Quartering his men along the east bank of the Rhine, in land recently taken from the Bavarians, the latter's commander appeared on the horizon in November and inflicted a terrible defeat on the French at the Battle of Tuttlingen. Fortunately for Condé, his name was not associated with the defeat, and he remained curiously isolated from any damage to his reputation. But the French army as a whole was less fortunate, as 1643 ended with the effective defeat of France's army in Germany and the virtual undoing of Condé triumph at Rocroi. Perhaps the sole silver lining for France was that Marshal Turenne, a rising star in the French army, was appointed to rebuild the army on the Rhine in place of Guébriant, who had been slain.[2]

The second point concerns the political context in France, when Condé's victory was learned of. On the other end of the urgent update was not Cardinal Richelieu, but his successor, another Cardinal by the name of Jules Mazarin. By late 1642, Richelieu had been prematurely aged by more than fifteen years of active political scheming, not to mention several campaigns against the enemies of France. He had preserved his political position by sheer force of will and tact, making use always of the firm friendship he enjoyed with the King. In his final significant act, Richelieu helped the King defeat the latest in a scheme fanned by Louis' brother, and a rising political star and favourite, the Marquis of Cinq-Mars. Louis' brother Gaston was humiliated one last time, and Cinq-Mars was executed. Thereafter, as he returned to Paris in November, Richelieu's health deteriorated, until, as Richard Lodge recorded:

> ...he relapsed into unconsciousness, which was only broken by occasional intervals till the following mid-day, when a groan and a last convulsion of the limbs announced that all was over, and that the man who had been for so many years the great motive- power in France had ceased to live.[3]

The great Cardinal was dead, and while the full extent of his impact upon France remains up for debate, what is not debateable is that Richelieu was wise enough to plan for a successor. In one of his final meetings with

Louis XIII in fact, he recommended that Jules Mazarin be given his position as France's de facto first minister. It was a request which the King, fortunately, determined to honour. Mazarin had arrived in France from Rome as Giulio Mazzarini, and in 1628 he had met Richelieu for the first time, and quickly impressed him. Mazarin was persuaded to join the papal service thereafter, and rose steadily up the ranks, being made Cardinal in 1641. Mazarin was ready, just in time it seemed, to pick up where Richelieu had left off, and the King's new minister would certainly have been buoyed by news of the victory at Rocroi, not least because the appointment of Condé to that front had been one of Richelieu's final political decisions.[4] The ghost of the late Cardinal was keenly felt, but Mazarin had little time to mourn, as he was confronted with a still more disconcerting death – that of the King himself.

During the campaigning season of 1642, Richelieu had accompanied the king to the front at Roussillon in the south, and the two had watched as the French army enjoyed several successes. Yet it was plain to Louis' entourage that the King's health was deteriorating, and some believed he would not even last the winter. His health had been poor for some time, and he had felt compelled to rely on Richelieu more and more, as gout, headaches, stomach disorders, and failing lungs rocked his constitution from 1640. The rigors of the war certainly had not helped, as the stress from campaigning increased the pain and reduced the time for leisure and rest which the King needed. Expressing his view of events to Richelieu on one occasion in 1641, the King commented pathetically that: 'All of these are simply thoughts that came to me, about which I tell you…to follow up the good ones and disregard the bad ones. I leave it all to your good judgment.'[5]

Richelieu had certainly become accustomed to this working relationship, but the task for Mazarin must have appeared daunting, especially since he had barely five months with the King before his death on 14 May 1643. There was precious little time to build any kind of lasting relationship, or to ensure that the King adhered to the late Richelieu's wishes. Plainly, if Mazarin wished to cling to his position, he would depend upon the powers granted to him through the regency, which had been established to protect and mould the regime of the infant King, Louis XIV. In time, Mazarin would come to recognise Louis XIV as one of the defining monarchs of his age, but in 1643, he was forced to rely on the mercies of Queen Anne, Louis XIII's widow, for support. Unfortunately for Mazarin, Anne happened to be not only the brother of the King of Spain, but also a committed enemy of the late Richelieu.

Again, Mazarin was fortunate that the widowed Queen listened to him and worked alongside him. The events of the next few years were to draw them even closer together. Back in Madrid, the preservation of Richelieu's policy could not have been expected, and some hoped that a turn in French policy, with the Spanish King's sister leading the charge, would follow. On 28 May 1643, King Philip himself wrote that:

...the death of King Louis should be enough to procure all that we desire in the making of an honest peace, since [among other things] France's allies will no longer be certain of her assistance, while I can offer myself as custodian, to defend the new King against any challenge to his authority which may arise within the kingdom.[6]

We may be tempted to criticise this view of France as naïve, considering how the course of the war was to play out. Yet, in the highly personal kingdoms of the period, such an expectation was not unusual, especially since a Habsburg relative sat in Paris. Indeed, historical precedent did exist, and history would repeat itself a century later, most famously in 1762, when the death of Empress Elizabeth and the ascension of Tsar Peter III effectively saved Frederick the Great's Prussia from disaster. Certainly, by summer 1643 it was only reasonable for Spain to pursue any avenue which might lead to peace. Rocroi was akin to the cherry on top of a cake which had become increasingly bitter and dangerous, but during the campaigning season of 1642 there had been cause enough to despair.[7]

Reportedly, when the fortress of Perpignan, in Roussillon fell to the forces of the French king late in 1642, Olivares threatened to throw himself out a window.[8] The threat was never made good, but Olivares would be relieved of his duties in January 1643. He had outlasted his great rival and counterpart in France by little more than a month, but while Richelieu was finally at peace, Olivares was destined to lead a restless, miserable retirement.[9] He lingered on for two more years before dying, perhaps taking solace from the fact that his successors proved no more capable at stemming the tide of defeat and decline than he had been. Olivares, as much as his successors, were hampered by the facts, and the facts were that Spain was running out of money as much as she was running out of options. With the eruption of the Portuguese war and the Catalan revolt in 1640, there were fewer and fewer resources to spare either for the Netherlands or for engaging with France. Indeed, the annual injection of monies sent to Brussels more than halved between 1639-43, and the subsidy to the Germans shrank with it. Considering the chronic neglect of that army, it is hardly surprising in retrospect that when a bankrupt Brussels sent out its army under de Melo in spring 1643, that the campaign was an utter disaster.[10]

Upon learning of the disaster at Rocroi, Spanish officials did not hide their sense of dread. While certainly not the triumphant, all-conquering victory which Condé and French propagandists would later claim – to the extent that the later Battle of Tuttlingen was effectively forgotten – Rocroi was critically important for one major reason.[11] If Rocroi had been a defeat of the French, then this ill-omen, coming a few days removed from the death of the King, could have been a catastrophe. According to Don Luis de Haro, Olivares' nephew and successor as Spanish favourite, Rocroi was 'Something which can never be called to mind without great sorrow' since it was 'a defeat which is giving rise in all parts to the consequences which we always feared.' Notwithstanding the historical debate surrounding Rocroi, one could thus argue that the loss was painfully felt in Madrid, and it added additional urgency to the cause of peace-making.[12] Regarding said debate on Rocroi, the historian David Parrott in his analysis of Richelieu's impact upon the army of France provides a perceptive evaluation of the significance of Rocroi, writing:

> The traditional argument that Rocroi first broke the myth of the invincibility of the Spanish tercios is not supported by a detailed overview of the period after 1635, where numerous examples were seen of Spanish armies going down to defeat at the hands of French opponents. The wider significance of Rocroi is also open to question, especially given the obvious circumstance that the battle occurred as a result of a Spanish invasion of France, not because of a French advance into the Spanish Netherlands. A Spanish victory at Rocroi, occurring in the context of a royal minority and uncertainty about the nature of the French governmental regime after the deaths of both Richelieu and Louis XIII, would have been more disastrous for France than the heavy loss of veteran infantry which was the main consequence for Spain of her defeat...There was no decisive French breakthrough in Italy or in Catalonia, though both received increased allocations of troops and funding through the mid-1640s...Even in the Empire, military progress was halted for a campaign after the setback of late 1643, when the army of Germany was surprised during the winter quarters and virtually destroyed at Tuttlingen. Only from 1645 was there evidence of real movement towards military/political objectives in this theatre.[13]

With the uninspiring returns from Rocroi, an empowered Mazarin determined to send representatives to the unfolding congress in Westphalia in time for spring 1644. He had delayed doing so throughout 1643, in the hope that military victories might improve the French negotiating position – a tactic which was to be used repeatedly over the next five years. With a lapsed German front, some gains made on the Pyrenean front at Roussillon, and his new regime to secure, Mazarin had a lot of his plate throughout the latter half of 1643, even without delegating responsibilities to French plenipotentiaries at Osnabruck and Münster. 'To a gentleman, any country is his homeland' was the famous remark Mazarin made in 1637, and he certainly lived that philosophy. Mazarin would spend the next two decades importing all manner of Italian influences to Paris, including its religious orders and opera singers. In short, the former Mazzarini was content to make himself at home, and his improving relationship with Queen Anne, rumoured to have been quite scandalously intimate, only aided his rise.[14]

Both Anne and Mazarin were outsiders in France; in fact, both had been born as subjects of Spain, before transferring their allegiance thereafter to the French Crown. In this respect, they held their origins in common, but that was where the similarities ended. Anne, at 42-years-old, was only nine months older than Mazarin, yet she pursued very different interests after her husband's death, mostly in the religious sphere, but above all in taking care of her son. In Mazarin, she found the ideal partner; Mazarin was not just the godfather of the young Louis XIV, he was also charged with the boy-king's education, and thus maintained an iron grip on his life until Louis came of age.[15]

Mazarin had left his native Rome behind for greater opportunities in France, and while he had risen high, he could not leave Rome or the Papacy firmly behind him. The mid-1640's were a turbulent time for said Papacy, and at a time when Europe truly needed a sincere mediator, this was particularly unfortunate. Yet, it had been made clear long before to Pope Urban VIII that nobody trusted him to be impartial, and though he was nominally a French Papal candidate, Urban was dismayed by consistent French intervention in Italy, beginning with the Mantuan wars and only escalating after 1635.[16]

But Urban did himself no favours; he took the opportunity in October 1641 to attack the small duchy of Castro. This provoked a war with the surrounding Italian powers, including Venice and Tuscany, who counterattacked the following autumn. As King Louis marched towards Roussillon, the Pope's forces were fighting their Italian brethren in bloody skirmishes, and Urban sacrificed his reputation on the battlefield as well as in the realm of mediation. Neither Urban's fortifications nor his impressive army of twenty thousand men proved sufficient for the task of resisting the combined might of his Italian foes.[17] One could hardly trust a figure who was so blatantly opportunistic and consumed by power politics, but upon Urban's death in July 1644, the situation became more urgent for Mazarin. As plague wracked Rome during the sweltering summer, and the Papal conclave met to elect a new leader, the Spanish managed, against Mazarin's expectations, to emerge successful from the contest. Pope Innocent X was Spain's candidate for Pope, and Mazarin could thus expect little in the way of sympathy or aid from his former home.

All this was to come for Mazarin in late 1643, but he was fortunate that the organisation and administration of France was beginning to tell. In the face of the forty-five thousand civil servants spread over innumerable judicial and financial departments, Spain had few answers. Mazarin effectively made a gamble in late 1643 then; he gambled that, expensive and painful though the war with Spain was bound to be, if pressure was maintained in all the vulnerable regions, Spain could be forced to make an unfavourable peace before the excesses of taxation on the French people became too much to bear. In other words, Mazarin bargained that Spain would be defeated before France collapsed in revolt; in fact, history would show that in the next sixteen years of war between France and Spain, revolts erupted on both sides, only for France still to pull ahead of its rival by the time a peace was made in 1659. Of course, this victory was not without a price. Richelieu, who was never fully versed in economic matters, still greatly feared the prospect of the people rising up in protest against increased taxes or greater governmental interference.[18] Near the end of his life in August 1642, Richelieu still took the time to opine:

> I have to say that I do not understand why you do not give more thought to the consequences of the decisions you take in the council of finance. It is easy to prevent misfortunes, even the worst, but when they strike, no remedy can be found...If the council of finance continues to allow the tax farmers and financiers full liberty to threat His Majesty's subjects according to their insatiable appetites, certainly France will fall victim to some disorder similar to that which has befallen Spain...By wishing to have too much we will create a situation where we shall have nothing at all.[19]

Due to his decision to take that gamble though, Mazarin neglected to heed his predecessor's advice. This was most visible in Mazarin's decision to farm out France's most important tax, *the taille*, to private financiers. The *taille* was a direct tax based on property, but it was particularly oppressive on the peasantry, who bore the greatest proportion of the burden. When collected by the government, the *taille* could be organised and calculated appropriately, its officers pay deducted from their takings. When privatised however, Mazarin did nothing less than create a class of men who engorged themselves on wealth and owed no loyalty to anyone. The full details of the disaster are not worth investigating, but it should be noted that the policy soured relations between the French people and the court, where Mazarin soon became infamous as the greedy foreign corrupter violating the sanctity of the French royal family.[20] By 1648, traditionally seen as a year of peace, these sentiments would erupt in a revolt known as the Frondes, which drew in countless citizens and civil servants, but also more distinguished men like Condé.[21]

Perhaps Mazarin's personal style was partially to blame? In contrast to Richelieu, Mazarin was privately warm and friendly, but utterly ruthless in the diplomatic sphere. He tended to pursue a policy which was governed less by principles and bound by the French interest. To Richelieu, this interest had revolved around the idea of creating leagues in Germany and Italy which France could influence directly. Mazarin allowed that idea to slip, instead pursuing power politics based on the familiar concept of territorial expansion. The more land France seized at the peace table, the more secure her realm would be in peacetime. There was reason enough to justify this logic; after all, France had been surrounded in previous years by Spanish possessions on virtually all its flanks save the Atlantic coast. By undermining Spanish authority in the Spanish Netherlands, Franche-Comte, Alsace, Lorraine and Italy, France would be much more secure along her borders.

Mazarin's goals loomed into view in the early years of the Westphalian congress. Mazarin's regime had built upon Richelieu's old policy, and like Richelieu, Mazarin believed Alsace could be and should be taken, but that Catalonia should be bargained away. Mazarin remained true to Richelieu's legacy in that he maintained the alliances with the Dutch and Swedes, but in the case of the former, he seems to have been somewhat tone deaf to Dutch concerns. From 1642, when the prospects for a Spanish reconquest of the Dutch Republic was effectively nil, the Dutch army was reduced in size. This reflected a feeling of exhaustion on the part of the regents, the wealthy merchant class, who chafed under the military leadership and incessant demands of Frederick Henry. The presence of a peace and war party in the Republic was nothing new, but Mazarin did not prove as sensitive to their existence as Richelieu had done. Instead, Richelieu's successor succeeded in offending Dutch sensibilities by intimating only a total victory in Flanders would suffice and requesting much more from the Dutch in military aid than Richelieu had ever asked for.

Mazarin also differed from Richelieu in his pursuit of that supposedly uniform goal of the late Cardinal – a universal peace. This was the idea that by making peace with all powers instead of each power piecemeal, the actual peace treaty would be a great deal more secure and long-lasting. Mazarin professed a belief in this concept, yet he took pleasure in threatening the Spanish that they would be excluded from the final Westphalian peace treaty, and a quick examination of what happened post-Westphalia shows that this threat was made good, with France and Spain only making peace in 1659. In respect to his other ally, the Swedes, Mazarin was more in tune with his vision for a universal peace. A running theme of the conference was to be the fear in Paris and in Stockholm that some dirty trick would be pulled to divide the two allies. These fears were fanned by Imperial, Spanish and Bavarian intrigues, but they never bore significant fruit. Mazarin was only genuinely interested in investment where there was a chance of a reasonable rate of return, and, surprisingly considering his origins, he was of the opinion that Italy was not such a place. He wrote to the French plenipotentiaries in 1644:

> It is next to impossible that the arms of the King can make any considerable progress in Italy...the next campaign will be the tenth since the declaration of war, yet we are still starting on the State of Milan, the places of which are so well fortified...that even supposing all prosperity for our arms, it would be a great deal to capture one every year, with enormous expense.[22]

This Italian perspective was likely inculcated in Mazarin further by the troubles with the Papacy in the early 1640's, and the arrival of a Spanish candidate as Pope. Following that development, Mazarin likely perceived that there were even fewer chances of success in Italy than ever before.

As we will see though, this did not prevent him from making further use of Spanish difficulties in the peninsula later in the decade.[23] Although his to-do list remained consistently long, diplomacy was Mazarin's overriding concern, and he thus took the time to delegate responsibility for other matters, such as finance and war, when he came into more power and money. These appointments, of men such as Le Tellier and the Colbert family, were to prove highly significant for France, as these families remained in power once Louis XIV came to his majority.[24]

France and Spain were not the only theatres to experience a change in leadership in 1643. Following the disaster of the previous year, Emperor Ferdinand delicately dismissed his brother Leopold William from the command of the main Imperial army in Germany, and replaced him with the long-serving Matthias Gallas, a veteran of Wallenstein's, but also, by 1643, an irredeemable alcoholic. Ferdinand was too desperate to care, but his subsequent efforts to rescue the Habsburg military situation in 1643 demonstrated that all was not yet lost. For one, the manpower pool remained impressive; Franz von Mercy commanded over twenty-two thousand Bavarians; in Cologne under Melchior von Hatzfeldt was another fifteen thousand, and Gallas had thirty-two thousand.

Were these armies to combine, a formidable, Swede-beating force might be created, but the troubles presented by the different fronts meant that this was, for the moment at least, impossible. Von Mercy was defending Bavaria and the middle Rhine against the French; the army in Cologne under Hatzfeldt was to guard against the Hessians, this left Gallas with the main army, and there was no mistaking his mission in 1643.[25] Little did Gallas know that while he had been given his orders, Torstenson had been given new orders of his own, and once the holes had been plugged and Sweden's defensive positions in Germany secured, these orders resembled nothing less than a retreat, in secret, back to Sweden. Chancellor Oxenstierna, it transpired, had eyed up a new target which was dearer to his heart and closer to home than those German outposts: Denmark.

TWO

Torstenson's War

On 5 June 1643, Chancellor Axel Oxenstierna wrote a letter to Lennart Torstenson, his commander in Germany, with a stark instruction. The Swedish commander must return to Sweden, and prepare for a war against Denmark, and he should ensure that Swedish interests in Germany were secure before he did so. Oxenstierna did not receive this letter until early October, but when he did, he may well have wished that he had never read it at all. After all, Torstenson could claim, Sweden was finally making some genuine progress against its Imperial enemies, and in the last year Torstenson had carved out a base for himself from Silesia and Moravia, placing him in the Habsburg's backyard. Facing him was Matthias Gallas, no doubt a competent soldier, leading capable officers, but plagued by rampant alcoholism which left him blind drunk on several occasions, and his army rudderless. Considering the circumstances, the moment seemed ideal to maintain the pressure, and plot new initiatives in the campaigning season of 1644. Here, though, was the Chancellor telling Torstenson that there was to be a change of plan. Whatever hesitation or irritation Torstenson may have exuded, these sentiments did not prevent him from obeying the veteran Chancellor. On 13 November 1643, Torstenson began his march from Upper Silesia across Brandenburg. The first stage of the war against Denmark had been set in motion.[26]

One might have asked why Oxenstierna believed that the conflict was necessary in the first place. Certainly, a panicked King Christian IV of Denmark would have wondered this when he learned that the Jutland Peninsula had been totally overrun for the second time in his reign, in January 1644. In fact, while Oxenstierna's decision might appear like a bolt from the blue, the act had been in the pipeline for some time. It was, in many respects, a continuation of the war which had come to an end in 1613. That conflict had been one of three which Gustavus Adolphus had inherited from his father, and ending it cost Sweden a million thalers, not to mention possession of Gothenburg, the island of Osel in the Baltic and recognition of Danish supremacy in the Baltic

Sea.[27] Thirty years later, Oxenstierna had not forgotten that defeat, but he had also watched as Denmark suffered a catastrophe of her own, with Wallenstein surging up the Jutland Peninsula in the late 1620s. The emergency which followed prompted Gustavus to move closer to his Danish foe, but this had not led to more amicable relations between the Scandinavian foes, especially when Gustavus defied all expectations and established a German bridgehead for Sweden.

But Christian had not sat still either. By 1631 he had settled his debts from the war with the Emperor, and moved closer to the Habsburgs, confirming his sons' possessions of the bishoprics of Bremen and Verden, just south of the Danish border. Thereafter, Christian tried to pose as mediator, intervening repeatedly as the Treaty of Hamburg was drawn up, and eventually signed in late 1641. This treaty stipulated the form which the Westphalian negotiations were to take, and Christian placed ten thousand men on the border to show he was serious. Indeed, his army had been allowed to grow even under the restrictions of the Danish royal council. By 1642 Christian could boast an army of more than twenty-two thousand militia, buoyed by a professional army of eleven thousand, an alliance with the neighbouring duke of Holstein, and a navy composed of thirty-five heavy warships.

This was a powerful force, and could make a difference if thrown into the balance against Sweden at a critical time, but even had he wanted to, Christian learned that after he had fired his best shot against the Emperor in the 1620s, a great deal of his freedom had been taken away. He was virtually forbidden from engaging in foreign wars without the prior approval of the Danish royal council, and it was this restriction that compelled the Imperial delegate to retire from Denmark in disgust by late 1641, having worked up to that point to bring Denmark into the war against Sweden and on the Emperor's side. Thus, Christian's army could only serve a defensive purpose, and by that logic, it was of no direct threat to Sweden. To Oxenstierna though, Denmark's military threat was less potent than the real impact her King could make on the peace negotiations as a mediator. For this reason, above all, the Swedish Chancellor believed Denmark needed to be stopped.[28]

Contrary to what he may have told his contemporaries, King Christian was not seeking to mediate out of the goodness of his heart. It was within his interest to intervene in the peace negotiations, because it granted him the chance to block Swedish possession of Pomerania. Sweden's expansion into Pomerania would grant her unrivalled control over the Baltic coast and would guarantee her a permanent seat in German affairs. But that was not all. Christian had been diplomatically active, sending embassies to Madrid, to Warsaw, to Moscow and to Paris, seeking support for his stance, and promising Danish rewards. Keeping these manoeuvres secret was impossible, but what Christian had managed to keep secret was just how miserably all of these initiatives had failed. Denmark was no closer to obtaining a foreign alliance in 1643 than it had been in 1635, when Sweden's position was most desperate.

The Emperor, who we may view as Christian's most natural ally, had been prevented from bringing Denmark into the war by Christian's royal council, but Christian had additional problems with cosying up to the Habsburg bloc. Christian was one of many figures who wanted the Palatinate restored to its pre-war status; he wanted control over several port tolls confirmed, and he wanted amnesty for Protestant German powers who might side with him against Sweden. And further problems had abounded with the Polish and Russian contacts. King Wladyslaw of Poland wanted Pomerania for himself, and the proposed marriage contract with Tsar Michael's daughter fell apart over disagreements regarding the religion of the ceremony and marriage itself. Christian had kept these failures quiet, but he had initiated them loudly, and the presence of his mediators at Westphalia was a further source of resentment and suspicion in Stockholm.

These slights were added to the tally of wrongdoing, but Oxenstierna could add a few more. The Sound, that passage which connected the Baltic to the North Sea, was monopolised by Denmark thanks to the accidents of geography, but Christian's aggressive squeezing of the tolls from the Sound had been no accident. The tolls themselves was not punishingly high, but the methods which Danish officers used generally were, and Christian continued to rankle Swedish opinion by claiming sovereignty over all of the Sound. The lucrative waterway was a part of his dominion as much as the Jutland peninsula and the Danish islands of Funen and Zealand, Christian claimed, and he alone was entitled to make use of it as he pleased.

By early 1643, these slights and threats to Swedish interests had accumulated sufficiently to persuade the Swedish Riksdag that the time had come to urge Oxenstierna to press for war with Denmark. Denmark's disingenuous mediation, her contacts with Sweden's rivals, her growing power and her offensive pursuance of the King's Sound entitlements were believed to be sufficient grounds for war.[29] To this was added a shot which Christian had fired across the bow of the Swedish royal family. Maria Eleanora of Brandenburg, the widow of Gustavus Adolphus, had become a source of some embarrassment and difficulty for the Swedish Chancellor and the regency government by 1640. When one of her letters was intercepted, and indicated a desire to improve relations with Denmark, Eleanora was effectively imprisoned.

Her captors evidently did not expect a frail and bothersome widow to be capable of escape from such a fortress, but escape she did in late July 1640, and she made her way to Denmark, where Christian IV was only too happy to house her, at least for a time. Scurrilous rumours even did the rounds that

Eleanora was in love with the 64-year-old Danish King! One can imagine the scandal and sense of shame that the event ingrained in Sweden, as King Christian could claim to have gotten one over on his rival even in death. Eleanora's Danish holiday lasted little more than a couple of years, before she moved home to Brandenburg and then back to Stockholm by 1648, but the incident had aroused even more hostility towards Christian, and this slight was included in the memorandum which announced Sweden's declaration of war in late January 1644, when the conflict was already a month old. Christian's decision to provide a Danish vessel for Eleanora's escape in the midsummer of 1640 was felt to be particularly insulting, and it certainly did Christian no favours in the long run.[30]

With their justification for war in hand, the true dilemma for Oxenstierna and the Swedish magnates was the fact that Sweden was already at war with, and heavily involved in, Germany. Could she manage a war on two fronts? Certainly not, if new campaigns were to be launched simultaneously. Some Swedish counsellors wished to establish alliances against Denmark, perhaps out of the pool of German princes that lived south of the Danish border. Others, led by Oxenstierna, emphasised the power of the surprise attack. And it certainly was a surprise – as Oxenstierna had added Christian's slights to the ledger, the Danish King carried on oblivious to the damage and resentment he had caused. The customary meeting of the Danish and Swedish monarchs in some border town was what Christian would have expected, if a war was to be proclaimed, but by the summer of 1643, Oxenstierna had planned to do away with such traditions.

The surprise was doubled thanks to Oxenstierna's decision to campaign in winter. This decision was taken due to logistical necessity as much as out of a desire to maintain the element of surprise. The war in Germany would effectively be on hold, as Gallas' men lay in winter quarters, and the Danes would in no sense expect an invasion of their lands during the winter, even if they had known that a Swedish force led by Torstenson was on its way. With these bases prepared, it still could not be denied that Oxenstierna and Torstenson were taking an immense risk. What would happen in the spring of 1644, when Christian realised what was happening, and called on the Emperor to aid him? Surely Gallas would have an easy time of it, and would capitalise upon Sweden's distraction by undoing all of Torstenson's gains of the last two years. Oxenstierna hoped it would not come to that, that Torstenson's defences would hold, and that Denmark could be crippled in record time, before the weight of an Imperial counterattack could tell. On 22 December 1643, to the utter surprise of Christian and his subjects, Torstenson crossed the border into Denmark, and began to advance up the Jutland Peninsula. Torstenson's War had begun.[31]

When Torstenson had informed his army of sixteen thousand where they were headed, he was faced with several protests. Many of these men were Germans and claimed they had not signed up to fight outside the Empire in Swedish service. This was a private war between Scandinavian powers, and they said they wanted no part in it. Torstenson tactfully appeased them by reminding them of an important fact – the Jutland Peninsula had been untouched since 1629, and was therefore likely to produce much healthier returns from looting than the aching lands they had been marching across since the mid-1630's. By crossing into Holstein on 22 December, Torstenson bullied its Duke into neutrality, which left Christian further isolated. It must have been an anxious Christmas season for the Danish King, made worse by the lack of clarity for the first month of the conflict. Torstenson had crossed into Danish lands as though he was a neutral party seeking quarters for his men, and the act had been so unexpected that the Swedish commander was not greeted by a Danish army, but by a Danish trumpeter, who asked Torstenson to explain himself. Torstenson delayed his answer for another month.

The formal declaration of war was not sent out until 28 January 1644, by which time Torstenson had more than capitalised on the rank confusion of his foe. The aggression and speed of the invader was eerily reminiscent of Wallenstein's advance up the peninsula, and like they had done fifteen years before, those Danes that could escape moved quickly either to the Danish islands or nearby German lands. Christian's army resided largely in those bishoprics maintained by his sons, and it would take a while to rally the ten thousand men there to defend the Danish homeland.[32] Having outmanoeuvred his foe, Torstenson effectively had the run of the peninsula, and surged through it, surprising even Oxenstierna, who contemplated conquering Denmark outright.[33]

As Danish defences were reeling, Oxenstierna revealed his trump card, and an army of ten thousand conscripts invaded the Danish province of Scania, in modern-day southern Sweden. This army was under the command of Gustav Horn, a veteran of the battles of Breitenfeld and Nordlingen, and a prisoner of the Imperials until his release in 1642. The move was a bold one, and if successful, would grant Sweden unfettered access to the Baltic by bypassing the Sound entirely. Danish possession of this Swedish land had been instrumental in insulating the Sound and protecting it from Swedish attack, but Horn's invasion in that direction in February 1644 demonstrated that Oxenstierna was not fighting simply to give Christian a bloody nose, but to overturn utterly the very balance of power within the Baltic. How could the aged Danish King respond to these successive attacks on his realm? After having left his kingdom in such a disadvantageous position, Christian sought redemption on the battlefield.

The initial acts of the war had been overwhelming and impressive, but by the time Gustav Horn's invasion stalled in the face of the resistance posed by a hastily rallied eight thousand Scanian militia, Oxenstierna may have begun to worry. The problem was logistical as much as geographic; Torstenson commanded the experienced veterans of the war, but he could do little now that the Jutland Peninsula was occupied. With the weather unseasonably warm, the crossings in between the Danish islands of Funen and Zealand had not frozen, and until naval supremacy could be brought to bear, Copenhagen could not be threatened. The mercies of geography had come to Christian's rescue, just as they had in the late 1620's, when a frustrated Wallenstein was able to go no further without a navy. The main front having stagnated, Gustav Horn was learning that his conscripts were more trouble than they were worth. They seemed more interested in plunder than in victory, and desertion also plagued his force. Horn was informed that, far from buckling under the invasion in Scania, counterattacks across the border into Swedish territory had been made by the Danes, and Oxenstierna had not accounted for this.

In the months before the invasion, Oxenstierna had instructed Sweden's agent in the Netherlands, Louis de Geer, to enlist a fleet of Dutch ships. The Dutch had also felt slighted by Danish monopolies over the Sound, and by Christian's heavy-handed exactions. As the masters of the Baltic entrepot trade, they could not allow their mercantile interests to be so undermined. They thus proved receptive to de Geer's requests for ships, but if Oxenstierna had hoped for the Dutch navy to rescue his lagging campaign, then he was to be disappointed. At Gothenburg, Sweden's old base on the Baltic Sea, wedged in between Norway and Scania, and sacked by Christian in 1612, a Danish fleet under King Christian IV himself sailed. The Swedish fleet and their smaller Dutch auxiliaries were defeated in July, only for Karl Gustav Wrangel, a new commander of some renown, to lead the Swedish navy to safety. Later in the month, in the inconclusive battle of Kolberger Heide off the coast of Holstein, King Christian got up close and personal with the battle, as a shell exploded on the deck of his ship, knocking him down and inflicting a reported twenty-three wounds on the aged King.

To the surprise of everyone, likely including himself, Christian bounced back to his feet, proclaiming that 'God has left me life and strength enough to fight for my people, so long as each will do his duty'. It was then that onlookers observed the King's right eye was missing.[34] The scene was immortalised by the Danish painter Vilhelm Nikolai Marstrand, who depicted the aged King standing in the centre of the scene of his flagship *Trinity*, with his right hand placed firmly on a sabre, which is stuck in the ground, and his left hand raised. A bandage covers the king's right eye, but his entourage are plainly impressed, as they take the time to raise their hats to their King and his bravery. The scene is obviously imagined and made much more glamorous than the awful conditions of battle would have allowed, but nonetheless, it provides a window into one of many incredible moments which the Thirty Years War produced.[35]

Notwithstanding the heroism and bravery of the Danish King, his stand did not represent the turning of the tide against Sweden, though the Danish home islands were saved from attack. It was in October 1644, at the battle of Fehmarn, that Sweden's navy surprised and then decisively defeated its Danish counterpart. Fehmarn had been a great relief to Oxenstierna because it granted Sweden the naval supremacy it needed to pursue the war on land against the Danish islands. But this optimism was short-lived, as it transpired that the Danish fleet remained a force to be reckoned with, and the route to Copenhagen was not clear.[36] In addition to these problems, by autumn 1644, the Danish King was no longer fighting alone; Emperor Ferdinand, as many Swedish counsellors had feared, sent eighteen thousand men Sweden's way to capitalise on the distraction, and rescue a potential Habsburg ally. Rather than besieging Copenhagen, or some other ambitious scheme, Oxenstierna would have to move Swedish forces to Pomerania or Mecklenburg, where they could be used to block the arrival of Matthias Gallas.[37]

The victory at Fehmarn had come just as Oxenstierna's strategy seemed to be falling apart. Swedish forces under Gustav Horn had been evicted from Scania; Norwegian counterattacks had poured across the border in the middle of Sweden, and Torstenson's army was in danger of being cut off altogether in the Jutland Peninsula. All eyes now moved to what Gallas would do, and whether he could cut Sweden off or launch some manoeuvre which would destroy Sweden's options. A more capable commander might have done so, but unfortunately for Christian, and fortunately for Oxenstierna, Matthias Gallas was no longer a capable commander. An alcoholic, Gallas happened to be blind drunk at the very moment when a tactician's mind was needed. His folly enabled Torstenson to move around him, and to unite with the Hessians and his subordinate Konigsmarck, who provided another five thousand men. Now outnumbered, Gallas elected to retreat back across the Elbe from the way they had come. Torstenson's soldiers pursued them all the way, until Gallas' army had collapsed along with his reputation. By the time he reached the Saxon town of Wittenberg far to the south-east, in December 1644, Gallas' army which had originally contained eighteen thousand men had been whittled down to just three thousand. Gallas obtained the unflattering epithet 'army wrecker' from his own soldiers, and he was relieved of command in late January 1645.

Had a more capable commander been at the helm, Oxenstierna's master plan could have landed Sweden in ruin. With Gallas' exit and no external threat to his position, Torstenson recouped his gains from the previous year, and hit at Christian where it hurt him most – his sons' inheritance, in the bishoprics of Verden and Bremen, which the Emperor had guaranteed to him in the Peace of Prague. The archbishoprics were all occupied by the spring of 1645, Holstein was detached from Denmark, and it was reported that Danish officials were no longer in a position to enforce the Sound tolls.[38] The middle portion of the story had been touch and go, but Oxenstierna had persevered, and the returns from a short sharp war with Denmark which he had envisioned had been wrested from the wounded Christian's hands. Sweden had made its point, with devastating consequences for the balance of power in the Baltic, and now it was time to make peace.[39]

The peace negotiations between Sweden and Denmark were something of a curious, if necessary, distraction from what were meant to have been the main peace negotiations at Westphalia. Predictably, it was impossible to consider a peace for the Thirty Years War when one of its major combatants was invested elsewhere. The French and the Dutch, as Sweden's allies in the struggle, had both reacted to the war differently. Mazarin had watched with alarm and irritation as it seemed Sweden was wasting its French subsidies on a hair-brained scheme, which very nearly backfired. The secret war against Denmark also left French forces alone to face the might of the Emperor and his German allies.

Yet, this irritation and apprehension could not last, especially since Mazarin wished to play a role in the peace which would follow. The Dutch perspective was more straightforward, and was aimed at undercutting the Danish Sound tolls, which had risen during the 1630s to Dutch irritation. After sailing through the Sound in July 1645, paying no tolls, it seemed apparent that this Dutch aim, at least, had been achieved. Neither France nor the Dutch wished to see Sweden replace Denmark in the Baltic, instead they wanted to leave the region divided, though with Sweden the clear benefactor. It was a delicate balance to maintain, but it essentially meant the protection of Danish independence...just about.[40]

The Peace of Bromsebro was facilitated by the Franco-Dutch mediators, and it was signed in mid-August 1645. The treaty was an unmitigated disaster for Christian and confirmed his worst fears about the extent to which the Baltic balance of power had shifted against him. As Michael Bregnsbo wrote: 'The Danish position as the leading power in the Baltic region and a middle-sized European power had come to an end. From then on, Denmark was unable to secure her own independence without the support of other powers.'[41] It is difficult to contest this claim. In the Scandinavian theatre, Denmark lost the Baltic islands of Gotland and Osel; she ceded the province of Halland on Sweden's south-western coast, granting Sweden a secure route to the North Sea in the process, and a slice of Norway was handed over, fattening the middle part of Sweden's land border with Norway and providing for greater security. It was in Germany that Christian was most seriously stung though, as his sons' archbishoprics were seized from him and granted to Sweden. On top of all of this, Christian promised to abandon his earlier commitment to serve as mediator. The aged Danish King, notwithstanding his heroic war wounds, withdrew from European affairs, and he died just before the Peace of Westphalia could be reached, in early 1648.[42]

Torstenson's War, as it would come to be known, was in some respects a close-run thing, but it had proved in the end a worthwhile distraction from the war in Germany, and a lucrative venture for Oxenstierna. Swedish prestige and income had been greatly inflated by the short conflict, while all efforts on the Emperor's side to arrange a lasting alliance between Denmark and Vienna had failed, tripping up, interestingly, on the same issue which had delayed the conclusion of a proper Franco-Swedish alliance for so long – the question of making peace. Ferdinand wanted Christian to pledge that he would remain in the war until the Emperor exited it, but the desperate, war-weary Danish King was keen to reach peace at any price.[43]

By the time peace was reached, Christian had a royal counterpart in Stockholm who was the opposite to him in virtually every sense, and not merely because she was Sweden's solitary Queen. Queen Christina came of age in November 1644, and from that point, wasted no time receiving communications from Oxenstierna, and advising where possible. She took care of the kingdom from February 1645 while Oxenstierna moved off to negotiate the peace with Denmark in person, and during that time began to flex her royal muscles freely, having been under the control of a regency for thirteen long years.[44] Just as Queen Christina's remarkable career was beginning, Sweden's war with its old foes was coming to an end; just, indeed, as the full consequences of her father's triumphs echoed in Copenhagen, this martial Queen, every bit her father's daughter, came into her majority.[45] After such a triumphant display of power, Oxenstierna and Queen Christina both were now more prepared than ever to bring the war in Germany to its conclusion. The Emperor had missed his chance to gain sweet revenge upon the distracted Swedes, and he was rapidly running out of chances himself.

THREE
Maintaining Pressure

Cardinal Mazarin had no choice but to grin and bear it. French isolation in 1644 was compounded by the Swedish preoccupation with Denmark, which meant that, for arguably the first time, the two branches of the Habsburg family theoretically had free reign to engage with and pressure the French positions. Mazarin may have envisioned nightmarish scenarios where France was overrun across the Rhine and Pyrenees, but the reality was far less disastrous, if somewhat unglamorous. In March and April 1644, French plenipotentiaries began to arrive at Münster and Osnabruck, as the Westphalian conference began without Danish mediation or enthusiastic Imperial participation. Weakly, the Emperor had tried to stall his plenipotentiaries, in the hope that this would demonstrate to the Danes his desire to let King Christian serve nobly as a mediator.

Pandering to the Danish King's ambitions, Ferdinand may have believed, could induce Denmark to formulate an alliance with Austria, thereby improving the Imperial position. Yet, the prospects of success for this policy varied immensely from the beginning of 1644 to the end, when in the latter part of the year, the initially impressive Danish resistance was overcome all at once. King Christian had left an agent behind in Osnabruck to oversee matters, but by the autumn he accepted that meaningful peace negotiations could begin without him. Furthermore, Christian displayed a continued hostility towards any concept of alliance with the Emperor – he did not wish to tie Denmark's hands, and limit his freedom of action. By the end of 1644 indeed, Ferdinand's opportunities for coercing Denmark into the Imperial camp would be lost, and the one source of military aid which was sent – the drunk Gallas and his eighteen thousand men – were outmanoeuvred and outmatched by their Swedish counterparts. It was a double disaster, but neither Ferdinand nor the French had sat still while the Danish drama unfolded.[46]

'Presently', wrote one French official in early 1644, 'the only thing we can all desire is to conserve the kingdom in its entirety and also the alliances that the late king Louis XIII has contracted.' This wasn't a particularly optimistic aim, but neither Mazarin nor his officials seemed to be aiming particularly high as 1644 dawned. 1643 had been a mixed bag as far as the military sphere had been concerned; Rocroi was a great victory, built upon by the capture of several places in the summer that followed, but the disaster at Tuttlingen in late November had destroyed French progress, killed the veteran French commander, and empowered the Bavarians in the region.[47] It had been kept relatively quiet, and as a consequence, Rocroi is known today, whereas Tuttlingen is largely not, but Mazarin could not escape the facts even if he had made effective use of the propaganda devices of the period.[48]

In military terms then, news that Sweden would henceforth devote the majority of its power to launching a pre-emptive strike against its old enemy for the campaigning season of 1644 greeted Mazarin like a bomb. The exit of her main ally in Germany was the very last thing he needed, and he was unsurprisingly irritated that Torstenson and Oxenstierna had acted without first consulting him. In the negotiations which were unfolding at Westphalia, Mazarin was frustrated by the Emperor's stalling, and by July 1644 he had instructed French negotiators to threaten to leave if the Habsburgs did not proceed with meaningful dialogue. The Swedes were similarly bothered by the Habsburg stalling at Osnabruck. For much of the year, Ferdinand's agents argued that it was a question of precedence, a thorny question indeed, but by September 1644, meaningful negotiations were entered into as the military situation turned against Denmark.[49] In the context of the Westphalian negotiations then, which would drag on for another four years, 1644 is an important case not just because it provides us with a great example of how issues of precedence could slow negotiations down, but also because we see how the stance of the plenipotentiaries shifted as the military situation changed. This latter point was to become especially important as the years progressed.

And what was the military situation in 1644? It was similar in many respects to the previous years, save for the absence of Sweden, and the theoretical opportunity it granted to the Emperor and the King of Spain to bring their superiority in arms to bear. Yet, in many respects, this superiority was merely theoretical. Spain was wholly occupied in the Spanish Netherlands, and it was here where French and Dutch arms would have great opportunities for success. The war had been brought to Spanish soil, and Madrid remained locked into a dual conflict with Portugal in the west, and Catalonia in the north. The former was aided intermittently by the Dutch, and the latter provided the French with a new front across the Pyrenees where the Spanish could be attacked. The new French King, the six-year-old Louis XIV, had been proclaimed Count of Barcelona as his father had been, thus confirming that there would be no break in the French protection of Catalonia which the deaths of Richelieu and Louis XIII had suggested.

This was disastrous for Spain, since she was unable to pursue the war outside of her own lands so long as the French were secure in Barcelona, and the Portuguese threatened in the west. Almost inevitably, one sees the Spanish influence in Germany begin to buckle especially from 1643 onwards, as money from Madrid was spent on shoring up local positions, or prioritising the Italian possessions over even the Netherlandish ones.[50] Since the departure of Olivares in early 1643, King Philip IV had taken it upon himself to seize the reins of government, and to direct policy with an energy and determination that his grandfather Philip II would certainly have recognised and approved of. But it was to be of little use, even if Philip remained largely positive of the prospects of success, seeing all small mercies as evidence of God's favour and the promise of eventual deliverance from his enemies. At some point in early 1643, Philip came into contact with the mystic abbess Mary of Jesus of Ágreda, confessing his sins and writing to her frequently for the next two decades of his life. Philip's piety and faith have thus provided us with a treasure trove of communications, where the Spanish King's innermost thoughts were often revealed to the so-called Lady in Blue.[51] In one particularly length letter, written in October 1644, Philip wrote:

> I write to you leaving a half margin, so that your reply may come on the same paper, and I enjoin and command you not to allow the contents of this to be communicated to anyone. Since the day that I was with you I have felt much encouraged by your promise to pray to God for me, and for the success of my realm; for the earnest attachment towards my well-being that I then recognised in you gave me great confidence and encouragement. As I told you, I left Madrid lacking all human resources, and trusting only to divine help, which is the sole way to obtain what we desire. Our Lord has already begun to work in my favour, bringing in the silver fleet, and relieving Oran [in Algiers] when we least expected it; whereby I have been able, though with infinite tardiness for want of money, to dispose my forces here so that we shall, I hope, start work with them this week. Although I beseech God and His most holy Mother to succour and aid us, I trust very little in myself; for I have offended and still offend very much, and I justly deserve the punishments and afflictions which I suffer. And so I appeal to you to fulfil your promise to me, to clamour to God to guide my actions and my arms to the end that the quietude of these realms may be secured, and peace may reign throughout Christendom. The Portuguese rebels still raid the frontiers of Portugal, acting against God and their natural sovereign. Affairs in Flanders are in great extremity, and there is risk of a rising unless God will intervene in my favour; and though affairs in Aragon have somewhat improved with my presence, I fear that unless we can gain some successes to encourage people here they are liable to lose heart and to take a course very injurious to the monarchy. The necessities, of course, are numerous and great; but I must confess that it is not that which distresses me most, but the certain conviction that they all arise from my having offended Our Lord. As He knows, I earnestly wish to please Him and to fulfil my duty

in all things; and I desire that, if by any means you arrive at a knowledge of what it is His holy will that I should do to placate Him, you will write to me here, for I am very anxious to do right, and I do not know in what I err. Some religious people give me to understand that they have revelations; and that God commands that I should punish certain persons, and that I should dismiss others from my service. But you know very well that in this matter of revelations one must be very careful, and particularly when these religious persons speak against those who are not really bad, and against whom I have never discovered anything injurious to me; whilst others are approved who are not usually well thought about. The general opinion about these persons is that they love turning things over and that their truth cannot be depended upon. I do hope that you will keep your word to me and will speak with all frankness as to a confessor, for we kings have much of the confessor in us. Do not let yourself be influenced by what the world says, for that is little to be depended upon, seeing the aims of those who move such discourse; but be guided solely by the inspiration of God, before whom I protest (and I have lately partaken of Him, in the Sacrament) that I desire in all things, and for all things, to fulfil His sacred law and the obligation He has laid upon me as a King. And I hope in His mercy that He will take pity on our pains and help us out of those afflictions. The greatest favour that I can receive from His holy hands is that the punishment He lays upon these realms may be laid upon me; for it is I and not they who deserve the punishment, for they have always been true and firm Catholics. I hope you will console me with your reply, and that I may have in you a true intercessor with Our Lord, that He may guide and enlighten me, and extricate me from the troubles in which I am now immersed. I the King. Saragossa, 4 October 1644.[52]

Such an incredible letter serves not only as a running commentary on the legion of woes which Philip IV faced, but also as a communication of his innermost fears and thoughts. He was a King who had done wrong, who had sinned many times against God, and Spanish disasters in the political and military sphere across his domains were what he perceived as his punishment. Desperate as he was to atone for these shortcomings, Philip begged Mary of Jesus to let him know urgently if she devised God's will and instructions for how he could make this situation right again. It is also little wonder that Philip wished Mary not to share any of these details with anyone, since as he bares his soul, Philip also reveals precisely how weak he truly felt his position to be – such an admission would have caused an unprecedented scandal in the proud, image-obsessed court of Madrid, and the confession of weakness could never become public knowledge. As Martin Hume perceived though, Philip's humility was intertwined with an unshakeable confidence that he was God's anointed, the Habsburg 'chosen one' who would lead Spain ever onward:

He was weak; he confesses to have no confidence in himself, although in his heart of hearts he is striving to live well and do his duty. He is unable to struggle successfully against the worldly pleasures that have captured him, and which he pursues still, whilst hating himself for doing so. Conscience haunted, he is the only sinner, and the terrible conviction forces itself upon him that his personal sins of omission and commission are to be visited in awful punishment upon whole nations of innocent people. His natural justice and his knowledge of men cause him to rebel against the suggestions that come to him, even under the cloak of religion, to punish those who in his eyes have done no ill; and behind the regal purple and the stately port of his great office we see the poor soul, so remorseful in the knowledge of its sin and insignificance as to feel unworthy even to pray without a poor nun's intercession to the appalling deity he thinks he has incensed. And yet, with all this humility, how the true Spaniard peeps out in the conviction that God has His eyes specially on *him*; how God's designs for the universe revolve around *his* fortunes, *his* acts, and *his* transgressions.[53]

But the world did not revolve around Philip IV of Spain. 'Affairs in Flanders are in great extremity' Philip had said, during the above letter, adding that 'there is risk of a rising unless God will intervene in my favour.' When he communicated these fears in October 1644, Frederick Henry was engaging in one of his final campaigns against the Spanish presence in the Netherlands. The town of Sas van Gent [or the sluice of Ghent] was captured in the late September of 1644, and with it, one of the most important river crossings of the River Scheldt was in Dutch hands. As one historian put it, Sas van Gent was the 'bulwark of Ghent and of Flanders, and gave to its possessors the command of one of the principal water-ways of the country.'[54] Thanks to the naval superiority of Admiral Martin Tromp, the hero of the Downs, the Dutch navy was able to snake its way along the Flanders coastline, aiding the French as they did so, and placing the beleaguered population of the Spanish Netherlands under unprecedented pressure.[55]

While on their way to Münster, the French delegates Abel Servien and Claude d'Avaux made a detour to The Hague, arriving there on 19 March 1644. While there a new arrangement between the French and Dutch was agreed, the last of its kind during the war, and the French negotiators worked to ensure that the Dutch would not leave the war without first consulting them. The end result was not quite what Mazarin had wanted though, as it permitted the Dutch and Spanish to negotiate separately in Münster, and only granted France the option of having a representative present during the talks – a French influence was not compulsory. In other words, if they managed to overcome their differences, it was possible that the Dutch could conclude a peace with Spain without French approval. As Abel Servien commented 'Their interests with the Spanish envoys can be solved in four days, and ours, which are composed of very important different points, are not even sketched out.' The French became obsessed with the idea that the Dutch would abandon them, while the Dutch became determined not to fight the Spanish for the sake of benefiting France.[56]

Included within the renewed alliance of March 1644 was a renewed commitment to partition the Spanish Netherlands in the event of the region being overrun by Franco-Dutch forces. Yet, it had become plain within the Dutch Republic that the erection of a common border with France would not be within the Dutch national interest. It would surely be better, then, to preserve Dutch gains, prop up the Spanish Netherlands as a buffer between France and the Netherlands, and maintain the French alliance. These were the aims which now motivated the peace party of the Dutch Republic,[57] and to a lesser extent, Frederick Henry, who led the war party. According to the French ambassador, the Dutch stadtholder was even heard to remark that French interests would be better served not by seizing all of Flanders, but by focusing its attentions more on Italy or Catalonia.[58] Coupled with this were new developments in Dutch policy, such as the keen desire to cling to Portuguese Brazil in any peace negotiations, and the concern in Holland that the Prince of Orange was acquiring too much power for himself.

Both of these concerns were reflected in the fact that the size of the Dutch army was actually reduced in 1642, from more than seventy thousand men to just under sixty thousand. It was a small reduction, but further efforts to reduce it in 1644 sent a message to Frederick Henry that the merchants and middle class who supported the war could not be relied upon forever,[59] especially now that the threat to national security posed by Spain – so apparently potent in the mid-1620s – had now vanished.[60] Nor was this all; the pervasive influence of the more intolerant Calvinist preachers in the Republic aroused much suspicion not only against Catholics, but also against Catholic France. One of the French negotiators, Claude d'Avaux, had not helped improve these sentiments when he made the admirably moderate, but strategically unwise, declaration to the State-General in late March 1644, to the effect that:

> The rigour which you use against them regarding the exercise of their religion, the strict prohibition of all religious assemblies, the covetousness of your commissioners and the scorn which they often show for those things which we hold most sacred, have caused some minds to become embittered. Would you win them back? Would you again join up this part of your state, which is now cleft from it? Would you make good citizens of them? Then soften the rigour of your edicts and ordinances. The names of Catholic and Hollander can go together. It is possible to be an enemy of the King of Spain without being a Protestant.[61]

Certainly, d'Avaux's master had provided good evidence for this latter point, as Catholic France continued to engage with Catholic Spain, largely across the Pyrenees in 1644, but also in the western portion of the Spanish Netherlands, where defences were traditionally weaker than they were along the border with the Dutch. Gaston d'Orléans, the rebellious brother of the late King, oversaw a campaign against the Spanish position in Flanders by seizing Gravelines in late July 1644, and Piccolomini, the Imperial general hired to salvage the situation there, could provide no answer. Impressive though the returns were for France, this campaign succeeded only to engender jealousy among the opponents of Frederick Henry.[62] One could be justified in wondering how the tottering Spanish regime in Flanders remained in place; a key reason was religious belief, and the fear among Catholics of the Spanish Netherlands that the increasingly hard-line Calvinist Contra-Remonstrants – who had done so much damage to common Dutch cooperation during the Twelve Years Truce period – would never grant them the right to worship freely. It would fair to assert then that a major opportunity for uniting the two Netherlands was lost in the early 1640s, as it had been lost the previous decade. Now, of course, there was the added wrinkle that where the Dutch were apparently unwilling to permit Catholic worship, the French certainly were.[63]

But the French had problems of greater urgency in 1644 than a desire to seize the Spanish Netherlands. 'We must hurt France' was how Maximillian of Bavaria described the goal of the Imperial cause in early 1644, during a conference at Passau. The plan was to send a mostly Bavarian army under the command of Franz von Mercy against Breisach, which had fallen in late 1638. Threatening this key French position would either compel the French to respond, whereupon von Mercy would defeat their army in the open, or Breisach would fall, and Bavaria would be secured. Confidence was high in the aftermath of Tuttlingen, which had shattered French confidence late in 1643, but it was also high because France was perceived to be at a distinct disadvantage with the Swedish war against Denmark. But Bavarian confidence was misplaced, as von Mercy began the campaign late, and was forced to besiege Freiburg before confronting Breisach. By the time he reached the latter in early August 1644, Condé, the victor of Rocroi, had arrived with reinforcements.[64]

By this point, Gallas was on his way northwards with an army of eighteen thousand. Any suggestion that the Emperor might sufficiently aid his Bavarian ally with an attack across the Upper Rhine was undone thanks to some deft diplomacy undertaken by Oxenstierna late in the previous year. Taking his cue from Gustavus Adolphus' negotiations with Muscovy in the previous decade, where the Tsar was entreated to attack the Polish King, therefore freeing Sweden to intervene in the Empire in 1630, here the Chancellor extended his feelers far to the east once more, this time to the Ottoman vassal of Transylvania. The partition of Hungary between the Habsburgs and Ottomans had left a royal Hungarian rump state for Vienna – through which the Crown of Hungary was claimed – but it also left two other states; occupied Hungary and the autonomous vassal of Transylvania. The Princes of Transylvania had intervened with great effect in the early phase of the Thirty Years War, and in spring 1644, thanks to secret negotiations undertaken by Swedish agents, Transylvanian Prince Georgy Racoczi was induced to invade once more.

The arrival of an army under Racoczi seriously hampered any immediate plans the Emperor might have had to jump quickly to Denmark's defence. The campaign which followed actually lasted only for half the year, as Racoczi found the newly Catholicised populace of Royal Hungary far less willing to join him than before. By June 1644, Racoczi had sued for peace, but the distraction had done its work, and occupied Imperial attention long enough to protect Torstenson's flank. He was ready for Gallas' army by the time it arrived, and the Transylvanian cameo meant that neither Sweden nor France suffered for their policies.[65] Furthermore, when Franz von Mercy's plan misfired, and after a bloody draw he failed to dislodge the French from Breisach, his battered army retreated in haste. Condé's army, in sufficient strength, went on to seize all manner of positions along the Main, including Philipsburg, Speyer, Mainz and Worms, the Rhinish heartland of the Empire, and a great cultural base.[66]

The French military position, in short, was greatly reinforced by the events of 1644. While there had been some disappointments, such as the replacement of Pope Urban VIII with the more Hispanophile Innocent X, sound military progress had been made in Flanders, along the Rhine and in Catalonia. The Spanish King continued to weaken, the agreement with the Dutch had been clarified, and French agents had arrived to begin the Westphalian negotiations. Further afield, Sweden's defeat of Denmark – made certain by the end of the year – could only serve as a boon to French fortunes, once the empowered Torstenson returned to focus solely on Germany.

In addition to these gains, French diplomacy had pinpointed Maximillian of Bavaria – the so-called soul of the Emperor's council – as the key to the German war. Much as Maximillian perceived the defeat of France as the key to a victory over Sweden, so too did Mazarin appreciate the central importance – in a strategic, political and economic sense – of Bavaria to the Emperor. The campaign which followed in 1644 demonstrated that Bavarian arms were not so potent as the victory at Tuttlingen had suggested. Yet, as French negotiators newly arrived in Münster understood, the battlefield was where the mettle of the foe would be tested, and any victories leveraged at the peace table.[67] As 1644 gave way to 1645, it was hoped that a turn in fortunes might present new opportunities in the already stuffed conference cities. Little did the French, Swedes, Bavarians, Habsburgs or anyone else know, following the stop-start year of 1644, precisely how important 1645 was destined to be.

Chapter 21 Notes

[1]Wilson, *Europe's Tragedy*, pp. 667-669.
[2]See Croxton, *Westphalia*, pp. 94-95.
[3]Richard Lodge, *Richelieu* (London: MacMillan, 1896), p. 219.
[4]C. V. Wedgwood, *Richelieu and the French Monarchy* (London: Hodder & Stoughton, 1949), pp. 193-194.
[5]Moote, *Louis XIII*, p. 244.
[6]Quoted in Croxton, *Westphalia*, p. 93.
[7]Parker, 'Why Did the Dutch Revolt Last Eighty Years?', p. 66.
[8]Geoffrey Treasure, *Richelieu and Mazarin*, p. 55.
[9]Hume, *The Court of Phillip IV: Spain in Decadence*, pp. 365-371.
[10]Parker, *Europe in Crisis*, pp. 265-266.
[11]See Wilson, *Europe's Tragedy*, p. 645.
[12]See Parker, Why Did the Dutch Revolt Last Eighty Years?', p. 67.
[13]Parrott, *Richelieu's Army*, pp. 162-163.
[14]See Parker, *Europe in Crisis*, pp. 270-271.
[15]Treasure, *Richelieu and Mazarin*, p. 12; Croxton, *Westphalia*, pp. 105-106.
[16]Wilson, *Europe's Tragedy*, p. 650.
[17]See W. Chandler Kirwin, *Powers Matchless: The Pontificate of Urban VIII, the Baldachin, and Gian Lorenzo Bernini* (New York: Peter Lang, 1997), pp. 74-77.
[18]Treasure, *Richelieu and Mazarin*, pp. 34-35.
[19]See Parker, *Europe in Crisis*, pp. 274-275.
[20]For additional details on the French taxation and the *taille* see *Ibid*, pp. 275-277.
[21]Moote, *Louis XIII, the Just*, pp. 251-252.
[22]Quoted in Croxton, *Westphalia*, p. 109. For Mazarin's perspectives on French goals see *Westphalia*, pp. 106-109.
[23]Parker, *Europe in Crisis*, p. 267.
[24]Treasure, *Richelieu and Mazarin*, p. 13.
[25]Wilson, *Europe's Tragedy*, pp. 641-642.
[26]Wilson, *Europe's Tragedy*, p. 685.
[27]See Oakley, *War and Peace in the Baltic, 1560-1790*, pp. 50-51.
[28]Wilson, *Europe's Tragedy*, p. 686.
[29]See Croxton, *Westphalia*, pp. 89-90.
[30]See Georgina Masson, *Queen Christina* (London: Sphere Books Ltd, 1974), pp. 61-63.
[31]Stomberg, *A History of Sweden*, pp. 384-385.
[32]See Wilson, *Europe's Tragedy*, pp. 687-688.
[33]Croxton, *Westphalia*, p. 91.
[34]See *Ibid*, p. 92.
[35]A copy of the painting is available at: https://upload.wikimedia.org/wikipedia/commons/5/5f/Christian_IV_by_Vilhelm_Marstrand.png
[36]Masson, *Queen Christina*, p. 66.
[37]Wilson, *Europe's Tragedy*, p. 689.
[38]*Ibid*, p. 690.
[39]Andersson, *A History of Sweden*, pp. 184-185.
[40]Stomberg, *A History of Sweden*, pp. 386-387.
[41]Michael Bregnsbo, 'Denmark and the Westphalian Peace', *Historische Zeitschrift. Beihefte*, New Series, Vol. 26, Der Westfälische Friede.Diplomatie – politische Zäsur – kulturelles Umfeld – Rezeptionsgeschichte (1998), pp. 361-367; p. 365.
[42]*Ibid*, pp. 366-367.
[43]Croxton, *Westphalia*, pp. 96-98.
[44]See Mary Elizabeth Ailes, *Courage and Grief: Women and Sweden's Thirty Years' War, Early Modern Cultural Studies* (Lincoln, NE: University of Nebraska Press, 2018), pp. 147-151.
[45]See Masson, *Queen Christina*, pp. 71-75.
[46]See Croxton, *Westphalia*, pp. 98-101.
[47]See Croxton, *Peacemaking in Early Modern Europe: Cardinal Mazarin and the Congress of Westphalia, 1643-1648* (Selinsgrove, PA: Susquehanna University Press, 1999), p. 108. Henceforth referred to as *Peacemaking*.

[48]No less a figure than Thomas Hobbes participated in these practices, see: Noel Malcolm, *Reason of State, Propaganda, and the Thirty Years' War: An Unknown Translation by Thomas Hobbes* (New York: Oxford University Press, 2007), pp. 74-92. It was also common for art to be used for propaganda purposes, see: Geoffrey Treasure, *Richelieu and Mazarin*, pp. 43-48.

[49]Croxton, *Peacemaking*, pp. 109-110.

[50]Parker, 'Spain, Her Enemies and the Revolt of the Netherlands 1559-1648', pp. 94-95.

[51]See R. Trevor Davies, *Spain in Decline, 1621-1700* (London: MacMillan, 1957), pp. 57-60.

[52]Quoted in *Ibid*, pp. 61-63.

[53]See Hume, *Court of Philip IV: Spain in Decadence*, pp. 384-385.

[54]Edmundson, 'Frederick Henry: Prince of Orange (continued)', p. 288.

[55]Geyl, *History of the Dutch-Speaking Peoples*, p. 416.

[56]Croxton, *Peacemaking*, p. 111.

[57]Parker, *Europe in Crisis*, pp. 277-278.

[58]Edmundson, 'Frederick Henry: Prince of Orange (continued)', pp. 286-287.

[59]See Croxton, *Westphalia*, p. 114.

[60]The struggle of the Prince of Orange with the Dutch regent party is examined in Geyl, *History of the Dutch-Speaking Peoples*, pp. 417-429, while his account of the impact which Orange relations with the House of Stuart and the Torstenson War had on the Republic's domestic politics is also provided by Geyl in 'Frederick Henry of Orange and King Charles I', pp. 365-381.

[61]Quoted in Geyl, *History of the Dutch-Speaking Peoples*, p. 431.

[62]Davies, *Spain in Decline*, p. 66.

[63]See Geyl, *History of the Dutch-Speaking Peoples*, pp. 432-434.

[64]Croxton, *Westphalia*, pp. 95-96.

[65]See Wilson, *Europe's Tragedy*, p. 696.

[66]See Derek Croxton, '"The Prosperity of Arms Is Never Continual": Military Intelligence, Surprise, and Diplomacy in 1640s Germany', *The Journal of Military History*, Vol. 64, No. 4 (Oct., 2000), pp. 981-1003; p. 986.

[67]See Croxton, *Peacemaking*, pp. 112-117.

(Top left) Hugo Grotius (Michiel an Mierevelt, 1631)
(Top right) Abel Servien (Amselm von Hulle, 1716)

(Top left) Adrian Pauw (Jan Baptista Floris, 1635)
(Top right) Henri de la Tour de Auvergne, Viscount Turenne (Philippe de Champaigne)

CHAPTER TWENTY-TWO
"The Long Road to Peace"

ONE: Arriving at Westphalia
TWO: The Different Parties
THREE: Yearning for Peace
FOUR: Dutch Loose Ends

ONE

Arriving at Westphalia

'During the negotiations leading up to the Congress of Westphalia', wrote the historian Kenneth Colegrove:

...a considerable number of problems of diplomatic procedure arose which occasioned serious delays in the conclusion of peace. The convoking of a general peace congress of the majority of the European states was a new departure in international practice; and in view of the great differences of these states in religion, politics, interests and language it was necessary to reach preliminary agreements on procedure before the actual work of making peace could begin. These agreements were not easily and quickly made; and the eight or nine years of negotiations which preceded the Congress of Westphalia are a good illustration of the fact that the diplomatic practice of today is the result of an evolutionary process.[1]

Colegrove was onto something, and he was ideally positioned to write on the evolution of the diplomatic practice, for at the time he wrote this article in July 1919 for the *American Journal of International Law*, the Treaty of Versailles had been signed. Among the great peacemaking processes in early modern history, one must consider the top three to include the Congress of Vienna, the Treaty of Versailles and the Peace of Westphalia. This was echoed by other contemporary historians who had lived through the Paris Peace Conference, who noted:

Great peace conferences are proverbially slow bodies. The negotiators of Münster and Osnabrück spent five years in elaborating the treaty of Westphalia; the conferences of Paris and Vienna laboured a year and a half at undoing the work of Napoleon. Judged by these standards, the Peace Conference of 1919 was an expeditious body.[2]

This Westphalian peace conference, which Colegrove and others wrote of, had plainly taught his contemporaries a great deal. The conclusion of a treaty nearly three hundred years after Westphalia, which brought the Great

War to an end, contained roadblocks and frustrations which Colegrove's forebears in the 1640s would have recognised. Issues of precedence, of secrecy, of communication, and even of accommodation, were all matters of great concern to statesmen in the mid-seventeenth century as much as the early twentieth.[3]

Indeed, to deal first with just one of these issues, that of accommodation, leads the historian into several fascinating rabbit holes regarding proper housing and the diplomat's struggle to find it in the rustic settings of Münster and Osnabruck. At their core, the Westphalian towns were provincial, isolated and in some respects quite unlike what the more privileged statesmen were used to. The geographic location of Osnabruck, reportedly, as roughly ten miles from the site where Arminius' German forces annihilated Varus' legions in 9AD, singled Westphalia out as, according to one priest, 'the image of ancient Germany: heathen, disagreeable, and full of bogs.' Münster's reputation was little better, since it was known for hosting one of the most violent and infamous explosions of religious conflict in 1534, when Anabaptists attempted to launch a revolution.[4]

The tale of the two Westphalian towns is rarely brought forward in narratives of the peacemaking, but it is worth dwelling for a moment on what the hosting of such a pivotal congress meant to Münster and Osnabruck. While we might expect that both towns would be pleased to have been selected for such an important task, the reality was much different. Hosting so many foreign dignitaries was crushingly expensive, and both derived little financial benefit from it. Instead, letters were sent in a kind of panic to Regensburg, which had hosted numerous Imperial Diets before, and the town council of Münster asked for advice regarding the provision of wine. Not wanting to appear cheap to their guests, new arrivals in the town were presented with free wine, and regularly given gifts as well. Such demonstrations of generosity cost a bomb, but since the new arrivals enjoyed diplomatic immunity, no new tax base could be drawn upon to pay for them. The gesture did not quite work anyway, since Westphalia's setting, as much as its appearance, did little to impress the new arrivals. The region's weather brought regular rain and could be bitterly cold, which on one occasion compelled the Spanish representative to spend 19 days in a row holed up in his room. It also turned the rudimentary roads of the towns into a morass of mud, which was quickly caked on the wagons and carriages, and the disgusted representatives themselves.[5]

Interestingly, Westphalia shared something else in common with the Paris Peace Conference of 1919 – the dispute over language.[6] Traditionally in the medieval art of peacemaking, Latin was the preferred language, but increasingly, national languages like German and French were coming to the fore, and diplomats were forced to compromise. It should go without saying that multilingual statesmen were easy to find in both Osnabruck and Münster.

Since few foreign dignitaries spoke either Dutch, Spanish or Swedish, German or French became the informal language of choice, but with the Imperial agent and the representative from the Papacy, Latin remained important for symbolic reasons. Among the powers, only France seemed to resist the general preference for Latin, as the French presented their first proposals in late 1644 in French rather than Latin. Similarly, some German figures wanted the final treaty to be written in German, as the Peace of Augsburg had been, but they had to make do only with a translation of the Latin treaty.

This created problems not just among the disgruntled plenipotentiaries, but also with the texts that were produced. Different translations could pose substantial problems to the jurist, where words or terms in one language could mean something very different in another. It is not too surprising therefore that lawyers were in demand during the negotiations, and interpretation became critically important for the sake of implementation. Many figures could understand more languages than they could comfortably speak themselves, and when it came time to compose official documents, it is unsurprising that individuals reverted to the language they were most comfortable with. Although it had a considerable legacy and history, Latin was increasingly falling out of favour as the language of international peacemaking, and some officials, in particular the French official Abel Servien, could not speak or understand Latin comfortably at all. This led to speculation about his mental fitness, which Servien pushed through, but he was little use when seated among those that reverted to Latin regularly, and he would even go as far as skipping meals on occasion because, according to his chaplain, 'he could not stomach so much fish and so much Latin.'[7]

Of course, it did not matter what language was used if the important messages which were pinged between the relevant cities could not be accessed in time. Westphalian diplomacy was reliant upon the rudimentary postage system, which the war had only served to undermine. On some occasions, privileged officials would rely on messengers: these were individuals employed solely for the purpose of absorbing information in one place, only to travel to another, and communicate all they had learned. This was useful for the sake of security, as there was no letter to intercept, but it was also expensive and inefficient, and depended on the memory of the messenger for vital details. Generally, then, letters were depended upon as a rule of the conference. Much of the Empire was covered by an Imperial postal service, under the control of the Taxis family, but although it had been expanded to include the Westphalia towns, the more distant regions such as Brandenburg were actually excluded from the service, and had to establish their own lines of communication. Further, the service operated on tried and tested traditions, and since the ten thousand or so residents of Osnabruck or Münster had never warranted a direct line to Vienna for instance, these direct lines had to be established, as would another line with Brussels, since Madrid was too far away from the negotiations for the Spanish to stay in the loop.

And staying in the loop was critical for the major powers if they were to have any impact or input into what was taking place in Westphalia. In this respect, they were at the mercy of the Taxis' postal service in the Empire in addition to whatever systems they had set up themselves. Geography played a critical role in determining how long communications might take. The Dutch were fortunate, as Westphalia was comparatively near their borders – indeed, the French had petitioned for Münster for the very reason that its close proximity to the Netherlands might encourage the Dutch to attend – but others suffered from the accidents of geography. It took letters a month to reach Madrid, two weeks to reach either Vienna or Stockholm, ten days to Paris, but only two days to reach The Hague. The system became more refined as the negotiations entered their second and third years, with the French receiving and sending their letters to Paris within a week, and Madrid three weeks, but the process could still be painfully slow.

Indeed, the process was hampered further by the slow machinery of bureaucracy which some powers also endured. A good example is provided by Spain, already at a disadvantage thanks to their distance from Westphalia. Haste rarely seemed to be within the vocabulary of Philip IV's regime, as one example of a letter arriving in June, and receiving a reply in September, proves. The Spanish agent on the ground in Westphalia found this intolerable, understandably, and marked letters as urgent when he required a faster turnaround, but this only improved the process slightly – one letter sent in early January was returned by mid-March, for example. Of course, upon enduring this maddening delay, it regularly transpired that the situation which the Spanish agent had been talking about had completely changed. Shorn of the wireless telegram services which powered the Paris Peace Conference negotiations, figures at Westphalia were not surprised to note that the lack of any sophisticated communications network let them down. After all, many had been enduring the hit and miss postal service long before attending at Westphalia.

Rudimentary concepts like diplomatic immunity, in their early stages at Westphalia, were ideally supposed to apply to diplomatic communications as well. Communication was hard enough without worrying whether one's enemy was intercepting these letters and revealing their secrets. Some made use of the equally rudimentary encryption methods, but simpler tools like wax seals were also still upheld, since one could at least be sure that the letter had travelled unspoiled if the seal was also unspoiled. This was often the best one could do, and the pressures of time meant that one was forced to rely on one's enemies for the safe passage of mail. The Spanish, again, come to mind, as Madrid made use of a land route for its communications that ran through French territory. A certain gentlemanly code was believed to apply, and improved as the negotiations progressed, but exceptions were made – military communications were fair game, and in the case of more sensitive communications, such as the confirmation of peace treaties that brought an end to wars the French wished to continue, Philip IV adapted. Thus, when the Peace of Münster brought the Spanish-Dutch War to an end, the Spanish King made sure to send four different copies of the ratified treaty through four different routes, in case the French attempted to seize these documents, and thus prolong the war to their advantage. These precautions proved worthwhile, as the French imprisoned the Spanish courier for ten days, but thankfully missed the couriers who were travelling by sea.[8]

Plenipotentiaries did not merely have to talk, they also had to live, and of course eat, during the numerous years where Westphalia was their home. Although a veritable army of diplomats had descended upon Osnabruck and Münster, these individuals were bound to have an easier time finding food than the actual common soldier, and they certainly ate better than he did. Larger embassies like the French and Imperials brought their own cooks, but many were not so fortunate. The leader of the French embassy brought 12 cooks and 5 bakers, but these culinary artists could not work miracles, and were limited by the availability of food, the North European climate, and general shortages aggravated by the war. Cooks tended to employ buyers to bring them the best quality foods and deals, beef and fish being the most popular meats, supplemented by birds and occasionally wild game. This contrasts with the soldier or humble peasant, who rarely ate meat, and survived on a diet largely composed of bread. Cabbages, turnips, potatoes, lemons, pears and cherries were available seasonally; but an official typically enjoyed a diet high in fat and alcohol, which tended to increase the cases of gout among the more well-to-do representatives.

Gout and other bouts of illness only served to underline the very rudimentary knowledge of the medical profession and indeed the human anatomy which seventeenth century science possessed. Surprisingly perhaps, this led to cooperation among even enemy delegations over the question of health, as the French would give their physicians on lend to the Spanish, and vice-versa. Some would blame the harsh climate for the poor health of the ambassadors, rarely considering the fact that many were the ideal candidates for gout, as middle-aged men on a diet high in fat and alcohol. Poor hygiene, rudimentary sanitation, a lack of antibiotics and a range of other factors played a role, as did simple accidents – Maximillian von Trauttmansdorff, the Imperial plenipotentiary, was unfortunate enough to suffer from a crab claw lodged in his windpipe, and took more than six months to recover from the consequences of such a trauma.

Nor would Trauttmansdorff be permitted to return home during the length of his illness. For the five years or so that the Westphalian negotiations were in session, Osnabruck and Münster became the new home for these dignitaries. It is therefore unsurprising that they did their best to make themselves at home. To some, this meant engaging in pleasures like the theatre or early representations of the ballet, but to others, it meant indulging in bouts of drinking and socialising. The French ordered so much wine from Bordeaux through the Netherlands – thirty thousand litres – that the Dutch attempted to charge import duties, as they suspected the French intended to sell this wine to their neighbours. Not so – the wine was consumed by the French embassy in Münster, and to the palpable horror of the Papal delegate, neither the French nor any other Northern European power kept with the southern tradition of mixing their wine with water. Wine was at least more palatable than beer, which not even Maximillian of Bavaria could claim to stomach.

Unfortunately, not everyone could handle their alcohol with equal sophistication. One is drawn to the example of the Transylvanian delegate, who caused quite a scene by becoming drunk at dinner, and shortly afterwards, threw up in a Dutch carriage. The Dutch were so offended that they refused to meet with him afterwards. Other delegates adopted methods of getting around the difficulties which alcohol caused; the French, for instance, insisted that by the afternoon, it was pointless to try and negotiate with Johan Oxenstierna, the Swedish representative, because he was always drunk by that time. Perhaps Oxenstierna had reason to indulge; his father, the Swedish Chancellor, ran a tight ship back in Stockholm, and while it was certainly invaluable to have one's father in so high a position, it could also be a curse. When Johan's wife died in August 1646, he understandably requested some leave for his bereavement: 'I am downright sick because of my blessed, dear wife's death, so that I don't even know what to do', he wrote, to the one person he believed might offer some sympathy, his father. But the Swedish Chancellor could not afford to bend the rules, even for his son. To leave the negotiations would delay everything, and who was to say that Johan would even return from his grief? Besides, as the senior Oxenstierna maintained, 'it would not be fitting to let you sink down on account of your domestic problem and let other judge contemptuously of you.'[9]

The Swedish Chancellor's comments certainly do not age well, but the senior Oxenstierna was not concerned merely for what other people might say of his son, he was also concerned for what they might think of Sweden. The question of prestige – or gauging which delegate represented the strongest, most influential, most important state – manifested itself in the order of precedence. Precedence was an important, but also maddening aspect of the negotiations, where pettiness and jealousies were allowed to mingle with interstate rivalries and personal feuds. It was a combination which threatened to unravel the negotiations before they had truly begun, but precedence also could not be ignored. It was by no means a new concept; in 1637, no less a figure than Hugo Grotius, representing Sweden, had engaged in a dispute with the English as his carriage attempted to enter Paris. This dispute over pre-eminence, or in this case, literally one of who would enter the city first, broke out into open conflict between the two embassies, and was only halted when the French themselves intervened. The dispute was not solved for several months though, and Grotius argued with his English counterpart over the grounds for pre-eminence, making use of points like who had converted to Christianity first. Grotius even disputed the French account of the dispute, because England's name was placed before that of Sweden.[10]

What are we to make of such a curious incident? What were the English and Swedes actually fighting about? Grotius, as a father of international law, was fighting for nothing less than Sweden's position in the pecking order of states. This pecking order could be reflected in the most surprising of ways; in 1637, it was a question of who was allowed into Paris first. At Westphalia, it was something as simple as who sat where on the long table where negotiations were held. It was also seen in the arrival of the dignitaries at Westphalia; the more powerful the state represented, it was said, the more extravagant the entourage of the dignitary. Take for instance the Duke of Longueville, leader of the French delegation, who arrived in Münster on 30 June 1645. Longueville's party was led by twelve mules, richly decorated with blankets embroidered with the family's coat of arms, followed by fifty finely dressed cavaliers, and twelve of the Duke's personal riding horses. Twenty-two of his pages followed this display, along with twelve members of his own private Swiss guard. Behind them, came the Duke himself, and the other French delegates guarded by a measly twenty horsemen. Longueville wanted to make it clear that France was the leader of the conference, by splendour alone, and that he was leader of its embassy.

Such a display announced to Münster that a powerful figure had arrived, but it also laid down the gauntlet to those that might challenge the image of France, such as her Spanish enemy. Surprisingly, given the Spanish propensity for ceremonials, Longueville's Spanish counterpart arrived in relative secrecy five days later, as did Trauttmansdorff, who arrived several months after him. Since the Spanish could not match the French display, they sought to avoid the whole practice entirely, but this was not always possible. When out and about, ambassadors tended to bring men or beasts with them as a symbol of their wealth and power, and when setting up shop, the pressure was also on to create a base worthy of their rank and name. Such displays could be practically useful, as it would inform the unaccustomed where he might stand, by measuring his own resources against the display.[11] This custom was recognised by contemporaries, such as the seventeenth century mathematician and philosopher Blaise Pascal (1623-1662), who noted in his *Pensées* that:

> How rightly do we distinguish men by external appearances rather than by internal qualities! Which of us two shall have precedence? Who will give place to the other? The least clever. But I am as clever as he. We should have to fight over this. He has four lackeys, and I have only one. This can be seen; we have only to count. It falls to me to yield, and I am a fool if I contest the matter. By this means we are at peace, which is the greatest of boons.[12]

It was not merely the size of one's deputation, but the form of government, that could affect the reception in Münster or Osnabruck. Thus the agents of republics, such as the Venetians or Dutch, would not be regarded as highly as those who represented Kings, such as the French, Swedish or Spanish, and the Imperials insisted that as representatives of the Emperor, they should reside in a plane all of their own. Such matters were in dispute, and solutions would often be found only when allies worked together, such as when the French and Dutch cooperated to minimise any potential source of conflict, and the Swedish and French did the same. When set against one's enemies though, the disputes could drag on endlessly, and even the form of address could produce mind-numbing questions or precedence and honour, which seem so wasteful and meaningless today. Insecurity had an additional role to play, so that ambassadors occasionally adopted the titles of their relatives or in-laws, such as Abel Servien, the French ambassador, who used his wife's title to assume the grand name of count de la Roche des Aubiers, while the Duke of Longueville attempted to claim that, as count of the tiny county of Nuechatel, he was entitled to the honorific 'Your Highness'.[13]

Questions of precedence and titles were encapsulated within the ideology of honour, on a personal and national level. As aristocratic representatives of their nations, the traditions of honour had been passed to these men, who were well-positioned either to make great progress with likeminded counterparts, or to tie themselves up on questions of precedence, and achieve virtually nothing. Costly disputes about rank and status were not harmless; there is reason to suppose that the French refusal to compromise with even their Dutch ally in this respect moved the latter to make a separate peace with the Spanish much quicker. We may wonder at the value which was placed upon something as ideological as honour; what was the tangible value of such a concept? Was pursuing the point worth it for the French or Swedish if it meant alienating one's allies and prolonging the costly war?

For some, precedence was an end all by itself, and was not simply a means by which statesmen could communicate their right to respect. As Axel Oxenstierna phrased it, 'next to God and one's own morality, nothing in the world is greater than to be worth an honourable and respectable name.' Even if this renown meant ruining his grieving son's mental health, or picking fights with potential allies, the Swedish Chancellor believed the price was worth paying. The renown of Sweden should be upheld at such a level that her foes and allies alike would be more willing to accommodate her statesmen in negotiations, thereby granting her more opportunities to achieve her objectives. And what were these objectives? For Sweden as much as for her contemporaries, they varied greatly, but all were forced to abide by the limitations placed upon their dignitaries, whether these limitations were caused by the rudimentary technology, the shortcomings in communications, or the ideology of the dignitaries themselves.[14]

TWO
The Different Parties

By 1645, the negotiations at Osnabruck and Münster had technically been ongoing for two years. In practice, however, 1645 and even 1646 were the years when the conference truly began for many. Much had also changed since these towns had opened their gates to the host of deputations and dignitaries. In Osnabruck, the Danish mediators had been comprehensively removed, following the defeat of Christian IV's kingdom in the Torstenson War.[15] Münster, where the Dutch-Spanish, Franco-Spanish and Franco-Imperial treaties were negotiated, contained two mediators by contrast – the Venetians and Papacy – and contained additional petitioners, such as the Portuguese.[16] The separation of the conference into the two towns had been decided upon in the 1641 Treaty of Hamburg, and on the surface, the decision had been taken owing to the refusal of the Papacy to deal fairly with Protestant powers.[17] Since 1641, profoundly optimistic predictions about when the powers would assemble were made, with March 1642 originally set as the beginning of the conference, before July 1643 was substituted instead. Not until 1645 though, with their Danish enemy removed, could the Swedish feel comfortable beginning their negotiations, while the Dutch did not arrive in Münster until spring 1646.[18] While the Westphalian peace negotiations did not seem to begin, or even end, at a strict point, one has an easier task measuring exactly what each of the powers wanted to achieve in their time there.[19]

We begin our examination with France, with Cardinal Mazarin running the government, and the boy king Louis XIV in the early phases of a reign which would take the country to legendary heights of power and glory. In 1645 though, few could have imagined how high Louis would rise, but Mazarin was determined to provide as beneficial a platform as possible for the young king, by first succeeding at Münster. Tasked with this mission were two very different diplomats, Abel Servien and Claude d'Avaux. Both had extensive experience in diplomacy and statesmanship, with Servien a former secretary for war, and d'Avaux prevalent in recent treaties like that truce brokered between Sweden and Poland in 1635. Unfortunately, these two hard-working Frenchmen could not stand one another, and they were also polar opposite personalities.

Servien was impersonable and irritable, d'Avaux friendly and engaging, but both seemed to combine the best aspects of Mazarin's personality, as they pursued a ruthlessly self-interested policy, while remaining on good terms with most of their counterparts. In fact, the two men couldn't get as far as Münster without falling out, thanks to an ill-advised speech which d'Avaux made in The Hague, where the Frenchman had advocated for Dutch Catholics and claimed to have Servien's support. Servien angrily disputed this assertion, and by the time they had reached Münster, they were publishing pamphlets attacking one another! Rather than recall either man, Mazarin sent a third figure, the Duke of Longueville, to lead the French delegation and balance them out. Longueville descended from an illegitimate son of Henry IV and imagined himself an influential French statesman of some repute, but he lacked the skill of his subordinates, and had only a minimal impact on the negotiations.

France's position in Westphalia was unique, because France was the only power at war with both branches of the Habsburgs – though the war with the Emperor had never been made official. This meant that not only had France several military fronts to worry about, in Catalonia, Italy, Flanders and the Rhine, but she also had several goals related to these theatres. Naturally, Mazarin prioritised his goals; he was willing enough to bargain away Catalonia, he was eager to receive lordship over Alsace, and thanks to the preponderance of French forces in the region and Dutch assistance, he expected to take additional portions of Flanders. For this reason, Mazarin worked to confound Maximillian of Bavaria and to gather as much intelligence about the latter's military plans as possible, with varying degrees of success. Mazarin believed that if Bavaria could be separated from the Emperor, either by military force or through a diplomatic arrangement, then the Imperials would be severely restricted.[20]

One of the guiding principles of Mazarin's regime was the Swedish alliance. Because the war against Spain was the 'main event', it was essential that Sweden, and therefore Oxenstierna, remain closely connected to France. Oxenstierna also adhered to this logic; the more distracted the Spanish were in their war with France, the less able they would be to support the Emperor. For his part, Oxenstierna helped Sweden's case by making separate peace agreements with the Protestant Electors before the guts of the negotiations at Osnabruck had even begun; peace was made with Brandenburg in 1644,[21] and with Saxony in 1646. Oxenstierna was well-connected to the negotiations in Osnabruck, thanks to the appointment of his son Johan, as one of the two plenipotentiaries there. We have already seen how the senior Oxenstierna refused to allow his grieving son to return home after the death of his wife, but notwithstanding this tough love, Johan and Axel forged a useful line of communication. His family's standing meant that the younger Oxenstierna was the head of the embassy, and outranked Johan Salvius, the other Swedish delegate. Other anecdotes testify to Johan Oxenstierna's inflated sense of self-importance, such as his insistence of having trumpets blare whenever he sat down to eat or retired to bed.[22] This was by no means unusual, as Johan Oxenstierna's contemporaries had long made use of trumpets during diplomacy, but still, it can't have endeared him to his colleague, or to those around him.[23]

Sweden's position had been greatly improved in the aftermath of the Torstenson War, which was brought to an end in August 1645. This not only removed Denmark as a mediator in Osnabruck, it also removed any opportunity which the Emperor might have had to distract Swedish attentions. With its old rival defeated and valuable tracts of land seized, Torstenson planned to focus his full attentions upon the Emperor, and events in the military sphere from 1645 would demonstrate that Sweden had finally recovered from the devastating aftermath of the defeat at Nordlingen a decade before. The recovery was fortunate, but neither Torstenson nor Oxenstierna were so naïve as to take it for granted; Nordlingen had taught Sweden a fierce lesson about the shifting nature of the war. What was to stop another Nordlingen once more ruining Swedish options? Shortly after the great Swedish triumph at Jankov in March 1645 (see below), news of the victory had reached Westphalia, and the Frenchman Abel Servien reflected on the event, noting that Torstenson...

...is now the master of the campaign, but it is necessary to reflect on what would have become of him had he been defeated in Bohemia, being so far from any secure retreat: our situation would be as bad as the Emperor's is, which goes to show that very little is required to change the state of affairs.[24]

This was an astute observation, but just as important to Oxenstierna as the continuing supremacy of Torstenson was the guarantee of Swedish territorial gains, above all in Pomerania. The aforementioned treaty with Brandenburg in June 1644 had guaranteed Brandenburg's neutrality and the payment of a large subsidy, but the Swedish possession of Pomerania remained out of Oxenstierna's grasp, and the wily Elector Frederick William would later manage to come into new territory, such as Mecklenburg, in return for that settlement. As confirmation on Pomerania's status was not forthcoming, it seemed that no one could decide whether Sweden should have half of or all of Pomerania, just as Sweden's policy towards Protestants was similarly up in the air. Axel and Johan Oxenstierna tended to push harder for greater religious concessions for Protestants, and for greater territorial demands, while Johan Salvius, in touch with Queen Christina since she had come into her majority in late 1644, opted for more moderate terms.[25]

The battlefield would improve the negotiating position of the French and Swedes, but both cooperated in the meantime to issue an interesting demand to the Emperor in early 1645: that the Imperial estates should be allowed to attend. On some level, this demand made sense. After all, it had proved impossible to prevent representatives of the Imperial estates from flocking into the Westphalian towns since 1643. According to the terms of the 1641 Treaty of Hamburg, the French and Swedes were entitled to invite their allies to attend and, they could both argue, several of their allies were among these estates. But did *all* estates, ranging from the small territory, to representatives of the free cities, to Imperial knights, to the larger Electors, all have to attend? Traditionally, such a wide attendance was only called for during an Imperial Diet, where every participant knew the pecking order and literally where they stood in the room. In the case of a peace conference involving powers outside of the Empire though, it was less clear what was to be done.

Furthermore, France and Sweden disagreed over the extent of the estates' representation – would the arrival of too many estates dilute the impact of others, and effectively paralyse the negotiations through sheer numbers alone? In April, the Emperor answered the question for them, at least partially, by ordering the Deputation Diet in Frankfurt to reconvene at Münster. This Diet had been in session for nearly two years and had served as the location for the Catholic estates allied to the Emperor to discuss matters of Imperial justice. That, at least, had been the intention, but these estates had spent much of the past two years debating over how to end the war, and by inviting them to Münster, the Emperor demonstrated that he was perhaps at last willing to listen. But to the Swedes and French, this was not good enough. For one, the reconvened Deputation Diet would contain virtually no Protestants, and no rebels, such as Hesse-Kassel, at all. It was also minimalist in its representation, as no Imperial Free Cities or Knights were represented. Sweden objected to the Deputation Diet moving to Münster as well, because this made Osnabruck appear less important, while both powers disputed the Emperor's decision to take religious matters out of that Diet's hands, by convening a separate Diet tasked solely with solving the religious question.

The issue of representation for the Estates had degenerated into something of a mess as 1645 progressed, but by 11 June, the two crowns had developed their proposals, and in the process, crossed a significant line of the negotiations. Unfortunately, the issue of the estates would drag the negotiations out for another six months, so that it was not until early 1646 that Westphalia began to host some truly meaningful negotiations. France had made some specific demands, such as placing a ban on electing an Emperor's successor in the current Emperor's lifetime – this was designed to break the grip on the Imperial office which the Habsburgs maintained. Sweden focused on the religious issue, which the French seemed unwilling to touch with a barge pole, since it would alienate potential allies in the Catholic camp, such as Bavaria, if the religious settlement in the Empire was turned back to 1618 as Sweden insisted. On questions of amnesty and satisfaction, neither the solution nor the methods were particularly clear, but the French and Swedes at least had a base from which they could negotiate from, and both had made a point of presenting these proposals on the same day in each town, so as to maintain the appearance of a strong, united alliance.

For the moment, Ferdinand seemed unwilling to approve of any widespread attendance by all estates of the Empire – he only consulted the Deputation Diet regarding these demands, even as Münster was beginning to fill up with representatives from the smallest loyal Imperial enclave to the more rebellious German state. This added an additional urgency to the debate, and over the summer several solutions were proposed, with the gathered estates effectively dividing themselves between the two towns. In practice, the division of these estates nullified what little influence they might have had, and the larger powers, such as the Electors, tended to dominate, while the views of the smaller entities were passed to the Emperor as protests. Ferdinand determined to resist the pull no longer, and on 29 August 1645, he relented and granted voting privileges to the estates, inviting them all to attend. The saga was by no means over, but Ferdinand had apparently come to the conclusion that it was better to accommodate the estates now than to resist. It would still have been impossible for the multitude of microstates to overwhelm the stance of the larger Electors, but these smaller voices would at least now be heard.[26] As Ferdinand himself wrote:

> You will be aware what was recently discussed and agreed between us and the electors and Estates of the Empire...We have followed this agreed Imperial Decision at all times and all and every elector and estate of the Empire can send their representatives to said peace talks to join and assist our imperial envoys with advice and thereby exercise their free rights of suffrage freely confessed and unhindered by us...Our Imperial envoys have already proposed proper peace terms at Münster and Osnabruck to the plenipotentiaries of both crowns, France and Sweden, who have also revealed their propositions on 11 June... and we have now given these propositions mature discussion and consideration and thereby found that they are of notable concern to the electors and estates of the Empire. We, however, do not want to detract from their current and customary rights and justice in the slightest, and are resolved once and for all and have instructed our envoys accordingly, that they should discuss with the electors and estates representatives, councillors and ambassadors and then respond to the plenipotentiaries of both crowns. Therefore, we have wanted to explain matters to you and wish, with your gracious request, that you, if you have not already done so, either send your envoy to the said negotiations with sufficient instructions and powers, or entrust another of the Imperial Estates with such powers, and instruct them to appear at the peace negotiations, and

on their arrival there to assemble and continue with the others in the three imperial curia as is customary in the Holy Roman Empire, as well as to assist our imperial envoys with true word and deed, because we do not want to delay promoting the said peace negotiations and, with God's help, bring them to the desired conclusion as far as the foreign crowns will be content with honourable, proper and Christian means.[27]

Interestingly, the more representative, Republican power at the peace negotiations, the Dutch, showed scant interest in the Imperial Estates debate, largely because the Dutch negotiators were focused utterly on Spain, and were at pains to emphasise that their quarrel was not with the Emperor. These Dutch representatives made their base in Münster, supposedly under the watchful eye of their French ally, but in practice, often far from them. Although eager to proclaim their disinterest in all matters relating to representative institutions in the Empire, the very form of the Dutch diplomatic mission to Münster told its own distinctive story about representative government, and of the sometimes-fractious nature of Dutch domestic politics. This was clearly evident in the fact that each of the seven provinces which constituted the Dutch Republic were permitted to send their own representatives, with Holland sending two owing to its larger size.

In practice, Holland and Zealand, as the two more powerful and influential provinces, led the Dutch delegation, and its agents proved the more important. The primary delegate from Holland was Adrian Pauw, a lawyer and former grand pensionary (similar to prime minister) of Holland; Zealand had sent Johan de Knuyt, a good friend of Frederick Henry. Traditionally, since Holland tended to bear most of the burden of cost for maintaining the army, its officials advocated reducing it, and had already done so by 1644. This tended to rub Zealand the wrong way, as the second largest province wished for the war to continue, and also tended to support the military commanders of the House of Orange most enthusiastically. By 1645, both provinces were animated by the pursuit of two main goals which the peace process could be expected to protect – a successful conclusion to the war with Spain, and the preservation of the Dutch colonial empire, which had exploded in size across the world since the turn of the century. [28]

With scant power and at small burden to the community, by means of the contributions of a small number of the inhabitants of this state, the operations of the Company have been carried out so successfully that the pride of Spain has not been able to withstand them, and it has plainly appeared therefrom in what wise this might sovereign may be damaged through his own resources, and the American treasures with which he has these many years plagued and kept in lasting unrest the whole of Christendom, be snatched from him or rendered useless. [29]

This optimistic account given by a Director of the West India Company in 1644 encapsulates this joint Dutch struggle against Spanish power abroad and closer to home. In 1630, a force of 65 ships, 3,780 sailors and 3,500 soldiers had landed at Olinda, Pernambuco, and ever since that date, the Dutch had effectively made themselves at home in modern-day Brazil. Pressure had mounted upon the Spanish to act in the name of their Portuguese client, but instead of removing the Dutch from the region, the investment from the rebels multiplied. From the late 1630s, when the Dutch managed to harness the sugar plantations and co-opt the support of the loyalist Portuguese population, healthy returns began to flow back to The Hague.[30] The Portuguese revolt in 1640 complicated the picture, but as the above quote explains, there was little reason to suppose that after a generation of trying, the Spanish or the Portuguese would be able to remove the Dutch now. But this hubris was to prove fatal. As the West India Company sought to reduce its costs and alleviate some of its debts, the decision was made to recall the Dutch governor of the region, John Maurice, who sailed out of the lucrative colony just in time for the whole place to degenerate into rebellion.[31]

Energised perhaps by the declaration of independence, loyalist Portuguese settlers overwhelmed the limited Dutch garrison, and before the end of 1645, the Dutch presence was reduced to the Recife, a spit of marshy land where the Dutch presence had originally been established fifteen years before. In the course of this retreat, the Portuguese settlers routed the Dutch in a skirmish at Tobocas, a short distance from the Recife refuge. In the context of the wider war, Geoffrey Parker writes:

> This minor engagement, fought six thousand miles from the Netherlands and involving under one thousand men on each side, was one of the most important 'actions' of the Eighty Years' War. It destroyed Dutch power in Brazil (only four toeholds on the coast, Recife the chief among them, remained). The great profits from the sugar trade were gone. The West India Company based on Zealand was therefore desperate to recover its lost empire and looked urgently at the means available.[32]

Could the colony be saved? Not so, said several relief fleets sent in 1646 and 1647; the only means to rescue the situation lay in a comprehensive defeat of Portugal, which was impossible so long as the Dutch and Spanish remained at war. Perhaps, some Dutch officials imagined, the Portuguese would be less able to support their Brazilian appendages once they were forced to take on Spain alone? But peace with Spain would present its own challenges, such as reduced incomes for the West and East India Companies from attacking Spanish shipping, and fewer opportunities elsewhere to encroach upon Spain's colonial holdings. Hard bargaining thus took place between representatives of Holland – eager to end the war with Spain – and Zealand – eager to reconquer Brazil for its Company.

By 1645, it was impossible to hide the fact that the war was not going well for Spain. 'It is indispensable to make peace', proclaimed the Count of Penaranda, the Spanish ambassador at Münster, adding with some urgency that:

> If I had to give instructions to a new ambassador, I would tell him to make a good peace, or a mediocre peace, or a bad peace, but to make peace, because there is no more time to delay, having arrived, as I believe, at the point when we no longer have any means of making war.[33]

Such a gloomy outlook seeped into the mood of the often irritable, often unwell, Spanish ambassador. Penaranda had never even been outside of Spain when he had been appointed as Spain's main representative in Münster. His orders were essentially to give away whatever the Dutch asked for, but to do his best to preserve some semblance – whatever it was – of King Philip IV's prestige. Spain's position in 1645 was a far cry from that of 1619, when Philip IV's father had ordered his soldiers into the Palatinate in support of Ferdinand III's father; indeed, it was a far cry even from the Spanish position of 1634, where the Cardinal-Infante had brought Spain's military contribution into Germany and destroyed a Swedish army at Nordlingen. These triumphs, and that activism, now seemed a distant memory. A gradual decline, punctuated by a series of defeats, and recently of revolutions, had been the Spanish story since the beginning of the Thirty Years War.

Neither Penaranda nor his peers back in Madrid expected this to markedly change, but they did hope that some beneficial arrangement might be squeezed out of the situation at Westphalia, perhaps by separating the Dutch or French from their ally, and pursuing the war with one or the other. Whatever naïve predictions might be made about the prospects of war with one of these powers, the prospects were infinitely better than those which plagued Spain currently. The Spanish Netherlands regime was kept together only by Leopold William (Ferdinand III's brother), but what truly preserved it was the lacklustre Dutch contributions since the fall of Breda in 1637. Evidently, with the fear of reconquest utterly banished, it was becoming difficult for the Dutch to muster enthusiasm to pursue the war any further; additionally, it was suspected within The Hague that any further battering upon the defences of Flanders could only be to the benefit of the French, who continued to seize new towns every year.

'France, enlarged by possession of the Spanish Netherlands, will be a dangerous neighbour for our country', commented the assembly in Holland. To avoid a border with the resurgent realm of Louis XIV, and to preserve a buffer between the nominal allies, Dutch strategists and officials argued that the advance should go no further.[34] This idea was hotly disputed, but as we have seen, the unconvinced could be coerced into cooperating by promising to make contributions elsewhere, where the Zealanders were persuaded to make peace with Spain in return for a Brazilian relief force paid for by Hollanders. Because Holland shouldered the burden of the war – more than 50% it was said – her officials were most eager to end it. Many merchants and regents in the Republic had become suspicious of Frederick Henry's intentions, especially once his son's marriage into the House of Stuart was confirmed. Was this scion of the House of Orange preparing himself to create a new monarchy at The Hague?

Hardly; at over 60 years old and in poor health, Frederick Henry mustered enough energy for one final campaign in 1645 – the capture of Hulst, a town just to the south of Zealand. Hulst had frustrated Frederick Henry before in 1640, but thanks to the aid of the French, the 2,500 Spanish were compelled to surrender in early November. The fall of Hulst marked a significant watershed moment in the history of the Dutch-Spanish War; this siege was destined to be not merely Frederick Henry's final campaign, but the final actual campaign of the eighty-year conflict. A glance at a map of the Netherlands today illustrates the strategic importance of Hulst; bordered to the South by Flanders, it is otherwise surrounded by the sea. It thus resembled a toehold in Flanders and enabled the Dutch to maintain control over the River Scheldt which flowed into the sea to the north-east.

This final gasp of the Dutch military machine, which had proved so effective in the hands of the House of Orange, underlined in Madrid that uncomfortable fact – that the continuation of the war simply meant additional losses. There were to be no opportunities, even with the Dutch colonial troubles, the relative division of the supposedly United Provinces, and the war weariness, for the Spanish to launch any resurgent campaigns.[35] The Army of Flanders, which had itself sucked in countless reserves of Spanish silver and manpower, seemed to be spluttering and stumbling towards its ignoble end by the mid-1640s, after years of chronic underinvestment and bitter defeats. 'Somewhat ironically' wrote the historian Jan Glete, 'the rebellious Dutch made Habsburg Spain more militarily powerful in Northern Europe than the monarchy would have been if these provinces had remained loyal but unwilling to support major military efforts.'[36] This military power had been used to great effect in the second half of the sixteenth century, and in the initial years of the Thirty Years War. However, by 1645, this irony was surely lost on the depleted Spanish, and as the war with the Dutch drew near to a close, what exactly did Madrid have to show for the eighty years of struggle, save an exhausted heartland, a broken treasury system and a shattered military reputation which had once been the terror of Europe? All Spain had was the prospect of peace. 'But to see the sufferings of so many poor innocent people in these wars and conflicts', lamented Philip IV, 'pierces me to the very heart, and if with my life's blood I could remedy it I would expend it most willingly.'[37]

Dutch independence was effectively secure, and as soon as the Spanish overcame their inbuilt stubbornness, it was expected that peace would at last be at hand between the two old enemies. It would certainly be more straightforward to reach peace with the Dutch, because the Dutch were at least recognised as plenipotentiaries; with Spain's Iberian neighbours up in revolt, both Catalonia and Portugal could be expected to send independent representatives of their own, with varying degrees of success. Portugal maintained a representative at Münster and Osnabruck, and these agents worked very hard for the five years that the towns were open for business, though the recent experiences of Portuguese diplomats had not boded well. The delegate in Rome had been attacked in broad daylight; the King's brother languished in a Spanish prison, and King John himself was the victim of an assassination attempt in 1647.[38] All the while, Portuguese representatives kept their eyes on the prize – that of including Portugal in whatever peace treaty might be signed between the Bourbons and Habsburgs, and of legitimising Portuguese sovereignty in the process.[39]

When one considers the exhaustion of the Bourbon and Habsburg parties, it is remarkable that the Spanish war with France dragged on until 1659, or that Portugal's wars with the Dutch and Spanish continued until 1663 and 1668 respectively. A key element in this morass of intrigue was a Spanish hope, seemingly against hope, that Cardinal Mazarin's grasping financial policies would eventually provoke a revolt against his authority from the French people.[40] For a time, this hope appeared desperately forlorn, and only Spanish dependencies in Naples and Sicily flocked to the standard of revolt. From 1648 though, a tear in the fabric of French society known as the Fronde did occur, and for the next four years this revolt grew, like a snowball rolling down a hill, until it included in its ranks disgruntled nobles, former commanders and even princes of the blood.[41] Whether Mazarin knew to expect the coming storm or not, he did recognise that separating the two Habsburg branches through war or peace was essential. In this task, the mission of settling with the Emperor appeared by far the more attainable.

THREE
Yearning for Peace

With the Danish War plan having plainly misfired, peace negotiations beginning, and the Swedish army under Torstenson enjoying a new sense of purpose, there was much for the Emperor's advisors to feel melancholy about when they gathered together in early 1645 to discuss their prospects. How much had changed in a decade; the simple patriotism which had moved his late father to urge all Germans to fight the invader would no longer suffice, and Ferdinand III now had to hear these men sigh that they no longer believed in a complete Imperial victory. Would victory be better and more cheaply gained at the peace table? Now that the Danes were excusing themselves as mediators, it was to be expected that the Swedes would contribute proper suggestions to any peace negotiations at Osnabruck.

With enough diplomatic dexterity, perhaps Sweden and France could be separated, the young Swedish Queen bought off with some trinkets, and the final disaster averted? Keeping the Swedes away from Bohemia was key, since Northern Germany was virtually emptied of potential allies whom the Emperor could count on, and the Bavarians were too distracted with the French to intervene there. As part of his dynasty's hereditary lands, Bohemia was a critical element in the source of the Austrian Habsburg power base. If this base was undermined, then the Habsburg hold on the office of Emperor could itself be threatened. There was thus much riding on the ability of the Imperial generalissimo Melchior von Hatzfeldt, who had replaced Matthias Gallas after the latter's poor showing the year before. Gallas had been criminally ineffective, not to mention roaring drunk, and he had failed to capitalise upon what was supposed to be a distracted Swedish host.

With that failure in mind, Hatzfeldt faced the formidable task of succeeding in the teeth not merely of fierce Swedish opposition, but also preparation. Torstenson was wholly focused on his Imperial foe in the campaigning season, and he had even moved south when the Danish War showed clear signs of winding down to meet whatever Imperial challenge the Emperor might send his way. Thanks to some diplomatic dexterity of his own, Chancellor Axel Oxenstierna had ensured that Transylvania ruined the Habsburg plans in 1644; perhaps, if Torstenson could show his hand to be a strong one, then the Prince of Transylvania would come knocking on the fragile Hungarian border again, thus undermining yet another source of the Austrian Habsburgs' power. All would depend on the outcome of battle; a victory would provide some shine to the Imperial delegates arriving at Westphalia, while a loss would enhance the Swedish negotiating position, perhaps to disastrous effect.

Thus began the Emperor's last great recruitment drive on such a massive scale, where all Germans were called to defend the Fatherland and repel the Swedes, as the Peace of Prague had advocated a decade before. Despite their creaking security position, John George of Saxony sent 1,500 cavalry, and Maximillian of Bavaria was persuaded to part with five thousand elite cavalry of his own. Hatzfeldt would thus command some eleven thousand horse, five thousand foot and twenty-six guns; five hundred dragoons were also added, to bring Hatzfeldt's force to nearly seventeen thousand. On paper, Sweden boasted more than forty thousand men in their pay in Germany by 1645, but a great portion of these remained occupied by the Danish War, and in particular with the task of pacifying and conquering the bishoprics of Bremen and Verden which King Christian IV of Denmark had once held for his sons. Under Torstenson's direct command was a force virtually equal to Hatzfeldt's, with nine thousand horse and six and a half thousand foot, but with nearly twice as many cannons, at sixty pieces. If Torstenson could bring this superiority of fire to bear upon his foe, then Hatzfeldt would suffer terribly.

But where to fight the battle? Torstenson knew he would have to find some means of drawing Hatzfeldt out, and to do this, he continued in his quest to seize as much of the Habsburg hereditary lands as he could. Olmutz in Moravia was his target, but it Hatzfeldt could not know whether he would make for that city by going north or south of Prague. Snows began to thaw in February, and the routes which had already been worn from three decades of war became impassable rivers of mud before long. In an effort to make it to comparative safety before the frozen ground melted completely, Torstenson took his men south of Prague to cross the still frozen Moldau River, a tributary of the Elbe, but Hatzfeldt anticipated the move and marched his men forwards to cut the Swedes off. Hatzfeldt arrived in the hills near the town of Jankau, and as Torstenson came to terms with his new position, he prepared to fight.

By all accounts, Hatzfeldt was lodged in a good defensive position. In front of him was the River Jankov which lent the nearby town its name, and this freezing stream would have to be crossed if the enemy was to meet him. Hills on his right and left secured the line, which was spread over two kilometres, but that was where Hatzfeldt's advantages ended. If Torstenson could overcome the stream and the network of ponds which it created, and if he could make use of his superiority in heavy guns, then Hatzfeldt's men would be battered into submission. Perhaps considering this, after a short skirmish in the morning, Hatzfeldt adjusted his line to account for Torstenson's rapidly moving forces, who seemed to be attempting a feint. By now Torstenson's army had moved over the river and was effectively facing down Hatzfeldt's men. The two lines had moved drastically, and victory would go to the commander who could think best on his feet.

At the crucial moment, the Bavarian cavalry elite which Maximillian had lent to Hatzfeldt charged, repelling their Swedish counterparts, but as happened so often during the era, these five thousand horse stayed behind to plunder the enemy's wares and women – nearly capturing Torstenson's wife in the process! Fortunately for the Swedish commander, he rallied the men back into the fray, and effectively repelled or captured Bavaria's finest cavalrymen. With the cavalry effectively absent, Torstenson had brought forward his superiority in gunfire, and quickly overwhelmed Hatzfeldt's batteries, which had been unable to secure themselves on the uneven ground. The combination of absent cavalry and a superiority in fire quickly began to tell, and the infantry in the Imperial centre began to crack. It was an echo of earlier battlefield situations like Rocroi and even Breitenfeld, and it underlined the importance of coordinating and maintaining the different arms of the army intact until the end of the day. Hatzfeldt had failed in this task, though he had given it his all. In the course of the terrible carnage, several senior ranking officers in the Imperial and Bavarian armies were slaughtered, and Hatzfeldt himself was captured, his horse simply running out of his steam as he sought to escape. It was like a cruel metaphor for the Imperial defence; after so many seasons of marching and fighting, this army had, it seemed, nothing left to give.[42]

The Battle of Jankau had been fought on 6 March 1645, and was arguably the last significant pitched battle of the war; what was not arguable was that the battle had been a disaster for the Emperor and his allies. The sting of defeat, it was painful because he had been in nominal command, as the figurehead in overall control of Hatzfeldt's men. Of course, Hatzfeldt commanded during the battle proper, and Ferdinand was in no position to make any difference to the outcome, but his association with the campaign, where he may have initially hoped for an outcome closer to Nordlingen a decade before, dulled that military aspect of his reputation which he had so highly valued. If the Emperor could not save his men, then who could? Ferdinand even made desperate overtures to the drunkard Gallas, but the disaster turned to emergency when the Prince of Transylvania signalled his intentions to try his luck again. Now that the Emperor was plainly reeling, it made sense to ignore the previous truce and strike into the soft Hungarian underbelly of the Habsburg domains. Like before, the Prince found fewer supporters among the thoroughly Catholicised Hungarian base, but he still posed a fearful security risk, and compelled the Emperor to flee to Graz, Austria's second city, two hundred kilometres southwest of Vienna.

The French also got in on the act, signing an alliance with Transylvania in April 1645, and attempting to follow up Torstenson's victory with some probing attacks of their own into Bavaria. In May, at the battle of Herbsthaus, near Bad Mergentheim (where the Teutonic Order was based for several centuries), the Bavarians beat the French back, and Turenne was himself nearly captured. The casualties were small, as were the size of the forces used, but the loss reminded Mazarin that he could not count Bavaria out, even if the Emperor was teetering. Undeterred, he tried again, this time with an army roughly similar in size to Torstenson's, at seventeen thousand. On 3 August 1645, this army under the joint command of the Prince of Condé and Turenne shattered its Bavarian counterpart at Allerheim, near the site where the Battle of Nordlingen had been fought a decade before, and Franz von Mercy, the Bavarian commander, was killed in the confrontation.

Here at last, so it seemed, was something of a turning point in the course of the war. That the negotiations at Westphalia were to last another three years demonstrates that the Habsburgs had not given up the ghost quite yet, but there could be no denying that, after a season of successive defeats, the well was running dry. Ferdinand had even fled Vienna at news of the re-entry into the war by Transylvania, and in November 1645, his representative finally arrived in Westphalia for the negotiations. By that time, John George of Saxony had officially thrown in the towel, formulating a truce with the Swedes on 6 September. The Emperor's representative was a pragmatist, and a realist. He was a veteran of court life, and had recommended moderation if it would bring about peace quicker; in fact had had spearheaded the approaches to Saxony a decade before in the Peace of Prague, and brought peace between the Emperor and Transylvania on numerous occasions. Who was this distinguished, accomplished diplomatist? It was Maximillian von Trauttmansdorff, by now in the twilight of his life and not in the best of health, but still the Imperial chief negotiator and Ferdinand's confidant. The very fact that Ferdinand saw it fit to send Trauttmansdorff to Westphalia demonstrated that he took these negotiations very seriously indeed, and as Geoffrey Parker noted, it was impossible to have expected the Emperor to do otherwise:

> The battle of Jankau...lasted longer than almost any other engagement in the war precisely because everyone recognised its decisive nature: The Emperor hazarded all his economic and military resources, the prestige of his house, and his own reputation as a commander of superior ability. The fact that he lost them all, through defeat, made it almost inevitable that the final peace settlement would be unfavourable to the Habsburgs. After Jankau and Allerheim, there was no longer any Catholic field army able to withstand the Swedes and their allies, and everyone knew it. [44]

There are few clearer indications of Ferdinand's desperation and yearning for peace than in the instructions which he communicated to his advisor in Latin in mid-October 1645, shortly after sending him on his mission to Westphalia. They make for depressing reading if one is a Habsburg, but they also demonstrate that the Emperor had effectively come to terms with the reality:

> I have considered the long duration of the present war, the ruin thereby inflicted on the Holy Roman Empire and on my hereditary kingdoms and lands in particular, the ever increasing enemy forces and strength against my own ever declining forces and strength and that of my allies, the almost exhausted means, the general sighs for peace and its necessity because of all this. I have also considered the good qualities, long experience in negotiations and the constant enthusiastic engagement for my and the common good displayed by Count Trauttmansdorff, my Senior Court Chamberlain. I am resolved...to appoint the said Count...to the peace negotiations in Münster and Osnabruck and to give him the following secret instructions, which he is to follow and to make peace as a last resort when nothing else can be done...

After introducing the circumstances, Ferdinand then outlined several of the issues which Trauttmansdorff was to try and solve, where he was to stand his ground, and where he was permitted to relent. Ferdinand's first demand set the tone for the others, when he noted:

> First, he is...to work zealously to ensure that the Estates of the Empire unite as members with myself as head and father, that the disrupted harmony of the Empire is restored, that the good old trust is re-established, and the proper combination of all Estates is consolidated again so that the foreign enemy crowns are brought to a proper peace, or that by forcing them back we can resist them more readily.

Ferdinand then dwelt on several other points, such as the question of a general amnesty. Originally, 1627 had been set as the key date but, as the Emperor himself now confessed, 'since it is likely that the Estates will not be satisfied by this', the amnesty can be granted 'in extreme cases to the year 1618, but then only in the Empire, but always excluding my kingdoms and hereditary provinces and the Palatine affair, of which more will be said later.' Indeed, Ferdinand declares his willingness to settle the Palatine affair – 'the cause of the war' – by granting an eighth electoral title. This settlement, in other words, would enable Maximillian to keep his Bavarian Electoral title, but Frederick V's offspring would be entitled to retain their electoral title as well. In return for this concession, Ferdinand declared that Trauttmansdorff should ask for a ninth electoral title to be 'created from our lands' but added that 'this can be relinquished if there is no other way.'

This proved to be a key suggestion in the peace negotiations, and it is significant to see them written here. At virtually every demand or request, Ferdinand added phrases like 'only to the last resort', 'only in the most desperate circumstances' and, as we have just seen, 'if there is no other way.' This underlined for Trauttmansdorff how far he was allowed to go with the negotiations, and addressed topics as varied as the ecclesiastical reservation, which had been created in 1555; the bill owed by Bavaria to the Palatine family; greater Lutheran participation in the Aulic Council, and satisfaction for Vienna's enemies. This latter issue was especially explosive, because it revolved for Sweden around Pomerania, and for France, Ferdinand suspected, around Alsace. As with all other cases, Ferdinand was willing to give away a great deal, but only if he absolutely had to. Thus, with the French, Ferdinand instructed Trauttmansdorff 'to grant them Alsace along the Rhine if they return the fortress of Breisach', but this was only if his position was strong enough. 'If this cannot be attained', Ferdinand instructed, then Trauttmansdorff should…

> …also attach Breisach and, if peace sticks solely on the Breisgau, finally to drop this as well, but only in the most desperate circumstances, especially as it is to be hoped that France will not ask for it, or at least will not insist on it, because up till now it has only claimed Alsace up to the Rhine.

Ferdinand was especially wary about handing over the Breisgau to the French, because under the terms of previous familiar arrangements signed by his father, the Breisgau technically did not belong to him. It actually belonged to his cousin, Ferdinand Karl – referred to henceforth as Karl to avoid confusion. Karl was the Archduke of the Breisgau, Alsace and the Tirol, because he had inherited these lands from his father in 1632. The arrangement, which Ferdinand II had authorised in 1626, had been intended to empower the cadet branches of the Habsburg family by giving them something to fight for and rule over, but now it was coming back to bite the Emperor, because if he wished to placate the French, it meant he might have to initiate a family feud which he could ill-afford. Indeed, the Emperor had even gone as far as ordering Trauttmansdorff to 'act before they [his Habsburg cousins] do', in the event that the latter proved unwilling to hand the Breisgau over. Was the Emperor so desperate for peace with his enemies that he was willing to rip his family apart? Apparently so and given this willingness to do all that was necessary, we should not be surprised to see him also work to hand anything to Brandenburg if its Elector would consent to granting Pomerania to Sweden.

The Pomeranian saga had been long and bitter for Brandenburg, thanks to the perfectly reasonable claim made by the late Elector of Brandenburg to the Duke of Pomerania's lucrative inheritance. Ferdinand II had even consented to this transfer of land and titles from Duke Bogislaw of Pomerania to George William of Brandenburg, but the arrival of the Swedes and their conquering of the region complicated this pretty picture. George William was denied his inheritance, and the Emperor was terminally unwilling to fight so far north for him. When their forces were defeated, the Swedes had retreated into their Pomeranian bridgehead, leaving no doubt in the Emperor's mind, or in Brandenburg's, that they intended to cling to the region for better or for worse. Per these instructions though, Ferdinand revealed his plan to make everyone happy; it involved nothing less than a plan to give Sweden everything it wanted – all of Pomerania, the bishoprics of Bremen and Verden, and the ports of Stralsund, Wismar and Rostock. As usual, Ferdinand was careful to clarify that 'it should be understood that all this is only to be conceded gradually one after the other and only as a matter of the last resort.' That begged the question, how was Brandenburg expected to agree to such a calamity?

Ferdinand believed he had the answer in other lands and duchies which Frederick William, the new Elector of Brandenburg, might want instead. While one might have expected Frederick William to fold his arms until he got what he wanted, Ferdinand rightly suspected that the new Elector was made of stronger, more strategic stuff than his late father. With the war plainly against the Habsburgs and his plans for Pomerania up in smoke, Frederick William would certainly prefer some inland German nuggets rather than nothing at all. 'It is likely that those that also want [Pomerania] will object', Ferdinand began, 'so Electoral Brandenburg can be offered my jurisdiction over the Duchy of Crossen together with a sum of money and so put off as long as possible.' The Duchy of Crossen was a small slice of land with a complicated history; it was in Bohemia but had been subject to the authority of the Electors of Brandenburg in the past, while still owing taxes to the Bohemian Crown, and thus to the Habsburgs. Granting the Duchy of Crossen would effectively simplify the situation, but Ferdinand was not so foolish as to imagine that Frederick William would be so easily bought off, and he had prepared a shopping list of duchies should he 'not be satisfied with this', and the Emperor remarked:

> ...it can be given Halberstadt as well, together with some districts from Magdeburg, meanwhile the holder of the archbishopric of Magdeburg, as well as Bremen and Mecklenburg, can be given financial compensation. The money must be provided by the Imperial Estates, instead of those that would have been given to Sweden...

By shuffling these interests around the board and drawing on new sources of tax to pay the disenfranchised, Ferdinand revealed an imaginative formula which would hopefully leave everyone happy. It was certainly a bold and controversial plan; if any of his relatives had gotten a hold of it, they would certainly have been upset to see their lands be nominated as potential pawns for a peace treaty. Even relatives as important as the Spanish were not out of bounds from the Emperor's considerations. Trauttmansdorff was instructed to deal 'in good faith and correspondence with the Spanish plenipotentiaries', but Ferdinand was unwilling to ruin Vienna for the sake of Madrid's doomed war, as he noted:

> It is known that all our enemies' plans, intentions, efforts and works [are] directed to separate the Germans from the Spanish and according to the principle divide and conquer, defeat one or the other both successively. Therefore, Count von Trauttmansdorff will above all ensure that it will not come to such a separation and will rather let all go to rack and ruin than this to happen. To avoid this danger, one must ensure that Spain is included in the peace.

These instructions were predictable, but while he wished for Spain and Austria to stand together, what Ferdinand wrote next demonstrated that he was only willing to stand with the Spanish for a certain length of time:

> Therefore…[the Count will stress] to them the danger, the impossibility of continuing the war, the necessity of peace and a swift conclusion. Should they reject this, however, or claim they have no instructions, he should indicate to them that I cannot leave this business, but will request that the King of Spain, my dearest cousin, brother in law and brother, with a previously agreed deadline will agree to the peace, or, if he does not, then he should not hold it against me that I can no longer assist him.

As far as Ferdinand was concerned, one could not afford to be sentimental, and all potential avenues for peace should be explored, if only as a final resort. If one's allies refused to see reason, then they should be informed, politely and gently, that the burden of the war was no longer sustainable here, and that since this was the case, continuing the war was impossible. Interestingly, this is what happened, as the Emperor made his peace with France in 1648, but the King of Spain carried on the war alone. It was important not to anticipate this rupture in 1645, however, and Ferdinand was plainly anxious to ensure that the enemy could never know just how far he was willing to go, and he trusted Trauttmansdorff to make the right call:

> And this is what I give to von Trauttmansdorff as instructions, that he realises that he is to proceed gradually in everything, and not concede this or that too hastily, but according to circumstances and the final stages only as the last resort in dire straits and when all hope is gone. I place my gracious trust in his prudence, skill, experience and loyalty, that he will observe the correct tempo and will not act too soon or too late. He and his family remain in my grace and I remain his gracious Emperor.[44]

Unfortunately for the Emperor, worse news was afoot. Ferdinand was virtually stripped of allies in Northern Germany; the Spanish continued to rumble forward with little hope of eventual success against their rebellious former subjects, not to mention the French, and the eastern border with Hungary was now volatile so long as the Prince of Transylvania was in the mix. Ferdinand may have hoped that, after all these years of solidarity, the last person who would be willing to abandon him was Maximillian of Bavaria, especially since the latter had gained so much from his participation in the war, being raised to an Elector, and expanding his landholdings into the Palatinate as he did so. But Maximillian was no fool, and as the ship began to sink, it was only to be expected that he would look for a lifeboat elsewhere. He believed he had found it not in the fickle fortunes of military adventure – Allerheim had put a stop to that – but in diplomacy, and through the French First Minister, Cardinal Mazarin.

We have already seen how the military events of 1645 turned against the Habsburgs, but something which deserves special mention is the fact that Bavaria faced down the vast majority of French incursions into the Empire. Thus, if the Bavarians collapsed, then this would open up the possibility for a joint Franco-Swedish assault on Vienna, or any other nightmarish scenario.[45] Bavarian contacts with France had been underway for many years, and as early as Gustavus Adolphus' first foray into Germany, Maximillian had worked to reach some form of arrangement with the French, though to no avail. Maximillian had been forced to watch his lands fall prey to the rapacious Swedes, but in the years after this catastrophe he continued to maintain limited contacts with Richelieu and then Mazarin, even with the French declaration of war on Spain in 1635 and the de facto open war with the Emperor from 1636.

In 1643, these contacts looked set to increase, as Maximillian contemplated sending his French confessor to treat with Mazarin in his name, only to back out at the last minute. Nor was he the only one to hesitate. Mazarin was deeply vexed over the possibility that the Swedes might find out about the negotiations, since he desperately needed Torstenson to maintain the pressure on Vienna while French forces met the Spanish in the numerous other theatres. Even after Rocroi suggested that a turning point had passed, the strategic situation for France was not so simple. Tuttlingen in late 1643 was a catastrophic mess for the French; In July 1644, the Spanish captured the town of Lleida from a Franco-Catalan garrison, and only a month after that fiasco, the Battle of Freiburg took place. Fought over three days in August 1644, Freiburg was an inconclusive, costly disaster, especially for the French who lost eight thousand casualties, to Franz von Mercy's two thousand.[46]

Plainly, the numerical superiority which was so evident in the French tax base and population had yet to produce an overwhelming successive campaign of attack; Mazarin banked on it being only a matter of time before this success was found, and he certainly gambled that it would bring France glory and triumph before her people rebelled under the choking pressure of taxes. The pressure finally began to tell by 1645, when the ripples caused by the defeat of Denmark were felt in the Empire, Jankau routed the Imperials, and Bavaria seemed to quake. In Münster, where many of the delegations had already arrived, France's agents reported to Mazarin that rumours of Franco-Bavarian negotiations were easy to come by. The French were forced to lie to their Swedish allies about these rumours, but in spring 1645, the planned trip by Maximillian's French confessor had come to pass, and it was inevitable that the truth would soon get out. For their part, the Frenchmen back in Münster were eager to communicate the point to Mazarin that secrecy should be maintained, whatever the situation on the battlefield might reveal:

> ...certainly, Monseigneur, France's situation seems to be so good in this war that we need only continue as we have while it lasts, and to keep all things in the state where they have been up until now. It could be dangerous to admit the slightest change.

But Jankau seemed to change all that. As Maximillian's confessor attempted in vain to gain some headway with the suspicious Mazarin, news of the Swedish triumph filtered through in early March 1645. With this news, efforts in Bavaria were turned towards making the French see how dangerous and powerful Sweden had become. When that failed, Maximillian requested that France take Bavaria under her protection, but only as a last resort. What he feared, evidently, was a repeat of that Swedish comeback in 1632, when Gustavus had rampaged across a helpless Bavaria, and all pleas to France fell on deaf ears. Maximillian wanted to ensure that Mazarin's ears were wide open this time around, and he was perfectly willing to leave the war if it meant saving his Electorate from catastrophe.[47]

During the summer, the initially impossible situation seemed to improve, at least for Bavaria, since Turenne was kept at bay in the Battle of Herbsthausen in July 1645. Unfortunately, this victory did not either dramatically improve Bavaria's bargaining position with France, nor did it solve Bavarian security problems along the Rhine for very long. Instead, the loss seems to have tarnished French credit in the mind of her Swedish ally, and Swedish representatives used the opportunity to push for greater religious concessions at Westphalia. The knock-on effects of battle upon the negotiations were clearly felt, but the impact was not allowed to rest for long, as the Battle of Allerheim a month later restored confidence in the French command, destroyed the Bavarian army and its commander Von Mercy, and fulfilled Maximillian's nightmare all in a single day.

This time there was no hesitation among Maximillian's officials; his council unanimously approved a plan to approach the French if it would save

Bavaria's situation. By now, Bavarian agents were approaching the French in secret in Münster and affirming their pledge to intervene favourably for French interests, essentially to vouch for them to the Emperor, if France would guarantee Bavaria and the position of its wily Elector. By 26 August 1645, the three main French plenipotentiaries laid out to the Bavarians what they desired. This included Breisach, the Breisgau, the Sundgau…

> …and the other lands and sovereign rights that "the House of Habsburg" had in Upper and Lower Alsace, and protection of the ten Imperial cities, with garrisons in the places where the King will judge necessary. And, last, that the estates immediate to the Empire and that were under the protection of the "Habsburgs" will remain in the Empire and will be under the protection of the King, and the mediate estates will be controlled by His Majesty as Landgrave of Alsace.[48]

Since we know the limits of what the Emperor was willing to concede (see his letter to Trauttmansdorff, above), we can deduce that the two sides were not far off guessing what the other side either wanted or was willing to concede. Certainly, Mazarin seemed to believe that France was winning the struggle; by early September 1645, in light of the triumph at Allerheim, he was writing that these advantageous circumstances enabled him to 'lay down the law just as you like to our opponents, and they will be forced to acquiesce to everything that we demand from them', but the Duke of Longueville, then in Münster, insisted matters were not so simple, and that 'we press as much as we can, but it is with little effect.'[49] Evidently, the peace negotiations, be they in secret between the French and Bavarians, or in the open at Westphalia, still had some way to go. 1645 had nonetheless demonstrated that the battlefield would decide the end result; no matter how long one spent determining where to sit at the peace table, what foods to import for one's place of residence, or even how to address one's fellow delegates, it was on the gritty, bloody, unpredictable battlefield that the truly momentous decisions could be gleaned.

FOUR
Dutch Loose Ends

Frederick Henry, Prince of Orange, was one of the defining commanders and innovators of his age. He had assumed the office of stadtholder of Holland from his brother Maurice in 1625, and at that time, the fate of the Dutch Republic seemed shrouded in uncertainty and defeat. Thanks to the leadership of the Spanish commander Ambrogio Spinola, the Army of Flanders had worked its way through the Dutch defences, capturing Breda before 1625 was out. Wedgewood provides an emotive account of Maurice's final moments, how his waning mental powers honed in on the threat posed by Spain, and how he feared his younger brother, mostly unknown in the Republic, would not be equal to the task in front of him. Maurice mustered enough strength to watch Frederick Henry at least leave his life as a bachelor behind, and at forty years old, marry one of the Bohemian ladies in waiting. At the very least, a dying Maurice could take solace in the fact that the House of Orange would continue. Just as he died in April 1625, Frederick Henry left his new bride behind to lead the assault of Spinola's outworks surrounding Breda, but the challenge was too great.[50]

Another, equally formidable challenge, was to expect Frederick Henry to succeed his brother as stadtholder for five of the seven Dutch provinces, and as supreme commander on land and at sea. Would this unknown Orange entity distinguish himself as his brother had done, in the field of military innovation and ingenuity, or was he merely riding to war on the name value of the House of Orange alone? The Dutch Republic was very fortunate indeed that Frederick Henry was a skilled, creative and learned commander of men. He had learned from, and been devoted to, his elder brother, but it is safe to say that he surpassed Maurice's exploits many times over. It would have been above Maurice's imagination to suppose that within twenty years, the Dutch position would be so transformed, and Spain so weakened. Yet it was in these last two decades that Frederick Henry had turned the tables on the Spanish; frequently, in fact, the stadtholder had provided the sole source of good news for the anti-Habsburg camp, as his well-drilled militias and professional soldiers undermined countless Spanish settlements, securing the borders of the Republic in the process, and removing the Spanish soldier from Dutch land.[51]

In 1625, indeed, the news was gloomy not only for the Dutch, but for all those who had determined to oppose the Emperor or the King of Spain. France remained controlled by a pro-Spanish regime, where Richelieu had yet to gain his footing. The English were more interested in a Spanish marriage than a Spanish War, and this had only recently begun to change with the death of King James. In 1625 also, the Danish King was poised to enter what he believed was bound to be a glorious showcase of his personal power, but it was to end in utter disaster. The Dutch were caught in the middle of these schemes, but as one Dutch observer saw it, 'Here, there is nothing but gloom for the present and fear for the future.'[52]

It is safe to say that Frederick Henry was the third in a run of three critically important Princes of Orange during the years of the Dutch Revolt. Frederick Henry assumed the role which Maurice had passed to him and Maurice had himself assumed the stadtholderate after succeeding from his father. William the Silent (1544-1584), the father of these two famed stadtholders, had raised the standard of revolt against Spain with some reluctance and much difficulty, but the act had had tremendous consequences.[53] The inheritance he left to Maurice was one of leadership, which all subsequent Princes of Orange would do their utmost to match. But it was also an inheritance of revolution; the Dutch revolted against the Spanish, and launched a revolution in finance, in trade, in entrepreneurship, in exploration, in exploitation, in military invention, in naval tactics,[54] and even in something as mundane as taxation.[55]

The conflict had the effect of supercharging the economy of an already lucrative corner of Europe, with the result that the seven provinces which eventually constituted the bulk of the revolt were forced to redefine their relationship with war finance to sustain their seemingly endless struggle.[56] The struggle paid off though, because it was thanks to their revolution, Spain suffered from a wound which never truly healed, and which sucked in resources and commitments far above and beyond what Madrid could have imagined when news of those rebellious Northerners was first learned of in the late 1560s.[57] The Dutch revolt shed its wholly Netherlandish character, as by the turn of the century the Dutch had been moved to establish foreign trading companies, and seize markets owned by the Spanish and Portuguese. As they bungled the war, the Spanish were faced with additional enemies; wars with the English and French were fought alongside that of the Dutch, and frequently spilled into the relevant zones of colonial influence. It was due to these considerations that the renowned historian Geoffrey Parker saw fit to label the Eighty Years War as the First World War of its age.[58]

In pursuit of their religious freedoms, the Dutch managed to inspire settlements in the New World, and the religious toleration its officials displayed while governing their colonies, such as Brazil,[59] may have gone some way towards influencing the religious pluralism of the United States.[60] Of course, the Dutch were not wholly free from bouts of religious extremism either, and the difficult experiences of division and suspicion during the years of the Twelve Years Truce[61] (1609-1621) in particular read like a warning to republics with a religiously diverse population.[62] To fight her enemies, the Dutch had become not merely adventurous seafarers, but also first-rate traders, with an entrepot trade network based in Amsterdam and snaking all over the world. The war had compelled the Dutch to improvise, to explore and to invest, with the result that, by the end of their war with Spain it was safe to proclaim that '...through our thrifty and shrewd management, we have sailed all nations off the seas, drawn almost all trade from other lands hither, and served the whole of Europe with our ships.' It was a grand claim to make, but few would have been able to dispute it.[63]

For eight decades the war with Spain had been maintained, and even during that aforementioned Twelve Years Truce which brought peace to Europe, the war was not paused in the New World, or anywhere else where the Dutch might perceive an advantage.[64] This conflict had carried on breathlessly from the middle of the sixteenth century to this scene, in 1647, when this great scion of the House of Orange lay dying. Frederick Henry – much like the war he had rescued, maintained and then pursued to victory – was nearing his end. In addition to all he had done for the Netherlands, the ailing stadtholder had also made another critically important dynastic decision which was to have an impact not only on his Republic, but also on his European neighbours, with consequences that are still felt today in Ireland, Britain and the Americas.

In 1642, Frederick Henry's son William was wedded to Mary Stuart, daughter of King Charles. By this act, the stadtholder demonstrated that the House of Orange – a curiously Dutch institution, and not quite royal – had been raised to parity with the actually royal House of Stuart.[65] Was Frederick Henry plotting to reimagine his House as the source of the country's Kings? Did he plan to launch some kind of royal coup? Certainly, he received no shortage of offers from Spain and occasionally from France which promised support for whatever grand dynastic ambitions he might have.[66] But Frederick Henry would not be drawn. Instead, he put his faith in the logic that his House would be raised up by the prestige of its connections, and his daughter Louisa was wed to Frederick William, the Elector of Brandenburg, in the weeks before his death. Frederick Henry certainly felt threatened in his position though; with the war over, would the Republic truly need his office?

Surely when peace with Spain came, his influence and that of his family would decline, since there would be no war to heap additional glory on his name. Indeed, the regent party in the Netherlands was already counting on this outcome, and in Holland in particular, rising political stars such as Johan de Witt were reaching for greater control over the country's policy. The result of this tension was that when Frederick Henry died on 14 March 1647, it seemed that few were in a position to pause for a moment and consider his incredible legacy, a legacy which had virtually saved the Dutch people from Spanish rule, and catapulted this small group of provinces to the forefront of the European concert of power.[67] Instead, his death occasioned the first of many showdowns between the regent party and Frederick Henry's son, William. The regent party had been suspicious of the French alliance, they had been eager for the war to end, and they had wanted to increase trade relations with all powers, even the Spanish, as soon as possible. In June 1647, only a few months after Frederick Henry's death, a truce was signed with the Spanish; by that point, in any event, the war in the Netherlands had wound down, with no activity of note since the late stadtholder's capture of Hulst in 1645. It could not have been guaranteed at the time, but this truce was to stick for another eight months, until in January 1648, it became an official peace.[68]

Thus, the war was effectively at an end by the time the new stadtholder assumed his title from his late father. But so long as William II remained in place, there was little chance to radically reimagine the government of the Republic. It was the occasion of William II's death from smallpox in 1650, therefore, that radically altered the history of the Republic. This provided the opportunity for the regent party to act, and to undermine the influence of the proto-monarchical House of Orange.[69] For more than twenty years after William II's death, the era of so-called 'true freedom' was at hand, where the office of stadtholder was left vacant in five of the seven provinces, and the regent class ruled the roost. This was a period of unrivalled prosperity and wealth for the Republic, but it could not last forever. The concerns regarding the French alliance proved valid, as an empowered French King Louis XIV launched a surprise attack in league with England in 1672. At the same time, a young Prince of Orange was rapidly coming of age. His name was William III, and he had been born a week after his father had died.

The challenges which faced his House and his countrymen were grave, but William III managed, by the end of the seventeenth century, to position himself firmly in opposition to the French, and more famously, to launch a bid for the British Crown in 1688 which was to redefine these Isles. William III was indeed a remarkable man, but he was granted such opportunities because of the exploits of his grandfather and granduncle, who fought for decades in the cause of Dutch independence.[70] The Thirty Years War seems to tidy up the story of the Eighty Years War, because the latter reached its climax and concluded within its parameters. Thanks to the interconnected nature of the war, and the heavy involvement from Dutch and Spanish allies, it was impossible for the results of the conflict not to spill over into the conflict between Spain and France or Sweden and the Emperor; indeed, the Dutch War is critical to our understanding of the Thirty Years War because of this.[71]

Central to keeping the Thirty Years War alive, by the mid-1640s the Dutch had notably moved to the periphery of the conflict. This was due to several factors, not least the utter distraction of their Spanish foe, following the eruption of revolts in Portugal and Catalonia. With the arrival of French support for a war within Spanish borders, Philip IV decided to prioritise the challenges facing his Crown, and since those in Iberia posed a direct security risk to Madrid, it was inevitable that the war with the Dutch slipped down his list of priorities. This in turn granted the Dutch new opportunities to defeat their foes in the Spanish Netherlands. The additional pressure applied by the French, who battered on the Spanish defences in Flanders to the west, while the Dutch operated in the east, could only produce one outcome.

The defences of the South Netherlands along the border with France had traditionally been weaker owing the decades of war between the Spanish and Dutch, and the diverting of resources to that front. The Brussels government therefore began to buckle in the face of these combined pressures, exacerbated by the chronic underinvestment from Madrid. Not even the efforts of the Emperor's brother, Leopold William, were enough to save the region from disaster. It seemed only a matter of time before the French and Dutch carved the area up between them, and it was arguably only Dutch fears of a French border that stopped this outcome.

If the war was not guaranteed to bring substantial returns, and if the Republic was not in present danger, then one could ask what the purpose of the war with Spain even was; or at the very least, the officials in Holland could complain that they no longer wished to foot the bill for such an enormous army that was effectively idle. It was necessary therefore to reach peace with the Spanish, but this goal contained two major problems. The first was that the Dutch were divided, ideologically but also literally, as the Dutch delegation was split between the seven provinces. Each province boasted a representative, which was sent to Münster, but these figures by no means always operated in tandem. This was because each representative hailed from a province that wished to pursue its own interests, as though it were an independent state. For the most part, these interests came down to where that province stood on the question of war with Spain.

For Holland, the war had gone on long enough, the House of Orange was becoming suspicious, the French dangerous, and the war wasteful. The merchants, entrepreneurs and middle-class burgers who had helped finance the war had grown tired of it, and they advocated peace as soon as possible. On the other side of the debate, the province of Zealand was against making peace, and was notably more pro-Orange. Zealand's mercantile interests were also aided by the wartime blockade of the River Scheldt, which choked the Spanish city of Antwerp, a blockade which would of course end to the detriment of these Zealand merchants once the war also ended. Embodying these two standpoints were the residents in Münster; Adrian Pauw for Holland, and Johan de Knuyt for Zealand. So long as these two officials disagreed about the nature of the peace treaty with Spain, or indeed the merits of making peace at all, the war with Spain would continue. Yet, as we have seen, a truce was reached in June 1647, which means that at some point in the eighteen months that the Dutch resided at Münster, common ground amongst themselves and with the Spanish was finally reached.

The second major problem the Dutch negotiators faced was that of the French. It was within the French interest to ensure that the war between the Dutch and Spanish continued, just as it was to ensure the war between Sweden and the Emperor continued. Many methods could be employed to exhaust and demoralise one's rival, and it only made sense to harness them to their full potential. The war with Spain had been a boon to French fortunes since its inception, and French Kings had intermittently supported the Dutch since the war began. By the mid-1640s, Mazarin was understandably anxious that the Dutch would make peace with Spain first, and thus undermine French leverage at the peace table, and potentially French security as well.

Mazarin wished to keep the Dutch close until peace could be made with the Spanish, and his agent, Abel Servien, went to remarkable lengths to disrupt their negotiations, at one point even accusing Adrian Pauw of bribery to undermine his position and potentially get him recalled. Pauw angrily denied the accusations, which were taken very seriously in the Republic. However, Servien might have been better served in this quest by examining the Zealand delegate, Johan de Knuyt, who was on record for accepting Spanish money. It is not known whether de Knuyt was a firm advocate for peace notwithstanding this secret income, but considering the fact that he represented Zealand, the more pro-war of the Dutch provinces, this would be an odd fit.[72] One imagines that Zealand would send a delegate that fit their outlook on the war, rather than send a potential ally of Holland to the negotiations. Pieter Geyl went as far as to call de Knuyt 'one of the most corrupt servants of the prince [of Orange]', so the jury seems mostly decided on that front.[73]

But Mazarin was more than capable of devising a scheme himself. In spring 1646 a damning secret plan was leaked by the Prince of Orange in The Hague, which contained a startling revelation about the intentions of the Republic's ally. Mazarin, Frederick Henry said, had schemed to swap the thankless province of Catalonia with Spain, in return for its possession of the Spanish Netherlands. This swap, Mazarin insisted, should not anger or even truly surprise the Dutch, because hadn't they made a deal in 1635 to divide the Spanish Netherlands between them? That they had, but the circumstances of that division were different indeed to the swap which Mazarin here had conceived. It would have placed the French, at a stroke, empowered and in possession of all the fortified places of Flanders, directly opposite the Dutch. There would be no question of the French having to fight for these gains, as they would be handed over unspoiled, with profound implications for the region. Perhaps, after more than a decade, this old offer was no longer as attractive to the Dutch as it had once been; Mazarin ought to have realised that swapping an exhausted Spanish regime for a reinvigorated French one would have been unpopular in The Hague, but instead of considering this, the wily Cardinal determined to contact the ailing stadtholder in late February 1646 with the terms.

This was a serious mistake; Frederick Henry was immediately burdened with the offer and recognised its dynamite qualities from the beginning. He asked Mazarin to keep the offer secret but seems to have accepted that the scheme would leak out, and would cast him in an unfavourable light with the anti-Orangist party. So, just as the Dutch delegates were returning to The Hague to try and bolster their negotiating position, news of the scheme was allowed to filter into the Dutch States-General. It caused a sensation – an anti-French sensation. On 28 February, the official statement condemning the plot had been published by the Dutch government:

> That France, being enlarged by the Spanish Netherlands, shall be a formidable body next to this state, that all states, at all times, have considered it dangerous to have neighbours who are too powerful; that the nature of the French is difficult and restless, and can scarcely be suffered except at a distance.

Yet, the official condemnation was not as inflammatory as the unofficial response from Dutch citizens. The news of the efforts of France to undermine the security of their ally by appearing on their doorstep overnight came accompanied by scurrilous rumours, which claimed that France also wished to inherit Philip IV's claims to overlordship over all the Netherlands, thereby inheriting a *casus belli* against the Dutch in one fell swoop. That latter rumour was in fact untrue, but it spread quickly, nonetheless. The Portuguese ambassador in The Hague even claimed that the Dutch, being at war with his state across the world, now hated France so much that they no longer had hatred to spare for Portugal, and it is certainly possible that this compelled the Dutch to take their focus off of Spain as well. In these circumstances, a lasting peace between the Dutch and Spanish suddenly seemed more possible than ever.

The Dutch delegates returned to Münster in May 1646, and shortly thereafter, they had intensified their negotiations with the Spanish. Originally willing to propose the equivalent of a twenty years truce, the Spanish were suddenly offered a comprehensive peace treaty by the Dutch delegates, containing 71 detailed articles. On 18 May 1646, the most substantial step forward in these negotiations were made, as the Spanish signalled their willingness to accept 60 of the 71 articles; the Dutch now had firm ground upon which they could negotiate, and they were determined to do so without the interference of the French.[74]

The Dutch delegation may have broadly favoured peace, but it was necessary still to smooth over any wrinkles in their united front. Thus, the delegates from Holland and Zealand led the charge, and would eventually reach a compromise in early 1647. This compromise saw Adrian Pauw promise to send a fleet and an army, funded by Holland, to recapture Brazil, if Johan de Knuyt promised publicly to agree to peace with Spain. It was through this largely forgotten arrangement, more than any other, that peace with Spain was facilitated. Certainly, it could not be said that the beleaguered Spanish had somehow pressured the Dutch to sign.[75] Even the Portuguese, nominally at war with the Dutch, managed to weigh in on the debate, despite possessing no officially recognised deputation at Münster.[76] The French and Portuguese were united in this quest to undermine a Dutch-Spanish peace, because it would free King Philip IV to focus more intently on their wars.

But if either King John of Portugal or Cardinal Mazarin feared that Spain would suddenly redirect her resources against them in the aftermath of the truce, then they were relieved to learn that King Philip faced yet another revolt in his lands, this time in the far-flung possessions in Naples. After a year of revolt, provoked by Spanish efforts to squeeze the Neapolitan tax base to the limit, the struggle was ended when Philip's illegitimate son captured the city in January 1648. At least one problem area of the Empire had been healed, but Philip was not particularly cheered by the news. With war destined to carry on with France and Portugal, and Catalonia still burning a hole in his coffers, he noted with dismay in summer 1648:

> It pierces my heart…to see the vicious state at which the world has arrived. I recognise it as clearly as you do, and as I cannot remedy it so quickly as I should like I am greatly troubled; although I do what I can. God grant that I may succeed in remedying it, and that I may begin by my own amendment; for there is no doubt that I need it more than anyone.[77]

At the very least, Philip could be encouraged that the war with the Dutch was over, and relations in trade and diplomacy could perhaps be normalised.[78] The Dutch, for their part, seemed more interested in taking the fight to the Portuguese, at least in the new world. Following on from the commitments which Holland had made to Zealand in early 1647, by the second half of the year, it was time for the flotilla targeting Brazil to set sail. Indeed, by August 1647, it would be fair to say that Holland and Zealand had already turned their attentions away from the negotiations at Westphalia, as a force of forty-one ships and six thousand men was assembled and prepared to sail in October. Even though various complications delayed the expedition until December, and even though this expedition itself produced no notable results, and certainly did not return the region to Dutch control, Zealand kept up her end of the bargain. The States (or assembly) in Zealand instructed her representative in Münster to make the truce official, and through this process, following a solemn ceremony on 30 January 1648, the Eighty Years War was officially brought to an end.[79]

There was nothing the Portuguese or French could do but fulminate at the Dutch decision; both powers were destined to remain locked in war with Spain for several more years. The Dutch, meanwhile, re-orientated their financial and political stance, to assume a more mutually beneficial relationship with the Spanish. Trade routes were opened up, border security with Flanders was relaxed, and money began to flow into the Dutch coffers like never before. A so-called 'special relationship' between the former enemies now began to blossom, with the result that the two powers became firm allies in the wars against France which the second half of the seventeenth century would host.[80] One significant chapter of the Eighty Years War, and therefore of the Thirty Years War, was now closed, but the other chapters which constituted this saga in peacemaking were far from finished yet.

Chapter 22 Notes

[1]Colegrove, 'Diplomatic Procedure Preliminary to the Congress of Westphalia', p. 450.
[2]Charles Homer Haskins and Robert Howard Lord, *Some Problems of the Peace Conference* (Cambridge: Harvard University Press, 1920), p. 3.
[3]For a useful examination of these issues see Sally Marks, 'Behind the Scenes at the Paris Peace Conference of 1919', *Journal of British Studies*, Vol. 9, No. 2 (May, 1970), pp. 154-180.
[4]See Croxton, *Westphalia*, pp. 127-128.
[5]*Ibid*, pp. 128-130.
[6]In 1919 Paris, Clemenceau lobbied for French to be the sole language of the conference, but the combined Anglo-American pressure eventually forced him to accept equal status for French and English, with allowances also made for Japanese and Italian, the language of the victors. See Council of Ten Minutes, *The Paris Peace Conference*, Volume III, pp. 440-454. Available: http://images.library.wisc.edu/FRUS/EFacs/1919Parisv03/reference/frus.frus1919parisv03.i0008.pdf Last accessed 12/10/2019
[7]See Croxton, *Westphalia*, pp. 164-167.
[8]See *Ibid*, pp. 155-157.
[9]*Ibid*, pp. 137-141.
[10]See Kenneth Colegrove, 'Diplomatic Procedure Preliminary to the Congress of Westphalia', 460-462.
[11]Croxton, *Westphalia*, pp. 142-145.
[12]Pascal, *Pensées*, part 319. Available: https://www.gutenberg.org/files/18269/18269-h/18269-h.htm
[13]Croxton, *Westphalia*, pp. 148-149.
[14]*Ibid*, pp. 152-153.
[15]Michael Bregnsbo, 'Denmark and the Westphalian Peace', pp. 366-367.
[16]Pedro Cardim, '"Portuguese Rebels" at Münster. The Diplomatic Self-Fashioning in mid-seventeenth Century European Politics', *Historische Zeitschrift. Beihefte*, New Series, Vol. 26, Der Westfälische Friede. Diplomatie – politische Zäsur – kulturelles Umfeld – Rezeptionsgeschichte (1998), pp. 293-333. Henceforth referred to as 'Portuguese Rebels'.
[17]Croxton, *Westphalia*, p. 174.
[18]Ward eds, *The Cambridge Modern History*, pp. 398-399.
[19]Croxton, *Westphalia*, pp. 185-186.
[20]Croxton, '"The Prosperity of Arms Is Never Continual": Military Intelligence, Surprise, and Diplomacy in 1640s Germany', pp. 990-992.
[21]See Wilson, *Sourcebook*, p. 281.
[22]Croxton, *Westphalia*, p. 112.
[23]See Stephen Rose, 'Trumpeters and diplomacy on the eve of the Thirty Years' War: the "album amicorum" of Jonas Kröschel', *Early Music*, Vol. 40, No. 3 (August 2012), pp. 379-392.
[24]Quoted in Croxton, *Westphalia*, p. 176.
[25]*Ibid*, pp. 112-113.
[26]The campaign for the representation of the estates is covered best by *Ibid*, pp. 197-205.
[27]Quoted in Wilson, *Sourcebook*, pp. 283-284.
[28]Croxton, *Westphalia*, pp. 114-116.
[29]Quoted in Geyl, *History of the Dutch-Speaking Peoples*, pp. 478-479.
[30]Daviken Studnicki-Gizbert, *A Nation upon the Ocean Sea: Portugal's Atlantic Diaspora and the Crisis of the Spanish Empire, 1492-1640* (New York: Oxford University Press, 2007), pp. 163-166.
[31]Geyl, *Dutch-Speaking Peoples*, pp. 480-485.
[32]Parker, 'Why Did the Dutch Revolt Last Eighty Years?', p. 71.
[33]Quoted in Croxton, *Westphalia*, p. 119.
[34]Parker, *Europe in Crisis*, pp. 277-278.
[35]Edmundson, 'Frederick Henry: Prince of Orange (continued)', pp. 289-290.
[36]Glete, *War and the State in Early Modern Europe*, p. 86.
[37]Quoted in Hume, *Court of Philip IV*, p. 398.
[38]Anderson, *The History of Portugal*, p. 116.
[39]Cardim, 'Portuguese Rebels', p. 298.
[40]See R. Trevor Davies, *Spain in Decline, 1621-1700*, pp. 54-67.
[41]Parker, *Europe in Crisis*, pp. 280-281.
[42]For details on the Battle of Jankau see Wilson, *Europe's Tragedy*, pp. 693-695. See also Parker, *Thirty Years War*, pp. 157-158.

[43]Parker, *Thirty Years War*, p. 158.

[44]All extracts of Emperor Ferdinand III's secret instructions to Count von Trauttmansdorff are taken from Wilson, *Sourcebook*, pp. 284-289.

[45]See Croxton, "The Prosperity of Arms is Never Continual", pp. 985-987.

[46]See W. P. Guthrie, *The Later Thirty Years' War: From the Battle of Wittstock to the Treaty of Westphalia* (Westport, 2003), pp. 212-213.

[47]See Croxton, *Peacemaking*, pp. 146-148.

[48]See *Ibid*, pp. 170-172.

[49]*Ibid*, p. 173.

[50]See Wedgewood, *Thirty Years War*, pp. 194-195.

[51]For Frederick Henry's early career see George Edmundson, 'Frederick Henry, Prince of Orange', *The English Historical Review*, Vol. 5, No. 17 (Jan., 1890), pp. 41-64.

[52]Quoted in Jonathan I. Israel, 'Frederick Henry and the Dutch Political Factions, 1625-1642', *The English Historical Review*, Vol. 98, No. 386 (Jan., 1983), pp. 1-27; p. 2.

[53]Herbert H. Rowen, 'The Dutch Revolt: What Kind of Revolution?', *Renaissance Quarterly*, Vol. 43, No. 3 (Autumn, 1990), pp. 570-590; pp. 571-572.

[54]Gordon Griffiths, 'The Revolutionary Character of the Revolt of the Netherlands', *Comparative Studies in Society and History*, Vol. 2, No. 4 (Jul., 1960), pp. 452-472.

[55]See James D. Tracy, *A Financial Revolution in the Habsburg Netherlands: "Renten" and "Renteniers" in the County of Holland, 1515-1565* (Berkeley: University of California Press, 1986); Wantje Fritschy, 'A 'Financial Revolution Reconsidered: Public Finance in Holland during the Dutch Revolt, 1568 1648', *Economic History Review*, Vol. 56 (2003), pp. 57-87.

[56]See Erik Swart, "'The field of finance": War and Taxation in Holland, Flanders, and Brabant, 1572-85', *The Sixteenth Century Journal*, Vol. 42, No. 4 (Winter 2011), pp. 1051-1071.

[57]Geoffrey Parker, 'Spain, Her Enemies and the Revolt of the Netherlands 1559-1648', pp. 93-95.

[58]Parker, 'Why Did the Dutch Revolt Last Eighty Years?', p. 72.

[59]Stuart B. Schwartz, 'Portuguese Attitudes of Religious Tolerance in Dutch Brazil', in *The Expansion of Tolerance: Religion in Dutch Brazil (1624-1654)*, by (eds.) Jonathan Israel and Stuart B. Schwartz (Amsterdam: Amsterdam University Press, 2007), pp. 35-59.

[60]George L. Smith, 'Guilders and Godliness: The Dutch Colonial Contribution to American Religious Pluralism', *Journal of Presbyterian History* (1962-1985), Vol. 47, No. 1 (MARCH 1969), pp. 1-30. See also: Jeremy Dupertuis Bangs, 'Dutch Contributions to Religious Toleration', *Church History*, Vol. 79, No. 3 (SEPTEMBER 2010), pp. 585-613.

[61]See Jasper van der Steen, 'A CONTESTED PAST. MEMORY WARS DURING THE TWELVE YEARS TRUCE (1609–21)', in *Memory before Modernity, Practices of Memory in Early Modern Europe*, by (eds.) Erika Kuijpers, Judith Pollmann, Johannes Müller, Jasper van der Steen (Brill, 2013), pp. 45-61.

[62]Carl Bangs, 'Dutch Theology, Trade, and War: 1590-1610', *Church History*, Vol. 39, No. 4 (Dec., 1970), pp. 470-482.

[63]See Geyl, *History of the Dutch-Speaking Peoples*, p. 448.

[64]Peter Brightwell, 'The Spanish System and the Twelve Years' Truce', *The English Historical Review*, Vol. 89, No. 351 (Apr., 1974), pp. 270-292.

[65]Edmundson, 'Frederick Henry: Prince of Orange (continued)', p. 284.

[66]See Croxton, *Westphalia*, p. 118.

[67]Edmundson, 'Frederick Henry: Prince of Orange (continued)', p. 290.

[68]See Parker, *Europe in Crisis*, p. 279.

[69]Geyl, 'Frederick Henry of Orange and Charles I', pp. 382-383.

[70]On the interconnected fates of the Dutch Republic and England after 1650 see Pieter Geyl, *House of Orange and Stuart 1641-1672*. Geyl takes the view that the Orange-Stuart marriage had disastrous consequences for both sides, but this idea has recently been revised, see Simon Groenveld, 'The House of Orange and the House of Stuart, 1639–1650: A Revision', *The Historical Journal* Vol. 34, No. 4 (1991), pp. 955-972.

[71]See Parker, 'Spain, Her Enemies and the Revolt of the Netherlands 1559-1648'; 'Why Did the Dutch Revolt Last Eighty Years?', both articles place the Dutch Revolt in the context of the wider Thirty Years War.

[72]Croxton, *Westphalia*, p. 170.

[73]Geyl, 'Frederick Henry of Orange and Charles I', p. 383.

[74]This incident is described in Croxton, *Westphalia*, pp. 229-232.

[75]Parker, 'Why Did the Dutch Revolt Last Eighty Years?', pp. 71-72.
[76]Pedro Cardrim, '"Portuguese Rebels" at Münster. The Diplomatic Self-Fashioning in mid-seventeenth Century European Politics', pp. 294-295.
[77]Quoted in Hume, *The Court of Philip IV: Spain in Decadence*, p. 406.
[78]*Ibid*, pp. 404-405.
[79]Parker, 'Why Did the Dutch Revolt Last Eighty Years?', p. 72.
[80]Parker, *Europe in Crisis*, p. 279.

(Top left) Maximillian von Trauttmansdorff (Jan Barbieri Floris, 1648)
(Top right) Karl Gustav Wrangel (Matthias Merian, 1662)

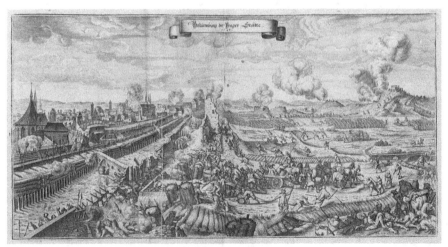

The Siege of Prague

CHAPTER TWENTY-THREE
"Endgame"

ONE: Satisfaction
TWO: Endurance
THREE: Conviction
FOUR: Vindication
FIVE: A Return to Prague

ONE

Satisfaction

By all accounts, Maximillian von Trauttmansdorff had arrived late to the party. He did not arrive under a pall of glory as his Spanish or French counterparts had done in Münster, instead he arrived on 25 November 1645 virtually in secret. He avoided the pomp and time-wasting one-upmanship, but Trauttmansdorff could not avoid the impression that his Emperor was weakening. Why else would he send his closest personal friend to the negotiations, after holding back for several years? The leader of the French delegation, the Duke of Longueville, was heard to welcome the arrival of Trauttmansdorff, because he likely suspected that this meant the Emperor was ready to give ground. For the French negotiators, pressure was easier to maintain on their enemies so long as the battlefield remained active, and for this reason, Longueville and his peers felt some anxiety that Trauttmansdorff had come to make a secret peace with the Swedes, which would isolate France, or that he had come to tell the Spanish that the Emperor was on his last legs, which would have been a blessing and a curse. When he met Trauttmansdorff, Longueville may have been tempted to judge a book by its cover – and what a cover it was. Trauttmansdorff, according to the description by Wedgewood, was a…

> …thick-set, tall, singularly ugly man, with nothing of the aristocrat in his appearance; he was flat-nosed, with high cheek-bones and dark, very deep-set eyes under thick, frowning brows, his face surmounted by a shabby wig combed forward in a fringe that overhung his eyebrows.

He must have been quite a sight, but if they were disarmed by his appearance, then the French were equally disarmed by Trauttmansdorff's good humour and evident command of the situation. Appearances, so it seemed, could be deceptive after all. And there was little mystery regarding what the French officials wanted.[1] Among other matters, Mazarin had focused his gaze on the Upper Rhine, which in geographical terms, formed roughly the middle portion of France's border with the Empire. Along this border region were important bishoprics and even some Electors, such as that of Mainz, but one of the more remarkable features of the landscape is the river itself. For the longest time, the Rhine formed the natural barrier of Empires, from the Roman to the French, and a key strategic possession was a well-defended crossing which could guarantee trade and the transport of soldiers. Strasbourg, the modern home of the European Parliament, was one such vital crossing, and the region where Strasbourg lay, known as Alsace, was high on Cardinal Mazarin's list. Unfortunately for Mazarin though, on more than one occasion, the Emperor had loudly proclaimed his refusal to give Alsace away.

Habsburg interest in Alsace, and its surrounding regions like the Breisgau – which surrounded Breisach – and the Black Forest, which was dotted with mineral mines, or the Upper Rhine itself, which contained no shortage of castles and strongholds that protected the crossings, had been expressed several times throughout the centuries. One Habsburg official in the early sixteenth century attempted to paint a vivid picture for Emperor Maximillian (r. 1508-1519), by detailing the potential extent of the Emperor's powers if he could only unite the disparate territories of the Upper Rhine together for the glory of the Habsburg dynasty. He explained:

> The elector Palatine, the bishop of Strasbourg, the city of Strasbourg, the margrave of Baden; and make out of these same lands, together with his [Majesty's own] lands of Alsace, Sundgau and Breisgau, and the Black Forest, a land which I consider would bear comparison with a powerful kingdom. If such were brought about, it would beyond doubt serve greatly to advance the holy Empire and the house of Austria. In my opinion, one would not find many powerful kings whose kingdoms had equal might to these lands with all their strength and fruitfulness.[2]

Maximillian's descendants evidently took this lesson to heart, because Ferdinand III initially refused to relinquish Alsace to the French, and as we have seen, he had even promised it to one of the cadet branches of the Habsburg family, the Innsbruck line. But then the war had changed, and the sheer threat which a continuation of the conflict represented compelled Ferdinand to moderate his stance. According to the secret instructions which Ferdinand had given Trauttmansdorff though, he was to give Alsace away only as a last resort. 'It is better to achieve a peace', Ferdinand opined, 'even if it excludes another line of my house, than to continue the war, the outcome of which is doubtful...' This Innsbruck line was essentially to be paid off or granted additional concessions in Carinthia if they proved obdurate. He would suggest other carrots first, but Ferdinand was adamant in his instructions to Trauttmansdorff that if Alsace was what stood between the Empire and peace, it would have to be handed over to the French.[3]

Where did this leave Trauttmansdorff in the negotiations with the French? He knew that he was empowered to concede it, and to bring French borders up to the Rhine in the process; what he did not know was whether the French would ask for all of Alsace, or merely parts of it, or what form of authority they would demand in either case. Certainly, there was a possibility that the confusing jumble of contracts which enabled the Emperor to govern Alsace might put the French off; perhaps they would demand only Strasbourg, so that crossing the river would be easier in the future? And if they demanded all of Alsace, what form of authority might they demand? Would they seek to annex all of it, or would they attempt to assume the Emperor's rights in the region, and maintain a halfway home of annexation by ruling Alsace as an Imperial fief? This latter option would grant France a seat at the Imperial Diet, and thus additional influence in the Empire's affairs, but it was certainly a complicated arrangement. Would it not be preferable to annex Alsace, and accept no infringements upon the French King's authority? On the other hand, would a bullish annexation not intimidate and alienate the moderate Germans who the French were attempting to court? It was a difficult balancing act, and as a dilemma it underlines the different way power and authority was considered. As Derek Croxton explained:

> It only makes sense if we appreciate the way authority in early modern Europe was cobbled together. Power did not flow from the people to the government, or from the ruler to the people, but instead consisted in something more like a bundle of contracts. These contracts granted a ruler (or other governing authority, such as a town council) rights: certain types of taxation, jurisdiction in particular cases, military protection and the right to garrison towns, and so forth. Each area had its own bundle of contracts that it had accumulated over time. Often, several towns, counties or other administrative units would be grouped together for some purposes, such as military protection, but they might have separate agreements on other subjects, such as taxation.[4]

This description of the situation in Alsace was often reflected on the micro and macro level across the Empire and could become especially confusing when considering the rights of inheritance or traditions within a given region. There is good reason to suspect that the French were confused by the situation in Alsace, as much as they were divided over how to proceed there. Being more a geographical than a legal entity, Alsace was governed by a complex arrangement of jurisdiction, city councils, and a division between Upper and Lower, which confusingly corresponded to the south and north of the territory respectively. Considering the venom which the region was to evoke in Franco-German relations into the future, we should perhaps not be surprised that the solution reached at Westphalia was vague and, in many respects, nonsensical.

Both sides assented to the creation of a treaty which resembled something of a word soup; after a summer of discussions and fact-finding, the French delegation had apparently arrived at their solution. According to these 'satisfaction articles', several estates in Alsace were left independent, but somehow, they were also to be subject to the authority of the French King. The contradictory arrangement, finalised in mid-September 1646, was created to grant the advantage to the side which was strong enough to press their claim, but it was also designed so that both sides could claim a victory. Viewing the situation objectively though, it is plain that the French had achieved something of a coup. Not only was Alsace now effectively theirs, but French jurisdiction had now been pushed right up to the Rhine, and French soldiers would henceforth be able to cross over Strasbourg's bridge into Germany.

And Alsace was not the only gain for France; Metz, Toul and Verdun, three bishoprics in the region, were also handed over, and a treaty was signed with the Elector of Trier, a French ally, whereby the fortress of Philipsburg would contain a French garrison. France also was allowed to retain Breisach and the Breisgau region which surrounded it, granting them the strongest position on the Upper Rhine, and any potential threats to their position, such as the fortresses of Saverne and Neuenburg were ordered destroyed. The Emperor waived his rights to the region, just as he had committed to do in secret with Trauttmansdorff, and the high price for peace with France was at last apparently paid.[5] Ferdinand even signalled his willingness to talk with the Spanish, and undo the provisions of the Onate Treaty from 1619 which had originally granted Spain so many strategic positions along the Upper Rhine, including Alsace and the Franche-Comté region to the south.[6]

Curiously though, even while the negotiation of this vast transferral of land to France had been concluded on 13 September, the treaty was not actually signed. One might have suspected that this was due to the French intention to gamble that the battlefield would grant greater opportunities to expand upon these gains, and perhaps Mazarin did not wish to close the door on further expansion just yet. He would have found that his own officials, chief among them Longueville, were wary at risking French gains on the battlefield. Longueville had written to Mazarin in April 1646, when the Alsatian situation seemed impossible to resolve, to the effect that:

> I believe that we should not precipitate or risk anything. [it] being certain that if things remain as they are...our enemies will be reduced to the positions that we desire of them; instead of which a defeat, however small, will make our peace conditions much worse.

This was a fundamental tenet of the Westphalian negotiations: making use of military pressure and military victories to wrest additional opportunities for concessions from the enemy. While the tide seemed broadly to be turning against the Emperor, and his Bavarian ally, it is therefore interesting that Longueville did not believe the risk was worth it. If the French were defeated, then the previous victory at Allerheim would be effectively undone, and additional pressures from Spain, or from the Dutch and Swedish peace negotiations, could compromise the French interest.[7]

The campaigning season of 1646 did not contain many opportunities to affect any fundamental changes in the strategic position of either side. Unlike 1645, there was no disintegration of the Emperor's allies, nor did the Swedes enjoy any great triumphs. If Longueville was nervous about French prospects on the battlefield, he was fortunate that there were few occasions in the year when much was truly put at risk. Perhaps this was because genuine progress was being made in Münster and Osnabruck, in contrast to previous years.

Since these satisfaction articles remain virtually unchanged in their incorporation of the Peace of Westphalia two years later, it seems likely that Mazarin delayed ratification for another reason other than military opportunism. Perhaps Mazarin wished to demonstrate some solidarity with his Swedish ally; according to their previous agreement after all, the French and Swedes were meant to resolve their negotiations with the Emperor at the same time. In practice of course, there were great benefits to be accrued from finishing up before your ally had done the same. For Mazarin, it meant that the pressure upon France was significantly reduced now that she had secured her major concessions from the Emperor. There was no longer any danger that either the Dutch or Swedish resolution would undermine French ambitions, and if anything, it meant that the Swedes were now under greater pressure to conclude their negotiations with the Emperor. But this was to be easier said than done; as complex and contradictory as the situation in Alsace had been, the Swedish tug-of-war over Pomerania appeared to defy all efforts at resolution.[8]

From the moment Gustavus Adolphus had arrived in Pomerania in 1630, the region had been entwined within Swedish demands. There was no escaping the fact that Swedish possession of Pomerania would grant her an unrivalled strategic position both to control the Baltic, and to interfere in Germany again in the future. It was to be her German base, within which some of the most lucrative ports could be controlled and squeezed for their tolls. Considering the legion of benefits which Sweden would accrue from her possession of the region, it is hardly surprising that a legion of powers lined up to oppose her. The Danes were eternally jealous of Swedish empowerment, the Dutch feared for their position in the Baltic trade routes, and the Poles did not want Sweden sharing another land border with them in Northern Europe. Though each of these powers were eager in their opposition, none was as bitter as the campaign mounted by the Elector of Brandenburg, Frederick William.

Since he succeeded his father in 1640, Frederick William had made it his mission to see that the Emperor respected the old commitments which bound Brandenburg to Pomerania by rights of inheritance. The childless Duke Bogislaw of Pomerania had not been allowed to pass his lands to Brandenburg as he had intended though; instead he had been bullied by the Swedish King into ceding it to his authority. When he died in 1637, the issue remained unresolved, and seemed even further from resolution when Brandenburg exited the war in 1642. Although no longer vulnerable to rampaging Swedish army, Frederick William's decision to leave the war meant that the Emperor would no longer be obliged to vouch for him at the peace negotiations.[9] The Pomeranian quarrel animated Swedish-Brandenburg hostility like no other, precisely because there was so much on the line. Possession of the region would propel Brandenburg to new heights of importance, power and influence in the Empire, and it was for these interests, as well as the sanctity of older treaties, that Frederick William campaigned.

One principle in seventeenth century peacemaking was that of demanding more than you intended to get in the end treaty, so that you could tactically give way on certain issues for the sake of retaining more valuable concessions. Sweden's delegation, led by Johan Oxenstierna and Johan Salvius, bought wholly into this approach. By late 1645 Sweden was officially laying claim to all of Pomerania, Silesia, the bishoprics of Bremen and Verden which were formerly owned by Denmark, some Baltic islands, and the ports of Rostock and Wismar.[10] So long as Brandenburg refused to give any ground on its claim to Pomerania either, Oxenstierna maintained this uncompromising stance. The French negotiators must have felt that their ally was content to fight the war forever, and demand subsidies from them as they did so. Once the French interests had been satisfied in mid-September then, the attentions of the French and of the Emperor turned to Pomerania with a renewed vigour.[11]

But could the intractable parties be brought to compromise? One advantage which the French had was that the Swedish delegation was becoming increasingly divided between this uncompromising stance advocated by the Swedish Chancellor on the one hand, and the more moderate, one could say peace hungry party, led by the young Swedish Queen, Christina. Anxious to preserve Sweden's relationship with France, ambassadors had been swapped between Paris and Stockholm to reach some kind of solution outside of the realm of the negotiations at Osnabruck. This certainly rubbed Chancellor Oxenstierna the wrong way, not least because it undercut his son who was attempting to bring the Brandenburg delegation to heel, with little success. Reportedly, in March 1646 when it was learned that Magnus De La Gardie had been sent in Sweden's name to Paris, by authorisation of the Queen, the embittered Chancellor refused even to see Queen Christina for nearly a week.[12]

But Christina was as determined to build a power base for herself at home in Stockholm, as she was to make her presence felt at Osnabruck. Once again, she did so by cutting between the official formula of the peace negotiations, and once again, this came at the expense of the Oxenstierna clan. Since Johan Oxenstierna was unlikely to be receptive to her approaches, the Queen focused her attentions upon Johan Adler Salvius, his second, and seems to have created in him a loyal agent. 'I put my entire confidence in you', Christina wrote in December 1646, 'that you will not allow yourself to be turned aside by anything, and by this I recommend to you very expressly the advancement of the peace.'[13] Soon she was even asking him for incredible favours; could Salvius arrange for the transfer of Benefeld, to Magnus De La Gardie? Benefeld was a Swedish enclave in Alsace, which the French wished to acquire, and which Sweden had little chance of clinging to – here, Christina apparently wished to kill two birds with one stone, by ceding this place to her heavily indebted favourite, regardless of the storm of controversy this would create.[14]

In early 1647, Christina and Oxenstierna engaged in a dispute about the religious state of Sweden, which only sharpened their additional disagreements over the shape of the peace negotiations. It seemed that Chancellor and Queen were destined always to argue and undermine one another; Christina would later tell the French ambassador that it was at this time she first thought of abdicating, but first she wished urgently to facilitate an end to the war. In April 1647, she wrote with some haste to her man in Osnabruck, Salvius, to the effect that:

> From your letters I know of your efforts to terminate a long, dangerous, and bloody war. I also know from many circumstances how a certain party who, not being able entirely to upset the treaties, is trying to delay them…I will conduct myself in such a way with this contrary party that the whole earth will know that the fault was not on my side. I will also make the whole universe see that the Royal Chancellor is not able, alone with his little finger, to make the world turn around.

As if proving her point, at the same time this gentle letter was sent to Salvius, the Queen sent a far more threatening message to that 'certain party', led by the junior Oxenstierna. No doubt, the letter was the end result of several months of conflict with the Chancellor back in Stockholm. It was certainly easier for the Queen to criticise her powerful Chancellor on the basis of his failure to make peace, than to properly challenge his domestic power base or alter his foreign policy course. The Queen's letter on 10 April 1647 thus reads:

...without trifling any more, you are to conduct negotiations to a desirable end...you are no longer to allow affairs to drag at length as has happened up to now. If this is not done it will be your business to see how you will be answerable to God, to the Estates of the Realm and to me. Do not allow yourselves to be turned from this end by the ideas of ambitious people, at least if you do not wish to incur my deepest displeasure and indignation...you may be sure that then neither authority nor the support of great families will prevent me from showing the whole world the displeasure that I feel for such proceedings which are destitute of judgement.[15]

By the summer of 1647, limited apologies were made, and Chancellor Oxenstierna warned the Queen of 'those who wish to create trouble between sovereigns and their servitors', but Christina did not dismantle her growing power base, which counted among its ranks the famed Marshal Torstenson, who had since retired due to poor health. Mazarin was by no means excluded from the gossip and rumour which swirled around Europe regarding the relationship between Chancellor and Queen; he recognised that the French influence was unpopular in Stockholm, that the Chancellor wished to protect his large brood of sons, and that Christina's marital prospects remained a hot topic. Yet, notwithstanding their disagreements, Mazarin wrote to his subordinates in Münster that:

The Chancellor Oxenstierna is so consummate a minister that although he seems to have lost credit, he will still continue to have a large part in the administration of the realm, and the Queen who desires to instruct herself in great affairs could not find a source of knowledge more lively and reliable than he.[16]

Indeed, whatever credit he had lost for his son's tardiness in making peace was surely recouped with the news that, by early February 1647, Brandenburg and Sweden had finally settled their differences over Pomerania. The compromise had been a long time coming and was a result of the Oxenstierna's effectively threatening to seize all of Pomerania if the Brandenburg Elector did not give some ground. In the end, with Trauttmansdorff indicating that he would accept Swedish occupation of all of Pomerania if it would bring about a lasting peace, Frederick William seems finally to have gotten the message.[17]

He switched his policy in a flash, from stubborn resilience to compromise, but the climbdown was far from a humiliation; after spending months fighting for Pomerania, the message had been received that only with large concessions and compensation would Brandenburg be actually happy to let it go. As a result, Frederick William received a litany of gains far in excess of what he could reasonably have expected in 1640. His policy of driving a hard bargain had made him few friends, but it had brought him new duchies in Mecklenburg, once owned by Wallenstein, and at Halberstadt, where Swedish Marshal Johan Baner had died in 1641. Brandenburg had also received its share of Pomerania in the east, a strip of coastal land more than twice the size of Sweden's Western Pomeranian portion, but less productive, and crucially excluding the lucrative city of Stettin, the old Pomeranian capital.

To compensate, Frederick William gained two additional bishoprics at Minden and Kammin, which he later secularised, thereby effectively expanding his writ into these former church lands. But Frederick William seemed unwilling to accept diplomatic carrots alone; he attempted to seize some for himself, by invading one of his German neighbours. Miniature conflicts among the German princes were irritating distractions for those at Westphalia, but there was relatively little the major powers could do. When Amalie-Elizabeth of Hesse-Kassel invaded her neighbour, Hesse-Darmstadt, in late 1644, she had forced the Emperor and then the Swedes to move troops around the board to compensate. It was also with the Elector of Brandenburg; his invasion of Berg in November 1646 threatened to derail sensitive discussions over the division of German territories, but in the end Frederick William's vaunted newly recruited and drilled army achieved practically little. [18]

Interestingly, this conflict among German princes was an outcome of the Julich-Cleve succession war, which had plagued anxious European onlookers as far back as 1608. Negotiations over who would succeed to the wealthy but disconnected duchies of Julich, Cleve, Mark, Berg and Ravensburg were animated by the appearance of Spain on one side and France on the other, but the conflict was eventually solved in 1614 with a treaty partitioning the lands in question. [19] Frederick William had invaded the lands of one of these recipients, Duke Wolfgang William of Pfalz-Neuburg, to settle disputes which dated back to this partition, but he was far from successful, gaining only a slice of Ravensburg for his troubles. The act also made him more vulnerable to Swedish threats, but few could deny that Frederick William, almost despite himself, had done well. By pushing and relenting at just the right time, Frederick William had expanded his realm by over a third, and had laid the foundations for the later expansion of Brandenburg-Prussia which were to pass into historical legend. [20]

As 1646 turned to 1647, it was evident that the Thirty Years War was approaching its end. France had been guaranteed Alsace, Sweden had been promised Pomerania, and the two more troubling challenges to the Emperor had thus been confronted and resolved. Further afield, the Dutch-Spanish War was also winding down, with a truce announced shortly after news of Sweden's satisfaction was gained, that proved durable enough to last the remainder of the war. Only in portions of Germany, where the Swedish army under its new commander Gustav Wrangel marched, or along the Pyrenees, where the Franco-Spanish conflict continued, did the war truly remain alive. In amongst these conflicts, opportunistic Germans continued to move, determined that the most troubling question of all – the fate of the Palatine family – should finally acquire its resolution.

TWO
Endurance

When Maximillian I took over from his father in 1597, as the Duke of Bavaria, he began a reign which was destined to be unlike anything the people of Bavaria or his contemporary rulers in Germany, had ever seen. By the end of his life in 1651, Maximillian would have transformed not just the reach of Bavaria, expanding its writ into his cousin's Palatine lands, but even his personal title and the Imperial hierarchy would be reimagined, with Bavaria as one of eight Electors. What Maximillian achieved during his tenure, and what he experienced, was nothing short of astounding. He was among a very small group of contemporaries to live through the full duration of the Thirty Years War, but by the time the conflict had begun, Maximillian had already been in power for more than 20 years. In that time, he had given an indication of his abilities by repairing the damage his father had inflicted upon Bavaria.

Maximillian had inherited one of the most indebted states in Germany; his father had been nearly 1.5 million guilders in debt by 1595, had only barely enough to spare for Maximillian's wedding, had been close to pawning the family's jewels, and was being advised to declare bankruptcy. Rather than face the music, Maximillian's father determined to abdicate, and put the reins of government in his son's hands. Maximillian had been learning under his father for two years, and by October 1597, he was declared Bavaria's sole ruling Duke; the Bavarian estates, whom he would have to petition for the payment of these extraordinary debts, had never been consulted about any of these decisions.

Through sheer determination and with a vision for balancing the books, Maximillian spent the next ten years squeezing the estates for additional incomes to reduce the debt. Through his frugal living, exhaustive piety and sensible if dogmatic governance, the estates were gradually made to see that their Duke was a reliable investment. Nor was his absolutist hand solely involved in finance, as the historian F. L. Carsten observed:

Maximillian exercised judicial and police authority without any interference and without being unduly hampered by the privileges of the nobility, who only exercised the lower jurisdiction on their estates. He controlled the Church, curtailed the jurisdiction of the bishops, intervened in its internal affairs, regulated religious festivals and processions, introduced the Roman rites, supervised the financial administration of the Church, and taxed the clergy and the monasteries.[21]

Aside from his financial acumen, Maximillian's piety distinguished him even in the era of Counter-Reformation as a uniquely rigorous son of the Church; he made the Virgin the patron of Bavaria in 1616, and dedicated himself to her through a vow which he wrote in his own blood, and which he displayed proudly in a tabernacle at the shrine of Altotting in 1645. His piety was thus a lifelong exercise, and as leader and financier of the Catholic League, he had also served as the Emperor's main military ally during the initial years of the war.[22] Though his service to his Emperor and patron were presented in noble terms, Maximillian was among the most handsomely rewarded of all the Emperor's allies, and he was also among the shortlist of German potentates who could afford to shoulder the burdens which Ferdinand's war against his enemies required.

Absolutist in his control of the Church, Maximillian's authority over Bavarian finances was equally absolute from the very beginning. He controlled everything, from the right to extend monopolies, to the lucrative salt monopoly, to the right to levy or increase tolls and duties. He viewed the Estates not as an early example of a representative body, but as a tool which he could use to raise finances, and thus raise Bavaria's standing. Just as remarkable as his ability to squeeze the Estates was the Estates' apparent willingness to cooperate; by 1605 his debts were reduced to 1 million guilders, by 1608 they disappeared, and by 1629 he boasted a surplus of more than 2 million guilders. All the while, the Bavarian Estates remained supplicant; in 1605 they granted him monies for six years, and in 1612, when Maximillian informed them he would not call on them for nine years, they granted him the funds regardless. In return for a vague promise that Maximillian would not take advantage of their cooperation to levy additional burdens, in 1605 the Estates agreed essentially to back their Duke to the hilt. The estates tripled his personal allowance to 150,000 guilders; they advanced 28,000 guilders for the maintenance of the Catholic League, and in 1607 when Maximillian annexed the Free City of Donauworth, his Estates willingly provided the 16,000 guilders necessary to finance the policy.

Evidently, the Bavarian nobility and their Estates had been in search of a strong-willed, determined Duke, but as a result of their support, Maximillian found that he needed them less and less. By virtue of his huge surplus and absolutist control over Bavaria, Maximillian was able to intervene in the initial years of the conflict and fulfil his ambitions in the process. As F. L. Carsten continued:

> He did not consult the Estates about the conclusion of alliances, nor about the declaration of war, and allowed them no influence in the sphere of administration and government. He was determined to govern himself and was his own first minister.[23]

Maximillian needed no Richelieu, nor Olivares, nor Oxenstierna; he was determined to control Bavarian affairs wholly by himself. His intentions do not seem to have been based on the pursuit of power for power's sake either: in 1623, Maximillian was confirmed as the Elector of Bavaria, having received the titles and honours of his distant, rebellious cousin, Frederick V, the Elector Palatine then living in exile in The Hague. We have already examined the inflammatory results of this policy; it effectively kept the conflict alive, long after Frederick V and Ferdinand II had died, and in the final years of the war, this Palatine Question presented arguably the most intractable problems of the peace congress.

Frederick V's son and heir Karl Ludwig (anglicised as Charles Louis) had been tireless in his petitioning for Palatine justice since the death of his father in 1632. He was defeated in battle in 1638, and was even imprisoned by Richelieu in 1639, but a decade later, Charles Louis' Palatine Question still required an answer, and depending on whom one asked, the answer would be very different at Westphalia. An important point to note is that Maximillian did not justify his acquisition of the Palatine titles on the act of conquest alone. First and foremost, Frederick V had rebelled against his Emperor and had the Imperial Ban invoked against him, thus forfeiting his position. In the second place, the relationship between the Palatine and Bavarian branches of the Wittelsbach family was something akin to dynastic competition, particularly once the Palatine Electors converted to Calvinism.

But religion was not the only source of contention; Maximillian actually had good reason to cry foul of the Palatine's very possession of the Electoral title. According to an agreement made between the two branches of the Wittelsbach families in 1329, Maximillian could note, the Electoral title was supposed to be shared between them; the Palatine and Bavarian leaders, in other words, committed to taking turns voting for the next Emperor. This arrangement was overturned in 1356, when the Golden Bull established the framework for an Emperor's election by detailing the seven Electors – Bavaria was not among them, and since then, Bavarian Dukes had been sensitive to the snub. As he balanced his budget and increased his prestige in the years before 1618, indeed, Maximillian had petitioned the Emperor for a reconsideration of this controversy. The eruption of the war plainly put such a debate on hold, but rather than wait for a peaceful resolution, the ambitious Bavarian Duke sought to harness his prowess and opportunities, not to mention the weakness and isolation of his once triumphant Palatine neighbour, to take what he believed was owed to him. Whether his contemporaries were convinced of the justice of this claim, dating back three hundred years, was another issue, and one which concerned Maximillian less than the actual fulfilment of his ambitions.[24]

However, it was precisely because the act of seizing the Palatine Electoral title looked like a mere smash and grab that Maximillian was still seeking to legitimise his position more than twenty years later. Maximillian would have to buy off potential objectors to his new position at Westphalia in the mid-1640s, just as the Emperor had been forced to do at Regensburg in 1623, when the announcement had originally been made. In 1623, Saxony and Brandenburg had been appeased through concessions in land and titles, while Papal envoys worked their magic convincing those hesitant Catholic figures who remained.[25] In 1646 and 1647 though, Maximillian believed that his best chances for coming out of the peace negotiations with his new titles and honours intact was through French support. The French negotiators at Münster, indeed, had privately promised the Imperial delegate, Trauttmansdorff, that they would intercede to moderate any Protestant demands made against Catholics.

Interestingly, this promise seems to have been made in full expectation that it would lead to friction between the French and Swedes. Yet, because the French had been satisfied in their demands by September 1646, they felt less pressure thereafter to rely upon Sweden, and were more willing to turn their attentions towards the Empire's religious settlement, where the Palatine Question was bound up. By February 1647 though, Sweden had also managed to satisfy its demands for Pomerania and other concessions, so its negotiators felt confident to focus their attentions on the Empire's religious settlement as well. With their immediate territorial demands satisfied, the Swedish and French delegates were to spend the remainder of 1647 working to bring some form of religious settlement to the table which all could agree on. This quest was easier said than done.[26]

As the debates at Westphalia rolled on, so too did the military manoeuvres. 1646 brought few inspiring returns for either side, but the tide was plainly turning against the Emperor. This meant that his allies, principally Bavaria, became more vulnerable. Indeed, with the creeping French advance to the Upper Rhine and the seizure of much of Alsace, French forces were in an ideal position to raid into the Swabian territory which bordered the Bavarian heartland. This was a substantial enough threat, but when combined with the Swedish decision to link up with Marshal Turenne for the campaigning season of 1646, the consequences threatened to be disastrous. Field Marshal Gustav Wrangel, who had replaced the ailing Torstenson, marched his army further south than ever before, reaching as far as Lake Constance along the northern border with Switzerland in the autumn. While there, Wrangel outmanoeuvred his foes, constructed a flotilla of boats of the picturesque lake, and stormed the island of Mainau where previously untouched treasures resided.

The mountain towns and passes gave way to the unexpected Swedish assaults, and among other successes, Wrangel wrested 4 million florins worth of booty from the city of Bregenz, on the Lake's eastern shore. The native Tirolese soldiers and militia who had been called to defend their homeland melted away, and Wrangel spent much of early 1647 rampaging through the previously unspoiled western portion of the Tyrol. That Wrangel could force his way through these lands and evoke no response from the Emperor was a telling fact for Maximillian; Wrangel was only a few days' march from Innsbruck, and a campaign into Inner Austria might rouse the once rebellious Austrian Estates into a repetition of their revolt which had consumed much Habsburg attention in the late 1620s. Ferdinand was plainly unable to stop the Swedes, and was frankly unsure how to combat Wrangel's invasion, losing first his brother as commander, who resigned, and then losing the alcoholic veteran commander Matthias Gallas, who was brought back in desperation in early 1647, only to die in April. The prospects for Imperial survival, let alone victory, appeared grim, and the allies seemed poised to choke Bavaria in a pincer movement before moving against Vienna. So it was that Maximillian consented, in December 1646, to negotiations for a truce with his enemies to begin.[27]

The Ulm Truce was signed in March 1647, a mere month after the Swedes had concluded their agreements for territorial satisfaction. With Bavaria's exit from the war, not only had a watershed moment passed, as his traditional ally finally abandoned him, but Ferdinand had now to face the fact that he was utterly alone against his enemies. Every other Elector had removed himself from the war, leaving the Habsburg Hereditary Lands, and Bohemia in particular, open for invasion by Wrangel's Swedes once they marched through the Palatinate in order to get there. But Wrangel was not particularly pleased at the Truce's arrival; he believed that the truce would only delay Maximillian's final defeat and would grant him a chance to catch his breath. With the French and Swedes no longer bearing down on him, Maximillian might repair his defences, rebuild his army, and be back on the field by the end of the year. Critics of Wrangel might have condemned these predictions as unrealistic, or cynical in the extreme, but the Swedish Field Marshal proved correct: by August, Maximillian would be back in the field. Just as he had resurrected his Duchy's fortunes at the time of his accession, now Maximillian sought to do so once more. This time, however, the results would be far less remarkable.

In the interim, while Bavaria was at peace with its rivals, it was the French who gained most. Mazarin was surprisingly risk averse and did not wish to gamble on the continued predominance of French arms over the Bavarians, particularly when France had been burned in previous campaigns. Rather than risk all in a campaign to achieve better terms, Mazarin was content to settle for the terms which were possible now, while the enemy was on the backfoot. Mazarin expressed these points in communications with Claude d'Avaux, the French delegate at Münster, saying 'It is no small skill to quit the game when one is winning, because one secures one's gain and one can count that which remains among one's possessions. In the name of God work for this with all your ability.'[28] He did not ignore France's superiority, but rather than harness this superiority to undo his foes, Mazarin noted that he was ready 'to sacrifice not only our hopes for future conquest, but even to cede a part of what we already have.' The Ulm Truce was a symptom of this approach and was fed by a lack of proper military intelligence on the ground in southern Germany, not to mention the fear that the cyclical patterns of military reversals would place France in a difficult position.[29]

These difficulties were especially pronounced because France suffered several successive setbacks in its war with Spain along the Pyrenees. Even as Naples and Sicily seemed poised to leave Spain's orbit for good, the Spanish army managed to dislodge the French from some Catalonian bases, and Mazarin was beginning to tire of Catalonia altogether. French efforts to capitalise on Spain's Italian troubles failed miserably thanks to poor planning and Mazarin's total surprise. By spring 1648, the region was back under Spanish control and the opportunity to strike a blow at Madrid in yet another theatre had been lost.[30] The French also seem to have missed some opportunities at Münster; they were unable to fight successfully for the rebellious Portuguese to gain recognition by the Spanish as anything more than rebels, while the Spanish launched a propaganda campaign of their own, accusing the French of dealing in bad faith, and having no interest in a lasting peace. Even the Portuguese lobbed some criticism France's way in this regard.

The French delegation seemed to have underestimated their Spanish counterparts, who had done enough research about the other delegations to appreciate how to get on their good side. The Venetian ambassador, for example, represented a country which was at war with the Ottomans and which was supposed to be serving as a mediator. The Spanish thus loudly proclaimed that they would send military aid in support of Venice, which seems to have moved Contarini, the Venetian delegate, to become considerably more pro-Spanish in his sympathies.[31] In the military sphere, furthermore, the arrival of a truce between the Spanish and Dutch liberated the army of Flanders after eighty years of conflict, and enabled its commander, Ferdinand's brother the Archduke Leopold William, to focus his attentions upon Marshal Turenne.[32]

And Mazarin had yet another very good reason to feel apprehensive about continuing the war indefinitely. His gamble that French society would support the crippling taxes to fund the war long enough to pay for worthwhile successes against Spain had failed. By May 1648, the domestic woes within France were erupting into the mainstream, and affecting Mazarin's ability to pursue the war against the Emperor.[33] Perhaps in anticipation of this threat, Mazarin approached the peace negotiations more willing to compromise than we might expect, especially once France's major goals in Alsace had been effectively granted. For all of these weaknesses and shortcomings though, the scales had long since set against Madrid. Although the strain on France was beginning to show, King Philip IV of Spain could not prevent his own royal couriers from speaking their mind about the desperate state of the country. One such courier wrote in the safety of his private memoirs that:

> The only place where the war was carried on with activity was here in Castile, and that in a most unheard-of way by disarming subjects and divesting them of their property on the pretext of the war. Even the treasury warrants which had been especially exempt from deduction were again seized and forced to yield a half. When those who had to pay were advised not to do so, because whilst the war lasted so long would the Government cut their purses and would soon take everything, a certain person asked: 'Why do they give habits?' (of knighthood). -'Because they are cloth,' was the reply. 'Why do they give keys?' (i.e. the office of chamberlain). -'Because they are iron.' 'Why do they give titles?'--'Because they are air.' 'Why do they not give money?'--'Because that is the essence and substance of everything, and they do not wish anyone to have it.' ... God save us from him who is liberal to vice and stingy to virtue, for the only people now who are comfortable and placed aloft are concubines and the women who look after them, low and common women, and those men who have been base enough to marry them.[34]

Such plain-speaking among Philip IV's own servants underlined the fact that Spain's decline was an open fact by the late 1640s, notwithstanding the last-minute rallies which her armed forces occasionally enjoyed. The war was turning broadly, and in some cases, gradually, against the Habsburgs, but it had unmistakably turned against them by now, and there were few in either Madrid or Vienna that imagined victory to be possible. Emperor Ferdinand's primary goal, indeed, was to avoid any further campaigning seasons out of fear of the consequences. These fears over what might befall his hereditary lands proved well-founded, as the Swedish commander Gustav Wrangel crossed into north-west Bohemia in the early summer of 1647 with reinforcements from Silesia. Armed not just with a formidable force of veterans, but also with a concrete plan to keep them provisioned and potent during the slim campaigning months, Wrangel conceived of nothing less than the ruin of the Emperor. Interestingly though, much as Bavaria's truce saved Maximillian, it also saved the Emperor from either having to rush to Bavaria's defence, or having to distribute soldiers to cover that flank. Bavaria, once an ally, could now be used as a buffer state against the French and Swedish ravages, and the Emperor could focus on preparing Austria and Bohemia for the campaign which was to come.

Tasked with defending what remained of the Emperor's realm was Gallas' successor as commander of Imperial forces, Count Peter Melander. Melander had at his disposal twenty thousand soldiers – the remnants of the Emperor's military arm in Germany – but he had also been led to hope that Bavaria's inactive army of nearly equal size might join him in a great defection. A curious scene followed, whereby some soldiers on the Bavarian side attempted to join their disenchanted commanders and defect to the Emperor, but this brought few returns. Maximillian even went as far as putting a price of ten thousand thalers on the head of Jan van Werth, his army's commanding officer, who had attempted to defect owing to his discontentment with the Ulm Truce. Melander waited in vain for Bavarian support, setting out late in August 1647 to meet Wrangel's army. In a minor skirmish on 22 August, Melander surprised Wrangel at his camp and inflicted around 1,300 casualties. Wrangel withdrew in good order, and little practically changed in the region, but the win was a vital one for the Emperor, and he attempted to use it to his advantage.[35]

As Melander had marched to meet Wrangel, back along the Rhine, Marshal Turenne had set his sights upon Luxemburg, yet another link in the chain that tied Madrid to Brussels. Turenne intended to bring his army to that duchy as a means of intercepting Leopold William's Army of Flanders. The Ulm Truce granted Turenne this opportunity, as Maximillian would not be sending any sorties across the Rhine for the foreseeable future. Something which Turenne had absolutely not foreseen, however, was the inclinations of his soldiers. Many of the Germans under his command were content only to campaign in Germany, and when rumours were put about that Turenne intended to march them to Catalonia to fight Mazarin's Spanish War, it seemed for many to be the final straw. Some of his best German troops, many of them veterans of Bernhard of Saxe-Weimar, fled from Turenne's command, and made their way to another Swedish commander at Westphalia. It was an unexpected and potentially fatal reversal which few could have imagined, but the Swedish Chancellor may well have viewed the incident as poetic justice for Richelieu's purchase of Bernhard's men a decade before.[36]

Turenne's uninspiring returns, combined with Melander's unexpected victory, seem to have persuaded Maximillian to engage in a stunning 180° in policy. On 7 September 1647, he announced that Bavaria would re-enter the war, but this time against only the Swedes. It was a bold move, and for a moment, it seemed that the Elector of Bavaria had done it again, harnessing just the right combination of opportunism, ambition and perception to have his way, but the initial optimism would not last the year. Compelled to focus on reaching a settlement in the Empire thanks to the increasing pressures of those aforementioned fronts, Mazarin was unwilling to allow another year to go to waste. 1648 would either be the year when France extricated herself from the war for good, or it would be the occasion when the wily Cardinal's sins finally caught up with him. Either way, Mazarin was determined that no power, least of all Maximillian of Bavaria, should be permitted to stand in his way.

THREE

Conviction

...the cardinal wanted everyone to believe that peace was not only his inclination, but also his interest; and he talked about it so much and with such strong expressions that he almost persuaded himself that he wanted [some] "peace" to which he was in fact averse.[37]

These were the words of Abraham de Wicquefort, a Dutch historian and diplomat, and contemporary of Mazarin's. Was this a fair estimation of Cardinal Mazarin's character? Historians have been somewhat puzzled by the ambitions and intentions of Richelieu's successor, with some suggesting he was animated by the struggle for Christendom; others declaring that he saved Catholic France from destruction by its enemies, and others still opining that Mazarin's aims for the Thirty Years War were all of a defensive character. He was, we are told, obsessed with preventing a repeat of 1636, when Paris was threatened by an army from the Spanish Netherlands. To guard against this, towns in Flanders must be seized, and Picardy itself heavily reinforced. Furthermore, by taking Alsace, the Spanish Road would be forever severed. Indeed it was because Mazarin had pushed for the absorption of Alsace that his plenipotentiaries in Münster were able to declare, in reference to the Spanish Road, that 'this dangerous communication of the forces of the House of Austria, which our fathers feared is now broken and discontinued...'

This was no small achievement, but to what end had Mazarin cut Spain off from Brussels. What were Mazarin's defining principles? Did he have one, or did he remain flexible, and ever watchful of the unfolding situation? Did he simply want to grab as much land for France as possible? Certainly, his vision seemed to grow as French prospects improved, but there was also an element of strategic sense behind the expansion. Without the fortress of Breisach, for example, Alsace would be that much harder to defend, so France would require both. Without the fortress of Philipsburg, it would be too easy to threaten Lorraine and cross the Rhine, so France would need that as well. Without the bishoprics of Metz, Toul and Verdun, it would be difficult to establish a permanent French base in the region, so these would also be seized. On the surface, capturing strategically placed fortresses might seem like the core of a defensive strategy; from here, minimal French garrisons would theoretically be able to halt or at least delay a larger army. Yet, as Mazarin well understood, the inverse was also true; a small French army could defend in their place, but a larger French army could also pass through them, and into Germany. This latter point, and the implications of it for the projection of French power into the Empire, cannot be ignored.

Not merely in his strategic conception of the French interest, but also in the diplomatic picture of Europe, Mazarin is difficult to figure out. Some have taken to calling him a Christian internationalist, who worked to defend a divided Christian West against the creeping Turkish threat. But is this a fair analysis? Mazarin was perfectly willing to provide soldiers to defend against the Turk, and even to ally with the Habsburgs in order to do it. He was even reported to have promised Emperor Ferdinand that France would support Vienna after the war against the Turk if it proved necessary, but this promise is less selfless than we might suspect. The Turks remained occupied by their war with Safavid Persia throughout the virtual entirety of the Thirty Years War, which was immensely fortunate for the Habsburgs. There is no indication, however, that if the circumstances had been different, Mazarin would not have emulated the old policy of French Kings, who had thought of France's interest before that of Christendom. Indeed, he is even recorded as having confessed to the French delegation in 1645, that any promise of military aid to the Habsburgs was merely a part of a wider strategy:

> …it would be useful not to lose any occasion to keep talking to the mediators and always assure them more that France will take marvellous action for the good of Christendom "against the Turks" provided that peace is made. It appears that this motive will cause them to put all of their effort into getting our enemies to concede the conditions that we desire.[38]

The litmus test for Mazarin would be Spain; he was not about to make peace with France's mortal enemy for the sake of aiding her against the Turks. But, by refraining from declaring one way or the other, Mazarin could keep Spain guessing, and therefore, hoping, that if the Habsburgs truly were threatened, France would rescue them in the name of the common Catholic interest. Some hints that he would not abandon a threatened Christendom had already been given; not only had he made that aforementioned promise to the Emperor's agents, Mazarin had also proposed a naval truce with Spain in 1645, and suggested soldiers could be sent to aid Spain as well. But Mazarin never went any further; money was never promised, and those famous French subsidies which powered the Swedish and Dutch would plainly never be seen by the Habsburgs in the event of a Turkish War. It could not be guaranteed that the Spanish would not simply horde these subsidies and use them against France. The provision of French soldiers, Mazarin admitted, was a less useful contribution than money, but as he pointed out, when the war ended, these soldiers would have to be used for something, so it may as well be to fight the infidel.[39]

From this, we can conclude that Mazarin's interest in defending Catholicism only went so far; certainly, he never felt restrained by his faith, which by all accounts was very real. He simply placed the interests of France above those of religion, though he was not above making statements to the contrary which would appease his critics. And Mazarin has been criticised, as a self-interested Italian, as a power-hungry Machiavellian, and as a faithless neorealist. Perhaps in some way, Mazarin was all of these things, but if so, then he was by no means different in those respects to his contemporaries. He was willing to come under criticism by the enemy, especially when discussing France's genuine desire for peace. As we have seen, Mazarin was averse to risking France's predominance on continued battlefield success and would have preferred a favourable peace as soon as it presented itself: this was especially true as the domestic situation in France deteriorated. He was also unwilling to relent when times were difficult, and was once heard to remark to Claude d'Avaux that:

> I am not at all unhappy that the Spanish accuse me of having an aversion to peace. It means, to judge it soundly, that I know their weakness and the good state of our affairs, and that I do not want to lose the great advantages that France can gain in such a conjuncture; and consequently they declare me by this accusation to be a very good Frenchman, as I effectively am.[40]

A good Frenchman he may have been, but Mazarin was not ignorant of the practical realities which governed geopolitics. He appreciated that maintaining the alliance with Sweden was vital if the Emperor was to be continually pressured, and France was to be permitted to focus most of its attentions on Spain. The war with Spain was, for Mazarin, the main event, and this explains why France's returns from the war into Germany were surprisingly minimal. With most of his attention on the King of Spain, Mazarin was anxious about changes in circumstance, such as a Swedish peace with the Emperor, or a Dutch peace with Spain. These developments would upset the balance, and potentially leave France alone to face the full might of the united, albeit depleted, Habsburg dynasty. On the other hand, if Mazarin could use the threat of peace with the Emperor in his negotiations with the Spanish, then this might net some valuable returns. It was in some senses a race to make peace, and Mazarin was altogether determined to make it over the finish line first.

Considering these interests, we may deduce that anything which threatened France's position in the war with Spain was to be avoided – this included offending the Emperor by making too mighty a demand. Offending the allies – or even the enemies – in your camp at this sensitive moment was a recipe for disaster. In his Bavarian negotiations, which arguably culminated in the conclusion of a truce in March 1647, Mazarin balanced the desire to create a Catholic party allied to France, with the danger of alienating the Swedes and the Protestant Germans.[41] This was a delicate balancing act indeed, made all the more so because during the spring and summer of 1647, the two sides seemed poised to settle the religious question once and for all. After posing as the friend of Protestant German liberties, as much as she was the natural ideological ally of German Catholics like Bavaria, how would France weigh in on this very weighted debate?

The debate was itself grounded in the ripples caused by the Reformation, but it had been codified with the 1555 Peace of Augsburg, which permitted the existence of the two denominations, the Protestants and Catholics. There was much that the Peace of Augsburg legislated for, but there was also much that it had left deliberately vague, so as to protect against the resumption of a religious war which had ripped through Germany in the first half of the sixteenth century. In a sense, this approach had worked, and the Empire had enjoyed relative peace until 1618, at least in comparison to her neighbours. With the need for a lasting peace foremost in the minds of the plenipotentiaries though, one could no longer afford to be vague when discussing religious matters, and this lack of freedom had the potential to delay the negotiations indefinitely. After three decades of war, there was a serious shortage of goodwill between the two denominations, and there were scores in need of settling which in some cases dated back to even before the Peace of Augsburg itself.

This was not the first time a solution to the religious problem had been debated; in the Peace of Prague in 1635 and at the Deputation Diet in 1640, the prospects for both religious groups were discussed, and in the case of the former, the then Emperor Ferdinand II made some important concessions. 1635 was an era ago however, compared to 1647; in that twelve-year period the war had been transformed from a conflict which united the Germans against the invader, to an exhausting slog which now counted only the Emperor himself as the sole German actor of note in the contest. Vienna's reliance on Spain as its source of power had been exposed, with the deterioration of Madrid following years of revolts and the arrival of the war with France on her very doorstep.[42] Perhaps the Emperor could draw from some of these earlier agreements which had been with the German princes, but he would certainly be unable to count on the kind of support his father had enjoyed.

There is little benefit to be accrued from examining the almost weekly fluctuations in the religious negotiations.[43] Broadly speaking, we can discern three phases in these negotiations. The first stage began once the negotiators arrived, and was characterised by the later arrival of the representatives for the German Estates, Trauttmansdorff taking the initiative even without the full consent of all parties, and input from Queen Christina, among others, who insisted that the negotiations be concluded briskly, and that concessions be made where possible. Christina may have leaned towards a sense of sympathy with the Catholics – as her later conversion would demonstrate – but she proved unable to fully persuade the more hard-line Protestant Germans, or even her more uncompromising subjects, such as Chancellor Oxenstierna. The first phase came tantalisingly close to resolving the situation, and in April 1647, preliminary treaties, containing the entirety of the issues already agreed to, were drawn up by the Emperor, France and Sweden. This optimism proved premature though, as in July 1647, after coming under fire for proceeding without the full consent of the parties, Trauttmansdorff left Münster for good. This was a seriously significant moment, as the Emperor's personal friend and delegate had been leading the charge in the realm of compromise and moderation since his arrival in November 1645. With his absence, would the negotiations be significantly delayed, or even collapse altogether?

In fact, the negotiations simply entered a new phase. During the summer of 1647, while the truce with Bavaria was in place, and Count Melander attempted to take Field Marshal Wrangel down a peg, the religious settlement was effectively put on hold. Now it was time for the armies to do the talking, as perhaps the final effort to wrest some leverage from the military situation followed. Melander, as we learned, repelled Wrangel in a limited skirmish, but of far more consequence was the apparent decline in relations between the Swedish and French high commands, which had culminated when Saxons under the command of Marshall Turenne had defected to a Swedish subordinate. Turenne's initial ambition to besiege Luxembourg and pre-empt the Spanish counterattack had to be abandoned, and in retaliation, Mazarin neglected to provide Sweden with its full subsidy for that quarter. This compelled the momentarily broke Wrangel to seek quarters in Saxony, and meant he was unable to strike back at the Emperor's forces for the remainder of 1647.

By the time these issues had matured, Maximillian of Bavaria had re-entered the war against Sweden, so he said, but his relations with the Emperor had suffered a knock as well. His leading commander Jan van Werth was effectively disowned as he attempted to defect to Melander's army, and Ferdinand was disappointed to learn that Maximillian had not decommissioned his army as he had expected. Certainly, Maximillian had learned that his greatest source of power and leverage lay in his army of nearly twenty thousand men, and when neither diplomatic nor religious settlements were forthcoming after the summer of operations, the Bavarian Elector took heed from the Emperor's apparent resurgence to attack Swedish positions in early September. These developments had a noted impact upon the negotiations at Münster and Osnabruck, particularly in light of the rapid progress made in Spanish-Dutch negotiations, which seemed to place pressure upon the French and the Emperor alike.

On 1 September 1647, Dutch delegates had returned to Münster after speaking with the States-General government in The Hague. On their return, they seemed invigorated with a new sense of purpose, but they too bumped into the question of religion. The Eighty Years War with Spain, after all, had been dominated by the religious differences of the Dutch, and the desire of the Dutch people to worship as they desired. Unfortunately for the Dutch though, one could not deny the presence of Catholics in their lands, especially in land which had recently been seized from the Spanish, and which lay outside the immediate writ of the seven United Provinces which constituted the Republic. While it may appear to be a minor issue, the talks stuck on the religious regime to be instituted in these conquered lands. The Dutch wanted Spain to acknowledge the Dutch spiritual authority over such land, but the Spanish claimed this was the Pope's prerogative, not the King of Spain's.

King Philip IV seemed to disagree, but rather than admit defeat, he passed the buck onto the governor of the Spanish Netherlands, who himself passed it to a group of bishops. This latter party eventually determined that giving up spiritual authority over land no longer in their possession should be done, but only if it proved worthwhile in the process of peacemaking. Even the Papal delegate, notoriously intolerant of concessions to Protestants, received the approval of the Pope, but he kept this fact secret in case the Spanish could get away with it. The Spanish delegate, Penaranda, was ill and desperate to return home, but he burst into tears at the Dutch intransigence – how could the Dutch willingly oppress these few Catholics, after the Dutch had spent eight decades fighting for their rights to religious liberty? The question was a valid one, but Penaranda would have known that at the centre of the debate was not the question of tolerance, but sovereignty. The Dutch wanted to strip every last vestige of authority from the Spanish government, as Derek Croxton discerned:

> ...it was not, of course, just about religious freedom; it was about the right to decide whether there was religious freedom or not. The Dutch wanted it to be absolutely clear that it was up to them to be tolerant; if the Spanish accepted that key point, the Dutch were willing to be tolerant of their own free will, but not because a treaty required them to be.

The solution to this deadlock was as typical as it was ridiculous; Penaranda consented to give up all of Spain's authority. The Dutch would insist that this included spiritual authority, and the Spanish would maintain that it did not. A halfway home, which effectively meant very little, was thus the proposed settlement to a problem that mattered very little on paper. 'It was', Croxton noted, 'another masterpiece of diplomatic wording, such as marked the negotiations in and around Westphalia.'[44] What happened next is relatively familiar to us; armed with this arrangement, the Dutch negotiators returned to The Hague once again, to see if the final peace treaty with the Spanish could at last be hammered out. There they met some opposition, principally from the province of Zeeland, but this was overcome with Holland's promise to finance the expedition to Brazil. On 30 November 1647, the Dutch negotiators were given approval to sign the peace treaty with Spain.

The Dutch moved rapidly towards peace after that, and its delegates did make some attempts to drag the French along with them, but these efforts were largely ineffective. After proposing some compromises and mediating between the French and Spanish – a remarkable state of affairs, since the Spanish and Dutch were technically still at war – the French delegation wrote home to Mazarin on 30 December requesting that he accept the terms. These terms included: French support for Portugal, but only in Iberia itself; continued French possession of Catalonia, with a French promise to build no new fortresses there; mediation of French conquests by the Dutch States-General, and the restoration of Duke Charles IV of Lorraine to his duchy, so long as he promised to forfeit his lands if he broke any treaties in the future. Of all of these terms, the status of Lorraine, like Alsace, animated the French delegates.[45]

Lorraine was to remain a problem for French Kings throughout the seventeenth and much of the eighteenth century. The independence of its Dukes proved a thorn in the side of Louis XIV in particular, who occupied the Duchy between 1670-97.[46] Despite his success in other ventures, Louis proved unable to conquer the territory in any of his wars. Unlike Alsace, the region had not fallen into French hands through the Peace of Westphalia either – far from it. In fact, Duke Charles IV of Lorraine would even find time to take an active interest in the plight of Ireland and its Catholics, then under the suppression of Cromwell's Protectorate.[47] The difficulties which the French had with the maintenance of an independent, self-interested, often-hostile Duke right on their doorstep is easy to understand, but their inability to conquer or annex the region dragged the question out late into the eighteenth century, when in 1766 it was annexed and reorganised as a province.

The question was apparently raw enough for German Chancellor Otto von Bismarck to annex the two provinces of Alsace and Lorraine in 1871.[48] Although by then its citizens seemed to have forgotten their independent past, the status of the region led to no end of confusion among academics writing during the First World War, leading one to ask in 1915, 'What is the point of view of Lorraine?'[49] While Mazarin may have cared very little about the answer to this question in 1648, detaching Lorraine from the Empire as he had done with Alsace was proving more difficult than he had anticipated. In the background, the Dutch, who had promised to renew their war with the Spanish if the latter proved unreasonable, watched nervously to see what would happen next. The compromise on Lorraine's status meant that the French might in fact agree, but Penaranda hoped they would not; interestingly, he believed that with the Dutch threat gone, Spain would be able to focus its full attentions upon the French, and wrest better terms from her. At the same time though, if the negotiations broke down because of the Spanish, then the Dutch might make good their threat and resume their war. Penaranda thus gambled that Mazarin would refuse to compromise on Lorraine, and to his great relief, the gamble paid off.

By standing firm, Mazarin may have believed that he was denying the Spanish the ability to save face, and that he was standing up for French interests. However, since we know that France did not fully hold Lorraine in its grasp until 1766, this determination to push the boundaries of France still further seems in retrospect like a bridge too far for Mazarin. It had the additional effect of releasing the Dutch from their bonds to France; now that Mazarin had torpedoed the negotiations over a Lorraine compromise himself, they were no longer prepared to make war against Spain in his name. On 30 January 1648, after much soul searching and last-minute hesitation, the Dutch and Spanish did sign their peace treaty at long last.

This was the Peace of Münster, and it brought officially to an end eight decades of conflict in the Low Countries. The sheer significance of the moment cannot have been lost on either Mazarin or his Spanish counterparts, but he almost certainly recognised an underlying message which came with the news. If France and Spain could not settle their differences while the Dutch element was in play – mediating, pressuring and cajoling as it attempted to bring both sides to the table – then what hope was there for a Franco-Spanish peace now that the Dutch element was suddenly absent?[50] Certainly, it was unlikely, but perhaps with the Dutch and Spanish appeased, there would now be time to focus more intently on the religious settlement. Phase three of that saga was about to begin.

One of the terms of Maximillian's re-entry into the war on Ferdinand's side was a promise from the Emperor to pursue and conclude the religious negotiations. Maximillian had come to see the religious issues as the truly knotty morass which delayed the final peace, rather than disagreement over territorial concessions. France (in September 1646) and Sweden (in February 1647) had already wrested what they wanted from the opposite side, and the religious settlement remained outstanding. The two pillars of Christendom met at Osnabruck, but this new act of the drama proved just as frustrating, with the Emperor hesitating, and Catholic delegates encouraged by the intransigence of the Papal delegate. A new tactic was tried, and a third party, led by the new

Elector of Mainz, spearheaded an assembly of interested parties at Osnabruck, which would meet free from either the Emperor or Swedish interference.

The Swedes were willing to cooperate, because their more extreme Protestant allies could not blame them for any concessions which emerged from that gathering. But the Emperor was opposed, arguing that such a gathering would undermine his authority. Maximillian of Bavaria had already advised him to harness this very authority in autumn 1647, to make a religious settlement in his capacity as Emperor, and to wait for the others to follow suit. A curious compromise was reached, which might permit those religious discussions to proceed. In one room, Johan Salvius, the Swedish delegate, would meet with Isaac Volmar, Trauttmasdorff's replacement. In a neighbouring room, the Protestant and Catholic estates, mediated by the Elector of Mainz, would assemble.

It was an idea just convoluted enough to work. With moderate Catholics and Protestants overwhelming the discussions, the more hard-line voices were largely drowned out. After so many years of war, it seemed that much of the venom had been sucked out of the German Estates. Of particular note was the Bavarian representative, who, as directed by Maximillian, swung determinedly to the side of the moderates. This proved effective, and the two sides worked quickly and continuously together, often presenting Salvius and Volmar with agreements that had already been signed, which gave neither man the time to let his pride get in the way. Throughout March 1648, great strides in the negotiations were made, and the representatives of the major powers, interestingly, were largely carried along with them.[51]

It was decided that 1 January 1624 was the 'normal date' for all secularised territories. This meant that all land in Protestant hands on that date was to remain Protestant or be restored to them if it had been occupied since. Old principles enshrined in the 1555 Peace of Augsburg were updated and refined; the ecclesiastical reservation which compelled a Catholic who converted to Protestantism to resign his bishopric was maintained, but it was also applied to Catholics. The principle that each independent territorial ruler had the right to determine the religion of his territory was reaffirmed, but it was also clarified so that the private faith of one's subjects would not be impacted. Limited toleration, respect for property and a recognition of Calvinism as standing legally alongside Lutheran and Catholic creeds were also accepted. In cases where there was some doubt over the faith of a ruler or region in 1624, toleration was recommended. The whole document was a considerable achievement and can be viewed as the de facto end of the religious wars which had divided Germans since Martin Luther's reformation had begun. Conflict had by no means been eliminated, and hard-line opinions could not be ignored in every circumstance, but the general tone of the settlement was certainly promising. As the historian John Gagliardo put it, the terms of the peace settlement...

...were also largely free of the vagueness and ambiguity which had deliberately been built into the Peace of Augsburg by an earlier and aggressively hopeful generation of Protestant and Catholic rulers who had sought to use equivocation to their own advantage; their descendants had finally learned, at great cost, that lack of clarity could be enormously harmful in many and unpredictable ways. They were determined to avoid it and this time they did.[52]

Such changes and intentions would mean little however, if the traditional institutions of the Empire, such as the Aulic Council or the Imperial Diet, were not also reformed to account for the religious equality. After more haggling, the two sides managed to reach agreement on something of a compromise, where the Catholics would retain a bare majority of 26 out of the 50 judges, but that in the event of a judgement being passed, an equal share of judges from both sides would be required. Such compromises maintained on paper the satisfaction for Catholics, and in practice satisfaction for Protestants. In the case of the Diet, that important Empire-wide assembly which had been torn asunder in the pre-war years by confessional divisions, a new form of procedure was developed, called *itio in partes*. This procedure ensured that religious issues which were put before the Imperial Diet would no longer be settled by a simple majority vote, which inevitably favoured the larger Catholic share of votes, but instead by a membership divided into Protestant and Catholic bodies, with an equal number of persons on each.

In all such decisions, the goal was to reduce the danger posed the Empire's stability in the event of a prince's conversion. Where once such a conversion could rupture the careful religious balance in a given region, and princes would act according to their own interpretation of the Peace of Augsburg, now all had a framework which would instruct them on the best way to proceed. In practice, interestingly, after 1648 cases of princes converting actually became quite rare, and the religious balance in the Empire appeared to have been, in many respects, set.[53] With the resolution of these issues in spring 1648, it seemed that the greatest hurdles to peace had been miraculously overcome. Thanks to the cooperation of the moderate Catholic and Protestant parties, the religious settlement was manufactured and advocated in such a manner as to persuade the Emperor and the Swedes to agree. It was indeed significant, that these moderates had acted to compromise, when in some instances – Bavaria for instance – they had once seemed like the greatest threat to the religious settlement. The war had persuaded them to give way, and their conviction had been transferred from their unbending religious dogma, to the peace party, with equal passion and resolve. With the religious settlement in hand, the pressing question now was whether the remaining issues could also be solved, and a fully comprehensive peace be signed. There remained no guarantees.

FOUR

Vindication

The end of the war between the Dutch Republic and Spain brought to an end eight decades of intermittent war in Europe and across the New World. The conflict had represented the core of Spain's military commitment, and it had compelled her rivals to take advantage of her distraction. At one point in the 1590s, we will recall, Spain was at war with England, France and the Dutch all at once – no state, however powerful, could sustain such a conflict for long. So it was that King Philip IV, likely with a mixture of relief and sadness, consented to officially release the Dutch Republic and recognise their independence. In the first article of the Peace of Münster, Philip IV recognised...

> ...that the Lords States-General of the United Provinces, and the respective Provinces thereof, with all their associated Territories, Towns and dependent Lands, are free and sovereign States, Provinces and Lands, unto which, as unto their aforesaid associated Territories, Towns and dependent Lands, he the Lord King makes no pretension, nor shall his heirs and successors for themselves, either nor or hereafter, evermore make any pretension thereunto.[54]

Through such a wordy statement, Philip IV effectively absolved himself of the war which had so animated and frustrated his father and grandfather. It seemed that Europe could breathe a sigh of relief at the conclusion of this ruinous war, but in fact, Europe was still attempting to catch its breath. Even within the very articles of the Peace of Münster, Philip referred to himself as the King of Castile, Aragon, Catalonia and Portugal. These latter two claims were then being feverishly disputed by Spain's enemies, and they served as something of a reminder that even while war was ending in some places, it was destined to continue in others.

In Catalonia and in Portugal, two peoples agitated for their freedom from Philip IV's yolk, with mixed fortunes. Due to a combination of factors, including the departure of the Dutch, and the eruption of the Fronde revolt in France (see below), Mazarin found he had precious little to spare for Catalonia, and by 1653, the region would be back under Spanish control. Portugal's fate was somewhat different, because it was in the awkward position of being in a state of war with the Dutch in the New World, and with Spain all over the world. Now that the Dutch had made peace with Spain, surely this meant her statesmen would devote more attention to the colonial conflict with Portugal? Indeed, in 1648, the expedition to Brazil which Holland had promised to Zeeland as the price for consenting to the Peace of Münster arrived off the coast of Pernambuco.

The expedition was ill-fated, but the message was still received loud and clear. The equally troubling other side of this dilemma was that Spain would turn its attentions to Portugal in Europe, now that the Dutch were appeased. This prospect became particularly acute once the Catalans had been defeated. King John thus instructed his ambassadors to cleave to the French alliance at all costs – so long as France maintained its armed struggle with Spain, there could be no question of Philip turning his full attention in Europe against Portugal. Should France and Spain conclude a separate peace without Portugal, however, the consequences for Portuguese independence could be dire. In the event, this is what happened; after making much noise about solidarity with their Portuguese ally, Mazarin decided to abandon that ally once it became convenient in 1659. To King John's relief though, Portugal was not reconquered like Catalonia had been; Portugal held out for another decade, concluding peace with the Dutch in 1663, and with Spain in 1668.[55]

The French had mixed feelings about the early exit of the Dutch from the war. On the one hand, it violated the terms of their treaty from 1644, which compelled both powers to make peace together. On the other, Mazarin could not afford to apportion blame to the Dutch, who had warned him repeatedly within the recent months that they planned on ending the conflict, and if France wished to be included, she ought to fall into line and compromise. Mazarin had been unable to compromise over the matter of Lorraine, but it soon became apparent that the war with Spain had lost some of its sheen. It seemed like years since French arms had won any signal triumphs against its Spanish foe – was Spain not supposed to be collapsing under the weight of its revolts and failures? Perhaps if France was able to focus solely on Spain, and not be repeatedly pulled into the conflict in Germany, she would be able to focus her superiority to gradually wear down Madrid. This granted a new urgency to the negotiations in Münster, but it also moved Mazarin to demand a victory from Marshal Turenne which would shore up France's negotiating position.

Mazarin initially thought Turenne might get one in the Spanish Netherlands. After the defection of those Germans in spring momentarily reduced his options, Turenne recovered sufficiently by the end of 1647, but missed his chance to strike before the Dutch had made peace. Just as the war with the Dutch was concluded, the revolt in Naples was crushed, and Spain seemed to enjoy something of a resurgence. The strategic situation as 1647 ended was therefore far from favourable for Mazarin, and this is before one considers the fact that the French army was 'in tatters, ill-fed and demoralised', according to Peter H. Wilson.[56] France's prospects for success would depend upon the Swedes, who would once again be expected to carry the majority of the responsibilities in Germany. For the best results, Marshal Turenne would have to rendezvous with his Swedish counterpart, Field Marshal Gustav Wrangel. If this could be arranged, the Emperor would surely be forced to the peace table, and Mazarin could focus all his energies on bringing Spain low. In early 1648 then, as the negotiations over the religious settlement were entering a critical phase, the French and Swedish armies were preparing for what ended up being their final campaign together.

As 1648 dawned, Sweden possessed an impressive sixty-three thousand soldiers under their banner, but this high number did not translate particularly well onto the field. The reason for this was that Sweden was holding onto a great deal of territory; the Baltic required a full third of these soldiers to serve as a garrison and to protect against a potential attack from Poland. Other forces were dotted around Franconia, Thuringia, Silesia and Moravia in case the Imperial army tried to break through. By the time all such issues were considered, Marshal Wrangel had at his fingertips just twelve and a half thousand horse and six thousand foot. Unlike the earlier phase of the war, cavalry had now occupied the pride of place within the army, as the mobility of the horse recommended it to commanders, who often marched across burnt territory, and the negotiators at Westphalia, who demanded quick returns which they could harness for leverage. The Swedish army as a whole also contained a greater proportion of Swedish conscripts than before, with 18,000 out of the 63,000-total consisting of Swedes, largely because Oxenstierna did not feel he could trust the Germans as wholly as before.[57]

Facing down Turenne and Wrangel was the Imperial commander, Melander, who had fourteen thousand Imperials and ten thousand Bavarians under his command. Melander's army of twenty-four thousand was similarly tasked with defending certain towns and bridgeheads, and he lacked the flexibility to recruit from further Germans lands, since many of these contained a smaller Swedish force. Turenne contributed only six thousand men to the campaign, crossing at Mainz in mid-February 1648, and while Melander managed to escape a potential pincer attack by the allies, he was powerless to stop them seizing several towns along the River Main. Before long, the allies had crossed the Main and had spilled into Franconia, bringing their force to Maximillian's doorstep once again. The mood in the allied camp was not entirely friendly, as disagreements over the pursuit of the war were made more bitter by the defection of many of Turenne's German units in the previous year.

Wrangel did not seem unduly fazed by the tension – he had his own plans for the Emperor, and he believed that the best results, in terms of pressure and of plunder, could be found by launching a new invasion of Bohemia. The idea had long been at the forefront of his mind, but setbacks, including the withdrawal of the French subsidy the previous spring, had hampered his plans. With Melander plainly unable to stop him though, Wrangel believed the moment had come to strike. He moved away from Turenne towards Eger on Bohemia's western border. After considering his prospects, however, Wrangel determined that once again, the time was not yet right for a Bohemian invasion, and he returned to link back up with Turenne. Instead, he determined that it would be more effective to remove Bavaria from the war once and for all, and to follow up that campaign by invading Austria along the Danube.

At 7AM on the morning of 17 May, the allies caught up with Melander's army at Zusmarshausen, near Augsburg, and after a short exchange, Melander was killed.[58] Imperial and Bavarian losses were minimal, but the baggage had been lost, the commander killed, and morale was at an all-time low. Bavaria's remaining forces withdrew across the River Lech to Ingolstadt, where Count Tilly had died in 1632, but the Imperial essentially disintegrated in the retreat. Only five thousand effective soldiers remained intact under the Emperor's command after Zusmarshausen; it seemed that the brittle hold which the Emperor maintained was finally breaking apart.

Maximillian's army fared little better, despite its escape. Morale was so low, and orders so confused thanks to the French relationship, that the Bavarian army also began to desert in droves. On 3 June, the Bavarian commander was even arrested due to his failures to stem these troubling tides, and Maximillian doubled down on punishing other equally unfaithful subjects. Commanders of minor towns who surrendered without a fight to the enemy were ordered hanged, but this was somewhat hypocritical of the Bavarian Elector, since he had followed his subjects in a retreat to Salzburg in the south-east, where the worst excesses of the coming invasion could hopefully be avoided. Maximillian would be safe, but the rest of his Duchy was not so lucky. Although even his former enemy Jan van Werth, last seen defecting to the Imperials with a price of his head, was welcomed back into the Bavarian command with six thousand Imperial reinforcements, these were insufficient to stop Turenne and Wrangel from plundering the region mercilessly with their army of twenty-four thousand. From now until the final peace was signed, Maximillian was effectively forced to watch helplessly as his homeland burned – a suitable penance, his enemies could proclaim, for the Bavarian Elector's sinful policy of the last three decades.[59]

As the armies marched, the Swedish plenipotentiary Johan Oxenstierna sought to tackle perhaps the prickliest of Sweden's demands at Osnabruck – the achievement of guaranteed pay for Sweden's army, to be supplied by the German Estates. In a similar case to the religious settlement, the objections of the Emperor, who wished to discuss the question of amnesty for former rebels first, was overcome by the initiatives of the Estates and Free Cities representatives. Large sums of money based on the size of the Swedish army were proposed, with Johan Oxenstierna originally pushing for twenty million thalers, but settling for five million. The issue was extremely inflammatory and difficult to traverse – this was why it had been postponed by Sweden until the last moment. If Sweden could get no money to satisfy its army, then tens of thousands of unpaid soldiers may rampage across Germany in pursuit of this pay, blackening Sweden's name in the process, and alienating her from Germany.

Sweden plainly did not have the resources to sustain or pay such a large force – this was illustrated by her dependence upon the French subsidy and the orders to live off the land. If the war ended before this could be settled, then the French subsidy and the opportunities for plunder would both vanish, and Sweden would be left with an impossible bill and an anxious multitude of hostile soldiers. The only chance to satisfy the soldiers was thus to wrest the monies from the Germans as part of a peace deal, but the results of this could be explosive. Why should the Germans princes have to pay for the Swedish soldiers' wages? In fact, so desperate were most of the estates for peace that the issue was not as controversial as we might have expected; we should remember also that a large proportion of this 'Swedish' army were actually Germans, and would have wanted to return home with their wage paid. On the other hand, though, Oxenstierna had to tread very carefully, as he quickly learned, when the Elector of Saxony became so offended by Swedish efforts to increase the bill and make German lands serve as collateral that he sent the Emperor a personal note.

Was Saxony about to re-enter the war? Not quite, but the point had been made. Over the summer of 1648, concluding on 10 July, an agreement was finally reached. Sweden's infamously underpaid, multinational army would be appeased with an immediate cash grant of 1.8 million thalers right away, while 1.2 million would be held in reserve. The remaining 2 million thalers would be raised and paid within two years after the conclusion of the peace. The Swedish Chancellor could breathe a sigh of relief – there would be no rampaging Swedish army in the Empire after all. In fact, it seemed like such a great idea that Maximillian of Bavaria, Hesse-Kassel, and even the Emperor attempted to seek some form of payment for their soldiery. But the Estates did not possess an infinite money pit; they determined that the Austrian and Bavarian Circles should pay the debts of the Emperor and Maximillian respectively, but they also ruled that those Circles should bear no responsibility for the Swedish bill, which was certainly a significant concession.

These developments told a fascinating story about the resilience and determination of the German Estates, who acted in unison against the stronger individual powers like Bavaria, Sweden and the Emperor. This strategy granted a voice to those smaller German powers who could afford to send a representative to Westphalia, but on one issue, even the Estates expected to have to tread carefully. The final question outstanding for the peacemakers, as the summer gave way to autumn, was that of amnesty. Isaac Volmar, the

Emperor's lead negotiator, had once proclaimed that permitting the Bohemian exiles to return was the equivalent of placing thirty thousand rebels in the Habsburg lands – it would be intolerable, and Volmar was anxious to avoid a compromise where so many had developed already.

It was important for the sake of Ferdinand's authority that he did not relent on this issue, but fortunately for him, the Swedes proved less enthusiastic than before when it came to discussing it. Amnesty was an issue they identified with, since many rebels and exiles fought for Sweden, but much like France would abandon Portugal for the sake of peace with Spain in 1659, the Swedes were willing to abandon these rebels in return for a limited amnesty, if it meant that peace was at hand. A new date of 1630 was set; any land lost by rebels before that date was gone forever, and this was as far as the Emperor was willing to go. In the last few days of July 1648, this was agreed. The final obstacle to peace had been overcome, could the negotiators now rejoice? In fact, the path to peace was paved with a few more bumps, most taking place in the battlefield. On the night of 25-26 July, for instance, the Swedes finally managed it, and through a combination of ingenuity and conspiracy, broke into Prague (see below). The storm of plunder and chaos which followed was destined to last until the final peace was signed, but it placed an acutely troubling exclamation point upon the negotiations. If Ferdinand did not make peace soon, then there might not be any of his Hereditary Lands left to rule over. As before though, the Thirty Years War hinged on more than just one theatre of war; in France, a brand-new campaign was unfolding with a terrifying ferocity that took Cardinal Mazarin completely off guard.[60]

An analysis of French fortunes in the Thirty Years War seems to contain two very distinct threads. On the one hand, France evidently won its war against Spain, expanded its writ to the Rhine by taking Alsace, and generally re-established its position of predominance following the ruinous Wars of Religion. On the other hand, though, French gains were not nearly as impressive as we might have expected, considering the Spanish weaknesses. Mazarin was forced to relent on Richelieu's aim to destroy the Habsburgs altogether, by making a separate peace with each branch of the family a decade apart. Above all though, one cannot deny that those victories and gains which France did enjoy were bought at an enormous expense. This was seen most notably in the near collapse of the regency regime of Louis XIV, as revolt spread among various influential and powerful French persons, until the young King's own relatives were implicated. Louis de Bourbon, also known as the Grand Condé, was the victor at the Battles of Rocroi in May 1643, and of Lens in August 1648, and counted himself among the Princes of the Blood, yet he was among the most high profile of those to defect, even fighting for the Spanish against his King as he did so.

Too often, one is drawn to the persons of Richelieu, Mazarin and Louis XIV, and we may be led to believe that French domination over its neighbours and rivals was painless, natural, or inevitable. Certainly, France enjoyed a great preponderance in resources, in manpower, in terms of its tax base, and in productivity, then any of its opponents in Western Europe. It was while the effort was made to harness these advantages though that the serious problems for Cardinal Mazarin began.[61] Furthermore, the disappointing returns on the battlefield for France between 1646-48 may have undermined its negotiating power at Westphalia, but of far more danger to this power was the eruption of the Fronde, that civic and societal revolt which ripped through the country, and very nearly killed Louis XIV's reign in its cradle.[62]

The disaster actually began in an atmosphere of triumph. The aforementioned Battle of Lens on 20 August 1648 marked one of the final occasions where French arms succeeded in the wider Thirty Years War. Under the command of Condé, a French army repelled a larger Spanish force of eighteen thousand at Lens, in the Pas-de-Calais region of north-east France. The Spanish, under the command of Leopold William, the Emperor's brother, had staked his fortunes on a daring invasion of France from Flanders, as had been attempted in 1636, but this time Condé was ready, and marched his army from Catalonia to meet him.[63] The victory did not merely add to Condé's legend, it also provided Mazarin with a much needed boost to his personal prestige, which had been waning thanks to the disappointing returns from the war. Rather than rest of his laurels though or use Lens as a bargaining chip for the negotiations with either the Emperor or Spain, Mazarin sought to take the opportunity to arrest some political opponents. It proved a fatal misstep, and riots erupted in Paris, which were to prove fertile ground for the Fronde revolt which emerged from them.[64] 'The Fronde', wrote Geoffrey Treasure,

> was the culmination, violent, widespread and confused, of many conflicts, the expression of many grievances, corporate and individual, the reaction to monarchy's absolutist trend and wartime financial expedients. In its first paroxysms and spreading effects it empowered the institutions and interests which the monarchy had struggled to subdue. In one aspect it was the greatest in the line of anti-fiscal revolts. In another, the constitutional, a set of claims, never reduced to a single programme but amounting to several alternative visions of government. Most dangerous to the crown was the determination of les Grands [powerful nobles] to recover their traditional place in council and, more realistically, in the province. where they had a territorial stake and wanted the authority and patronage associated with the potent office of governor. They wanted not so much to reduce monarchy's powers as to share in its resources.[65]

The Fronde also added to the mid-seventeenth century's image of hellish disruption, which frequently leaked into the language used by the pamphleteers.[66] As if to reflect this state of affairs, 'revolution' as a term first began to enter into the lexicon of the French language between 1649-53. Considering their own experiences, not to mention the fate of the Stuart royal family next door in Britain at this time, this is not too surprising.[67] Initially powered by the *Parlement* of Paris, in its second year the Fronde drew in the French nobility, who participated depending on factors as broad as their corporate loyalties, ties of marriage, and patronage.[68] Mazarin was initially in grave danger from the nobility which he had attempted to keep at arm's length for so long, but against such overwhelming odds, the wily Cardinal clung to power.[69] Animated by their claims to be fighting against the unsuitable regency led by Mazarin and Anne of Austria, these arguments were outmanoeuvred when Louis XIV was declared to be in his majority in 1651. From that point, even if the political passions receded, the religious fervour which had attached itself to the conflict did not.[70]

The eruption of revolts in France was a hardly a new feature; Richelieu had rallied against reluctant taxpayers, and the more dangerous Huguenots, during much of his tenure in office. Mazarin, for his part, had dealt with judges anxious to protect their privileges, and nobility concerned that the creeping absolutism of Louis XIV's regime might undermine their local authority.[71] The Fronde can be seen as the culmination of these concerns; as we have seen, it was akin to a jack of all trades revolt, and a banner was available for anyone with a grievance against Mazarin's regime. This struggle for the future of France and its regency was serious, but when combined with France's existing wars with the Emperor and Spain, a repetition of the opening years of the war where France had suffered invasion on all sides was again possible.

It was essential that Mazarin meet these threats head-on; if the King of Spain would not bend, then he would at least conclude peace with the Emperor. It was imperative that this was done before the worst excesses of the Fronde became known; it was one thing to complain of a tax-revolt, quite another to host a battle for the survival of one's regime. Mazarin could not expect the Emperor to agree to a favourable peace if the Fronde became a crisis. Mercifully for him, the sinister scenes of defection by the nobility, and the crumbling authority of the Crown, were not visible for another two years. Much like he been averse to risking French fortunes on the battlefield, however, Mazarin was unwilling to bet that the Fronde would not escalate further and undermine the French negotiating position. The final agreements, on satisfaction, amnesty, religion and many more matters besides, had been concluded, but a curious period of wait and see now seemed to begin. Mazarin anxiously looked on, but he would be rescued from infamy from an unlikely source – the Swedish army. As the Parisians erected their barricades and Mazarin's authority crumbled, Swedish and German soldiers were returning to the scene of crime: Prague, where, more than thirty years before, the contagion of war had first escaped.

FIVE

A Return to Prague

Can he make peace without even asking me? Does he not owe all his victories to me? Have I not shot down the Swedish king? Have I not conquered Saxony? Have I not earned my reputation in Denmark? How would the battle on White Mountain have ended without me? What glory have I not earned in the battle with Grand Turk? Fie upon you! Get out of my sight; for I get mortally vexed when I fly into a real rage: overpowered by hot and boiling wrath and savage ire I am capable of seizing the spire of St Stephen's Cathedral in Vienna and bending it down so hard that the whole world will turn upside down like a skittle ball.[72]

This is an extract of a comedy drama, penned by contemporary Silesian poet Andreas Gryphius. Gryphius clearly had an eye for the dramatic and the sarcastic, but he was also sensitive enough to the circumstances of the late 1640s to delay the official release of the play. It would not be performed until the early 1660s – perhaps Gryphius believed it was too dangerous to poke fun at the peacemakers so long as the peace was developing. But Gryphius needn't have worried; by August 1648, the final steps towards peace were being taken, and there could be no going back. After several false starts, the endurance of some incredibly time-consuming protocols, and navigation through some immensely bloated egos, it seemed that the Emperor and his foes would at last be brought conclusively to the peace table.

At Westphalia, there was more than enough tragicomedy to go around; a message from the Emperor, urging his delegates to agree to the peace terms, had arrived. Unfortunately, his delegates mislaid the cipher needed to decode his message, and so 'the document which was to end the sufferings of the last thirty years' carnage lay unread' as the Emperor's agents 'searched frantically' for the key.[73] What is not in doubt is that the Emperor had instructed his agents to agree to the peace terms; by now, after all, the French, Swedes and Imperial delegates had fulfilled their goals. Sweden had acquired the sum of 5 million thalers for the payment of its troops, and the Pomeranian knot had been cut in its favour; France had had its rights in Alsace recognised, and both approved of the religious settlement. So it was that on 6 August 1648, Imperial delegates visited Johan Oxenstierna's quarters, and proceeded to read the preliminary agreements out loud. Sweden could not sign the peace treaty yet, Oxenstierna reminded them, because they were compelled to make peace alongside France. However, Oxenstierna did go as far as to consummate the agreement with a handshake, and he promised not to demand any alterations to the treaty as it now stood.[74]

It was just as well Oxenstierna had made such a commitment, because many miles away from this scene in Osnabruck, Swedish soldiers were converging on Prague. Johan Christophe von Konigsmarck, a senior Swedish commander who had fought under the Emperor and the Elector of Brandenburg, orchestrated a brilliant piece of deception, which facilitated a horrendous scene. Prague was destined to be the city where the Thirty Years War both erupted and concluded; no shortage of bloody unrest was to be found in each case. Thanks to the help of a disgruntled Imperial soldier, on the night of 25-26 July, Konigsmarck's three thousand soldiers broke into the western portion of the city. The River Moldau and its Charles Bridge now separated Konigsmarck from the rest of the city, including its prosperous New Town district, but he was content to let his soldiers loose in that portion of the city which he did control.

Over the last few days of July 1648, we are told that more than two hundred citizens were killed by the rampaging Swedes. There was a sense among the soldiery that this was their last true chance to plunder the enemy's wares, and they did not hold back. Priceless art collections and libraries, some gathered by the late Emperor Rudolf II in the beginning of the century, others even older, fell into their hands, and were shipped home to Sweden, where the would-be art connoisseur Queen Christina eagerly awaited their arrival. Konigsmarck managed to squeeze some 7 million thalers from the city, but try as he might, he was unable to break across the bridge and seize the New Town. But help was at hand; over the next month, additional reinforcements of opportunistic Swedes and Germans arrived, drawn like moths to a flame, all desperate to seize some wealth before the war was brought to an end.

Charles Gustav, the Queen's cousin and heir brought six thousand men, and eight thousand came from Saxony. A siege of what remained of Prague was attempted, but Imperial reinforcements were en route. These three and a half thousand Imperial reinforcements made use of the River Moldau to arrive within the New Town before the Swedes, and they put steel into the resilient citizens, who were determined to outlast the invader by holding out until the peace was finally signed. Konigsmarck and Charles Gustav were thus challenged to seize all of Prague before their licence to plunder expired with the arrival of peace. On 11 October, it seemed that the besiegers might break through, but the resistance held out – after handing Prague over in 1620, 1631 and 1632, it seemed that this epicentre of the Thirty Years War was determined to avoid any more harm. Against all these odds, its citizens and soldiers were successful; news of peace arrived in the city on 5 November, and in vain did the Swedes attempt to break in anyway over the next few days, before Imperial reinforcements came to turf them out once and for all.[75]

It had been an incredibly close-run thing, but the end of the war had saved Prague from further destruction. There was something profoundly poetic about the return of the war to its source in its final moments, three decades after it had first erupted from the windows of Hradschin Castle and escaped its Pandora's Box. As Imperial soldiers filed into Bohemia, and the Swedes began their lumbering journey northwards, it must have been difficult for all involved to believe that their war was over. We might imagine that there would be rejoicing and revelling in the camps, but the peace did not greet everyone as good news. 'I was born in war', wailed a female camp follower at Olmutz, in Moravia, 'I have no home, no country and no friends, war is all my wealth and now whither shall I go?' As a stark contrast was the behaviour of the town's burghers, who gathered for a thanksgiving service in the remnants of their church to sing:

> At Thy rebuke they fled, at the voice of Thy thunder they hasted away. They go up by the mountains; they go down by the valleys unto the place which Thou hast founded for them. Thou hast set a bound that they may not pass over; that they turn not again to cover the earth.[76]

But beneath the proclamations, innumerable fears abounded that in fact, the soldiers might return to 'cover the earth' after all. How, one might ask, were the hundreds of thousands of men in Imperial or Swedish service to be demobilised? Could these disgruntled Germans, who might have missed their opportunity to enrich themselves, be expected to take matters into their own hands? What if the satisfaction Sweden had acquired for its soldiers proved insufficient? And what of Charles Gustav, the cousin of the Swedish Queen? He had been appointed to succeed Field Marshal Wrangel, and though it was not yet known why he had been appointed – to increase his profile and make Queen Christina's abdication easier as a result – it was known that he had come in search of glory, but had arrived when only weeks remained in the war. In 1654, Charles Gustav would succeed Christina as Charles X,[77] and thereafter, he would make his name in a momentous war with all his neighbours,[78] but as matters stood in autumn 1648, all felt nervous at the intentions of this 'young, ambitious and warlike' prince, who undoubtedly had much to prove.[79]

But Charles was not present at Westphalia, and it was here that the most important decisions were taken. Notwithstanding the gentleman's agreement between the Imperial and Swedish delegates on 6 August, there remained some wrinkles to iron out before the final signatures could be ascribed to the peace treaties. Evidently, since these signatures were not given until the evening of 24 October, there was a great deal of time remaining for quarrels to emerge and feelings to be hurt. There was plenty for the peacemakers to find issue with, be it with protocol or when clarifying previous statements, but few wished to genuinely jeopardise the negotiations.

For Cardinal Mazarin, indeed, it seemed that the situation in France was more than grave enough to jeopardise the negotiations, without her delegates at Westphalia also acting out. Throughout August 1648, the Cardinal had urged the revolting Parlement in Paris to reconsider its position, to refrain from opposing the tax farming practices which had been established for more than twelve years, and to consider the 'necessities of the war', in light of their opposition. This was the prelude to the Fronde which would erupt later in the month, and although it could not yet be known just how serious the Fronde would be, on 24 August, Mazarin was already confessing to a peer that this 'small domestic war' was keeping him very busy. He had high hopes for French arms applying additional pressure upon the enemy, but recent news, such as the informal peace between Sweden and the Emperor on 6 August, had troubled him.[80] Two days later, when he received news of Condé's triumph at Lens, Mazarin overstepped and provoked the very conflict he feared.

The consequences were grave, but while he had overestimated its impact, the victory at Lens was a crucial last stab in the heart of Imperial resilience. This was Leopold William's third defeat in a row as governor of the Spanish Netherlands, and it virtually guaranteed that the Emperor would have to make peace without Spain. It also persuaded the Estates in the Empire to motor on ahead of the Emperor's delegate, Isaac Volmar, who waited in Münster for the French delegate to meet with him, only to be disappointed. In fact, Abel Servien – the only French plenipotentiary of some importance who remained to represent France – had stayed in Osnabruck, while the German Estates negotiated with him in private. Just as they had done several times in recent memory, these Estates revolted against the slow-moving procedures of their Emperor's representatives and took matters into their own hands. The Estates committed to make peace without Spain, who they had little love for in any case, and by 15 September, France and the Empire had signed their final agreement. The next day the Swedes followed suit. Now all that was needed was the Emperor's signature for the whole process to be made official.

Emperor Ferdinand did not want to exclude Spain from the peace, but recent events on the battlefield had only served to highlight his vulnerability. His brother was a proven loser in warfare, and Prague was on its last reserves. To save against any worse disasters, Ferdinand elected to ignore the Spanish warnings, and sent orders on 30 September to the effect that he would sign. Interestingly, the peacemakers had already made plans to ignore him if he proved difficult. The Estates had presented their fait accompli, and had outmanoeuvred the Emperor, so that if he refused to consent, he would be left alone with an eroded support base, to continue the war against France. There was no prospect of the Estates supporting their Emperor now – they had decided firmly on peace, from the smallest principality to the largest Electorate, and they would not continue this ruinous war for the sake of Spain.

When Isaac Volmar received these instructions from the Emperor to relent, and sign the peace, Volmar stalled, perhaps hoping to wrest some final concessions, but it was quickly brought home to the Emperor's representative that he no longer controlled either the narrative, or the negotiations. Before long, Volmar was forced to follow the lead of the Estates, who had rallied around the cause of peace without regard for the Emperor's interests. In the eleventh hour, the prickly matter of Alsace was raised, because Spain owned some claim to it according to the Onate Treaty of 1617. The Estates overcame this with the incredible concession that until Spain relinquished its claim upon the region, France could keep the indemnity it was meant to pay the Habsburgs for it. This placed a serious onus upon Imperial negotiators to persuade the Spanish to give way; if they could not manage it, they would be poorer as a result, but the peace negotiations would not be allowed to suffer. Predictably, Volmar issued his objections, but by this point the Estates were ignoring him, and he, as well as the Habsburgs generally, had 'lost all control of the negotiations.'[81]

The final weeks of the war were a remarkable blur of final complaints and quarrels over precedence. After all their work getting the peace over the finish line, the Estates were curiously aloof from the moment when the final signatures were ascribed. There were sound technical reasons for this; the morass of representatives which the Estates had provided had worked diligently, but many potentates in Germany had neglected to send any representatives or had left before the end of the process. It was thus important not to make the legitimacy of the peace contingent on the signature of every power, college, body or institution, minor or major, within the Empire. A halfway home was arrived at, whereby fifteen of the most important Estates provided their signatures, and additional Estates were allowed to affix their names for the sake of prestige, but no more than those fifteen would be required to make the treaty valid.

Even the day of peacemaking, 24 October, did not proceed smoothly. So obsessed with the issues of precedence were the peacemakers, that they could not appear in public to sign as Volmar had wanted. Instead, the process was carried out in private, just as the preceding years of negotiations had been. The Swedes granted a significant concession and agreed to abandon Osnabruck to sign with their friends and foes together in Münster. This certainly gave the peace treaty the appearance of unity, but it did not mean the Swedes were beginning to see things the French way. The most delicate arrangements and ridiculous procedures had to be prepared to avoid any semblance of superiority; copies of the treaty were signed simultaneously, and one's dignity was carefully guarded. Swapping between different rooms, affixing their signatures, the necessary copies of the treaties were produced by 9PM, and when this was learned, the 70-gun salute was fired, announcing that the Treaties of Osnabruck and of Münster had been signed, and that the Thirty Years War was officially over. The war may have been over, but the struggle was not.[82]

> Be it known to each and everyone it may concern in whatever way: that after the disputes and internal troubles which began many years ago in the Roman Empire and spread to such an extent that they drew in not only all Germany, but also several neighbouring kingdoms, especially Sweden and France, thereby causing a long and bitter war...Consequently, the plenipotentiary envoys of both sides gathered at the appointed place and time...and agreed in the presence of, and with the acceptance and consent of the Electors, Princes and Estates of the Holy Roman Empire to the honour of God and the salvation of Christendom, the following terms of peace and friendship.[83]

This opening preamble of the Treaty of Osnabruck was copied into the Treaty of Münster, in addition to the following point, Article 1, on the subject of Universal Peace – a somewhat hollow claim, considering the continuation of the Franco-Spanish War, but a significant declaration nonetheless. Article 1 read:

> That there be a Christian, universal and perpetual peace, and a true and sincere friendship and amity between his sacred imperial majesty, the House of Austria, and all his allies and adherents, and the heirs and successors of each and everyone of them, chiefly the Catholic King of Spain and the Electors, Princes and Estates of the Empire, on the one side; and her sacred royal majesty, the kingdom of Sweden, her allies and adherents, and the heirs and successors of each of them, especially his most Christian majesty of France, and the relevant Electors, Princes and Estates of the Empire on the other side; and that this peace shall be observed and cultivated sincerely and seriously, so that each party promotes the other's benefit, honour and advantage, and that a true neighbourliness, sincere peace and genuine friendship grows afresh and flourishes between the Roman Empire and the Kingdom of Sweden.[84]

These were high-minded goals indeed, but was it truly realistic to suppose that the end of the war could bring about the transformation of relations? Could enemies become allies so quickly? The Spanish and Dutch had managed the transition with an impressive degree of realism and finesse, but both those powers had active interests in repairing their relationship and resuming their natural relations as mutually beneficial trading partners. There was no indication that between the Emperor and France, or the Emperor and Sweden, the story would be similar. And indeed, it was hard to imagine that France would never again threaten the equilibrium of Germany, particularly with a young King growing in age and ambition, and soon to come into his majority. The same, arguably, was true of Sweden, where Charles X was destined to ascend; with two new monarchs at the helm, could Germany truly be safe from their individual quests for glory and renown? Perhaps not, but there were certainly enough interests at stake aside from the French or Swedish variety to make peace appear attractive.

It proved impossible, ultimately, to end three decades of war instantaneously through the mere signatures on treaties. This was not due to misplaced bitterness, necessarily, or because France and Sweden wished to maintain pressure and wrest additional concessions. By and large, the Franco-Swedish alliance had provided incredibly lucrative returns for the two partners. France had pushed its borders to the Rhine with the acquisition of Alsace, in addition to Metz, Toul, Verdun and Philipsburg. The Emperor had been separated from his Spanish cousin, which surely meant that the war with Spain would be easier. Sweden had gained extensive rights over Pomerania, and the formerly Danish-owned bishoprics of Bremen and Verden, while her soldiery would be paid not from the Swedish taxpayer, but by the Empire's organisation. Five million thalers would be sent from the Estates, and Sweden could husband its resources and rebuild its shattered finances after eighteen years of continuous conflict.

There seemed some apprehension over ratifying and implementing the terms of the peace treaties; so long as trust was in short supply, it was very difficult for either side to relinquish the only source of power they possessed, their army, and to allow goodwill and mutual exhaustion to do its work. Indeed, the ending of the war did not result in the armies being discarded. Although according to Article XVI of the Treaty of Osnabruck the armies were supposed to be demobilised within two months, that prediction proved far too optimistic to be practical.[85] It was understandable why the French armies were not demobilised; these soldiers were to be redirected against Spain, where Mazarin intended they be used to wrest additional victories and concessions. For the people of France, this meant that the gloom of war and the impossible taxation would have to be endured indefinitely, a prospect which they blamed upon the foreign Cardinal, who it was said was disdaining peace for his own personal gain.[86]

But what of the soldiers under the Imperial or Swedish command; what need was there for these men to remain at arms? A combination of factors, including hesitation on the part of the commanders, distrust of one's enemies and the complications arising from suddenly releasing tens of thousands of men from their service into civilian life all served to delay the demobilisation process. A quick survey of events following the signing of the peace seem to suggest that no one was in any particular hurry; the first conference which the commanders hosted took place in Prague on 17 November 1648, but the topic of demobilisation was less pressing than the question of how these soldiers were to be continually supplied.

In all, one hundred and fifty thousand men were under arms across the Empire, be they Swedes, French, Hessians, Bavarians, Imperials or others, and until it could be certain that the peace treaties were ratified and their terms implemented, the soldiers would not be released from their service. Again, one is struck by the poetic nature of the dilemma; for years, the citizen had been terrorised by the soldier, and now it was the statesman who urgently worked to find some solution so that the soldier would not terrorise him. The debate dragged on well into the following year, even as compromises over where the armies were to quartered were reached, and limited restitution of church land took place. In mid-February 1649, the treaties were ratified, but this did little to resolve matters.

Instead, it would require yet another gathering of potentates, and it was decided that the potentates should meet at Nuremburg to work through the remaining disputes, including Charles Gustav's newfound passion for the Palatine cause, which could only worry the Imperials. Demobilisation remained the order of the day however, and the terms of the recent peace treaties were upheld and respected. Amidst a worsening situation in France, Mazarin found that his leverage declined with the increased focus on Spain and the retreat from German territory. Grave warnings about the fate of his regime were received in January 1649, when King Charles was executed, ushering in a new phase of the revolution sweeping across the British Isles, which was soon to place the realm in Cromwell's hands. Further afield in Poland, the beginnings of the rupture which was to end in utter destruction and ruin were being felt amidst the Cossack revolt. Notwithstanding these ill-omens, the need was sufficient to open this unofficial sequel to the Westphalian negotiations, and all gathered at Nuremburg in November 1649. Nuremburg was not left in peace until summer 1651, yet even then, the work was not completed. Swedish soldiers remained in portions of Germany well into the early 1650s for various reasons, and were likely only fully returned to the Baltic by 1654 because Sweden's new king planned a glorious new war. This meant that, in effect, it took nearly six years for the soldiers to be fully demobilised, and for the final remnants of the Thirty Years War to be definitively put to be.

On 25 October 1648, Münster's town council had authorised a thanksgiving service to take place, followed by the secretary's journey through the streets. As he went through the town, accompanied by a military drummer and eight trumpeters, the arrival of peace was proclaimed, and details provided.[87] Considering the unceasing activity which followed this proclamation, one could surely argue that any celebrations which marked the end of the Thirty Years War in October 1648 appear premature. Yet, just as the citizen wished to welcome the end of the war, so too must the historian mark the end point of this series of wars somewhere. At the very least, while the list of issues in need of resolution remained legion in October 1648, the hostilities which had ruined the Empire for three decades had finally come to an end. Germany was under threat of foreign invaders, and was at war with its neighbours, no longer. Citizens and soldiers alike would no longer be forced to pick a side, and face ruin for the consequences. The great quest between God or the Devil was mercifully over, however imperfectly it had ended. To many contemporaries, this was just cause indeed for celebration.

Chapter 23 Notes

[1]Wedgewood, *Thirty Years War*, pp. 469-470.
[2]Quoted in Tom Scott, *Regional Identity and Economic Change: The Upper Rhine, 1450-1600* (Oxford: Oxford University, 1997), pp. 49-50.
[3]See Wilson, *Sourcebook*, pp. 287-288.
[4]Croxton, *Westphalia*, pp. 238-239.
[5]*Ibid*, pp. 240-241.
[6]For the central role which Alsace played in the Austro-Spanish negotiations from 1617-19, see: Magdalena S. Sanchez, 'A House Divided: Spain, Austria, and the Bohemian and Hungarian Successions', *The Sixteenth Century Journal*, Vol. 25, No. 4 (Winter, 1994), pp. 887-903.
[7]See Croxton, '"The Prosperity of Arms is Never Continual"', pp. 999-1000.
[8]See Croxton, *Westphalia*, pp. 241-242.
[9]See *The Columbia Encyclopaedia*, 6th ed. (Columbia University Press, 2018), "Pomerania," http://www.questia.com/read/1E1-Pomerani/pomerania.
[10]Croxton, *Peacemaking*, p. 236.
[11]See Georgina Masson, *Queen Christina*, pp. 88-89.
[12]*Ibid*, p. 91.
[13]Quoted in *Ibid*, p. 95.
[14]*Ibid*, p. 96.
[15]Both quoted in *Ibid*, p. 100.
[16]See *Ibid*, p. 102.
[17]Croxton, *Westphalia*, pp. 258-262.
[18]Wilson, *Europe's Tragedy*, p. 716.
[19]See Sutherland, 'The Origins of the Thirty Years War and the Structure of European Politics', pp. 603-607.
[20]See Wilson, *Europe's Tragedy*, pp. 716-717.
[21]See F. L. Carsten, *Princes and Parliaments in Germany: From the Fifteenth to the Eighteenth Century* (Oxford: Clarendon Press, 1959), pp. 392-393.
[22]See Wilson, *Europe's Tragedy*, pp. 219-220.
[23]Carsten, *Princes and Parliaments in Germany*, pp. 393-395.
[24]See Croxton, *Westphalia*, pp. 269-270.
[25]See Parker, *Europe in Crisis*, pp. 181-182.
[26]Croxton, *Westphalia*, pp. 271-279 examines the religious struggle in the most accessible and comprehensive way.
[27]See Wilson, *Europe's Tragedy*, pp. 714-715.
[28]Quoted in Croxton, *Peacemaking*, p. 236.
[29]See Croxton, '"The Prosperity of Arms is Never Continual"', p. 1001.
[30]Hume, *Court of Philip IV*, pp. 405-406.
[31]See Pedro Cardim, '"Portuguese Rebels" at Münster', pp. 307-312.
[32]Davies, *Spain in Decline*, pp. 66-67.
[33]Treasure, *Richelieu and Mazarin*, pp. 61-64.
[34]Quoted in Hume, *Court of Philip IV*, pp. 406-407.
[35]See Wilson, *Europe's Tragedy*, pp. 723-725.
[36]Wolfgang Menzel, *The History of Germany: From the Earliest Period to the Present Time*, trans. George Horrocks, vol. 2 (London: Bell & Daldy, 1871), p. 391.
[37]Quoted in Croxton, *Peacemaking*, p. 271.
[38]Quoted in *Ibid*, pp. 273-274.
[39]Croxton, *Peacemaking*, pp. 271-279 provides the best analysis of Mazarin's character, and we have drawn on it for this section.
[40]Quoted in *Ibid*, p. 275.
[41]See *Ibid*, pp. 275-281.
[42]Ogg, Europe in the Seventeenth Century, pp. 372-373; Parker, *Europe in Crisis*, pp. 263-266.
[43]One would do well to see Croxton, *Westphalia*, pp. 285-295 for the most comprehensive examination of these negotiations. We have drawn on Croxton's analysis heavily for this section of the book.
[44]See Croxton, *Westphalia*, p. 297.
[45]*Ibid*, pp. 299-300.

[46]See Philip McCluskey, 'From Regime Change to Réunion: Louis XIV's Quest for Legitimacy in Lorraine, 1670—97', *The English Historical Review*, Vol. 126, No. 523 (DECEMBER 2011), pp. 1386-1407.

[47]Micheál Ó. Siochrú, 'The Duke of Lorraine and the International Struggle for Ireland, 1649-1653', *The Historical Journal*, Vol. 48, No. 4 (Dec., 2005), pp. 905-932.

[48]Dan P. Silverman, 'The Economic Consequences of Annexation: Alsace-Lorraine and Imperial Germany, 1871-1918', *Central European History*, Vol. 4, No. 1 (Mar., 1971), pp. 34-53.

[49]T. B. Rudmose-Brown, 'Alsace-Lorraine: A Problem of Nationality', *Studies: An Irish Quarterly Review*, Vol. 4, No. 15 (Sep., 1915), pp. 367-383; p. 367. Other contemporary notes on the situation can be found in C. C. Eckhardt, 'The Alsace-Lorraine Question', *The Scientific Monthly*, Vol. 6, No. 5 (May, 1918), pp. 431-443; Lucien Gallois, 'Alsace-Lorraine and Europe', *Geographical Review*, Vol. 6, No. 2 (Aug., 1918), pp. 89-115.

[50]See Croxton, *Westphalia*, pp. 300-301.

[51]See *Ibid*, pp. 302-305.

[52]Gagliardo, *Germany under the Old Regime*, p. 84.

[53]*Ibid*, pp. 84-85.

[54]Quoted in Geyl, *History of the Dutch-Speaking Peoples*, p. 442.

[55]See Pedro Cardim, '"Portuguese Rebels" at Münster. The Diplomatic Self-Fashioning in mid-seventeenth Century European Politics', pp. 329-333.

[56]Wilson, *Europe's Tragedy*, p. 736.

[57]The numbers and dispositions of the soldiers are provided by W. P. Guthrie, *The Later Thirty Years War* (Westport, 2003), pp. 257-260.

[58]Croxton, '"The Prosperity of Arms is Never Continual"', p. 988.

[59]Wilson, *Europe's Tragedy*, pp. 741-743.

[60]See Croxton, *Westphalia*, pp. 309-313.

[61]Paul Sonnino, 'Prelude to the Fronde. The French Delegation at the Peace of Westphalia', *Historische Zeitschrift. Beihefte*, New Series, Vol. 26, Der Westfälische Friede.Diplomatie – politische Zäsur – kulturelles Umfeld – Rezeptionsgeschichte (1998), pp. 217-233; p. 217.

[62]Lucien Bély, 'The Peace Treaties of Westphalia and the French Domestic Crisis', *Historische Zeitschrift. Beihefte*, New Series, Vol. 26, Der Westfälische Friede.Diplomatie – politische Zäsur – kulturelles Umfeld – Rezeptionsgeschichte (1998), pp. 235-252; pp. 235-236.

[63]Guthrie, *Later Thirty Years War*, p. 192.

[64]Wilson, *Europe's Tragedy*, p. 737.

[65]Geoffrey Treasure, "Mazarin and the Fronde," *History Review*, no. 28 (1997); Available: http://www. questia.com/read/1G1-19805554/mazarin-and-the-fronde.

[66]See Adrianna E. Bakos, 'Images of Hell in the Pamphlets of the Fronde', *Historical Reflections / Réflexions Historiques*, Vol. 26, No. 2, The Last Things (Summer 2000), pp. 335-353.

[67]See Ilan Rachum, 'The Entrance of the Word "Revolution" into French Political Discourse (1648-1653)', *Historical Reflections / Réflexions Historiques*, Vol. 23, No. 2 (Spring 1997), pp.229-249.

[68]Sharon Kettering, 'Patronage and Politics during the Fronde', *French Historical Studies*, Vol. 14, No. 3 (Spring, 1986), pp. 409-441.

[69]Richard Bonney, 'Cardinal Mazarin and the Great Nobility during the Fronde', *The English Historical Review*, Vol. 96, No. 381 (Oct., 1981), pp. 818-833.

[70]Richard M. Golden, *The Godly Rebellion: Parisian Cures and the Religious Fronde, 1652-1662* (Chapel Hill, NC: University of North Carolina Press, 1981).

[71]William H. Beik, 'Magistrates and Popular Uprisings in France before the Fronde: The Case of Toulouse', *The Journal of Modern History*, Vol. 46, No. 4 (Dec., 1974), pp. 585-608.

[72]Quoted in Wilson, *Sourcebook*, p. 263.

[73]The scene is recorded in Masson, *Queen Christina*, p. 109. See also Wedgewood, *Thirty Years War*, p. 484.

[74]See Croxton, *Westphalia*, p. 313.

[75]See Wilson, *Europe's Tragedy*, pp. 744-746.

[76]See Wedgewood, *Thirty Years War*, p. 485.

[77]Masson, *Queen Christina*, pp. 215-216.

[78]Charles X would launch the Northern War in 1655, a conflict which ruined Poland in particular, and which saw Sweden push the limits of its conquests at the expense of European opinion. In spite of his undeniable successes against the Danes, Poles and Russians, the conflict cost Charles X his life in 1659, and only highlighted the shortcomings of an Empire supported by the sword. See Haumant, "Chapter XI- The Struggle for Baltic Supremacy- Sweden, Denmark, and Prussia," in *Europe in the Seventeenth*

Century, by David Ogg, 6th Rev. ed. (London: Adam & Charles Black, 1954), pp. 447-451.

[79]Wedgewood, *Thirty Years War*, p. 487.

[80]See Lucien Bély, 'The Peace Treaties of Westphalia and the French Domestic Crisis', p. 243.

[81]See Croxton, *Westphalia*, p. 319; see pp. 314-319 for a concise summary of the final stages in the negotiations.

[82]*Ibid*, pp. 319-320.

[83]Quoted in Wilson, *Sourcebook*, pp. 304-305.

[84]Quoted in *Ibid*, p. 305.

[85]Wilson, *Sourcebook*, p. 318.

[86]Bély, 'The Peace Treaties of Westphalia and the French Domestic Crisis', pp. 251-252.

[87]See Croxton, *Westphalia*, pp. 321-328.

CONCLUSION

> They say the terrible war is now over. But there is still no sign of a peace. Everywhere there is envy, hatred and greed: that's what the war has taught us...We live like animals, eating bark and grass. No one could have imagined that anything like this would happen to us. Many people say that there is no God...But we still believe that God has not abandoned us. We must all stand together and help each other.[1]

This entry was scrawled into the Bible of a Swabian family, and is dated 17 January 1647. Evidently, the war was not over yet, but the confusion which the unfortunate family felt and the desperation they had for peace is palpable. Indeed, if the passage of time had not played its role, we would expect to find a myriad of diary entries similar to this one. The war had lasted a generation, and the peace process had dragged throughout the 1640s, beginning in 1643 and continuing at an inconsistent pace, until it ended on 24 October 1648. And even then, the aftermath of the war continued to haunt its contemporaries. Soldiers in Swedish service would not return to the Baltic until 1654; many in French service turned to face Spain, and the Emperor preserved a force of twenty-five thousand to stock the depleted frontier with the Ottomans, which had been ominously quiet during the war's ravages. The war had underlined the pivotal importance of maintaining such a force, and indeed, some of its regiments were to remain in service until the final collapse of the Habsburg patrimony in 1918.[2] Rising stars in Habsburg service, such as the two Italian commanders Ottavio Piccolomini (1599-1656) and Raimondo Montecuccoli (1609-1680), were destined to carry the standards of this army well into the seventeenth century, against Turks, French and other Germans.[3]

But what of the war which had ravaged Europe, however unequally, for three decades? For anyone born in the period 1618-1648, the war would have been a constant fixture of their lives. Some, like Maximillian of Bavaria, Chancellor Axel Oxenstierna of Sweden, or John George of Saxony, had lived through every wretched year of the conflict, but this was statistically very rare. Most, including the vast majority of the soldiers employed, had been born into an era when the Thirty Years War was already a fact of life. These individuals knew nothing other than the state of affairs where the Empire and war were common bedfellows. It was difficult to imagine any other state of affairs existing; how was the Empire now to act? How were bankrupted, homeless, grieving families now to move on? Could those that had made a fortune in war protect these gains in peacetime? Was it possible to conceive of a system where justice prevailed? Was it possible to trust one's rulers, or one's neighbours, that conflict would not be resorted to again as a means to solve any outstanding disputes? These were questions which normally followed every conflict, but there was little about the Thirty Years War that could be classified as normal.

First and foremost, it was a conflict composed of several interconnected wars. Even those conflicts which did not spill into the main war in Germany, such as that between Sweden and Poland (fought intermittently from 1611-1629),[4] between rival claimants to the Duchy of Mantua in North Italy (1627-31),[5] between Poland and Muscovy (1632-34),[6] between Denmark and Sweden (1643-45),[7] between the Ottomans and Venice (1645-1669),[8] or more painfully for Cardinal Mazarin, the domestic and foreign crisis known as the Fronde (1648-54),[9] all had an impact upon the Thirty Years War itself.

Considering these varied conflicts, both connected and unrelated to the Thirty Years War, one could be forgiven for wondering whether a classification of that conflict would even be possible. The conflict defies easy classification, and it does not fit neatly into a box; was it a world war, since conflicts were fought over distant colonies owned by the interested powers, such as the Spanish, Portuguese and Dutch? Was it a German War, since the conflict between the Emperor and his enemies was waged mostly on German soil? Maybe it would be helpful to view the war as originating in the power and ambitions of the Habsburg dynasty, while the states who intervened in the Empire represented 'wild cards', altering the status of the conflict as they did so.[10] Perhaps it was a civil war, since the conflict had first erupted out of a Bohemian succession issue within the Holy Roman Empire, and it had been prolonged by the Palatine question. Others underline the religious aspects of the conflict, and note that the Thirty Years War was primarily religious in nature, that the peace was religiously oriented, and that Europe never saw a war for religious questions of its kind again.[11] Others still believe that the very concept of the Thirty Years War is flawed, and that by viewing these conflicts as one, we do the historical record a disservice.[12]

The Thirty Years War was all of these things to varying degrees; it was rooted in disagreements over the Empire's constitution and religious makeup which dated back to the Reformation; it was aggravated and prolonged by the intervention of interested foreign powers, like the Danes (1625), Swedes (1630) and French (1635). It was shaped by the intervention of these powers, just as it was shaped by the distraction of normally active states like Poland,

England and the Ottoman Empire. It was complemented, if such a term could be used, by the maintenance of the simultaneous Eighty Years War between the Dutch and Spain. It provided the platform for the latest confrontation between the House of Bourbon and the House of Habsburg, which did not end until 1659, and which was resumed a few years after that. While we may be assured of the validity of the term 'Thirty Years War', we may also be assured that attempting to classify such an event is an impossible task.[13]

It is possible to view the Holy Roman Empire as the centre of the conflict, or the 'main event', since the majority of the decisive campaigns were fought here, and the war itself began within the boundaries of this realm in 1618. Furthermore, the Peace of Westphalia focused intently upon leaving the Empire in a state of peace, by settling the religious and civil issues which had plagued her states since the Reformation. Resolving such dilemmas dragged the negotiations out, but they also enabled the Habsburg Emperors to husband their resources in the aftermath of the war, and consolidate their strength in their hereditary lands, leading as a result to the conception of 'Austria' as a great European power.[14]

It was within the Empire that peace proved most durable, but a lasting Christian peace covering all of Europe was an illusion, nor did contemporaries of the peace genuinely expect an end to war. All they could truly hope for was that things would get better, as one prayed in 1642:

> ...the lord grant that our sons grow up in their youth like plants and our daughters like the bay trees, and that our palaces and magazines be full, so that they can produce one supply after another, that our sheep bear a thousand and a hundred thousand in our villages.

Those that lived through the worst excesses of the war had spent its final years willing it to end. Having yearned for peace, or news of some breakthrough which would facilitate peace, it is little surprise that Germans in particular would have 'sighed' and 'shouted with joy' at news of the Peace of Westphalia.[15] However, if such optimists had looked a little closer at the final document, then several signal truths would have been obvious, as John Gagliardo noted...

> ...they might have seen the evacuations of troops from their fatherland for what it really was: a respite from war, not eternal absolution from it. The treaty reflected no conscious desire to create conditions for perpetual peace, but only every participant's determination to protect his own interests and position to the degree permitted by others under the circumstances of the moment.[16]

Indeed, far from ending war, the Thirty Years War had 'forced all European states to place intolerable pressures on their subjects', and it had 'exported disorder to the whole of Europe.'[17] Much of this disorder had to do with the towering number of soldiers under arms at any one time, relying invariably upon the resources of the Empire for their succour, where insufficient supply lines made regular provisioning impossible. The nature of the conflict meant that military service became something of a scramble for the best contracts and terms; loyalty was in short supply, especially when a favoured tactic was to coerce the defeated army to re-enlist with your side. If soldiers were in short supply, then all from the conscripted peasant to the released felon was fair game.[18] The breakdown in the recruitment system which had generally satisfied the demands of previous wars facilitated an upturn in the recruitment of mercenaries. Famously, Scots distinguished themselves under the banner of the Swedish King,[19] but they were equally active in Habsburg service,[20] as were their Irish neighbours.[21]

Service in foreign armies, according to an unsympathetic chronicler writing in the early nineteenth century, was hardly something to be proud of:

> Shame on the pack of these mercenary swordsmen! [T]hey have made the name of Scot through all Europe equivalent to that of a pitiful mercenary, who knows neither honour nor principle but his month's pay, who transfers his allegiance from standard to standard, at the pleasure of fortune or the highest bidder …Scottish soldiers of fortune, who had served in the German wars until they had lost almost all distinction of political principle, and even of country, in the adoption of the mercenary faith.[22]

Yet, one must be careful not to judge military service by the same standards as the nineteenth or indeed the twenty-first centuries. Some chose to enlist in foreign armies due to religious or political conviction, others because they felt compelled to because of economic circumstance, and others still because it was safer to be employed and drag one's family along with the army than it was to take one's chances as a civilian.[23] An availability of mercenaries does not suggest an absence of conviction of the part of those that enlisted. Robert Monro, author of the first historical record of a military regiment,[24] and a contemporary of Gustavus Adolphus, served the allies of Protestantism faithfully, and never considered crossing over to fight for the Emperor.[25] Whatever one might conclude about the loyalties of mercenaries or one's soldiers, these individuals made the Thirty Years War possible, and contributed to its destructive, harrowing qualities like no other factor.

Like a plague of locusts, the swarms of soldiers criss-crossed over parts of Europe, wresting contributions from towns, raiding storehouses, seizing livestock and taking advantage of the absence of the law to act, in some cases, reprehensively. A recent study investigating the woman's experience in Sweden's warpath reveals some shocking, but unfortunately, predictable, findings.[26] Rape, for instance, was a widely accepted consequence of war, and while efforts were made to clamp down on excesses,[27] instances where soldiers were punished for their heinous crimes were rare. This was not solely due to chauvinism, but also to the practical difficulties of gaining proof while the army was constantly on the march. Justice was thus in short supply, and even those soldiers that were meant to be allied to the native population could behave horrendously. One such example was in the town of Erfurt. Although it was allied to Sweden, this did not stop an officer from attempting to rape a bride on her wedding day in 1641. The assault was not successful, but the unrepentant officer offended again several times, likely taking advantage of his rank to skirt the law.[28]

In addition to the terror which the spectre of an approaching army presented, the practical dilemmas which characterised the Thirty Years War exacerbated the crisis. The balance between supply and demand of foodstuffs was by its very nature seasonal and delicate, prone to severe disruption in the event of a conflict which drew away the labourer and ravaged the land. The peasant grabbed what he could and moved away from the combat zone; if he was lucky, the approaching army would be provisioned and would not have to live off his land. As we have learned though, the likelihood of any army receiving sufficient supplies which could sustain it throughout the duration of a campaign was statistically rare. The larger the army was, the more unlikely it was that the government had the means to provision it.

Thus, an example is given of two thousand English and Scottish soldiers who enlisted to fight for the King of Denmark and defended his fortress of Gluckstadt over the winter of 1627-28. This smaller, more manageable force was provisioned with an impressive 313,000 kg of bread, 33,500 kg of cheese, and 9,000 kg of bacon, in addition to 36 barrels of butter, 8 barrels of mutton, 7 barrels of beef, 8 barrels of herring, 37 barrels of salt to preserve it all, and 1,674 barrels of beer to wash it down. If a force of two thousand men could require and consume so much food, one need only imagine what a force of ten thousand, twenty thousand or even one hundred thousand men might require. Because an army generally fielded cavalry as well, provisions would be required for men and beast alike. If an army marched with twenty thousand horses, for example, these would require not only 9,000 kg of fodder, but also four hundred good acres of grazing land.

Because of these requirements, armies on the march would literally strip the ground bare, and any prospect of provisioning them directly was out of the question. Sweden was not in a position to pay its soldiers wages, so one imagines that paying for provisions was something akin to a pipe dream. It was also in the interest of states to live off the land, since it was cheaper than providing resources themselves. The downside was that the system was unreliable, and armies would be less flexible, but generally, commanders had little choice, and planned their campaigns around the availability of such commodities as grass for the horses, which tended to grow back in spring.[29]

With these aspects of the war in mind, one should not be surprised when confronted by such a large butcher's bill by 1648. Taking the parameters of 1600 to 1650, we can deduce that the population of Spain declined from 7.6 million to 5.2 million; that Russia declined from 11 million to 9.5 million; that Italy dipped from 13 million to 12 million; that Germany's population declined from 15 million to 11 million, and that Bohemia's population contracted by nearly half, from 4 million to 2.25 million. All told, some 20 million souls vanished from Europe during the first half of the century.[30] Of course, we cannot blame all of these losses upon the Thirty Years War; across Europe, everything from the Time of Troubles in Russia, to the appearance of a miniature ice age, where the temperature dropped by 1 degrees, with dramatic consequences, must be taken into consideration.[31] This is to show that although the Thirty Years War is generally accepted to have cost eight million lives, the unfortunate peoples caught in the war's furies could be killed by all manner of causes, be it starvation, famine, disease, murder, or exposure. Death on the battlefield, revealingly, represented a proportionally small number of those killed overall.[32]

Yet, one could argue that, just as important as the casualties it caused, were the wars it directly or indirectly fanned into being. We should not confine our analysis merely to the wars which erupted during the conflict, such as the Franco-Spanish War (1635-59). Instead, historians have assessed the impact of the Thirty Years War in the context of early modern history; to what extent, for instance, was the Thirty Years War responsible for facilitating the later showdown between Austria and Prussia, between Poland and Russia, or between France and England?[33] It is in fact difficult to pinpoint precisely where the ripples and waves caused by the Thirty Years War actually end, but if we take a moment to consider that the conflict was a feature of European realties for three decades, then this would only make sense. Much as they disagree over its classification, historians also disagree over the extent of the Thirty Years War's impact. Wolfgang Menzel believed that the conflict had a decisively negative impact upon the unity of Germany, and that it fatally weakened the Empire and its Emperor, writing that:

> One portion after another of the Holy German empire was thus ceded to her foes. The remaining provinces still retained their ancient form but hung too loosely together to withstand another storm. The ancient empire existed merely in name; the more powerful princes virtually possessed the power and rendered themselves completely independent, and the supremacy of the emperor, and with it the unity of the body of the state, sank to a mere shadow.[34]

Yet, the outcome of the conflict was by no means this clear cut. The more measured conclusions of other historians are perhaps more valuable then, because rather than attempting to discern the ending of one era and the arrival of a new thanks to the conclusion of the war, they view history as more fluid and, essentially, messy.[35] If an accurate examination of the full impact of the war remains difficult, but prone to simplification, then the peace congress at Westphalia suffers similar problems. Indeed, perhaps few myths in history are as stale as that which proclaims 1648 as the beginning of an era of sovereignty, the end phase of religious wars, of conflict in general, or as the arrival of modernity. Contemporaries possessed no such high-minded goals and wished only to bring to an end a conflict which had twisted and turned through various phases since 1618. The 'Westphalian system' which was supposedly created in 1648 is, we are told, under threat. But this system was not the natural outcome of 1648; indeed, it was only conceived of in the 1960s,[36] and has begun to come under deserved criticism since as a flawed lens through which the last three and a half centuries of international relations should not be viewed.[37]

Significant though it certainly was, for it provided a guidebook for later peace efforts in the seventeenth century,[38] Westphalia was not diplomacy's ultimate answer to conflict, nor was it reason's reply to fundamentalism. Religion did not cease to be a factor in politics, as demonstrated by Louis XIV's decision to expel all Huguenots from France in 1685 – the tail-end of a conflict which Richelieu would have recognised in his own time. In 1688, British subjects deposed their Catholic King with the help of his Protestant Dutch replacement. Religion remained a mark of loyalty in Ireland and in Britain, where in 1695 Penal Laws were imposed to reduce opportunities for advancement so long as one adhered to Catholicism.[39] On the continent, meanwhile, the old bugbear of a Catholic Universal Monarchy and 'Black Legend' which had once been ascribed to Spain was simply transferred to France.[40]

Westphalia's significance for religion may be contentious, but the case of sovereignty presents additionally frustrating questions to the reader. While one might assume that the treaties which constitute the Peace of Westphalia – Osnabruck and Münster – would be filled with references to sovereignty and convenient definitions of the concept as a seventeenth century statesman understood it, in fact the term is missing from the document almost entirely.[41] It would be incorrect then, to view Westphalia as the moment when European sovereignty was enshrined in a document, and all involved stood up and took notice. This, indeed, was not how sovereignty worked. Even had the Peace of Westphalia contained pages of detail about sovereignty and its importance, this would not have fundamentally changed how Europeans conducted themselves.

At most, such a hypothetical inclusion of sovereignty would signal that states *should* have sovereignty, and therefore authority to rule exclusively over their own lands. But 'should have' and 'do have' were very different matters, and in the seventeenth century the best means to ensure one's authority was respected was to rely upon the traditional means of legitimation and power; be that through armed force, or from agreements and contracts already made.[42] It would be incorrect, in other words, to imagine the contemporaries at Westphalia sneaking in some revolutionary new resolution on sovereignty, and expecting all involved to respect the new concept. Just as it would be incorrect to conceive of Westphalia as 'the end of an epoch and the opening of another...the majestic portal which leads from the old into the new world.'[43]

If Westphalia had been such a 'majestic portal', then we would expect some fundamental changes to the state system to appear – perhaps Europeans would discover a newfound respect for the sovereignty of their neighbours, and refrain from attacking them so often? Such a revelation was not forthcoming though, in spite of the claims from innumerable historians that Westphalia 'explicitly recognized a society of states based on the principle of territorial sovereignty'.[44] We should not imagine that sovereignty was unknown to Europe by 1648; in fact it had been a recognised concept for three centuries before the Thirty Years War had even begun. In the high middle ages, thanks to the deteriorating powers of the Papacy and concepts of national identity, rulers over independent states came to see themselves as sovereign and their neighbours responded through a developing lexicon of political devices, such as feudalism or absolutism, and not through a sudden or profound declaration in a treaty. The simplistic notion that sovereignty was declared in 1648 suggests that those at the Westphalian negotiations did not recognise one another as such before the treaty was signed, which in practice makes little sense.

Indeed, Westphalia neglected to create either sovereignty or sovereign states, retaining the old oaths which the German states had previously made to the Emperor, and denying these potentates full rights of authority over their lands. Although in practice some of the larger and more powerful states in the Empire could ignore what this implied, the device remained a fundamental part of how the Empire was conceived, and did not vanish overnight with the passage of Westphalia.[45] Nevertheless, the claim to have founded sovereignty at Westphalia seems to have been based more on the propaganda of the anti-Habsburg powers, who claimed to have fought against the absolutist intentions of the Emperor. According to this propaganda, it was the Swedes and French who 'saved' the independence of the European states from the domineering ambitions of the Habsburgs – this despite the fact that neither Ferdinand II nor his son was ever powerful enough to take over all of Europe.

Indeed, Ferdinand II had had to mortgage his own lands in order to bribe potential allies to his side, and he only defeated his Palatine enemy in the first phase of the war by effectively rupturing the constitutional settlement upon which the Empire was based. Considering the absence of any ringing declarations on sovereignty, and the impact which anti-Habsburg propaganda has had on our whole conceptualisation of the Thirty Years War, it seems that it is time to reconsider what we know about what the conflict and its conclusion actually means.[46] It is more useful to view the Peace of Westphalia, first and foremost, as a significant historical event, if only because it brought to an end thirty years of conflict in the Holy Roman Empire. Beyond that though, one should view Westphalia not as the end of one era, and the beginning of another; instead, Westphalia was the latest chapter in a century which contained no shortage of conflict, peacemaking and crises.[47]

The Thirty Years War and the Peace of Westphalia reside in a century which included, among other events, the massive expansion of French power under its Bourbon dynasty, the rise of Prussia, the decline of Poland, the expansion of Russia and the last siege of Vienna by an Ottoman Empire army. The very dynamism of the century underlines the fact that very little time after the conclusion of the Peace of Westphalia was allowed to pass before additional great and terrible eruptions followed. Only a few years after Sweden's soldiers had evacuated Germany and returned to the Baltic, in 1655 they had invaded a new foe, this time in Poland, and a new conflict was instigated with the Danes, Dutch, Brandenburg and Emperor in the process. Consider also the case of France, where an ambitious new King, jealous of his glory, was coming of age. Barely eight years after France and Spain concluded peace in 1659, Louis XIV's armies had invaded the Spanish Netherlands; in 1672, his armies invaded the Dutch Republic, provoking yet another war with the Emperor. In 1686, Louis was at it again, this time over his rights in the Palatinate and his late wife's inheritance. In 1700, the prospect of inheriting the Spanish Crown compelled him to make war on the English, Dutch and Emperor for the final time.[48]

What are we to make of this period in history, after following the conflict from its roots to its famous end? The Thirty Years War left a changed Europe in its wake, and left some grizzled veteran statesmen and rulers at the helm. To men like Maximillian of Bavaria, John George of Saxony or Chancellor Oxenstierna, the experience must have felt akin to a marathon, but their tenure in office would arguably have been less successful without the opportunities to gain which war provided. There can be little doubt that the Thirty Years War provided commanders with an unparalleled opportunity for experimentation, enrichment and fame, but the coming period of the century – where the wars of Louis XIV were to dominate – would prove just as pivotal in honing the fundamentals of the drill, perfecting defensive fortification techniques, and fine-tuning the administrative capabilities of concerned governments. The Military Revolution was destined to continue, and additional revolutions in technology, theory and tactics continued to flow from Europe's military academies.

Much like the terrible scenes of Magdeburg in 1631 did not compel contemporaries to stop the war immediately, not even the horrors of the Thirty Years War could put a stop to European war. War remained just as favoured a tool of foreign policy as before 1618 – the sheen had not worn off. In fact, the war had opened up new opportunities for those that had participated in its furies, opportunities which could be capitalised upon in the future. For the populations that would continue to be caught in the middle, this meant yet more terrible dilemmas, where the actors might have been different, but the choice was virtually the same. New Gods and new Devils had simply taken the place of the old.

For God or the Devil

Conclusion Notes

[1] Quoted in Parker, *Thirty Years War*, p. 160.

[2] *Ibid*, p. 169.

[3] Basset, *For God and Kaiser*, pp. 75-78.

[4] See Francis J. Bowman, 'Sweden's Wars, 1611-32', *The Journal of Modern History*, Vol. 14, No. 3 (Sep., 1942), pp. 357-369.

[5] David Parrott, 'The Mantuan Succession, 1627-31: A Sovereignty Dispute in Early Modern Europe', *The English Historical Review*, Vol. 112, No. 445 (Feb., 1997), pp. 20-65.

[6] Porshnev, *Muscovy and Sweden*, pp. 208-238.

[7] Oakley, *War and Peace in the Baltic*, pp. 75-77.

[8] Croxton, *Westphalia*, p. 208.

[9] Richard Bonney, 'Cardinal Mazarin and the Great Nobility during the Fronde', *The English Historical Review*, Vol. 96, No. 381 (Oct., 1981), pp. 818-833.

[10] Myron P. Gutmann, 'The Origins of the Thirty Years' War', *The Journal of Interdisciplinary History*, Vol. 18, No. 4, The Origin and Prevention of Major Wars (Spring, 1988), pp. 749-770; pp. 768-769.

[11] Croxton, *Westphalia*, pp. 344-345.

[12] See Sutherland, 'The Origins of the Thirty Years War and the Structure of European Politics', *The English Historical Review*, Vol. 107, No. 424 (Jul., 1992), pp. 587-625; especially pp. 587-589. See also S. H. Steinberg, 'The Thirty Years War: A New Interpretation', *History*, xxxii (1947), pp. 87-102.

[13] Contrary to the claims of both Sutherland and Steinburg, the term Thirty Years War was in use at the time, and contemporaries did indeed recognise it. See Mortimer, 'Did Contemporaries Recognize a 'Thirty Years War'?', *The English Historical Review*, Vol. 116, No. 465 (Feb., 2001), pp. 124-136.

[14] See Wilson, 'The Causes of the Thirty Years War 1618-48', pp. 585-586.

[15] See John Theibault, 'The Rhetoric of Death and Destruction in the Thirty Years War', p. 285.

[16] Gagliardo, *Germany under the Old Regime*, p. 88.

[17] Sheilagh C. Ogilvie, 'Germany and the Seventeenth-Century Crisis', *The Historical Journal*, Vol. 35, No. 2 (Jun., 1992), pp. 417-441; p. 441.

[18] See Parker ed., *Thirty Years War*, pp. 172-73.

[19] James Miller, *Swords for Hire: the Scottish Mercenary* (Birmingham: Birlinn Limited, 2007), chapters 7-11.

[20] David Worthington, *Scots in Habsburg Service, 1618-1648* (Boston: Brill, 2003).

[21] John Hennig, 'Irish Soldiers in the Thirty Years War', *The Journal of the Royal Society of Antiquaries of Ireland*, Vol. 82, No. 1 (1952), pp. 28-36.

[22] W. Scott, *A Legend of Montrose* (New York: 1819), pp. 160-178.

[23] Parker, *Thirty Years War*, p. 174.

[24] An edited version of his account is available from William S. Brockington ed. *Monro, His Expedition with the Worthy Scots Regiment called MacKeyes Regiment* (Westport: 1999).

[25] See William S. Brockington, "9: Robert Monro: Professional Soldier, Military Historian and Scotsman," in *Scotland and the Thirty Years' War, 1618-1648*, ed. Steve Murdoch (Boston: Brill, 2001), p. 218.

[26] Mary Elizabeth Ailes, *Courage and Grief: Women and Sweden's Thirty Years' War*.

[27] Parker, *Thirty Years War*, pp. 179-181.

[28] Ailes, *Courage and Grief*, pp. 28-29.

[29] Parker, *Thirty Years War*, pp. 178-179.

[30] Figures provided by Parker, *Europe in Crisis*, p. 23.

[31] *Ibid*, pp. 22-24.

[32] Wilson, *Europe's Tragedy*, p. 4.

[33] See Lyudmila Ivonina, 'The Results of the Thirty Years' War in Russia and Ukraine and the Pereyaslave Treaty of 1654', *Historische Zeitschrift. Beihefte*, New Series, Vol. 26, Der Westfälische Friede.Diplomatie – politische Zäsur – kulturelles Umfeld – Rezeptionsgeschichte (1998), pp. 413-420.

[34] Wolfgang Menzel, *The History of Germany*, trans. George Horrocks, pp. 394-395.

[35] One such examination is provided by Graham Darby, "The 30 Years' War: Graham Darby Examines the Nature and Effects of the War That Dominated the First Half of the Seventeenth Century. (the Unpredictable Past)," *History Review*, 2001. Available: http://www.questia.com/read/1G1-80678819/the-30-years-war-graham-darby-examines-the-nature.

[36] Sebastian Schmidt, 'To Order the Minds of Scholars: The Discourse of the Peace of Westphalia in International Relations Literature', *International Studies Quarterly*, Vol. 55, No. 3 (September 2011), pp. 601-623.

[37]Stephen D. Krasner, 'Compromising Westphalia', *International Security*, Vol. 20, No. 3 (Winter, 1995-1996), pp. 115-151.

[38]Croxton, *Westphalia*, pp. 331-333.

[39]A good overview on the subject is available: Louis Cullen, 'Catholics under the Penal Laws', *Eighteenth-Century Ireland / Iris an dá chultúr*, Vol. 1 (1986), pp. 23-36.

[40]Croxton, *Westphalia*, 335-337.

[41]Derek Croxton, 'The Peace of Westphalia of 1648 and the Origins of Sovereignty', *The International History Review*, Vol. 21, No. 3 (Sep., 1999), pp. 569-591.

[42]*Ibid*, p. 570.

[43]See Leo Gross, 'The Peace of Westphalia, 1648-1948', *The American Journal of International Law*, Vol. 42, No. 1 (Jan., 1948), pp. 20-41; p. 28.

[44]Graham Evans, and Jeffrey Newnham, *The Dictionary of World Politics: A Reference Guide Concepts, Ideas, and Institutions* (Hemel, Hempstead: Harvester. 1990), p. 420.

[45]See Andrew MacRae, "Counterpoint: The Westphalia Overstatement," *International Social Science Review* 80, no. 3-4 (2005), Available: http://www.questia.com/read/1G1-140744240/counterpoint-the-westphalia-overstatement.

[46]The most useful revisionist account is provided by Andreas Osiander, 'Sovereignty, International Relations, and the Westphalian Myth', *International Organization*, Vol. 55, No. 2 (Spring, 2001), pp. 251-287; see especially pp. 258-263.

[47]Those interested in learning more about the debate on the Peace of Westphalia should seek out my podcast series on the question 'Is Westphalia Overrated'; the first of three episodes is available: https://play.acast.com/s/whendiplomacyfails/2af42a9a-1956-42bf-bc69-5b6722f153a9

[48]A good summary of the second half of the seventeenth century and its related conflicts is available: Enid M. G. Routh, 'The Attempts to Establish a Balance of Power in Europe during the Second Half of the Seventeenth Century (1648-1702): (Alexander Prize, 1903)', *Transactions of the Royal Historical Society*, New Series, Vol. 18 (1904), pp. 33-76. See also David Onnekink (eds.) *War and Religion after Westphalia, 1648-1713*, Politics and Culture in North-Western Europe, 1650-1720 (Burlington, VT: Ashgate Publishing. 2009).

The Hanging Tree by Jacques Callot

THIRTY YEARS WAR BIBLIOGRAPHY
A note on sources

This book would not have been possible without the considerable body of work available to me. Those interested in further reading should follow relevant sources below; this bibliography is in itself a testament to the debt I owe to the wider scholarship on the Thirty Years War. Such extensive research would not possible without access to considerable resources, and I am indebted to the online platforms of Questia and JSTOR, in addition to my wife, for allowing me to crowd our apartment with so many books, both borrowed and bought. I have depended upon too many sources and scholars to possibly give credit to them all, but I did find the surveys by Geoffrey Parker, Peter H. Wilson and C. V. Wedgewood particularly helpful. All offer something different to the reader, and all are useful and enjoyable in their own way.

I am perhaps particularly attached to Parker's accounts of the conflict, since his was the first book I ever read of the conflict, and my interest and enthusiasm were ignited within the first few pages. This was before I even realised precisely how significant Parker's contribution to our understanding of Dutch history, Spanish history or the Military Revolution was. This book would be less lively and assessible without his works, and I can only hope that I will play a role in igniting the passions of another potential scholar as he did for me.

Special credit should also be paid to Peter H. Wilson. *'For God or the Devil'* has been greatly enriched by his edited edition of primary sources relating to the Thirty Years War – the *Sourcebook* – which I have drawn upon heavily. It has to be said that, as a historian lacking in a second or third language, Wilson's work in translating and editing primary sources, in the process bringing them forward to an English-speaking audience, has been invaluable. Any shortcomings or errors in referencing these works are those of my own making.

It is perhaps my sole regret that I was not fortunate enough to be proficient in French, Spanish, Italian or German when researching for this work. I am as a result more dependent upon those pioneers in their field, who have shed new light upon oft neglected periods of the war. Derek Croxton and his invaluable work illuminating the period of the Westphalian negotiations spring immediately to mind. Indeed, it struck me as I researched the latter period of the war that from 1643 onwards, I could merely place directions for the reader to find Croxton's defining work *Westphalia: The Last Christian Peace*, rather than research it myself. It is thanks to Croxton that the traditionally scant coverage of the final stage of the conflict – normally a by-product of long and exhausting researching projects like these – is absent here.

Additional thanks should be given to other authors who have engaged in similarly pioneering works. I found the following works particularly useful and enlightening: the account of Frederick V, by Brennan Pursell; Porshnev's account of Muscovy and Sweden in the Thirty Years War, edited and translated by Paul Dukes and Brian Pearce respectively; and the detailed biography of Gustavus Adolphus by Michael Roberts. Indeed, without the work of the latter in envisioning the thought-provoking, hotly-debated Military Revolution theory, the first section of this book would be considerably thinner. Thus, notwithstanding one's views of his theory, scholars and enthusiasts of military history in the seventeenth century owe the late Mr Roberts a debt which can scarcely be repaid.

Bibliography
Books

- Aaron, Melissa D. *Global Economics: A History of the Theatre Business, the Chamberlain's/King's Men, and Their Plays, 1599–1642*. Newark, DE: University of Delaware Press, 2003.
- Allison, Rayne. *A Monarchy of Letters: Royal Correspondence and English Diplomacy in the Reign of Elizabeth I*. London: Springer, 2012.
- Arblaster, Paul. "Our Valiant Dunkirk Romans": Glorifying the Habsburg War at Sea, 1622–1629', in *News Networks in Early Modern Europe* by Joad Raymond, Noah Moxham eds. Brill, 2016.
- Benecke, Gerhard. *Society and Politics in Germany 1500-1700*. London, 1974.
- Berenger, Jean and Simpson, C. A. *A History of the Habsburg Empire 1273-1700*. London: Routledge, 2014.
- Bergin, Joseph. *Cardinal Richelieu: Power and the Pursuit of Wealth*. New Haven CT: Yale University Press, 1990.
- Black, Jeremy. *A Military Revolution? Military Change and European Society, 1550-1800*. NJ: Atlantic Highlands, 1991.
- Blanchard, Jean-Vincent. *Eminence: Cardinal Richelieu and the Rise of France*. New York: Walker Books, 2013.
- Blanning, Tim. *Frederick the Great, King of Prussia*. London: Penguin, 2016.
- Bussmann, Klaus and Schilling, Heinz eds., *1648: War and Peace*, 3 vols. Munich, 1999.
- Chandler, David. *The Art of Warfare in the Age of Marlborough*. New York, 1976.
- Charles Homer Haskins and Robert Howard Lord, *Some Problems of the Peace Conference* (Cambridge: Harvard University Press, 1920).
- Chudoba, Bohdan. *Spain and the Empire*. Chicago: Chicago University Press, 1952.
- Clark, Christopher. *Iron Kingdom, the Rise and Downfall of Prussia 1600-1947*. London: Penguin, 2007.
- Clark, G. N. *War and Society in the seventeenth Century*. Cambridge, 1958.
- Clark, Jack Aden. *Huguenot Warrior: The Life and Times of Henri de Rohan 1579-1638*. The Hague: Springer, 1967.
- Cramer, Kevin. *The Thirty Years' War and German Memory in the Nineteenth Century*. Lincoln, NE: University of Nebraska Press, 2010.
- Croxton, Derek. *Westphalia: The Last Christian Peace*. New York: Palgrave Macmillan, 2013.
- Davies, R. Trevor. *The Golden Century of Spain 1501-1621*. London: Macmillan and Co Ltd, 1967.
- Derry, T. K. *History of Scandinavia: Norway, Sweden, Denmark, Finland, and Iceland*. Minneapolis: University of Minnesota Press, 1979.
- Elliot, J. H. *Richelieu and Olivares*. Cambridge, 1984.
- Elliot, J. H. *The Count-Duke of Olivares: The Statesman in an Age of Decline*. Yale: Yale University Press, 1989.
- Ergang, Robert. *The Myth of the All-Destructive Fury of the Thirty Years' War*. Pocono Pines: PA, 1956.
- Evans, Graham and Newnham, Jeffrey. *The Dictionary of World Politics: A Reference Guide Concepts, Ideas, and Institutions*. Hemel, Hempstead: Harvester. 1990.

- Faulkner, James. *Marshal Vauban and the Defence of Louis XIV's France*. South Yorkshire: Pen & Sword Military, 2011.
- Faulkner, James. *The War of the Spanish Succession 1701-1714*. South Yorkshire; Pen & Sword Books, 2015.
- Fraser, Antonia. *King Charles II*. London: Phoenix, 2011.
- Frost, Robert I. *The Northern Wars: War, State and Society in North-Eastern Europe, 1558 – 1721*. London: Routledge, 2014.
- Gardiner, Samuel Rawlinson. *History of England from the Accession of James I to the Outbreak of the Civil War*, vol. 1. London, 1884.
- Geyl, Pieter. *A History of the Dutch-Speaking Peoples 1555-1648*. London: Phoenix Press, 2001.
- Geyl, Pieter. *House of Orange and Stuart 1641-1672*. London: W&N New Edition, 2001.
- Guthrie, W. P. *Battles of the Thirty Years War: from White Mountain to Nordlingen, 1618-1635*. CT: Greenwood Publishing Group, 2002.
- Guthrie, W. P. *The Later Thirty Years' War: From the Battle of Wittstock to the Treaty of Westphalia*. CT: Greenwood Publishing Group, 2003.
- Harrison, G. B. *A Jacobean Journal, Being a Record of those Things Most Talked of during the Years 1603-1616*. London, 1941.
- Holden Hutton, William. *Constantinople: The Story of the Old Capital of the Empire*. London: J.M. Dent & Co, 1900.
- Howard Carter, Charles. *The Secret Diplomacy of the Habsburgs 1598-1625*. New York: Columbia University Press, 1964.
- Israel, Jonathan and Schwartz, Stuart B. eds. *The Expansion of Tolerance: Religion in Dutch Brazil (1624-1654)*. Amsterdam: Amsterdam University Press, 2007.
- Keegan, John. *The Face of Battle*. London: Penguin Books, 1988.
- Kenyon, J. P. *Stuart England*, 2nd ed. New York: Penguin, 1985.
- Kirby, David. *Northern Europe in the Early Modern Period: The Baltic World 1492-1772*. London: Routledge, 2014.
- Kirwin, W. Chandler. *Powers Matchless: The Pontificate of Urban VIII, the Baldachin, and Gian Lorenzo Bernini*. New York: Peter Lang, 1997.
- Klima, Arnost. "Inflation in Bohemia in the Early Stage of the seventeenth Century", in Michael Flinn, ed., *Seventh International Economic History Congress*. Edinburgh, 1978.
- Levi, Anthony. *Cardinal Richelieu and the Making of France*. Cambridge MA: Da Capo Press, 2001.
- Lockhart, Paul Douglas. *Denmark, 1513-1660: The Rise and Decline of a Renaissance Monarchy: The Rise and Decline of a Renaissance Monarchy*. Oxford: Oxford University Press, 2007.
- Lynch, John. *Spain under the Hapsburgs: Empire and Absolutism 1516-1598*. New York, 1964.
- Manning, Roger B. *An Apprenticeship in Arms: The Origins of the British Army 1585-1702*. New York: Oxford University Press, 2006.
- Masson, Georgina. *Queen Christina*. London: Sphere Books Ltd, 1974.
- Mathew, David. *The Age of Charles I*. London: Eyre & Spottiswoode, 1951.
- Meyerson, Mark D. *The Muslims of Valencia in the Age of Fernando and Isabel: Between Coexistence and Crusade*. Berkeley: University of California Press, 1991.
- Miller, James. *Swords for Hire: the Scottish Mercenary*. Birmingham: Birlinn Limited, 2007, chapters 7-11.
- Montefiore, Simon Sebag. *The Romanovs 1613-1918*. London: Penguin Random House, 2016.
- Nicolle, David. *Forces of the Hanseatic League: thirteenth–fifteenth Centuries*. London: Osprey Publishing, 2014.
- Oman, Sir Charles. *The Art of War in the Sixteenth Century*. London: E.P Dutton and Co., 1937.
- Pages, Georges. *The Thirty Years War 1618-1648*. London: Adam and Charles Black, 1970.
- Parker, Geoffrey ed., *The Thirty Years War* 2nd Edition. London: Routledge, 1997.
- Parker, Geoffrey. *Europe in Crisis 1598-1648*. London: Fontana Paperbacks, 1979.
- Parker, Geoffrey. *The Military Revolution: Military Innovation and the Rise of the West, 1500-1800*. Cambridge: Cambridge University Press, 1988; rev. ed., 1999.
- Pollard, Albert Frederick. *The Jesuits in Poland*. London, 1892.
- Porshnev, B. F. *Muscovy and Sweden in the Thirty Years War 1630-1635* ed. Paul Dukes, trans. Brian Pearce. Cambridge: Cambridge University Press, 2012.

- Pursell, Brennan C. *The Winter King: Frederick V of the Palatinate and the Coming of the Thirty Years War*. Burlington VT: Ashgate Publishing Company, 2003.
- Reid, Peter. *A Brief History of Medieval Warfare: The Rise and Fall of the English Supremacy at Arms 1314-1485*. London: Constable and Robinson, 2007.
- Reuter, Timothy. *Germany in the Early Middle Ages 800–1056*. MA: Addison Wesley Longman, 1991.
- Roberts, Michael. *Gustavus Adolphus: A History of Sweden 1611-1632*, vol. II. London: Longmans, Green and Co. Ltd, 1958.
- Saul, Nigel. *For Honour and Fame: Chivalry in England 1066-1500*. London: Pimlico, 2012.
- Scott, W. *A Legend of Montrose*. New York: 1819.
- Sommerville, Johan P. ed. *King James VI & I: Political Writings*. Cambridge: Cambridge University Press, 1994.
- Spurr, John. *English Puritanism, 1603–1689*. London: Palgrave Macmillan, 1998.
- Steinberg, S. H. *The 'Thirty Years War' and the Conflict for European Hegemony 1600-1660*. London, 1966.
- Stevens, Carol. *Russia's Wars of Emergence 1460-1730*. London: Routledge, 2013.
- Stokes, David Robert. *A Failed Alliance And Expanding Horizons: Relations Between The Austrian Habsburgs And The Safavid Persians In The Sixteenth And Seventeenth Centuries*. PhD Thesis, University of St Andrews, 2014.
- Stoye, John. *The Siege of Vienna*. Edinburgh: Birlinn, 2000.
- Tracy, James D. *A Financial Revolution in the Habsburg Netherlands: "Renten' and "Renteniers" in the County of Holland, 1515-1565*. Berkeley: University of California Press, 1986.
- Vincent, John. *Switzerland at the Beginning of the Sixteenth Century*. Baltimore, 1904; reprint New York, 1974.
- Wander, Karl Friedrich Wilhelm. *German Proverb Lexicon* Bd. II. Leipzig: F. A. Brockhaus, 1870.
- Wedgewood, C. V. *The King's Peace*. London: Collins-Fontana, 1966.
- Wedgewood, C. V. *The King's War*. London: Collins-Fontana, 1966.
- Wedgewood, C. V. *The Thirty Years War*. London: Pimlico, 1992.
- Wedgwood, C. V. *Richelieu and the French Monarchy*. London: Hodder & Stoughton, 1949.
- Wheatcroft, Andrew. *The Habsburgs: Embodying Empire*. London: Penguin Books, 1996.
- Williams, Hywel. *The Emperor of the West: Charlemagne and the Carolingian Empire*. London: Quercus, 2010.
- Williamson Murray and McGregor Knox, *The Dynamics of Military Revolution, 1300-2050*. New York: Cambridge University Press, 2001.
- Wilson, J. Dover. *The Library*, Fourth Series, 11 (1930).
- Wilson, Peter H. *Europe's Tragedy, A New History of the Thirty Years War*. London: Penguin, 2010.
- Wilson, Peter H. *The Holy Roman Empire: A Thousand Years of Europe's History*. London: Penguin Books, 2017.
- Wilson, Peter H. *The Thirty Years War, A Sourcebook*. New York: Palgrave Macmillan, 2010.
- Worthington, David. *Scots in Habsburg Service, 1618-1648*. Boston: Brill, 2003.

E-books

Google e-books

- Basset, Richard. *For God and Kaiser: The Imperial Austrian Army*, 1619-1918. London: Yale University Press, 2015.
- Bertram Hill, Henry. (trans.) *The Political Testament of Cardinal Richelieu, The Significant Chapters and Supporting Sections*. London: University of Wisconsin Press, 1961.
- Black, Jeremy. *Beyond the Military Revolution, War in the Seventeenth Century World*. New York: Palgrave Macmillan, 2011.
- Burckhardt, Carl J. (trans. and abbr. by Edwin and Willa Muir), *Richelieu: His Rise to Power*. Borodino Books reprint from 1940; Virginia, 2017.

- Dodge, Theodore Ayrault. *Gustavus Adolphus: A History of the Art of War from Its Revival After the Middle Ages to the End of the Spanish Succession War, With a Detailed Account of the Campaigns of the Great Swede, and of the Most Famous Campaigns of Turenne, Condé, Eugene and Marlborough*. Houghton, Mifflin and Company, 1895; republished for Tales End Press, 2012.
- Matusiak, John. *Europe in Flames: The Crisis of the Thirty Years War* (Gloucestershire: The History Press, 2018.
- Mortimer, Geoff. *Wallenstein, The Enigma of the Thirty Years War*. New York: Palgrave Macmillan, 2010.
- Paget, John. *Hungary and Transylvania, with Remarks on their Condition, Social, Political and Economical* Vol. II (London: John Murray, 1839.
- Robson, William. *The Life of Cardinal Richelieu*. London: Routledge, 1875.
- Ward, Sir Adolphus William. *The House of Austria in the Thirty Years War*. London: Macmillan and Co, 1869.
- Wilson, Peter H. *Great Battles – Lutzen*. London; Oxford University Press, 2018.

Questia

- Ahnlund, Nils. *Gustav Adolf, the Great*. Translated by Michael Roberts. Princeton: Princeton University Press; American-Scandinavian Foundation, 1940. http://www.questia.com/read/91243183/gustav-adolf-the-great.
- Ailes, Mary Elizabeth. *Courage and Grief: Women and Sweden's Thirty Years' War*. Early Modern Cultural Studies. Lincoln, NE: University of Nebraska Press, 2018. http://www.questia.com/read/126837776/courage-and-grief-women-and-sweden-s-thirty-years.
- Anderson, James M. *The History of Portugal*. Westport, CT: Greenwood Press, 2000. http://www.questia.com/read/14295391/the-history-of-portugal.
- Andersson, Ingvar. *A History of Sweden*. Translated by Carolyn Hannay. New York: Praeger, 1956. http://www.questia.com/read/9548132/a-history-of-sweden.
- Bachrach, Bernard S. "A History of the Late Medieval Siege, 1200-1500." *Cithara* 50, no. 2 (2011): 39+. http://www.questia.com/read/1P3-2373201941/a-history-of-the-late-medieval-siege-1200-1500.
- Baumgartner, Frederic J. *From Spear to Flintlock: A History of War in Europe and the Middle East to the French Revolution*. New York: Praeger Publishers, 1991. http://www.questia.com/read/23110757/from-spear-to-flintlock-a-history-of-war-in-europe.
- Bonney, Richard. *The European Dynastic States, 1494-1660*. Oxford: Oxford University Press, 1991. http://www.questia.com/read/13819719/the-european-dynastic-states-1494-1660.
- Cameron, Keith, and Elizabeth Woodrough, eds. *Ethics and Politics in Seventeenth-Century France*. Exeter, England: University of Exeter Press, 1996. http://www.questia.com/read/120554730/ethics-and-politics-in-seventeenth-century-france.
- Carsten, F. L. *Princes and Parliaments in Germany: From the Fifteenth to the Eighteenth Century*. Oxford: Clarendon Press, 1959. http://www.questia.com/read/55414667/princes-and-parliaments-in-germany-from-the-fifteenth.
- Collier, James Lincoln. *Gunpowder and Weaponry*. New York: Benchmark Books, 2004. http://www.questia.com/read/122746325/gunpowder-and-weaponry.
- Cramer, Kevin. *The Thirty Years' War and German Memory in the Nineteenth Century*. Lincoln, NE: University of Nebraska Press, 2010. http://www.questia.com/read/120822144/the-thirty-years-war-and-german-memory-in-the-nineteenth.
- Croxton, Derek. *Peacemaking in Early Modern Europe: Cardinal Mazarin and the Congress of Westphalia, 1643-1648*. Selinsgrove, PA: Susquehanna University Press, 1999. http://www.questia.com/read/119094031/peacemaking-in-early-modern-europe-cardinal-mazarin.
- Cust, Richard. *Charles I: A Political Life*. New York: Routledge, 2014. http://www.questia.com/read/126062506/charles-i-a-political-life.
- Darby, Graham. "The 30 Years' War: Graham Darby Examines the Nature and Effects of the War That Dominated the First Half of the Seventeenth Century. (the Unpredictable Past)." *History Review*, 2001, 3+. http://www.questia.com/read/1G1-80678819/the-30-years-war-graham-darby-examines-the-nature.
- Dastrup, Boyd L. *The Field Artillery: History and Sourcebook*. Westport, CT: Greenwood

Press, 1994. http://www.questia.com/read/9175413/the-field-artillery-history-and-sourcebook.

- Davies, R. Trevor. *Spain in Decline, 1621-1700*. London: MacMillan, 1957. http://www. questia.com/read/94951519/spain-in-decline-1621-1700.

- Dixon, C. Scott. *Protestants: A History from Wittenberg to Pennsylvania, 1517-1740*. Malden, MA: Wiley-Blackwell, 2010. http://www.questia.com/read/123542197/protestants-a-history-from-wittenberg-to-pennsylvania.

- Ekberg, Carl J. *The Failure of Louis XIV's Dutch War*. Chapel Hill, NC: University of North Carolina Press, 1979. http://www.questia.com/read/8105638/the-failure-of-louis-xiv-s-dutch-war.

- Elliott, J. H. *The Revolt of the Catalans: A Study in the Decline of Spain (1598-1640)*. Cambridge: University Press, 1963. http://www.questia.com/read/13962911/the-revolt-of-the-catalans-a-study-in-the-decline.

- Farr, Jason. "Point: The Westphalia Legacy and the Modern Nation-State." *International Social Science Review* 80, no. 3-4 (2005): 156+. http://www.questia.com/read/1G1-140744239/point-the-westphalia-legacy-and-the-modern-nation-state.

- Fletcher, C. R. L. *Gustavus Adolphus and the Struggle of Protestantism for Existence*. New York: G. P. Putnam's Sons, 1890. http://www.questia.com/read/1420928/gustavus-adolphus-and-the-struggle-of-protestantism.

- Folmer, Henry D. *Franco-Spanish Rivalry in North America, 1524-1763*. Glendale, CA: Arthur H. Clark, 1953. http://www.questia.com/read/59404669/franco-spanish-rivalry-in-north-america-1524-1763.

- Forster, Marc R. *Catholic Revival in the Age of the Baroque: Religious Identity in Southwest Germany, 1550-1750*. Cambridge, England: Cambridge University Press, 2001. http://www. questia.com/read/104999503/catholic-revival-in-the-age-of-the-baroque-religious.

- Gagliardo, John G. *Germany under the Old Regime, 1600-1790*. London: Longman, 1991. http://www.questia.com/read/54794651/germany-under-the-old-regime-1600-1790.

- Glete, Jan. *War and the State in Early Modern Europe: Spain, the Dutch Republic, and Sweden as Fiscal-Military States, 1500-1660*. London: Routledge, 2002. http://www.questia.com/read/108416665/war-and-the-state-in-early-modern-europe-spain.

- Golden, Richard M. *The Godly Rebellion: Parisian Cures and the Religious Fronde, 1652-1662*. Chapel Hill, NC: University of North Carolina Press, 1981. http://www.questia.com/read/105837613/the-godly-rebellion-parisian-cures-and-the-religious.

- Greenspan, Nicole. "David Randall. English Military News Pamphlets, 1513-1637." *Seventeenth-Century News* 71, no. 3-4 (2013): 135+. http://www.questia.com/read/1G1-359213145/david-randall-english-military-news-pamphlets-1513-1637.

- Hassall, Arthur. *Louis XIV and the Zenith of the French Monarchy*. New York: G. P. Putnam's Sons, 1895. http://www.questia.com/read/1209597/louis-xiv-and-the-zenith-of-the-french-monarchy.

- Hebron, Malcolm. *The Medieval Siege: Theme and Image in Middle English Romance*. Oxford: Clarendon Press, 1997. http://www.questia.com/read/62222368/the-medieval-siege-theme-and-image-in-middle-english.

- Hume, Martin. *The Court of Phillip IV: Spain in Decadence*. New York: G. P. Putnam's Sons, 1907. http://www.questia.com/read/98592773/the-court-of-phillip-iv-spain-in-decadence.

- Kotilaine, Jarmo, and Marshall Poe, eds. *Modernizing Muscovy: Reform and Social Change in Seventeenth-Century Russia*. New York: RoutledgeCurzon, 2004. http://www.questia.com/read/108236295/modernizing-muscovy-reform-and-social-change-in.

- Livermore, H. V. *A History of Portugal*. Cambridge, England: Cambridge University Press, 1947. http://www.questia.com/read/96255716/a-history-of-portugal.

- Lodge, Richard. *Richelieu*. London: MacMillan, 1896. http://www.questia.com/read/13578476/richelieu.

- Lund, Erik A. *War for the Every Day: Generals, Knowledge, and Warfare in Early Modern Europe, 1680-1740*. Westport, CT: Greenwood Press, 1999. http://www.questia.com/read/28817428/war-for-the-every-day-generals-knowledge-and-warfare.

- MacRae, Andrew. "Counterpoint: The Westphalia Overstatement." *International Social Science Review* 80, no. 3-4 (2005): 159+. http://www.questia.com/read/1G1-140744240/counterpoint-the-westphalia-overstatement.

- Malcolm, Noel. *Reason of State, Propaganda, and the Thirty Years' War: An Unknown Translation by Thomas Hobbes ; Noel Malcolm*. New York: Oxford University Press, 2007.

http://www.questia.com/read/121989094/reason-of-state-propaganda-and-the-thirty-years.

- Manning, Roger B. *An Apprenticeship in Arms: The Origins of the British Army 1585-1702.* New York: Oxford University Press, 2006. http://www.questia.com/read/121167611/an-apprenticeship-in-arms-the-origins-of-the-british.

- Mathew, David. *The Age of Charles I.* London: Eyre & Spottiswoode, 1951. http://www.questia.com/read/3618055/the-age-of-charles-i.

- Menzel, Wolfgang. *The History of Germany: From the Earliest Period to the Present Time.* Translated by George Horrocks. Vol. 2. London: Bell & Daldy, 1871. http://www.questia.com/read/8484749/the-history-of-germany-from-the-earliest-period-to.

- Moote, A. Lloyd. *Louis XIII, the Just.* Berkeley, CA: University of California Press, 1989. http://www.questia.com/read/124979247/louis-xiii-the-just.

- Murdoch, Steve, ed. *Scotland and the Thirty Years' War, 1618-1648.* Boston: Brill, 2001. http://www.questia.com/read/109286924/scotland-and-the-thirty-years-war-1618-1648.

- Nowell, Charles E. *A History of Portugal.* New York: D. Van Nostrand, 1952. http://www.questia.com/read/89102811/a-history-of-portugal.

- Oakley, Stewart P. *War and Peace in the Baltic, 1560-1790.* New York: Routledge, 1992. http://www.questia.com/read/108714865/war-and-peace-in-the-baltic-1560-1790.

- O'Connell, Robert L. *Of Arms and Men: A History of War, Weapons, and Aggression.* New York: Oxford University Press, 1989. http://www.questia.com/read/78884437/of-arms-and-men-a-history-of-war-weapons-and-aggression.

- Ogg, David. *Europe in the Seventeenth Century.* 6th Rev. ed. London: Adam & Charles Black, 1954. http://www.questia.com/read/73973843/europe-in-the-seventeenth-century.

- Parrott, David. *Richelieu's Army: War, Government, and Society in France, 1624-1642.* Cambridge, England: Cambridge University Press, 2001. http://www.questia.com/read/105940145/richelieu-s-army-war-government-and-society-in.

- Petrie, Charles. *Earlier Diplomatic History, 1492-1713.* New York: Macmillan, 1949. http://www.questia.com/read/73973537/earlier-diplomatic-history-1492-1713.

- Ranum, Orest A. *Richelieu and the Councillors of Louis XIII: A Study of the Secretaries of State and Superintendents of Finance in the Ministry of Richelieu, 1635-1642.* Oxford, England: Clarendon Press, 1963. http://www.questia.com/read/33741930/richelieu-and-the-councillors-of-louis-xiii-a-study.

- Rogers, Clifford J., ed. *The Military Revolution Debate: Readings on the Military Transformation of Early Modern Europe.* Boulder, CO: Westview Press, 1995. http://www.questia.com/read/89742370/the-military-revolution-debate-readings-on-the-military.

- Satterfield, George. *Princes, Posts and Partisans: The Army of Louis XIV and Partisan Warfare in the Netherlands (1673-1678).* History of Warfare. Boston: Brill, 2003. http://www.questia.com/read/120473314/princes-posts-and-partisans-the-army-of-louis-xiv.

- Schiller, Friedrich. *The Works of Frederick Schiller: Historical.* Translated by A. J. W. Morrison. London: Bell & Daldy, 1873. http://www.questia.com/read/10987752/the-works-of-frederick-schiller-historical.

- Scott, Tom. *Regional Identity and Economic Change: The Upper Rhine, 1450-1600.* Oxford: Oxford University, 1997. http://www.questia.com/read/49490784/regional-identity-and-economic-change-the-upper-rhine.

- Stevens, John L. *History of Gustavus Adolphus.* New York: G. P. Putnam's Sons, 1884. http://www.questia.com/read/54736637/history-of-gustavus-adolphus.

- Stomberg, Andrew A. *A History of Sweden.* New York: Macmillan, 1931. http://www.questia.com/read/537624/a-history-of-sweden.

- Stoye, John. *The Siege of Vienna.* Edinburgh: Birlinn, 2000. http://www.questia.com/read/119675052/the-siege-of-vienna.

- Studnicki-Gizbert, Daviken. *A Nation upon the Ocean Sea: Portugal's Atlantic Diaspora and the Crisis of the Spanish Empire, 1492-1640.* New York: Oxford University Press, 2007. http://www.questia.com/read/121609841/a-nation-upon-the-ocean-sea-portugal-s-atlantic.

- Tallett, Frank. *War and Society in Early-Modern Europe: 1495-1715.* New York: Routledge, 1997. http://www.questia.com/read/103448222/war-and-society-in-early-modern-europe-1495-1715.

- Taylor, Philip M. *Munitions of the Mind: A History of Propaganda from the Ancient World to the Present Era.* 3rd ed. Manchester, England: Manchester University Press, 2003. http://www.questia.com/read/117223929/munitions-of-the-mind-a-history-of-propaganda-from.

- Thorp, Malcolm R., and Arthur J. Slavin. *Politics, Religion & Diplomacy in Early Modern Europe: Essays in Honor of Delamar Jensen.* Kirksville, MO: Sixteenth Century Journal Publishers, 1994. http://www.questia.com/read/25432178/politics-religion-diplomacy-in-early-modern-europe.
- Treasure, Geoffrey. "Mazarin and the Fronde." *History Review,* no. 28 (1997): 8+. http://www.questia.com/read/1G1-19805554/mazarin-and-the-fronde.
- Treasure, Geoffrey. *Richelieu and Mazarin.* London: Routledge, 1998. http://www.questia.com/read/103835297/richelieu-and-mazarin.
- Ward, A. W., G. W. Prothero, and Stanley Leathes, eds. *The Cambridge Modern History.* Vol. 4. Cambridge: University Press, 1902. http://www.questia.com/read/100053841/the-cambridge-modern-history.
- Wedgwood, C. V. *Richelieu and the French Monarchy.* London: Hodder & Stoughton, 1949. http://www.questia.com/read/3020767/richelieu-and-the-french-monarchy.
- Wieland, Christian. "War and Religion after Westphalia, 1648-1713." *The Catholic Historical Review* 97, no. 4 (2011): 816+. http://www.questia.com/read/1P3-2489341431/war-and-religion-after-westphalia-1648-1713.

Articles

- Abou-El-Haj, Rifa'at A. Ottoman Diplomacy at Karlowitz. *Journal of the American Oriental Society,* Vol. 87, No. 4 (Oct. - Dec., 1967), pp. 498-512.
- Abou-El-Haj, Rifa'at A. The Narcissism of Mustafa II (1695-1703): A Psychohistorical Study. *Studia Islamica,* No. 40 (1974), pp. 115-131.
- ÁGOSTON, GÁBOR. Firearms and Military Adaptation: The Ottomans and the European Military Revolution, 1450-1800. *Journal of World History,* Vol. 25, No. 1 (March 2014), pp. 85-124.
- Ailes, Mary Elizabeth. Power, Status, and Wealth: British Officers in Seventeenth-Century Sweden. *Scandinavian Studies,* Vol. 71, No. 2 (Summer 1999), pp. 221-240.
- ANASTÁCIO, Vanda. Fragmenting Iberia: Images of Castile in Seventeenth-Century Portuguese Pamphlets. *Portuguese Studies,* Vol. 25, No. 2 (2009), pp. 199-214.
- Armitage, David. The Elizabethan Idea of Empire. *Transactions of the Royal Historical Society,* Vol. 14 (2004), pp. 269-277.
- Arnold, Thomas F. Gonzaga Fortifications and the Mantuan Succession Crisis of 1613-1631. *Mediterranean Studies,* Vol. 4 (1994), pp. 113-130.
- Bachrach, Bernard S. Medieval Siege Warfare: A Reconnaissance. *The Journal of Military History,* Vol. 58, No. 1 (Jan., 1994), pp. 119-133.
- Backus III, Oswald P. The Problem of Unity in the Polish-Lithuanian State. *Slavic Review,* Vol. 22, No. 3 (Sep., 1963), pp. 411-431.
- Bakos, Adrianna E. Images of Hell in the Pamphlets of the Fronde. *Historical Reflections / Réflexions Historiques,* Vol. 26, No. 2, The Last Things (Summer 2000), pp. 335-353.
- Bangs, Carl. Dutch Theology, Trade, and War: 1590-1610. *Church History,* Vol. 39, No. 4 (Dec., 1970), pp. 470-482.
- Bangs, Jeremy Dupertuis Dutch Contributions to Religious Toleration. *Church History,* Vol. 79, No. 3 (SEPTEMBER 2010), pp. 585-613.
- Baumer, Franklin L. England, the Turk, and the Common Corps of Christendom. *The American Historical Review,* Vol. 50, No. 1 (Oct., 1944), pp. 26-48.
- Beik, William H. Magistrates and Popular Uprisings in France before the Fronde: The Case of Toulouse. *The Journal of Modern History,* Vol. 46, No. 4 (Dec., 1974), pp. 585-608.
- Beik, William. The Culture of Protest in Seventeenth-Century French Towns. *Social History,* Vol. 15, No. 1 (Jan., 1990), pp. 1-23.
- Beller, E. A. Recent Studies on the Thirty Years' War. *The Journal of Modern History,* Vol. 3, No. 1 (Mar., 1931), pp. 72-83.
- Bély, Lucien. The Peace Treaties of Westphalia and the French Domestic Crisis. *Historische Zeitschrift. Beihefte,* New Series, Vol. 26, Der Westfälische Friede.Diplomatie – politische Zäsur – kulturelles Umfeld – Rezeptionsgeschichte (1998), pp. 235-252.
- Berg, Joseph. "De iniustitia belli: Violence Against Civilians in the Thirty Years War": Honour's Thesis. *Loyola Marymount University.* 5-5-2016.

- Bergeron, David M. "Are we turned Turks?": English Pageants and the Stuart Court. *Comparative Drama*, Vol. 44, No. 3 (Fall 2010), pp. 255-275.
- Betts, R. R. Social and Constitutional Development in Bohemia in the Hussite Period. *Past & Present*, No. 7 (Apr., 1955), pp. 37-54.
- Bewes, Wyndham A. Gathered Notes on the Peace of Westphalia of 1648. *Transactions of the Grotius Society*, Vol. 19, Problems of Peace and War, Papers Read before the Society in the Year 1933 (1933), pp. 61-73.
- Bireley, Robert. The Peace of Prague (1635) and the Counterreformation in Germany. *The Journal of Modern History*, Vol. 48, No. 1, On Demand Supplement (Mar.,1976), pp. 31-70.
- Bonney, Richard. Cardinal Mazarin and the Great Nobility during the Fronde. *The English Historical Review*, Vol. 96, No. 381 (Oct., 1981), pp. 818-833.
- Borschberg, Peter. The Seizure of the Sta. Catarina Revisited: The Portuguese Empire in Asia, VOC Politics and the Origins of the Dutch-Johor Alliance (1602-c.1616). *Journal of Southeast Asian Studies*, Vol. 33, No. 1 (Feb., 2002), pp. 31-62.
- Bourke, E. Irish Levies for the Army of Sweden (1609-1610). *The Irish Monthly*, Vol. 46, No. 541 (Jul., 1918), pp. 396-404.
- Bowman, Francis J. Sweden's Wars, 1611-32. *The Journal of Modern History*, Vol. 14, No. 3 (Sep., 1942), pp. 357-369.
- Bowman, Francis J. The European Naval Situation during the Early Years of the Thirty Years' War. *Pacific Historical Review*, Vol. 2, No. 2 (Jun., 1933), pp. 170-179.
- Boxer, C. R. Portuguese and Spanish Rivalry in the Far East during the seventeenth century. *The Journal of the Royal Asiatic Society of Great Britain and Ireland*, No. 2 (Dec.,1946), pp. 150-164.
- Brady, Andrea. Dying with Honour: Literary Propaganda and the Second English Civil War. *The Journal of Military History*, Vol. 70, No. 1 (Jan., 2006), pp. 9-30.
- Brainhard, Alfred P. POLISH-LITHUANIAN CAVALRY IN THE LATE SEVENTEENTH CENTURY. *The Polish Review*, Vol. 36, No. 1 (1991), pp. 69-82.
- Bregnsbo, Michael. Denmark and the Westphalian Peace. *Historische Zeitschrift Beihefte*, New Series, Vol. 26, Der Westfälische Friede.Diplomatie – politische Zäsur – kulturelles Umfeld – Rezeptionsgeschichte (1998), pp. 361-367
- Brennan C. Pursell, 'Elector Palatine Friedrich V and the Question of Influence Revisited', *The Court Historian* vol. 6, (2001), pp. 123-139.
- Brightwell, Peter. The Spanish System and the Twelve Years' Truce. *The English Historical Review*, Vol. 89, No. 351 (Apr., 1974), pp. 270-292.
- Brodek, Theodor V. Socio-Political Realities in the Holy Roman Empire. *The Journal of Interdisciplinary History*, Vol. 1, No. 3 (Spring, 1971), pp. 395-405.
- Burgess, Glenn. Was the English Civil War a War of Religion? The Evidence of Political Propaganda. *Huntington Library Quarterly*, Vol. 61, No. 2 (1998), pp. 173-201.
- Burke, James. The New Model Army and the Problems of Siege Warfare, 1648-51. *Irish Historical Studies*, Vol. 27, No. 105 (May, 1990), pp. 1-29.
- Cantoni, Davide. ADOPTING A NEW RELIGION: THE CASE OF PROTESTANTISM IN sixteenth CENTURY GERMANY. *The Economic Journal*, Vol. 122, No. 560, CONFERENCE PAPERS (MAY 2012), pp. 502-531.
- Capponi, Niccolò. Le Palle di Marte: Military Strategy and Diplomacy in the Grand Duchy of Tuscany under Ferdinand II de' Medici (1621-1670). *The Journal of Military History*, Vol. 68, No. 4 (Oct., 2004), pp. 1105-1141.
- Cardim, Pedro. "Portuguese Rebels" at Münster. The Diplomatic Self-Fashioning in mid-seventeenth Century European Politics. *Historische Zeitschrift. Beihefte*, New Series, Vol. 26, Der Westfälische Friede.Diplomatie – politische Zäsur – kulturelles Umfeld – Rezeptionsgeschichte (1998), pp. 293-333
- Carlson, Christina Marie. The Rhetoric of Providence: Thomas Middleton's A Game at Chess (1624) and Seventeenth-Century Political Engraving. *Renaissance Quarterly*, Vol. 67, No. 4 (Winter 2014), pp. 1224-1264.
- Carter, Charles H. Belgian "Autonomy" under the Archdukes, 1598-1621. *The Journal of Modern History*, Vol. 36, No. 3 (Sep., 1964), pp. 245-259.
- Carter, Charles Howard. Gondomar: Ambassador to James I. *The Historical Journal*, Vol. 7, No. 2 (1964), pp. 189-208.
- Casey, James. Moriscos and the Depopulation of Valencia. *Past & Present*, No. 50 (Feb., 1971),

pp. 19-40.

- Cassidy, Ben. Machiavelli and the Ideology of the Offensive: Gunpowder Weapons in "The Art of War". *The Journal of Military History*, Vol. 67, No. 2 (Apr., 2003), pp. 381-404.
- Chevedden, Paul E. The Invention of the Counterweight Trebuchet: A Study in Cultural Diffusion. *Dumbarton Oaks Papers*, Vol. 54 (2000), pp. 71-116.
- Christensen, Carl C. John of Saxony's Diplomacy, 1529-1530: Reformation or Realpolitik? *The Sixteenth Century Journal*, Vol. 15, No. 4 (Winter, 1984), pp. 419-430.
- Church, William F. Publications on Cardinal Richelieu since 1945: A Bibliographical Study. *The Journal of Modern History*, Vol. 37, No. 4 (Dec., 1965), pp. 421-444.
- Close, Christopher W. Augsburg, Zurich, and the Transfer of Preachers during the Schmalkaldic War. Central European History, Vol. 42, No. 4 (DECEMBER 2009), pp. 595-619
- Cogswell, Thomas. Foreign Policy and Parliament: The Case of La Rochelle, 1625-1626. *The English Historical Review*, Vol. 99, No. 391 (Apr., 1984), pp. 241-267.
- Cogswell, Thomas. Thomas Middleton and the Court, 1624: "A Game at Chess" in Context. *Huntington Library Quarterly*, Vol. 47, No. 4 (Autumn, 1984), pp. 273-288.
- Colegrove, Kenneth. Diplomatic Procedure Preliminary to the Congress of Westphalia. *The American Journal of International Law*, Vol. 13, No. 3 (Jul., 1919), pp. 450-482.
- Como, David R. Secret Printing, the Crisis of 1640, and the Origins of Civil War Radicalism. *Past & Present*, No. 196 (Aug., 2007), pp. 37-82.
- Cook, Weston F. Jr. The Cannon Conquest of Nasrid Spain and the End of the Reconquista. *The Journal of Military History*, Vol. 57, No. 1 (Jan., 1993), pp. 43-70.
- Cressy, David. Conflict, Consensus, and the Willingness to Wink: The Erosion of Community in Charles I's England. *Huntington Library Quarterly*, Vol. 61, No. 2 (1998), pp. 131-149.
- Cressy, David. Revolutionary England 1640-1642. *Past & Present*, No. 181 (Nov., 2003), pp. 35-71.
- Croft, Pauline. Trading with the Enemy 1585-1604. *The Historical Journal*, Vol. 32, No. 2 (Jun., 1989), pp. 281-302.
- Croxton, Derek. "The Prosperity of Arms Is Never Continual": Military Intelligence, Surprise, and Diplomacy in 1640s Germany. *The Journal of Military History*, Vol. 64, No. 4 (Oct., 2000), pp. 981-1003.
- Croxton, Derek. The Peace of Westphalia of 1648 and the Origins of Sovereignty. *The International History Review*, Vol. 21, No. 3 (Sep., 1999), p. 569-591.
- Cust, Richard. News and Politics in Early Seventeenth-Century England. *Past & Present*, No. 112 (Aug., 1986), pp. 60-90.
- Cust, Richard. Prince Charles and the Second Session of the 1621 Parliament. *The English Historical Review*, Vol. 122, No. 496 (Apr., 2007), pp. 427-441.
- Dart, Thurston. Two English Musicians at Heidelberg in 1613. *The Musical Times*, Vol. 111, No. 1523 (Jan., 1970), pp. 29+31-32
- Davies, Brian. Village into Garrison: The Militarized Peasant Communities of Southern Muscovy. *The Russian Review*, Vol. 51, No. 4 (Oct., 1992), pp. 481-501.
- Davies, Siriol and Davis, Jack L. Greeks, Venice, and the Ottoman Empire. *Hesperia Supplements*, Vol. 40, Between Venice and Istanbul: Colonial Landscapes in Early Modern Greece (2007), pp. 25-31.
- Davis, Garold. Anglo-German Cultural Relations and the Thirty Years' War. *The Bulletin of the Rocky Mountain Modern Language Association*, Vol. 22, No. 2 (Jun., 1968), pp. 22-29.
- De Brito, Pedro. Knights, Squires and Foot Soldiers in Portugal during the Sixteenth-Century Military Revolution. *Mediterranean Studies*, Vol. 17 (2008), pp. 118-147.
- De Leon, Fernando Gonzalez. "Doctors of the Military Discipline": Technical Expertise and the Paradigm of the Spanish Soldier in the Early Modern Period. *The Sixteenth Century Journal*, Vol. 27, No. 1 (Spring, 1996), pp. 61-85.
- De Silva, Filipa Ribeiro. Crossing Empires: Portuguese, Sephardic, and Dutch Business Networks in the Atlantic Slave Trade, 1580-1674. *The Americas*, Vol. 68, No. 1 (July 2011), pp. 7-32.
- De Witt, David. Rembrandt and the Climate of Religious Conflict in the 1620s. *Jahrbuch der Berliner Museen*, 51. Bd., Beiheft. Rembrandt — Wissenschaft aufder Suche. Beiträge des Internationalen Symposiums Berlin — 4. und 5. November 2006 (2009), pp. 17-24.
- Deshpande, Anirudh. Limitations of Military Technology: Naval Warfare on the West Coast, 1650-1800. *Economic and Political Weekly*, Vol. 27, No. 17 (Apr. 25, 1992), pp. 900-904.

- Doelman, James. Claimed by Two Religions: The Elegy on Thomas Washington, 1623, and Middleton's "A Game at Chesse" *Studies in Philology*, Vol. 110, No. 2 (Spring, 2013), pp. 318-349.
- Doran, Susan. Religion and Politics at the Court of Elizabeth I: The Habsburg Marriage Negotiations of 1559-1567. *The English Historical Review*, Vol. 104, No. 413 (Oct., 1989), pp. 908-926.
- Downing, Brian M. Constitutionalism, Warfare, and Political Change in Early Modern Europe. *Theory and Society*, Vol. 17, No. 1 (Jan., 1988), pp. 7-56.
- Drelichman, Mauricio and Voth, Hans-Joachim. The Sustainable Debts of Philip II: A Reconstruction of Castile's Fiscal Position, 1566-1596. *The Journal of Economic History*, Vol. 70, No. 4 (DECEMBER 2010), pp. 813-842.
- Duffy, Eamon P. The Siege and Surrender of Galway 1651-1652. *Journal of the Galway Archaeological and Historical Society*, Vol. 39 (1983/1984), pp. 115-142.
- Duke, Alastair. From King and Country to King or Country? Loyalty and Treason in the Revolt of the Netherlands. *Transactions of the Royal Historical Society*, Vol. 32 (1982), pp. 113-135.
- Dunning, Chester and Caesar, Dmitrii. Tsar Dmitrii's Bellicose Letter to King Karl IX of Sweden. *The Slavonic and East European Review*, Vol. 87, No. 2 (April 2009), pp. 322-336
- Eckhardt, C. C. The Alsace-Lorraine Question. *The Scientific Monthly*, Vol. 6, No. 5 (May, 1918), pp. 431-443.
- Edie, Carolyn A. Tactics and Strategies: Parliament's Attack upon the Royal Dispensing Power 1597-1689. *The American Journal of Legal History*, Vol. 29, No. 3 (Jul., 1985), pp. 197-234.
- Edie, Carolyn A. Tactics and Strategies: Parliament's Attack upon the Royal Dispensing Power 1597-1689. *The American Journal of Legal History*, Vol. 29, No. 3 (Jul., 1985), pp. 197-234.
- Edmundson, George. Frederick Henry, Prince of Orange (Continued). *The English Historical Review*, Vol. 5, No. 18 (Apr., 1890), pp. 264-292.
- Edmundson, George. Frederick Henry, Prince of Orange. *The English Historical Review*, Vol. 5, No. 17 (Jan., 1890), pp. 41-64.
- Ekman, Ernst. Three Decades of Research on Gustavus Adolphus. *The Journal of Modern History*, Vol. 38, No. 3 (Sep., 1966), pp. 243-255.
- Ekman, Ernst. Three Decades of Research on Gustavus Adolphus. *The Journal of Modern History*, Vol. 38, No. 3 (Sep., 1966), pp. 243-255.
- Elliott, J. H. A Question of Reputation? Spanish Foreign Policy in the Seventeenth Century. *The Journal of Modern History*, Vol. 55, No. 3 (Sep., 1983), pp. 475-483.
- Elliott, J. H. Self-Perception and Decline in Early Seventeenth-Century Spain. *Past & Present*, No. 74 (Feb., 1977), pp. 41-61.
- Esper, Thomas. The Replacement of the Longbow by Firearms in the English Army. *Technology and Culture*, Vol. 6, No. 3 (Summer, 1965), pp. 382-393.
- Eutropia. Richelieu and His Policy: A Contemporary Dialogue. *The English Historical Review*, Vol. 17, No. 65 (Jan., 1902), pp. 20-49.
- Evans, Richard J. W. A Czech Historian in Troubled Times: J. V. Polišenský. *Past & Present*, No. 176 (Aug., 2002), pp. 257-274.
- Fincham, Kenneth and Lake, Peter. The Ecclesiastical Policy of King James I. *Journal of British Studies*, Vol. 24, No. 2, Politics and Religion in the Early Seventeenth Century: New Voices (Apr., 1985), pp. 169-207.
- Finkel, C. F. French Mercenaries in the Habsburg-Ottoman War of 1593-1606: The Desertion of the Papa Garrison to the Ottomans in 1600. *Bulletin of the School of Oriental and African Studies*, University of London, Vol.55, No. 3 (1992), pp. 451-471.
- Finlayson, J. Caitlin. Jacobean Foreign Policy, London's Civic Polity, and John Squire's Lord Mayor's Show, "The Tryumphs of Peace" (1620). *Studies in Philology*, Vol. 110, No. 3 (Summer, 2013), pp. 584-610.
- Forde, Steven. Hugo Grotius on Ethics and War. *The American Political Science Review*, Vol. 92, No. 3 (Sep., 1998), pp. 639-648.
- France, John. Close Order and Close Quarter: The Culture of Combat in the West. *The International History Review*, Vol. 27, No. 3 (Sep., 2005), pp. 498-517.
- Friedman, Ellen G. North African Piracy on the Coasts of Spain in the Seventeenth Century: A New Perspective on the Expulsion of the Moriscos. *The International History Review*, Vol. 1, No. 1 (Jan., 1979), pp. 1-16.
- Fuchs, Ralf-Peter. The Supreme Court of the Holy Roman Empire: The State of Research and

the Outlook. *The Sixteenth Century Journal*, Vol. 34, No. 1 (Spring, 2003), pp. 9-27.

- Gajda, Alexandra. DEBATING WAR AND PEACE IN LATE ELIZABETHAN ENGLAND. *The Historical Journal*, Vol. 52, No. 4 (DECEMBER 2009), pp. 851-878.
- Gallois, Lucien. Alsace-Lorraine and Europe. *Geographical Review*, Vol. 6, No. 2 (Aug., 1918), pp. 89-115.
- Geevers, Liesbeth. Family Matters: William of Orange and the Habsburgs after the Abdication of Charles V (1555–67). *Renaissance Quarterly*, Vol. 63, No. 2 (Summer 2010), pp. 459-490.
- Geyl, Peiter. Frederick Henry of Orange and King Charles I. *The English Historical Review*, Vol. 38, No. 151 (Jul., 1923), pp. 355-383.
- Geyl, Pieter. Frederick Henry of Orange and King Charles I. *The English Historical Review*, Vol. 38, No. 151 (Jul., 1923), pp. 355-383.
- Ghica, Demetrius Ion. MICHEL V., SURNAMED "THE BRAVE," PRINCE OF WALLACHIA. 1593—1601. *The Numismatic Chronicle and Journal of the Numismatic Society*, New Series, Vol. 16 (1876), pp. 161-176.
- Giry-Deloison, Charles. France and Elizabethan England. *Transactions of the Royal Historical Society*, Vol. 14 (2004), pp. 223-242.
- Griffiths, Gordon. The Revolutionary Character of the Revolt of the Netherlands. *Comparative Studies in Society and History*, Vol. 2, No. 4 (Jul., 1960), pp. 452-472.
- Groenveld, Simon. The English Civil Wars As a Cause of the First Anglo-Dutch War, 1640-1652. *The Historical Journal*, Vol. 30, No. 3 (Sep., 1987), pp. 541-566.
- Gross, Leo. The Peace of Westphalia, 1648-1948. *The American Journal of International Law*, Vol. 42, No. 1 (Jan., 1948), pp. 20-41.
- Guilmartin, John F. Jr. Ideology and Conflict: The Wars of the Ottoman Empire, 1453-1606. *The Journal of Interdisciplinary History*, Vol. 18, No. 4, The Origin and Prevention of Major Wars (Spring, 1988), pp. 721-747.
- Gunn, Steven. ARCHERY PRACTICE IN EARLY TUDOR ENGLAND. *Past & Present*, No. 209 (NOVEMBER 2010), pp. 53-81.
- Gutmann, Myron P. The Origins of the Thirty Years' War. *The Journal of Interdisciplinary History*, Vol. 18, No. 4, The Origin and Prevention of Major Wars (Spring, 1988), pp. 749-770
- Hackett, Kimberly J. The English Reception of Oldenbarnevelt's Fall. *Huntington Library Quarterly*, Vol. 77, No. 2 (Summer 2014), pp. 157-176.
- Hamilton, Charles L. The Basis for Scottish Efforts to Create a Reformed Church in England, 1640-41. *Church History*, Vol. 30, No. 2 (Jun., 1961), pp. 171-178.
- Harari, Yuval Noah. The Concept of "Decisive Battles" in World History. *Journal of World History*, Vol. 18, No. 3 (Sep., 2007), pp. 251-266.
- Harris, Tim. Revisiting the Causes of the English Civil War. *Huntington Library Quarterly*, Vol. 78, No. 4 (Winter 2015), pp. 615-635.
- Haug-Moritz, Gabriele. The Holy Roman Empire, the Schmalkald League, and the Idea of Confessional Nation-Building. *Proceedings of the American Philosophical Society*, Vol. 152, No. 4 (Dec., 2008), pp. 427-439.
- Havelock, H. The Cossacks in the Early Seventeenth Century. *The English Historical Review*, Vol. 13, No. 50 (Apr., 1898), pp. 242-260.
- Havran, Martin J. The Character and Principles of an English King: The Case of Charles I. *The Catholic Historical Review*, Vol. 69, No. 2 (Apr., 1983), pp. 169-208.
- Hayden, J. Michael. Continuity in the France of Henry IV and Louis XIII: French Foreign Policy, 1598-1615. *The Journal of Modern History*, Vol. 45, No. 1 (Mar., 1973), pp. 1-23.
- Hayes-McCoy, G. A. Strategy and Tactics in Irish Warfare, 1593-1601. *Irish Historical Studies*, Vol. 2, No. 7 (Mar., 1941), pp. 255-279.
- Hayes-McCoy, G. A. The Early History of Guns in Ireland. *Journal of the Galway Archaeological and Historical Society*, Vol. 18, No. 1/2(1938), pp. 43-65.
- Hayes-McCoy, G. A. The Irish Pike. *Journal of the Galway Archaeological and Historical Society*, Vol. 20, No. 3/4(1943), pp. 99-128.
- Heaver, Andrew H. Music in the Service of Counter-Reformation Politics: The Immaculate Conception at the Habsburg Court of Ferdinand III (1637-1657). *Music & Letters*, Vol. 87, No. 3 (Aug., 2006), pp. 361-378.
- Hennig, John. Irish Soldiers in the Thirty Years War. *The Journal of the Royal Society of Antiquaries of Ireland*, Vol. 82, No. 1 (1952), pp. 28-36.
- Herr, Richard. Honor versus Absolutism: Richelieu's Fight against Duelling. *The Journal of*

Modern History, Vol. 27, No. 3 (Sep., 1955), pp. 281-285.

- Hess, Andrew C. The Battle of Lepanto and Its Place in Mediterranean History. *Past & Present*, No. 57 (Nov., 1972), pp. 53-73.
- Hess, Andrew C. The Moriscos: An Ottoman Fifth Column in Sixteenth-Century Spain. *The American Historical Review*, Vol. 74, No. 1 (Oct., 1968), pp. 1-25.
- Hess, Andrew C. The Moriscos: An Ottoman Fifth Column in Sixteenth-Century Spain. *The American Historical Review*, Vol. 74, No. 1 (Oct., 1968), pp. 1-25.
- Heymann, Frederick G. The Impact of Martin Luther upon Bohemia. *Central European History*, Vol. 1, No. 2 (Jun., 1968), pp. 107-130.
- Heywood, James. Narrative of the Transference of the German Weimarian Army to the Crown of France in the Seventeenth Century. *Transactions of the Royal Historical Society*, Vol. 9 (1881), pp. 216-223.
- Hoffman, Philip T. Why Was It Europeans Who Conquered the World? *The Journal of Economic History*, Vol. 72, No. 3 (SEPTEMBER 2012), pp. 601-633.
- Howard-Hill, T. H. Buc and the Censorship of Sir John Van Olden Barnavelt in 1619. *The Review of English Studies*, Vol. 39, No. 153 (Feb., 1988), pp. 39-63.
- Howard-Hill, T. H. Political Interpretations of Middleton's 'A Game at Chess' (1624). *The Yearbook of English Studies*, Vol. 21, Politics, Patronage and Literature in England 1558-1658 Special Number (1991), pp. 274-285.
- Hussey, Ronald Dennis. America in European Diplomacy, 1597-1604. *Revista de Historia de América*, No. 41 (Jun., 1956), pp. 1-30.
- Israel, Jonathan I. Central European Jewry during the Thirty Years' War. *Central European History*, Vol. 16, No. 1 (Mar., 1983), pp. 3-30.
- Israel, Jonathan I. Frederick Henry and the Dutch Political Factions, 1625-1642. *The English Historical Review*, Vol. 98, No. 386 (Jan., 1983), pp. 1-27.
- Israel, Jonathan I. The Politics of International Trade Rivalry during the Thirty Years War: Gabriel de Roy and Olivares' Mercantilist Projects, 1621-1645. *The International History Review*, Vol. 8, No. 4 (Nov., 1986), pp. 517-549.
- Ivonia, Lyudmila. The Results of the Thirty Years' War in Russia and Ukraine and the Pereyaslave Treaty of 1654. *Historische Zeitschrift. Beihefte*, New Series, Vol. 26, Der Westfälische Friede. Diplomatie – politische Zäsur – kulturelles Umfeld – Rezeptionsgeschichte (1998), pp. 413-420.
- Janssen, Geert H. Political Ambiguity and Confessional Diversity in the Funeral Processions of Stadholders in the Dutch Republic. *The Sixteenth Century Journal*, Vol. 40, No. 2 (Summer, 2009), pp. 283-301.
- Janssen, Geert H. Quo Vadis? Catholic Perceptions of Flight and the Revolt of the Low Countries, 1566–1609. *Renaissance Quarterly*, Vol. 64, No. 2 (Summer 2011), pp. 472-499.
- Jennings, Brendan. Melchior de Burgo A Connaught Soldier of Fortune in the Low Countries in the Seventeenth Century. *Journal of the Galway Archaeological and Historical Society*, Vol. 22, No. 3/4(1947), pp. 174-181.
- Jespersen, Knud J. V. Social Change and Military Revolution in Early Modern Europe: Some Danish Evidence. *The Historical Journal*, Vol. 26, No. 1 (Mar., 1983), pp. 1-13.
- Kamen, Henry. The Economic and Social Consequences of the Thirty Years' War. *Past & Present*, No. 39 (Apr., 1968), pp. 44-61.
- Kea, R. A. Firearms and Warfare on the Gold and Slave Coasts from the Sixteenth to the Nineteenth Centuries. *The Journal of African History*, Vol. 12, No. 2 (1971), pp. 185-213.
- Kennedy, Mark E. Legislation, Foreign Policy, and the "Proper Business" of the Parliament of 1624. *Albion: A Quarterly Journal Concerned with British Studies*, Vol. 23, No. 1(Spring, 1991), pp. 41-60.
- Kent, Barry C. More on Gunflints. *Historical Archaeology*, Vol. 17, No. 2 (1983), pp. 27-40
- Kepler, J. S. Fiscal Aspects of the English Carrying Trade during the Thirty Years War. *The Economic History Review*, Vol. 25, No. 2 (May, 1972), pp. 261-283.
- Kettering, Sharon. Patronage and Politics during the Fronde. *French Historical Studies*, Vol. 14, No. 3 (Spring, 1986), pp. 409-441.
- Kindleberger, Charles P. The Economic Crisis of 1619 to 1623. *The Journal of Economic History*, Vol. 51, No. 1 (Mar., 1991), pp. 149-175.
- King, Peter. The Episcopate during the Civil Wars, 1642-1649. *The English Historical Review*, Vol. 83, No. 328 (Jul., 1968), pp. 523-537.

- Kingra, Mahinder S. The Trace Italienne and the Military Revolution During the Eighty Years' War, 1567-1648. *The Journal of Military History*, Vol. 57, No. 3 (Jul., 1993), pp. 431-446.
- Kleinschmidt, Harald. Using the Gun: Manual Drill and the Proliferation of Portable Firearms. *The Journal of Military History*, Vol. 63, No. 3 (Jul., 1999), pp. 601-630.
- Kooi, Christine. Popish Impudence: The Perseverance of the Roman Catholic Faithful in Calvinist Holland, 1572-1620. *The Sixteenth Century Journal*, Vol. 26, No. 1 (Spring, 1995), pp. 75-85.
- Kortepeter, C. M. Ġāzī Girāy II, Khan of the Crimea, and Ottoman Policy in Eastern Europe and the Caucasus, 1588-94. *The Slavonic and East European Review*, Vol. 44, No. 102 (Jan., 1966), pp. 139-166.
- Krasner, Stephen D. Compromising Westphalia. *International Security*, Vol. 20, No. 3 (Winter, 1995-1996), pp. 115-151.
- Krodel, Gottfried G. Law, Order, and the Almighty Taler: The Empire in Action at the 1530 Diet of Augsburg. *The Sixteenth Century Journal*, Vol. 13, No. 2 (Summer, 1982), pp. 75-106.
- Lake, P. G. Constitutional Consensus and Puritan Opposition in the 1620s: Thomas Scott and the Spanish Match. *The Historical Journal*, Vol. 25, No. 4 (Dec., 1982), pp. 805-825.
- Larminie, Vivienne. The Jacobean Diplomatic Fraternity and the Protestant Cause: Sir Isaac Wake and the View from Savoy. *The English Historical Review*, Vol. 121, No. 494 (Dec., 2006), pp. 1300-1326.
- Lawson-Peebles, Robert. A Conjoined Commonwealth: The Implications of the Accession of James VI and I. *The Yearbook of English Studies*, Vol. 46, Writing the Americas, 1480–1826 (2016), pp. 56-74.
- Lee, Maurice Jr. The Jacobean Diplomatic Service. *The American Historical Review*, Vol. 72, No. 4 (Jul., 1967), pp. 1264-1282.
- Lockhart, Paul Douglas. Denmark and the Empire: A Reassessment of Danish Foreign Policy under King Christian IV. *Scandinavian Studies,* Vol. 64, No. 3 (Summer 1992), pp. 390-416.
- Lockhart, Paul Douglas. Religion and Princely Liberties: Denmark's Intervention in the Thirty Years War, 1618-1625. *The International History Review*, Vol. 17, No. 1 (Feb., 1995), pp. 1-22.
- Loomie, Albert J. Alonso de Cárdenas and the Long Parliament, 1640-1648. *The English Historical Review*, Vol. 97, No. 383 (Apr., 1982), pp. 289-307.
- Loomie, Albert J. Gondomar's Selection of English Officers in 1622. *The English Historical Review*, Vol. 88, No. 348 (Jul., 1973), pp. 574-581.
- Loomie, Albert J. King James I's Catholic Consort. *Huntington Library Quarterly*, Vol. 34, No. 4 (Aug., 1971), pp. 303-316.
- Loomie, Albert J. Toleration and Diplomacy: The Religious Issue in Anglo-Spanish Relations, 1603-1605. *Transactions of the American Philosophical Society*, Vol. 53, No. 6 (1963), pp. 1-60.
- Love, Ronald S. "All the King's Horsemen": The Equestrian Army of Henri IV, 1585-1598. *The Sixteenth Century Journal*, Vol. 22, No. 3 (Autumn, 1991), pp. 510-533.
- Lynn, John A. Recalculating French Army Growth during the Grand Siecle, 1610-1715. *French Historical Studies*, Vol. 18, No. 4 (Autumn, 1994), pp. 881-906.
- Lynn, John A. Tactical Evolution in the French Army, 1560-1660. *French Historical Studies*, Vol. 14, No. 2 (Autumn, 1985), pp. 176-191.
- Lynn, John A. The Evolution of Army Style in the Modern West, 800-2000. *The International History Review*, Vol. 18, No. 3 (Aug., 1996), pp. 505-545.
- Lynn, John A. The Trace Italienne and the Growth of Armies: The French Case. *The Journal of Military History*, Vol. 55, No. 3 (Jul., 1991), pp. 297-330.
- MacHardy, Karin J. The Rise of Absolutism and Noble Rebellion in Early Modern Habsburg Austria, 1570 to 1620. *Comparative Studies in Society and History*, Vol. 34, No. 3 (Jul., 1992), pp. 407-438.
- Manning, Roger B. Styles of Command in Seventeenth Century English Armies. *The Journal of Military History*, Vol. 71, No. 3 (Jul., 2007), pp. 671-699.
- Marshall, P. J. Western Arms in Maritime Asia in the Early Phases of Expansion. *Modern Asian Studies*, Vol. 14, No. 1 (1980), pp. 13-28.
- McCluskey, Philip. From Regime Change to Réunion: Louis XIV's Quest for Legitimacy in Lorraine, 1670—97. *The English Historical Review*, Vol. 126, No. 523 (DECEMBER 2011), pp. 1386-1407.
- McCoog, Thomas M. The English Jesuit Mission and the French Match, 1579-1581. *The*

Catholic Historical Review, Vol. 87, No. 2 (Apr., 2001), pp. 185-213.
- Mears, John A. THE EMERGENCE OF THE STANDING PROFESSIONAL ARMY IN SEVENTEENTH-CENTURY EUROPE. *Social Science Quarterly*, Vol. 50, No. 1 (JUNE, 1969), pp. 106-115.
- Mears, John A. The Thirty Years' War, the "General Crisis," and the Origins of a Standing Professional Army in the Habsburg Monarchy. *Central European History*, Vol. 21, No. 2 (Jun., 1988), pp. 122-141.
- Medick, Hans and Selwyn, Pamela. Historical Event and Contemporary Experience: The Capture and Destruction of Magdeburgin 1631. *History Workshop Journal*, No. 52 (Autumn, 2001), pp. 23-48.
- Melammed, Renée Levine. Judeo-conversas and Moriscas in sixteenth-century Spain: a study of parallels. *Jewish History*, Vol. 24, No. 2 (2010), pp. 155-168.
- Merrick, Jeffrey. The Cardinal and the Queen: Sexual and Political Disorders in the Mazarinades. *French Historical Studies*, Vol. 18, No. 3 (Spring, 1994), pp. 667-699.
- Meyer, Judith Pugh. La Rochelle and the Failure of the French Reformation. *The Sixteenth Century Journal*, Vol. 15, No. 2 (Summer, 1984), pp. 169-183.
- Moote, A. Lloyd. The Parlementary Fronde and Seventeenth-Century Robe Solidarity. *French Historical Studies*, Vol. 2, No. 3 (Spring, 1962), pp. 330-355.
- Morillo, Stephen. Guns and Government: A Comparative Study of Europe and Japan. *Journal of World History*, Vol. 6, No. 1 (Spring, 1995), pp. 75-106.
- Mortimer, Geoff. 'Did Contemporaries Recognize a 'Thirty Years War'?', *The English Historical Review*, Vol. 116, No. 465 (Feb., 2001), pp. 124-136.
- Mortimer, Geoff. Did Contemporaries Recognize a 'Thirty Years War'?. *The English Historical Review*, Vol. 116, No. 465 (Feb., 2001), pp. 124-136.
- Motomura, Akira. The Best and Worst of Currencies: Seigniorage and Currency Policy in Spain, 1597-1650. *The Journal of Economic History*, Vol. 54, No. 1 (Mar., 1994), pp. 104-127.
- Mueller, Guenther H. S. 'The "Thirty Years' War" or Fifty Years of War', *The Journal of Modern History*, Vol. 50, No. 1, On Demand Supplement (Mar.,1978), pp. D1053-D1056.
- Mueller, Guenther H. S. The "Thirty Years' War" or Fifty Years of War. *The Journal of Modern History*, Vol. 50, No. 1, On Demand Supplement (Mar.,1978), pp. D1053-D1056.
- Najam, Edward W. "Europe": Richelieu's Blueprint for Unity and Peace. *Studies in Philology*, Vol. 53, No. 1 (Jan., 1956), pp. 25-34.
- Nef, John U. Limited Warfare and the Progress of European Civilization: 1640-1740. *The Review of Politics*, Vol. 6, No. 3 (Jul., 1944), pp. 275-314.
- Neill, Donald A. Ancestral Voices: The Influence of the Ancients on the Military Thought of the Seventeenth and Eighteenth Centuries. *The Journal of Military History*, Vol. 62, No. 3 (Jul., 1998), pp. 487-520.
- Neu, Tim. Rhetoric and Representation: Reassessing Territorial Diets in Early Modern Germany. *Central European History*, Vol. 43, No. 1 (MARCH 2010), pp. 1-24.
- Nischan, Bodo. Calvinism, the Thirty Years' War, and the Beginning of Absolutism in Brandenburg: The Political Thought of John Bergius. *Central European History*, Vol. 15, No. 3 (Sep., 1982), pp. 203-223
- Nischan, Bodo. Calvinism, the Thirty Years' War, and the Beginning of Absolutism in Brandenburg: The Political Thought of John Bergius. *Central European History*, Vol. 15, No. 3 (Sep., 1982), pp. 203-223.
- Nischan, Bodo. The Second Reformation in Brandenburg: Aims and Goals. *The Sixteenth Century Journal*, Vol. 14, No. 2 (Summer, 1983), pp. 173-187.
- Nolan, John S. The Militarization of the Elizabethan State. *The Journal of Military History*, Vol. 58, No. 3 (Jul., 1994), pp. 391-420.
- Ó. Siochrú, Micheál Atrocity, Codes of Conduct and the Irish in the British Civil Wars 1641-1653. *Past & Present*, No. 195 (May, 2007), pp. 55-86.
- Ó. Siochrú, Micheál The Duke of Lorraine and the International Struggle for Ireland, 1649-1653. *The Historical Journal*, Vol. 48, No. 4 (Dec., 2005), pp. 905-932.
- Odložilík, Otakar. Karel of Žerotín and the English Court (1564-1636). *The Slavonic and East European Review*, Vol. 15, No. 44 (Jan., 1937), pp. 413-425.
- Ogilvie, Sheilagh C. Germany and the Seventeenth-Century Crisis. *The Historical Journal*, Vol. 35, No. 2 (Jun., 1992), pp. 417-441.
- Ohlmeyer, Jane. Driving a Wedge within Gaeldom: Ireland & Scotland in the Seventeenth

Century. *History Ireland*, Vol. 7, No. 3, Scotland and Ireland through the Ages (Autumn,1999), pp. 27-31.

- Orchard, G. Edward. The Election of Michael Romanov. *The Slavonic and East European Review*, Vol. 67, No. 3 (Jul., 1989), pp. 378-402.
- Osiander, Andreas. Sovereignty, International Relations, and the Westphalian Myth. *International Organization*, Vol. 55, No. 2 (Spring, 2001), pp. 251-287.
- Paas, John Roger. The Changing Image of Gustavus Adolphus on German Broadsheets, 1630-3. *Journal of the Warburg and Courtauld Institutes*, Vol. 59 (1996), pp. 205-244.
- Paas, John Roger. The Changing Image of Gustavus Adolphus on German Broadsheets, 1630-3. *Journal of the Warburg and Courtauld Institutes*, Vol. 59 (1996), pp. 205-244.
- Palm, Franklin Charles. The Siege and Capture of La Rochelle in 1628: Its Economic Significance. *Journal of Political Economy*, Vol. 31, No. 1 (Feb., 1923), pp. 114-127.
- Palmitessa, James R. The Prague Uprising of 1611: Property, Politics, and Catholic Renewal in the Early Years of Habsburg Rule. *Central European History*, Vol. 31, No. 4 (1998), pp. 299-328.
- Parker, Charles H. To the Attentive, Nonpartisan Reader: The Appeal to History and National Identity in the Religious Disputes of the Seventeenth-Century Netherlands. *The Sixteenth Century Journal*, Vol. 28, No. 1 (Spring, 1997), pp. 57-78.
- Parker, Geoffrey and de Schepper, Hugo. The Formation of Government Policy in the Catholic Netherlands under 'The Archdukes', 1596-1621. *The English Historical Review*, Vol. 91, No. 359 (Apr., 1976), pp. 241-254.
- Parker, Geoffrey. Crisis and Catastrophe: The Global Crisis of the Seventeenth Century Reconsidered. *The American Historical Review*, Vol. 113, No. 4 (Oct., 2008), pp. 1053-1079.
- Parker, Geoffrey. Mutiny and Discontent in the Spanish Army of Flanders 1572-1607. *Past & Present*, No. 58 (Feb., 1973), pp. 38-52.
- Parker, Geoffrey. Spain, Her Enemies and the Revolt of the Netherlands 1559-1648. *Past & Present*, No. 49 (Nov., 1970), pp. 72-95.
- Parker, Geoffrey. The "Military Revolution," 1560-1660--a Myth? *The Journal of Modern History*, Vol. 48, No. 2 (Jun., 1976), pp. 195-214.
- Parker, Geoffrey. The Limits to Revolutions in Military Affairs: Maurice of Nassau, the Battle of Nieuwpoort (1600), and the Legacy. *The Journal of Military History*, Vol. 71, No. 2 (Apr., 2007), pp. 331-372.
- Parker, Geoffrey. Why Did the Dutch Revolt Last Eighty Years? *Transactions of the Royal Historical Society*, Vol. 26 (1976), pp. 53-72.
- Parrott, David. The Mantuan Succession, 1627-31: A Sovereignty Dispute in Early Modern Europe. *The English Historical Review*, Vol. 112, No. 445 (Feb., 1997), pp. 20-65.
- Partner, Peter. Papal Financial Policy in the Renaissance and Counter-Reformation. *Past & Present*, No. 88 (Aug., 1980), pp. 17-62.
- Paul, Michael C. The Military Revolution in Russia, 1550-1682. *The Journal of Military History*, Vol. 68, No. 1 (Jan., 2004), pp. 9-45.
- Pekař, Josef. Wallenstein and the Habsburgs. *The Slavonic and East European Review*, Vol. 16, No. 47 (Jan., 1938), pp. 412-424.
- Perceval-Maxwell, M. Strafford, the Ulster-Scots and the Covenanters. *Irish Historical Studies*, Vol. 18, No. 72 (Sep., 1973), pp. 524-551
- Philips, Carla Rahn. The Moriscos of La Mancha, 1570-1614. *The Journal of Modern History*, Vol. 50, No. 2, On Demand Supplement (Jun.,1978), pp. D1067-D1095.
- Philips, Gervase. Longbow and Hackbutt: Weapons Technology and Technology Transfer in Early Modern England. *Technology and Culture*, Vol. 40, No. 3 (Jul., 1999), pp. 576-593.
- Philpott, Daniel. The Religious Roots of Modern International Relations. *World Politics*, Vol. 52, No. 2 (Jan., 2000), pp. 206-245.
- Piirimäe, Pärtel. Just War in Theory and Practice: The Legitimation of Swedish Intervention in the Thirty Years War. *The Historical Journal*, Vol. 45, No. 3 (Sep., 2002), pp. 499-523.
- Pike, Ruth. An Urban Minority: The Moriscos of Seville. *International Journal of Middle East Studies*, Vol. 2, No. 4 (Oct., 1971), pp. 368-377.
- Poe, Marshall. The Consequences of the Military Revolution in Muscovy: A Comparative Perspective. *Comparative Studies in Society and History*, Vol. 38, No. 4 (Oct., 1996), pp. 603-618.

- Polišenský, J. V. The Thirty Years' War and the Crises and Revolutions of Seventeenth-Century Europe. *Past & Present*, No. 39 (Apr., 1968), pp. 34-43.
- Potter, D. L. Foreign Policy in the Age of the Reformation: French Involvement in the Schmalkaldic War, 1544-1547. *The Historical Journal*, Vol. 20, No. 3 (Sep., 1977), pp. 525-544.
- Potter, David. The International Mercenary Market in the Sixteenth Century: Anglo-French Competition in Germany, 1543-50. *The English Historical Review*, Vol. 111, No. 440 (Feb., 1996), pp. 24-58.
- Press, Volker. The Habsburg Court as Center of the Imperial Government. *The Journal of Modern History*, Vol. 58, Supplement: Politics and Society in the Holy Roman Empire, 1500-1806 (Dec., 1986), pp. S23-S45.
- Pursell, Brennan C. The End of the Spanish Match. *The Historical Journal*, Vol. 45, No. 4 (Dec., 2002), pp. 699-726.
- Questier, Michael. Arminianism, Catholicism, and Puritanism in England during the 1630s. *The Historical Journal*, Vol. 49, No. 1 (Mar., 2006), pp. 53-78.
- Questier, Michael. Catholic Loyalism in Early Stuart England. *The English Historical Review*, Vol. 123, No. 504 (Oct., 2008), pp. 1132-1165.
- Rabb, Theodore K. Artists and Warfare: A Study of Changing Values in Seventeenth-Century Europe. *Transactions of the American Philosophical Society*, New Series, Vol. 75, No. 6, The Visual Arts and Sciences: A Symposium Held at the American Philosophical Society (1985), pp. 79-106.
- Rabb, Theodore K. The Effects of the Thirty Years' War on the German Economy. *The Journal of Modern History*, Vol. 34, No. 1 (Mar., 1962), pp. 40-51.
- Rachum, Ilan. The Entrance of the Word "Revolution" into French Political Discourse (1648-1653). *Historical Reflections / Réflexions Historiques*, Vol. 23, No. 2 (Spring 1997), pp.229-249.
- Raitt, Jill. The Emperor and the Exiles: The Clash of Religion and Politics in the Late Sixteenth Century. *Church History*, Vol. 52, No. 2 (Jun., 1983), pp. 145-156.
- Ranum, Orest. Richelieu and the Great Nobility: Some Aspects of Early Modern Political Motives. *French Historical Studies*, Vol. 3, No. 2 (Autumn, 1963), pp. 184-204.
- Raudzens, George. War-Winning Weapons: The Measurement of Technological Determinism in Military History. *The Journal of Military History*, Vol. 54, No. 4 (Oct., 1990), pp. 403-434.
- Redworth, Glyn. Of Pimps and Princes: Three Unpublished Letters from James I and the Prince of Wales Relating to the Spanish Match. *The Historical Journal*, Vol. 37, No. 2 (Jun., 1994), pp. 401-409.
- Reeve, L. J. and de Quiroga, Diego. Quiroga's Paper of 1631: A Missing Link in Anglo-Spanish Diplomacy during the Thirty Years War. *The English Historical Review*, Vol. 101, No. 401 (Oct., 1986), pp. 913-926.
- Reeves, Jesse S. THE LIFE AND WORK OF HUGO GROTIUS. *Proceedings of the American Society of International Law at Its Annual Meeting*. (1921-1969), Vol. 19 (APRIL 23-25, 1925), pp. 48-58.
- Rein, Nathan Baruch. Faith and Empire: Conflicting Visions of Religion in a Late Reformation Controversy: The Augsburg "Interim" and Its Opponents, 1548-50. *Journal of the American Academy of Religion*, Vol. 71, No. 1 (Mar., 2003), pp. 45-74.
- Reiss, Timothy J. Descartes, the Palatinate, and the Thirty Years War: Political Theory and Political Practice. *Yale French Studies*, No. 80, Baroque Topographies: Literature/History/Philosophy (1991), pp. 108-145.
- Riches, Daniel. Early Modern Military Reform and the Connection Between Sweden and Brandenburg-Prussia. *Scandinavian Studies*, Vol. 77, No. 3 (Fall 2005), pp. 347-364
- Roberts, Michael. The Political Objectives of Gustavus Adolphus in Germany 1630-1632. *Transactions of the Royal Historical Society*, Vol. 7 (1957), pp. 19-46.
- Root, Deborah. Speaking Christian: Orthodoxy and Difference in Sixteenth-Century Spain. *Representations*, No. 23 (Summer, 1988), pp. 118-134.
- Rose, Stephen. Trumpeters and diplomacy on the eve of the Thirty Years' War: the "album amicorum" of Jonas Kröschel. *Early Music*, Vol. 40, No. 3 (August 2012), pp. 379-392.
- Rosier, Bart. The Victories of Charles V: A Series of Prints by Maarten van Heemskerck, 1555-56. *Simiolus: Netherlands Quarterly for the History of Art*, Vol. 20, No. 1 (1990 -1991), pp. 24-38.

- Routh, Enid M. G. The Attempts to Establish a Balance of Power in Europe during the Second Half of the Seventeenth Century (1648-1702): (Alexander Prize, 1903). *Transactions of the Royal Historical Society*, New Series, Vol. 18 (1904), pp. 33-76.
- Rowe, Erin Kathleen. St. Teresa and Olivares: Patron Sainthood, Royal Favourites, and the Politics of Plurality in Seventeenth-Century Spain. *The Sixteenth Century Journal*, Vol. 37, No. 3 (Fall, 2006), pp. 721-737.
- Rowen, Herbert H. The Dutch Revolt: What Kind of Revolution? *Renaissance Quarterly*, Vol. 43, No. 3 (Autumn, 1990), pp. 570-590.
- Rudmose-Brown , T. B. Alsace-Lorraine: A Problem of Nationality. *Studies: An Irish Quarterly Review*, Vol. 4, No. 15 (Sep., 1915), pp. 367-383.
- Samson, Alexander. Changing Places: The Marriage and Royal Entry of Philip, Prince of Austria, and Mary Tudor, July-August 1554. *The Sixteenth Century Journal*, Vol. 36, No. 3 (Fall, 2005), pp. 761-784.
- Sanchez, Magdalena S. A House Divided: Spain, Austria, and the Bohemian and Hungarian Successions. *The Sixteenth Century Journal*, Vol. 25, No. 4 (Winter, 1994), pp. 887-903.
- Schmidt, Sebastian. To Order the Minds of Scholars: The Discourse of the Peace of Westphalia in International Relations Literature. *International Studies Quarterly*, Vol. 55, No. 3 (September 2011), pp. 601-623.
- Schreiber, Roy E. The First Carlisle Sir James Hay, First Earl of Carlisle as Courtier, Diplomat and Entrepreneur, 1580-1636. *Transactions of the American Philosophical Society*, Vol. 74, No. 7 (1984), pp. 1-202.
- Schwartz, Marc L. James I and the Historians: Toward a Reconsideration. *Journal of British Studies*, Vol. 13, No. 2 (May, 1974), pp. 114-134.
- Schwartz, Stuart B. The Voyage of the Vassals: Royal Power, Noble Obligations, and Merchant Capital before the Portuguese Restoration of Independence, 1624-1640. *The American Historical Review*, Vol. 96, No. 3 (Jun., 1991), pp. 735-762.
- Senning, Calvin F. Piracy, Politics, and Plunder under James I: The Voyage of the "Pearl" and Its Aftermath,1611-1615. *Huntington Library Quarterly*, Vol. 46, No. 3 (Summer, 1983), pp. 187-222.
- Shagan, Ethan Howard. Constructing Discord: Ideology, Propaganda, and English Responses to the Irish Rebellion of 1641. *Journal of British Studies*, Vol. 36, No. 1 (Jan., 1997), pp. 4-34.
- Shimp, Robert E. A Catholic Marriage for an Anglican Prince. *Historical Magazine of the Protestant Episcopal Church*, Vol. 50, No. 1 (March,1981), pp. 3-18.
- Shoenberger, Cynthia Grant. The Development of the Lutheran Theory of Resistance: 1523-1530. *The Sixteenth Century Journal*, Vol. 8, No. 1 (Apr., 1977), pp. 61-76.
- Showalter, Dennis E. Caste, Skill, and Training: The Evolution of Cohesion in European Armies from the Middle Ages to the Sixteenth Century. *The Journal of Military History*, Vol. 57, No. 3 (Jul., 1993), pp. 407-430.
- Silke, John J. Spain and the Invasion of Ireland, 1601-2. *Irish Historical Studies*, Vol. 14, No. 56 (Sep., 1965), pp. 295-312.
- Silverman, Dan P. The Economic Consequences of Annexation: Alsace-Lorraine and Imperial Germany, 1871-1918. *Central European History*, Vol. 4, No. 1 (Mar., 1971), pp. 34-53.
- Simon, Róbert. Muslims and Christians in Spain as Seen by Ibn Khaldoun. *Mediterranean Studies*, Vol. 1, Iberia & the Mediterranean (1989), pp. 19, 21-32.
- Singer, P. W. "The Ultimate Military Entrepreneur". *MHQ: Military History Quarterly*, Spring 2003, p. 6-15.
- Skarsten, Trygve R. The Reception of the Augsburg Confession in Scandinavia. *The Sixteenth Century Journal*, Vol. 11, No. 3, 450th Anniversary Augsburg Confession (Jun. 25, 1980), pp. 86-98.
- Sluiter, Engel. Dutch Maritime Power and the Colonial Status Quo, 1585-1641. *Pacific Historical Review*, Vol. 11, No. 1 (Mar., 1942), pp. 29-41.
- Sluiter, Engel. Dutch-Spanish Rivalry in the Caribbean Area, 1594-1609. *The Hispanic American Historical Review*, Vol. 28, No. 2 (May, 1948), pp. 165-196.
- Smith, David L. The Fourth Earl of Dorset and the Personal Rule of Charles I. *Journal of British Studies*, Vol. 30, No. 3 (Jul., 1991), pp. 257-287.
- Smith, George L. GUILDERS AND GODLINESS: THE DUTCH COLONIAL CONTRIBUTION TO AMERICAN RELIGIOUS PLURALISM. *Journal of Presbyterian History (1962-1985)*, Vol. 47, No. 1 (MARCH 1969), pp. 1-30.

- Sonnino, Paul. Prelude to the Fronde. The French Delegation at the Peace of Westphalia. *Historische Zeitschrift. Beihefte*, New Series, Vol. 26, Der Westfälische Friede.Diplomatie – politische Zäsur – kulturelles Umfeld – Rezeptionsgeschichte (1998), pp. 217-233.
- Soucek, Svatopluk, Navals Aspects of the Ottoman Conquests of Rhodes, Cyprus and Crete. *Studia Islamica*, No. 98/99 (2004), pp. 219-261.
- Stankiewicz, W. J. The Huguenot Downfall: The Influence of Richelieu's Policy and Doctrine. *Proceedings of the American Philosophical Society*, Vol. 99, No. 3 (Jun. 15, 1955), pp. 146-168.
- Stearns, S. J. A Problem of Logistics in the Early seventeenth Century: The Siege of Re. *Military Affairs*, Vol. 42, No. 3 (Oct., 1978), pp. 121-126.
- Stein, Leon. Religion and Patriotism in German Peace Dramas during the Thirty Years' War. *Central European History*, Vol. 4, No. 2 (Jun., 1971), pp. 131-148.
- Steinberg, S. H. 'The Thirty Years War: A New Interpretation', *History*, xxxii (1947), pp. 89-102.
- Stewart, Laura A. M. English Funding of the Scottish Armies in England and Ireland, 1640-1648. *The Historical Journal*, Vol. 52, No. 3 (Sep., 2009), pp. 573-593.
- Stone, John. Technology, Society, and the Infantry Revolution of the Fourteenth Century. *The Journal of Military History*, Vol. 68, No. 2 (Apr., 2004), pp. 361-380.
- Stone, John. Technology, Society, and the Infantry Revolution of the Fourteenth Century. The *Journal of Military History*, Vol. 68, No. 2 (Apr., 2004), pp. 361-380.
- Stradling, R. A. Olivares and the Origins of the Franco-Spanish War, 1627-1635. The English *Historical Review*, Vol. 101, No. 398 (Jan., 1986), pp. 68-94.
- Stradling, R. A. Prelude to Disaster; the Precipitation of the War of the Mantuan Succession, 1627-29. *The Historical Journal*, Vol. 33, No. 4 (Dec., 1990), pp. 769-785.
- Subrahmanyam, Sanjay. Holding the World in Balance: The Connected Histories of the Iberian Overseas Empires,1500-1640. *The American Historical Review*, Vol. 112, No. 5 (Dec., 2007), pp. 1359-1385.
- Surtz, Ronald E. Morisco Women, Written Texts, and the Valencia Inquisition. *The Sixteenth Century Journal*, Vol. 32, No. 2 (Summer, 2001), pp. 421-433.
- Sutherland, N. M. The Origins of the Thirty Years War and the Structure of European Politics. *The English Historical Review*, Vol. 107, No. 424 (Jul., 1992), pp. 587-625.
- Swart, Erik. "The field of finance": War and Taxation in Holland, Flanders, and Brabant, 1572—85. *The Sixteenth Century Journal*, Vol. 42, No. 4 (Winter 2011), pp. 1051-1071.
- Swope, Kenneth M. Crouching Tigers, Secret Weapons: Military Technology Employed during the Sino-Japanese-Korean War, 1592-1598. *The Journal of Military History*, Vol. 69, No. 1 (Jan., 2005), pp. 11-41.
- Tarssuk, Leonid. The Cabinet d'Armes of Louis XIII: Some Firearms and Related Problems. *Metropolitan Museum Journal*, Vol. 21 (1986), pp. 65-122.
- Tarver, W. T. S. The Traction Trebuchet: A Reconstruction of an Early Medieval Siege Engine. *Technology and Culture*, Vol. 36, No. 1 (Jan., 1995), pp. 136-167.
- Terry, Elizabeth and C. Sanford. Charles I and Alexander Leslie. *The English Historical Review*, Vol. 16, No. 61 (Jan., 1901), pp. 115-120.
- Theibault, John. Jeremiah in the Village: Prophecy, Preaching, Pamphlets, and Penance in the Thirty Years' War. *Central European History*, Vol. 27, No. 4 (1994), pp. 441-460.
- Theibault, John. The Rhetoric of Death and Destruction in the Thirty Years War. *Journal of Social History*, Vol. 27, No. 2 (Winter, 1993), pp. 271-290.
- Thompson, William R. The Military Superiority Thesis and the Ascendancy of Western Eurasia in the World System. *Journal of World History*, Vol. 10, No. 1 (Spring, 1999), pp. 143-178.
- Thomson, Erik. Axel Oxenstierna and Books. *The Sixteenth Century Journal*, Vol. 38, No. 3 (Fall, 2007), pp. 705-729.
- Tingle, Elizabeth. Nantes and the Origins of the Catholic League of 1589. *The Sixteenth Century Journal*, Vol. 33, No. 1 (Spring, 2002), pp. 109-128.
- Tracy, James D. With and Without the Counter-Reformation: The Catholic Church in the Spanish Netherlands and the Dutch Republic, 1580-1650: A Review of the Literature since 1945. *The Catholic Historical Review*, Vol. 71, No. 4 (Oct., 1985), pp. 547-575.
- Tucker, Treva J. Eminence over Efficacy: Social Status and Cavalry Service in Sixteenth-Century France. *The Sixteenth Century Journal*, Vol. 32, No. 4 (Winter, 2001), pp. 1057-1095.
- Tueller, James B. The Assimilating Morisco: Four Families in Valladolid prior to the Expulsion

of 1610. *Mediterranean Studies*, Vol. 7 (1998), pp. 167-177.

- Turchetti, Mario. Religious Concord and Political Tolerance in Sixteenth- and Seventeenth-Century France. *The Sixteenth Century Journal*, Vol. 22, No. 1 (Spring, 1991), pp. 15-25.
- Unger, Richard W. Warships and Cargo Ships in Medieval Europe. *Technology and Culture*, Vol. 22, No. 2 (Apr., 1981), pp. 233-252.
- Ungerer, Gustav. The Spanish and English Chronicles in King James's and Sir George Buc's Dossiers on the Anglo-Spanish Peace Negotiations. *Huntington Library Quarterly*, Vol. 61, No. 3/4 (1998), pp. 309-324.
- Valentin, Veit. Wallenstein, after Three Centuries. *The Slavonic and East European Review*, Vol. 14, No. 40 (Jul., 1935), pp. 154-162.
- Vallance, Edward. Preaching to the Converted: Religious Justifications for the English Civil War. *Huntington Library Quarterly*, Vol. 65, No. 3/4 (2002), pp. 395-419.
- Van der Steen, Jasper. Chapter Title: A CONTESTED PAST. MEMORY WARS DURING THE TWELVE YEARS TRUCE (1609–21). *In Memory before Modernity: Practices of Memory in Early Modern Europe*. Eds Erika Kuijpers, Judith Pollmann, Johannes Müller, Jasper van der Steen. Brill, 2013.
- Van Eerde, Katherine S. The Spanish Match through an English Protestant's Eyes. *Huntington Library Quarterly*, Vol. 32, No. 1 (Nov., 1968), pp. 59-75.
- Vreeland Jr, Hamilton. Hugo Grotius, Diplomatist. *The American Journal of International Law*, Vol. 11, No. 3 (Jul., 1917), pp. 580-606.
- Waureghen, Sarah. Covenanter Propaganda and Conceptualizations of the Public during the Bishops Wars, 1638-1640. *The Historical Journal*, Vol. 52, No. 1 (Mar., 2009), pp. 63-86.
- Westergaard, Waldemar. The Hansa Towns and Scandinavia on the Eve of Swedish Independence. *The Journal of Modern History*, Vol. 4, No. 3 (Sep., 1932), pp. 349-360.
- Wiegers, Gerard. MANAGING DISASTER: NETWORKS OF THE MORISCOS DURING THE PROCESS OF THE EXPULSION FROM THE IBERIAN PENINSULA AROUND 1609. *Journal of Medieval Religious Cultures*, Vol. 36, No. 2 (2010), pp. 141-168.
- Willson, David Harris. Summoning and Dissolving Parliament, 1603-25. *The American Historical Review*, Vol. 45, No. 2 (Jan., 1940), pp. 279-300.
- Wilson, Edward M and Turner, Olga. The Spanish Protest against "A Game at Chesse". The *Modern Language Review*, Vol. 44, No. 4 (Oct., 1949), pp. 476-482.
- Wilson, Peter H. Dynasty, Constitution, and Confession: The Role of Religion in the Thirty Years War. *The International History Review*, Vol. 30, No. 3 (Sep., 2008), pp. 473-514.
- Wilson, Peter H. The Causes of the Thirty Years War 1618-48. *The English Historical Review*, Vol. 123, No. 502 (Jun., 2008), pp. 554-586.
- Wilson, Peter H. The German 'Soldier Trade' of the Seventeenth and Eighteenth Centuries: A Reassessment. *The International History Review*, Vol. 18, No. 4 (Nov., 1996), pp. 757-792.
- Wormald, Jenny. Gunpowder, Treason, and Scots. *Journal of British Studies*, Vol. 24, No. 2, Politics and Religion in the Early Seventeenth Century: New Voices (Apr., 1985), pp. 141-168.
- Worthington, David. Towards a Bibliography of the Irish in Central Europe, 1618-48. *Archivium Hibernicum*, Vol. 56 (2002), pp. 206-227.
- Wright, Louis B. Propaganda against James I's "Appeasement" of Spain. *Huntington Library Quarterly*, Vol. 6, No. 2 (Feb., 1943), pp. 149-172.
- Zaller, Robert. "Interest of State": James I and the Palatinate. *Albion: A Quarterly Journal Concerned with British Studies*, Vol. 6, No. 2(Summer, 1974), pp. 144-175.

INDEX

Bourbon, Armand de (Prince of Conde) 657, 930, 952, 954, 955, 956, 957, 960, 978, 979, 1005, 1060, 1061, 1066
Brandenburg 146, 182, 189, 248, 299, 300, 362, 411, 440, 458, 473, 487, 537, 546, 577, 578, 645, 650, 653, 721, 725, 731, 744, 773, 778, 781, 788, 797, 799, 801, 848, 583, 856, 867, 903, 905, 916, 917, 921, 927, 929, 965, 980, 981, 982, 987, 1005, 1008, 1029, 1036, 1037, 1076, 1078, 1084
Brandenburg, Elector Frederick William 15, 24, 123, 189, 219, 227, 234, 240, 241, 297, 404, 450, 570, 571, 618, 633, 725, 729, 782, 783, 788, 789, 791, 794, 795, 805, 852, 863, 968, 979, 980, 981, 1059, 1075, 1079, 1110
Brandenburg, George William 457, 585, 608, 646, 796, 812, 847, 849, 850, 852, 856, 863, 868, 870, 906, 912, 916, 928, 968, 979, 980, 1050, 1051
Brandenburg, Maria Elenore 992, 1007
Breda 458, 487, 533, 633, 634, 635, 636, 638, 640, 643, 656, 671, 884, 885, 891, 897, 898, 943, 999, 1013
Breisach 600, 893, 894, 909, 918, 922, 923, 978, 979, 1007, 1012, 1028, 1030, 1045
Breitenfeld 33, 57, 112, 114, 119, 120, 128, 131, 132, 133, 137, 138, 141, 142, 159, 181, 733, 773, 774 – 783, 790, 793, 796, 798, 799, 801, 802, 805, 806, 807, 817, 820, 830, 832, 833, 841, 856, 868, 875, 876, 948, 955, 967, 1004
Calvin, John 213
Catholic League 159, 161, 162, 201, 226, 230, 231, 232, 235, 272, 298, 325, 337, 347, 348, 378, 392, 397, 402, 403, 405, 407, 418, 422, 427, 428, 429, 431, 435, 447, 451, 522, 556, 557, 561, 565, 566, 578, 590, 603, 626, 648, 659, 695, 697, 698, 699, 721, 736, 750, 756, 768, 769, 778, 814, 856, 878, 912, 925, 1037
Charles I (England) 166, 415, 516, 527, 536, 539, 659, 674, 747, 902, 905, 940
Charles II (England) 811, 842
Charles II (Gonzaga, Duke of Mantua and Montferrat & Duke of Nevers) 172, 173, 330, 658, 663, 664, 665, 666, 669
Charles V 24, 204, 205, 206, 207, 208, 212, 214, 237, 239, 266, 304, 313, 329, 352, 379, 424, 425, 426, 433, 525, 623, 665, 757, 877, 878, 879, 880, 885, 890, 917, 925, 946, 999
Charles V (Lorraine) 580, 661, 817, 832, 885, 888, 891, 942
Charles IX (Sweden) 286, 306, 309, 311, 355, 724
Charles Emmanuel (Savoy) 387, 669, 688, 689
Christian IV (Denmark) 111, 161, 285, 309, 311, 312, 430, 437, 515, 540, 551, 552, 553, 554, 556, 557, 559, 560, 566, 567, 571, 575, 576, 580, 582, 585, 592, 602, 605, 606, 616, 634, 658, 726, 735, 765, 814, 873, 882, 926, 945, 963, 965, 968
Christian I (Anhalt) 231, 288, 293, 294, 298, 302, 343, 344, 345, 346, 347,

About the Author

Zachary Twamley is an author, history podcaster, former University lecturer, and History PhD candidate at Trinity College Dublin, with a keen interest in early modern Europe, modern British history, and all things Otto von Bismarck. His past works include a book examining the British decision to enter the First World War: A Matter of Honour (2016), and in addition to the written word, he has also produced multiple history podcast projects through his When Diplomacy Fails Podcast. These projects include The July Crisis, The Korean War, The Versailles Anniversary Project and the podcast series upon which this book is based, The Thirty Years War. You can find Zachary Twamley and his podcasts at his website www.wdfpodcast.com To access the free, extensive audio library which When Diplomacy Fails Podcast has to offer, please subscribe by searching for the show on your favourite podcasting app.